HMO/PPO
Directory®

2012
Twenty-Fourth Edition

HMO/PPO
Directory®

Detailed Profiles of U.S. Managed Healthcare
Organizations & Key Decision Makers

A SEDGWICK PRESS Book

Grey House
Publishing

PUBLISHER: Leslie Mackenzie
EDITORIAL DIRECTOR: Laura Mars
ASSOCIATE EDITOR: Diana Delgado

PRODUCTION MANAGER: Kristen Thatcher
COMPOSITION: David Garoogian
MARKETING DIRECTOR: Jessica Moody

A Sedgwick Press Book
Grey House Publishing, Inc.
4919 Route 22
Amenia, NY 12501
518.789.8700
FAX 845.373.6390
www.greyhouse.com
e-mail: books @greyhouse.com

First edition published 1987
Twenty-fourth edition published 2011
Printed in the USA

HMO/PPO directory -- 1986-
    586 v. 28 cm.
    Annual
    HMO PPO directory
    Includes index.
    ISSN: 0887-4484
1. Health maintenance organizations--United States--Directories. 2. Preferred provider organizations (Medical care)--United States--Directories. I. Title: HMO PPO directory.

RA413.5.U5 H58
362.1'0425—dc21

ISBN: 978-1-59237-761-9 Softcover

Table of Contents

Introduction

This 24th edition of the *HMO/PPO Directory* profiles 1,183 managed care organizations in the United States, and lists important, current, and comprehensive information for HMO, PPO, POS, and Vision & Dental Plans.

In addition to detailed profiles of **Managed Healthcare Organizations**, it includes an **Implementation Timeline** that explains how and when the provisions of the health reform law will be implemented over the next several years. Plus, a **State Statistics and Rankings** section provides state-by-state numbers of individuals covered by type of health plans, and also ranks states by number of individuals enrolled in health plans.

Praise for *HMO/PPO Directory:*

> *"...designed primarily for...businesses seeking to make decisions about plans to offer employee health care coverage...also valuable for individuals seeking information about different states as they enter into job searches...recommended for corporate, large public and academic, medical and law libraries."*
> —American Reference Books Annual, 2011

Arrangement of State Chapters

Plan profiles are arranged alphabetically by state. An important feature of each state chapter is the state summary chart of Health Insurance Coverage Status and Type of Coverage by Age. This chart is broken down into 13 categories from "Covered by some type of health insurance" to "Not covered at any time during the year."

Directly following the State Summary, plan listings provide crucial contact information, including key executives, often with direct phones and e-mails, fax numbers, web sites and hundreds of e-mail addresses. Each profile provides a detailed summary of the plan, including the following:

- Type of Plan, including Specialty and Benefits
- Type of Coverage
- Type of Payment Plan
- Subscriber Information
- Financial History
- Average Compensation Information
- Employer References
- Current Member Enrollment
- Hospital Affiliations
- Number of Primary Care and Specialty Physicians
- Federal Qualification Status
- For Profit Status
- Specialty Managed Care Partners
- Regional Business Coalitions
- Employer References
- Peer Review Information
- Accreditation Information

The 1,183 plan profiles, combined, include 5,777 key executives, 798 fax numbers, 1,176 web sites, and 1,237 emails—8,988 ways to directly access the health care information needed by you and your business.

Additional Features

In addition to the educational material in the front matter, state statistics and detailed plan profiles, *HMO/PPO Directory* includes two Appendices and five Indexes.

- Appendix A: Glossary of Health Insurance Terms — Includes more than 150 terms such as Aggregate Indemnity, Diagnostic Related Groups, Non-participating Provider, and Waiting Period.
- Appendix B: Industry Web Sites — Contains dozens of the most valuable health care web sites and a detailed description, from Alliance of Community Health Plans to National Quality Forum to National Society of Certified Healthcare Business Consultants.
- Plan Index: Alphabetical list of insurance plans by seven plan types: HMO; PPO; HMO/PPO; Dental; Vision; Medicare; and Multiple.
- Personnel Index: Alphabetical list of all executives listed in the directory, with their affiliated organization.
- Membership Enrollment Index: List of organizations in the directory by member enrollment.
- Primary Care Physician Index: List of organizations in the directory by their number of primary care physicians.
- Referral/Specialty Care Physician Index: List of organizations in the directory by their number of referral and specialty care physicians.

To broaden its availability, the *HMO/PPO Directory* is also available for subscription online at http://gold.greyhouse.com. Subscribers can search by plan details, geographic area, number of members, personnel name, title and much more. Users can print out prospect sheets or download data into their own spreadsheet or database. This database is a must for anyone in need of immediate access to contacts in the US managed care marketplace. Plus, buyers of the print directory get a free 30-day trial of the online database. Call (800) 562-2139 x118 to start your trial.

User Guide

Descriptive listings in the *HMO/PPO Directory* are organized by state, then alphabetically by health plan. Each numbered item is described in the User Key on the following pages. Terms are defined in the Glossary.

---

1. → **U Healthcare**
2. → **3000 Riverside Road**
   Sharon, CT 06069
3. → **Toll Free: 060-364-0000**
4. → **Phone: 060-364-0001**
5. → **Fax: 060-364-0002**
6. → Info@uhealth.com
7. → www.uhealth.com
8. → Mailing Address: PO Box 729 Sharon, CT 06069-0729
9. → Subsidiary of: USA Healthcare
10. → For Profit: Yes
11. → Year Founded: 1992
12. → Physician Owned: No
13. → Owned by an IDN: No
14. → Federally Qualified: Yes 08/01/82
15. → Number of Affiliated Hospitals: 2,649
16. → Number of Primary Physicians: 4,892
17. → Number of Referral/Specialty Physicians: 6,246
18. → Current Member Enrollment: 204,000 (as of 7/1/01)
19. → State Member Enrollment: 29,000

Healthplan and Services Defined

20. → Plan Type: HMO
21. → Model Type: Staff, IPA, Group, Network
22. → Plan Specialty: ASO, Chiropractic, Dental, Disease Management, Lab, Vision, Radiology
23. → Benefits Offered: Chiropractic, Dental, Disease Management, Vision, Wellness
24. → Offers a Demand Management Patient Information Service: Yes
    DMPI Services Offered: Vision Works, Medical Imaging Institute

25. → **Type of Coverage**
    Commercial, Medicare, Supplemental Medicare, Medicaid
    Catastrophic Illness Benefit: Varies by case

26. → **Type of Payment Plans Offered**
    POS, Capitated, FFS, Combination FFS & DFFS

27. → **Geographic Areas Served**
    Connecticut, Maryland, New Jersey, Vermont, New York

Subscriber Information

28. → Average Monthly Fee Per Subscriber (Employee & Employer Contribution):
    Employee Only (Self): $8.00
    Employee & 1 Family Member: $10.00
    Employee & 2 Family Members: $15.00
    Medicare: $ 10.00
29. → Average Annual Deductible Per Subscriber:
    Employee Only (Self): $200.00

Employee & 1 Family Member: $250.00
Employee & 2 Family Members: $500.00
Medicare: $200.00

30.➤ Average Subscriber Co-Payment:
Primary Care Physician: $8.00
Non-Network Physician: $10.00
Prescription Drugs: $5.00
Hospital ER: $50.00
Home Health Care: $25.00
Home Health Care Max Days Covered/Visits: 30 days
Nursing Home: $5.00
Nursing Home Max Days/Visits Covered: 365 days

31.➤ **Network Qualifications**
Minimum Years of Practice: 10
Pre-Admission Certification: Yes

32.➤ **Peer Review Type**
Utilization Review: Yes
Second Surgical Opinion: No
Case Management: Yes

33.➤ **Accreditation Certification**
JCAHO, AAHC (formerly URAC), NCQA
Publishes and Distributes a Report Card: Yes

34.➤ **Key Personnel**
CFO...........................David Williams
Marketing.....................Clarence J. Fist
Medical Affairs...............Samantha Johnson, MD
Provider Services.............Laura Falk

Average Claim Compensation
35.➤ Physician's Fee's Charged: 22%
36.➤ Hospital's Fee Charged: 34%

37.➤ **Specialty Managed Care Partners**
AMBI, Pharmaceutical Treatment, OxiTherapy

38.➤ **Enters into Contracts with Regional Business Coalitions: Yes**
New York Healthcare

39.➤ **Employer References**
Life Science Corporation

User Key

1. → **Health Plan:** Formal name of health plan
2. → **Address:** Physical location
3. → **Toll Free:** Toll free number
4. → **Phone:** Main number of organization
5. → **Fax:** Fax number
6. → **E-mail:** Main e-mail address of health plan, if provided
7. → **Website:** Main website address of health plan, if provided
8. → **Mailing Address:** If different from physical address, above.
9. → **Subsidiary of:** Corporation the health plan is legally affiliated with
10. → **For Profit:** Indicates if the organization was formed to make a financial profit. Non-profit organizations can make a profit, but the profits must be used to benefit the organization or purpose the corporation was created to help
11. → **Year Founded:** The year the organization was recognized as a legal entity
12. → **Physician Owned:** Notes if the organization is owned by a group of physicians who are recognized as a legal entity
13. → **Owned by an IDN:** Notes if the organization is owned by an Integrated Delivery Network
14. → **Federally Qualified:** Shows if and when the plan received federally qualified status
15. → **Number of Affiliated Hospitals:** In-network hospitals contracted with the health plans
16. → **Number of Primary Physicians:** In-network primary physicians contracted with the health plan
17. → **Number of Referral/Specialty Physicians:** In-network referral/specialty physicians contracted with the health plan
18. → **Current Member Enrollment:** The number of health plan members or subscribers using health plan benefits, and date of last enrollment count
19. → **State Member Enrollment:** The number of health plan members or subscribers using health plan benefits in that state, and date of last enrollment count
20. → **Plan Type:** Identifies the health plan as an HMO, PPO, Other (neither an HMO or PPO) or Multiple (both an HMO and PPO, or an HMO and TPA or POS; see Glossary for definitions of terms). Note: If a plan is both an HMO and PPO with different product information, i.e. number of hospitals or physicians, the plan is listed as two separate entries
21. → **Model Type:** Describes the relationship between the health plan and its physicians
22. → **Plan Specialty:** Indicates specialized services provided by the plan
23. → **Benefits Offered:** Indicates specialized benefits offered in addition to standard coverage for physician services, hospitalization, diagnostic testing, and prescription drugs
24. → **Offers Demand Management Patient Information Services:** Notes if Triage and other services are offered to help plan members find the most appropriate type and level of care, and what those services are
25. → **Type of Coverage:** Lines of business offered
26. → **Type of Payment Plans Offered:** How the insuror pays its contracted providers
27. → **Geographical Areas Served:** Geographical areas the health plan services
28. → **Average Monthly Fee Per Subscriber:** Monthly premium due to the carrier for each member
29. → **Annual Average Deductible Per Subscriber:** The deductible each member must meet before expenses can be reimbursed
30. → **Average Subscriber Co-Payment:** The co-payment each member must pay at the time services are rendered
31. → **Network Qualifications:** Qualifications a physician must meet to contract with the plan
32. → **Peer Review Type:** The type of on-going peer review process used by the health plan

33. ➔**Accreditation Certification:** Specific certifications the health plan achieved after rigorous review of its policies, procedures, and clinical outcomes

34. ➔**Key Personnel:** Key Executives in the most frequently contacted departments within the plans, with phone and e-mails when provided

35. ➔**Physician's Fees Charged:** The percentage of physicians' billed charges that is actually paid out by the plan

36. ➔**Hospital's Fees Charged:** The percentage of hospitals' billed charges that is actually paid out by the plan

37. ➔**Specialty Managed Care Partners:** Specialty carve-out companies that are contracted with the health plan to offer a broader array of health services to members

38. ➔**Regional Business Coalitions:** Notes if physician or business entities have formed for the sole purpose of achieving economies of scale when purchasing supplies and services, and the names of those businesses

39. ➔**Employer References:** Large employers that have contracted with the health plan and are willing to serve as references for the health plan

Health Reform Implementation Timeline

Provisions by Year

2010 (26 total, 26 in effect)

Review of Health Plan Premium Increases

Requires the federal government to create a process, in conjunction with states, where insurers have to justify unreasonable premium increases. Provides grants to states for reviewing premium increases.

Implementation: Plan year 2010

Implementation update: On August 16, 2010, HHS Secretary Kathleen Sebelius announced the award of $46 million to 45 states and the District of Columbia to improve their processes for reviewing health plan premium increases. On December 21, HHS issued a proposed rule on premium rate reviews. HHS announced the availability of another $199 million in grants to states on February 24, 2011. A fact sheet on rate reviews was issued on December 22, 2010. On May 19, 2011, the final rule for the insurance rate review program was published in the Federal Register. On July 7, 2011, HHS released a list of states and territories with effective review programs in the private small group and individual markets; CMS will conduct the reviews in states without the authority or resources. On September 1, 2011, states and HHS will begin reviewing proposed premium increases for 2012.

Changes in Medicare Provider Rates

Reduces annual market basket updates for inpatient and outpatient hospital services, long-term care hospitals, inpatient rehabilitation facilities, and psychiatric hospitals and units and adjusts payments for productivity.

Implementation: Beginning fiscal year 2010; productivity adjustments added to market basket update in 2012

Implementation update: The Centers for Medicare and Medicaid Services has issued several proposed and final rules reducing annual market basket updates for different provider types: inpatient hospital services (Final Rule August 16, 2010; Proposed Rule for FY 2012 issued April 20, 2011), outpatient hospital services (Final Rule November 3, 2010), long-term care hospitals (Final Rule August 16, 2010; Proposed Rule for FY 2012 issued April 20, 2011), inpatient rehabilitation facilities and psychiatric hospitals and units (Proposed Rule January 27, 2011).

Qualifying Therapeutic Discovery Project Credit

Provides tax credits or grants to employers with 250 or fewer employees for up to 50% of the investments costs in projects that have the potential to produce new therapies, reduce long-term cost growth, or advance the goal of curing cancer within 30 years. The grant or tax is available for investments made in 2009 or 2010.

Implementation: Program established within 60 days of enactment

Implementation update: On June 18, 2010, the IRS announced the availability of tax credits and grants through the program. On May 21, 2010, the IRS released guidance for the program. Applications were due by July 21, 2010 and awards were announced on October 29, 2010. Nearly $1 billion in tax credits and grants have been provided through the program as of November 2010.

Medicaid and CHIP Payment Advisory Commission

Provides funding for and expands the role of the Medicaid and CHIP Payment and Access Commission to include assessments of adult services in Medicaid.

Implementation: Funding appropriated for fiscal year 2010

Implementation update: On December 23, 2009, GAO announced the appointment of 17 members to MACPAC. MACPAC held its first public meeting on September 23 and 24, 2010. On March 15, 2011, MACPAC released its first report, establishing the development of key baseline data and information on Medicaid and CHIP. The MACPAC website is available at http://www.macpac.gov/

Comparative Effectiveness Research

Establishes a non-profit Patient-Centered Outcomes Research Institute to conduct research that compares the clinical effectiveness of medical treatments.

Implementation: Funding appropriated beginning fiscal year 2010.

Implementation update: On September 23, 2010, The General Accounting Office announced the appointment of 19 members to the Board of Governors for the new Patient-Centered Outcomes Research Institute (PCORI). In addition, the Director of the Agency for Healthcare Research and Quality and the Director of the National Institutes of Health will serve on the 21-member Board. The PCORI website is available at http://www.pcori.org/

Prevention and Public Health Fund

Appropriates $5 billion for fiscal years 2010 through 2014 and $2 billion for each subsequent fiscal year to support prevention and public health programs.

Implementation: Funding appropriated beginning fiscal year 2010.

Implementation update: The Department of Health and Human Services has allocated $500 million in funding from the Prevention and Public Health Fund for fiscal year 2010. Half of this funding is dedicated to improving the supply of primary care providers and half will support public health and prevention priorities. On February 11, 2011, HHS announces $750 million in funds from the

Prevention and Public Health Fund to help prevent tobacco use, obesity, heart disease, stroke and cancer; and to increase immunizations.

Medicare Beneficiary Drug Rebate

Provides a $250 rebate to Medicare beneficiaries who reach the Part D coverage gap in 2010. Further subsidies and discounts that ultimately close the coverage gap begin in 2011.

Implementation: January 1, 2010.

Implementation update: In May 2010, CMS issued a consumer brochure with information about the Medicare Part D coverage gap. In June 2010, the first rebate checks were sent to Medicare beneficiaries who reached the Medicare Part D coverage gap, more commonly known as the "doughnut hole." As of March 22, 2011, 3.8 million beneficiaries had received a $250 check to close the coverage gap, according to an HHS report.

Small Business Tax Credits

Provides tax credits to small employers with no more than 25 employees and average annual wages of less than $50,000 that provide health insurance for employees. Phase I (2010 2013): tax credit up to 35% (25% for non-profits) of employer cost; Phase II (2014 and later): tax credit up to 50% (35% for non-profits) of employer cost if purchased through an insurance Exchange for two years.

Implementation: January 1, 2010

Implementation update: The Internal Revenue Service (IRS) sent postcards to small businesses alerting them to the availability of the new tax credit. The IRS also created a fact sheet for small businesses to determine whether they are eligible for the tax credit and a draft form for claiming the tax credit. On December 2, 2010, the IRS released guidance on the tax credits and the form that small businesses can use to claim the credits.

Medicaid Drug Rebate

Increases the Medicaid drug rebate percentage for brand name drugs to 23.1% (except the rebate for clotting factors and drugs approved exclusively for pediatric use increases to 17.1%) and to 13% of average manufacturer price for non-innovator, multiple source drugs. Extends the drug rebate to Medicaid managed care plans.

Implementation: January 1, 2010 for increase in Medicaid drug rebate percentage; March 23, 2010 for extension of drug rebate to Medicaid managed care plans

Implementation update: The Centers for Medicare and Medicaid Services issued a State Medicaid Directors Letter on April 22, 2010 explaining the new rules. On August 11, 2010 and September 28, 2010, CMS issued letters to state Medicaid directors with additional guidance on the prescription drug rebates. On January 6, 2011, CMS issued another letter with further changes pursuant to the ACA.

Coordinating Care for Dual Eligibles

Establishes the Federal Coordinated Health Care Office to improve care coordination for dual eligibles (people eligible for both Medicare and Medicaid).

Implementation: March 1, 2010

Implementation update: The Federal Coordinated Health Care Office was created in September 2010. On December 30, 2010, CMS issued a notice in the Federal Register announcing the establishment of the Federal Coordinated Health Care Office.

Generic Biologic Drugs

Authorizes the Food and Drug Administration to approve generic versions of biologic drugs and grant biologics manufacturers 12 years of exclusive use before generics can be developed.

Implementation: March 23, 2010

Implementation update: On November 2-3, 2010, the Food and Drug Administration held a public hearing to obtain input on the issues and challenges related to implementing the Biologics Price Competition and Innovation Act of 2009, which was included in the health reform law. On October 5, 2010, HHS issued a request for comment notice in the Federal Register on the approval process for biosimilar drugs.

New Requirements on Non-profit Hospitals

Imposes additional requirements on non-profit hospitals to conduct community needs assessments and develop a financial assistance policy and impose a tax of $50,000 per year for failure to meet these requirements.

Implementation: March 23, 2010

Implementation update: On May 27, 2010, the Internal Revenue Service issued a notice requesting comment on the new requirements for non-profit hospitals.

Medicaid Coverage for Childless Adults

Creates a state option to provide Medicaid coverage to childless adults with incomes up to 133% of the federal poverty level. (States will be required to provide this coverage in 2014.)

Implementation: April 1, 2010

Implementation update: On April 9, 2010, the Centers for Medicare and Medicaid Services issued a letter to State Health Officials and Medicaid Directors providing guidance on the new optional Medicaid coverage for childless adults with incomes up to 133% of the federal poverty level. Connecticut, the District of Columbia, and Minnesota have received approval to provide this optional coverage.

Reinsurance Program for Retiree Coverage

Creates a temporary reinsurance program for employers providing health insurance coverage to retirees over age 55 who are not eligible for Medicare.

Implementation: 90 days following enactment until January 1, 2014

Implementation update: The Department of Health and Human Services began accepting applications for the Early Retiree Reinsurance Program on June 29, 2010 and approved more than 5,000 employer and union plans by the end of December 2010. HHS is continuing to accept until May 5, 2011. The program is slated to close by the end of 2013; however, the program may terminate early if the $5 billion assigned funds are spent sooner.

Pre-existing Condition Insurance Plan

Creates a temporary program to provide health coverage to individuals with pre-existing medical conditions who have been uninsured for at least six months. The plan will be operated by the states or the federal government.

Implementation: Enrollment into the federal plan began July 1, 2010; implementation dates for the state-operated plans vary

Implementation update: The federal government is operating PCIP programs in 23 states and the District of Columbia, while the remaining states are running their own programs. On July 30, HHS released interim rules for the PCIP programs. On November 5, 2010, HHS announced new plan options for 2011 that include lower premiums for the federally administered programs. As of March 2011, 18,000 individuals had enrolled in a PCIP program. Learn more: Learn more about the PCIP plans in this FAQ and view the enrollment data for PCIP plans in all 50 states at Statehealthfacts.org.

New Prevention Council

Creates the National Prevention, Health Promotion and Public Health Council to develop a national prevention, health promotion and public health strategy.

Implementation: First report due July 1, 2010

Implementation update: On June 10, 2010, President Obama signed an Executive Order creating the National Prevention, Health Promotion, and Public Health Council (National Prevention Council). The Council is chaired by the Surgeon General. On July 1, 2010, the Council released its first report. On September 15, 2010, the Council approved draft framework to guide development of the National Prevention Strategy. On June 16, 2011, the Council released the National Prevention Strategy.

Consumer Website

Requires the Department of Health and Human Services to develop an internet website to help residents identify health coverage options.

Implementation: July 1, 2010

Implementation update: On July 1, 2010, HHS launched a new consumer-focused health care website, healthcare.gov, and on September 8, 2010, HHS launched a Spanish-language version of the site. On October 1, 2010, HHS added new information on private insurance coverage and premiums to the site.

Tax on Indoor Tanning Services

Imposes a tax of 10% on the amount paid for indoor tanning services.

Implementation: July 1, 2010

Implementation update: On June 15, 2010, the Internal Revenue Service issued regulations implementing the new tax on indoor tanning services effective July 1, 2010. The first payments were due November 1, 2010.

Expansion of Drug Discount Program

Expands eligibility for the 340(B) drug discount program to sole-community hospitals, critical access hospitals, certain children's hospitals, and other entities.

Implementation: Applications accepted beginning August 2, 2010

Implementation update: On June 28, 2010, the Health Resources and Services Administration began enrolling newly eligible organizations into the 340(B) drug discount program.

Adult Dependent Coverage to Age 26

Extends dependent coverage for adult children up to age 26 for all individual and group policies.

Implementation: Plan or policy years beginning on or after September 23, 2010

Implementation update: On May 13, 2010, the Office of Consumer Information and Insurance Oversight (OCIIO) issued regulations allowing adult children to remain on their parents' health plan until age 26. This new provision takes effect for new plans and existing plans when they renew on or after September 23, 2010. Learn more: How does the provision that allows young adults to remain on a parent's insurance work? Learn more with this FAQ.

Consumer Protections in Insurance

Prohibits individual and group health plans from placing lifetime limits on the dollar value of coverage, rescinding coverage except in cases of fraud, and from denying children coverage based on pre-existing medical conditions or from including pre-existing condition exclusions for children. Restricts annual limits on the dollar value of coverage (and eliminates annual limits in 2014)

Implementation: Plan or policy years beginning on or after September 23, 2010 (annual limits eliminated in 2014)

Implementation update: On June 28, 2010, the Office of Consumer Information and Insurance Oversight (OCIIO) issued regulations implementing several consumer protection provisions in the health reform law. Certain of the provisions take effect for new plans and existing plans when they renew on or after September 23, 2010, while other provisions only apply to new plans established on or after September 23, 2010.

Insurance Plan Appeals Process

Requires new health plans to implement an effective process for allowing consumers to appeal health plan decisions and requires new plans to establish an external review process.

Implementation: Plan or policy years beginning on or after September 23, 2010

Implementation update: On July 23, 2010, the Office of Consumer Information and Insurance Oversight (OCIIO) issued regulations requiring standardized internal and external processes for consumers to appeal health plan decisions. These rules apply to new plans established on or after September 23, 2010. On November 17, 2010, HHS issued a request for information notice on the external review of health insurance claims. On August 4, 2011, HHS released a list of states with approved external review processes.

Coverage of Preventive Benefits

Requires new health plans to provide at a minimum coverage without cost-sharing for preventive services rated A or B by the U.S. Preventive Services Task Force, recommended immunizations, preventive care for infants, children, and adolescents, and additional preventive care and screenings for women.

Implementation: Plan or policy years beginning on or after September 23, 2010

Implementation update: On July 19, 2010, the Office of Consumer Information and Insurance Oversight (OCIIO) issued regulations on the new preventive benefits coverage requirements. These rules apply to new plans established on or after September 23, 2010. On August 1, 2010, the U.S. Preventative Services Task Force released its recommendations. On July 19, 2011, the Institute of Medicine released a report that recommended several women's preventive services that should be included in health plans with no cost-sharing. On August 1, 2011, HHS issued interim final regulations on preventive services, including requirements that insurers cover birth control with no cost-sharing. On August 3, 2011, HHS issued an amendment to the final regulations.

Health Centers and the National Health Service Corps

Permanently authorizes the federally qualified health centers and NHSC programs and increases funding for FQHCs and for the NHSC for fiscal years 2010-2015.

Implementation: Funding appropriated beginning fiscal year 2010

Implementation update: On October 8, 2010, HHS announced grant awards of $727 million to 143 community health centers for infrastructure improvements and on October 26, 2010, HHS announced the availability of an addition $335 million for existing community health centers to expand medical services.

Health Care Workforce Commission

Establishes the National Health Care Workforce Commission to coordinate federal workforce activities and make recommendations on workforce goals and policies and establishes the National Center for Health Workforce Analysis to undertake state and regional workforce data collection and analysis.

Implementation: Initial appointments to the National Health Care Workforce made by September 30, 2010

Implementation update: On September 30, 2010, the Government Accountability Office announced the appointment of 15 members of the National Health Care Workforce Commission.

Medicaid Community-Based Services

Provides states with new options for offering home and community-based services through a Medicaid state plan amendment to certain individuals and permits states to extend full Medicaid benefits to individuals receiving home and community-based services under a state plan.

Implementation: October 1, 2010

Implementation update: On August 6, 2010, the Centers for Medicare and Medicaid Services issued a letter to State Medicaid Directors providing guidance on the new flexibility to provide home and community-based services through Medicaid.

2011 (21 total, 18 in effect)

Minimum Medical Loss Ratio for Insurers

Requires health plans to report the proportion of premium dollars spent on clinical services, quality, and other costs and provide rebates to consumers if the share of the premium spent on clinical services and quality is less than 85% for plans in the large group market and 80% for plans in the individual and small group markets.

Implementation: Requirement to provide rebates begins for coverage purchased in 2011, with the rebates issued to enrollees the year following (e.g., 2011 rebates will be provided in 2012).

Implementation update: On November 22, 2010, the Department of Health and Human Services issued an interim final rule on medical loss ratio (MLR) calculations that will apply to plans in the small and large group markets and individual insurance companies. Several states have gotten temporary waivers from CCIIO and will be exempt from the MLR requirements for a specific period of time.

Closing the Medicare Drug Coverage Gap

Requires pharmaceutical manufacturers to provide a 50% discount on brand-name prescriptions filled in the Medicare Part D coverage gap beginning in 2011 and begins phasing-in federal subsidies for generic prescriptions filled in the Medicare Part D coverage gap.

Implementation: January 1, 2011

Implementation update: On December 17, 2010, CMS sent a letter to pharmaceutical companies providing operational guidance for pharmaceutical manufacturers participating in the Medicare Coverage Gap Discount Program. According to the guidance, the Discount Program became effective January 1, 2011. On June 28, 2011, CMS announced that nearly 500,000 people had received a discount on their brand-name prescription drugs, with an average savings of $545 per beneficiary. As of August 4, 2011, 900,000 Medicare beneficiaries who hit the prescription drug doughnut hole received a 50 percent discount on their prescription drugs.

Medicare Payments for Primary Care

Provides a 10% Medicare bonus payment for primary care services; also, provides a 10% Medicare bonus payment to general surgeons practicing in health professional shortage areas.

Implementation: January 1, 2011 through December 31, 2015

Implementation update: On November 29, 2010, CMS published a final rule that implements the 10 percent incentive payment for primary care services.

Medicare Prevention Benefits

Eliminates cost-sharing for Medicare-covered preventive services that are recommended (rated A or B) by the U.S. Preventive Services Task Force and waives the Medicare deductible for colorectal cancer screening tests; authorizes Medicare coverage for a personalized prevention plan, including a comprehensive health risk assessment.

Implementation: January 1, 2011

Implementation update: On November 29, 2010, CMS published a final rule that will augment the benefits for the "Initial Preventive

Physical Examination," an annual visit for the purposes of developing a prevention plan for the patient. On December 2010, CMS released a Medicare Consumer Guide to Preventative Services, including services that will no longer require cost-sharing (co-pays) in 2011 as a result of the health reform law. As of October 6, 2011, CMS reported that 20.5 million people had participated in the free Annual Wellness Visit or received other preventive services with no cost-sharing.

Center for Medicare and Medicaid Innovation

Creates the Center for Medicare and Medicaid Innovation to test new payment and delivery system models that reduce costs while maintaining or improving quality.

Implementation: Center established by January 1, 2011

Implementation update: On November 17, 2010, CMS issued a notice announcing the establishment of the Center for Medicare and Medicaid Innovation in its organization.

Medicare Premiums for Higher-Income Beneficiaries

Freezes the income threshold for income-related Medicare Part B premiums for 2011 through 2019 at 2010 levels resulting in more people paying income-related premiums, and reduces the Medicare Part D premium subsidy for those with incomes above $85,000/individual and $170,000/couple.

Implementation: January 1, 2011

Implementation update: On November 4, 2010, CMS issued a fact sheet with Medicare premium information for 2011 reflecting higher premiums for Medicare beneficiaries whose incomes exceed a set threshold. In January 2011, the Social Security Administration released a consumer publication reflecting the changes.

Medicare Advantage Payment Changes

Restructures payments to private Medicare Advantage plans by phasing-in payments set at increasingly smaller percentages of Medicare fee-for-service rates; freezes 2011 payments at 2010 levels; and prohibits Medicare Advantage plans from imposing higher cost-sharing requirements for some Medicare covered benefits than is required under the traditional fee-for-service program.

Implementation: January 1, 2011

Implementation update: The Centers for Medicare and Medicaid Services issued a letter to Medicare Advantage plans on April 5, 2010 announcing the freeze in 2011 payment rates at 2010 levels. On November 22, 2010, CMS issued a proposed rule updating the Medicare Advantage program. On April 15, 2011, CMS issued a final rule updating the Medicare Advantage program.

Medicaid Health Homes

Creates a new Medicaid state option to permit certain Medicaid enrollees to designate a provider as a health home and provides states taking up the option with 90% federal matching payments for two years for health home-related services.

Implementation: January 1, 2011

Implementation update: On November 11, 2010, CMS issued guidance to State Medicaid Directors regarding health homes for Medicaid enrollees.

Chronic Disease Prevention in Medicaid

Provides 3-year grants to states to develop programs to provide Medicaid enrollees with incentives to participate in comprehensive health lifestyle programs and meet certain health behavior targets.

Implementation: January 1, 2011

Implementation update: On February 24, 2011, the Centers for Medicare and Medicaid Services announced the availability of $100 million in grants for states to offer incentives to Medicaid beneficiaries who participate in prevention programs and demonstrate improvements in health risk and outcomes.

CLASS Program

Establishes a national, voluntary insurance program for purchasing community living assistance services and supports (CLASS program).

Implementation: January 1, 2011

Implementation update: On January 28, 2011, HHS issued a notice establishing the Office of Community Living Assistance Services and Supports (CLASS). CLASS website: http://www.aoa.gov/AoARoot/CLASS/index.aspx Learn more: How will the new program designed to provide long term care assistance to people who are functionally disabled work? Understand more about the CLASS Act in this video.

National Quality Strategy

Requires the Secretary of the federal Department of Health and Human Services to develop and update annually a national quality improvement strategy that includes priorities to improve the delivery of health care services, patient health outcomes, and population health.

Implementation: Initial strategy due to Congress by January 1, 2011

Implementation update: On September 11, 2010, HHS issued a request for comment notice on the National Health Care Quality Strategy and Plan. On March 21, 2011, HHS released a report to Congress outlining the priorities set by the National Quality Strategy.

Changes to Tax-Free Savings Accounts

Excludes the costs for over-the-counter drugs not prescribed by a doctor from being reimbursed through a Health Reimbursement Account or health Flexible Spending Account and from being reimbursed on a tax-free basis through a Health Savings Account or Archer Medical Savings Account. Increases the tax on distributions from a health savings account or an Archer MSA that are not used for qualified medical expenses to 20% of the amount used.

Implementation: January 1, 2011

Implementation update: On September 3, 2010, the IRS issued guidance regarding changes on health flexible spending accounts including Health Reimbursement Accounts and health Flexible Spending Accounts noting that over-the-counter medicines prescribed by a doctor could be reimbursed by these tax-savings accounts.

Grants to Establish Wellness Programs
Provides grants for up to five years to small employers that establish wellness programs.

Implementation: Funding authorized beginning in fiscal year 2011

Teaching Health Centers
Establishes Teaching Health Centers and provides payments for primary care residency programs in community-based ambulatory patient care centers.

Implementation: Funding appropriated for five years beginning in fiscal year 2011

Implementation update: On November 29, 2010, HRSA issued guidelines for community-based ambulatory patient care settings that operate a primary care residency program to apply for grants to establish teaching health centers. On January 25, 2011, HHS announced the designation of 11 new Teaching Health Centers.

Medical Malpractice Grants
Authorizes $50 million for five-year demonstration grants to states to develop, implement, and evaluate alternatives to current tort litigations.

Implementation: Authorizes funding beginning fiscal year 2011

Funding for Health Insurance Exchanges
Provides grants to states to begin planning for the establishment of American Health Benefit Exchanges and Small Business Health Options Program Exchanges, which facilitate the purchase of insurance by individuals and small employers.

Implementation: Grants awarded starting March 23, 2011; enrollment in Exchanges begins January 1, 2014

Implementation update: On September 30, 2010, HHS awarded states $49 million to help plan the health insurance Exchanges. On February 17, 2011, HHS awarded "early innovator" grants to seven states. On August 12, 2011, HHS awarded $185 million in grants to 13 states and the District of Columbia to help them build their exchanges.

Learn more: Which states have received grants to establish their health insurance exchanges? Browse exchange data on Statehealthfacts.org.

Nutritional Labeling
Requires disclosure of the nutritional content of standard menu items at chain restaurants and food sold from vending machines.

Implementation: By March 23, 2011

Implementation update: On January 21, 2011, the Food and Drug Administration withdrew the draft guidance it had previously issued and announced it will issue a notice and comment rulemaking process. On April 6, 2011, the FDA published two proposed rules in the Federal Register on nutritional labeling for vending machines and chain restaurants. Establishments whose primary purpose is not selling food, such as movie theaters and bowling alleys, were exempted from the regulations.

Medicaid Payments for Hospital-Acquired Infections
Prohibits federal payments to states for Medicaid services related to certain hospital-acquired infections.

Implementation: July 1, 2011

Implementation update: On February 17, 2011, the Centers for Medicare and Medicaid Services issued a proposed rule that would prohibit federal Medicaid payments to states for health care-acquired infections.

Graduate Medical Education
Increases the number of Graduate Medical Education (GME) training positions by redistributing currently unused slots and promotes training in outpatient settings.

Implementation: July 1, 2011

Implementation update: On November 29, 2010, the Department of Health and Human Services issued a final rule establishing a methodology for determining payments to hospitals for the direct costs of approved graduate medical education programs. The final rule also clarifies whether hospitals can be paid for situations in which one hospital incurs the costs of training medical residents at nonprovider settings. On March 14, 2011, CMS issued an interim final rule making revisions to the reductions and increases to caps on payments to hospitals for residents.

Medicare Independent Payment Advisory Board
Establishes an Independent Advisory Board, comprised of 15 members, to submit legislative proposals containing recommendations to reduce the per capita rate of growth in Medicare spending if spending exceeds targeted growth rates.

Implementation: Funding available October 1, 2011; first recommendations due January 15, 2014

Medicaid Long-Term Care Services
Creates the State Balancing Incentive Program in Medicaid to provide enhanced federal matching payments to increase non-institutionally based long-term care services and establishes the Community First Choice Option in Medicaid to provide community-based attendant support services to certain people with disabilities.

Implementation: October 1, 2011

Implementation update: On February 22, 2011, the Centers for Medicare and Medicaid Services issued a proposed rule to allow states to provide home and community-based attendant services and supports through the Community First Choice Medicaid State plan option.

2012 (10 total, 5 in effect)

Accountable Care Organizations in Medicare
Allows providers organized as accountable care organizations (ACOs) that voluntarily meet quality thresholds to share in the cost savings they achieve for the Medicare program.

Implementation: January 1, 2012

Implementation update: On April 7, 2011, the Department of Health and Human Services published a proposed rule in the Federal Register defining Accountable Care Organizations and set out requirements for governance, legal structure, transparency efforts and the incorporation of evidence-based medicine and quality efforts. HHS also released facts sheets for providers and consumers, as well as fact sheets on legal issues and quality scoring in ACOs. The Federal Trade Commission and Department of Justice issued a joint policy statement on antitrust issues related to ACOs. On May 20, 2011, CMS issued a request for applications for the Pioneer ACO Program, which is targeted at organizations that can demonstrate the improvements in quality and cost-savings of a mature ACO.

Medicare Advantage Plan Payments
Reduces rebates paid to Medicare Advantage plans and provides bonus payments to high-quality plans.

Implementation: January 1, 2012.

Implementation update: On February 28, 2011, the Centers for Medicare and Medicaid Services issued a letter to Medicare Advantage plans announcing payment rates for 2012 that included changes included in the health reform law. On November 22, 2010, CMS announced a proposed rule updating Medicare Advantage plan payments.

Medicare Independence at Home Demonstration
Creates the Independence at Home demonstration program to provide high-need Medicare beneficiaries with primary care services in their home.

Implementation: January 1, 2012

Medicare Provider Payment
Changes Adds a productivity adjustment to the market basket update for certain providers, resulting in lower rates than otherwise would have been paid.

Implementation: Begins calendar, fiscal, or rate year 2012, as appropriate

Fraud and Abuse Prevention
Establishes procedures for screening, oversight, and reporting for providers and suppliers that participate in Medicare, Medicaid, and CHIP; requires additional entities to register under Medicare.

Implementation: January 1, 2012.

Implementation update: On February 2, 2011, the Centers for Medicare and Medicaid Services issued a final rule implementing fraud and abuse prevention initiatives in Medicare, Medicaid, and CHIP. On March 23, 2011, CMS published a notice regarding the fee that new providers and providers updating their information would have to pay in order to fund fraud screening efforts.

Annual Fees on the Pharmaceutical Industry
Imposes new annual fees on the pharmaceutical manufacturing sector.

Implementation: January 1, 2012.

Implementation update: On August 15, 2011, the Internal Revenue Service issued temporary regulations that provide guidance on the annual fee imposed on pharmaceutical companies.

Medicaid Payment Demonstration Projects
Creates new demonstration projects in Medicaid for up to eight states to pay bundled payments for episodes of care that include hospitalizations and to allow pediatric medical providers organized as accountable care organizations to share in cost-savings.

Implementation: January 1, 2012 through December 31, 2016

Data Collection to Reduce Health Care Disparities
Requires enhanced collection and reporting of data on race, ethnicity, sex, primary language, disability status, and for underserved rural and frontier populations.

Implementation: March 23, 2012

Implementation update: On June 30, 2011, HHS published a request for comment in the Federal Register on the proposed data collection standards for race, ethnicity, sex, primary language and disability status.

Medicare Value-Based Purchasing
Establishes a hospital value-based purchasing program in Medicare to pay hospitals based on performance on quality measures and requires plans to be developed to implement value-based purchasing programs for skilled nursing facilities, home health agencies, and ambulatory surgical centers.

Implementation: October 1, 2012.

Implementation update: On January 13, 2011, the Centers for Medicare and Medicaid Services issued a proposed rule that would implement a value-based purchasing program for hospitals in Medicare. On May 6, 2011, CMS published a final rule on the value-based purchasing program.

Reduced Medicare Payments for Hospital Readmissions
Reduces Medicare payments that would otherwise be made to hospitals to account for excess (preventable) hospital readmissions.

Implementation: October 1, 2012

2013 (13 total, 1 in effect)

State Notification Regarding Exchanges
States indicate to the Secretary of HHS whether they will operate an American Health Benefit Exchange.

Implementation: January 1, 2013

Closing the Medicare Drug Coverage Gap
Begins phasing-in federal subsidies for brand-name prescriptions filled in the Medicare Part D coverage gap (reducing coinsurance from 100% in 2010 to 25% in 2020, in addition to the 50% manufacturer brand-name discount).

Implementation: January 1, 2013

Medicare Bundled Payment Pilot Program

Establishes a national Medicare pilot program to develop and evaluate making bundled payments for acute, inpatient hospital services, physician services, outpatient hospital services, and post-acute care services for an episode of care.

Implementation: January 1, 2013

Medicaid Coverage of Preventive Services

Provides a one percentage point increase in federal matching payments for preventive services in Medicaid for states that offer Medicaid coverage with no patient cost sharing for services recommended (rated A or B) by the U.S. Preventive Services Task Force and recommended immunizations.

Implementation: January 1, 2013

Medicaid Payments for Primary Care

Increases Medicaid payments for primary care services provided by primary care doctors to 100% of the Medicare payment rate for 2013 and 2014 (financed with 100% federal funding).

Implementation: January 1, 2013 through December 31. 2014

Itemized Deductions for Medical Expenses

Increases the threshold for the itemized deduction for unreimbursed medical expenses from 7.5% of adjusted gross income to 10% of adjusted gross income; waives the increase for individuals age 65 and older for tax years 2013 through 2016.

Implementation: January 1, 2013

Flexible Spending Account Limits

Limits the amount of contributions to a flexible spending account for medical expenses to $2,500 per year, increased annually by the cost of living adjustment.

Implementation: January 1, 2013

Medicare Tax Increase

Increases the Medicare Part A (hospital insurance) tax rate on wages by 0.9% (from 1.45% to 2.35%) on earnings over $200,000 for individual taxpayers and $250,000 for married couples filing jointly and imposes a 3.8% assessment on unearned income for higher-income taxpayers.

Implementation: January 1, 2013

Employer Retiree Coverage Subsidy

Eliminates the tax-deduction for employers who receive Medicare Part D retiree drug subsidy payments.

Implementation: January 1, 2013

Tax on Medical Devices

Imposes an excise tax of 2.3% on the sale of any taxable medical device.

Implementation: January 1, 2013

Financial Disclosure

Requires disclosure of financial relationships between health entities, including physicians, hospitals, pharmacists, other providers, and manufacturers and distributors of covered drugs, devices, biologicals, and medical supplies.

Implementation: Report to Congress due April 1, 2013

CO-OP Health Insurance Plans

Creates the Consumer Operated and Oriented Plan (CO-OP) to foster the creation of non profit, member-run health insurance companies.

Implementation: CO-OPs established by July 1, 2013

Implementation update: On March 14, 2011, the Department of Health and Human Services (HHS) issued a report on the Consumer Operated and Oriented Plan Program. The report included recommendations by the CO-OP Advisory Board on governance, finance, infrastructure, and compliance. On July 18, 2011, HHS published a proposed rule that would implement the CO-OP program.

Extension of CHIP

Extends authorization and funding for the Children's Health Insurance Program (CHIP) through 2015 (current authorization is through 2013).

Implementation: Fiscal year 2013

2014 (19 total, 0 in effect)

Expanded Medicaid Coverage

Expands Medicaid to all individuals not eligible for Medicare under age 65 (children, pregnant women, parents, and adults without dependent children) with incomes up to 133% FPL and provides enhanced federal matching payments for new eligibles.

Implementation: January 1, 2014 (states have the option to expand coverage to childless adults beginning April 1, 2010)

Presumptive Eligibility for Medicaid

Allows all hospitals participating in Medicaid to make presumptive eligibility determinations for all Medicaid-eligible populations.

Implementation: January 1, 2014

Individual Requirement to Have Insurance

Requires U.S. citizens and legal residents to have qualifying health coverage (there is a phased-in tax penalty for those without coverage, with certain exemptions).

Implementation: January 1, 2014 Learn more: How will the requirement that people be insured or pay a penalty work under the health reform law? This simple infographic explains how "the individual mandate" works.

Health Insurance Exchanges

Creates state-based American Health Benefit Exchanges and Small Business Health Options Program (SHOP) Exchanges, administered by a governmental agency or non-profit organization, through which individuals and small businesses with up to 100 employees can purchase qualified coverage. Exchanges will have a single form for applying for health programs, including coverage through the Exchanges and Medicaid and CHIP programs.

Implementation: January 1, 2014

Implementation update: On July 11, 2011, HHS issued two proposed rules on the health insurance exchanges. The first rule detailed the specifics of how states may set up their exchanges, while the second rule focused on the standards related to risk adjustment, risk corridors and reinsurance provisions. On August 17, 2011, HHS, the Department of the Treasury and the Department of Labor issued three proposed regulations regarding the exchanges, including a rule that expands and simplifies Medicaid eligibility and promotes a system that coordinates coverage between Medicaid and the exchanges, a rule that provides standards for determining eligibility and calculating advance payments for the premium tax credits, and a rule that proposes standards and systems for applying for and enrolling in the insurance plans in the exchanges.

Learn more: Where are states in establishing and implementing their health insurance exchanges? Track state actions with the Exchange Monitor on Statehealthfacts.org.

Health Insurance Premium and Cost Sharing Subsidies

Provides refundable and advanceable tax credits and cost sharing subsidies to eligible individuals. Premium subsidies are available to families with incomes between 133-400% of the federal poverty level to purchase insurance through the Exchanges, while cost sharing subsidies are available to those with incomes up to 250% of the poverty level.

Implementation: January 1, 2014

Guaranteed Availability of Insurance

Requires guarantee issue and renewability of health insurance regardless of health status and allows rating variation based only on age (limited to a 3 to 1 ratio), geographic area, family composition, and tobacco use (limited to 1.5. to 1 ratio) in the individual and the small group market and the Exchanges.

Implementation: January 1, 2014

No Annual Limits on Coverage

Prohibits annual limits on the dollar value of coverage.

Implementation: January 1, 2014

Essential Health Benefits

Creates an essential health benefits package that provides a comprehensive set of services, limiting annual cost-sharing to the Health Savings Account limits ($5,950/individual and $11,900/family in 2010). Creates four categories of plans to be offered through the Exchanges, and in the individual and small group markets, varying based on the proportion of plan benefits they cover.

Implementation: January 1, 2014

Multi-State Health Plans

Requires the Office of Personnel Management to contract with insurers to offer at least two multi-state plans in each Exchange. At least one plan must be offered by a non-profit entity and at least one plan must not provide coverage for abortions beyond those permitted by federal law.

Implementation: January 1, 2014

Temporary Reinsurance Program for Health Plans

Creates a temporary reinsurance program to collect payments from health insurers in the individual and group markets to provide payments to plans in the individual market that cover high-risk individuals.

Implementation: January 1, 2014 through December 31, 2016

Basic Health Plan

Permits states the option to create a Basic Health Plan for uninsured individuals with incomes between 133-200% FPL who would otherwise be eligible to receive premium subsidies in the Exchange.

Implementation: January 1, 2014

Employer Requirements

Assesses a fee of $2,000 per full-time employee, excluding the first 30 employees, on employers with more than 50 employees that do not offer coverage and have at least one full-time employee who receives a premium tax credit. Employers with more than 50 employees that offer coverage but have at least one full-time employee receiving a premium tax credit, will pay the lesser of $3,000 for each employee receiving a premium credit or $2,000 for each full-time employee, excluding the first 30 employees.

Implementation: January 1, 2014 Learn more: Larger employers will have to pay a penalty if they don't provide comprehensive, affordable coverage to their employees. Find out how employer responsibilities will work with this simple infographic.

Medicare Advantage Plan Loss Ratios

Requires Medicare Advantage plans to have medical loss ratios no lower than 85%.

Implementation: January 1, 2014

Wellness Programs in Insurance

Permits employers to offer employees rewards of up to 30%, potentially increasing to 50%, of the cost of coverage for participating in a wellness program and meeting certain health-related standards; establishes 10-state pilot programs to permit participating states to apply similar rewards for participating in wellness programs in the individual market.

Implementation: Changes to employer wellness plans effective January 1, 2014; 10-state pilot programs established by July 1, 2014

Fees on Health Insurance Sector

Imposes new fees on the health insurance sector.

Implementation: January 1, 2014

Medicare Independent Payment Advisory Board Report

Establishes an Independent Advisory Board, comprised of 15 members, to submit legislative proposals containing recommendations to reduce the per capita rate of growth in Medicare spending if spending exceeds a target growth rate.

Implementation: First recommendations due January 15, 2014 (Funding available October 1, 2011)

Medicare Disproportionate Share Hospital Payments

Reduces Medicare Disproportionate Share Hospital (DSH) payments initially by 75% and subsequently increases payments based on the percent of the population uninsured and the amount of uncompensated care provided.

Implementation: October 1, 2014

Medicaid Disproportionate Share Hospital Payments

Reduces states' Medicaid Disproportionate Share Hospital (DSH) allotments and requires the Secretary to develop a methodology for distributing the DSH reductions.

Implementation: October 1, 2014

Medicare Payments for Hospital-Acquired Infections

Reduces Medicare payments to certain hospitals for hospital-acquired conditions by 1%.

Implementation: Fiscal Year 2015

2015 (1 total, 0 in effect)

Increase Federal Match for CHIP

Provides for a 23 percentage point increase in the Children's Health Insurance Program (CHIP) match rate up to a cap of 100%.

Implementation: October 1, 2015

2016 (1 total, 0 in effect)

Health Care Choice Compacts

Permits states to form health care choice compacts and allows insurers to sell policies in any state participating in the compact.

Implementation: January 1, 2016

2018 (1 total, 0 in effect)

Tax on High-Cost Insurance

Imposes an excise tax on insurers of employer-sponsored health plans with aggregate expenses that exceed $10,200 for individual coverage and $27,500 for family coverage.

Implementation: January 1, 2018

Source: Implementation Timeline, healthreform.kff.org, The Henry J. Kaiser Family Foundation

This information was reprinted with permission from the Henry J. Kaiser Family Foundation. The Kaiser Family Foundation, a leader in health policy analysis, health journalism and communication, is dedicated to filling the need for trusted, independent information on the biggest health issues facing our nation and its people. The Foundation is a non-profit private operating foundation based in Menlo Park, California.

State Statistics & Rankings

Covered by Some Type of Health Insurance

All Persons		Under 18 Years		Under 65 Years		65 Years and Over	
State	**Percent[1]**	**State**	**Percent[1]**	**State**	**Percent[1]**	**State**	**Percent[1]**
Massachusetts	94.4 (0.6)	Hawaii	97.7 (0.7)	Massachusetts	93.7 (0.7)	New Hampshire	100.0 (0.0)
Hawaii	92.3 (0.7)	West Virginia	97.3 (0.8)	Hawaii	91.2 (0.9)	Colorado	99.8 (0.2)
Maine	90.6 (0.7)	Massachusetts	96.2 (1.0)	Vermont	89.2 (0.9)	Kansas	99.8 (0.2)
Wisconsin	90.6 (0.8)	Vermont	95.9 (1.1)	Wisconsin	89.1 (0.9)	Missouri	99.8 (0.2)
Vermont	90.5 (0.8)	Maine	95.6 (0.9)	Maine	88.8 (0.9)	Oklahoma	99.8 (0.2)
Minnesota	90.2 (0.6)	Wisconsin	95.4 (0.7)	Minnesota	88.8 (0.7)	Oregon	99.8 (0.2)
New Hampshire	89.7 (0.7)	District of Columbia	94.9 (1.3)	New Hampshire	88.2 (0.9)	South Dakota	99.7 (0.3)
Connecticut	89.0 (0.7)	Michigan	94.9 (0.7)	Connecticut	87.7 (0.8)	Kentucky	99.6 (0.3)
Pennsylvania	89.0 (0.7)	Rhode Island	94.7 (1.0)	Delaware	87.3 (1.0)	Maine	99.6 (0.3)
Delaware	88.7 (0.9)	New Hampshire	94.5 (1.0)	Pennsylvania	87.1 (0.9)	North Dakota	99.5 (0.5)
Rhode Island	88.6 (0.9)	Washington	94.1 (0.9)	Rhode Island	86.9 (1.0)	Utah	99.5 (0.5)
Iowa	87.7 (1.1)	Connecticut	94.0 (0.9)	District of Columbia	86.2 (1.2)	Vermont	99.4 (0.4)
District of Columbia	87.5 (1.1)	Delaware	94.0 (1.0)	Iowa	86.2 (1.3)	Minnesota	99.3 (0.3)
Kansas	87.3 (1.1)	Indiana	94.0 (1.6)	Colorado	85.5 (0.9)	Pennsylvania	99.3 (0.3)
Colorado	87.0 (0.8)	Minnesota	94.0 (0.9)	Maryland	85.5 (1.0)	Tennessee	99.1 (0.5)
Michigan	87.0 (0.7)	South Dakota	93.4 (1.1)	Kansas	85.3 (1.3)	West Virginia	99.1 (0.4)
South Dakota	87.0 (0.8)	Kentucky	93.2 (1.2)	Michigan	85.1 (0.8)	Wisconsin	99.1 (0.6)
Maryland	86.9 (0.9)	Arkansas	92.6 (1.7)	Nebraska	85.1 (0.9)	Washington	99.0 (0.6)
North Dakota	86.9 (0.9)	Iowa	92.6 (1.7)	North Dakota	85.0 (1.0)	Idaho	98.9 (0.8)
Nebraska	86.7 (0.8)	Kansas	92.5 (1.6)	South Dakota	85.0 (1.0)	Michigan	98.9 (0.5)
Indiana	86.6 (1.0)	Illinois	92.4 (1.1)	Utah	84.8 (1.2)	Mississippi	98.9 (0.7)
West Virginia	86.5 (1.4)	Colorado	92.2 (1.1)	Indiana	84.7 (1.2)	North Carolina	98.9 (0.6)
Utah	86.4 (1.1)	New York	92.1 (1.0)	Ohio	84.5 (0.9)	Nebraska	98.6 (0.9)
Ohio	86.3 (0.8)	Tennessee	92.1 (1.5)	West Virginia	84.5 (1.7)	Rhode Island	98.6 (0.7)
Washington	86.2 (1.0)	Pennsylvania	91.8 (1.4)	Virginia	84.3 (0.9)	Virginia	98.6 (0.5)
Missouri	86.0 (1.1)	Ohio	91.7 (1.0)	Washington	84.3 (1.0)	Wyoming	98.6 (0.8)
Virginia	85.9 (0.8)	Virginia	91.7 (1.2)	Missouri	83.9 (1.3)	Massachusetts	98.5 (0.7)
Tennessee	85.3 (1.1)	Montana	91.2 (1.5)	Illinois	83.4 (1.0)	South Carolina	98.5 (0.6)
Illinois	85.2 (0.9)	Alabama	91.1 (2.5)	New York	83.3 (0.7)	Hawaii	98.4 (0.7)
Kentucky	85.1 (1.2)	Missouri	91.1 (2.5)	Tennessee	83.3 (1.2)	Indiana	98.4 (0.6)
New York	85.0 (0.7)	Idaho	91.0 (1.9)	Kentucky	83.0 (1.4)	Iowa	98.4 (0.9)
Alabama	84.6 (1.3)	Louisiana	91.0 (1.8)	Alabama	82.6 (1.6)	Montana	98.4 (0.8)
New Jersey	84.6 (1.0)	Maryland	90.8 (1.4)	New Jersey	82.6 (1.2)	Ohio	98.3 (0.7)
Oregon	83.8 (1.1)	New Jersey	90.8 (1.2)	United States	81.6 (0.2)	Illinois	98.1 (0.6)
United States	83.7 (0.1)	North Carolina	90.8 (1.2)	Oregon	81.3 (1.3)	Nevada	98.1 (0.8)
North Carolina	83.0 (1.0)	United States	90.2 (0.2)	Alaska	80.7 (1.2)	United States	98.0 (0.1)
Oklahoma	83.0 (1.3)	Georgia	90.1 (1.4)	North Carolina	80.7 (1.1)	Louisiana	97.9 (1.2)
Wyoming	82.7 (0.9)	North Dakota	89.8 (1.7)	Wyoming	80.7 (1.1)	Maryland	97.9 (0.6)
Alaska	82.0 (1.1)	Wyoming	89.8 (1.5)	Oklahoma	80.3 (1.5)	New Jersey	97.9 (0.7)
Montana	81.9 (1.2)	Nebraska	89.7 (1.5)	Arizona	78.8 (1.4)	Connecticut	97.8 (0.8)
Arkansas	81.3 (1.5)	Oregon	89.6 (1.5)	Arkansas	78.8 (1.8)	New Mexico	97.8 (1.0)
Arizona	80.9 (1.3)	California	89.3 (0.7)	Georgia	78.8 (1.3)	Delaware	97.7 (0.8)
Idaho	80.8 (1.5)	Utah	88.6 (1.6)	Montana	78.7 (1.5)	Florida	97.7 (0.4)
California	80.6 (0.5)	Oklahoma	88.1 (1.6)	California	78.6 (0.5)	Georgia	97.6 (0.9)
Georgia	80.6 (1.2)	Mississippi	86.6 (2.8)	Idaho	78.3 (1.7)	District of Columbia	96.9 (0.9)
Louisiana	80.0 (1.2)	Alaska	86.3 (2.1)	Louisiana	77.6 (1.4)	New York	96.9 (0.9)
South Carolina	79.4 (1.1)	New Mexico	86.3 (2.3)	South Carolina	76.3 (1.3)	Alabama	96.8 (2.1)
Florida	79.2 (0.8)	Florida	85.8 (1.3)	Nevada	76.1 (1.6)	Alaska	96.8 (1.3)
Mississippi	78.9 (1.3)	South Carolina	85.8 (2.1)	Mississippi	75.9 (1.4)	Arizona	96.6 (1.0)
Nevada	78.7 (1.4)	Arizona	85.0 (2.3)	Florida	75.4 (0.9)	California	96.3 (0.5)
New Mexico	78.4 (1.5)	Texas	83.7 (0.9)	New Mexico	75.3 (1.7)	Texas	96.0 (0.7)
Texas	75.4 (0.8)	Nevada	82.5 (2.0)	Texas	73.1 (0.9)	Arkansas	95.5 (1.6)

Note: (1) Standard error appears in parenthesis; figures cover 2010; (b) base less than 75,000; (x) not applicable
Source: U.S. Census Bureau, Current Population Survey, 2011 Annual Social and Economic Supplement. Table HI05. Health Insurance Coverage Status and Type of Coverage by State and Age for All People: 2010

Covered by Private Health Insurance

All Persons		Under 18 Years		Under 65 Years		65 Years and Over	
State	Percent[1]	State	Percent[1]	State	Percent[1]	State	Percent[1]
New Hampshire	77.6 (1.2)	New Hampshire	82.5 (1.8)	New Hampshire	80.6 (1.3)	North Dakota	74.4 (3.6)
North Dakota	75.2 (1.4)	Minnesota	74.4 (1.9)	Massachusetts	76.0 (1.6)	Oregon	73.5 (3.4)
Minnesota	74.8 (1.1)	Massachusetts	73.6 (2.9)	Utah	75.9 (1.7)	Iowa	73.4 (4.4)
Massachusetts	74.6 (1.4)	North Dakota	73.0 (2.4)	Connecticut	75.4 (1.3)	Minnesota	71.9 (3.1)
Wisconsin	74.3 (1.5)	Utah	73.0 (2.6)	Minnesota	75.3 (1.3)	Wisconsin	70.2 (3.6)
Connecticut	74.1 (1.2)	Wisconsin	72.5 (1.8)	North Dakota	75.3 (1.3)	Pennsylvania	69.8 (2.3)
Iowa	74.0 (1.5)	Connecticut	72.0 (2.0)	Wisconsin	75.1 (1.5)	Kansas	69.5 (3.1)
Utah	73.8 (1.8)	Virginia	71.0 (2.0)	Iowa	74.1 (1.5)	Nebraska	68.7 (3.7)
Maryland	73.2 (1.3)	Iowa	69.8 (2.8)	Maryland	74.0 (1.4)	South Dakota	68.5 (4.2)
Nebraska	72.7 (1.4)	New Jersey	69.4 (2.3)	Nebraska	73.3 (1.4)	Maryland	67.6 (2.3)
Pennsylvania	72.2 (1.1)	South Dakota	69.0 (3.0)	Pennsylvania	72.6 (1.2)	Wyoming	67.5 (4.2)
South Dakota	70.7 (1.7)	Colorado	68.9 (1.9)	Hawaii	72.0 (1.6)	Idaho	67.2 (4.5)
Kansas	70.6 (2.0)	Maryland	68.1 (2.6)	Colorado	71.9 (1.4)	Missouri	67.2 (3.2)
Virginia	70.6 (1.3)	Missouri	67.2 (2.8)	Virginia	71.8 (1.4)	Washington	67.1 (3.1)
Hawaii	70.4 (1.5)	Nebraska	66.5 (2.6)	South Dakota	71.1 (1.7)	Michigan	66.8 (2.8)
Colorado	70.0 (1.4)	Pennsylvania	66.1 (2.1)	New Jersey	70.9 (1.6)	Massachusetts	66.6 (3.5)
New Jersey	69.7 (1.5)	Michigan	65.8 (2.1)	Kansas	70.8 (2.1)	Connecticut	65.0 (3.0)
Missouri	69.1 (2.0)	Rhode Island	65.7 (2.7)	Delaware	69.6 (1.6)	Illinois	65.0 (2.6)
Delaware	68.7 (1.5)	Maine	65.0 (2.6)	Rhode Island	69.5 (1.5)	Delaware	63.4 (3.3)
Oregon	68.4 (1.7)	Ohio	64.8 (2.5)	Missouri	69.4 (2.1)	Maine	63.3 (2.8)
Michigan	68.3 (1.3)	Indiana	64.3 (3.2)	Ohio	68.8 (1.8)	North Carolina	62.9 (2.5)
Vermont	68.0 (1.6)	Kansas	64.2 (3.1)	Vermont	68.8 (1.7)	Vermont	62.4 (3.7)
Wyoming	67.8 (1.6)	Delaware	64.1 (2.5)	Michigan	68.5 (1.3)	Indiana	61.6 (4.5)
Ohio	67.5 (1.7)	Wyoming	63.7 (2.8)	Maine	68.0 (1.5)	New Jersey	61.6 (2.7)
Rhode Island	67.5 (1.4)	Vermont	63.2 (2.5)	Wyoming	67.8 (1.8)	Hawaii	61.2 (2.7)
Maine	67.2 (1.5)	Idaho	63.1 (2.9)	Oregon	67.6 (1.9)	Virginia	61.1 (3.0)
Indiana	66.7 (1.6)	West Virginia	63.0 (4.5)	Indiana	67.4 (2.0)	Kentucky	61.0 (4.2)
Illinois	66.2 (1.2)	Hawaii	62.6 (2.8)	Alabama	66.5 (2.2)	Montana	59.0 (5.5)
Washington	66.1 (1.7)	Oregon	62.5 (3.3)	Illinois	66.3 (1.3)	Ohio	58.8 (3.0)
Alabama	65.4 (1.9)	Nevada	62.2 (2.6)	Washington	66.0 (1.8)	Alabama	58.3 (3.1)
Idaho	64.8 (1.8)	Montana	60.7 (4.8)	United States	64.9 (0.2)	New Hampshire	58.0 (3.0)
United States	64.0 (0.2)	Alabama	60.5 (3.3)	Nevada	64.7 (1.8)	United States	57.9 (0.5)
Kentucky	63.5 (2.7)	New York	60.1 (2.1)	Idaho	64.5 (2.0)	West Virginia	57.2 (3.6)
Nevada	63.0 (1.7)	United States	59.6 (0.4)	New York	64.3 (1.1)	Oklahoma	56.6 (3.1)
New York	62.7 (1.0)	Illinois	59.1 (1.9)	Kentucky	63.8 (2.9)	District of Columbia	55.9 (3.1)
Oklahoma	62.6 (1.7)	Kentucky	58.8 (3.6)	Oklahoma	63.5 (1.9)	Utah	55.5 (5.6)
Montana	62.4 (2.4)	Tennessee	58.3 (2.5)	Alaska	63.3 (2.0)	Rhode Island	55.4 (3.3)
Alaska	62.3 (1.9)	Georgia	56.7 (2.9)	District of Columbia	63.2 (1.6)	Arizona	55.0 (3.5)
District of Columbia	62.3 (1.5)	Alaska	56.4 (3.1)	Tennessee	63.1 (1.8)	Colorado	54.5 (3.3)
West Virginia	61.9 (2.4)	South Carolina	56.2 (2.9)	Montana	63.0 (2.6)	South Carolina	54.1 (3.8)
Tennessee	61.5 (1.5)	Oklahoma	56.0 (3.0)	West Virginia	62.6 (2.9)	New York	51.9 (2.2)
North Carolina	60.1 (1.4)	Florida	55.3 (1.9)	Georgia	61.2 (1.9)	Mississippi	51.7 (4.5)
Georgia	59.8 (1.8)	Washington	55.3 (2.9)	California	60.3 (0.8)	Louisiana	51.4 (6.0)
California	59.1 (0.7)	California	55.1 (1.2)	South Carolina	60.0 (1.8)	Alaska	50.9 (4.9)
South Carolina	59.1 (1.6)	Arizona	53.1 (3.0)	North Carolina	59.7 (1.5)	Tennessee	50.1 (4.8)
Arizona	57.8 (1.7)	Arkansas	52.5 (3.7)	Florida	59.1 (1.2)	California	49.9 (1.5)
Florida	57.2 (1.1)	North Carolina	50.8 (2.5)	Arizona	58.1 (1.9)	Nevada	49.9 (3.3)
Arkansas	55.7 (2.2)	District of Columbia	47.4 (3.0)	Arkansas	58.1 (2.9)	Texas	48.4 (2.3)
Texas	55.1 (1.1)	New Mexico	47.4 (4.1)	Texas	55.9 (1.2)	Florida	48.1 (2.0)
Louisiana	54.2 (2.3)	Texas	47.1 (1.4)	Louisiana	54.6 (2.3)	Georgia	46.4 (3.4)
Mississippi	53.9 (1.5)	Louisiana	45.4 (3.7)	Mississippi	54.3 (1.3)	New Mexico	45.3 (3.6)
New Mexico	52.4 (2.2)	Mississippi	43.9 (2.3)	New Mexico	53.6 (2.5)	Arkansas	41.9 (6.2)

Note: (1) Standard error appears in parenthesis; figures cover 2010; (b) base less than 75,000; (x) not applicable
Source: U.S. Census Bureau, Current Population Survey, 2011 Annual Social and Economic Supplement. Table HI05. Health Insurance Coverage Status and Type of Coverage by State and Age for All People: 2010

Covered by Private Health Insurance: Employment Based

All Persons		Under 18 Years		Under 65 Years		65 Years and Over	
State	Percent[1]	State	Percent[1]	State	Percent[1]	State	Percent[1]
New Hampshire	68.4 (1.3)	New Hampshire	75.3 (2.0)	New Hampshire	73.5 (1.4)	Hawaii	50.9 (2.7)
Utah	65.7 (2.1)	Wisconsin	69.7 (1.9)	Connecticut	69.7 (1.4)	Maryland	48.3 (3.0)
Maryland	65.6 (1.3)	Massachusetts	68.9 (3.0)	Utah	69.4 (2.0)	District of Columbia	42.7 (2.9)
Connecticut	65.2 (1.4)	Connecticut	67.7 (2.3)	Massachusetts	69.1 (1.7)	Delaware	42.4 (3.5)
Massachusetts	64.7 (1.6)	Minnesota	67.7 (1.8)	Maryland	67.9 (1.4)	West Virginia	42.3 (4.0)
Hawaii	63.9 (1.6)	Utah	67.7 (3.0)	Wisconsin	67.9 (1.7)	Michigan	41.2 (3.2)
New Jersey	62.3 (1.5)	New Jersey	65.3 (2.5)	Minnesota	67.7 (1.3)	New Jersey	40.5 (2.8)
Iowa	62.0 (1.4)	Virginia	65.3 (1.8)	Iowa	66.9 (1.4)	Alaska	40.1 (4.4)
Wisconsin	61.9 (1.6)	Iowa	63.8 (2.2)	Hawaii	66.2 (1.7)	Kentucky	39.9 (3.7)
Minnesota	61.8 (1.2)	Maryland	63.7 (2.5)	Pennsylvania	66.0 (1.3)	Maine	39.9 (2.7)
Virginia	61.4 (1.3)	North Dakota	63.1 (2.6)	New Jersey	65.5 (1.7)	Ohio	38.8 (2.8)
Delaware	61.1 (1.6)	Pennsylvania	62.6 (2.0)	Virginia	64.5 (1.3)	Massachusetts	38.6 (3.5)
Pennsylvania	61.1 (1.2)	South Dakota	62.1 (3.5)	Delaware	64.2 (1.8)	Virginia	37.0 (2.7)
Ohio	60.2 (1.7)	Rhode Island	61.3 (2.7)	Rhode Island	63.9 (1.6)	New York	36.5 (2.1)
Indiana	59.5 (1.7)	Michigan	61.2 (2.1)	Kansas	63.5 (2.1)	Indiana	35.6 (3.8)
Michigan	59.5 (1.4)	Ohio	60.8 (2.6)	Nebraska	63.4 (1.9)	North Dakota	35.5 (3.5)
North Dakota	59.2 (1.7)	West Virginia	60.8 (4.4)	Ohio	63.4 (1.8)	Connecticut	35.4 (2.8)
Rhode Island	58.7 (1.5)	Maine	60.7 (2.6)	Indiana	63.2 (2.1)	Pennsylvania	35.2 (2.1)
Vermont	58.7 (1.7)	Indiana	60.6 (3.3)	Vermont	63.2 (1.8)	New Hampshire	35.1 (3.0)
Nebraska	58.6 (1.8)	Nebraska	60.4 (2.7)	North Dakota	62.7 (1.9)	Oklahoma	34.3 (3.4)
Colorado	58.4 (1.3)	Missouri	60.1 (3.0)	Michigan	62.4 (1.4)	Illinois	33.9 (2.6)
Maine	58.3 (1.5)	Delaware	60.0 (2.7)	Maine	62.0 (1.6)	New Mexico	33.7 (3.2)
Wyoming	58.3 (1.8)	Colorado	59.7 (2.1)	South Dakota	61.9 (2.2)	Utah	33.4 (5.8)
Alaska	58.2 (2.1)	Kansas	58.9 (3.2)	Wyoming	61.7 (1.8)	Alabama	33.2 (4.0)
Kansas	58.1 (1.9)	Wyoming	58.3 (2.7)	Colorado	61.6 (1.4)	United States	32.5 (0.5)
West Virginia	57.9 (2.5)	Vermont	57.8 (2.4)	Missouri	61.0 (2.1)	Wyoming	32.0 (4.0)
Illinois	57.4 (1.1)	Hawaii	57.7 (2.7)	Illinois	60.7 (1.3)	Colorado	31.7 (2.7)
Missouri	57.0 (1.8)	New York	56.9 (2.3)	West Virginia	60.3 (2.9)	North Carolina	31.3 (3.0)
Kentucky	56.6 (2.4)	Nevada	56.7 (2.6)	Alabama	60.0 (2.6)	Missouri	31.2 (2.8)
New York	56.5 (1.0)	Kentucky	56.0 (3.5)	Oregon	59.9 (1.9)	Oregon	30.7 (4.2)
Alabama	56.4 (2.7)	Alabama	55.8 (3.3)	Alaska	59.8 (2.2)	Washington	30.4 (3.0)
South Dakota	56.2 (2.1)	Oregon	55.5 (3.4)	New York	59.5 (1.1)	Louisiana	30.2 (6.5)
Oregon	55.9 (1.7)	United States	54.8 (0.4)	Kentucky	59.1 (2.6)	Georgia	30.0 (3.1)
Washington	55.4 (1.6)	Illinois	54.6 (1.8)	Washington	59.1 (1.7)	Nevada	30.0 (2.9)
United States	55.3 (0.2)	Alaska	54.4 (3.3)	United States	58.6 (0.2)	Texas	30.0 (2.2)
Oklahoma	55.2 (1.6)	Montana	53.6 (4.0)	Oklahoma	58.5 (1.7)	California	29.9 (1.3)
District of Columbia	54.8 (1.4)	Tennessee	52.1 (2.6)	Nevada	57.3 (1.8)	Florida	28.5 (1.7)
Nevada	54.2 (1.8)	Oklahoma	51.9 (2.6)	Tennessee	56.8 (2.0)	Vermont	28.5 (3.6)
Tennessee	52.6 (1.7)	Georgia	51.5 (3.0)	District of Columbia	56.6 (1.6)	Rhode Island	27.9 (2.7)
Georgia	52.3 (1.8)	Idaho	50.9 (2.9)	Georgia	54.7 (1.9)	Wisconsin	27.4 (2.5)
North Carolina	51.6 (1.4)	Florida	50.6 (1.8)	North Carolina	54.5 (1.5)	Arizona	27.1 (3.5)
California	50.2 (0.7)	South Carolina	50.6 (2.7)	South Carolina	54.2 (1.9)	Iowa	26.7 (3.0)
Idaho	50.2 (1.5)	Washington	50.4 (2.6)	Idaho	53.8 (1.7)	Mississippi	26.5 (3.7)
South Carolina	50.0 (1.7)	California	49.1 (1.1)	Arkansas	52.9 (2.7)	South Carolina	24.9 (3.5)
Arizona	49.3 (1.8)	Arkansas	48.5 (3.8)	California	52.9 (0.8)	Idaho	24.6 (3.7)
Texas	49.2 (1.1)	Arizona	47.3 (2.8)	Florida	52.8 (1.2)	Nebraska	24.3 (3.2)
Florida	48.6 (1.0)	North Carolina	46.9 (2.5)	Montana	52.8 (2.5)	Montana	23.5 (3.7)
Montana	48.1 (2.5)	New Mexico	44.8 (3.9)	Arizona	52.2 (1.9)	Kansas	23.1 (2.2)
Arkansas	47.7 (2.4)	Texas	44.3 (1.4)	Texas	51.4 (1.2)	Minnesota	22.6 (2.7)
Louisiana	46.6 (2.3)	District of Columbia	43.6 (2.9)	Louisiana	48.9 (2.2)	Tennessee	22.6 (3.3)
New Mexico	46.4 (2.1)	Louisiana	40.6 (3.4)	New Mexico	48.4 (2.3)	South Dakota	20.4 (3.4)
Mississippi	45.2 (1.7)	Mississippi	40.4 (2.3)	Mississippi	48.0 (1.6)	Arkansas	17.8 (2.6)

Note: (1) Standard error appears in parenthesis; figures cover 2010; (b) base less than 75,000; (x) not applicable
Source: U.S. Census Bureau, Current Population Survey, 2011 Annual Social and Economic Supplement. Table HI05. Health Insurance Coverage Status and Type of Coverage by State and Age for All People: 2010

Covered by Private Health Insurance: Own Employment Based

All Persons		Under 18 Years		Under 65 Years		65 Years and Over	
State	**Percent[1]**	**State**	**Percent[1]**	**State**	**Percent[1]**	**State**	**Percent[1]**
District of Columbia	38.7 (1.0)	Indiana	0.7 (0.3)	District of Columbia	38.9 (1.1)	Hawaii	40.9 (2.7)
Hawaii	37.4 (1.0)	Minnesota	0.7 (0.3)	Hawaii	36.7 (1.1)	District of Columbia	37.0 (2.6)
Maryland	34.2 (0.8)	District of Columbia	0.6 (0.4)	Maryland	33.9 (0.8)	Maryland	36.3 (2.6)
Massachusetts	32.1 (1.0)	Maryland	0.6 (0.3)	New Hampshire	33.4 (0.8)	Michigan	32.2 (2.6)
New Hampshire	32.1 (0.8)	Arizona	0.5 (0.3)	Pennsylvania	33.1 (0.7)	Maine	32.0 (2.4)
Pennsylvania	31.9 (0.6)	Florida	0.4 (0.1)	Iowa	33.0 (1.1)	New Jersey	31.9 (2.3)
Maine	31.8 (0.9)	Maine	0.4 (0.2)	Minnesota	32.9 (0.9)	Kentucky	31.1 (3.1)
North Dakota	31.7 (1.3)	Massachusetts	0.4 (0.2)	North Dakota	32.7 (1.4)	West Virginia	31.1 (3.0)
Iowa	31.6 (1.0)	Nebraska	0.4 (0.3)	Kansas	32.4 (1.0)	Delaware	30.2 (2.5)
Delaware	31.5 (0.9)	Oklahoma	0.4 (0.3)	Massachusetts	32.4 (1.0)	Massachusetts	29.9 (2.8)
Alaska	31.4 (1.2)	West Virginia	0.4 (0.4)	Connecticut	32.0 (0.8)	Alaska	29.0 (3.7)
Connecticut	31.4 (0.7)	Connecticut	0.3 (0.2)	Wisconsin	32.0 (1.0)	Ohio	28.1 (2.0)
Ohio	31.0 (0.8)	Illinois	0.3 (0.1)	Alaska	31.7 (1.2)	Wyoming	28.1 (3.8)
Wyoming	31.0 (1.0)	Mississippi	0.3 (0.3)	Delaware	31.7 (1.0)	New York	27.8 (1.7)
Kentucky	30.9 (1.3)	New York	0.3 (0.1)	Maine	31.7 (0.9)	Virginia	27.7 (2.3)
Minnesota	30.8 (0.8)	Ohio	0.3 (0.1)	Washington	31.7 (0.8)	Connecticut	27.5 (2.2)
Kansas	30.5 (0.8)	Alabama	0.2 (0.2)	Oregon	31.6 (1.1)	Oklahoma	27.5 (3.1)
Washington	30.5 (0.8)	California	0.2 (0.1)	Vermont	31.6 (1.0)	Indiana	26.9 (3.2)
Missouri	30.2 (1.1)	Kansas	0.2 (0.2)	Ohio	31.4 (0.8)	Illinois	26.7 (2.1)
Virginia	30.2 (0.8)	Kentucky	0.2 (0.2)	Wyoming	31.4 (0.9)	Pennsylvania	25.5 (1.7)
Illinois	30.0 (0.6)	Michigan	0.2 (0.2)	Nebraska	31.3 (1.2)	North Carolina	25.2 (2.6)
New Jersey	30.0 (0.7)	Nevada	0.2 (0.1)	Missouri	31.2 (1.3)	North Dakota	25.1 (2.0)
Oregon	30.0 (0.9)	New Mexico	0.2 (0.2)	South Dakota	31.2 (1.1)	United States	24.5 (0.4)
Colorado	29.9 (0.7)	North Dakota	0.2 (0.2)	Kentucky	30.9 (1.3)	Louisiana	24.4 (5.4)
Vermont	29.9 (1.0)	Texas	0.2 (0.1)	Colorado	30.8 (0.7)	New Mexico	24.2 (2.4)
Wisconsin	29.8 (0.9)	United States	0.2 (0.0)	Illinois	30.5 (0.7)	Missouri	23.7 (2.4)
West Virginia	29.7 (1.2)	Virginia	0.2 (0.1)	Virginia	30.5 (0.8)	Alabama	23.6 (2.9)
Oklahoma	29.5 (1.2)	Washington	0.2 (0.1)	Rhode Island	30.4 (0.9)	New Hampshire	23.3 (2.0)
Alabama	29.4 (1.8)	Wisconsin	0.2 (0.1)	Alabama	30.3 (1.8)	Arizona	23.2 (3.2)
Nebraska	29.4 (1.2)	Alaska	0.1 (0.1)	North Carolina	29.9 (0.9)	Georgia	23.2 (2.5)
North Carolina	29.3 (0.9)	Arkansas	0.1 (0.1)	Oklahoma	29.9 (1.2)	Utah	23.1 (4.5)
New York	29.1 (0.5)	Colorado	0.1 (0.1)	New Jersey	29.7 (0.8)	Colorado	23.0 (2.0)
Indiana	28.9 (0.8)	Georgia	0.1 (0.1)	Tennessee	29.5 (1.2)	Texas	22.9 (1.8)
South Dakota	28.9 (1.1)	Iowa	0.1 (0.1)	West Virginia	29.5 (1.5)	Washington	22.6 (2.2)
Rhode Island	28.8 (0.9)	Louisiana	0.1 (0.1)	Nevada	29.4 (1.0)	California	22.3 (1.1)
United States	28.6 (0.1)	Missouri	0.1 (0.1)	New York	29.3 (0.6)	Iowa	22.0 (3.1)
Nevada	28.5 (1.0)	New Hampshire	0.1 (0.1)	Indiana	29.2 (1.0)	Nevada	21.7 (2.4)
Michigan	28.2 (0.7)	New Jersey	0.1 (0.1)	United States	29.2 (0.1)	Florida	21.5 (1.5)
Utah	28.0 (1.0)	North Carolina	0.1 (0.1)	Florida	28.7 (0.7)	Mississippi	20.4 (2.5)
Tennessee	27.9 (1.0)	Oregon	0.1 (0.1)	Utah	28.6 (0.9)	Oregon	19.8 (3.0)
Florida	27.4 (0.6)	Pennsylvania	0.1 (0.1)	South Carolina	28.4 (1.0)	Rhode Island	19.4 (2.1)
South Carolina	26.8 (1.0)	Utah	0.1 (0.1)	Arkansas	27.9 (1.4)	Vermont	18.8 (2.5)
California	25.9 (0.4)	Wyoming	0.1 (0.1)	Michigan	27.5 (0.7)	Kansas	18.1 (2.0)
Georgia	25.9 (0.9)	Delaware	0.0 (0.0)	California	26.3 (0.4)	Idaho	17.5 (2.2)
Arizona	25.7 (0.9)	Hawaii	0.0 (0.0)	Montana	26.3 (1.3)	South Carolina	17.5 (2.5)
Arkansas	25.7 (1.2)	Idaho	0.0 (0.0)	Arizona	26.1 (1.0)	Wisconsin	17.4 (1.7)
Texas	25.6 (0.6)	Montana	0.0 (0.0)	Georgia	26.1 (0.9)	Minnesota	16.9 (2.0)
Mississippi	25.1 (0.9)	Rhode Island	0.0 (0.0)	Texas	25.9 (0.6)	Tennessee	16.2 (2.7)
Montana	24.6 (1.4)	South Carolina	0.0 (0.0)	Mississippi	25.8 (0.9)	Montana	16.0 (2.7)
Idaho	24.3 (0.8)	South Dakota	0.0 (0.0)	Idaho	25.3 (0.8)	Nebraska	15.6 (1.9)
New Mexico	23.8 (1.0)	Tennessee	0.0 (0.0)	New Mexico	23.8 (1.2)	South Dakota	14.3 (2.7)
Louisiana	23.4 (1.5)	Vermont	0.0 (0.0)	Louisiana	23.3 (1.2)	Arkansas	13.1 (1.9)

Note: (1) Standard error appears in parenthesis; figures cover 2010; (b) base less than 75,000; (x) not applicable
Source: U.S. Census Bureau, Current Population Survey, 2011 Annual Social and Economic Supplement. Table HI05. Health Insurance Coverage Status and Type of Coverage by State and Age for All People: 2010

Covered by Private Health Insurance: Direct Purchase

All Persons		Under 18 Years		Under 65 Years		65 Years and Over	
State	Percent[1]	State	Percent[1]	State	Percent[1]	State	Percent[1]
North Dakota	18.1 (1.6)	Idaho	16.0 (2.3)	North Dakota	13.7 (1.4)	Minnesota	54.5 (3.1)
South Dakota	17.4 (1.6)	North Dakota	12.0 (2.1)	Idaho	12.9 (1.4)	South Dakota	53.9 (5.5)
Idaho	16.7 (1.3)	Colorado	10.8 (1.3)	Nebraska	11.6 (1.0)	Iowa	51.8 (5.5)
Nebraska	16.0 (0.9)	New Hampshire	10.0 (1.5)	South Dakota	11.6 (1.4)	Kansas	51.0 (2.8)
Minnesota	15.5 (0.7)	Missouri	9.9 (1.7)	Colorado	11.2 (1.2)	Nebraska	47.9 (2.7)
Montana	15.1 (1.4)	Oregon	9.4 (1.3)	Montana	10.7 (1.7)	Wisconsin	47.5 (4.4)
Missouri	14.5 (1.0)	South Dakota	9.2 (1.8)	Missouri	10.4 (1.2)	North Dakota	47.1 (5.1)
Oregon	14.1 (1.1)	Nebraska	9.1 (1.3)	Minnesota	9.7 (0.7)	Oregon	46.4 (5.2)
Pennsylvania	14.0 (0.7)	Minnesota	9.0 (1.1)	Maryland	9.3 (0.9)	Idaho	43.8 (4.4)
Kansas	13.8 (0.6)	Iowa	7.4 (1.6)	Pennsylvania	9.2 (0.7)	Missouri	40.8 (3.2)
Iowa	13.5 (1.7)	Tennessee	7.2 (1.3)	Connecticut	9.1 (0.8)	Vermont	39.8 (3.6)
Colorado	12.9 (1.2)	Maryland	7.0 (1.0)	Oregon	9.0 (0.8)	Washington	39.3 (2.9)
Wisconsin	12.7 (1.0)	Nevada	6.9 (1.3)	New Hampshire	8.5 (0.8)	Pennsylvania	39.2 (2.2)
Connecticut	12.3 (0.9)	California	6.7 (0.5)	Iowa	8.2 (1.1)	Wyoming	38.7 (4.7)
Washington	11.8 (0.9)	Connecticut	6.7 (1.1)	Hawaii	8.1 (1.0)	Montana	37.6 (4.3)
Maryland	11.3 (0.9)	Montana	6.7 (1.9)	Utah	8.1 (1.2)	Illinois	36.1 (2.5)
Tennessee	10.9 (1.1)	Kansas	6.6 (1.5)	District of Columbia	8.0 (0.8)	North Carolina	35.6 (3.2)
Maine	10.7 (0.8)	Pennsylvania	6.4 (1.0)	Kansas	8.0 (0.7)	Connecticut	33.7 (3.1)
New Hampshire	10.7 (0.9)	Arizona	6.3 (1.3)	Tennessee	7.9 (0.9)	Massachusetts	32.2 (3.8)
Vermont	10.6 (0.8)	Hawaii	6.1 (2.1)	Nevada	7.8 (0.9)	Indiana	31.9 (4.2)
Alabama	10.5 (1.1)	Florida	6.0 (0.7)	Washington	7.7 (0.7)	Oklahoma	31.7 (2.8)
Michigan	10.2 (0.8)	Maine	6.0 (1.1)	California	7.6 (0.3)	Tennessee	31.7 (4.4)
Mississippi	10.1 (1.1)	Virginia	6.0 (1.3)	Virginia	7.6 (0.9)	Mississippi	31.1 (5.3)
Illinois	10.0 (0.6)	New Jersey	5.8 (1.1)	Alabama	7.4 (1.0)	Rhode Island	31.0 (2.9)
Indiana	10.0 (0.9)	North Carolina	5.7 (1.0)	Michigan	7.3 (0.8)	South Carolina	31.0 (3.0)
North Carolina	10.0 (0.8)	United States	5.7 (0.2)	Maine	7.2 (0.8)	Alabama	30.4 (4.8)
Utah	9.9 (1.1)	Utah	5.7 (1.3)	Florida	7.1 (0.5)	Arizona	30.3 (3.6)
United States	9.8 (0.1)	Georgia	5.6 (1.0)	United States	7.1 (0.1)	United States	28.8 (0.5)
Virginia	9.8 (0.9)	Illinois	5.6 (0.9)	Mississippi	6.9 (1.2)	Michigan	28.7 (2.8)
Wyoming	9.8 (0.7)	Alabama	5.5 (1.5)	Arizona	6.7 (0.8)	Maine	28.2 (2.7)
Florida	9.7 (0.6)	Vermont	5.5 (1.2)	Indiana	6.6 (0.8)	Virginia	27.5 (2.4)
Nevada	9.7 (0.9)	Michigan	5.4 (1.0)	New Jersey	6.6 (0.7)	Colorado	27.3 (2.7)
Massachusetts	9.6 (0.9)	New York	5.2 (0.7)	Wisconsin	6.6 (0.7)	Arkansas	26.4 (5.5)
Arizona	9.5 (0.9)	Wyoming	5.1 (0.7)	Illinois	6.4 (0.6)	Maryland	26.0 (2.4)
Oklahoma	9.5 (0.9)	South Carolina	4.9 (1.3)	North Carolina	6.4 (0.6)	New Jersey	25.8 (2.4)
Rhode Island	9.5 (0.8)	Delaware	4.8 (1.2)	Louisiana	6.3 (0.9)	Utah	25.8 (3.7)
South Carolina	9.3 (0.8)	Louisiana	4.8 (1.2)	Georgia	6.2 (0.7)	New Hampshire	25.4 (2.9)
California	9.2 (0.3)	Indiana	4.6 (0.9)	New York	6.2 (0.5)	Delaware	24.2 (2.8)
Hawaii	9.1 (1.0)	Oklahoma	4.5 (1.2)	Vermont	6.2 (0.8)	Nevada	23.9 (3.2)
New Jersey	9.1 (0.7)	Washington	4.5 (0.9)	Wyoming	6.1 (0.7)	Louisiana	23.2 (3.7)
Arkansas	9.0 (1.1)	Arkansas	4.4 (1.2)	Arkansas	6.0 (1.0)	Kentucky	23.0 (3.9)
District of Columbia	8.9 (0.8)	District of Columbia	4.4 (1.0)	Oklahoma	6.0 (0.9)	Florida	22.4 (1.7)
Delaware	8.5 (0.8)	Ohio	4.3 (0.7)	Delaware	5.9 (0.8)	California	21.8 (1.3)
Louisiana	8.3 (0.8)	Massachusetts	4.0 (0.9)	Ohio	5.9 (0.5)	Ohio	20.9 (2.7)
Ohio	7.9 (0.7)	Mississippi	3.5 (1.3)	Rhode Island	5.9 (0.8)	Texas	20.8 (1.6)
New York	7.7 (0.5)	Rhode Island	3.5 (0.9)	Massachusetts	5.8 (0.7)	Georgia	18.4 (2.8)
Georgia	7.3 (0.7)	Kentucky	3.1 (1.1)	South Carolina	5.6 (0.8)	New York	18.0 (1.3)
Kentucky	7.0 (1.1)	Wisconsin	3.1 (0.6)	Kentucky	4.7 (0.9)	West Virginia	15.8 (2.6)
Texas	6.1 (0.4)	Texas	3.0 (0.4)	New Mexico	4.7 (0.9)	District of Columbia	15.1 (2.2)
New Mexico	5.7 (0.9)	New Mexico	2.9 (1.1)	Texas	4.5 (0.4)	Hawaii	14.7 (2.1)
Alaska	4.4 (0.7)	Alaska	2.2 (0.7)	Alaska	3.7 (0.6)	Alaska	12.8 (3.5)
West Virginia	4.1 (0.6)	West Virginia	1.7 (0.8)	West Virginia	2.2 (0.5)	New Mexico	12.0 (2.4)

Note: (1) Standard error appears in parenthesis; figures cover 2010; (b) base less than 75,000; (x) not applicable
Source: U.S. Census Bureau, Current Population Survey, 2011 Annual Social and Economic Supplement. Table HI05. Health Insurance Coverage Status and Type of Coverage by State and Age for All People: 2010

Covered by Government Health Insurance

All Persons		Under 18 Years		Under 65 Years		65 Years and Over	
State	Percent[1]	State	Percent[1]	State	Percent[1]	State	Percent[1]
Maine	40.9 (1.5)	District of Columbia	52.6 (2.9)	Maine	30.0 (1.5)	Oklahoma	98.2 (0.7)
New Mexico	37.9 (2.0)	Louisiana	52.5 (3.3)	New Mexico	28.9 (2.1)	Kansas	98.1 (0.8)
West Virginia	37.8 (1.8)	Arkansas	50.8 (3.3)	Vermont	28.8 (1.5)	South Dakota	97.7 (1.0)
Vermont	37.6 (1.5)	Mississippi	49.5 (4.7)	West Virginia	28.7 (1.9)	Oregon	97.3 (0.8)
Hawaii	37.1 (1.5)	New Mexico	48.7 (3.6)	Louisiana	27.9 (1.4)	Vermont	97.1 (1.1)
Arkansas	36.0 (1.7)	Washington	47.6 (2.8)	Hawaii	27.6 (1.6)	Minnesota	97.0 (0.8)
Kentucky	35.7 (2.0)	Hawaii	46.7 (3.0)	Alaska	27.2 (2.0)	Kentucky	96.9 (1.0)
Mississippi	35.6 (1.6)	North Carolina	46.6 (3.1)	District of Columbia	27.2 (1.4)	Iowa	96.8 (1.3)
Louisiana	35.2 (1.4)	Oklahoma	44.9 (3.1)	Kentucky	26.8 (2.0)	Utah	96.3 (1.4)
Tennessee	35.2 (1.4)	Vermont	44.6 (2.6)	Tennessee	26.6 (1.6)	Montana	96.1 (1.0)
District of Columbia	34.9 (1.3)	Alaska	44.1 (3.5)	Mississippi	26.5 (1.5)	New Hampshire	96.1 (1.2)
Oklahoma	34.8 (1.5)	Kentucky	44.0 (3.7)	Arkansas	26.2 (1.5)	Tennessee	96.1 (1.2)
Florida	34.3 (0.8)	West Virginia	43.9 (4.3)	North Carolina	25.5 (2.1)	West Virginia	96.0 (1.5)
North Carolina	34.2 (1.8)	Maine	43.1 (2.8)	Arizona	25.4 (1.8)	Wisconsin	95.8 (1.0)
Washington	33.8 (1.6)	Texas	41.8 (1.3)	Washington	24.8 (1.8)	Maine	95.7 (1.0)
Indiana	33.7 (1.5)	Tennessee	41.6 (2.4)	Oklahoma	24.7 (1.6)	Nebraska	95.7 (1.2)
Montana	33.7 (2.1)	Georgia	41.0 (2.8)	Indiana	24.4 (1.6)	Mississippi	95.6 (1.3)
Arizona	33.5 (1.7)	Indiana	40.6 (3.5)	New York	24.3 (1.1)	North Carolina	95.5 (1.3)
New York	33.2 (1.0)	Illinois	40.4 (2.1)	Delaware	23.3 (1.5)	South Carolina	95.5 (1.2)
Delaware	33.1 (1.5)	California	40.3 (1.1)	Georgia	23.1 (1.5)	Missouri	95.2 (1.1)
Rhode Island	33.1 (1.4)	Montana	39.9 (4.4)	Alabama	22.9 (2.1)	Rhode Island	95.2 (1.1)
Massachusetts	32.7 (1.5)	Florida	38.9 (1.6)	Massachusetts	22.9 (1.7)	Colorado	94.5 (1.3)
Michigan	32.4 (1.2)	New York	38.9 (2.3)	Michigan	22.6 (1.2)	Pennsylvania	94.5 (0.9)
Alabama	32.3 (1.8)	United States	37.9 (0.3)	Rhode Island	22.6 (1.4)	Arizona	94.4 (1.4)
Alaska	32.1 (2.0)	Alabama	37.5 (4.2)	California	22.5 (0.6)	Michigan	94.3 (1.1)
South Carolina	32.1 (1.3)	Delaware	37.5 (2.8)	Florida	22.0 (0.9)	Washington	94.3 (1.3)
Pennsylvania	31.5 (0.9)	Kansas	37.3 (3.0)	United States	21.9 (0.2)	Florida	94.2 (0.7)
Kansas	31.2 (2.0)	Rhode Island	37.2 (2.7)	Montana	21.6 (1.9)	Ohio	94.1 (1.1)
Wisconsin	31.2 (1.2)	Arizona	36.9 (3.2)	South Carolina	21.5 (1.3)	North Dakota	93.8 (1.5)
South Dakota	31.0 (1.3)	Michigan	36.7 (2.3)	Illinois	21.3 (1.0)	Idaho	93.7 (1.9)
United States	31.0 (0.2)	South Carolina	36.3 (3.0)	Kansas	20.8 (2.3)	Nevada	93.6 (1.5)
California	30.5 (0.6)	Idaho	35.6 (2.9)	Texas	20.8 (0.6)	Indiana	93.5 (1.6)
Illinois	29.9 (1.0)	Wyoming	35.2 (2.9)	South Dakota	20.5 (1.2)	New Mexico	93.5 (1.8)
Georgia	29.6 (1.4)	South Dakota	34.6 (2.4)	Colorado	19.8 (1.0)	United States	93.5 (0.2)
Missouri	29.4 (1.5)	Ohio	33.8 (2.2)	Wisconsin	19.8 (1.2)	Connecticut	93.4 (1.3)
Ohio	29.4 (1.1)	Oregon	32.8 (2.6)	Ohio	19.6 (1.3)	Virginia	93.3 (1.4)
Minnesota	29.2 (1.1)	Iowa	32.3 (2.2)	Pennsylvania	19.5 (0.9)	Wyoming	92.9 (1.6)
Oregon	29.1 (1.4)	Pennsylvania	32.1 (2.1)	Missouri	19.1 (1.7)	Illinois	92.5 (1.1)
Texas	27.9 (0.7)	Colorado	31.4 (1.9)	Minnesota	19.0 (1.1)	Delaware	92.4 (1.6)
Colorado	27.8 (1.1)	Missouri	31.3 (1.9)	Virginia	18.9 (1.0)	New York	92.4 (1.1)
Idaho	27.8 (1.2)	Wisconsin	31.1 (2.2)	Idaho	18.6 (1.3)	Georgia	92.3 (1.4)
Nebraska	27.5 (1.1)	Nebraska	30.4 (2.1)	Oregon	18.3 (1.2)	Arkansas	92.2 (2.3)
Virginia	27.4 (1.1)	New Jersey	29.5 (2.3)	Wyoming	18.3 (1.7)	Massachusetts	91.8 (1.6)
Iowa	27.0 (1.1)	Virginia	29.1 (1.9)	Nebraska	18.0 (1.1)	Texas	91.5 (1.0)
Wyoming	26.7 (1.8)	Massachusetts	28.2 (3.1)	Iowa	17.4 (1.0)	Alabama	91.2 (2.6)
Connecticut	26.4 (1.1)	Minnesota	28.1 (1.8)	Nevada	16.4 (1.1)	New Jersey	91.2 (1.4)
North Dakota	26.2 (1.1)	Maryland	27.8 (2.4)	Connecticut	16.3 (1.0)	California	91.1 (0.8)
New Jersey	25.8 (1.1)	Nevada	27.4 (2.5)	Maryland	16.1 (1.1)	Hawaii	90.3 (1.7)
Nevada	25.3 (1.1)	Connecticut	26.6 (1.9)	New Jersey	16.1 (1.1)	Maryland	89.8 (1.4)
Maryland	25.0 (1.1)	North Dakota	25.3 (2.8)	North Dakota	15.9 (1.2)	Alaska	89.2 (2.6)
Utah	23.0 (1.4)	Utah	22.1 (2.6)	Utah	14.5 (1.4)	Louisiana	88.7 (2.3)
New Hampshire	22.3 (1.0)	New Hampshire	17.6 (1.7)	New Hampshire	11.1 (0.9)	District of Columbia	88.2 (1.8)

Note: (1) Standard error appears in parenthesis; figures cover 2010; (b) base less than 75,000; (x) not applicable
Source: U.S. Census Bureau, Current Population Survey, 2011 Annual Social and Economic Supplement. Table HI05. Health Insurance Coverage Status and Type of Coverage by State and Age for All People: 2010

Covered by Government Health Insurance: Medicaid

All Persons		Under 18 Years		Under 65 Years		65 Years and Over	
State	Percent[1]	State	Percent[1]	State	Percent[1]	State	Percent[1]
Vermont	23.4 (1.2)	District of Columbia	50.4 (3.0)	Vermont	25.0 (1.4)	Alaska	16.5 (2.6)
District of Columbia	23.0 (1.2)	Arkansas	49.3 (3.0)	District of Columbia	24.7 (1.4)	Maine	16.2 (2.2)
Maine	21.7 (1.3)	Louisiana	49.0 (3.2)	New Mexico	23.6 (1.7)	California	15.6 (1.1)
New Mexico	21.1 (1.4)	Mississippi	46.9 (5.0)	Maine	22.8 (1.4)	Mississippi	15.4 (2.5)
Louisiana	20.6 (1.1)	New Mexico	45.9 (3.4)	Louisiana	22.1 (1.3)	Massachusetts	13.7 (3.1)
Massachusetts	20.3 (1.5)	Vermont	43.0 (2.5)	Massachusetts	21.4 (1.7)	New York	13.3 (1.3)
New York	20.3 (1.0)	Kentucky	41.3 (3.8)	New York	21.4 (1.1)	Vermont	12.5 (2.7)
Mississippi	20.0 (2.1)	West Virginia	40.7 (4.5)	Mississippi	20.7 (2.2)	Kentucky	11.5 (2.6)
Kentucky	19.1 (1.6)	North Carolina	40.4 (2.3)	Kentucky	20.3 (1.8)	Texas	11.4 (1.1)
California	18.8 (0.5)	Oklahoma	39.5 (3.0)	Arkansas	20.2 (1.2)	District of Columbia	11.3 (2.0)
Arizona	18.3 (1.4)	Washington	39.5 (2.5)	West Virginia	20.1 (1.6)	Oklahoma	11.3 (2.6)
Arkansas	18.3 (1.0)	Illinois	39.3 (2.2)	Arizona	19.8 (1.5)	Florida	11.1 (1.3)
West Virginia	18.3 (1.4)	Hawaii	38.9 (2.8)	California	19.2 (0.6)	North Carolina	9.9 (1.5)
Tennessee	17.4 (1.2)	Texas	38.7 (1.4)	Michigan	18.9 (1.1)	Hawaii	9.8 (2.0)
North Carolina	17.1 (0.8)	California	38.3 (1.2)	Tennessee	18.8 (1.4)	Louisiana	9.8 (1.8)
Michigan	17.0 (1.0)	Maine	38.0 (2.9)	Rhode Island	18.5 (1.3)	Alabama	9.3 (2.2)
Rhode Island	16.7 (1.1)	New York	37.7 (2.3)	Delaware	18.4 (1.4)	United States	9.2 (0.3)
Illinois	16.6 (0.8)	Indiana	37.0 (3.5)	Illinois	18.2 (0.9)	Washington	9.2 (1.6)
Indiana	16.6 (1.2)	Tennessee	36.4 (2.6)	North Carolina	18.1 (0.9)	Nevada	8.9 (2.0)
Delaware	16.5 (1.2)	Michigan	36.0 (2.3)	Indiana	17.9 (1.4)	Oregon	8.9 (2.4)
Hawaii	16.4 (1.2)	Alabama	35.3 (4.2)	Hawaii	17.6 (1.3)	Nebraska	8.8 (1.3)
Oklahoma	16.2 (1.1)	Rhode Island	35.3 (2.6)	Oklahoma	17.0 (1.2)	Colorado	8.1 (2.2)
United States	15.9 (0.1)	Montana	35.1 (3.9)	United States	16.9 (0.2)	South Dakota	7.8 (2.2)
Texas	15.8 (0.6)	Florida	34.8 (1.6)	Wisconsin	16.8 (1.1)	Indiana	7.7 (1.8)
Washington	15.1 (0.9)	United States	34.8 (0.3)	Texas	16.3 (0.6)	South Carolina	7.7 (2.7)
Wisconsin	15.0 (1.0)	Delaware	34.7 (2.9)	Pennsylvania	16.1 (0.9)	Tennessee	7.6 (1.7)
Florida	14.5 (0.6)	Arizona	34.5 (3.1)	Washington	16.0 (1.1)	Arkansas	7.5 (1.7)
Alaska	14.3 (1.7)	Idaho	33.8 (2.8)	Ohio	15.5 (1.1)	Montana	7.5 (2.0)
Minnesota	14.3 (0.9)	South Carolina	33.6 (3.0)	Minnesota	15.4 (1.0)	Arizona	7.0 (1.6)
Pennsylvania	14.3 (0.8)	Georgia	32.4 (2.1)	Missouri	15.3 (1.2)	Minnesota	6.8 (1.5)
Ohio	14.2 (1.1)	Ohio	31.9 (2.3)	Florida	15.2 (0.6)	Maryland	6.5 (1.2)
Missouri	14.1 (1.0)	Kansas	31.8 (3.4)	Montana	15.1 (1.6)	West Virginia	6.5 (1.7)
Montana	13.9 (1.4)	Oregon	31.8 (2.6)	South Carolina	14.8 (1.2)	New Jersey	6.3 (1.3)
Alabama	13.8 (1.2)	Wyoming	31.5 (2.8)	Oregon	14.6 (1.0)	Georgia	6.2 (1.6)
Oregon	13.8 (0.9)	Pennsylvania	31.4 (2.1)	Alabama	14.5 (1.3)	Missouri	6.2 (1.6)
South Carolina	13.8 (1.0)	South Dakota	30.4 (2.4)	Georgia	14.4 (0.9)	Virginia	6.1 (1.9)
Georgia	13.6 (0.8)	Missouri	30.1 (1.8)	Idaho	14.3 (1.2)	Idaho	6.0 (1.8)
Idaho	13.3 (1.1)	Alaska	29.7 (3.8)	Alaska	14.1 (1.8)	New Mexico	5.9 (2.0)
Iowa	13.0 (0.7)	Wisconsin	29.7 (2.1)	Iowa	14.0 (0.8)	Rhode Island	5.8 (1.0)
South Dakota	12.8 (1.0)	Iowa	29.3 (1.8)	Connecticut	13.6 (1.0)	Iowa	5.7 (1.2)
New Jersey	12.6 (0.9)	New Jersey	29.1 (2.3)	Kansas	13.6 (1.5)	Delaware	5.5 (1.6)
Connecticut	12.4 (0.8)	Massachusetts	28.0 (3.1)	New Jersey	13.5 (1.0)	North Carolina	5.5 (1.8)
Kansas	12.2 (1.3)	Nebraska	26.4 (2.0)	South Dakota	13.5 (1.1)	Ohio	5.4 (1.1)
Colorado	12.1 (0.8)	Minnesota	26.3 (1.8)	Wyoming	12.9 (1.3)	Utah	5.4 (2.4)
Wyoming	12.0 (1.2)	Connecticut	25.8 (1.9)	Colorado	12.6 (0.7)	Wyoming	5.1 (1.4)
Maryland	11.4 (0.9)	Maryland	25.2 (2.4)	Maryland	12.1 (1.0)	Michigan	5.0 (1.3)
Nebraska	11.3 (0.8)	Colorado	24.6 (1.6)	Nebraska	11.7 (0.8)	Pennsylvania	5.0 (0.9)
Nevada	9.8 (0.8)	Nevada	21.7 (2.4)	North Dakota	10.1 (1.0)	Illinois	4.9 (0.9)
North Dakota	9.5 (0.8)	North Dakota	20.7 (2.5)	Nevada	9.9 (0.9)	Connecticut	4.8 (1.1)
Utah	9.5 (1.0)	Virginia	19.3 (1.8)	Utah	9.9 (1.1)	Wisconsin	4.6 (1.7)
Virginia	8.3 (0.8)	Utah	17.7 (2.1)	Virginia	8.6 (0.7)	Kansas	3.5 (1.2)
New Hampshire	6.5 (0.6)	New Hampshire	16.0 (1.7)	New Hampshire	7.0 (0.7)	New Hampshire	3.0 (0.9)

Note: (1) Standard error appears in parenthesis; figures cover 2010; (b) base less than 75,000; (x) not applicable
Source: U.S. Census Bureau, Current Population Survey, 2011 Annual Social and Economic Supplement. Table HI05. Health Insurance Coverage Status and Type of Coverage by State and Age for All People: 2010

Covered by Medicaid and Private Health Insurance

All Persons		Under 18 Years		Under 65 Years		65 Years and Over	
State	Percent[1]	State	Percent[1]	State	Percent[1]	State	Percent[1]
Vermont	5.6 (0.6)	Vermont	11.2 (1.6)	Vermont	5.9 (0.7)	Alaska	5.5 (1.8)
Maine	5.4 (0.5)	Arkansas	9.6 (2.2)	Maine	5.6 (0.5)	Hawaii	4.6 (1.2)
Kentucky	4.3 (0.8)	Oklahoma	9.4 (1.9)	Massachusetts	4.5 (0.6)	Maine	4.3 (1.1)
Massachusetts	4.2 (0.6)	Maine	8.9 (1.7)	Kentucky	4.4 (0.9)	Oregon	4.2 (1.4)
Oklahoma	4.0 (0.6)	Indiana	8.4 (1.5)	New Mexico	4.3 (0.9)	Oklahoma	3.9 (1.3)
Indiana	3.8 (0.5)	Iowa	8.3 (1.2)	New York	4.0 (0.4)	Vermont	3.9 (1.4)
New York	3.8 (0.3)	South Dakota	8.0 (1.3)	Oklahoma	4.0 (0.7)	Nevada	3.8 (1.4)
Hawaii	3.7 (0.5)	New Jersey	7.8 (1.1)	Wisconsin	4.0 (0.6)	North Dakota	3.8 (1.4)
New Mexico	3.7 (0.8)	New Mexico	7.8 (2.0)	Michigan	3.9 (0.5)	South Dakota	3.8 (1.4)
Wisconsin	3.6 (0.5)	Kentucky	7.7 (1.5)	Indiana	3.8 (0.6)	Indiana	3.5 (1.5)
Iowa	3.5 (0.3)	Hawaii	7.6 (1.3)	Arkansas	3.7 (0.7)	Nebraska	3.5 (1.4)
Michigan	3.5 (0.4)	West Virginia	7.6 (1.5)	Iowa	3.7 (0.4)	Kentucky	3.1 (1.0)
Arkansas	3.4 (0.6)	Michigan	7.4 (1.1)	Minnesota	3.6 (0.5)	Washington	2.9 (1.0)
Minnesota	3.4 (0.5)	Minnesota	7.3 (1.3)	Hawaii	3.5 (0.5)	Texas	2.7 (0.6)
South Dakota	3.4 (0.5)	Rhode Island	7.1 (1.2)	Rhode Island	3.5 (0.5)	Massachusetts	2.6 (1.0)
Alaska	3.3 (0.6)	Wisconsin	7.1 (1.3)	South Dakota	3.3 (0.5)	New York	2.6 (0.7)
Delaware	3.1 (0.5)	Alaska	7.0 (1.5)	Delaware	3.2 (0.5)	California	2.5 (0.4)
Rhode Island	3.1 (0.4)	Illinois	6.9 (1.1)	New Jersey	3.2 (0.4)	Delaware	2.5 (1.0)
District of Columbia	3.0 (0.5)	Missouri	6.8 (1.4)	Pennsylvania	3.2 (0.3)	Florida	2.5 (0.6)
North Dakota	3.0 (0.5)	Wyoming	6.8 (1.3)	West Virginia	3.2 (0.6)	North Carolina	2.5 (0.8)
Pennsylvania	3.0 (0.3)	Montana	6.3 (1.5)	Alaska	3.1 (0.6)	District of Columbia	2.3 (0.8)
California	2.9 (0.2)	Idaho	6.2 (1.3)	District of Columbia	3.1 (0.5)	Colorado	2.2 (1.0)
Illinois	2.9 (0.4)	Delaware	6.1 (1.1)	Illinois	3.1 (0.4)	Idaho	2.2 (1.3)
Missouri	2.9 (0.4)	New York	6.1 (0.8)	Connecticut	3.0 (0.4)	Minnesota	2.2 (0.8)
New Jersey	2.9 (0.4)	Pennsylvania	6.0 (0.8)	Missouri	3.0 (0.5)	Wyoming	2.2 (1.1)
West Virginia	2.9 (0.6)	Alabama	5.9 (1.3)	Utah	3.0 (0.7)	South Carolina	2.1 (1.0)
Colorado	2.8 (0.5)	Florida	5.9 (0.9)	California	2.9 (0.2)	Missouri	2.0 (0.5)
Connecticut	2.8 (0.4)	Ohio	5.7 (0.8)	Colorado	2.9 (0.5)	United States	2.0 (0.1)
Oregon	2.8 (0.3)	United States	5.7 (0.2)	North Dakota	2.9 (0.5)	Arkansas	1.9 (1.3)
United States	2.8 (0.1)	Washington	5.7 (1.2)	United States	2.9 (0.1)	Connecticut	1.8 (0.8)
Utah	2.8 (0.6)	Massachusetts	5.6 (1.3)	Florida	2.7 (0.3)	Alabama	1.7 (1.1)
Nebraska	2.7 (0.4)	South Carolina	5.5 (1.3)	Montana	2.7 (0.5)	Iowa	1.7 (0.6)
Florida	2.6 (0.3)	Louisiana	5.4 (1.6)	Tennessee	2.7 (0.4)	Pennsylvania	1.6 (0.5)
Tennessee	2.6 (0.4)	California	5.3 (0.4)	Idaho	2.6 (0.5)	Georgia	1.3 (0.8)
Washington	2.6 (0.4)	Kansas	5.3 (1.0)	Nebraska	2.6 (0.3)	Ohio	1.3 (0.4)
Idaho	2.5 (0.4)	Tennessee	5.2 (0.9)	Oregon	2.6 (0.4)	Tennessee	1.3 (0.8)
Wyoming	2.5 (0.4)	Colorado	5.1 (0.9)	Washington	2.6 (0.5)	West Virginia	1.3 (0.9)
Montana	2.4 (0.5)	North Dakota	5.1 (1.2)	Wyoming	2.6 (0.4)	Kansas	1.2 (0.6)
Kansas	2.3 (0.4)	Mississippi	5.0 (2.1)	Kansas	2.5 (0.4)	Mississippi	1.2 (1.1)
Louisiana	2.3 (0.5)	New Hampshire	4.8 (0.9)	Louisiana	2.5 (0.6)	Montana	1.2 (0.7)
Mississippi	2.3 (0.6)	Nebraska	4.7 (0.8)	Ohio	2.5 (0.3)	Wisconsin	1.2 (0.6)
Ohio	2.3 (0.2)	Oregon	4.7 (1.4)	Maryland	2.4 (0.5)	New Jersey	1.1 (0.5)
Alabama	2.2 (0.3)	Utah	4.7 (1.2)	Mississippi	2.4 (0.7)	Arizona	0.9 (0.5)
Maryland	2.2 (0.4)	North Carolina	4.3 (1.0)	Alabama	2.2 (0.4)	Michigan	0.9 (0.4)
North Carolina	2.2 (0.4)	Connecticut	4.2 (1.0)	Arizona	2.2 (0.5)	Illinois	0.8 (0.2)
South Carolina	2.2 (0.4)	Georgia	4.2 (0.7)	South Carolina	2.2 (0.5)	Maryland	0.8 (0.4)
Arizona	2.0 (0.4)	Arizona	4.0 (1.3)	North Carolina	2.1 (0.4)	Utah	0.8 (0.5)
Georgia	2.0 (0.3)	Maryland	4.0 (0.9)	Georgia	2.0 (0.4)	Virginia	0.8 (0.6)
Nevada	2.0 (0.4)	Virginia	3.7 (0.8)	New Hampshire	2.0 (0.3)	Louisiana	0.5 (0.3)
New Hampshire	1.8 (0.3)	Texas	3.6 (0.4)	Nevada	1.7 (0.4)	Rhode Island	0.4 (0.3)
Texas	1.8 (0.2)	District of Columbia	3.5 (1.1)	Texas	1.7 (0.2)	New Hampshire	0.3 (0.3)
Virginia	1.5 (0.2)	Nevada	3.5 (1.0)	Virginia	1.6 (0.3)	New Mexico	0.2 (0.2)

Note: (1) Standard error appears in parenthesis; figures cover 2010; (b) base less than 75,000; (x) not applicable
Source: U.S. Census Bureau, Current Population Survey, 2011 Annual Social and Economic Supplement. Table HI05. Health Insurance Coverage Status and Type of Coverage by State and Age for All People: 2010

Covered by Government Health Insurance: Medicare

All Persons		Under 18 Years		Under 65 Years		65 Years and Over	
State	Percent[1]	State	Percent[1]	State	Percent[1]	State	Percent[1]
Maine	19.2 (0.9)	Utah	2.6 (1.3)	West Virginia	6.8 (0.8)	Kansas	97.5 (1.0)
Florida	18.8 (0.5)	South Dakota	2.5 (1.2)	Alabama	5.0 (0.5)	South Dakota	97.1 (1.1)
West Virginia	18.8 (1.1)	Nevada	2.4 (1.1)	Arkansas	4.9 (0.5)	Vermont	97.1 (1.1)
Arkansas	17.7 (1.1)	Hawaii	1.9 (1.0)	South Carolina	4.4 (0.5)	Oklahoma	96.9 (0.9)
Pennsylvania	17.7 (0.6)	South Carolina	1.7 (0.8)	Tennessee	4.4 (0.4)	Iowa	96.8 (1.3)
Montana	17.4 (1.1)	Ohio	1.4 (0.6)	Louisiana	4.2 (0.5)	Minnesota	96.5 (0.9)
South Carolina	17.4 (0.9)	District of Columbia	1.2 (0.6)	Maine	4.2 (0.5)	Utah	96.3 (1.4)
Alabama	16.6 (0.9)	Arizona	1.1 (0.7)	Michigan	4.2 (0.4)	Oregon	96.2 (1.0)
Rhode Island	16.6 (0.9)	California	1.1 (0.2)	Kentucky	4.1 (0.6)	Kentucky	96.0 (1.3)
Wisconsin	16.6 (0.6)	New Hampshire	1.1 (0.5)	Missouri	4.1 (0.8)	Nebraska	95.7 (1.2)
Michigan	16.5 (0.7)	Oklahoma	1.1 (0.7)	New Hampshire	3.5 (0.5)	New Hampshire	95.7 (1.1)
Missouri	16.4 (0.9)	Iowa	1.0 (0.4)	Florida	3.4 (0.3)	Tennessee	95.7 (1.3)
South Dakota	16.0 (0.9)	Maryland	1.0 (0.4)	Rhode Island	3.4 (0.4)	Mississippi	95.6 (1.3)
Kentucky	15.8 (1.1)	Nebraska	1.0 (0.5)	South Dakota	3.3 (0.7)	West Virginia	95.6 (1.6)
New Hampshire	15.7 (0.8)	New York	1.0 (0.3)	Nevada	3.2 (0.4)	Wisconsin	95.6 (1.1)
Oklahoma	15.7 (0.8)	Tennessee	1.0 (0.5)	Ohio	3.2 (0.3)	Maine	95.3 (1.0)
Tennessee	15.7 (0.9)	Arkansas	0.9 (0.6)	Pennsylvania	3.2 (0.3)	North Carolina	95.3 (1.3)
Hawaii	15.6 (0.9)	Illinois	0.9 (0.4)	Vermont	3.2 (0.4)	Missouri	95.2 (1.1)
Kansas	15.6 (0.8)	Kentucky	0.9 (0.4)	Arizona	3.0 (0.5)	South Carolina	95.1 (1.3)
Massachusetts	15.6 (0.8)	Louisiana	0.9 (0.4)	Mississippi	3.0 (0.4)	Rhode Island	95.0 (1.1)
Oregon	15.6 (0.8)	Michigan	0.9 (0.4)	Kansas	2.9 (0.5)	Montana	94.8 (1.2)
Vermont	15.4 (0.8)	Texas	0.9 (0.2)	Massachusetts	2.9 (0.5)	Pennsylvania	94.3 (0.9)
Delaware	15.2 (0.8)	Kansas	0.8 (0.4)	New Jersey	2.9 (0.3)	Michigan	94.1 (1.1)
Mississippi	15.2 (0.7)	Rhode Island	0.8 (0.3)	New York	2.9 (0.2)	Washington	94.1 (1.4)
Ohio	15.1 (0.6)	United States	0.8 (0.1)	North Carolina	2.9 (0.3)	Ohio	93.9 (1.1)
Indiana	15.0 (0.9)	Wisconsin	0.8 (0.4)	Oklahoma	2.9 (0.6)	North Dakota	93.8 (1.5)
New Mexico	15.0 (1.0)	Alabama	0.7 (0.4)	United States	2.9 (0.1)	Colorado	93.6 (1.4)
Minnesota	14.7 (0.7)	Connecticut	0.7 (0.4)	Indiana	2.8 (0.3)	Nevada	93.6 (1.5)
New York	14.5 (0.4)	Maine	0.6 (0.3)	Oregon	2.8 (0.4)	Arizona	93.5 (1.6)
United States	14.5 (0.1)	Missouri	0.6 (0.4)	Illinois	2.7 (0.3)	Florida	93.5 (0.8)
North Carolina	14.4 (0.7)	Washington	0.6 (0.4)	Iowa	2.7 (0.5)	Indiana	93.5 (1.6)
Louisiana	14.3 (0.6)	Florida	0.5 (0.2)	New Mexico	2.7 (0.4)	Connecticut	93.4 (1.3)
New Jersey	14.2 (0.6)	Massachusetts	0.5 (0.3)	Wisconsin	2.7 (0.3)	Idaho	93.2 (2.0)
North Dakota	14.2 (0.8)	Minnesota	0.5 (0.3)	Nebraska	2.6 (0.5)	United States	93.1 (0.2)
Connecticut	14.0 (0.7)	North Dakota	0.5 (0.2)	Utah	2.6 (0.7)	Wyoming	92.9 (1.6)
Iowa	14.0 (0.8)	Virginia	0.5 (0.3)	Delaware	2.5 (0.4)	Georgia	92.3 (1.4)
Nebraska	14.0 (0.7)	West Virginia	0.5 (0.5)	Idaho	2.5 (0.4)	Virginia	92.3 (1.6)
Washington	14.0 (0.8)	Alaska	0.4 (0.2)	California	2.4 (0.1)	New Mexico	92.1 (2.0)
Idaho	13.7 (0.7)	Georgia	0.4 (0.3)	Georgia	2.4 (0.4)	New York	92.1 (1.1)
Arizona	13.6 (0.8)	New Jersey	0.4 (0.2)	Minnesota	2.4 (0.3)	Illinois	91.8 (1.1)
Nevada	13.6 (0.8)	Idaho	0.2 (0.2)	Montana	2.4 (0.4)	Delaware	91.7 (1.7)
Illinois	13.5 (0.5)	Indiana	0.2 (0.2)	Texas	2.4 (0.2)	Massachusetts	91.7 (1.6)
District of Columbia	13.0 (0.8)	Montana	0.2 (0.2)	Colorado	2.2 (0.3)	Arkansas	91.3 (2.3)
California	12.6 (0.3)	Pennsylvania	0.2 (0.2)	District of Columbia	2.2 (0.4)	New Jersey	91.2 (1.4)
Maryland	12.6 (0.5)	Colorado	0.1 (0.1)	Hawaii	2.2 (0.5)	Texas	91.1 (1.1)
Virginia	12.5 (0.7)	North Carolina	0.1 (0.1)	Maryland	2.2 (0.3)	California	90.4 (0.8)
Utah	12.4 (1.0)	Vermont	0.1 (0.1)	Virginia	2.2 (0.3)	Alabama	90.3 (2.5)
Colorado	12.0 (0.8)	Delaware	0.0 (0.0)	Connecticut	2.1 (0.3)	Hawaii	90.1 (1.7)
Wyoming	11.7 (0.9)	Mississippi	0.0 (0.0)	North Dakota	2.1 (0.4)	Maryland	89.0 (1.4)
Texas	11.3 (0.4)	New Mexico	0.0 (0.0)	Washington	1.9 (0.3)	Louisiana	88.7 (2.3)
Georgia	10.9 (0.6)	Oregon	0.0 (0.0)	Alaska	1.8 (0.3)	Alaska	88.0 (2.8)
Alaska	8.6 (0.6)	Wyoming	0.0 (0.0)	Wyoming	1.4 (0.3)	District of Columbia	87.0 (1.8)

Note: (1) Standard error appears in parenthesis; figures cover 2010; (b) base less than 75,000; (x) not applicable
Source: U.S. Census Bureau, Current Population Survey, 2011 Annual Social and Economic Supplement. Table HI05. Health Insurance Coverage Status and Type of Coverage by State and Age for All People: 2010

Covered by Medicare and Private Health Insurance

All Persons		Under 18 Years		Under 65 Years		65 Years and Over	
State	Percent[1]	State	Percent[1]	State	Percent[1]	State	Percent[1]
Pennsylvania	11.3 (0.6)	Nevada	1.3 (0.8)	West Virginia	2.2 (0.5)	Iowa	71.8 (4.7)
Wisconsin	10.8 (0.8)	Connecticut	0.5 (0.4)	Michigan	1.6 (0.3)	Oregon	70.3 (3.4)
Maine	10.7 (0.7)	District of Columbia	0.3 (0.3)	Alabama	1.5 (0.3)	Minnesota	69.3 (2.9)
Oregon	10.4 (0.7)	Iowa	0.3 (0.2)	South Carolina	1.3 (0.3)	North Dakota	68.8 (3.8)
Michigan	9.9 (0.6)	North Dakota	0.3 (0.2)	Maine	1.2 (0.2)	Kansas	67.2 (3.6)
Kansas	9.7 (0.7)	Ohio	0.3 (0.3)	Kentucky	1.1 (0.3)	Wisconsin	66.7 (3.2)
Minnesota	9.7 (0.6)	South Carolina	0.3 (0.3)	Missouri	1.1 (0.3)	Nebraska	65.8 (3.7)
North Dakota	9.6 (0.7)	Alabama	0.2 (0.2)	Pennsylvania	1.1 (0.2)	South Dakota	65.8 (4.4)
South Dakota	9.6 (0.9)	Florida	0.2 (0.1)	Tennessee	1.1 (0.2)	Pennsylvania	65.0 (2.5)
Missouri	9.4 (0.8)	Georgia	0.2 (0.2)	Arkansas	1.0 (0.3)	Missouri	62.6 (3.4)
Montana	9.4 (1.0)	Michigan	0.2 (0.1)	Delaware	1.0 (0.2)	Washington	62.4 (3.2)
Iowa	9.3 (1.0)	Minnesota	0.2 (0.2)	Louisiana	1.0 (0.3)	Michigan	62.2 (2.9)
Massachusetts	9.2 (0.6)	New Jersey	0.2 (0.1)	Nebraska	1.0 (0.3)	Idaho	62.0 (5.0)
West Virginia	9.2 (0.8)	Rhode Island	0.2 (0.2)	Nevada	1.0 (0.3)	Wyoming	61.8 (4.2)
Delaware	9.1 (0.7)	South Dakota	0.2 (0.2)	New Hampshire	1.0 (0.2)	Connecticut	60.6 (3.0)
Nebraska	8.9 (0.6)	Texas	0.2 (0.1)	New Jersey	1.0 (0.2)	Vermont	60.1 (3.5)
Hawaii	8.6 (0.6)	Utah	0.2 (0.2)	Oregon	1.0 (0.2)	Massachusetts	59.9 (3.4)
Alabama	8.5 (0.8)	Virginia	0.2 (0.1)	Wisconsin	1.0 (0.2)	North Carolina	59.3 (2.6)
Connecticut	8.5 (0.6)	California	0.1 (0.1)	Maryland	0.9 (0.2)	Maryland	59.2 (2.6)
South Carolina	8.4 (0.6)	Hawaii	0.1 (0.1)	North Carolina	0.9 (0.2)	Illinois	59.1 (2.7)
Vermont	8.4 (0.7)	Indiana	0.1 (0.1)	Kansas	0.8 (0.2)	Maine	59.0 (3.0)
Kentucky	8.3 (0.9)	Maryland	0.1 (0.1)	Massachusetts	0.8 (0.2)	Delaware	58.1 (3.4)
Washington	8.3 (0.8)	New Hampshire	0.1 (0.1)	Minnesota	0.8 (0.2)	Kentucky	57.5 (4.5)
Indiana	8.2 (0.8)	New York	0.1 (0.1)	Mississippi	0.8 (0.2)	Indiana	56.7 (4.2)
Rhode Island	8.2 (0.7)	North Carolina	0.1 (0.1)	New York	0.8 (0.1)	Montana	55.9 (5.5)
Florida	8.1 (0.4)	Oklahoma	0.1 (0.1)	Rhode Island	0.8 (0.2)	Virginia	55.3 (3.0)
Idaho	8.1 (0.8)	United States	0.1 (0.0)	South Dakota	0.8 (0.2)	New Jersey	54.9 (2.7)
North Carolina	8.1 (0.6)	Vermont	0.1 (0.1)	United States	0.8 (0.0)	Ohio	54.6 (2.9)
New Hampshire	8.0 (0.6)	Wisconsin	0.1 (0.1)	Connecticut	0.7 (0.2)	Oklahoma	54.5 (3.4)
Oklahoma	8.0 (0.6)	Alaska	0.0 (0.0)	Florida	0.7 (0.1)	West Virginia	54.0 (4.3)
Maryland	7.9 (0.5)	Arizona	0.0 (0.0)	Indiana	0.7 (0.2)	New Hampshire	53.7 (2.9)
New Jersey	7.9 (0.5)	Arkansas	0.0 (0.0)	Iowa	0.7 (0.2)	United States	53.2 (0.5)
Illinois	7.6 (0.5)	Colorado	0.0 (0.0)	Utah	0.7 (0.2)	Hawaii	53.1 (2.6)
Ohio	7.6 (0.5)	Delaware	0.0 (0.0)	Vermont	0.7 (0.2)	Alabama	52.7 (3.0)
United States	7.5 (0.1)	Idaho	0.0 (0.0)	Virginia	0.7 (0.1)	Utah	52.2 (5.7)
Wyoming	7.2 (0.7)	Illinois	0.0 (0.0)	Arizona	0.6 (0.2)	Arizona	52.0 (3.6)
Mississippi	7.1 (0.8)	Kansas	0.0 (0.0)	California	0.6 (0.1)	Rhode Island	52.0 (3.2)
New York	6.9 (0.4)	Kentucky	0.0 (0.0)	Colorado	0.6 (0.1)	South Carolina	50.7 (3.5)
Virginia	6.9 (0.5)	Louisiana	0.0 (0.0)	District of Columbia	0.6 (0.2)	Colorado	49.1 (3.4)
Tennessee	6.7 (0.7)	Maine	0.0 (0.0)	Hawaii	0.6 (0.2)	Mississippi	48.4 (4.6)
Arizona	6.6 (0.6)	Massachusetts	0.0 (0.0)	Idaho	0.6 (0.2)	New York	47.4 (2.1)
Arkansas	6.6 (1.0)	Mississippi	0.0 (0.0)	North Dakota	0.6 (0.2)	Tennessee	46.7 (4.3)
District of Columbia	6.5 (0.6)	Missouri	0.0 (0.0)	Oklahoma	0.6 (0.2)	District of Columbia	46.6 (3.2)
Nevada	6.2 (0.6)	Montana	0.0 (0.0)	Alaska	0.5 (0.2)	Nevada	45.4 (3.4)
Utah	6.1 (0.6)	Nebraska	0.0 (0.0)	Georgia	0.5 (0.1)	California	44.4 (1.5)
New Mexico	6.0 (0.6)	New Mexico	0.0 (0.0)	Illinois	0.5 (0.1)	Florida	44.1 (2.0)
Louisiana	5.9 (0.7)	Oregon	0.0 (0.0)	Montana	0.5 (0.3)	Texas	43.8 (2.2)
Colorado	5.8 (0.4)	Pennsylvania	0.0 (0.0)	New Mexico	0.5 (0.2)	Alaska	42.9 (5.3)
California	5.6 (0.2)	Tennessee	0.0 (0.0)	Ohio	0.5 (0.1)	Louisiana	42.2 (5.5)
Texas	4.8 (0.3)	Washington	0.0 (0.0)	Texas	0.4 (0.1)	Georgia	41.0 (3.5)
Georgia	4.3 (0.4)	West Virginia	0.0 (0.0)	Wyoming	0.3 (0.1)	New Mexico	39.9 (3.4)
Alaska	3.8 (0.5)	Wyoming	0.0 (0.0)	Washington	0.2 (0.1)	Arkansas	38.6 (6.0)

Note: (1) Standard error appears in parenthesis; figures cover 2010; (b) base less than 75,000; (x) not applicable
Source: U.S. Census Bureau, Current Population Survey, 2011 Annual Social and Economic Supplement. Table HI05. Health Insurance Coverage Status and Type of Coverage by State and Age for All People: 2010

Covered by Medicaid and Medicare

All Persons		Under 18 Years		Under 65 Years		65 Years and Over	
State	Percent[1]	State	Percent[1]	State	Percent[1]	State	Percent[1]
Maine	4.5 (0.5)	South Dakota	2.5 (1.2)	Maine	2.2 (0.3)	Maine	16.2 (2.2)
Massachusetts	3.7 (0.6)	Hawaii	1.6 (1.0)	Massachusetts	2.1 (0.4)	California	15.4 (1.1)
Vermont	3.3 (0.5)	South Carolina	1.4 (0.7)	Rhode Island	2.1 (0.3)	Mississippi	15.4 (2.5)
Florida	2.9 (0.2)	Nebraska	1.0 (0.5)	Missouri	2.0 (0.5)	Alaska	15.3 (2.6)
Mississippi	2.9 (0.4)	Oklahoma	1.0 (0.7)	South Dakota	1.9 (0.5)	Massachusetts	13.6 (3.1)
California	2.7 (0.2)	Arkansas	0.9 (0.6)	Vermont	1.9 (0.3)	New York	13.0 (1.3)
South Dakota	2.7 (0.5)	Illinois	0.8 (0.4)	West Virginia	1.9 (0.3)	Vermont	12.5 (2.7)
Missouri	2.6 (0.4)	Kentucky	0.8 (0.4)	New Mexico	1.6 (0.5)	Texas	11.3 (1.1)
New York	2.6 (0.2)	Maryland	0.7 (0.4)	Michigan	1.5 (0.3)	Kentucky	11.0 (2.4)
Rhode Island	2.6 (0.3)	Ohio	0.7 (0.3)	Iowa	1.4 (0.3)	District of Columbia	10.7 (2.0)
Kentucky	2.5 (0.4)	Tennessee	0.7 (0.4)	South Carolina	1.4 (0.3)	Florida	10.7 (1.2)
West Virginia	2.5 (0.4)	Arizona	0.6 (0.5)	Tennessee	1.4 (0.3)	Oklahoma	10.4 (2.2)
Louisiana	2.3 (0.3)	California	0.6 (0.2)	Arkansas	1.3 (0.3)	North Carolina	9.9 (1.5)
South Carolina	2.3 (0.4)	Kansas	0.6 (0.4)	Florida	1.3 (0.1)	Hawaii	9.8 (2.0)
Arkansas	2.2 (0.4)	Rhode Island	0.6 (0.3)	Kansas	1.3 (0.3)	Louisiana	9.8 (1.8)
Hawaii	2.2 (0.5)	Connecticut	0.5 (0.4)	Louisiana	1.3 (0.2)	Washington	9.2 (1.6)
New Mexico	2.2 (0.4)	Maine	0.5 (0.3)	Wisconsin	1.3 (0.2)	United States	9.0 (0.3)
Alaska	2.1 (0.4)	Michigan	0.5 (0.3)	Kentucky	1.2 (0.3)	Nevada	8.9 (2.0)
District of Columbia	2.1 (0.3)	Missouri	0.5 (0.4)	California	1.1 (0.1)	Oregon	8.9 (2.4)
North Carolina	2.1 (0.3)	New Hampshire	0.5 (0.4)	Colorado	1.1 (0.3)	Alabama	8.8 (2.2)
Oklahoma	2.1 (0.4)	New York	0.5 (0.2)	Illinois	1.1 (0.2)	Nebraska	8.8 (1.3)
Tennessee	2.1 (0.3)	United States	0.5 (0.0)	Nebraska	1.1 (0.2)	Colorado	7.9 (2.2)
United States	2.1 (0.0)	Wisconsin	0.5 (0.3)	Nevada	1.1 (0.2)	South Dakota	7.8 (2.2)
Michigan	2.0 (0.3)	Minnesota	0.4 (0.3)	New Hampshire	1.1 (0.3)	Indiana	7.7 (1.8)
Nebraska	2.0 (0.3)	North Dakota	0.4 (0.1)	New York	1.1 (0.1)	Tennessee	7.6 (1.7)
Nevada	2.0 (0.3)	Texas	0.4 (0.2)	Pennsylvania	1.1 (0.2)	South Carolina	7.4 (2.7)
Oregon	2.0 (0.4)	Washington	0.4 (0.3)	United States	1.1 (0.0)	Arkansas	7.3 (1.7)
Texas	2.0 (0.2)	District of Columbia	0.3 (0.3)	Alaska	1.0 (0.3)	Montana	7.1 (2.0)
Alabama	1.9 (0.5)	Florida	0.3 (0.1)	Arizona	1.0 (0.3)	Arizona	6.5 (1.5)
Colorado	1.9 (0.4)	Massachusetts	0.3 (0.3)	Idaho	1.0 (0.3)	West Virginia	6.5 (1.7)
Iowa	1.9 (0.3)	New Jersey	0.3 (0.2)	Mississippi	1.0 (0.3)	Maryland	6.4 (1.1)
Montana	1.9 (0.4)	Alabama	0.2 (0.2)	North Carolina	1.0 (0.2)	Minnesota	6.4 (1.5)
Indiana	1.8 (0.3)	Alaska	0.2 (0.2)	Texas	1.0 (0.1)	New Jersey	6.3 (1.3)
Wisconsin	1.8 (0.3)	Georgia	0.2 (0.2)	Alabama	0.9 (0.3)	Georgia	6.2 (1.6)
Arizona	1.7 (0.4)	Idaho	0.2 (0.2)	District of Columbia	0.9 (0.2)	Missouri	6.2 (1.6)
Minnesota	1.7 (0.2)	Iowa	0.2 (0.1)	Hawaii	0.9 (0.4)	Idaho	6.0 (1.8)
Pennsylvania	1.7 (0.2)	Montana	0.2 (0.2)	Indiana	0.9 (0.2)	Virginia	5.8 (1.9)
Washington	1.7 (0.2)	Nevada	0.2 (0.1)	Minnesota	0.9 (0.2)	Iowa	5.7 (1.2)
Idaho	1.6 (0.3)	Pennsylvania	0.2 (0.2)	Ohio	0.9 (0.2)	Rhode Island	5.7 (1.0)
Kansas	1.6 (0.3)	Utah	0.2 (0.2)	Oregon	0.9 (0.2)	New Mexico	5.6 (2.0)
Illinois	1.5 (0.2)	Colorado	0.1 (0.1)	Georgia	0.8 (0.2)	North Dakota	5.5 (1.8)
Maryland	1.5 (0.2)	Indiana	0.1 (0.1)	Maryland	0.8 (0.2)	Ohio	5.4 (1.1)
Ohio	1.5 (0.2)	North Carolina	0.1 (0.1)	Montana	0.8 (0.2)	Utah	5.4 (2.4)
New Hampshire	1.4 (0.3)	Delaware	0.0 (0.0)	Oklahoma	0.8 (0.3)	Wyoming	5.1 (1.4)
New Jersey	1.4 (0.2)	Louisiana	0.0 (0.0)	New Jersey	0.7 (0.2)	Pennsylvania	5.0 (0.9)
Georgia	1.3 (0.3)	Mississippi	0.0 (0.0)	Connecticut	0.6 (0.2)	Delaware	4.9 (1.4)
Connecticut	1.2 (0.2)	New Mexico	0.0 (0.0)	Delaware	0.6 (0.2)	Connecticut	4.8 (1.1)
Delaware	1.2 (0.2)	Oregon	0.0 (0.0)	North Dakota	0.6 (0.2)	Michigan	4.7 (1.3)
North Dakota	1.2 (0.3)	Vermont	0.0 (0.0)	Utah	0.6 (0.2)	Wisconsin	4.6 (1.7)
Utah	1.1 (0.3)	Virginia	0.0 (0.0)	Washington	0.6 (0.2)	Illinois	4.4 (0.8)
Virginia	1.1 (0.3)	West Virginia	0.0 (0.0)	Wyoming	0.6 (0.2)	Kansas	3.3 (1.2)
Wyoming	1.1 (0.2)	Wyoming	0.0 (0.0)	Virginia	0.5 (0.1)	New Hampshire	3.0 (0.9)

Note: (1) Standard error appears in parenthesis; figures cover 2010; (b) base less than 75,000; (x) not applicable
Source: U.S. Census Bureau, Current Population Survey, 2011 Annual Social and Economic Supplement. Table HI05. Health Insurance Coverage Status and Type of Coverage by State and Age for All People: 2010

Covered by Government Health Insurance: Military

All Persons		Under 18 Years		Under 65 Years		65 Years and Over	
State	**Percent[1]**	**State**	**Percent[1]**	**State**	**Percent[1]**	**State**	**Percent[1]**
Alaska	12.7 (1.5)	Alaska	14.5 (2.1)	Alaska	12.7 (1.6)	Nevada	17.9 (3.0)
Virginia	9.6 (0.8)	Georgia	10.0 (2.1)	Hawaii	9.3 (1.3)	Arizona	16.0 (3.1)
Hawaii	8.9 (1.1)	Virginia	9.9 (1.3)	Virginia	9.2 (0.8)	Arkansas	15.8 (2.4)
Washington	8.7 (1.5)	Washington	8.7 (2.7)	Washington	8.2 (1.8)	Montana	15.1 (4.0)
Georgia	8.1 (1.4)	Hawaii	8.4 (1.8)	Georgia	7.9 (1.4)	South Dakota	15.1 (2.4)
South Dakota	7.5 (0.9)	Colorado	7.4 (1.2)	Maine	6.6 (0.8)	Wyoming	14.7 (3.2)
Oklahoma	7.3 (1.5)	North Carolina	7.4 (2.6)	Colorado	6.5 (0.7)	Oklahoma	13.8 (3.2)
Maine	7.2 (0.8)	Maine	6.1 (1.1)	Oklahoma	6.3 (1.3)	Utah	13.6 (3.0)
Montana	7.1 (1.1)	Oklahoma	6.0 (2.0)	South Dakota	6.3 (0.8)	Kansas	13.1 (2.9)
Kansas	7.0 (2.5)	Kansas	5.8 (3.0)	North Carolina	6.1 (2.1)	Alaska	12.8 (3.0)
Colorado	6.8 (0.7)	South Dakota	5.3 (1.2)	Kansas	6.0 (2.5)	Vermont	12.7 (3.1)
Nevada	6.8 (0.7)	Montana	5.2 (1.6)	Alabama	5.6 (1.1)	Virginia	12.6 (2.4)
Florida	6.3 (0.7)	Nebraska	5.2 (1.0)	Nebraska	5.6 (0.7)	Washington	11.9 (2.0)
North Carolina	6.1 (2.0)	Tennessee	5.2 (2.5)	Montana	5.5 (0.9)	New Hampshire	11.2 (2.2)
Wyoming	6.1 (1.0)	Florida	4.9 (0.9)	Florida	5.4 (0.7)	New Mexico	10.9 (3.5)
Nebraska	5.9 (0.7)	Nevada	4.9 (1.1)	Tennessee	5.4 (1.8)	Texas	10.7 (1.1)
New Mexico	5.9 (1.5)	North Dakota	4.8 (0.9)	Nevada	5.3 (0.7)	Maine	10.6 (2.1)
Indiana	5.7 (0.8)	West Virginia	4.4 (0.9)	Indiana	5.1 (0.8)	Florida	10.5 (1.3)
Alabama	5.6 (1.0)	Indiana	4.2 (1.1)	New Mexico	5.1 (1.4)	Oregon	10.5 (3.3)
Arizona	5.6 (0.8)	Alabama	4.1 (1.4)	Wyoming	5.0 (1.0)	Kentucky	10.0 (2.2)
Tennessee	5.6 (1.5)	Wyoming	4.0 (1.2)	North Dakota	4.9 (0.8)	South Carolina	9.8 (2.2)
West Virginia	5.4 (0.7)	Kentucky	3.7 (0.9)	West Virginia	4.9 (0.7)	Indiana	9.5 (1.9)
Kentucky	5.3 (0.7)	Louisiana	3.6 (1.2)	Kentucky	4.6 (0.7)	Georgia	9.3 (1.9)
Arkansas	5.1 (0.9)	Delaware	3.5 (1.2)	Arizona	4.2 (0.8)	Missouri	9.3 (2.0)
North Dakota	5.0 (0.7)	United States	3.3 (0.2)	South Carolina	4.2 (0.7)	Idaho	9.0 (2.3)
South Carolina	5.0 (0.7)	New Mexico	3.2 (1.5)	Mississippi	4.1 (1.0)	Colorado	8.8 (2.2)
Mississippi	4.3 (1.0)	Arizona	2.9 (0.9)	Louisiana	3.8 (0.7)	California	8.5 (1.0)
United States	4.2 (0.1)	Mississippi	2.9 (0.9)	United States	3.6 (0.1)	United States	8.1 (0.3)
Texas	4.1 (0.4)	Texas	2.9 (0.5)	Delaware	3.5 (0.8)	West Virginia	8.1 (2.3)
Delaware	4.0 (0.8)	South Carolina	2.7 (0.9)	Arkansas	3.3 (0.8)	Nebraska	7.9 (1.8)
Idaho	4.0 (0.8)	Maryland	2.6 (0.7)	Idaho	3.3 (0.8)	Wisconsin	7.7 (2.0)
Vermont	4.0 (0.6)	Arkansas	2.3 (1.3)	Texas	3.3 (0.4)	Rhode Island	7.5 (1.6)
Utah	3.8 (0.8)	Idaho	2.3 (0.8)	Rhode Island	3.0 (0.6)	Tennessee	7.5 (1.9)
Louisiana	3.7 (0.7)	Iowa	2.3 (0.8)	Maryland	2.9 (0.5)	Hawaii	6.6 (1.3)
Rhode Island	3.7 (0.5)	Minnesota	2.0 (0.6)	Utah	2.7 (0.7)	District of Columbia	6.5 (1.5)
Maryland	3.3 (0.4)	Rhode Island	2.0 (0.7)	Vermont	2.7 (0.5)	Delaware	6.4 (1.6)
Missouri	3.2 (0.5)	Utah	2.0 (0.7)	Iowa	2.6 (0.3)	Maryland	6.4 (1.4)
Oregon	3.2 (0.6)	California	1.8 (0.4)	Minnesota	2.4 (0.4)	Ohio	6.3 (1.8)
Wisconsin	3.1 (0.5)	Vermont	1.8 (0.7)	California	2.3 (0.3)	North Carolina	6.2 (1.8)
California	3.0 (0.3)	Wisconsin	1.6 (0.7)	Wisconsin	2.3 (0.4)	Pennsylvania	6.0 (1.2)
New Hampshire	3.0 (0.4)	Missouri	1.4 (0.5)	Missouri	2.2 (0.4)	Minnesota	5.9 (1.3)
Minnesota	2.8 (0.4)	Ohio	1.4 (0.4)	Ohio	2.1 (0.4)	Illinois	5.8 (1.3)
Iowa	2.7 (0.3)	District of Columbia	1.3 (0.7)	Oregon	2.0 (0.4)	Alabama	5.6 (1.7)
Ohio	2.7 (0.4)	Illinois	1.3 (0.4)	Illinois	1.8 (0.4)	Michigan	5.6 (1.5)
Pennsylvania	2.4 (0.3)	New Hampshire	1.0 (0.4)	New Hampshire	1.8 (0.4)	Mississippi	5.5 (2.0)
Illinois	2.3 (0.4)	Oregon	1.0 (0.6)	Pennsylvania	1.7 (0.3)	North Dakota	5.2 (1.6)
District of Columbia	1.9 (0.3)	New York	0.9 (0.3)	Connecticut	1.4 (0.3)	Connecticut	3.9 (1.2)
Michigan	1.8 (0.3)	Pennsylvania	0.9 (0.4)	New York	1.4 (0.3)	Iowa	3.5 (1.4)
Connecticut	1.7 (0.3)	Connecticut	0.7 (0.3)	District of Columbia	1.2 (0.3)	Louisiana	3.5 (1.6)
New York	1.6 (0.3)	Michigan	0.5 (0.2)	Michigan	1.2 (0.2)	Massachusetts	3.3 (1.2)
Massachusetts	1.3 (0.3)	New Jersey	0.5 (0.3)	Massachusetts	1.0 (0.3)	New York	3.0 (0.7)
New Jersey	0.8 (0.2)	Massachusetts	0.4 (0.3)	New Jersey	0.6 (0.2)	New Jersey	1.8 (0.8)

Note: (1) Standard error appears in parenthesis; figures cover 2010; (b) base less than 75,000; (x) not applicable
Source: U.S. Census Bureau, Current Population Survey, 2011 Annual Social and Economic Supplement. Table HI05. Health Insurance Coverage Status and Type of Coverage by State and Age for All People: 2010

Not Covered by Health Insurance at any Time During the Year

All Persons		Under 18 Years		Under 65 Years		65 Years and Over	
State	Percent[1]	State	Percent[1]	State	Percent[1]	State	Percent[1]
Texas	24.6 (0.8)	Nevada	17.5 (2.0)	Texas	26.9 (0.9)	Arkansas	4.5 (1.6)
New Mexico	21.6 (1.5)	Texas	16.3 (0.9)	New Mexico	24.7 (1.7)	Texas	4.0 (0.7)
Nevada	21.3 (1.4)	Arizona	15.0 (2.3)	Florida	24.6 (0.9)	California	3.7 (0.5)
Mississippi	21.1 (1.3)	Florida	14.2 (1.3)	Mississippi	24.1 (1.4)	Arizona	3.4 (1.0)
Florida	20.8 (0.8)	South Carolina	14.2 (2.1)	Nevada	23.9 (1.6)	Alabama	3.2 (2.1)
South Carolina	20.6 (1.1)	Alaska	13.7 (2.1)	South Carolina	23.7 (1.3)	Alaska	3.2 (1.3)
Louisiana	20.0 (1.2)	New Mexico	13.7 (2.3)	Louisiana	22.4 (1.4)	District of Columbia	3.1 (0.9)
California	19.4 (0.5)	Mississippi	13.4 (2.8)	Idaho	21.7 (1.7)	New York	3.1 (0.9)
Georgia	19.4 (1.2)	Oklahoma	11.9 (1.6)	California	21.4 (0.5)	Georgia	2.4 (0.9)
Idaho	19.2 (1.5)	Utah	11.4 (1.6)	Montana	21.3 (1.5)	Delaware	2.3 (0.8)
Arizona	19.1 (1.3)	California	10.7 (0.7)	Arizona	21.2 (1.4)	Florida	2.3 (0.4)
Arkansas	18.7 (1.5)	Oregon	10.4 (1.5)	Arkansas	21.2 (1.8)	Connecticut	2.2 (0.8)
Montana	18.1 (1.2)	Nebraska	10.3 (1.5)	Georgia	21.2 (1.3)	New Mexico	2.2 (1.0)
Alaska	18.0 (1.1)	North Dakota	10.2 (1.7)	Oklahoma	19.7 (1.5)	Louisiana	2.1 (1.2)
Wyoming	17.3 (0.9)	Wyoming	10.2 (1.5)	Alaska	19.3 (1.2)	Maryland	2.1 (0.6)
North Carolina	17.0 (1.0)	Georgia	9.9 (1.4)	North Carolina	19.3 (1.1)	New Jersey	2.1 (0.7)
Oklahoma	17.0 (1.3)	United States	9.8 (0.2)	Wyoming	19.3 (1.1)	United States	2.0 (0.1)
United States	16.3 (0.1)	Maryland	9.2 (1.4)	Oregon	18.7 (1.3)	Illinois	1.9 (0.6)
Oregon	16.2 (1.1)	New Jersey	9.2 (1.2)	United States	18.4 (0.2)	Nevada	1.9 (0.8)
Alabama	15.4 (1.3)	North Carolina	9.2 (1.2)	Alabama	17.4 (1.6)	Ohio	1.7 (0.7)
New Jersey	15.4 (1.0)	Idaho	9.0 (1.9)	New Jersey	17.4 (1.2)	Hawaii	1.6 (0.7)
New York	15.0 (0.7)	Louisiana	9.0 (1.8)	Kentucky	17.0 (1.4)	Indiana	1.6 (0.6)
Kentucky	14.9 (1.2)	Alabama	8.9 (2.5)	New York	16.7 (0.7)	Iowa	1.6 (0.9)
Illinois	14.8 (0.9)	Missouri	8.9 (2.5)	Tennessee	16.7 (1.2)	Montana	1.6 (0.8)
Tennessee	14.7 (1.1)	Montana	8.8 (1.5)	Illinois	16.6 (1.0)	Massachusetts	1.5 (0.7)
Virginia	14.1 (0.8)	Ohio	8.3 (1.0)	Missouri	16.1 (1.3)	South Carolina	1.5 (0.6)
Missouri	14.0 (1.1)	Virginia	8.3 (1.2)	Virginia	15.7 (0.9)	Nebraska	1.4 (0.9)
Washington	13.8 (1.0)	Pennsylvania	8.2 (1.4)	Washington	15.7 (1.0)	Rhode Island	1.4 (0.7)
Ohio	13.7 (0.8)	New York	7.9 (1.0)	Ohio	15.5 (0.9)	Virginia	1.4 (0.5)
Utah	13.6 (1.1)	Tennessee	7.9 (1.5)	West Virginia	15.5 (1.7)	Wyoming	1.4 (0.8)
West Virginia	13.5 (1.4)	Colorado	7.8 (1.1)	Indiana	15.3 (1.2)	Idaho	1.1 (0.8)
Indiana	13.4 (1.0)	Illinois	7.6 (1.1)	Utah	15.2 (1.2)	Michigan	1.1 (0.5)
Nebraska	13.3 (0.8)	Kansas	7.5 (1.6)	North Dakota	15.0 (1.0)	Mississippi	1.1 (0.7)
Maryland	13.1 (0.9)	Arkansas	7.4 (1.7)	South Dakota	15.0 (1.0)	North Carolina	1.1 (0.6)
North Dakota	13.1 (0.9)	Iowa	7.4 (1.7)	Michigan	14.9 (0.8)	Washington	1.0 (0.6)
Colorado	13.0 (0.8)	Kentucky	6.8 (1.2)	Nebraska	14.9 (0.9)	Tennessee	0.9 (0.5)
Michigan	13.0 (0.7)	South Dakota	6.6 (1.1)	Kansas	14.7 (1.3)	West Virginia	0.9 (0.4)
South Dakota	13.0 (0.8)	Connecticut	6.0 (0.9)	Colorado	14.5 (0.9)	Wisconsin	0.9 (0.6)
Kansas	12.7 (1.1)	Delaware	6.0 (1.0)	Maryland	14.5 (1.0)	Minnesota	0.7 (0.3)
District of Columbia	12.5 (1.1)	Indiana	6.0 (1.6)	District of Columbia	13.8 (1.2)	Pennsylvania	0.7 (0.3)
Iowa	12.3 (1.1)	Minnesota	6.0 (0.9)	Iowa	13.8 (1.3)	Vermont	0.6 (0.4)
Rhode Island	11.4 (0.9)	Washington	5.9 (0.9)	Rhode Island	13.1 (1.0)	North Dakota	0.5 (0.5)
Delaware	11.3 (0.9)	New Hampshire	5.5 (1.0)	Pennsylvania	12.9 (0.9)	Utah	0.5 (0.5)
Connecticut	11.0 (0.7)	Rhode Island	5.3 (1.0)	Delaware	12.7 (1.0)	Kentucky	0.4 (0.3)
Pennsylvania	11.0 (0.7)	District of Columbia	5.1 (1.3)	Connecticut	12.3 (0.8)	Maine	0.4 (0.3)
New Hampshire	10.3 (0.7)	Michigan	5.1 (0.7)	New Hampshire	11.8 (0.9)	South Dakota	0.3 (0.3)
Minnesota	9.8 (0.6)	Wisconsin	4.6 (0.7)	Maine	11.2 (0.9)	Colorado	0.2 (0.2)
Vermont	9.5 (0.8)	Maine	4.4 (0.9)	Minnesota	11.2 (0.7)	Kansas	0.2 (0.2)
Maine	9.4 (0.7)	Vermont	4.1 (1.1)	Wisconsin	10.9 (0.9)	Missouri	0.2 (0.2)
Wisconsin	9.4 (0.8)	Massachusetts	3.8 (1.0)	Vermont	10.8 (0.9)	Oklahoma	0.2 (0.2)
Hawaii	7.7 (0.7)	West Virginia	2.7 (0.8)	Hawaii	8.8 (0.9)	Oregon	0.2 (0.2)
Massachusetts	5.6 (0.6)	Hawaii	2.3 (0.7)	Massachusetts	6.3 (0.7)	New Hampshire	0.0 (0.0)

Note: (1) Standard error appears in parenthesis; figures cover 2010; (b) base less than 75,000; (x) not applicable
Source: U.S. Census Bureau, Current Population Survey, 2011 Annual Social and Economic Supplement. Table HI05. Health Insurance Coverage Status and Type of Coverage by State and Age for All People: 2010

Managed Care Organizations Ranked by Total Enrollment

State	Total Enrollment	Organization	Plan Type
Alabama	75,000,000	UnitedHealthCare of Alabama	HMO/PPO
Alabama	54,000,000	Delta Dental of Alabama	Dental
Alabama	8,000,000	United Concordia: Alabama	Dental
Alabama	4,500,000	CompBenefits: Alabama	Multiple
Alabama	3,200,000	Blue Cross & Blue Shield of Alabama	HMO
Alabama	3,200,000	Blue Cross Preferred Care	PPO
Alabama	502,000	Behavioral Health Systems	PPO
Alabama	80,000	VIVA Health	HMO
Alabama	66,000	North Alabama Managed Care Inc	PPO
Alabama	47,000	Assurant Employee Benefits: Alabama	Multiple
Alabama	45,000	Health Choice of Alabama	PPO
Alabama	30,000	HealthSpring of Alabama	Medicare
Alabama	8,147	Great-West Healthcare Alabama	HMO/PPO
Alaska	75,000,000	UnitedHealthCare of Alaska	HMO/PPO
Alaska	11,596,230	Aetna Health of Alaska	PPO
Alaska	1,500,000	ODS Alaska	Multiple
Alaska	187,000	Premera Blue Cross Blue Shield of Alaska	PPO
Alaska	8,097	Humana Health Insurance of Alaska	HMO/PPO
Alaska	1,003	CCN: Alaska	PPO
Arizona	75,000,000	UnitedHealthCare of Arizona	HMO/PPO
Arizona	60,000,000	Preferred Therapy Providers	PPO
Arizona	55,000,000	VSP: Vision Service Plan of Arizona	Vision
Arizona	54,000,000	Delta Dental of Arizona	Dental
Arizona	8,000,000	United Concordia: Arizona	Dental
Arizona	7,000,000	Outlook Vision Service	Vision
Arizona	2,000,000	Avesis: Corporate Headquarters	PPO
Arizona	1,100,000	CoreSource: Arizona	Multiple
Arizona	1,000,000	Blue Cross & Blue Shield of Arizona	HMO/PPO
Arizona	300,000	Mercy Care Plan/Mercy Care Advantage	Medicare
Arizona	175,000	Arizona Foundation for Medical Care	Multiple
Arizona	127,564	Humana Health Insurance of Arizona	HMO/PPO
Arizona	120,000	Employers Dental Services	Dental
Arizona	119,000	Health Net of Arizona	HMO
Arizona	115,000	Health Choice Arizona	HMO
Arizona	109,089	Aetna Health of Arizona	HMO
Arizona	103,561	CIGNA HealthCare of Arizona	HMO/PPO
Arizona	98,500	Action Healthcare Management Services	PPO
Arizona	80,000	Magellan Health Services Arizona	PPO
Arizona	55,000	SecureCare Dental	Dental
Arizona	50,715	Maricopa Integrated Health System/Maricopa Health Plan	HMO
Arizona	37,459	Great-West Healthcare Arizona	HMO/PPO
Arizona	7,000	Pima Health System	HMO
Arizona	3,000	Abrazo Advantage Health Plan	Multiple
Arkansas	75,000,000	UnitedHealthCare of Arkansas	HMO/PPO
Arkansas	54,000,000	Delta Dental of Arkansas	Dental
Arkansas	11,596,230	Aetna Health of Arkansas	PPO
Arkansas	1,100,000	CoreSource: Arkansas	Multiple
Arkansas	475,000	HealthSCOPE Benefits	Other
Arkansas	460,448	CIGNA HealthCare of Arkansas	HMO
Arkansas	400,000	Arkansas Blue Cross and Blue Shield	Multiple

State	Total Enrollment	Organization	Plan Type
Arkansas	200,000	Arkansas Managed Care Organization	PPO
Arkansas	73,000	Mercy Health Plans: Arkansas	HMO
Arkansas	50,000	American Denticare	HMO
Arkansas	36,000	QualChoice/QCA Health Plan	HMO/PPO
Arkansas	7,000	Arkansas Community Care	Medicare
California	94,000,000	American Specialty Health	HMO
California	75,000,000	UnitedHealthCare of Northern California	HMO/PPO
California	75,000,000	UnitedHealthCare of Southern California	HMO/PPO
California	55,000,000	VSP: Vision Service Plan	Vision
California	55,000,000	VSP: Vision Service Plan of California	Vision
California	54,000,000	Delta Dental of California	Dental
California	43,000,000	United Behavioral Health	Other
California	16,000,000	Beech Street Corporation: Corporate Office	PPO
California	12,225,000	Beech Street Corporation: Northeast Region	PPO
California	12,225,000	Beech Street Corporation: Western Region	HMO
California	10,000,000	Managed Health Network	PPO
California	10,000,000	CIGNA HealthCare of Northern California	HMO
California	10,000,000	CIGNA HealthCare of Southern California	HMO
California	8,569,000	Kaiser Permanente Health Plan: Corporate Office	HMO
California	8,000,000	United Concordia: California	Dental
California	6,700,000	Health Net Medicare Plan	Medicare
California	6,600,000	Dental Benefit Providers: California	Dental
California	6,000,000	Health Net: Corporate Headquarters	HMO
California	3,500,000	Blue Shield of California	HMO/PPO
California	3,284,000	Kaiser Permanente Health Plan of Southern California	HMO
California	3,223,235	Kaiser Permanente Health Plan of Northern California	HMO
California	2,900,000	Interplan Health Group	PPO
California	2,000,000	Superior Vision Services, Inc.	Vision
California	1,915,829	PacifiCare Health Systems	HMO
California	1,800,000	March Vision Care	Vision
California	1,800,000	SafeGuard Health Enterprises: Corporate Office	Dental
California	1,400,000	Molina Healthcare: Corporate Office	HMO
California	1,283,000	PacifiCare of California	HMO
California	1,100,000	Orange County Foundation for Medical Care	PPO
California	1,100,000	Physical Therapy Provider Network	Multiple
California	1,000,000	California Foundation for Medical Care	PPO
California	950,000	Bright Now! Dental	Dental
California	857,252	L.A. Care Health Plan	HMO
California	700,000	Los Angeles County Public Healthcare	HMO
California	650,000	Pacific Dental Benefits	Dental
California	540,000	Health Net Dental	Dental
California	461,773	Inland Empire Health Plan	HMO
California	427,039	Aetna Health of California	HMO
California	402,000	CalOptima	HMO
California	390,000	Dental Alternatives Insurance Services	Dental
California	338,000	Pacific Health Alliance	PPO
California	315,440	Western Dental Services	Dental
California	300,000	Pacific Foundation for Medical Care	Multiple
California	291,000	Care 1st Health Plan: California	HMO
California	250,000	Lakeside Community Healthcare Network	HMO
California	234,072	CIGNA HealthCare of California	HMO
California	204,077	Great-West Healthcare California	HMO/PPO
California	200,473	Golden West Dental & Vision Plan	Multiple
California	200,000	Community Health Plan of Los Angeles County	HMO
California	190,000	Central California Alliance for Health	HMO

16

State	Total Enrollment	Organization	Plan Type
California	150,000	Landmark Healthplan of California	HMO/PPO
California	140,462	PacifiCare Dental and Vision Administrators	Multiple
California	130,000	Alameda Alliance for Health	HMO
California	128,272	SCAN Health Plan	HMO
California	125,000	Premier Access Insurance/Access Dental	PPO
California	123,880	Access Dental Services	Dental
California	121,794	Santa Clara Family Health Plan	HMO
California	116,000	Community Health Group	HMO
California	109,000	Health Plan of San Joaquin	HMO
California	100,000	Contra Costa Health Plan	HMO
California	97,000	Kern Family Health Care	HMO
California	93,000	Partnership HealthPlan of California	Medicare
California	90,000	BEST Life and Health Insurance Co.	PPO
California	90,000	Dental Health Services of California	Dental
California	87,740	Health Plan of San Mateo	HMO
California	70,819	Western Health Advantage	HMO
California	60,000	Foundation for Medical Care for Kern & Santa Barbara County	PPO
California	55,000	Arta Medicare Health Plan	Medicare
California	55,000	San Francisco Health Plan	HMO
California	49,000	Sharp Health Plan	HMO
California	47,000	Assurant Employee Benefits: California	Multiple
California	41,266	Coastal Healthcare Administrators	PPO
California	34,000	Foundation for Medical Care for Mendocino and Lake Counties	PPO
California	17,000	Primecare Dental Plan	Dental
California	14,600	Inter Valley Health Plan	Multiple
California	13,582	Chinese Community Health Plan	HMO
California	8,000	Easy Choice Health Plan	Medicare
California	3,000	Central Health Medicare Plan	Medicare
California	1,000	On Lok Lifeways	HMO
Colorado	75,000,000	UnitedHealthCare of Colorado	HMO/PPO
Colorado	55,000,000	VSP: Vision Service Plan of Colorado	Vision
Colorado	54,000,000	Delta Dental of Colorado	Dental
Colorado	8,000,000	United Concordia: Colorado	Dental
Colorado	2,000,000	Great-West/One Health Plan	HMO/PPO
Colorado	880,475	Anthem Blue Cross & Blue Shield of Colorado	HMO/PPO
Colorado	522,000	Kaiser Permanente Health Plan of Colorado	HMO
Colorado	328,000	PacifiCare of Colorado	HMO
Colorado	270,000	CNA Insurance Companies: Colorado	PPO
Colorado	180,000	Rocky Mountain Health Plans	HMO/PPO
Colorado	160,000	Colorado Health Partnerships	HMO
Colorado	126,000	HMO Colorado	HMO
Colorado	123,472	Great-West PPO	HMO/PPO
Colorado	113,229	Humana Health Insurnace of Colorado	HMO/PPO
Colorado	60,000	Boulder Valley Individual Practice Association	PPO
Colorado	56,000	Beta Health Plan	Multiple
Colorado	47,000	Assurant Employee Benefits: Colorado	Multiple
Colorado	36,611	CIGNA HealthCare of Colorado	HMO
Colorado	36,423	Aetna Health of Colorado	HMO
Colorado	15,000	Denver Health Medical Plan Inc	HMO
Colorado	5,000	Colorado Choice Health Plans	HMO
Connecticut	75,000,000	UnitedHealthCare of Connecticut	HMO/PPO
Connecticut	54,000,000	Delta Dental of New Jersey & Connecticut	Dental
Connecticut	18,602,000	Aetna Health, Inc. Corporate Headquarters	HMO
Connecticut	1,600,000	Oxford Health Plans: Corporate Headquarters	HMO/PPO

State	Total Enrollment	Organization	Plan Type
Connecticut	1,535,753	Anthem Blue Cross & Blue Shield Connecticut	HMO/PPO
Connecticut	1,200,000	Health Plan of New York: Connecticut	HMO/PPO
Connecticut	240,000	ConnectiCare	HMO/PPO
Connecticut	169,000	Health Net of the Northeast	HMO
Connecticut	29,506	CIGNA HealthCare of Connecticut	HMO
Delaware	75,000,000	UnitedHealthCare of the Mid-Atlantic	HMO/PPO
Delaware	54,000,000	Delta Dental of the Mid-Atlantic	Dental
Delaware	400,000	Blue Cross & Blue Shield of Delaware	HMO/PPO
Delaware	265,000	AmeriHealth HMO	HMO/PPO
Delaware	180,000	Mid Atlantic Medical Services: Delaware	HMO/PPO
Delaware	100,000	Coventry Health Care of Delaware	HMO/PPO
Delaware	27,179	Aetna Health of Delaware	HMO
Delaware	2,718	Great-West Healthcare Delaware	HMO/PPO
Delaware	984	CIGNA HealthCare of Delaware	HMO
District of Columbia	75,000,000	UnitedHealthCare of the District of Columbia	HMO/PPO
District of Columbia	54,000,000	Delta Dental of the Mid-Atlantic	Dental
District of Columbia	550,000	CareFirst Blue Cross Blue Shield	HMO/PPO
District of Columbia	211,156	Aetna Health District of Columbia	HMO
District of Columbia	180,000	Mid Atlantic Medical Services: DC	HMO/PPO
District of Columbia	109,186	CIGNA HealthCare of the Mid-Atlantic	HMO/PPO
District of Columbia	90,000	Quality Plan Administrators	HMO/PPO
District of Columbia	70,000	DC Chartered Health Plan	HMO
Florida	75,000,000	UnitedHealthCare of Florida	HMO/PPO
Florida	75,000,000	UnitedHealthCare of South Florida	HMO/PPO
Florida	55,000,000	VSP: Vision Service Plan of Florida	Vision
Florida	54,000,000	Delta Dental of Florida	Dental
Florida	8,000,000	United Concordia: Florida	Dental
Florida	4,500,000	CompBenefits: Florida	Multiple
Florida	2,200,000	WellCare Health Plans	Medicare
Florida	1,900,000	Amerigroup Florida	HMO
Florida	1,800,000	SafeGuard Health Enterprises: Florida	Dental
Florida	1,547,873	Blue Cross & Blue Shield of Florida: Jacksonville	HMO/PPO
Florida	1,400,000	Molina Healthcare: Florida	HMO
Florida	900,000	CompCare: Comprehensive Behavioral Care	Multiple
Florida	521,696	Aetna Health of Florida	HMO
Florida	400,000	Dimension Health PPO	PPO
Florida	320,000	First Medical Health Plan of Florida	Medicare
Florida	310,000	Coventry Health Care of Florida	HMO/PPO
Florida	300,000	AvMed Health Plan: Gainesville	HMO
Florida	300,000	AvMed Health Plan: Jacksonville	HMO
Florida	300,000	AvMed Health Plan: Orlando	HMO
Florida	300,000	AvMed Health Plan: Tampa	HMO
Florida	300,000	AvMed Health Plan: Corporate Office	HMO
Florida	300,000	AvMed Health Plan: Fort Lauderdale	HMO
Florida	194,944	CIGNA HealthCare of Florida	HMO
Florida	125,000	Humana Health Insurance of Tampa - Pinellas	HMO/PPO
Florida	125,000	Humana Health Insurance of Jacksonville	HMO/PPO
Florida	113,000	Capital Health Plan	HMO
Florida	108,000	Neighborhood Health Partnership	HMO
Florida	105,000	JMH Health Plan	HMO
Florida	81,822	Great-West Healthcare Florida	HMO/PPO
Florida	69,000	Vista Healthplan of South Florida, Inc	Multiple
Florida	67,440	Florida Health Care Plan	HMO

State	Total Enrollment	Organization	Plan Type
Florida	63,700	Health First Health Plans	HMO
Florida	62,000	CarePlus Health Plans, Inc	HMO
Florida	56,000	Humana Health Insurance of Orlando	HMO/PPO
Florida	54,000	Citrus Health Care	Medicare
Florida	54,000	Blue Cross & Blue Shield of Florida: Pensacola	HMO/PPO
Florida	52,000	Preferred Medical Plan	HMO
Florida	47,000	Assurant Employee Benefits: Florida	Multiple
Florida	45,000	Preferred Care Partners	Multiple
Florida	35,000	Healthchoice Orlando	PPO
Florida	27,000	Leon Medical Centers Health Plan	HMO
Florida	19,000	Quality Health Plans	Medicare
Florida	12,000	Medica HealthCare Plans, Inc	Medicare
Florida	10,000	Total Health Choice	HMO
Florida	6,000	Avalon Healthcare	PPO
Georgia	75,000,000	UnitedHealthCare of Georgia	HMO/PPO
Georgia	55,000,000	VSP: Vision Service Plan of Georgia	Vision
Georgia	54,000,000	Delta Dental of Georgia	Dental
Georgia	8,000,000	United Concordia: Georgia	Dental
Georgia	4,500,000	CompBenefits Corporation	Multiple
Georgia	3,300,000	Blue Cross & Blue Shield of Georgia	HMO
Georgia	2,000,000	Avesis: Georgia	PPO
Georgia	1,900,000	Amerigroup Georgia	HMO
Georgia	1,000,000	National Better Living Association	PPO
Georgia	270,000	CNA Insurance Companies: Georgia	PPO
Georgia	257,819	Kaiser Permanente of Georgia	HMO
Georgia	150,000	Coventry Health Care of GA	HMO/PPO
Georgia	116,375	Aetna Health of Georgia	HMO
Georgia	73,000	Humana Health Insurance of Georgia	HMO/PPO
Georgia	68,000	Secure Health PPO Newtork	PPO
Georgia	49,984	Great-West Healthcare Georgia	HMO/PPO
Georgia	47,000	Assurant Employee Benefits: Georgia	Multiple
Georgia	42,000	Northeast Georgia Health Partners	PPO
Georgia	25,769	CIGNA HealthCare of Georgia	HMO
Georgia	23,241	Athens Area Health Plan Select	HMO
Georgia	15,000	Alliant Health Plans	HMO/PPO
Hawaii	75,000,000	UnitedHealthCare of Hawaii	HMO/PPO
Hawaii	55,000,000	VSP: Vision Service Plan of Hawaii	Vision
Hawaii	11,596,230	Aetna Health of Hawaii	PPO
Hawaii	556,000	Hawaii Medical Services Association	PPO
Hawaii	223,795	Kaiser Permanente Health Plan of Hawaii	HMO
Hawaii	75,000	AlohaCare	HMO
Hawaii	42,000	Hawaii Medical Assurance Association	PPO
Hawaii	36,505	University Health Alliance	PPO
Hawaii	2,407	CIGNA HealthCare of Hawaii	HMO
Hawaii	368	Great-West Healthcare Hawaii	HMO/PPO
Idaho	75,000,000	UnitedHealthCare of Idaho	HMO/PPO
Idaho	54,000,000	Delta Dental of Idaho	Dental
Idaho	11,596,230	Aetna Health of Idaho	PPO
Idaho	2,500,000	Regence BlueShield of Idaho	Multiple
Idaho	563,000	Blue Cross of Idaho Health Service, Inc.	HMO/PPO
Idaho	456,719	IHC: Intermountain Healthcare Health Plan	HMO
Idaho	280,000	PacificSource Health Plans: Idaho	HMO/PPO
Idaho	27,000	CIGNA HealthCare of Idaho	PPO

State	Total Enrollment	Organization	Plan Type
Idaho	14,000	Primary Health Plan	Multiple
Illinois	75,000,000	UnitedHealthCare of Illinois	HMO/PPO
Illinois	55,000,000	VSP: Vision Service Plan of Illinois	Vision
Illinois	54,000,000	Delta Dental of Illinois	Dental
Illinois	12,400,000	Health Care Service Corporation	HMO/PPO
Illinois	6,500,000	Blue Cross & Blue Shield of Illinois	HMO/PPO
Illinois	6,200,000	Dental Network of America	Dental
Illinois	4,500,000	CompBenefits: Illinois	Multiple
Illinois	1,500,000	OSF Healthcare	HMO
Illinois	1,100,000	CoreSource: Corporate Headquarters	Multiple
Illinois	763,175	Humana Health Insurance of Illinois	HMO/PPO
Illinois	475,000	Trustmark Companies	PPO
Illinois	470,623	HealthSmart Preferred Care	PPO
Illinois	316,465	Health Alliance Medical Plans	HMO/PPO
Illinois	316,000	Preferred Network Access	PPO
Illinois	300,000	First Commonwealth	HMO
Illinois	270,000	CNA Insurance Companies: Illinois	PPO
Illinois	255,494	Health Alliance Medicare	Medicare
Illinois	145,000	Unicare: Illinois	HMO/PPO
Illinois	115,313	Great-West Healthcare Illinois	HMO/PPO
Illinois	77,000	PersonalCare	HMO
Illinois	64,973	OSF HealthPlans	PPO
Illinois	47,000	Assurant Employee Benefits: Illinois	Multiple
Illinois	45,014	Aetna Health of Illinois	HMO
Illinois	45,000	Medical Associates Health Plan	HMO
Illinois	18,588	CIGNA HealthCare of Illinois	HMO
Indiana	75,000,000	UnitedHealthCare of Indiana	HMO/PPO
Indiana	55,000,000	VSP: Vision Service Plan of Indiana	Vision
Indiana	54,000,000	Delta Dental of Michigan, Ohio and Indiana	Dental
Indiana	36,500,000	Magellan Health Services Indiana	PPO
Indiana	35,000,000	WellPoint: Corporate Office	HMO
Indiana	28,000,000	Anthem Dental Services	Dental
Indiana	2,000,000	Avesis: Indiana	PPO
Indiana	1,600,818	Anthem Blue Cross & Blue Sheild of Indiana	HMO
Indiana	900,000	Anthem Blue Cross & Blue Shield of Indiana	HMO/PPO
Indiana	664,318	Encore Health Network	PPO
Indiana	500,000	Meritain Health: Indiana	PPO
Indiana	360,561	Sagamore Health Network	PPO
Indiana	200,000	Health Resources, Inc.	Dental
Indiana	140,000	Deaconess Health Plans	PPO
Indiana	102,506	Humana Health Insurance of Indiana	HMO/PPO
Indiana	90,000	Parkview Total Health	PPO
Indiana	86,000	Advantage Health Solutions	HMO
Indiana	45,014	Aetna Health of Indiana	HMO
Indiana	43,620	Great-West Healthcare Indiana	HMO/PPO
Indiana	43,000	Physicians Health Plan of Northern Indiana	HMO
Indiana	40,000	Cardinal Health Alliance	HMO/PPO
Indiana	38,515	Welborn Health Plans	HMO
Indiana	15,153	American Health Network of Indiana	PPO
Indiana	10,231	Southeastern Indiana Health Organization	HMO
Indiana	9,678	CIGNA HealthCare of Indiana	HMO
Indiana	8,000	Arnett Health Plans	HMO
Iowa	75,000,000	UnitedHealthCare of Iowa	HMO/PPO

State	Total Enrollment	Organization	Plan Type
Iowa	54,000,000	Delta Dental of Iowa	Dental
Iowa	11,596,230	Aetna Health of Iowa	PPO
Iowa	7,000,000	Humana Health Insurance of Iowa	HMO/PPO
Iowa	2,000,000	Avesis: Iowa	PPO
Iowa	250,000	Wellmark Health Plan of Iowa	HMO
Iowa	50,000	Sanford Health Plan	HMO
Iowa	47,000	Coventry Health Care of Iowa	HMO/PPO
Iowa	45,000	Medical Associates Health Plan: West	HMO
Iowa	34,284	CIGNA HealthCare of Iowa	HMO
Iowa	10,082	Great-West Healthcare Iowa	HMO/PPO
Kansas	75,000,000	UnitedHealthCare of Kansas	HMO/PPO
Kansas	55,000,000	VSP: Vision Service Plan of Kansas	Vision
Kansas	54,000,000	Delta Dental of Kansas	Dental
Kansas	11,596,230	Aetna Health of Kansas	PPO
Kansas	5,000,000	PCC Preferred Chiropractic Care	PPO
Kansas	1,100,000	CoreSource: Kansas (FMH CoreSource)	Multiple
Kansas	898,111	Blue Cross & Blue Shield of Kansas	HMO
Kansas	400,000	Preferred Mental Health Management	Multiple
Kansas	152,000	ProviDRs Care Network	PPO
Kansas	145,000	Unicare: Kansas	HMO/PPO
Kansas	135,000	Advance Insurance Company of Kansas	Multiple
Kansas	100,000	Preferred Vision Care	Vision
Kansas	95,000	Health Partners of Kansas	PPO
Kansas	84,841	Humana Health Insurance of Kansas	HMO/PPO
Kansas	83,151	Preferred Plus of Kansas	HMO
Kansas	73,000	Coventry Health Care of Kansas	HMO/PPO
Kansas	73,000	Mercy Health Plans: Kansas	HMO
Kansas	47,000	Assurant Employee Benefits: Kansas	Multiple
Kansas	33,153	Preferred Health Systems Insurance Company	PPO
Kansas	21,580	Great-West Healthcare Kansas	HMO/PPO
Kansas	9,848	CIGNA HealthCare of Kansas	HMO
Kentucky	75,000,000	UnitedHealthCare of Kentucky	HMO/PPO
Kentucky	54,000,000	Delta Dental of Kentucky	Dental
Kentucky	11,596,230	Aetna Health of Kentucky	PPO
Kentucky	4,000,000	Humana Medicare Plan	Medicare
Kentucky	894,531	Anthem Blue Cross & Blue Shield of Kentucky	HMO
Kentucky	500,000	Meritain Health: Kentucky	PPO
Kentucky	190,000	CHA Health	HMO
Kentucky	159,730	Passport Health Plan	HMO
Kentucky	136,472	Bluegrass Family Health	HMO/PPO
Kentucky	110,000	Preferred Health Plan Inc	PPO
Louisiana	75,000,000	UnitedHealthCare of Louisiana	HMO/PPO
Louisiana	54,000,000	Delta Dental Insurance Company	Dental
Louisiana	11,596,230	Aetna Health of Louisiana	PPO
Louisiana	1,172,000	Blue Cross & Blue Shield of Louisiana	HMO/PPO
Louisiana	500,000	Meritain Health: Louisiana	PPO
Louisiana	142,000	Humana Health Insurance of Louisiana	HMO/PPO
Louisiana	137,000	Calais Health	Multiple
Louisiana	42,000	Peoples Health	Medicare
Louisiana	41,000	Tenet Choices	HMO
Louisiana	30,000	Coventry Health Care of Louisiana	HMO
Louisiana	30,000	DINA Dental Plans	Dental
Louisiana	30,000	Health Plus of Louisiana	HMO

State	Total Enrollment	Organization	Plan Type
Louisiana	14,000	Vantage Medicare Advantage	Medicare
Louisiana	14,000	Vantage Health Plan	HMO
Maine	75,000,000	UnitedHealthCare of Maine	HMO/PPO
Maine	1,100,000	Harvard Pilgrim Health Care: Maine	Multiple
Maine	545,610	Anthem Blue Cross & Blue Shield of Maine	HMO/PPO
Maine	85,000	Martin's Point HealthCare	Multiple
Maine	22,417	Aetna Health of Maine	HMO
Maine	8,184	Great-West Healthcare Maine	HMO/PPO
Maine	6,343	CIGNA HealthCare of Maine	HMO
Maryland	75,000,000	UnitedHealthCare of the Mid-Atlantic	HMO/PPO
Maryland	54,000,000	Delta Dental of the Mid-Atlantic	Dental
Maryland	36,500,000	Magellan Health Services: Corporate Headquarters	Multiple
Maryland	17,000,000	Spectera	Multiple
Maryland	8,000,000	United Concordia: Maryland	Dental
Maryland	6,600,000	Dental Benefit Providers	Dental
Maryland	5,000,000	Coventry Health Care: Corporate Headquarters	HMO/PPO
Maryland	3,000,000	Block Vision	Vision
Maryland	3,000,000	Catalyst Health Solutions Inc	HMO
Maryland	2,000,000	Avesis: Maryland	PPO
Maryland	1,900,000	Amerigroup Maryland	HMO
Maryland	1,100,000	CoreSource: Maryland	Multiple
Maryland	970,000	OneNet PPO	PPO
Maryland	960,000	Alliance PPO, LLC	PPO
Maryland	471,360	Kaiser Permanente Health Plan of the Mid-Atlantic States	HMO
Maryland	360,000	Bravo Health: Corporate Headquarters	Medicare
Maryland	211,156	Aetna Health of Maryland	HMO
Maryland	185,000	Priority Partners Health Plans	HMO
Maryland	161,000	Mid Atlantic Medical Services: Corporate Office	HMO/PPO
Maryland	151,000	Optimum Choice	HMO
Maryland	141,000	American Postal Workers Union (APWU) Health Plan	HMO/PPO
Maryland	109,186	CIGNA HealthCare of the Mid-Atlantic	HMO/PPO
Maryland	101,900	Mid Atlantic Psychiatric Services (MAMSI)	Multiple
Maryland	10,000	Denta-Chek of Maryland	Multiple
Maryland	8,000	Graphic Arts Benefit Corporation	HMO/PPO
Massachusetts	75,000,000	UnitedHealthCare of Massachusetts	HMO/PPO
Massachusetts	55,000,000	VSP: Vision Service Plan of Massachusetts	Vision
Massachusetts	14,000,000	Dentaquest	Dental
Massachusetts	3,000,000	Blue Cross & Blue Shield of Massachusetts	HMO
Massachusetts	2,000,000	Avesis: Massachusetts	PPO
Massachusetts	2,000,000	Great-West Healthcare of Massachusetts	HMO/PPO
Massachusetts	1,200,000	Health Plan of New York: Massachusetts	HMO/PPO
Massachusetts	1,079,674	Harvard Pilgrim Health Care	Multiple
Massachusetts	737,411	Tufts Health Plan	HMO/PPO
Massachusetts	240,890	Boston Medical Center Healthnet Plan	HMO
Massachusetts	240,000	ConnectiCare of Massachusetts	HMO/PPO
Massachusetts	186,000	Neighborhood Health Plan	HMO
Massachusetts	178,000	Fallon Community Health Plan	HMO/PPO
Massachusetts	106,000	Health New England	HMO
Massachusetts	80,000	Unicare: Massachusetts	HMO/PPO
Massachusetts	47,000	Assurant Employee Benefits: Massachusetts	Multiple
Massachusetts	12,000	Health Plans, Inc.	Other
Massachusetts	11,121	Aetna Health of Massachusetts	HMO
Massachusetts	10,315	CIGNA HealthCare of Massachusetts	PPO

State	Total Enrollment	Organization	Plan Type
Massachusetts	6,443	Harvard University Group Health Plan	HMO
Michigan	75,000,000	UnitedHealthCare of Michigan	HMO/PPO
Michigan	55,000,000	VSP: Vision Service Plan of Michigan	Vision
Michigan	54,000,000	Delta Dental: Corporate Headquarters	Dental
Michigan	11,596,230	Aetna Health of Michigan	PPO
Michigan	8,000,000	United Concordia: Michigan	Dental
Michigan	4,500,000	DenteMax	Dental
Michigan	4,300,000	Blue Cross Blue Shield of Michigan	PPO
Michigan	2,500,000	Cofinity	PPO
Michigan	1,700,000	Unicare: Michigan	HMO
Michigan	1,400,000	Molina Healthcare: Michigan	HMO
Michigan	1,100,000	CoreSource: Michigan (NGS CoreSource)	Multiple
Michigan	620,000	Blue Care Network of Michigan: Corporate Headquarters	HMO
Michigan	620,000	Blue Care Network: Ann Arbor	HMO
Michigan	620,000	Blue Care Network: Flint	HMO
Michigan	620,000	Blue Care Network: Great Lakes, Muskegon Heights	HMO
Michigan	596,220	Priority Health: Corporate Headquarters	HMO
Michigan	500,000	Health Alliance Plan	HMO/PPO
Michigan	500,000	Meritain Health: Michigan	PPO
Michigan	390,000	SVS Vision	Vision
Michigan	383,000	Health Alliance Medicare	Medicare
Michigan	250,863	Health Plan of Michigan	HMO
Michigan	220,000	M-Care	PPO
Michigan	215,000	Great Lakes Health Plan	HMO
Michigan	200,000	HealthPlus of Michigan: Flint	HMO
Michigan	200,000	HealthPlus of Michigan: Saginaw	HMO
Michigan	200,000	HealthPlus of Michigan: Troy	HMO
Michigan	187,000	Paramount Care of Michigan	HMO/PPO
Michigan	185,000	American Community Mutual Insurance Company	PPO
Michigan	130,000	Golden Dental Plans	Dental
Michigan	112,011	Humana Health Insurance of Michigan	HMO/PPO
Michigan	90,000	Total Health Care	HMO
Michigan	68,942	Physicians Health Plan of Mid-Michigan	HMO
Michigan	50,000	OmniCare: A Coventry Health Care Plan	HMO
Michigan	50,000	CareSource: Michigan	HMO
Michigan	47,000	Assurant Employee Benefits: Michigan	Multiple
Michigan	35,992	Great-West Healthcare Michigan	HMO/PPO
Michigan	25,278	Upper Peninsula Health Plan	HMO
Michigan	17,000	ConnectCare	PPO
Michigan	14,000	HealthPlus Senior Medicare Plan	Medicare
Michigan	8,000	Grand Valley Health Plan	HMO
Minnesota	75,000,000	UnitedHealthCare of Minnesota	HMO/PPO
Minnesota	75,000,000	UnitedHealthCare of Wisconsin: Central	HMO/PPO
Minnesota	60,000,000	OptumHealth Care Solutions: Physical Health	Multiple
Minnesota	55,000,000	Security Life Insurance Company of America	Multiple
Minnesota	55,000,000	VSP: Vision Service Plan of Minnesota	Vision
Minnesota	54,000,000	Delta Dental of Minnesota	Dental
Minnesota	11,596,230	Aetna Health of Minnesota	PPO
Minnesota	2,700,000	Blue Cross & Blue Shield of Minnesota	HMO
Minnesota	2,000,000	Avesis: Minnesota	PPO
Minnesota	1,600,000	Medica: Corporate Office	PPO
Minnesota	1,250,000	HealthPartners	HMO
Minnesota	500,000	Meritain Health: Minnesota	PPO
Minnesota	250,000	Araz Group	PPO

State	Total Enrollment	Organization	Plan Type
Minnesota	200,000	UCare Minnesota	HMO/PPO
Minnesota	97,800	PreferredOne	HMO/PPO
Minnesota	80,000	Patient Choice	PPO
Minnesota	75,000	UCare Medicare Plan	Medicare
Minnesota	64,977	CIGNA HealthCare of Minnesota	HMO
Minnesota	47,000	Assurant Employee Benefits: Minnesota	Multiple
Minnesota	21,000	Metropolitan Health Plan	HMO
Minnesota	18,556	Great-West Healthcare Minnesota	HMO/PPO
Minnesota	3,971	Evercare Health Plans	Medicare
Mississippi	75,000,000	UnitedHealthCare of Mississippi	HMO/PPO
Mississippi	54,000,000	Delta Dental Insurance Company	Dental
Mississippi	11,596,230	Aetna Health of Mississippi	PPO
Mississippi	155,070	Health Link PPO	PPO
Mississippi	78,600	Humana Health Insurance of Mississippi	HMO/PPO
Mississippi	64,997	CIGNA HealthCare of Mississippi	HMO
Missouri	75,000,000	UnitedHealthCare of Missouri	HMO/PPO
Missouri	54,000,000	Delta Dental of Missouri	Dental
Missouri	1,700,000	Dental Health Alliance	Dental
Missouri	1,450,000	Centene Corporation	HMO
Missouri	1,400,000	Molina Healthcare: Missouri	HMO
Missouri	1,159,875	BlueChoice	HMO
Missouri	1,100,000	Anthem Blue Cross & Blue Shield of Missouri	PPO
Missouri	1,000,000	Blue Cross & Blue Shield of Kansas City	PPO
Missouri	1,000,000	HealthLink HMO	HMO
Missouri	942,000	American Health Care Alliance	PPO
Missouri	900,000	GEHA-Government Employees Hospital Association	Multiple
Missouri	500,000	Meritain Health: Missouri	PPO
Missouri	330,000	GHP Coventry Health Plan	HMO/PPO
Missouri	238,976	Preferred Care Blue	PPO
Missouri	185,375	Healthcare USA of Missouri	HMO
Missouri	119,600	Mid America Health	HMO/PPO
Missouri	73,000	Mercy Health Plans: Corporate Office	HMO
Missouri	67,308	Great-West Healthcare Missouri	HMO/PPO
Missouri	49,976	Children's Mercy Family Health Partners	HMO
Missouri	47,000	Assurant Employee Benefits: Corporate Headquarters	Multiple
Missouri	10,885	Aetna Health of Missouri	HMO
Missouri	8,049	CIGNA HealthCare of St. Louis	HMO
Missouri	7,000	Community Health Improvement Solutions	HMO
Missouri	5,000	Cox Healthplans	HMO/PPO
Montana	75,000,000	UnitedHealthCare of Montana	HMO/PPO
Montana	54,000,000	Delta Dental of Montana	Dental
Montana	11,596,230	Aetna Health of Montana	PPO
Montana	236,000	Blue Cross & Blue Shield of Montana	HMO
Montana	80,000	Health InfoNet	PPO
Montana	43,000	New West Health Services	HMO/PPO
Montana	43,000	New West Medicare Plan	Medicare
Montana	7,642	CIGNA HealthCare of Montana	HMO
Montana	4,970	Great-West Healthcare Montana	HMO/PPO
Nebraska	75,000,000	UnitedHealthCare of Nebraska	HMO/PPO
Nebraska	54,000,000	Delta Dental of Nebraska	Dental
Nebraska	11,596,230	Aetna Health of Nebraska	PPO
Nebraska	2,543,705	Ameritas Group	Dental

State	Total Enrollment	Organization	Plan Type
Nebraska	717,000	Blue Cross & Blue Shield of Nebraska	PPO
Nebraska	615,000	Midlands Choice	PPO
Nebraska	54,418	Mutual of Omaha Health Plans	HMO/PPO
Nebraska	54,000	Coventry Health Care of Nebraska	HMO/PPO
Nebraska	18,322	CIGNA HealthCare of Nebraska	PPO
Nevada	54,000,000	Delta Dental of Nevada	Dental
Nevada	14,000,000	Anthem Blue Cross & Blue Shield of Nevada	HMO/PPO
Nevada	1,900,000	Amerigroup Nevada	HMO
Nevada	600,000	Behavioral Healthcare Options, Inc.	HMO/PPO
Nevada	580,000	UnitedHealthcare Nevada	HMO/PPO
Nevada	418,000	Health Plan of Nevada	HMO/PPO
Nevada	150,000	Nevada Preferred Healthcare Providers	HMO/PPO
Nevada	150,000	Nevada Preferred Healthcare Providers	PPO
Nevada	109,089	Aetna Health of Nevada	HMO
Nevada	32,000	Hometown Health Plan	Multiple
Nevada	26,000	PacifiCare of Nevada	HMO
Nevada	15,000	Saint Mary's Health Plans	HMO
Nevada	3,000	NevadaCare	HMO
New Hampshire	75,000,000	UnitedHealthCare of New Hampshire	HMO/PPO
New Hampshire	54,000,000	Delta Dental Northeast	Dental
New Hampshire	11,596,230	Aetna Health of New Hampshire	PPO
New Hampshire	1,100,000	Harvard Pilgrim Health Care of New England	Multiple
New Hampshire	750,000	MVP Health Care: New Hampshire	HMO/PPO
New Hampshire	560,000	Anthem Blue Cross & Blue Shield of New Hampshire	HMO
New Hampshire	23,559	CIGNA HealthCare of New Hampshire	HMO
New Jersey	75,000,000	UnitedHealthCare of New Jersey	HMO/PPO
New Jersey	55,000,000	VSP: Vision Service Plan of New Jersey	Vision
New Jersey	54,000,000	Delta Dental of New Jersey & Connecticut	Dental
New Jersey	5,183,333	Aetna Health of New Jersey	HMO
New Jersey	3,600,000	Horizon Blue Cross & Blue Shield of New Jersey	HMO/PPO
New Jersey	3,600,000	Horizon Healthcare of New Jersey	HMO/PPO
New Jersey	1,900,000	Amerigroup New Jersey	HMO
New Jersey	975,000	CHN PPO	PPO
New Jersey	750,000	QualCare	HMO/PPO
New Jersey	500,000	HealthFirst New Jersey Medicare Plan	Medicare
New Jersey	467,000	Horizon NJ Health	PPO
New Jersey	332,840	Oxford Health Plans: New Jersey	HMO
New Jersey	300,000	Block Vision of New Jersey	Vision
New Jersey	265,000	AmeriHealth HMO	HMO/PPO
New Jersey	200,871	AmeriChoice by UnitedHealthCare	HMO
New Jersey	150,000	Atlanticare Health Plans	HMO/PPO
New Jersey	68,935	CIGNA HealthCare of New Jersey	HMO
New Jersey	47,000	Assurant Employee Benefits: New Jersey	Multiple
New Jersey	21,000	Rayant Insurance Company	Dental
New Jersey	12,317	WellChoice	HMO
New Mexico	75,000,000	UnitedHealthCare of New Mexico	HMO/PPO
New Mexico	54,000,000	Delta Dental of New Mexico	Dental
New Mexico	11,596,230	Aetna Health of New Mexico	PPO
New Mexico	8,000,000	United Concordia: New Mexico	Dental
New Mexico	1,900,000	Amerigroup New Mexico	HMO
New Mexico	1,400,000	Molina Healthcare: New Mexico	HMO
New Mexico	400,000	Presbyterian Health Plan	HMO

State	Total Enrollment	Organization	Plan Type
New Mexico	367,000	Blue Cross & Blue Shield of New Mexico	HMO/PPO
New Mexico	200,000	Lovelace Medicare Health Plan	HMO/PPO
New Mexico	163,000	Lovelace Health Plan	HMO
New Mexico	10,816	Great-West Healthcare New Mexico	HMO/PPO
New York	75,000,000	UnitedHealthCare of New York	HMO/PPO
New York	55,000,000	Davis Vision	Vision
New York	54,000,000	Delta Dental of the Mid-Atlantic	Dental
New York	19,000,000	MultiPlan, Inc.	PPO
New York	8,000,000	United Concordia: New York	Dental
New York	4,450,116	Coalition America's National Preferred Provider Network	PPO
New York	2,000,000	Healthplex	Dental
New York	2,000,000	Universal American Medicare Plans	Medicare
New York	1,900,000	Amerigroup New York	HMO
New York	1,850,000	National Medical Health Card	Multiple
New York	1,700,000	Excellus Blue Cross Blue Shield: Central New York	HMO
New York	1,700,000	Excellus Blue Cross Blue Shield: Rochester Region	HMO
New York	1,700,000	Excellus Blue Cross Blue Shield: Utica Region	HMO
New York	1,700,000	Univera Healthcare	HMO
New York	1,601,000	Group Health Incorporated (GHI)	HMO/PPO
New York	1,500,000	Oxford Health Plans: New York	HMO
New York	1,326,000	MagnaCare	PPO
New York	1,200,000	Health Plan of New York	HMO/PPO
New York	750,000	MVP Health Care: Buffalo Region	HMO/PPO
New York	750,000	MVP Health Care: Central New York	HMO/PPO
New York	750,000	MVP Health Care: Corporate Office	HMO/PPO
New York	750,000	MVP Health Care: Mid-State Region	HMO/PPO
New York	750,000	MVP Health Care: Western New York	HMO/PPO
New York	625,000	Fidelis Care	Multiple
New York	555,405	Blue Cross & Blue Shield of Western New York	HMO/PPO
New York	553,000	HealthNow New York	HMO
New York	500,000	Meritain Health: Corporate Headquarters	PPO
New York	400,000	CDPHP Medicare Plan	Medicare
New York	365,000	Independent Health	HMO
New York	350,000	CDPHP: Capital District Physicians' Health Plan	HMO/PPO
New York	332,128	MetroPlus Health Plan	HMO
New York	240,000	ConnectiCare of New York	HMO/PPO
New York	205,677	Guardian Life Insurance Company	HMO/PPO
New York	200,000	Vytra Health Plans	HMO/PPO
New York	193,498	BlueShield of Northeastern New York	HMO/PPO
New York	171,028	Empire Blue Cross & Blue Shield	HMO/PPO
New York	154,162	Aetna Health of New York	PPO
New York	134,837	Affinity Health Plan	HMO
New York	107,387	AmeriChoice by UnitedHealthCare	HMO
New York	81,000	Humana Health Insurance of New York	HMO/PPO
New York	80,000	NOVA Healthcare Administrators	Other
New York	53,000	GHI Medicare Plan	Medicare
New York	52,000	Island Group Administration, Inc.	Multiple
New York	40,319	CIGNA HealthCare of New York	HMO
New York	30,000	Atlantis Health Plan	HMO
New York	28,785	Great-West Healthcare New York	HMO/PPO
New York	19,000	Quality Health Plans of New York	Medicare
New York	16,000	Elderplan	Medicare
New York	11,000	Touchstone Health HMO	Medicare
New York	9,000	Perfect Health Insurance Company	PPO

State	Total Enrollment	Organization	Plan Type
North Carolina	75,000,000	UnitedHealthCare of North Carolina	HMO/PPO
North Carolina	54,000,000	Delta Dental of North Carolina	Dental
North Carolina	50,000,000	Mid Atlantic Medical Services: North Carolina	HMO/PPO
North Carolina	8,000,000	United Concordia: North Carolina	Dental
North Carolina	5,000,000	Catalyst RX	PPO
North Carolina	3,718,355	Blue Cross & Blue Shield of North Carolina	HMO/PPO
North Carolina	1,100,000	CoreSource: North Carolina	Multiple
North Carolina	1,000,000	OptiCare Managed Vision	Vision
North Carolina	670,000	MedCost	PPO
North Carolina	494,200	Humana Health Insurance of North Carolina	HMO/PPO
North Carolina	160,000	WellPath: A Coventry Health Care Plan	HMO
North Carolina	56,422	Great-West Healthcare North Carolina	HMO/PPO
North Carolina	47,000	Assurant Employee Benefits: North Carolina	Multiple
North Carolina	40,000	Crescent Preferred Provider Organization	PPO
North Carolina	29,583	CIGNA HealthCare of North Carolina	HMO
North Carolina	18,960	Aetna Health of the Carolinas	HMO
North Carolina	13,000	FirstCarolinaCare	HMO
North Dakota	75,000,000	UnitedHealthCare of North Dakota	HMO/PPO
North Dakota	54,000,000	Delta Dental of North Dakota	Dental
North Dakota	11,596,230	Aetna Health of North Dakota	PPO
North Dakota	1,600,000	Medica: North Dakota	HMO
North Dakota	434,000	Noridian Insurance Services	PPO
North Dakota	1,000	Heart of America Health Plan	HMO
North Dakota	884	Great-West Healthcare North Dakota	HMO/PPO
Ohio	159,000,000	EyeMed Vision Care	Vision
Ohio	75,000,000	UnitedHealthCare of Ohio: Columbus	HMO/PPO
Ohio	75,000,000	UnitedHealthCare of Ohio: Dayton & Cincinnati	HMO/PPO
Ohio	55,000,000	VSP: Vision Service Plan of Ohio	Vision
Ohio	54,000,000	Delta Dental of Michigan, Ohio and Indiana	Dental
Ohio	3,000,000	Anthem Blue Cross & Blue Shield of Ohio	PPO
Ohio	1,900,000	Amerigroup Ohio	HMO
Ohio	1,400,000	Molina Healthcare: Ohio	HMO
Ohio	1,107,000	Medical Mutual of Ohio	HMO/PPO
Ohio	1,100,000	CoreSource: Ohio	Multiple
Ohio	1,000,000	Interplan Health Group	PPO
Ohio	840,000	CareSource	HMO
Ohio	500,000	Aultcare Corporation	HMO/PPO
Ohio	500,000	Meritain Health: Ohio	PPO
Ohio	380,000	The Health Plan of the Upper Ohio Valley	HMO/PPO
Ohio	370,000	Ohio Health Choice	PPO
Ohio	269,392	The Dental Care Plus Group	Dental
Ohio	187,000	Paramount Health Care	HMO/PPO
Ohio	187,000	Paramount Elite Medicare Plan	Medicare
Ohio	159,375	Aetna Health of Ohio	HMO
Ohio	155,000	SummaCare Health Plan	HMO/PPO
Ohio	110,000	Kaiser Permanente Health Plan Ohio	HMO
Ohio	108,000	HealthSpan	PPO
Ohio	103,000	Unison Health Plan of Ohio	HMO
Ohio	100,000	Humana Health Insurance of Ohio	HMO/PPO
Ohio	100,000	OhioHealth Group	PPO
Ohio	52,000	Ohio State University Health Plan Inc.	Multiple
Ohio	47,000	Assurant Employee Benefits: Ohio	Multiple
Ohio	28,125	Mount Carmel Health Plan Inc (MediGold)	Medicare
Ohio	26,000	SummaCare Medicare Advantage Plan	Medicare

State	Total Enrollment	Organization	Plan Type
Oklahoma	75,000,000	UnitedHealthCare of Oklahoma	HMO/PPO
Oklahoma	54,000,000	Delta Dental of Oklahoma	Dental
Oklahoma	600,000	Blue Cross & Blue Shield of Oklahoma	HMO/PPO
Oklahoma	522,248	BlueLincs HMO	HMO
Oklahoma	250,000	CommunityCare Managed Healthcare Plans of Oklahoma	HMO/PPO
Oklahoma	73,000	Mercy Health Plans: Oklahoma	HMO
Oklahoma	47,000	Assurant Employee Benefits: Oklahoma	Multiple
Oklahoma	43,000	PacifiCare of Oklahoma	HMO
Oklahoma	31,363	Aetna Health of Oklahoma	HMO
Oklahoma	18,335	Great-West Healthcare Oklahoma	HMO/PPO
Oregon	75,000,000	UnitedHealthCare of Oregon	HMO/PPO
Oregon	55,000,000	VSP: Vision Service Plan of Oregon	Vision
Oregon	11,596,230	Aetna Health of Oregon	PPO
Oregon	8,000,000	United Concordia: Oregon	Dental
Oregon	2,500,000	Regence Blue Cross & Blue Shield of Oregon	PPO
Oregon	1,500,000	Lifewise Health Plan of Oregon	PPO
Oregon	1,500,000	ODS Health Plan	Multiple
Oregon	471,000	Kaiser Permanente Health Plan Northwest	HMO
Oregon	350,000	Providence Health Plans	HMO/PPO
Oregon	280,000	PacificSource Health Plans: Corporate Headquarters	HMO/PPO
Oregon	131,096	CareOregon Health Plan	Medicare
Oregon	129,120	Managed HealthCare Northwest	PPO
Oregon	126,000	CIGNA HealthCare of Oregon	PPO
Oregon	123,000	Health Net Health Plan of Oregon	HMO/PPO
Oregon	47,000	Assurant Employee Benefits: Oregon	Multiple
Oregon	39,334	Great-West Healthcare Oregon	HMO/PPO
Oregon	35,000	Clear One Health Plans	Multiple
Oregon	30,000	Samaritan Health Plan	Multiple
Oregon	29,000	PacifiCare of Oregon	HMO
Oregon	2,000	FamilyCare Health Medicare Plan	Medicare
Pennsylvania	75,000,000	UnitedHealthCare of Pennsylvania	HMO/PPO
Pennsylvania	54,000,000	Delta Dental of the Mid-Atlantic	Dental
Pennsylvania	22,000,000	Value Behavioral Health of Pennsylvania	PPO
Pennsylvania	11,000,000	CIGNA: Corporate Headquarters	HMO
Pennsylvania	8,000,000	United Concordia	Dental
Pennsylvania	4,700,000	Highmark Blue Cross & Blue Shield	HMO/PPO
Pennsylvania	3,400,000	Keystone Health Plan East	HMO/PPO
Pennsylvania	3,300,000	Independence Blue Cross	HMO/PPO
Pennsylvania	3,100,000	American WholeHealth Network	PPO
Pennsylvania	3,000,000	Devon Health Services	PPO
Pennsylvania	1,100,000	CoreSource: Pennsylvania	Multiple
Pennsylvania	700,000	InterGroup Services Corporation	PPO
Pennsylvania	600,000	Blue Cross of Northeastern Pennsylvania	HMO/PPO
Pennsylvania	600,000	Highmark Blue Shield	PPO
Pennsylvania	500,000	HealthAmerica	Multiple
Pennsylvania	500,000	HealthAmerica Pennsylvania	Multiple
Pennsylvania	409,265	Aetna Health of Pennsylvania	HMO
Pennsylvania	360,000	Bravo Health: Pennsylvania	Medicare
Pennsylvania	250,000	Geisinger Health Plan	HMO/PPO
Pennsylvania	244,000	Gateway Health Plan	HMO
Pennsylvania	186,425	Preferred Care	PPO
Pennsylvania	180,000	Mid Atlantic Medical Services: Pennsylvania	HMO/PPO
Pennsylvania	174,309	Valley Preferred	Multiple

State	Total Enrollment	Organization	Plan Type
Pennsylvania	160,000	Unison Health Plan of Pennsylvania	Multiple
Pennsylvania	154,000	Health Partners Medicare Plan	Medicare
Pennsylvania	143,488	CIGNA HealthCare of Pennsylvania	HMO
Pennsylvania	121,000	Capital Blue Cross	HMO/PPO
Pennsylvania	115,400	First Priority Health	HMO
Pennsylvania	101,000	UPMC Health Plan	Multiple
Pennsylvania	93,000	Keystone Health Plan Central	HMO
Pennsylvania	80,316	Preferred Health Care	PPO
Pennsylvania	71,000	Americhoice of Pennsylvania	Multiple
Pennsylvania	60,353	Berkshire Health Partners	PPO
Pennsylvania	60,000	American Health Care Group	HMO/PPO
Pennsylvania	56,000	South Central Preferred	PPO
Pennsylvania	50,000	Blue Ridge Health Network	PPO
Pennsylvania	47,000	Assurant Employee Benefits: Pennsylvania	Multiple
Pennsylvania	45,000	Susquehanna Health Care	PPO
Pennsylvania	33,000	Prime Source Health Network	PPO
Pennsylvania	26,411	Great-West Healthcare Pennsylvania	HMO/PPO
Pennsylvania	20,000	Preferred Healthcare System	PPO
Pennsylvania	18,500	Penn Highlands Health Plan	PPO
Pennsylvania	15,700	SelectCare Access Corporation	PPO
Pennsylvania	12,700	Central Susquehanna Healthcare Providers	PPO
Pennsylvania	2,375	Val-U-Health	PPO
Puerto Rico	75,000,000	UnitedHealthCare of Puerto Rico	HMO/PPO
Puerto Rico	370,000	Humana Health Insurance of Puerto Rico	HMO/PPO
Puerto Rico	300,000	Medical Card System (MCS)	Multiple
Puerto Rico	180,000	First Medical Health Plan	Multiple
Puerto Rico	126,000	MMM Healthcare	Multiple
Puerto Rico	100,000	Triple-S Salud Blue Cross Blue Shield of Puerto Rico	Multiple
Puerto Rico	53,000	PMC Medicare Choice	Medicare
Rhode Island	75,000,000	CVS CareMark	Other
Rhode Island	75,000,000	UnitedHealthCare of Rhode Island	HMO/PPO
Rhode Island	54,000,000	Delta Dental of Rhode Island	Dental
Rhode Island	11,596,230	Aetna Health of Rhode Island	PPO
Rhode Island	737,411	Tufts Health Plan: Rhode Island	HMO/PPO
Rhode Island	600,000	Blue Cross & Blue Shield of Rhode Island	HMO
Rhode Island	76,000	Neighborhood Health Plan of Rhode Island	HMO
South Carolina	75,000,000	UnitedHealthCare of South Carolina	HMO/PPO
South Carolina	55,000,000	VSP: Vision Service Plan of South Carolina	Vision
South Carolina	54,000,000	Delta Dental of South Carolina	Dental
South Carolina	950,000	Blue Cross & Blue Shield of South Carolina	HMO/PPO
South Carolina	205,000	BlueChoice Health Plan of South Carolina	Multiple
South Carolina	200,000	Select Health of South Carolina	HMO
South Carolina	144,000	Medical Mutual Services	PPO
South Carolina	123,000	Carolina Care Plan	HMO
South Carolina	47,000	Assurant Employee Benefits: South Carolina	Multiple
South Carolina	39,000	Unison Health Plan of South Carolina	HMO
South Carolina	30,000	InStil Health	Medicare
South Carolina	19,468	Kanawha Healthcare Solutions	PPO
South Carolina	18,960	Aetna Health of the Carolinas	HMO
South Carolina	16,852	Great-West Healthcare South Carolina	HMO/PPO
South Carolina	14,341	CIGNA HealthCare of South Carolina	HMO
South Dakota	75,000,000	UnitedHealthCare of South Dakota	HMO/PPO

State	Total Enrollment	Organization	Plan Type
South Dakota	54,000,000	Delta Dental of South Dakota	Dental
South Dakota	11,596,230	Aetna Health of South Dakota	PPO
South Dakota	1,600,000	Medica: South Dakota	HMO
South Dakota	199,000	Wellmark Blue Cross & Blue Shield of South Dakota	PPO
South Dakota	118,600	DakotaCare	HMO
South Dakota	87,000	First Choice of the Midwest	PPO
South Dakota	18,000	Avera Health Plans	HMO
South Dakota	8,135	CIGNA HealthCare of South Dakota	PPO
South Dakota	1,685	Great-West Healthcare South Dakota	HMO/PPO
Tennessee	75,000,000	UnitedHealthCare of Tennessee	HMO/PPO
Tennessee	3,000,000	Blue Cross & Blue Shield of Tennessee	HMO/PPO
Tennessee	1,900,000	Amerigroup Tennessee	HMO
Tennessee	1,200,000	Delta Dental of Tennessee	Dental
Tennessee	551,309	John Deere Health	HMO/PPO
Tennessee	518,000	Health Choice LLC	PPO
Tennessee	423,244	Baptist Health Services Group	Other
Tennessee	345,000	HealthSpring: Corporate Offices	Medicare
Tennessee	229,356	CIGNA HealthCare of Tennessee	HMO
Tennessee	200,000	Initial Group	PPO
Tennessee	172,000	Humana Health Insurance of Tennessee	HMO/PPO
Tennessee	80,000	Signature Health Alliance	PPO
Tennessee	75,000	Windsor Medicare Extra	Medicare
Tennessee	73,000	Cariten Healthcare	Multiple
Tennessee	50,919	Cariten Preferred	PPO
Tennessee	48,477	HealthPartners	PPO
Tennessee	47,000	Assurant Employee Benefits: Tennessee	Multiple
Tennessee	24,054	Aetna Health of Tennessee	HMO
Texas	75,000,000	UnitedHealthCare of Texas	HMO/PPO
Texas	55,000,000	VSP: Vision Service Plan of Texas	Vision
Texas	54,000,000	Delta Dental of Texas	Dental
Texas	8,000,000	United Concordia: Texas	Dental
Texas	5,427,579	USA Managed Care Organization	PPO
Texas	5,000,000	MHNet Behavioral Health	Multiple
Texas	4,000,000	Blue Cross & Blue Shield of Texas: Houston	HMO/PPO
Texas	3,800,000	HMO Blue Texas	HMO
Texas	3,645,891	Blue Cross & Blue Shield of Texas	HMO/PPO
Texas	3,200,000	Galaxy Health Network	PPO
Texas	2,000,000	Avesis: Texas	PPO
Texas	1,900,000	Amerigroup Texas	HMO
Texas	1,800,000	SafeGuard Health Enterprises: Texas	Dental
Texas	1,400,000	Molina Healthcare: Texas	HMO
Texas	1,080,000	HAS-Premier Providers	PPO
Texas	1,080,000	Texas True Choice	PPO
Texas	470,623	HealthSmart Preferred Care	PPO
Texas	360,000	Bravo Health: Texas	Medicare
Texas	300,000	WellPoint NextRx	Multiple
Texas	294,566	Aetna Health of Texas	HMO
Texas	230,000	Texas Community Care	Medicare
Texas	203,856	Great-West Healthcare Texas	HMO/PPO
Texas	202,000	Scott & White Health Plan	HMO
Texas	172,000	Humana Health Insurance of Corpus Christi	HMO/PPO
Texas	172,000	Humana Health Insurance of San Antonio	HMO/PPO
Texas	170,000	Parkland Community Health Plan	HMO
Texas	146,000	PacifiCare of Texas	HMO

State	Total Enrollment	Organization	Plan Type
Texas	130,000	First Care Health Plans	Multiple
Texas	120,000	Horizon Health Corporation	PPO
Texas	111,877	CIGNA HealthCare of South Texas	HMO
Texas	111,877	CIGNA HealthCare of North Texas	HMO/PPO
Texas	110,000	Community First Health Plans	HMO/PPO
Texas	107,539	Healthcare Partners of East Texas	PPO
Texas	80,000	Alliance Regional Health Network	PPO
Texas	73,000	Mercy Health Plans: Texas	HMO
Texas	65,300	Brazos Valley Health Network	PPO
Texas	47,000	Assurant Employee Benefits: Texas	Multiple
Texas	42,000	TexanPlus Medicare Advantage HMO	Medicare
Texas	38,000	Unicare: Texas	HMO/PPO
Texas	30,000	Concentra: Corporate Office	HMO/PPO
Texas	22,000	Valley Baptist Health Plan	HMO
Texas	15,000	Seton Health Plan	HMO
Texas	1,000	UTMB HealthCare Systems	HMO
Texas	1,000	Legacy Health Plan	HMO
Utah	75,000,000	UnitedHealthCare of Utah	HMO/PPO
Utah	54,000,000	Delta Dental of Utah	Dental
Utah	11,596,230	Aetna Health of Utah	PPO
Utah	1,400,000	Molina Healthcare: Utah	HMO
Utah	500,000	Meritain Health: Utah	PPO
Utah	402,000	SelectHealth	HMO
Utah	320,000	Regence Blue Cross & Blue Shield of Utah	PPO
Utah	177,854	Public Employees Health Program	PPO
Utah	150,000	Opticare of Utah	Vision
Utah	148,000	Altius Health Plans	Multiple
Utah	86,000	University Health Plans	HMO/PPO
Utah	47,724	CIGNA HealthCare of Utah	HMO/PPO
Utah	6,000	Educators Mutual	HMO/PPO
Vermont	75,000,000	UnitedHealthCare of Vermont	HMO/PPO
Vermont	54,000,000	Delta Dental of Vermont	Dental
Vermont	11,596,230	Aetna Health of Vermont	PPO
Vermont	750,000	MVP Health Care: Vermont	HMO/PPO
Vermont	180,000	Blue Cross & Blue Shield of Vermont	PPO
Virginia	75,000,000	UnitedHealthCare of Virginia	HMO/PPO
Virginia	54,000,000	Delta Dental of Virginia	Dental
Virginia	24,000,000	Dominion Dental Services	Dental
Virginia	8,000,000	United Concordia: Virginia	Dental
Virginia	3,400,000	CareFirst Blue Cross & Blue Shield of Virginia	HMO/PPO
Virginia	2,800,000	Anthem Blue Cross & Blue Shield of Virginia	HMO
Virginia	1,900,000	Amerigroup Corporation	HMO
Virginia	415,000	Optima Health Plan	HMO/PPO
Virginia	324,600	CIGNA HealthCare of Virginia	HMO
Virginia	211,156	Aetna Health of Virginia	HMO
Virginia	200,000	Coventry Health Care Virginia	HMO/PPO
Virginia	180,000	Mid Atlantic Medical Services: Virginia	HMO/PPO
Virginia	143,725	Virginia Premier Health Plan	HMO
Virginia	105,200	Trigon Health Care	HMO
Virginia	100,000	National Capital PPO	PPO
Virginia	88,366	Virginia Health Network	PPO
Virginia	53,000	Peninsula Health Care	HMO/PPO
Virginia	30,000	Piedmont Community Health Plan	PPO

State	Total Enrollment	Organization	Plan Type
Washington	75,000,000	UnitedHealthCare of Washington	HMO/PPO
Washington	55,000,000	VSP: Vision Service Plan of Washington	Vision
Washington	54,000,000	Delta Dental of Washington	Dental
Washington	11,596,230	Aetna Health of Washington	PPO
Washington	8,000,000	United Concordia: Washington	Dental
Washington	1,500,000	Lifewise Health Plan of Washington	PPO
Washington	1,400,000	Molina Healthcare: Washington	HMO
Washington	1,300,000	Premera Blue Cross	PPO
Washington	1,117,128	Regence Blue Shield	PPO
Washington	600,000	Group Health Cooperative	Multiple
Washington	270,000	Community Health Plan of Washington	Multiple
Washington	240,000	PacifiCare Benefit Administrators	PPO
Washington	120,000	CIGNA HealthCare of Washington	PPO
Washington	47,000	Assurant Employee Benefits: Washington	Multiple
Washington	45,000	PacifiCare of Washington	HMO
West Virginia	75,000,000	UnitedHealthCare of West Virginia	HMO/PPO
West Virginia	54,000,000	Delta Dental of the Mid-Atlantic	Dental
West Virginia	11,596,230	Aetna Health of West Virginia	PPO
West Virginia	400,000	Mountain State Blue Cross Blue Shiled	PPO
West Virginia	180,000	Mid Atlantic Medical Services: West Virginia	HMO/PPO
West Virginia	100,000	Coventry Health Care of West Virginia	HMO/PPO
West Virginia	80,000	Unicare: West Virginia	HMO/PPO
West Virginia	65,000	SelectNet Plus, Inc.	PPO
West Virginia	35,316	CIGNA HealthCare of West Virginia	PPO
West Virginia	11,745	Great-West Healthcare West Virginia	HMO/PPO
Wisconsin	75,000,000	UnitedHealthCare of Wisconsin: Central	HMO/PPO
Wisconsin	54,000,000	Delta Dental of Wisconsin	Dental
Wisconsin	11,596,230	Aetna Health of Wisconsin	PPO
Wisconsin	5,000,000	Vision Insurance Plan of America	Vision
Wisconsin	820,000	HealthEOS	PPO
Wisconsin	247,881	Dean Health Plan	Multiple
Wisconsin	200,000	Care Plus Dental Plans	Dental
Wisconsin	187,000	Security Health Plan of Wisconsin	Multiple
Wisconsin	175,000	Wisconsin Physician's Service	PPO
Wisconsin	150,000	ChiroCare of Wisconsin	PPO
Wisconsin	130,000	Managed Health Services	HMO
Wisconsin	119,712	Prevea Health Network	PPO
Wisconsin	118,000	Network Health Plan of Wisconsin	HMO/PPO
Wisconsin	112,000	Physicians Plus Insurance Corporation	HMO/PPO
Wisconsin	95,000	Group Health Cooperative of Eau Claire	HMO
Wisconsin	90,000	Gundersen Lutheran Health Plan	HMO
Wisconsin	90,000	Unity Health Insurance	Multiple
Wisconsin	72,853	CIGNA HealthCare of Wisconsin	PPO
Wisconsin	61,000	Group Health Cooperative of South Central Wisconsin	HMO
Wisconsin	49,000	Humana Health Insurance of Wisconsin	HMO/PPO
Wisconsin	47,000	Assurant Employee Benefits: Wisconsin	Multiple
Wisconsin	45,000	Medical Associates Health Plan: East	HMO
Wisconsin	34,000	Health Tradition	HMO
Wisconsin	30,000	MercyCare Health Plans	HMO
Wisconsin	28,619	Great-West Healthcare Wisconsin	HMO/PPO
Wisconsin	24,000	ABRI Health Plan, Inc.	Multiple
Wisconsin	5,000	Trilogy Health Insurance	PPO

State	Total Enrollment	Organization	Plan Type
Wyoming	75,000,000	UnitedHealthCare of Wyoming	HMO/PPO
Wyoming	54,000,000	Delta Dental of Wyoming	Dental
Wyoming	11,596,230	Aetna Health of Wyoming	PPO
Wyoming	100,000	Blue Cross & Blue Shield of Wyoming	PPO
Wyoming	11,234	CIGNA HealthCare of Wyoming	PPO
Wyoming	11,000	WINhealth Partners	Multiple

Managed Care Organizations Ranked by State Enrollment

State	State Enrollment	Organization	Plan Type
Alabama	3,200,000	Blue Cross & Blue Shield of Alabama	HMO
Alabama	2,842,000	Blue Cross Preferred Care	PPO
Alabama	831,000	Beech Street Corporation: Alabama	PPO
Alabama	107,210	UnitedHealthCare of Alabama	HMO/PPO
Alabama	80,000	VIVA Health	HMO
Alabama	45,000	Health Choice of Alabama	PPO
Alabama	17,844	HealthSpring of Alabama	Medicare
Alabama	6,662	Great-West Healthcare Alabama	HMO/PPO
Alaska	187,000	Premera Blue Cross Blue Shield of Alaska	PPO
Alaska	6,000	Beech Street: Alaska	PPO
Arizona	1,270,000	UnitedHealthCare of Arizona	HMO/PPO
Arizona	1,000,000	Blue Cross & Blue Shield of Arizona	HMO/PPO
Arizona	435,000	Delta Dental of Arizona	Dental
Arizona	300,000	Mercy Care Plan/Mercy Care Advantage	Medicare
Arizona	120,000	Employers Dental Services	Dental
Arizona	103,561	CIGNA HealthCare of Arizona	HMO/PPO
Arizona	100,000	Phoenix Health Plan	HMO
Arizona	80,000	Magellan Health Services Arizona	PPO
Arizona	60,500	Health Net of Arizona	HMO
Arizona	39,997	Maricopa Integrated Health System/Maricopa Health Plan	HMO
Arizona	26,120	Humana Health Insurance of Arizona	HMO/PPO
Arizona	7,000	Pima Health System	HMO
Arizona	5,048	Great-West Healthcare Arizona	HMO/PPO
Arkansas	1,000,000	Delta Dental of Arkansas	Dental
Arkansas	400,000	Arkansas Blue Cross and Blue Shield	Multiple
Arkansas	200,000	Arkansas Managed Care Organization	PPO
Arkansas	92,995	UnitedHealthCare of Arkansas	HMO/PPO
Arkansas	84,176	QualChoice/QCA Health Plan	HMO/PPO
California	6,700,000	Health Net Medicare Plan	Medicare
California	6,400,000	Kaiser Permanente Health Plan: Corporate Office	HMO
California	3,500,000	Blue Shield of California	HMO/PPO
California	3,284,540	Kaiser Permanente Health Plan of Southern California	HMO
California	3,223,235	Kaiser Permanente Health Plan of Northern California	HMO
California	2,300,000	UnitedHealthCare of Northern California	HMO/PPO
California	2,300,000	UnitedHealthCare of Southern California	HMO/PPO
California	1,700,000	Interplan Health Group	PPO
California	1,345,473	PacifiCare Health Systems	HMO
California	836,724	L.A. Care Health Plan	HMO
California	773,000	Beech Street Corporation: Northeast Region	PPO
California	653,000	Beech Street Corporation: Corporate Office	PPO
California	653,000	Beech Street Corporation: Western Region	HMO
California	461,773	Inland Empire Health Plan	HMO
California	450,000	CIGNA HealthCare of Northern California	HMO
California	450,000	CIGNA HealthCare of Southern California	HMO
California	427,039	Aetna Health of California	HMO
California	402,000	CalOptima	HMO
California	250,000	Lakeside Community Healthcare Network	HMO
California	234,072	CIGNA HealthCare of California	HMO
California	200,000	Community Health Plan of Los Angeles County	HMO

State	State Enrollment	Organization	Plan Type
California	197,000	Pacific Health Alliance	PPO
California	190,000	Central California Alliance for Health	HMO
California	121,794	Santa Clara Family Health Plan	HMO
California	116,000	Community Health Group	HMO
California	110,000	Alameda Alliance for Health	HMO
California	109,000	Health Plan of San Joaquin	HMO
California	100,000	Contra Costa Health Plan	HMO
California	90,074	Kern Family Health Care	HMO
California	87,740	Health Plan of San Mateo	HMO
California	70,819	Western Health Advantage	HMO
California	57,459	Great-West Healthcare California	HMO/PPO
California	55,000	Arta Medicare Health Plan	Medicare
California	55,000	San Francisco Health Plan	HMO
California	49,000	Sharp Health Plan	HMO
California	34,000	Foundation for Medical Care for Mendocino and Lake Counties	PPO
California	12,283	SCAN Health Plan	HMO
California	8,000	Easy Choice Health Plan	Medicare
California	6,336	Chinese Community Health Plan	HMO
California	942	On Lok Lifeways	HMO
Colorado	735,900	UnitedHealthCare of Colorado	HMO/PPO
Colorado	522,000	Kaiser Permanente Health Plan of Colorado	HMO
Colorado	180,000	Rocky Mountain Health Plans	HMO/PPO
Colorado	160,000	Colorado Health Partnerships	HMO
Colorado	115,262	Great-West/One Health Plan	HMO/PPO
Colorado	113,229	Humana Health Insurnace of Colorado	HMO/PPO
Colorado	100,000	Delta Dental of Colorado	Dental
Colorado	60,270	Anthem Blue Cross & Blue Shield of Colorado	HMO/PPO
Colorado	36,611	CIGNA HealthCare of Colorado	HMO
Colorado	36,423	Aetna Health of Colorado	HMO
Colorado	15,000	Denver Health Medical Plan Inc	HMO
Connecticut	391,301	Anthem Blue Cross & Blue Shield Connecticut	HMO/PPO
Connecticut	356,844	Health Net of the Northeast	HMO
Connecticut	160,000	ConnectiCare	HMO/PPO
Connecticut	70,139	Oxford Health Plans: Corporate Headquarters	HMO/PPO
Connecticut	61,677	Aetna Health, Inc. Corporate Headquarters	HMO
Connecticut	29,506	CIGNA HealthCare of Connecticut	HMO
Delaware	400,000	Blue Cross & Blue Shield of Delaware	HMO/PPO
Delaware	27,179	Aetna Health of Delaware	HMO
Delaware	20,538	UnitedHealthCare of the Mid-Atlantic	HMO/PPO
Delaware	2,508	Great-West Healthcare Delaware	HMO/PPO
Delaware	984	CIGNA HealthCare of Delaware	HMO
District of Columbia	176,000	UnitedHealthCare of the District of Columbia	HMO/PPO
District of Columbia	90,000	Quality Plan Administrators	HMO/PPO
District of Columbia	70,000	DC Chartered Health Plan	HMO
Florida	2,200,000	WellCare Health Plans	Medicare
Florida	1,373,917	Blue Cross & Blue Shield of Florida: Jacksonville	HMO/PPO
Florida	870,159	UnitedHealthCare of Florida	HMO/PPO
Florida	521,696	Aetna Health of Florida	HMO
Florida	400,000	Dimension Health PPO	PPO
Florida	320,000	First Medical Health Plan of Florida	Medicare
Florida	300,000	AvMed Health Plan: Corporate Office	HMO

State	State Enrollment	Organization	Plan Type
Florida	300,000	AvMed Health Plan: Fort Lauderdale	HMO
Florida	300,000	AvMed Health Plan: Gainesville	HMO
Florida	300,000	AvMed Health Plan: Jacksonville	HMO
Florida	300,000	AvMed Health Plan: Orlando	HMO
Florida	300,000	AvMed Health Plan: Tampa	HMO
Florida	295,000	UnitedHealthCare of South Florida	HMO/PPO
Florida	237,000	Amerigroup Florida	HMO
Florida	194,944	CIGNA HealthCare of Florida	HMO
Florida	141,178	Neighborhood Health Partnership	HMO
Florida	105,024	Capital Health Plan	HMO
Florida	105,000	JMH Health Plan	HMO
Florida	63,700	Health First Health Plans	HMO
Florida	62,000	CarePlus Health Plans, Inc	HMO
Florida	54,000	Citrus Health Care	Medicare
Florida	39,776	Preferred Medical Plan	HMO
Florida	39,511	Florida Health Care Plan	HMO
Florida	35,000	Healthchoice Orlando	PPO
Florida	15,347	Total Health Choice	HMO
Florida	1,771	Great-West Healthcare Florida	HMO/PPO
Georgia	1,051,334	UnitedHealthCare of Georgia	HMO/PPO
Georgia	500,733	Blue Cross & Blue Shield of Georgia	HMO
Georgia	257,819	Kaiser Permanente of Georgia	HMO
Georgia	150,000	Coventry Health Care of GA	HMO/PPO
Georgia	116,375	Aetna Health of Georgia	HMO
Georgia	82,000	Humana Health Insurance of Georgia	HMO/PPO
Georgia	68,000	Secure Health PPO Newtork	PPO
Georgia	42,000	Northeast Georgia Health Partners	PPO
Georgia	25,769	CIGNA HealthCare of Georgia	HMO
Georgia	23,241	Athens Area Health Plan Select	HMO
Georgia	15,000	Alliant Health Plans	HMO/PPO
Georgia	1,545	Great-West Healthcare Georgia	HMO/PPO
Hawaii	414,370	Hawaii Medical Services Association	PPO
Hawaii	223,795	Kaiser Permanente Health Plan of Hawaii	HMO
Hawaii	42,000	Hawaii Medical Assurance Association	PPO
Hawaii	3,902	UnitedHealthCare of Hawaii	HMO/PPO
Hawaii	1,602	CIGNA HealthCare of Hawaii	HMO
Hawaii	213	Great-West Healthcare Hawaii	HMO/PPO
Idaho	2,500,000	Regence BlueShield of Idaho	Multiple
Idaho	563,000	Blue Cross of Idaho Health Service, Inc.	HMO/PPO
Idaho	296,175	IHC: Intermountain Healthcare Health Plan	HMO
Idaho	40,618	UnitedHealthCare of Idaho	HMO/PPO
Illinois	12,400,000	Health Care Service Corporation	HMO/PPO
Illinois	6,500,000	Blue Cross & Blue Shield of Illinois	HMO/PPO
Illinois	763,175	Humana Health Insurance of Illinois	HMO/PPO
Illinois	646,192	UnitedHealthCare of Illinois	HMO/PPO
Illinois	585,000	First Health	PPO
Illinois	316,000	Preferred Network Access	PPO
Illinois	59,830	PersonalCare	HMO
Illinois	45,014	Aetna Health of Illinois	HMO
Illinois	37,792	Medical Associates Health Plan	HMO
Illinois	18,588	CIGNA HealthCare of Illinois	HMO
Illinois	9,662	Great-West Healthcare Illinois	HMO/PPO

State	State Enrollment	Organization	Plan Type
Illinois	2,732	OSF HealthPlans	PPO
Indiana	450,000	Meritain Health: Indiana	PPO
Indiana	244,441	UnitedHealthCare of Indiana	HMO/PPO
Indiana	132,000	Deaconess Health Plans	PPO
Indiana	61,064	Advantage Health Solutions	HMO
Indiana	48,000	Physicians Health Plan of Northern Indiana	HMO
Indiana	45,086	Arnett Health Plans	HMO
Indiana	40,136	Anthem Blue Cross & Blue Sheild of Indiana	HMO
Indiana	10,231	Southeastern Indiana Health Organization	HMO
Indiana	9,678	CIGNA HealthCare of Indiana	HMO
Indiana	900	Humana Health Insurance of Indiana	HMO/PPO
Indiana	718	Great-West Healthcare Indiana	HMO/PPO
Iowa	250,000	Wellmark Health Plan of Iowa	HMO
Iowa	74,000	Delta Dental of Iowa	Dental
Iowa	41,644	Coventry Health Care of Iowa	HMO/PPO
Iowa	28,259	CIGNA HealthCare of Iowa	HMO
Iowa	14,412	Medical Associates Health Plan: West	HMO
Iowa	8,337	Great-West Healthcare Iowa	HMO/PPO
Kansas	1,000,000	Preferred Vision Care	Vision
Kansas	880,000	Delta Dental of Kansas	Dental
Kansas	680,466	Blue Cross & Blue Shield of Kansas	HMO
Kansas	132,716	Coventry Health Care of Kansas	HMO/PPO
Kansas	95,000	Health Partners of Kansas	PPO
Kansas	82,778	Preferred Plus of Kansas	HMO
Kansas	40,800	Humana Health Insurance of Kansas	HMO/PPO
Kansas	31,453	Preferred Health Systems Insurance Company	PPO
Kansas	17,258	Great-West Healthcare Kansas	HMO/PPO
Kentucky	570,000	Delta Dental of Kentucky	Dental
Kentucky	450,000	Meritain Health: Kentucky	PPO
Kentucky	159,730	Passport Health Plan	HMO
Kentucky	135,106	UnitedHealthCare of Kentucky	HMO/PPO
Kentucky	110,000	Preferred Health Plan Inc	PPO
Kentucky	67,948	CHA Health	HMO
Kentucky	65,428	Bluegrass Family Health	HMO/PPO
Kentucky	63,698	Anthem Blue Cross & Blue Shield of Kentucky	HMO
Louisiana	1,172,000	Blue Cross & Blue Shield of Louisiana	HMO/PPO
Louisiana	450,000	Meritain Health: Louisiana	PPO
Louisiana	272,972	UnitedHealthCare of Louisiana	HMO/PPO
Louisiana	155,722	Humana Health Insurance of Louisiana	HMO/PPO
Louisiana	71,716	Coventry Health Care of Louisiana	HMO
Louisiana	30,000	Health Plus of Louisiana	HMO
Louisiana	14,000	Vantage Health Plan	HMO
Louisiana	4,707	Tenet Choices	HMO
Maine	85,917	Anthem Blue Cross & Blue Shield of Maine	HMO/PPO
Maine	67,000	Harvard Pilgrim Health Care: Maine	Multiple
Maine	22,417	Aetna Health of Maine	HMO
Maine	8,078	Great-West Healthcare Maine	HMO/PPO
Maine	6,343	CIGNA HealthCare of Maine	HMO
Maryland	471,360	Kaiser Permanente Health Plan of the Mid-Atlantic States	HMO

State	State Enrollment	Organization	Plan Type
Maryland	185,000	Priority Partners Health Plans	HMO
Maryland	176,000	UnitedHealthCare of the Mid-Atlantic	HMO/PPO
Massachusetts	3,000,000	Blue Cross & Blue Shield of Massachusetts	HMO
Massachusetts	240,890	Boston Medical Center Healthnet Plan	HMO
Massachusetts	135,581	Fallon Community Health Plan	HMO/PPO
Massachusetts	106,000	Health New England	HMO
Massachusetts	65,000	Harvard Pilgrim Health Care	Multiple
Massachusetts	25,804	Neighborhood Health Plan	HMO
Massachusetts	19,053	Great-West Healthcare of Massachusetts	HMO/PPO
Massachusetts	11,121	Aetna Health of Massachusetts	HMO
Massachusetts	10,315	CIGNA HealthCare of Massachusetts	PPO
Massachusetts	9,000	ConnectiCare of Massachusetts	HMO/PPO
Michigan	4,300,000	Blue Cross Blue Shield of Michigan	PPO
Michigan	620,000	Blue Care Network of Michigan: Corporate Headquarters	HMO
Michigan	620,000	Blue Care Network: Ann Arbor	HMO
Michigan	620,000	Blue Care Network: Flint	HMO
Michigan	620,000	Blue Care Network: Great Lakes, Muskegon Heights	HMO
Michigan	500,000	Health Alliance Plan	HMO/PPO
Michigan	450,000	Meritain Health: Michigan	PPO
Michigan	250,863	Health Plan of Michigan	HMO
Michigan	215,000	Great Lakes Health Plan	HMO
Michigan	207,319	UnitedHealthCare of Michigan	HMO/PPO
Michigan	200,000	HealthPlus of Michigan: Flint	HMO
Michigan	200,000	HealthPlus of Michigan: Saginaw	HMO
Michigan	200,000	HealthPlus of Michigan: Troy	HMO
Michigan	146,000	Priority Health	HMO/PPO
Michigan	102,752	Care Choices	HMO
Michigan	90,000	Total Health Care	HMO
Michigan	68,942	Physicians Health Plan of Mid-Michigan	HMO
Michigan	50,000	CareSource: Michigan	HMO
Michigan	50,000	OmniCare: A Coventry Health Care Plan	HMO
Michigan	47,400	Humana Health Insurance of Michigan	HMO/PPO
Michigan	36,000	ConnectCare	PPO
Michigan	31,314	Great-West Healthcare Michigan	HMO/PPO
Michigan	26,599	Grand Valley Health Plan	HMO
Michigan	25,278	Upper Peninsula Health Plan	HMO
Michigan	20,000	Dencap Dental Plans	Dental
Michigan	14,000	HealthPlus Senior Medicare Plan	Medicare
Michigan	3,944	M-Care	PPO
Minnesota	3,500,000	Delta Dental of Minnesota	Dental
Minnesota	2,700,000	Blue Cross & Blue Shield of Minnesota	HMO
Minnesota	450,000	Meritain Health: Minnesota	PPO
Minnesota	392,782	UnitedHealthCare of Wisconsin: Central	HMO/PPO
Minnesota	349,070	HealthPartners	HMO
Minnesota	216,150	PreferredOne	HMO/PPO
Minnesota	160,000	Araz Group	PPO
Minnesota	53,490	CIGNA HealthCare of Minnesota	HMO
Minnesota	17,322	Great-West Healthcare Minnesota	HMO/PPO
Minnesota	3,971	Evercare Health Plans	Medicare
Mississippi	53,490	CIGNA HealthCare of Mississippi	HMO
Mississippi	2,900	Humana Health Insurance of Mississippi	HMO/PPO

State	State Enrollment	Organization	Plan Type
Missouri	1,400,000	Delta Dental of Missouri	Dental
Missouri	1,000,000	Blue Cross & Blue Shield of Kansas City	PPO
Missouri	900,000	Anthem Blue Cross & Blue Shield of Missouri	PPO
Missouri	860,000	American Health Care Alliance	PPO
Missouri	450,000	Meritain Health: Missouri	PPO
Missouri	395,996	HealthLink HMO	HMO
Missouri	330,000	GHP Coventry Health Plan	HMO/PPO
Missouri	185,375	Healthcare USA of Missouri	HMO
Missouri	68,070	BlueChoice	HMO
Missouri	60,000	UnitedHealthCare of Missouri	HMO/PPO
Missouri	49,976	Children's Mercy Family Health Partners	HMO
Missouri	47,367	Great-West Healthcare Missouri	HMO/PPO
Missouri	26,000	Med-Pay	Other
Missouri	25,335	Community Health Improvement Solutions	HMO
Missouri	10,885	Aetna Health of Missouri	HMO
Missouri	8,049	CIGNA HealthCare of St. Louis	HMO
Missouri	1,964	Cox Healthplans	HMO/PPO
Montana	236,000	Blue Cross & Blue Shield of Montana	HMO
Montana	56,000	Health InfoNet	PPO
Montana	43,000	New West Health Services	HMO/PPO
Montana	43,000	New West Medicare Plan	Medicare
Montana	17,853	UnitedHealthCare of Montana	HMO/PPO
Montana	5,008	CIGNA HealthCare of Montana	HMO
Montana	3,405	Great-West Healthcare Montana	HMO/PPO
Nebraska	818,531	Ameritas Group	Dental
Nebraska	717,000	Blue Cross & Blue Shield of Nebraska	PPO
Nebraska	602,578	Mutual of Omaha DentaBenefits	Dental
Nebraska	63,000	Coventry Health Care of Nebraska	HMO/PPO
Nebraska	44,000	UnitedHealthCare of Nebraska	HMO/PPO
Nebraska	28,978	Mutual of Omaha Health Plans	HMO/PPO
Nebraska	15,405	CIGNA HealthCare of Nebraska	PPO
Nevada	600,000	Behavioral Healthcare Options, Inc.	HMO/PPO
Nevada	154,503	Anthem Blue Cross & Blue Shield of Nevada	HMO/PPO
Nevada	150,000	Nevada Preferred Healthcare Providers	HMO/PPO
Nevada	150,000	Nevada Preferred Healthcare Providers	PPO
Nevada	107,963	UnitedHealthcare Nevada	HMO/PPO
Nevada	28,591	PacifiCare of Nevada	HMO
Nevada	25,576	Health Plan of Nevada	HMO/PPO
Nevada	19,642	NevadaCare	HMO
Nevada	10,000	Hometown Health Plan	Multiple
New Hampshire	700,000	Delta Dental Northeast	Dental
New Hampshire	400,000	Anthem Blue Cross & Blue Shield of New Hampshire	HMO
New Hampshire	139,000	Harvard Pilgrim Health Care of New England	Multiple
New Hampshire	23,559	CIGNA HealthCare of New Hampshire	HMO
New Jersey	3,600,000	Horizon Blue Cross & Blue Shield of New Jersey	HMO/PPO
New Jersey	3,000,000	Horizon Healthcare of New Jersey	HMO/PPO
New Jersey	750,000	QualCare	HMO/PPO
New Jersey	518,333	Aetna Health of New Jersey	HMO
New Jersey	500,000	HealthFirst New Jersey Medicare Plan	Medicare
New Jersey	467,000	Horizon NJ Health	PPO
New Jersey	431,833	UnitedHealthCare of New Jersey	HMO/PPO

State	State Enrollment	Organization	Plan Type
New Jersey	199,018	AmeriChoice by UnitedHealthCare	HMO
New Jersey	150,000	Atlanticare Health Plans	HMO/PPO
New Jersey	115,000	Family Choice Health Alliance	PPO
New Jersey	105,000	Amerigroup New Jersey	HMO
New Jersey	77,761	AmeriHealth HMO	HMO/PPO
New Jersey	68,935	CIGNA HealthCare of New Jersey	HMO
New Jersey	59,800	Oxford Health Plans: New Jersey	HMO
New Jersey	30,000	Managed Healthcare Systems of New Jersey	HMO
New Jersey	12,317	WellChoice	HMO
New Mexico	400,000	Presbyterian Health Plan	HMO
New Mexico	367,000	Blue Cross & Blue Shield of New Mexico	HMO/PPO
New Mexico	200,000	Delta Dental of New Mexico	Dental
New Mexico	120,937	UnitedHealthCare of New Mexico	HMO/PPO
New Mexico	83,000	Molina Healthcare: New Mexico	HMO
New Mexico	68,674	Lovelace Health Plan	HMO
New Mexico	7,417	Great-West Healthcare New Mexico	HMO/PPO
New York	2,475,666	Group Health Incorporated (GHI)	HMO/PPO
New York	1,700,000	Excellus Blue Cross Blue Shield: Central New York	HMO
New York	1,700,000	Excellus Blue Cross Blue Shield: Rochester Region	HMO
New York	1,700,000	Excellus Blue Cross Blue Shield: Utica Region	HMO
New York	1,700,000	Univera Healthcare	HMO
New York	928,200	MagnaCare	PPO
New York	625,000	Fidelis Care	Multiple
New York	553,000	HealthNow New York	HMO
New York	450,000	Meritain Health: Corporate Headquarters	PPO
New York	365,000	Independent Health	HMO
New York	350,000	CDPHP: Capital District Physicians' Health Plan	HMO/PPO
New York	332,128	MetroPlus Health Plan	HMO
New York	295,841	Dentcare Delivery Systems	Dental
New York	222,000	UnitedHealthCare of New York	HMO/PPO
New York	200,000	National Health Plan Corporation	PPO
New York	197,194	Blue Cross & Blue Shield of Western New York	HMO/PPO
New York	154,162	Aetna Health of New York	PPO
New York	134,837	Affinity Health Plan	HMO
New York	100,000	NOVA Healthcare Administrators	Other
New York	76,753	Coalition America's National Preferred Provider Network	PPO
New York	76,213	Vytra Health Plans	HMO/PPO
New York	72,563	BlueShield of Northeastern New York	HMO/PPO
New York	40,319	CIGNA HealthCare of New York	HMO
New York	30,000	Atlantis Health Plan	HMO
New York	24,502	Great-West Healthcare New York	HMO/PPO
New York	15,000	Elderplan	Medicare
New York	3,000	Perfect Health Insurance Company	PPO
North Carolina	3,718,355	Blue Cross & Blue Shield of North Carolina	HMO/PPO
North Carolina	822,170	Preferred Care Select	PPO
North Carolina	670,000	MedCost	PPO
North Carolina	357,768	UnitedHealthCare of North Carolina	HMO/PPO
North Carolina	325,000	Catalyst RX	PPO
North Carolina	160,000	WellPath: A Coventry Health Care Plan	HMO
North Carolina	53,379	Great-West Healthcare North Carolina	HMO/PPO
North Carolina	40,000	Crescent Preferred Provider Organization	PPO
North Carolina	29,583	CIGNA HealthCare of North Carolina	HMO
North Carolina	17,400	Humana Health Insurance of North Carolina	HMO/PPO

State	State Enrollment	Organization	Plan Type
North Carolina	13,000	FirstCarolinaCare	HMO
North Dakota	2,049	Heart of America Health Plan	HMO
North Dakota	503	Great-West Healthcare North Dakota	HMO/PPO
Ohio	3,000,000	Anthem Blue Cross & Blue Shield of Ohio	PPO
Ohio	952,000	Delta Dental of Michigan, Ohio and Indiana	Dental
Ohio	501,086	CareSource	HMO
Ohio	450,000	Meritain Health: Ohio	PPO
Ohio	404,052	Humana Health Insurance of Ohio	HMO/PPO
Ohio	380,000	The Health Plan of the Upper Ohio Valley	HMO/PPO
Ohio	370,000	Ohio Health Choice	PPO
Ohio	300,000	Emerald Health PPO	PPO
Ohio	159,375	Aetna Health of Ohio	HMO
Ohio	155,000	SummaCare Health Plan	HMO/PPO
Ohio	135,000	Superior Dental Care	Dental
Ohio	134,949	Kaiser Permanente Health Plan Ohio	HMO
Ohio	100,000	OhioHealth Group	PPO
Ohio	82,000	UnitedHealthCare of Ohio: Columbus	HMO/PPO
Ohio	82,000	UnitedHealthCare of Ohio: Dayton & Cincinnati	HMO/PPO
Ohio	81,760	HealthSpan	PPO
Ohio	73,724	SummaCare Medicare Advantage Plan	Medicare
Ohio	55,000	HMO Health Ohio	HMO
Ohio	52,000	Ohio State University Health Plan Inc.	Multiple
Ohio	28,125	Mount Carmel Health Plan Inc (MediGold)	Medicare
Ohio	5,151	Aultcare Corporation	HMO/PPO
Oklahoma	700,000	Delta Dental of Oklahoma	Dental
Oklahoma	600,000	Blue Cross & Blue Shield of Oklahoma	HMO/PPO
Oklahoma	250,000	CommunityCare Managed Healthcare Plans of Oklahoma	HMO/PPO
Oklahoma	177,243	UnitedHealthCare of Oklahoma	HMO/PPO
Oklahoma	78,785	PacifiCare of Oklahoma	HMO
Oklahoma	31,363	Aetna Health of Oklahoma	HMO
Oklahoma	22,300	CIGNA HealthCare of Oklahoma	HMO/PPO
Oklahoma	16,882	Great-West Healthcare Oklahoma	HMO/PPO
Oklahoma	15,248	BlueLincs HMO	HMO
Oregon	1,500,000	ODS Health Plan	Multiple
Oregon	800,000	Regence Blue Cross & Blue Shield of Oregon	PPO
Oregon	471,000	Kaiser Permanente Health Plan Northwest	HMO
Oregon	350,000	Providence Health Plans	HMO/PPO
Oregon	231,125	UnitedHealthCare of Oregon	HMO/PPO
Oregon	131,096	CareOregon Health Plan	Medicare
Oregon	129,120	Managed HealthCare Northwest	PPO
Oregon	82,000	Lifewise Health Plan of Oregon	PPO
Oregon	49,455	PacifiCare of Oregon	HMO
Oregon	35,000	Clear One Health Plans	Multiple
Oregon	30,000	Samaritan Health Plan	Multiple
Oregon	17,100	Health Net Health Plan of Oregon	HMO/PPO
Oregon	3,487	Great-West Healthcare Oregon	HMO/PPO
Pennsylvania	4,700,000	Highmark Blue Cross & Blue Shield	HMO/PPO
Pennsylvania	3,300,000	Independence Blue Cross	HMO/PPO
Pennsylvania	3,000,000	Devon Health Services	PPO
Pennsylvania	2,600,000	Keystone Health Plan East	HMO/PPO
Pennsylvania	600,000	Blue Cross of Northeastern Pennsylvania	HMO/PPO

State	State Enrollment	Organization	Plan Type
Pennsylvania	409,265	Aetna Health of Pennsylvania	HMO
Pennsylvania	395,000	HealthAmerica Pennsylvania	Multiple
Pennsylvania	375,300	Highmark Blue Shield	PPO
Pennsylvania	283,106	UnitedHealthCare of Pennsylvania	HMO/PPO
Pennsylvania	244,000	Gateway Health Plan	HMO
Pennsylvania	209,211	UPMC Health Plan	Multiple
Pennsylvania	174,209	Valley Preferred	Multiple
Pennsylvania	154,000	Health Partners Medicare Plan	Medicare
Pennsylvania	146,000	Preferred Care	PPO
Pennsylvania	116,465	Capital Blue Cross	HMO/PPO
Pennsylvania	110,736	Americhoice of Pennsylvania	Multiple
Pennsylvania	60,353	Berkshire Health Partners	PPO
Pennsylvania	56,000	South Central Preferred	PPO
Pennsylvania	50,000	Blue Ridge Health Network	PPO
Pennsylvania	45,000	Susquehanna Health Care	PPO
Pennsylvania	33,000	Prime Source Health Network	PPO
Pennsylvania	21,997	Great-West Healthcare Pennsylvania	HMO/PPO
Pennsylvania	18,500	Penn Highlands Health Plan	PPO
Pennsylvania	12,700	Central Susquehanna Healthcare Providers	PPO
Pennsylvania	11,969	CIGNA: Corporate Headquarters	HMO
Pennsylvania	13	CIGNA HealthCare of Pennsylvania	HMO
Puerto Rico	180,000	First Medical Health Plan	Multiple
Puerto Rico	100,000	Triple-S Salud Blue Cross Blue Shield of Puerto Rico	Multiple
Rhode Island	620,000	Delta Dental of Rhode Island	Dental
Rhode Island	92,000	UnitedHealthCare of Rhode Island	HMO/PPO
Rhode Island	76,000	Neighborhood Health Plan of Rhode Island	HMO
South Carolina	950,000	Blue Cross & Blue Shield of South Carolina	HMO/PPO
South Carolina	205,000	BlueChoice Health Plan of South Carolina	Multiple
South Carolina	200,000	Select Health of South Carolina	HMO
South Carolina	148,404	UnitedHealthCare of South Carolina	HMO/PPO
South Carolina	123,000	Carolina Care Plan	HMO
South Carolina	19,468	Kanawha Healthcare Solutions	PPO
South Carolina	15,452	Great-West Healthcare South Carolina	HMO/PPO
South Carolina	14,341	CIGNA HealthCare of South Carolina	HMO
South Dakota	275,053	Wellmark Blue Cross & Blue Shield of South Dakota	PPO
South Dakota	245,000	Americas PPO	PPO
South Dakota	204,000	Delta Dental of South Dakota	Dental
South Dakota	29,748	Avera Health Plans	HMO
South Dakota	25,000	First Choice of the Midwest	PPO
South Dakota	24,310	DakotaCare	HMO
South Dakota	6,570	CIGNA HealthCare of South Dakota	PPO
South Dakota	1,430	Great-West Healthcare South Dakota	HMO/PPO
Tennessee	3,000,000	Blue Cross & Blue Shield of Tennessee	HMO/PPO
Tennessee	518,000	Health Choice LLC	PPO
Tennessee	379,224	Signature Health Alliance	PPO
Tennessee	270,665	UnitedHealthCare of Tennessee	HMO/PPO
Tennessee	251,418	John Deere Health	HMO/PPO
Tennessee	229,356	CIGNA HealthCare of Tennessee	HMO
Tennessee	106,364	Initial Group	PPO
Tennessee	50,919	Cariten Preferred	PPO
Tennessee	48,477	HealthPartners	PPO

State	State Enrollment	Organization	Plan Type
Tennessee	35,800	Humana Health Insurance of Tennessee	HMO/PPO
Tennessee	24,054	Aetna Health of Tennessee	HMO
Tennessee	17,844	HealthSpring: Corporate Offices	Medicare
Tennessee	14,477	Cariten Healthcare	Multiple
Texas	4,000,000	Block Vision of Texas	Vision
Texas	3,200,000	Galaxy Health Network	PPO
Texas	2,720,162	Blue Cross & Blue Shield of Texas: Houston	HMO/PPO
Texas	1,862,466	UnitedHealthCare of Texas	HMO/PPO
Texas	1,118,582	USA Managed Care Organization	PPO
Texas	1,080,000	HAS-Premier Providers	PPO
Texas	1,080,000	Texas True Choice	PPO
Texas	394,011	HealthSmart Preferred Care	PPO
Texas	310,853	Blue Cross & Blue Shield of Texas	HMO/PPO
Texas	294,566	Aetna Health of Texas	HMO
Texas	275,000	Interplan Health Group	PPO
Texas	202,000	Scott & White Health Plan	HMO
Texas	177,539	Healthcare Partners of East Texas	PPO
Texas	130,000	First Care Health Plans	Multiple
Texas	111,877	CIGNA HealthCare of North Texas	HMO/PPO
Texas	111,877	CIGNA HealthCare of South Texas	HMO
Texas	110,000	Community First Health Plans	HMO/PPO
Texas	79,500	Alliance Regional Health Network	PPO
Texas	78,139	Brazos Valley Health Network	PPO
Texas	65,000	Medical Care Referral Group	PPO
Texas	47,755	PacifiCare of Texas	HMO
Texas	12,334	Great-West Healthcare Texas	HMO/PPO
Texas	12,004	Valley Baptist Health Plan	HMO
Texas	1,500	Dental Source: Dental Health Care Plans	Dental
Utah	450,000	Meritain Health: Utah	PPO
Utah	231,824	Regence Blue Cross & Blue Shield of Utah	PPO
Utah	177,854	Public Employees Health Program	PPO
Utah	150,000	Opticare of Utah	Vision
Utah	109,709	UnitedHealthCare of Utah	HMO/PPO
Utah	84,000	Altius Health Plans	Multiple
Utah	65,000	Educators Mutual	HMO/PPO
Utah	50,000	University Health Plans	HMO/PPO
Utah	4,198	CIGNA HealthCare of Utah	HMO/PPO
Vermont	54,023	Blue Cross & Blue Shield of Vermont	PPO
Virginia	2,800,000	Anthem Blue Cross & Blue Shield of Virginia	HMO
Virginia	415,000	Optima Health Plan	HMO/PPO
Virginia	400,000	Dominion Dental Services	Dental
Virginia	200,000	Coventry Health Care Virginia	HMO/PPO
Virginia	88,366	Virginia Health Network	PPO
Virginia	81,803	Virginia Premier Health Plan	HMO
Virginia	55,017	Peninsula Health Care	HMO/PPO
Virginia	44,458	National Capital PPO	PPO
Virginia	30,000	Piedmont Community Health Plan	PPO
Virginia	28,460	CIGNA HealthCare of Virginia	HMO
Washington	2,000,000	Delta Dental of Washington	Dental
Washington	1,300,000	Premera Blue Cross	PPO
Washington	624,000	UnitedHealthCare of Washington	HMO/PPO

State	State Enrollment	Organization	Plan Type
Washington	270,000	Community Health Plan of Washington	Multiple
Washington	263,795	Molina Healthcare: Washington	HMO
Washington	87,000	Lifewise Health Plan of Washington	PPO
Washington	52,186	PacifiCare of Washington	HMO
Washington	49,135	CIGNA HealthCare of Washington	PPO
Washington	21,633	Regence Blue Shield	PPO
Washington	7,550	PacifiCare Benefit Administrators	PPO
West Virginia	400,000	Mountain State Blue Cross Blue Shiled	PPO
West Virginia	100,000	Coventry Health Care of West Virginia	HMO/PPO
West Virginia	50,000	SelectNet Plus, Inc.	PPO
West Virginia	27,783	CIGNA HealthCare of West Virginia	PPO
West Virginia	10,417	Great-West Healthcare West Virginia	HMO/PPO
Wisconsin	700,000	HealthEOS	PPO
Wisconsin	392,782	UnitedHealthCare of Wisconsin: Central	HMO/PPO
Wisconsin	223,000	Wisconsin Physician's Service	PPO
Wisconsin	187,000	Security Health Plan of Wisconsin	Multiple
Wisconsin	164,700	Managed Health Services	HMO
Wisconsin	112,000	Physicians Plus Insurance Corporation	HMO/PPO
Wisconsin	95,000	Group Health Cooperative of Eau Claire	HMO
Wisconsin	90,000	Gundersen Lutheran Health Plan	HMO
Wisconsin	75,000	Unity Health Insurance	Multiple
Wisconsin	67,812	Network Health Plan of Wisconsin	HMO/PPO
Wisconsin	53,255	CIGNA HealthCare of Wisconsin	PPO
Wisconsin	48,202	Group Health Cooperative of South Central Wisconsin	HMO
Wisconsin	40,000	Health Tradition	HMO
Wisconsin	22,450	Great-West Healthcare Wisconsin	HMO/PPO
Wisconsin	15,706	Prevea Health Network	PPO
Wisconsin	8,527	Medical Associates Health Plan: East	HMO
Wyoming	100,000	Blue Cross & Blue Shield of Wyoming	PPO
Wyoming	21,919	UnitedHealthCare of Wyoming	HMO/PPO
Wyoming	9,864	WINhealth Partners	Multiple
Wyoming	3,334	CIGNA HealthCare of Wyoming	PPO

HMO/PPO Profiles

Health Insurance Coverage Status and Type of Coverage by Age

Category	All Persons		Under 18 years		Under 65 years		65 years and over	
	Number	%	Number	%	Number	%	Number	%
Total population	4,672	-	1,137	-	4,034	-	638	-
Covered by some type of health insurance	3,951 (71)	84.6 (1.3)	1,035 (33)	91.1 (2.5)	3,334 (109)	82.6 (1.6)	618 (55)	96.8 (2.1)
Covered by private health insurance	3,054 (93)	65.4 (1.9)	687 (39)	60.5 (3.3)	2,682 (120)	66.5 (2.2)	372 (45)	58.3 (3.1)
Employment based	2,634 (130)	56.4 (2.7)	634 (38)	55.8 (3.3)	2,422 (132)	60.0 (2.6)	212 (31)	33.2 (4.0)
Own employment based	1,372 (90)	29.4 (1.8)	3 (2)	0.2 (0.2)	1,222 (88)	30.3 (1.8)	151 (20)	23.6 (2.9)
Direct purchase	491 (49)	10.5 (1.1)	63 (17)	5.5 (1.5)	297 (42)	7.4 (1.0)	194 (40)	30.4 (4.8)
Covered by government health insurance	1,508 (82)	32.3 (1.8)	426 (48)	37.5 (4.2)	926 (87)	22.9 (2.1)	582 (49)	91.2 (2.6)
Covered by Medicaid	644 (54)	13.8 (1.2)	401 (48)	35.3 (4.2)	585 (53)	14.5 (1.3)	59 (13)	9.3 (2.2)
Also by private insurance	101 (16)	2.2 (0.3)	67 (15)	5.9 (1.3)	90 (16)	2.2 (0.4)	11 (7)	1.7 (1.1)
Covered by Medicare	776 (44)	16.6 (0.9)	8 (4)	0.7 (0.4)	200 (22)	5.0 (0.5)	576 (49)	90.3 (2.5)
Also by private insurance	399 (37)	8.5 (0.8)	2 (2)	0.2 (0.2)	62 (13)	1.5 (0.3)	337 (38)	52.7 (3.0)
Also by Medicaid	91 (21)	1.9 (0.5)	2 (2)	0.2 (0.2)	35 (10)	0.9 (0.3)	56 (13)	8.8 (2.2)
Covered by military health care	261 (44)	5.6 (1.0)	47 (16)	4.1 (1.4)	226 (44)	5.6 (1.1)	36 (11)	5.6 (1.7)
Not covered at any time during the year	720 (62)	15.4 (1.3)	101 (29)	8.9 (2.5)	700 (59)	17.4 (1.6)	21 (14)	3.2 (2.1)

Note: Numbers in thousands; figures cover 2010; standard error appears in parenthesis; (b) base less than 75,000; (x) not applicable
Source: U.S. Census Bureau, Current Population Survey, 2011 Annual Social and Economic Supplement. Table HI05. Health Insurance Coverage Status and Type of Coverage by State and Age for All People: 2010

Alabama

1 **Aetna Health of Alabama**
Partnered with eHealthInsurance Services Inc.

2 **Assurant Employee Benefits: Alabama**
3595 Grandview Parkway
Suite 1
Birmingham, AL 35243-1934
Toll-Free: 866-909-1955
Phone: 205-909-5872
Fax: 205-909-5646
benefits@assurant.com
www.assurantemployeebenefits.com
Subsidiary of: Assurant, Inc
For Profit Organization: Yes
Number of Primary Care Physicians: 112,000
Total Enrollment: 47,000

Healthplan and Services Defined
  PLAN TYPE: Multiple
  Plan Specialty: Dental, Vision, Long & Short-Term Disability
  Benefits Offered: Dental, Vision, Wellness, AD&D, Life, LTD, STD,
    Long & Short-Term Disability

Type of Coverage
  Commercial, Indemnity, Individual Dental Plans

Geographic Areas Served
  Statewide

Subscriber Information
  Average Monthly Fee Per Subscriber
    (Employee + Employer Contribution):
    Employee Only (Self): Varies by plan

Key Personnel
  President/CEO.............................John S Roberts
  Executive Vice President ....James J Brinkerhoff

3 **Beech Street Corporation: Alabama**
Acquired by MultiPlan

4 **Behavioral Health Systems**
2 Metroplex Drive
Suite 500
Birmingham, AL 35209
Toll-Free: 800-245-1150
Phone: 205-879-1150
Fax: 205-879-1178
info@behavioralhealthsystems.com
www.behavioralhealthsystems.com
For Profit Organization: Yes
Physician Owned Organization: No
Federally Qualified: No
Number of Affiliated Hospitals: 617
Number of Primary Care Physicians: 11,000
Total Enrollment: 502,000

Healthplan and Services Defined
  PLAN TYPE: PPO
  Benefits Offered: Behavioral Health, Psychiatric, Worker's
    Compensation, EAP, Drug Testing

Type of Coverage
  Commercial

Geographic Areas Served
  Nationwide

Network Qualifications
  Minimum Years of Practice: 5
  Pre-Admission Certification: Yes

Peer Review Type
  Utilization Review: Yes
  Case Management: Yes

Publishes and Distributes Report Card: Yes

Accreditation Certification
  AAAHC, TJC
  Utilization Review, Pre-Admission Certification, Quality Assurance
    Program

Key Personnel
  Founder, Chairman & CEO ....Deborah L Stephens
  CQO...Pat Friedley
  COO ....Kyle Strange
  CFO..Mark Gordon
  Dir, Business Development....................Judi Braswell
  VP, Public Relations ....Shannon Flanagan
    205-443-5483

Specialty Managed Care Partners
  State of Alabama, Drummond Co, MTD Products
  Enters into Contracts with Regional Business Coalitions: Yes
  Employers Coalition on Healthcare Options (ECHO), Louisiana
    Business Group on Health (LBGH)

5 **Blue Cross & Blue Shield of Alabama**
450 Riverchase Parkway East
Birmingham, AL 35244
Toll-Free: 888-267-2955
Phone: 205-220-5400
www.bcbsal.com
Year Founded: 1936
Total Enrollment: 3,200,000
State Enrollment: 3,200,000

Healthplan and Services Defined
  PLAN TYPE: HMO

Type of Coverage
  Commercial, Individual, Supplemental Medicare

Geographic Areas Served
  Alabama

Accreditation Certification
  URAC

Key Personnel
  President/CEO ....Terry D Kellogg
  Senior VP Finance ....Dan Mallea
  Media Contact...............................Koko Mackin
    205-220-2713

6 **Blue Cross Preferred Care**
450 Riverchase Parkway East
Birmingham, AL 35298
Toll-Free: 800-213-7930
Phone: 205-988-2200
www.bcbsal.com
Non-Profit Organization: Yes
Year Founded: 1936
Number of Affiliated Hospitals: 130
Number of Primary Care Physicians: 9,000
Total Enrollment: 3,200,000
State Enrollment: 2,842,000

Healthplan and Services Defined
  PLAN TYPE: PPO
  Model Type: Network
  Plan Specialty: Behavioral Health, Chiropractic, Dental, Disease
    Management, Lab, Radiology, UR
  Benefits Offered: Behavioral Health, Chiropractic, Dental, Disease
    Management, Home Care, Inpatient SNF, Long-Term Care,
    Physical Therapy, Podiatry, Prescription, Psychiatric, Transplant,
    Vision, Wellness, AD&D, Life, LTD, STD, Hospital, Miscellaneous

Type of Coverage
Commercial, Individual, Medicare, Supplemental Medicare

Type of Payment Plans Offered
DFFS

Publishes and Distributes Report Card: Yes

Accreditation Certification
URAC

Key Personnel
President/CEO . . . . .Terry Kellogg
SVP/CFO. . . . . .Cynthia Mizell
SVP/CIO . . . . .Scott McGlaun
Media Contact. . . . . .Koko Mackin
205-220-2713

7 CompBenefits: Alabama
2204 Lakeshore Drive
Suite 100
Birmingham, AL 35209
Toll-Free: 888-879-7374
Phone: 205-879-7374
Fax: 205-879-5307
www.compbenefits.com
Subsidiary of: Humana
Year Founded: 1978
Owned by an Integrated Delivery Network (IDN): Yes
Total Enrollment: 4,500,000

Healthplan and Services Defined
PLAN TYPE: Multiple
Model Type: Network, HMO, PPO, POS, TPA
Plan Specialty: ASO, Dental, Vision
Benefits Offered: Dental, Vision

Type of Coverage
Commercial, Individual, Indemnity

Type of Payment Plans Offered
DFFS, Capitated, FFS

Geographic Areas Served
Alabama, Arkansas, Illinois, Indiana, Georgia, Florida, Mississippi, Missouri, Kentucky, Kansas, North Carolina, South Carolina, West Virginia, Texas, Tennessee, Ohio, Louisiana

Publishes and Distributes Report Card: Yes

Specialty Managed Care Partners
Enters into Contracts with Regional Business Coalitions: Yes

8 Delta Dental of Alabama
Two Perimeter Park
Suite 440 West
Birmingham, AL 35243
Toll-Free: 800-322-7976
Phone: 205-969-5755
Fax: 205-969-5777
alsales@delta.org
www.deltadentalins.com
Non-Profit Organization: Yes
Total Enrollment: 54,000,000

Healthplan and Services Defined
PLAN TYPE: Dental
Other Type: Dental PPO
Plan Specialty: Dental
Benefits Offered: Dental

Type of Coverage
Commercial

Geographic Areas Served
Statewide

Key Personnel
President/CEO. . . . . .Gary D Radine

Manager. . . . . .Mary Ray
VP, Public & Govt Affairs . . . . .Jeff Album
415-972-8418

9 eHealthInsurance Services Inc.
11919 Foundation Place
Gold River, CA 95670
Toll-Free: 800-977-8860
info@ehealthinsurance.com
www.e.healthinsurance.com
Year Founded: 1997

Healthplan and Services Defined
PLAN TYPE: HMO/PPO
Benefits Offered: Dental, Life, STD

Type of Coverage
Commercial, Individual, Medicare

Geographic Areas Served
All 50 states in the USA and District of Columbia

Key Personnel
Chairman & CEO . . . . .Gary L. Lauer
EVP/Business & Corp. Dev. .Bruce Telkamp
EVP/Chief Technology .Dr. Sheldon X. Wang
SVP & CFO . . . . .Stuart M. Huizinga
Pres. of eHealth Gov. Sys . . . . .Samuel C. Gibbs
SVP of Sales & Operations . . . . .Robert S. Hurley
Director Public Relations. .Nate Purpura
650-210-3115

10 Great-West Healthcare Alabama
Acquired by CIGNA

11 Health Choice of Alabama
3201 Fourth Avenue S
Birmingham, AL 35222
Toll-Free: 866-508-4800
Phone: 205-715-4800
Fax: 205-715-4802
email@bhsala.com
www.healthchoiceofalabama.com
Mailing Address: PO Box 830605, Birmingham, AL 35283
Subsidiary of: Alabama Premier Network (APN)
Non-Profit Organization: Yes
Year Founded: 1984
Number of Affiliated Hospitals: 90
Number of Primary Care Physicians: 4,538
Number of Referral/Specialty Physicians: 2,681
Total Enrollment: 45,000
State Enrollment: 45,000

Healthplan and Services Defined
PLAN TYPE: PPO
Model Type: Group, Network
Plan Specialty: Chiropractic
Benefits Offered: Chiropractic

Type of Coverage
Commercial

Type of Payment Plans Offered
POS, DFFS, FFS

Geographic Areas Served
Statewide

Key Personnel
President/CEO . . . . .Joe Oaks
CMO/Director. . . . . .Alan Goldstein
Marketing . . . . .Joe Oaks
Medical Affairs. . . . . .Alan Goldstein, MD
Director Provider Services .Cherie Pardi

Specialty Managed Care Partners
Aetna, Superien, MNHO

12 HealthSpring of Alabama

2 Chase Corporate Drive
Suite 300
Birmingham, AL 35244
Toll-Free: 800-888-7647
Phone: 205-423-1000
Fax: 205-968-2277
moreinfo@healthspring.com
www.healthspringofalabama.com
Subsidiary of: The Oath of Alabama
For Profit Organization: Yes
Year Founded: 2000
Number of Affiliated Hospitals: 50
Total Enrollment: 30,000
State Enrollment: 17,844

Healthplan and Services Defined
 PLAN TYPE: Medicare
 Model Type: Network
 Plan Specialty: Disease Management, Lab, MSO, Vision, Radiology,
  UR, Group Medical
 Benefits Offered: Behavioral Health, Chiropractic, Disease
  Management, Home Care, Inpatient SNF, Long-Term Care,
  Physical Therapy, Podiatry, Prescription, Psychiatric, Transplant,
  Wellness

Type of Coverage
 Commercial, Individual, Medicare

Type of Payment Plans Offered
 DFFS

Geographic Areas Served
 Autauga, Baldwin, Bibb, Blount, Bullock, Butler, Calhoun,
 Cherokee, Chilton, Clarke, Clay, Cleburn, Colbert, Conecuh, Coosa,
 Cullman, Dallas, DeKalb, Elmore, Escambia, Etowah, Fayette,
 Franklin, Green, Hale, Jefferson, Lamar, Lauderdale, Lawrence,
 Lowndes, Macon, Madison, Marion, Marshall, Mobile, Monroe,
 Montgomery, Morgan, Perry, Pickens, Randolph, Saint Clair, Shelby,
 Talladega, Tucaloosa, Walker, Washington, Wilcox, Winston counties

Accreditation Certification
 NCQA
 TJC Accreditation

Key Personnel
 President . . . . Bob Dawson
 CFO . . . . David Beauchaine

Specialty Managed Care Partners
 MHNet, Express Script

Employer References
 Hertz, USX, Public Education Employees Health Plan

13 Humana Health Insurance of Alabama

600 Boulevard Street
Suite 104
Huntsville, AL 35802
Toll-Free: 800-942-0605
Phone: 256-705-3551
Fax: 205-879-5307
www.humana.com
Secondary Address: 2100 Southbridge Parkway, Suite 650,
 Birmingham, AL 35209
For Profit Organization: Yes

Healthplan and Services Defined
 PLAN TYPE: HMO/PPO

Type of Coverage
 Commercial, Individual

Accreditation Certification
 URAC, NCQA, CORE

14 North Alabama Managed Care Inc

699 A Gallatin Street
PO Box 18788
Huntsville, AL 35801
Toll-Free: 800-636-2624
Phone: 256-532-2755
Fax: 256-532-2756
beth.couch@compone.org
www.namci.com
Mailing Address: PO Box 18788, Huntsville, AL 35804
Non-Profit Organization: Yes
Year Founded: 1991
Number of Affiliated Hospitals: 31
Number of Primary Care Physicians: 498
Number of Referral/Specialty Physicians: 1,014
Total Enrollment: 66,000

Healthplan and Services Defined
 PLAN TYPE: PPO
 Model Type: Network
 Plan Specialty: Group Health
 Benefits Offered: PPO Network

Type of Coverage
 Commercial, Individual

Type of Payment Plans Offered
 Combination FFS & DFFS

Geographic Areas Served
 Alabama counties: Madison, Morgan, Marshall, Jackson, Colbert,
 Limestone, Lauderdale, and Franklin. Also Lincoln county,
 Tennessee, Tishomingo, MS

Subscriber Information
 Average Subscriber Co-Payment:
  Primary Care Physician: Varies by plan
  Nursing Home: Varies

Network Qualifications
 Pre-Admission Certification: Yes

Key Personnel
 Operations Manager . . . . Brenda Willoughby
  256-532-2754
  brenda.willoughby@namci.com
 Credentialing Claims Spec . . . . Nichelle Russell
  256-532-2759
 Sales/Marketing . . . . Beth Couch
  beth.couch@compone.org
 Media Contact . . . . Beth Couch
  256-532-2756

Specialty Managed Care Partners
 Enters into Contracts with Regional Business Coalitions: Yes
 ECHO

Employer References
 Huntsville HospitalSunshine Homes

15 United Concordia: Alabama

400 Vestavia Parkway
Suite 205
Birmingham, AL 35216
Toll-Free: 800-554-6155
Fax: 205-822-1653
ucproducer@ucci.com
www.secure.ucci.com
For Profit Organization: Yes
Year Founded: 1971
Number of Primary Care Physicians: 111,000
Total Enrollment: 8,000,000

Healthplan and Services Defined
  PLAN TYPE: Dental
  Plan Specialty: Dental
  Benefits Offered: Dental

Type of Coverage
  Commercial, Individual

Geographic Areas Served
  Military personnel and their families, nationwide

Key Personnel
  Chief Dental Officer. . . . . James Bramson
  Account Representataive . . . . David Belrose

16   UnitedHealthCare of Alabama

33 Inverness Center Parkway
Suite 350
Birmingham, AL 35242
Toll-Free: 800-345-1520
www.uhc.com
Subsidiary of: UnitedHealth Group
For Profit Organization: Yes
Year Founded: 1991
Total Enrollment: 75,000,000
State Enrollment: 107,210

Healthplan and Services Defined
  PLAN TYPE: HMO/PPO
  Plan Specialty: Dental, Vision
  Benefits Offered: Dental, Vision

Geographic Areas Served
  Statewide

Key Personnel
  President/CEO . . . . Glen Golemi
  Chairman . . . . Richard Burke, Sr
  CFO . . . . Frank Ulibarri
  Media Contact. . . . . Roger Rollman
     roger_f_rollman@uhc.com

17   VIVA Health

1222 14th Avenue South
Birmingham, AL 35205
Toll-Free: 800-633-1542
Phone: 205-939-1718
Fax: 205-558-7546
vivamemberhelp@uabmc.edu
www.vivahealth.com
Mailing Address: PO Box 55209, Birmingham, AL 35255
Subsidiary of: Triton Health Systems or UAB Health Systems
Total Enrollment: 80,000
State Enrollment: 80,000

Healthplan and Services Defined
  PLAN TYPE: HMO
  Other Type: Medicare
  Plan Specialty: Medicare
  Benefits Offered: Medicare

Type of Coverage
  Medicare, Supplemental Medicare

Geographic Areas Served
  Alabama

Key Personnel
  CEO . . . . Brad Rollow
  COO. . . . . Card Feagin
  VP of Provider Services . . . . Terry Knight
  VP, Network Development. . . . . Terry Knight
  VP, Corporate Development . . . . Libba Yates
  VP, Information Systems. Ryan Kramer
  VP, Provider Relations . . . . Terry Knight

Health Insurance Coverage Status and Type of Coverage by Age

Category	All Persons		Under 18 years		Under 65 years		65 years and over	
	Number	%	Number	%	Number	%	Number	%
Total population	693	-	186	-	638	-	55	-
Covered by some type of health insurance	568 *(8)*	82.0 *(1.1)*	161 *(4)*	86.3 *(2.1)*	515 *(10)*	80.7 *(1.2)*	53 *(4)*	96.8 *(1.3)*
Covered by private health insurance	432 *(13)*	62.3 *(1.9)*	105 *(6)*	56.4 *(3.1)*	404 *(13)*	63.3 *(2.0)*	28 *(3)*	50.9 *(4.9)*
Employment based	403 *(14)*	58.2 *(2.1)*	101 *(6)*	54.4 *(3.3)*	382 *(14)*	59.8 *(2.2)*	22 *(3)*	40.1 *(4.4)*
Own employment based	218 *(8)*	31.4 *(1.2)*	0 *(0)*	0.1 *(0.1)*	202 *(8)*	31.7 *(1.2)*	16 *(2)*	29.0 *(3.7)*
Direct purchase	31 *(5)*	4.4 *(0.7)*	4 *(1)*	2.2 *(0.7)*	24 *(4)*	3.7 *(0.6)*	7 *(2)*	12.8 *(3.5)*
Covered by government health insurance	223 *(14)*	32.1 *(2.0)*	82 *(7)*	44.1 *(3.5)*	174 *(13)*	27.2 *(2.0)*	49 *(4)*	89.2 *(2.6)*
Covered by Medicaid	99 *(12)*	14.3 *(1.7)*	55 *(7)*	29.7 *(3.8)*	90 *(11)*	14.1 *(1.8)*	9 *(2)*	16.5 *(2.6)*
Also by private insurance	23 *(4)*	3.3 *(0.6)*	13 *(3)*	7.0 *(1.5)*	20 *(4)*	3.1 *(0.6)*	3 *(1)*	5.5 *(1.8)*
Covered by Medicare	60 *(4)*	8.6 *(0.6)*	1 *(0)*	0.4 *(0.2)*	12 *(2)*	1.8 *(0.3)*	48 *(4)*	88.0 *(2.8)*
Also by private insurance	27 *(3)*	3.8 *(0.5)*	0 *(0)*	0.0 *(0.0)*	3 *(1)*	0.5 *(0.2)*	23 *(3)*	42.9 *(5.3)*
Also by Medicaid	15 *(3)*	2.1 *(0.4)*	0 *(0)*	0.2 *(0.2)*	7 *(2)*	1.0 *(0.3)*	8 *(2)*	15.3 *(2.6)*
Covered by military health care	88 *(11)*	12.7 *(1.5)*	27 *(4)*	14.5 *(2.1)*	81 *(10)*	12.7 *(1.6)*	7 *(2)*	12.8 *(3.0)*
Not covered at any time during the year	125 *(8)*	18.0 *(1.1)*	25 *(4)*	13.7 *(2.1)*	123 *(8)*	19.3 *(1.2)*	2 *(1)*	3.2 *(1.3)*

Note: Numbers in thousands; figures cover 2010; standard error appears in parenthesis; (b) base less than 75,000; (x) not applicable
Source: U.S. Census Bureau, Current Population Survey, 2011 Annual Social and Economic Supplement. Table HI05. Health Insurance Coverage Status and Type of Coverage by State and Age for All People: 2010

Alaska

18　Aetna Health of Alaska

151 Farmington Avenue
Hartford, CT 06156
Toll-Free: 866-582-9629
www.aetna.com
For Profit Organization: Yes
Total Enrollment: 11,596,230

Healthplan and Services Defined
　PLAN TYPE: PPO
　Other Type: POS
　Plan Specialty: EPO
　Benefits Offered: Dental, Disease Management, Long-Term Care,
　　Prescription, Wellness, Life, LTD, STD

Type of Coverage
　Commercial, Individual

Type of Payment Plans Offered
　POS, FFS

Geographic Areas Served
　Statewide

Subscriber Information
　Average Monthly Fee Per Subscriber
　　(Employee + Employer Contribution):
　　　Employee Only (Self): Varies
　　　Employee & 2 Family Members: Varies
　Average Annual Deductible Per Subscriber:
　　　Employee Only (Self): Varies
　　　Employee & 2 Family Members: Varies
　Average Subscriber Co-Payment:
　　　Primary Care Physician: Varies
　　　Prescription Drugs: Varies

Key Personnel
　CEO . . . . .Ronald A Williams
　President. . . . . .Mark T Bertolini
　SVP, General Counsel . . . . .William J Casazza
　EVP, CFO. . . . . .Joseph M Zubretsky
　Head, M&A Integration .Kay Mooney
　SVP, Marketing. . . . . .Robert E Mead
　Chief Medical Officer . . . . .Lonny Reisman, MD
　SVP, Human Resources. . . . . .Elease E Wright
　SVP, CIO. . . . . .Meg McCarthy

19　Beech Street: Alaska

Acquired by MultiPlan

20　CCN: Alaska

Acquired by First Health/Coventry

21　CIGNA HealthCare of Alaska

3900 East Mexico Avenue
Suite 1100
Denver, CO 80210
Toll-Free: 800-832-3211
Phone: 303-782-1500
Fax: 303-691-3197
www.cigna.com
For Profit Organization: Yes
Number of Affiliated Hospitals: 200

Healthplan and Services Defined
　PLAN TYPE: HMO
　Plan Specialty: Behavioral Health, Dental, Vision
　Benefits Offered: Behavioral Health, Dental, Disease Management,
　　Prescription, Transplant, Vision, Wellness, Life

Type of Coverage
　Commercial

Type of Payment Plans Offered
　POS, FFS

Geographic Areas Served
　Montana

Key Personnel
　Director At Cigna . . . . .Sallie Vanasdale
　VP Provider Relations . . . . .William Cetti
　VP Client Relations . . . . .Gregg Prussing

22　eHealthInsurance Services Inc.

11919 Foundation Place
Gold River, CA 95670
Toll-Free: 800-977-8860
info@ehealthinsurance.com
www.e.healthinsurance.com
Year Founded: 1997

Healthplan and Services Defined
　PLAN TYPE: HMO/PPO
　Benefits Offered: Dental, Life, STD

Type of Coverage
　Commercial, Individual, Medicare

Geographic Areas Served
　All 50 states in the USA and District of Columbia

Key Personnel
　Chairman & CEO. . . . . .Gary L. Lauer
　EVP/Business & Corp. Dev.. . . . . .Bruce Telkamp
　EVP/Chief Technology. . . . . .Dr. Sheldon X. Wang
　SVP & CFO . . . . .Stuart M. Huizinga
　Pres. of eHealth Gov. Sys . . . . .Samuel C. Gibbs
　SVP of Sales & Operations . . . . .Robert S. Hurley
　Director Public Relations. .Nate Purpura
　　650-210-3115

23　Great-West Healthcare Alaska

Acquired by CIGNA

24　Humana Health Insurance of Alaska

1498 SE Tech Center Place
Suite 300
Vancouver, WA 98683
Toll-Free: 800-781-4203
Phone: 360-253-7523
Fax: 360-253-7524
www.humana.com
For Profit Organization: Yes
Year Founded: 1961
Federally Qualified: Yes
Total Enrollment: 8,097

Healthplan and Services Defined
　PLAN TYPE: HMO/PPO
　Model Type: IPA
　Benefits Offered: Behavioral Health, Chiropractic, Dental,
　　Prescription, Psychiatric, Transplant, Vision, Worker's
　　Compensation

Type of Coverage
　Commercial, Individual

Geographic Areas Served
　Nationwide

Accreditation Certification
　TJC, URAC, NCQA, CORE

Key Personnel
　President/CEO . . . . .Michael McCallister

25   Liberty Health Plan: Alaska

2700 Gambell Street
Suite 405
Anchorage, AK 99503-2835
Toll-Free: 866-893-1541
Phone: 907-561-2030
Fax: 800-254-5728
customerservice.center@libertynorthwest.com
www.libertynorthwest.com
For Profit Organization: Yes
Year Founded: 1983

Healthplan and Services Defined
  PLAN TYPE: PPO
  Model Type: Group
  Plan Specialty: Worker's Compensation, Property & Casualty
  Benefits Offered: Prescription, Property & Casualty

Type of Payment Plans Offered
  POS, DFFS, FFS, Combination FFS & DFFS

Geographic Areas Served
  Statewide

Network Qualifications
  Pre-Admission Certification: Yes

Peer Review Type
  Case Management: Yes

Publishes and Distributes Report Card: No

Specialty Managed Care Partners
  Enters into Contracts with Regional Business Coalitions: No

26   ODS Alaska

601 W Fifth Avenue
Suite 510
Anchorage, AK 99501
Toll-Free: 877-299-9062
www.odscompanies.com
Secondary Address: 601 SW Second Avenue, Portland, OR 97240
Year Founded: 1955
Total Enrollment: 1,500,000

Healthplan and Services Defined
  PLAN TYPE: Multiple
  Other Type: PPO, POS, Dental
  Plan Specialty: Dental
  Benefits Offered: Chiropractic, Dental, Disease Management, Home
    Care, Inpatient SNF, Physical Therapy, Podiatry, Prescription,
    Psychiatric, Vision, Wellness

Type of Coverage
  Commercial, Individual, Medicare

Subscriber Information
  Average Monthly Fee Per Subscriber
    (Employee + Employer Contribution):
      Employee Only (Self): Varies
      Medicare: Varies
  Average Annual Deductible Per Subscriber:
      Employee Only (Self): Varies
      Medicare: Varies
  Average Subscriber Co-Payment:
      Primary Care Physician: Varies
      Non-Network Physician: Varies
      Prescription Drugs: Varies
      Hospital ER: Varies
      Home Health Care: Varies
      Home Health Care Max. Days/Visits Covered: Varies
      Nursing Home: Varies
      Nursing Home Max. Days/Visits Covered: Varies

Key Personnel
  President/CEO . . . . .Kim Volk
  Dir Applications Mgmt . . . . .Sam Hart

VP Marketing . . . . .Tom Dolatowski

27   Premera Blue Cross Blue Shield of Alaska

2550 Denali Street
Suite 1404
Anchorage, AK 99503
Toll-Free: 888-669-2583
Phone: 907-258-5065
www.premera.com
For Profit Organization: Yes
Year Founded: 1952
Total Enrollment: 187,000
State Enrollment: 187,000

Healthplan and Services Defined
  PLAN TYPE: PPO
  Other Type: EPO
  Plan Specialty: Dental
  Benefits Offered: Dental, Long-Term Care, Vision, Life

Type of Coverage
  Supplemental Medicare

Key Personnel
  President . . . . .Cameron Pelly
  EVP, Health Care Services . . . . .Brian Ancell
  EVP, Operations . . . . .Karen Bartlett
  EVP, Chief Financial Offc . . . . .Kent Marquardt
  SVP, Health Care Delivery . . . . .Richard Maturi
  SVP, Legislative Affairs . . . . .Jack McRae
  EVP, Legal Public Policy . . . . .Yoram Milo
  EVP, Chief Marketing Offc . . . . .Heyward Donigan
  SVP, Chief Medical Offc . . . . .Roki Chauhan, MD
  SVP, Human Resources .Barbara Magusin
  SVP, CIO . . . . .Kirsten Simonitsch
  SVP, General Counsel . . . . .John Pierce
  Media Relations Manager .Eric Earling
    425-918-3297
    eric.earling@premera.com

28   UnitedHealthCare of Alaska

7632 SW Durham Road
Tigard, OR 97224
Toll-Free: 866-432-5992
www.uhc.com
Subsidiary of: UnitedHealth Group
For Profit Organization: Yes
Total Enrollment: 75,000,000

Healthplan and Services Defined
  PLAN TYPE: HMO/PPO

Geographic Areas Served
  Statewide

Key Personnel
  Chief Executive Officer . . . . .David Hansen
  Marketing . . . . .Lya Selby
  Medical Director . . . . .Roger Muller, MD
  Media Contact . . . . .Will Shanley
    will.shanley@uhc.com

Health Insurance Coverage Status and Type of Coverage by Age

Category	All Persons		Under 18 years		Under 65 years		65 years and over	
	Number	%	Number	%	Number	%	Number	%
Total population	6,703	-	1,781	-	5,915	-	788	-
Covered by some type of health insurance	5,420 (91)	80.9 (1.3)	1,514 (45)	85.0 (2.3)	4,659 (98)	78.8 (1.4)	761 (46)	96.6 (1.0)
Covered by private health insurance	3,872 (115)	57.8 (1.7)	945 (51)	53.1 (3.0)	3,439 (116)	58.1 (1.9)	433 (35)	55.0 (3.5)
Employment based	3,301 (118)	49.3 (1.8)	843 (49)	47.3 (2.8)	3,088 (117)	52.2 (1.9)	214 (30)	27.1 (3.5)
Own employment based	1,724 (62)	25.7 (0.9)	9 (6)	0.5 (0.3)	1,541 (61)	26.1 (1.0)	183 (27)	23.2 (3.2)
Direct purchase	636 (63)	9.5 (0.9)	113 (22)	6.3 (1.3)	398 (47)	6.7 (0.8)	239 (30)	30.3 (3.6)
Covered by government health insurance	2,248 (113)	33.5 (1.7)	657 (60)	36.9 (3.2)	1,504 (106)	25.4 (1.8)	744 (48)	94.4 (1.4)
Covered by Medicaid	1,229 (93)	18.3 (1.4)	614 (57)	34.5 (3.1)	1,174 (90)	19.8 (1.5)	55 (12)	7.0 (1.6)
Also by private insurance	134 (29)	2.0 (0.4)	72 (22)	4.0 (1.3)	127 (30)	2.2 (0.5)	7 (4)	0.9 (0.5)
Covered by Medicare	911 (54)	13.6 (0.8)	19 (12)	1.1 (0.7)	175 (30)	3.0 (0.5)	737 (48)	93.5 (1.6)
Also by private insurance	445 (38)	6.6 (0.6)	0 (0)	0.0 (0.0)	34 (11)	0.6 (0.2)	410 (37)	52.0 (3.6)
Also by Medicaid	112 (24)	1.7 (0.4)	11 (9)	0.6 (0.5)	61 (18)	1.0 (0.3)	51 (11)	6.5 (1.5)
Covered by military health care	375 (51)	5.6 (0.8)	52 (16)	2.9 (0.9)	249 (46)	4.2 (0.8)	126 (28)	16.0 (3.1)
Not covered at any time during the year	1,283 (86)	19.1 (1.3)	267 (41)	15.0 (2.3)	1,256 (85)	21.2 (1.4)	27 (8)	3.4 (1.0)

Note: Numbers in thousands; figures cover 2010; standard error appears in parenthesis; (b) base less than 75,000; (x) not applicable
Source: U.S. Census Bureau, Current Population Survey, 2011 Annual Social and Economic Supplement. Table HI05. Health Insurance Coverage Status and Type of Coverage by State and Age for All People: 2010

Arizona

29 Abrazo Advantage Health Plan

7878 North 16th Street
Suite 105
Phoenix, AZ 85020
Toll-Free: 888-864-1114
Phone: 602-824-3900
Fax: 602-674-6680
www.abrazoadvantage.com
Mailing Address: PO Box 81200, Phoenix, AZ 85069
Subsidiary of: An Affiliate of Abrazo Health Care
Total Enrollment: 3,000

Healthplan and Services Defined
PLAN TYPE: Multiple
Benefits Offered: Chiropractic, Home Care, Inpatient SNF, Physical
Therapy, Podiatry, Prescription, Vision, Wellness, Mental Health,
Hospice

Type of Coverage
Supplemental Medicare

Geographic Areas Served
Arizona

Key Personnel
CEO . . . . .Jeff Egbert
CFO . . . . .Brian Steines

30 Action Healthcare Management Services

6245 N 24th Parkway
Suite 112
Phoenix, AZ 85016
Toll-Free: 800-433-6915
Phone: 602-265-0681
Fax: 602-265-0202
jeanr@actionhealthcare.com
www.actionhealthcare.com
For Profit Organization: Yes
Year Founded: 1987
Physician Owned Organization: No
Federally Qualified: No
Total Enrollment: 98,500

Healthplan and Services Defined
PLAN TYPE: PPO
Model Type: Medical Mgmt Company
Plan Specialty: Disease Management
Benefits Offered: Behavioral Health, Disease Management, Home
Care, Inpatient SNF, Long-Term Care, Podiatry, Psychiatric,
Transplant, Wellness, Worker's Compensation

Type of Coverage
Commercial, Self-Funded Healthcare Benefits

Geographic Areas Served
Nationwide

Network Qualifications
Pre-Admission Certification: No

Peer Review Type
Utilization Review: Yes

Publishes and Distributes Report Card: No

Accreditation Certification
TJC

Key Personnel
President/CEO . . . . .Jean Rice
Medical Director . . . . .Joel V Brill, MD
Clinical Operations Mgr. . . . . Mary Kim Brown, RN-BC

Specialty Managed Care Partners
Enters into Contracts with Regional Business Coalitions: No

31 Aetna Health of Arizona

2625 Shadelands Drive
Suite 240
Walnut Creek, CA 94598
Toll-Free: 866-582-9629
Fax: 602-427-2176
www.aetna.com
For Profit Organization: Yes
Year Founded: 1988
Number of Affiliated Hospitals: 44
Number of Primary Care Physicians: 1,554
Number of Referral/Specialty Physicians: 4,374
Total Enrollment: 109,089

Healthplan and Services Defined
PLAN TYPE: HMO
Other Type: POS
Benefits Offered: Dental, Disease Management, Long-Term Care,
Prescription, Wellness, LTD, STD
Offers Demand Management Patient Information Service: Yes

Type of Coverage
Commercial, Individual

Type of Payment Plans Offered
POS, Capitated, Combination FFS & DFFS

Geographic Areas Served
Statewide

Network Qualifications
Minimum Years of Practice: 2
Pre-Admission Certification: Yes

Peer Review Type
Utilization Review: Yes

Publishes and Distributes Report Card: Yes

Accreditation Certification
NCQA

Specialty Managed Care Partners
Behavioral Health, Prescription, Dental, Vision

32 Arizona Foundation for Medical Care

326 East Coronado Road
Phoenix, AZ 85004-1576
Toll-Free: 800-624-4277
Phone: 602-252-4042
Fax: 602-254-3086
marketing@azfmc.com
www.azfmc.com
Non-Profit Organization: Yes
Year Founded: 1969
Number of Affiliated Hospitals: 73
Number of Primary Care Physicians: 13,000
Total Enrollment: 175,000

Healthplan and Services Defined
PLAN TYPE: Multiple
Other Type: HMO, PPO, POS, EPO
Model Type: Group, Network
Plan Specialty: Chiropractic, Disease Management, EPO, Worker's
Compensation, PPO, POS, Medical Management, Case
Management, Utilization Management, Wellness Services, 24/7
Nurse Line
Benefits Offered: Disease Management, Wellness, Maternity
Management
Offers Demand Management Patient Information Service: Yes
DMPI Services Offered: 24-Hour Nurse Care Line

Type of Coverage
Commercial, Individual, Indemnity

Type of Payment Plans Offered
POS

Geographic Areas Served
Arizona (Statewide)

Network Qualifications
Pre-Admission Certification: Yes

Peer Review Type
Utilization Review: Yes
Case Management: Yes

Key Personnel
Executive VP . . . . Anthony Mitten
Director of Operations . . . . Daniel Mitten
Administration/Finance . . . . Sandra D Flowers
Claims Operations. . . . . Terry Murphy
Dir, Network Management . . . . Coleen Hamilton
Manager. . . . . Kay Banda
Mgr, Bus Implementation . . . . Ashley Rogers
Business Relations/Comm. . . . . Jennifer Robinson
Medical Management . . . . Kerry Kovaleski
Information Services . . . . Tracy Mitchell

33 Arizona Physicians IPA

3141 North Third Avenue
Phoenix, AZ 85013
Phone: 602-651-6127
www.myapipa.com
Subsidiary of: AmeriChoice, A UnitedHealth Group Company
For Profit Organization: Yes

Healthplan and Services Defined
PLAN TYPE: HMO

Type of Coverage
Medicare, Supplemental Medicare, Medicaid

Geographic Areas Served
Apache, Cochise, Coconino, Graham, Greenlee, La Paz, Maricopa, Mohave, Navajo, Pima, Santa Cruz, Yavapai, Yuma

Key Personnel
Principal . . . . Donna Payne
Media Contact. . . . . Jeff Smith
952-931-5685
jeff.smith@uhc.com

34 Avesis: Corporate Headquarters

3030 N Central Avenue
Suite 300
Phoenix, AZ 85012
Toll-Free: 800-522-0258
Phone: 602-241-3400
Fax: 602-240-9100
www.avesis.com
Year Founded: 1978
Number of Primary Care Physicians: 18,000
Total Enrollment: 2,000,000

Healthplan and Services Defined
PLAN TYPE: PPO
Other Type: Vision, Dental
Model Type: Network
Plan Specialty: Dental, Vision, Hearing
Benefits Offered: Dental, Vision

Type of Coverage
Commercial

Type of Payment Plans Offered
POS, Capitated, Combination FFS & DFFS

Geographic Areas Served
Nationwide and Puerto Rico

Publishes and Distributes Report Card: Yes

Accreditation Certification
AAAHC

TJC Accreditation

Key Personnel
Vice Chairman . . . . William Cohen
Chief Information Officer. . . . . Laura Gill
Chief Operations Officer. . . . . Linda Chirichella
Chief Marketing Officer . . . . Michael Reamer
Chief Information Officer. . . . . Laura Gill
Government Sales. . . . . Josh Cohn
410-581-8700
jcohn@avesis.com

35 Banner MediSun Medicare Plan

13632 N 99th Avenue
Sun City, AZ 85351
Toll-Free: 800-446-8331
Phone: 623-974-7430
www.bannerhealth.com

Healthplan and Services Defined
PLAN TYPE: Medicare

Type of Coverage
Medicare, Supplemental Medicare

Geographic Areas Served
Maricopa County

36 Blue Cross & Blue Shield of Arizona

2444 West Las Palmaritas Drive
Phoenix, AZ 85021
Toll-Free: 800-232-2345
Phone: 602-864-4400
Fax: 602-864-5160
www.bcbsaz.com
Secondary Address: 1500 E Cedar Avenue, Suite 56, Flagstaff, AZ 86004
Non-Profit Organization: Yes
Year Founded: 1939
Number of Affiliated Hospitals: 65
Number of Primary Care Physicians: 1,611
Total Enrollment: 1,000,000
State Enrollment: 1,000,000

Healthplan and Services Defined
PLAN TYPE: HMO/PPO
Model Type: Network
Benefits Offered: Behavioral Health, Chiropractic, Dental, Prescription, Wellness

Type of Coverage
Commercial, Individual, Indemnity, Supplemental Medicare

Geographic Areas Served
Statewide

Accreditation Certification
TJC Accreditation, Medicare Approved, Utilization Review, Pre-Admission Certification, State Licensure, Quality Assurance Program

Key Personnel
President/CEO. . . . . Richard L Boals
EVP, External Operations. . . . . Sandra Lee Gibson
EVP, Internal Operations . . . . Susan Navran
Sr VP Claims Services . . . . H Jody Chandler
SVP, Chief Financial Offc . . . . Karen Abraham
SVP, General Counsel . . . . Deanna Salazar
602-864-5870
SVP, Business Development. . . . . Tony M Astorga
SVP, Marketing & Prov Aff. . . . . Richard M Hannon
SVP, Chief Medical Offc . . . . Vishu J Jhaveri, MD
SVP, Finance & Admin . . . . Karen Abraham
SVP, Chief Info Officer . . . . Elizabeth A Messina

Dir, Public Relations . . . . .Regena Frieden
602-864-4046
rfrieden@phx1.bcbsaz.com
Public Relations Spec. . . . . .Renee Hunt
602-864-5182
rhunt@phx1.bcbsaz.com

37 Care 1st Health Plan: Arizona

2355 East Camelback Road
Suite 300
Phoenix, AZ 85016
Toll-Free: 866-560-4042
Phone: 602-778-1800
Fax: 602-778-8939
www.care1st.com
For Profit Organization: Yes
Year Founded: 1994

Healthplan and Services Defined
PLAN TYPE: HMO
Benefits Offered: Disease Management, Wellness

Type of Coverage
Supplemental Medicare, Medicaid

Geographic Areas Served
Maricopa County

Accreditation Certification
NCQA

Key Personnel
Chief Admin Officer. . . . . .Scott Cummings
Chief Operating Officer . . . . .Susan Cordier
CFO/COO . . . . .Brenda Hanserd
Director, Claims. . . . . .Steffanie Costal
Dir, Pharmacy. . . . . .Nirali Soni, RPh, CDE
Dir, Sales & Marketing. . . . . .Anna Maria Maldonado
Dir, Quality Management . . . . .Pat Seabert, RN
Dir, Member Services . . . . .Rachel McDonald
Dir, Information Tech . . . . .Kathy Thurman
Dir, Provider Network . . . . .Jessica Sedita-Igneri

38 CIGNA HealthCare of Arizona

11001 North Black Canyon Highway
Suite 400
Phoenix, AZ 85029
Toll-Free: 800-801-7257
Phone: 602-942-4462
Fax: 602-371-2625
www.cigna.com
Secondary Address: Great-West Healthcare, now part of CIGNA, 6909
East Greenway Parkway, Suite 180, Scottsdale, AZ 85254,
480-922-6508
For Profit Organization: Yes
Year Founded: 1972
Number of Primary Care Physicians: 1,150
Number of Referral/Specialty Physicians: 3,180
Total Enrollment: 103,561
State Enrollment: 103,561

Healthplan and Services Defined
PLAN TYPE: HMO/PPO
Other Type: POS
Model Type: IPA, Network
Benefits Offered: Behavioral Health, Chiropractic, Complementary
Medicine, Disease Management, Home Care, Inpatient SNF,
Long-Term Care, Physical Therapy, Podiatry, Prescription,
Psychiatric, Transplant, Vision, Wellness

Type of Coverage
Commercial, Individual, Medicare

Type of Payment Plans Offered
POS

Accreditation Certification
NCQA

Key Personnel
President/General Manager . . . . .Kurt A Weimer
COO . . . . .Bill Carroll
Principal . . . . .Lavon Carriveau
Network Manager. . . . . .Wendy Woske
Pharmacy Compliance Offc. . . . . .David Hu
Marketing Manager . . . . .Jay Headley
VP, Sales . . . . .Frank Benedetto

39 CoreSource: Arizona

7830 E Broadway Blvd
Tucson, AZ 85710
Toll-Free: 800-888-7202
Phone: 520-290-4600
www.coresource.com
Subsidiary of: Trustmark
Year Founded: 1980
Total Enrollment: 1,100,000

Healthplan and Services Defined
PLAN TYPE: Multiple
Other Type: TPA
Model Type: Network
Plan Specialty: Claims Administration, TPA
Benefits Offered: Behavioral Health, Home Care, Prescription,
Transplant

Type of Coverage
Commercial

Geographic Areas Served
Nationwide

Accreditation Certification
Utilization Review, Pre-Admission Certification

Key Personnel
Office Manager. . . . . .Kathy Mitchell
Manager . . . . .Jane Bergman

40 Delta Dental of Arizona

5656 West Talavi Blvd
Glendale, AZ 85306
Toll-Free: 800-352-6132
Phone: 602-938-3131
Fax: 602-588-3636
www.deltadentalaz.com
Mailing Address: PO Box 43000, Phoenix, AZ 85080-3000
Non-Profit Organization: Yes
Year Founded: 1972
Number of Primary Care Physicians: 2,700
Total Enrollment: 54,000,000
State Enrollment: 435,000

Healthplan and Services Defined
PLAN TYPE: Dental
Other Type: Dental PPO
Model Type: Network
Plan Specialty: Dental, Vision
Benefits Offered: Dental, Vision

Type of Coverage
Commercial, Indemnity

Type of Payment Plans Offered
FFS

Geographic Areas Served
Statewide

Key Personnel
Chairman. . . . . .James Davis

Vice Chairman . . . . Karen Berrigan
Chairman . . . . Wesley A Harper, DDS
Media Contact . . . . Shannon Keller
    602-346-2575
    shannonk@barclaycomm.com

41   Desert Canyon Community Care

3767 Karicio Lane
Suite D
Prescott, AZ 86303
Toll-Free: 800-887-6177
Phone: 928-777-9226
Fax: 928-777-9243
www.desertcanyoncommunitycare.com
Subsidiary of: Arcadian Health Plans

Healthplan and Services Defined
    PLAN TYPE: Medicare

Type of Coverage
    Medicare

42   eHealthInsurance Services Inc.

11919 Foundation Place
Gold River, CA 95670
Toll-Free: 800-977-8860
info@ehealthinsurance.com
www.e.healthinsurance.com
Year Founded: 1997

Healthplan and Services Defined
    PLAN TYPE: HMO/PPO
    Benefits Offered: Dental, Life, STD

Type of Coverage
    Commercial, Individual, Medicare

Geographic Areas Served
    All 50 states in the USA and District of Columbia

Key Personnel
    Chairman & CEO . . . . Gary L. Lauer
    EVP/Business & Corp. Dev. Bruce Telkamp
    EVP/Chief Technology . . . . Dr. Sheldon X. Wang
    SVP & CFO . . . . Stuart M. Huizinga
    Pres. of eHealth Gov. Sys . . . . Samuel C. Gibbs
    SVP of Sales & Operations . . . . Robert S. Hurley
    Director Public Relations . . . . Nate Purpura
    650-210-3115

43   Employers Dental Services

3430 E Sunrise Dr
Suite 160
Tucson, AZ 85718
Toll-Free: 800-722-9772
Phone: 520-696-4343
Fax: 520-696-4311
edscs@mydentalplan.net
www.mydentalplan.net
Mailing Address: PO Box 36600, Tucson, AZ 85740
Year Founded: 1974
Owned by an Integrated Delivery Network (IDN): Yes
Number of Primary Care Physicians: 1,340
Total Enrollment: 120,000
State Enrollment: 120,000

Healthplan and Services Defined
    PLAN TYPE: Dental
    Model Type: Group, Individual
    Plan Specialty: Dental
    Benefits Offered: Dental, Prepaid

Type of Coverage
    DHMO

Geographic Areas Served
    Arizona Statewide

Peer Review Type
    Utilization Review: Yes
    Case Management: Yes

Accreditation Certification
    Utilization Review, Quality Assurance Program

Key Personnel
    VP Finance . . . . Cynthia Weeks
    CCO. . . . . Elizabeth Stambaugh, SPHR
    CFO . . . . Todd Laporte, CPA

Specialty Managed Care Partners
    Enters into Contracts with Regional Business Coalitions: Yes

44   Fortified Provider Network

8096 N 85th Way
Suite 103
Scottsdale, AZ 85258
Toll-Free: 866-955-4376
Phone: 480-607-0222
Fax: 480-607-2199
fpn@fortifiedprovider.com
www.fortifiedprovider.com
Year Founded: 1997

Healthplan and Services Defined
    PLAN TYPE: PPO

Key Personnel
    President . . . . Michael Reagan
    Vice President Operations . . . . Tom Flynn
    VP Contracting . . . . Michael Olson

45   Great-West Healthcare Arizona

Acquired by CIGNA

46   Health Choice Arizona

401 N 44th Street
Suite 900
Phoenix, AZ 85008
Toll-Free: 800-322-8670
Phone: 480-968-6866
Fax: 480-784-2933
hch_comments/hch@iasishealthcare.com
www.healthchoiceaz.com
Subsidiary of: IASIS Healthcare
For Profit Organization: Yes
Year Founded: 1990
Number of Affiliated Hospitals: 16
Number of Primary Care Physicians: 400
Total Enrollment: 115,000

Healthplan and Services Defined
    PLAN TYPE: HMO
    Model Type: IPA
    Plan Specialty: Services to AHCCCS members
    Benefits Offered: Behavioral Health, Dental, Disease Management,
        Prescription, Wellness, Care Coordination, Maternal Child Health

Type of Coverage
    Medicaid, Managed Medicaid

Geographic Areas Served
    Apache, Coconino, Gila, Maricopa, Mohave, Navajo, Pima, Pinal
    counties

Network Qualifications
    Pre-Admission Certification: Yes

Peer Review Type
Utilization Review: Yes
Second Surgical Opinion: Yes
Case Management: Yes

Accreditation Certification
TJC Accreditation, Utilization Review

Key Personnel
President/CEO.................................Carolyn Rose
Claims.......................................Adrian Brown
Member Services..............................Suzan Irmer
CIO..Mike Uchrin
Information Systems.......................Jesse Perlmutter

47 Health Net of Arizona

1230 West Washington Street
Suite 401
Tempe, AZ 85281
Toll-Free: 800-289-2818
Phone: 602-794-1400
Fax: 602-286-9244
www.healthnet.com
Subsidiary of: Health Net
For Profit Organization: Yes
Year Founded: 1981
Number of Affiliated Hospitals: 52
Number of Primary Care Physicians: 1,200
Number of Referral/Specialty Physicians: 3,800
Total Enrollment: 119,000
State Enrollment: 60,500

Healthplan and Services Defined
PLAN TYPE: HMO
Model Type: Network
Plan Specialty: Behavioral Health, Chiropractic, Disease
Management, Lab, MSO, PBM, Vision, Radiology, UR
Benefits Offered: Behavioral Health, Chiropractic, Complementary
Medicine, Dental, Disease Management, Home Care, Inpatient
SNF, Physical Therapy, Podiatry, Prescription, Psychiatric,
Transplant, Vision, Wellness, AD&D, Life, Alternative Medicine

Type of Coverage
Commercial, Individual, Indemnity, Medicare

Type of Payment Plans Offered
POS, DFFS, Combination FFS & DFFS

Geographic Areas Served
Apache, Cochise, Coconino, Gila, Graham, Greenlee, La Paz,
Maricipa, Mohave, Navajo, Pima, Pinal, Santa Cruz, Yuma counties

Subscriber Information
Average Monthly Fee Per Subscriber
(Employee + Employer Contribution):
Employee Only (Self): Varies
Employee & 1 Family Member: Varies
Employee & 2 Family Members: Varies
Medicare: Varies
Average Annual Deductible Per Subscriber:
Employee Only (Self): Varies
Employee & 1 Family Member: Varies
Employee & 2 Family Members: Varies
Medicare: Varies

Network Qualifications
Minimum Years of Practice: 3
Pre-Admission Certification: Yes

Peer Review Type
Utilization Review: Yes
Second Surgical Opinion: Yes
Case Management: Yes

Accreditation Certification
NCQA

Medicare Approved, Utilization Review, Pre-Admission Certification,
State Licensure, Quality Assurance Program

Key Personnel
President ....Brett A Morris
CFO ....Alec Mahmood
Regional CFO ....Lorry Bottrill
Chief Medical Officer ....Richard Jacobs, MD
VP Provider Services.........................Carolyn Pace
Mgr, Public Relations..........................Lori Rieger
602-794-1415
lori.rieger@healthnet.com

Specialty Managed Care Partners
Preferred Home Care, Infusion Care Systems, Catalina Behavioral
Health Services, Sonoma Quest Laboratory, Health South,
Southwest Footcare

Employer References
FEHB, IBM

48 Humana Health Insurance of Arizona

20860 N Tatum Boulevard
Suite 400
Phoenix, AZ 85050
Toll-Free: 800-889-0301
Phone: 480-515-6400
Fax: 480-515-6681
www.humana.com
Secondary Address: 5120 E Williams Circle, Suite 200, Tucson, AZ
85711
For Profit Organization: Yes
Year Founded: 1984
Number of Affiliated Hospitals: 33
Number of Primary Care Physicians: 500
Total Enrollment: 127,564
State Enrollment: 26,120

Healthplan and Services Defined
PLAN TYPE: HMO/PPO
Model Type: IPA
Benefits Offered: Dental, Disease Management, Prescription,
Transplant, Vision, Wellness, Life, LTD, STD

Type of Coverage
Commercial, Individual

Type of Payment Plans Offered
POS, Combination FFS & DFFS

Geographic Areas Served
Apache, Cochise, Coconino, Gila, Graham, Greenlee, La Paz,
Maricipa, Mohave, Navajo, Pima, Pinal, Santa Cruz, Yavapai, Yuma
counties

Subscriber Information
Average Monthly Fee Per Subscriber
(Employee + Employer Contribution):
Employee Only (Self): Varies
Employee & 1 Family Member: Varies
Employee & 2 Family Members: Varies
Medicare: Varies
Average Subscriber Co-Payment:
Prescription Drugs: Varies

Network Qualifications
Pre-Admission Certification: Yes

Peer Review Type
Utilization Review: Yes
Second Surgical Opinion: Yes
Case Management: Yes

Publishes and Distributes Report Card: Yes

Accreditation Certification
URAC, NCQA, CORE
TJC Accreditation

Key Personnel
President/CEO . . . . Michael McCallister
COO Market & Business . . . . James Murray
VP Chief Actuary . . . . John Bertko, FSA MAAA
Sr VP CFO/Treasurer . . . . James Bloem
Sr VP General Counsel . . . . Arthur Hipwell
Sr VP Corporate Develop . . . . Thomas Liston
Sr VP Human Resources . . . . Bonita Hathcock
Sr VP Marketing Officer . . . . Steven Moya
Sr VP Government Relation . . . . Heidi Margulis
Sr VP Innovation Officer . . . . Jonathan Lord, MD
VP/Controller . . . . Steven McCulley
Sr VP CSO/CIO . . . . Bruce Goodman

Specialty Managed Care Partners
Enters into Contracts with Regional Business Coalitions: Yes

---

49   Magellan Health Services Arizona
4129 E Van Buren Street
Suite 250
Phoenix, AZ 85008
Toll-Free: 800-564-5465
www.magellanofaz.com
For Profit Organization: Yes
Total Enrollment: 80,000
State Enrollment: 80,000

Healthplan and Services Defined
PLAN TYPE: PPO

Type of Coverage
Medicaid, Title XXI/KidsCare

Accreditation Certification
URAC, NCQA

Key Personnel
CEO . . . . Chris Carson
Deputy CEO . . . . Jeff Boldizsar
Chief of Adult Services . . . . David Covington
Chief Operations Officer . . . . Dale Villani
Chief Financial Officer . . . . Brian Karr
Chief Comm Relations Offc . . . . Andrea Smiley
Chief Medical Officer . . . . Robert Sack, MD
Chief of Child Services . . . . Shawn Thiele
Dir, Public Relations . . . . Greg Taylor
    602-652-8282
    gataylor@magellanhealth.com

**50   Maricopa Integrated Health
System/Maricopa Health Plan**
2601 East Roosevelt Street
Phoenix, AZ 85008
Toll-Free: 800-582-8686
Phone: 302-344-8760
Fax: 602-344-5190
copanet@hcs.maricopa.gov
www.mihs.org
Subsidiary of: University Physicians Health Plans
Non-Profit Organization: Yes
Year Founded: 1981
Number of Affiliated Hospitals: 10
Number of Primary Care Physicians: 124
Number of Referral/Specialty Physicians: 317
Total Enrollment: 50,715
State Enrollment: 39,997

Healthplan and Services Defined
PLAN TYPE: HMO
Model Type: Network
Plan Specialty: Lab, Radiology
Benefits Offered: Dental, Physical Therapy, Prescription, Wellness

Type of Coverage
Individual, Medicare, Medicaid

Type of Payment Plans Offered
Capitated, FFS

Geographic Areas Served
Maricopa County

Network Qualifications
Pre-Admission Certification: Yes

Peer Review Type
Utilization Review: Yes
Second Surgical Opinion: No
Case Management: Yes

Publishes and Distributes Report Card: Yes

Accreditation Certification
TJC Accreditation, Medicare Approved, Utilization Review,
    Pre-Admission Certification, State Licensure, Quality Assurance
    Program

Key Personnel
President . . . . Thomas G McKinley
    602-344-1818
    tom.mckinley@mihs.org
Dir, Network Development . . . . Mary Consie
    602-344-8389
    mconsie@uph.org
Provider Relations Rep . . . . Connie Leonardo
    602-344-8387
    cleonardo@uph.org

Specialty Managed Care Partners
Enters into Contracts with Regional Business Coalitions: Yes

---

51   Mercy Care Plan/Mercy Care Advantage
4350 East Cotton Center Blvd
Bldg D
Phoenix, AZ 85040
Toll-Free: 800-624-3879
Phone: 602-263-3000
Fax: 602-263-2098
www.mercycareplan.com
Subsidiary of: Southwest Catholic Health Network
Non-Profit Organization: Yes
Year Founded: 1985
Total Enrollment: 300,000
State Enrollment: 300,000

Healthplan and Services Defined
PLAN TYPE: Medicare
Model Type: Group
Benefits Offered: Disease Management, Prescription, Wellness

Type of Coverage
Medicare, Medicaid

Geographic Areas Served
Cochise, Gila, Graham, Greenlee, La Paz, Maricopa, Pima, Pinal,
Santa Cruz, Yavapai, Yuma counties

Key Personnel
Chief Executive Officer . . . . Mark Fisher
Chief Operating Officer . . . . Lorry Bottrill
Chief Financial Officer . . . . Chuck Sowers

---

52   Novasys Health
10801 Executive Center Drive
Suite 305
Little Rock, AZ 72211-4353
Toll-Free: 800-294-3557
Phone: 501-219-4444
Fax: 501-219-4455
www.novasyshealth.com

Mailing Address: PO Box 25230, Little Rock, AR 72221

Healthplan and Services Defined
 PLAN TYPE: PPO

Key Personnel
 President . . . . .John Glassford
 Executive Director/Claims .Michael Boone
 CEO . . . . .John Ryan
 VP of IT . . . . .Scott Shell

53 Outlook Vision Service

1 North MacDonald Street
Suite 312
Mesa, AZ 85201
Toll-Free: 800-342-7188
Phone: 480-461-9001
Fax: 480-461-9021
customerservice@outlookvision.com
www.outlookvision.com
Year Founded: 1990
Federally Qualified: Yes
Total Enrollment: 7,000,000

Healthplan and Services Defined
 PLAN TYPE: Vision
 Plan Specialty: Vision
 Benefits Offered: Prescription, Vision, Hearing

Type of Coverage
 Commercial, Individual

Geographic Areas Served
 Nationwide

Key Personnel
 Owner/President . . . . .Ron Johnson
 Dir Provider Services . . . . .Joan Vander Pluym

54 PacifiCare of Arizona

United Healthcare

55 Phoenix Health Plan

7878 North 16th Street
Suite 105
Phoenix, AZ 85020
Toll-Free: 800-747-7997
Phone: 602-824-3700
Fax: 602-674-6659
www.php-cc.com
Mailing Address: PO Box 81000, Phoenix, AZ 85069
Non-Profit Organization: Yes
Year Founded: 1982
Number of Affiliated Hospitals: 27
Number of Primary Care Physicians: 300
State Enrollment: 100,000

Healthplan and Services Defined
 PLAN TYPE: HMO
 Model Type: IPA
 Benefits Offered: Behavioral Health, Dental, Disease Management,
  Prescription, Wellness
 Offers Demand Management Patient Information Service: Yes
 DMPI Services Offered: 24 Hour Nurse Hotline

Type of Coverage
 Medicaid

Type of Payment Plans Offered
 POS, Combination FFS & DFFS

Geographic Areas Served
 Apache, Coconino, Gila, Maricopa, Mohave, Najavo, Pima, Pinal,
 Yavapai counties

Publishes and Distributes Report Card: Yes

Accreditation Certification
 NCQA
 TJC Accreditation, Medicare Approved, Utilization Review,
  Pre-Admission Certification, State Licensure, Quality Assurance
  Program

Key Personnel
 President/CEO . . . . .Nancy Novick
 CFO . . . . .Deena Sigel
 Marketing . . . . .Mark Sands
 Medical Affairs . . . . .Nancy Hirst
 Information Systems . . . . .James Mathew
 Provider Services . . . . .Mark Jokisch

Specialty Managed Care Partners
 Enters into Contracts with Regional Business Coalitions: Yes

56 Pima Health System

3950 S Country Club Road, Suite 400
Herbert K Abrams Public Health Center
Tucson, AZ 85714
Toll-Free: 800-423-3801
Phone: 520-243-8060
Fax: 520-243-8314
www.pimahealthsystem.org
Secondary Address: 857 W Bell Road, Suite 5, Nogales, AZ 85621
Non-Profit Organization: Yes
Year Founded: 1982
Number of Affiliated Hospitals: 1
Number of Primary Care Physicians: 350
Total Enrollment: 7,000
State Enrollment: 7,000

Healthplan and Services Defined
 PLAN TYPE: HMO
 Model Type: Group
 Benefits Offered: Disease Management, Long-Term Care,
  Prescription, Wellness, Home Support Programs

Type of Coverage
 Medicaid

Type of Payment Plans Offered
 Capitated, FFS

Geographic Areas Served
 Pima, Santa Cruz counties

Subscriber Information
 Average Subscriber Co-Payment:
  Nursing Home Max. Days/Visits Covered: Fully covered

Publishes and Distributes Report Card: Yes

Accreditation Certification
 TJC Accreditation, Medicare Approved, Utilization Review,
  Pre-Admission Certification, State Licensure, Quality Assurance
  Program

Key Personnel
 President/CEO . . . . .Karen Fields
 CFO . . . . .Donna Terry
 Materials Management . . . . .Mona Berkowitz
 Medical Affairs . . . . .Fred Miller, Md
 Member Services . . . . .Virginia Rountree

57 Preferred Therapy Providers

23460 North 19th Avenue, Suite 250
CenterPointe Deer Valley
Phoenix, AZ 85027
Toll-Free: 800-664-5240
Phone: 623-869-9101
Fax: 623-869-9102
preferred@preferredtherapy.com
www.preferredtherapy.com

For Profit Organization: Yes
Year Founded: 1992
Physician Owned Organization: No
Federally Qualified: No
Number of Referral/Specialty Physicians: 3,000
Total Enrollment: 60,000,000

Healthplan and Services Defined
PLAN TYPE: PPO
Model Type: Network
Plan Specialty: Physical, Occupational, Speech Therapies
Benefits Offered: Physical Therapy, Ocupational Therapy, Speech
  Therapy
Offers Demand Management Patient Information Service: No

Type of Coverage
Commercial

Geographic Areas Served
35 states

Network Qualifications
Pre-Admission Certification: No

Publishes and Distributes Report Card: No

Accreditation Certification
NCQA, AAPPO

Key Personnel
President . . . . Jaxene Hillebert
VP . . . . Christy Beauchamp
General Manager. . . . . Sam Cega
Contracts Associate. . . . . Anne Singer
Network Services . . . . Alma Neira
Credentialing Coordinator . . . . Christi Hemmele
Operations Coordinator. Dawn Wilson
Finance Coordinator. . . . . Sandy Dodt
Payor Reports Coordinator . . . . Pat Petersen
Client Service Specialist . . . . Julie Jones
Provider Relations Rep . . . . Kay Banda

Specialty Managed Care Partners
Enters into Contracts with Regional Business Coalitions: No

58 SecureCare Dental

3625 North 16th Street
Suite 206
Phoenix, AZ 85016
Toll-Free: 888-429-0914
Phone: 602-241-0914
Fax: 602-285-0121
quotes@securedental.com
www.securecaredental.com
Mailing Address: PO Box 29697, Phoenix, AZ 85038-9697
Year Founded: 1987
Number of Primary Care Physicians: 1,850
Total Enrollment: 55,000

Healthplan and Services Defined
PLAN TYPE: Dental
Other Type: Dental PPO
Model Type: Network
Plan Specialty: Dental
Benefits Offered: Dental

Type of Coverage
Commercial, Group

Type of Payment Plans Offered
FFS, Combination FFS & DFFS

Geographic Areas Served
Arizona and Nevada

Key Personnel
President. . . . . Mark Popejoy
Principal . . . . Thomas Abrams
Partner . . . . David Popejoy

59 Total Dental Administrators

2111 E Highland Avenue
Suite 250
Phoenix, AZ 85016-4735
Toll-Free: 888-422-1995
Phone: 602-266-1995
Fax: 602-266-1948
www.tdadental.com

Healthplan and Services Defined
PLAN TYPE: Dental

Key Personnel
President . . . . Christopher Jehle
Chief Operating Officer . . . . Scott Clark
VP, Technology . . . . Chad Cranston
Mgr Of Info Systems . . . . Chris Parrott
Dental Director. . . . . Donald Peterson

60 United Concordia: Arizona

2198 E Camelback Road
Suite 260
Phoenix, AZ 85016
Toll-Free: 800-998-8224
ucproducer@ucci.com
www.ucci.com
For Profit Organization: Yes
Year Founded: 1971
Number of Primary Care Physicians: 111,000
Total Enrollment: 8,000,000

Healthplan and Services Defined
PLAN TYPE: Dental
Plan Specialty: Dental
Benefits Offered: Dental

Type of Coverage
Commercial, Individual

Geographic Areas Served
Military personnel and their families, nationwide

61 UnitedHealthCare of Arizona

2390 E Camelback Road
Suite 300
Phoenix, AZ 85016
Toll-Free: 800-985-2356
www.uhc.com
Secondary Address: 6245 E Broadway, #600, Tucson, AZ 85711,
  866-374-6057
Subsidiary of: UnitedHealth Group
For Profit Organization: Yes
Total Enrollment: 75,000,000
State Enrollment: 1,270,000

Healthplan and Services Defined
PLAN TYPE: HMO/PPO

Geographic Areas Served
Statewide

Key Personnel
Chief Executive Officer . . . . Benton Davis
Marketing. . . . . Janet Bollman
Senior Medical Director. . . . . Robert Beauchamp, MD
Media Contact . . . . Will Shanley
  will.shanley@uhc.com

62 University Family Care Health Plan

2701 E Elvira Road
Tucson, AZ 85756
Toll-Free: 800-582-8686

Phone: 520-874-5290
Fax: 866-465-8340
www.ufcaz.com
Subsidiary of: University Physicians Health Plans
Non-Profit Organization: Yes

Healthplan and Services Defined
   PLAN TYPE: HMO

Geographic Areas Served
   Maricopa County

Key Personnel
   Dir, Network Development . . . . .Mary Consie
      602-344-8389
   Provider Relations Rep . . . . .Connie Leonardo
      602-344-8387
      cleonardo@uph.org

---

63   **VSP: Vision Service Plan of Arizona**
2111 E Highland Avenue
Suite B160
Phoenix, AZ 85016-4757
Toll-Free: 800-877-7195
Phone: 602-956-1820
webmaster@vsp.com
www.vsp.com
Year Founded: 1955
Number of Primary Care Physicians: 26,000
Total Enrollment: 55,000,000

Healthplan and Services Defined
   PLAN TYPE: Vision
   Plan Specialty: Vision
   Benefits Offered: Vision

Type of Payment Plans Offered
   Capitated

Geographic Areas Served
   Statewide

Network Qualifications
   Pre-Admission Certification: Yes

Peer Review Type
   Utilization Review: Yes

Accreditation Certification
   Utilization Review, Quality Assurance Program

Health Insurance Coverage Status and Type of Coverage by Age

Category	All Persons		Under 18 years		Under 65 years		65 years and over	
	Number	%	Number	%	Number	%	Number	%
Total population	2,880	-	710	-	2,452	-	428	-
Covered by some type of health insurance	2,341 *(48)*	81.3 *(1.5)*	658 *(15)*	92.6 *(1.7)*	1,933 *(55)*	78.8 *(1.8)*	408 *(31)*	95.5 *(1.6)*
Covered by private health insurance	1,604 *(64)*	55.7 *(2.2)*	373 *(28)*	52.5 *(3.7)*	1,425 *(79)*	58.1 *(2.9)*	179 *(29)*	41.9 *(6.2)*
Employment based	1,372 *(70)*	47.7 *(2.4)*	344 *(28)*	48.5 *(3.8)*	1,296 *(74)*	52.9 *(2.7)*	76 *(13)*	17.8 *(2.6)*
Own employment based	741 *(35)*	25.7 *(1.2)*	1 *(1)*	0.1 *(0.1)*	685 *(37)*	27.9 *(1.4)*	56 *(10)*	13.1 *(1.9)*
Direct purchase	260 *(32)*	9.0 *(1.1)*	31 *(9)*	4.4 *(1.2)*	147 *(25)*	6.0 *(1.0)*	113 *(25)*	26.4 *(5.5)*
Covered by government health insurance	1,036 *(50)*	36.0 *(1.7)*	361 *(22)*	50.8 *(3.3)*	641 *(36)*	26.2 *(1.5)*	394 *(30)*	92.2 *(2.3)*
Covered by Medicaid	528 *(29)*	18.3 *(1.0)*	350 *(20)*	49.3 *(3.0)*	496 *(27)*	20.2 *(1.2)*	32 *(8)*	7.5 *(1.7)*
Also by private insurance	98 *(19)*	3.4 *(0.6)*	68 *(15)*	9.6 *(2.2)*	90 *(18)*	3.7 *(0.7)*	8 *(6)*	1.9 *(1.3)*
Covered by Medicare	509 *(34)*	17.7 *(1.1)*	6 *(4)*	0.9 *(0.6)*	119 *(14)*	4.9 *(0.5)*	390 *(30)*	91.3 *(2.3)*
Also by private insurance	189 *(30)*	6.6 *(1.0)*	0 *(0)*	0.0 *(0.0)*	24 *(6)*	1.0 *(0.3)*	165 *(28)*	38.6 *(6.0)*
Also by Medicaid	64 *(10)*	2.2 *(0.4)*	6 *(4)*	0.9 *(0.6)*	33 *(8)*	1.3 *(0.3)*	31 *(7)*	7.3 *(1.7)*
Covered by military health care	147 *(25)*	5.1 *(0.9)*	16 *(9)*	2.3 *(1.3)*	80 *(18)*	3.3 *(0.8)*	67 *(12)*	15.8 *(2.4)*
Not covered at any time during the year	539 *(43)*	18.7 *(1.5)*	52 *(12)*	7.4 *(1.7)*	519 *(44)*	21.2 *(1.8)*	19 *(7)*	4.5 *(1.6)*

Note: Numbers in thousands; figures cover 2010; standard error appears in parenthesis; (b) base less than 75,000; (x) not applicable
Source: U.S. Census Bureau, Current Population Survey, 2011 Annual Social and Economic Supplement. Table HI05. Health Insurance Coverage Status and Type of Coverage by State and Age for All People: 2010

Arkansas

64   Aetna Health of Arkansas

Partnered with eHealthInsurance Services Inc.

65   American Denticare

1525 Merrill Drive
Little Rock, AR 72211
Toll-Free: 877-537-6453
marketing@aiba.com
www.americandenticare.com
For Profit Organization: Yes
Year Founded: 1985
Number of Primary Care Physicians: 70
Number of Referral/Specialty Physicians: 25
Total Enrollment: 50,000

Healthplan and Services Defined
  PLAN TYPE: HMO
  Model Type: IPA
  Plan Specialty: Dental
  Benefits Offered: Dental
  Offers Demand Management Patient Information Service: Yes

Type of Coverage
  Commercial, Individual

Type of Payment Plans Offered
  POS, Capitated

Geographic Areas Served
  Arkansas, Chicot, Columbia, Craighead, Crawford, Crittenden,
  Cross, Desha, Faulkner, Garland, Hot Springs, Jackson, Jefferson,
  Lincoln, Lonoke, Miller, Mississippi, Poinsette, Pope, Pulaski,
  Saline, Sebastian, St. Francis, Union, Washington, White counties

Network Qualifications
  Pre-Admission Certification: Yes

Peer Review Type
  Second Surgical Opinion: Yes
  Case Management: Yes

Publishes and Distributes Report Card: Yes

Accreditation Certification
  URAC
  Quality Assurance Program

Key Personnel
  President . . . . .J Matt Lile III, RHU

66   Arkansas Blue Cross and Blue Shield

601 S Gaines Street
Little Rock, AR 72201
Toll-Free: 800-238-8379
Phone: 501-278-2000
Fax: 501-378-3258
sitetech@arkbluecross.com
www.arkansasbluecross.com
Mailing Address: PO Box 2181, Little Rock, AR 72203-2181
Total Enrollment: 400,000
State Enrollment: 400,000

Healthplan and Services Defined
  PLAN TYPE: Multiple
  Other Type: HMO, Medicare
  Benefits Offered: Chiropractic, Dental, Home Care, Inpatient SNF,
    Physical Therapy, Podiatry, Prescription, Vision, Worker's
    Compensation, Life, Mental Health, Substance Abuse, Emergency

Type of Coverage
  Commercial, Individual, Medicare, Supplemental Medicare
  Catastrophic Illness Benefit: Varies per case

Geographic Areas Served
  Arkansas

Subscriber Information
  Average Subscriber Co-Payment:
    Hospital ER: $250.00
    Home Health Care: Varies
    Nursing Home: Varies

Key Personnel
  Chairman of the Board . . . . .Robert L Shoptaw
  President & CEO . . . . .Mark White
  Executive VP & COO . . . . .Mike Brown
  EVP, Internal Operations . . . . .David Bridges
  Vice Chairman . . . . .George K Mitchell, MD
  VP, Human Resources . . . . .Richard Cooper
  SVP, Chief Info Officer . . . . .Joseph Smith
  SVP, Chief Financial Offc . . . . .Steve Short
  VP, Alliance Management . . . . .Steve Abell
  SVP, National Business Rl . . . . .Jim Bailey
  VP, Medical Officer .James Adamson, MD
  SVP, Statewide Business . . . . .Ron DeBerry
  VP, Financial Services . . . . .Gray Dillard
  SVP, Law & Govt Relations .Lee Douglass
  SVP, Chief Medical Offc . . . . .Robert Griffin, MD
  Media Contact . . . . .Max Heuer
    501-378-2131
    mxheuer@arkbluecross.com
  VP, Communications . . . . .Karen Raley

67   Arkansas Community Care

10025 West Markham Street
Suite 220
Little Rock, AR 72205
Toll-Free: 800-705-0766
Phone: 501-223-9088
lhenry@arcadianhealth.com
www.arkansascommunitycare.com
Subsidiary of: Arcadian Health Plans
Year Founded: 1998
Physician Owned Organization: Yes
Total Enrollment: 7,000

Healthplan and Services Defined
  PLAN TYPE: Medicare
  Plan Specialty: Dental, Vision
  Benefits Offered: Dental, Prescription, Vision

Type of Coverage
  Medicare, Supplemental Medicare

Geographic Areas Served
  Benton, Carroll, Lonoke, Madison, Pulaski, Saline, Washington, and
  White counties

Key Personnel
  President . . . . .John Austin, MD
  Executive Director. . . . . .Ray Blaylock
  Vice President . . . . .Nancy Freeman
  Member Services . . . . .Lisa Henry
    lhenry@arcadianhealth.com

68   Arkansas Managed Care Organization

10 Corporate Hill Drive
Suite 200
Little Rock, AR 72205
Toll-Free: 800-278-8470
Phone: 501-225-8470
Fax: 501-225-7954
info@amcoppo.com
www.amcoppo.com
Non-Profit Organization: Yes
Year Founded: 1993

Owned by an Integrated Delivery Network (IDN): Yes
Number of Affiliated Hospitals: 100
Number of Primary Care Physicians: 1,000
Number of Referral/Specialty Physicians: 5,000
Total Enrollment: 200,000
State Enrollment: 200,000

Healthplan and Services Defined
PLAN TYPE: PPO
Model Type: Network
Plan Specialty: ASO, Behavioral Health, Chiropractic, Lab, PBM,
   Vision, Radiology, Burns, Cardiovascular Care, Neonatal Intensive
   Care, Neurological & Physical Rehabilitation, Organ Transplants
Benefits Offered: Behavioral Health, Chiropractic, Home Care,
   Long-Term Care, Physical Therapy, Podiatry, Transplant, Vision

Type of Coverage
Commercial, Individual

Accreditation Certification
TJC Accreditation, Medicare Approved, State Licensure

Key Personnel
Associate Executive Dir. . . . . Jo Anna Gist
Director Of Network Serv. . . . . Denese Montes
Director, Customer Serv. . . . . Pamela Loux
Dir/Network Services . . . . Daryl Whitehead
Credentialing Coordinator. . . . . Michelle Townsend
Dir/Contract Reimbursment . . . . Denise Lewis

Specialty Managed Care Partners
Enters into Contracts with Regional Business Coalitions: Yes

69   CIGNA HealthCare of Arkansas
3400 Players Club Parkway
Suite 140
Memphis, TN 38125
Toll-Free: 866-438-2446
Phone: 901-748-4100
Fax: 901-748-4104
www.cigna.com
For Profit Organization: Yes
Year Founded: 1985
Number of Affiliated Hospitals: 31
Number of Primary Care Physicians: 300
Number of Referral/Specialty Physicians: 1,668
Total Enrollment: 460,448

Healthplan and Services Defined
PLAN TYPE: HMO
Model Type: IPA
Benefits Offered: Behavioral Health, Disease Management, Home
   Care, Physical Therapy, Prescription, Psychiatric, Transplant,
   Vision, Wellness
Offers Demand Management Patient Information Service: Yes
DMPI Services Offered: Language Links Service, 24 hour Health
   Information Line, Health Information Library, Automated
   ReferralLine

Type of Coverage
Commercial
Catastrophic Illness Benefit: Varies per case

Type of Payment Plans Offered
POS

Geographic Areas Served
Cannon, Cheatham, Coffee, Davidson, DeKalb, Dickson, Franlin,
   Hickney, Maury, Montgomery, Overton, Robertson, Rutherford,
   Smith, Sumner, Warren, Williamson and Wilson counties, Tennessee

Subscriber Information
Average Subscriber Co-Payment:
   Primary Care Physician: $10.00
   Non-Network Physician: $10.00
   Prescription Drugs: $10.00
   Hospital ER: $500.00

Publishes and Distributes Report Card: Yes
Accreditation Certification
NCQA
TJC Accreditation, Medicare Approved

Key Personnel
President/CEO. . . . . David Mathis
CFO . . . . Stuart Wright
Network Contracting. . . . . David Mathis
In House Formulary . . . . Tim Moore
Medical Affairs. . . . . Frederick Buckwold
Member Services . . . . Chuck Utterbeck

Average Claim Compensation
Physician's Fees Charged: 82%
Hospital's Fees Charged: 56%

Specialty Managed Care Partners
Enters into Contracts with Regional Business Coalitions: Yes

70   CoreSource: Arkansas
1811 Rahling Road
Suite 100
Little Rock, AR 72223
Toll-Free: 888-604-9397
Phone: 501-221-9905
www.coresource.com
Subsidiary of: Trustmark
Year Founded: 1980
Total Enrollment: 1,100,000

Healthplan and Services Defined
PLAN TYPE: Multiple
Other Type: TPA
Model Type: Network
Plan Specialty: Claims Administration, TPA
Benefits Offered: Behavioral Health, Home Care, Prescription,
   Transplant

Type of Coverage
Commercial

Geographic Areas Served
Nationwide

Accreditation Certification
Utilization Review, Pre-Admission Certification

71   Delta Dental of Arkansas
1513 Country Club Road
Sherwood, AR 72120
Toll-Free: 800-462-5410
Phone: 501-835-3400
Fax: 501-992-1899
www.deltadentalar.com
Non-Profit Organization: Yes
Year Founded: 1982
Total Enrollment: 54,000,000
State Enrollment: 1,000,000

Healthplan and Services Defined
PLAN TYPE: Dental
Other Type: Dental\Vision PPO
Model Type: Network
Plan Specialty: Dental, Vision
Benefits Offered: Dental, Vision

Type of Coverage
Commercial

Type of Payment Plans Offered
DFFS

Geographic Areas Served
Statewide

Subscriber Information
Average Monthly Fee Per Subscriber
(Employee + Employer Contribution):
Employee Only (Self): $17
Employee & 2 Family Members: $50
Average Annual Deductible Per Subscriber:
Employee Only (Self): $150
Employee & 2 Family Members: $50
Average Subscriber Co-Payment:
Primary Care Physician: 80%
Non-Network Physician: 50%

Network Qualifications
Pre-Admission Certification: Yes

Publishes and Distributes Report Card: Yes

Key Personnel
President/CEO.................................Eddie Choate
Chairman ....Ron Ownbey
Vice Chairman.............................Robert Gladden
Media Contact ....Melissa Masingill
501-992-1666
mmasingill@ddpar.com

---

72 eHealthInsurance Services Inc.

11919 Foundation Place
Gold River, CA 95670
Toll-Free: 800-977-8860
info@ehealthinsurance.com
www.e.healthinsurance.com
Year Founded: 1997

Healthplan and Services Defined
PLAN TYPE: HMO/PPO
Benefits Offered: Dental, Life, STD

Type of Coverage
Commercial, Individual, Medicare

Geographic Areas Served
All 50 states in the USA and District of Columbia

Key Personnel
Chairman & CEO.............................Gary L. Lauer
EVP/Business & Corp. Dev....................Bruce Telkamp
EVP/Chief Technology.................Dr. Sheldon X. Wang
SVP & CFO ....Stuart M. Huizinga
Pres. of eHealth Gov. Sys ....Samuel C. Gibbs
SVP of Sales & Operations ....Robert S. Hurley
Director Public Relations.......................Nate Purpura
650-210-3115

---

73 HealthSCOPE Benefits

27 Corporate Hill Drive
Little Rock, AR 72205
Toll-Free: 800-972-3025
Phone: 501-218-7578
Fax: 501-218-7799
www.healthscopebenefits.com
Mailing Address: PO Box 1224, Little Rock, AR 72203
For Profit Organization: Yes
Year Founded: 1985
Total Enrollment: 475,000

Healthplan and Services Defined
PLAN TYPE: Other
Model Type: IPA, Group, Network, PHO
Plan Specialty: ASO, Behavioral Health, Chiropractic, Dental,
Disease Management, EPO, Lab, PBM, Vision, Radiology, UR,
COBRA, HIPAA, FSA, Retiree
Benefits Offered: Behavioral Health, Chiropractic, Complementary
Medicine, Dental, Disease Management, Home Care, Inpatient
SNF, Physical Therapy, Podiatry, Prescription, Psychiatric,
Transplant, Vision, Wellness, STD

Type of Coverage
Medicare, Catastrophic
Catastrophic Illness Benefit: Maximum $1M

Type of Payment Plans Offered
POS, DFFS, FFS, Combination FFS & DFFS

Geographic Areas Served
Nationwide

Network Qualifications
Minimum Years of Practice: 3
Pre-Admission Certification: Yes

Peer Review Type
Utilization Review: Yes
Second Surgical Opinion: Yes
Case Management: Yes

Accreditation Certification
URAC
Utilization Review, State Licensure

Key Personnel
CEO...Joe Edwards
President............................Mary Catherine Person
VP, Operations ....Darren Ashby
Director, Claims Admin ....Cathleen Armstrong
Regional VP.....................................Carol Gaines
Regional VP....................................Susan Johnson
Regional VP..................................Paula Thompson
Reg Dir, Business Dev ....Scott Barnes
VP, Business Development ....Bob Bracy
VP, Network Services ....Mike Castleberry
Director, Operations ....Mel Cox
Director, Benefits Admin......................Ross Johnston
Director, Business System ....Ed Grooms
VP, Provider Services ....Rebecca McSwain
VP, Sales.......................................Kevin Ryan

Specialty Managed Care Partners
American Health Holdings, PHCS, Advance PCS, Caremark, CCN
Enters into Contracts with Regional Business Coalitions: Yes
Alaska Business Coalition

Employer References
American Greetings, Alcoa, MedCath, Whirlpool

---

74 Humana Health Insurance of Little Rock

650 S Shackleford
Suite 125
Little Rock, AR 72211
Toll-Free: 800-941-4951
Phone: 501-223-6048
Fax: 501-223-2094
www.humana.com
For Profit Organization: Yes

Healthplan and Services Defined
PLAN TYPE: HMO/PPO

Type of Coverage
Commercial, Individual

Accreditation Certification
URAC, NCQA, CORE

---

75 Mercy Health Plans: Arkansas

521 President Clinton Ave
Suite 700
Little Rock, AR 72201
Toll-Free: 866-647-1551
Phone: 501-372-0065
Fax: 501-372-0211
www.mercyhealthplans.com
Non-Profit Organization: Yes
Total Enrollment: 73,000

Healthplan and Services Defined
  PLAN TYPE: HMO

Type of Coverage
  Commercial, Individual

76   QualChoice/QCA Health Plan

12615 Chenal Parkway
Suite 300
Little Rock, AR 72211
Toll-Free: 800-235-7111
Phone: 501-228-7111
Fax: 501-801-2972
www.qualchoice.com
Secondary Address: 4100 Corporate Center Drive, Suite 102,
  Springdale, AR 72762
Year Founded: 1994
Number of Affiliated Hospitals: 80
Number of Primary Care Physicians: 3,200
Total Enrollment: 36,000
State Enrollment: 84,176

Healthplan and Services Defined
  PLAN TYPE: HMO/PPO
  Other Type: POS
  Benefits Offered: Behavioral Health, Dental, Prescription, Worker's
    Compensation

Type of Coverage
  Commercial, Individual, Indemnity

Geographic Areas Served
  Statewide

Key Personnel
  President . . . . Francis Browning
  VP, COO, CIO . . . . M Haley Wilson
  Chief Financial Officer . . . . Randall A Crow
  VP, Compliance . . . . Jim Couch
  Dir, Network Services. . . . . Rose Anne Cato
  VP, Underwriting . . . . Jon Foose
  VP, Operations . . . . Joni S Daniels
  VP, Pharmacy . . . . Barry Fielder, PharmD
  VP, Sales & Marketing . . . . BJ Himes
  Dir, Actuarial Services . . . . Graham Sutherlin
  VP, Medical Affairs . . . . Richard Armstrong, MD
  VP, Quality & Care Mgmt . . . . Cindy Reese Furgerson, RN
  Director, Underwriting . . . . Kenneth W Bowen, Jr
  Director, Human Resources . . . . Karin J Ward
  VP Sales/Marketing. . . . . Roy Lamm

Specialty Managed Care Partners
  Express Scripts

77   Secure Horizons

PO Box 29675
Hot Springs, AR 71903-9801
Toll-Free: 800-577-5623
www.securehorizons.com
Subsidiary of: UnitedHealthCare
For Profit Organization: Yes

Healthplan and Services Defined
  PLAN TYPE: Medicare
  Model Type: Network
  Benefits Offered: Prescription

Type of Coverage
  Medicare, Supplemental Medicare

Publishes and Distributes Report Card: Yes

Key Personnel
  Chairman/CEO Health Sys. . . . . Howard Phanstiel
  CFO . . . . Greg Scott
  President/CEO Health Plan . . . . Brad Bowlus

Exec VP/Specialty Plans . . . . Jacqueline Kosecoff
Exec VP/Enterprise Svce. . . . . Sharon Garrett
Exec VP/General Counsel . . . . Joseph Konowiecki
Exec VP/Secure Horizons . . . . Kathy Feeny
Exec VP/Major Accounts . . . . James Frey
Exec VP/Chief Med Officer. . . . . Sam Ho
Pres/CEO Behavioral Healt. . . . . Jerome V Vaccaro, MD
Sr VP/Human Resources . . . . Carol Black

Specialty Managed Care Partners
  Enters into Contracts with Regional Business Coalitions: Yes

78   UnitedHealthCare of Arkansas

415 N McKinley Street
Suite 820
Little Rock, AR 72205
Toll-Free: 800-678-3176
Phone: 501-664-7700
Fax: 501-664-7768
www.uhc.com
Subsidiary of: UnitedHealth Group
For Profit Organization: Yes
Year Founded: 1991
Total Enrollment: 75,000,000
State Enrollment: 92,995

Healthplan and Services Defined
  PLAN TYPE: HMO/PPO
  Model Type: IPA
  Benefits Offered: Dental, Disease Management, Prescription, Vision,
    Wellness, LTD, STD

Type of Coverage
  Commercial, Individual, Indemnity, Medicare

Type of Payment Plans Offered
  POS, FFS

Geographic Areas Served
  Statewide

Network Qualifications
  Pre-Admission Certification: Yes

Peer Review Type
  Utilization Review: Yes

Publishes and Distributes Report Card: Yes

Accreditation Certification
  TJC Accreditation, Medicare Approved, Utilization Review,
    Pre-Admission Certification, State Licensure, Quality Assurance
    Program

Key Personnel
  CEO . . . . Ken Hoverman
  Marketing . . . . David Johnson
  Sales. . . . . David Johnson
  Media Contact. . . . . Roger Rollman
    roger_f_rollman@uhc.com

Specialty Managed Care Partners
  Enters into Contracts with Regional Business Coalitions: Yes

Health Insurance Coverage Status and Type of Coverage by Age

Category	All Persons		Under 18 years		Under 65 years		65 years and over	
	Number	%	Number	%	Number	%	Number	%
Total population	37,223	-	9,549	-	32,918	-	4,305	-
Covered by some type of health insurance	30,014 *(179)*	80.6 *(0.5)*	8,530 *(72)*	89.3 *(0.7)*	25,870 *(192)*	78.6 *(0.5)*	4,145 *(101)*	96.3 *(0.5)*
Covered by private health insurance	22,007 *(267)*	59.1 *(0.7)*	5,260 *(111)*	55.1 *(1.2)*	19,860 *(265)*	60.3 *(0.8)*	2,147 *(85)*	49.9 *(1.5)*
Employment based	18,702 *(264)*	50.2 *(0.7)*	4,693 *(108)*	49.1 *(1.1)*	17,415 *(261)*	52.9 *(0.8)*	1,286 *(66)*	29.9 *(1.3)*
Own employment based	9,629 *(143)*	25.9 *(0.4)*	20 *(6)*	0.2 *(0.1)*	8,671 *(137)*	26.3 *(0.4)*	958 *(54)*	22.3 *(1.1)*
Direct purchase	3,440 *(130)*	9.2 *(0.3)*	642 *(44)*	6.7 *(0.5)*	2,501 *(109)*	7.6 *(0.3)*	939 *(57)*	21.8 *(1.3)*
Covered by government health insurance	11,338 *(207)*	30.5 *(0.6)*	3,852 *(108)*	40.3 *(1.1)*	7,417 *(196)*	22.5 *(0.6)*	3,921 *(99)*	91.1 *(0.8)*
Covered by Medicaid	6,999 *(194)*	18.8 *(0.5)*	3,657 *(111)*	38.3 *(1.2)*	6,330 *(183)*	19.2 *(0.6)*	670 *(50)*	15.6 *(1.1)*
Also by private insurance	1,065 *(67)*	2.9 *(0.2)*	510 *(42)*	5.3 *(0.4)*	956 *(62)*	2.9 *(0.2)*	109 *(16)*	2.5 *(0.4)*
Covered by Medicare	4,675 *(109)*	12.6 *(0.3)*	108 *(21)*	1.1 *(0.2)*	785 *(48)*	2.4 *(0.1)*	3,890 *(97)*	90.4 *(0.8)*
Also by private insurance	2,100 *(83)*	5.6 *(0.2)*	12 *(5)*	0.1 *(0.1)*	189 *(24)*	0.6 *(0.1)*	1,911 *(82)*	44.4 *(1.5)*
Also by Medicaid	1,019 *(62)*	2.7 *(0.2)*	62 *(16)*	0.6 *(0.2)*	357 *(36)*	1.1 *(0.1)*	662 *(49)*	15.4 *(1.1)*
Covered by military health care	1,120 *(99)*	3.0 *(0.3)*	174 *(35)*	1.8 *(0.4)*	753 *(86)*	2.3 *(0.3)*	368 *(44)*	8.5 *(1.0)*
Not covered at any time during the year	7,209 *(178)*	19.4 *(0.5)*	1,019 *(66)*	10.7 *(0.7)*	7,049 *(176)*	21.4 *(0.5)*	160 *(22)*	3.7 *(0.5)*

Note: Numbers in thousands; figures cover 2010; standard error appears in parenthesis; (b) base less than 75,000; (x) not applicable
Source: U.S. Census Bureau, Current Population Survey, 2011 Annual Social and Economic Supplement. Table HI05. Health Insurance Coverage Status and Type of Coverage by State and Age for All People: 2010

California

79 Access Dental Services
8890 Cal Center Drive
Sacramento, CA 95826-3200
Toll-Free: 866-682-9904
Phone: 916-922-5000
Fax: 916-646-9000
info@accessdental.com
www.accessdental.com
Mailing Address: PO Box 659005, Sacramento, CA 95865-9005
For Profit Organization: Yes
Year Founded: 1989
Number of Primary Care Physicians: 2,000
Total Enrollment: 123,880

Healthplan and Services Defined
PLAN TYPE: Dental
Model Type: Staff
Plan Specialty: Dental
Benefits Offered: Dental

Type of Coverage
Commercial, Individual, Medicare, Supplemental Medicare, Medicaid

Geographic Areas Served
Statewide

Key Personnel
President . . . . Terri Abbaszadeh, DDS
CEO . . . . Reza Abbaszadeh
Vice President. . . . . Maria Torres

80 Aetna Health of California
2625 Shadelands Drive
Suite 1100, MSF915
Walnut Creek, CA 94598
Toll-Free: 866-582-9629
www.aetna.com
For Profit Organization: Yes
Total Enrollment: 427,039
State Enrollment: 427,039

Healthplan and Services Defined
PLAN TYPE: HMO
Plan Specialty: EPO
Benefits Offered: Dental, Disease Management, Long-Term Care, Prescription, Wellness, Life, LTD, STD

Type of Coverage
Commercial, Individual

Type of Payment Plans Offered
POS, FFS

Geographic Areas Served
Statewide

81 Alameda Alliance for Health
1240 S Loop Road
Alameda, CA 94502
Toll-Free: 877-932-2738
Phone: 510-747-4500
Fax: 877-747-4502
providerservices@alamedaalliance.org
www.alamedaalliance.org
Secondary Address: 475 14th Street, Suite 730, Oakland, CA 94612
Non-Profit Organization: Yes
Year Founded: 1996
Federally Qualified: Yes
Number of Affiliated Hospitals: 15
Number of Primary Care Physicians: 1,700

Total Enrollment: 130,000
State Enrollment: 110,000

Healthplan and Services Defined
PLAN TYPE: HMO
Model Type: Network
Plan Specialty: Dental
Benefits Offered: Dental, Prescription, Vision, Medi-Cal, Healthy Families, Alliance Group Care, Alliance CompleteCare

Type of Coverage
Individual, Government Sponsored Programs

Type of Payment Plans Offered
POS

Geographic Areas Served
California

Peer Review Type
Second Surgical Opinion: Yes

Accreditation Certification
State Licensure

Key Personnel
CEO . . . . Ingrid Lamirault
COO. . . . . Zina Glover
Chief Health Plan Svs Off. . . . . Marie Barrett
Chief Medical Officer . . . . Lily Boris, MD
Marketing/Sales Executive. . . . . Amanda Flores-Witte

82 American Specialty Health
10221 Waterridge Circle
San Diego, CA 92131
Toll-Free: 800-848-3555
Fax: 619-237-3859
service@ashn.com
www.ashcompanies.com
For Profit Organization: Yes
Year Founded: 1987
Total Enrollment: 94,000,000

Healthplan and Services Defined
PLAN TYPE: HMO
Model Type: Network
Plan Specialty: Chiropractic
Benefits Offered: Chiropractic, Complementary Medicine, Acupuncture

Type of Coverage
Commercial, Supplemental Medicare

Type of Payment Plans Offered
POS, Capitated

Geographic Areas Served
Nationwide - ASH Network, California - ASH Plans

Network Qualifications
Pre-Admission Certification: Yes

Peer Review Type
Utilization Review: Yes
Case Management: Yes

Accreditation Certification
URAC

Key Personnel
Chairman/President/CEO . . . . George DeVries
President/COO. . . . . Robert White
EVP, CFO . . . . William M Comer, Jr
Chief Health Services Ofc. . . . . R Douglas Metz, DC
Medical Director, VP . . . . Mary Jane Osmick
Chief Wellness Oper Offc. . . . . Julie Jennings
Chief Information Officer . . . . Kevin Kujawa
SVP, Marketing. . . . . Debby Clark
800-848-3555
debbyc@ashn.com

Specialty Managed Care Partners
Enters into Contracts with Regional Business Coalitions: Yes

83 Arcadian Health Plans
500 12th Street
Suite 350
Oakland, CA 94607
Phone: 510-832-0311
Fax: 510-832-0170
www.arcadianhealth.com
For Profit Organization: Yes

Healthplan and Services Defined
PLAN TYPE: HMO/PPO

Key Personnel
Chairman & CEO . . . . Robert Falhman
Chief Financial Officer . . . . Les Granow
CFO/MSO . . . . Richard Greene
VP, Market Development. Chase Milbrandt
SVP, General Counsel . . . . James Novello
SVP, Operations . . . . Patrick Ross
SVP, Human Capital . . . . Heidi Sullivan
SVP, Chief Sales & Mktg . . . . Garrison Rios
Chief Medical Officer. . . . . Frank Apgar, MD
Chief Information Officer . . . . Rick Click

84 Arta Medicare Health Plan
3333 Michelson Drive
Suite 750
Irvine, CA 92612
Toll-Free: 866-844-2170
www.artamedicare.com
Year Founded: 1995
Number of Affiliated Hospitals: 15
Number of Primary Care Physicians: 800
Total Enrollment: 55,000
State Enrollment: 55,000

Healthplan and Services Defined
PLAN TYPE: Medicare
Other Type: HMO

Type of Coverage
Individual, Medicare, Supplemental Medicare

85 Assurant Employee Benefits: California
2399 Gateway Oaks Drive
#120
Sacramento, CA 95833-4251
Phone: 916-929-5526
Fax: 916-929-0269
benefits@assurant.com
www.assurantemployeebenefits.com
Subsidiary of: Assurant, Inc
For Profit Organization: Yes
Number of Primary Care Physicians: 112,000
Total Enrollment: 47,000

Healthplan and Services Defined
PLAN TYPE: Multiple
Plan Specialty: Dental, Vision, Long & Short-Term Disability
Benefits Offered: Dental, Vision, Wellness, AD&D, Life, LTD, STD

Type of Coverage
Commercial, Indemnity, Individual Dental Plans

Geographic Areas Served
Statewide

Subscriber Information
Average Monthly Fee Per Subscriber
(Employee + Employer Contribution):

Employee Only (Self): Varies by plan

Key Personnel
Vice President . . . . Fred Brook
Business Manager. . . . . Kyle See
PR Specialist. . . . . Megan Hutchison
816-556-7815
megan.hutchinson@assurant.com

86 Basic Chiropractic Health Plan
2027 Grand Canal Blvd
Suite 21
Stockton, CA 95207
Toll-Free: 866-224-7462
Phone: 209-476-1435
www.bchpinc.com
Year Founded: 1999

Healthplan and Services Defined
PLAN TYPE: PPO
Plan Specialty: Chiropractic
Benefits Offered: Chiropractic

Key Personnel
President . . . . Don Smallie, DC
dsmallie@bchpinc.com
CEO/COO. . . . . David Moscovic
david@bchpinc.com
Accounting Manager . . . . Venus Giacomotti
venus@bchpinc.com
Member Services. . . . . Kimberly Randolph
kimberly@bchpinc.com
Provider Relations. . . . . Kimberly Randolph
kimberly@bchpinc.com

87 Beech Street Corporation: Corporate Office
Acquired by MultiPlan

88 Beech Street Corporation: Northeast Region
Acquired by MultiPlan

89 Beech Street Corporation: Western Region
Acquired by MultiPlan

90 BEST Life and Health Insurance Co.
2505 McCabe Way
Irvine, CA 92614
Toll-Free: 888-210-2378
Fax: 949-553-0883
info@bestlife.com
www.bestlife.com
For Profit Organization: Yes
Year Founded: 1970
Number of Affiliated Hospitals: 5,005
Number of Primary Care Physicians: 772,292
Total Enrollment: 90,000

Healthplan and Services Defined
PLAN TYPE: PPO
Model Type: PPO/Indemnity
Benefits Offered: Dental, Disease Management, Vision, Wellness, Life, STD

Type of Coverage
Commercial

Geographic Areas Served
AK, AL, AR, AZ, CA, CO, DC, FL, GA, HI, ID, IL, IN, KS, KY, LA, MD, MI, MS, MO, MT, NC, ND, NE, NM, NV, OH, OK, OR, PA, SC, SD, TN, TX, UT, VA, WA, WY

Network Qualifications
Pre-Admission Certification: Yes

Peer Review Type
Case Management: Yes

Accreditation Certification
URAC, NCQA
Quality Assurance Program

Key Personnel
Vice President . . . . .Steve Course
scourse@bestlife.com
Sales Manager . . . . .Jennifer Bolton
jbolton@bestlife.com
Underwriting Coordinator . . . . .Heidi Lazar
hlazar@bestlife.com

91   Blue Shield of California
50 Beale Street
San Francisco, CA 94105-1808
Toll-Free: 888-568-3560
Phone: 415-229-5000
www.blueshieldca.com
Secondary Address: 6300 Canoga Avenue, Individual, Small Group &
Govt Business, Woodland Hills, CA 91367
Subsidiary of: California Physicians' Service, Inc
Non-Profit Organization: Yes
Year Founded: 1939
Number of Affiliated Hospitals: 354
Number of Primary Care Physicians: 67,000
Total Enrollment: 3,500,000
State Enrollment: 3,500,000

Healthplan and Services Defined
PLAN TYPE: HMO/PPO
Benefits Offered: Home Care, Prescription

Type of Coverage
Supplemental Medicare

Geographic Areas Served
California

Accreditation Certification
NCQA

Key Personnel
Chairman, President & CEO . . . . .Bruce G Bodaken
Executive VP & CFO . . . . .Heidi Fields
Executive VP & COO . . . . .Paul Markovich
SVP, Chief Actuary . . . . .Ed Cymerys
SVP, Network Management. .Juan Davila
SVP, Indiv, Sm Grp & Govt . . . . .Mark Gastineau
SVP, Customer Operations . . . . .Rob Geyer
SVP, General Counsel. . . . . .Seth A Jacobs, Esq
VP, Corporate Marketing. . . . . .Doug Biehn
SVP, LgGrp & Spec Benefit. . . . . .David S Joyner
Chief Medical Officer . . . . .Meredith Mathews, MD
Senior VP, Human Resource . . . . .Marianne Jackson
SVP, Chief Info Officer. . . . . .Elinor MacKinnon
SVP, Public & Strat Accts . . . . .Janet Widmann
VP, Direct Sales. . . . . .John Reinke
Media Contact . . . . .Erica Perng
415-229-6171
publicaffairs@blueshieldca.com
VP, Public Affairs . . . . .Tom Epstein

92   Brand New Day HMO
1680 E Hill Street
Signal Hill, CA 90755
Toll-Free: 866-255-4795
Fax: 562-981-5818
www.hmocalif.com

Healthplan and Services Defined
PLAN TYPE: HMO
Plan Specialty: Behavioral Health
Benefits Offered: Behavioral Health, Dental, Disease Management,
Prescription, Psychiatric, Vision, Wellness

Type of Coverage
Individual, Medicare, Medicaid

93   Bright Now! Dental
201 E Sandpointe
Suite 800
Santa Ana, CA 92707
Toll-Free: 800-497-6453
Phone: 714-668-1300
Fax: 714-428-1300
www.brightnow.com
Secondary Address: 8105 Irvine Center Drive, Suite 1500, Irvine, CA
92618
Subsidiary of: Smile Brands
Year Founded: 1998
Number of Primary Care Physicians: 300
Number of Referral/Specialty Physicians: 416
Total Enrollment: 950,000

Healthplan and Services Defined
PLAN TYPE: Dental
Model Type: Staff, Network
Plan Specialty: Dental
Benefits Offered: Dental

Type of Payment Plans Offered
Capitated

Geographic Areas Served
Nationwide

Subscriber Information
Average Monthly Fee Per Subscriber
(Employee + Employer Contribution):
Employee Only (Self): $40.00
Employee & 1 Family Member: $75.00
Employee & 2 Family Members: $110.00

Network Qualifications
Pre-Admission Certification: Yes

Key Personnel
President/CEO. . . . . .Steven Bilt
sbilt@brightnow.com
CFO . . . . .Bradley Schmidt
COO. . . . . .Roy Smith
Credentialing . . . . .Lanchi Hua
VP Dental Affairs .Charles Stirewalt, DDS
cstirewalt@brightnow.com
Medical Affairs . . . . .Charles Stirewalt, DMD
Member Services . . . . .Lanchi Hua
Provider Services . . . . .Lanchi Hua

Specialty Managed Care Partners
Enters into Contracts with Regional Business Coalitions: No

94   California Dental Network
1971 E 4th Street
Suite 184
Santa Ana, CA 92705
Toll-Free: 877-433-6825
Fax: 714-479-0779
www.caldental.net

Healthplan and Services Defined
PLAN TYPE: Dental
Plan Specialty: Dental
Benefits Offered: Dental

Type of Coverage
Individual

Key Personnel
Chairman . . . . .James Lindsey
President . . . . .Steven Casey

95 California Foundation for Medical Care

3993 Jurupa Avenue
Riverside, CA 92506
Toll-Free: 800-334-7341
Phone: 951-686-9049
Fax: 951-686-1692
support@cfmcnet.org
www.cfmcnet.org
Non-Profit Organization: Yes
Year Founded: 1983
Number of Affiliated Hospitals: 300
Number of Primary Care Physicians: 34,000
Number of Referral/Specialty Physicians: 5,500
Total Enrollment: 1,000,000

Healthplan and Services Defined
PLAN TYPE: PPO
Other Type: EPO and Workers Comp
Plan Specialty: Behavioral Health, Lab, Worker's Compensation, UR
Benefits Offered: Worker's Compensation, EPO

Geographic Areas Served
California

Key Personnel
President. . . . . .Steve Beargeon
559-734-1321
steve@tkfmc.org
CEO . . . . .Dolores L Green
951-686-9094
dgreen@rcmanet.org
Dir Of Administration . . . . .Ester M Sanchez
951-686-9049
esanchez@rfasi.com
Network Coordinator .Bianca Scarborough
951-686-9049
bscraborough@rfasi.com

96 CalOptima

1120 W La Veta Avenue
Suite 200
Orange, CA 92868
Toll-Free: 888-587-8088
Phone: 714-246-8400
Fax: 714-246-8492
www.caloptima.org
For Profit Organization: Yes
Year Founded: 1995
Owned by an Integrated Delivery Network (IDN): Yes
Number of Primary Care Physicians: 3,500
Total Enrollment: 402,000
State Enrollment: 402,000

Healthplan and Services Defined
PLAN TYPE: HMO
Model Type: Group
Plan Specialty: ASO, Behavioral Health, Chiropractic, Dental,
Disease Management, EPO, Lab, MSO, PBM, Vision, Radiology,
Worker's Compensation
Benefits Offered: Prescription

Type of Coverage
Individual, Supplemental Medicare, Medicaid, Medi-Cal

Geographic Areas Served
Orange County

Key Personnel
Chief Executive Officer . . . . .Richard Chambers
Chief Operating Officer . . . . .Greg Buckert, MD, MPH
Chief Counsel. . . . . .Gary Crockett, Esq
Chief Medical Officer. . . . . .Trudi Carter, MD
Chief Financial Officer . . . . .Michael P Engelhard
Chief Administrative Offc . . . . .Kim Cunningham, SPHR
Exec Dir, OneCare. . . . . .Kurt Hubler
Exec Dir, Medi-Cal. . . . . .Ray Jankowski
Exec Dir, CalOptima Care. . . . . .Javier Sanchez
Exec Dir, Public Affairs .Margaret Tatar
Exec Dir, Operations . . . . .Ruth Watson
Exec Dir, Infomation Sys . . . . .Eileen Moscaritolo
Public Affairs . . . . .Vy Truong
714-246-8682
vtruong@caloptima.org

97 Care 1st Health Plan: California

601 Potrero Grande Drive
Monterey Park, CA 91755
Toll-Free: 800-847-1222
Phone: 323-889-6638
Fax: 323-889-6255
www.care1st.com
Secondary Address: 3131 Camino del Rio North, Suite 350, San Diego,
CA 92108
For Profit Organization: Yes
Year Founded: 1995
Number of Affiliated Hospitals: 69
Number of Primary Care Physicians: 3,000
Total Enrollment: 291,000

Healthplan and Services Defined
PLAN TYPE: HMO
Benefits Offered: Disease Management, Wellness

Type of Coverage
Supplemental Medicare, Medicaid

Geographic Areas Served
Southern California & Arizona

Accreditation Certification
NCQA

Key Personnel
CEO . . . . .Anna Tran
Chief Financial Offier. . . . . .Janet Jan
Chief Operation Officer .Mitchell Brodsky
VP, Legal & Regulator Ser . . . . .Alan Bloom
VP, Administration . . . . .Brooks Jones
VP, Management Info Sys .Herbert Woo
VP, Medical Services .Josie Wong, RN
VP, Pharmacy & Medicare .Jamie Ueoka
Dir, Legal & Regulatory . . . . .Gamini Gunawardane, PhD
Assoc VP, Quality Improve. . . . . .David Wedemeyer
Chief Medical Officer . . . . .Jorge Weingarten, Md
Assoc VP, Member Services . . . . .Tracie Howell
Chief Information Officer .Michael Rowan
Medical Dir, Informatics. . . . . .Daryl Leong
VP, Business Development .Walter Gray
Dir, Medicare Sales . . . . .Ed Gorner

98 CareMore Health Plan

12900 Park Plaza Drive
Suite 150
Cerritos, CA 90703
Toll-Free: 800-499-2793
Fax: 562-741-4393
www.caremore.com

Healthplan and Services Defined
PLAN TYPE: Medicare

Type of Coverage
Medicare

Geographic Areas Served
Arizona, California, Nevada

Key Personnel
Chairman & CEO...............................Alan Hoops
President, Health Plan ....Leeba Lessin
Pres, Management Services........................John Kao
CFO...Brendan Baker
GM, Senior Vice President......................Eric Van Horn
SVP, Corp Development ....Sergio Zaldivar
SVP, Operations..............................Chuck Weber
VP, Touch ....Joyce Furlough
Chief Sales & Marketing ....Dawn Maroney
General Counsel ....Michael C Foster
Chief Medical Officer ....Ken Kim, MD
Regional Medical Officer.................Charles Holzner, MD
Chief Information Officer....................Kerry Matsumoto
VP, Clinical Outcomes ....Doug Allen

99 CenCal Health: The Regional Health Authority

4050 Calle Real
Santa Barbara, CA 93110
Toll-Free: 800-421-2560
Phone: 805-685-9525
webmaster@cencalhealth.org
www.cencalhealth.org
Non-Profit Organization: Yes

Healthplan and Services Defined
PLAN TYPE: HMO
Benefits Offered: Complementary Medicine, Disease Management, Prescription, Wellness

Type of Coverage
Individual, Medicare, Medicaid, Medi-Cal, Healthly Families

Geographic Areas Served
Santa Barbara and San Luis Obispo counties

Key Personnel
Chief Executive Officer ....R Lyle Luman, MBA
lluman@cencalhealth.org
Dir, Human Resources ....Debbie Horne, SPHR
dhorne@cencalhealth.org
Chief Medical Officer................Irwin E Harris, MD, MBA
iharris@cencalhealth.org
Chief Financial Officer ....David Ambrose
dambrose@cencalhealth.org
Chief Operating Officer ....Michael Schrader
mschrader@cencalhealth.org

100 Central California Alliance for Health

1600 Green Hills Road
Suite 101
Scotts Valley, CA 95066-4981
Toll-Free: 800-700-3874
Phone: 831-430-5500
www.ccah-alliance.org
Secondary Address: 339 Pajaro Street, Suite E, Salinas, CA 93901-3400
Non-Profit Organization: Yes
Year Founded: 1996
Physician Owned Organization: No
Federally Qualified: No
Number of Primary Care Physicians: 1,590
Total Enrollment: 190,000
State Enrollment: 190,000

Healthplan and Services Defined
PLAN TYPE: HMO
Model Type: County Org Health System
Benefits Offered: Medi-Cal, Healthy Families, Healthy Kids, Alliance Care Access for Infants and Mothers, Alliance Care IHSS
Offers Demand Management Patient Information Service: No

Geographic Areas Served
Santa Cruz, Monterey and Merced counties

Network Qualifications
Pre-Admission Certification: No

Publishes and Distributes Report Card: No

Key Personnel
Executive Director ....Alan McCay
Chief Financial Officer ....Patti McFarland
Chief Operating Officer ....Rachael Nava
Provider Services Dir..................Stephanie Sonnenshine
Finance Director ....Frank Souza
Utilization Management ....Christine Gerbo, RN
Human Resources Director ....Scott Fortner
Pharmacy Director ....Richard Johnson, PharmD
Quality Improvement Dir...................Barbara Flynn, RN
Reg Dir, Monterey County....................Lilia Chagolla
Medical Director ....Richard Helmer, MD
Assoc Medical Director ....David Altman, MD
Information Tech Director ....Bob Chernis
Govt Relations Director ....Danita Carlson
Reg Dir, Merced County..................Jennifer Mockus, RN
Business Devlopment Mgr ....Traci Webb
831-430-5500
press@ccah-alliance.org
Member Services Director ....Jan Wolf

Specialty Managed Care Partners
Enters into Contracts with Regional Business Coalitions: No

101 Central Health Medicare Plan

1540 Bridgegate Drive
Diamond Bar, CA 91765
Toll-Free: 866-314-2427
www.centralhealthplan.com
Subsidiary of: Central Health Plan of California, Inc
Year Founded: 2004
Total Enrollment: 3,000

Healthplan and Services Defined
PLAN TYPE: Medicare
Other Type: HMO
Benefits Offered: Chiropractic, Dental, Home Care, Inpatient SNF, Podiatry, Vision, Wellness

Type of Coverage
Medicare, Supplemental Medicare

Geographic Areas Served
Los Angeles, San Bernardino, Orange counties

Subscriber Information
Average Monthly Fee Per Subscriber
(Employee + Employer Contribution):
Employee Only (Self): $89.00
Average Subscriber Co-Payment:
Primary Care Physician: $5.00/10.00
Prescription Drugs: Varies
Hospital ER: $50.00
Home Health Care: Varies
Nursing Home: Varies

102 Chinese Community Health Plan

445 Grant Avenue
Suite 700
San Francisco, CA 94108
Toll-Free: 888-775-7888

Phone: 415-955-8800
Fax: 415-955-8818
mktginfo@cchphmo.com
www.cchphmo.com
Secondary Address: 835 Jackson Street, Member Services
Department, San Francisco, CA 94133
For Profit Organization: Yes
Year Founded: 1986
Owned by an Integrated Delivery Network (IDN): Yes
Number of Affiliated Hospitals: 5
Number of Primary Care Physicians: 160
Number of Referral/Specialty Physicians: 144
Total Enrollment: 13,582
State Enrollment: 6,336

Healthplan and Services Defined
PLAN TYPE: HMO
Model Type: IPA
Benefits Offered: Prescription, Acupuncture Services, Worldwide
Emergency

Type of Coverage
Medicare

Geographic Areas Served
San Francisco, Northern San Mateo

Subscriber Information
Average Monthly Fee Per Subscriber
(Employee + Employer Contribution):
Employee Only (Self): $218.00
Employee & 1 Family Member: $419.00
Employee & 2 Family Members: $384.53
Average Subscriber Co-Payment:
Primary Care Physician: $10.00
Non-Network Physician: Not covered
Prescription Drugs: $6.00
Hospital ER: $25.00
Home Health Care Max. Days/Visits Covered: None except
mental
Nursing Home Max. Days/Visits Covered: 10 days

Network Qualifications
Pre-Admission Certification: Yes

Peer Review Type
Utilization Review: Yes
Second Surgical Opinion: Yes
Case Management: Yes

Accreditation Certification
TJC Accreditation, Medicare Approved, Utilization Review,
Pre-Admission Certification, State Licensure, Quality Assurance
Program

Key Personnel
CEO/Executive Director . . . . Richard Loosn
CFO . . . . Steve Tsang
Executive Director . . . . Tom Tsang
Claims Manager . . . . Amy Lee
Dir, Business Development . . . . Deena Louie
Manager, Sales . . . . Yolanda Lee
Dir, Clinical Services . . . . Dana Samples
Chief Medical Officer . . . . Edward Chow, MD
Member Services Manager . . . . Irene Louie
IT Manager . . . . JC Tucker
Provider Services Manager . . . . Heather Brandenburg

Specialty Managed Care Partners
Enters into Contracts with Regional Business Coalitions: No

103 Chiropractic Health Plan of California
5356 Clayton Road #201
Concord, CA 94521
Toll-Free: 800-995-2442

Phone: 925-844-3100
Fax: 925-844-3124
info@chpc.com
www.chpc.com
Mailing Address: PO Box 190, Clayton, CA 94517
For Profit Organization: Yes
Year Founded: 1986
Number of Primary Care Physicians: 795

Healthplan and Services Defined
PLAN TYPE: PPO
Model Type: Network
Plan Specialty: ASO, Chiropractic, EPO, Worker's Compensation, UR
Benefits Offered: Chiropractic, Worker's Compensation, Group
Health

Type of Coverage
Commercial

Type of Payment Plans Offered
POS, DFFS, FFS, Combination FFS & DFFS

Geographic Areas Served
California, Nevada, Texas

Network Qualifications
Pre-Admission Certification: Yes

Peer Review Type
Utilization Review: Yes

Key Personnel
President/CEO . . . . Ronald S Cataldo, DC
CFO . . . . Jeanette Cataldo
Claims . . . . Gloria Spahn
Network Contracting . . . . Ronald S Cataldo, Jr
Credentialing . . . . Todd Cataldo
Medical Affairs . . . . Ronald Cataldo, DC
Provider Services . . . . Ronald Cataldo, DC

Specialty Managed Care Partners
Enters into Contracts with Regional Business Coalitions: Yes

104 ChiroSource Inc
5356 Clayton Road
Suite 201
Concord, CA 94521
Toll-Free: 800-680-9997
Fax: 925-844-3124
info@chirosource.com
www.chirosource.com
Mailing Address: PO Box 130, Clayton, CA 94517
Subsidiary of: Discover Health, A Product of ChiroSource, Inc.
For Profit Organization: Yes
Year Founded: 1993
Number of Primary Care Physicians: 2,133

Healthplan and Services Defined
PLAN TYPE: Multiple
Model Type: Network
Plan Specialty: Chiropractic, Physical Medicine, Accupuncture,
Massage
Benefits Offered: Worker's Compensation, Health-Group &
Individual, Medicare Advantage, IME Networks

Type of Coverage
PPO, EPO, POS, MPN, HCN, IME

Type of Payment Plans Offered
FFS

Geographic Areas Served
National

Network Qualifications
Pre-Admission Certification: Yes

Peer Review Type
Utilization Review: Yes

Publishes and Distributes Report Card: No
Key Personnel
President/CEO..........................Ronald S Cataldo, DC
CFO......................................Jeanette Cataldo
Claims..................................Glorie Spahn
Network Contracting..........................Todd Cataldo
Specialty Managed Care Partners
Enters into Contracts with Regional Business Coalitions: Yes

---

105 CIGNA HealthCare of California

400 North Brand Blvd
Suite 400
Glendale, CA 91203
Toll-Free: 866-438-2446
Phone: 818-500-6262
www.cigna.com
For Profit Organization: Yes
Total Enrollment: 234,072
State Enrollment: 234,072

Healthplan and Services Defined
PLAN TYPE: HMO
Other Type: POS

Type of Coverage
Commercial

---

106 CIGNA HealthCare of Northern California

1 Front Street
7th Floor
San Francisco, CA 94111
Toll-Free: 888-802-4462
Phone: 415-374-2500
Fax: 860-298-2443
www.cigna.com
Secondary Address: Great-West Healthcare, now part of CIGNA, 1340 Treat Blvd, Suite 599, Walnut Creek, CA 94597, 925-938-7788
For Profit Organization: Yes
Year Founded: 1929
Number of Affiliated Hospitals: 100
Number of Primary Care Physicians: 52,300
Number of Referral/Specialty Physicians: 20,766
Total Enrollment: 10,000,000
State Enrollment: 450,000

Healthplan and Services Defined
PLAN TYPE: HMO
Model Type: Network
Plan Specialty: ASO, HMO, POS, PPO, CDHP, Fully Insured Funding, Minimum Premium Funding
Benefits Offered: Chiropractic, Dental, Disease Management, Home Care, Physical Therapy, Podiatry, Psychiatric, Transplant, Vision, Wellness, Behavioral Health, Pharmacy, Radiology

Type of Coverage
Commercial, Individual, Indemnity
Catastrophic Illness Benefit: Covered

Type of Payment Plans Offered
DFFS, Capitated, FFS, Combination FFS & DFFS

Geographic Areas Served
Northern and Southern California, Nationwide

Subscriber Information
Average Monthly Fee Per Subscriber
(Employee + Employer Contribution):
Employee Only (Self): $140
Employee & 1 Family Member: $280
Employee & 2 Family Members: $420
Average Subscriber Co-Payment:
Primary Care Physician: $10.00
Prescription Drugs: $7.00/14.00

Hospital ER: $50.00
Network Qualifications
Pre-Admission Certification: Yes
Peer Review Type
Utilization Review: Yes
Case Management: Yes
Publishes and Distributes Report Card: Yes
Accreditation Certification
NCQA
TJC Accreditation, Medicare Approved, Utilization Review, Pre-Admission Certification, State Licensure, Quality Assurance Program
Key Personnel
President/CEO...............................Peter Welch
CFO.....................................Ryan Mcgroarty
Claims....................................Doug Stewart
Network Contracting ....Ben Katz
Dental.....................................Ron Bolden
Marketing.................................Lincoln Acholonu
Medical Affairs ....Steven Halpern, MD
Member Services............................Doug Stewart
Provider Services ....Ben Katz
Sales....................................Kirby Hutson
VP Sales...................................Peter Welch
Specialty Managed Care Partners
CIGNA Dental, CIGNA Vision, CIGNA Voluntary, CIGNA Behavioral
Employer References
Intel, Cisco, Safeway

---

107 CIGNA HealthCare of Southern California

26 Executive Park
Suite 200
Irvine, CA 92614
Phone: 949-255-1400
Fax: 949-255-1483
www.cigna.com
Secondary Address: 400 North Brand Blvd, Suite 400, Glendale, CA 91203, 818-500-6262
Subsidiary of: CIGNA
For Profit Organization: Yes
Year Founded: 1929
Owned by an Integrated Delivery Network (IDN): Yes
Number of Affiliated Hospitals: 234
Number of Primary Care Physicians: 52,300
Number of Referral/Specialty Physicians: 20,766
Total Enrollment: 10,000,000
State Enrollment: 450,000

Healthplan and Services Defined
PLAN TYPE: HMO
Model Type: Network
Plan Specialty: ASO, HMO, POS, PPO, CDHP, Fully Insured Funding, Minimum Premium Funding
Benefits Offered: Behavioral Health, Chiropractic, Dental, Disease Management, Home Care, Physical Therapy, Podiatry, Psychiatric, Transplant, Vision, Wellness, Pharmacy, Radiology

Type of Coverage
Commercial, Individual, Indemnity
Catastrophic Illness Benefit: Varies per case

Type of Payment Plans Offered
DFFS, Capitated, FFS, Combination FFS & DFFS

Geographic Areas Served
Northern and Southern California, Nationwide

Network Qualifications
Pre-Admission Certification: Yes

Peer Review Type
Utilization Review: Yes
Case Management: Yes

Publishes and Distributes Report Card: Yes

Accreditation Certification
NCQA

Key Personnel
President.....................................Chris De Rosa
CFO..Ryan Mcgroarty
Claims.......................................Doug Stewart
Network Contracting ....Michelle DeMonteverde
Dental.......................................Ron Bolden
Marketing...................................Lincoln Acholonu
Medical Affairs ....Steven Halpern, MD
Member Services............................Doug Stewart
Provider Services ....Randy Mathews
Sales ....Laura Hosmer

Specialty Managed Care Partners
CIGNA Behavioral, CIGNA Dental, CIGNA Vision, CIGNA
Voluntary

Employer References
Disney, Los Angeles School District, County of Orange

---

108   **Citizens Choice Healthplan**
17315 Studebaker Road
Suite #200
Cerritos, CA 90703
Toll-Free: 866-646-2247
Phone: 323-728-7232
Fax: 323-728-8494
info@mycchp.com
www.citizenschoicehealth.com
Year Founded: 2005

Healthplan and Services Defined
PLAN TYPE: HMO

Type of Coverage
Supplemental Medicare

Geographic Areas Served
California

Key Personnel
Media Contact..............................Mayra Merrick
323-728-7232

---

109   **Coastal Healthcare Administrators**
928 East Blanco Road
Suite 235
Salinas, CA 93901
Toll-Free: 800-564-7475
Phone: 831-754-3800
Fax: 831-754-3830
info@coastalmgmt.com
www.coastalmgmt.com
Mailing Address: PO Box 80308, Salinas, CA 93912
For Profit Organization: Yes
Year Founded: 1961
Number of Affiliated Hospitals: 21
Number of Primary Care Physicians: 2,594
Number of Referral/Specialty Physicians: 3,241
Total Enrollment: 41,266

Healthplan and Services Defined
PLAN TYPE: PPO
Model Type: PPO Network
Benefits Offered: Prescription, PPO Network

Type of Coverage
Commercial

Catastrophic Illness Benefit: Unlimited

Type of Payment Plans Offered
FFS

Geographic Areas Served
Monterey, San Benito, San Luis Obispo, Santa Clara and Santa Cruz
counties

Subscriber Information
Average Subscriber Co-Payment:
Primary Care Physician: $20.00
Prescription Drugs: $10.00
Home Health Care Max. Days/Visits Covered: 120 days
Nursing Home Max. Days/Visits Covered: 60 days

Peer Review Type
Utilization Review: No
Second Surgical Opinion: Yes
Case Management: No

Accreditation Certification
NCQA

Key Personnel
President/CEO ....Debi Hardwick
831-754-3800
dhardwick@coastalmgmt.com
CFO..Peggy Kalekos
831-754-3800
Dir Network Management......................Betty Yancey
831-754-3800
byancey@coastalmgmt.com
Provider Relations Rep ....Betty Yancey
831-754-3800
byancey@coastalmgmt.com

Average Claim Compensation
Physician's Fees Charged: 70%
Hospital's Fees Charged: 85%

---

110   **Community Health Group**
740 Bay Boulevard
Chula Vista, CA 91910
Toll-Free: 800-840-0089
Phone: 619-422-0422
Fax: 619-213-1008
info@chgsd.com
www.chgsd.com
Mailing Address: PO Box 1177, Chula Vista, CA 91912
Non-Profit Organization: Yes
Year Founded: 1982
Number of Affiliated Hospitals: 28
Number of Primary Care Physicians: 488
Number of Referral/Specialty Physicians: 1,820
Total Enrollment: 116,000
State Enrollment: 116,000

Healthplan and Services Defined
PLAN TYPE: HMO
Model Type: Network
Plan Specialty: Behavioral Health, Disease Management, Lab, Vision,
Radiology, UR
Benefits Offered: Behavioral Health, Disease Management, Home
Care, Inpatient SNF, Physical Therapy, Podiatry, Prescription,
Psychiatric, Transplant, Wellness
Offers Demand Management Patient Information Service: Yes

Type of Coverage
Medi-Cal, Healthy Families, SNP
Catastrophic Illness Benefit: None

Type of Payment Plans Offered
Capitated, FFS

Geographic Areas Served
San Diego and Riverside counties

Network Qualifications
Pre-Admission Certification: Yes

Peer Review Type
Utilization Review: Yes
Second Surgical Opinion: Yes
Case Management: Yes

Publishes and Distributes Report Card: Yes

Accreditation Certification
NCQA
Utilization Review, Pre-Admission Certification, State Licensure, Quality Assurance Program

Key Personnel
CEO . . . . .Norma Diaz
CFO . . . . .Bill Rice
COO . . . . .Joseph Garcia
In House Formulary . . . . .Noreen Koizumi, PharmD
Chief Marketing Officer . . . . .Joseph Garcia
Chief Medical Officer . . . . .Edward Hutt, MD, MPH
Member Services . . . . .Nora Pintado
Chief Info System Officer . . . . .Jonathan Tamayo
Provider Services . . . . .Ann Warrren

Specialty Managed Care Partners
Enters into Contracts with Regional Business Coalitions: No

111 Community Health Plan of Los Angeles County
1100 Corporate Center Drive
Monterey Park, CA 91754
Toll-Free: 800-450-5550
Fax: 626-299-7258
http://chp.dhs.lacounty.gov
Non-Profit Organization: Yes
Total Enrollment: 200,000
State Enrollment: 200,000

Healthplan and Services Defined
PLAN TYPE: HMO
Offers Demand Management Patient Information Service: Yes
DMPI Services Offered: 24-hour Nurse Line

Type of Coverage
Individual, Medicare, Medicaid

Key Personnel
Chief Executive Officer. . . . . .Teri Daly Lauenstein

112 CONCERN: Employee Assistance Program
1503 Grant Road
Suite 120
Mountain View, CA 94040-3293
Phone: 650-940-7100
Fax: 650-966-9291
info@concern-eap.com
www.concern-eap.com

Healthplan and Services Defined
PLAN TYPE: Other
Other Type: EAP

Type of Coverage
Commercial, EAP

Key Personnel
Chief Executive Officer . . . . .Cecile Currier
Chief Technology Officer . . . . .Jim Carroll

113 Contra Costa Health Plan
595 Center Avenue
Suite 100
Martinez, CA 94553

Toll-Free: 877-661-6230
Phone: 925-313-6000
Fax: 925-313-6047
3chp@hsd.cccounty.us
www.cchealth.org
Non-Profit Organization: Yes
Year Founded: 1973
Federally Qualified: Yes
Number of Affiliated Hospitals: 7
Number of Primary Care Physicians: 150
Number of Referral/Specialty Physicians: 210
Total Enrollment: 100,000
State Enrollment: 100,000

Healthplan and Services Defined
PLAN TYPE: HMO
Model Type: Staff, Network
Benefits Offered: Disease Management, Wellness

Geographic Areas Served
Contra Costa County

Subscriber Information
Average Monthly Fee Per Subscriber
(Employee + Employer Contribution):
Employee Only (Self): $389.00
Employee & 1 Family Member: $985.00
Employee & 2 Family Members: $1530.00
Average Annual Deductible Per Subscriber:
Employee Only (Self): $0.00
Employee & 1 Family Member: $0.00
Employee & 2 Family Members: $0.00
Average Subscriber Co-Payment:
Primary Care Physician: $15.00
Non-Network Physician: $15.00
Prescription Drugs: $15/30
Hospital ER: $35.00
Nursing Home: $100.00
Nursing Home Max. Days/Visits Covered: 100.00/200.00 max

Network Qualifications
Pre-Admission Certification: No

Peer Review Type
Utilization Review: Yes
Second Surgical Opinion: Yes
Case Management: Yes

Publishes and Distributes Report Card: Yes

Accreditation Certification
URAC Accredition
TJC Accreditation, Medicare Approved, Utilization Review, State Licensure, Quality Assurance Program

Key Personnel
CEO . . . . .Patricia Tanquary, MPH, PhD
CFO/COO . . . . .Patrick Godley
925-957-5405
Director/Health Officer . . . . .William Walker, MD
925-957-5403
Manager Claims . . . . .Cindy Shelby
925-957-5185
In-House Formulary . . . . .Curt Le
925-957-7260
Marketing/Sales Manger .Wendy Mailer
800-211-8040
Communications Officer . . . . .Kate Fowlie
925-313-6268
kate.fowlie@hsd.cccounty.us

Specialty Managed Care Partners
Enters into Contracts with Regional Business Coalitions: Yes

114 CorVel Corporation
2010 Main Street
Suite 600

Irvine, CA 92614
Toll-Free: 888-726-7835
Phone: 949-851-1473
Fax: 949-851-1469
marketing@corvel.com
www.corvel.com
For Profit Organization: Yes
Year Founded: 1988

Healthplan and Services Defined
PLAN TYPE: PPO
Benefits Offered: Disease Management, Wellness, Worker's
Compensation

Type of Coverage
Commercial, Indemnity

Geographic Areas Served
Nationwide

Accreditation Certification
URAC

Key Personnel
Chairman . . . . .Gordon Clemons
CEO, President & COO .Daniel J Starck
CFO. . . . . .Scott McCloud
Director, Legal Services . . . . .Sharon O'Connor
Secretary . . . . .Richard Schweppe
Chief Information Officer . . . . .Donald C McFarlane
Vice President, Sales. . . . . .Diane J Blaha

115   Delta Dental of California
12898 Towne Center Drive
Cerritos, CA 90703-8546
Toll-Free: 800-422-4234
Phone: 562-403-4040
Fax: 562-924-3172
scasales@delta.org
www.deltadentalca.org
Mailing Address: PO Box 997330, Sacramento, CA 95899-7330
Non-Profit Organization: Yes
Year Founded: 1955
Number of Primary Care Physicians: 2,476
Number of Referral/Specialty Physicians: 924
Total Enrollment: 54,000,000

Healthplan and Services Defined
PLAN TYPE: Dental
Other Type: Dental PPO
Model Type: Network
Plan Specialty: Dental
Benefits Offered: Dental

Type of Coverage
Commercial, Dental Benefits

Type of Payment Plans Offered
DFFS, Capitated, FFS

Geographic Areas Served
Statewide

Subscriber Information
Average Monthly Fee Per Subscriber
(Employee + Employer Contribution):
Employee Only (Self): Varies
Employee & 1 Family Member: Varies
Employee & 2 Family Members: Varies
Medicare: Varies
Average Annual Deductible Per Subscriber:
Employee Only (Self): Varies
Average Subscriber Co-Payment:
Primary Care Physician: Varies
Non-Network Physician: Varies

Network Qualifications
Pre-Admission Certification: No

Peer Review Type
Utilization Review: Yes
Second Surgical Opinion: Yes
Case Management: Yes

Publishes and Distributes Report Card: Yes

Key Personnel
President/CEO. . . . . .Gary Radine
415-972-8300
CFO. . . . . .Elizabeth Russell
415-972-8300
Sr VP Dental . . . . .Marilynn Belek, DMD
415-972-8300
Director Product Mtkg/Dev . . . . .Lynette Crosby
415-972-8300
Information Systems. . . . . .Martin Whelan
415-972-8300
VP Sales . . . . .John Crooms, Jr.
415-972-8300
VP, Public & Govt Affairs .Jeff Album
415-972-8418
Dir/Media & Public Affair . . . . .Elizabeth Risberg
415-972-8423

Specialty Managed Care Partners
PMI Dental Health Plan
Enters into Contracts with Regional Business Coalitions: Yes

116   Dental Alternatives Insurance Services
3720 S Susan Street
2nd Floor, Suite 102
Santa Ana, CA 92704
Toll-Free: 800-445-8119
Phone: 714-429-0200
Fax: 714-429-1261
info@gotodais.com
www.gotodais.com
For Profit Organization: Yes
Year Founded: 1979
Total Enrollment: 390,000

Healthplan and Services Defined
PLAN TYPE: Dental
Model Type: IPA
Plan Specialty: Dental
Benefits Offered: Dental
Offers Demand Management Patient Information Service: Yes

Network Qualifications
Pre-Admission Certification: Yes

Peer Review Type
Utilization Review: Yes
Second Surgical Opinion: Yes
Case Management: Yes

Publishes and Distributes Report Card: Yes

Accreditation Certification
NCQA

Specialty Managed Care Partners
Enters into Contracts with Regional Business Coalitions: Yes

117   Dental Benefit Providers: California
425 Market Street
12th Floor, Mail Route CA035-1200
San Francisco, CA 94105
Toll-Free: 800-445-9090
Phone: 415-778-3800
Fax: 415-778-3833
networkrecruit@uhc.com
www.dbp.com
Secondary Address: 6220 Old Dobbin Lane, Columbia, MD 21045

For Profit Organization: Yes
Year Founded: 1984
Number of Primary Care Physicians: 125,000
Total Enrollment: 6,600,000

Healthplan and Services Defined
PLAN TYPE: Dental
Model Type: IPA
Plan Specialty: ASO, Dental, EPO, DHMO, PPO, CSO, Preventive, Claims Repricing and Network Access
Benefits Offered: Dental

Type of Coverage
Indemnity, Medicare, Medicaid

Type of Payment Plans Offered
POS, DFFS, Capitated, FFS

Geographic Areas Served
48 states including District of Columbia, Puerto Rico and Virgin Islands

Accreditation Certification
NCQA

Key Personnel
Chief Administrator . . . . Jill Schultze-Evans

118 Dental Health Services of California

3833 Atlantic Avenue
Long Beach, CA 90807
Toll-Free: 800-637-6453
Phone: 562-595-6000
Fax: 562-424-0150
www.dentalhealthservices.com
Secondary Address: 2515 Camino del Rio S, #242A, San Diego, CA 92108
For Profit Organization: Yes
Year Founded: 1974
Physician Owned Organization: Yes
Federally Qualified: Yes
Number of Primary Care Physicians: 1,000
Number of Referral/Specialty Physicians: 400
Total Enrollment: 90,000

Healthplan and Services Defined
PLAN TYPE: Dental
Model Type: Network
Plan Specialty: Dental
Benefits Offered: Dental

Type of Coverage
Commercial, Individual
Catastrophic Illness Benefit: None

Type of Payment Plans Offered
DFFS

Geographic Areas Served
California and Washington

Subscriber Information
Average Monthly Fee Per Subscriber
(Employee + Employer Contribution):
Employee Only (Self): Varies
Employee & 1 Family Member: Varies
Employee & 2 Family Members: Varies

Network Qualifications
Pre-Admission Certification: Yes

Peer Review Type
Second Surgical Opinion: Yes
Case Management: Yes

Publishes and Distributes Report Card: Yes

Accreditation Certification
Dhm
TJC Accreditation, Utilization Review, State Licensure, Quality Assurance Program

Key Personnel
Marketing . . . . Gary Pernell
Member Services . . . . Karen Phillips
Information Services . . . . Del Ziegler

Specialty Managed Care Partners
United Association, 7up
Enters into Contracts with Regional Business Coalitions: No

119 Dentistat

900 Lafayette Street
Suite 201
Santa Clara, CA 95050
Toll-Free: 800-336-8250
Phone: 408-244-1102
Fax: 408-244-4889
info@dentistat.com
www.dentistat.com
For Profit Organization: Yes
Year Founded: 1968
Number of Primary Care Physicians: 80,000

Healthplan and Services Defined
PLAN TYPE: Dental
Model Type: Network
Plan Specialty: Dental
Benefits Offered: Dental

Type of Payment Plans Offered
DFFS, Capitated, FFS, Combination FFS & DFFS

Geographic Areas Served
Nationwide

Accreditation Certification
NCQA
Utilization Review, Quality Assurance Program

Key Personnel
President . . . . Bret Guenther
Chief Information Officer . . . . Sondra Zambino

Specialty Managed Care Partners
Enters into Contracts with Regional Business Coalitions: Yes

120 Easy Choice Health Plan

180 E Ocean Blvd
Suite 700
Long Beach, CA 90802
Toll-Free: 866-999-3945
Phone: 562-343-9710
Fax: 877-999-3945
info@easychoicehp.com
www.easychoicehealthplan.com
Mailing Address: PO Box 22653, Long Beach, CA 90801
Total Enrollment: 8,000
State Enrollment: 8,000

Healthplan and Services Defined
PLAN TYPE: Medicare
Benefits Offered: Dental, Disease Management, Prescription, Vision, Wellness

Type of Coverage
Medicare

Geographic Areas Served
Los Angeles & Orange County

Key Personnel
President . . . . Eric E Spencer, MBA
COO & CFO . . . . Frank Vo
Medical Director . . . . M Nicole Jamali, MD
Vice President . . . . Joya Bond
562-343-9715
jbond@easychoicehp.com

121 eHealthInsurance Services Inc.

11919 Foundation Place
Gold River, CA 95670
Toll-Free: 800-977-8860
info@ehealthinsurance.com
www.e.healthinsurance.com
Year Founded: 1997

Healthplan and Services Defined
   PLAN TYPE: HMO/PPO
   Benefits Offered: Dental, Life, STD

Type of Coverage
   Commercial, Individual, Medicare

Geographic Areas Served
   All 50 states in the USA and District of Columbia

Key Personnel
   Chairman & CEO . . . . .Gary L. Lauer
   EVP/Business & Corp. Dev. .Bruce Telkamp
   EVP/Chief Technology . . . . .Dr. Sheldon X. Wang
   SVP & CFO . . . . .Stuart M. Huizinga
   Pres. of eHealth Gov. Sys . . . . .Samuel C. Gibbs
   SVP of Sales & Operations . . . . .Robert S. Hurley
   Director Public Relations. . . . . .Nate Purpura
      650-210-3115

122 eHealthInsurance Services Inc. Corporate Office

440 E Middlefield Road
Mountainview, CA 94043
Toll-Free: 877-456-7180
headquarters@ehealth.com
www.e.healthinsurance.com
Year Founded: 1997

Healthplan and Services Defined
   PLAN TYPE: HMO/PPO
   Benefits Offered: Dental, Life, STD

Type of Coverage
   Commercial, Individual, Medicare

Geographic Areas Served
   All 50 states in the USA and District of Columbia

Key Personnel
   Chairman & CEO . . . . .Gary L. Lauer
   EVP/Business & Corp. Dev. .Bruce Telkamp
   EVP/Chief Technology . . . . .Dr. Sheldon X. Wang
   SVP & CFO . . . . .Stuart M. Huizinga
   Pres. of eHealth Gov. Sys . . . . .Samuel C. Gibbs
   SVP of Sales & Operations . . . . .Robert S. Hurley
   Director Public Relations. . . . . .Nate Purpura
      650-210-3115

123 Foundation for Medical Care for Kern & Santa Barbara County

5701 Truxton Avenue
Suite 100
Bakersfield, CA 93309
Toll-Free: 800-322-5709
Phone: 661-327-7581
Fax: 661-327-5129
ctemple@kernfmc.com
www.kernfmc.com
Non-Profit Organization: Yes
Year Founded: 1983
Physician Owned Organization: Yes
Number of Affiliated Hospitals: 400
Number of Primary Care Physicians: 30,000
Number of Referral/Specialty Physicians: 7,000

Total Enrollment: 60,000

Healthplan and Services Defined
   PLAN TYPE: PPO
   Model Type: IPA, Group, Network
   Benefits Offered: Prescription
   Offers Demand Management Patient Information Service: Yes

Type of Payment Plans Offered
   POS, DFFS, FFS, Combination FFS & DFFS

Geographic Areas Served
   Kern, Santa Barbara, Mono and Inyo counties

Network Qualifications
   Pre-Admission Certification: Yes

Peer Review Type
   Utilization Review: Yes
   Second Surgical Opinion: Yes
   Case Management: Yes

Accreditation Certification
   TJC Accreditation, Medicare Approved, Utilization Review,
      Pre-Admission Certification, State Licensure

Key Personnel
   CEO. . . . . .Carolyn J Temple
      ctemple@kernfmc.com
   COO. . . . . .Lori Howell
      lhowell@kernfmc.com
   Dir, Admin & Finance . . . . .Elizabeth Maynard
      lizmaynard@kernfmc.com
   Chief Marketing Officer . . . . .George Stephenson, II
      gstephenson@kernfmc.com
   Executive Assistant . . . . .Lisa Garzelli
      lgarzelli@kernfmc.com
   Manager, Customer Service . . . . .Ellen Wright
      ewright@kernfmc.com
   Provider Relations . . . . .D'Ln Brown
      dbrown@kernfmc.com
   Mgr, Provider Relations . . . . .Jeanne Simpson
      jsimpson@kernfmc.com
   Sales & Mktg Supervisor . . . . .Keith Salyards
      ksalyards@kernfmc.com
   Exec Admin Supervisor . . . . .Lisa Garzelli
      lgarzelli@kernfmc.com

Specialty Managed Care Partners
   Enters into Contracts with Regional Business Coalitions: No

124 Foundation for Medical Care for Mendocino and Lake Counties

620 S Dora Street
Suite 201
Ukiah, CA 95482
Toll-Free: 800-273-3762
Phone: 707-462-7607
Fax: 707-462-1206
mendolake_counties@sbcglobal.net
www.mendolake-physicians.com
Subsidiary of: California Foundation for Medical Care
Non-Profit Organization: Yes
Year Founded: 1962
Number of Affiliated Hospitals: 5
Number of Primary Care Physicians: 350
Number of Referral/Specialty Physicians: 5,500
Total Enrollment: 34,000
State Enrollment: 34,000

Healthplan and Services Defined
   PLAN TYPE: PPO
   Model Type: PPO
   Benefits Offered: Prescription
   Offers Demand Management Patient Information Service: Yes

Geographic Areas Served
Lake & Mendocino counties

Network Qualifications
Pre-Admission Certification: Yes

Peer Review Type
Utilization Review: Yes
Second Surgical Opinion: No
Case Management: No

Accreditation Certification
TJC Accreditation, Utilization Review, Pre-Admission Certification, State Licensure, Quality Assurance Program

Key Personnel
Executive Director . . . . .Kathy King
CEO . . . . .Gene Draper
Controller . . . . .Shawn Lowry
Medical Affairs . . . . .Mark Apfel, MD

125 GEMCare Health Plan
4550 California Avenue
Suite 100
Bakersfield, CA 93309
Toll-Free: 877-697-2464
Phone: 661-716-8800
info@gemcarehealthplan.com
www.gemcarehealthplan.com

Healthplan and Services Defined
PLAN TYPE: Medicare

Type of Coverage
Medicare, Supplemental Medicare

Geographic Areas Served
Kern County

Key Personnel
President/CEO. . . . . .Michael R Myers

126 Golden West Dental & Vision Plan
PO Box 5347
Oxnard, CA 93031
Toll-Free: 800-995-4124
Phone: 805-987-6110
Fax: 805-987-7491
www.goldenwestdental.com
Subsidiary of: WellPoint
For Profit Organization: Yes
Year Founded: 1974
Number of Primary Care Physicians: 2,011
Number of Referral/Specialty Physicians: 733
Total Enrollment: 200,473

Healthplan and Services Defined
PLAN TYPE: Multiple
Model Type: IPA, Network
Plan Specialty: Dental, Vision
Benefits Offered: Dental, Vision
Offers Demand Management Patient Information Service: Yes

Type of Payment Plans Offered
Capitated, Combination FFS & DFFS

Geographic Areas Served
Statewide

Subscriber Information
Average Monthly Fee Per Subscriber
(Employee + Employer Contribution):
Employee Only (Self): Varies
Employee & 1 Family Member: Varies
Employee & 2 Family Members: Varies
Medicare: Varies

Peer Review Type
Second Surgical Opinion: Yes

Publishes and Distributes Report Card: Yes

Key Personnel
Marketing . . . . .Chris McConathy
Dental Director . . . . .Karen Feldman

Average Claim Compensation
Physician's Fees Charged: 80%

Specialty Managed Care Partners
Enters into Contracts with Regional Business Coalitions: Yes

127 Great-West Healthcare California
Acquired by CIGNA

128 Great-West Healthcare Los Angeles
Acquired by CIGNA

129 Great-West Healthcare Northern California
Acquired by CIGNA

130 Health Net Dental
21650 Oxnard Street
Woodland Hills, CA 91367
Toll-Free: 800-291-6911
Phone: 818-676-6000
www.yourdentalplan.com/healthnet
Mailing Address: PO Box 30930, Laguna Hills, CA 92654-0930
For Profit Organization: Yes
Year Founded: 1972
Number of Primary Care Physicians: 2,700
Total Enrollment: 540,000

Healthplan and Services Defined
PLAN TYPE: Dental
Plan Specialty: Dental
Benefits Offered: Dental

Key Personnel
Presdient/CEO. . . . . .Jay M Gellert
Mgr, Public Relations . . . . .Brad Kieffer
818-676-6833
brad.kieffer@healthnet.com

131 Health Net Medicare Plan
21650 Oxnard Street
Woodland Hills, CA 91367
Toll-Free: 888-747-2424
Phone: 800-845-8829
www.healthnet.com/portal/medicare/home.do
Mailing Address: PO Box 10198, Van Nuys, CA 91410-0198
Year Founded: 1978
Total Enrollment: 6,700,000
State Enrollment: 6,700,000

Healthplan and Services Defined
PLAN TYPE: Medicare
Benefits Offered: Chiropractic, Dental, Disease Management, Home Care, Inpatient SNF, Physical Therapy, Podiatry, Prescription, Psychiatric, Vision, Wellness

Type of Coverage
Individual, Medicare

Geographic Areas Served
Available in multiple states

Subscriber Information
Average Monthly Fee Per Subscriber
(Employee + Employer Contribution):
Employee Only (Self): Varies

Medicare: Varies
Average Annual Deductible Per Subscriber:
Employee Only (Self): Varies
Medicare: Varies
Average Subscriber Co-Payment:
Primary Care Physician: Varies
Non-Network Physician: Varies
Prescription Drugs: Varies
Hospital ER: Varies
Home Health Care: Varies
Home Health Care Max. Days/Visits Covered: Varies
Nursing Home: Varies
Nursing Home Max. Days/Visits Covered: Varies

Key Personnel
President/CEO . . . . Jay M Gellert
SVP/Speciality Services . . . . Gerald V Coil
Regional Health Plans . . . . Stephen D Lynch
SVP/Organization Mgmt. . . . . Karin D Mayhew
SVP/Communications . . . . David W Olson
EVP/CFO . . . . Anthony S Piszel
SVP/Chief Medical Officer . . . . Jonathan H Scheff, MD/MBA
Pharmaceutical Division . . . . John P Sivori
SVP/General Counsel . . . . B Curtis Westen, Esq
President/Government Svcs . . . . James E Woys
Dir, Communications . . . . Amy Sheyer
818-676-8304
amy.l.sheyer@healthnet.org

132 Health Net: Corporate Headquarters

21650 Oxnard Street
Woodland Hills, CA 91367
Toll-Free: 800-291-6911
Phone: 818-676-6000
www.healthnet.com
Mailing Address: PO Box 9103, Van Nuys, CA 91409-9103
For Profit Organization: Yes
Year Founded: 1979
Number of Affiliated Hospitals: 419
Number of Primary Care Physicians: 1,207
Total Enrollment: 6,000,000

Healthplan and Services Defined
PLAN TYPE: HMO
Model Type: IPA, Group
Benefits Offered: Disease Management, Prescription, Wellness
Offers Demand Management Patient Information Service: Yes

Type of Coverage
Catastrophic Illness Benefit: Covered

Type of Payment Plans Offered
POS, DFFS, FFS

Geographic Areas Served
Alameda, Amador, Butte, Calaveras, Colusa, Contra Costa, El
Dorado, Fresno, Glenn, Humboldt, Kern, Kings, Lake, Lassen, Los
Angeles, Madera, Marin, Mariposa, Mendocino, Merced, Napa,
Nevada, Orange, Placer, Plumas, Riverside, Sacramento, San
Bernardino, San Diego, San Francisco, San Joaquin, San Luis
Obispo, San Mateo, Santa Barbara, Santa Clara, Santa Cruz, Shasta,
Sierra, Solano, Sonoma, Stanislaus, Sutter, Tehama, Trinity, Tulare,
Tuolumne, Ventura, Yolo & Yuba

Subscriber Information
Average Monthly Fee Per Subscriber
(Employee + Employer Contribution):
Employee Only (Self): $139.08
Employee & 1 Family Member: $305.98/236.44
Employee & 2 Family Members: $403.34
Medicare: $0-52.00
Average Subscriber Co-Payment:
Primary Care Physician: $10.00
Non-Network Physician: Not covered
Prescription Drugs: $6.00

Hospital ER: $35.00
Home Health Care Max. Days/Visits Covered: Unlimited
Nursing Home Max. Days/Visits Covered: 100 days

Network Qualifications
Pre-Admission Certification: Yes

Peer Review Type
Utilization Review: Yes
Second Surgical Opinion: Yes
Case Management: Yes

Publishes and Distributes Report Card: Yes

Accreditation Certification
NCQA
TJC Accreditation, Medicare Approved, Utilization Review,
Pre-Admission Certification, State Licensure, Quality Assurance
Program

Key Personnel
President/Ceo . . . . Jay M Gellert
SVP, General Counsel . . . . Angelee F Bouchard, Esq
EVP, Chief Financial Offc . . . . Joseph C Capezza, CPA
SVP, Chief Regulatory Ofc . . . . Patricia T Clarey
Chief Govt Prog Officer . . . . Scott R Kelly
SVP, Org. Effectiveness . . . . Karin D Mayhew
VP, Treasurer. . . . . Jonathan Rollins, CFA
Health Care Svcs Officer . . . . John P Sivori
VP, Ext Communications . . . . Margita Thompson
818-676-7912
margita.thompson@healthnet.com
President, Govt Programs . . . . Steven D Tough
Chief Operating Officer . . . . James E Woys
Mgr, Public Relations . . . . Brad Kieffer
818-676-6833
brad.kieffer@healthnet.com
Corporate Communications . . . . Lori Hillman
818-676-8684
lori.a.hillman@healthnet.com

Specialty Managed Care Partners
Enters into Contracts with Regional Business Coalitions: Yes

133 Health Plan of San Joaquin

7751 South Manthey Road
French Camp, CA 95231
Toll-Free: 888-936-7526
Phone: 209-942-6300
Fax: 209-942-6305
www.hpsj.com
Mailing Address: PO Box 30490, Stockton, CA 95213-0490
Non-Profit Organization: Yes
Year Founded: 1996
Number of Primary Care Physicians: 180
Number of Referral/Specialty Physicians: 1,400
Total Enrollment: 109,000
State Enrollment: 109,000

Healthplan and Services Defined
PLAN TYPE: HMO
Benefits Offered: Inpatient SNF, Podiatry, Vision, Wellness
Offers Demand Management Patient Information Service: Yes
DMPI Services Offered: 24 Hour Nurse Advice Hotline

Type of Coverage
Commercial, Medicaid

Geographic Areas Served
San Joaquin county

Key Personnel
CEO . . . . John Hackworth, PhD
209-461-2211
jhackworth@hpsj.com

CFO ....Paul Antigua
209-461-2268
pantigua@hpsj.com
COO...Kathryn Kutz
Marketing Director ....David Hurst
209-461-2241
dhurst@hpsj.com
Medical Director...........................Dale Bishop, MD
209-461-2281
dbishop@hpsj.com
Dir, Marketing ....David Hurst
209-491-2241
dhurst@hpsj.com

134   Health Plan of San Mateo
701 Gateway Boulevard
Suite 400
South San Francisco, CA 94080
Toll-Free: 800-750-4776
Phone: 650-616-0050
Fax: 650-616-0060
info@hpsm.org
www.hpsm.org
Non-Profit Organization: Yes
Year Founded: 1987
Number of Affiliated Hospitals: 12
Number of Primary Care Physicians: 197
Total Enrollment: 87,740
State Enrollment: 87,740

Healthplan and Services Defined
PLAN TYPE: HMO
Model Type: IPA
Benefits Offered: Disease Management, Prescription, Wellness

Type of Coverage
Medi-Cal, Healthy Families

Type of Payment Plans Offered
Capitated, FFS

Geographic Areas Served
San Mateo county

Key Personnel
Executive Director ....Maya Altman
Finance Director.............................Ron Robinson
MIS Director ....Eben Yong
Dir, Systems Improvement...................Chris Baughman
Dir, Compliance & Regul ....Ellen Dunn-Malhotra
Medical Director ....Mary Giammona, MD
Member Services Director ....Carolyn Thon
Human Resources Director......................Cindy Lem
Provider Services Dir ....Mari Baca

135   Humana Health Insurance of Northern California
1676 N California Blvd
Suite 600
Walnut Creek, CA 94596
Toll-Free: 888-486-0257
Phone: 925-934-0284
Fax: 925-934-1347
www.humana.com
For Profit Organization: Yes

Healthplan and Services Defined
PLAN TYPE: HMO/PPO

Type of Coverage
Commercial, Individual

Accreditation Certification
URAC, NCQA, CORE

136   Humana Health Insurance of Southern California
5421 Avenida Encinas
Suite N
Carlsbad, CA 92008
Toll-Free: 800-795-2403
Phone: 760-918-0152
Fax: 760-918-0654
www.humana.com
For Profit Organization: Yes

Healthplan and Services Defined
PLAN TYPE: HMO
Model Type: POS

Type of Coverage
Commercial, Individual

Accreditation Certification
URAC, NCQA, CORE

137   Inland Empire Health Plan
303 East Vanderbilt Way
San Bernardino, CA 92408
Toll-Free: 800-440-4347
Phone: 909-890-2000
Fax: 909-890-2003
member_services@iehp.org
www.iehp.org
Mailing Address: P.O. Box 19026, San Bernardino, CA 92423
Non-Profit Organization: Yes
Year Founded: 1996
Number of Affiliated Hospitals: 27
Number of Primary Care Physicians: 1,700
Total Enrollment: 461,773
State Enrollment: 461,773

Healthplan and Services Defined
PLAN TYPE: HMO
Model Type: Staff, IPA
Benefits Offered: Inpatient SNF, Physical Therapy, Prescription, Transplant, Vision, Wellness

Type of Coverage
Commercial, Medicaid

Geographic Areas Served
San Bernardino and Riverside counties

Accreditation Certification
NCQA

Key Personnel
CEO ....Bradley P Gilbert, MD
CFO...Chet Uma
Chief Operations Officer ....Phil Branstetter
Chief Marketing Officer...................Susan Arcidiacono
Chief Medical Officer...................William Henning, MD
Marketing Director...........................Thomas Pham
909-890-2176
pham-t@iehp.org

138   Inter Valley Health Plan
300 S Park Avenue
PO Box 6002
Pomona, CA 91769-6002
Toll-Free: 800-251-8191
Phone: 909-623-6333
info@ivhp.com
www.ivhp.com
Non-Profit Organization: Yes
Year Founded: 1979
Owned by an Integrated Delivery Network (IDN): No

Federally Qualified: Yes
Number of Affiliated Hospitals: 24
Number of Primary Care Physicians: 1,161
Number of Referral/Specialty Physicians: 4,791
Total Enrollment: 14,600

Healthplan and Services Defined
  PLAN TYPE: Multiple
  Model Type: Network
  Benefits Offered: Behavioral Health, Home Care, Inpatient SNF,
    Physical Therapy, Prescription, Psychiatric, Transplant, Wellness

Type of Coverage
  Medicare
  Catastrophic Illness Benefit: Unlimited

Type of Payment Plans Offered
  Capitated

Geographic Areas Served
  Southern California counties including Los Angeles, Riverside, San
  Bernardino

Subscriber Information
  Average Subscriber Co-Payment:
    Primary Care Physician: $7/15/30/55
    Hospital ER: $50.00
    Nursing Home: $40/day,day 2/thru100
    Nursing Home Max. Days/Visits Covered: 100

Network Qualifications
  Pre-Admission Certification: No

Peer Review Type
  Utilization Review: Yes
  Second Surgical Opinion: Yes
  Case Management: Yes

Accreditation Certification
  URAC, PBGH, CCHRI
  TJC Accreditation, Medicare Approved, Utilization Review, State
    Licensure, Quality Assurance Program

Key Personnel
  President and CEO . . . . .Ron Bolding
  CFO . . . . .Donald D McCain
  Claims Manager . . . . .Trina Alexander
  VP, Marketing . . . . .Cyndie O'Brien
  Member Services. . . . . .Judy Johnson

Average Claim Compensation
  Physician's Fees Charged: 75%
  Hospital's Fees Charged: 55%

Specialty Managed Care Partners
  Vision Service Plan

---

139 Interplan Health Group
Acquired by HealthSmart

---

140 Kaiser Permanente Health Plan of Northern California
1950 Franklin Street
Oakland, CA 94612-2911
Phone: 510-987-1000
Fax: 510-271-6493
marc.t.brown@kp.org
www.kaiserpermanente.org
Non-Profit Organization: Yes
Year Founded: 1945
Number of Affiliated Hospitals: 35
Number of Primary Care Physicians: 15,129
Total Enrollment: 3,223,235
State Enrollment: 3,223,235

Healthplan and Services Defined
  PLAN TYPE: HMO
  Model Type: Group, Network

Benefits Offered: Disease Management, Home Care, Inpatient SNF,
  Long-Term Care, Physical Therapy, Podiatry, Prescription,
  Psychiatric, Transplant, Vision, Wellness

Type of Payment Plans Offered
  POS, Combination FFS & DFFS

Geographic Areas Served
  Alameda, Amador, Contra Costa, El Dorado, Francisco, San Joaquin,
  San Mateo, Santa Clara, Solano, Sonoma, Sutter, Tulcare, Yolo &
  Yuba counties

Subscriber Information
  Average Monthly Fee Per Subscriber
    (Employee + Employer Contribution):
      Employee Only (Self): Varies by plan
  Average Subscriber Co-Payment:
      Home Health Care: $5.00
      Home Health Care Max. Days/Visits Covered: Unlimited
      Nursing Home Max. Days/Visits Covered: 100 days

Network Qualifications
  Pre-Admission Certification: Yes

Publishes and Distributes Report Card: Yes

Accreditation Certification
  TJC Accreditation, Medicare Approved, Utilization Review,
    Pre-Admission Certification, State Licensure, Quality Assurance
    Program

Key Personnel
  CEO . . . . .George C Halvorson
  CFO/Executive VP . . . . .Kathy Lancaster
  Sr VP/Community Benefit. . . . . .Raymond J Baxter, PhD
  SVP, Corp Development. . . . . .Chris Grant
  SVP, Chief Diversity Offc . . . . .Ronald Knox
  Consultant . . . . .Louise L Liang, MD
  Exec VP/Health Plan Ops. . . . . .Bernard J Tyson
  Exec Dir, Clinical Care. . . . . .Scott Young, MD
  EVP/Health Plan Operation . . . . .Arthur M Southam, MD
  SVP, Communications . . . . .Diane Gage Lofgren
  SVP, General Counsel. . . . . .Steven Zatkin
  SVP, Human Resources . . . . .Paul Records
  SVP, Chief Info Officer . . . . .Phil Fasano
  SVP, Quality Care . . . . .Jed Weissberg, MD
  CEO, Northern Calif Reg. . . . . .Robert M Pearl, MD
  Media Contact. . . . . .Marc Brown
    510-987-4672
    marc.t.brown@kp.org
  Pres, Northern Calif Reg . . . . .Gregory A Adams

Specialty Managed Care Partners
  Enters into Contracts with Regional Business Coalitions: Yes

---

141 Kaiser Permanente Health Plan of Southern California
393 E Walnut Street
Pasadena, CA 91188
Toll-Free: 800-464-4000
Phone: 626-405-5000
Fax: 626-405-6239
www.kaiserpermanente.org
Non-Profit Organization: Yes
Year Founded: 1945
Physician Owned Organization: Yes
Federally Qualified: Yes
Number of Affiliated Hospitals: 32
Number of Primary Care Physicians: 13,729
Total Enrollment: 3,284,000
State Enrollment: 3,284,540

Healthplan and Services Defined
  PLAN TYPE: HMO
  Model Type: Group

Plan Specialty: Behavioral Health, Chiropractic, Dental, Disease Management, Lab, PBM, Vision, Radiology, Worker's Compensation, UR, All Types of Medical Services

Benefits Offered: Behavioral Health, Chiropractic, Complementary Medicine, Dental, Disease Management, Home Care, Inpatient SNF, Long-Term Care, Physical Therapy, Podiatry, Prescription, Psychiatric, Transplant, Vision, Wellness, Worker's Compensation, AD&D, Life

Offers Demand Management Patient Information Service: Yes

Type of Coverage
Commercial, Individual, Indemnity, Medicare, Supplemental Medicare, Catastrophic
Catastrophic Illness Benefit: Unlimited

Type of Payment Plans Offered
POS

Geographic Areas Served
East Bay, Fresno, Golden Gate, North East Bay, South Bay, Sanislaus, Coachella Valley, Inland Empire, Metropolitan Los Angeles/West Los Angeles, Orange, San Diego, Tri-Central and Western Ventura counties

Subscriber Information
Average Monthly Fee Per Subscriber
 (Employee + Employer Contribution):
  Employee Only (Self): Varies by plan
Average Subscriber Co-Payment:
  Home Health Care Max. Days/Visits Covered: Unlimited
  Nursing Home Max. Days/Visits Covered: 100 days

Network Qualifications
Pre-Admission Certification: Yes

Peer Review Type
Utilization Review: Yes
Second Surgical Opinion: No
Case Management: Yes

Publishes and Distributes Report Card: Yes

Accreditation Certification
NCQA
TJC Accreditation, Medicare Approved, Utilization Review, State Licensure, Quality Assurance Program

Key Personnel
CEO . . . . .George C Halvorson
CFO/Executive VP . . . . .Kathy Lancaster
Sr VP/Community Benefit . . . . .Raymond J Baxter, PhD
SVP, Corp Development. . . . . .Chris Grant
SVP, Chief Diversity Offc .Ronald Knox
Consultant . . . . .Louise L Liang, MD
Exec VP/Health Plan Ops .Bernard J Tyson
Exec Dir, Clinical Care . . . . .Scott Young, MD
EVP/Health Plan Operation . . . . .Arthur M Southam, MD
SVP, Communications . . . . .Diane Gage Lofgren
SVP, General Counsel. . . . . .Steven Zatkin
SVP, Human Resources . . . . .Paul Records
SVP, Chief Info Officer . . . . .Phil Fasano
SVP, Quality Care . . . . .Jed Weissberg, MD
Exec Med Dir, South Calif . . . . .Jeffery A Weisz, MD
Media Contact. . . . . .Jim Anderson
  626-405-5157
  jim.h.anderson@kp.org
Pres, Southern Calif Reg . . . . .Benjamin K Chu, MPH

Specialty Managed Care Partners
Enters into Contracts with Regional Business Coalitions: Yes

---

142   Kaiser Permanente Health Plan: Corporate Office
One Kaiser Plaza
Oakland, CA 94612-3610
Phone: 510-271-5910
Fax: 510-271-5820

newscenter@kp.org
www.kaiserpermanente.org
Non-Profit Organization: Yes
Year Founded: 1945
Number of Affiliated Hospitals: 35
Number of Primary Care Physicians: 15,129
Total Enrollment: 8,569,000
State Enrollment: 6,400,000

Healthplan and Services Defined
 PLAN TYPE: HMO
 Model Type: Group
 Benefits Offered: Disease Management, Home Care, Inpatient SNF, Long-Term Care, Physical Therapy, Podiatry, Prescription, Psychiatric, Transplant, Vision, Wellness
 Offers Demand Management Patient Information Service: Yes

Type of Coverage
Catastrophic Illness Benefit: Covered

Type of Payment Plans Offered
POS

Geographic Areas Served
The 12 Kaiser Permanente Regions cover service areas in 16 states and the District of Columbia: portions of California, Colorado, Connecticut, Washington, DC, Georgia, Hawaii, Idaho, Kansas, Maryland, Massachusetts, Missouri, New York, North Carolina, Ohio, Oregon, South Carolina, Texas, Virginia, Vermont & Washington

Network Qualifications
Pre-Admission Certification: Yes

Peer Review Type
Utilization Review: Yes
Second Surgical Opinion: Yes
Case Management: Yes

Publishes and Distributes Report Card: Yes

Accreditation Certification
NCQA
TJC Accreditation, Medicare Approved, Utilization Review, Pre-Admission Certification, State Licensure, Quality Assurance Program

Key Personnel
CEO . . . . .George C Halvorson
CFO/Executive VP . . . . .Kathy Lancaster
Sr VP/Community Benefit . . . . .Raymond J Baxter, PhD
SVP, Corp Development. . . . . .Chris Grant
SVP, Chief Diversity Offc .Ronald Knox
Consultant . . . . .Louise L Liang, MD
Exec VP/Health Plan Ops .Bernard J Tyson
Exec Dir, Clinical Care . . . . .Scott Young, MD
EVP/Health Plan Operation . . . . .Arthur M Southam, MD
SVP, Communications . . . . .Diane Gage Lofgren
SVP, General Counsel. . . . . .Steven Zatkin
SVP, Human Resources . . . . .Paul Records
SVP, Chief Info Officer . . . . .Phil Fasano
SVP, Quality Care . . . . .Jed Weissberg, MD
Media Contact. . . . . .Danielle Cass
  510-267-5354
  newscenter@kp.org

Specialty Managed Care Partners
Enters into Contracts with Regional Business Coalitions: No

---

143   Kaiser Permanente Medicare Plan
1950 Franklin Street
Oakland, CA 94612
Toll-Free: 866-681-3592
Phone: 510-987-1000
http://medicare.kaiserpermanente.org

Healthplan and Services Defined
 PLAN TYPE: Medicare

Benefits Offered: Chiropractic, Dental, Disease Management, Home Care, Inpatient SNF, Physical Therapy, Podiatry, Prescription, Psychiatric, Vision, Wellness

Type of Coverage
Individual, Medicare

Geographic Areas Served
Available within multiple states

Subscriber Information
Average Monthly Fee Per Subscriber
(Employee + Employer Contribution):
Employee Only (Self): Varies
Medicare: Varies
Average Annual Deductible Per Subscriber:
Employee Only (Self): Varies
Medicare: Varies
Average Subscriber Co-Payment:
Primary Care Physician: Varies
Non-Network Physician: Varies
Prescription Drugs: Varies
Hospital ER: Varies
Home Health Care: Varies
Home Health Care Max. Days/Visits Covered: Varies
Nursing Home: Varies
Nursing Home Max. Days/Visits Covered: Varies

Key Personnel
CEO . . . . .George C Halvorson
CFO/Executive VP . . . . .Kathy Lancaster
Sr VP/Community Benefit . . . . .Raymond J Baxter, PhD
SVP, Corp Development. . . . . .Chris Grant
SVP, Chief Diversity Offc . . . . .Ronald Knox
Consultant . . . . .Louise L Liang, MD
Exec VP/Health Plan Ops . . . . .Bernard J Tyson
Exec Dir, Clinical Care . . . . .Scott Young, MD
EVP/Health Plan Operation . . . . .Arthur M Southam, MD
SVP, Communications . . . . .Diane Gage Lofgren
SVP, General Counsel. . . . . .Steven Zatkin
SVP, Human Resources . . . . .Paul Records
SVP, Chief Info Officer . . . . .Phil Fasano
SVP, Quality Care . . . . .Jed Weissberg, MD

144   Kern Family Health Care
9700 Stockdale Highway
Bakersfield, CA 93311
Toll-Free: 800-391-2000
Phone: 661-664-5000
www.kernfamilyhealthcare.com
Subsidiary of: Kern Health Systems
Non-Profit Organization: Yes
Year Founded: 1996
Number of Affiliated Hospitals: 9
Number of Primary Care Physicians: 213
Number of Referral/Specialty Physicians: 400
Total Enrollment: 97,000
State Enrollment: 90,074

Healthplan and Services Defined
PLAN TYPE: HMO
Model Type: Network
Benefits Offered: Disease Management, Wellness
Offers Demand Management Patient Information Service: Yes
DMPI Services Offered: 24 Hour Nurse Advice Hotline

Type of Coverage
Individual, Medicaid

Key Personnel
Chief Executive Officer .Carol Sorrell, RN
Chief Financial Officer .Keith Quinlinvan
Chief Operations Officer. . . . . .Becky Davenport
Chief Compliance Officer . . . . .Clayton Carlos, MPA

Manager, Marketing . . . . .Louis Iturriria
661-664-5120
louiei@khs-net.com
Associate Medical Dir . . . . .G. Remmington Brooks, MD
Health Services Officer. . . . . .Bob Woodard
Manager, Marketing . . . . .Louis Iturriria
661-664-5120
louiei@khs-net.com

145   L.A. Care Health Plan
555 West 5th Street
29th Floor
Los Angeles, CA 90013-3036
Toll-Free: 888-452-2273
Phone: 213-694-1250
Fax: 213-694-1246
webmaster@lacare.org
www.lacare.org
Non-Profit Organization: Yes
Year Founded: 1994
Number of Affiliated Hospitals: 83
Number of Primary Care Physicians: 3,555
Number of Referral/Specialty Physicians: 6,286
Total Enrollment: 857,252
State Enrollment: 836,724

Healthplan and Services Defined
PLAN TYPE: HMO
Model Type: Staff
Benefits Offered: Dental, Vision, Comprehensive Health Coverage, Medical

Type of Coverage
Medicaid, Healthy Families, L.A. Care's Healt

Geographic Areas Served
Los Angeles County

Key Personnel
Chief Executive Officer . . . . .Howard A Kahn
Chief Legal Officer .Augustavia J Haydel
Chief Financial Officer . . . . .W Randy Stone
Chief Medical Officer . . . . .Elaine Batchlor, MD
Public Relations Spec. .Marissa Jiminez
213-694-1250
mjiminez@lacare.org

146   Lakeside Community Healthcare Network
777A Flower Street
Glendale, CA 91201
Toll-Free: 888-472-7787
Phone: 808-637-2000
info@lakesidecommunityhealthcare.com
www.lakesidecommunityhealthcare.com
For Profit Organization: Yes
Year Founded: 1997
Number of Primary Care Physicians: 300
Number of Referral/Specialty Physicians: 1,500
Total Enrollment: 250,000
State Enrollment: 250,000

Healthplan and Services Defined
PLAN TYPE: HMO
Model Type: IPA

Key Personnel
President/CEO. . . . . .Francesco Federico, MD
EVP, Corporate Dev . . . . .Keith S Richman, MD
COO. . . . . .Joan Rose, MPH
CFO. . . . . .Kermit Newman
SVP, Medical Operations . . . . .Jeffrey Hay
Medical Director. . . . . .Ziad Dabuni, MD
Chief Medical Officer. . . . . .Bernard Siegel, MD

Media Contact . . . . .Pamela Pollock
pam.pollock@lakesidecommunityhealthcare.

147 Landmark Healthplan of California

1750 Howe Avenue
Suite 300
Sacramento, CA 95825-3369
Toll-Free: 800-638-4557
Phone: 916-646-3477
Fax: 916-929-2293
info@LMhealthcare.com
www.landmarkhealthcare.com
For Profit Organization: Yes
Year Founded: 1985
Number of Referral/Specialty Physicians: 4,500
Total Enrollment: 150,000

Healthplan and Services Defined
PLAN TYPE: HMO/PPO
Model Type: IPA, Network
Plan Specialty: Chiropractic, Acupuncture
Benefits Offered: Chiropractic, Acupuncture

Type of Payment Plans Offered
Combination FFS & DFFS

Geographic Areas Served
California

Network Qualifications
Pre-Admission Certification: Yes

Peer Review Type
Utilization Review: Yes
Case Management: Yes

Key Personnel
President/CEO . . . . .George W Vieth, Jr
VP/CFO. . . . . .Thomas P Klammer
VP Operations/COO . . . . .Debra Tull
VP, Sales & Marketing . . . . .Guy Shields
VP/Chief Clinical Officer .Joel Stevans, DC
Sales Account Manager . . . . .Michelle Kulton
800-638-4557
mkulton@lmhealthcare.com

148 Liberty Dental Plan

3200 El Camino Real
Suite 290
Irvine, CA 92602
Toll-Free: 888-703-6999
www.libertydentalplan.com
For Profit Organization: Yes

Healthplan and Services Defined
PLAN TYPE: Dental
Other Type: Dental HMO
Plan Specialty: Dental
Benefits Offered: Dental

Type of Coverage
Commercial

Key Personnel
Chairman & CEO . . . . .Amir Neshat, DDS
Executive Vice President. . . . . .John Carvelli
Chief Operating Officer . . . . .Stu Gray
VP, Liberty Nevada. . . . . .Randy Brecher
VP, Business Development. .Bill Henderson
Chief Financial Officer. . . . . .Maja Kapic
Dental Director .Richard Hague, DMD, MPA
VP, Client Services. . . . . .Marsha Hazlewood
Dental Dir, Utiliz Mgmt. . . . . .Brian Benjamin, DDS
Dir, Administrative Svcs . . . . .Rob Linfield
Gen Mgr, Nevada Operation. . . . . .Terry Allen

149 Los Angeles County Public Healthcare

313 N Figueroa Street
6th Floor W
Los Angeles, CA 90012-2659
Toll-Free: 800-427-8700
Phone: 800-475-5550
Fax: 626-299-7251
www.ladhs.org
Subsidiary of: Los Angeles County Department of Health Services
Non-Profit Organization: Yes
Year Founded: 1983
Federally Qualified: Yes
Number of Affiliated Hospitals: 12
Number of Primary Care Physicians: 800
Total Enrollment: 700,000

Healthplan and Services Defined
PLAN TYPE: HMO
Model Type: Staff
Benefits Offered: Prescription

Type of Coverage
Catastrophic Illness Benefit: Unlimited

Geographic Areas Served
Los Angeles County

Subscriber Information
Average Monthly Fee Per Subscriber
(Employee + Employer Contribution):
Employee Only (Self): $143.05
Employee & 1 Family Member: $286.15
Employee & 2 Family Members: $332.01
Average Subscriber Co-Payment:
Primary Care Physician: $5.00
Prescription Drugs: $4.00
Home Health Care Max. Days/Visits Covered: Unlimited
Nursing Home Max. Days/Visits Covered: 60 days

Network Qualifications
Pre-Admission Certification: Yes

Peer Review Type
Utilization Review: Yes
Second Surgical Opinion: Yes
Case Management: Yes

Accreditation Certification
TJC Accreditation, Medicare Approved, Utilization Review, State
Licensure, Quality Assurance Program

Key Personnel
Interim Director. . . . . .John F Schunhoff, PhD
Interim Admin Deputy .Gregory Polk, MPA
Planning & Prog Oversight . . . . .Cheri Todoroff, MPH
Chief Network Officer . . . . .Carol Meyer
Interim Chief Medical Off. . . . . .Gail V Anderson Jr, MD
Chief Nursing Officer . . . . .Vivian C Branchick, RN
Director, Ambulatory Care . . . . .Gretchen McGinley
Chief Information Officer. . . . . .Kevin Lynch, MS

150 Managed Health Network

2370 Kerner Blvd
San Rafael, CA 94901
Toll-Free: 800-327-2133
Phone: 714-898-8311
Fax: 714-934-5555
marketing@mhn.com
www.mhn.com
Subsidiary of: Health Net Inc
For Profit Organization: Yes
Year Founded: 1974
Number of Affiliated Hospitals: 1,400
Number of Primary Care Physicians: 44,000
Total Enrollment: 10,000,000

Healthplan and Services Defined
  PLAN TYPE: PPO
  Model Type: IPA, Group
  Plan Specialty: Behavioral Health, Disease Management
  Benefits Offered: Behavioral Health, Disease Management,
    Prescription, Substance Abuse

Type of Coverage
  Commercial, TRICARE, EAP

Type of Payment Plans Offered
  POS, FFS

Geographic Areas Served
  Nationwide

Network Qualifications
  Pre-Admission Certification: Yes

Peer Review Type
  Case Management: Yes

Publishes and Distributes Report Card: Yes

Accreditation Certification
  URAC, NCQA

Key Personnel
  President/CEO . . . . .Juanell Hefner
  Chief Medical Officer . . . . .Ian A Schaffer
  Chief Sales Officer. . . . . .Gidget Peddie
  Media Contact. . . . . .Gina Clemente
    415-460-8054
    gina.clemente@mhn.com
  Media Contact . . . . .Margita Thompson
    818-676-7912
    margita.thompson@healthnet.com

Specialty Managed Care Partners
  Enters into Contracts with Regional Business Coalitions: Yes

151 March Vision Care
6701 Center Drive West
Suite 790
Los Angeles, CA 90045
Toll-Free: 888-493-4070
marchinfo@marchvisioncare.com
www.marchvisioncare.com
For Profit Organization: Yes
Total Enrollment: 1,800,000

Healthplan and Services Defined
  PLAN TYPE: Vision
  Plan Specialty: Vision
  Benefits Offered: Vision

Type of Coverage
  Commercial

Geographic Areas Served
  Nationwide

Key Personnel
  Founder & CEO. . . . . .Glenville A March, Jr, MD
  Founder & EVP . . . . .Cabrini T March, MD

152 MD Care Healthplan
1640 E Hill Street
Signal Hill, CA 90755
Toll-Free: 888-322-2730
Phone: 562-344-3400
Fax: 866-237-3578
www.mdcareadvantage.com

Healthplan and Services Defined
  PLAN TYPE: Medicare

Type of Coverage
  Medicare

Key Personnel
  Principal . . . . .Minh N Nguyen

153 Medfocus Radiology Network
2811 Wilshire Boulevard
Suite 900
Santa Monica, CA 90403
Toll-Free: 800-398-8999
Phone: 310-828-4472
Fax: 800-950-4700
webmaster@medfocus.net
www.medfocuslogin.net
Year Founded: 1988
Number of Primary Care Physicians: 3,400

Healthplan and Services Defined
  PLAN TYPE: PPO
  Model Type: Network
  Plan Specialty: UR

Geographic Areas Served
  42 States, including District of Columbia and Puerto Rico

Peer Review Type
  Utilization Review: Yes
  Second Surgical Opinion: Yes

Accreditation Certification
  NCQA

Key Personnel
  President/CEO . . . . .Catherine Lewis
  CFO. . . . . .Gus Grouel
  Marketing . . . . .Brandon Beaver
    bbeaver@medfocus.net
  Medical Affairs . . . . .Stephen Meisel, MD
  Provider Services . . . . .Steven Casper
  Sales . . . . .Tom Quinn

154 Mida Dental Plan
Acquired by United Concordia

155 Molina Healthcare: Corporate Office
200 Oceangate
Suite 100
Long Beach, CA 90802
Toll-Free: 888-562-5442
Phone: 562-435-3666
Fax: 562-499-0790
www.molinahealthcare.com
Secondary Address: 2277 Fair Oaks Blvd, Suite 195, Sacramento, CA
  95825
For Profit Organization: Yes
Year Founded: 1980
Physician Owned Organization: Yes
Number of Affiliated Hospitals: 84
Number of Primary Care Physicians: 2,167
Number of Referral/Specialty Physicians: 6,184
Total Enrollment: 1,400,000

Healthplan and Services Defined
  PLAN TYPE: HMO
  Model Type: Network
  Benefits Offered: Chiropractic, Dental, Home Care, Inpatient SNF,
    Long-Term Care, Podiatry, Vision

Type of Coverage
  Commercial, Medicare, Supplemental Medicare, Medicaid

Geographic Areas Served
  Los Angeles, Riverside, San Bernardino, Sacramento, Yolo and San
  Diego counties

Accreditation Certification
URAC, NCQA

Key Personnel
President.................................J Mario Molina, MD
Executive VP/CFO.........................John C Molina, JD
COO.......................................Terry T Bayer, JD
VP Legal Affairs...........................Mark L Andrews
VP Research & Development..............Martha Bernadett, MD
VP Medical Affairs.....................Richard A Helmer, MD
Chief Information Officer...................David W Erickson
VP Finance.................................Harvey A Fein
Chief Marketing Officer......................Janice Hopkins
Chief Medical Officer...................James W Howatt, MD

156 Omni IPA/Medcore Medical Group

2609 E Hammer Lane
Stockton, CA 95210
Toll-Free: 877-963-2673
Phone: 209-320-2600
Fax: 209-320-2644
webmaster@medcoreipa.com
www.medcoreipa.com
Year Founded: 1985
Number of Primary Care Physicians: 400

Healthplan and Services Defined
PLAN TYPE: Other
Other Type: IPA

Geographic Areas Served
San Joaquin County

157 On Lok Lifeways

1333 Bush Street
San Francisco, CA 94109
Phone: 415-292-8888
Fax: 415-292-8745
info@onlok.org
www.onlok.org
Non-Profit Organization: Yes
Year Founded: 1971
Number of Affiliated Hospitals: 7
Number of Primary Care Physicians: 10
Number of Referral/Specialty Physicians: 100
Total Enrollment: 1,000
State Enrollment: 942

Healthplan and Services Defined
PLAN TYPE: HMO
Model Type: Staff
Benefits Offered: Home Care, Long-Term Care, Physical Therapy,
Prescription, Vision, Wellness

Type of Coverage
Medicaid
Catastrophic Illness Benefit: Covered

Geographic Areas Served
San Francisco, Fremont, Newark, Union City and Santa Clara County

Subscriber Information
Average Monthly Fee Per Subscriber
(Employee + Employer Contribution):
Employee & 1 Family Member: None if medicare/med
Medicare: $2100.00
Average Subscriber Co-Payment:
Home Health Care Max. Days/Visits Covered: Unlimited
Nursing Home Max. Days/Visits Covered: Unlimited

Accreditation Certification
TJC Accreditation, Medicare Approved, Utilization Review,
Pre-Admission Certification, State Licensure, Quality Assurance
Program

Key Personnel
Executive Director/CEO..................Robert E Edmondson
CFO...Sue Wong
Chief Administrative Offc.........................Amy Shin
Dir, Policy & Govt Rel.....................Eileen Kunz, MPH
Dir, Program Operations.......................Grace Li, MHA
Dir, Regulatory Affairs...........................Jerry Hill
Chief Medical Officer.....................Cheryl Phillips, MD
Dir, Technical Assistance...............Gretchen Brickson, MPH

158 Orange County Foundation for Medical Care

300 S Flower Street
Orange, CA 92868
Toll-Free: 800-345-8643
Phone: 714-978-5048
Fax: 714-634-4167
info@ocfmc.com
www.ocfmc.com
Non-Profit Organization: Yes
Year Founded: 1959
Number of Affiliated Hospitals: 283
Number of Primary Care Physicians: 6,000
Total Enrollment: 1,100,000

Healthplan and Services Defined
PLAN TYPE: PPO
Other Type: EPO
Model Type: Network
Plan Specialty: Medical
Benefits Offered: Claims Management/Utilization Management, Case
Management/Claims Repricing/Customer Service/Provider
Services/Cobra
Offers Demand Management Patient Information Service: Yes

Type of Payment Plans Offered
DFFS

Geographic Areas Served
Orange County, Los Angeles County and Statewide

Subscriber Information
Average Monthly Fee Per Subscriber
(Employee + Employer Contribution):
Employee Only (Self): $5.00
Employee & 1 Family Member: $5.00
Employee & 2 Family Members: $5.00
Average Annual Deductible Per Subscriber:
Employee Only (Self): $500.00
Employee & 1 Family Member: $500.00
Employee & 2 Family Members: $250.00
Average Subscriber Co-Payment:
Primary Care Physician: $10.00
Non-Network Physician: $35.00
Hospital ER: $50.00

Network Qualifications
Pre-Admission Certification: Yes

Peer Review Type
Utilization Review: Yes
Second Surgical Opinion: Yes
Case Management: Yes

Accreditation Certification
URAC
TJC Accreditation, Medicare Approved, Utilization Review, State
Licensure, Quality Assurance Program

Key Personnel
Medical Director.......................Mark E Krugman, MD
Sales ....Jaime Abreu
714-941-5468
jabreu@ocfmc.com

159 Pacific Dental Benefits

Acquired by UnitedHealthcare Dental

160 Pacific Foundation for Medical Care

3033 Cleveland Avenue
104
Santa Rosa, CA 95403
Toll-Free: 800-548-7677
Phone: 707-525-4281
Fax: 707-525-4311
jnacol@rhs.org
www.pfmc.org
Non-Profit Organization: Yes
Year Founded: 1957
Number of Affiliated Hospitals: 75
Number of Primary Care Physicians: 3,000
Number of Referral/Specialty Physicians: 4,430
Total Enrollment: 300,000

Healthplan and Services Defined
  PLAN TYPE: Multiple
  Model Type: Network
  Plan Specialty: EPO, PPO, LOCO

Geographic Areas Served
  Sonoma, Alameda, Contra Costa, El Dorado, Imperial, Napa,
  Nevada, Placer, Sacramento, San Diego, Solano, Marin and Yolo
  counties. Butte, Colusa, Glenn, Lassen, Modoc, Pluma, Shasta,
  Sierra, Siskiquou, Sutter counties

Network Qualifications
  Pre-Admission Certification: Yes

Peer Review Type
  Utilization Review: Yes
  Second Surgical Opinion: Yes
  Case Management: Yes

Publishes and Distributes Report Card: No

Key Personnel
  Chief Executive Officer . . . . .John Nacol
    707-525-4370
    jnacol@rhs.org
  Medical Director . . . . .William Pitt
  Claims. . . . . .Sandy Sylvers
  Network Contracting. . . . . .Kathy Pass
  Medical Review Services .Nancy Manchee
    619-401-6843
    nmanchee@rhs.org
  Marketing Manager. . . . . .Kathy Pass
  Medical Affairs . . . . .William Pitt, MD
  Member Services. . . . . .Kathy Pass
    707-525-4281
    kpass@rhs.org
  Provider Services. . . . . .Kathy Pass
    707-525-4281
    kpass@rhs.org

Specialty Managed Care Partners
  Enters into Contracts with Regional Business Coalitions: No

161 Pacific Health Alliance

1350 Old Bayshore Highway
Suite 560
Burlingame, CA 94010
Toll-Free: 800-533-4742
Phone: 650-375-5800
Fax: 650-375-5820
pha@pacifichealthalliance.com
www.pacifichealthalliance.com
For Profit Organization: Yes
Year Founded: 1986

Number of Affiliated Hospitals: 300
Number of Primary Care Physicians: 38,000
Number of Referral/Specialty Physicians: 1,500
Total Enrollment: 338,000
State Enrollment: 197,000

Healthplan and Services Defined
  PLAN TYPE: PPO
  Model Type: Group
  Plan Specialty: Behavioral Health, Chiropractic, EPO, Lab, Worker's
    Compensation, UR
  Benefits Offered: Behavioral Health, Chiropractic, Dental, Home
    Care, Inpatient SNF, Long-Term Care, Physical Therapy, Podiatry,
    Psychiatric, Transplant, Vision, Worker's Compensation

Type of Coverage
  Commercial, Individual, Indemnity

Type of Payment Plans Offered
  DFFS, FFS

Geographic Areas Served
  California, Nevada

Network Qualifications
  Pre-Admission Certification: Yes

Peer Review Type
  Utilization Review: Yes
  Second Surgical Opinion: Yes
  Case Management: Yes

Publishes and Distributes Report Card: No

Accreditation Certification
  TJC Accreditation, Medicare Approved, Utilization Review,
    Pre-Admission Certification, State Licensure, Quality Assurance
    Program

Key Personnel
  President/CEO . . . . .Lawrence Cappel, PhD
    mail4pha@aol.com
  Director . . . . .Denis Collins
  COO . . . . .Robert Mackler, MA
  Director of Claims . . . . .Alison Sparks
    asparks@pacifichealthalliance.com
  Network Contracting . . . . .Alison Sparks
  Credentialing . . . . .Lauren Bellone
  Marketing . . . . .Lawrence Cappel
  Medical Affairs . . . . .John Clark, MD
  Executive VP . . . . .Robert Mackler, MA
    rmackler@pacifichealthalliance.com
  Pharmacy . . . . .Robert Mackler

Average Claim Compensation
  Physician's Fees Charged: 70%
  Hospital's Fees Charged: 75%

Specialty Managed Care Partners
  Daughters of Charity, Saint Rose Hospital, San Monterry
  Enters into Contracts with Regional Business Coalitions: No

162 Pacific IPA

9700 Flair Drive
El Monte, CA 91731
Toll-Free: 888-888-7472
Phone: 626-652-3526
Fax: 626-401-1670
admin@pacificipa.com
http://pacificipa.net
Year Founded: 1986
Number of Primary Care Physicians: 800

Healthplan and Services Defined
  PLAN TYPE: Other
  Other Type: IPA
  Model Type: IPA
  Benefits Offered: Disease Management, Wellness

163 PacifiCare Dental and Vision Administrators

3110 Lake Center Drive
Mail Stop LC05-131
Santa Ana, CA 92704-6921
Toll-Free: 800-228-3384
Fax: 714-513-6486
www.pacificare-dental.com
Mailing Address: PO Box 30968, Salt Lake City, UT 84130-0968
Subsidiary of: UnitedHealthCare
For Profit Organization: Yes
Year Founded: 1973
Number of Primary Care Physicians: 8,986
Number of Referral/Specialty Physicians: 2,705
Total Enrollment: 140,462

Healthplan and Services Defined
  PLAN TYPE: Multiple
  Model Type: IPA
  Plan Specialty: Dental, Vision
  Benefits Offered: Dental, Vision

Type of Coverage
  Commercial, Individual, Indemnity, Medicare

Type of Payment Plans Offered
  POS, Capitated, FFS

Geographic Areas Served
  Arizona, California, Colorado, Nevada, Oklahoma, Oregon, Texas
  and Washington

Network Qualifications
  Pre-Admission Certification: Yes

Peer Review Type
  Utilization Review: Yes

Key Personnel
  President/CEO . . . . .Jerome V Vaccaro, MD
  VP/General Manager. . . . . .Claire L Hannan, CPA
  CFO . . . . .Christopher D Boles
  VP Information Services. . . . . .Kerry Matsumoto
  VP Sales/Marketing . . . . .John W Whalley

164 PacifiCare Health Systems

5995 Plaza Drive
Cypress, CA 90630
Toll-Free: 800-411-0191
Phone: 714-952-1121
Fax: 714-236-5803
www.pacificare.com
Mailing Address: PO Box 6006, Cypress, CA 90630-0006
Subsidiary of: UnitedHealthCare
For Profit Organization: Yes
Year Founded: 1978
Number of Affiliated Hospitals: 305
Number of Primary Care Physicians: 1,050
Number of Referral/Specialty Physicians: 1,791
Total Enrollment: 1,915,829
State Enrollment: 1,345,473

Healthplan and Services Defined
  PLAN TYPE: HMO
  Model Type: Network
  Benefits Offered: Disease Management, Prescription, Wellness

Type of Coverage
  Commercial, Individual, Indemnity, Medicare

Geographic Areas Served
  California, Texas, Oklahoma, Oregon & Washington

Peer Review Type
  Second Surgical Opinion: Yes

Publishes and Distributes Report Card: Yes

Accreditation Certification
  TJC Accreditation, Medicare Approved, Utilization Review,
    Pre-Admission Certification, State Licensure, Quality Assurance
    Program

Key Personnel
  Chairman/CEO . . . . .Howard Phanstiel
  Exec VP/CFO. . . . . .Gregory W Scott
  Vice President . . . . .Edward Cymerys
  Facilities Mangager. . . . . .Pam Palumbo
  Chief Medical Officer . . . . .Sam Ho
  Director Member Services. . . . . .Judu Bernauer
  Chief Information Officer. . . . . .Mike Connelly
  Provider Services . . . . .Carol Ackerman

Specialty Managed Care Partners
  Enters into Contracts with Regional Business Coalitions: Yes

165 PacifiCare of California

5995 Plaza Drive
Cypress, CA 90630
Toll-Free: 800-624-8822
Phone: 909-274-3045
www.pacificare.com
Mailing Address: PO Box 6006, Cypress, CA 90963
Subsidiary of: UnitedHealthCare
For Profit Organization: Yes
Year Founded: 1978
Number of Affiliated Hospitals: 304
Number of Primary Care Physicians: 8,271
Number of Referral/Specialty Physicians: 1,466
Total Enrollment: 1,283,000

Healthplan and Services Defined
  PLAN TYPE: HMO
  Model Type: Network
  Benefits Offered: Behavioral Health, Dental, Prescription, Vision, Life

Type of Coverage
  Commercial, Individual, Indemnity, Medicare

Type of Payment Plans Offered
  POS, DFFS, Capitated, FFS, Combination FFS & DFFS

Geographic Areas Served
  Licensed in areas comprising 90% of California's population

Subscriber Information
  Average Monthly Fee Per Subscriber
    (Employee + Employer Contribution):
      Employee Only (Self): $139.68
      Employee & 1 Family Member: $312.69
      Employee & 2 Family Members: $428.93
      Medicare: $19.80
  Average Subscriber Co-Payment:
      Primary Care Physician: $5.00
      Prescription Drugs: $5.00
      Hospital ER: $35.00
      Home Health Care: $5.00
      Home Health Care Max. Days/Visits Covered: As necessary

Network Qualifications
  Pre-Admission Certification: Yes

Peer Review Type
  Utilization Review: Yes
  Case Management: Yes

Publishes and Distributes Report Card: Yes

Accreditation Certification
  NCQA
  TJC Accreditation, Medicare Approved, Utilization Review,
    Pre-Admission Certification, State Licensure, Quality Assurance
    Program

Key Personnel
President . . . . James Frey
james.frey@phs.com

166 Partnership HealthPlan of California

360 Campus Lane
Suite 100
Fairfield, CA 94534-1400
Toll-Free: 800-863-4144
Phone: 707-863-4100
Fax: 707-863-4117
www.partnershiphp.org
Non-Profit Organization: Yes
Year Founded: 1994
Total Enrollment: 93,000

Healthplan and Services Defined
PLAN TYPE: Medicare
Other Type: Medicare HMO
Benefits Offered: Chiropractic, Inpatient SNF, Long-Term Care, Vision

Type of Coverage
Individual, Medicare, Medicaid

Geographic Areas Served
Miami-Dade, Broward and Palm Beach counties

Accreditation Certification
NCQA

Key Personnel
CEO. . . . . Jack Horn
Director, Health Services . . . . Peggy Hoover
Chief Financial Officer . . . . Gary Erickson
Director, Claims . . . . Paula Frederickson
Deputy Exective Director . . . . Elizabeth Gibboney
Director, Human Resources . . . . Sue Monez
Chief Medical Officer . . . . Ronald W Chapman, MD
Director, Member Services . . . . Deborah Shafer
Chief Information Officer . . . . Todd Morgan
Dir, Provider Relations . . . . Mary Kerlin

167 Physical Therapy Provider Network

26635 W Agoura Road
Suite 250
Calabasas, CA 91302
Toll-Free: 800-766-7876
Phone: 818-883-7876
Fax: 818-737-0270
info@ptpn.com
www.ptpn.com
For Profit Organization: Yes
Year Founded: 1985
Physician Owned Organization: No
Federally Qualified: No
Number of Referral/Specialty Physicians: 1,200
Total Enrollment: 1,100,000

Healthplan and Services Defined
PLAN TYPE: Multiple
Model Type: Network
Benefits Offered: Physical Therapy, Occupational Therapy, Hand Therapy, Pediatric Therapy and Speech/Language Therapy
Offers Demand Management Patient Information Service: No

Geographic Areas Served
Arizona, California, Colorado, Florida, Georgia, Louisiana, Massachusetts, Maryland, Maine, Michigan, Missouri, Mississippi, New Hampshire, New Jersey, New York, Ohio, Oklahoma, Pennsylvania, Rhode Island, Tennessee, Texas, Vermont, West Virginia

Network Qualifications
Pre-Admission Certification: Yes

Peer Review Type
Utilization Review: Yes
Case Management: Yes

Publishes and Distributes Report Card: No

Accreditation Certification
State Licensure

Key Personnel
President/CEO . . . . Michael Weinper
Director, Claims . . . . Nancy Rothenberg
Network Contracting . . . . Stephen Moore
Medical Officer . . . . Mitchel Kaye
Information Services . . . . Kevin Gentry
Media Director . . . . Stephen Moore
smoore@ptpn.com

Specialty Managed Care Partners
Enters into Contracts with Regional Business Coalitions: No

168 Preferred Utilization Management Inc

5356 Clayton Road
Suite 201
Concord, CA 94521
Phone: 925-844-3100
Fax: 925-844-3124
www.pumi.com
For Profit Organization: Yes
Year Founded: 1982

Healthplan and Services Defined
PLAN TYPE: Other
Other Type: VRO
Model Type: URO
Plan Specialty: Chiropractic
Benefits Offered: Concurrent Review and Retro-Review, prospective review

Type of Coverage
Health & Workers Comp, Pers Injury

Geographic Areas Served
Nationwide

Peer Review Type
Utilization Review: Yes

Key Personnel
President/CEO . . . . Ronald Cataldo, DC
CFO. . . . . Jeanette Cataldo

Specialty Managed Care Partners
ChiroSource Inc, Chiropractic Health Plan of California Inc, Basic Chiropractic Health Plan Inc, Preferred Therapy Provider of America
Enters into Contracts with Regional Business Coalitions: Yes

169 Premier Access Insurance/Access Dental

8890 Cal Center Drive
Sacramento, CA 95826-3200
Toll-Free: 888-715-0760
Phone: 916-646-9000
Fax: 916-563-0488
customerservice@premierlife.com
www.premierppo.com
Mailing Address: PO Box 659010, Sacramento, CA 95865-9010
For Profit Organization: Yes
Year Founded: 1998
Number of Primary Care Physicians: 1,000
Total Enrollment: 125,000

Healthplan and Services Defined
PLAN TYPE: PPO

Model Type: Network
Plan Specialty: Dental
Benefits Offered: Dental

Type of Payment Plans Offered
FFS

Geographic Areas Served
California and outside of California

Accreditation Certification
TJC Accreditation, Medicare Approved, Utilization Review, Pre-Admission Certification, State Licensure, Quality Assurance Program

Key Personnel
President . . . . .Reza Abbaszadeh, DDS
CFO. . . . . .Katherine Smith
VP, Plan Administrator . . . . .Terri Abbaszaden
Dental . . . . .Kerry Hanson, MD
Chief Marketing Officer .Richard Fulton
Director Membership Accounts . . . . .Marie Brandon
Information Tech Manager . . . . .Hideo Kakiuchi
Sr Network Administrator . . . . .Will Woodsone
Director, Sales . . . . .Daryl Webster

170 Primecare Dental Plan

9500 Haven Avenue
Suite 125
Rancho Cucamonga, CA 91730
Toll-Free: 800-937-3400
Phone: 909-483-8310
Fax: 909-483-5351
info@primecaredental.net
www.primecaredental.net
Subsidiary of: Jaimini Health Inc. Companies, Healthdent of California
For Profit Organization: Yes
Year Founded: 1983
Physician Owned Organization: Yes
Number of Referral/Specialty Physicians: 3,700
Total Enrollment: 17,000

Healthplan and Services Defined
PLAN TYPE: Dental
Model Type: Staff
Plan Specialty: Dental
Benefits Offered: Dental
Offers Demand Management Patient Information Service: Yes

Type of Coverage
Commercial, Individual

Type of Payment Plans Offered
DFFS, Capitated

Geographic Areas Served
Alameda, Butte, Colusa, Contra Costa, El Dorado, Fresno, Glenn, Kern, Kings, Los Angeles, Madera, Mariposa, Merced Monterey, Napa, Nevada, Orange, Placer, Riverside, Sacramento, San Benito, San Bernardino, San Diego, San Francisco, San Joaquin, San Luis Opispo, San Mateo, Santa Barbara, Santa Clara, Santa Cruz, Shasta, Siskiyou, Solano, Sonoma, Stanislaus, Sutter, Tehama, Tuolumne, Tulare, Ventura, Yolo, and Yuba counties

Subscriber Information
Average Monthly Fee Per Subscriber
(Employee + Employer Contribution):
Employee Only (Self): $9.50
Employee & 1 Family Member: $12.00
Employee & 2 Family Members: $14.00

Network Qualifications
Pre-Admission Certification: Yes

Peer Review Type
Utilization Review: Yes

Publishes and Distributes Report Card: No

Accreditation Certification
URAC, NCQA
Utilization Review

Key Personnel
President and CEO . . . . .Mohender Narula
CFO . . . . .Mahesh Manchandia
COO . . . . .Carolyn Brodt

Specialty Managed Care Partners
Enters into Contracts with Regional Business Coalitions: No

171 PTPN

26635 W Agoura Road
Suite 250
Calabasas, CA 91302
Toll-Free: 800-766-7876
www.ptpn.com
Year Founded: 1985
Number of Primary Care Physicians: 1,200

Healthplan and Services Defined
PLAN TYPE: PPO
Other Type: Rehab Network
Model Type: Network
Plan Specialty: Outpatient Rehabilitation (Physical, Occupational and Speech Therapy)
Benefits Offered: Physical Therapy, Worker's Compensation, Occupational Therapy, Speech Therapy, Physical Therapy, Hand Therapy, Speech/Language Therapy and Pediatric Therapy.

Type of Payment Plans Offered
DFFS

Geographic Areas Served
Nationwide

Network Qualifications
Minimum Years of Practice: 3

Peer Review Type
Utilization Review: Yes

Accreditation Certification
NCQA

Key Personnel
President and CEO . . . . .Michael Weinper, PT
VP . . . . .Nancy Rothenberg
Quality Assurance. . . . . .Michael Kaye
Media Contact. . . . . .Ruben Marroquin
818-737-0207
rmarroquin@ptpn.com

172 SafeGuard Health Enterprises: Corporate Office

95 Enterprise
Suite 200
Aliso Viejo, CA 92656
Toll-Free: 800-880-1800
Phone: 949-425-4300
Fax: 949-425-4308
www.safeguard.net
Subsidiary of: MetLife
For Profit Organization: Yes
Year Founded: 1974
Number of Primary Care Physicians: 2,073
Number of Referral/Specialty Physicians: 2,030
Total Enrollment: 1,800,000

Healthplan and Services Defined
PLAN TYPE: Dental
Other Type: Dental HMO
Model Type: IPA

Plan Specialty: ASO, Dental, Vision
Benefits Offered: Dental, Vision

Type of Coverage
Individual, Indemnity, Medicaid

Type of Payment Plans Offered
DFFS, Capitated

Geographic Areas Served
California, Texas, Florida

Subscriber Information
Average Annual Deductible Per Subscriber:
Employee Only (Self): $50.00
Employee & 1 Family Member: $100.00
Employee & 2 Family Members: $150.00

Network Qualifications
Pre-Admission Certification: Yes

Peer Review Type
Utilization Review: Yes

Publishes and Distributes Report Card: No

Key Personnel
Chairman/CEO ....James E Buncher
949-425-4500
President/COO ....Stephen J Baker
SVP/CFO ....Dennis L Gates
VP/CIO ....Michael J Lauffenburger
SVP/General Counsel ....Ronald I Brendzel
Dir/Human Resources ....William Wolff
Director ....Jack R Anderson

Specialty Managed Care Partners
Enters into Contracts with Regional Business Coalitions: Yes

Employer References
State of California, Boeing, County of Los Angeles, Farmers Insurance, Automobile Club

173 San Francisco Health Plan
201 Third Street
7th Floor
San Francisco, CA 94103
Toll-Free: 800-883-7347
Phone: 415-547-7818
Fax: 415-547-7826
memberservices@sfhp.org
www.sfhp.org
Non-Profit Organization: Yes
Year Founded: 1994
Number of Affiliated Hospitals: 6
Number of Primary Care Physicians: 2,300
Total Enrollment: 55,000
State Enrollment: 55,000

Healthplan and Services Defined
PLAN TYPE: HMO
Benefits Offered: Disease Management, Wellness

Type of Coverage
Medicare, Medicaid, Medi-Cal, Healthy Families, Healthy

Geographic Areas Served
San Francisco

Key Personnel
Chief Executive Officer....................John F Grgurina, Jr
Chief Financial Officer.......................John Gregoire
Chief Operating Officer ....Deena Louie
Chief Information Officer ....Sunny Cooper
Compliance Officer..........................Nina Maruyama
Medical Director ....Kelly Pfeifer, MD
General Counsel...........................Richard Rubinstein
Human Res Consultant........................Kate Gormley
Dir, Marketing & Comm......................Bob Menezes
Dir, Clinical Services ....Alison Lum, PharmD

Dir, Clinical Informatics ....Kimberley Higgins-Mays
Dir, Finance ....Skip Bishop
Dir, Technology Services ....Cecil Newton
Dir, Business Services ....Van Wong
Dir, Qual & Performance ....Tammy Fisher
Media Contact ....Bob Memezes
bmenezes@sfhp.org

174 Santa Clara Family Health Plan
210 East Hacienda Avenue
Campbell, CA 95008-6617
Toll-Free: 800-260-2055
Phone: 408-376-2000
Fax: 408-376-2191
mainoffice@scfhp.com
www.scfhp.com
Secondary Address: Mi Pueblo Plaza, 1775 Story Road, Suite 130, San Jose, CA 95122
Non-Profit Organization: Yes
Year Founded: 1997
Number of Affiliated Hospitals: 8
Number of Primary Care Physicians: 890
Number of Referral/Specialty Physicians: 2,309
Total Enrollment: 121,794
State Enrollment: 121,794

Healthplan and Services Defined
PLAN TYPE: HMO
Benefits Offered: Behavioral Health, Disease Management, Prescription, Wellness
Offers Demand Management Patient Information Service: Yes
DMPI Services Offered: 24 hour nurse advice line

Type of Coverage
Commercial, Medicaid, Medicare Advantage SNP, Medi-Cal, H

Geographic Areas Served
Santa Clara County

Subscriber Information
Average Monthly Fee Per Subscriber
(Employee + Employer Contribution):
Employee & 2 Family Members: $18 max per family

Key Personnel
President/CEO ....Christopher Dawes
COO..Jane Ogle
CFO.............................Michael Weatherford
CMO ....R Dennis Collins, MD
General Counsel...........................Sheila Maloney
Provider Relations..........................Lisa Kraymer
Marketing ....Janie Tyre
Member Relations ....Pat McClelland
Pharmacy Director..........................Angeli Garg
Public Relations ....Elisabeth Handler

Specialty Managed Care Partners
Medimpact

175 SCAN Health Plan
3800 Kilroy Airport Way
Suite 100
Long Beach, CA 90806
Toll-Free: 800-247-5091
Phone: 562-989-5100
Fax: 562-989-5200
sstanislaw@scanhealthplan.com
www.scanhealthplan.com
Non-Profit Organization: Yes
Year Founded: 1983
Number of Affiliated Hospitals: 151
Number of Primary Care Physicians: 6,560
Number of Referral/Specialty Physicians: 17,186

Total Enrollment: 128,272
State Enrollment: 12,283

Healthplan and Services Defined
 PLAN TYPE: HMO
  Plan Specialty: Medicare

Type of Coverage
 Medicare

Geographic Areas Served
 California & Arizona

Subscriber Information
 Average Annual Deductible Per Subscriber:
  Medicare: $0
 Average Subscriber Co-Payment:
  Primary Care Physician: $0-$5
  Hospital ER: $50
  Home Health Care: $0
  Nursing Home: $0
  Nursing Home Max. Days/Visits Covered: 100

Key Personnel
 CEO . . . . .Dave Schmidt
 CFO . . . . .Dennis Eder
 Chief Medical Officer . . . . .Timothy Schwab, MD
 CIO . . . . .Merlin Swackhamer
 SVP, Network Management. . . . . .Elizabeth S Russell
 President, SCAN Arizona . . . . .Tom Lescault
 SVP, General Counsel . . . . .Douglas A Jacques, Esq
 SVP, Compliance Officer . . . . .Rebecca Mauritson Learner
 SVP, Business Development . . . . .Henry Osowski
 SVP, Health Care Services . . . . .Deborah A Miller
 SVP, Operations . . . . .Sherry L Stanislaw
 SVP, Human Resources . . . . .Marc J Radner
 SVP, Compliance Officer . . . . .Rebecca Mauritson Learner
 SVP, Sales/Membership .Roger L Lapp

176   Sharp Health Plan

4305 University Ave
Suite 200
San Diego, CA 92105-1694
Toll-Free: 800-359-2002
Phone: 619-228-2429
commercial.sales@sharp.com
www.sharphealthplan.com
Subsidiary of: Sharp HealthCare
Non-Profit Organization: Yes
Total Enrollment: 49,000
State Enrollment: 49,000

Healthplan and Services Defined
 PLAN TYPE: HMO

Geographic Areas Served
 San Diego and Southern Riverside counties

Key Personnel
 CEO & President . . . . .Melissa Hayden Cook
 Chief Business Dev Offc. . . . . .Janet Hoy
 Network Contracting . . . . .Rita Datko
 Mgr, Marketing & Comm . . . . .Roxane Helstrom
 VP, Chief Medical Officer . . . . .Nora Faine, MD
 Member Services . . . . .Leslie Pels Beck
 Sales Director . . . . .Janey Hoy
 Mgr, Marekting & Comm . . . . .Roxane Helstrom
  619-228-2371
  roxane.helstrom@sharp.com

177   Stanislaus Foundation for Medical Care

2339 St Pauls Way
Modesto, CA 95355-3309
Phone: 209-527-1704
Fax: 209-527-5861

sms@stanislausmedicalsociety.com
www.stanislausmedicalsociety.com
Mailing Address: PO Box 576007, Modesto, CA 95357
Non-Profit Organization: Yes
Year Founded: 1957
Number of Affiliated Hospitals: 400
Number of Primary Care Physicians: 27,000
Number of Referral/Specialty Physicians: 5,000

Healthplan and Services Defined
 PLAN TYPE: PPO
  Model Type: Network
  Benefits Offered: Prescription
  Offers Demand Management Patient Information Service: Yes

Geographic Areas Served
 Stanislaus, Tuolumne counties

Network Qualifications
 Pre-Admission Certification: Yes

Publishes and Distributes Report Card: No

Key Personnel
 President . . . . .Krystyna Belski, MD
 President-Elect. . . . . .Peter Broderick, MD
 Treasurer . . . . .C. Alan Yates, MD
 Secretary . . . . .Amarjit Dhaliwal, MD

Specialty Managed Care Partners
 Enters into Contracts with Regional Business Coalitions: No

178   Superior Vision Services, Inc.

11101 White Rock Road
Suite 150
Rancho Cordova, CA 95670
Toll-Free: 800-923-6766
Phone: 9166-852-2290
Fax: 916-852-2290
www.superiorvision.com
Secondary Address: 1855 W Katella Avenue, Suite 100, Orange, CA 92867
For Profit Organization: Yes
Year Founded: 1993
Number of Primary Care Physicians: 46,000
Total Enrollment: 2,000,000

Healthplan and Services Defined
 PLAN TYPE: Vision
  Model Type: Group
  Plan Specialty: Vision, Vision Benefits, Exams, Glasses, Contact Lenses
  Benefits Offered: Vision, Managed Vision Care

Type of Coverage
 Commercial, Indemnity, Medicaid, Catastrophic

Geographic Areas Served
 Nationwide

Subscriber Information
 Average Monthly Fee Per Subscriber
  (Employee + Employer Contribution):
   Employee Only (Self): Varies
   Employee & 1 Family Member: Varies
   Employee & 2 Family Members: Varies
   Medicare: Varies

Accreditation Certification
 AAPI, NCQA

Key Personnel
 President/CEO . . . . .Rick P Corbett
 SVP/Oper & Accts Mgmt . . . . .Kimberley Hess
 SVP/CFO . . . . .Joanna Freeman, CPa
 VP/Prod Dev & Compliance . . . . Lori Hemmingsen-Souza, RN
 VP, Strategic Alliances . . . . .Joy Rausch
 Natl VP/Sales . . . . .Rick Kjerstad, CEBS
 Reg VP/Sales . . . . .Dan Moore

Reg VP/Sales . . . . Roger Watson
Reg VP/Sales . . . . Greg Beck
Reg VP/Sales . . . . Kristi Lockwood
VP/Provider Relations . . . . Zon Dunn

179 UDC Dental Care of California

6310 Greenwich Drive
Suite 210
San Diego, CA 92122
Toll-Free: 800-821-1294
Phone: 858-812-8230
Fax: 858-678-0692
www.udcdentalcalifornia.com
For Profit Organization: Yes

Healthplan and Services Defined
PLAN TYPE: Dental
Other Type: Prepaid Dental Plan
Plan Specialty: Dental
Benefits Offered: Dental

Type of Coverage
Commercial

180 United Behavioral Health

425 Market Street
27th Floor
San Francisco, CA 94105
Toll-Free: 800-888-2998
Phone: 415-547-5000
www.unitedbehavioralhealth.com
Subsidiary of: UnitedHealth Group
Year Founded: 1997
Number of Affiliated Hospitals: 3,500
Number of Primary Care Physicians: 85,000
Total Enrollment: 43,000,000

Healthplan and Services Defined
PLAN TYPE: Other
Other Type: EAP
Model Type: Network
Plan Specialty: Behavioral Health
Benefits Offered: Behavioral Health, Prescription, Psychiatric
Offers Demand Management Patient Information Service: Yes

Type of Payment Plans Offered
POS

Geographic Areas Served
Nationwide

Peer Review Type
Case Management: Yes

Publishes and Distributes Report Card: Yes

Accreditation Certification
TJC, URAC, NCQA

Key Personnel
CEO . . . . Gregory A Bayer, PhD
CFO . . . . Randall Odzer
VP, Human Capital . . . . Pamela Russo
COO . . . . Jim Hudak
Chief Strategy Officer . . . . David Whitehouse, MD
Chief Medical Officer . . . . Rhonda Robinson-Beale, MD
Human Capital Partner . . . . Pamela Russo
Chief Information Officer . . . . Kerry Matsumoto
Media Relations . . . . Brad Lotterman
714-445-0453

Specialty Managed Care Partners
Enters into Contracts with Regional Business Coalitions: Yes

181 United Concordia: California

21700 Oxnard Street
Suite 500
Woodland Hills, CA 91367
Toll-Free: 800-876-6432
Fax: 925-463-4869
ucproducer@ucci.com
www.secure.ucci.com
Secondary Address: 4370 La Jolla Village Drive, Suite 429, San Diego, CA 92122, 858-646-3041
For Profit Organization: Yes
Year Founded: 1971
Number of Primary Care Physicians: 111,000
Total Enrollment: 8,000,000

Healthplan and Services Defined
PLAN TYPE: Dental
Plan Specialty: Dental
Benefits Offered: Dental

Type of Coverage
Commercial, Individual

Geographic Areas Served
Military personnel and their families, nationwide

182 UnitedHealthCare of Northern California

5757 Plaza Drive
Cypress, CA 90630
Toll-Free: 800-357-0978
www.uhc.com
Secondary Address: 8880 Cal Center Drive, Suite 300, Sacramento, CA 95826, 866-288-4993
Subsidiary of: UnitedHealth Group
For Profit Organization: Yes
Year Founded: 1986
Total Enrollment: 75,000,000
State Enrollment: 2,300,000

Healthplan and Services Defined
PLAN TYPE: HMO/PPO
Model Type: Network
Benefits Offered: Disease Management, Prescription, Wellness
Offers Demand Management Patient Information Service: Yes

Type of Coverage
Catastrophic Illness Benefit: Covered

Type of Payment Plans Offered
DFFS, Capitated

Geographic Areas Served
Statewide

Subscriber Information
Average Monthly Fee Per Subscriber
(Employee + Employer Contribution):
Employee Only (Self): $120.00
Employee & 1 Family Member: $240.00
Employee & 2 Family Members: $375.00
Average Annual Deductible Per Subscriber:
Employee & 2 Family Members: Varies
Average Subscriber Co-Payment:
Primary Care Physician: $5.00-10.00
Prescription Drugs: $5.00/10.00/25.00
Hospital ER: $50.00
Nursing Home Max. Days/Visits Covered: 120 per year

Publishes and Distributes Report Card: Yes

Accreditation Certification
NCQA
TJC Accreditation, Utilization Review, State Licensure

Key Personnel
President/CEO . . . . Dan Rosenthal
Chief Financial Officer . . . . Peter Horn

Marketing . . . . Devon Waggoner
CMO/West Region . . . . Sandra Nichols, MD
Media Contact . . . . Will Shanley
    will.shanley@uhc.com

Specialty Managed Care Partners
Enters into Contracts with Regional Business Coalitions: Yes

183   UnitedHealthCare of Southern California

5757 Plaza Drive
Cypress, CA 90630
Toll-Free: 800-357-0978
www.uhc.com
Secondary Address: 505 N Brand Blvd, Suite 1200, Glendale, CA
91203
Subsidiary of: UnitedHealth Group
For Profit Organization: Yes
Year Founded: 1987
Total Enrollment: 75,000,000
State Enrollment: 2,300,000

Healthplan and Services Defined
  PLAN TYPE: HMO/PPO
  Model Type: IPA
  Benefits Offered: Disease Management, Prescription, Wellness
  Offers Demand Management Patient Information Service: Yes

Type of Coverage
  Catastrophic Illness Benefit: Unlimited

Type of Payment Plans Offered
  POS

Geographic Areas Served
  Statewide

Subscriber Information
  Average Monthly Fee Per Subscriber
    (Employee + Employer Contribution):
      Employee Only (Self): $120.00
      Employee & 1 Family Member: $240.00
      Employee & 2 Family Members: $370.00
  Average Subscriber Co-Payment:
      Primary Care Physician: $10.00
      Prescription Drugs: $5.00
      Hospital ER: $50.00

Network Qualifications
  Pre-Admission Certification: Yes

Peer Review Type
  Utilization Review: Yes
  Second Surgical Opinion: Yes
  Case Management: Yes

Publishes and Distributes Report Card: Yes

Accreditation Certification
  NCQA
  TJC Accreditation, Medicare Approved, Utilization Review,
    Pre-Admission Certification, State Licensure, Quality Assurance
    Program

Key Personnel
  Chief Executive Officer . . . . David Anderson
  Chief Financial Officer. . . . . Alex Uhm
  Marketing . . . . Devon Waggoner
  Chief Medical Officer . . . . Sandra Nichols, MD
  Media Contact . . . . Will Shanley
    will.shanley@uhc.com

Specialty Managed Care Partners
Enters into Contracts with Regional Business Coalitions: Yes

184   Ventura County Health Care Plan

2323 Knoll Drive
Ventura, CA 93003

Phone: 805-981-5050
Fax: 805-981-5051
vchcp.memberservices@ventura.org
www.vchealthcareplan.org
Non-Profit Organization: Yes
Year Founded: 1993

Healthplan and Services Defined
  PLAN TYPE: HMO
  Benefits Offered: Disease Management, Prescription, Wellness

Geographic Areas Served
  Ventura County

185   Vision Plan of America

3255 Wilshire Boulevard
Suite 1610
Los Angeles, CA 90010
Toll-Free: 800-400-4872
Phone: 213-384-2600
Fax: 213-384-0084
visionplan@yahoo.com
www.visionplanofamerica.com
Subsidiary of: The Camden Insurance Agency
For Profit Organization: Yes
Year Founded: 1986
Number of Primary Care Physicians: 700
Number of Referral/Specialty Physicians: 165

Healthplan and Services Defined
  PLAN TYPE: Vision
  Model Type: IPA
  Plan Specialty: Vision
  Benefits Offered: Vision

Type of Coverage
  Commercial, Individual

Type of Payment Plans Offered
  POS, Capitated

Geographic Areas Served
  Statewide

Peer Review Type
  Case Management: Yes

Key Personnel
  President and CEO . . . . Stuart Needleman, OD
  CFO. . . . . Phillip Needleman
  Manager . . . . Milori Lopez Duarte
  Optometric Director . . . . Adolphus Lages, OD
  Provider Relations. . . . . Mayra Castillo

186   VSP: Vision Service Plan

3333 Quality Drive
Rancho Cordova, CA 95670
Toll-Free: 800-852-7600
Phone: 916-851-5000
Fax: 916-851-4858
webmaster@vsp.com
www.vsp.com
Secondary Address: 3400 Morse Crossing, Columbus, OH 43219
Year Founded: 1955
Number of Primary Care Physicians: 26,000
Total Enrollment: 55,000,000

Healthplan and Services Defined
  PLAN TYPE: Vision
  Plan Specialty: Vision
  Benefits Offered: Vision

Type of Payment Plans Offered
  Capitated

Geographic Areas Served
Nationwide

Network Qualifications
Pre-Admission Certification: Yes

Peer Review Type
Utilization Review: Yes

Accreditation Certification
Utilization Review, Quality Assurance Program

Key Personnel
President/CEO . . . . .Rob Lynch
CEO, Marchon Eyewear. . . . . .Al Berg
President, Vision Care . . . . .Gary Brooks
Pres/Opthalmic Operations. . . . . .Donald Oakley
Pres/Practice Solutions . . . . .Jim McGrann
Chairman. . . . . .Tim Jankowski
CFO. . . . . .Donald Ball, Jr
VSP, Public Relations . . . . .Pat McNeil
        patrmc@vps.com

---

187 VSP: Vision Service Plan of California
1 Market Plaza
Suite 2625
San Francisco, CA 94105-1101
Phone: 415-957-0977
Fax: 415-546-9755
webmaster@vsp.com
www.vsp.com
Year Founded: 1955
Number of Primary Care Physicians: 26,000
Total Enrollment: 55,000,000

Healthplan and Services Defined
  PLAN TYPE: Vision
  Plan Specialty: Vision
  Benefits Offered: Vision

Type of Payment Plans Offered
Capitated

Geographic Areas Served
Statewide

Network Qualifications
Pre-Admission Certification: Yes

Peer Review Type
Utilization Review: Yes

Accreditation Certification
Utilization Review, Quality Assurance Program

Key Personnel
Regional Vice President. . . . . .Janet Findlay
Regional Manager. . . . . .Daniel Morgan
Marketing Manager . . . . .Phyllis Moore

---

188 Western Dental Services
530 S Main Street
Orange, CA 92868
Toll-Free: 800-417-4444
Phone: 714-480-3000
Fax: 714-480-3001
corporate@westerndental.com
www.westerndental.com
For Profit Organization: Yes
Year Founded: 1984
Number of Primary Care Physicians: 1,700
Number of Referral/Specialty Physicians: 1,400
Total Enrollment: 315,440

Healthplan and Services Defined
  PLAN TYPE: Dental
  Other Type: Dental HMO

Model Type: Staff, IPA
Plan Specialty: Dental
Benefits Offered: Dental

Type of Coverage
Indemnity

Type of Payment Plans Offered
POS, Combination FFS & DFFS

Geographic Areas Served
California and Arizona

Subscriber Information
Average Monthly Fee Per Subscriber
  (Employee + Employer Contribution):
    Employee Only (Self): $10.28
    Employee & 1 Family Member: $19.48
    Employee & 2 Family Members: $25.62

Network Qualifications
Pre-Admission Certification: Yes

Peer Review Type
Utilization Review: Yes
Second Surgical Opinion: Yes
Case Management: Yes

Publishes and Distributes Report Card: No

Accreditation Certification
Utilization Review

Key Personnel
President/CEO . . . . .Samuel H Gruenbaum
CFO. . . . . .David Joe
Chief Accounting Officer. . . . . .Bradley Rodgers
General Counsel . . . . .Sandra Lau
VP, Call Center. . . . . .Kittrick Ireland
VP Real Estate/Facilities . . . . .Tony Roxstrom
Chief Dental Director . . . . .Louis J Amendola, DDS
Chief Operating Officer . . . . .Phil Runnoe, DDS
Dir, Marketing Finance . . . . .Anna Yang
Director, Recruiting. . . . . .Kenneth W Kirsch, DDS
VP, Human Resources . . . . .Cody R Decamp
Chief Information Officer. . . . . .Daniel Treves
VP, Collections . . . . .Richard Montgomery
Sr VP/Chief Sales Officer. . . . . .Wayne Butts

Average Claim Compensation
Physician's Fees Charged: 80%

Specialty Managed Care Partners
Enters into Contracts with Regional Business Coalitions: No

---

189 Western Health Advantage
2349 Gateway Oaks Drive
Suite 100
Sacramento, CA 95833
Toll-Free: 888-563-2250
Phone: 916-563-2250
Fax: 916-568-0126
memberservices@westernhealth.com
www.westernhealth.com
Non-Profit Organization: Yes
Total Enrollment: 70,819
State Enrollment: 70,819

Healthplan and Services Defined
  PLAN TYPE: HMO

Geographic Areas Served
Sacramento, Yolo, Solano, western El Dorado, western Placer
counties

Key Personnel
President & CEO . . . . .Garry Maisel
Dir, Community Relations . . . . .Rick Heron
Finance Director. . . . . .Jill Camancho

Health Insurance Coverage Status and Type of Coverage by Age

Category	All Persons		Under 18 years		Under 65 years		65 years and over	
	Number	%	Number	%	Number	%	Number	%
Total population	5,050	-	1,252	-	4,507	-	542	-
Covered by some type of health insurance	4,393 *(45)*	87.0 *(0.8)*	1,154 *(17)*	92.2 *(1.1)*	3,852 *(57)*	85.5 *(0.9)*	541 *(33)*	99.8 *(0.2)*
Covered by private health insurance	3,534 *(72)*	70.0 *(1.4)*	863 *(25)*	68.9 *(1.9)*	3,239 *(79)*	71.9 *(1.4)*	296 *(21)*	54.5 *(3.3)*
Employment based	2,949 *(70)*	58.4 *(1.3)*	747 *(28)*	59.7 *(2.1)*	2,777 *(72)*	61.6 *(1.4)*	172 *(17)*	31.7 *(2.7)*
Own employment based	1,512 *(36)*	29.9 *(0.7)*	2 *(1)*	0.1 *(0.1)*	1,387 *(38)*	30.8 *(0.7)*	125 *(14)*	23.0 *(2.0)*
Direct purchase	651 *(60)*	12.9 *(1.2)*	135 *(17)*	10.8 *(1.3)*	503 *(57)*	11.2 *(1.2)*	148 *(15)*	27.3 *(2.7)*
Covered by government health insurance	1,405 *(53)*	27.8 *(1.1)*	394 *(23)*	31.4 *(1.9)*	893 *(45)*	19.8 *(1.0)*	512 *(32)*	94.5 *(1.3)*
Covered by Medicaid	611 *(38)*	12.1 *(0.8)*	308 *(20)*	24.6 *(1.6)*	567 *(33)*	12.6 *(0.7)*	44 *(12)*	8.1 *(2.2)*
Also by private insurance	143 *(25)*	2.8 *(0.5)*	64 *(11)*	5.1 *(0.9)*	131 *(22)*	2.9 *(0.5)*	12 *(5)*	2.2 *(1.0)*
Covered by Medicare	607 *(38)*	12.0 *(0.8)*	2 *(2)*	0.1 *(0.1)*	100 *(15)*	2.2 *(0.3)*	507 *(32)*	93.6 *(1.4)*
Also by private insurance	291 *(23)*	5.8 *(0.4)*	0 *(0)*	0.0 *(0.0)*	25 *(7)*	0.6 *(0.1)*	266 *(20)*	49.1 *(3.4)*
Also by Medicaid	94 *(18)*	1.9 *(0.4)*	2 *(2)*	0.1 *(0.1)*	51 *(12)*	1.1 *(0.3)*	43 *(12)*	7.9 *(2.2)*
Covered by military health care	342 *(34)*	6.8 *(0.7)*	93 *(15)*	7.4 *(1.2)*	294 *(31)*	6.5 *(0.7)*	48 *(12)*	8.8 *(2.2)*
Not covered at any time during the year	656 *(41)*	13.0 *(0.8)*	98 *(14)*	7.8 *(1.1)*	655 *(41)*	14.5 *(0.9)*	1 *(1)*	0.2 *(0.2)*

Note: Numbers in thousands; figures cover 2010; standard error appears in parenthesis; (b) base less than 75,000; (x) not applicable
Source: U.S. Census Bureau, Current Population Survey, 2011 Annual Social and Economic Supplement. Table HI05. Health Insurance Coverage Status and Type of Coverage by State and Age for All People: 2010

Colorado

190 Aetna Health of Colorado
Partnered with eHealthInsurance Services Inc.

191 American Dental Group
PO Box 25517
Colorado Springs, CO 80917
Toll-Free: 800-633-3010
Phone: 719-633-3000
www.americandentalgroup.org
For Profit Organization: Yes
Year Founded: 1991
Physician Owned Organization: Yes
Number of Primary Care Physicians: 54,000
Number of Referral/Specialty Physicians: 60

Healthplan and Services Defined
  PLAN TYPE: Dental
  Model Type: Group
  Plan Specialty: Dental
  Benefits Offered: Dental, Vision

Type of Coverage
  Commercial, Individual

Type of Payment Plans Offered
  DFFS, FFS, Combination FFS & DFFS

Geographic Areas Served
  Allen Park, Ann Arbor, Bloomfield Hills, Brighton, Canton, Clinton Twp, Dearborn, Dearborn Hts, Detroit, Eastpointe, Farmington Hills, Flint, Grand Blanc, Gross Pointe, Lansing, Livonia, Monroe, Novi, Oak Park, Pontiac, Rochester Hills, Rochester, Roseville, Southfield, Shelby Twp, Southgate, Sterling Hts, Troy, Walled Lakes, Warren, Waterford, Wayne, W Bloomfield. Also, Toledo, OH; Richmond, VA and Atlanta, Douglasville, Kennesaw, Lawrenceville, Marietta, GA

Subscriber Information
  Average Monthly Fee Per Subscriber
    (Employee + Employer Contribution):
      Employee Only (Self): $9.59/month
      Employee & 1 Family Member: $16.95/mont
  Average Annual Deductible Per Subscriber:
      Employee Only (Self): $0
      Employee & 1 Family Member: $0
      Employee & 2 Family Members: $0
      Medicare: $0

Key Personnel
  President/CEO . . . . T McGinty
  Owner . . . . Don Whaley

192 Anthem Blue Cross & Blue Shield of Colorado
700 Broadway
Denver, CO 80273
Toll-Free: 866-293-2892
Phone: 303-831-2131
Fax: 303-894-9385
www.anthem.com
Secondary Address: 555 Middlecreek Parkway, Colorado Springs, CO 80921
For Profit Organization: Yes
Total Enrollment: 880,475
State Enrollment: 60,270

Healthplan and Services Defined
  PLAN TYPE: HMO/PPO
  Plan Specialty: Dental, Vision
  Benefits Offered: Dental, Disease Management, Prescription, Vision, Wellness, Life

Type of Coverage
  Commercial, Individual, Medicare

Type of Payment Plans Offered
  POS, FFS

Geographic Areas Served
  Colorado

Key Personnel
  CEO . . . . Larry Glasscock
  COO . . . . Donna Lee Boreing
  CFO . . . . Michael Smith
  CMO . . . . Dr Lisa Latts
  General Counsel . . . . Dave Harris
  Provider Relations . . . . Dr Robert London
  Marketing . . . . Joseph Hoffman
  Member Relations . . . . Dana Held
  Pharmacy Director . . . . James Lang
  Public Relations . . . . Deborah New
  Media Contact . . . . Joyzelle Davis
    303-831-2005
    joyzelle.davis@anthem.com

193 Assurant Employee Benefits: Colorado
8101 E Prentice Avenue
Greenwood Village, CO 80111-2909
Phone: 303-796-7990
Fax: 303-796-2769
benefits@assurant.com
www.assurantemployeebenefits.com
Subsidiary of: Assurant, Inc
For Profit Organization: Yes
Number of Primary Care Physicians: 112,000
Total Enrollment: 47,000

Healthplan and Services Defined
  PLAN TYPE: Multiple
  Plan Specialty: Dental, Vision, Long & Short-Term Disability
  Benefits Offered: Dental, Vision, Wellness, AD&D, Life, LTD, STD

Type of Coverage
  Commercial, Indemnity, Individual Dental Plans

Geographic Areas Served
  Statewide

Subscriber Information
  Average Monthly Fee Per Subscriber
    (Employee + Employer Contribution):
      Employee Only (Self): Varies by plan

Key Personnel
  Manager . . . . David Churchill
  PR Specialist . . . . Megan Hutchison
    816-556-7815
    megan.hutchison@assurant.com

194 Behavioral Healthcare
155 Inverness Drive West
Suite 201
Englewood, CO 80112
Phone: 720-490-4400
Fax: 720-490-4395
www.bhicares.org

Healthplan and Services Defined
  PLAN TYPE: Other
  Model Type: Network
  Plan Specialty: Behavioral Health
  Benefits Offered: Behavioral Health

Type of Coverage
  Medicaid

Geographic Areas Served
  Arapahoe, Adams, Douglas counties

195   Beta Health Plan

9725 E Hampden Avenue
Suite 400
Denver, CO 80231
Toll-Free: 800-807-0706
Phone: 303-744-3007
Fax: 303-744-2890
www.betadental.com
Subsidiary of: Beta Health Association Inc
For Profit Organization: Yes
Year Founded: 1990
Physician Owned Organization: Yes
Number of Primary Care Physicians: 480
Number of Referral/Specialty Physicians: 120
Total Enrollment: 56,000

Healthplan and Services Defined
   PLAN TYPE: Multiple
   Model Type: Discount FFS Network
   Plan Specialty: Dental, Vision
   Benefits Offered: Dental, Vision

Type of Coverage
   Commercial, Individual, Indemnity
   Catastrophic Illness Benefit: Unlimited

Geographic Areas Served
   Statewide

Subscriber Information
   Average Monthly Fee Per Subscriber
      (Employee + Employer Contribution):
         Employee Only (Self): $11.00
         Employee & 1 Family Member: $21.75
         Employee & 2 Family Members: $31.75

Network Qualifications
   Pre-Admission Certification: No

Publishes and Distributes Report Card: Yes

Accreditation Certification
   State Dental Board

Key Personnel
   President . . . . .Joseph Jurak
   Senior Account Executive . . . . .Linda Krueger
   VP . . . . .Gail Burk

Specialty Managed Care Partners
   Enters into Contracts with Regional Business Coalitions: Yes

196   Boulder Valley Individual Practice Association

6676 Gunpark Drive
Suite B
Boulder, CO 80301
Phone: 303-530-3405
Fax: 303-530-2441
www.bvipa.com
Non-Profit Organization: Yes
Year Founded: 1978
Physician Owned Organization: Yes
Number of Affiliated Hospitals: 2
Number of Primary Care Physicians: 92
Number of Referral/Specialty Physicians: 171
Total Enrollment: 60,000

Healthplan and Services Defined
   PLAN TYPE: PPO
   Model Type: IPA
   Offers Demand Management Patient Information Service: Yes

Type of Payment Plans Offered
   POS

Geographic Areas Served
   Boulder, Lafayette, Longmont & Louisville

Network Qualifications
   Pre-Admission Certification: Yes

Peer Review Type
   Utilization Review: Yes
   Second Surgical Opinion: Yes
   Case Management: Yes

Publishes and Distributes Report Card: No

Accreditation Certification
   TJC Accreditation, Utilization Review, State Licensure

Key Personnel
   President. . . . . .Susan Roach, MD
   Executive Director .Catherine Higgins, CPA
      chiggins@bvipa.com
   Referral/PreCertification . . . . .Jennifer Kohlscheen
      jkohlscheen@bvipa.com
   Finance/Accounting . . . . .Wendy Saltarelli
      wsaltarelli@bvipa.com
   Medical Director. . . . . .Laird Cagan, MD
      lcagan@bvipa.com
   Prov Relations/Credent . . . . .Barbara Massey
      bmassey@bvipa.com

Specialty Managed Care Partners
   Enters into Contracts with Regional Business Coalitions: No

197   CIGNA HealthCare of Colorado

3900 E Mexico Avenue
Suite 1100
Denver, CO 80210
Toll-Free: 800-245-2471
Phone: 303-782-1500
Fax: 303-782-1577
www.cigna.com
Secondary Address: Great-West Healthcare, now part of CIGNA, 5445
   DTC Parkway, Suite 400, Greenwood Village, CO 80111,
   303-323-0000
For Profit Organization: Yes
Year Founded: 1986
Number of Affiliated Hospitals: 18
Number of Primary Care Physicians: 500
Total Enrollment: 36,611
State Enrollment: 36,611

Healthplan and Services Defined
   PLAN TYPE: HMO
   Other Type: POS
   Model Type: IPA, Network
   Plan Specialty: Behavioral Health, Dental, Vision
   Benefits Offered: Behavioral Health, Dental, Disease Management,
      Prescription, Vision, Wellness, Life, LTD, STD
   Offers Demand Management Patient Information Service: Yes

Type of Coverage
   Commercial, Individual
   Catastrophic Illness Benefit: Covered

Type of Payment Plans Offered
   POS, Combination FFS & DFFS

Geographic Areas Served
   Adams, Arapahoe, Boulder, Denver, Douglas, El Paso, Elbert,
   Jefferson, Larimer, Pueblo, Teller and Weld counties

Subscriber Information
   Average Monthly Fee Per Subscriber
      (Employee + Employer Contribution):
         Employee Only (Self): $128.00
         Medicare: $396.00
      Average Subscriber Co-Payment:
         Primary Care Physician: $10.00
         Prescription Drugs: $5.00

Hospital ER: $50.00

Network Qualifications
Pre-Admission Certification: Yes

Peer Review Type
Utilization Review: Yes
Second Surgical Opinion: Yes
Case Management: Yes

Publishes and Distributes Report Card: Yes

Accreditation Certification
NCQA
TJC Accreditation, Medicare Approved, Utilization Review,
Pre-Admission Certification, State Licensure, Quality Assurance
Program

Key Personnel
President.....................................Daryl Edmunds
Director At Cigna............................Sallie Vanasdale
VP Provider Relations..........................William Cetti
VP Client Relations ....Gregg Prussing

Specialty Managed Care Partners
Enters into Contracts with Regional Business Coalitions: Yes

198 CNA Insurance Companies: Colorado
10375 Park Meadows Drive
Suite 300
Littleton, CO 80124
Phone: 303-858-4100
Fax: 303-858-4427
cna_help@cna.com
www.cna.com
Year Founded: 1986
Number of Affiliated Hospitals: 57
Number of Primary Care Physicians: 3,400
Total Enrollment: 270,000

Healthplan and Services Defined
PLAN TYPE: PPO

Geographic Areas Served
Metro Denver area

Key Personnel
Chairman/CEO ....Thomas F Motamed
President/COO ....Bob Lindemann
EVP, Chief Actuary.........................Larry A Haefner
EVP, Worldwide P&C Claim ....George R Fay
EVP, General Counsel.....................Johathan D Kantor
EVP/CFO ....D Craig Mense
EVP, Chief Admin Officer..................Thomas Pontarelli
President, COO CNA Spec ....Peter W Wilson
President, Field Oper........................Tim Szerlong
SVP, CNA Select Risk ....John Angerami
SVP, Business Insurance ....Michael W Covne
Mid-Atlantic Zone Officer.....................George Agven
Western Zone Officer ....Steve Stonehouse
Central Zone Officer ....Greg Vezzosi
Northern Zone Officer ....Steve Wachtel
Media Contact...........................Katrina W Parker
312-822-5167

199 Colorado Access
10065 E Harvard Avenue
Suite 600
Denver, CO 80231
Toll-Free: 800-511-5010
Phone: 303-751-2657
www.coaccess.com

Healthplan and Services Defined
PLAN TYPE: HMO

Type of Coverage
Medicare, Medicaid

Key Personnel
President/CEO/CMO ....Marshall Thomas, MD
Chief Financial Officer ....Philip J Reed
Chief Operating Officer ....Marie Steckbeck, MBA
VP, Clinical Services.................Mike L McKitterick, RN
Dir, Human Ressources........................Rene Gallegos
VP, Public Policy...........Gretchen Flanders McGinnis, MSPH
VP, Behavioral Health ....Alexis Giese, MD

200 Colorado Choice Health Plans
700 Main Street
Suite 100
Alamosa, CO 81101
Toll-Free: 800-475-8466
Phone: 718-589-3696
Fax: 719-589-4901
www.slvhmo.com
For Profit Organization: Yes
Year Founded: 1972
Total Enrollment: 5,000

Healthplan and Services Defined
PLAN TYPE: HMO
Benefits Offered: Dental, Disease Management, Prescription, Vision,
Wellness, Life

Type of Coverage
Commercial, Individual, Medicare

Geographic Areas Served
San Luis Valley, Arkansas Valley, Durango, Pueblo, Colorado Springs,
Denver

Key Personnel
CEO ....Cynthia Palmer
CFO.................................Lisa A Sandoval, CPA
VP, Development ....Lynn Borup
Sales Director ....Paul Roberts

201 Colorado Health Partnerships
7150 Campus Drive
Suite 300
Colorado Springs, CO 80920
Toll-Free: 800-804-5008
www.coloradohealthpartnerships.com
Non-Profit Organization: Yes
Year Founded: 1995
Number of Affiliated Hospitals: 8
Total Enrollment: 160,000
State Enrollment: 160,000

Healthplan and Services Defined
PLAN TYPE: HMO
Plan Specialty: Behavioral Health
Benefits Offered: Behavioral Health

Type of Coverage
Medicaid

Geographic Areas Served
Alamosa, Archleta, Baca, Bent, Chaffee, Conejos, Costilla, Crowley,
Custer, Delta, Dolores, Eagle, El Paso, Fremont, Garfield, Grand,
Gunnison, Hinsdale, Huerfano, Jackson, Kiowa, Lake, La Plata, Las
Animas, Mesa, Mineral, Moffat, Montezuma, Montrose, Otero, Ouray,
Park, Pitkin, Pueblo, Prowers, Rio Blanco, Rio Grande, Routt,
Saguache, San Juan, San Miguel, Summit, Teller counties

202 Delta Dental of Colorado
4582 S Ulster Street
Suite 800

Denver, CO 80237
Toll-Free: 800-233-0860
Phone: 303-741-9300
Fax: 303-741-4233
customer_service@ddpco.com
www.deltadentalco.com
Mailing Address: PO Box 5468, Denver, CO 80217-5468
Non-Profit Organization: Yes
Year Founded: 1958
Total Enrollment: 54,000,000
State Enrollment: 100,000

Healthplan and Services Defined
PLAN TYPE: Dental
Other Type: Dental PPO
Model Type: Network
Plan Specialty: Dental
Benefits Offered: Dental

Type of Coverage
Commercial

Type of Payment Plans Offered
DFFS

Geographic Areas Served
Statewide

Subscriber Information
Average Monthly Fee Per Subscriber
(Employee + Employer Contribution):
Employee Only (Self): $17
Employee & 2 Family Members: $50
Average Annual Deductible Per Subscriber:
Employee Only (Self): $150
Employee & 2 Family Members: $50
Average Subscriber Co-Payment:
Primary Care Physician: 80%
Non-Network Physician: 50%

Network Qualifications
Pre-Admission Certification: Yes

Publishes and Distributes Report Card: Yes

Key Personnel
President & CEO . . . . Katherine Paul
General Counsel/VP Admin . . . . Barbara B Springer, JD
VP, Finance . . . . Russell J Scherier
Chief Operating Officer . . . . Linda M Arneson
Dental Director . . . . Fiona Collins, DDS
VP, Sales & Marketing . . . . Jean Lawhead

203   Denver Health Medical Plan Inc

990 Bannock Street
Courtyard
Denver, CO 80204-4507
Phone: 303-436-7253
Fax: 303-436-5131
public_relations@dhha.org
www.denverhealthmedicalplan.com
Secondary Address: Mail: 777 Bannock Street, Mail Code 6000,
Denver, CO 80204-4507
For Profit Organization: Yes
Year Founded: 1997
Number of Primary Care Physicians: 5,000
Total Enrollment: 15,000
State Enrollment: 15,000

Healthplan and Services Defined
PLAN TYPE: HMO
Benefits Offered: Chiropractic, Home Care, Inpatient SNF, Physical
Therapy, Podiatry, Psychiatric, Transplant, Vision, Wellness

Type of Coverage
Commercial, Medicare, Medicare Advantage, CHP+

Key Personnel
CEO . . . . Leann Donovan
Prescription Plan Manger . . . . Beth Henchel

204   eHealthInsurance Services Inc.

11919 Foundation Place
Gold River, CA 95670
Toll-Free: 800-977-8860
info@ehealthinsurance.com
www.e.healthinsurance.com
Year Founded: 1997

Healthplan and Services Defined
PLAN TYPE: HMO/PPO
Benefits Offered: Dental, Life, STD

Type of Coverage
Commercial, Individual, Medicare

Geographic Areas Served
All 50 states in the USA and District of Columbia

Key Personnel
Chairman & CEO . . . . Gary L. Lauer
EVP/Business & Corp. Dev. Bruce Telkamp
EVP/Chief Technology . . . . Dr. Sheldon X. Wang
SVP & CFO . . . . Stuart M. Huizinga
Pres. of eHealth Gov. Sys . . . . Samuel C. Gibbs
SVP of Sales & Operations . . . . Robert S. Hurley
Director Public Relations . . . . Nate Purpura
650-210-3115

205   Great-West Healthcare Colorado
Acquired by CIGNA

206   Great-West PPO
Acquired by CIGNA

207   Great-West/One Health Plan
Acquired by CIGNA

208   HMO Colorado

700 Broadway
9th Floor
Denver, CO 80203
Toll-Free: 800-654-9338
Phone: 303-831-2131
Fax: 303-831-2011
www.anthem.com
Subsidiary of: Anthem Blue Cross/Blue Shield
For Profit Organization: Yes
Year Founded: 1979
Owned by an Integrated Delivery Network (IDN): Yes
Number of Affiliated Hospitals: 66
Number of Primary Care Physicians: 1,941
Number of Referral/Specialty Physicians: 5,454
Total Enrollment: 126,000

Healthplan and Services Defined
PLAN TYPE: HMO
Model Type: IPA
Benefits Offered: Behavioral Health, Chiropractic, Complementary
Medicine, Dental, Disease Management, Home Care, Inpatient
SNF, Long-Term Care, Physical Therapy, Podiatry, Prescription,
Psychiatric, Transplant, Vision, Wellness, AD&D, Life, LTD, STD

Type of Coverage
Commercial, Individual, Indemnity, Medicare, Supplemental
Medicare, Medicaid, Catastrophic
Catastrophic Illness Benefit: Maximum $1M

Type of Payment Plans Offered
POS, FFS, Combination FFS & DFFS

Geographic Areas Served
Adams, Araphoe, Denver, Douglas and Jefferson counties

Network Qualifications
Pre-Admission Certification: Yes

Peer Review Type
Utilization Review: Yes
Second Surgical Opinion: Yes
Case Management: Yes

Publishes and Distributes Report Card: No

Accreditation Certification
NCQA
TJC Accreditation, Medicare Approved, Utilization Review, Pre-Admission Certification, State Licensure, Quality Assurance Program

Key Personnel
Vice President . . . . .Blair Christianson
Senior Vice President . . . . .Beverly Sloan

Specialty Managed Care Partners
Enters into Contracts with Regional Business Coalitions: No

Employer References
Proprietary

209 Humana Health Insurnace of Colorado

8033 N Academy Blvd
Colorado Springs, CO 80920
Toll-Free: 800-871-6270
Phone: 719-598-1317
Fax: 719-531-7089
www.humana.com
Secondary Address: 7400 E Orchard Road, Suite 1000 N, Greenwood Village, CO 80111
For Profit Organization: Yes
Year Founded: 1987
Number of Affiliated Hospitals: 72
Number of Primary Care Physicians: 2,811
Number of Referral/Specialty Physicians: 3,653
Total Enrollment: 113,229
State Enrollment: 113,229

Healthplan and Services Defined
PLAN TYPE: HMO/PPO
Plan Specialty: ASO, Dental, Vision, Fully Insured
Benefits Offered: Dental, Disease Management, Transplant, Vision, Personal Nurse, Case Management, On-Site Hospital Review, Utilization Management, Transplant Management, Humana First

Type of Coverage
Commercial, Individual, Group, Medicare

Geographic Areas Served
Colorado

Accreditation Certification
URAC, NCQA

Key Personnel
Market President . . . . .Leslie Andrews
Market Vice President . . . . .Richard W Jones
Provider Contracting VP. . . . . .Rich Powers
Director Large Group Sale . . . . .David Fingers
Director Small Group Sale . . . . .Robb Scheele

210 Kaiser Permanente Health Plan of Colorado

10350 E Dakota Avenue
Denver, CO 80247
Toll-Free: 888-681-7878
Phone: 303-338-3700
Fax: 303-338-3797

www.kaiserpermanente.org
Subsidiary of: Kaiser Permanente
Non-Profit Organization: Yes
Year Founded: 1969
Physician Owned Organization: Yes
Federally Qualified: Yes
Number of Affiliated Hospitals: 35
Number of Primary Care Physicians: 15,129
Total Enrollment: 522,000
State Enrollment: 522,000

Healthplan and Services Defined
PLAN TYPE: HMO
Model Type: Staff
Plan Specialty: Behavioral Health, Chiropractic, Dental, Disease Management, Vision, Radiology, UR
Benefits Offered: Behavioral Health, Chiropractic, Dental, Disease Management, Home Care, Inpatient SNF, Long-Term Care, Physical Therapy, Podiatry, Prescription, Psychiatric, Transplant, Vision, Wellness
Offers Demand Management Patient Information Service: Yes

Type of Coverage
Major Medical Plan
Catastrophic Illness Benefit: Unlimited

Geographic Areas Served
Denver, Boulder, Longmont metropolitan area and Colorado Springs

Publishes and Distributes Report Card: Yes

Accreditation Certification
NCQA

Key Personnel
Regional President . . . . .Donna Lynne, DrPH
VP, Govt Relations. . . . . .Jandel Allen-Davis, MD
Med Dir, Quality. . . . . .Michael D Chase, MD
Exec Dir, Colorado Spr . . . . .Mark Iorio
Med Dir, Network. . . . . .Elizabeth Kincannon, MD
VP, Health Plan Admin . . . . .Anne McDow
VP, Primary Care. . . . . .Ginny McLain
VP, Finance. . . . . .Rick Newsome
VP, Business Operations . . . . .Kerry Kohnen
Med Dir, Clinical Process .Bill Marsh, MD
Exec Medical Director. . . . . .William Wright, MD
Med Dir, Human Resources . . . . .Rudy Kadota, MD
VP, Human Resources . . . . .Robin Sadler
Med Dir, Primary Care. . . . . .Scott Smith
VP, Sales & Marketing. . . . . .Jean Barker
Mgr, Integrated Communic. . . . . .Art Luebke
303-344-7619
arthur.j.luebke@kp.org
Media Contact. . . . . .Amy D Whited
303-344-7763

Specialty Managed Care Partners
Dental, Prescription, Vision, Good Samaritan, Saint Joseph
Enters into Contracts with Regional Business Coalitions: Yes

211 PacifiCare of Colorado

6455 S Yosemite Street
Greenwood Village, CO 80111
Phone: 303-714-3427
www.pacificare.com
Mailing Address: PO Box 4306, Englewood, CO 80155
Subsidiary of: UnitedHealthCare
For Profit Organization: Yes
Year Founded: 1974
Number of Affiliated Hospitals: 43
Number of Primary Care Physicians: 1,100
Number of Referral/Specialty Physicians: 2,400
Total Enrollment: 328,000

Healthplan and Services Defined
PLAN TYPE: HMO

Model Type: Network
Benefits Offered: Prescription

Type of Coverage
Commercial, Individual, Indemnity, Medicare
Catastrophic Illness Benefit: Covered

Type of Payment Plans Offered
DFFS, Capitated, FFS, Combination FFS & DFFS

Geographic Areas Served
Adams, Arapahoe, Boulder, Broomfield, Clear Creek, Denver,
Douglas, Elbert, El Paso, Fremont, Gilpin, Jefferson, Larimer,
Lincoln, Logan, Morgan, Park, Teller, Washington and Weld counties

Subscriber Information
Average Monthly Fee Per Subscriber
(Employee + Employer Contribution):
Employee Only (Self): $148.11
Employee & 2 Family Members: $473.96
Average Subscriber Co-Payment:
Primary Care Physician: $10.00
Non-Network Physician: 30%
Prescription Drugs: $10.00
Hospital ER: $50.00
Home Health Care: $0
Nursing Home: $0
Nursing Home Max. Days/Visits Covered: 120/yr.

Network Qualifications
Pre-Admission Certification: Yes

Peer Review Type
Utilization Review: Yes
Case Management: Yes

Accreditation Certification
NCQA
TJC Accreditation, Medicare Approved, Utilization Review,
Pre-Admission Certification, State Licensure, Quality Assurance
Program

Key Personnel
Chairman/CEO . . . . .Howard Phanstiel
Executive VP/CFO. . . . . .Greg Scott
VP/Chief Medical Officer . . . . .Sam Ho

Average Claim Compensation
Physician's Fees Charged: 1%
Hospital's Fees Charged: 1%

Specialty Managed Care Partners
Enters into Contracts with Regional Business Coalitions: Yes

212 Pueblo Health Care

400 West 16th Street
Pueblo, CO 81003
Phone: 719-584-4806
Fax: 719-584-4038
www.pueblohealthcare.com
Number of Primary Care Physicians: 245

Healthplan and Services Defined
PLAN TYPE: PPO
Model Type: Network

Key Personnel
Executive Director . . . . .Ann Bellah
719-584-4371
ann_bellah@parkviewmc.com
Provider Relations . . . . .Sandra Proud
719-584-4642
sandra_proud@parkviewmc.com
Provider Relations. . . . . .Christie Velasco
719-584-4642
cnv@parkviewmc.com

213 Rocky Mountain Health Plans

2775 Crossroads Boulevard
Grand Junction, CO 81506
Toll-Free: 800-453-2981
Phone: 970-244-7800
Fax: 970-244-7880
customer_service@rmph.org
www.rmhp.org
Secondary Address: 6251 Greenwood Plaza Blvd, Suite 300,
Greenwood Village, CO 80111
Subsidiary of: Rocky Mountain Health Maintenance Organization
Non-Profit Organization: Yes
Year Founded: 1974
Owned by an Integrated Delivery Network (IDN): Yes
Number of Affiliated Hospitals: 100
Number of Primary Care Physicians: 2,558
Number of Referral/Specialty Physicians: 5,621
Total Enrollment: 180,000
State Enrollment: 180,000

Healthplan and Services Defined
PLAN TYPE: HMO/PPO
Other Type: HSA
Model Type: Mixed
Benefits Offered: Disease Management, Home Care, Prescription,
Wellness

Type of Coverage
Commercial, Individual, Medicare, Supplemental Medicare, Medicaid
Catastrophic Illness Benefit: Unlimited

Type of Payment Plans Offered
FFS

Geographic Areas Served
Plan are available throughout Colorado

Subscriber Information
Average Subscriber Co-Payment:
Primary Care Physician: $20.00
Home Health Care Max. Days/Visits Covered: Unlimited

Network Qualifications
Minimum Years of Practice: 3
Pre-Admission Certification: Yes

Peer Review Type
Utilization Review: Yes
Second Surgical Opinion: Yes
Case Management: Yes

Publishes and Distributes Report Card: Yes

Accreditation Certification
NCQA
Medicare Approved, Utilization Review, Pre-Admission Certification,
State Licensure, Quality Assurance Program

Key Personnel
President/CEO . . . . .Steven Erkenbrack
COO. . . . . .Laurel Walters
CFO. . . . . .Pat Duncan
VP, Human Resources. . . . . .Jan Rohr
VP, GM Front Range Oper. . . . . .Jim Swayze
VP, Legal & Govt Affairs . . . . .Mike Huotari
Chief Marketing Officer . . . . .Neil Waldron
Chief Medical Officer . . . . .Kevin R Fitzgerald, MD
Dir, Marketing. . . . . .Kayla Arnesen
970-244-7967

Specialty Managed Care Partners
Delta Dental, Landmark Chiropractic, Vision Service Plan, Life
Strategies

214 United Concordia: Colorado

999 18th Street
Suite 3023

Denver, CO 80202
Phone: 303-357-2388
Fax: 303-357-2389
ucproducer@ucci.com
www.secure.ucci.com
For Profit Organization: Yes
Year Founded: 1971
Number of Primary Care Physicians: 111,000
Total Enrollment: 8,000,000

Healthplan and Services Defined
    PLAN TYPE: Dental
    Plan Specialty: Dental
    Benefits Offered: Dental

Type of Coverage
    Commercial, Individual

Geographic Areas Served
    Military personnel and their families, nationwide

215 UnitedHealthCare of Colorado

6465 S Greenwood Plaza Boulevard
Suite 300
Centennial, CO 80111
Toll-Free: 800-516-3344
Phone: 303-267-3300
Fax: 303-267-3597
www.uhc.com
Subsidiary of: UnitedHealth Group
For Profit Organization: Yes
Year Founded: 1986
Number of Affiliated Hospitals: 47
Number of Primary Care Physicians: 1,600
Number of Referral/Specialty Physicians: 3,500
Total Enrollment: 75,000,000
State Enrollment: 735,900

Healthplan and Services Defined
    PLAN TYPE: HMO/PPO
    Model Type: Mixed Model
    Plan Specialty: MSO
    Benefits Offered: Behavioral Health, Chiropractic, Complementary
      Medicine, Dental, Disease Management, Home Care, Inpatient
      SNF, Long-Term Care, Physical Therapy, Podiatry, Prescription,
      Psychiatric, Transplant, Vision, Wellness, AD&D, Life

Type of Coverage
    Commercial, Individual, Medicaid, Commercial Group

Type of Payment Plans Offered
    DFFS, FFS, Combination FFS & DFFS

Geographic Areas Served
    HMO: Front Range Colorado; PPO/POS statewide

Subscriber Information
    Average Monthly Fee Per Subscriber
      (Employee + Employer Contribution):
        Employee Only (Self): Varies
    Average Subscriber Co-Payment:
        Primary Care Physician: $10
        Prescription Drugs: $10/15/30
        Hospital ER: $50

Network Qualifications
    Pre-Admission Certification: Yes

Peer Review Type
    Case Management: Yes

Publishes and Distributes Report Card: Yes

Accreditation Certification
    URAC, NCQA
    State Licensure, Quality Assurance Program

Key Personnel
    CEO . . . . .Beth Sorberg

Marketing . . . . .Janet Bollman
Senior Medical Director . . . . .Christopher Stanley, MD
VP Small Business Sales . . . . .Chad Zecheil
VP Key Account Sales . . . . .Cory Foreman
Media Contact . . . . .Will Shanley
    will.shanley@uhc.com

Average Claim Compensation
    Physician's Fees Charged: 70%
    Hospital's Fees Charged: 55%

Specialty Managed Care Partners
    United Behavioral Health
    Enters into Contracts with Regional Business Coalitions: No

216 VSP: Vision Service Plan of Colorado

1050 17th Street
Suite 1430
Denver, CO 80265-1501
Phone: 303-892-7663
webmaster@vsp.com
www.vsp.com
Year Founded: 1955
Number of Primary Care Physicians: 26,000
Total Enrollment: 55,000,000

Healthplan and Services Defined
    PLAN TYPE: Vision
    Plan Specialty: Vision
    Benefits Offered: Vision

Type of Payment Plans Offered
    Capitated

Geographic Areas Served
    Statewide

Network Qualifications
    Pre-Admission Certification: Yes

Peer Review Type
    Utilization Review: Yes

Accreditation Certification
    Utilization Review, Quality Assurance Program

Key Personnel
    Manager . . . . .Paula Palmer

Health Insurance Coverage Status and Type of Coverage by Age

Category	All Persons		Under 18 years		Under 65 years		65 years and over	
	Number	%	Number	%	Number	%	Number	%
Total population	3,497	-	819	-	3,042	-	455	-
Covered by some type of health insurance	3,113 *(31)*	89.0 *(0.7)*	770 *(11)*	94.0 *(0.9)*	2,668 *(37)*	87.7 *(0.8)*	445 *(21)*	97.8 *(0.8)*
Covered by private health insurance	2,591 *(45)*	74.1 *(1.2)*	589 *(18)*	72.0 *(2.0)*	2,295 *(48)*	75.4 *(1.3)*	296 *(19)*	65.0 *(3.0)*
Employment based	2,281 *(49)*	65.2 *(1.4)*	554 *(20)*	67.7 *(2.3)*	2,120 *(50)*	69.7 *(1.4)*	161 *(14)*	35.4 *(2.8)*
Own employment based	1,099 *(26)*	31.4 *(0.7)*	2 *(1)*	0.3 *(0.2)*	974 *(26)*	32.0 *(0.8)*	125 *(11)*	27.5 *(2.2)*
Direct purchase	431 *(31)*	12.3 *(0.9)*	54 *(9)*	6.7 *(1.1)*	278 *(25)*	9.1 *(0.8)*	153 *(16)*	33.7 *(3.1)*
Covered by government health insurance	922 *(37)*	26.4 *(1.1)*	218 *(16)*	26.6 *(1.9)*	497 *(30)*	16.3 *(1.0)*	425 *(21)*	93.4 *(1.3)*
Covered by Medicaid	435 *(29)*	12.4 *(0.8)*	211 *(16)*	25.8 *(1.9)*	413 *(29)*	13.6 *(1.0)*	22 *(5)*	4.8 *(1.1)*
Also by private insurance	99 *(14)*	2.8 *(0.4)*	34 *(8)*	4.2 *(1.0)*	90 *(13)*	3.0 *(0.4)*	8 *(4)*	1.8 *(0.8)*
Covered by Medicare	490 *(23)*	14.0 *(0.7)*	6 *(3)*	0.7 *(0.4)*	65 *(9)*	2.1 *(0.3)*	425 *(21)*	93.4 *(1.3)*
Also by private insurance	298 *(20)*	8.5 *(0.6)*	4 *(3)*	0.5 *(0.4)*	23 *(5)*	0.7 *(0.2)*	276 *(19)*	60.6 *(3.0)*
Also by Medicaid	41 *(7)*	1.2 *(0.2)*	4 *(3)*	0.5 *(0.4)*	20 *(5)*	0.6 *(0.2)*	22 *(5)*	4.8 *(1.1)*
Covered by military health care	59 *(11)*	1.7 *(0.3)*	5 *(3)*	0.7 *(0.3)*	41 *(10)*	1.4 *(0.3)*	18 *(5)*	3.9 *(1.2)*
Not covered at any time during the year	384 *(26)*	11.0 *(0.7)*	49 *(7)*	6.0 *(0.9)*	374 *(26)*	12.3 *(0.8)*	10 *(3)*	2.2 *(0.8)*

Note: Numbers in thousands; figures cover 2010; standard error appears in parenthesis; (b) base less than 75,000; (x) not applicable
Source: U.S. Census Bureau, Current Population Survey, 2011 Annual Social and Economic Supplement. Table HI05. Health Insurance Coverage Status and Type of Coverage by State and Age for All People: 2010

Connecticut

217 Aetna Health, Inc. Corporate Headquarters

151 Farmington Avenue
Hartford, CT 06156
Toll-Free: 866-582-9629
Phone: 860-273-0123
Fax: 860-273-4764
www.aetna.com
Secondary Address: 1000 Middle Street, Middletown, CT 06457
For Profit Organization: Yes
Year Founded: 1853
Number of Affiliated Hospitals: 5,200
Number of Primary Care Physicians: 546,000
Number of Referral/Specialty Physicians: 981,000
Total Enrollment: 18,602,000
State Enrollment: 61,677

Healthplan and Services Defined
PLAN TYPE: HMO
Other Type: POS
Plan Specialty: Dental, Lab, PBM, Vision, Radiology
Benefits Offered: Behavioral Health, Dental, Disease Management,
Long-Term Care, Physical Therapy, Podiatry, Prescription,
Psychiatric, Vision, Life

Type of Coverage
Commercial, Individual

Type of Payment Plans Offered
FFS

Geographic Areas Served
Nationwide

Key Personnel
CEO . . . . Ronald A Williams
President. . . . . Mark T Bertolini
SVP, General Counsel . . . . William J Casazza
EVP, CFO . . . . Joseph M Zubretsky
Head, M&A Integration . . . . Kay Mooney
SVP, Marketing. . . . . Robert E Mead
Chief Medical Officer . . . . Lonny Reisman, MD
SVP, Human Resources. . . . . Elease E Wright
SVP, CIO. . . . . Meg McCarthy

218 Aetna Health, Inc. Medicare Plan

Aetna Golden Medicare Plan
151 Farmington Avenue
Hartford, CT 06156
Toll-Free: 866-582-9629
Phone: 860-273-0123
www.aetnamedicare.com

Healthplan and Services Defined
PLAN TYPE: Medicare
Benefits Offered: Chiropractic, Dental, Disease Management, Home
Care, Inpatient SNF, Physical Therapy, Podiatry, Prescription,
Psychiatric, Vision, Wellness

Type of Coverage
Individual, Medicare

Geographic Areas Served
Available in multiple states

Subscriber Information
Average Monthly Fee Per Subscriber
(Employee + Employer Contribution):
Employee Only (Self): Varies
Medicare: Varies
Average Annual Deductible Per Subscriber:
Employee Only (Self): Varies
Medicare: Varies
Average Subscriber Co-Payment:

Primary Care Physician: Varies
Non-Network Physician: Varies
Prescription Drugs: Varies
Hospital ER: Varies
Home Health Care: Varies
Home Health Care Max. Days/Visits Covered: Varies

Key Personnel
CEO . . . . Ronald A Williams
President. . . . . Mark T Bertolini
SVP, General Counsel . . . . William J Casazza
EVP, CFO . . . . Joseph M Zubretsky
Head, M&A Integration . . . . Kay Mooney
SVP, Marketing. . . . . Robert E Mead
Chief Medical Officer . . . . Lonny Reisman, MD
SVP, Human Resources. . . . . Elease E Wright
SVP, CIO. . . . . Meg McCarthy

219 AmeriChoice by UnitedHealthcare

400 Capital Blvd
Rocky Hill, CT 06067
www.americhoice.com
Subsidiary of: UnitedHealth Group

Healthplan and Services Defined
PLAN TYPE: HMO

Key Personnel
Media Contact. . . . . Alice Ferreira
203-459-7775
aferreira@uhc.com

220 Anthem Blue Cross & Blue Shield Connecticut

370 Bassett Road
Building Three, Fourth Floor
North Haven, CT 06473
Toll-Free: 800-545-0948
Phone: 203-239-4911
www.anthem.com
Subsidiary of: Wellpoint
For Profit Organization: Yes
Total Enrollment: 1,535,753
State Enrollment: 391,301

Healthplan and Services Defined
PLAN TYPE: HMO/PPO
Benefits Offered: Behavioral Health, Chiropractic, Complementary
Medicine, Disease Management, Home Care, Inpatient SNF,
Physical Therapy, Podiatry, Prescription, Psychiatric, Transplant,
Vision, Wellness

Type of Coverage
Commercial, Individual, Supplemental Medicare, Medicaid

Type of Payment Plans Offered
POS, FFS

Geographic Areas Served
Connecticut

Network Qualifications
Pre-Admission Certification: Yes

Peer Review Type
Utilization Review: Yes

Publishes and Distributes Report Card: Yes

Accreditation Certification
NCQA

Key Personnel
CEO. . . . . Larry Glasscock
President . . . . Marjorie Dorr
COO . . . . Claudia Lindsey
CFO . . . . Guy W Marszalek

CMO . . . . Dr Eleanor Seiler
General Counsel . . . . Alfred Jarvis
Provider Relations . . . . DiJuana Lewis
Marketing . . . . Dave Fusco
Member Relations . . . . Rita Marcinkus
Pharmacy Director . . . . Glen Smyth
Public Relations . . . . Deborah New
Media Contact . . . . Sarah Yeager
203-234-5402
sarah.yeager@anthem.com

Average Claim Compensation
Physician's Fees Charged: 40%
Hospital's Fees Charged: 33%

Specialty Managed Care Partners
Psychiatric Management, Quest Diagnostics
Enters into Contracts with Regional Business Coalitions: Yes

221 Charter Oak Health Plan
C/O Department of Social Services
25 Sigourney Street
Hartford, CT 06106-5033
Toll-Free: 877-772-8625
dss.healthcare@ct.gov
www.charteroakhealthplan.com
Subsidiary of: Community Health Network of Connecticut
Year Founded: 2008

Healthplan and Services Defined
PLAN TYPE: HMO
Benefits Offered: Behavioral Health, Disease Management,
Prescription, Wellness

Type of Coverage
Individual
Catastrophic Illness Benefit: Maximum $1M

Subscriber Information
Average Monthly Fee Per Subscriber
(Employee + Employer Contribution):
Employee Only (Self): $307
Average Annual Deductible Per Subscriber:
Employee Only (Self): Varies
Average Subscriber Co-Payment:
Primary Care Physician: $25
Non-Network Physician: $35
Prescription Drugs: $10
Hospital ER: $100

222 CIGNA HealthCare of Connecticut
900 Cottage Grove Road
C8NAS
Hartford, CT 06152-7314
Toll-Free: 866-438-2446
Phone: 860-226-6000
Fax: 860-226-2333
www.cigna.com
For Profit Organization: Yes
Year Founded: 1986
Number of Affiliated Hospitals: 28
Number of Primary Care Physicians: 11,300
Number of Referral/Specialty Physicians: 4,500
Total Enrollment: 29,506
State Enrollment: 29,506

Healthplan and Services Defined
PLAN TYPE: HMO
Model Type: IPA
Benefits Offered: Dental, Disease Management, Prescription,
Transplant, Wellness

Type of Coverage
Commercial, Individual

Catastrophic Illness Benefit: Varies per case
Type of Payment Plans Offered
FFS

Geographic Areas Served
Fairfield, Hartford, Litchfield, Middlesex, New Haven, New London,
Tolland, Windham counties

Subscriber Information
Average Annual Deductible Per Subscriber:
Employee Only (Self): $0
Employee & 1 Family Member: $0
Employee & 2 Family Members: $0
Medicare: $0
Average Subscriber Co-Payment:
Primary Care Physician: $5.00-15.00
Prescription Drugs: $10.00
Hospital ER: $50.00
Home Health Care Max. Days/Visits Covered: Based on medical
nec
Nursing Home Max. Days/Visits Covered: Varies

Publishes and Distributes Report Card: Yes

Accreditation Certification
NCQA
TJC Accreditation

Key Personnel
President . . . . David Cordani
CEO . . . . H Edward Hanway
CFO . . . . Michael W Bell

223 ConnectiCare
175 Scott Swamp Road
PO Box 4050
Farmington, CT 06034-4050
Toll-Free: 800-251-7722
Phone: 860-674-5757
Fax: 860-674-2011
info@connecticare.com
www.connecticare.com
For Profit Organization: Yes
Year Founded: 1981
Owned by an Integrated Delivery Network (IDN): Yes
Number of Affiliated Hospitals: 126
Number of Primary Care Physicians: 5,580
Number of Referral/Specialty Physicians: 11,800
Total Enrollment: 240,000
State Enrollment: 160,000

Healthplan and Services Defined
PLAN TYPE: HMO/PPO
Other Type: POS
Model Type: IPA, HMO, POS
Plan Specialty: Disease Management, Vision, UR
Benefits Offered: Behavioral Health, Chiropractic, Complementary
Medicine, Dental, Disease Management, Home Care, Inpatient
SNF, Physical Therapy, Podiatry, Prescription, Psychiatric,
Transplant, Vision, Wellness, Medical

Type of Coverage
Commercial, Individual, Medicare, Medicare Advantage
Catastrophic Illness Benefit: Unlimited

Type of Payment Plans Offered
Capitated, FFS

Geographic Areas Served
All of Connecticut, Hampshire, Hampden, Franklin and Berkshire
counties in Massachusetts, Westchester, Rockland, Putnam and
Orange counties in New York

Subscriber Information
Average Monthly Fee Per Subscriber
(Employee + Employer Contribution):
Employee Only (Self): Proprietary

Employee & 1 Family Member: Proprietary
Employee & 2 Family Members: Proprietary
Medicare: Proprietary
Average Subscriber Co-Payment:
  Non-Network Physician: $10.00
  Prescription Drugs: $10.00
  Hospital ER: $25.00
  Nursing Home Max. Days/Visits Covered: 90

Network Qualifications
Pre-Admission Certification: Yes

Peer Review Type
Utilization Review: Yes
Second Surgical Opinion: Yes
Case Management: Yes

Publishes and Distributes Report Card: Yes

Accreditation Certification
TJC, NCQA
Utilization Review, Pre-Admission Certification, State Licensure,
  Quality Assurance Program

Key Personnel
President/CEO . . . . Michael Wise
VP Network Operations . . . . Kathleen Madden
Credentialing Manager . . . . Joyce Vagts
Pharmacy Serv Director . . . . Jeff Casberg, RPh
Marketing Director . . . . Ezio Sabatino
VP/CIO . . . . Mark Verre
Media Contact . . . . Stephen Jewett
  publicrelations@connecticare.com

Average Claim Compensation
Physician's Fees Charged: 100%
Hospital's Fees Charged: 100%

Specialty Managed Care Partners
United Behavioral Health, Express Scripts
Enters into Contracts with Regional Business Coalitions: No

Employer References
Federal Government, Hartford Insurance Company, United
  Technologies, State of Connecticut

224 Delta Dental of New Jersey & Connecticut
1639 Route 10
PO Box 222
Parsippany, NJ 07054-0222
Toll-Free: 800-452-9310
Phone: 973-285-4000
Fax: 973-285-4141
marketing@deltadentalnj.com
www.deltadentalnj.com
Non-Profit Organization: Yes
Year Founded: 1969
Total Enrollment: 54,000,000

Healthplan and Services Defined
  PLAN TYPE: Dental
  Other Type: Dental HMO/PPO/POS
  Model Type: Staff
  Plan Specialty: Dental
  Benefits Offered: Dental

Type of Coverage
Commercial

Type of Payment Plans Offered
POS, DFFS, Capitated, FFS, Combination FFS & DFFS

Geographic Areas Served
New Jersey and Connecticut

Key Personnel
President/CEO . . . . Walter VenBrunt
CFO . . . . James Suleski
Senior Vice President . . . . Bruce Silverman

Vice President . . . . Scott Navarro, DDS
Vice President . . . . Mark Nadeau
Dir/Media & Public Affair . . . . Elizabeth Risberg
  415-972-8423

225 Great-West Healthcare Connecticut
Acquired by CIGNA

226 Health Net of the Northeast
One Far Mill Crossing
PO Box 904
Shelton, CT 06484-0944
Toll-Free: 800-848-4747
Phone: 203-402-4200
www.healthnet.com
Subsidiary of: Health Net
For Profit Organization: Yes
Year Founded: 1975
Federally Qualified: Yes
Number of Affiliated Hospitals: 248
Number of Primary Care Physicians: 28,538
Number of Referral/Specialty Physicians: 118,089
Total Enrollment: 169,000
State Enrollment: 356,844

Healthplan and Services Defined
  PLAN TYPE: HMO
  Plan Specialty: ASO, EPO
  Benefits Offered: Behavioral Health, Chiropractic, Disease
    Management, Home Care, Inpatient SNF, Physical Therapy,
    Podiatry, Prescription, Psychiatric, Transplant, Vision, Wellness
  DMPI Services Offered: Nurse Advice Line, Disease Management,
    Wellness Program

Type of Coverage
Medicare, Medicaid, HMO, POS, PPO, HSA

Type of Payment Plans Offered
POS

Geographic Areas Served
Connecticut and New Jersey for commercial business; New York:
  Bronx, Dutchess, Kings, Nassau, New York, Orange, Putnam, Queens,
  Richmond, Rockland, Suffolk and Westchester counties; For
  Medicare, the following counties are covered: Connecticut: Fairfield,
  Hartford and New Haven, Litchfield, Middlesex, New London,
  Tollond, Windham

Subscriber Information
Average Monthly Fee Per Subscriber
  (Employee + Employer Contribution):
    Employee Only (Self): $395.15
    Employee & 1 Family Member: $790.30
    Medicare: $83.99
Average Subscriber Co-Payment:
    Primary Care Physician: $15
    Prescription Drugs: Varies
    Home Health Care: Varies
    Nursing Home: Varies

Network Qualifications
Pre-Admission Certification: No

Peer Review Type
Utilization Review: Yes
Case Management: Yes

Key Personnel
President . . . . Linda V Tiano, Esq
Manager, Communications . . . . Lauralee Heckman
  203-225-8583
  lauralee.heckman@healthnet.com

Average Claim Compensation
Physician's Fees Charged: 50%
Hospital's Fees Charged: 45%

Specialty Managed Care Partners
　　Caremark, National Imaging Association, Express Scripts, MHN

Employer References
　　General Dynamics, EB Division, IBM Inc, Altria, American Express

---

227 Health Plan of New York: Connecticut

55 Water Street
New York, NY 10041
Toll-Free: 800-447-8255
Phone: 646-447-5900
Fax: 646-447-3011
www.hipusa.com
Subsidiary of: An Emblem Health Company
Total Enrollment: 1,200,000

Healthplan and Services Defined
　　PLAN TYPE: HMO/PPO
　　Other Type: POS, EPO, ASO
　　Benefits Offered: Chiropractic, Dental, Disease Management, Home
　　　　Care, Inpatient SNF, Physical Therapy, Podiatry, Prescription,
　　　　Psychiatric, Vision, Wellness

Type of Coverage
　　Individual, Medicare

Geographic Areas Served
　　New York, Connecticut, Massachusetts

Subscriber Information
　　Average Monthly Fee Per Subscriber
　　　　(Employee + Employer Contribution):
　　　　　　Employee Only (Self): Varies
　　　　　　Medicare: Varies
　　Average Annual Deductible Per Subscriber:
　　　　　　Employee Only (Self): Varies
　　　　　　Medicare: Varies
　　Average Subscriber Co-Payment:
　　　　　　Primary Care Physician: Varies
　　　　　　Non-Network Physician: Varies
　　　　　　Prescription Drugs: Varies
　　　　　　Hospital ER: Varies
　　　　　　Home Health Care: Varies
　　　　　　Home Health Care Max. Days/Visits Covered: Varies
　　　　　　Nursing Home: Varies
　　　　　　Nursing Home Max. Days/Visits Covered: Varies

---

228 Humana Health Insurance of Connecticut

1 International Blvd
Suite 400
Mahwah, NJ 07495
Toll-Free: 800-967-2370
Phone: 201-512-8818
www.humana.com
For Profit Organization: Yes

Healthplan and Services Defined
　　PLAN TYPE: HMO/PPO

Type of Coverage
　　Commercial, Individual

Accreditation Certification
　　URAC, NCQA, CORE

---

229 Oxford Health Plans: Corporate Headquarters

48 Monroe Turnpike
Trumbull, CT 06611
Toll-Free: 800-444-6222
Phone: 203-459-6000
Fax: 203-459-6464
groupservices@oxfordhealth.com

---

www.oxhp.com
Subsidiary of: UnitedHealthCare
For Profit Organization: Yes
Year Founded: 1984
Owned by an Integrated Delivery Network (IDN): Yes
Number of Affiliated Hospitals: 219
Number of Primary Care Physicians: 17,000
Total Enrollment: 1,600,000
State Enrollment: 70,139

Healthplan and Services Defined
　　PLAN TYPE: HMO/PPO
　　Model Type: IPA, Network, POS
　　Benefits Offered: Behavioral Health, Chiropractic, Complementary
　　　　Medicine, Dental, Disease Management, Home Care, Inpatient
　　　　SNF, Podiatry, Prescription, Psychiatric, Transplant, Vision,
　　　　Wellness
　　Offers Demand Management Patient Information Service: Yes

Type of Coverage
　　Commercial, Individual, Indemnity, Medicare, Catastrophic
　　Catastrophic Illness Benefit: Varies per case

Type of Payment Plans Offered
　　FFS

Geographic Areas Served
　　Connecticut: Fairfield, New Haven, Litchfield, Hartford, Middlesex,
　　　　New London, Tolland & Windham counties; New Jersey: Essex,
　　　　Hudson, Middlesex, Monmouth, Morris, Ocean, Passaic & Somerset
　　　　counties; New York: Bronx, Dutchess, Kings, Nassau, New York,
　　　　Putnam, Queens, Richmond, Rockland, Suffolk, & Westchester
　　　　counties

Subscriber Information
　　Average Monthly Fee Per Subscriber
　　　　(Employee + Employer Contribution):
　　　　　　Employee Only (Self): Varies
　　　　　　Employee & 1 Family Member: Varies
　　　　　　Employee & 2 Family Members: Varies
　　　　　　Medicare: Varies
　　Average Annual Deductible Per Subscriber:
　　　　　　Employee Only (Self): Varies
　　　　　　Employee & 1 Family Member: Varies
　　　　　　Employee & 2 Family Members: Varies
　　　　　　Medicare: Varies

Network Qualifications
　　Pre-Admission Certification: Yes

Peer Review Type
　　Utilization Review: Yes
　　Second Surgical Opinion: Yes
　　Case Management: Yes

Publishes and Distributes Report Card: Yes

Accreditation Certification
　　NCQA
　　TJC Accreditation, Medicare Approved, Utilization Review,
　　　　Pre-Admission Certification, State Licensure, Quality Assurance
　　　　Program

Key Personnel
　　Chairman . . . . Norman Payson, MD
　　CFO . . . . Kurt Thompson

Specialty Managed Care Partners
　　Enters into Contracts with Regional Business Coalitions: Yes

---

230 UnitedHealthCare of Connecticut

185 Asylum Street
Hartford, CT 06103
Toll-Free: 877-832-7734
Phone: 860-702-5000
www.uhc.com
Subsidiary of: UnitedHealth Group
For Profit Organization: Yes

Year Founded: 1991
Total Enrollment: 75,000,000

Healthplan and Services Defined
  PLAN TYPE: HMO/PPO

Key Personnel
  Media Contact . . . . Mary McElrath-Jones
    914-467-2039
    mary_r_mcelrath-jones@uhc.com

Health Insurance Coverage Status and Type of Coverage by Age

Category	All Persons		Under 18 years		Under 65 years		65 years and over	
	Number	%	Number	%	Number	%	Number	%
Total population	881	-	209	-	756	-	125	-
Covered by some type of health insurance	782 *(10)*	88.7 *(0.9)*	197 *(3)*	94.0 *(1.0)*	660 *(11)*	87.3 *(1.0)*	122 *(7)*	97.7 *(0.8)*
Covered by private health insurance	606 *(15)*	68.7 *(1.5)*	134 *(5)*	64.1 *(2.5)*	526 *(15)*	69.6 *(1.6)*	79 *(6)*	63.4 *(3.3)*
Employment based	539 *(15)*	61.1 *(1.6)*	126 *(6)*	60.0 *(2.7)*	486 *(15)*	64.2 *(1.8)*	53 *(5)*	42.4 *(3.5)*
Own employment based	278 *(9)*	31.5 *(0.9)*	0 *(0)*	0.0 *(0.0)*	240 *(9)*	31.7 *(1.0)*	38 *(4)*	30.2 *(2.5)*
Direct purchase	75 *(7)*	8.5 *(0.8)*	10 *(2)*	4.8 *(1.2)*	45 *(6)*	5.9 *(0.8)*	30 *(4)*	24.2 *(2.8)*
Covered by government health insurance	291 *(14)*	33.1 *(1.5)*	78 *(6)*	37.5 *(2.8)*	176 *(11)*	23.3 *(1.5)*	115 *(7)*	92.4 *(1.6)*
Covered by Medicaid	146 *(10)*	16.5 *(1.2)*	73 *(6)*	34.7 *(2.9)*	139 *(10)*	18.4 *(1.4)*	7 *(2)*	5.5 *(1.6)*
Also by private insurance	27 *(4)*	3.1 *(0.5)*	13 *(2)*	6.1 *(1.1)*	24 *(4)*	3.2 *(0.5)*	3 *(1)*	2.5 *(1.0)*
Covered by Medicare	134 *(8)*	15.2 *(0.8)*	0 *(0)*	0.0 *(0.0)*	19 *(3)*	2.5 *(0.4)*	115 *(7)*	91.7 *(1.7)*
Also by private insurance	80 *(6)*	9.1 *(0.7)*	0 *(0)*	0.0 *(0.0)*	8 *(2)*	1.0 *(0.2)*	73 *(6)*	58.1 *(3.4)*
Also by Medicaid	11 *(2)*	1.2 *(0.2)*	0 *(0)*	0.0 *(0.0)*	5 *(1)*	0.6 *(0.2)*	6 *(2)*	4.9 *(1.4)*
Covered by military health care	35 *(7)*	4.0 *(0.8)*	7 *(3)*	3.5 *(1.2)*	27 *(6)*	3.5 *(0.8)*	8 *(2)*	6.4 *(1.6)*
Not covered at any time during the year	99 *(8)*	11.3 *(0.9)*	12 *(2)*	6.0 *(1.0)*	96 *(8)*	12.7 *(1.0)*	3 *(1)*	2.3 *(0.8)*

Note: Numbers in thousands; figures cover 2010; standard error appears in parenthesis; (b) base less than 75,000; (x) not applicable
Source: U.S. Census Bureau, Current Population Survey, 2011 Annual Social and Economic Supplement. Table HI05. Health Insurance Coverage Status and Type of Coverage by State and Age for All People: 2010

Delaware

231 Aetna Health of Delaware
151 Farmington Avenue
Conveyer ASB2
Hartford, CT 06156
Toll-Free: 866-582-9629
www.aetna.com
For Profit Organization: Yes
Total Enrollment: 27,179
State Enrollment: 27,179

Healthplan and Services Defined
PLAN TYPE: HMO
Other Type: POS
Plan Specialty: EPO
Benefits Offered: Dental, Disease Management, Long-Term Care,
Prescription, Wellness, Life, LTD, STD

Type of Coverage
Commercial, Individual

Type of Payment Plans Offered
POS, FFS

Geographic Areas Served
Statewide

Key Personnel
CEO . . . . Ronald A Williams
President . . . . Mark T Bertolini
SVP, General Counsel . . . . William J Casazza
EVP, CFO . . . . Joseph M Zubretsky
Head, M&A Integration . . . . Kay Mooney
SVP, Marketing . . . . Robert E Mead
Chief Medical Officer . . . . Lonny Reisman, MD
SVP, Human Resources . . . . Elease E Wright
SVP, CIO . . . . Meg McCarthy

232 AmeriHealth HMO
Mellon Bank Center
919 Market Street, Suite 1200
Wilmington, DE 19801
Toll-Free: 800-444-6282
Phone: 302-777-6400
Fax: 302-777-6444
www.amerihealth.com
Year Founded: 1995
Number of Affiliated Hospitals: 230
Number of Primary Care Physicians: 37,000
Total Enrollment: 265,000

Healthplan and Services Defined
PLAN TYPE: HMO/PPO
Model Type: IPA
Plan Specialty: Health Insurance
Benefits Offered: Dental, Disease Management, Prescription, Vision,
Wellness, HMO, POS, PPO, HSA

Type of Coverage
Commercial

Geographic Areas Served
Delaware, New Jersey, Pennsylvania

Subscriber Information
Average Subscriber Co-Payment:
Primary Care Physician: $10.00

Network Qualifications
Pre-Admission Certification: Yes

Peer Review Type
Utilization Review: Yes
Second Surgical Opinion: Yes
Case Management: Yes

Publishes and Distributes Report Card: No

Accreditation Certification
NCQA
TJC Accreditation, Medicare Approved, Utilization Review,
Pre-Admission Certification, State Licensure, Quality Assurance
Program

Key Personnel
Chairman and CEO . . . . Joseph Frick
CFO . . . . John Foos
Network Contracting . . . . Christine Sick
Marketing . . . . Robin Colantuono
Media Contact . . . . Kate Wilhelmi
856-778-6552

233 Blue Cross & Blue Shield of Delaware
800 Delaware Ave
Wilmington, DE 19801
Toll-Free: 800-633-2563
Phone: 302-421-3000
Fax: 302-421-3110
info@bcbsde.com
www.bcbsde.com
Non-Profit Organization: Yes
Year Founded: 1935
Number of Affiliated Hospitals: 11
Number of Primary Care Physicians: 762
Number of Referral/Specialty Physicians: 826
Total Enrollment: 400,000
State Enrollment: 400,000

Healthplan and Services Defined
PLAN TYPE: HMO/PPO
Other Type: POS
Model Type: IPA, Network
Benefits Offered: Dental, Disease Management, Prescription, Vision,
Wellness

Type of Coverage
Commercial, Individual, Medicare, Supplemental Medicare

Type of Payment Plans Offered
Combination FFS & DFFS

Geographic Areas Served
Statewide

Key Personnel
President . . . . Timothy J Constantine
302-421-3210
tconstantine@bcbsde.com
Director of Real Estate . . . . Jeff Putz
Claims . . . . Keith Richard
302-421-3263
krichard@bcbsde.com
Network Contracting . . . . Sally Retzko
302-421-2621
sretzko@bcbsde.com
Community Relations . . . . Melissa Lukach
VP Operations . . . . George English
302-421-3290
genglish@bcbsde.com
Information Technology . . . . Marty Hayburn
Provider Services . . . . Diana Ortiz
302-421-3117
dortiz@bcbsde.com

234 CIGNA HealthCare of Delaware
1777 Sentry Parkway West
Gwynedd Hall, Suite 100
Blue Bell, PA 19422
Toll-Free: 800-441-7150
Phone: 215-283-3300

www.cigna.com
For Profit Organization: Yes
Federally Qualified: Yes
Total Enrollment: 984
State Enrollment: 984

Healthplan and Services Defined
    PLAN TYPE: HMO
    Other Type: POS
    Model Type: IPA, Group, Network
    Benefits Offered: Disease Management, Prescription, Transplant,
        Wellness

Type of Coverage
    Commercial

Publishes and Distributes Report Card: Yes

Accreditation Certification
    NCQA
    TJC Accreditation, Medicare Approved, Utilization Review,
        Pre-Admission Certification, State Licensure, Quality Assurance
        Program

Key Personnel
    AVP National Contracting . . . . Diane Exline Van De Beek
    General Manager . . . . Vincent Sobocinski
    Care Senior Associate . . . . Lorraine Gray

235 Coventry Health Care of Delaware

2751 Centerville Road
Suite 400
Wilmington, DE 19808
Toll-Free: 800-833-7423
Phone: 302-995-6100
Fax: 302-633-4044
http://chcdelaware.coventryhealthcare.com
Secondary Address: 211 Lake Drive, Newark, DE 19702
For Profit Organization: Yes
Year Founded: 1986
Number of Affiliated Hospitals: 120
Number of Primary Care Physicians: 24,000
Total Enrollment: 100,000

Healthplan and Services Defined
    PLAN TYPE: HMO/PPO
    Other Type: POS
    Model Type: Group, Individual
    Benefits Offered: Behavioral Health, Worker's Compensation

Type of Coverage
    Medicare, Medicaid

Geographic Areas Served
    Delaware, Maryland, southern Pennsylvania, southern New Jersey

Accreditation Certification
    URAC

Key Personnel
    Chief Executive Officer . . . . Mark Malloy
    Executive Director . . . . Timothy Nonal
    Chief Financial Officer . . . . James Hinek

236 Delta Dental of the Mid-Atlantic

One Delta Drive
Mechanicsburg, PA 17055-6999
Toll-Free: 800-471-7091
Fax: 717-766-8719
www.deltadentalins.com
Non-Profit Organization: Yes
Total Enrollment: 54,000,000

Healthplan and Services Defined
    PLAN TYPE: Dental
    Other Type: Dental PPO

Type of Coverage
    Commercial

Geographic Areas Served
    Statewide

Key Personnel
    President/CEO . . . . Gary D Radine
    VP, Public & Govt Affairs . . . . Jeff Album
        415-972-8418
    Dir/Media & Public Affair . . . . Elizabeth Risberg
        415-972-8423

237 eHealthInsurance Services Inc.

11919 Foundation Place
Gold River, CA 95670
Toll-Free: 800-977-8860
info@ehealthinsurance.com
www.e.healthinsurance.com
Year Founded: 1997

Healthplan and Services Defined
    PLAN TYPE: HMO/PPO
    Benefits Offered: Dental, Life, STD

Type of Coverage
    Commercial, Individual, Medicare

Geographic Areas Served
    All 50 states in the USA and District of Columbia

Key Personnel
    Chairman & CEO . . . . Gary L. Lauer
    EVP/Business & Corp. Dev. Bruce Telkamp
    EVP/Chief Technology . . . . Dr. Sheldon X. Wang
    SVP & CFO . . . . Stuart M. Huizinga
    Pres. of eHealth Gov. Sys . . . . Samuel C. Gibbs
    SVP of Sales & Operations . . . . Robert S. Hurley
    Director Public Relations . . . . Nate Purpura
        650-210-3115

238 Great-West Healthcare Delaware

Acquired by CIGNA

239 Humana Health Insurance of Delaware

1 International Blvd
Suite 400
Mahwah, NJ 07495
Toll-Free: 800-967-2370
Phone: 201-512-8818
www.humana.com
For Profit Organization: Yes

Healthplan and Services Defined
    PLAN TYPE: HMO/PPO

Type of Coverage
    Commercial, Individual

Accreditation Certification
    URAC, NCQA, CORE

240 Mid Atlantic Medical Services: Delaware

2 West Rolling Crossroads
Suite 11
Baltimore, MD 21228
Toll-Free: 800-782-1966
Phone: 410-869-7400
Fax: 410-869-7583
masales99@uhc.com
www.mamsiunitedhealthcare.com
Subsidiary of: United Healthcare/United Health Group
Year Founded: 1986

Number of Affiliated Hospitals: 342
Number of Primary Care Physicians: 3,276
Total Enrollment: 180,000

Healthplan and Services Defined
PLAN TYPE: HMO/PPO
Model Type: IPA, Network
Benefits Offered: Disease Management, Prescription, Wellness

Type of Payment Plans Offered
Combination FFS & DFFS

Geographic Areas Served
Delaware, Maryland, North Carolina, Pennsylvania, Virginia, Washington DC, West Virginia

Network Qualifications
Pre-Admission Certification: Yes

Peer Review Type
Utilization Review: Yes
Second Surgical Opinion: Yes
Case Management: Yes

Publishes and Distributes Report Card: No

Accreditation Certification
TJC, NCQA

Key Personnel
President/CEO . . . . Thomas P Barbera
CFO. . . . . Robert E Foss
EVP/CIO. . . . . R Larry Mauzy

Specialty Managed Care Partners
Enters into Contracts with Regional Business Coalitions: Yes

241 Unison Health Plan of Delaware

3844 Kennett Pike
Powder Mill Square, Suite 210
Greenville, DE 19807
Phone: 302-429-7800
Fax: 866-915-0309
www.uhccommunityplan.com
Subsidiary of: AmeriChoice, A UnitedHealth Group Company

Healthplan and Services Defined
PLAN TYPE: HMO

Type of Coverage
Supplemental Medicare

Key Personnel
Marketing Director. . . . . Dorinda Borer
Chief Medical Officer. . . . . H. Guerra-Garcia, MD
Sales Director. . . . . Dorinda Borer
Media Contact. . . . . Jeff Smith
952-931-5685
jeff.smith@uhc.com

242 UnitedHealthCare of the Mid-Atlantic

6095 Marshalee Drive
Suite 200
Elkridge, MD 21075
Toll-Free: 800-307-7820
Phone: 410-379-3402
Fax: 410-379-3446
www.uhc.com
Subsidiary of: UnitedHealth Group
Non-Profit Organization: Yes
Year Founded: 1976
Number of Affiliated Hospitals: 58
Number of Primary Care Physicians: 2,559
Number of Referral/Specialty Physicians: 8,300
Total Enrollment: 75,000,000
State Enrollment: 20,538

Healthplan and Services Defined
PLAN TYPE: HMO/PPO
Model Type: Network
Benefits Offered: Disease Management, Prescription, Wellness
Offers Demand Management Patient Information Service: Yes

Geographic Areas Served
Statewide

Subscriber Information
Average Monthly Fee Per Subscriber
(Employee + Employer Contribution):
Employee Only (Self): $104.00-135.00
Employee & 1 Family Member: $143.00-184.00
Employee & 2 Family Members: $331.00-440.00
Medicare: $112.00-156.00
Average Annual Deductible Per Subscriber:
Employee Only (Self): $100.00-250.00
Employee & 1 Family Member: $500.00-1500.00
Employee & 2 Family Members: $200.00-500.00
Medicare: $0
Average Subscriber Co-Payment:
Primary Care Physician: $5.00/10.00
Non-Network Physician: Deductible
Prescription Drugs: $5.00/10.00
Hospital ER: $25.00/50.00
Home Health Care: $5.00/10.00

Network Qualifications
Pre-Admission Certification: Yes

Peer Review Type
Utilization Review: Yes
Second Surgical Opinion: Yes
Case Management: Yes

Publishes and Distributes Report Card: Yes

Accreditation Certification
TJC Accreditation, Medicare Approved, Utilization Review, Pre-Admission Certification, State Licensure, Quality Assurance Program

Specialty Managed Care Partners
Enters into Contracts with Regional Business Coalitions: Yes

Health Insurance Coverage Status and Type of Coverage by Age

Category	All Persons		Under 18 years		Under 65 years		65 years and over	
	Number	%	Number	%	Number	%	Number	%
Total population	608	-	114	-	531	-	77	-
Covered by some type of health insurance	532 *(7)*	87.5 *(1.1)*	108 *(2)*	94.9 *(1.3)*	457 *(8)*	86.2 *(1.2)*	75 *(4)*	96.9 *(0.9)*
Covered by private health insurance	379 *(9)*	62.3 *(1.5)*	54 *(3)*	47.4 *(3.0)*	336 *(9)*	63.2 *(1.6)*	43 *(3)*	55.9 *(3.1)*
Employment based	333 *(9)*	54.8 *(1.4)*	50 *(3)*	43.6 *(2.9)*	300 *(9)*	56.6 *(1.6)*	33 *(3)*	42.7 *(2.9)*
Own employment based	235 *(7)*	38.7 *(1.0)*	1 *(0)*	0.6 *(0.4)*	206 *(7)*	38.9 *(1.1)*	29 *(2)*	37.0 *(2.6)*
Direct purchase	54 *(5)*	8.9 *(0.8)*	5 *(1)*	4.4 *(1.0)*	42 *(4)*	8.0 *(0.8)*	12 *(2)*	15.1 *(2.2)*
Covered by government health insurance	212 *(8)*	34.9 *(1.3)*	60 *(3)*	52.6 *(2.9)*	144 *(7)*	27.2 *(1.4)*	68 *(4)*	88.2 *(1.8)*
Covered by Medicaid	140 *(7)*	23.0 *(1.2)*	58 *(3)*	50.4 *(3.0)*	131 *(7)*	24.7 *(1.4)*	9 *(2)*	11.3 *(2.0)*
Also by private insurance	18 *(3)*	3.0 *(0.5)*	4 *(1)*	3.5 *(1.1)*	16 *(3)*	3.1 *(0.5)*	2 *(1)*	2.3 *(0.8)*
Covered by Medicare	79 *(5)*	13.0 *(0.8)*	1 *(1)*	1.2 *(0.6)*	11 *(2)*	2.2 *(0.4)*	67 *(4)*	87.0 *(1.8)*
Also by private insurance	39 *(3)*	6.5 *(0.6)*	0 *(0)*	0.3 *(0.3)*	3 *(1)*	0.6 *(0.2)*	36 *(3)*	46.6 *(3.2)*
Also by Medicaid	13 *(2)*	2.1 *(0.3)*	0 *(0)*	0.3 *(0.3)*	5 *(1)*	0.9 *(0.2)*	8 *(2)*	10.7 *(2.0)*
Covered by military health care	11 *(2)*	1.9 *(0.3)*	1 *(1)*	1.3 *(0.7)*	6 *(2)*	1.2 *(0.3)*	5 *(1)*	6.5 *(1.5)*
Not covered at any time during the year	76 *(7)*	12.5 *(1.1)*	6 *(1)*	5.1 *(1.3)*	73 *(6)*	13.8 *(1.2)*	2 *(1)*	3.1 *(0.9)*

Note: Numbers in thousands; figures cover 2010; standard error appears in parenthesis; (b) base less than 75,000; (x) not applicable
Source: U.S. Census Bureau, Current Population Survey, 2011 Annual Social and Economic Supplement. Table HI05. Health Insurance Coverage Status and Type of Coverage by State and Age for All People: 2010

District of Columbia

243 Aetna Health District of Columbia
151 Farmintgon Avenue
Conveyer ASB2
Hartford, CT 06156
Toll-Free: 866-582-9629
www.aetna.com
For Profit Organization: Yes
Year Founded: 1986
Number of Affiliated Hospitals: 64
Number of Primary Care Physicians: 1,898
Total Enrollment: 211,156

Healthplan and Services Defined
PLAN TYPE: HMO
Benefits Offered: Disease Management, Wellness

Geographic Areas Served
Statewide

Accreditation Certification
TJC Accreditation, Medicare Approved, Utilization Review,
Pre-Admission Certification, State Licensure, Quality Assurance
Program

Key Personnel
CEO . . . . .Ronald A Williams
President. . . . . .Mark T Bertolini
SVP, General Counsel . . . . .William J Casazza
EVP, CFO . . . . .Joseph M Zubretsky
Head, M&A Integration . . . . .Kay Mooney
SVP, Marketing. . . . . .Robert E Mead
Chief Medical Officer .Lonny Reisman, MD
SVP, Human Resources. .Elease E Wright
SVP, CIO. . . . . .Meg McCarthy

244 CareFirst Blue Cross Blue Shield
840 First Street NE
Union Center Plaza
Washington, DC 20065
Toll-Free: 866-520-6099
Phone: 202-484-9100
www.carefirst.com
Non-Profit Organization: Yes
Year Founded: 1984
Number of Affiliated Hospitals: 165
Number of Primary Care Physicians: 4,500
Total Enrollment: 550,000

Healthplan and Services Defined
PLAN TYPE: HMO/PPO
Model Type: Network
Benefits Offered: Prescription

Type of Coverage
Commercial, Individual, Medicare
Catastrophic Illness Benefit: Unlimited

Geographic Areas Served
Areas of Fairfax and Prince William counties, Maryland, District of
Columbia, Arlington county, town of Vienna and the cities of
Alexandria and Fairfax

Accreditation Certification
NCQA
TJC Accreditation, Medicare Approved, Utilization Review,
Pre-Admission Certification, State Licensure, Quality Assurance
Program

Key Personnel
Chairman/CEO . . . . .Chester Burrell
CFO . . . . .Mark Chaney
Executive Director, NCA . . . . .Maynard McAlpin
In-House Formulary . . . . .Winston Wong, MD

Specialty Managed Care Partners
Enters into Contracts with Regional Business Coalitions: Yes

245 CIGNA HealthCare of the Mid-Atlantic
10490 Little Patuxent Parkway
60 Corporate Center Suite 400
Columbia, MD 21044
Toll-Free: 866-438-2446
Phone: 410-884-2500
Fax: 800-657-3073
www.cigna.com
For Profit Organization: Yes
Year Founded: 1984
Physician Owned Organization: No
Number of Affiliated Hospitals: 54
Number of Primary Care Physicians: 2,032
Number of Referral/Specialty Physicians: 5,028
Total Enrollment: 109,186

Healthplan and Services Defined
PLAN TYPE: HMO/PPO
Model Type: IPA
Benefits Offered: Disease Management, Prescription, Transplant,
Wellness
Offers Demand Management Patient Information Service: Yes

Type of Coverage
Commercial

Type of Payment Plans Offered
Combination FFS & DFFS

Geographic Areas Served
District of Columbia, Maryland, Virginia

Network Qualifications
Pre-Admission Certification: Yes

Peer Review Type
Utilization Review: Yes
Second Surgical Opinion: Yes
Case Management: Yes

Publishes and Distributes Report Card: Yes

Accreditation Certification
NCQA

Specialty Managed Care Partners
CIGNA Dental, CIGNA Behavioral Health
Enters into Contracts with Regional Business Coalitions: No

246 DC Chartered Health Plan
1025 15th Street NW
Washington, DC 20005-4205
Toll-Free: 800-408-7511
Phone: 202-408-4720
Fax: 202-408-4730
member-services@chartered-health.com
www.chartered-health.com
For Profit Organization: Yes
Year Founded: 1987
Total Enrollment: 70,000
State Enrollment: 70,000

Healthplan and Services Defined
PLAN TYPE: HMO
Model Type: IPA
Benefits Offered: Prescription

Type of Coverage
Medicaid

Geographic Areas Served
District of Columbia

Publishes and Distributes Report Card: Yes

Accreditation Certification
    NCQA

Key Personnel
    President/CEO...............................Gabriel J Hanna
    Acting CFO ....Joel Neil Lowry, CPA
    COO ....Robert E Watkins
    SVP, General Counsel ....Francis S Smith
    SVP, Health Plan Services...................Leslie Lyles Smith
    Chief Medical Officer....................Lavdena Adams, MD
    SVP, Chief Tech Officer.....................Khalil Bouharoun

Specialty Managed Care Partners
    Enters into Contracts with Regional Business Coalitions: Yes

247   Delta Dental of the Mid-Atlantic
One Delta Drive
Mechanicsburg, PA 17055-6999
Toll-Free: 800-471-7091
Fax: 717-766-8719
www.deltadentalins.com
Non-Profit Organization: Yes
Total Enrollment: 54,000,000

Healthplan and Services Defined
    PLAN TYPE: Dental
    Other Type: Dental PPO

Type of Coverage
    Commercial

Geographic Areas Served
    Statewide

Key Personnel
    President/CEO...............................Gary D Radine
    VP, Public & Govt Affairs ....Jeff Album
        415-972-8418
    Dir/Media & Public Affair ....Elizabeth Risberg
        415-972-8423

248   eHealthInsurance Services Inc.
11919 Foundation Place
Gold River, CA 95670
Toll-Free: 800-977-8860
info@ehealthinsurance.com
www.e.healthinsurance.com
Year Founded: 1997

Healthplan and Services Defined
    PLAN TYPE: HMO/PPO
    Benefits Offered: Dental, Life, STD

Type of Coverage
    Commercial, Individual, Medicare

Geographic Areas Served
    All 50 states in the USA and District of Columbia

Key Personnel
    Chairman & CEO ....Gary L. Lauer
    EVP/Business & Corp. Dev.....................Bruce Telkamp
    EVP/Chief Technology...................Dr. Sheldon X. Wang
    SVP & CFO ....Stuart M. Huizinga
    Pres. of eHealth Gov. Sys ....Samuel C. Gibbs
    SVP of Sales & Operations ....Robert S. Hurley
    Director Public Relations.......................Nate Purpura
        650-210-3115

249   Humana Health Insurance of D.C.
1 International Blvd
Suite 400
Mahwah, NJ 07495

Toll-Free: 8000-967-2370
Phone: 201-512-8818
www.humana.com
For Profit Organization: Yes

Healthplan and Services Defined
    PLAN TYPE: HMO/PPO

Type of Coverage
    Commercial, Individual

Accreditation Certification
    URAC, NCQA, CORE

250   Mid Atlantic Medical Services: DC
3 Taft Court
Rockville, MD 20850
Toll-Free: 800-884-5188
Phone: 301-545-5300
Fax: 301-545-5380
masales99@uhc.com
www.mamsiunitedhealthcare.com
Subsidiary of: United Healthcare/United Health Group
Year Founded: 1986
Number of Affiliated Hospitals: 342
Number of Primary Care Physicians: 3,276
Total Enrollment: 180,000

Healthplan and Services Defined
    PLAN TYPE: HMO/PPO
    Model Type: IPA, Network
    Benefits Offered: Disease Management, Prescription, Wellness

Type of Payment Plans Offered
    Combination FFS & DFFS

Geographic Areas Served
    Delaware, Maryland, North Carolina, Pennsylvania, Virginia,
    Washington DC, West Virginia

Network Qualifications
    Pre-Admission Certification: Yes

Peer Review Type
    Utilization Review: Yes
    Second Surgical Opinion: Yes
    Case Management: Yes

Publishes and Distributes Report Card: No

Accreditation Certification
    TJC, NCQA

Specialty Managed Care Partners
    Enters into Contracts with Regional Business Coalitions: Yes

251   Quality Plan Administrators
7824 Eastern Avenue NW
Suite 100
Washington, DC 20012
Toll-Free: 800-900-4112
Phone: 202-722-2744
Fax: 202-291-5703
qpa2000@aol.com
www.qualityplanadmin.com
For Profit Organization: Yes
Year Founded: 1986
Number of Primary Care Physicians: 175
Total Enrollment: 90,000
State Enrollment: 90,000

Healthplan and Services Defined
    PLAN TYPE: HMO/PPO
    Other Type: Dental/Vision
    Plan Specialty: Dental, Vision
    Benefits Offered: Dental, Vision

Key Personnel
President/CEO . . . . Milton Bernard, DDS
CFO . . . . Alphonzo L Davidson, DDS
Manager . . . . Barry Scott
Credentialing . . . . Grace Coward
Dental Manager . . . . Martha McClary
Materials Management . . . . Desi Bernard
Member Services . . . . Nasia Eudell
Information Systems . . . . Wilfred Welsh

Employer References
DC Chartered Health Plan, Healthright, Vision Plan for DC
  Government, Health Services for Children with Special Needs, DC
  Healthcare Alliance, DC Healthy Smiles (Medicaid)

---

252 Unison Health Plan of the Capital Area

1001 Pennsylvania Ave NW
Suite 600 South
Washington, DC
Toll-Free: 877-856-6444
www.unisonhealthplan.com
Subsidiary of: AmeriChoice, A UnitedHealth Group Company

Healthplan and Services Defined
PLAN TYPE: HMO

Key Personnel
Media Contact . . . . Jeff Smith
  952-931-5685
  jeff.smith@uhc.com

---

253 UnitedHealthCare of the District of Columbia

4416 East West Highway
Suite 310
Bethesda, MD 20814
Toll-Free: 800-307-7820
www.uhc.com
Subsidiary of: UnitedHealth Group
Non-Profit Organization: Yes
Year Founded: 1976
Number of Affiliated Hospitals: 58
Number of Primary Care Physicians: 2,559
Number of Referral/Specialty Physicians: 8,300
Total Enrollment: 75,000,000
State Enrollment: 176,000

Healthplan and Services Defined
PLAN TYPE: HMO/PPO
Model Type: Network
Benefits Offered: Disease Management, Prescription, Wellness
Offers Demand Management Patient Information Service: Yes

Geographic Areas Served
Statewide

Subscriber Information
Average Monthly Fee Per Subscriber
  (Employee + Employer Contribution):
    Employee Only (Self): $104.00-135.00
    Employee & 1 Family Member: $143.00-184.00
    Employee & 2 Family Members: $331.00-440.00
    Medicare: $112.00-156.00
Average Annual Deductible Per Subscriber:
    Employee Only (Self): $100.00-250.00
    Employee & 1 Family Member: $500.00-1500.00
    Employee & 2 Family Members: $200.00-500.00
    Medicare: $0
Average Subscriber Co-Payment:
    Primary Care Physician: $5.00/10.00
    Non-Network Physician: Deductible
    Prescription Drugs: $5.00/10.00
    Hospital ER: $25.00/50.00

Home Health Care: $5.00/10.00

Network Qualifications
Pre-Admission Certification: Yes

Peer Review Type
Utilization Review: Yes
Second Surgical Opinion: Yes
Case Management: Yes

Publishes and Distributes Report Card: Yes

Accreditation Certification
TJC Accreditation, Medicare Approved, Utilization Review,
  Pre-Admission Certification, State Licensure, Quality Assurance
  Program

Specialty Managed Care Partners
Enters into Contracts with Regional Business Coalitions: Yes

Health Insurance Coverage Status and Type of Coverage by Age

Category	All Persons		Under 18 years		Under 65 years		65 years and over	
	Number	%	Number	%	Number	%	Number	%
Total population	18,531	-	4,042	-	15,369	-	3,162	-
Covered by some type of health insurance	14,677 *(155)*	79.2 *(0.8)*	3,466 *(58)*	85.8 *(1.3)*	11,587 *(158)*	75.4 *(0.9)*	3,090 *(94)*	97.7 *(0.4)*
Covered by private health insurance	10,608 *(203)*	57.2 *(1.1)*	2,234 *(78)*	55.3 *(1.9)*	9,087 *(184)*	59.1 *(1.2)*	1,521 *(88)*	48.1 *(2.0)*
Employment based	9,015 *(194)*	48.6 *(1.0)*	2,045 *(76)*	50.6 *(1.8)*	8,115 *(183)*	52.8 *(1.2)*	900 *(64)*	28.5 *(1.7)*
Own employment based	5,084 *(120)*	27.4 *(0.6)*	17 *(6)*	0.4 *(0.1)*	4,404 *(107)*	28.7 *(0.7)*	680 *(54)*	21.5 *(1.5)*
Direct purchase	1,805 *(108)*	9.7 *(0.6)*	241 *(29)*	6.0 *(0.7)*	1,099 *(79)*	7.1 *(0.5)*	707 *(59)*	22.4 *(1.7)*
Covered by government health insurance	6,363 *(158)*	34.3 *(0.8)*	1,571 *(64)*	38.9 *(1.6)*	3,384 *(143)*	22.0 *(0.9)*	2,979 *(92)*	94.2 *(0.7)*
Covered by Medicaid	2,691 *(108)*	14.5 *(0.6)*	1,409 *(63)*	34.8 *(1.6)*	2,340 *(97)*	15.2 *(0.6)*	351 *(41)*	11.1 *(1.3)*
Also by private insurance	489 *(49)*	2.6 *(0.3)*	238 *(37)*	5.9 *(0.9)*	409 *(46)*	2.7 *(0.3)*	80 *(18)*	2.5 *(0.6)*
Covered by Medicare	3,482 *(89)*	18.8 *(0.5)*	18 *(7)*	0.5 *(0.2)*	525 *(42)*	3.4 *(0.3)*	2,957 *(91)*	93.5 *(0.8)*
Also by private insurance	1,507 *(82)*	8.1 *(0.4)*	7 *(4)*	0.2 *(0.1)*	112 *(22)*	0.7 *(0.1)*	1,395 *(84)*	44.1 *(2.0)*
Also by Medicaid	531 *(46)*	2.9 *(0.2)*	11 *(5)*	0.3 *(0.1)*	192 *(22)*	1.3 *(0.1)*	339 *(39)*	10.7 *(1.2)*
Covered by military health care	1,167 *(128)*	6.3 *(0.7)*	198 *(37)*	4.9 *(0.9)*	834 *(112)*	5.4 *(0.7)*	333 *(41)*	10.5 *(1.3)*
Not covered at any time during the year	3,854 *(144)*	20.8 *(0.8)*	576 *(51)*	14.2 *(1.3)*	3,782 *(143)*	24.6 *(0.9)*	72 *(12)*	2.3 *(0.4)*

Note: Numbers in thousands; figures cover 2010; standard error appears in parenthesis; (b) base less than 75,000; (x) not applicable
Source: U.S. Census Bureau, Current Population Survey, 2011 Annual Social and Economic Supplement. Table HI05. Health Insurance Coverage Status and Type of Coverage by State and Age for All People: 2010

Florida

254 Aetna Health of Florida
11675 Great Oaks Way
Alpharetta, GA 30022
Toll-Free: 866-582-9629
www.aetna.com
For Profit Organization: Yes
Total Enrollment: 521,696
State Enrollment: 521,696

Healthplan and Services Defined
PLAN TYPE: HMO
Other Type: POS
Plan Specialty: EPO
Benefits Offered: Dental, Disease Management, Long-Term Care,
Prescription, Wellness, Life, LTD, STD

Type of Coverage
Commercial, Individual

Type of Payment Plans Offered
POS, FFS

Geographic Areas Served
Statewide

255 American Pioneer Life Insurance Co
1001 Heathrow Park Lane
Suite 5001
Lake Mary, FL 32741
Toll-Free: 800-538-1053
www.amerpion.com
Subsidiary of: Universal American
For Profit Organization: Yes
Year Founded: 1961

Healthplan and Services Defined
PLAN TYPE: Medicare

Type of Coverage
Medicare, Supplemental Medicare

Key Personnel
Chairman of the Board . . . . .Richard A Barasch
President & CEO. . . . . .Gary W Bryant, CPA
Executive Vice President. . . . . .Theodore M Carpenter, Jr
VP, Marketing . . . . .Harry Jenkins
EVP, CFO . . . . .Robert A Waegelein
VP, Marketing & Staff Op . . . . .Mark E Yeager
SVP, Project Management . . . . .Dana Adams
VP, Marketing Support .Nancy Walko
VP, Financial Reporting .William H Cushman
VP, Underwriting . . . . .James Kalmer
SVP, Finance & Treasurer . . . . .John Squarok, CPA
VP, Product Filing. . . . . .Michelle Doherty
SVP, Managed Care . . . . .Gary M Jacobs
VP, Market Conduct. . . . . .John T Mackin, Jr
SVP, Operations. . . . . .Roslind Nelles

256 Amerigroup Florida
4200 W Cypress Street
Suite 900
Tampa, FL 33607
Phone: 813-830-6900
Fax: 813-314-2050
www.amerigroupcorp.com
Secondary Address: 621 NW 53rd Street, Suite 175, Boca Raton, FL
33487
Subsidiary of: Amerigroup Corporation
For Profit Organization: Yes
Owned by an Integrated Delivery Network (IDN): Yes

Number of Affiliated Hospitals: 30
Number of Primary Care Physicians: 1,000
Total Enrollment: 1,900,000
State Enrollment: 237,000

Healthplan and Services Defined
PLAN TYPE: HMO
Model Type: Network
Plan Specialty: ASO, Behavioral Health, Chiropractic, Dental,
Disease Management, EPO, Lab, MSO, PBM, Vision, Radiology,
Medicaid
Benefits Offered: Behavioral Health, Chiropractic, Complementary
Medicine, Dental, Disease Management, Home Care, Inpatient
SNF, Long-Term Care, Physical Therapy, Podiatry, Prescription,
Psychiatric, Transplant, Vision, Wellness, AD&D, Medicaid
Offers Demand Management Patient Information Service: Yes

Type of Coverage
Individual, Medicare, Medicaid, Healthy kids

Geographic Areas Served
Tampa, Orlando and Miami-Fort Lauderdale areas

Publishes and Distributes Report Card: Yes

Key Personnel
CEO . . . . .Don Gilmore
813-830-6900
Marketing President. . . . . .David Rodriguez
Chief Medical Officer. . . . . .John Knispel

Specialty Managed Care Partners
Enters into Contracts with Regional Business Coalitions: Yes

257 Assurant Employee Benefits: Florida
5401 W Kennedy Blvd
Suite 760
Tampa, FL 33609-2428
Phone: 813-286-7736
Fax: 813-289-8315
benefits@assurant.com
www.assurantemployeebenefits.com
Subsidiary of: Assurant, Inc
For Profit Organization: Yes
Number of Primary Care Physicians: 112,000
Total Enrollment: 47,000

Healthplan and Services Defined
PLAN TYPE: Multiple
Plan Specialty: Dental, Vision, Long & Short-Term Disability
Benefits Offered: Dental, Vision, Wellness, AD&D, Life, LTD, STD

Type of Coverage
Commercial, Indemnity, Individual Dental Plans

Geographic Areas Served
Statewide

Subscriber Information
Average Monthly Fee Per Subscriber
(Employee + Employer Contribution):
Employee Only (Self): Varies by plan

Key Personnel
Account Manager . . . . .Matt Beaulieu
PR Specialist. . . . . .Megan Hutchison
816-556-7815
megan.hutchison@assurant.com

258 Avalon Healthcare
3030 North Rocky Point Drive West #800
Rocky Point Center
Tampa, FL 33607
Toll-Free: 877-280-0010
info@avalonhealthcare.com
www.avalonhealthcare.com
For Profit Organization: Yes

Total Enrollment: 6,000

Healthplan and Services Defined
    PLAN TYPE: PPO
    Benefits Offered: Dental, Prescription, Vision

Type of Coverage
    Commercial, Individual

Key Personnel
    Chairman, COO . . . . .Andrew Cassidy
    Founder . . . . .Charles O'Neill
    Chief Executive Officer . . . . .Debye Saxinger Norwig

259   AvMed Health Plan: Corporate Office

9400 S Dadeland Boulevard
Corporate Headquarters
Miami, FL 33156
Toll-Free: 800-477-8768
Phone: 305-671-5437
Fax: 305-671-4764
rxcoaching@avmed.com
www.avmed.org
Subsidiary of: SanteFe Healthcare, Inc.
Non-Profit Organization: Yes
Year Founded: 1973
Number of Affiliated Hospitals: 126
Number of Primary Care Physicians: 2,061
Number of Referral/Specialty Physicians: 7,629
Total Enrollment: 300,000
State Enrollment: 300,000

Healthplan and Services Defined
    PLAN TYPE: HMO
    Model Type: IPA
    Benefits Offered: Disease Management, Prescription, Wellness

Type of Payment Plans Offered
    POS

Geographic Areas Served
    Dade county

Subscriber Information
    Average Annual Deductible Per Subscriber:
        Employee Only (Self): $0
        Employee & 1 Family Member: $0
        Employee & 2 Family Members: $0
        Medicare: $0

Network Qualifications
    Pre-Admission Certification: Yes

Peer Review Type
    Utilization Review: Yes
    Second Surgical Opinion: Yes
    Case Management: Yes

Publishes and Distributes Report Card: Yes

Accreditation Certification
    NCQA
    TJC Accreditation, Medicare Approved, Utilization Review,
        Pre-Admission Certification, State Licensure, Quality Assurance
        Program

Key Personnel
    CEO . . . . .Michael P Gallagher
    President/COO . . . . .Ed Hannum
    SVP, General Counsel . . . . .Stephen J DeMontmollin
    VP, CFO . . . . .Randall L Stuart
    SVP, Network . . . . .Susan Knapp Pinnas
    SVP, Sales & Marketing . . . . .Greg Fischer
    SVP, Chief Medical Offc . . . . .Kirk Cianciolo
    SVP, Member Services . . . . .Kay Ayers
    Sales . . . . .Edwin Hannum
    Director, Communications . . . . .Conchita Ruiz-Topinka
        305-671-7306

Specialty Managed Care Partners
    Enters into Contracts with Regional Business Coalitions: No

260   AvMed Health Plan: Fort Lauderdale

13450 W Sunrise Boulevard
Suite 370
Fort Lauderdale, FL 33323
Toll-Free: 800-368-9189
Phone: 954-462-2520
www.avmed.org
Non-Profit Organization: Yes
Year Founded: 1973
Federally Qualified: Yes
Number of Affiliated Hospitals: 22
Number of Primary Care Physicians: 328
Number of Referral/Specialty Physicians: 564
Total Enrollment: 300,000
State Enrollment: 300,000

Healthplan and Services Defined
    PLAN TYPE: HMO
    Model Type: IPA
    Benefits Offered: Disease Management, Prescription, Wellness

Geographic Areas Served
    Broward county

Subscriber Information
    Average Monthly Fee Per Subscriber
        (Employee + Employer Contribution):
            Employee Only (Self): $145.00
            Employee & 1 Family Member: $320.00
            Employee & 2 Family Members: $410.00
            Medicare: $0
    Average Subscriber Co-Payment:
        Primary Care Physician: $5.00/10.00/15.00
        Prescription Drugs: $5.00/7.00/12.00
        Hospital ER: $30.00/50.00

Accreditation Certification
    TJC, NCQA

Key Personnel
    President/CEO . . . . .Robert Hudson
    Claims . . . . .Doug Cueny
    In House Formulary . . . . .Robert Wilson
    Marketing . . . . .Jill Richardi
    Materials Management . . . . .Bill Waters
    Medical Affairs . . . . .James Moffat, MD
    Information Systems . . . . .Winston Lonsdale
    Provider Services . . . . .Cindy Scavone
    Dir, Communications . . . . .Conchita Ruiz-Topinka
        305-671-7306

261   AvMed Health Plan: Gainesville

4300 NW 89th Boulevard
Gainesville, FL 32606
Toll-Free: 800-346-0231
Phone: 352-372-8400
www.avmed.org
Non-Profit Organization: Yes
Year Founded: 1986
Number of Affiliated Hospitals: 11
Number of Primary Care Physicians: 219
Number of Referral/Specialty Physicians: 596
Total Enrollment: 300,000
State Enrollment: 300,000

Healthplan and Services Defined
    PLAN TYPE: HMO
    Model Type: IPA
    Benefits Offered: Disease Management, Prescription, Wellness
    Offers Demand Management Patient Information Service: Yes

Type of Coverage
Catastrophic Illness Benefit: Unlimited

Type of Payment Plans Offered
POS, DFFS, Combination FFS & DFFS

Geographic Areas Served
Alachua, Bradford, Citrus, Columbia, Dixie, Gilchrist, Hamilton, Levy, Marion, Suwannee and Union counties

Subscriber Information
Average Monthly Fee Per Subscriber
(Employee + Employer Contribution):
Employee Only (Self): $110.00-135.00
Employee & 1 Family Member: $385.00-460.00
Employee & 2 Family Members: $220.00-260.00
Average Annual Deductible Per Subscriber:
Employee Only (Self): $0
Employee & 1 Family Member: $0
Employee & 2 Family Members: $0
Medicare: $0
Average Subscriber Co-Payment:
Primary Care Physician: $5.00-15.00
Prescription Drugs: $7.00/12.00
Hospital ER: $30.00/50.00
Home Health Care: $0
Nursing Home: $0
Nursing Home Max. Days/Visits Covered: 20

Network Qualifications
Minimum Years of Practice: 5
Pre-Admission Certification: Yes

Peer Review Type
Utilization Review: Yes
Second Surgical Opinion: Yes
Case Management: Yes

Publishes and Distributes Report Card: Yes

Accreditation Certification
NCQA
TJC Accreditation, Medicare Approved, Utilization Review, Pre-Admission Certification, State Licensure, Quality Assurance Program

Key Personnel
President/CEO . . . . .Robert Hudson
CFO. . . . . .Donald Hairston
Director . . . . .Helen Creech
Network Contracting . . . . .Barry Wagner
Medical Affairs. . . . . .Bruce Weiss, MD
Member Services . . . . .Kay Ayers
Provider Services . . . . .Barry Wagner
Sales. . . . . .Ed Hannum
Dir, Communications. . . . . .Conchita Ruiz-Topinka
305-671-7306

Average Claim Compensation
Physician's Fees Charged: 85%
Hospital's Fees Charged: 70%

Specialty Managed Care Partners
Enters into Contracts with Regional Business Coalitions: No

262 AvMed Health Plan: Jacksonville
1300 Riverplace Boulevard
Suite 640
Jacksonville, FL 32207
Toll-Free: 800-227-4184
Phone: 904-858-1300
Fax: 904-858-1355
www.avmed.org
Non-Profit Organization: Yes
Year Founded: 1969
Federally Qualified: Yes
Number of Affiliated Hospitals: 12

Number of Primary Care Physicians: 267
Total Enrollment: 300,000
State Enrollment: 300,000
Healthplan and Services Defined
PLAN TYPE: HMO
Model Type: IPA
Benefits Offered: Disease Management, Prescription, Wellness

Type of Coverage
Commercial, Individual, Supplemental Medicare

Geographic Areas Served
Baker, Clay, Duval, Nassau, & St. Johns counties

Subscriber Information
Average Subscriber Co-Payment:
Primary Care Physician: $10.00
Non-Network Physician: Not covered
Prescription Drugs: $7.00
Hospital ER: $50.00

Peer Review Type
Second Surgical Opinion: Yes
Case Management: Yes

Publishes and Distributes Report Card: Yes

Accreditation Certification
NCQA

Key Personnel
President/CEO . . . . .Michael P Gallagher
Dir, Communications. . . . . .Conchita Ruiz-Topinka
305-671-7306

263 AvMed Health Plan: Orlando
1800 Pembrook Drive
Suite 190
Orlando, FL 32810
Toll-Free: 800-227-4848
Phone: 407-539-0007
www.avmed.org
Non-Profit Organization: Yes
Year Founded: 1988
Number of Primary Care Physicians: 1,400
Number of Referral/Specialty Physicians: 775
Total Enrollment: 300,000
State Enrollment: 300,000
Healthplan and Services Defined
PLAN TYPE: HMO
Model Type: IPA
Plan Specialty: ASO, Behavioral Health, Chiropractic, Disease Management, EPO, Lab, Vision, Radiology, UR
Benefits Offered: Disease Management, Prescription, Wellness
Offers Demand Management Patient Information Service: Yes

Type of Coverage
Commercial

Type of Payment Plans Offered
FFS, Combination FFS & DFFS

Geographic Areas Served
Orange, Osceola and Seminole counties

Subscriber Information
Average Subscriber Co-Payment:
Primary Care Physician: $5.00/10.00/15.00
Prescription Drugs: $5.00/7.00/12.00
Hospital ER: $30.00/50.00

Network Qualifications
Pre-Admission Certification: Yes

Peer Review Type
Second Surgical Opinion: Yes

Publishes and Distributes Report Card: Yes

Accreditation Certification
TJC, NCQA
Utilization Review, Quality Assurance Program

Key Personnel
CFO . . . . .Don Hairston
In House Formulary . . . . .James Moffat, MD
Marketing . . . . .David Wells
Materials Management . . . . .Bill Waters
Medical Affairs. . . . . .Marc Edelstein, MD
Provider Services . . . . .Kay Ayers
Sales . . . . .Edwin Hannum
Dir, Communications. . . . . .Conchita Ruiz-Topinka
305-671-7306

Specialty Managed Care Partners
Enters into Contracts with Regional Business Coalitions: Yes

264   AvMed Health Plan: Tampa
1511 North WestShore Blvd
Suite 450
Tampa, FL 33607
Toll-Free: 800-257-2273
Phone: 813-281-5650
Fax: 813-288-3336
www.avmed.org
Non-Profit Organization: Yes
Year Founded: 1969
Federally Qualified: Yes
Number of Affiliated Hospitals: 14
Number of Primary Care Physicians: 240
Number of Referral/Specialty Physicians: 550
Total Enrollment: 300,000
State Enrollment: 300,000

Healthplan and Services Defined
PLAN TYPE: HMO
Model Type: IPA
Benefits Offered: Disease Management, Prescription, Wellness
Offers Demand Management Patient Information Service: Yes

Geographic Areas Served
Hernando, Hillsborough, Lee, Pasco, Pinellas, Polk and Sarasota
counties

Subscriber Information
Average Monthly Fee Per Subscriber
(Employee + Employer Contribution):
Employee Only (Self): Varies
Employee & 1 Family Member: Varies
Employee & 2 Family Members: Varies
Average Annual Deductible Per Subscriber:
Employee Only (Self): Varies
Employee & 1 Family Member: Varies
Employee & 2 Family Members: Varies
Average Subscriber Co-Payment:
Primary Care Physician: Varies
Non-Network Physician: Varies
Prescription Drugs: Varies
Hospital ER: Varies

Network Qualifications
Pre-Admission Certification: Yes

Peer Review Type
Utilization Review: Yes
Second Surgical Opinion: Yes

Publishes and Distributes Report Card: Yes

Accreditation Certification
AAAHC, TJC, NCQA

Key Personnel
President/CEO . . . . .Robert Hudson
Marketing . . . . .James Moffat, MD

Information Systems . . . . .Winston Lonsdale
Sales . . . . .Edwin Hannum
Dir, Communications. . . . . .Conchita Ruiz-Topinka
305-671-7306

Specialty Managed Care Partners
Enters into Contracts with Regional Business Coalitions: Yes

265   AvMed Medicare Preferred
9400 South Dadeland Boulevard
Miami, FL 33156
Toll-Free: 800-782-8633
Phone: 305-671-5437
www.avmed.org
Non-Profit Organization: Yes
Year Founded: 1969
Federally Qualified: Yes

Healthplan and Services Defined
PLAN TYPE: Medicare

Type of Coverage
Medicare, Supplemental Medicare

Key Personnel
President & CEO. . . . . .Bob Hudson
avmedpresident@avmed.org

266   Blue Cross & Blue Shield of Florida: Jacksonville
4800 Deerwood Campus Parkway
Jacksonville, FL 32246
Toll-Free: 800-477-3736
Phone: 904-791-6111
Fax: 904-905-6638
corporatecommunications@bcbsfl.com
www.bcbsfl.com
Mailing Address: PO Box 1798, Jacksonville, FL 32231-0014
Non-Profit Organization: Yes
Year Founded: 1985
Owned by an Integrated Delivery Network (IDN): Yes
Number of Affiliated Hospitals: 211
Number of Primary Care Physicians: 8,977
Number of Referral/Specialty Physicians: 18,451
Total Enrollment: 1,547,873
State Enrollment: 1,373,917

Healthplan and Services Defined
PLAN TYPE: HMO/PPO
Benefits Offered: Behavioral Health, Chiropractic, Complementary
Medicine, Disease Management, Home Care, Inpatient SNF,
Physical Therapy, Podiatry, Prescription, Psychiatric, Transplant,
Wellness
Offers Demand Management Patient Information Service: Yes
DMPI Services Offered: Nurse Line 24x7x365, Health Coaching,
Support for Chronic Conditions, Health Risk Assessments, Web
Tools & Resources

Type of Coverage
Commercial, Individual, Indemnity, Medicare

Type of Payment Plans Offered
FFS

Geographic Areas Served
State of Florida

Subscriber Information
Average Subscriber Co-Payment:
Primary Care Physician: Varies
Non-Network Physician: Varies
Prescription Drugs: Varies
Hospital ER: Varies
Home Health Care: Varies
Nursing Home: Varies

Network Qualifications
Pre-Admission Certification: Yes

Peer Review Type
Utilization Review: Yes

Publishes and Distributes Report Card: No

Accreditation Certification
Utilization Review

Key Personnel
CEO/Chairman . . . . Robert I Lufrano, MD
SVP General Counsel & Sec. Charles Joseph
CFO. . . . . R Chris Doerr
VP Pharmacy Programs . . . . Lowell Sterler
Group VP Marketing. . . . . R John Kaegi
Chief Medical Officer . . . . Jonathan B Gavras, MD
Group VP Service Org . . . . Darnell Smith
Executive VP Business Ops . . . . Duke Livermore
VP Provider Services . . . . Elana Schrader, MD
Group VP Sales/Distrib . . . . Michael Guyette
Director of Sales Compen . . . . Bill Price
Media Contact. . . . . Lauralee W Shapiro
904-905-0461

Specialty Managed Care Partners
Prime Therapeutics, LLC-PBM and Mental Health Network
(MHnet), Health Dialog, Accordant and Quest Diagnostics
Enters into Contracts with Regional Business Coalitions: Yes

Employer References
State of Florida, Gevity HR (formerly Staff Leasing), Publix,
Lincare, Miami Dade County

267 Blue Cross & Blue Shield of Florida: Pensacola

2190 Airport Boulevard
Suite 3000
Pensacola, FL 32504-8907
Toll-Free: 800-477-3736
Phone: 904-791-6111
Fax: 904-905-6638
corporatecommunications@bcbsfl.com
www.bcbsfl.com
Mailing Address: PO Box 1798, Jacksonville, FL 32231-0014
Subsidiary of: Blue Cross Blue Shield
For Profit Organization: Yes
Year Founded: 1985
Number of Affiliated Hospitals: 7
Number of Primary Care Physicians: 240
Number of Referral/Specialty Physicians: 350
Total Enrollment: 54,000

Healthplan and Services Defined
PLAN TYPE: HMO/PPO
Model Type: IPA
Plan Specialty: Worker's Compensation
Benefits Offered: Dental, Disease Management, Prescription,
Wellness, Worker's Compensation, AD&D, Life

Type of Coverage
Commercial, Individual, Medicare, Supplemental Medicare
Catastrophic Illness Benefit: Unlimited

Type of Payment Plans Offered
POS, DFFS, Capitated, FFS, Combination FFS & DFFS

Geographic Areas Served
Escambia, Okaloosa, Walton and Santa Rosa counties

Subscriber Information
Average Subscriber Co-Payment:
Primary Care Physician: $10.00
Non-Network Physician: $10.00
Prescription Drugs: $7.00/14.00
Hospital ER: $50.00

Home Health Care Max. Days/Visits Covered: Unlimited

Network Qualifications
Pre-Admission Certification: Yes

Peer Review Type
Utilization Review: Yes
Second Surgical Opinion: Yes
Case Management: Yes

Publishes and Distributes Report Card: Yes

Accreditation Certification
NCQA
TJC Accreditation, Medicare Approved, Utilization Review,
Pre-Admission Certification, State Licensure, Quality Assurance
Program

Key Personnel
CEO . . . . Robert I Lufrano, MD
CFO. . . . . R Chris Doerr
EVP & COO. . . . . Arnold Livermore
Sr VP/CIO. . . . . Duke Livermore
Sales Manager . . . . Steve Macomber

268 Capital Health Plan

2140 Centerville Place
Tallahassee, FL 32317-5349
Toll-Free: 800-390-1434
Phone: 850-383-3400
Fax: 850-383-1031
www.capitalhealth.com
Mailing Address: PO Box 15349, Tallahaseee, FL 32317-5349
Subsidiary of: Blue Cross Blue Shield of Florida
Non-Profit Organization: Yes
Year Founded: 1982
Owned by an Integrated Delivery Network (IDN): Yes
Number of Affiliated Hospitals: 4
Number of Primary Care Physicians: 120
Number of Referral/Specialty Physicians: 186
Total Enrollment: 113,000
State Enrollment: 105,024

Healthplan and Services Defined
PLAN TYPE: HMO
Model Type: Staff, Mixed Model
Plan Specialty: Chiropractic, Lab, Vision, Radiology, UR
Benefits Offered: Behavioral Health, Chiropractic, Disease
Management, Home Care, Inpatient SNF, Physical Therapy,
Podiatry, Prescription, Psychiatric, Transplant, Vision, Wellness

Type of Coverage
Commercial, Medicare, Supplemental Medicare, Catastrophic
Catastrophic Illness Benefit: Unlimited

Geographic Areas Served
Leon, Gadsden, Jefferson and Wakulla counties

Subscriber Information
Average Annual Deductible Per Subscriber:
Employee Only (Self): $0
Employee & 1 Family Member: $0
Employee & 2 Family Members: $0
Medicare: $0
Average Subscriber Co-Payment:
Primary Care Physician: $15.00
Prescription Drugs: $7.00
Hospital ER: $50.00
Nursing Home Max. Days/Visits Covered: 60

Peer Review Type
Second Surgical Opinion: Yes

Publishes and Distributes Report Card: Yes

Accreditation Certification
NCQA

Key Personnel
```
Principal.................................Summer Knight
CFO/COO ................................Kearney Pool
Director of Claims...........................Amy Adams
Network Development..........................Eric Smith
Chief Marketing Officer.........................Sue Conte
Chief Medical Officer ................Nancy Van Vessem, MD
Chief Information Officer .......................Eric Smith
```

Specialty Managed Care Partners
Enters into Contracts with Regional Business Coalitions: Yes

---

269 CarePlus Health Plans, Inc

11430 NW 20th Street
Suite 300
Doral, FL 33172
Toll-Free: 800-793-9808
CPHP_memberservices@careplus-hp.com
www.careplus-hp.com
Year Founded: 2003
Total Enrollment: 62,000
State Enrollment: 62,000

Healthplan and Services Defined
PLAN TYPE: HMO
Plan Specialty: Dental, Vision
Benefits Offered: Dental, Prescription, Vision, Transportation in some areas

Type of Coverage
Medicare, Supplemental Medicare

Geographic Areas Served
Miami-Dade, Broward, Palm Beach, Hillsborough, Pinellas, Pasco, Polk, Seminole, Orange, Osceola, Brevard, Okeechobee and Saint Lucie counties. 2010 expansion to Indian River, Martin, Lake, Marion, Charlotte, Lee and Sarasota

---

270 CIGNA HealthCare of Florida

255 Primera Blvd
Suite 264
Lake Mary, FL 32746
Toll-Free: 800-942-2471
Phone: 954-514-6600
Fax: 813-282-0356
www.cigna.com
Secondary Address: 1571 Sawgrass Corporate Parkway, Suite 140, Sunrise, FL 33323, 954-514-6600
For Profit Organization: Yes
Year Founded: 1981
Number of Affiliated Hospitals: 28
Number of Primary Care Physicians: 32,300
Number of Referral/Specialty Physicians: 797
Total Enrollment: 194,944
State Enrollment: 194,944

Healthplan and Services Defined
PLAN TYPE: HMO
Other Type: POS
Model Type: Network
Benefits Offered: Disease Management, Prescription, Transplant, Vision, Wellness, Life, LTD, STD

Type of Coverage
Commercial

Type of Payment Plans Offered
POS, DFFS, FFS, Combination FFS & DFFS

Geographic Areas Served
Tampa

Network Qualifications
Minimum Years of Practice: 3

Peer Review Type
Second Surgical Opinion: Yes
Case Management: Yes

Publishes and Distributes Report Card: Yes

Accreditation Certification
NCQA
TJC Accreditation, Medicare Approved, Utilization Review, Pre-Admission Certification, State Licensure, Quality Assurance Program

Key Personnel
Chief Medical Officer ....William Alexander, MD

---

271 Citrus Health Care

5420 Bay Center Drive
Suite 250
Tampa, FL 33609
Toll-Free: 877-624-8787
Phone: 813-490-8900
Fax: 813-490-8909
www.citrushc.com
Mailing Address: PO Box 690670, San Antonio, TX 78269-0670
Subsidiary of: Physicians Health Choice/WellMed Medical Management
For Profit Organization: Yes
Year Founded: 2003
Physician Owned Organization: Yes
Total Enrollment: 54,000
State Enrollment: 54,000

Healthplan and Services Defined
PLAN TYPE: Medicare
Other Type: HMO
Benefits Offered: Disease Management, Wellness

Type of Coverage
Commercial, Medicare, Medicaid, Long Term Care

Geographic Areas Served
Florida

Key Personnel
```
President ...................................Dan J Comrie
VP, Marketing & Dev...........................Jeff White
Chief Medical Officer .................Robert S Grossman, MD
VP, Customer Service.......................Donna L Debner
Compliance Officer ........................Laura Ketterman
VP, Sales ........................Tamara Schumacher-Konick
```

---

272 CompBenefits: Florida

5775 Blue Lagoon Drive
Suite 400
Miami, FL 33126-1333
Toll-Free: 800-223-6447
Phone: 305-262-1333
Fax: 305-269-2118
www.compbenefits.com
Secondary Address: 1511 North Westshore Blvd, Suite 1000, Tampa, FL 33607
Subsidiary of: Humana
Year Founded: 1978
Owned by an Integrated Delivery Network (IDN): Yes
Total Enrollment: 4,500,000

Healthplan and Services Defined
PLAN TYPE: Multiple
Model Type: Network, HMO, PPO, POS, TPA
Plan Specialty: ASO, Dental, Vision
Benefits Offered: Dental, Vision

Type of Coverage
Commercial, Individual, Indemnity

Type of Payment Plans Offered
DFFS, Capitated, FFS

Geographic Areas Served
Alabama, Arkansas, Illinois, Indiana, Georgia, Florida, Mississippi, Missouri, Kentucky, Kansas, North Carolina, South Carolina, West Virginia, Texas, Tennessee, Ohio, Louisiana

Publishes and Distributes Report Card: Yes

Specialty Managed Care Partners
Enters into Contracts with Regional Business Coalitions: Yes

273 CompCare: Comprehensive Behavioral Care
3405 W Dr Martin Luther King Jr Blvd
Suite 101
Tampa, FL 33607
Toll-Free: 800-435-5348
Phone: 813-288-4808
Fax: 813-288-4844
info@compcare.com
www.compcare.com
For Profit Organization: Yes
Year Founded: 1986
Total Enrollment: 900,000

Healthplan and Services Defined
PLAN TYPE: Multiple
Model Type: Network
Plan Specialty: ASO, Behavioral Health, Disease Management, PBM
Benefits Offered: Behavioral Health
Offers Demand Management Patient Information Service: Yes

Type of Coverage
Commercial, Medicare, Medicaid

Type of Payment Plans Offered
POS, DFFS, Capitated, FFS, Combination FFS & DFFS

Geographic Areas Served
Nationwide and Puerto Rico

Peer Review Type
Utilization Review: Yes
Second Surgical Opinion: Yes

Publishes and Distributes Report Card: Yes

Accreditation Certification
TJC, NCQA

Key Personnel
Chairman & CEO . . . . .Clark Marcus
Chief Financial Officer. . . . . .Joe Crisafi, CPA
Chief Accounting Officer .Robert J Landis
SVP, Corp Development. . . . . .Richard L Powers
Corporate Communications . . . . .Darnell Albarado
813-367-4519
dalbarado@compcare.com

274 Coventry Health Care of Florida
1340 Concord Terrace
Sunrise, FL 33323
Toll-Free: 866-847-8235
Phone: 954-858-3000
Fax: 954-846-0331
www.chcflorida.com
Secondary Address: 3611 Queen Palm Drive, Suite 200, Tampa, FL 33619
For Profit Organization: Yes
Number of Affiliated Hospitals: 16
Number of Primary Care Physicians: 1,500
Total Enrollment: 310,000

Healthplan and Services Defined
PLAN TYPE: HMO/PPO
Other Type: Other Health Plans

Benefits Offered: Disease Management, Wellness

Type of Coverage
Commercial, Individual, Medicare, Medicaid

Type of Payment Plans Offered
POS

Geographic Areas Served
Hernando, Pasco, Pinellas, Hillsborough, St. Lucie, Martin, Palm Beach, Broward, Miami-Dade counties

Key Personnel
CEO. . . . . .Ronald J Berding
COO. . . . . .Michael Hogan, MD
CFO . . . . .Tom Wyss
CMO. . . . . .Mark Bloom, MD
General Counsel . . . . .Gerald Cohen
Provider Relations. . . . . .Duell Wise
Marketing . . . . .Peter Joseph
Member Relations. . . . . .Frank Appel
Pharmacy Director. . . . . .Hal Goldman
Public Relations. . . . . .Pam Gadinsky

275 Delta Dental of Florida
258 Southhall Lane
Suite 350
Maitland, FL 32751
Toll-Free: 800-662-9034
Phone: 407-660-9034
Fax: 407-660-2899
flsales@delta.org
www.deltadentalins.com
Secondary Address: 5200 Blue Lagoon Drive, Suite 110, Miami, FL 33126
Non-Profit Organization: Yes
Total Enrollment: 54,000,000

Healthplan and Services Defined
PLAN TYPE: Dental
Other Type: Dental PPO

Type of Coverage
Commercial

Geographic Areas Served
Statewide

Key Personnel
VP, Public & Govt Affairs . . . . .Jeff Album
415-972-8418
Dir/Media & Public Affair . . . . .Elizabeth Risberg
415-972-8423

276 Dimension Health PPO
5881 NW 151st Street
Suite 201
Miami Lakes, FL 33014
Toll-Free: 800-483-4992
Phone: 305-823-7664
Fax: 305-818-8814
info@dimensionhealth.com
www.dimensionhealth.com
Year Founded: 1985
Number of Affiliated Hospitals: 34
Number of Primary Care Physicians: 6,000
Number of Referral/Specialty Physicians: 3,660
Total Enrollment: 400,000
State Enrollment: 400,000

Healthplan and Services Defined
PLAN TYPE: PPO
Model Type: Network, PPO
Benefits Offered: Disease Management, Wellness, Worker's Compensation

Type of Coverage
Commercial

Type of Payment Plans Offered
POS, DFFS, Capitated, FFS, Combination FFS & DFFS

Geographic Areas Served
Monroe, Dade, Broward and Palm Beach counties

Network Qualifications
Pre-Admission Certification: Yes

Peer Review Type
Utilization Review: Yes
Second Surgical Opinion: Yes
Case Management: Yes

Publishes and Distributes Report Card: No

Key Personnel
President/CEO . . . . .Charles Lindgren
  clindgren@dimensionhealth.com
Assistant to CEO . . . . .Rosemary Osorio
  rosorio@dimensionhealth.com
VP, Network Development . . . . .Leslie Glazer
  lglazer@dimensionhealth.com
Medical Director . . . . .Ray Mummery, MD
  rmummery@dimensionhealth.com
Dir, Provider Relations . . . . .Creta Diehs
  cdiehs@dimensionhealth.com

Average Claim Compensation
Physician's Fees Charged: 110%

Specialty Managed Care Partners
Enters into Contracts with Regional Business Coalitions: No

---

277 eHealthInsurance Services Inc.
11919 Foundation Place
Gold River, CA 95670
Toll-Free: 800-977-8860
info@ehealthinsurance.com
www.e.healthinsurance.com
Year Founded: 1997

Healthplan and Services Defined
PLAN TYPE: HMO/PPO
Benefits Offered: Dental, Life, STD

Type of Coverage
Commercial, Individual, Medicare

Geographic Areas Served
All 50 states in the USA and District of Columbia

Key Personnel
Chairman & CEO . . . . .Gary L. Lauer
EVP/Business & Corp. Dev. .Bruce Telkamp
EVP/Chief Technology .Dr. Sheldon X. Wang
SVP & CFO . . . . .Stuart M. Huizinga
Pres. of eHealth Gov. Sys . . . . .Samuel C. Gibbs
SVP of Sales & Operations . . . . .Robert S. Hurley
Director Public Relations . . . . .Nate Purpura
  650-210-3115

---

278 First Medical Health Plan of Florida
5960 NW Seventh Street
Miami, FL 33126
Toll-Free: 888-364-7535
Phone: 303-269-7995
www.firstmedicalflorida.com
For Profit Organization: Yes
Year Founded: 1977
Number of Primary Care Physicians: 5,000
Total Enrollment: 320,000
State Enrollment: 320,000

Healthplan and Services Defined
PLAN TYPE: Medicare

Benefits Offered: Behavioral Health, Prescription, Wellness

Type of Coverage
Medicare, Supplemental Medicare

Geographic Areas Served
Southern Florida and Puerto Rico

Key Personnel
President . . . . .Patricia Serrano

---

279 Florida Health Care Plan
1340 Ridgewood Avenue
Holly Hill, FL 32117
Toll-Free: 800-352-9823
Phone: 386-676-7100
Fax: 386-676-7119
www.floridahealthcares.com
Subsidiary of: Blue Cross Blue Shield
Non-Profit Organization: Yes
Year Founded: 1974
Owned by an Integrated Delivery Network (IDN): Yes
Federally Qualified: Yes
Number of Affiliated Hospitals: 7
Number of Primary Care Physicians: 71
Number of Referral/Specialty Physicians: 241
Total Enrollment: 67,440
State Enrollment: 39,511

Healthplan and Services Defined
PLAN TYPE: HMO
Model Type: Mixed
Benefits Offered: Behavioral Health, Chiropractic, Dental, Disease
  Management, Home Care, Inpatient SNF, Podiatry, Prescription,
  Psychiatric, Transplant, Vision, Wellness
Offers Demand Management Patient Information Service: Yes
DMPI Services Offered: Asthma Disease Management, Complex Case
  Management, Diabetes Health Management, Depression Healing
  Management, Congestive Heart Failure

Type of Coverage
Commercial, Medicare, Supplemental Medicare, Healthy Kids
Catastrophic Illness Benefit: Varies per case

Geographic Areas Served
Volusia and Flagler counties, Florida

Subscriber Information
Average Annual Deductible Per Subscriber:
  Employee Only (Self): $0
  Employee & 1 Family Member: $0
  Employee & 2 Family Members: $0
  Medicare: $0

Peer Review Type
Utilization Review: Yes
Second Surgical Opinion: Yes
Case Management: Yes

Publishes and Distributes Report Card: Yes

Accreditation Certification
TJC

Key Personnel
CEO . . . . .Edward F Simpson, Jr
  386-676-7100
CFO . . . . .David Schandel
  386-676-7100
Chief Marketing Officer . . . . .Mikelle Streicher, RN
Pharmacy Administrator. . . . . .Gary Klein, RPh
  386-676-7100
Adm. Membership/Retention . . . . .Pamela C Mims
  386-676-7110
Materials Management . . . . .Tom Beall
President Medical Affairs. . . . . .Wendy Myers, MD
  386-676-7100

Member Service Manager. . . . . .Mickey Linse-weiss
386-676-7100
CIO. . . . . .Roy Kloystermeyer
386-238-3200
Administrator of Contact . . . . .Sherri Hutchinson
386-676-7100
Sales. . . . . .Pamela C Mims
386-676-7100

Specialty Managed Care Partners
Enters into Contracts with Regional Business Coalitions: Yes

Employer References
State of Florida, Volusia County School District, City of Daytona
Beach, Florida, Publix Super-Markets, Walgreen Company

280 Freedom Health, Inc

PO Box 151137
Tampa, FL 33684
Toll-Free: 888-796-0946
Fax: 813-506-6150
contact@freedomhealth.com
www.freedomhealth.com
Physician Owned Organization: Yes

Healthplan and Services Defined
PLAN TYPE: Medicare
Benefits Offered: Dental, Prescription, Vision, Hearing, and
Preventative health care services

Type of Coverage
Supplemental Medicare, Medicaid

Geographic Areas Served
Broward, Hillsborough, Pasco, Sumter, Dade, Lake, Pinellas,
Hernando, Marion and Orange counties

281 Great-West Healthcare Florida

Acquired by CIGNA

282 Health First Health Plans

6450 US Highway 1
Rockledge, FL 32955
Toll-Free: 800-716-7737
Phone: 321-434-5665
Fax: 321-434-4362
hfhpinfo@health-first.org
www.health-first.org/health_plans
Subsidiary of: Health First
Non-Profit Organization: Yes
Year Founded: 1995
Number of Affiliated Hospitals: 5
Number of Primary Care Physicians: 228
Number of Referral/Specialty Physicians: 537
Total Enrollment: 63,700
State Enrollment: 63,700

Healthplan and Services Defined
PLAN TYPE: HMO
Other Type: POS
Model Type: IPA, Network
Plan Specialty: Fully Insured HMO
Benefits Offered: Behavioral Health, Chiropractic, Disease
Management, Home Care, Inpatient SNF, Long-Term Care,
Physical Therapy, Podiatry, Prescription, Psychiatric, Transplant,
Vision, Wellness

Type of Coverage
Commercial, Medicare
Catastrophic Illness Benefit: Covered

Type of Payment Plans Offered
FFS

Geographic Areas Served
All of Brevard County, the town of Sebastian in Indian River County

Subscriber Information
Average Subscriber Co-Payment:
Primary Care Physician: $15.00
Prescription Drugs: $2.00/7/15/35/70
Hospital ER: $75
Home Health Care: $0
Nursing Home: $0
Nursing Home Max. Days/Visits Covered: 60 days

Peer Review Type
Utilization Review: Yes
Second Surgical Opinion: Yes
Case Management: Yes

Accreditation Certification
NCQA

Key Personnel
CEO . . . . .Peter J Weiss, MD
VP/Finance . . . . .Roberta Stoner
In-House Formulary . . . . .Bill Anderson, PharmD
Marketing/Sales . . . . .Angela Handa
Medical Affairs . . . . .Joseph Collins, MD
Provider Services . . . . .Katie Fleming

Average Claim Compensation
Physician's Fees Charged: 110%

Specialty Managed Care Partners
SXC, Ameripharm

Employer References
Boeing/McDonnell Douglas Corp., ITT, Computer Science Raytheon,
Intersil Corp.

283 Health First Medicare Plans

6450 US Highway 1
Rockledge, FL 32955
Toll-Free: 800-716-7737
Phone: 321-434-5665
Fax: 321-434-4362
www.health-first.org/health_plans/medicare
Subsidiary of: Health First
Year Founded: 1997

Healthplan and Services Defined
PLAN TYPE: Medicare

Type of Coverage
Medicare, MA and MA-PD

Geographic Areas Served
Brevard county, zip codes of 32957, 32958, 32978 and in the city of
Sebastian in Indian River county

Key Personnel
Chairman . . . . .Nicholas E Pellegrino
Vice Chairman . . . . .Larry F Garrison

284 Healthchoice Orlando

102 W Pineloch Avenue
Suite 23
Orlando, FL 32806
Toll-Free: 800-635-4345
Phone: 407-481-7100
Fax: 321-843-6034
hcweb@orlandohealth.com
www.healthchoiceorlando.org
Subsidiary of: Orlando Health
For Profit Organization: Yes
Year Founded: 1984
Number of Affiliated Hospitals: 16
Number of Primary Care Physicians: 2,000
Number of Referral/Specialty Physicians: 2,221

Total Enrollment: 35,000
State Enrollment: 35,000

Healthplan and Services Defined
  PLAN TYPE: PPO
  Model Type: IPA
  Plan Specialty: Worker's Compensation, UR
  Benefits Offered: Disease Management
  Offers Demand Management Patient Information Service: Yes

Type of Coverage
  Commercial
  Catastrophic Illness Benefit: Varies per case

Type of Payment Plans Offered
  FFS

Geographic Areas Served
  PPO: Brevard, Orange, Osceola, Seminole and Lake counties; EPO:
  Orange, Osceola, Seminole, and Lake counties

Network Qualifications
  Pre-Admission Certification: Yes

Peer Review Type
  Utilization Review: Yes
  Second Surgical Opinion: Yes
  Case Management: Yes

Publishes and Distributes Report Card: Yes

Accreditation Certification
  AAAHC
  TJC Accreditation, Medicare Approved, Utilization Review,
    Pre-Admission Certification, State Licensure, Quality Assurance
    Program

Key Personnel
  Vice President . . . . Christy Pearson
  Medical Director . . . . Michael Howell, MD
  Marketing/Sales . . . . Stephanie Scarbrough

Specialty Managed Care Partners
  Enters into Contracts with Regional Business Coalitions: Yes

285   HealthSun Health Plans

1205 SW 37th Ave
2nd Floor
Miami, FL 33135
Toll-Free: 877-207-4900
Phone: 305-234-9292
Fax: 305-444-9148
info@healthsun.com
www.health-sun.com

Healthplan and Services Defined
  PLAN TYPE: Medicare
  Other Type: HMO

Type of Coverage
  Medicare

Geographic Areas Served
  Miami-Dade and Broward counties

286   Humana Health Insurance of Jacksonville

76 S Laura Street
10th Floor
Jacksonville, FL 32202
Toll-Free: 800-639-1133
Phone: 904-376-1234
Fax: 904-376-1270
www.humana.com
For Profit Organization: Yes
Year Founded: 1985
Owned by an Integrated Delivery Network (IDN): Yes
Number of Affiliated Hospitals: 13
Number of Primary Care Physicians: 3,200

Total Enrollment: 125,000

Healthplan and Services Defined
  PLAN TYPE: HMO/PPO
  Model Type: IPA
  Plan Specialty: ASO, Behavioral Health, Chiropractic, Dental,
    Disease Management, EPO, Lab, Vision, Radiology, Worker's
    Compensation
  Benefits Offered: Behavioral Health, Chiropractic, Complementary
    Medicine, Dental, Disease Management, Home Care, Inpatient
    SNF, Physical Therapy, Podiatry, Prescription, Psychiatric,
    Transplant, Vision, Worker's Compensation
  Offers Demand Management Patient Information Service: Yes

Type of Coverage
  Commercial, Individual, Indemnity, Medicare, Catastrophic
  Catastrophic Illness Benefit: Maximum $1M

Geographic Areas Served
  Statewide

Peer Review Type
  Utilization Review: Yes
  Second Surgical Opinion: Yes

Accreditation Certification
  TJC, URAC, NCQA, CORE

Key Personnel
  President/CEO . . . . Alan Guzzino
  CFO . . . . Michael Lynch
  Marketing . . . . Monica Colquette
  Medical Affairs . . . . Robert Blalock, MD
  Sales . . . . Laura Taravaglia

Specialty Managed Care Partners
  University of Florida

287   Humana Health Insurance of Orlando

385 Douglas Avenue
Suite 1050
Alamonte Springs, FL 32714
Toll-Free: 800-797-2273
Phone: 407-772-3140
Fax: 407-862-0355
www.humana.com
For Profit Organization: Yes
Year Founded: 1962
Number of Affiliated Hospitals: 12
Number of Primary Care Physicians: 250
Total Enrollment: 56,000

Healthplan and Services Defined
  PLAN TYPE: HMO/PPO
  Model Type: IPA
  Benefits Offered: Disease Management, Prescription, Wellness

Type of Coverage
  Commercial, Individual

Type of Payment Plans Offered
  POS

Geographic Areas Served
  Alachua, Lake, Marion, Orange, Osceola & Seminole counties

Subscriber Information
  Average Annual Deductible Per Subscriber:
    Employee Only (Self): $0
    Medicare: $0
  Average Subscriber Co-Payment:
    Primary Care Physician: $10.00
    Prescription Drugs: $7.00
    Hospital ER: $25.00

Network Qualifications
  Pre-Admission Certification: Yes

Peer Review Type
  Utilization Review: Yes

Second Surgical Opinion: Yes
Case Management: Yes

Publishes and Distributes Report Card: Yes

Accreditation Certification
URAC, NCQA, CORE
TJC Accreditation, Medicare Approved, Utilization Review,
Pre-Admission Certification, State Licensure, Quality Assurance
Program

Key Personnel
President/CEO . . . . .Nancy Smith
CFO . . . . .Brenda Radhe
In House Formulary . . . . .Mauro Florentine
Marketing . . . . .Michelle McPhail
Materials Management . . . . .Kathy Basher
Medical Affairs . . . . .Mark Reinecke, MD
Provider Services . . . . .Julie Brown

Specialty Managed Care Partners
Enters into Contracts with Regional Business Coalitions: Yes

288 Humana Health Insurance of Tampa - Pinellas

430 Park Place Blvd
Suite 100
Tampa, FL 33759
Toll-Free: 800-443-1702
Phone: 727-725-8080
Fax: 727-791-7846
tmoore@humana.com
www.humana.com
For Profit Organization: Yes
Year Founded: 1984
Number of Affiliated Hospitals: 29
Number of Primary Care Physicians: 600
Total Enrollment: 125,000

Healthplan and Services Defined
PLAN TYPE: HMO/PPO
Model Type: Staff, IPA, Network
Benefits Offered: Disease Management, Prescription, Wellness

Type of Coverage
Commercial, Individual
Catastrophic Illness Benefit: Varies per case

Type of Payment Plans Offered
DFFS, Capitated

Geographic Areas Served
Citrus, DeSoto, Hardee, Highlands, Hillsborough, Hernando,
Manatee, Pasco, Pinellas, Polk, Sarasota counties

Subscriber Information
Average Monthly Fee Per Subscriber
(Employee + Employer Contribution):
Employee Only (Self): Varies
Employee & 1 Family Member: Varies
Employee & 2 Family Members: Varies
Medicare: Varies
Average Annual Deductible Per Subscriber:
Employee Only (Self): Varies
Employee & 1 Family Member: Varies
Employee & 2 Family Members: Varies
Medicare: Varies
Average Subscriber Co-Payment:
Primary Care Physician: Varies
Non-Network Physician: Varies
Prescription Drugs: Varies
Hospital ER: Varies
Home Health Care: Varies
Home Health Care Max. Days/Visits Covered: Varies
Nursing Home: Varies
Nursing Home Max. Days/Visits Covered: Varies

Publishes and Distributes Report Card: Yes

Accreditation Certification
AAAHC, URAC, NCQA
TJC Accreditation, State Licensure

Key Personnel
Chairman of The Board/CEO . . . . .Michael B McCallister
COO . . . . .James E Murray
SVP/CFO/Treasurer . . . . .James H Bloem
In House Formulary . . . . .Richard Nissenbaum, RPh

Specialty Managed Care Partners
Enters into Contracts with Regional Business Coalitions: Yes

289 JMH Health Plan

155 South Miami Avenue
Suite 110
Miami, FL 33130
Toll-Free: 800-721-2993
Phone: 305-575-3640
Fax: 305-575-3730
inquiries@jmhhp.com
www.jmhhp.com
Subsidiary of: Jackson Health System
Non-Profit Organization: Yes
Year Founded: 1985
Number of Affiliated Hospitals: 32
Number of Primary Care Physicians: 3,000
Total Enrollment: 105,000
State Enrollment: 105,000

Healthplan and Services Defined
PLAN TYPE: HMO
Model Type: Staff, Group
Benefits Offered: Prescription

Type of Coverage
Catastrophic Illness Benefit: Covered

Type of Payment Plans Offered
POS, DFFS, Capitated

Geographic Areas Served
Broward and Miami-Dade counties

Subscriber Information
Average Subscriber Co-Payment:
Primary Care Physician: $10.00
Prescription Drugs: $5.00
Hospital ER: $25.00
Home Health Care: $0
Home Health Care Max. Days/Visits Covered: 60 days
Nursing Home: $0
Nursing Home Max. Days/Visits Covered: 90 days

Network Qualifications
Pre-Admission Certification: No

Peer Review Type
Utilization Review: Yes
Second Surgical Opinion: Yes
Case Management: Yes

Accreditation Certification
AAAHC
TJC Accreditation

Key Personnel
President/CEO . . . . .Joseph Rogers
CFO . . . . .Asif Jamal
Medical Affairs . . . . .Eugene Edynak, MD
Information Systems . . . . .Todd S Roberts
Provider Services . . . . .Serge Boisette

Average Claim Compensation
Physician's Fees Charged: 30%
Hospital's Fees Charged: 19%

290 Leon Medical Centers Health Plan

11401 SW 40th Street
Suite 400
Miami, FL 33165
Toll-Free: 866-393-5366
Phone: 305-559-5366
questions@leonmedicalcenters.com
www.lmchealthplans.com
Subsidiary of: HealthSpring
For Profit Organization: Yes
Year Founded: 1996
Number of Affiliated Hospitals: 5
Number of Primary Care Physicians: 1,200
Total Enrollment: 27,000

Healthplan and Services Defined
   PLAN TYPE: HMO

Type of Coverage
   Supplemental Medicare, Medicare Advantage

Geographic Areas Served
   Miami-Dade County

Key Personnel
   President . . . . Albert Maury
      305-644-2135
      albert.maury@lmchealthplans.com
   Director, Finance . . . . Mercy Kirkpatrick
      305-631-4435
      mercy.marill-kirkpatrick@lmchealthplans
   Vice President, Claims . . . . Luis Fernandez
      305-631-5337
      luis.fernandez@lmchealthplans.com
   Human Resources . . . . Carolina M Garcia
      305-631-5934
      carolina.garcia@lmchealthplans.com
   SVP, Utilization Mgmt . . . . Henry Hernandez
      305-642-1140
      henry.hernandez@lmchealthplans.com
   Medical Director . . . . Alina Campos, MD
      305-642-1149
      alina.campos@lmchealthplans.com
   Member Administration . . . . Sandra Rivera
      305-631-5937
      sandra.rivera@lmchealthplans.com
   VP, MIS . . . . Jennifer Puglisi
      305-644-2152
      jen.puglisi@lmchealthplans.com
   Provider Relations Coord . . . . Marta Perez
      305-646-3776
      marta.perez@lmchealthplans.com
   VP, Sales . . . . Manuel Chica
      305-631-5898
      manuel.chica@lmchealthplans.com

291 Medica HealthCare Plans, Inc

4000 Ponce de Leon Blvd
Suite 650
Coral Gables, FL 33146
Toll-Free: 800-407-9069
Phone: 305-460-0600
Fax: 305-460-0613
membersvc@medicaplans.com
www.medicaplans.com
Total Enrollment: 12,000

Healthplan and Services Defined
   PLAN TYPE: Medicare
   Benefits Offered: Disease Management, Wellness

Type of Coverage
   Medicare, Supplemental Medicare

Geographic Areas Served
   Florida

292 Molina Healthcare: Florida

8300 NW 3rd Street
Suite 400
Miami, FL 33122
Toll-Free: 866-422-2541
www.molinahealthcare.com
For Profit Organization: Yes
Year Founded: 1980
Physician Owned Organization: Yes
Number of Affiliated Hospitals: 84
Number of Primary Care Physicians: 2,167
Number of Referral/Specialty Physicians: 6,184
Total Enrollment: 1,400,000

Healthplan and Services Defined
   PLAN TYPE: HMO
   Model Type: Network
   Benefits Offered: Chiropractic, Dental, Home Care, Inpatient SNF,
      Long-Term Care, Podiatry, Vision

Type of Coverage
   Commercial, Medicare, Supplemental Medicare, Medicaid

Accreditation Certification
   URAC, NCQA

293 Neighborhood Health Partnership

7600 Corporate Center Drive
Miami, FL 33126
Toll-Free: 800-354-0222
Phone: 305-715-2500
www.neighborhood-health.com
Subsidiary of: UnitedHealthcare
For Profit Organization: Yes
Year Founded: 1993
Number of Affiliated Hospitals: 29
Number of Primary Care Physicians: 1,282
Total Enrollment: 108,000
State Enrollment: 141,178

Healthplan and Services Defined
   PLAN TYPE: HMO
   Other Type: POS

Type of Coverage
   Commercial, Medicare

Type of Payment Plans Offered
   Capitated

Geographic Areas Served
   Miami-Dade, Broward and Palm Beach counties

Peer Review Type
   Utilization Review: Yes

Publishes and Distributes Report Card: Yes

Accreditation Certification
   NCQA

Key Personnel
   President & CEO . . . . Daniel Rosenthal
   Chief Financial Officer . . . . Ramon Coto
   VP, Provider Relations . . . . Maritza Borrajero

294 Optimum HealthCare, Inc

5403 North Churc Ave
Tampa, FL 33614
Toll-Free: 866-245-5360
contact@youroptimumhealthcare.com
www.youroptimumhealthcare.com
Secondary Address: 8373 Northcliffe Blvd, Springhill, FL 34606

Healthplan and Services Defined
  PLAN TYPE: Medicare

Geographic Areas Served
  Brevard, Broward, Charlotte, Citrus, Clay, Collier, Dade, De Sota, Duval, Escambia, Hernando, Hillsborough, Indian River, Lake, Lee, Manatee, Marion, Martin, Orange, Osceola, Palm Beach, Pasco, Pinellas, Polk, Sarasota, Seminole, St. Lucie, Sumter and Volusia counties

295   Physicians United Plan
483 North Semoran Blvd
Winter Park, FL 32792
Toll-Free: 866-571-0693
memberservices@pupcorp.com
www.pupcorp.com
Secondary Address: 1124 1st Street South, Winter Haven, FL 33880
Year Founded: 2005

Healthplan and Services Defined
  PLAN TYPE: Multiple
  Other Type: HMO, Medicare

Type of Coverage
  Supplemental Medicare

Geographic Areas Served
  Lake, Marion, Orange, Osceola, Polk, Seminole and Sumter counties

Key Personnel
  Chief Executive Officer . . . . James Kollefrath
  President . . . . Sandeep Bajaj
  Chief Financial Officer . . . . Aaron S Henry
  Compliance Officer . . . . Paul Christy
  Dir, Enrollment . . . . Ryan Horbal
  Human Resources Manager . . . . Jennifer Blue
  VP, Sales & Operations . . . . Shawn Holt
  Media Contact . . . . Ana Handshuh
    407-619-3016
    ahandshuh@pupcorp.com

296   Preferred Care Partners
PO Box 56-5748
Miami, FL 33256-5748
Toll-Free: 866-231-7201
Phone: 305-670-8437
Fax: 888-659-0618
memberservices@mypreferredcare.com
www.mypreferredcare.com
Number of Affiliated Hospitals: 27
Number of Primary Care Physicians: 1,500
Total Enrollment: 45,000

Healthplan and Services Defined
  PLAN TYPE: Multiple
  Benefits Offered: Dental, Prescription, Vision, Hearing, Transportation, Fitness Programs

Type of Coverage
  Supplemental Medicare

Geographic Areas Served
  Miami-Dade, Broward, Marion, Lake & Sumter counties

Key Personnel
  President . . . . Justo Luis Pozo
  CEO . . . . Joseph L Caruncho
  CFO . . . . Eladio Gil
  SVP, COO . . . . Roger Rodriguez
  SVP/Chief Compliance Offc . . . . Annette C Onorati, Esq
  Chairman, CMO . . . . Orlando Lopez-Fernandez, Jr, MD
  SVP, Chief Info Officer . . . . Doug Cormany

297   Preferred Medical Plan
4950 SW 8th Street
Coral Gables, FL 33134
Toll-Free: 800-767-5551
Phone: 305-447-8373
Fax: 305-648-0420
www.pmphmo.com
For Profit Organization: Yes
Year Founded: 1975
Number of Affiliated Hospitals: 30
Number of Primary Care Physicians: 600
Total Enrollment: 52,000
State Enrollment: 39,776

Healthplan and Services Defined
  PLAN TYPE: HMO
  Model Type: Staff, Group
  Benefits Offered: Disease Management, Prescription, Wellness

Geographic Areas Served
  Dade, Broward counties

Accreditation Certification
  AAAHC

Key Personnel
  President/CEO . . . . Tamara Meyerson
  CFO . . . . Albert Arca
  COO . . . . Nancy Garcia
  Marketing . . . . Estella Ginoris
  Dir, Patient Relations . . . . Rosie Lopez-Casiro
  Chief Information Officer . . . . Paul Bell

298   Quality Health Plans
4010 Gunn Highway
Suite 220
Tampa, FL 33618
Toll-Free: 866-747-2700
Phone: 727-945-8400
www.qualityhealthplans.com
Year Founded: 2003
Physician Owned Organization: Yes
Total Enrollment: 19,000

Healthplan and Services Defined
  PLAN TYPE: Medicare

Type of Coverage
  Supplemental Medicare

Geographic Areas Served
  13 counties in Florida

Key Personnel
  President . . . . Haider A Khan, MD
  CEO & CMO . . . . Nazeer H Khan, MD
  COO . . . . Sabiha Khan, MBA
  Medical Director . . . . Trevor A Rose, MD, MS MMM
  Reg Mgr, Network Services . . . . Dawn R Smith
  Director, Finance . . . . David A Sherwin
  Corp Services Manager . . . . Farrah Sanabria, PHR
  Director, Medical Affairs . . . . Lisa Cierpka, RN
  Dir, Business Development . . . . Amber R Clements
  Dir, Compliance . . . . Angela Hart
  Medical Director . . . . Michael Yanuck, MD
  Medical Director . . . . Richard Bonanno, MD
  Media Contact . . . . Mike Worley
    866-747-2700
    mworley@qualityhealthplans.comm

299   SafeGuard Health Enterprises: Florida
95 Enterprise
Suite 200

Aliso Viejo, CA 92656
Toll-Free: 800-880-1800
www.safeguard.net
Subsidiary of: MetLife
For Profit Organization: Yes
Year Founded: 1974
Number of Primary Care Physicians: 2,073
Number of Referral/Specialty Physicians: 2,030
Total Enrollment: 1,800,000

Healthplan and Services Defined
  PLAN TYPE: Dental
  Other Type: Dental HMO
  Model Type: IPA
  Plan Specialty: ASO, Dental, Vision
  Benefits Offered: Dental, Vision

Type of Coverage
  Individual, Indemnity, Medicaid

Type of Payment Plans Offered
  DFFS, Capitated

Geographic Areas Served
  California, Texas, Florida

Subscriber Information
  Average Annual Deductible Per Subscriber:
    Employee Only (Self): $50.00
    Employee & 1 Family Member: $100.00
    Employee & 2 Family Members: $150.00

Network Qualifications
  Pre-Admission Certification: Yes

Peer Review Type
  Utilization Review: Yes

Publishes and Distributes Report Card: No

Key Personnel
  Chairman/CEO . . . . James E Buncher
    949-425-4500
  President/COO . . . . Stephen J Baker
  SVP/CFO . . . . Dennis L Gates
  VP/CIO . . . . Michael J Lauffenburger
  SVP/General Counsel . . . . Ronald I Brendzel
  Dir/Human Resources . . . . William Wolff
  Director . . . . Jack R Anderson

Specialty Managed Care Partners
  Enters into Contracts with Regional Business Coalitions: Yes

Employer References
  State of California, Boeing, County of Los Angeles, Farmers
    Insurance, Automobile Club

---

300   Total Health Choice

PO Box 830010
Miami, FL 33283-0010
Toll-Free: 800-887-6888
Phone: 305-408-5700
Fax: 305-408-5858
info@thc-online.com
www.totalhealthchoiceonline.com
Subsidiary of: Total Health Care, Inc. of Michigan
Non-Profit Organization: Yes
Year Founded: 1997
Owned by an Integrated Delivery Network (IDN): Yes
Number of Affiliated Hospitals: 28
Number of Primary Care Physicians: 600
Number of Referral/Specialty Physicians: 1,200
Total Enrollment: 10,000
State Enrollment: 15,347

Healthplan and Services Defined
  PLAN TYPE: HMO
  Model Type: Group

Plan Specialty: Disease Management, Worker's Compensation,
    Prescription
Benefits Offered: Behavioral Health, Chiropractic, Disease
    Management, Physical Therapy, Podiatry, Prescription, Wellness,
    Worker's Compensation, Life, LTD

Type of Coverage
  Commercial, Individual, Supplemental Medicare, Medicaid,
    Catastrophic
  Catastrophic Illness Benefit: Varies per case

Type of Payment Plans Offered
  POS, DFFS, FFS

Geographic Areas Served
  Broward, Miami-Dade counties

Subscriber Information
  Average Subscriber Co-Payment:
    Primary Care Physician: $5.00
    Prescription Drugs: $5.00

Network Qualifications
  Pre-Admission Certification: Yes

Peer Review Type
  Utilization Review: No
  Second Surgical Opinion: Yes
  Case Management: Yes

Publishes and Distributes Report Card: Yes

Accreditation Certification
  AAAHC
  Medicare Approved, State Licensure, Quality Assurance Program

Key Personnel
  Owner. . . . . Kenneth Rimmer
  CEO . . . . Michael Ross
  CFO . . . . Gerry Hammond
  Marketing . . . . Carlos Martinez
  Medical Affairs . . . . Robyn Arrington, MD
  Provider Services . . . . Sergie Covas

Specialty Managed Care Partners
  Enters into Contracts with Regional Business Coalitions: Yes

---

301   United Concordia: Florida

1408 N Westshore Blvd
Suite 512
Tampa, FL
Toll-Free: 888-441-8585
Phone: 813-287-1823
Fax: 813-287-1819
ucproducer@ucci.com
www.secure.ucci.com
For Profit Organization: Yes
Year Founded: 1971
Number of Primary Care Physicians: 111,000
Total Enrollment: 8,000,000

Healthplan and Services Defined
  PLAN TYPE: Dental
  Plan Specialty: Dental
  Benefits Offered: Dental

Type of Coverage
  Commercial, Individual

Geographic Areas Served
  Military personnel and their families, nationwide

---

302   UnitedHealthCare of Florida

10151 Deerwood Park
Bldg 100, Suite 420
Jacksonville, FL 32256
Toll-Free: 800-250-6178
www.uhc.com

Secondary Address: 495 North Keller Road, Maitland, FL 32751, 407-659-6900
Subsidiary of: UnitedHealth Group
For Profit Organization: Yes
Owned by an Integrated Delivery Network (IDN): Yes
Total Enrollment: 75,000,000
State Enrollment: 870,159

Healthplan and Services Defined
　PLAN TYPE: HMO/PPO
　Model Type: Group
　Plan Specialty: Full Service
　Benefits Offered: Behavioral Health, Chiropractic, Dental, Disease Management, Home Care, Inpatient SNF, Physical Therapy, Podiatry, Prescription, Psychiatric, Transplant, Vision, Wellness, AD&D, Life, LTD, STD

Type of Coverage
　Commercial

Geographic Areas Served
　Central/North Florida

Subscriber Information
　Average Monthly Fee Per Subscriber
　　(Employee + Employer Contribution):
　　　Employee Only (Self): Varies

Peer Review Type
　Case Management: Yes

Accreditation Certification
　TJC, NCQA

Key Personnel
　President/CEO . . . . Matthew Davies
　Media Contact. . . . . Roger Rollman
　　roger_f_rollman@uhc.com

Specialty Managed Care Partners
　Own Network
　Enters into Contracts with Regional Business Coalitions: Yes

303　UnitedHealthCare of South Florida

13621 NW 12th Street
Sunrise, FL 33323
Toll-Free: 800-825-8792
Phone: 954-858-4000
Fax: 954-858-3815
www.uhc.com
Secondary Address: 9009 Corporate Lake Drive, Suite 200, Tampa, FL 33634, 813-890-4500
Subsidiary of: UnitedHealth Group
For Profit Organization: Yes
Year Founded: 1970
Number of Affiliated Hospitals: 58
Number of Primary Care Physicians: 2,500
Number of Referral/Specialty Physicians: 4,500
Total Enrollment: 75,000,000
State Enrollment: 295,000

Healthplan and Services Defined
　PLAN TYPE: HMO/PPO
　Model Type: Network
　Plan Specialty: ASO, Behavioral Health, Chiropractic, Dental, Disease Management
　Benefits Offered: Behavioral Health, Chiropractic, Complementary Medicine, Dental, Disease Management, Physical Therapy, Podiatry, Prescription, Psychiatric, Vision, Wellness, AD&D, Life, LTD, STD
　Offers Demand Management Patient Information Service: Yes

Type of Coverage
　Commercial
　Catastrophic Illness Benefit: Varies per case

Type of Payment Plans Offered
　POS, DFFS, Capitated, FFS, Combination FFS & DFFS

Geographic Areas Served
　Palm Beach, Broward & Dade counties

Subscriber Information
　Average Subscriber Co-Payment:
　　Primary Care Physician: $5.00-15.00
　　Non-Network Physician: Varies
　　Prescription Drugs: $5.00-10.00
　　Hospital ER: $100.00

Network Qualifications
　Pre-Admission Certification: Yes

Peer Review Type
　Utilization Review: Yes
　Second Surgical Opinion: Yes
　Case Management: Yes

Publishes and Distributes Report Card: Yes

Accreditation Certification
　AAAHC, URAC, NCQA
　TJC Accreditation, Medicare Approved, Utilization Review, Pre-Admission Certification, State Licensure, Quality Assurance Program

Key Personnel
　CEO . . . . Dan Rosenthal
　CFO. . . . . Jon Schwarz
　Network Contracting . . . . Jonathan Gavras, MD
　Marketing. . . . . Lawrence J Kissner
　Medical Affairs . . . . Jonathan Gavras, MD
　Sales. . . . . Albert Fernandez
　Media Contact. . . . . Roger Rollman
　　roger_f_rollman@uhc.com

Specialty Managed Care Partners
　Enters into Contracts with Regional Business Coalitions: No

304　Universal Health Care Group

100 Central Ave
Suite 200
St Petersburg, FL 33701
Toll-Free: 866-690-4842
www.univhc.com
Secondary Address: 2713 Forest Road, Spring Hill, FL 34606

Healthplan and Services Defined
　PLAN TYPE: Medicare

Type of Coverage
　Individual, Medicare, Supplemental Medicare, Medicaid

Key Personnel
　Chairman & CEO . . . . A.K. Desai, MD, MPH
　Chief Operating Officer. . . . . James P O'Drobinak
　General Counsel . . . . Sandip Patel
　Chief Financial Officer . . . . Dennis Kant
　SVP, Sales & Marketing . . . . Jeff Ludy

305　Vista Healthplan of South Florida, Inc

Acquired by Coventry Health Care of Florida

306　VSP: Vision Service Plan of Florida

3001 N Rocky Point Drive East
Suite 200
Tampa, FL 33607-5806
Phone: 813-281-4605
webmaster@vsp.com
www.vsp.com
Year Founded: 1955
Number of Primary Care Physicians: 26,000
Total Enrollment: 55,000,000

Healthplan and Services Defined
　PLAN TYPE: Vision

Plan Specialty: Vision
Benefits Offered: Vision

Type of Payment Plans Offered
Capitated

Geographic Areas Served
Statewide

Network Qualifications
Pre-Admission Certification: Yes

Peer Review Type
Utilization Review: Yes

Accreditation Certification
Utilization Review, Quality Assurance Program

---

307 WellCare Health Plans

PO Box 31372
Tampa, FL 33631-3372
Toll-Free: 866-530-9491
Phone: 813-290-6200
Fax: 813-262-2802
www.wellcare.com
For Profit Organization: Yes
Year Founded: 1985
Number of Affiliated Hospitals: 83
Number of Primary Care Physicians: 2,091
Total Enrollment: 2,200,000
State Enrollment: 2,200,000

Healthplan and Services Defined
  PLAN TYPE: Medicare
  Model Type: IPA
  Benefits Offered: Disease Management, Prescription, Wellness

Type of Coverage
  Medicare, Medicaid
  Catastrophic Illness Benefit: Unlimited

Type of Payment Plans Offered
  POS, Combination FFS & DFFS

Geographic Areas Served
  Connecticut, Florida, Georgia, Hawaii, Illinois, Indiana, Missouri,
  New Jersey, New York, Ohio, Texas

Subscriber Information
  Average Subscriber Co-Payment:
    Primary Care Physician: $10.00
    Prescription Drugs: $8.00
    Hospital ER: $35.00
    Home Health Care: $10.00
    Home Health Care Max. Days/Visits Covered: Unlimited
    Nursing Home Max. Days/Visits Covered: 120 days

Network Qualifications
  Pre-Admission Certification: Yes

Peer Review Type
  Utilization Review: Yes
  Second Surgical Opinion: Yes
  Case Management: Yes

Publishes and Distributes Report Card: Yes

Accreditation Certification
  NCQA
  TJC Accreditation, Medicare Approved, Utilization Review,
    Pre-Admission Certification, State Licensure, Quality Assurance
    Program

Key Personnel
  Executive Chairman . . . . Charles G Berg
  Chief Executive Officer . . . . Alec Cunningham
  SVP/COO . . . . Rex M Adams
  President, FL & HI Div . . . . Christina C Cooper
  SVP/Chief Marketing Offc . . . . Walter W Cooper
  SVP/Health Care Delivery . . . . Scott D Law
  President, North Division . . . . Dan Parietti

SVP/General Counsel . . . . Timothy S Susanin
SVP/Chief Complaince Offc . . . . Blair W Todt
SVP/CFO . . . . Thomas L Tran
Chief Medical Officer . . . . Ann O Wehr

HMO/PPO DIRECTORY — GEORGIA

Health Insurance Coverage Status and Type of Coverage by Age

Category	All Persons		Under 18 years		Under 65 years		65 years and over	
	Number	%	Number	%	Number	%	Number	%
Total population	9,832	-	2,589	-	8,900	-	932	-
Covered by some type of health insurance	7,927 (135)	80.6 (1.2)	2,332 (40)	90.1 (1.4)	7,018 (135)	78.8 (1.3)	909 (48)	97.6 (0.9)
Covered by private health insurance	5,879 (186)	59.8 (1.8)	1,467 (79)	56.7 (2.9)	5,446 (175)	61.2 (1.9)	432 (39)	46.4 (3.4)
Employment based	5,146 (187)	52.3 (1.8)	1,332 (81)	51.5 (3.0)	4,867 (177)	54.7 (1.9)	279 (34)	30.0 (3.1)
Own employment based	2,542 (91)	25.9 (0.9)	2 (2)	0.1 (0.1)	2,326 (82)	26.1 (0.9)	216 (27)	23.2 (2.5)
Direct purchase	722 (67)	7.3 (0.7)	145 (26)	5.6 (1.0)	551 (65)	6.2 (0.7)	171 (26)	18.4 (2.8)
Covered by government health insurance	2,913 (143)	29.6 (1.4)	1,061 (71)	41.0 (2.8)	2,053 (141)	23.1 (1.5)	860 (46)	92.3 (1.4)
Covered by Medicaid	1,340 (81)	13.6 (0.8)	838 (54)	32.4 (2.1)	1,283 (78)	14.4 (0.9)	57 (15)	6.2 (1.6)
Also by private insurance	194 (33)	2.0 (0.3)	110 (18)	4.2 (0.7)	182 (33)	2.0 (0.4)	12 (7)	1.3 (0.8)
Covered by Medicare	1,074 (60)	10.9 (0.6)	11 (8)	0.4 (0.3)	215 (32)	2.4 (0.4)	860 (46)	92.3 (1.4)
Also by private insurance	426 (38)	4.3 (0.4)	6 (6)	0.2 (0.2)	44 (11)	0.5 (0.1)	382 (38)	41.0 (3.5)
Also by Medicaid	126 (25)	1.3 (0.3)	5 (6)	0.2 (0.2)	68 (20)	0.8 (0.2)	57 (15)	6.2 (1.6)
Covered by military health care	792 (138)	8.1 (1.4)	260 (55)	10.0 (2.1)	705 (129)	7.9 (1.4)	86 (19)	9.3 (1.9)
Not covered at any time during the year	1,905 (111)	19.4 (1.2)	257 (36)	9.9 (1.4)	1,883 (112)	21.2 (1.3)	22 (9)	2.4 (0.9)

Note: Numbers in thousands; figures cover 2010; standard error appears in parenthesis; (b) base less than 75,000; (x) not applicable
Source: U.S. Census Bureau, Current Population Survey, 2011 Annual Social and Economic Supplement. Table HI05. Health Insurance Coverage Status and Type of Coverage by State and Age for All People: 2010

147

Georgia

308 Aetna Health of Georgia
11675 Great Oaks Way
-9629
Atlanta, GA 30022
Toll-Free: 866-582-9629
Phone: 770-346-4300
Fax: 770-346-4490
www.aetna.com
For Profit Organization: Yes
Year Founded: 1986
Number of Affiliated Hospitals: 28
Number of Primary Care Physicians: 469
Number of Referral/Specialty Physicians: 1,200
Total Enrollment: 116,375
State Enrollment: 116,375

Healthplan and Services Defined
  PLAN TYPE: HMO
  Model Type: IPA
  Benefits Offered: Disease Management, Prescription, Wellness

Type of Coverage
  Catastrophic Illness Benefit: Unlimited

Type of Payment Plans Offered
  DFFS, Capitated

Geographic Areas Served
  Statewide

Subscriber Information
  Average Annual Deductible Per Subscriber:
      Employee Only (Self): $0
      Employee & 2 Family Members: $0
  Average Subscriber Co-Payment:
      Primary Care Physician: $10.00
      Non-Network Physician: Not covered
      Prescription Drugs: $5.00
      Hospital ER: $35.00
      Home Health Care: $0
      Home Health Care Max. Days/Visits Covered: Unlimited
      Nursing Home: $0
      Nursing Home Max. Days/Visits Covered: 100/yr.

Network Qualifications
  Pre-Admission Certification: Yes

Peer Review Type
  Second Surgical Opinion: Yes
  Case Management: Yes

Accreditation Certification
  NCQA
  TJC Accreditation, Pre-Admission Certification

Key Personnel
  President/CEO . . . . .Joseph Wild
  CFO . . . . .Pamela Woodley
  In House Formulary . . . . .Sandra Williams
  Marketing . . . . .Dan Feruck
  Medical Affairs . . . . .Richard Hart, MD
  Member Services . . . . .Deborah Moorman
  Provider Services. . . . . .Laurel Levy

Specialty Managed Care Partners
  Enters into Contracts with Regional Business Coalitions: No

309 Alere Health
3200 Windy Hill Road
Suite 300E
Altanta, GA 30339
Toll-Free: 800-456-4060
salesinquiry@alere.com
www.alere.com/alerehealth

Secondary Address: 10615 Professional Circle, Reno, NV 89521
For Profit Organization: Yes
Year Founded: 2008
Number of Primary Care Physicians: 1,200

Healthplan and Services Defined
  PLAN TYPE: PPO

Key Personnel
  CEO . . . . .Thomas D Underwood
  President, Free & Clear . . . . .Tim Kilgallon
  President, Health Improv. . . . . .Michael L Cotton
  President, Women's Health . . . . .Gregg E Raybuck
  EVP, Technology Solutions .Douglas Albro
  EVP, General Counsel . . . . .Craig Apolinsky
  EVP, Performance . . . . .Julie Griffin
  SVP, Enterprise Marketing . . . . .Scott McClintock
  Chief Innovation Officer . . . . .Gordon K Norman, MD/MBA
  Media Contact. . . . . .Jan McClure
    770-559-1016
    janm@mccluremedia.com

310 Alliant Health Plans
401 S Wall Street
Suite 201
Calhoun, GA 30701
Toll-Free: 800-664-8480
Phone: 706-629-8848
Fax: 706-629-3593
general.info@alliantplans.com
www.alliantplans.com
Non-Profit Organization: Yes
Year Founded: 1998
Physician Owned Organization: Yes
Number of Affiliated Hospitals: 9,999
Number of Primary Care Physicians: 500,000
Total Enrollment: 15,000
State Enrollment: 15,000

Healthplan and Services Defined
  PLAN TYPE: HMO/PPO
  Model Type: PSHCC
  Benefits Offered: Groupd & Individual

Key Personnel
  CEO . . . . .Judy Pair
  CFO. . . . . .Sara Carpenter
  COO . . . . .Al Ertel
  VP/Sales & Marketing. . . . . .Mark Mixer

311 Amerigroup Georgia
303 Perimeter Center North
Suite 400
Atlanta, GA 30346
Toll-Free: 888-423-6765
www.realsolutions.com
Secondary Address: 621 Northwest Frontage Road, Suite 100,
  Augusta, GA 30907
For Profit Organization: Yes
Year Founded: 2006
Total Enrollment: 1,900,000

Healthplan and Services Defined
  PLAN TYPE: HMO

Type of Coverage
  Medicaid, PeachCare

312 Assurant Employee Benefits: Georgia
780 Johnson Ferry Road NE
Atlanta, GA 30342-1434
benefits@assurant.com

www.assurantemployeebenefits.com
Subsidiary of: Assurant, Inc
For Profit Organization: Yes
Number of Primary Care Physicians: 112,000
Total Enrollment: 47,000

Healthplan and Services Defined
    PLAN TYPE: Multiple
    Plan Specialty: Dental, Vision, Long & Short-Term Disability
    Benefits Offered: Dental, Vision, Wellness, AD&D, Life, LTD, STD

Type of Coverage
    Commercial, Indemnity, Individual Dental Plans

Geographic Areas Served
    Statewide

Subscriber Information
    Average Monthly Fee Per Subscriber
        (Employee + Employer Contribution):
            Employee Only (Self): Varies by plan

Key Personnel
    Partner . . . . .Pace Schuchmann
    VP, Sales & Marketing. . . . . .Mike Geren
    PR Specialist. . . . . .Megan Hutchison
        816-556-7815
        megan.hutchison@assurant.com

313   Athens Area Health Plan Select

295 West Clayton Street
Athens, GA 30601
Toll-Free: 800-293-6260
Phone: 706-549-0549
Fax: 706-549-8004
memberservices@aahps.com
www.aahps.com
Subsidiary of: Athens Regional Health Services
Non-Profit Organization: Yes
Year Founded: 1997
Number of Primary Care Physicians: 1,000
Total Enrollment: 23,241
State Enrollment: 23,241

Healthplan and Services Defined
    PLAN TYPE: HMO
    Other Type: POS
    Benefits Offered: Disease Management, Prescription, Wellness,
        Durable Medical Equipment
    Offers Demand Management Patient Information Service: Yes
    DMPI Services Offered: 24 hour nurse line

Type of Coverage
    Commercial, Self-Insured

Geographic Areas Served
    Georgia

Accreditation Certification
    URAC

Key Personnel
    President . . . . .W Larry Webb
    Chief Executive Officer . . . . .Jeff Kunkle
    COO. . . . . .Raymond Donovan
    Medical Director . . . . .Fred Young, MD
    Member Relations . . . . .Deborah Hinshaw

314   Avesis: Georgia

2398 Lenora Church Road
Suite 200
Snellville, GA 30078-3600
Toll-Free: 800-522-4925
Phone: 770-979-3600
www.avesis.com
Year Founded: 1978

Number of Primary Care Physicians: 18,000
Total Enrollment: 2,000,000

Healthplan and Services Defined
    PLAN TYPE: PPO
    Other Type: Vision, Dental
    Model Type: Network
    Plan Specialty: Dental, Vision, Hearing
    Benefits Offered: Dental, Vision

Type of Coverage
    Commercial

Type of Payment Plans Offered
    POS, Capitated, Combination FFS & DFFS

Geographic Areas Served
    Nationwide and Puerto Rico

Publishes and Distributes Report Card: Yes

Accreditation Certification
    AAAHC
    TJC Accreditation

Key Personnel
    Manager. . . . . .Merl Inabnit

315   Blue Cross & Blue Shield of Georgia

3350 Peachtree Road NE
Atlanta, GA 30326
Toll-Free: 800-441-2273
Phone: 404-842-8000
Fax: 404-842-8100
www.bcbsga.com
Secondary Address: 2357 Warm Springs Road, Suite 375, Columbus,
    GA 31909
For Profit Organization: Yes
Year Founded: 1937
Number of Affiliated Hospitals: 196
Number of Primary Care Physicians: 19,000
Total Enrollment: 3,300,000
State Enrollment: 500,733

Healthplan and Services Defined
    PLAN TYPE: HMO
    Model Type: Network
    Plan Specialty: ASO, Behavioral Health, Chiropractic, Dental,
        Disease Management, EPO, Lab, MSO, PBM, Vision, Radiology,
        Worker's Compensation, UR
    Benefits Offered: Behavioral Health, Chiropractic, Complementary
        Medicine, Dental, Disease Management, Home Care, Inpatient
        SNF, Physical Therapy, Podiatry, Prescription, Psychiatric,
        Transplant, Vision, Wellness, AD&D, Life
    Offers Demand Management Patient Information Service: Yes

Type of Coverage
    Commercial, Individual, Indemnity, Medicare, Supplemental
    Medicare

Type of Payment Plans Offered
    POS, DFFS, Capitated, FFS

Geographic Areas Served
    Statewide

Network Qualifications
    Pre-Admission Certification: Yes

Peer Review Type
    Utilization Review: Yes
    Case Management: Yes

Publishes and Distributes Report Card: Yes

Accreditation Certification
    AAAHC, URAC, NCQA
    TJC Accreditation, Medicare Approved, Utilization Review,
        Pre-Admission Certification, State Licensure, Quality Assurance
        Program

Key Personnel

President . . . . .Morgan Kendrick
VP CFO . . . . .Greg Chandler
VP, Operations . . . . .Doris Anderson
VP . . . . .Kevin Leninhan
Manager . . . . .Fred Leathers, Jr.
Credentialing . . . . .Bob McCormack, MD
Chief Pharmacy Officer . . . . .Rob Seidman
VP Mktg/Adv. . . . . .Steve Miller
VP Procurement . . . . .Bill Cook
Medical Affairs . . . . .Wayne Hollman, MD
Member Services . . . . .Kevin Lenihamy
VP Information Tech. .John Kludt, MD
Provider Services . . . . .Monye Hollman, MD
VP Large Group Sales .David Goodrow
Media Contact . . . . .Cheryl Monkhouse
404-842-8516
cheryl.monkhouse@bcbsga.com

Average Claim Compensation

Physician's Fees Charged: 1%
Hospital's Fees Charged: 1%

Specialty Managed Care Partners

Wellpoint Dental Services, Greater Georgia Life, Wellpoint
Pharmacy Management, Wellpoint Behavioral Health
Enters into Contracts with Regional Business Coalitions: Yes

316 CIGNA HealthCare of Georgia

3500 Piedmont Road NE
Suite 200
Atlanta, GA 30305
Toll-Free: 800-526-5481
Phone: 404-443-8800
Fax: 404-443-8932
www.cigna.com
Mailing Address: PO Box 740022, Atlanta, GA 30374
Subsidiary of: CIGNA Corporation
For Profit Organization: Yes
Year Founded: 1981
Owned by an Integrated Delivery Network (IDN): Yes
Number of Primary Care Physicians: 16,000
Number of Referral/Specialty Physicians: 7,683
Total Enrollment: 25,769
State Enrollment: 25,769

Healthplan and Services Defined
PLAN TYPE: HMO
Other Type: POS
Model Type: IPA
Plan Specialty: ASO, Behavioral Health, Chiropractic, Dental,
Disease Management, EPO, Lab, MSO, PBM, Vision, Radiology,
UR
Benefits Offered: Behavioral Health, Chiropractic, Dental, Disease
Management, Home Care, Inpatient SNF, Physical Therapy,
Podiatry, Prescription, Psychiatric, Transplant, Vision, Wellness,
Life

Type of Coverage
Commercial

Type of Payment Plans Offered
FFS, Combination FFS & DFFS

Geographic Areas Served
Atlanta & Metro Area

Subscriber Information
Average Annual Deductible Per Subscriber:
Employee Only (Self): $0
Employee & 1 Family Member: $0
Employee & 2 Family Members: $0
Average Subscriber Co-Payment:
Primary Care Physician: $15.00
Non-Network Physician: Varies

Prescription Drugs: $10.00
Hospital ER: $50.00
Home Health Care: $0

Network Qualifications
Pre-Admission Certification: Yes

Peer Review Type
Utilization Review: Yes
Second Surgical Opinion: Yes
Case Management: Yes

Publishes and Distributes Report Card: Yes

Accreditation Certification
NCQA
TJC Accreditation, Utilization Review, Pre-Admission Certification,
State Licensure, Quality Assurance Program

Key Personnel
President/General Manager . . . . .Robert A Yungk
CFO . . . . .Lauren O'Brien
Network Contracting . . . . .Vernice Gailey
Credentialing . . . . .Rita Rakestraw
In House Formulary . . . . .Marybeth Luptowski
Marketing . . . . .Stephen Joiner
Chief Medical Officer . . . . .Mary Caufield, MD
Provider Services . . . . .Karen Little
Sales . . . . .Raplh Stokes

Specialty Managed Care Partners
Enters into Contracts with Regional Business Coalitions: No

317 CNA Insurance Companies: Georgia

2435 Commerce Avenue
Building 2200 Satellite Place
Duluth, GA 30096
Toll-Free: 800-282-7084
Phone: 678-473-3700
Fax: 866-512-2301
cna_help@cna.com
www.cna.com
Year Founded: 1897
Number of Affiliated Hospitals: 57
Number of Primary Care Physicians: 3,400
Total Enrollment: 270,000

Healthplan and Services Defined
PLAN TYPE: PPO
Model Type: Network
Plan Specialty: Worker's Compensation
Benefits Offered: Prescription

Type of Coverage
Catastrophic Illness Benefit: Varies per case

Type of Payment Plans Offered
POS, DFFS, Capitated, FFS, Combination FFS & DFFS

Geographic Areas Served
Nationwide

Network Qualifications
Pre-Admission Certification: Yes

Peer Review Type
Utilization Review: Yes
Second Surgical Opinion: Yes
Case Management: Yes

Accreditation Certification
TJC Accreditation, Medicare Approved, Utilization Review,
Pre-Admission Certification, State Licensure, Quality Assurance
Program

Key Personnel
Chairman/CEO . . . . .Thomas F Motamed
President/COO . . . . .Bob Lindemann
EVP, Chief Actuary . . . . .Larry A Haefner
EVP, Worldwide P&C Claim . . . . .George R Fay

EVP, General Counsel . . . . Johnathan D Kantor
EVP/CFO . . . . D Craig Mense
EVP, Chief Admin Officer . . . . Thomas Pontarelli
President, COO CNA Spec . . . . Peter W Wilson
President, Field Oper . . . . Tim Szerlong
SVP, CNA Select Risk . . . . John Angerami
SVP, Business Insurance . . . . Michael W Covne
Mid-Atlantic Zone Officer . . . . George Agven
Western Zone Officer . . . . Steve Stonehouse
Central Zone Officer . . . . Greg Vezzosi
Northern Zone Officer . . . . Steve Wachtel
Media Contact . . . . Katrina W Parker
    312-822-5167

Specialty Managed Care Partners
Enters into Contracts with Regional Business Coalitions: No

318 CompBenefits Corporation

100 Mansell Court East
Suite 400
Roswell, GA 30076-4859
Toll-Free: 800-633-1262
Phone: 770-998-8936
Fax: 770-998-6871
www.compbenefits.com
Subsidiary of: Humana
Year Founded: 1978
Owned by an Integrated Delivery Network (IDN): Yes
Total Enrollment: 4,500,000

Healthplan and Services Defined
  PLAN TYPE: Multiple
  Model Type: Network, HMO, PPO, POS, TPA
  Plan Specialty: ASO, Dental, Vision
  Benefits Offered: Dental, Vision

Type of Coverage
  Commercial, Individual, Indemnity

Type of Payment Plans Offered
  DFFS, Capitated, FFS

Geographic Areas Served
  Alabama, Arkansas, Illinois, Indiana, Georgia, Florida, Mississippi, Missouri, Kentucky, Kansas, North Carolina, South Carolina, West Virginia, Texas, Tennessee, Ohio, Louisiana

Publishes and Distributes Report Card: Yes

Key Personnel
  President/CEO . . . . Kirk Rothrock
    770-552-7101
    krothrock@compbenefits.com
  Exec VP/CFO . . . . George Dunaway
  Sr VP Operations . . . . Mary Kay Gilbert
  Dir, Vice Chairman . . . . Stanley Shapiro
  SVP . . . . Judith Herron
  Director . . . . Larry Fisher
  National Dental Director . . . . Kenneth J Hammer, DDS,MBA
  Sr VP Marketing . . . . Judith Herron
  Exec VP Sales . . . . Steven K Isaacs, LLIF
    770-552-7101

Specialty Managed Care Partners
Enters into Contracts with Regional Business Coalitions: Yes

319 Coventry Health Care of GA

1100 Circle 75 Parkway
Suite 1400
Atlanta, GA 30339
Toll-Free: 800-470-2004
Phone: 678-202-2100
Fax: 866-599-3720
cpbush@cvty.com

http://chcgeorgia.coventryhealthcare.com
Secondary Address: 7402 Hodgson Memorial Drive, 1st Floor, Suite 105, Savannah, GA 31406
For Profit Organization: Yes
Year Founded: 1994
Number of Affiliated Hospitals: 86
Number of Primary Care Physicians: 17,000
Total Enrollment: 150,000
State Enrollment: 150,000

Healthplan and Services Defined
  PLAN TYPE: HMO/PPO
  Other Type: POS
  Model Type: Group, Individual, Medicare Adv
  Benefits Offered: Disease Management, Prescription, Wellness

Geographic Areas Served
  71 counties in Georgia

Publishes and Distributes Report Card: Yes

Accreditation Certification
  AAAHC

Key Personnel
  CEO . . . . Thomas Davis
  CFO . . . . Paul Farrell
  COO . . . . Angela Meoli
  Director . . . . Mark Norato
  VP Sales . . . . Cory Scott

Specialty Managed Care Partners
Enters into Contracts with Regional Business Coalitions: Yes

320 Delta Dental of Georgia

1130 Sanctuary Parkway
Suite 600
Alpharetta, GA 30004
Toll-Free: 888-858-5252
Phone: 770-645-8700
Fax: 770-518-4757
4gasales@delta.org
www.deltadentalins.com
Mailing Address: PO Box 1809, Alpharetta, GA 30023-1809
Non-Profit Organization: Yes
Number of Primary Care Physicians: 198,000
Total Enrollment: 54,000,000

Healthplan and Services Defined
  PLAN TYPE: Dental
  Other Type: Dental PPO
  Plan Specialty: Dental
  Benefits Offered: Dental

Type of Coverage
  Commercial

Type of Payment Plans Offered
  POS, DFFS, FFS

Geographic Areas Served
  Statewide

Key Personnel
  CEO . . . . Gary D Radine
  VP, Public & Govt Affairs . . . . Jeff Album
    415-972-8418
  Dir/Media & Public Affair . . . . Elizabeth Risberg
    415-972-8423

321 eHealthInsurance Services Inc.

11919 Foundation Place
Gold River, CA 95670
Toll-Free: 800-977-8860
info@ehealthinsurance.com
www.e.healthinsurance.com
Year Founded: 1997

Healthplan and Services Defined
  PLAN TYPE: HMO/PPO
  Benefits Offered: Dental, Life, STD

Type of Coverage
  Commercial, Individual, Medicare

Geographic Areas Served
  All 50 states in the USA and District of Columbia

Key Personnel
  Chairman & CEO . . . . Gary L. Lauer
  EVP/Business & Corp. Dev. Bruce Telkamp
  EVP/Chief Technology . . . . Dr. Sheldon X. Wang
  SVP & CFO . . . . Stuart M. Huizinga
  Pres. of eHealth Gov. Sys . . . . Samuel C. Gibbs
  SVP of Sales & Operations . . . . Robert S. Hurley
  Director Public Relations . . . . Nate Purpura
    650-210-3115

322 Great-West Healthcare Georgia
Acquired by CIGNA

323 Humana Health Insurance of Georgia
6 Concourse Parkway
Suite 1440
Atlanta, GA 30328
Toll-Free: 800-671-4055
Phone: 770-829-3820
Fax: 770-730-9732
www.humana.com
For Profit Organization: Yes
Year Founded: 1961
Number of Affiliated Hospitals: 144
Number of Primary Care Physicians: 3,464
Number of Referral/Specialty Physicians: 6,452
Total Enrollment: 73,000
State Enrollment: 82,000

Healthplan and Services Defined
  PLAN TYPE: HMO/PPO
  Model Type: Network
  Benefits Offered: Behavioral Health, Chiropractic, Dental, Disease
    Management, Prescription, Psychiatric, Transplant, Wellness,
    Worker's Compensation

Type of Coverage
  Commercial, Individual, Medicare, Supplemental Medicare

Geographic Areas Served
  Statewide

Accreditation Certification
  URAC, NCQA, CORE

Key Personnel
  Chairman . . . . David A Jones, Jr
  Executive Director . . . . Dan Feruck

324 Kaiser Permanente of Georgia
3495 Piedmont Road
Piedmont Center, Building 9
Atlanta, GA 30305-1736
Toll-Free: 800-611-1811
Phone: 404-364-7000
Fax: 404-364-4906
billy.auer@kp.org
www.kaiserpermanente.org
Non-Profit Organization: Yes
Year Founded: 1985
Number of Affiliated Hospitals: 35
Number of Primary Care Physicians: 15,129
Total Enrollment: 257,819

State Enrollment: 257,819

Healthplan and Services Defined
  PLAN TYPE: HMO
  Model Type: Group
  Benefits Offered: Disease Management, Prescription, Wellness
  Offers Demand Management Patient Information Service: Yes

Geographic Areas Served
  Metro-Atlanta Area

Subscriber Information
  Average Subscriber Co-Payment:
    Primary Care Physician: $10.00
    Prescription Drugs: $10.00
    Hospital ER: $50.00
    Home Health Care: $10.00
    Nursing Home Max. Days/Visits Covered: 100/yr.

Publishes and Distributes Report Card: Yes

Accreditation Certification
  NCQA
  TJC Accreditation, Medicare Approved, Utilization Review,
    Pre-Admission Certification, State Licensure, Quality Assurance
    Program

Key Personnel
  President, KP Georgia . . . . Peter Andruszkiewicz
  Exec Medical Director . . . . Rob Schreiner, MD
  Media Contact . . . . Bill Auer
    404-869-5952
    billy.auer@kp.org

325 National Better Living Association
5425 Peachtree Parkway
Norcross, GA 30092
Toll-Free: 888-774-0848
Phone: 770-448-4677
Fax: 888-774-0456
www.mynbla.com
Year Founded: 1994
Number of Affiliated Hospitals: 5,500
Total Enrollment: 1,000,000

Healthplan and Services Defined
  PLAN TYPE: PPO
  Model Type: Network
  Plan Specialty: Chiropractic, Dental, Lab, PBM, Vision, Radiology,
    Act Med
  Benefits Offered: Chiropractic, Complementary Medicine, Dental,
    Home Care, Long-Term Care, Physical Therapy, Prescription,
    Vision, Wellness, AD&D, LTD, Indemnity

Type of Coverage
  Commercial, Individual, Indemnity, Medicare, Catastrophic, Discount
    Programs
  Catastrophic Illness Benefit: Maximum $2M

Type of Payment Plans Offered
  DFFS

Geographic Areas Served
  Nationwide

Subscriber Information
  Average Monthly Fee Per Subscriber
    (Employee + Employer Contribution):
      Employee Only (Self): $150.00
      Employee & 1 Family Member: $250.00
      Employee & 2 Family Members: $350.00
    Average Annual Deductible Per Subscriber:
      Employee Only (Self): $0
      Employee & 1 Family Member: $0
      Employee & 2 Family Members: $6

Network Qualifications
  Minimum Years of Practice: 3
  Pre-Admission Certification: Yes

Publishes and Distributes Report Card: No

Accreditation Certification
NCQA, Internally Performed
Pre-Admission Certification, State Licensure, Quality Assurance
Program

Key Personnel
President . . . . .George E Spalding, Jr, CPA
   800-669-8682
   gspalding@corpsavershealthcare.com
CEO . . . . .Dan Sewert, III
   800-669-8682
   dsiewert@corpsavershealthcare.com
COO . . . . .Timothy Siewert
   800-669-8682
   tsiewert@corpsavershealthcare.com
VP Provider Relations .Susan Spalding

Specialty Managed Care Partners
Guardian Life Insurance Co, Coalition America
Enters into Contracts with Regional Business Coalitions: Yes

Employer References
Aegon Financial Services, Memberworks, Ses, Goodhealth Services
LLC, Global Care

---

326   Northeast Georgia Health Partners

1405 Jesse Jewell Parkway
Gainesville, GA 30501
Phone: 770-219-6600
Fax: 770-219-6609
steven.mcneilly@nghs.com
www.healthpartnersnetwork.com
Subsidiary of: Northeat Georgia Health System
Non-Profit Organization: Yes
Number of Affiliated Hospitals: 8
Number of Primary Care Physicians: 500
Number of Referral/Specialty Physicians: 35
Total Enrollment: 42,000
State Enrollment: 42,000

Healthplan and Services Defined
   PLAN TYPE: PPO
Benefits Offered: Behavioral Health, Home Care, Prescription,
Psychiatric, Wellness

Type of Coverage
Commercial

Geographic Areas Served
Banks, Barrow, Dawson, Forsyth, Gwinnet, Habersham, Hall,
Jackson, Lumplin, Rabun, Stephens, Towns, Union and White
counties

Accreditation Certification
NCQA

Key Personnel
Sales/Marketing Director . . . . .Steven McNeilly
   678-897-6601
   steven.mcneilly@nghs.com
QI Specialist. . . . . .Janet Lathem
   janet.lathem@nghs.com
Credentialing Coordinator . . . . .Pam Short
   pam.short@nghs.com
Sales & Marketing Dir . . . . .Steven McNeilly
   770-219-6601
   steven.mcneilly@nghs.com
Provider Relations Rep . . . . .Melissa D Corral
   melissa.corral@nghs.com

---

327   Secure Health PPO Newtork

577 Mulberry Street
Suite 1000
Macon, GA 31201
Toll-Free: 800-648-7563
Phone: 478-314-2400
Fax: 478-314-2428
www.shpg.com
Mailing Address: PO Box 4088, Macon, GA 31028
For Profit Organization: Yes
Year Founded: 1992
Physician Owned Organization: Yes
Number of Affiliated Hospitals: 16
Number of Primary Care Physicians: 950
Total Enrollment: 68,000
State Enrollment: 68,000

Healthplan and Services Defined
   PLAN TYPE: PPO
Other Type: TPA
Benefits Offered: Disease Management, Prescription, Wellness, EAP

Type of Coverage
Commercial

Geographic Areas Served
Georgia

Peer Review Type
Utilization Review: Yes
Case Management: Yes

Key Personnel
President/CEO. . . . . .Robert Morton

---

328   Southeast Community Care

3920 Arkwright Road
Suite 370
Macon, GA 31210
Toll-Free: 888-701-2678
Phone: 478-474-2678
Fax: 484-477-9958
www.southeastcommunitycare.com
Subsidiary of: Arcadian Health Plans

Healthplan and Services Defined
   PLAN TYPE: Medicare

Type of Coverage
Medicare

---

329   United Concordia: Georgia

Three Northwinds Center
2500 Northwinds Parkway, Suite 360
Alpharetta, GA 30009
Toll-Free: 888-340-2001
Phone: 678-893-8650
Fax: 678-297-9920
ucproducer@ucci.com
www.secure.ucci.com
For Profit Organization: Yes
Year Founded: 1971
Number of Primary Care Physicians: 111,000
Total Enrollment: 8,000,000

Healthplan and Services Defined
   PLAN TYPE: Dental
Plan Specialty: Dental
Benefits Offered: Dental

Type of Coverage
Commercial, Individual

Geographic Areas Served
Military personnel and their families, nationwide

330 UnitedHealthCare of Georgia

3720 Davinci Court
Suite 300
Norcross, GA 30092
Toll-Free: 800-842-6219
Phone: 770-300-3501
Fax: 770-300-4362
www.uhc.com
Subsidiary of: UnitedHealth Group
For Profit Organization: Yes
Year Founded: 1980
Number of Affiliated Hospitals: 47
Number of Primary Care Physicians: 2,200
Number of Referral/Specialty Physicians: 4,000
Total Enrollment: 75,000,000
State Enrollment: 1,051,334

Healthplan and Services Defined
  PLAN TYPE: HMO/PPO
  Model Type: Network
  Benefits Offered: Disease Management, Physical Therapy,
    Prescription, Wellness
  Offers Demand Management Patient Information Service: Yes

Type of Coverage
  Catastrophic Illness Benefit: Unlimited

Type of Payment Plans Offered
  POS, FFS

Geographic Areas Served
  Statewide

Network Qualifications
  Pre-Admission Certification: Yes

Peer Review Type
  Utilization Review: Yes
  Case Management: Yes

Publishes and Distributes Report Card: Yes

Accreditation Certification
  NCQA
  TJC Accreditation, Medicare Approved, Utilization Review,
    Pre-Admission Certification, State Licensure, Quality Assurance
    Program

Key Personnel
  Regional CEO . . . . .Daniel Laurence Ohman
  CEO . . . . .Rick Elliott
  Media Contact. . . . . .Roger Rollman
    roger_f_rollman@uhc.com

Specialty Managed Care Partners
  Enters into Contracts with Regional Business Coalitions: Yes

331 VSP: Vision Service Plan of Georgia

3091 Governors Lake Drive
#240
Norcross, GA 30071-1143
Phone: 770-447-6128
Fax: 770-263-6008
webmaster@vsp.com
www.vsp.com
Year Founded: 1955
Number of Primary Care Physicians: 26,000
Total Enrollment: 55,000,000

Healthplan and Services Defined
  PLAN TYPE: Vision
  Plan Specialty: Vision
  Benefits Offered: Vision

Type of Payment Plans Offered
  Capitated

Geographic Areas Served
  Statewide

Network Qualifications
  Pre-Admission Certification: Yes

Peer Review Type
  Utilization Review: Yes

Accreditation Certification
  Utilization Review, Quality Assurance Program

Key Personnel
  Manager . . . . .Cheryl Rains

HMO/PPO DIRECTORY

HAWAII

Health Insurance Coverage Status and Type of Coverage by Age

Category	All Persons		Under 18 years		Under 65 years		65 years and over	
	Number	%	Number	%	Number	%	Number	%
Total population	1,257	-	296	-	1,065	-	192	-
Covered by some type of health insurance	1,160 *(13)*	92.3 *(0.7)*	289 *(4)*	97.7 *(0.7)*	972 *(16)*	91.2 *(0.9)*	188 *(11)*	98.4 *(0.7)*
Covered by private health insurance	885 *(20)*	70.4 *(1.5)*	185 *(9)*	62.6 *(2.8)*	768 *(20)*	72.0 *(1.6)*	117 *(8)*	61.2 *(2.7)*
Employment based	803 *(21)*	63.9 *(1.6)*	171 *(8)*	57.7 *(2.7)*	705 *(21)*	66.2 *(1.7)*	97 *(7)*	50.9 *(2.7)*
Own employment based	470 *(14)*	37.4 *(1.0)*	0 *(0)*	0.0 *(0.0)*	391 *(14)*	36.7 *(1.1)*	78 *(6)*	40.9 *(2.7)*
Direct purchase	114 *(13)*	9.1 *(1.0)*	18 *(6)*	6.1 *(2.1)*	86 *(11)*	8.1 *(1.0)*	28 *(4)*	14.7 *(2.1)*
Covered by government health insurance	467 *(20)*	37.1 *(1.5)*	138 *(9)*	46.7 *(3.0)*	294 *(17)*	27.6 *(1.6)*	173 *(10)*	90.3 *(1.7)*
Covered by Medicaid	206 *(14)*	16.4 *(1.2)*	115 *(9)*	38.9 *(2.8)*	187 *(13)*	17.6 *(1.3)*	19 *(4)*	9.8 *(2.0)*
Also by private insurance	46 *(6)*	3.7 *(0.5)*	23 *(4)*	7.6 *(1.3)*	38 *(6)*	3.5 *(0.5)*	9 *(2)*	4.6 *(1.2)*
Covered by Medicare	196 *(12)*	15.6 *(0.9)*	6 *(3)*	1.9 *(1.0)*	24 *(5)*	2.2 *(0.5)*	173 *(10)*	90.1 *(1.7)*
Also by private insurance	108 *(8)*	8.6 *(0.6)*	0 *(0)*	0.1 *(0.1)*	7 *(2)*	0.6 *(0.2)*	102 *(7)*	53.1 *(2.6)*
Also by Medicaid	28 *(6)*	2.2 *(0.5)*	5 *(3)*	1.6 *(1.0)*	9 *(4)*	0.9 *(0.4)*	19 *(4)*	9.8 *(2.0)*
Covered by military health care	112 *(14)*	8.9 *(1.1)*	25 *(5)*	8.4 *(1.8)*	99 *(14)*	9.3 *(1.3)*	13 *(2)*	6.6 *(1.3)*
Not covered at any time during the year	97 *(9)*	7.7 *(0.7)*	7 *(2)*	2.3 *(0.7)*	93 *(9)*	8.8 *(0.9)*	3 *(1)*	1.6 *(0.7)*

Note: Numbers in thousands; figures cover 2010; standard error appears in parenthesis; (b) base less than 75,000; (x) not applicable
Source: U.S. Census Bureau, Current Population Survey, 2011 Annual Social and Economic Supplement. Table HI05. Health Insurance Coverage Status and Type of Coverage by State and Age for All People: 2010

Hawaii

332 Aetna Health of Hawaii
Partnered with eHealthInsurance Services Inc.

333 AlohaCare
1357 Kapiolani Boulevard
Suite 1250
Honolulu, HI 96814
Toll-Free: 800-434-1002
Phone: 808-973-1650
Fax: 808-973-0726
customerservice@alohacarehawaii.org
www.alohacarehawaii.org
Non-Profit Organization: Yes
Year Founded: 1994
Number of Primary Care Physicians: 3,000
Total Enrollment: 75,000

Healthplan and Services Defined
  PLAN TYPE: HMO

Type of Coverage
  Medicare, Supplemental Medicare

Peer Review Type
  Case Management: Yes

Publishes and Distributes Report Card: Yes

Key Personnel
  President . . . . .Dana Howeth
  Vice President . . . . .David Bess
  Vice President. . . . . .Richard Bettini
  Medical Director. . . . . .Rio Banner, MD
  Marketing Director. . . . . .Greg Irion
    808-973-1569
    girion@alohacarehawaii.org

334 CIGNA HealthCare of Hawaii
1 Front Street
7th Floor
San Francisco, CA 94111
Toll-Free: 888-802-4462
Fax: 860-298-2443
www.cigna.com
For Profit Organization: Yes
Total Enrollment: 2,407
State Enrollment: 1,602

Healthplan and Services Defined
  PLAN TYPE: HMO
  Benefits Offered: Disease Management, Prescription, Transplant,
  Wellness

Type of Coverage
  Commercial

Type of Payment Plans Offered
  POS, FFS

Geographic Areas Served
  Hawaii

335 eHealthInsurance Services Inc.
11919 Foundation Place
Gold River, CA 95670
Toll-Free: 800-977-8860
info@ehealthinsurance.com
www.e.healthinsurance.com
Year Founded: 1997

Healthplan and Services Defined
  PLAN TYPE: HMO/PPO

Benefits Offered: Dental, Life, STD
Type of Coverage
  Commercial, Individual, Medicare

Geographic Areas Served
  All 50 states in the USA and District of Columbia

Key Personnel
  Chairman & CEO . . . . .Gary L. Lauer
  EVP/Business & Corp. Dev.. . . . . .Bruce Telkamp
  EVP/Chief Technology . . . . .Dr. Sheldon X. Wang
  SVP & CFO . . . . .Stuart M. Huizinga
  Pres. of eHealth Gov. Sys .Samuel C. Gibbs
  SVP of Sales & Operations .Robert S. Hurley
  Director Public Relations. . . . . .Nate Purpura
    650-210-3115

336 Great-West Healthcare Hawaii
Acquired by CIGNA

337 Hawaii Medical Assurance Association
737 Bishop Street
Suite 1200
Honolulu, HI 96813
Toll-Free: 800-621-6998
Phone: 808-591-0088
Fax: 808-591-0463
www.hmaa.com
For Profit Organization: Yes
Year Founded: 1989
Number of Primary Care Physicians: 1,874
Total Enrollment: 42,000
State Enrollment: 42,000

Healthplan and Services Defined
  PLAN TYPE: PPO
  Benefits Offered: Dental, Prescription, Vision, Wellness, AD&D, Life

Type of Coverage
  Commercial

Key Personnel
  Chairman/President/CEO .John Henry Felix

338 Hawaii Medical Services Association
818 Keeaumoku Street
Honolulu, HI 96814
Phone: 808-948-6111
Fax: 808-948-5567
www.hmsa.com
Mailing Address: PO Box 860HI 96808-0860
Subsidiary of: Blue Cross/Blue Shield
Non-Profit Organization: Yes
Year Founded: 1938
Total Enrollment: 556,000
State Enrollment: 414,370

Healthplan and Services Defined
  PLAN TYPE: PPO

Accreditation Certification
  NCQA

Key Personnel
  President/CEO. . . . . .Robert P Hiam
  Exec VP/COO . . . . .Michael A Gold
  Exec VP/CFO/Treasurer .Steve Van Ribbink
  Executive Vice President .Gwen S Miyasato
  Senior Vice President . . . . .Michael Cheng
  Senior Vice President .Richard S Chung, MD
  Media Relations. . . . . .Chuck Marshall
    chuck_marshall@hmsa.com

339   Humana Health Insurance of Hawaii

500 Ala Moana Blvd, 7 Waterfront Plaza
Suite 400
Honolulu, HI 96813
Phone: 808-543-2080
Fax: 808-543-2085
www.humana.com
For Profit Organization: Yes

Healthplan and Services Defined
   PLAN TYPE: HMO/PPO

Type of Coverage
   Commercial, Individual

Accreditation Certification
   URAC, NCQA, CORE

340   Kaiser Permanente Health Plan of Hawaii

711 Kapiolani Boulevard
Honolulu, HI 96813-5249
Toll-Free: 800-966-5955
Phone: 808-432-5955
Fax: 808-432-5300
jan,kagehiro@kp.org
www.kaiserpermanente.org
Non-Profit Organization: Yes
Year Founded: 1958
Number of Affiliated Hospitals: 35
Number of Primary Care Physicians: 15,129
Total Enrollment: 223,795
State Enrollment: 223,795

Healthplan and Services Defined
   PLAN TYPE: HMO
   Model Type: Group
   Benefits Offered: Chiropractic, Complementary Medicine, Disease
      Management, Prescription, Vision, Wellness, Worker's
      Compensation
   Offers Demand Management Patient Information Service: Yes

Type of Coverage
   Commercial, Individual, Medicare, Medicaid
   Catastrophic Illness Benefit: Unlimited

Type of Payment Plans Offered
   POS, Capitated, FFS

Geographic Areas Served
   Big Island of Hawaii, Kauai, Maui & Oahu

Subscriber Information
   Average Subscriber Co-Payment:
      Home Health Care Max. Days/Visits Covered: Unlimited
      Nursing Home: Skilled nursing fac.
      Nursing Home Max. Days/Visits Covered: Skilled nursing fac.

Network Qualifications
   Pre-Admission Certification: No

Peer Review Type
   Utilization Review: Yes
   Case Management: Yes

Publishes and Distributes Report Card: Yes

Accreditation Certification
   NCQA
   TJC Accreditation, Medicare Approved, Utilization Review, State
      Licensure, Quality Assurance Program

Key Personnel
   Hawaii Region President . . . . .Janet Liang
   Exec Medical Director . . . . .Geoffrey S Sewell, MD
   Media Contact . . . . .Jan Kagehiro
      808-432-5460
      jan.kagehiro@kp.org

Specialty Managed Care Partners
   Enters into Contracts with Regional Business Coalitions: Yes

341   UnitedHealthCare of Hawaii

5757 Plaza Drive
Cypress, CA 90630
Toll-Free: 800-343-2608
www.uhc.com
Subsidiary of: UnitedHealth Group
For Profit Organization: Yes
Year Founded: 1986
Total Enrollment: 75,000,000
State Enrollment: 3,902

Healthplan and Services Defined
   PLAN TYPE: HMO/PPO
   Model Type: Network
   Benefits Offered: Disease Management, Prescription, Wellness
   Offers Demand Management Patient Information Service: Yes

Type of Coverage
   Catastrophic Illness Benefit: Covered

Type of Payment Plans Offered
   DFFS, Capitated

Geographic Areas Served
   Statewide

Subscriber Information
   Average Monthly Fee Per Subscriber
      (Employee + Employer Contribution):
         Employee Only (Self): $120.00
         Employee & 1 Family Member: $240.00
         Employee & 2 Family Members: $375.00
   Average Annual Deductible Per Subscriber:
      Employee & 2 Family Members: Varies
   Average Subscriber Co-Payment:
      Primary Care Physician: $5.00-10.00
      Prescription Drugs: $5.00/10.00/25.00
      Hospital ER: $50.00
      Nursing Home Max. Days/Visits Covered: 120 per year

Publishes and Distributes Report Card: Yes

Accreditation Certification
   NCQA
   TJC Accreditation, Utilization Review, State Licensure

Specialty Managed Care Partners
   Enters into Contracts with Regional Business Coalitions: Yes

342   University Health Alliance

700 Bishop Street
Suite 300, Bishop Street Tower
Honolulu, HI 96813
Toll-Free: 800-458-4600
Phone: 808-532-4000
Fax: 866-572-4393
www.uhahealth.com
For Profit Organization: Yes
Year Founded: 1996
Total Enrollment: 36,505

Healthplan and Services Defined
   PLAN TYPE: PPO
   Benefits Offered: Dental, Prescription, Vision, Wellness

Type of Coverage
   Commercial

Accreditation Certification
   URAC, HUM

Key Personnel
   President/CEO. . . . . .Howard K Lee, MD
   SVP/CFO . . . . .Charles Murray
   SVP, Chief Mktng Officer. .Linda Kalahiki

```
SVP/Chief Medical Officer. . . . . . . . . . . George O McPheeters, MD
Medical Director . . . . . . . . . . . . . . . . . . . . . . . Glenn Ishikawa, MD
SVP, Chief HR Officer. . . . . . . . . . . . . . . . . . . . . . . Emily Weaver
SVP, Chief Info Officer . . . . . . . . . . . . . . . . . . . . . . . . Chad Lee
SVP, Chief Sales Officer . . . . . . . . . . . . . . . . . . Lance Kaneshiro
```

343 VSP: Vision Service Plan of Hawaii

1003 Bishop Street
Suite 890
Honolulu, HI 96813-6426
Phone: 808-532-1600
Fax: 808-533-0604
webmaster@vsp.com
www.vsp.com
Year Founded: 1955
Number of Primary Care Physicians: 26,000
Total Enrollment: 55,000,000

Healthplan and Services Defined
  PLAN TYPE: Vision
  Plan Specialty: Vision
  Benefits Offered: Vision

Type of Payment Plans Offered
  Capitated

Geographic Areas Served
  Statewide

Network Qualifications
  Pre-Admission Certification: Yes

Peer Review Type
  Utilization Review: Yes

Accreditation Certification
  Utilization Review, Quality Assurance Program

Key Personnel
  Manager . . . . Paula Palmer

Health Insurance Coverage Status and Type of Coverage by Age

Category	All Persons		Under 18 years		Under 65 years		65 years and over	
	Number	%	Number	%	Number	%	Number	%
Total population	1,531	-	418	-	1,344	-	188	-
Covered by some type of health insurance	1,238 *(25)*	80.8 *(1.5)*	380 *(9)*	91.0 *(1.9)*	1,052 *(28)*	78.3 *(1.7)*	186 *(11)*	98.9 *(0.8)*
Covered by private health insurance	993 *(28)*	64.8 *(1.8)*	264 *(13)*	63.1 *(2.9)*	866 *(29)*	64.5 *(2.0)*	126 *(11)*	67.2 *(4.5)*
Employment based	769 *(24)*	50.2 *(1.5)*	213 *(13)*	50.9 *(2.9)*	723 *(26)*	53.8 *(1.7)*	46 *(7)*	24.6 *(3.7)*
Own employment based	372 *(12)*	24.3 *(0.8)*	0 *(0)*	0.0 *(0.0)*	339 *(12)*	25.3 *(0.8)*	33 *(4)*	17.5 *(2.2)*
Direct purchase	256 *(19)*	16.7 *(1.3)*	67 *(9)*	16.0 *(2.3)*	173 *(18)*	12.9 *(1.4)*	82 *(10)*	43.8 *(4.4)*
Covered by government health insurance	425 *(18)*	27.8 *(1.2)*	149 *(12)*	35.6 *(2.9)*	249 *(18)*	18.6 *(1.3)*	176 *(11)*	93.7 *(1.9)*
Covered by Medicaid	204 *(17)*	13.3 *(1.1)*	141 *(11)*	33.8 *(2.8)*	193 *(16)*	14.3 *(1.2)*	11 *(4)*	6.0 *(1.8)*
Also by private insurance	39 *(7)*	2.5 *(0.4)*	26 *(6)*	6.2 *(1.3)*	35 *(6)*	2.6 *(0.5)*	4 *(3)*	2.2 *(1.3)*
Covered by Medicare	209 *(11)*	13.7 *(0.7)*	1 *(1)*	0.2 *(0.2)*	34 *(5)*	2.5 *(0.4)*	175 *(11)*	93.2 *(2.0)*
Also by private insurance	125 *(12)*	8.1 *(0.8)*	0 *(0)*	0.0 *(0.0)*	8 *(2)*	0.6 *(0.2)*	116 *(12)*	62.0 *(5.0)*
Also by Medicaid	25 *(5)*	1.6 *(0.3)*	1 *(1)*	0.2 *(0.2)*	14 *(3)*	1.0 *(0.3)*	11 *(4)*	6.0 *(1.8)*
Covered by military health care	61 *(12)*	4.0 *(0.8)*	10 *(3)*	2.3 *(0.8)*	45 *(10)*	3.3 *(0.8)*	17 *(4)*	9.0 *(2.3)*
Not covered at any time during the year	294 *(23)*	19.2 *(1.5)*	38 *(8)*	9.0 *(1.9)*	292 *(23)*	21.7 *(1.7)*	2 *(2)*	1.1 *(0.8)*

Note: Numbers in thousands; figures cover 2010; standard error appears in parenthesis; (b) base less than 75,000; (x) not applicable
Source: U.S. Census Bureau, Current Population Survey, 2011 Annual Social and Economic Supplement. Table HI05. Health Insurance Coverage Status and Type of Coverage by State and Age for All People: 2010

Idaho

344 Aetna Health of Idaho
Partnered with eHealthInsurance Services Inc.

345 Blue Cross of Idaho Health Service, Inc.
3000 East Pine Avenue
Meridian, ID 83642
Toll-Free: 800-274-4018
Phone: 208-345-4550
Fax: 208-331-7311
www.bcidaho.com
Mailing Address: PO Box 7408, Boise, ID 83707
Subsidiary of: Blue Cross and Blue Shield Association
Non-Profit Organization: Yes
Year Founded: 1945
Number of Affiliated Hospitals: 44
Number of Primary Care Physicians: 1,631
Total Enrollment: 563,000
State Enrollment: 563,000

Healthplan and Services Defined
PLAN TYPE: HMO/PPO
Model Type: IPA, Group, Network
Plan Specialty: ASO, Chiropractic, Dental, Disease Management
Benefits Offered: Chiropractic, Dental, Disease Management,
Prescription, Vision, Wellness

Type of Coverage
Commercial, Individual, Indemnity, Medicare, Supplemental
Medicare

Type of Payment Plans Offered
POS, DFFS, FFS

Geographic Areas Served
Statewide

Subscriber Information
Average Subscriber Co-Payment:
Prescription Drugs: Varies
Hospital ER: Varies
Home Health Care: Varies
Nursing Home: Varies

Network Qualifications
Pre-Admission Certification: Yes

Peer Review Type
Utilization Review: Yes
Case Management: Yes

Publishes and Distributes Report Card: Yes

Accreditation Certification
TJC Accreditation, Pre-Admission Certification, State Licensure

Key Personnel
President/CEO . . . . Ray Flachbart
Chairman. . . . . Jack Gustavel
Vice Chairman . . . . Michael Shirlely
VP Actuarial Services . . . . David Hutchins
VP/Human Resources . . . . Debra M Henry
SVP/Chief Marketing Offc . . . . Jerry Dworak
Dir Pharmacy Management . . . . Stephen J Brocksome
SVP/Chief Medical Officer . . . . Bruce Croffy, MD
VP Benefits Management . . . . Drew S Forney
VP Chief Information Offc . . . . Lance Hatfield
VP Provider Services . . . . Jeff Crouch
VP Account Management . . . . Dennis Warren
Corp & Media Relations . . . . Karen Early
208-387-6920
kearly@bcidaho.com
Dir Human Resources. . . . . Doug Bullock

Specialty Managed Care Partners
Wellpoint Pharmacy Management, Dental through Blue Cross of
Idaho, Vision through VSP, Life Insurance, EAP through Business
Psychology Associates
Enters into Contracts with Regional Business Coalitions: No

346 CIGNA HealthCare of Idaho
701 Fifth Avenue
Suite 4900
Seattle, WA 98104
Toll-Free: 866-438-2446
Phone: 206-625-8892
Fax: 206-625-8880
www.cigna.com
For Profit Organization: Yes
Total Enrollment: 27,000

Healthplan and Services Defined
PLAN TYPE: PPO
Model Type: Consumer Driven
Benefits Offered: Behavioral Health, Dental, Prescription, Medical

Type of Coverage
Commercial

Type of Payment Plans Offered
POS, FFS

Geographic Areas Served
Idaho

Network Qualifications
Pre-Admission Certification: Yes

Key Personnel
President & General Mgr . . . . Chris Blanton

347 Delta Dental of Idaho
555 East Parkcenter Blvd
Boise, ID 83706
Toll-Free: 800-356-7586
Phone: 208-489-3580
customerservice@deltadentalid.com
www.deltadentalid.com
Mailing Address: PO Box 2870, Boise, ID 83701
Non-Profit Organization: Yes
Year Founded: 1971
Total Enrollment: 54,000,000

Healthplan and Services Defined
PLAN TYPE: Dental
Other Type: Dental PPO
Model Type: Network
Plan Specialty: Dental
Benefits Offered: Dental

Type of Coverage
Commercial

Type of Payment Plans Offered
DFFS

Geographic Areas Served
Statewide

Subscriber Information
Average Monthly Fee Per Subscriber
(Employee + Employer Contribution):
Employee Only (Self): $17
Employee & 2 Family Members: $50
Average Annual Deductible Per Subscriber:
Employee Only (Self): $150
Employee & 2 Family Members: $50
Average Subscriber Co-Payment:
Primary Care Physician: 80%
Non-Network Physician: 50%

Network Qualifications
Pre-Admission Certification: Yes

Publishes and Distributes Report Card: Yes

Key Personnel
President & CEO . . . . .Tamara Brandstetter
Dir/Media & Public Affair . . . . .Elizabeth Risberg
415-972-8423

348 eHealthInsurance Services Inc.

11919 Foundation Place
Gold River, CA 95670
Toll-Free: 800-977-8860
info@ehealthinsurance.com
www.e.healthinsurance.com
Year Founded: 1997

Healthplan and Services Defined
PLAN TYPE: HMO/PPO
Benefits Offered: Dental, Life, STD

Type of Coverage
Commercial, Individual, Medicare

Geographic Areas Served
All 50 states in the USA and District of Columbia

Key Personnel
Chairman & CEO . . . . .Gary L. Lauer
EVP/Business & Corp. Dev.. . . . . .Bruce Telkamp
EVP/Chief Technology . . . . .Dr. Sheldon X. Wang
SVP & CFO . . . . .Stuart M. Huizinga
Pres. of eHealth Gov. Sys . . . . .Samuel C. Gibbs
SVP of Sales & Operations . . . . .Robert S. Hurley
Director Public Relations. . . . . .Nate Purpura
650-210-3115

349 Great-West Healthcare of Idaho

Acquired by CIGNA

350 Humana Health Insurance of Idaho

3006 E Goldstone Drive
Suite 118
Meridian, ID 83642
Phone: 208-350-7307
www.humana.com
For Profit Organization: Yes

Healthplan and Services Defined
PLAN TYPE: HMO/PPO

Type of Coverage
Commercial, Individual

Accreditation Certification
URAC, NCQA, CORE

351 IHC: Intermountain Healthcare Health Plan

Acquired by SelectHealth

352 Liberty Health Plan: Idaho

6213 North Cloverdale Road
Suite 150
Boise, ID 93713-2215
Toll-Free: 800-283-4456
Phone: 208-322-3339
Fax: 800-256-3853
customerservice.center@libertynorthwest.com
www.libertynorthwest.com
Mailing Address: PO Box 50098, Idaho Falls, ID 83405
For Profit Organization: Yes
Year Founded: 1983

Healthplan and Services Defined
PLAN TYPE: PPO
Model Type: Group
Plan Specialty: Worker's Compensation
Benefits Offered: Prescription

Type of Payment Plans Offered
POS, DFFS, FFS, Combination FFS & DFFS

Geographic Areas Served
Statewide

Network Qualifications
Pre-Admission Certification: Yes

Peer Review Type
Case Management: Yes

Publishes and Distributes Report Card: No

Specialty Managed Care Partners
Enters into Contracts with Regional Business Coalitions: No

353 PacificSource Health Plans: Idaho

800 Park Blvd
Suite 760
Boise, ID 83712
Toll-Free: 888-492-2875
Phone: 208-342-3709
Fax: 208-342-4508
www.pacificsource.com
Secondary Address: 110 West Park Place, Suite 221, Coeur d'Alene, ID
83814
Non-Profit Organization: Yes
Year Founded: 1933
Number of Primary Care Physicians: 34,000
Total Enrollment: 280,000

Healthplan and Services Defined
PLAN TYPE: HMO/PPO
Benefits Offered: Dental, Disease Management, Prescription, Vision,
Wellness

Type of Coverage
Commercial, Individual

Type of Payment Plans Offered
POS, Combination FFS & DFFS

Geographic Areas Served
Oregon and Idaho

Key Personnel
President & CEO. . . . . .Ken Provencher
SVP, Reg Director ID & WA. .Dave Self
Media Contact. . . . . .Colleen Thompson
541-684-5453
cthompson@pacificsource.com

Specialty Managed Care Partners
Caremark Rx

354 Primary Health Plan

Acquired by PacificSource Health Plans

355 Regence BlueShield of Idaho

1602 21st Avenue
PO Box 1106
Lewiston, ID 83501
Toll-Free: 800-632-2022
Phone: 208-746-2671
Fax: 208-798-2097
www.id.regence.com
Total Enrollment: 2,500,000
State Enrollment: 2,500,000

Healthplan and Services Defined
 PLAN TYPE: Multiple

Type of Coverage
 Supplemental Medicare

Geographic Areas Served
 Idaho; Asotin and Garfield counties in Washington

Key Personnel
 President & CEO...............................Mark B Ganz
 EVP, Corporate Services ....Kerry E Barnett
 EVP, Health Care Oper ....Bill Barr
 Pres, Reg BlueShield ID.........................Scott Kreiling

356 UnitedHealthCare of Idaho

5757 Plaza Drive
Cypress, CA 90630
Toll-Free: 800-343-2608
www.uhc.com
Subsidiary of: UnitedHealth Group
For Profit Organization: Yes
Year Founded: 1986
Total Enrollment: 75,000,000
State Enrollment: 40,618

Healthplan and Services Defined
 PLAN TYPE: HMO/PPO
 Model Type: Network
 Benefits Offered: Disease Management, Prescription, Wellness
 Offers Demand Management Patient Information Service: Yes

Type of Coverage
 Catastrophic Illness Benefit: Covered

Type of Payment Plans Offered
 DFFS, Capitated

Geographic Areas Served
 Statewide

Subscriber Information
 Average Monthly Fee Per Subscriber
  (Employee + Employer Contribution):
   Employee Only (Self): $120.00
   Employee & 1 Family Member: $240.00
   Employee & 2 Family Members: $375.00
 Average Annual Deductible Per Subscriber:
   Employee & 2 Family Members: Varies
 Average Subscriber Co-Payment:
   Primary Care Physician: $5.00-10.00
   Prescription Drugs: $5.00/10.00/25.00
   Hospital ER: $50.00
   Nursing Home Max. Days/Visits Covered: 120 per year

Publishes and Distributes Report Card: Yes

Accreditation Certification
 NCQA
 TJC Accreditation, Utilization Review, State Licensure

Specialty Managed Care Partners
 Enters into Contracts with Regional Business Coalitions: Yes

HMO/PPO DIRECTORY
ILLINOIS

Health Insurance Coverage Status and Type of Coverage by Age

Category	All Persons		Under 18 years		Under 65 years		65 years and over	
	Number	%	Number	%	Number	%	Number	%
Total population	12,901	-	3,137	-	11,337	-	1,564	-
Covered by some type of health insurance	10,986 *(122)*	85.2 *(0.9)*	2,897 *(45)*	92.4 *(1.1)*	9,452 *(140)*	83.4 *(1.0)*	1,534 *(62)*	98.1 *(0.6)*
Covered by private health insurance	8,537 *(157)*	66.2 *(1.2)*	1,854 *(65)*	59.1 *(1.9)*	7,519 *(163)*	66.3 *(1.3)*	1,017 *(58)*	65.0 *(2.6)*
Employment based	7,407 *(157)*	57.4 *(1.1)*	1,712 *(59)*	54.6 *(1.8)*	6,876 *(159)*	60.7 *(1.3)*	531 *(45)*	33.9 *(2.6)*
Own employment based	3,874 *(89)*	30.0 *(0.6)*	11 *(4)*	0.3 *(0.1)*	3,456 *(84)*	30.5 *(0.7)*	418 *(37)*	26.7 *(2.1)*
Direct purchase	1,287 *(78)*	10.0 *(0.6)*	176 *(29)*	5.6 *(0.9)*	723 *(62)*	6.4 *(0.6)*	564 *(47)*	36.1 *(2.5)*
Covered by government health insurance	3,861 *(124)*	29.9 *(1.0)*	1,266 *(66)*	40.4 *(2.1)*	2,415 *(117)*	21.3 *(1.0)*	1,446 *(62)*	92.5 *(1.1)*
Covered by Medicaid	2,143 *(108)*	16.6 *(0.8)*	1,234 *(68)*	39.3 *(2.2)*	2,067 *(106)*	18.2 *(0.9)*	76 *(14)*	4.9 *(0.9)*
Also by private insurance	368 *(49)*	2.9 *(0.4)*	217 *(34)*	6.9 *(1.1)*	357 *(48)*	3.1 *(0.4)*	12 *(4)*	0.8 *(0.2)*
Covered by Medicare	1,744 *(64)*	13.5 *(0.5)*	30 *(13)*	0.9 *(0.4)*	308 *(33)*	2.7 *(0.3)*	1,436 *(61)*	91.8 *(1.1)*
Also by private insurance	984 *(59)*	7.6 *(0.5)*	0 *(0)*	0.0 *(0.0)*	59 *(14)*	0.5 *(0.1)*	925 *(58)*	59.1 *(2.7)*
Also by Medicaid	196 *(29)*	1.5 *(0.2)*	26 *(12)*	0.8 *(0.4)*	127 *(26)*	1.1 *(0.2)*	68 *(13)*	4.4 *(0.8)*
Covered by military health care	300 *(52)*	2.3 *(0.4)*	41 *(14)*	1.3 *(0.4)*	210 *(46)*	1.8 *(0.4)*	90 *(21)*	5.8 *(1.3)*
Not covered at any time during the year	1,914 *(112)*	14.8 *(0.9)*	239 *(33)*	7.6 *(1.1)*	1,884 *(112)*	16.6 *(1.0)*	30 *(9)*	1.9 *(0.6)*

Note: Numbers in thousands; figures cover 2010; standard error appears in parenthesis; (b) base less than 75,000; (x) not applicable
Source: U.S. Census Bureau, Current Population Survey, 2011 Annual Social and Economic Supplement. Table HI05. Health Insurance Coverage Status and Type of Coverage by State and Age for All People: 2010

Illinois

357 Aetna Health of Illinois

1 South Wacker Drive
Mail Stop F643
Chicago, IL 60606
Toll-Free: 866-582-9629
www.aetna.com
For Profit Organization: Yes
Total Enrollment: 45,014
State Enrollment: 45,014

Healthplan and Services Defined
  PLAN TYPE: HMO
  Other Type: POS
  Plan Specialty: EPO
  Benefits Offered: Dental, Disease Management, Long-Term Care,
    Prescription, Wellness, Life, LTD, STD

Type of Coverage
  Commercial, Individual

Type of Payment Plans Offered
  POS, FFS

Geographic Areas Served
  Statewide

358 Assurant Employee Benefits: Illinois

1 Tower Lane
Suite 2410
Oakbrook Terrace, IL 60181-4639
Phone: 630-954-5700
Fax: 630-954-1365
benefits@assurant.com
www.assurantemployeebenefits.com
Subsidiary of: Assurant, Inc
For Profit Organization: Yes
Number of Primary Care Physicians: 112,000
Total Enrollment: 47,000

Healthplan and Services Defined
  PLAN TYPE: Multiple
  Plan Specialty: Dental, Vision, Long & Short-Term Disability
  Benefits Offered: Dental, Vision, Wellness, AD&D, Life, LTD, STD

Type of Coverage
  Commercial, Indemnity, Individual Dental Plans

Geographic Areas Served
  Statewide

Subscriber Information
  Average Monthly Fee Per Subscriber
    (Employee + Employer Contribution):
      Employee Only (Self): Varies by plan

Key Personnel
  Business Manager . . . . Paul Sweatman
  PR Specialist . . . . Megan Hutchison
    816-556-7815
    megan.hutchison@assurant.com

359 Blue Cross & Blue Shield of Illinois

300 East Randolph Street
Chicago, IL 60601-5099
Toll-Free: 800-654-7385
Phone: 312-653-6000
Fax: 312-938-3868
www.bcbsil.com
Subsidiary of: Health Care Service Corporation
Non-Profit Organization: Yes
Total Enrollment: 6,500,000

State Enrollment: 6,500,000

Healthplan and Services Defined
  PLAN TYPE: HMO/PPO
  Benefits Offered: Disease Management, Physical Therapy, Wellness

Type of Coverage
  Commercial, Supplemental Medicare, Medicaid

Type of Payment Plans Offered
  POS, FFS

Geographic Areas Served
  Illinois

Key Personnel
  President & CEO . . . . Patricia Hemingway Hall
  Chairman . . . . Milton Carrollux
  EVP & COO . . . . Colleen Reitan
  CFO . . . . Denise Bujak
  CMO . . . . Stanley Borg, DO
  General Counsel . . . . Hugo Tagli
  Provider Relations . . . . Brad Buxton
  Marketing . . . . Dennis Hooker
  Member Relations . . . . Raymond Angeli
  Pharmacy Director . . . . Kevin Slavik, RPh/MHA
  Public Relations . . . . Robert Kieckhefer
  Sr Mgr, Media Relations . . . . Mary Ann Schultz
    312-653-6701
    maryann_schultz@bcbsil.com

Specialty Managed Care Partners
  Prime Therapeutics

360 Blue Cross and Blue Shield Association

225 North Michigan Avenue
BCBS Association Headquarters
Chicago, IL 60601
Phone: 312-297-6000
Fax: 312-297-6609
www.bcbs.com/medicare
Secondary Address: 1310 G Street NW, Washington, DC 20005

Healthplan and Services Defined
  PLAN TYPE: Medicare
  Benefits Offered: Chiropractic, Disease Management, Home Care,
    Inpatient SNF, Physical Therapy, Podiatry, Prescription, Psychiatric,
    Wellness

Type of Coverage
  Individual, Medicare

Geographic Areas Served
  Available in multiple states. Go to Web/URL provided to view state by
  state availability of Medicare Plans which also provides direct Web
  links to state plans each with detailed information on coverages
  available and contact info for that state

Subscriber Information
  Average Monthly Fee Per Subscriber
    (Employee + Employer Contribution):
      Employee Only (Self): Varies
      Medicare: Varies
  Average Annual Deductible Per Subscriber:
      Employee Only (Self): Varies
      Medicare: Varies
  Average Subscriber Co-Payment:
      Primary Care Physician: Varies
      Non-Network Physician: Varies
      Prescription Drugs: Varies
      Hospital ER: Varies
      Home Health Care: Varies
      Home Health Care Max. Days/Visits Covered: Varies
      Nursing Home: Varies
      Nursing Home Max. Days/Visits Covered: Varies

Key Personnel
  President/CEO . . . . Scott P Serota

VP/Deputy General Counsel . . . . .Paul F Brown
SVP/Human Resources . . . . .William A Colbourne
VP/Inter-Plan Programs . . . . .Frank C Coyne
VP/Federal Relations . . . . .Jack Ericksen
Legislation/Reg. Policy . . . . .Alissa Fox
SVP National Programs . . . . .Stephen W Gammarino
SVP/Chief Medical Officer . . . . .Allan M Korn, MD
VP/Business Informatics . . . . .Shirley S Lady
VP/Chief Tech Officer . . . . .William B O'Loughlin
SVP/Strategic Services .Maureen E Sullivan
SVP/Chief Info Officer . . . . .Doug Porter
General Counsel . . . . .Roger G Wilson
SVP/Chief Financial Offc .Robert Kolodgy
VP/Brand Strategy . . . . .Jennifer Vachon
Exec Dir, Ext Affairs . . . . .Jeff Smokler
   jeff.smokler@bcbsa.com

361 CIGNA HealthCare of Illinois

525 W Monroe Street
Suite 300
Chicago, IL 60661
Toll-Free: 800-832-3211
Phone: 312-648-2460
Fax: 312-648-3617
www.cigna.com
For Profit Organization: Yes
Year Founded: 1986
Total Enrollment: 18,588
State Enrollment: 18,588

Healthplan and Services Defined
   PLAN TYPE: HMO
   Other Type: POS
   Model Type: IPA, Network
   Plan Specialty: ASO, Behavioral Health, Dental
   Benefits Offered: Behavioral Health, Complementary Medicine,
      Dental, Disease Management, Prescription, Transplant, Vision,
      Wellness

Type of Coverage
   Commercial, Indemnity

Type of Payment Plans Offered
   POS, DFFS, FFS

Geographic Areas Served
   Illinois: Bureau, Coles, Cook, DuPage, Grundy, Kane, Kankakee,
   Lake, LaSalle, Livingston, Madison, Massac, McHenry, Monroe,
   Saint Clair, Shelby, Vermilion, Will counties

Network Qualifications
   Pre-Admission Certification: Yes

Peer Review Type
   Utilization Review: Yes

Publishes and Distributes Report Card: Yes

Accreditation Certification
   NCQA
   TJC Accreditation, Medicare Approved, Utilization Review,
      Pre-Admission Certification, State Licensure, Quality Assurance
      Program

Key Personnel
   President/CEO . . . . .H Edward Hanway
   Sales Manager . . . . .Sue Povbielski

362 CNA Insurance Companies: Illinois

CNA Plaza
333 S Wabash
Chicago, IL 60604
Toll-Free: 800-262-4473
Phone: 312-822-5000
Fax: 312-817-1237

cna_help@cna.com
www.cna.com
Year Founded: 1987
Owned by an Integrated Delivery Network (IDN): Yes
Number of Affiliated Hospitals: 57
Number of Primary Care Physicians: 3,400
Total Enrollment: 270,000

Healthplan and Services Defined
   PLAN TYPE: PPO
   Model Type: Network
   Plan Specialty: Dental, Disease Management, Lab, MSO, Vision,
      Radiology, Worker's Compensation, UR
   Benefits Offered: Behavioral Health, Chiropractic, Dental, Disease
      Management, Home Care, Inpatient SNF, Long-Term Care,
      Physical Therapy, Podiatry, Prescription, Psychiatric, Transplant,
      Vision, Wellness, Worker's Compensation, AD&D, Life, LTD, STD

Type of Coverage
   Commercial, Individual, Indemnity, Medicaid, Catastrophic

Type of Payment Plans Offered
   POS

Network Qualifications
   Pre-Admission Certification: Yes

Peer Review Type
   Utilization Review: Yes
   Case Management: Yes

Publishes and Distributes Report Card: Yes

Accreditation Certification
   URAC
   TJC Accreditation, Pre-Admission Certification

Key Personnel
   Chairman/CEO . . . . .Thomas F Motamed
   President/COO . . . . .Bob Lindemann
   EVP, Chief Actuary . . . . .Larry A Haefner
   EVP, Worldwide P&C Claim . . . . .George R Fay
   EVP, General Counsel .Johathan D Kantor
   EVP/CFO . . . . .D Craig Mense
   EVP, Chief Admin Officer . . . . .Thomas Pontarelli
   President, COO CNA Spec . . . . .Peter W Wilson
   President, Field Oper . . . . .Tim Szerlong
   SVP, CNA Select Risk .John Angerami
   SVP, Business Insurance . . . . .Michael W Covne
   Mid-Atlantic Zone Officer . . . . .George Agven
   Western Zone Officer .Steve Stonehouse
   Central Zone Officer . . . . .Greg Vezzosi
   Northern Zone Officer .Steve Wachtel
   Media Contact . . . . .Katrina W Parker
      312-822-5167

Specialty Managed Care Partners
   Enters into Contracts with Regional Business Coalitions: Yes

363 CompBenefits: Illinois

200 W Jackson Blvd
9th Floor
Chicago, IL 60606
Toll-Free: 800-837-2341
Phone: 312-261-6200
Fax: 312-427-9665
www.compbenefits.com
Subsidiary of: Humana
Year Founded: 1978
Owned by an Integrated Delivery Network (IDN): Yes
Total Enrollment: 4,500,000

Healthplan and Services Defined
   PLAN TYPE: Multiple
   Model Type: Network, HMO, PPO, POS, TPA
   Plan Specialty: ASO, Dental, Vision
   Benefits Offered: Dental, Vision

Type of Coverage
Commercial, Individual, Indemnity

Type of Payment Plans Offered
DFFS, Capitated, FFS

Geographic Areas Served
Alabama, Arkansas, Illinois, Indiana, Georgia, Florida, Mississippi, Missouri, Kentucky, Kansas, North Carolina, South Carolina, West Virginia, Texas, Tennessee, Ohio, Louisiana

Publishes and Distributes Report Card: Yes

Specialty Managed Care Partners
Enters into Contracts with Regional Business Coalitions: Yes

364 CoreSource: Corporate Headquarters

400 Field Drive
Lake Forest, IL 60045
Toll-Free: 800-832-3332
Phone: 847-604-9200
www.coresource.com
Secondary Address: 18401 Maple Creek Drive, Suite 300, Tinley Park, IL 60477
Subsidiary of: Trustmark
Year Founded: 1980
Total Enrollment: 1,100,000

Healthplan and Services Defined
  PLAN TYPE: Multiple
  Other Type: TPA
  Model Type: Network
  Plan Specialty: Claims Administration, TPA
  Benefits Offered: Behavioral Health, Home Care, Prescription, Transplant

Type of Coverage
Commercial

Geographic Areas Served
Nationwide

Accreditation Certification
Utilization Review, Pre-Admission Certification

Key Personnel
President . . . . .Nancy Eckrich
VP, Chief Financial Offc . . . . .Clare Smith
Chief Operating Officer . . . . .Lloyd Sarrel
VP, Product Management . . . . .Rob Corrigan
VP, Healthcare Management. . . . . .Donna Heiser
VP, Marketing. . . . . .Sean McManamy
SVP, Communications . . . . .Melanie A Morgan
  601-208-2979
  melanie.morgan@trustmark.com

365 Delta Dental of Illinois

111 Shuman Blvd
Naperville, IL 60532
Toll-Free: 800-323-1743
Phone: 630-964-2400
Fax: 630-964-2596
askdelta@deltadentalil.com
www.deltadentalil.com
Mailing Address: PO Box 5402, Lisle, IL 60532
Non-Profit Organization: Yes
Year Founded: 1967
Total Enrollment: 54,000,000

Healthplan and Services Defined
  PLAN TYPE: Dental
  Other Type: Dental PPO
  Model Type: Network
  Benefits Offered: Dental

Type of Coverage
Commercial

Geographic Areas Served
Statewide

Peer Review Type
Utilization Review: Yes

Key Personnel
President/CEO . . . . .Bernard Glossy
CFO . . . . .David Behnke
Chief Admin Officer. . . . . .Stacey Bonn
VP Sales . . . . .Jeanette Battista
Dir, Corp Communications . . . . .Ann Marie Walker
  630-718-4739
  awalker@deltadentalil.com
Dir/Media & Public Affair . . . . .Elizabeth Risberg
  415-972-8423

366 Dental Network of America

Two TransAm Plaza Drive
Oakbrook Terrace, IL 60181-4275
Toll-Free: 800-323-6840
Phone: 630-691-1133
Fax: 630-495-0575
general_inquiry@dnoa.com
www.dnoa.com
Subsidiary of: Health Care Service Corporation
For Profit Organization: Yes
Year Founded: 1985
Federally Qualified: Yes
Number of Primary Care Physicians: 80,000
Total Enrollment: 6,200,000

Healthplan and Services Defined
  PLAN TYPE: Dental
  Other Type: TPA, Dental PPO
  Plan Specialty: ASO, Dental, Dental, Fully Insured
  Benefits Offered: Dental

Type of Coverage
Commercial, Individual, Indemnity, Group

Type of Payment Plans Offered
Capitated

Geographic Areas Served
Nationwide

Network Qualifications
Pre-Admission Certification: Yes

Peer Review Type
Utilization Review: Yes

Key Personnel
President & CEO. . . . . .John Doyle
CFO. . . . . .Craig Simundza
VP, Risk Management. . . . . .Christopher Stevens
Exec Dir, Operations. . . . . .Thomas McNally
Exec Dir, Finance . . . . .Craig Simundza
Dental Director . . . . .Timothy J Custer
VP, Dental Networks . . . . .Mike Miller
VP, Sales & Marketing. . . . . .Chip Huffman
Exec Dir, Project Mgmt. . . . . .Justin Majcher
Exec Dir, Human Resources. . . . . .Rachel Poormon Garrido
Executive Director, IT. . . . . .Tom Kimrey
Marketing. . . . . .Lynne Culberson
  630-691-0302
  lculberson@dnoa.com

367 eHealthInsurance Services Inc.

11919 Foundation Place
Gold River, CA 95670
Toll-Free: 800-977-8860
info@ehealthinsurance.com
www.e.healthinsurance.com

Year Founded: 1997

Healthplan and Services Defined
   PLAN TYPE: HMO/PPO
   Benefits Offered: Dental, Life, STD

Type of Coverage
   Commercial, Individual, Medicare

Geographic Areas Served
   All 50 states in the USA and District of Columbia

Key Personnel
   Chairman & CEO . . . . Gary L. Lauer
   EVP/Business & Corp. Dev. Bruce Telkamp
   EVP/Chief Technology . . . . Dr. Sheldon X. Wang
   SVP & CFO . . . . Stuart M. Huizinga
   Pres. of eHealth Gov. Sys . . . . Samuel C. Gibbs
   SVP of Sales & Operations . . . . Robert S. Hurley
   Director Public Relations. . . . . Nate Purpura
    650-210-3115

---

368   First Commonwealth
Acquired by Guardian Life Insurance Company

---

369   First Health
3200 Highland Avenue
Downers Grove, IL 60515
Toll-Free: 800-226-5116
Phone: 630-737-7900
Fax: 405-843-0956
www.firsthealth.com
Subsidiary of: A Coventry Health Care Company
For Profit Organization: Yes
Year Founded: 1984
Number of Affiliated Hospitals: 134
Number of Primary Care Physicians: 1,923
Number of Referral/Specialty Physicians: 5,744
State Enrollment: 585,000

Healthplan and Services Defined
   PLAN TYPE: PPO
   Model Type: Network
   Benefits Offered: Disease Management, Wellness

Type of Payment Plans Offered
   DFFS

Geographic Areas Served
   State of Oklahoma and contiguous border cities of Missouri,
   Arkansas, Kansas and Texas

Key Personnel
   President . . . . George E Bennett
   COO & CFO . . . . R. Blaine Faulkner II
   VP, Sales & Marketing. . . . . Colleen West
   VP, Account Management. . . . . Susan Korth

Average Claim Compensation
   Physician's Fees Charged: 72%
   Hospital's Fees Charged: 62%

---

370   Great-West Healthcare Illinois
Acquired by CIGNA

---

371   Health Alliance Medical Plans
301 S Vine Street
Urbana, IL 61801
Toll-Free: 800-851-3379
Phone: 217-337-8000
Fax: 217-337-8093
www.healthalliance.org
For Profit Organization: Yes
Year Founded: 1979

Physician Owned Organization: Yes
Federally Qualified: Yes
Total Enrollment: 316,465

Healthplan and Services Defined
   PLAN TYPE: HMO/PPO
   Benefits Offered: Disease Management, Wellness

Type of Coverage
   Medicare

Geographic Areas Served
   Illinois and Central Iowa

Subscriber Information
   Average Monthly Fee Per Subscriber
    (Employee + Employer Contribution):
     Employee Only (Self): $329.00
     Employee & 2 Family Members: $1053.00
   Average Subscriber Co-Payment:
    Primary Care Physician: $20.00
    Prescription Drugs: $10.00-15.00

Publishes and Distributes Report Card: Yes

Accreditation Certification
   NCQA

Key Personnel
   CEO . . . . Jeffrey C Ingrum
   CFO . . . . Gordon Salm
   Chief Medical Officer. Robert Parker, MD
   General Counsel . . . . Lori Cowdrey
   Marketing/Sales . . . . Lori Rudd
   Member Relations . . . . Angela Beitelman
   Pharmacy Director . . . . Christina Barrington
   Public Relations . . . . Jane Hayes
   Marketing/Sales. . . . . Todd Hutchison
   Communications Coord. . . . . Nichole Evans
    217-255-4694

---

372   Health Alliance Medicare
301 S Vine Street
Urbana, IL 61801
Toll-Free: 888-382-9771
www.healthalliancemedicare.org
Year Founded: 1997
Number of Primary Care Physicians: 3,000
Total Enrollment: 255,494

Healthplan and Services Defined
   PLAN TYPE: Medicare
   Other Type: HMO/PPO
   Benefits Offered: Prescription

Type of Coverage
   Medicare, Supplemental Medicare

Accreditation Certification
   NCQA

---

373   Health Care Service Corporation
300 East Randolph Street
Chicago, IL 60601-5099
Phone: 312-653-6000
Fax: 312-819-1323
www.hcsc.com
Subsidiary of: A Mutual Legal Reserve Company
For Profit Organization: Yes
Year Founded: 1975
Owned by an Integrated Delivery Network (IDN): Yes
Total Enrollment: 12,400,000
State Enrollment: 12,400,000

Healthplan and Services Defined
   PLAN TYPE: HMO/PPO
   Other Type: POS, HSA, HCA

Model Type: Network
Plan Specialty: Chiropractic, Dental, Disease Management, Lab, Vision, Radiology, UR
Benefits Offered: Chiropractic, Dental, Disease Management, Home Care, Inpatient SNF, Physical Therapy, Podiatry, Prescription, Psychiatric, Transplant, Vision, Wellness, AD&D, Life, LTD, STD

Type of Coverage
Commercial, Individual, Indemnity, Supplemental Medicare, Catastrophic, Major Medical Plan

Type of Payment Plans Offered
Capitated

Geographic Areas Served
Illinois, New Mexico, Oklahoma, Texas

Peer Review Type
Second Surgical Opinion: Yes

Accreditation Certification
NCQA

Key Personnel
President/CEO .Patricia A Hemingway Hall
EVP, President Plan Oper . . . . .Martin G Foster
EVP/COO . . . . .Colleen Reitan
EVP, Corporate Services. . . . . Tara Dowd Gurber
Sr VP Chief Legal Officer. . . . . Deborah Dorman-Rodriguez
SVP, Chief Actuary. . . . . .Kenneth Avner
SVP, Chief Financial Off. . . . . .Denise Bujak
Media Contact . . . . .Kim Lane
972-766-8304
kim_lane@hcsc.net
Media Contact. . . . . .Ross Blackstone
972-766-1735
ross_blackstone@hcsc.net

374 HealthSmart Preferred Care

2400 Cabot Drive
Suite 300
Lisle, IL 60532
Toll-Free: 800-268-5209
Phone: 630-493-9570
Fax: 630-493-3865
info.cms@healthsmart.com
www.healthsmart.com
Secondary Address: 2002 West Loop 289, Suite 110, Lubbock, TX 79407
For Profit Organization: Yes
Year Founded: 1983
Number of Affiliated Hospitals: 63
Number of Primary Care Physicians: 400,000
Total Enrollment: 470,623

Healthplan and Services Defined
PLAN TYPE: PPO

Key Personnel
Chairman & Founder . . . . .Ted Parker
SVP, Operations . . . . .Jane Williamson, RN
Regional VP, Sales. . . . . .Clay Timmons
VP, Network Development. . . . . .Jim Sabolik
SVP, Product Development .Reagan Bruce
VP, Sales & Marketing . . . . .John Farnsley

375 HealthSpring of Illinois

9701 W Higgins Road
Suite 360
Rosemont, IL 60018
Toll-Free: 888-588-4827
Phone: 847-318-8844
info@healthspringofillinois.com
www.healthspring.com

Physician Owned Organization: Yes

Healthplan and Services Defined
PLAN TYPE: Medicare

Type of Coverage
Medicare, Supplemental Medicare

Geographic Areas Served
Cook, DeKalb, DuPage, Kane, Kendall, Lake, McHenry, and Will counties

Key Personnel
President . . . . .Randy Fike
Corp Mgr, Media Relations .Jolene Sharp
615-234-6710
jolene.sharp@healthspring.com

376 Humana Benefit Plan of Illinois

7915 N Hale Avenue
Suite D
Peoria, IL 61615
Toll-Free: 877-677-8205
Phone: 309-677-8200
Fax: 309-677-8295
member@osfhealthcare.org
www.osfmedicare.com
Secondary Address: 6957 Olde Creek Road, Suite 2300, Rockford, IL 61114
Subsidiary of: A Humana Afilliate
Year Founded: 1878

Healthplan and Services Defined
PLAN TYPE: Medicare

Type of Coverage
Medicare, Supplemental Medicare

Geographic Areas Served
CARE PREFERRED ONLY: Stephenson, Winnebago, Boone, Ogle, Whiteside, Lee, La Salle, Putnam, Bureau, Henry, Mercer, Warren, Hancock, McDonough, Fulton, Schuyler, Brown, Cass and De Witt; CARE PREFERRED & CARE ADVANTAGE: Knox, Stark, Marshall, Peoria, Woodford, Tazewell, McLean, and Livingston

Accreditation Certification
URAC, NCQA, CORE

Key Personnel
Marketing & Communication . . . . .James Farrell
309-655-2856
james.farrell@osfhealthcare.org

377 Humana Health Insurance of Illinois

550 W Adams Street
7th Floor
Chicago, IL 60661
Toll-Free: 800-230-6825
Phone: 312-441-9111
Fax: 312-441-5086
www.humana.com
Secondary Address: 2301 W 22nd Street, Suite 301, Oak Brook, IL 60523
For Profit Organization: Yes
Year Founded: 1972
Number of Affiliated Hospitals: 437
Number of Primary Care Physicians: 21,070
Total Enrollment: 763,175
State Enrollment: 763,175

Healthplan and Services Defined
PLAN TYPE: HMO/PPO
Model Type: Network
Plan Specialty: Behavioral Health, Chiropractic, Dental, Disease Management, Lab, PBM, Vision, Worker's Compensation, UR

Benefits Offered: Behavioral Health, Chiropractic, Complementary Medicine, Dental, Disease Management, Home Care, Inpatient SNF, Long-Term Care, Physical Therapy, Prescription, Psychiatric, Transplant, Vision, Wellness, Worker's Compensation, AD&D, Life, LTD, STD

Type of Coverage
Commercial, Individual, Indemnity, Medicare, Supplemental Medicare, Medicaid, Catastrophic

Type of Payment Plans Offered
POS, DFFS, Capitated, FFS

Geographic Areas Served
18 States and Puerto Rico

Network Qualifications
Pre-Admission Certification: Yes

Peer Review Type
Utilization Review: Yes
Second Surgical Opinion: Yes
Case Management: Yes

Publishes and Distributes Report Card: Yes

Accreditation Certification
URAC, NCQA, CORE
TJC Accreditation, Medicare Approved, Utilization Review, Pre-Admission Certification, State Licensure, Quality Assurance Program

Key Personnel
President/CEO ....Mike McCallister
Sr VP Innovation Officer ....Jack Lord, MD
Sr VP/CFO...............................James Bloem
Sr VP Senior Products ....Douglas Carlisle
Sr VP General Counsel ....Art Hipwell
Sr VP Corporate Develop......................Tom Liston
VP Market Operations........................Stefen Brueckner
Sr VP Human Resources......................Bonnie Hathcock
COO Market/Business ....Jim Murray
Sr VP Government Relation ....Heidi Margulis
Sr VP Corporate Communica ....Tom Noland
Sr VP/CSO/CIO ....Bruce Goodman
Sr VP National Contracts ....Bruce Perkins
Sr VP Marketing Officer ....Steve Moya

Specialty Managed Care Partners
Behavioral Health, Disease Management, PBM, Worker's Compensation
Enters into Contracts with Regional Business Coalitions: Yes
Midwest Business Group on Health, Mercer Coalition

378   Medical Associates Health Plan

1500 Associates Drive
Dubuque, IA 52002
Toll-Free: 800-747-8900
Phone: 563-556-8070
Fax: 563-556-5134
www.mahealthcare.com
Non-Profit Organization: Yes
Year Founded: 1982
Physician Owned Organization: Yes
Total Enrollment: 45,000
State Enrollment: 37,792

Healthplan and Services Defined
PLAN TYPE: HMO
Other Type: EPO, POS
Plan Specialty: EPO, TPA
Benefits Offered: Behavioral Health, Chiropractic, Complementary Medicine, Home Care, Inpatient SNF, Physical Therapy, Podiatry, Prescription, Psychiatric, Transplant, Vision, Wellness

Type of Coverage
Commercial, Indemnity, Medicare, Supplemental Medicare

Type of Payment Plans Offered
POS

Geographic Areas Served
Illinois: Jo Daviess County. Iowa: Allamakee, Clayton, Delaware, Dubuque, Jackson, Jones counties

Peer Review Type
Utilization Review: Yes
Case Management: Yes

Accreditation Certification
NCQA
Pre-Admission Certification

Key Personnel
Executive Director ....Alan Avery
CEO ....John Tallent

Specialty Managed Care Partners
Express Scripts

379   OSF Healthcare

800 NE Glen Oak Avenue
Peoria, IL 61603-3200
Phone: 309-655-2850
www.osfhealthcare.org
Subsidiary of: Sisters of the Third Order of St Francis
Non-Profit Organization: Yes
Number of Affiliated Hospitals: 6
Number of Primary Care Physicians: 210
Number of Referral/Specialty Physicians: 50
Total Enrollment: 1,500,000

Healthplan and Services Defined
PLAN TYPE: HMO
Model Type: Network
Plan Specialty: Integrated Healthcare Network of Facilities
Benefits Offered: Disease Management, Wellness

Geographic Areas Served
Illinois and Michigan

Key Personnel
CEO ....James Moore
SVP, Marketing ....James G Farrell
   309-655-2856
   james.g.farrell@osfhealthcare.org
SVP, Marketing ....James Farell
   309-655-2856
   james.farrell@osfhealthcare.org

380   OSF HealthPlans

7915 North Hale Avenue
Suite D
Peoria, IL 61615
Toll-Free: 800-673-4699
Phone: 309-677-8200
Fax: 309-677-8295
member@osfhealthcare.org
www.osfhealthplans.com
Secondary Address: 6957 Olde Creek Road, Suite 2300, Rockford, IL 61114
Subsidiary of: A Humana Affiliate
For Profit Organization: Yes
Year Founded: 1995
Number of Affiliated Hospitals: 21
Number of Primary Care Physicians: 485
Number of Referral/Specialty Physicians: 1,133
Total Enrollment: 64,973
State Enrollment: 2,732

Healthplan and Services Defined
PLAN TYPE: PPO
Model Type: Network

Plan Specialty: ASO, Chiropractic, Dental, Disease Management, EPO, Lab, PBM, Vision, Radiology, UR

Benefits Offered: Chiropractic, Home Care, Inpatient SNF, Physical Therapy, Prescription, Psychiatric, Transplant, Wellness

Offers Demand Management Patient Information Service: Yes

Type of Coverage
Commercial, Medicare

Type of Payment Plans Offered
POS

Geographic Areas Served
Boone, Bureau, DeKalb, DeWitt, Fulton, Hancock, Henderson, Henry, Kane, Knox, LaSalle, Lee, Livingston, Marshall, McDonough, McHenry, McLean, Mercer, Ogle, Peoria, Putnam, Stark, Stephenson, Tazewell, Warren, Whiteside, Winnebago, Woodford counties

Publishes and Distributes Report Card: Yes

Accreditation Certification
NCQA

Key Personnel
Vice Chairperson & CEO . . . . .James Moore
President & Director. . . . . .Diane McGrew
VP Operations. . . . . .Melody Berry
VP Chief Medical Officer . . . . Ralph Velazquez, MD

Specialty Managed Care Partners
McHelson

381 PersonalCare

2110 Fox Drive
Suite A
Champaign, IL 61820
Toll-Free: 800-431-1211
Phone: 217-366-5551
Fax: 217-366-5410
info@personalcare.org
www.personalcare.org
Secondary Address: 4507 Sterling Avenue, Suite 205, Peoria, IL 61615
Subsidiary of: Coventry Health Care
For Profit Organization: Yes
Year Founded: 1984
Number of Affiliated Hospitals: 20
Number of Primary Care Physicians: 274
Number of Referral/Specialty Physicians: 711
Total Enrollment: 77,000
State Enrollment: 59,830

Healthplan and Services Defined
PLAN TYPE: HMO
Model Type: Network
Plan Specialty: ASO
Benefits Offered: Behavioral Health, Chiropractic, Disease Management, Home Care, Inpatient SNF, Physical Therapy, Podiatry, Prescription, Psychiatric, Transplant, Vision
Offers Demand Management Patient Information Service: Yes

Type of Coverage
Commercial, Individual, Supplemental Medicare

Type of Payment Plans Offered
POS, DFFS, Capitated, FFS, Combination FFS & DFFS

Geographic Areas Served
Bond, Boone, Calhoun, Champaign, Christian, Clark, Clinton, Coles, Crawford, Cumberland, DeWitt, Douglas, Edgar, Effingham, Fayette, Ford, Greene, Iroquois, Jasper, Jersey, Kankakee, LaSalle, Lee, Logan, Macon, Macoupin, Madison, Marshall, McLean, Menard, Monroe, Montgomery, Morgan, Moultrie, Ogle, Peoria, Piatt, Sangaman, Saint Clair, Shelby, Stark, Stephenson, Tazewell, Vermilion, Washington, Whiteside, Will, Winnebago, Woodford counties

Network Qualifications
Pre-Admission Certification: Yes

Peer Review Type
Utilization Review: Yes
Second Surgical Opinion: Yes
Case Management: Yes

Accreditation Certification
NCQA
TJC Accreditation, Medicare Approved, Utilization Review, Pre-Admission Certification, State Licensure, Quality Assurance Program

Key Personnel
CEO . . . . .Todd Petersen
President . . . . .Randy Hoffman
Manager . . . . .Mary Ellen Stinde
Credentialing Manager . . . . .Debbie Weiman
Marketing Director . . . . .Darcy Sementi
Medical Director. . . . . .Richard Grassy
Member Relations. . . . . .Toni Sauter
Information Tech Manager . . . . .Chuck Wallbaum

Employer References
Horace Mann, Verizon, Pepsi, Sarah Bush Lincoln Health, Walgreen's

382 Preferred Network Access

1510 West 75th Street
Suite 250
Darien, IL 60561
Toll-Free: 888-476-2776
Phone: 630-493-0905
Fax: 630-493-0912
www.pna-usa.com
For Profit Organization: Yes
Year Founded: 1995
Number of Affiliated Hospitals: 113
Number of Primary Care Physicians: 34,000
Number of Referral/Specialty Physicians: 250
Total Enrollment: 316,000
State Enrollment: 316,000

Healthplan and Services Defined
PLAN TYPE: PPO
Plan Specialty: Group, Health
Benefits Offered: Home Care, Physical Therapy, Wellness, Worker's Compensation, Occupational Health

Type of Coverage
Commercial

Geographic Areas Served
Illinois, Indiana, Iowa, Wisconsin

Key Personnel
President . . . . .Joseph M Zerega

383 SXC Health Solutions Corp

2441 Warrenville Road
Suite 610
Lisle, IL 60532-3642
Toll-Free: 800-282-3232
Phone: 630-577-3100
Fax: 630-577-3101
sales.marketing@sxc.com
www.sxc.com

Healthplan and Services Defined
PLAN TYPE: Other
Other Type: PBM

Key Personnel
President & CEO . . . . .Mark A Thierer
EVP/CFO. . . . . .Jeffrey Park
investors@sxc.com

EVP, General Manager . . . . .Greg Buscetto
SVP, General Counsel . . . . .Cliff Berman
SVP, Mail & Specialty .Mark A Adkison
SVP, PBM Operations . . . . .Kelly Kettlewell
EVP, Research & Dev, CTO . . . . .John Romza
EVP, Healthcare Info Tech . . . . .Mike Bennof
SVP, Industry Relations . . . . .Russell Annunziata
Vice President, Sales . . . . .Mark Mateka

384 Trustmark Companies

400 Field Drive
Lake Forest, IL 60045
Toll-Free: 800-877-9077
Phone: 847-615-1500
Fax: 847-615-3910
www.trustmarkcompanies.com
For Profit Organization: Yes
Year Founded: 1913
Federally Qualified: Yes
Total Enrollment: 475,000

Healthplan and Services Defined
PLAN TYPE: PPO
Other Type: Self-funded
Model Type: Network
Plan Specialty: Behavioral Health, Dental, Lab
Benefits Offered: Behavioral Health, Dental, Disease Management, Prescription, Wellness, AD&D, Life, LTD, STD, Major Medical, Nurse Line, Health Advocacy Service

Type of Coverage
Commercial, Indemnity

Type of Payment Plans Offered
FFS

Geographic Areas Served
Nationwide

Network Qualifications
Pre-Admission Certification: Yes

Peer Review Type
Utilization Review: Yes
Second Surgical Opinion: Yes

Accreditation Certification
TJC Accreditation, Utilization Review, State Licensure

Key Personnel
Chairman . . . . .J Grover Thomas, Jr
President, CEO . . . . .Joseph L. Pray
SVP, CFO . . . . .Phil Goss, CPA
SVP, Employer Medical .John Anderson
Media Contact . . . . .Cindy Gallaher
847-283-4065
cindy.gallaher@trustmarkins.com

385 Unicare: Illinois

233 South Wacker Drive
Suite 3900
Chicago, IL 60606
Toll-Free: 800-543-0675
Phone: 312-234-8000
Fax: 312-234-8001
direct.sales@wellpoint.com
www.unicare.com
Subsidiary of: WellPoint
For Profit Organization: Yes
Year Founded: 1995
Number of Affiliated Hospitals: 30
Total Enrollment: 145,000

Healthplan and Services Defined
PLAN TYPE: HMO/PPO

Model Type: Network
Benefits Offered: Behavioral Health, Dental, Disease Management, Long-Term Care, Prescription, Vision, Wellness, Life, LTD, STD

Type of Coverage
Commercial, Individual, Medicare, Supplemental Medicare

Type of Payment Plans Offered
POS

Geographic Areas Served
Illinois: Cook, DuPage, Kane, Kankakee, Kendall, Lake, McHenry, Will counties. Indiana: Lake, Porter counties

Network Qualifications
Pre-Admission Certification: Yes

Peer Review Type
Utilization Review: Yes
Second Surgical Opinion: Yes

Accreditation Certification
NCQA
TJC Accreditation, State Licensure

Key Personnel
President/CEO . . . . .David Fields
Sales Director . . . . .Paul Nobile
paul.nobile@wellpoint.com
Media Contact . . . . .Tony Felts
317-287-6036
tony.felts@wellpoint.com

Specialty Managed Care Partners
Enters into Contracts with Regional Business Coalitions: Yes

386 UnitedHealthCare of Illinois

233 North Michigan Ave
Chicago, IL 60601
Toll-Free: 800-627-0687
Phone: 312-424-4460
Fax: 888-311-4599
www.uhc.com
Subsidiary of: UnitedHealth Group
For Profit Organization: Yes
Total Enrollment: 75,000,000
State Enrollment: 646,192

Healthplan and Services Defined
PLAN TYPE: HMO/PPO

Geographic Areas Served
Statewide

Key Personnel
CEO . . . . .Thomas Wiffler
Director . . . . .Julie Ward
Medical Director . . . . .David Stumpf
Media Contact . . . . .Greg Thompson
312-424-6913
gregory_a_thompson@uhc.com

387 VSP: Vision Service Plan of Illinois

222 S Riverside Plaza
#2210
Chicago, IL 60606-5808
Phone: 312-466-1601
Fax: 312-466-1733
webmaster@vsp.com
www.vsp.com
Year Founded: 1955
Number of Primary Care Physicians: 26,000
Total Enrollment: 55,000,000

Healthplan and Services Defined
PLAN TYPE: Vision
Plan Specialty: Vision

Benefits Offered: Vision

Type of Payment Plans Offered
Capitated

Geographic Areas Served
Statewide

Network Qualifications
Pre-Admission Certification: Yes

Peer Review Type
Utilization Review: Yes

Accreditation Certification
Utilization Review, Quality Assurance Program

Key Personnel
President....................................Roger Valine
Manager ....John Trybual

Health Insurance Coverage Status and Type of Coverage by Age

Category	All Persons		Under 18 years		Under 65 years		65 years and over	
	Number	%	Number	%	Number	%	Number	%
Total population	6,359	-	1,610	-	5,508	-	852	-
Covered by some type of health insurance	5,505 *(75)*	86.6 *(1.0)*	1,513 *(29)*	94.0 *(1.6)*	4,667 *(91)*	84.7 *(1.2)*	838 *(52)*	98.4 *(0.6)*
Covered by private health insurance	4,239 *(109)*	66.7 *(1.6)*	1,035 *(54)*	64.3 *(3.2)*	3,715 *(126)*	67.4 *(2.0)*	525 *(54)*	61.6 *(4.5)*
Employment based	3,784 *(114)*	59.5 *(1.7)*	976 *(56)*	60.6 *(3.3)*	3,482 *(126)*	63.2 *(2.1)*	303 *(39)*	35.6 *(3.8)*
Own employment based	1,836 *(49)*	28.9 *(0.8)*	11 *(6)*	0.7 *(0.3)*	1,607 *(64)*	29.2 *(1.0)*	229 *(34)*	26.9 *(3.2)*
Direct purchase	634 *(58)*	10.0 *(0.9)*	74 *(14)*	4.6 *(0.9)*	362 *(44)*	6.6 *(0.8)*	272 *(40)*	31.9 *(4.2)*
Covered by government health insurance	2,141 *(94)*	33.7 *(1.5)*	653 *(55)*	40.6 *(3.5)*	1,344 *(92)*	24.4 *(1.6)*	796 *(54)*	93.5 *(1.6)*
Covered by Medicaid	1,054 *(77)*	16.6 *(1.2)*	596 *(56)*	37.0 *(3.5)*	988 *(79)*	17.9 *(1.4)*	66 *(16)*	7.7 *(1.8)*
Also by private insurance	241 *(34)*	3.8 *(0.5)*	135 *(24)*	8.4 *(1.5)*	211 *(34)*	3.8 *(0.6)*	30 *(14)*	3.5 *(1.5)*
Covered by Medicare	953 *(56)*	15.0 *(0.9)*	3 *(3)*	0.2 *(0.2)*	157 *(18)*	2.8 *(0.3)*	796 *(54)*	93.5 *(1.6)*
Also by private insurance	524 *(49)*	8.2 *(0.8)*	2 *(2)*	0.1 *(0.1)*	41 *(10)*	0.7 *(0.2)*	483 *(52)*	56.7 *(4.2)*
Also by Medicaid	113 *(22)*	1.8 *(0.3)*	1 *(1)*	0.1 *(0.1)*	47 *(10)*	0.9 *(0.2)*	66 *(16)*	7.7 *(1.8)*
Covered by military health care	360 *(48)*	5.7 *(0.8)*	68 *(17)*	4.2 *(1.1)*	279 *(46)*	5.1 *(0.8)*	81 *(16)*	9.5 *(1.9)*
Not covered at any time during the year	855 *(64)*	13.4 *(1.0)*	97 *(26)*	6.0 *(1.6)*	841 *(64)*	15.3 *(1.2)*	13 *(5)*	1.6 *(0.6)*

Note: Numbers in thousands; figures cover 2010; standard error appears in parenthesis; (b) base less than 75,000; (x) not applicable
Source: U.S. Census Bureau, Current Population Survey, 2011 Annual Social and Economic Supplement. Table HI05. Health Insurance Coverage Status and Type of Coverage by State and Age for All People: 2010

Indiana

388 Advantage Health Solutions
9045 River Road
Suite 200
Indianapolis, IN 46240
Toll-Free: 800-553-8933
Phone: 317-573-6228
Fax: 317-580-8009
www.advantageplan.com
For Profit Organization: Yes
Year Founded: 2000
Number of Affiliated Hospitals: 37
Number of Primary Care Physicians: 754
Number of Referral/Specialty Physicians: 4,151
Total Enrollment: 86,000
State Enrollment: 61,064

Healthplan and Services Defined
PLAN TYPE: HMO
Benefits Offered: Behavioral Health, Chiropractic, Complementary
  Medicine, Dental, Home Care, Inpatient SNF, Podiatry,
  Prescription, Psychiatric, Transplant, Vision, Wellness

Type of Coverage
Commercial, Medicare

Accreditation Certification
NCQA

Key Personnel
President/CEO . . . . Vicki F Perry
  v.perry@advantageplan.com
CFO . . . . Jennifer Ponski
Chief Operating Officer . . . . Jan Teal
VP, Medical Affairs . . . . Issac Myers
Quality Improvement Mgr . . . . Trudy Perkins, LPN
Medical Management Mgr . . . . Linda York
  317-587-8461
Provider Relations . . . . Candace Ervin
  317-573-6218
VP, Sales . . . . Robert Balash

Specialty Managed Care Partners
PharmaCare Management Services

389 Aetna Health of Indiana
Partnered with eHealthInsurance Services Inc.

390 American Health Network of Indiana
10333 N Meridian Street
Suite 450
Indianapolis, IN 46290
Toll-Free: 888-255-2246
Phone: 317-580-6309
Fax: 317-580-6388
Debbie_Pehler@ahni.com
www.ahni.com
Secondary Address: 2500 Corporate Exchange, Suite 100, Columbus,
  OH 43229
Year Founded: 1994
Number of Affiliated Hospitals: 70
Total Enrollment: 15,153

Healthplan and Services Defined
PLAN TYPE: PPO
Benefits Offered: Prescription

Type of Payment Plans Offered
Capitated

Geographic Areas Served
Indiana and Ohio

Subscriber Information
Average Annual Deductible Per Subscriber:
  Employee Only (Self): $250
Average Subscriber Co-Payment:
  Prescription Drugs: 100% post deductible
  Home Health Care: 60% post deductible

Accreditation Certification
TJC Accreditation, State Licensure

Key Personnel
President/CEO . . . . Gerald Dewester
Marketing . . . . Dona Stohler

391 Anthem Blue Cross & Blue Sheild of Indiana
120 Monument Circle
Indianapolis, IN 46204
Toll-Free: 800-548-3394
Phone: 317-488-6000
Fax: 317-488-6028
www.anthem.com
Secondary Address: 1099 North Meridian Street, Indianapolis, IN
  46204
For Profit Organization: Yes
Year Founded: 1988
Owned by an Integrated Delivery Network (IDN): Yes
Number of Affiliated Hospitals: 6
Number of Primary Care Physicians: 110
Number of Referral/Specialty Physicians: 363
Total Enrollment: 1,600,818
State Enrollment: 40,136

Healthplan and Services Defined
PLAN TYPE: HMO
Model Type: IPA
Plan Specialty: ASO, Behavioral Health, Chiropractic, Dental,
  Disease Management, Lab, PBM, Vision, Radiology
Benefits Offered: Dental, Disease Management, Prescription, Vision,
  Wellness, Life
Offers Demand Management Patient Information Service: Yes

Type of Coverage
Commercial, Individual, Medicare

Type of Payment Plans Offered
DFFS

Geographic Areas Served
Daviess, Dubois, Gibson, Knox, Martin, Perry, Pike, Posey, Spencer,
  Vanderburgh, & Warrick

Subscriber Information
Average Subscriber Co-Payment:
  Primary Care Physician: $10.00
  Non-Network Physician: 20%
  Prescription Drugs: $7.00
  Hospital ER: $40.00
  Home Health Care: 20%
  Nursing Home: 20%

Network Qualifications
Pre-Admission Certification: Yes

Publishes and Distributes Report Card: Yes

Accreditation Certification
URAC, NCQA
Utilization Review, Quality Assurance Program

Key Personnel
CEO . . . . Larry Glasscock
  317-488-6000
President . . . . Keith Faller
COO . . . . Jane Niederberger
CFO . . . . George Walker
Chief Medical Officer . . . . Samuel Cramer, MD
General Counsel . . . . Sandra H Miller
Provider Relations . . . . Robert McIntire

Pharmacy Director . . . . John Klasner
Marketing/Sales . . . . Dennis Casey
Member Relations . . . . Susan Cummins
Specialty Pharmacy . . . . Matt Totterdale
Public Relations . . . . Deborah New
Media Contact . . . . Tony Felts
    317-287-6036
    tony.felts@wellpoint.com

Specialty Managed Care Partners
Enters into Contracts with Regional Business Coalitions: No

---

392 Anthem Blue Cross & Blue Shield of Indiana

120 Monument Circle
Suite 200
Indianapolis, IN 46204
Toll-Free: 800-331-1476
Phone: 317-488-6000
Fax: 317-287-5582
anthem.corporate.communications@anthem.com
www.anthem.com
Secondary Address: 220 Virginia Avenue, Indianapolis, In 46204
Subsidiary of: WellPoint
For Profit Organization: Yes
Year Founded: 1990
Number of Affiliated Hospitals: 105
Number of Primary Care Physicians: 3,532
Number of Referral/Specialty Physicians: 8,475
Total Enrollment: 900,000

Healthplan and Services Defined
  PLAN TYPE: HMO/PPO
  Model Type: Network
  Benefits Offered: Behavioral Health, Chiropractic, Complementary
    Medicine, Dental, Disease Management, Home Care, Inpatient
    SNF, Physical Therapy, Podiatry, Prescription, Psychiatric,
    Transplant, Vision, Wellness

Type of Payment Plans Offered
  DFFS, FFS, Combination FFS & DFFS

Geographic Areas Served
  Statewide

Subscriber Information
  Average Annual Deductible Per Subscriber:
    Employee Only (Self): Varies $250-$5000
    Employee & 2 Family Members: Varies $2500-$10000
  Average Subscriber Co-Payment:
    Primary Care Physician: Varies $25/20%
    Non-Network Physician: 20%
    Prescription Drugs: Varies $15/$30/$0
    Hospital ER: 20%
    Home Health Care: 20%
    Home Health Care Max. Days/Visits Covered: 100 days
    Nursing Home Max. Days/Visits Covered: 60 days

Network Qualifications
  Pre-Admission Certification: Yes

Peer Review Type
  Utilization Review: Yes
  Second Surgical Opinion: No
  Case Management: Yes

Publishes and Distributes Report Card: Yes

Accreditation Certification
  URAC, NCQA
  TJC Accreditation, Medicare Approved, Utilization Review,
    Pre-Admission Certification, State Licensure, Quality Assurance
    Program

Key Personnel
  President . . . . Dennis W Casey
  Media Relations . . . . Ed West

Media Relations . . . . Deborah New
  mediarelations@wellpoint.com
Media Relations . . . . James Kappel

---

393 Anthem Dental Services

120 Monument Circle
Indianapolis, IN 46204
Phone: 317-488-6000
www.anthem.com
Mailing Address: PO Box 37180, Dental Claims, Louisville, KY
  40233-7180
Subsidiary of: Anthem Blue Cross & Blue Shield
For Profit Organization: Yes
Year Founded: 1972
Total Enrollment: 28,000,000

Healthplan and Services Defined
  PLAN TYPE: Dental
  Other Type: Dental PPO
  Model Type: Network
  Plan Specialty: Dental
  Benefits Offered: Dental
  Offers Demand Management Patient Information Service: Yes

Type of Payment Plans Offered
  POS, Capitated, FFS

Geographic Areas Served
  Colorado, Connecticut, Georgia, Indiana, Kentucky, Maine, Missouri,
  Nevada, New Hampshire, Ohio, Virginia, Wisconsin

Network Qualifications
  Pre-Admission Certification: Yes

Peer Review Type
  Utilization Review: Yes
  Second Surgical Opinion: Yes
  Case Management: Yes

Publishes and Distributes Report Card: Yes

Accreditation Certification
  Utilization Review, Pre-Admission Certification, State Licensure,
    Quality Assurance Program

---

394 Arnett Health Plans

Acquired by UnitedHealthCare

---

395 Avesis: Indiana

1493 Golfview Court
Lawrenceburg, IN 47025
Toll-Free: 800-522-0258
www.avesis.com
Year Founded: 1978
Number of Primary Care Physicians: 18,000
Total Enrollment: 2,000,000

Healthplan and Services Defined
  PLAN TYPE: PPO
  Other Type: Vision, Dental
  Model Type: Network
  Plan Specialty: Dental, Vision, Hearing
  Benefits Offered: Dental, Vision

Type of Coverage
  Commercial

Type of Payment Plans Offered
  POS, Capitated, Combination FFS & DFFS

Geographic Areas Served
  Nationwide and Puerto Rico

Publishes and Distributes Report Card: Yes

Accreditation Certification
  AAAHC
  TJC Accreditation

396 Cardinal Health Alliance

300 North Pauline Avenue
Muncie, IN 47303
Phone: 765-286-2150
Fax: 765-751-3051
www.cardinalcare.com
For Profit Organization: Yes
Year Founded: 1996
Number of Affiliated Hospitals: 11
Number of Primary Care Physicians: 200
Number of Referral/Specialty Physicians: 215
Total Enrollment: 40,000

Healthplan and Services Defined
  PLAN TYPE: HMO/PPO
  Other Type: EPO
  Model Type: Network
  Plan Specialty: ASO, Disease Management, PBM, Worker's
    Compensation, UR
  Benefits Offered: Behavioral Health, Disease Management, Home
    Care, Inpatient SNF, Physical Therapy, Podiatry, Prescription,
    Psychiatric, Wellness, Worker's Compensation

Type of Coverage
  Commercial
  Catastrophic Illness Benefit: Varies per case

Type of Payment Plans Offered
  POS

Geographic Areas Served
  Indiana, Ohio

Peer Review Type
  Utilization Review: Yes
  Second Surgical Opinion: Yes
  Case Management: Yes

Accreditation Certification
  Utilization Review, State Licensure, Quality Assurance Program

Key Personnel
  President and CEO . . . . .Karen Popovich
  CFO . . . . .Kathy Edwards
  Director . . . . .Pam Livingston
  Claims . . . . .Tiffany Ridge
  Network Contracting. . . . . .Karen Popovich
  Credentialing. . . . . .Tiffany Ridge
  In-House Formulary . . . . .Mark Barnhart
  Medical Affairs . . . . .Charles Routh, MD
  Provider Services . . . . .Tiffany Ridge

Specialty Managed Care Partners
  Enters into Contracts with Regional Business Coalitions: Yes

397 CIGNA HealthCare of Indiana

11595 North Meridian Street
Suite 500
Carmel, IN 46032
Toll-Free: 866-438-2446
Phone: 317-208-3230
Fax: 317-208-3241
www.cigna.com
Secondary Address: Great-West Healthcare, now part of CIGNA, 9025
  North River Road, Suite 104, Indianapolis, IN 46240, 317-575-0022
For Profit Organization: Yes
Year Founded: 1993
Number of Affiliated Hospitals: 72
Number of Primary Care Physicians: 2,000
Number of Referral/Specialty Physicians: 2,000
Total Enrollment: 9,678
State Enrollment: 9,678

Healthplan and Services Defined
  PLAN TYPE: HMO

Other Type: POS
Model Type: Network
Plan Specialty: ASO, Behavioral Health, Chiropractic, Dental,
  Disease Management, EPO, Lab, MSO, PBM, Vision, Radiology,
  UR
Benefits Offered: Behavioral Health, Dental, Disease Management,
  Prescription, Transplant, Vision, Wellness, Life, LTD, STD

Type of Coverage
  Commercial

Geographic Areas Served
  Adams, Allen, Boone, Cass, Clay, DeKalb, Grant, Hamilton, Hancock,
  Henricks, Howard, Huntington, Johnson, Kosciusko, Madison,
  Marion, Marshall, Miami, Montgomery, Morgan, Noble, Owen,
  Putnam, Saint Joseph, Shelby, Tipton, Wabash, Wells, Whitley,
  Michigan counties of Berrien, Cass and Van Buren

Network Qualifications
  Pre-Admission Certification: Yes

Peer Review Type
  Utilization Review: Yes

Publishes and Distributes Report Card: Yes

Accreditation Certification
  NCQA
  TJC Accreditation, Medicare Approved, Utilization Review,
    Pre-Admission Certification, State Licensure, Quality Assurance
    Program

Key Personnel
  Chief Medical Officer. . . . . .Asiam Khan, MD

Average Claim Compensation
  Physician's Fees Charged: 82%
  Hospital's Fees Charged: 85%

398 Deaconess Health Plans

350 W Columbia
Suite 400
Evansville, IN 47710
Toll-Free: 800-374-8993
Phone: 812-450-7265
Fax: 812-450-2030
www.deaconess.com
Subsidiary of: Deaconess Health System
Year Founded: 1985
Physician Owned Organization: Yes
Number of Affiliated Hospitals: 17
Number of Primary Care Physicians: 900
Number of Referral/Specialty Physicians: 555
Total Enrollment: 140,000
State Enrollment: 132,000

Healthplan and Services Defined
  PLAN TYPE: PPO
  Model Type: Network
  Plan Specialty: Behavioral Health, Chiropractic
  Benefits Offered: Disease Management, Wellness

Type of Coverage
  Individual

Type of Payment Plans Offered
  POS, FFS

Geographic Areas Served
  Northwestern Kentucky, Southeastern Illinois, Southwestern Indiana

Network Qualifications
  Pre-Admission Certification: Yes

Peer Review Type
  Utilization Review: Yes
  Second Surgical Opinion: No
  Case Management: Yes

Accreditation Certification
TJC Accreditation, Medicare Approved, Utilization Review, Pre-Admission Certification, State Licensure, Quality Assurance Program

Key Personnel
CEO . . . . .Joyce Hudson
   joyce_hudson@deaconess.com
Provider Credentialing . . . . .Mindi Alvey
Provider Credentialing. . . . . .Jamie Montgomery
Provider Credentialing . . . . .Elizabeth Patberg
Marketing . . . . .Tina Hazelip
Member Services . . . . .Vicky Berneking
   vicky_berneking@deaconess.com
Provider Relations . . . . .Jolee Miller
Provider Relations . . . . .Nicole Hensley
Sales . . . . .Beth Deters

Average Claim Compensation
Physician's Fees Charged: 1%
Hospital's Fees Charged: 1%

399 Delta Dental of Michigan, Ohio and Indiana

5875 Castle Creek Parkway, N Drive
Suite 191
Indianapolis, IN 46250
Phone: 3178424022
www.deltadentalin.com
Total Enrollment: 54,000,000

Healthplan and Services Defined
PLAN TYPE: Dental
Other Type: Dental PPO
Plan Specialty: Dental
Benefits Offered: Dental

Geographic Areas Served
Michigan, Ohio, Indiana

Key Personnel
President/CEO . . . . .Thomas Fleszar, DDS
   517-349-6000
   tfleszar@ddpmi.com
CFO. . . . . .Laura L Czelada, CPA
VP/Chief Actuary . . . . .William T Billard
VP/Administration .Judge Patrick T Cahill
VP/Operations . . . . .Sherry L Crisp
VP/Corporate Affairs. . . . . .Nancy E Hostetler
Dental Director . . . . .Jed J Jacobson, DDS
VP/Sales . . . . .Charles D Floyd, CEBS
VP/Marketing . . . . .E Craig Lesley
Communications Admin . . . . .Ari B Adler
   517-347-5292
   aadler@deltadentalmi.com
Dir/Media & Public Affair . . . . .Elizabeth Risberg
   415-972-8423

400 eHealthInsurance Services Inc.

11919 Foundation Place
Gold River, CA 95670
Toll-Free: 800-977-8860
info@ehealthinsurance.com
www.e.healthinsurance.com
Year Founded: 1997

Healthplan and Services Defined
PLAN TYPE: HMO/PPO
Benefits Offered: Dental, Life, STD

Type of Coverage
Commercial, Individual, Medicare

Geographic Areas Served
All 50 states in the USA and District of Columbia

Key Personnel
Chairman & CEO . . . . .Gary L. Lauer
EVP/Business & Corp. Dev. . . . . .Bruce Telkamp
EVP/Chief Technology . . . . .Dr. Sheldon X. Wang
SVP & CFO . . . . .Stuart M. Huizinga
Pres. of eHealth Gov. Sys . . . . .Samuel C. Gibbs
SVP of Sales & Operations . . . . .Robert S. Hurley
Director Public Relations. . . . . .Nate Purpura
   650-210-3115

401 Encircle Network

1776 North Meridian Street
Suite 200
Indianpolis, IN 46202-1404
Toll-Free: 888-574-8180
Phone: 317-963-9852
Fax: 317-963-9850
www.encoreconnect.com
Subsidiary of: Encore Connect, The HealthCare Group, LLC
For Profit Organization: Yes
Year Founded: 2003
Number of Affiliated Hospitals: 43
Number of Primary Care Physicians: 14,000

Healthplan and Services Defined
PLAN TYPE: Other
Other Type: EPO

Type of Coverage
Commercial, Individual

Geographic Areas Served
Select Indiana Markets

Key Personnel
President . . . . .Bruce Smiley
   317-963-9825
   bsmiley@encoreppo.com

402 Encore Health Network

1776 North Meridian Street
Suite 200
Indianapolis, IN 46202-1404
Toll-Free: 888-574-8180
Phone: 317-963-9852
Fax: 317-963-9850
www.encoreconnect.com
Subsidiary of: The Healthcare Group LLC
Year Founded: 1999
Number of Affiliated Hospitals: 176
Number of Primary Care Physicians: 29,000
Number of Referral/Specialty Physicians: 2,200
Total Enrollment: 664,318

Healthplan and Services Defined
PLAN TYPE: PPO
Model Type: Group
Plan Specialty: Medical PPO
Benefits Offered: Chiropractic, Complementary Medicine, Vision, Wellness, Worker's Compensation, Alternative Heath Care Management, Health Savings Plans, HealthyRoads

Type of Coverage
Fully insured & self-funded

Type of Payment Plans Offered
DFFS

Geographic Areas Served
All of Indiana, Chicago area, MI, IL & OH bordering couties & northern KY

Peer Review Type
Utilization Review: Yes
Case Management: Yes

Key Personnel
President . . . . .Bruce Smiley
   317-963-9825
   bsmiley@encoreppo.com
Dir Sales & Marketing. . . . . .Shawn Gibbons
   317-963-9733
   sgibbons@encoreppo.com
Sales Account Executive . . . . .Rochelle Forrest, RN
   317-963-9723
   rforrest@encoreppo.com

Average Claim Compensation
Physician's Fees Charged: 36%
Hospital's Fees Charged: 29%

Specialty Managed Care Partners
Enters into Contracts with Regional Business Coalitions: Yes

Employer References
Marsh Supermarkets, Reid Hospital, Deaconness Development Corporation, Suburu-Isuzu, Group Dekko/Multi-Kare

403 Great-West Healthcare Indiana South
Acquired by CIGNA

404 Great-West Healthcare Indiana
Acquired by CIGNA

405 Health Resources, Inc.
5010 Carriage Drive
PO Box 15660
Evansville, IN 47716-0660
Toll-Free: 800-727-1444
Phone: 812-424-1444
Fax: 812-424-2096
info@hri-dho.com
www.hri-dho.com
For Profit Organization: Yes
Year Founded: 1986
Physician Owned Organization: Yes
Number of Primary Care Physicians: 1,800
Total Enrollment: 200,000

Healthplan and Services Defined
   PLAN TYPE: Dental
   Model Type: Network
   Plan Specialty: Dental
   Benefits Offered: Dental

Type of Payment Plans Offered
FFS

Geographic Areas Served
Northern, Southwest & Central Indiana, Western Kentucky

Subscriber Information
Average Annual Deductible Per Subscriber:
   Employee Only (Self): $0
   Employee & 1 Family Member: $0
   Employee & 2 Family Members: $0

Network Qualifications
Pre-Admission Certification: No

Accreditation Certification
Utilization Review

Key Personnel
President/CEO . . . . .Allan Reid
COO . . . . .Cynthia Kuester
Marketing Director. . . . . .Chad Decker

Specialty Managed Care Partners
Dental

Employer References
University of Notre Dame, Old National Bank, University of Southern Indiana, Integra

406 Healthy Indiana Plan
401 West Washington Street
PO Box 7083
Indianapolis, IN 46207-7083
Toll-Free: 877-438-4479
Phone: 317-655-3304
www.in.gov/fssa/hip
Subsidiary of: AmeriChoice, A UnitedHealth Group Company

Healthplan and Services Defined
   PLAN TYPE: HMO
   Benefits Offered: Behavioral Health, Disease Management, Home Care, Inpatient SNF, Prescription, Wellness

Type of Coverage
Individual

Key Personnel
Media Contact. . . . . .Jeff Smith
   952-931-5685
   jeff.smith@uhc.com

407 Humana Health Insurance of Indiana
8888 Keystone Crossing
Suite 700
Indianapolis, IN 46240
Toll-Free: 866-355-6170
Phone: 317-841-1196
Fax: 317-816-9121
www.humana.com
Secondary Address: 6319 Mutual Drive, Fort Wayne, IN 46825
Non-Profit Organization: Yes
Year Founded: 1986
Total Enrollment: 102,506
State Enrollment: 900

Healthplan and Services Defined
   PLAN TYPE: HMO/PPO
   Model Type: IPA
   Benefits Offered: Disease Management, Wellness

Type of Coverage
Commercial, Individual, Medicare, Medicaid

Geographic Areas Served
(Southern Indiana) Boone, Clark, Crawford, Delaware, Dubois, Floyd, Gibson, Hamilton, Hancock, Harrison, Hendricks, Howard, Jackson, Jefferson, Jennings, Johnson, Knox, Lake, LaPorte, Madison, Marrion, Morgan, Orange, Pike, Porter, Posey, Scott, Shelby, Spencer, Tipton, Vanderburgh, Warrick, Washington

Accreditation Certification
URAC, NCQA, CORE

408 Magellan Health Services Indiana
9265 Counselor's Road
Suite 118
Indianapolis, IN 46240
Phone: 317-815-1356
www.magellanhealth.com
Secondary Address: Magellan RSC of The Northwest, 1501 Market Street, Suite 200, Tacoma, WA 98411
For Profit Organization: Yes
Year Founded: 1986
Number of Affiliated Hospitals: 45
Total Enrollment: 36,500,000

Healthplan and Services Defined
   PLAN TYPE: PPO

Model Type: Staff
Plan Specialty: Behavioral Health, Disease Management, EAP
Benefits Offered: Behavioral Health, Disease Management,
  Prescription, Psychiatric, Wellness, EAP
Offers Demand Management Patient Information Service: Yes

Geographic Areas Served
Statewide

Network Qualifications
Pre-Admission Certification: Yes

Peer Review Type
Utilization Review: Yes
Second Surgical Opinion: Yes
Case Management: Yes

Publishes and Distributes Report Card: Yes

Accreditation Certification
URAC, NCQA
TJC Accreditation, Utilization Review, Pre-Admission Certification,
  State Licensure

Key Personnel
President/COO . . . . Rene Lerer, MD
Chairman/CEO . . . . Steven J Shulman
CFO . . . . Mark S Demilio
CIO . . . . Jeff D Emerson
General Counsel . . . . Daniel N Gregoire
Chief Clinical Officer . . . . Anthony M Kotin, MD
Chief HR Officer . . . . Caskie Lewis-Clapper
Chief Growth Officer . . . . Eric Reimer
Chief Medical Officer . . . . Alex R Rodriguez, MD

Specialty Managed Care Partners
Enters into Contracts with Regional Business Coalitions: Yes

409 Meritain Health: Indiana

111 Southeast Third Street
Suite 101
Evansville, IN 47708
Toll-Free: 866-828-1338
sales@meritain.com
www.meritain.com
Secondary Address: 9254 N Meridian Street, Indianapolis, IN 46240
For Profit Organization: Yes
Year Founded: 1983
Number of Affiliated Hospitals: 110
Number of Primary Care Physicians: 3,467
Number of Referral/Specialty Physicians: 5,720
Total Enrollment: 500,000
State Enrollment: 450,000

Healthplan and Services Defined
PLAN TYPE: PPO
Model Type: Network
Plan Specialty: Dental, Disease Management, Vision, Radiology, UR
Benefits Offered: Prescription
Offers Demand Management Patient Information Service: Yes

Type of Coverage
Commercial

Geographic Areas Served
Nationwide

Subscriber Information
Average Monthly Fee Per Subscriber
  (Employee + Employer Contribution):
    Employee Only (Self): Varies by plan

Accreditation Certification
URAC
TJC Accreditation, Medicare Approved, Utilization Review,
  Pre-Admission Certification, State Licensure, Quality Assurance
  Program

Key Personnel
Regional President . . . . Chris Reef

Average Claim Compensation
Physician's Fees Charged: 78%
Hospital's Fees Charged: 90%

Specialty Managed Care Partners
Express Scripts, LabOne, Interactive Health Solutions

410 Parkview Total Health

10501 Corporate Drive
Fort Wayne, IN 46845
Toll-Free: 800-666-4449
Phone: 260-373-9100
Fax: 260-373-9004
signaturecarewebmaster@parkview.com
www.parkviewtotalhealth.com
Mailing Address: PO Box 5548, Fort Wayne, IN 46895-5548
For Profit Organization: Yes
Year Founded: 1992
Number of Affiliated Hospitals: 77
Number of Primary Care Physicians: 9,000
Total Enrollment: 90,000

Healthplan and Services Defined
PLAN TYPE: PPO
Other Type: EAP
Model Type: Network, IPA
Benefits Offered: Disease Management, Wellness

Type of Coverage
Commercial

Geographic Areas Served
Indiana & Northwestern Ohio

Network Qualifications
Pre-Admission Certification: Yes

Peer Review Type
Utilization Review: Yes
Second Surgical Opinion: No
Case Management: Yes

Accreditation Certification
TJC Accreditation, Medicare Approved, Utilization Review,
  Pre-Admission Certification, State Licensure, Quality Assurance
  Program

Employer References
Parkview Hospitals, East Allen County Schools, Guardian Industries,
  Chore Timer Brook, Tomkins

411 Physicians Health Plan of Northern Indiana

8101 W Jefferson Boulevard
Fort Wayne, IN 46804-4163
Toll-Free: 800-982-6257
Phone: 260-432-6690
Fax: 260-432-0493
custsvc@phpni.com
www.phpni.com
Non-Profit Organization: Yes
Year Founded: 1983
Physician Owned Organization: Yes
Federally Qualified: Yes
Number of Affiliated Hospitals: 40
Number of Primary Care Physicians: 2,000
Number of Referral/Specialty Physicians: 1,174
Total Enrollment: 43,000
State Enrollment: 48,000

Healthplan and Services Defined
PLAN TYPE: HMO
Model Type: IPA
Benefits Offered: Behavioral Health, Dental, Disease Management,
  Home Care, Physical Therapy, Podiatry, Prescription, Psychiatric,
  Transplant, Vision, Wellness, AD&D, Life, LTD, STD

Offers Demand Management Patient Information Service: Yes

Type of Coverage
Commercial
Catastrophic Illness Benefit: Unlimited

Type of Payment Plans Offered
POS, DFFS, FFS, Combination FFS & DFFS

Geographic Areas Served
Northern Indiana, Southwest Michigan, Northwest Ohio. counties covered include: Berrien, Cass, St. Joseph, Branch, La Porte, Elkhart, LaGrange, Steuben, Starke, Marshall, Kosciusko, Noble, DeKalb, Newton, Jasper, Pulaski, Fulton, Whitley, Allen, Benton, White, Cass, Miami, Wabash, Huntington, Wells, Adams, Benton, Carroll, Warren, Foundtain, Tippecanoe, Montgomery, Clinton, Boone, Howard, Tipton, Hamilton, Grant, Blackford, Jay, Delaware, Randolph, Defiance, Mercer

Subscriber Information
Average Monthly Fee Per Subscriber
  (Employee + Employer Contribution):
    Employee Only (Self): $210.25
    Employee & 1 Family Member: $384.50
    Employee & 2 Family Members: $610.74 family
Average Annual Deductible Per Subscriber:
    Employee Only (Self): $250.00
    Employee & 1 Family Member: $500.00
    Employee & 2 Family Members: $500.00 family
Average Subscriber Co-Payment:
    Primary Care Physician: $15.00
    Non-Network Physician: Pos=20%
    Prescription Drugs: $15.00
    Hospital ER: $75.00
    Home Health Care: 100%
    Home Health Care Max. Days/Visits Covered: 60 per year
    Nursing Home Max. Days/Visits Covered: 30 per year

Network Qualifications
Pre-Admission Certification: Yes

Peer Review Type
Utilization Review: Yes
Case Management: Yes

Publishes and Distributes Report Card: Yes

Accreditation Certification
Utilization Review, Pre-Admission Certification, State Licensure, Quality Assurance Program

Key Personnel
President & CEO . . . . .Jay Gilbert
Vice President, COO . . . . .Cheryl Lee
VP, Chief Medical Officer . . . . .Angela Pippin
Media Contact . . . . .Vicki Johnson
  260-432-6690
  vjohnson@phpni.com

Specialty Managed Care Partners
Enters into Contracts with Regional Business Coalitions: Yes

412 Sagamore Health Network

11555 N Meridian Street
Suite 400
Carmel, IN 46032
Toll-Free: 800-364-3469
Phone: 317-573-2886
mps@sagamorehn.com
www.sagamorehn.com
Subsidiary of: A CIGNA Company
Year Founded: 1985
Number of Affiliated Hospitals: 257
Number of Primary Care Physicians: 15,059
Number of Referral/Specialty Physicians: 39,212
Total Enrollment: 360,561

Healthplan and Services Defined
  PLAN TYPE: PPO
  Model Type: IPA

Geographic Areas Served
Entire state of Indiana, Kentucky, Illinois, Michigan and Ohio

Accreditation Certification
  URAC
  TJC Accreditation, Medicare Approved, Utilization Review, Pre-Admission Certification, State Licensure, Quality Assurance Program

Key Personnel
  President . . . . .Ronald Vance

413 Southeastern Indiana Health Organization

417 Washington Street
PO Box 1787
Columbus, IN 47202-1787
Toll-Free: 800-443-2980
Phone: 812-378-7000
Fax: 812-378-7048
www.siho.org
Secondary Address: 222 South Walnut Street, Bloomington, IN 47404
Non-Profit Organization: Yes
Year Founded: 1987
Physician Owned Organization: Yes
Number of Affiliated Hospitals: 101
Number of Primary Care Physicians: 2,316
Number of Referral/Specialty Physicians: 4,722
Total Enrollment: 10,231
State Enrollment: 10,231

Healthplan and Services Defined
  PLAN TYPE: HMO
  Model Type: IPA, Network, POS
  Plan Specialty: ASO, Dental, Disease Management, Vision
  Benefits Offered: Behavioral Health, Chiropractic, Dental, Disease Management, Home Care, Inpatient SNF, Long-Term Care, Physical Therapy, Prescription, Transplant, Vision, Wellness, AD&D, Life, STD

Type of Coverage
Individual, Indemnity, Medicaid
Catastrophic Illness Benefit: Unlimited

Type of Payment Plans Offered
POS, DFFS, FFS

Geographic Areas Served
Bartholomew, Brown, Clark, Crawford, Davies, Decatur, Dubois, Gibson, Jackson, Jefferson, Jennings, Johnson, Knox, Lawrence, Martin, Monroe, Orange, Perry, Pike, Posey, Ripley, Scott, Shelby, Switzerland, Vanderburgh, Warrick, Washington

Subscriber Information
Average Subscriber Co-Payment:
    Primary Care Physician: $15.00
    Non-Network Physician: 40%
    Prescription Drugs: $10/20/30
    Hospital ER: $75.00

Network Qualifications
Pre-Admission Certification: Yes

Peer Review Type
Utilization Review: Yes
Case Management: Yes

Publishes and Distributes Report Card: Yes

Accreditation Certification
TJC Accreditation, Utilization Review, Pre-Admission Certification, State Licensure

Key Personnel

President and CEO . . . . David S Barker
  812-378-7024
  david.barker@siho.org

CFO . . . . Marc Rothbart, BSN
  812-348-7458

COO. . . . . Ronald Sewell
  812-378-7021

VP Claims . . . . Jennifer Cutsinger
  812-378-7030

Network Contracting. . . . . Randy Mills
  812-378-7000

In-House Formulary . . . . Joseph Sheehy, MD
  812-378-7067

Medical Director . . . . Joseph Sheehy, MD
  812-378-7067

Manager Member Services. . . . . Cathy Dykes

VP Information Services . . . . Mike Clancy
  812-378-7052

Sales Representative. . . . . Mike Ketron
  812-348-4575
  mike.ketron@siho.org

Media Contact . . . . Chris Asher
  812-378-7028
  chris.asher@siho.org

Media Contact . . . . Alan Clark
  812-348-4581
  alan.clark@siho.org

Specialty Managed Care Partners

Caremark Rx

Enters into Contracts with Regional Business Coalitions: Yes

Employer References

Columbus Regional Hospital, Enkei America, Seymour Memorial
  Hospital, Seymour Tubing

414   UnitedHealthCare of Indiana

7440 Woodland Drive
Department 100
Indianapolis, IN 46278
Toll-Free: 800-382-5445
Fax: 317-405-3895
www.uhc.com
Secondary Address: 180 E Ocean Blvd, Suite 500, Long Beach, CA
  90802, 888-283-9847
Subsidiary of: UnitedHealth Group
For Profit Organization: Yes
Year Founded: 1986
Number of Affiliated Hospitals: 66
Number of Primary Care Physicians: 1,208
Number of Referral/Specialty Physicians: 1,983
Total Enrollment: 75,000,000
State Enrollment: 244,441

Healthplan and Services Defined
  PLAN TYPE: HMO/PPO
  Model Type: IPA, Network
  Benefits Offered: Chiropractic, Dental, Home Care, Inpatient SNF,
    Long-Term Care, Podiatry, Psychiatric, Transplant, Vision,
    Wellness

Type of Coverage
  Commercial

Type of Payment Plans Offered
  POS

Geographic Areas Served
  Statewide

Subscriber Information
  Average Monthly Fee Per Subscriber
    (Employee + Employer Contribution):
      Employee Only (Self): Varies per plan

Employee & 2 Family Members: Variers per plan
Average Annual Deductible Per Subscriber:
  Employee Only (Self): Varies per plan
  Employee & 2 Family Members: Varies per plan
Average Subscriber Co-Payment:
  Primary Care Physician: Varies per plan

Accreditation Certification
  TJC

Key Personnel
  CEO . . . . Charles Price
  Medical Director . . . . Alan Grimes, MD
  Media Contact . . . . Greg Thompson
    312-424-6913
    gregory_a_thompson@uhc.com

415   VSP: Vision Service Plan of Indiana

201 N Illinois Street
#2075
Indianpolis, IN 46204-1904
Phone: 317-686-1066
Fax: 317-686-1140
webmaster@vsp.com
www.vsp.com
Year Founded: 1955
Number of Primary Care Physicians: 26,000
Total Enrollment: 55,000,000

Healthplan and Services Defined
  PLAN TYPE: Vision
  Plan Specialty: Vision
  Benefits Offered: Vision

Type of Payment Plans Offered
  Capitated

Geographic Areas Served
  Statewide

Network Qualifications
  Pre-Admission Certification: Yes

Peer Review Type
  Utilization Review: Yes

Accreditation Certification
  Utilization Review, Quality Assurance Program

Key Personnel
  Administrator. . . . . Kathy Maxey
  Senior Account Executive . . . . Linda Stevens

416   Welborn Health Plans

101 SE Third Street
Evansville, IN 47708
Toll-Free: 800-521-0265
Phone: 812-426-6600
Fax: 716-541-6335
memberservices@welbornhealthplans.com
www.welbornhealthplans.com
For Profit Organization: Yes
Year Founded: 1986
Physician Owned Organization: No
Number of Affiliated Hospitals: 27
Number of Primary Care Physicians: 300
Number of Referral/Specialty Physicians: 1,000
Total Enrollment: 38,515

Healthplan and Services Defined
  PLAN TYPE: HMO
  Model Type: Network
  Plan Specialty: Health & Wellness, Diabetes, Hyperlipidemia,
    Hypertension, Heart Failure, Asthma, COPD, Migraine,
    Depression, Case Mgmt
  Benefits Offered: HMO, POS/PPO-Type, Medicare Advantage

Offers Demand Management Patient Information Service: Yes

Type of Coverage
Medicare, Group Health, Pharmacy
Catastrophic Illness Benefit: Unlimited

Type of Payment Plans Offered
POS, DFFS, Capitated, FFS

Geographic Areas Served
IN counties: Vanderburgh, Posey, Warrick, Spencer, Perry, Gibson, Pike, Dubois, Knox, Daviess   KY counties: Henderson, Union, Daviess, Hancock, Breckinridge, Webster, McLean, Ohio, Hopkins, Muhlenberg, Crittenden, Caldwell, Butler, Edmonson, Livingston, Lyon, McCracken, Ballard, Carlisle, Hickman, Fulton, Graves, Marshall, Calloway, Trigg, Christian, Todd, Logan, Simpson, Allen, Warren, Barren, Metalfe, Monroe

Subscriber Information
Average Annual Deductible Per Subscriber:
 Medicare: $90.00

Network Qualifications
Pre-Admission Certification: Yes

Peer Review Type
Utilization Review: Yes
Second Surgical Opinion: Yes
Case Management: Yes

Publishes and Distributes Report Card: Yes

Key Personnel
Regional President, CEO . . . . .Chris Reef
Chief Financial Officer . . . . .Debby Sidener
COO, Evansville Ops Lead .Claudia Winsett
Director of Operations . . . . .Heather Burns
Mgr, Quality Mgmt & Cred . . . . .Lynda Ensner
Pharmacy Tech . . . . .Su Quinn
 812-773-0376
Chief Marketing Officer . . . . .Janet Burnett
Chief Medical Director . . . . .Roy Arnold, MD
Director of Technology . . . . .Jeremy Mathews

Average Claim Compensation
Physician's Fees Charged: 75%
Hospital's Fees Charged: 80%

Specialty Managed Care Partners
Enters into Contracts with Regional Business Coalitions: Yes

---

417 WellPoint: Corporate Office

120 Monument Circle
Indianapolis, IN 46204
Phone: 317-532-6000
Fax: 317-488-6028
www.wellpoint.com
For Profit Organization: Yes
Year Founded: 2004
Total Enrollment: 35,000,000

Healthplan and Services Defined
PLAN TYPE: HMO

Type of Coverage
Commercial

Key Personnel
President & CEO . . . . .Angela F Braly
EVP, General Counsel . . . . .John Cannon, III
EVP, CFO . . . . .Wayne S DeVeydt
EVP, Chief Strategy Offc . . . . .Brad M Fluegel
Pres, Comm Business Unit . . . . .Ken Goulet
Pres,Comp Health Solution . . . . .Dijuana Lewis
EVP, Integration Mgmt . . . . .Cynthia S Miller
Pres, Consumer Business . . . . .Brian A Sassi
EVP, Chief Medical Offc . . . . .Samuel R Nussbaum, MD
Media Contact . . . . .Cheryl Leamon
 317-488-6748
 cheryl.leamon@wellpoint.com

HMO/PPO DIRECTORY
IOWA

Health Insurance Coverage Status and Type of Coverage by Age

Category	All Persons		Under 18 years		Under 65 years		65 years and over	
	Number	%	Number	%	Number	%	Number	%
Total population	2,962	-	714	-	2,605	-	357	-
Covered by some type of health insurance	2,597 *(45)*	87.7 *(1.1)*	661 *(18)*	92.6 *(1.7)*	2,245 *(42)*	86.2 *(1.3)*	351 *(23)*	98.4 *(0.9)*
Covered by private health insurance	2,192 *(49)*	74.0 *(1.5)*	498 *(24)*	69.8 *(2.8)*	1,930 *(42)*	74.1 *(1.5)*	262 *(27)*	73.4 *(4.4)*
Employment based	1,837 *(45)*	62.0 *(1.4)*	455 *(18)*	63.8 *(2.2)*	1,742 *(44)*	66.9 *(1.4)*	95 *(14)*	26.7 *(3.0)*
Own employment based	937 *(33)*	31.6 *(1.0)*	0 *(0)*	0.1 *(0.1)*	859 *(32)*	33.0 *(1.1)*	78 *(14)*	22.0 *(3.1)*
Direct purchase	399 *(50)*	13.5 *(1.7)*	53 *(11)*	7.4 *(1.6)*	214 *(28)*	8.2 *(1.1)*	185 *(26)*	51.8 *(5.5)*
Covered by government health insurance	800 *(37)*	27.0 *(1.1)*	230 *(15)*	32.3 *(2.2)*	454 *(26)*	17.4 *(1.0)*	346 *(22)*	96.8 *(1.3)*
Covered by Medicaid	384 *(21)*	13.0 *(0.7)*	209 *(13)*	29.3 *(1.8)*	364 *(21)*	14.0 *(0.8)*	20 *(4)*	5.7 *(1.2)*
Also by private insurance	103 *(10)*	3.5 *(0.3)*	59 *(9)*	8.3 *(1.2)*	97 *(9)*	3.7 *(0.4)*	6 *(2)*	1.7 *(0.6)*
Covered by Medicare	415 *(25)*	14.0 *(0.8)*	7 *(3)*	1.0 *(0.4)*	70 *(13)*	2.7 *(0.5)*	346 *(22)*	96.8 *(1.3)*
Also by private insurance	274 *(30)*	9.3 *(1.0)*	2 *(1)*	0.3 *(0.2)*	18 *(5)*	0.7 *(0.2)*	256 *(27)*	71.8 *(4.7)*
Also by Medicaid	57 *(8)*	1.9 *(0.3)*	1 *(1)*	0.2 *(0.1)*	37 *(8)*	1.4 *(0.3)*	20 *(4)*	5.7 *(1.2)*
Covered by military health care	79 *(8)*	2.7 *(0.3)*	17 *(6)*	2.3 *(0.8)*	66 *(9)*	2.6 *(0.3)*	13 *(5)*	3.5 *(1.4)*
Not covered at any time during the year	366 *(33)*	12.3 *(1.1)*	53 *(11)*	7.4 *(1.7)*	360 *(35)*	13.8 *(1.3)*	6 *(3)*	1.6 *(0.9)*

Note: Numbers in thousands; figures cover 2010; standard error appears in parenthesis; (b) base less than 75,000; (x) not applicable
Source: U.S. Census Bureau, Current Population Survey, 2011 Annual Social and Economic Supplement. Table HI05. Health Insurance Coverage Status and Type of Coverage by State and Age for All People: 2010

Iowa

418 Aetna Health of Iowa
Partnered with eHealthInsurance Services Inc.

419 American Republic Insurance Company
PO Box 9371
Des Moines, IA 50306-9371
Toll-Free: 800-247-2190
www.americanrepublic.com
For Profit Organization: Yes
Year Founded: 1929

Healthplan and Services Defined
PLAN TYPE: HMO

Type of Coverage
Commercial, Individual, Medicare

Geographic Areas Served
Alabama, Arizona, Arkansas, Colorado, Delaware, Florida, Georgia, Illinois, Indiana, Iowa, Kansas, Kentucky, Louisiana, Michigan, Mississippi, Missouri, Montana, Nebraska, Nevada, New Mexico, North Carolina, North Dakota, Ohio, Oklahoma, Pennsylvania, South Carolina, South Daokga, Tennessee, Virginia, West Virginia, Wisconsin, Wyoming

420 Avesis: Iowa
317 Sixth Avenue
Suite 1040
Des Moines, IA 50309
Phone: 515-244-6282
www.avesis.com
Year Founded: 1978
Number of Primary Care Physicians: 18,000
Total Enrollment: 2,000,000

Healthplan and Services Defined
PLAN TYPE: PPO
Other Type: Vision, Dental
Model Type: Network
Plan Specialty: Dental, Vision, Hearing
Benefits Offered: Dental, Vision

Type of Coverage
Commercial

Type of Payment Plans Offered
POS, Capitated, Combination FFS & DFFS

Geographic Areas Served
Nationwide and Puerto Rico

Publishes and Distributes Report Card: Yes

Accreditation Certification
AAAHC
TJC Accreditation

421 CIGNA HealthCare of Iowa
525 West Monroe Street
Suite 300
Chicago, IL 60661
Toll-Free: 800-832-3211
Phone: 312-648-2460
Fax: 312-648-3617
www.cigna.com
For Profit Organization: Yes
Total Enrollment: 34,284
State Enrollment: 28,259

Healthplan and Services Defined
PLAN TYPE: HMO

Benefits Offered: Disease Management, Prescription, Transplant, Wellness

Type of Coverage
Commercial

Type of Payment Plans Offered
POS, FFS

Geographic Areas Served
Iowa

Key Personnel
Vice President . . . . Sherry Husa
VP Network Services . . . . Thomas Golias
VP National Accounts . . . . Karen Weaver

422 Coventry Health Care of Iowa
4320 114th Street
Urbandale, IA 50322
Toll-Free: 800-470-6352
Phone: 515-225-1234
Fax: 515-223-0097
csia@cvty.com
http://chciowa.coventryhealthcare.com
For Profit Organization: Yes
Year Founded: 1986
Number of Affiliated Hospitals: 152
Number of Primary Care Physicians: 3,500
Total Enrollment: 47,000
State Enrollment: 41,644

Healthplan and Services Defined
PLAN TYPE: HMO/PPO
Other Type: POS
Model Type: Group
Benefits Offered: Disease Management, Home Care, Inpatient SNF, Long-Term Care, Physical Therapy, Podiatry, Prescription, Psychiatric, Transplant, Vision, Wellness, Worker's Compensation

Type of Coverage
Commercial, Individual, Medicare, Supplemental Medicare, Medicaid

Type of Payment Plans Offered
POS

Geographic Areas Served
Sioux City, Waterloo/Cedar Falls, Cedar Rapids and Central Iowa

Peer Review Type
Utilization Review: Yes

Accreditation Certification
NCQA

423 Delta Dental of Iowa
9000 Northpark Drive
Johnson, IA 50131
Toll-Free: 877-423-3582
Fax: 515-261-5573
marketing@deltadentalia.com
www.deltadentalia.com
Mailing Address: PO Box 9010, Johnson, IA 50130-9010
Non-Profit Organization: Yes
Year Founded: 1970
Total Enrollment: 54,000,000
State Enrollment: 74,000

Healthplan and Services Defined
PLAN TYPE: Dental
Other Type: Dental PPO
Model Type: Network
Plan Specialty: Dental
Benefits Offered: Dental

Type of Coverage
Commercial

Type of Payment Plans Offered
DFFS

Geographic Areas Served
Statewide

Subscriber Information
Average Monthly Fee Per Subscriber
(Employee + Employer Contribution):
Employee Only (Self): $17
Employee & 2 Family Members: $50
Average Annual Deductible Per Subscriber:
Employee Only (Self): $150
Employee & 2 Family Members: $50
Average Subscriber Co-Payment:
Primary Care Physician: 80%
Non-Network Physician: 50%

Network Qualifications
Pre-Admission Certification: Yes

Publishes and Distributes Report Card: Yes

Key Personnel
VP, Chief Operating Offc . . . . Cheryl Harding
Dir/Media & Public Affair . . . . Elizabeth Risberg
415-972-8423

---

424 eHealthInsurance Services Inc.

11919 Foundation Place
Gold River, CA 95670
Toll-Free: 800-977-8860
info@ehealthinsurance.com
www.e.healthinsurance.com
Year Founded: 1997

Healthplan and Services Defined
PLAN TYPE: HMO/PPO
Benefits Offered: Dental, Life, STD

Type of Coverage
Commercial, Individual, Medicare

Geographic Areas Served
All 50 states in the USA and District of Columbia

Key Personnel
Chairman & CEO . . . . Gary L. Lauer
EVP/Business & Corp. Dev. Bruce Telkamp
EVP/Chief Technology . . . . Dr. Sheldon X. Wang
SVP & CFO . . . . Stuart M. Huizinga
Pres. of eHealth Gov. Sys . . . . Samuel C. Gibbs
SVP of Sales & Operations . . . . Robert S. Hurley
Director Public Relations . . . . Nate Purpura
650-210-3115

---

425 Great-West Healthcare Iowa

Acquired by CIGNA

---

426 Healthy & Well Kids in Iowa

PO Box 71336
Des Moines, IA 50325
Toll-Free: 800-257-8563
www.hawk-i.org
Subsidiary of: AmeriChoice, A UnitedHealth Group Company

Healthplan and Services Defined
PLAN TYPE: HMO

Key Personnel
Chairman . . . . Kim Carson
Vice Chairman . . . . Selden Spencer, MD

---

427 Humana Health Insurance of Iowa

5107 Utica Ridge Road
Davenport, IA 52807

Toll-Free: 866-653-7275
Phone: 563-388-7920
Fax: 563-388-6295
www.humana.com
For Profit Organization: Yes
Year Founded: 1961
Federally Qualified: Yes
Total Enrollment: 7,000,000

Healthplan and Services Defined
PLAN TYPE: HMO/PPO
Model Type: Staff
Plan Specialty: Dental
Benefits Offered: Behavioral Health, Chiropractic, Dental, Disease
Management, Prescription, Psychiatric, Wellness, Worker's
Compensation, Life, LTD, STD

Type of Coverage
Commercial, Individual, Supplemental Medicare

Geographic Areas Served
15 states and Puerto Rico

Accreditation Certification
URAC, NCQA, CORE

Key Personnel
Chairman . . . . David A Jones, Jr
President/CEO . . . . Michael B McCallister
Sr VP Innovation Officer . . . . Jack Lord, MD
COO Market/Business . . . . Jim Murray
Sr VP/CFO . . . . James Bloem
Sr VP General Counsel . . . . Art Hipwell
Sr VP Human Resources . . . . Bonnie Hathcock
Sr VP Corporate Develop . . . . Tom Liston
Sr VP Government Relation . . . . Hiedi Margulis
Sr VP/CSO/CIO . . . . Bruce Goodman
Sr VP Corporate Communica . . . . Tom Noland
Sr VP Marketing Officer . . . . Steve Moya

---

428 Medical Associates Health Plan: West

1500 Associates Drive
Dubuque, IA 52002
Toll-Free: 800-648-6868
Phone: 563-584-3000
Fax: 563-556-5134
www.mahealthcare.com
For Profit Organization: Yes
Year Founded: 1982
Physician Owned Organization: Yes
Federally Qualified: Yes
Total Enrollment: 45,000
State Enrollment: 14,412

Healthplan and Services Defined
PLAN TYPE: HMO
Other Type: EPO, POS
Model Type: Staff
Plan Specialty: Behavioral Health, Disease Management, Lab, MSO,
Vision, Radiology, UR
Benefits Offered: Home Care, Inpatient SNF, Physical Therapy,
Podiatry, Prescription, Psychiatric, Transplant, Vision, Wellness
Offers Demand Management Patient Information Service: Yes

Type of Coverage
Commercial, Indemnity, Medicare, Supplemental Medicare,
Catastrophic
Catastrophic Illness Benefit: Varies per case

Type of Payment Plans Offered
POS

Geographic Areas Served
Iowa: Allamakee, Clayton, Delaware, Dubuque, Jackson, Jones
counties. Illinois: JoDaviess County

Network Qualifications
Pre-Admission Certification: Yes

Peer Review Type
Utilization Review: Yes
Case Management: Yes

Publishes and Distributes Report Card: Yes

Accreditation Certification
NCQA
TJC Accreditation, Medicare Approved, Utilization Review, Pre-Admission Certification, State Licensure, Quality Assurance Program

Key Personnel
Executive Director . . . . Alan Avery
CEO . . . . John Tallent

Specialty Managed Care Partners
Enters into Contracts with Regional Business Coalitions: Yes

429 Mercy Health Network
1111 Sixth Avenue
Suite 201
Des Moines, IA 50314
Phone: 515-643-5300
Fax: 515-643-5350
info@mercyhealthnetwork.com
www.mercyhealthnetwork.com
Subsidiary of: Catholic Health Initiatives, Trinity Health
Year Founded: 1998
Number of Affiliated Hospitals: 33

Healthplan and Services Defined
PLAN TYPE: HMO
Plan Specialty: Lab, Cardiac Care
Benefits Offered: Disease Management, Home Care, Physical Therapy, Prescription, Wellness

Type of Coverage
Individual

Geographic Areas Served
Clinton, Des Moines, Dubuque, North Iowa, Sioux City

Key Personnel
CEO . . . . Steven Kukla

430 Sanford Health Plan
300 Cherapa Place
Suite 201
Sioux Falls, SD 57103
Toll-Free: 877-305-5463
Phone: 605-328-6868
Fax: 605-328-1577
memberservices@sanfordhealth.org
www.sanfordhealthplan.com
Mailing Address: PO Box 91110, Sioux Falls, SD 57109-1110
Non-Profit Organization: Yes
Year Founded: 1996
Total Enrollment: 50,000

Healthplan and Services Defined
PLAN TYPE: HMO
Model Type: IPA
Plan Specialty: Commercial Group
Benefits Offered: Disease Management, Home Care, Long-Term Care, Prescription, Wellness

Type of Coverage
Commercial, Individual, Medicare, Supplemental Medicare, Sec 125, TPA, Individual, Lg Group

Geographic Areas Served
Northwest Iowa, Southwest Minnesota, South Dakota

Key Personnel
Executive Director . . . . Jerome Freeman, MD
Administrative Director . . . . Ellen Schellinger, MA
Director, Planning & Reg . . . . Lisa Carlson
605-328-6859
Media Strategy Manager . . . . Stacy Bauer Jones
605-328-7056
stacy.jones@sanfordhealth.org

431 UnitedHealthCare of Iowa
11141 Aurora Avenue
Des Moines, IA 50322
Toll-Free: 800-669-1830
www.uhc.com
Secondary Address: 2540 106th Street, Suite 201, Urbandale, IA 50322, 800-669-1812
Subsidiary of: UnitedHealth Group
For Profit Organization: Yes
Year Founded: 1984
Number of Affiliated Hospitals: 4,500
Number of Primary Care Physicians: 470,000
Total Enrollment: 75,000,000

Healthplan and Services Defined
PLAN TYPE: HMO/PPO
Model Type: Network
Plan Specialty: Dental, Vision
Benefits Offered: Dental, Disease Management, Prescription, Vision, Wellness, Life, LTD, STD

Type of Coverage
Commercial, Individual, Indemnity

Type of Payment Plans Offered
POS, DFFS, FFS

Geographic Areas Served
Statewide

Network Qualifications
Pre-Admission Certification: Yes

Peer Review Type
Utilization Review: Yes
Second Surgical Opinion: Yes
Case Management: Yes

Publishes and Distributes Report Card: Yes

Accreditation Certification
TJC Accreditation, Medicare Approved, Utilization Review, Pre-Admission Certification, State Licensure, Quality Assurance Program

Key Personnel
President . . . . Daniel Kuter
Administrator . . . . Julia Arnett
Media Contact . . . . Greg Thompson
312-424-6913
gregory_a_thompson@uhc.com

432 Wellmark Health Plan of Iowa
636 Grand Avenue
PO Box 9232
Des Moines, IA 50309-2565
Toll-Free: 800-524-9242
Phone: 515-245-4500
Fax: 515-245-5090
www.wellmark.com
Year Founded: 1939
Number of Affiliated Hospitals: 117
Number of Primary Care Physicians: 2,500
Total Enrollment: 250,000
State Enrollment: 250,000

Healthplan and Services Defined
  PLAN TYPE: HMO
  Model Type: IPA
  Plan Specialty: ASO, Chiropractic, Disease Management, Lab,
    Vision, Radiology, UR
  Benefits Offered: Chiropractic, Disease Management, Home Care,
    Inpatient SNF, Physical Therapy, Podiatry, Prescription,
    Psychiatric, Transplant, Vision, Wellness
  Offers Demand Management Patient Information Service: Yes

Type of Coverage
  Commercial, Individual, Indemnity, Medicare, Supplemental
    Medicare, Medicaid

Type of Payment Plans Offered
  POS, Capitated

Geographic Areas Served
  Statewide except Alamakee, Winneshiek, Fayette, Des Moines and
    Dubuque counties

Network Qualifications
  Pre-Admission Certification: Yes

Peer Review Type
  Utilization Review: Yes

Publishes and Distributes Report Card: Yes

Accreditation Certification
  URAC, NCQA
  TJC Accreditation, Medicare Approved, Utilization Review,
    Pre-Admission Certification, State Licensure, Quality Assurance
    Program

Key Personnel
  Chairman/CEO . . . . John Forsyth
  Sr VP Finance . . . . Richard Anderson
  VP Investments . . . . Mike Crowley
  VP Claims Administration . . . . Elaine Palmer
  Associate General Counsel . . . . Michele Druker
  EVP Human Resources . . . . Marcelle Chickering
  VP Actuarial . . . . Patricia Huffman
  Sr VP Human Resources . . . . Laura Jackson
  VP Marketing. . . . . Tim Weber
  VP Health Networks . . . . Michael D Fay
  Chief Medical Officer . . . . Paul Karajia
  EVP Chief Admin Officer . . . . Ellen J Gaucher
  VP Information Systems. . . . . Sandy Nelson
  VP Customer Service . . . . Scott Froyen
  Sr VP Sales & Marketing. . . . . Keith Heckel
  Media Contact . . . . Rob Schweers
    515-248-5683
    schweersr@wellmark.com
  EVP Chief Info Officer . . . . Denis J Roy

Health Insurance Coverage Status and Type of Coverage by Age

Category	All Persons		Under 18 years		Under 65 years		65 years and over	
	Number	%	Number	%	Number	%	Number	%
Total population	2,757	-	707	-	2,387	-	371	-
Covered by some type of health insurance	2,407 (43)	87.3 (1.1)	654 (13)	92.5 (1.6)	2,037 (44)	85.3 (1.3)	370 (18)	99.8 (0.2)
Covered by private health insurance	1,947 (61)	70.6 (2.0)	453 (21)	64.2 (3.1)	1,690 (59)	70.8 (2.1)	258 (15)	69.5 (3.1)
Employment based	1,601 (61)	58.1 (1.9)	416 (22)	58.9 (3.2)	1,516 (60)	63.5 (2.1)	86 (9)	23.1 (2.2)
Own employment based	840 (27)	30.5 (0.8)	2 (2)	0.2 (0.2)	773 (28)	32.4 (1.0)	67 (8)	18.1 (2.0)
Direct purchase	381 (17)	13.8 (0.6)	47 (11)	6.6 (1.5)	191 (16)	8.0 (0.7)	189 (13)	51.0 (2.8)
Covered by government health insurance	861 (57)	31.2 (2.0)	264 (22)	37.3 (3.0)	497 (55)	20.8 (2.3)	364 (18)	98.1 (0.8)
Covered by Medicaid	337 (34)	12.2 (1.3)	224 (25)	31.8 (3.4)	324 (33)	13.6 (1.5)	13 (5)	3.5 (1.2)
Also by private insurance	64 (11)	2.3 (0.4)	38 (7)	5.3 (1.0)	60 (10)	2.5 (0.4)	4 (2)	1.2 (0.6)
Covered by Medicare	430 (21)	15.6 (0.8)	6 (3)	0.8 (0.4)	69 (12)	2.9 (0.5)	361 (18)	97.5 (1.0)
Also by private insurance	268 (18)	9.7 (0.7)	0 (0)	0.0 (0.0)	19 (6)	0.8 (0.2)	249 (17)	67.2 (3.6)
Also by Medicaid	43 (8)	1.6 (0.3)	4 (2)	0.6 (0.4)	31 (6)	1.3 (0.3)	12 (5)	3.3 (1.2)
Covered by military health care	193 (69)	7.0 (2.5)	41 (21)	5.8 (3.0)	144 (61)	6.0 (2.5)	49 (11)	13.1 (2.9)
Not covered at any time during the year	350 (29)	12.7 (1.1)	53 (11)	7.5 (1.6)	350 (29)	14.7 (1.3)	1 (1)	0.2 (0.2)

Note: Numbers in thousands; figures cover 2010; standard error appears in parenthesis; (b) base less than 75,000; (x) not applicable
Source: U.S. Census Bureau, Current Population Survey, 2011 Annual Social and Economic Supplement. Table HI05. Health Insurance Coverage Status and Type of Coverage by State and Age for All People: 2010

Kansas

433 **Advance Insurance Company of Kansas**
1133 SW Topeka Blvd
Topeka, KS 66629
Toll-Free: 800-530-5989
Phone: 785-273-9804
Fax: 785-290-0727
csc-advance@advanceinsurance.com
www.advanceinsurance.com
Subsidiary of: Blue Cross & Blue Shield of Kansas
For Profit Organization: Yes
Total Enrollment: 135,000

Healthplan and Services Defined
  PLAN TYPE: Multiple

Key Personnel
  Chairman of the Board . . . . Andrew C Corbin
  President . . . . Beryl Lowery-Born
  Chief Operating Officer . . . . Jennifer Rose-Long

434 **Aetna Health of Kansas**
151 Farmington Avenue
Hartford, CT 06156
Toll-Free: 866-582-9629
www.aetna.com
For Profit Organization: Yes
Total Enrollment: 11,596,230

Healthplan and Services Defined
  PLAN TYPE: PPO
  Other Type: POS
  Plan Specialty: EPO
  Benefits Offered: Dental, Disease Management, Long-Term Care, Prescription, Wellness, Life, LTD, STD

Type of Coverage
  Commercial, Individual

Type of Payment Plans Offered
  POS, FFS

Geographic Areas Served
  Statewide

Key Personnel
  CEO . . . . Ronald A Williams
  President. . . . . Mark T Bertolini
  SVP, General Counsel . . . . William J Casazza
  EVP, CFO . . . . Joseph M Zubretsky
  Head, M&A Integration . . . . Kay Mooney
  SVP, Marketing. . . . . Robert E Mead
  Chief Medical Officer . . . . Lonny Reisman, MD
  SVP, Human Resources. . . . . Elease E Wright
  SVP, CIO. . . . . Meg McCarthy

435 **Assurant Employee Benefits: Kansas**
8300 College Blvd
Suite 120
Shawnee Mission, KS 66210-2603
Phone: 913-469-8090
Fax: 913-469-8091
benefits@assurant.com
www.assurantemployeebenefits.com
Subsidiary of: Assurant, Inc
For Profit Organization: Yes
Number of Primary Care Physicians: 112,000
Total Enrollment: 47,000

Healthplan and Services Defined
  PLAN TYPE: Multiple
  Plan Specialty: Dental, Vision, Long & Short-Term Disability

Benefits Offered: Dental, Vision, Wellness, AD&D, Life, LTD, STD

Type of Coverage
  Commercial, Indemnity, Individual Dental Plans

Geographic Areas Served
  Statewide

Subscriber Information
  Average Monthly Fee Per Subscriber
    (Employee + Employer Contribution):
      Employee Only (Self): Varies by plan

Key Personnel
  Office Manager. . . . . Kristen Stine
  PR Specialist. . . . . Megan Hutchison
    816-556-7815
    megan.hutchison@assurant.com

436 **Blue Cross & Blue Shield of Kansas**
1133 Southwest Topeka Boulevard
Topeka, KS 66629-0001
Toll-Free: 800-432-0216
Phone: 785-291-4180
Fax: 785-291-8295
csc@bcbsks.com
www.bcbsks.com
For Profit Organization: Yes
Year Founded: 1941
Number of Affiliated Hospitals: 120
Total Enrollment: 898,111
State Enrollment: 680,466

Healthplan and Services Defined
  PLAN TYPE: HMO
  Model Type: Staff
  Benefits Offered: Chiropractic, Disease Management, Inpatient SNF, Podiatry, Psychiatric, Wellness

Type of Coverage
  Commercial, Individual

Geographic Areas Served
  All Kansas counties except Johnson and Wyandotte

Subscriber Information
  Average Annual Deductible Per Subscriber:
    Employee Only (Self): $1,000
    Employee & 2 Family Members: $2,000
  Average Subscriber Co-Payment:
    Primary Care Physician: $15.00
    Prescription Drugs: $5.00
    Hospital ER: $50.00

Accreditation Certification
  TJC

Key Personnel
  Chairman. . . . . Gary D. Shorman, Hays
  President/CEO. . . . . Andrew C. Corbin
  VP Public Relations. . . . . S Graham Bailey
  VP Finance. . . . . Beryl Lowery Born
  VP/General Counsel. . . . . Jane Chandler Holt
  VP, Sales & Marketing. . . . . Mark G Dolsky
  VP, Operations . . . . Shelley Pittman
  Chief Medical Officer . . . . Michael D Atwood, MD
  VP, Information Services . . . . Julie Hinrichsen
  VP, Prov Rel & Med Affrs . . . . Frederick D Palenske
  Mgr Corp Communications . . . . Mary Beth Chambers
    785-291-8869
    mary.beth.chambers@bcbsks.com

437 **CIGNA HealthCare of Kansas**
7400 West 110th Street
Suite 400
Overland Park, KS 66210

Toll-Free: 866-438-2446
Phone: 913-339-4700
Fax: 913-339-4705
www.cigna.com
For Profit Organization: Yes
Total Enrollment: 9,848

Healthplan and Services Defined
PLAN TYPE: HMO
Other Type: POS

Type of Coverage
Commercial

---

438   CoreSource: Kansas (FMH CoreSource)

13160 Foster Street
Suite 150
Overland Park, KS 66213
Toll-Free: 800-990-9058
Phone: 913-685-4740
www.coresource.com; www.f-m-h.com
Subsidiary of: Trustmark
Year Founded: 1980
Total Enrollment: 1,100,000

Healthplan and Services Defined
PLAN TYPE: Multiple
Other Type: TPA
Model Type: Network
Plan Specialty: Claims Administration, TPA
Benefits Offered: Behavioral Health, Home Care, Prescription,
Transplant

Type of Coverage
Commercial

Geographic Areas Served
Nationwide

Accreditation Certification
Utilization Review, Pre-Admission Certification

---

439   Coventry Health Care of Kansas

8320 Ward Parkway
Kansas City, KS 64114
Toll-Free: 800-969-3343
Phone: 816-941-3030
Fax: 816-941-8516
www.chckansas.com
Secondary Address: 8301 East 21st Street North, Suite 300, Wichita,
KS 67206
For Profit Organization: Yes
Year Founded: 1988
Number of Affiliated Hospitals: 100
Number of Primary Care Physicians: 4,800
Number of Referral/Specialty Physicians: 731
Total Enrollment: 73,000
State Enrollment: 132,716

Healthplan and Services Defined
PLAN TYPE: HMO/PPO
Other Type: POS
Model Type: IPA
Benefits Offered: Complementary Medicine, Disease Management,
Prescription, Vision, Wellness, Alternative and complementary
care services include discounts on massage therapy, acupuncture
and chiropractic services.
Offers Demand Management Patient Information Service: Yes

Type of Coverage
Catastrophic Illness Benefit: Covered

Type of Payment Plans Offered
DFFS

Geographic Areas Served
Kansas, Missouri, Oklahoma

Subscriber Information
Average Monthly Fee Per Subscriber
(Employee + Employer Contribution):
Employee Only (Self): Varies
Average Annual Deductible Per Subscriber:
Employee & 2 Family Members: None
Average Subscriber Co-Payment:
Primary Care Physician: $10.00
Prescription Drugs: $5.00/15.00
Hospital ER: $50
Home Health Care: None
Nursing Home: None

Peer Review Type
Second Surgical Opinion: Yes
Case Management: Yes

Publishes and Distributes Report Card: Yes

Accreditation Certification
NCQA
Medicare Approved, Utilization Review, Pre-Admission Certification,
State Licensure, Quality Assurance Program

Key Personnel
President.............................Thomas P McDonough
CEO...................................Dale B Wolf
EVP................................Harvey C DeMovick, Jr
EVP/Operations.......................Francis S Soistman, Jr
EVP/CFO...............................Richard Kleinner

Specialty Managed Care Partners
Enters into Contracts with Regional Business Coalitions: Yes

---

440   Delta Dental of Kansas

1619 North Waterfront Parkway
PO Box 789769
Wichita, KS 67278-9769
Toll-Free: 800-234-3375
Phone: 316-264-4511
Fax: 316-462-3392
moreinfo@deltadentalks.com
www.deltadentalks.com
Non-Profit Organization: Yes
Year Founded: 1972
Number of Primary Care Physicians: 1,200
Number of Referral/Specialty Physicians: 250
Total Enrollment: 54,000,000
State Enrollment: 880,000

Healthplan and Services Defined
PLAN TYPE: Dental
Other Type: Dental PPO
Model Type: Network
Plan Specialty: Dental
Benefits Offered: Dental

Type of Coverage
Commercial

Type of Payment Plans Offered
DFFS

Geographic Areas Served
Statewide

Subscriber Information
Average Monthly Fee Per Subscriber
(Employee + Employer Contribution):
Employee Only (Self): $17
Employee & 2 Family Members: $50
Average Annual Deductible Per Subscriber:
Employee Only (Self): $150
Employee & 2 Family Members: $50
Average Subscriber Co-Payment:

Primary Care Physician: 80%
Non-Network Physician: 50%

Network Qualifications
Pre-Admission Certification: Yes

Publishes and Distributes Report Card: Yes

Key Personnel
CEO . . . . Linda Brantner
   316-264-1099
   lbrantner@deltadentalks.com
Chief Financial Officer . . . . Michael Herbert
Chief Operations Officer . . . . Frank Clepper
VP, Professional Relation . . . . Junetta Everett
In-House Counsel . . . . Mindy McPheeters
VP, Dental Director . . . . Jon W Tilton, DDS
Chief Mktg & Sales Offc . . . . Dean Newton
VP, Human Resources . . . . Amy Ellison
VP, Information Tech . . . . Bob Ebenkamp
Communications Coord . . . . Sarah Pritchard
   316-264-1099
   spritchard@deltadentalks.com
Dir/Media & Public Affair . . . . Elizabeth Risberg
   415-972-8423

441 eHealthInsurance Services Inc.
11919 Foundation Place
Gold River, CA 95670
Toll-Free: 800-977-8860
info@ehealthinsurance.com
www.e.healthinsurance.com
Year Founded: 1997

Healthplan and Services Defined
PLAN TYPE: HMO/PPO
Benefits Offered: Dental, Life, STD

Type of Coverage
Commercial, Individual, Medicare

Geographic Areas Served
All 50 states in the USA and District of Columbia

Key Personnel
Chairman & CEO . . . . Gary L. Lauer
EVP/Business & Corp. Dev. . . . . Bruce Telkamp
EVP/Chief Technology . . . . Dr. Sheldon X. Wang
SVP & CFO . . . . Stuart M. Huizinga
Pres. of eHealth Gov. Sys . . . . Samuel C. Gibbs
SVP of Sales & Operations . . . . Robert S. Hurley
Director Public Relations . . . . Nate Purpura
   650-210-3115

442 Great-West Healthcare Kansas
Acquired by CIGNA

443 Health Partners of Kansas
550 North Lorraine Street
Wichita, KS 67214
Toll-Free: 800-633-9917
Phone: 316-652-1327
Fax: 316-652-1345
gaylee.dolloff@wesleymc.com
www.hpkansas.com
For Profit Organization: Yes
Year Founded: 1987
Number of Affiliated Hospitals: 149
Number of Primary Care Physicians: 1,000
Number of Referral/Specialty Physicians: 6,000
Total Enrollment: 95,000
State Enrollment: 95,000

Healthplan and Services Defined
PLAN TYPE: PPO
Model Type: IPA, Network
Benefits Offered: Worker's Compensation, Network Rental, Provider Servicing, Provider Credentialing

Type of Coverage
Catastrophic Illness Benefit: Maximum $1M

Type of Payment Plans Offered
POS, DFFS, Capitated, FFS, Combination FFS & DFFS

Geographic Areas Served
Statewide

Network Qualifications
Pre-Admission Certification: Yes

Peer Review Type
Utilization Review: Yes
Second Surgical Opinion: Yes
Case Management: Yes

Key Personnel
President . . . . Gaylee Dolloff
   gaylee.dolloff@wesleymc.com
Credentialing . . . . Sandra Johnson
   sandra.johnson@wesleymc.com
VP Provider Services . . . . Teresa Montenegro
   teresa.montenegro@wesleymc.com

Specialty Managed Care Partners
Enters into Contracts with Regional Business Coalitions: No

444 Humana Health Insurance of Kansas
7311 W 132nd Street
Suite 200
Overland Park, MO 66213
Toll-Free: 800-842-6188
Phone: 913-217-3333
Fax: 913-217-3245
www.humana.com
Secondary Address: 1313 N Webb Road, Suite 230, Wichita, KS 67206
For Profit Organization: Yes
Year Founded: 1985
Number of Affiliated Hospitals: 8
Number of Primary Care Physicians: 1,300
Total Enrollment: 84,841
State Enrollment: 40,800

Healthplan and Services Defined
PLAN TYPE: HMO/PPO
Model Type: IPA
Benefits Offered: Disease Management, Prescription, Wellness

Type of Coverage
Commercial, Individual

Geographic Areas Served
Kansas City metro area

Subscriber Information
Average Monthly Fee Per Subscriber
  (Employee + Employer Contribution):
    Employee Only (Self): $150.44
    Employee & 1 Family Member: $354.06
    Employee & 2 Family Members: $354.06
    Medicare: $196.48
Average Subscriber Co-Payment:
    Primary Care Physician: $5.00
    Non-Network Physician: Not covered
    Prescription Drugs: $5.00
    Hospital ER: $25.00
    Home Health Care: $0
    Nursing Home: $0
    Nursing Home Max. Days/Visits Covered: 60 days

Accreditation Certification
URAC, NCQA, CORE

Key Personnel
President/CEO . . . . Michael B McCallister
COO . . . . James E Murray
CFO . . . . James H Bloem
Chief Marketing Officer. Steven O Moya

Average Claim Compensation
Physician's Fees Charged: 70%
Hospital's Fees Charged: 60%

Specialty Managed Care Partners
Enters into Contracts with Regional Business Coalitions: Yes

445 Mercy Health Plans: Kansas
14528 South Outer 40
Suite 300
Chesterfield, MO 63017-5743
Toll-Free: 800-830-1918
Phone: 314-214-8100
Fax: 314-214-8101
www.mercyhealthplans.com
Non-Profit Organization: Yes
Total Enrollment: 73,000

Healthplan and Services Defined
PLAN TYPE: HMO

Type of Coverage
Commercial, Individual

Key Personnel
Interim CEO . . . . Chris Knackstedt
EVP, COO. . . . . Mike Treash
Executive Vice President . . . . Janet Pursley
CFO, Treasurer . . . . George Schneider
VP, General Counsel . . . . Charles Gilham
Chief Medical Officer . . . . Stephen Spurgeon, MD
VP, Human Resources . . . . Donna McDaniel
VP, Mission & Ethics . . . . Michael Doyle
VP, Sales & Service. . . . . Carl Schultz

446 PCC Preferred Chiropractic Care
555 North McLean Boulevard
Suite 200
Wichita, KS 67203
Toll-Free: 800-611-3048
Phone: 316-263-7800
Fax: 316-263-7814
marketing@pccnetwork.com
www.pccnetwork.com
For Profit Organization: Yes
Year Founded: 1984
Physician Owned Organization: No
Federally Qualified: No
Number of Primary Care Physicians: 3,500
Total Enrollment: 5,000,000

Healthplan and Services Defined
PLAN TYPE: PPO
Model Type: Network
Plan Specialty: Chiropractic
Benefits Offered: Chiropractic, Disease Management, Wellness, Worker's Compensation
Offers Demand Management Patient Information Service: Yes
DMPI Services Offered: Chiropractic, Physical Therapy

Type of Coverage
Medicaid

Type of Payment Plans Offered
POS, DFFS, Capitated, FFS, Combination FFS & DFFS

Geographic Areas Served
All continental states

Subscriber Information
Average Subscriber Co-Payment:
Primary Care Physician: 20%
Non-Network Physician: 50%

Network Qualifications
Pre-Admission Certification: No

Peer Review Type
Utilization Review: Yes
Second Surgical Opinion: Yes
Case Management: No

Publishes and Distributes Report Card: No

Accreditation Certification
URAC, NCQA

Key Personnel
President and CEO . . . . Brad Dopps, DC
CFO . . . . Mark Dopps, DC
COO. . . . . Robert Dopps, DC
Claims Manager . . . . Jacque Fox
316-263-7800
jfox@pccnetwork.com
Credentialing . . . . Kay Lukens
Marketing . . . . Beth Dauner
bdauner@pccnetwork.com
Member Services . . . . John Dopps, DC
Provider Services. . . . . Kay Lukens
316-263-7800
kaylukens@pccnetwork.com

Average Claim Compensation
Physician's Fees Charged: 80%

Specialty Managed Care Partners
Enters into Contracts with Regional Business Coalitions: Yes

Employer References
Preferred Health Systems, fiserv, Health Partners of Kansas

447 Preferred Health Systems Insurance Company
8535 East 21st Street N
Wichita, KS 67206
Toll-Free: 800-990-0345
Phone: 316-609-2345
Fax: 316-609-2346
phsimail@phsystems.com
www.phsystems.com
Subsidiary of: A Coventry Health Care Plan
For Profit Organization: Yes
Year Founded: 1996
Number of Affiliated Hospitals: 140
Number of Primary Care Physicians: 1,386
Number of Referral/Specialty Physicians: 1,870
Total Enrollment: 33,153
State Enrollment: 31,453

Healthplan and Services Defined
PLAN TYPE: PPO
Model Type: Group
Plan Specialty: ASO, Behavioral Health, Chiropractic, Disease Management, EPO, PBM, Vision, Radiology, UR, Medicare Supplement
Benefits Offered: Behavioral Health, Chiropractic, Dental, Disease Management, Home Care, Inpatient SNF, Physical Therapy, Podiatry, Prescription, Psychiatric, Transplant, Vision, AD&D, Life

Type of Coverage
Commercial, Supplemental Medicare
Catastrophic Illness Benefit: Maximum $2M

Type of Payment Plans Offered
FFS

Geographic Areas Served
Kansas: Statewide

Subscriber Information
Average Monthly Fee Per Subscriber
(Employee + Employer Contribution):
Employee Only (Self): $307.11
Employee & 1 Family Member: $625.79
Employee & 2 Family Members: $758.37
Average Annual Deductible Per Subscriber:
Employee Only (Self): $1151.20
Employee & 1 Family Member: $2302.40
Employee & 2 Family Members: $2302.40
Average Subscriber Co-Payment:
Primary Care Physician: $20.00
Non-Network Physician: Ded/coinsurance
Prescription Drugs: $10/30/50
Hospital ER: $150.00
Home Health Care: $0 up to $2500 max
Home Health Care Max. Days/Visits Covered: Varies
Nursing Home Max. Days/Visits Covered: Varies

Network Qualifications
Pre-Admission Certification: Yes

Peer Review Type
Utilization Review: Yes
Second Surgical Opinion: Yes
Case Management: Yes

Publishes and Distributes Report Card: No

Accreditation Certification
URAC
Utilization Review, Pre-Admission Certification, State Licensure,
Quality Assurance Program

Key Personnel
CEO/President/Director . . . . Marlon R Dauner
CFO . . . . Todd Kasitz
COO. . . . . Brad Clothier
Director . . . . Robert Kenargy
Director. . . . . Ken Griggs
Director. . . . . George Fahnestock
Coord, Payer Relations . . . . Tracy Biglow
Senior Marketing Exec . . . . Jeremy Gilson
Senior Marketing Exec. Jennifer Elliot
Mgr, Sales & Medicare . . . . Dennis Manson
Medical Director . . . . Paul Huser
Coord, Customer Service. Ivy McCray
Human Resources Officer . . . . Raedina Campbell
Mgr, Payer/Medicare Mktg . . . . Dennis Manson
Director Sales & Mktg . . . . Brian Rose
Administrative Specialist . . . . Jessica Warren
316-609-2431
jwarren@phsystems.com

Average Claim Compensation
Physician's Fees Charged: 67%
Hospital's Fees Charged: 52%

Specialty Managed Care Partners
Express Scripts

Employer References
Royal Valley USD 337, Ark City USD 470, Chance Rides
Manufacturing, Butler Community College

448 Preferred Mental Health Management
401 East Douglas Avenue
Suite 505
Wichita, KS 67202
Toll-Free: 800-819-9571
Phone: 316-262-0444
info@pmhm.com
www.pmhm.com
Year Founded: 1987

Number of Affiliated Hospitals: 1,900
Number of Primary Care Physicians: 10,500
Number of Referral/Specialty Physicians: 4,000
Total Enrollment: 400,000
Healthplan and Services Defined
PLAN TYPE: Multiple
Model Type: Network
Plan Specialty: Mental Health
Benefits Offered: Behavioral Health, Prescription, Psychiatric
Offers Demand Management Patient Information Service: Yes

Type of Coverage
Work

Geographic Areas Served
All 50 states and Puerto Rico

Network Qualifications
Minimum Years of Practice: 6
Pre-Admission Certification: Yes

Peer Review Type
Utilization Review: Yes

Publishes and Distributes Report Card: Yes

Accreditation Certification
TJC Accreditation, Utilization Review, Pre-Admission Certification,
State Licensure, Quality Assurance Program

Key Personnel
President and CEO. . . . . Les Ruthven, PhD
316-262-0444
EVP . . . . Courtney Ruthven
Director Operations . . . . Angie Byrd

Specialty Managed Care Partners
Enters into Contracts with Regional Business Coalitions: No

449 Preferred Plus of Kansas
8535 East 21st Street North
Wichita, KS 67206
Toll-Free: 800-660-8114
Phone: 316-609-2345
Fax: 316-609-2346
phsimail@phsystems.com
www.phsystems.com
Subsidiary of: Preferred Health Systems/A Coventry Health Care Plan
For Profit Organization: Yes
Year Founded: 1991
Physician Owned Organization: No
Federally Qualified: No
Number of Affiliated Hospitals: 34
Number of Primary Care Physicians: 416
Number of Referral/Specialty Physicians: 1,197
Total Enrollment: 83,151
State Enrollment: 82,778

Healthplan and Services Defined
PLAN TYPE: HMO
Model Type: IPA
Plan Specialty: Behavioral Health, Chiropractic, Disease
Management, Lab, PBM, Vision, Radiology, UR
Benefits Offered: Behavioral Health, Chiropractic, Dental, Disease
Management, Home Care, Inpatient SNF, Physical Therapy,
Podiatry, Prescription, Psychiatric, Transplant, Vision, Wellness,
AD&D, Life
Offers Demand Management Patient Information Service: Yes
DMPI Services Offered: Diabetes, High Risk Pregnancy, Transplants,
Catastrophic Case Management

Type of Coverage
Commercial
Catastrophic Illness Benefit: Maximum $2M

Type of Payment Plans Offered
DFFS, Capitated, FFS, Combination FFS & DFFS

Geographic Areas Served
Kansas: Butler, Chase, Chautauqua, Cowley, Dickenson, Elk, Greenwood, Harper, Harvey, Kingman, Marion, McPherson, Morris, Reno, Saline, Sedgwick and Sumner counties; Oklahoma: Kay county

Subscriber Information
Average Monthly Fee Per Subscriber
(Employee + Employer Contribution):
Employee Only (Self): $312.11
Employee & 1 Family Member: $674.23
Employee & 2 Family Members: $784.98
Average Annual Deductible Per Subscriber:
Employee Only (Self): $46.05
Employee & 1 Family Member: $92.09
Employee & 2 Family Members: $92.09
Average Subscriber Co-Payment:
Primary Care Physician: $19.64
Non-Network Physician: Not covered
Prescription Drugs: $10/30/50
Hospital ER: $127.15
Home Health Care: $0 up to $2500 max
Home Health Care Max. Days/Visits Covered: Varies
Nursing Home Max. Days/Visits Covered: Varies

Network Qualifications
Pre-Admission Certification: Yes

Peer Review Type
Utilization Review: Yes
Case Management: Yes

Publishes and Distributes Report Card: No

Accreditation Certification
URAC, URAC
TJC Accreditation, Medicare Approved, Utilization Review, Pre-Admission Certification, State Licensure, Quality Assurance Program

Key Personnel
CEO/President/Director . . . . Marlon R Dauner
CFO . . . . Todd Kasitz
COO. . . . . Brad Clothier
Director . . . . Robert Kenargy
Director. . . . . Ken Griggs
Director. . . . . George Fahnestock
Coord, Payer Relations . . . . Tracy Biglow
Senior Marketing Exec . . . . Jeremy Gilson
Senior Marketing Exec. . . . . Jennifer Elliot
Mgr, Sales & Medicare . . . . Dennis Manson
Medical Director . . . . Paul Huser
Coord, Customer Service. . . . . Ivy McCray
Human Resources Officer . . . . Raedina Campbell
Mgr, Payer/Medicare Mktg . . . . Dennis Manson
Director Sales & Mktg . . . . Brian Rose
Administrative Specialist . . . . Jessica Warren
316-609-2431
jwarren@phsystems.com

Average Claim Compensation
Physician's Fees Charged: 61%
Hospital's Fees Charged: 36%

Specialty Managed Care Partners
Express Scripts
Enters into Contracts with Regional Business Coalitions: No

Employer References
Boeing, General Electric, Lear Jet, Spirit AeroSystems, ViaChrish Health System

---

450   **Preferred Vision Care**
PO Box 26025
Overland Park, KS 66225-6025
Toll-Free: 888-635-7874

Phone: 913-451-1672
Fax: 913-451-1704
customerservice@preferredvisioncare.com
www.preferredvisioncare.com
For Profit Organization: Yes
Year Founded: 1987
Owned by an Integrated Delivery Network (IDN): Yes
Number of Primary Care Physicians: 10,000
Total Enrollment: 100,000
State Enrollment: 1,000,000

Healthplan and Services Defined
PLAN TYPE: Vision
Model Type: Network
Plan Specialty: Vision
Benefits Offered: Vision

Type of Coverage
Commercial, Individual, Indemnity, Medicare, Supplemental Medicare, Medicaid, Catastrophic
Catastrophic Illness Benefit: Unlimited

Type of Payment Plans Offered
POS, DFFS

Geographic Areas Served
US, Puerto Rico, Guam, & VI

Subscriber Information
Average Monthly Fee Per Subscriber
(Employee + Employer Contribution):
Employee Only (Self): Varies
Employee & 1 Family Member: Varies
Employee & 2 Family Members: Varies

Network Qualifications
Pre-Admission Certification: No

Peer Review Type
Utilization Review: Yes
Second Surgical Opinion: Yes
Case Management: Yes

Publishes and Distributes Report Card: Yes

Accreditation Certification
URAC
Quality Assurance Program

Key Personnel
CEO. . . . . Michele G Disser, RN
Operations . . . . E J Disser
Marketing . . . . P J Disser

Specialty Managed Care Partners
Enters into Contracts with Regional Business Coalitions: Yes

---

451   **ProviDRs Care Network**
1102 South Hillside
Wichita, KS 67211
Toll-Free: 800-801-9772
Phone: 316-683-4111
Fax: 316-683-6255
customerservice@providrscare.net
www.providrscare.net
Subsidiary of: Medical Society Medical Review Foundation
For Profit Organization: Yes
Year Founded: 1985
Physician Owned Organization: Yes
Number of Affiliated Hospitals: 139
Number of Primary Care Physicians: 4,500
Number of Referral/Specialty Physicians: 1,275
Total Enrollment: 152,000

Healthplan and Services Defined
PLAN TYPE: PPO
Model Type: Group

Benefits Offered: Behavioral Health, Chiropractic, Home Care,
Physical Therapy, Podiatry, Psychiatric, Transplant, Worker's
Compensation

Type of Coverage
Commercial, Individual

Type of Payment Plans Offered
POS

Geographic Areas Served
Kansas and Southwest Missouri

Subscriber Information
Average Monthly Fee Per Subscriber
(Employee + Employer Contribution):
Employee Only (Self): $3.00
Employee & 1 Family Member: $3.00
Employee & 2 Family Members: $3.00
Average Annual Deductible Per Subscriber:
Employee Only (Self): Varies
Employee & 1 Family Member: Varies
Average Subscriber Co-Payment:
Primary Care Physician: Varies
Non-Network Physician: Varies
Prescription Drugs: Varies
Hospital ER: Varies

Network Qualifications
Pre-Admission Certification: Yes

Peer Review Type
Utilization Review: Yes
Second Surgical Opinion: Yes
Case Management: No

Publishes and Distributes Report Card: No

Accreditation Certification
URAC
TJC Accreditation, Medicare Approved, Utilization Review,
Pre-Admission Certification, State Licensure, Quality Assurance
Program

Key Personnel
COO . . . . .Karen Cox
karencox@providrscare.net
Dir, Care Utilization . . . . Shirley Sisco-Creed, RN
shirleycreed@providrscare.net
Director, Claims . . . . .Jeanne Hingst
jeannehingst@providrscare.net
Prov Credentialing Spec .Mary Ann Morand
316-683-4111
maryannmorand@providrscare.net
Client Services Rep . . . . .Cheryl Tibbetts
Infomation Systems Admin. . . . . .Nikki Sade
nikkisade@providrscare.net
Dir, Provider Services . . . . .Marsha Fisher
316-683-4111
marshafisher@providrscare.net

Specialty Managed Care Partners
Enters into Contracts with Regional Business Coalitions: No

Employer References
Western Resources, Kansas Health Insurance Association,
Medicalodges, County of Reno Kansas, National Cooperative of
Refineries Association

---

452 Unicare: Kansas
825 Kansas Avenue
Suite 101
Topeka, KS 67214
Toll-Free: 877-864-2273
www.unicare.com
Secondary Address: 327 North Hillside Road, Wichita, KS 67214
Subsidiary of: WellPoint
For Profit Organization: Yes

Year Founded: 1995
Total Enrollment: 145,000
Healthplan and Services Defined
PLAN TYPE: HMO/PPO
Model Type: Network
Benefits Offered: Behavioral Health, Chiropractic, Complementary
Medicine, Dental, Disease Management, Home Care, Inpatient
SNF, Long-Term Care, Physical Therapy, Podiatry, Prescription,
Psychiatric, Transplant, Vision, Wellness, Life, LTD, STD

Type of Coverage
Commercial, Individual, Medicare, Supplemental Medicare, Medicaid

Type of Payment Plans Offered
POS

Geographic Areas Served
Illinois: Cook, DuPage, Kane, Kankakee, Kendall, Lake, McHenry,
Will counties. Indiana: Lake, Porter counties

Network Qualifications
Pre-Admission Certification: Yes

Peer Review Type
Utilization Review: Yes
Second Surgical Opinion: Yes
Case Management: Yes

Publishes and Distributes Report Card: Yes

Accreditation Certification
NCQA
TJC Accreditation, Utilization Review, Pre-Admission Certification,
State Licensure, Quality Assurance Program

Key Personnel
CEO . . . . .David Fields
Media Contact . . . . .Tony Felts
317-287-6036
tony.felts@wellpoint.com

Specialty Managed Care Partners
WellPoint Pharmacy Management, WellPoint Dental Services,
WellPoint Behavioral Health
Enters into Contracts with Regional Business Coalitions: Yes

---

453 UnitedHealthCare of Kansas
9900 West 109th Street
Suite 200
Overland Park, KS 66210
Toll-Free: 888-340-9716
Phone: 913-663-6500
www.uhc.com
Subsidiary of: UnitedHealth Group
For Profit Organization: Yes
Total Enrollment: 75,000,000

Healthplan and Services Defined
PLAN TYPE: HMO/PPO

Geographic Areas Served
Statewide

Key Personnel
Media Contact . . . . .Greg Thompson
312-424-6913
gregory_a_thompson@uhc.com

---

454 VSP: Vision Service Plan of Kansas
9393 W 110th Street
Suite 500
Shawnee Mission, KS 66210-1464
Phone: 913-451-6730
Fax: 913-451-6976
webmaster@vsp.com
www.vsp.com
Year Founded: 1955

Number of Primary Care Physicians: 26,000
Total Enrollment: 55,000,000

Healthplan and Services Defined
  PLAN TYPE: Vision
  Plan Specialty: Vision
  Benefits Offered: Vision

Type of Payment Plans Offered
  Capitated

Geographic Areas Served
  Statewide

Network Qualifications
  Pre-Admission Certification: Yes

Peer Review Type
  Utilization Review: Yes

Accreditation Certification
  Utilization Review, Quality Assurance Program

Key Personnel
  Manager . . . . .Susan Young

Health Insurance Coverage Status and Type of Coverage by Age

Category	All Persons		Under 18 years		Under 65 years		65 years and over	
	Number	%	Number	%	Number	%	Number	%
Total population	4,292	-	1,017	-	3,747	-	545	-
Covered by some type of health insurance	3,653 (62)	85.1 (1.2)	948 (14)	93.2 (1.2)	3,110 (75)	83.0 (1.4)	543 (43)	99.6 (0.3)
Covered by private health insurance	2,724 (122)	63.5 (2.7)	598 (39)	58.8 (3.6)	2,391 (120)	63.8 (2.9)	333 (32)	61.0 (4.2)
Employment based	2,430 (112)	56.6 (2.4)	569 (37)	56.0 (3.5)	2,213 (111)	59.1 (2.6)	218 (26)	39.9 (3.7)
Own employment based	1,326 (58)	30.9 (1.3)	2 (2)	0.2 (0.2)	1,157 (56)	30.9 (1.3)	170 (21)	31.1 (3.1)
Direct purchase	300 (47)	7.0 (1.1)	31 (12)	3.1 (1.1)	175 (34)	4.7 (0.9)	125 (22)	23.0 (3.9)
Covered by government health insurance	1,531 (81)	35.7 (2.0)	447 (36)	44.0 (3.7)	1,003 (75)	26.8 (2.0)	528 (43)	96.9 (1.0)
Covered by Medicaid	821 (69)	19.1 (1.6)	420 (38)	41.3 (3.8)	759 (66)	20.3 (1.8)	63 (16)	11.5 (2.6)
Also by private insurance	183 (33)	4.3 (0.8)	79 (15)	7.7 (1.5)	166 (34)	4.4 (0.9)	17 (6)	3.1 (1.0)
Covered by Medicare	679 (47)	15.8 (1.1)	9 (4)	0.9 (0.4)	155 (23)	4.1 (0.6)	523 (44)	96.0 (1.3)
Also by private insurance	355 (36)	8.3 (0.9)	0 (0)	0.0 (0.0)	42 (9)	1.1 (0.3)	313 (34)	57.5 (4.5)
Also by Medicaid	106 (18)	2.5 (0.4)	8 (4)	0.8 (0.4)	45 (12)	1.2 (0.3)	60 (15)	11.0 (2.4)
Covered by military health care	226 (32)	5.3 (0.7)	37 (9)	3.7 (0.9)	171 (27)	4.6 (0.7)	55 (13)	10.0 (2.2)
Not covered at any time during the year	640 (52)	14.9 (1.2)	69 (12)	6.8 (1.2)	637 (52)	17.0 (1.4)	2 (2)	0.4 (0.3)

Note: Numbers in thousands; figures cover 2010; standard error appears in parenthesis; (b) base less than 75,000; (x) not applicable
Source: U.S. Census Bureau, Current Population Survey, 2011 Annual Social and Economic Supplement. Table HI05. Health Insurance Coverage Status and Type of Coverage by State and Age for All People: 2010

Kentucky

455 Aetna Health of Kentucky

Partnered with eHealthInsurance Services Inc.

456 Anthem Blue Cross & Blue Shield of Kentucky

9901 Linn Station Road
Louisville, KY 40223
Toll-Free: 800-880-2583
Phone: 502-889-4600
www.anthem.com
Secondary Address: 1945 Scottsville Road, Bowling Green, KY 42104
Non-Profit Organization: Yes
Year Founded: 1999
Number of Affiliated Hospitals: 117
Number of Primary Care Physicians: 2,212
Number of Referral/Specialty Physicians: 3,952
Total Enrollment: 894,531
State Enrollment: 63,698

Healthplan and Services Defined
  PLAN TYPE: HMO
  Model Type: Network, PHO
  Benefits Offered: Dental, Disease Management, Prescription, Vision, Wellness, Life

Type of Coverage
  Individual, Medicare, Supplemental Medicare

Type of Payment Plans Offered
  DFFS, FFS, Combination FFS & DFFS

Geographic Areas Served
  Statewide

Subscriber Information
  Average Annual Deductible Per Subscriber:
    Employee Only (Self): $500
    Employee & 2 Family Members: $1000
  Average Subscriber Co-Payment:
    Primary Care Physician: 30%
    Non-Network Physician: 50%
    Prescription Drugs: $15/$500 max annual
    Hospital ER: 30%

Network Qualifications
  Pre-Admission Certification: Yes

Peer Review Type
  Utilization Review: Yes
  Case Management: Yes

Publishes and Distributes Report Card: Yes

Accreditation Certification
  URAC
  TJC Accreditation, Medicare Approved, Utilization Review, Pre-Admission Certification, State Licensure, Quality Assurance Program

457 Bluegrass Family Health

651 Perimeter Drive
Suite 300
Lexington, KY 40517
Toll-Free: 800-787-2680
Phone: 859-269-4475
Fax: 859-335-3700
cservice@bgfh.com
www.bgfh.com
Secondary Address: 2630 Elm Hill Pike, Suite 110, Nashville, TN 37214
Subsidiary of: Baptist Health Care Systems

Non-Profit Organization: Yes
Year Founded: 1993
Number of Affiliated Hospitals: 40
Number of Primary Care Physicians: 764
Number of Referral/Specialty Physicians: 1,000
Total Enrollment: 136,472
State Enrollment: 65,428

Healthplan and Services Defined
  PLAN TYPE: HMO/PPO
  Other Type: POS
  Model Type: Network
  Plan Specialty: ASO, Behavioral Health, Dental, EPO, MSO, PBM, Vision
  Benefits Offered: Chiropractic, Disease Management, Home Care, Physical Therapy, Podiatry, Prescription, Transplant, Wellness

Type of Coverage
  Commercial

Type of Payment Plans Offered
  POS, Combination FFS & DFFS

Geographic Areas Served
  Kentucky, Indiana and Tenessee

Peer Review Type
  Second Surgical Opinion: Yes
  Case Management: Yes

Publishes and Distributes Report Card: Yes

Accreditation Certification
  TJC Accreditation, Medicare Approved, Utilization Review, Pre-Admission Certification, State Licensure, Quality Assurance Program

Key Personnel
  President and CEO . . . . James S Fritz
    859-269-4475
  CFO . . . . Art Lowe
    859-269-4475
  CMO . . . . Garry Ramsey
    859-269-4475
  Claims Director . . . . Leonard Hornsley
    859-269-4475
    leonard.hornsley@bgfh.com
  Network Contracting Dir . . . . Chris Bulger
    859-269-4475
    chris.bulger@bgfh.com
  Credentialing . . . . Barbara Farrell
    859-269-4475
  VP, COO . . . . Carl Felix
  Marketing Director . . . . Nancy Atkins
    859-269-4475
    nancy.atkins@bgfh.com
  Info Services Director . . . . Preston Gorman
    859-269-4475
    preston.gorman@bgfh.com
  Provider Svs Director . . . . Chris Bulger
    859-269-4475
    chris.bulger@bgfh.com

458 CHA Health

Acquired by Humana

459 CIGNA HealthCare of Kentucky

1000 Corporate Center Drive
Suite 500
Franklin, TN 37067
Toll-Free: 866-438-2446
Phone: 615-595-3383
Fax: 615-595-3287
www.cigna.com
For Profit Organization: Yes

Healthplan and Services Defined
  PLAN TYPE: HMO

Type of Coverage
  Commercial

460 Coventry Medicare

PO Box 7154
Coventry Health Care, Inc.
London, KY 40742-7154
Toll-Free: 866-386-2330
Fax: 866-386-2329
http://coventry-medicare.coventryhealthcare.com
Secondary Address: Coventry Health Care, Inc., 3200 Highland
  Avenue, Downers Grove, IL 60515
Subsidiary of: Coventry Health Care, Inc

Healthplan and Services Defined
  PLAN TYPE: HMO/PPO
  Other Type: POS
  Benefits Offered: Chiropractic, Dental, Home Care, Inpatient SNF,
    Podiatry, Prescription, Vision, Wellness

Type of Coverage
  Medicare, Supplemental Medicare

Type of Payment Plans Offered
  FFS

Geographic Areas Served
  Kentucky

Subscriber Information
  Average Subscriber Co-Payment:
    Primary Care Physician: Varies
    Hospital ER: Varies
    Home Health Care: Varies
    Home Health Care Max. Days/Visits Covered: Varies
    Nursing Home: Varies
    Nursing Home Max. Days/Visits Covered: Varies

461 Delta Dental of Kentucky

10100 Linn Station Rd
Suite 700
Louisville, KY 40223-3861
Toll-Free: 800-955-2030
Phone: 502-736-5000
Fax: 502-736-4839
marketing@deltadental.com
www.deltadentalky.com
Non-Profit Organization: Yes
Year Founded: 1966
Total Enrollment: 54,000,000
State Enrollment: 570,000

Healthplan and Services Defined
  PLAN TYPE: Dental
  Other Type: Dental PPO
  Model Type: IPA
  Plan Specialty: Dental
  Benefits Offered: Dental

Type of Coverage
  Commercial

Type of Payment Plans Offered
  DFFS

Geographic Areas Served
  Statewide

Subscriber Information
  Average Monthly Fee Per Subscriber
    (Employee + Employer Contribution):
      Employee Only (Self): $13.50
      Employee & 1 Family Member: $27.00
      Employee & 2 Family Members: $42.75

Average Annual Deductible Per Subscriber:
  Employee Only (Self): $25.00
  Employee & 1 Family Member: $50.00
  Employee & 2 Family Members: $75.00

Network Qualifications
  Pre-Admission Certification: No

Peer Review Type
  Utilization Review: Yes
  Second Surgical Opinion: Yes
  Case Management: Yes

Publishes and Distributes Report Card: Yes

Key Personnel
  CEO . . . . .Clifford Maesaka
  CFO . . . . .Curt Ladig
  VP, Provider Relations . . . . .Angie Nenni
  VP, Marketing . . . . .Stephen Day
  VP, Public & Govt Affairs . . . . .Jeff Album
    415-972-8418

Specialty Managed Care Partners
  Enters into Contracts with Regional Business Coalitions: Yes

462 eHealthInsurance Services Inc.

11919 Foundation Place
Gold River, CA 95670
Toll-Free: 800-977-8860
info@ehealthinsurance.com
www.e.healthinsurance.com
Year Founded: 1997

Healthplan and Services Defined
  PLAN TYPE: HMO/PPO
  Benefits Offered: Dental, Life, STD

Type of Coverage
  Commercial, Individual, Medicare

Geographic Areas Served
  All 50 states in the USA and District of Columbia

Key Personnel
  Chairman & CEO . . . . .Gary L. Lauer
  EVP/Business & Corp. Dev. .Bruce Telkamp
  EVP/Chief Technology .Dr. Sheldon X. Wang
  SVP & CFO . . . . .Stuart M. Huizinga
  Pres. of eHealth Gov. Sys . . . . .Samuel C. Gibbs
  SVP of Sales & Operations . . . . .Robert S. Hurley
  Director Public Relations . . . . .Nate Purpura
    650-210-3115

463 Humana Health Insurance of Kentucky

Corporate Headquarters
500 West Main Street
Louisville, KY 40202
Toll-Free: 800-486-2620
Phone: 502-580-1000
Fax: 502-318-1451
www.humana.com
For Profit Organization: Yes

Healthplan and Services Defined
  PLAN TYPE: HMO/PPO
  Benefits Offered: Prescription

Type of Coverage
  Commercial, Individual, Supplemental Medicare

Geographic Areas Served
  Kentucky

Subscriber Information
  Average Subscriber Co-Payment:
    Prescription Drugs: $4.00-$30.00

Accreditation Certification
URAC, NCQA

Key Personnel
Chairman/President/CEO . . . . Michael B McCallister
COO . . . . James E Murray
SVP/CFO/Treasurer . . . . James H Bloem
SVP/Chief Strategy Offc . . . . Paul B Kusserow
SVP, Senior Products . . . . Thomas J Liston
SVP, Public Affairs . . . . Heidi S Marqulis
VP, Controller . . . . Steven E McCulley
SVP, General Counsel . . . . Christopher M Todoroff
SVP/Innovation & Mktg Ofc . . . . Raja Rajamannar
SVP/Ch Human Resources Of . . . . Bonita C Hathcock
SVP/Ch Service & Info Ofc . . . . Brian LeClaire
Corp Media Relations . . . . Jim Turner
502-580-3221
jturner2@humana.com

464 Humana Medicare Plan

Humana Corporate Headquarters
500 West Main Street
Louisville, KY 40202
Toll-Free: 800-645-7322
Phone: 502-580-3644
Fax: 502-580-3677
www.humana-medicare.com
For Profit Organization: Yes
Total Enrollment: 4,000,000

Healthplan and Services Defined
PLAN TYPE: Medicare
Benefits Offered: Chiropractic, Dental, Home Care, Inpatient SNF, Physical Therapy, Podiatry, Prescription, Psychiatric, Vision, Wellness

Type of Coverage
Commercial, Individual, Medicare

Geographic Areas Served
Available in multiple states

Subscriber Information
Average Monthly Fee Per Subscriber
(Employee + Employer Contribution):
Employee Only (Self): Varies
Medicare: Varies
Average Annual Deductible Per Subscriber:
Employee Only (Self): Varies
Medicare: Varies
Average Subscriber Co-Payment:
Primary Care Physician: Varies
Non-Network Physician: Varies
Prescription Drugs: Varies
Hospital ER: Varies
Home Health Care: Varies
Home Health Care Max. Days/Visits Covered: Varies
Nursing Home: Varies
Nursing Home Max. Days/Visits Covered: Varies

Accreditation Certification
URAC, NCQA, CORE

Key Personnel
President/CEO . . . . Michael B McCallister
Chief Operating Officer . . . . James E Murray
SVP/CFO and Treasurer . . . . James H Bloem
VP/Chief Actuary . . . . John M Bertko
SVP/CIO. . . . . Bruce J Goodman
SVP/Strategy & Dvlpmnt. . . . . Thomas J Liston
SVP/Government Relations. . . . . Heidi S Marqulis
SVP/Chief Mktg Officer . . . . Steven O Moya
VP Investor Relations. Regina C Nethery

Corporate Communications. . . . . Jeff Blunt
513-826-7094
jblunt@humana.com

465 Meritain Health: Kentucky

1830 Destiny Lane
Suite 108
Bowling Green, KY 42104
Toll-Free: 800-570-6745
Fax: 800-646-9360
sales@meritain.com
www.meritain.com
For Profit Organization: Yes
Year Founded: 1983
Number of Affiliated Hospitals: 110
Number of Primary Care Physicians: 3,467
Number of Referral/Specialty Physicians: 5,720
Total Enrollment: 500,000
State Enrollment: 450,000

Healthplan and Services Defined
PLAN TYPE: PPO
Model Type: Network
Plan Specialty: Dental, Disease Management, Vision, Radiology, UR
Benefits Offered: Prescription
Offers Demand Management Patient Information Service: Yes

Type of Coverage
Commercial

Geographic Areas Served
Nationwide

Subscriber Information
Average Monthly Fee Per Subscriber
(Employee + Employer Contribution):
Employee Only (Self): Varies by plan

Accreditation Certification
URAC
TJC Accreditation, Medicare Approved, Utilization Review, Pre-Admission Certification, State Licensure, Quality Assurance Program

Key Personnel
Regional President . . . . Chris Reef

Average Claim Compensation
Physician's Fees Charged: 78%
Hospital's Fees Charged: 90%

Specialty Managed Care Partners
Express Scripts, LabOne, Interactive Health Solutions

466 Passport Health Plan

305 West Broadway
Third Floor, Fincastle Building
Louisville, KY 40202
Toll-Free: 800-578-0603
Phone: 502-585-7900
www.passporthealthplan.com
Subsidiary of: AmeriHealth Mercy Health Plan
Total Enrollment: 159,730
State Enrollment: 159,730

Healthplan and Services Defined
PLAN TYPE: HMO

Geographic Areas Served
Jefferson, Oldham, Trimble, Carroll, Henry, Shelby, Spencer, Bullitt, Nelson, Washington, Marion, Larue, Hardin, Grayson, Meade, Breckenridge counties

Accreditation Certification
NCQA

Key Personnel

Chairman/CEO . . . . Larry N Cook, MD
Executive Vice President. . . . . Shannon R Turner, JD
Assoc Vice President . . . . Nici C Gaines
VP, Chief Financial Offc. . . . . David A Stanley
VP, Health Plan Operation. . . . . DeDe Davis
VP, Public Affairs. . . . . Jill J Bell
  502-585-7983
  jill.bell@amerihealthmercy.org

467 Preferred Health Plan Inc

9520 Ormsby Station Road
#3
Louisville, KY 40223-5017
Toll-Free: 800-832-8212
Phone: 502-339-7500
Fax: 502-339-8716
www.phpinc.com
For Profit Organization: Yes
Year Founded: 1983
Number of Affiliated Hospitals: 23
Number of Primary Care Physicians: 500
Number of Referral/Specialty Physicians: 1,500
Total Enrollment: 110,000
State Enrollment: 110,000

Healthplan and Services Defined
  PLAN TYPE: PPO
  Other Type: TPA
  Model Type: Network
  Plan Specialty: ASO, Dental, PBM, Vision, UR
  Benefits Offered: TPA Services

Type of Coverage
  Commercial

Type of Payment Plans Offered
  DFFS

Geographic Areas Served
  Nationwide

Network Qualifications
  Pre-Admission Certification: Yes

Publishes and Distributes Report Card: No

Accreditation Certification
  Medicare Approved, Utilization Review, Pre-Admission
    Certification, State Licensure, Quality Assurance Program

Key Personnel
  CEO . . . . Rick Mitchum
    rickm@phpinc.com
  President. . . . . Paula Barr
  Executive Director. . . . . Bernard Tamme
  Dir, Finance . . . . Dennis Stovall
  Dir, Operations . . . . Mary Stivers
  Dir, Marketing . . . . Rich McAuliffe

Specialty Managed Care Partners
  Enters into Contracts with Regional Business Coalitions: No

468 Rural Carrier Benefit Plan

PO Box 7404
London, KY 40742
Toll-Free: 800-638-8432
www.rcbp.coventryhealthcare.com
Subsidiary of: Coventry Health Care

Healthplan and Services Defined
  PLAN TYPE: PPO
  Benefits Offered: Disease Management, Vision, Wellness, Cancer
    Treatment, Kidney Dialysis, 24-hour Nurse Line, Travel
    Assistance Program, Healthy Maternity, Lab One

Type of Coverage
  Commercial, Individual

Type of Payment Plans Offered
  Capitated, FFS

Geographic Areas Served
  specific groups

Subscriber Information
  Average Monthly Fee Per Subscriber
    (Employee + Employer Contribution):
      Employee Only (Self): $105.71
      Employee & 2 Family Members: $187.89
  Average Annual Deductible Per Subscriber:
      Employee & 2 Family Members: $350.00
  Average Subscriber Co-Payment:
      Primary Care Physician: 10%
      Prescription Drugs: $20 - $30
      Hospital ER: $0

469 UnitedHealthCare of Kentucky

2424 Harrodsburg Road
Suite 300
Lexington, KY 40503
Toll-Free: 800-495-5285
Phone: 859-260-3600
Fax: 859-260-3619
www.uhc.com
Secondary Address: 301 North Huntsborne Parkway, Suite 100,
  Louisville, KY 40222, 800-307-4959
Subsidiary of: UnitedHealth Group
For Profit Organization: Yes
Year Founded: 1986
Number of Affiliated Hospitals: 66
Number of Primary Care Physicians: 1,208
Number of Referral/Specialty Physicians: 1,983
Total Enrollment: 75,000,000
State Enrollment: 135,106

Healthplan and Services Defined
  PLAN TYPE: HMO/PPO
  Model Type: IPA, Network
  Plan Specialty: Dental, Vision
  Benefits Offered: Chiropractic, Dental, Disease Management,
    Prescription, Vision, Wellness, Life, LTD, STD
  Offers Demand Management Patient Information Service: Yes

Type of Coverage
  Catastrophic Illness Benefit: Maximum $1M

Type of Payment Plans Offered
  POS

Geographic Areas Served
  Central Kentucky: 99 counties

Subscriber Information
  Average Monthly Fee Per Subscriber
    (Employee + Employer Contribution):
      Employee Only (Self): $139.00
      Employee & 1 Family Member: $282.00
      Employee & 2 Family Members: $445.00
      Medicare: $0
  Average Annual Deductible Per Subscriber:
      Employee Only (Self): $0
      Employee & 1 Family Member: $0
      Employee & 2 Family Members: $0
  Average Subscriber Co-Payment:
      Primary Care Physician: $10.00
      Non-Network Physician: Not covered
      Prescription Drugs: $7.00
      Hospital ER: $50.00
      Home Health Care: 20%
      Nursing Home: Not covered

Network Qualifications
Pre-Admission Certification: Yes

Peer Review Type
Utilization Review: Yes
Second Surgical Opinion: No
Case Management: Yes

Publishes and Distributes Report Card: Yes

Accreditation Certification
TJC Accreditation, Utilization Review, Pre-Admission Certification,
State Licensure, Quality Assurance Program

Key Personnel
President . . . . Walter W Wakefield
CFO . . . . Richard Dunlop
Director Communications. . . . . Mark Lindsay
Media Contact . . . . Greg Thompson
312-424-6913
gregory_a_thompson@uhc.com

Average Claim Compensation
Physician's Fees Charged: 1%
Hospital's Fees Charged: 1%

Specialty Managed Care Partners
Enters into Contracts with Regional Business Coalitions: Yes

Health Insurance Coverage Status and Type of Coverage by Age

Category	All Persons		Under 18 years		Under 65 years		65 years and over	
	Number	%	Number	%	Number	%	Number	%
Total population	4,432	-	1,166	-	3,901	-	531	-
Covered by some type of health insurance	3,545 (65)	80.0 (1.2)	1,061 (21)	91.0 (1.8)	3,025 (73)	77.6 (1.4)	520 (26)	97.9 (1.2)
Covered by private health insurance	2,402 (111)	54.2 (2.3)	529 (43)	45.4 (3.7)	2,129 (107)	54.6 (2.3)	273 (31)	51.4 (6.0)
Employment based	2,067 (111)	46.6 (2.3)	474 (39)	40.6 (3.4)	1,906 (99)	48.9 (2.2)	161 (32)	30.2 (6.5)
Own employment based	1,039 (70)	23.4 (1.5)	2 (2)	0.1 (0.1)	909 (52)	23.3 (1.2)	130 (27)	24.4 (5.4)
Direct purchase	367 (35)	8.3 (0.8)	56 (14)	4.8 (1.2)	244 (34)	6.3 (0.9)	123 (22)	23.2 (3.7)
Covered by government health insurance	1,558 (57)	35.2 (1.4)	612 (37)	52.5 (3.3)	1,087 (52)	27.9 (1.4)	471 (29)	88.7 (2.3)
Covered by Medicaid	912 (47)	20.6 (1.1)	572 (37)	49.0 (3.2)	860 (48)	22.1 (1.3)	52 (10)	9.8 (1.8)
Also by private insurance	102 (24)	2.3 (0.5)	63 (18)	5.4 (1.6)	99 (24)	2.5 (0.6)	3 (2)	0.5 (0.3)
Covered by Medicare	636 (28)	14.3 (0.6)	11 (5)	0.9 (0.4)	164 (21)	4.2 (0.5)	471 (29)	88.7 (2.3)
Also by private insurance	262 (30)	5.9 (0.7)	0 (0)	0.0 (0.0)	38 (13)	1.0 (0.3)	224 (29)	42.2 (5.5)
Also by Medicaid	104 (14)	2.3 (0.3)	0 (0)	0.0 (0.0)	52 (10)	1.3 (0.2)	52 (10)	9.8 (1.8)
Covered by military health care	165 (30)	3.7 (0.7)	43 (13)	3.6 (1.2)	147 (29)	3.8 (0.7)	18 (9)	3.5 (1.6)
Not covered at any time during the year	886 (52)	20.0 (1.2)	105 (22)	9.0 (1.8)	875 (50)	22.4 (1.4)	11 (6)	2.1 (1.2)

Note: Numbers in thousands; figures cover 2010; standard error appears in parenthesis; (b) base less than 75,000; (x) not applicable
Source: U.S. Census Bureau, Current Population Survey, 2011 Annual Social and Economic Supplement. Table HI05. Health Insurance Coverage Status and Type of Coverage by State and Age for All People: 2010

Louisiana

470 Aetna Health of Louisiana
151 Farmington Avenue
Hartford, CT 06156
Toll-Free: 866-582-9629
www.aetna.com
For Profit Organization: Yes
Total Enrollment: 11,596,230

Healthplan and Services Defined
PLAN TYPE: PPO
Other Type: POS
Plan Specialty: EPO
Benefits Offered: Dental, Disease Management, Long-Term Care, Prescription, Wellness, Life, LTD, STD

Type of Coverage
Commercial, Individual

Type of Payment Plans Offered
POS, FFS

Geographic Areas Served
Statewide

Key Personnel
CEO . . . . .Ronald A Williams
President . . . . .Mark T Bertolini
SVP, General Counsel . . . . .William J Casazza
EVP, CFO . . . . .Joseph M Zubretsky
Head, M&A Integration . . . . .Kay Mooney
SVP, Marketing . . . . .Robert E Mead
Chief Medical Officer . . . . .Lonny Reisman, MD
SVP, Human Resources . . . . .Elease E Wright
SVP, CIO . . . . .Meg McCarthy

471 Arcadian Community Care
Pierremont Office Park III
920 Pierremont Road, Suite 506
Shreveport, LA 71106
Toll-Free: 888-261-1061
Phone: 318-865-1061
Fax: 318-865-1232
www.arcadiancommunitycare.com
Subsidiary of: Arcadian Health Plans

Healthplan and Services Defined
PLAN TYPE: Medicare

Type of Coverage
Medicare

472 Blue Cross & Blue Shield of Louisiana
5525 Reitz Avenue
PO Box 98029
Baton Rouge, LA 70898-9029
Toll-Free: 800-599-2583
Phone: 225-295-3307
Fax: 225-295-2054
help@bcbsla.com
www.bcbsla.com
Secondary Address: 4508 Coliseum Blvd, Suite A, Alexandria, LA 71303
For Profit Organization: Yes
Year Founded: 1933
Number of Affiliated Hospitals: 39
Number of Primary Care Physicians: 962
Number of Referral/Specialty Physicians: 2,219
Total Enrollment: 1,172,000
State Enrollment: 1,172,000

Healthplan and Services Defined
PLAN TYPE: HMO/PPO
Model Type: Network
Benefits Offered: Disease Management, Prescription, Wellness

Type of Coverage
Catastrophic Illness Benefit: Maximum $2M

Geographic Areas Served
New Orleans, Baton Rouge and Shreveport Metropolitan areas

Subscriber Information
Average Subscriber Co-Payment:
Primary Care Physician: 10%/20%
Home Health Care: Varies

Network Qualifications
Pre-Admission Certification: Yes

Peer Review Type
Utilization Review: Yes

Publishes and Distributes Report Card: No

Accreditation Certification
NCQA
TJC Accreditation, Medicare Approved, Utilization Review, Pre-Admission Certification, State Licensure, Quality Assurance Program

Key Personnel
President & CEO . . . . .Mike Reitz
SVP/CIO . . . . .Ob Soonthornsima
EVP/COO/CFO . . . . .Peggy Scott
VP, Benefits Admin/Claims . . . . .Karen Lagrone
VP, Network Admin . . . . .Dawn Cantrell
SVP, Healthcare Sys Qual . . . . .Sabrina Heltz
VP, Chief Actuary . . . . .Brian Small
VP, Pharmacy Services .Milam Ford
SVP, Chief Mktg Officer . . . . .Brian Keller
VP, Customer Engagement . . . . .Laura Landry
Interim Chief Medical Ofc . . . . .Dwight Brower, MD
SVP, Human Resources . . . . .Todd Schexnayder
VP Healthcare Informatics . . . . .Barry Zajac
VP, Benefits Admin . . . . .Jacqueline Addison
VP, Sales . . . . .Gregory Cross
VP, Corp Communications . . . . .John Maginnis
225-295-2405
corporate.communications@bcbsla.com
VP, Compliance, Privacy . . . . .Darrell Langlois

Specialty Managed Care Partners
Enters into Contracts with Regional Business Coalitions: Yes

473 Calais Health
5745 Essen Lane
Suite 220
Baton Rouge, LA 70810
Toll-Free: 800-572-6983
Phone: 225-765-6570
Fax: 225-765-9463
webmaster@calaishealth.com
www.calaishealth.com
Subsidiary of: Calais Health
For Profit Organization: Yes
Year Founded: 2000
Number of Affiliated Hospitals: 11
Number of Referral/Specialty Physicians: 99
Total Enrollment: 137,000

Healthplan and Services Defined
PLAN TYPE: Multiple
Model Type: Network
Plan Specialty: Behavioral Health, Worker's Compensation, UR
Benefits Offered: Behavioral Health, Disease Management, Psychiatric, EAP

Type of Payment Plans Offered
POS, Capitated, FFS

Geographic Areas Served
Louisiana, Oklahoma and Mississippi

Network Qualifications
Pre-Admission Certification: Yes

Peer Review Type
Utilization Review: Yes
Case Management: Yes

Accreditation Certification
State Licensure

Key Personnel
Mgr Information Services . . . . Ted Nguyen
    225-765-6829
VP/ Health Services. . . . . Helen Granger
Director CCM/FMC. . . . . Laura Hebert
    225-765-6882
Business Development . . . . Ann Sellars
CFO . . . . Michael Whittington
Human Resources Director. Leslie Yander
    225-765-6827

Employer References
City of East Baton Rouge Parish, East Baton Rouge Parish School
    System, Our Lady of the Lake Hospital, The Advocate/Capitol
    City Press, Woman's Hospital

---

474   CIGNA HealthCare of Louisiana

2700 Post Oak Blvd
Suite 700
Houston, TX 77056
Toll-Free: 866-438-2446
Phone: 713-576-4300
Fax: 866-530-3585
www.cigna.com
For Profit Organization: Yes

Healthplan and Services Defined
    PLAN TYPE: HMO

Type of Coverage
Commercial

---

475   Coventry Health Care of Louisiana

3838 North Causeway
Suite 3350
Metairie, LA 70002
Toll-Free: 800-341-6613
Fax: 504-828-6433
http://chclouisiana.coventryhealthcare.com
Secondary Address: 1720 South Sykes Drive, Bismarck, ND 58504
Subsidiary of: Coventry Health Care
For Profit Organization: Yes
Number of Primary Care Physicians: 2,000
Total Enrollment: 30,000
State Enrollment: 71,716

Healthplan and Services Defined
    PLAN TYPE: HMO
    Benefits Offered: Disease Management, Wellness

Geographic Areas Served
Louisiana

Key Personnel
CEO . . . . Michael Kasper
COO . . . . George Bucher
CMO . . . . Lynn Williamson, MD
Provider Relations . . . . Clay Bittner
Marketing. . . . . Carson Meehan
CFO . . . . Angela Meoli

---

476   Delta Dental Insurance Company

1130 Sanctuary Parkway
Suite 600
Alpharetta, GA 30004
Toll-Free: 888-858-5252
Phone: 770-645-8700
Fax: 770-518-4757
www.deltadentalins.com
Mailing Address: PO Box 1809, Alpharetta, GA 30023-1809
Non-Profit Organization: Yes
Number of Primary Care Physicians: 198,000
Total Enrollment: 54,000,000

Healthplan and Services Defined
    PLAN TYPE: Dental
    Other Type: Dental PPO
    Plan Specialty: Dental
    Benefits Offered: Dental

Type of Coverage
Commercial

Type of Payment Plans Offered
POS, DFFS, FFS

Geographic Areas Served
Statewide

Key Personnel
CEO. . . . . Gary D Radine
VP, Public & Govt Affairs . . . . Jeff Album
    415-972-8418
Dir/Media & Public Affair . . . . Elizabeth Risberg
    415-972-8423

---

477   DINA Dental Plans

11969 Bricksome Avenue
Baton Rouge, LA 70816
Toll-Free: 800-376-3462
Phone: 225-291-3172
Fax: 225-292-3075
info@dinadental.com
www.dinadental.com
For Profit Organization: Yes
Year Founded: 1978
Total Enrollment: 30,000

Healthplan and Services Defined
    PLAN TYPE: Dental
    Model Type: Group, Individual
    Plan Specialty: Dental
    Benefits Offered: Dental

Type of Coverage
Commercial, Individual

Geographic Areas Served
Statewide

Subscriber Information
Average Monthly Fee Per Subscriber
    (Employee + Employer Contribution):
        Employee Only (Self): $13.00-20.00
        Employee & 1 Family Member: $21.00-38.00
        Employee & 2 Family Members: $28.00-60.00
        Medicare: $30.00
Average Annual Deductible Per Subscriber:
        Employee Only (Self): $50.00
        Employee & 1 Family Member: $50.00
        Employee & 2 Family Members: $50.00

Network Qualifications
Pre-Admission Certification: Yes

Peer Review Type
Second Surgical Opinion: Yes

Publishes and Distributes Report Card: No

Key Personnel

President . . . . .James Taylor
CFO . . . . .Patrick Stoner
COO. . . . . .Rick Barrett

Specialty Managed Care Partners

Enters into Contracts with Regional Business Coalitions: No

---

478 eHealthInsurance Services Inc.

11919 Foundation Place
Gold River, CA 95670
Toll-Free: 800-977-8860
info@ehealthinsurance.com
www.e.healthinsurance.com
Year Founded: 1997

Healthplan and Services Defined
PLAN TYPE: HMO/PPO
Benefits Offered: Dental, Life, STD

Type of Coverage
Commercial, Individual, Medicare

Geographic Areas Served
All 50 states in the USA and District of Columbia

Key Personnel

Chairman & CEO . . . . .Gary L. Lauer
EVP/Business & Corp. Dev. .Bruce Telkamp
EVP/Chief Technology . . . . .Dr. Sheldon X. Wang
SVP & CFO . . . . .Stuart M. Huizinga
Pres. of eHealth Gov. Sys . . . . .Samuel C. Gibbs
SVP of Sales & Operations . . . . .Robert S. Hurley
Director Public Relations. .Nate Purpura
650-210-3115

---

479 Health Plus of Louisiana

2219 Line Avenue
Shreveport, LA 71104-2128
Toll-Free: 800-331-5055
Phone: 318-212-8800
Fax: 318-676-3372
webmaster@wkhealthplus.com
www.wkhealthplus.com
Mailing Address: PO Box 32625, Shreveport, LA 71130-2625
Subsidiary of: Willis-Knighton Health System
Non-Profit Organization: Yes
Year Founded: 1994
Physician Owned Organization: Yes
Total Enrollment: 30,000
State Enrollment: 30,000

Healthplan and Services Defined
PLAN TYPE: HMO
Model Type: IPA
Benefits Offered: Prescription
Offers Demand Management Patient Information Service: Yes

Type of Payment Plans Offered
POS

Geographic Areas Served
Northern Louisiana

Subscriber Information
Average Monthly Fee Per Subscriber
(Employee + Employer Contribution):
Employee Only (Self): $0
Employee & 1 Family Member: $0
Employee & 2 Family Members: $0
Medicare: $0

Peer Review Type
Case Management: Yes

Accreditation Certification
TJC, NCQA

Key Personnel

President and CEO . . . . .Patrick Bicknell
VP/CFO . . . . .Larry Knighton
Business Office Director . . . . .Patty Fuller
Claims/Operations Manager .Sandy Brown
Compliance Director . . . . .Jim Frantz
Business Office Assistant . . . . .Owen Rigby
Member Relations. . . . . .Teri Graves
Human Resources Manager .Debbie Forston
Dir, Sales & Marketing. . . . . .Scott Johnson
VP, Chief Medical Officer .Carey Allison
Medical Director . . . . .Bendel Johnson
Director Medical Staff. . . . . .Marion Morrison
Credential Analyst . . . . .Cynthia Blanchard
Credential Coordinator .Camissa Decker
Peer Review Coordinator . . . . .Joan Rigby

Specialty Managed Care Partners
Enters into Contracts with Regional Business Coalitions: Yes

---

480 Humana Health Insurance of Louisiana

1 Galleria Boulevard
Suite 1000
Metairie, LA 70001
Toll-Free: 800-284-8110
Phone: 504-219-6600
Fax: 504-219-5142
www.humana.com
Secondary Address: 910 Pierremont Road, Suite 410, Shreveport, LA 71106
For Profit Organization: Yes
Year Founded: 1985
Physician Owned Organization: Yes
Federally Qualified: Yes
Number of Affiliated Hospitals: 60
Number of Primary Care Physicians: 3,500
Number of Referral/Specialty Physicians: 2,427
Total Enrollment: 142,000
State Enrollment: 155,722

Healthplan and Services Defined
PLAN TYPE: HMO/PPO
Model Type: IPA, mixed
Benefits Offered: Behavioral Health, Chiropractic, Disease
Management, Home Care, Inpatient SNF, Physical Therapy,
Podiatry, Prescription, Psychiatric, Transplant, Vision, Wellness

Type of Coverage
Commercial, Individual, Indemnity, Medicare
Catastrophic Illness Benefit: Unlimited

Type of Payment Plans Offered
POS, Combination FFS & DFFS

Geographic Areas Served
Louisiana, excluding Monroe

Subscriber Information
Average Monthly Fee Per Subscriber
(Employee + Employer Contribution):
Employee Only (Self): $189.31
Employee & 1 Family Member: $378.62
Employee & 2 Family Members: $530.07
Average Subscriber Co-Payment:
Primary Care Physician: $15.00
Prescription Drugs: $10/$25/$40
Home Health Care Max. Days/Visits Covered: 60 days

Network Qualifications
Pre-Admission Certification: Yes

Peer Review Type
Utilization Review: Yes

Second Surgical Opinion: Yes
Case Management: Yes

Publishes and Distributes Report Card: Yes

Accreditation Certification
URAC, NCQA, CORE
Medicare Approved, Utilization Review, Pre-Admission
Certification, State Licensure, Quality Assurance Program

Key Personnel
President and CEO . . . . Hassan Rifaat

Specialty Managed Care Partners
CMS Healthcare, Medimpact
Enters into Contracts with Regional Business Coalitions: Yes
Chamber of Commerce

Employer References
State Of Louisiana, Exxon-Mobil, Shell, Chevron, Sears

---

481 Meritain Health: Louisiana

PO Box 70100
Shreveport, LA 71137
Toll-Free: 800-258-2657
Fax: 318-424-9702
sales@meritain.com
www.meritain.com
For Profit Organization: Yes
Year Founded: 1983
Number of Affiliated Hospitals: 110
Number of Primary Care Physicians: 3,467
Number of Referral/Specialty Physicians: 5,720
Total Enrollment: 500,000
State Enrollment: 450,000

Healthplan and Services Defined
PLAN TYPE: PPO
Model Type: Network
Plan Specialty: Dental, Disease Management, Vision, Radiology, UR
Benefits Offered: Prescription
Offers Demand Management Patient Information Service: Yes

Type of Coverage
Commercial

Geographic Areas Served
Nationwide

Subscriber Information
Average Monthly Fee Per Subscriber
(Employee + Employer Contribution):
Employee Only (Self): Varies by plan

Accreditation Certification
URAC
TJC Accreditation, Medicare Approved, Utilization Review,
Pre-Admission Certification, State Licensure, Quality Assurance
Program

Average Claim Compensation
Physician's Fees Charged: 78%
Hospital's Fees Charged: 90%

Specialty Managed Care Partners
Express Scripts, LabOne, Interactive Health Solutions

---

482 Peoples Health

3838 North Causeway Blvd
Suite 2200, Three Lakeway Center
Metairie, LA 70002
Toll-Free: 800-631-8443
Phone: 504-849-4500
Fax: 504-464-1015
www.peopleshealth.com
Year Founded: 1994
Physician Owned Organization: Yes

Total Enrollment: 42,000

Healthplan and Services Defined
PLAN TYPE: Medicare
Other Type: HMO-POS

Type of Coverage
Medicare, Supplemental Medicare

Geographic Areas Served
Choices 65 (HMO): Jefferson, Orleans, Plaquemines, St. Tammany;
Choices Plus (HMO-POS): Ascension, East Baton Rouge, Livingston,
St. Bernard, St. Charles, St. James, St. John, West Baton Rouge;
Choice Select (HMO-POS): Tangipahoa, Washington; SecureHealth
(HMO SNP): Ascension, East Baton Rouge, Jefferson, Livingston,
Orleans, Plaquemines, St. Bernard, St. Charles, St. James, St.
Tammany, Tangipahoa, Washington, West Baton Rouge

Key Personnel
Chief Executive Officer. . . . . Carol A Soloman
Chief Operating Officer . . . . Warren Murrell
Chief Financial Officer . . . . Kim Eller
VP, Plan & Development . . . . Macon Moore
VP, Network Development . . . . Janice Ortega
VP, Audit & Compliance. . . . . Michael J Robert
Asst VP, Decision Support . . . . Kristie Marino
Chief Marketing Officer . . . . Mike Putiak
Medical Director Benefits . . . . Frank N Deus, MD
VP, Medical Affairs. . . . . Kevin J Roache, MD
Director, Human Resources . . . . Greg Ruppert
Chief Information Officer . . . . Colin Hulin
Director, Communications. . . . . Suzanne M Whitaker, APR
504-681-8978
suzanne.whitaker@peopleshealth.com

---

483 Tenet Choices

Acquired by Peoples Health

---

484 UnitedHealthCare of Louisiana

3838 N. Causeway Boulevard
Suite 2600
Metairie, LA 70002
Toll-Free: 800-826-1981
Phone: 225-923-0550
Fax: 504-849-1540
www.uhc.com
Subsidiary of: UnitedHealth Group
For Profit Organization: Yes
Year Founded: 1986
Number of Affiliated Hospitals: 42
Number of Primary Care Physicians: 356
Number of Referral/Specialty Physicians: 877
Total Enrollment: 75,000,000
State Enrollment: 272,972

Healthplan and Services Defined
PLAN TYPE: HMO/PPO
Model Type: IPA
Benefits Offered: Disease Management, Prescription, Wellness

Geographic Areas Served
Ascension, Assumption, East Baton Rouge, East Feliciana, Iberville,
Jefferson, LaFourche, Livingston, Orleans, Plaquemines, Point
Coupee, St. Bernard, St. Charles, St. Helena, St. James, St. Tammany,
Tangipahoa, Terrabona, West Baton Rouge, West Feliciana

Subscriber Information
Average Monthly Fee Per Subscriber
(Employee + Employer Contribution):
Employee Only (Self): $129.45
Employee & 1 Family Member: $261.04
Employee & 2 Family Members: $422.40
Average Annual Deductible Per Subscriber:
Employee Only (Self): $5.00

Average Subscriber Co-Payment:
Primary Care Physician: $10.00
Prescription Drugs: $10.00
Hospital ER: $50.00

Network Qualifications
Pre-Admission Certification: Yes

Peer Review Type
Utilization Review: Yes

Publishes and Distributes Report Card: No

Accreditation Certification
TJC Accreditation, Medicare Approved, Utilization Review,
Pre-Admission Certification, State Licensure, Quality Assurance
Program

Key Personnel
CFO....................................Steve Cunningham
Marketing ....Glen Golemi
Medical Affairs ....Debbie Bates, MD
Member Services............................Kathy Magby
Information Systems ....Heidi Chapman
Provider Services ....Charles Brewer
Media Contact.............................Roger Rollman
roger_f_rollman@uhc.com

Specialty Managed Care Partners
Enters into Contracts with Regional Business Coalitions: No

---

485 Vantage Health Plan
130 DeSiard Street
Suite 300
Monroe, LA 71201
Toll-Free: 888-823-1910
Phone: 318-361-0900
Fax: 318-361-2159
www.vhpla.com
Secondary Address: 855 Pierremont Road, Suite 109, Shreveport, LA
71106
For Profit Organization: Yes
Year Founded: 1994
Number of Affiliated Hospitals: 4
Total Enrollment: 14,000
State Enrollment: 14,000

Healthplan and Services Defined
PLAN TYPE: HMO
Plan Specialty: Lab, Radiology
Benefits Offered: Behavioral Health, Chiropractic, Disease
Management, Home Care, Inpatient SNF, Physical Therapy,
Prescription, Wellness, Durable Medical Equipment

Type of Coverage
Commercial

Geographic Areas Served
Louisiana

Network Qualifications
Pre-Admission Certification: Yes

Key Personnel
CEO ....P Gary Jones, MD
COO....................................Wendy Poe, RN
CFO ....Mike Briard
Provider Relations ....Annette Napier
Marketing ....Billy Justice

Specialty Managed Care Partners
Caremark Rx

---

486 Vantage Medicare Advantage
130 DeSiard Street
Suite 300
Monroe, LA 71201
Toll-Free: 888-823-1910

Phone: 318-361-0900
Fax: 318-361-2159
www.vhp-medicare.com
Secondary Address: 855 Pierremont Road, Suite 109, Shreveport, LA
71106
Year Founded: 1994
Total Enrollment: 14,000

Healthplan and Services Defined
PLAN TYPE: Medicare
Other Type: Medicare PPO
Benefits Offered: Home Care, Inpatient SNF, Prescription

Type of Coverage
Medicare, Supplemental Medicare

Geographic Areas Served
Bossier, Caddo, Caldwell, Jackson, Lincoln, Morehouse, Rapides,
Ouachita, richland, and Union Parishes

Health Insurance Coverage Status and Type of Coverage by Age

Category	All Persons		Under 18 years		Under 65 years		65 years and over	
	Number	%	Number	%	Number	%	Number	%
Total population	1,285	-	262	-	1,073	-	212	-
Covered by some type of health insurance	1,164 *(12)*	90.6 *(0.7)*	250 *(4)*	95.6 *(0.9)*	952 *(15)*	88.8 *(0.9)*	211 *(11)*	99.6 *(0.3)*
Covered by private health insurance	864 *(20)*	67.2 *(1.5)*	170 *(7)*	65.0 *(2.6)*	730 *(20)*	68.0 *(1.5)*	134 *(9)*	63.3 *(2.8)*
Employment based	749 *(20)*	58.3 *(1.5)*	159 *(7)*	60.7 *(2.6)*	665 *(21)*	62.0 *(1.6)*	85 *(7)*	39.9 *(2.7)*
Own employment based	408 *(12)*	31.8 *(0.9)*	1 *(1)*	0.4 *(0.2)*	340 *(12)*	31.7 *(0.9)*	68 *(6)*	32.0 *(2.4)*
Direct purchase	137 *(10)*	10.7 *(0.8)*	16 *(3)*	6.0 *(1.1)*	77 *(8)*	7.2 *(0.8)*	60 *(6)*	28.2 *(2.7)*
Covered by government health insurance	525 *(20)*	40.9 *(1.5)*	113 *(7)*	43.1 *(2.8)*	322 *(16)*	30.0 *(1.5)*	203 *(10)*	95.7 *(1.0)*
Covered by Medicaid	279 *(16)*	21.7 *(1.3)*	99 *(8)*	38.0 *(2.9)*	245 *(14)*	22.8 *(1.4)*	34 *(5)*	16.2 *(2.2)*
Also by private insurance	69 *(6)*	5.4 *(0.5)*	23 *(4)*	8.9 *(1.7)*	60 *(6)*	5.6 *(0.5)*	9 *(2)*	4.3 *(1.1)*
Covered by Medicare	247 *(12)*	19.2 *(0.9)*	2 *(1)*	0.6 *(0.3)*	45 *(6)*	4.2 *(0.5)*	202 *(10)*	95.3 *(1.0)*
Also by private insurance	138 *(9)*	10.7 *(0.7)*	0 *(0)*	0.0 *(0.0)*	13 *(2)*	1.2 *(0.2)*	125 *(8)*	59.0 *(3.0)*
Also by Medicaid	58 *(7)*	4.5 *(0.5)*	1 *(1)*	0.5 *(0.3)*	23 *(4)*	2.2 *(0.3)*	34 *(5)*	16.2 *(2.2)*
Covered by military health care	93 *(10)*	7.2 *(0.8)*	16 *(3)*	6.1 *(1.1)*	70 *(9)*	6.6 *(0.8)*	22 *(4)*	10.6 *(2.1)*
Not covered at any time during the year	121 *(9)*	9.4 *(0.7)*	12 *(2)*	4.4 *(0.9)*	120 *(9)*	11.2 *(0.9)*	1 *(1)*	0.4 *(0.3)*

Note: Numbers in thousands; figures cover 2010; standard error appears in parenthesis; (b) base less than 75,000; (x) not applicable
Source: U.S. Census Bureau, Current Population Survey, 2011 Annual Social and Economic Supplement. Table HI05. Health Insurance Coverage Status and Type of Coverage by State and Age for All People: 2010

Maine

487 Aetna Health of Maine

151 Farmington Avenue
Conveyer ASB2
Hartford, CT 06156
Toll-Free: 866-582-9629
www.aetna.com
For Profit Organization: Yes
Year Founded: 1996
Federally Qualified: Yes
Total Enrollment: 22,417
State Enrollment: 22,417

Healthplan and Services Defined
PLAN TYPE: HMO
Other Type: POS
Model Type: Network
Plan Specialty: PBM
Benefits Offered: Chiropractic, Home Care, Prescription, Psychiatric, Vision, Wellness

Type of Coverage
Commercial, Individual

Geographic Areas Served
Statewide

Subscriber Information
Average Monthly Fee Per Subscriber
(Employee + Employer Contribution):
Employee Only (Self): $73.42
Employee & 1 Family Member: $168.89

Key Personnel
CEO . . . . Ronald A Williams
President . . . . Mark T Bertolini
SVP, General Counsel . . . . William J Casazza
EVP, CFO . . . . Joseph M Zubretsky
Head, M&A Integration . . . . Kay Mooney
SVP, Marketing . . . . Robert E Mead
Chief Medical Officer . . . . Lonny Reisman, MD
SVP, Human Resources . . . . Elease E Wright
SVP, CIO . . . . Meg McCarthy

488 Anthem Blue Cross & Blue Shield of Maine

330 Civic Center Drive
Suite 3
Augusta, ME 04330
Toll-Free: 888-399-8706
Phone: 207-822-7000
www.anthem.com
Secondary Address: One Merchants Plaza, Bangor, ME 04401
For Profit Organization: Yes
Year Founded: 1985
Number of Affiliated Hospitals: 42
Number of Primary Care Physicians: 971
Number of Referral/Specialty Physicians: 1,604
Total Enrollment: 545,610
State Enrollment: 85,917

Healthplan and Services Defined
PLAN TYPE: HMO/PPO
Model Type: Staff
Plan Specialty: ASO, Behavioral Health, Chiropractic, Disease Management, Lab, PBM, Vision, Radiology, Worker's Compensation, UR
Benefits Offered: Behavioral Health, Chiropractic, Dental, Disease Management, Home Care, Inpatient SNF, Physical Therapy, Podiatry, Prescription, Psychiatric, Transplant, Vision, Wellness, Worker's Compensation, Life

Type of Coverage
Commercial, Individual, Supplemental Medicare

Type of Payment Plans Offered
POS, DFFS, Capitated, FFS

Geographic Areas Served
Statewide

Network Qualifications
Pre-Admission Certification: Yes

Peer Review Type
Utilization Review: Yes
Second Surgical Opinion: Yes
Case Management: Yes

Publishes and Distributes Report Card: Yes

Accreditation Certification
NCQA
TJC Accreditation, Medicare Approved, Utilization Review, Pre-Admission Certification, State Licensure, Quality Assurance Program

Key Personnel
President . . . . Marjorie Dorr
CEO . . . . Larry Glasscock
COO . . . . Claudia Lindsey
CFO . . . . Guy Marszalek
Provider Relations . . . . DiJuana Lewis
Pharmacy Director . . . . James Lang
Chief Medical Officer . . . . Sheila Hanley, MD
Member Relations . . . . Karen Andrews
Public Relations . . . . Deborah New
Sales Executive . . . . James Parker
Media Contact . . . . Chris Dugan
603-695-7202
chris.dugan@anthem.com

Specialty Managed Care Partners
Green Spring Health Service

Employer References
Maine Education Association, State of Maine Employees Benefits Trust, Sappi Fine Paper, Maine Medical Center, Maine General Health

489 CIGNA HealthCare of Maine

500 Southborough Drive
Suite 302, Rtg 596
South Portland, ME 04106
Toll-Free: 866-438-2446
Phone: 207-828-9700
Fax: 207-728-9717
www.cigna.com
For Profit Organization: Yes
Year Founded: 1986
Owned by an Integrated Delivery Network (IDN): Yes
Number of Affiliated Hospitals: 39
Number of Primary Care Physicians: 900
Number of Referral/Specialty Physicians: 1,200
Total Enrollment: 6,343
State Enrollment: 6,343

Healthplan and Services Defined
PLAN TYPE: HMO
Other Type: POS
Model Type: IPA
Plan Specialty: Dental, Vision
Benefits Offered: Behavioral Health, Chiropractic, Disease Management, Home Care, Inpatient SNF, Long-Term Care, Physical Therapy, Podiatry, Prescription, Transplant, Vision, Wellness
Offers Demand Management Patient Information Service: Yes

Type of Coverage
Commercial

Type of Payment Plans Offered
POS, DFFS

Geographic Areas Served
CIGNA @ Maine serves the counties of Aroostook, Cumberland, Hancock, Kennebec, Knox, Penobscot, Piscataquis, Somerset, Waldo, and York

Subscriber Information
Average Annual Deductible Per Subscriber:
Employee Only (Self): $0
Employee & 1 Family Member: $0
Employee & 2 Family Members: $0
Average Subscriber Co-Payment:
Primary Care Physician: $10.00
Prescription Drugs: $5.00/10.00/20.00
Hospital ER: $25.00

Network Qualifications
Pre-Admission Certification: Yes

Peer Review Type
Utilization Review: Yes
Second Surgical Opinion: Yes
Case Management: Yes

Publishes and Distributes Report Card: Yes

Accreditation Certification
NCQA
TJC Accreditation, Medicare Approved, Utilization Review, Pre-Admission Certification, State Licensure, Quality Assurance Program

Key Personnel
Chairman and CEO . . . . H Edward Hanway
215-762-6002
h.edward.hanway@cigna.com
CFO . . . . Michael W Bell
Chief Marketing Officer . . . . Robert G Romasco
Human Resources . . . . Donald M Levinson
Chief Information Officer . . . . Andrea Anania

Specialty Managed Care Partners
CIGNA Behavioral Health

Employer References
BIW, UNUM

490 eHealthInsurance Services Inc.
11919 Foundation Place
Gold River, CA 95670
Toll-Free: 800-977-8860
info@ehealthinsurance.com
www.e.healthinsurance.com
Year Founded: 1997

Healthplan and Services Defined
PLAN TYPE: HMO/PPO
Benefits Offered: Dental, Life, STD

Type of Coverage
Commercial, Individual, Medicare

Geographic Areas Served
All 50 states in the USA and District of Columbia

Key Personnel
Chairman & CEO . . . . Gary L. Lauer
EVP/Business & Corp. Dev. Bruce Telkamp
EVP/Chief Technology . . . . Dr. Sheldon X. Wang
SVP & CFO . . . . Stuart M. Huizinga
Pres. of eHealth Gov. Sys . . . . Samuel C. Gibbs
SVP of Sales & Operations . . . . Robert S. Hurley
Director Public Relations . . . . Nate Purpura
650-210-3115

491 Great-West Healthcare Maine
Acquired by CIGNA

492 Harvard Pilgrim Health Care: Maine
1 Market Street
Third Floor
Portland, ME 04101
Toll-Free: 888-888-4742
www.harvardpilgrim.org
Non-Profit Organization: Yes
Year Founded: 1977
Number of Affiliated Hospitals: 135
Number of Primary Care Physicians: 28,000
Total Enrollment: 1,100,000
State Enrollment: 67,000

Healthplan and Services Defined
PLAN TYPE: Multiple
Model Type: Network
Plan Specialty: ASO, Behavioral Health, Chiropractic, Dental, Disease Management, EPO, Lab, MSO, PBM, Vision, Radiology, Worker's Compensation, UR
Benefits Offered: Behavioral Health, Chiropractic, Disease Management, Home Care, Inpatient SNF, Long-Term Care, Physical Therapy, Podiatry, Prescription, Psychiatric, Transplant, Vision, Wellness
Offers Demand Management Patient Information Service: Yes
DMPI Services Offered: Clinical Program, Specialty On-Line, Case Management, Cybernurse, On-Line A-Z

Type of Coverage
Commercial, Individual, Indemnity, Medicare, Supplemental Medicare, Medicaid

Type of Payment Plans Offered
POS, Combination FFS & DFFS

Geographic Areas Served
Mass.: All counties; Rhode Island: All counties; New Hampshire: Sullivan, Belknap, Merrimack, Strafford, Cheshire, Hillsborough, Rockingham counties, parts of Coos, Grafton and Carroll counties; Vermont: Windham, Windsor and Caledonia county

Subscriber Information
Average Monthly Fee Per Subscriber
(Employee + Employer Contribution):
Employee Only (Self): $5.50
Average Annual Deductible Per Subscriber:
Employee Only (Self): $1000.00
Employee & 1 Family Member: $2000.00
Employee & 2 Family Members: $2000.00
Average Subscriber Co-Payment:
Primary Care Physician: $20.00
Non-Network Physician: 20%
Prescription Drugs: $10.00
Hospital ER: $50.00-50.00
Home Health Care: $0
Home Health Care Max. Days/Visits Covered: Subject to review
Nursing Home: $0
Nursing Home Max. Days/Visits Covered: 60 days

Network Qualifications
Pre-Admission Certification: Yes

Peer Review Type
Utilization Review: Yes
Second Surgical Opinion: Yes
Case Management: Yes

Publishes and Distributes Report Card: Yes

Accreditation Certification
NCQA
TJC Accreditation, Medicare Approved, Utilization Review, Pre-Admission Certification, State Licensure, Quality Assurance Program

Key Personnel
President & CEO . . . . Eric H Schultz
VP, Maine Operations . . . . Ed Kane
SVP, Provider Network . . . . Rick Weisblatt, PhD

VP, Marketing & Comm . . . . Dana Rashti
VP, Customer Service . . . . Lynn Bowman
Chief Information Officer . . . . Deborah Norton
SVP, Sales & Cust Service . . . . Vincent Capozzi
Dir, Media Relations . . . . Sharon Torgerson
   617-509-7458
   sharon_torgerson@hphc.org

Average Claim Compensation
Physician's Fees Charged: 51%
Hospital's Fees Charged: 40%

Specialty Managed Care Partners
Mass General, Brigham And Women Hospital, Boston Medical,
Value Options, MedImpact
Enters into Contracts with Regional Business Coalitions: No

Employer References
Commonwealth of Massachusetts, City of Boston, Harvard
University

493 Martin's Point HealthCare

331 Veranda Street
PO Box 9746
Portland, ME 04104-5040
Toll-Free: 800-322-0280
Phone: 207-774-5801
gainfo@martinspoint.org
www.martinspoint.org
Non-Profit Organization: Yes
Year Founded: 1981
Total Enrollment: 85,000

Healthplan and Services Defined
PLAN TYPE: Multiple
Benefits Offered: Disease Management, Prescription, Wellness, No
co-pay for: routine physical exams/hearing tests/eye
exams/mammograms/prostrate & pap exams/bone mass/flu
vaccines.

Type of Coverage
Commercial, Medicare, Military

Geographic Areas Served
Maine, New Hampshire, Vermont, northeastern New York

Subscriber Information
Average Monthly Fee Per Subscriber
(Employee + Employer Contribution):
Employee Only (Self): Varies
Medicare: Varies
Average Annual Deductible Per Subscriber:
Employee Only (Self): Varies
Medicare: Varies
Average Subscriber Co-Payment:
Primary Care Physician: Varies
Prescription Drugs: Varies
Hospital ER: Varies

Key Personnel
President/CEO . . . . David H Howes, MD
Chief Operating Officer . . . . Dale Bradford
Chief Admin Officer . . . . Sandra Monfiletto
Chief Deliver Systems Off . . . . Dan Olsten
Chief Financial Officer . . . . Dennis Reese, CPA
Chief Medical Officer . . . . Elizabeth H Johnson, MD
VP, Corporate Affairs . . . . Andrea Cianchette Maker
   207-791-3711
   andrea.maker@martinspoint.org

494 Northeast Community Care

49 Atlantic Place
South Portland, ME 04106-2316
Toll-Free: 800-998-3056

Phone: 207-773-3920
Fax: 207-773-3990
www.northeastcommunitycare.com
Subsidiary of: Arcadian Health Plans

Healthplan and Services Defined
PLAN TYPE: Medicare

Type of Coverage
Medicare

495 UnitedHealthCare of Maine

5901 Lincoln Drive
Edina, MN 55436
Toll-Free: 800-842-3585
www.uhc.com
Subsidiary of: UnitedHealth Group
Year Founded: 1977
Number of Affiliated Hospitals: 4,200
Number of Primary Care Physicians: 460,000
Total Enrollment: 75,000,000

Healthplan and Services Defined
PLAN TYPE: HMO/PPO
Model Type: IPA, Group, Network
Plan Specialty: Lab, Radiology
Benefits Offered: Chiropractic, Dental, Physical Therapy,
Prescription, Wellness, AD&D, Life, LTD, STD
Offers Demand Management Patient Information Service: Yes

Type of Coverage
Commercial, Individual, Indemnity, Medicare

Geographic Areas Served
Statewide

Network Qualifications
Pre-Admission Certification: Yes

Peer Review Type
Utilization Review: Yes
Second Surgical Opinion: Yes
Case Management: Yes

Publishes and Distributes Report Card: Yes

Accreditation Certification
TJC, NCQA

Specialty Managed Care Partners
Enters into Contracts with Regional Business Coalitions: Yes

Health Insurance Coverage Status and Type of Coverage by Age

Category	All Persons		Under 18 years		Under 65 years		65 years and over	
	Number	%	Number	%	Number	%	Number	%
Total population	5,727	-	1,355	-	5,037	-	690	-
Covered by some type of health insurance	4,979 (58)	86.9 (0.9)	1,230 (25)	90.8 (1.4)	4,305 (63)	85.5 (1.0)	675 (31)	97.9 (0.6)
Covered by private health insurance	4,193 (83)	73.2 (1.3)	923 (38)	68.1 (2.6)	3,728 (81)	74.0 (1.4)	466 (27)	67.6 (2.3)
Employment based	3,754 (83)	65.6 (1.3)	864 (37)	63.7 (2.5)	3,421 (80)	67.9 (1.4)	333 (24)	48.3 (3.0)
Own employment based	1,956 (49)	34.2 (0.8)	9 (4)	0.6 (0.3)	1,706 (45)	33.9 (0.8)	250 (20)	36.3 (2.6)
Direct purchase	646 (50)	11.3 (0.9)	95 (13)	7.0 (1.0)	467 (43)	9.3 (0.9)	180 (20)	26.0 (2.4)
Covered by government health insurance	1,430 (60)	25.0 (1.1)	377 (32)	27.8 (2.4)	811 (54)	16.1 (1.1)	619 (28)	89.8 (1.4)
Covered by Medicaid	655 (49)	11.4 (0.9)	342 (32)	25.2 (2.4)	610 (48)	12.1 (1.0)	45 (8)	6.5 (1.2)
Also by private insurance	125 (23)	2.2 (0.4)	54 (13)	4.0 (0.9)	119 (23)	2.4 (0.5)	6 (2)	0.8 (0.4)
Covered by Medicare	724 (29)	12.6 (0.5)	13 (5)	1.0 (0.4)	110 (13)	2.2 (0.3)	614 (28)	89.0 (1.4)
Also by private insurance	455 (28)	7.9 (0.5)	1 (1)	0.1 (0.1)	47 (9)	0.9 (0.2)	408 (26)	59.2 (2.6)
Also by Medicaid	85 (12)	1.5 (0.2)	10 (5)	0.7 (0.4)	41 (8)	0.8 (0.2)	44 (8)	6.4 (1.1)
Covered by military health care	192 (24)	3.3 (0.4)	36 (9)	2.6 (0.7)	147 (24)	2.9 (0.5)	44 (10)	6.4 (1.4)
Not covered at any time during the year	747 (50)	13.1 (0.9)	125 (19)	9.2 (1.4)	733 (49)	14.5 (1.0)	15 (4)	2.1 (0.6)

Note: Numbers in thousands; figures cover 2010; standard error appears in parenthesis; (b) base less than 75,000; (x) not applicable
Source: U.S. Census Bureau, Current Population Survey, 2011 Annual Social and Economic Supplement. Table HI05. Health Insurance Coverage Status and Type of Coverage by State and Age for All People: 2010

Maryland

496 Aetna Health of Maryland

151 Farmington Avenue
Conveyer ASB2
Hartford, CT 06156
Toll-Free: 866-582-9629
www.aetna.com
For Profit Organization: Yes
Year Founded: 1987
Number of Affiliated Hospitals: 50
Number of Primary Care Physicians: 10,032
Total Enrollment: 211,156

Healthplan and Services Defined
PLAN TYPE: HMO
Other Type: POS
Model Type: Network
Plan Specialty: EPO
Benefits Offered: Behavioral Health, Dental, Disease Management,
Prescription, Vision
Offers Demand Management Patient Information Service: Yes

Type of Coverage
Commercial, Individual, Medicare

Type of Payment Plans Offered
Capitated, FFS

Geographic Areas Served
Statewide

Subscriber Information
Average Monthly Fee Per Subscriber
(Employee + Employer Contribution):
Employee Only (Self): $67.32
Employee & 1 Family Member: $157.54

Network Qualifications
Pre-Admission Certification: Yes

Peer Review Type
Utilization Review: Yes

Publishes and Distributes Report Card: Yes

Accreditation Certification
NCQA

Key Personnel
CEO . . . . .Ronald A Williams
President. . . . . .Mark T Bertolini
SVP, General Counsel . . . . .William J Casazza
EVP, CFO . . . . .Joseph M Zubretsky
Head, M&A Integration .Kay Mooney
SVP, Marketing. . . . . .Robert E Mead
Chief Medical Officer .Lonny Reisman, MD
SVP, Human Resources. . . . . .Elease E Wright
SVP, CIO. . . . . .Meg McCarthy

Specialty Managed Care Partners
Enters into Contracts with Regional Business Coalitions: Yes

497 Alliance PPO, LLC

4 Taft Court
First Floor
Rockville, MD 20850
Toll-Free: 800-884-5188
Phone: 301-360-8063
Fax: 301-545-5380
masales99@uhc.com
www.mamsiunitedhealthcare.com/w/d/ps/ppomedical.jsp
Subsidiary of: United Healthcare / United Health Group
For Profit Organization: Yes
Year Founded: 1988
Number of Affiliated Hospitals: 350

Number of Primary Care Physicians: 57,000
Total Enrollment: 960,000

Healthplan and Services Defined
PLAN TYPE: PPO
Model Type: IPA
Plan Specialty: Behavioral Health, Worker's Compensation
Benefits Offered: Behavioral Health, Dental, Prescription, Vision,
Worker's Compensation, Life, STD, Accident, Disability
Offers Demand Management Patient Information Service: Yes

Type of Payment Plans Offered
Capitated

Geographic Areas Served
Delaware, Maryland, North Carolina, Virginia, Pennsylvania, West
Virginia, & Washington, DC

Subscriber Information
Average Monthly Fee Per Subscriber
(Employee + Employer Contribution):
Employee Only (Self): $4.25
Average Subscriber Co-Payment:
Primary Care Physician: $15.00

Network Qualifications
Minimum Years of Practice: 2
Pre-Admission Certification: Yes

Peer Review Type
Utilization Review: Yes
Second Surgical Opinion: Yes
Case Management: Yes

Publishes and Distributes Report Card: Yes

Accreditation Certification
Quality Assurance Program

Key Personnel
President/CEO . . . . .Thomas P Barbera
SEVP/CFO/Director. . . . . .Robert E Foss
EVP/CIO. . . . . .R Larry Mauzy

Specialty Managed Care Partners
Enters into Contracts with Regional Business Coalitions: Yes

498 American Postal Workers Union (APWU) Health Plan

799 Cromwell Park Drive
Suites K-Z
Glen Burnie, MD 21061
Toll-Free: 800-222-2798
Phone: 410-424-2852
Fax: 410-424-1588
custser@apwuhp.com
www.apwuhp.com
Subsidiary of: American Postal Workers Union / AFL-CIO
Year Founded: 1960
Number of Affiliated Hospitals: 6,000
Number of Primary Care Physicians: 600,000
Total Enrollment: 141,000

Healthplan and Services Defined
PLAN TYPE: HMO/PPO
Benefits Offered: Disease Management, Wellness
Offers Demand Management Patient Information Service: Yes
DMPI Services Offered: 24 Hour Nurse Advisory Line

Type of Payment Plans Offered
FFS

Geographic Areas Served
Nationwide - APWU/The American Postal Workers Union Health
Plan is health insurance for federal employees and retirees

Subscriber Information
Average Monthly Fee Per Subscriber
(Employee + Employer Contribution):
Employee Only (Self): $36.80-177.20 varies

Employee & 2 Family Members: $82.80-398.66 varies
Average Annual Deductible Per Subscriber:
Employee Only (Self): $250
Average Subscriber Co-Payment:
Primary Care Physician: 15%
Prescription Drugs: 25%
Hospital ER: 15% - 30%
Home Health Care Max. Days/Visits Covered: 10 - 30%

Key Personnel
President, APWU . . . . .William Burrus
Director. . . . . .William J Kaczor, Jr
Executive Vice President . . . . .CJ Guffey

499 Amerigroup Maryland
7550 Teague Road
Suite 500
Hanover, MD 21076
Toll-Free: 800-977-7388
www.realsolutions.com
For Profit Organization: Yes
Year Founded: 1999
Total Enrollment: 1,900,000

Healthplan and Services Defined
PLAN TYPE: HMO

Type of Coverage
Medicare, Medicaid, SCHIP, SSI

500 Avesis: Maryland
10324 S Dolfiled Road
Owings Mills, MD 21117
Toll-Free: 800-522-0258
www.avesis.com
Year Founded: 1978
Number of Primary Care Physicians: 18,000
Total Enrollment: 2,000,000

Healthplan and Services Defined
PLAN TYPE: PPO
Other Type: Vision, Dental
Model Type: Network
Plan Specialty: Dental, Vision, Hearing
Benefits Offered: Dental, Vision

Type of Coverage
Commercial

Type of Payment Plans Offered
POS, Capitated, Combination FFS & DFFS

Geographic Areas Served
Nationwide and Puerto Rico

Publishes and Distributes Report Card: Yes

Accreditation Certification
AAAHC
TJC Accreditation

501 Block Vision
120 West Fayette Street
Suite 700
Baltimore, MD 21201
Toll-Free: 800-243-1401
Phone: 410-752-0121
Fax: 410-752-8969
www.blockvision.com
Secondary Address: 6737 West Washington Street, Suite 2202, PO
Box 44077, Milwaukee, WI 53214-7077
Subsidiary of: Block Vision Holdings Corporation
For Profit Organization: Yes
Year Founded: 1990

Number of Primary Care Physicians: 18,000
Total Enrollment: 3,000,000

Healthplan and Services Defined
PLAN TYPE: Vision
Plan Specialty: Vision
Benefits Offered: Vision

Type of Coverage
Commercial, Medicare, Medicaid

Key Personnel
President/CEO . . . . .Andrew Alcorn
Sr VP/COO/CFO. . . . . .Ernest A Viscuso
Sr VP/General Counsel . . . . .Audrey M Weinstein
SVP, Business Development. . . . . .Stephanie Lucas
slucas@blockvision.com
Sr VP/Clinical Director . . . . .Howard Levin, OD
VP, Group Sales . . . . .Steven Fleischer
866-246-9589
sfleischer@blockvision.com
VP, Sales . . . . .Mark Wallner
800-883-5747
mwallner@visionplans.com

502 Bravo Health: Corporate Headquarters
3601 O'Donnell Street
Baltimore, MD 21224
Toll-Free: 800-235-9188
www.bravohealth.com
Year Founded: 1996
Number of Primary Care Physicians: 30,000
Total Enrollment: 360,000

Healthplan and Services Defined
PLAN TYPE: Medicare

Type of Coverage
Medicare, Supplemental Medicare

Geographic Areas Served
Delaware, Maryland, Pennslyvania, Texas, Washington DC, New
Jersey

Key Personnel
Chairman & CEO. . . . . .Jeff Folick
EVP, CFO . . . . .Scott Tabakin
EVP, Chief Admin Officer . . . . .Thomas Rekart
Founder & Govt Relations . . . . .David Carliner
SVP, Bravo Pennsylvania . . . . .Jason Feuerman
SVP, Bravo Texas . . . . .Patrick Feyen
SVP, Development . . . . .Kristen Krzyzewski
SVP, General Counsel . . . . .Frances Woodward
EVP, Marketing. . . . . .Scott Ptacek
SVP, Phamarcy. . . . . .Tom Rim
SVP, Bravo Mid-Atlantic . . . . .Chuck Kanach
SVP, General Counsel . . . . .Frances Woodward
SVP, Govt Relations . . . . .Julia Ciorletti
SVP, Medicaid . . . . .Mark Puente
EVP, Sales. . . . . .Gil Miller
Media Contact. . . . . .Lisa Trapani
410-245-0094
ltrapani@rosecomm.com
SVP, Chief Compliance Ofc . . . . .Ena Authur Pierce

503 Catalyst Health Solutions Inc
800 King Farm Boulevard
Rockville, MD 20850
Toll-Free: 800-323-6640
Phone: 301-548-2900
Fax: 301-548-2991
rxcsinfo@catalystrx.com
www.catalysthealthsolutions.com
For Profit Organization: Yes

Year Founded: 1986
Owned by an Integrated Delivery Network (IDN): Yes
Number of Primary Care Physicians: 54,000
Total Enrollment: 3,000,000

Healthplan and Services Defined
PLAN TYPE: HMO
Model Type: Group
Plan Specialty: PBM
Benefits Offered: Prescription, Worker's Compensation

Type of Coverage
Commercial, Medicare, Supplemental Medicare, Catastrophic
Catastrophic Illness Benefit: Varies per case

Type of Payment Plans Offered
POS

Geographic Areas Served
Nationwide with concentration in Southeast

Network Qualifications
Pre-Admission Certification: Yes

Peer Review Type
Utilization Review: Yes
Second Surgical Opinion: No
Case Management: No

Publishes and Distributes Report Card: Yes

Accreditation Certification
TJC Accreditation, Utilization Review, State Licensure

Key Personnel
Chief Executive Officer . . . . David T Blair
President/COO . . . . Richard Bates
Treasurer/CFO. . . . . Hai Tran
General Counsel . . . . Bruce Metge
Chief Financial Officer . . . . Hai Tran
301-548-2900
htran@chsi.com

Specialty Managed Care Partners
Catalyst Rx
Enters into Contracts with Regional Business Coalitions: Yes

504 CIGNA HealthCare of the Mid-Atlantic

10490 Little Patuxent Parkway
60 Corporate Center Suite 400
Columbia, MD 21044
Toll-Free: 866-438-2446
Phone: 410-884-2500
www.cigna.com
Secondary Address: Great-West Healthcare, now part of CIGNA, 6701 Democracy Blvd, Suite 401, Bethesda, MD 20817, 301-841-0950
For Profit Organization: Yes
Year Founded: 1984
Physician Owned Organization: No
Number of Affiliated Hospitals: 54
Number of Primary Care Physicians: 2,032
Number of Referral/Specialty Physicians: 5,028
Total Enrollment: 109,186

Healthplan and Services Defined
PLAN TYPE: HMO/PPO
Model Type: IPA
Benefits Offered: Disease Management, Prescription, Transplant, Wellness
Offers Demand Management Patient Information Service: Yes

Type of Coverage
Commercial

Type of Payment Plans Offered
Combination FFS & DFFS

Geographic Areas Served
District of Columbia, Maryland, Virginia

Network Qualifications
Pre-Admission Certification: Yes

Peer Review Type
Utilization Review: Yes
Second Surgical Opinion: Yes
Case Management: Yes

Publishes and Distributes Report Card: Yes

Accreditation Certification
NCQA

Key Personnel
President . . . . Mike Triplett
Government Affairs . . . . Katie Wade
Medical Director . . . . Nicholas Gettas, MD
Sales . . . . Ron Vance Jr
Provider Relations . . . . Yvonne Van Lowe

Specialty Managed Care Partners
CIGNA Dental, CIGNA Behavioral Health
Enters into Contracts with Regional Business Coalitions: No

505 CoreSource: Maryland

4940 Campbell Blvd
Suite 200
Baltimore, MD 21236
Toll-Free: 800-624-7130
Phone: 410-931-5060
www.coresource.com
Subsidiary of: Trustmark
Year Founded: 1980
Total Enrollment: 1,100,000

Healthplan and Services Defined
PLAN TYPE: Multiple
Other Type: TPA
Model Type: Network
Plan Specialty: Claims Administration, TPA
Benefits Offered: Behavioral Health, Home Care, Prescription, Transplant

Type of Coverage
Commercial

Geographic Areas Served
Nationwide

Accreditation Certification
Utilization Review, Pre-Admission Certification

506 Coventry Health Care: Corporate Headquarters

6705 Rockledge Drive
Suite 900
Bethesda, MD 20817
Toll-Free: 800-843-7421
Phone: 301-581-0600
Fax: 301-493-0743
info-de@cvty.com
www.coventryhealthcare.com
For Profit Organization: Yes
Year Founded: 1987
Total Enrollment: 5,000,000

Healthplan and Services Defined
PLAN TYPE: HMO/PPO
Other Type: POS, ASO
Model Type: IPA
Plan Specialty: Behavioral Health, Dental, Disease Management, Worker's Compensation
Benefits Offered: Behavioral Health, Dental, Disease Management, Prescription, Wellness, Worker's Compensation

Type of Coverage
Commercial, Individual, Medicare, Supplemental Medicare, Medicaid

Type of Payment Plans Offered
POS, DFFS, Capitated, FFS, Combination FFS & DFFS

Geographic Areas Served
Nationwide

Subscriber Information
Average Annual Deductible Per Subscriber:
Employee Only (Self): Varies
Employee & 1 Family Member: Varies
Employee & 2 Family Members: Varies
Medicare: Varies
Average Subscriber Co-Payment:
Primary Care Physician: $10.00
Non-Network Physician: Varies
Prescription Drugs: $5.00
Hospital ER: Varies
Home Health Care: Varies
Nursing Home: Varies
Nursing Home Max. Days/Visits Covered: Varies

Network Qualifications
Pre-Admission Certification: Yes

Peer Review Type
Utilization Review: Yes
Second Surgical Opinion: Yes
Case Management: Yes

Publishes and Distributes Report Card: No

Accreditation Certification
NCQA
TJC Accreditation, Utilization Review, Pre-Admission Certification, State Licensure, Quality Assurance Program

Key Personnel
Chief Executive Officer . . . . Allen F Wise
Director . . . . Dale B Wolf
Interim CFO . . . . John Stelben
301-581-5729
SVP, Corporate Finance . . . . Drew Asher
301-581-5717
SVP/Chief Human Resources. . . . . Patrisha L Davis
SVP/Chief Info Officer . . . . Maria Fitzpatrick
SVP/Customer Service . . . . James E McGarry
SVP/Corporate Controller . . . . John L Ruhlmann
EVP/General Counsel . . . . Thomas C Zielinski

Specialty Managed Care Partners
Enters into Contracts with Regional Business Coalitions: No

---

507   Delta Dental of the Mid-Atlantic
One Delta Drive
Mechanicsburg, PA 17055-6999
Toll-Free: 800-471-7091
Fax: 717-766-8719
www.deltadentalins.com
Non-Profit Organization: Yes
Total Enrollment: 54,000,000

Healthplan and Services Defined
PLAN TYPE: Dental
Other Type: Dental PPO

Type of Coverage
Commercial

Geographic Areas Served
Statewide

Key Personnel
President/CEO. . . . . Gary D Radine
VP, Public & Govt Affairs . . . . Jeff Album
415-972-8418

Dir/Media & Public Affair . . . . Elizabeth Risberg
415-972-8423

---

508   Denta-Chek of Maryland
7125 Thomas Edison Drive
Suite 105
Columbia, MD 21046
Toll-Free: 888-478-8833
Phone: 410-997-3300
Fax: 410-997-3796
info@dentachek.com
www.dentachek.com
Non-Profit Organization: Yes
Year Founded: 1981
Number of Primary Care Physicians: 300
Number of Referral/Specialty Physicians: 200
Total Enrollment: 10,000

Healthplan and Services Defined
PLAN TYPE: Multiple
Model Type: IPA
Plan Specialty: Dental
Benefits Offered: Dental

Type of Coverage
Catastrophic Illness Benefit: None

Type of Payment Plans Offered
POS, Combination FFS & DFFS

Geographic Areas Served
Statewide

Subscriber Information
Average Monthly Fee Per Subscriber
(Employee + Employer Contribution):
Employee Only (Self): $15.00
Employee & 1 Family Member: $20.00
Employee & 2 Family Members: $25.00
Medicare: $0
Average Annual Deductible Per Subscriber:
Employee Only (Self): $0
Employee & 1 Family Member: $0
Employee & 2 Family Members: $0
Medicare: $0
Average Subscriber Co-Payment:
Primary Care Physician: $5.00
Non-Network Physician: $0
Prescription Drugs: $0
Hospital ER: $0
Home Health Care: $0
Nursing Home: $0

Network Qualifications
Pre-Admission Certification: Yes

Peer Review Type
Utilization Review: Yes
Second Surgical Opinion: Yes
Case Management: Yes

Publishes and Distributes Report Card: No

Accreditation Certification
State Licensure, Quality Assurance Program

Key Personnel
President. . . . . Robert D Sacks
CFO . . . . Mary Pflueger
VP . . . . Joel Sacks

Specialty Managed Care Partners
Enters into Contracts with Regional Business Coalitions: No

---

509   Dental Benefit Providers
6220 Old Dobbin Lane
Columbia, MD 21045

Toll-Free: 800-638-3895
Phone: 240-632-8000
info@dbp.com
www.dbp.com
Secondary Address: 425 Market Street, 12th Floor, San Francisco, CA
94105
For Profit Organization: Yes
Year Founded: 1984
Number of Primary Care Physicians: 125,000
Total Enrollment: 6,600,000

Healthplan and Services Defined
PLAN TYPE: Dental
Model Type: IPA
Plan Specialty: ASO, Dental, EPO, DHMO, PPO, CSO, Preventive,
Claims Repricing and Network Access
Benefits Offered: Dental

Type of Coverage
Indemnity, Medicare, Medicaid

Type of Payment Plans Offered
POS, DFFS, Capitated, FFS

Geographic Areas Served
48 states including District of Columbia, Puerto Rico and Virgin
Islands

Accreditation Certification
NCQA

Key Personnel
CEO . . . . .Dawn Owens
President & COO. . . . . .Karen Schievelbein
COO . . . . .Kevin Ruth
VP . . . . .Ben Davis
CEO . . . . .David Hall
COO. . . . . .Karen Schievelbein

510   eHealthInsurance Services Inc.

11919 Foundation Place
Gold River, CA 95670
Toll-Free: 800-977-8860
info@ehealthinsurance.com
www.e.healthinsurance.com
Year Founded: 1997

Healthplan and Services Defined
PLAN TYPE: HMO/PPO
Benefits Offered: Dental, Life, STD

Type of Coverage
Commercial, Individual, Medicare

Geographic Areas Served
All 50 states in the USA and District of Columbia

Key Personnel
Chairman & CEO . . . . .Gary L. Lauer
EVP/Business & Corp. Dev. .Bruce Telkamp
EVP/Chief Technology. . . . . .Dr. Sheldon X. Wang
SVP & CFO . . . . .Stuart M. Huizinga
Pres. of eHealth Gov. Sys . . . . .Samuel C. Gibbs
SVP of Sales & Operations . . . . .Robert S. Hurley
Director Public Relations. . . . . .Nate Purpura
650-210-3115

511   Graphic Arts Benefit Corporation

64 11 Ivy Lane
Suite 700
Greenbelt, MD 20770-1411
Phone: 301-474-7950
Fax: 301-474-3197
gtoner@gabchealth.org
www.gabchealth.org
Non-Profit Organization: Yes

Total Enrollment: 8,000

Healthplan and Services Defined
PLAN TYPE: HMO/PPO
Benefits Offered: Dental, Prescription, Vision, AD&D, Life, STD

Type of Coverage
Commercial, Individual

Geographic Areas Served
Maryland, Virginia, District of Columbia

512   Great-West Healthcare of Maryland
Acquired by CIGNA

513   Humana Health Insurance of Maryland

1 International Blvd
Suite 400
Mahwah, NJ 07495
Toll-Free: 800-967-2370
Phone: 201-512-8818
www.humana.com
For Profit Organization: Yes

Healthplan and Services Defined
PLAN TYPE: HMO/PPO

Type of Coverage
Commercial, Individual

Accreditation Certification
URAC, NCQA, CORE

514   Kaiser Permanente Health Plan of the Mid-Atlantic States

2101 E Jefferson Street
Rockville, MD 20852
Toll-Free: 800-777-7902
Phone: 301-468-6000
Fax: 301-816-7478
beverlie.brinson@kp.org
www.kaiserpermanente.org
Non-Profit Organization: Yes
Year Founded: 1980
Number of Affiliated Hospitals: 35
Number of Primary Care Physicians: 15,129
Total Enrollment: 471,360
State Enrollment: 471,360

Healthplan and Services Defined
PLAN TYPE: HMO
Model Type: Group
Benefits Offered: Disease Management, Prescription, Wellness
Offers Demand Management Patient Information Service: Yes

Type of Payment Plans Offered
POS, DFFS, FFS, Combination FFS & DFFS

Geographic Areas Served
Metro Baltimore & Metro Washington

Subscriber Information
Average Annual Deductible Per Subscriber:
Employee Only (Self): $0
Employee & 1 Family Member: $0
Employee & 2 Family Members: $0
Medicare: $0

Peer Review Type
Case Management: Yes

Publishes and Distributes Report Card: Yes

Accreditation Certification
NCQA
Medicare Approved, Quality Assurance Program

Key Personnel
Pres, Kaiser Foundation.....................Marilyn Kawamura
Pres/CEO, Mid-Atlantic....................Robert M Pearl, MD
Media Contact ....Beverlie Brinson
301-816-6264
beverlie.brinson@kp.org

Specialty Managed Care Partners
Enters into Contracts with Regional Business Coalitions: Yes

---

515 Magellan Health Services: Corporate Headquarters

6950 Columbia Gateway Drive
Columbia, MD 21046
Toll-Free: 800-410-8312
Phone: 410-953-1000
Fax: 410-953-5200
www.magellanhealth.com
Non-Profit Organization: Yes
Year Founded: 1998
Owned by an Integrated Delivery Network (IDN): Yes
Number of Affiliated Hospitals: 5,000
Number of Primary Care Physicians: 67,000
Number of Referral/Specialty Physicians: 45,000
Total Enrollment: 36,500,000

Healthplan and Services Defined
PLAN TYPE: Multiple
Model Type: Network
Plan Specialty: Behavioral Health
Benefits Offered: Behavioral Health, Psychiatric
Offers Demand Management Patient Information Service: Yes
DMPI Services Offered: Behavioral Health Managment, EAP

Type of Coverage
Behavioral Health

Geographic Areas Served
National

Peer Review Type
Utilization Review: Yes
Case Management: Yes

Accreditation Certification
AAAHC, URAC, NCQA

Key Personnel
Chairman & CEO ....Rene Lerer, MD
Pres, Health Services ....Karen S Rohan
Chief Financial Officer ....Jonathan N Rubin
CEO, Natl Imaging Assoc ....Tina Blasi
Chief Oper & Finance Offc ....Edward J Christie
General Counsel ....Daniel N Gregoire
SVP, Comm Behav Health ....Suzanne Kunis
President, ICORE ....Alan M Lotvin, MD
SVP, Marketing & Comm ....David W Carter
SVP, Public Sector..........................Anne M McCabe
Chief Medical Officer ....Anthony M Kotin, MD
Chief Human Res Officer ....Caskie Lewis-Clapper
Chief Information Offc.....................Gary D Anderson
Pres, Medicaid Adminstr ....Tim Nolan
Chief Corp Dev Officer..................Prakash R Patel, MD

---

516 Mid Atlantic Medical Services: Corporate Office

4 Taft Court
Rockville, MD 20850
Toll-Free: 800-884-5188
Phone: 301-762-8205
Fax: 301-545-5380
masales99@uhc.com
www.mamsiunitedhealthcare.com

Secondary Address: 6095 Marshalee Drive South, Suite 200, Baltimore, MD 21075
Subsidiary of: United HealthGroup
For Profit Organization: Yes
Year Founded: 1979
Number of Affiliated Hospitals: 340
Number of Primary Care Physicians: 45,000
Number of Referral/Specialty Physicians: 45,000
Total Enrollment: 161,000

Healthplan and Services Defined
PLAN TYPE: HMO/PPO
Other Type: POS
Model Type: IPA
Benefits Offered: Dental, Disease Management, Home Care, Prescription, Vision, Wellness, Life, STD

Type of Coverage
Catastrophic Illness Benefit: Varies per case

Type of Payment Plans Offered
POS, FFS, Combination FFS & DFFS

Geographic Areas Served
Delaware, Washington DC, Maryland and Virginia

Subscriber Information
Average Monthly Fee Per Subscriber
(Employee + Employer Contribution):
Employee Only (Self): $129.03
Employee & 1 Family Member: $245.15
Employee & 2 Family Members: $390.96
Average Annual Deductible Per Subscriber:
Employee Only (Self): $0
Employee & 1 Family Member: $0
Employee & 2 Family Members: $0
Medicare: $0
Average Subscriber Co-Payment:
Primary Care Physician: $10.00
Prescription Drugs: $10.00/20.00
Hospital ER: $50.00
Home Health Care Max. Days/Visits Covered: Varies
Nursing Home Max. Days/Visits Covered: 60 days

Network Qualifications
Pre-Admission Certification: Yes

Peer Review Type
Utilization Review: Yes
Second Surgical Opinion: Yes
Case Management: Yes

Publishes and Distributes Report Card: Yes

Accreditation Certification
NCQA
TJC Accreditation, Medicare Approved, Utilization Review, Pre-Admission Certification, State Licensure, Quality Assurance Program

Key Personnel
SVP, Controller ....Christopher Mackail
Senior Vice President ....Debbie Hulen
Vice President.............................Wayne Monroe

Specialty Managed Care Partners
Enters into Contracts with Regional Business Coalitions: Yes

---

517 Mid Atlantic Psychiatric Services (MAMSI)

Acquired by UnitedHealthcare/A UnitedHealth Group

---

518 OneNet PPO

800 King Farm Blvd
6th Floor
Rockville, MD 20850
Toll-Free: 800-884-5188

Phone: 814-336-1782
Fax: 866-563-8071
www.onenetppo.com
Subsidiary of: UnitedHealth Group
For Profit Organization: Yes
Year Founded: 1988
Number of Affiliated Hospitals: 26
Number of Primary Care Physicians: 950
Total Enrollment: 970,000

Healthplan and Services Defined
  PLAN TYPE: PPO
  Model Type: Network
  Benefits Offered: Prescription

Type of Payment Plans Offered
  POS

Geographic Areas Served
  Southwestern Pennsylvania, Delaware, Washington DC, Maryland, West Virginia, Virginia, Central North Carolina

Subscriber Information
  Average Monthly Fee Per Subscriber
    (Employee + Employer Contribution):
      Employee Only (Self): $2.00
  Average Annual Deductible Per Subscriber:
      Employee Only (Self): $100.00
      Employee & 1 Family Member: $200.00
      Employee & 2 Family Members: $200.00
  Average Subscriber Co-Payment:
      Primary Care Physician: Varies
      Non-Network Physician: Varies

Publishes and Distributes Report Card: Yes

Key Personnel
  President/CEO . . . . .Jerry Alonge
  Marketing . . . . .Mike Ebert

519   Optimum Choice
Acquired by UnitedHealthcare/A UnitedHealth Group

520   Priority Partners Health Plans
6704 Curtis Court
Glen Burnie, MD 21060-9949
Toll-Free: 800-654-9728
Phone: 410-424-4611
Fax: 410-424-4883
ppcustomerservice@jhhc.com
www.hopkinsmedicine.org/priority_partners
Subsidiary of: John Hopkins HealthCare LLC/Maryland Community Health System
Non-Profit Organization: Yes
Year Founded: 1996
Total Enrollment: 185,000
State Enrollment: 185,000

Healthplan and Services Defined
  PLAN TYPE: HMO

Type of Coverage
  Medicaid

Type of Payment Plans Offered
  Capitated, FFS

Peer Review Type
  Second Surgical Opinion: Yes

Publishes and Distributes Report Card: Yes

Accreditation Certification
  TJC, NCQA, JACHO, HMO

Key Personnel
  Chairman . . . . .C Michael Armstrong
  President. . . . . .Patricia M.C. Brown

Medical Director . . . . .Chester Schmidt, MD
Communications Dept . . . . .Deb Chase
  dchase@jhhc.com

521   Spectera
6220 Old Dobbin Lane
Liberty 6, Suite 200
Columbia, MD 21045
Toll-Free: 800-638-3120
Phone: 410-265-5872
Fax: 410-944-5903
scox@spectera.com
www.spectera.com
Subsidiary of: United Health Group
For Profit Organization: Yes
Year Founded: 1964
Number of Primary Care Physicians: 24,000
Total Enrollment: 17,000,000

Healthplan and Services Defined
  PLAN TYPE: Multiple
  Model Type: Network
  Plan Specialty: Vision
  Benefits Offered: Disease Management, Vision

Type of Coverage
  Commercial, Individual

Type of Payment Plans Offered
  POS, DFFS, Capitated

Geographic Areas Served
  Continental United States

Subscriber Information
  Average Monthly Fee Per Subscriber
    (Employee + Employer Contribution):
      Employee Only (Self): Varies
  Average Annual Deductible Per Subscriber:
      Employee & 2 Family Members: Varies
  Average Subscriber Co-Payment:
      Primary Care Physician: Varies

Network Qualifications
  Pre-Admission Certification: Yes

Publishes and Distributes Report Card: Yes

Key Personnel
  CEO. . . . . .Paul Gaulstrand
  COO . . . . .Tom Rekart
  CFO . . . . .Kyle Stern
  General Counsel . . . . .Jennifer Lewis
  SVP, Marketing. . . . . .Susan E Cox
    800-638-3895
    susan_cox@uhc.com
  Chief Sales Officer. . . . . .Laurida Mackenzie
  Media Contact . . . . .Susan Cox
    800-638-3895
    susan_cox@uhc.com

Specialty Managed Care Partners
  United Heath Group
  Enters into Contracts with Regional Business Coalitions: No

522   United Concordia: Maryland
Longview Executive Park
309 International Circle, Suite 130
Hunt Valley, MD 21030
Toll-Free: 800-272-8865
Phone: 443-866-9500
Fax: 443-886-9525
ucproducer@ucci.com
www.secure.ucci.com
For Profit Organization: Yes

Year Founded: 1971
Number of Primary Care Physicians: 111,000
Total Enrollment: 8,000,000

Healthplan and Services Defined
  PLAN TYPE: Dental
  Plan Specialty: Dental
  Benefits Offered: Dental

Type of Coverage
  Commercial, Individual

Geographic Areas Served
  Military personnel and their families, nationwide

---

523   UnitedHealthCare of the Mid-Atlantic

6095 Marshalee Drive
Suite 200
Elkridge, MD 21075
Toll-Free: 800-307-7820
Phone: 410-379-3402
Fax: 410-379-3446
midatlantic_pr_team@uhc.com
www.uhc.com
Subsidiary of: UnitedHealth Group
Non-Profit Organization: Yes
Year Founded: 1976
Number of Affiliated Hospitals: 58
Number of Primary Care Physicians: 2,559
Number of Referral/Specialty Physicians: 8,300
Total Enrollment: 75,000,000
State Enrollment: 176,000

Healthplan and Services Defined
  PLAN TYPE: HMO/PPO
  Model Type: Network
  Benefits Offered: Disease Management, Prescription, Wellness
  Offers Demand Management Patient Information Service: Yes

Geographic Areas Served
  Baltimore Metro Area, Washington DC Metro Area, Eastern Shore, Southern Maryland, Western Maryland

Subscriber Information
  Average Monthly Fee Per Subscriber
    (Employee + Employer Contribution):
      Employee Only (Self): $104.00-135.00
      Employee & 1 Family Member: $143.00-184.00
      Employee & 2 Family Members: $331.00-440.00
      Medicare: $112.00-156.00
  Average Annual Deductible Per Subscriber:
      Employee Only (Self): $100.00-250.00
      Employee & 1 Family Member: $500.00-1500.00
      Employee & 2 Family Members: $200.00-500.00
      Medicare: $0
  Average Subscriber Co-Payment:
      Primary Care Physician: $5.00/10.00
      Non-Network Physician: Deductible
      Prescription Drugs: $5.00/10.00
      Hospital ER: $25.00/50.00
      Home Health Care: $5.00/10.00

Network Qualifications
  Pre-Admission Certification: Yes

Peer Review Type
  Utilization Review: Yes
  Second Surgical Opinion: Yes
  Case Management: Yes

Publishes and Distributes Report Card: Yes

Accreditation Certification
  TJC Accreditation, Medicare Approved, Utilization Review, Pre-Admission Certification, State Licensure, Quality Assurance Program

Key Personnel
  President and CEO . . . . Richard Zoretic
  CFO . . . . John Dell Erba
  Network Contracting . . . . Marie Carpenter
  Marketing . . . . David Yalowitz, MD
  Member Services . . . . Laverne Smith-boykin
  Provider Services . . . . Theresa Farasce
  Media Contact . . . . Debora Spano
    401-732-7374
    debora_m_spano@uhc.com

Specialty Managed Care Partners
  Enters into Contracts with Regional Business Coalitions: Yes

HMO/PPO DIRECTORY

Health Insurance Coverage Status and Type of Coverage by Age

Category	All Persons		Under 18 years		Under 65 years		65 years and over	
	Number	%	Number	%	Number	%	Number	%
Total population	6,616	-	1,443	-	5,671	-	945	-
Covered by some type of health insurance	6,246 (57)	94.4 (0.6)	1,389 (25)	96.2 (1.0)	5,315 (68)	93.7 (0.7)	930 (52)	98.5 (0.7)
Covered by private health insurance	4,937 (103)	74.6 (1.4)	1,062 (41)	73.6 (2.9)	4,308 (106)	76.0 (1.6)	629 (44)	66.6 (3.5)
Employment based	4,280 (115)	64.7 (1.6)	994 (42)	68.9 (3.0)	3,916 (112)	69.1 (1.7)	364 (36)	38.6 (3.5)
Own employment based	2,121 (70)	32.1 (1.0)	5 (3)	0.4 (0.2)	1,838 (65)	32.4 (1.0)	283 (28)	29.9 (2.8)
Direct purchase	633 (61)	9.6 (0.9)	58 (13)	4.0 (0.9)	328 (40)	5.8 (0.7)	305 (39)	32.2 (3.8)
Covered by government health insurance	2,164 (101)	32.7 (1.5)	407 (46)	28.2 (3.1)	1,296 (94)	22.9 (1.7)	868 (51)	91.8 (1.6)
Covered by Medicaid	1,346 (98)	20.3 (1.5)	404 (46)	28.0 (3.1)	1,216 (93)	21.4 (1.7)	130 (31)	13.7 (3.1)
Also by private insurance	280 (39)	4.2 (0.6)	81 (18)	5.6 (1.3)	255 (36)	4.5 (0.6)	24 (10)	2.6 (1.0)
Covered by Medicare	1,032 (55)	15.6 (0.8)	8 (5)	0.5 (0.3)	167 (28)	2.9 (0.5)	866 (51)	91.7 (1.6)
Also by private insurance	610 (43)	9.2 (0.6)	0 (0)	0.0 (0.0)	44 (13)	0.8 (0.2)	566 (41)	59.9 (3.4)
Also by Medicaid	248 (40)	3.7 (0.6)	5 (4)	0.3 (0.3)	120 (25)	2.1 (0.4)	128 (31)	13.6 (3.1)
Covered by military health care	88 (21)	1.3 (0.3)	6 (4)	0.4 (0.3)	56 (17)	1.0 (0.3)	32 (12)	3.3 (1.2)
Not covered at any time during the year	370 (40)	5.6 (0.6)	54 (15)	3.8 (1.0)	356 (40)	6.3 (0.7)	14 (6)	1.5 (0.7)

Note: Numbers in thousands; figures cover 2010; standard error appears in parenthesis; (b) base less than 75,000; (x) not applicable
Source: U.S. Census Bureau, Current Population Survey, 2011 Annual Social and Economic Supplement. Table HI05. Health Insurance Coverage Status and Type of Coverage by State and Age for All People: 2010

Massachusetts

524 Aetna Health of Massachusetts

Partnered with eHealthInsurance Services Inc.

525 Assurant Employee Benefits: Massachusetts

33 Boston Post Road West
#590
Marlborough, MA 01752-1867
Phone: 508-870-2200
Fax: 508-382-3750
benefits@assurant.com
www.assurantemployeebenefits.com
Subsidiary of: Assurant, Inc
For Profit Organization: Yes
Number of Primary Care Physicians: 112,000
Total Enrollment: 47,000

Healthplan and Services Defined
 PLAN TYPE: Multiple
 Plan Specialty: Dental, Vision, Long & Short-Term Disability
 Benefits Offered: Dental, Vision, Wellness, AD&D, Life, LTD, STD

Type of Coverage
 Commercial, Indemnity, Individual Dental Plans

Geographic Areas Served
 Statewide

Subscriber Information
 Average Monthly Fee Per Subscriber
  (Employee + Employer Contribution):
   Employee Only (Self): Varies by plan

Key Personnel
 President . . . . .Michael Germain
 Regional Sales Manager. . . . . .David Fraser
 PR Specialist. . . . . .Megan Hutchison
  816-556-7815
  megan.hutchison@assurant.com

526 Avesis: Massachusetts

790 Turnpike Street
Suite 202
North Andover, MA 01845
Toll-Free: 800-522-4834
www.avesis.com
Year Founded: 1978
Number of Primary Care Physicians: 18,000
Total Enrollment: 2,000,000

Healthplan and Services Defined
 PLAN TYPE: PPO
 Other Type: Vision, Dental
 Model Type: Network
 Plan Specialty: Dental, Vision, Hearing
 Benefits Offered: Dental, Vision

Type of Coverage
 Commercial

Type of Payment Plans Offered
 POS, Capitated, Combination FFS & DFFS

Geographic Areas Served
 Nationwide and Puerto Rico

Publishes and Distributes Report Card: Yes

Accreditation Certification
 AAAHC
 TJC Accreditation

527 Blue Cross & Blue Shield of Massachusetts

Landmark Center
401 Park Drive
Boston, MA 02215-3326
Toll-Free: 800-262-2583
Phone: 617-246-5000
Fax: 617-832-4832
www.bcbsma.com
Non-Profit Organization: Yes
Year Founded: 1937
Number of Affiliated Hospitals: 77
Number of Primary Care Physicians: 20,266
Total Enrollment: 3,000,000
State Enrollment: 3,000,000

Healthplan and Services Defined
 PLAN TYPE: HMO
 Model Type: Network
 Plan Specialty: Dental, Group Medical
 Benefits Offered: Behavioral Health, Chiropractic, Complementary
  Medicine, Dental, Disease Management, Home Care, Inpatient
  SNF, Long-Term Care, Physical Therapy, Podiatry, Prescription,
  Psychiatric, Transplant, Vision, Wellness, AD&D, Life, LTD, STD
 Offers Demand Management Patient Information Service: Yes
 DMPI Services Offered: 24-Hour Nurse Care Line

Type of Coverage
 Group Insurance

Type of Payment Plans Offered
 FFS

Geographic Areas Served
 Massachusetts & Southern New Hampshire

Subscriber Information
 Average Monthly Fee Per Subscriber
  (Employee + Employer Contribution):
   Employee Only (Self): Varies by plan
 Average Annual Deductible Per Subscriber:
  Employee Only (Self): $0
  Employee & 1 Family Member: $0
  Employee & 2 Family Members: $0
 Average Subscriber Co-Payment:
  Primary Care Physician: $10.00
  Non-Network Physician: 20%
  Prescription Drugs: $5.00/10.00
  Hospital ER: $25.00
  Nursing Home: Not covered

Network Qualifications
 Pre-Admission Certification: Yes

Peer Review Type
 Utilization Review: Yes

Accreditation Certification
 NCQA
 TJC Accreditation, Medicare Approved, Utilization Review,
  Pre-Admission Certification, State Licensure

Key Personnel
 President & CEO . . . . .Andrew Dreyfus
 SVP, Govt Affairs . . . . .Jay Curley
 EVP, CFO . . . . .Allen P Maltz
 SVP/Chief Physician Exec .John Fallon, MD
 EVP, Chief Legal Officer . . . . .Sandra L Jesse
 SVP, Strategic Services . . . . .Deborah Devaux
 SVP, Health Care Services. . . . . .Patrick Gilligan
 VP, Corp Communications. .Jay McQuaide
 SVP, Sales Division . . . . .Tim O'Brien
 SVP, Human Resources . . . . .Ann S Anderson
 SVP, Chief Info Officer. .William Fandricch
 SVP, Corp Relations . . . . .Fredi Shonkoff
 Dir, Public Relations . . . . .Tara Murray
  617-246-4841
  tara.murray@bcbsma.com

Specialty Managed Care Partners
Express Scripts

---

528   Boston Medical Center Healthnet Plan
2 Copley Place
Suite 600
Boston, MA 02116
Toll-Free: 888-566-0010
memberquestions@bmchp.org
www.bmchp.org
Year Founded: 1997
Number of Affiliated Hospitals: 60
Number of Primary Care Physicians: 3,000
Number of Referral/Specialty Physicians: 12,000
Total Enrollment: 240,890
State Enrollment: 240,890

Healthplan and Services Defined
   PLAN TYPE: HMO
   Benefits Offered: Disease Management, Prescription, Wellness

Type of Coverage
   Individual

Key Personnel
   Chief Executive Officer . . . . Kate Walsh
   Vice President . . . . Thomas Traylor
   Executive Director . . . . Karen Fifer Ferry
   Chief/Public Partnerships . . . . John Cragin
   Chief Medical Officer . . . . Stanley Hochberg, MD
   Chief Financial Officer . . . . Scott O'Gorman
   Chief Operating Officer . . . . Michael Schrader
   Chief/Operational Excell. . . . . Raymond Sessler
   Chief/Human Resources . . . . Anna Trask

---

529   CIGNA HealthCare of Massachusetts
Three Newton Executive Park
2223 Washington Street, Suite 200
Newton, MA 02462
Toll-Free: 866-438-2446
Phone: 617-630-4300
Fax: 617-630-4383
www.cigna.com
Secondary Address: Great-West Healthcare, now part of CIGNA, 130
   Turner Street, Bldg 3, Suite 610, Waltham, MA 02453, 781-893-0370
For Profit Organization: Yes
Total Enrollment: 10,315
State Enrollment: 10,315

Healthplan and Services Defined
   PLAN TYPE: PPO
   Benefits Offered: Disease Management, Prescription, Transplant,
   Wellness

Type of Coverage
   Commercial

Type of Payment Plans Offered
   POS, FFS

Geographic Areas Served
   Massachusetts

Key Personnel
   President . . . . Donald M Curry
   CMO . . . . Dr Rob Hockmuth

---

530   ConnectiCare of Massachusetts
175 Scott Swamp Road
PO Box 4050
Farmington, CT 06034-4050
Toll-Free: 800-251-7772

Phone: 860-574-5757
Fax: 860-674-2030
info@connecticare.com
www.connecticare.com
For Profit Organization: Yes
Year Founded: 1981
Number of Affiliated Hospitals: 126
Number of Primary Care Physicians: 22,000
Total Enrollment: 240,000
State Enrollment: 9,000

Healthplan and Services Defined
   PLAN TYPE: HMO/PPO
   Other Type: POS
   Plan Specialty: Lab, Radiology
   Benefits Offered: Dental, Disease Management, Physical Therapy,
      Prescription, Wellness

Type of Coverage
   Commercial, Individual, Medicare

Type of Payment Plans Offered
   POS

Geographic Areas Served
   Massachusetts

Key Personnel
   President . . . . Michael Wise
   COO . . . . Ida Schnipper
   CFO . . . . Tom Tran
   CMO . . . . Paul Bluestein, MD
   General Counsel . . . . Gail Bogossian
   Marketing . . . . Paul Philpott
   Pharmacy Director . . . . Jeff Casberg
   Public Relations . . . . Deb Hoyt
   Media Contact . . . . Stephen Jewett
      publicrelations@connecticare.com

Specialty Managed Care Partners
Express Scripts

---

531   Dentaquest
465 Medford Street
Boston, MA 02129-1454
Toll-Free: 888-788-8600
webmaster@dentaquest.com
www.dentaquest.com
Subsidiary of: DentaQuest Ventures
Year Founded: 1980
Number of Primary Care Physicians: 750
Total Enrollment: 14,000,000

Healthplan and Services Defined
   PLAN TYPE: Dental
   Plan Specialty: Dental
   Benefits Offered: Dental

Geographic Areas Served
   District of Columbia, Florida, Maryland, Virginia

Key Personnel
   CEO . . . . Fay Donohue
   CFO . . . . Gary Guengerich
   Chief Dental Officer . . . . Doyle Williams
   Communications Manager . . . . Amy Nelson
      262-834-3727

---

532   eHealthInsurance Services Inc.
11919 Foundation Place
Gold River, CA 95670
Toll-Free: 800-977-8860
info@ehealthinsurance.com
www.e.healthinsurance.com
Year Founded: 1997

Healthplan and Services Defined
  PLAN TYPE: HMO/PPO
  Benefits Offered: Dental, Life, STD

Type of Coverage
  Commercial, Individual, Medicare

Geographic Areas Served
  All 50 states in the USA and District of Columbia

Key Personnel
  Chairman & CEO . . . . .Gary L. Lauer
  EVP/Business & Corp. Dev.. .Bruce Telkamp
  EVP/Chief Technology. . . . . .Dr. Sheldon X. Wang
  SVP & CFO . . . . .Stuart M. Huizinga
  Pres. of eHealth Gov. Sys . . . . .Samuel C. Gibbs
  SVP of Sales & Operations . . . . .Robert S. Hurley
  Director Public Relations. . . . . .Nate Purpura
    650-210-3115

---

533 Fallon Community Health Plan

10 Chestnut Street
Worcester, MA 01608
Toll-Free: 800-333-2535
Phone: 508-799-2100
Fax: 508-831-1137
contactcustomerservice@fchp.org
www.fchp.org
Non-Profit Organization: Yes
Year Founded: 1977
Federally Qualified: Yes
Number of Affiliated Hospitals: 57
Number of Primary Care Physicians: 1,291
Number of Referral/Specialty Physicians: 3,504
Total Enrollment: 178,000
State Enrollment: 135,581

Healthplan and Services Defined
  PLAN TYPE: HMO/PPO
  Model Type: Network
  Plan Specialty: ASO, Behavioral Health, Chiropractic, Dental,
    Disease Management, Lab, PBM, Vision, Worker's Compensation,
    HMO, PPO, POS
  Benefits Offered: Behavioral Health, Chiropractic, Complementary
    Medicine, Dental, Disease Management, Home Care, Inpatient
    SNF, Physical Therapy, Podiatry, Prescription, Psychiatric,
    Transplant, Vision, Wellness

Type of Coverage
  Commercial, Individual, Indemnity, Medicare, Medicaid
  Catastrophic Illness Benefit: Covered

Type of Payment Plans Offered
  POS, DFFS, Capitated, FFS, Combination FFS & DFFS

Geographic Areas Served
  Worcester, Norfolk, Plymouth, Hampshire, Middlesex, Bristol,
  Franklin, Essex, Suffolk and Hampden counties

Subscriber Information
  Average Monthly Fee Per Subscriber
    (Employee + Employer Contribution):
      Employee Only (Self): $306.00
      Employee & 1 Family Member: $623.00
      Employee & 2 Family Members: $802.00
      Medicare: $223.00
  Average Annual Deductible Per Subscriber:
      Employee Only (Self): $316.00
      Employee & 1 Family Member: $633.00
      Employee & 2 Family Members: $561.00
      Medicare: $512.00
  Average Subscriber Co-Payment:
      Primary Care Physician: $12.97
      Non-Network Physician: $10.00
      Prescription Drugs: $14.83
      Hospital ER: $51.00

Home Health Care: $0
Nursing Home: $0
Nursing Home Max. Days/Visits Covered: 100days/year

Peer Review Type
  Utilization Review: Yes
  Second Surgical Opinion: Yes
  Case Management: Yes

Publishes and Distributes Report Card: Yes

Accreditation Certification
  NCQA
  Medicare Approved, Utilization Review, Pre-Admission Certification,
    State Licensure, Quality Assurance Program

Key Personnel
  President/CEO . . . . .Patrick Hughes
    patrick.hughes@fchp.org
  EVP/CFO . . . . .Charley Goheen
    charles.goheen@fchp.org
  Div Pres, Senior Care . . . . .Richard P Burke
  Div Pres, Health Plan Op. . . . . .W Patrick Hughes
  EVP/Chief Compliance Offc . . . . .Anne Doyle
  Chiel Legal Counsel. . . . . .Jesse M Caplan, Esq
  VP, Operations . . . . .Richard Commander
  VP, Strategy & Planning. . . . . .Mary C Ritter
  VP, Marketing. . . . . .Janis Liepins
  SVP, Chief Medical Offc . . . . .Elizabeth Malko, MD
  Community Relations . . . . .Kate McEvoy-Zdonczyk
    508-368-9523
    kate.mcevoy-zdonczyk@fcph.org
  EVP, Human Resources . . . . .Teena Osgood
  VP, Sales . . . . .David Przesiek
  Public Relations . . . . .Christine Cassidy
    508-368-9502
    mediainfo@fchp.org

Average Claim Compensation
  Physician's Fees Charged: 125%

Specialty Managed Care Partners
  American Specialty Health Networks, Beacon Health Strategies,
    Pharma Care, Dental Benefits
  Enters into Contracts with Regional Business Coalitions: Yes
  West Suburban Health Group, Reserves Management Inc, Minuteman
    Nashoba Health Group, Municipalities of Regional
    Effectiveness(MORE)

Employer References
  Federal Employees Benefit Program, Commomwealth of
    Massachusetts, City of Worcester, Wyman Gordon, National Grid

---

534 Fallon Community Medicare Plan

10 Chestnut Street
Worcester, MA 01608
Toll-Free: 800-333-2535
Phone: 508-799-2100
Fax: 508-797-9621
seniorplan@fchp.org
www.fchp.org
Non-Profit Organization: Yes
Year Founded: 1977

Healthplan and Services Defined
  PLAN TYPE: Medicare
  Benefits Offered: Chiropractic, Dental, Disease Management, Home
    Care, Inpatient SNF, Physical Therapy, Podiatry, Prescription,
    Psychiatric, Vision, Wellness

Type of Coverage
  Individual, Medicare

Geographic Areas Served
  Available for Massachusetts only

Subscriber Information
Average Monthly Fee Per Subscriber
(Employee + Employer Contribution):
Employee Only (Self): Varies
Medicare: Varies
Average Annual Deductible Per Subscriber:
Employee Only (Self): Varies
Medicare: Varies
Average Subscriber Co-Payment:
Primary Care Physician: Varies
Non-Network Physician: Varies
Prescription Drugs: Varies
Hospital ER: Varies
Home Health Care: Varies
Home Health Care Max. Days/Visits Covered: Varies
Nursing Home: Varies
Nursing Home Max. Days/Visits Covered: Varies

Key Personnel
President/CEO . . . . .Patrick Hughes
   patrick.hughes@fchp.org
EVP/CFO . . . . .Charley Goheen
   charles.goheen@fchp.org
Div Pres, Senior Care . . . . Richard P Burke
Div Pres, Health Plan Op . . . . W Patrick Hughes
EVP/Chief Compliance Offc . . . . Anne Doyle
Chiel Legal Counsel . . . . .Jesse M Caplan, Esq
VP, Operations . . . . .Richard Commander
VP, Strategy & Planning . . . . .Mary C Ritter
VP, Marketing . . . . .Janis Liepins
SVP, Chief Medical Offc . . . . Elizabeth Malko, MD
Community Relations . . . . Kate McEvoy-Zdonczyk
   508-368-9523
   kate.mcevoy-zdonczyk@fcph.org
EVP, Human Resources . . . . .Teena Osgood
VP, Sales . . . . .David Przesiek
Public Relations . . . . .Christine Cassidy
   508-368-9502
   mediainfo@fchp.org

535   Great-West Healthcare of Massachusetts
Acquired by CIGNA

536   Harvard Pilgrim Health Care
93 Worcester Street
Wellesley, MA 02481
Toll-Free: 888-888-4742
Phone: 617-745-1000
Fax: 617-509-0049
www.harvardpilgrim.org
Secondary Address: 1600 Crown Colony Drive, Quincy, MA 02169
Non-Profit Organization: Yes
Year Founded: 1977
Number of Affiliated Hospitals: 135
Number of Primary Care Physicians: 28,000
Total Enrollment: 1,079,674
State Enrollment: 65,000
Healthplan and Services Defined
   PLAN TYPE: Multiple
   Model Type: Network
   Plan Specialty: ASO, Behavioral Health, Chiropractic, Dental,
      Disease Management, EPO, Lab, MSO, PBM, Vision, Radiology,
      Worker's Compensation, UR
   Benefits Offered: Behavioral Health, Chiropractic, Disease
      Management, Home Care, Inpatient SNF, Long-Term Care,
      Physical Therapy, Podiatry, Prescription, Psychiatric, Transplant,
      Vision, Wellness
   Offers Demand Management Patient Information Service: Yes
   DMPI Services Offered: Clinical Program, Specialty On-Line, Case
      Management, Cybernurse, On-Line A-Z

Type of Coverage
   Commercial, Individual, Indemnity, Medicare, Supplemental
      Medicare, Medicaid
Type of Payment Plans Offered
   POS, Combination FFS & DFFS
Geographic Areas Served
   Mass.: All counties; Rhode Island: All counties; New Hampshire:
      Sullivan, Belknap, Merrimack, Strafford, Cheshire, Hillsborough,
      Rockingham counties, parts of Coos, Grafton and Carroll counties;
      Vermont: Windham, Windsor and Caledonia county
Subscriber Information
   Average Monthly Fee Per Subscriber
      (Employee + Employer Contribution):
      Employee Only (Self): $5.50
   Average Annual Deductible Per Subscriber:
      Employee Only (Self): $1000.00
      Employee & 1 Family Member: $2000.00
      Employee & 2 Family Members: $2000.00
   Average Subscriber Co-Payment:
      Primary Care Physician: $20.00
      Non-Network Physician: 20%
      Prescription Drugs: $10.00
      Hospital ER: $50.00-50.00
      Home Health Care: $0
      Home Health Care Max. Days/Visits Covered: Subject to review
      Nursing Home: $0
      Nursing Home Max. Days/Visits Covered: 60 days
Network Qualifications
   Pre-Admission Certification: Yes
Peer Review Type
   Utilization Review: Yes
   Second Surgical Opinion: Yes
   Case Management: Yes
Publishes and Distributes Report Card: Yes
Accreditation Certification
   NCQA
   TJC Accreditation, Medicare Approved, Utilization Review,
      Pre-Admission Certification, State Licensure, Quality Assurance
      Program
Key Personnel
   CEO . . . . .Eric Schultz
      888-333-4742
   CFO . . . . .James DuCharme
   COO/Chief Medical Officer . . . . .Roberta Herman
   SVP Sales & Cust Service . . . . .Vincent Capozzi
   Chief Human Resources Ofc .Jack Lane
   Manager Regional Claims . . . . .Barbara Chapman
   Medical Director . . . . .Carolyn Langer
   Chief Legal Officer . . . . .Laura S Peabody
   VP, Marketing . . . . .Dana Rashti
   VP, Policy & Govt Affairs . . . . .William J Graham
   SVP Provider Network . . . . .Rick Weisblatt, PhD
   VP, Customer Service . . . . .Lynn Bowman
      lynn_bowman@hphc.org
   Chief Information Officer .Deborah Norton
   SVP, Actuarial Services . . . . .Gary H Lin
   Media Contact . . . . .Sharon Torgerson
      617-509-7458
      sharon_torgerson@hphc.org
Average Claim Compensation
   Physician's Fees Charged: 51%
   Hospital's Fees Charged: 40%
Specialty Managed Care Partners
   Mass General, Brigham And Women Hospital, Boston Medical, Value
      Options, MedImpact
   Enters into Contracts with Regional Business Coalitions: No
Employer References
   Commonwealth of Massachusetts, City of Boston, Harvard University

537 Harvard University Group Health Plan

75 Mount Auburn Street
Cambridge, MA 02138
Phone: 617-495-2008
Fax: 617-496-6125
mservices@uhs.harvard.edu
www.hughp.harvard.edu
Non-Profit Organization: Yes
Year Founded: 1973
Number of Affiliated Hospitals: 4
Number of Primary Care Physicians: 430
Number of Referral/Specialty Physicians: 60
Total Enrollment: 6,443

Healthplan and Services Defined
  PLAN TYPE: HMO
  Other Type: POS
  Model Type: Staff
  Benefits Offered: Prescription

Type of Payment Plans Offered
  POS

Geographic Areas Served
  Harvard University faculty, staff and their families

Subscriber Information
  Average Annual Deductible Per Subscriber:
    Employee Only (Self): $0
  Average Subscriber Co-Payment:
    Primary Care Physician: $10.00
    Prescription Drugs: $10/$20/$35
    Hospital ER: $0
    Home Health Care: $0
    Nursing Home: $0

Network Qualifications
  Pre-Admission Certification: Yes

Peer Review Type
  Utilization Review: Yes
  Second Surgical Opinion: No
  Case Management: Yes

Publishes and Distributes Report Card: No

Accreditation Certification
  TJC Accreditation, Medicare Approved, Utilization Review,
    Pre-Admission Certification, State Licensure, Quality Assurance
    Program

Key Personnel
  Director...........................David S Rosenthal, MD
  CFO ....Marc Pollack
  Director of Health Plan...........................Paula Fiore
  In House Formulary.......................Maureen McCarthy
  Marketing ....Catherine Lukas
  Materials Management ....Art Strauss
  Medical Affairs ....Christopher Coley, MD
  Director of Health Plan...........................Paula Fiore
  Information Systems ....Marc Pollack
  Director of Health Plan...........................Paula Fiore

Specialty Managed Care Partners
  Enters into Contracts with Regional Business Coalitions: No

538 Health New England

One Monarch Place
Suite 1500
Springfield, MA 01144-1500
Toll-Free: 800-842-4464
Phone: 413-787-4000
Fax: 413-734-3356
jcampbell@hne.com
www.hne.com
For Profit Organization: Yes

Year Founded: 1985
Number of Affiliated Hospitals: 14
Number of Primary Care Physicians: 4,310
Number of Referral/Specialty Physicians: 3,000
Total Enrollment: 106,000
State Enrollment: 106,000

Healthplan and Services Defined
  PLAN TYPE: HMO
  Model Type: IPA
  Plan Specialty: ASO, Disease Management
  Benefits Offered: Behavioral Health, Chiropractic, Complementary
    Medicine, Dental, Disease Management, Home Care, Inpatient
    SNF, Physical Therapy, Podiatry, Prescription, Psychiatric,
    Transplant, Vision, Wellness

Type of Coverage
  Commercial, Catastrophic, HMO Unlimited
  Catastrophic Illness Benefit: Maximum $1M

Type of Payment Plans Offered
  POS

Geographic Areas Served
  Western Massachusetts (Berkshire, Franklin, Hampden, and
    Hampshire counties as well as parts of Worcester county)

Subscriber Information
  Average Subscriber Co-Payment:
    Primary Care Physician: $15.00
    Non-Network Physician: Not covered
    Prescription Drugs: $15.00/25.00/45.00
    Hospital ER: $50.00
    Nursing Home Max. Days/Visits Covered: 100 days

Network Qualifications
  Pre-Admission Certification: Yes

Peer Review Type
  Utilization Review: Yes
  Second Surgical Opinion: Yes
  Case Management: Yes

Publishes and Distributes Report Card: Yes

Accreditation Certification
  NCQA
  TJC Accreditation, Medicare Approved, Utilization Review,
    Pre-Admission Certification, State Licensure, Quality Assurance
    Program

Key Personnel
  President/CEO..............................Peter F Straley
  VP Finance/CFO..............................Robert A Kosior
  VP, General Counsel..........................James Kessler
  VP Marketing..............................Maura McCaffrey
  Chief Medical Officer ....Thomas H Ebert, MD
  VP, Human Resources ....Amy Trombley
  VP Information Technology ....Philip M Lacombe
  VP Sales..............................Juan A Campbell
  RFP Analyst..............................Laurie Beebe
    413-233-3244
    lbeebe@hne.com

Average Claim Compensation
  Physician's Fees Charged: 59%
  Hospital's Fees Charged: 49%

Specialty Managed Care Partners
  Enters into Contracts with Regional Business Coalitions: No

539 Health Plan of New York: Massachusetts

55 Water Street
New York, NY 10041
Toll-Free: 800-447-8255
Phone: 646-447-5900
Fax: 646-447-3011
www.hipusa.com
Subsidiary of: An Emblem Health Company

Total Enrollment: 1,200,000

Healthplan and Services Defined
PLAN TYPE: HMO/PPO
Other Type: POS, EPO, ASO
Benefits Offered: Chiropractic, Dental, Disease Management, Home
Care, Inpatient SNF, Physical Therapy, Podiatry, Prescription,
Psychiatric, Vision, Wellness

Type of Coverage
Individual, Medicare

Geographic Areas Served
New York, Connecticut, Massachusetts

Subscriber Information
Average Monthly Fee Per Subscriber
(Employee + Employer Contribution):
Employee Only (Self): Varies
Medicare: Varies
Average Annual Deductible Per Subscriber:
Employee Only (Self): Varies
Medicare: Varies
Average Subscriber Co-Payment:
Primary Care Physician: Varies
Non-Network Physician: Varies
Prescription Drugs: Varies
Hospital ER: Varies
Home Health Care: Varies
Home Health Care Max. Days/Visits Covered: Varies
Nursing Home: Varies
Nursing Home Max. Days/Visits Covered: Varies

540 Health Plans, Inc.

1500 West Park Drive
Suite 330, PO Box 5199
Westborough, MA 01581
Toll-Free: 800-532-7575
Phone: 508-752-2480
Fax: 508-754-9664
info@healthplansinc.com
www.healthplansinc.com
Secondary Address: 300 TradeCenter, Suite 2500, Woburn, MA 01801
Subsidiary of: A Harvard Pilgrim Company
For Profit Organization: Yes
Year Founded: 1981
Number of Affiliated Hospitals: 12
Number of Primary Care Physicians: 1,700
Total Enrollment: 12,000

Healthplan and Services Defined
PLAN TYPE: Other
Other Type: TPA
Model Type: Network
Plan Specialty: ASO, Behavioral Health, Chiropractic, Dental,
Disease Management, EPO, Lab, PBM, Vision, Radiology, UR
Benefits Offered: Home Care, Inpatient SNF, Long-Term Care,
Physical Therapy, Podiatry, Prescription, Psychiatric, Transplant,
Vision, Wellness, Worker's Compensation, AD&D, Life, LTD,
STD

Type of Coverage
Employer Self Funded

Geographic Areas Served
Statewide

Subscriber Information
Average Monthly Fee Per Subscriber
(Employee + Employer Contribution):
Employee Only (Self): $2.00
Employee & 1 Family Member: $2.00
Employee & 2 Family Members: $2.00
Average Subscriber Co-Payment:
Primary Care Physician: $5.00
Non-Network Physician: $250.00

Prescription Drugs: $4.00
Hospital ER: $25.00
Home Health Care: $0
Nursing Home: $250.00

Accreditation Certification
TJC Accreditation, Pre-Admission Certification

Key Personnel
President/CEO . . . . William R Breidenbach
Marketing . . . . Debra Hovagimian
Medical Affairs . . . . Michael Galica, MD
Sales . . . . Deb Hoges

Specialty Managed Care Partners
Care Management Service

541 Humana Health Insurance of Massachusetts

1 International Blvd
Suite 400
Mahwah, NJ 07495
Toll-Free: 800-967-2370
Phone: 201-512-8818
www.humana.com
For Profit Organization: Yes

Healthplan and Services Defined
PLAN TYPE: HMO/PPO

Type of Coverage
Commercial, Individual

Accreditation Certification
URAC, NCQA, CORE

542 Neighborhood Health Plan

253 Summer Street
Boston, MA 02210
Toll-Free: 800-433-5556
Phone: 617-772-5500
Fax: 617-772-5513
MemberServices@nhp.org
www.nhp.org
Non-Profit Organization: Yes
Year Founded: 1986
Owned by an Integrated Delivery Network (IDN): Yes
Number of Affiliated Hospitals: 41
Number of Primary Care Physicians: 2,800
Number of Referral/Specialty Physicians: 10,400
Total Enrollment: 186,000
State Enrollment: 25,804

Healthplan and Services Defined
PLAN TYPE: HMO
Model Type: Network
Plan Specialty: ASO, Behavioral Health, Disease Management,
Medicaid Focus
Benefits Offered: Behavioral Health, Complementary Medicine,
Disease Management, Home Care, Prescription, Vision, Wellness

Type of Coverage
Commercial, Medicaid
Catastrophic Illness Benefit: Covered

Geographic Areas Served
Most of Massachusetts counties

Subscriber Information
Average Subscriber Co-Payment:
Primary Care Physician: $0
Prescription Drugs: $5.00
Hospital ER: $0
Home Health Care: $0

Network Qualifications
Pre-Admission Certification: Yes

Peer Review Type
Utilization Review: Yes
Second Surgical Opinion: Yes
Case Management: Yes

Publishes and Distributes Report Card: Yes

Accreditation Certification
State Of Ma
TJC Accreditation, Medicare Approved, Utilization Review, Pre-Admission Certification, State Licensure, Quality Assurance Program

Key Personnel
President/CEO ....Deborah C Enos
VP Business Development ....Carla Bettano
Chief Medical Officer.....................Paul Mendis, MD
Chief Financial Officer.......................Harold Putnam
Chief Information Officer ....Marilyn Daly
VP Human Resources ....Joanne Derr
VP Operations ....Joanne Landry
Chief Operating Officer.......................David Segal
VP Quality & Compliance ....Pam Siren
Director, Marketing..........................Rhian Gregory
617-772-5660

Specialty Managed Care Partners
Beacon Health Strategies
Enters into Contracts with Regional Business Coalitions: No

543 Tufts Health Medicare Plan

705 Mt Auburn Street
Watertown, MA 02472
Toll-Free: 800-462-0024
Phone: 617-972-9400
www.tuftshealthplan.com
Secondary Address: 1441 Main Street, 9th Floor, Springfield, MA 01103
Year Founded: 1979

Healthplan and Services Defined
PLAN TYPE: Medicare
Benefits Offered: Chiropractic, Dental, Disease Management, Home Care, Inpatient SNF, Physical Therapy, Podiatry, Prescription, Psychiatric, Vision, Wellness

Type of Coverage
Individual, Medicare

Geographic Areas Served
Available within Massachusetts, Connecticut, New Hampshire, Rhode Island and Vermont

Subscriber Information
Average Monthly Fee Per Subscriber
(Employee + Employer Contribution):
Employee Only (Self): Varies
Medicare: Varies
Average Annual Deductible Per Subscriber:
Employee Only (Self): Varies
Medicare: Varies
Average Subscriber Co-Payment:
Primary Care Physician: Varies
Non-Network Physician: Varies
Prescription Drugs: Varies
Hospital ER: Varies
Home Health Care: Varies
Home Health Care Max. Days/Visits Covered: Varies
Nursing Home: Varies
Nursing Home Max. Days/Visits Covered: Varies

Key Personnel
President and CEO ....James Roosevelt, Jr
COO..................................Thomas A Croswell
SVP/CIO...................................Tricia Trebino
SVP/Senior Products ....Patty Blake
SVP/Human Resources...................Lois Dehls Cornell

SVP/Marketing ....Rob Egan
Chief Medical Officer.......................Pual Kasuba, MD
SVP/CFO ....Umesh Kurpad
SVP/Sales & Client Svcs ....Brian P Pagliaro

544 Tufts Health Plan

705 Mt Auburn Street
Watertown, MA 02472
Toll-Free: 800-462-0224
Phone: 617-972-9400
www.tuftshealthplan.com
Secondary Address: 1441 Main Street, 9th Floor, Springfield, MA 01103
Non-Profit Organization: Yes
Year Founded: 1979
Number of Affiliated Hospitals: 90
Number of Primary Care Physicians: 25,000
Number of Referral/Specialty Physicians: 12,500
Total Enrollment: 737,411

Healthplan and Services Defined
PLAN TYPE: HMO/PPO
Other Type: POS
Model Type: IPA
Plan Specialty: ASO, Behavioral Health, Chiropractic, Disease Management, EPO, Lab, PBM, Vision, Radiology, UR, Pharmacy
Benefits Offered: Behavioral Health, Chiropractic, Complementary Medicine, Disease Management, Home Care, Inpatient SNF, Physical Therapy, Podiatry, Prescription, Psychiatric, Transplant, Vision, Wellness

Type of Coverage
Commercial, Individual, Medicare, Supplemental Medicare, HSA, HRA

Type of Payment Plans Offered
POS, DFFS, FFS, Combination FFS & DFFS

Geographic Areas Served
Massachusetts, New Hampshire and Rhode Island

Subscriber Information
Average Monthly Fee Per Subscriber
(Employee + Employer Contribution):
Employee Only (Self): $190.00-220.00
Employee & 2 Family Members: $800.00-950.00
Medicare: $150.00
Average Annual Deductible Per Subscriber:
Employee Only (Self): $1000.00
Employee & 1 Family Member: $500.00
Employee & 2 Family Members: $3000.00
Average Subscriber Co-Payment:
Primary Care Physician: $10.00
Non-Network Physician: 20%
Prescription Drugs: $10/20/35
Hospital ER: $50.00
Home Health Care: $0
Home Health Care Max. Days/Visits Covered: 120 days
Nursing Home: $0
Nursing Home Max. Days/Visits Covered: 120 days

Network Qualifications
Pre-Admission Certification: No

Peer Review Type
Utilization Review: Yes
Case Management: Yes

Publishes and Distributes Report Card: Yes

Accreditation Certification
TJC, AAPI, NCQA

Key Personnel
President and CEO ....James Roosevelt, Jr
COO..................................Thomas A Croswell
SVP/CIO...................................Tricia Trebino

SVP/Senior Products . . . . Patty Blake
SVP/Human Resources. Lois Dehls Cornell
SVP/Marketing . . . . Rob Egan
Chief Medical Officer. . . . . Pual Kasuba, MD
SVP/CFO . . . . Umesh Kurpad
SVP/Sales & Client Svcs . . . . Brian P Pagliaro

Average Claim Compensation
Physician's Fees Charged: 75%
Hospital's Fees Charged: 70%

Specialty Managed Care Partners
Advance PCS, Private Healthe Care Systems

Employer References
Commonwealth of Massachuestts, Fleet Boston, Roman Catholic
Archdiocese of Boston, City of Boston, State Street Corporation

545 Unicare: Massachusetts

Brickstone Square
8th Floor
Andover, MA 01810-0916
Toll-Free: 800-862-9988
Phone: 978-470-1795
Fax: 978-247-6599
www.unicare.com
Year Founded: 1985
Number of Affiliated Hospitals: 102
Number of Primary Care Physicians: 3,500
Number of Referral/Specialty Physicians: 8,000
Total Enrollment: 80,000

Healthplan and Services Defined
PLAN TYPE: HMO/PPO
Model Type: Network
Benefits Offered: Chiropractic, Physical Therapy, Prescription

Geographic Areas Served
Massachusetts, Southern New Hampshire & Rhode Island

Subscriber Information
Average Monthly Fee Per Subscriber
(Employee + Employer Contribution):
Employee Only (Self): Varies
Employee & 1 Family Member: Varies
Employee & 2 Family Members: Varies
Medicare: Varies
Average Annual Deductible Per Subscriber:
Employee Only (Self): Varies
Employee & 1 Family Member: Varies
Employee & 2 Family Members: Varies
Medicare: Varies
Average Subscriber Co-Payment:
Primary Care Physician: Varies
Non-Network Physician: Varies
Prescription Drugs: Varies
Hospital ER: Varies
Home Health Care: Varies
Home Health Care Max. Days/Visits Covered: Varies
Nursing Home: Varies
Nursing Home Max. Days/Visits Covered: Varies

Network Qualifications
Pre-Admission Certification: Yes

Peer Review Type
Utilization Review: Yes
Second Surgical Opinion: Yes
Case Management: Yes

Publishes and Distributes Report Card: No

Accreditation Certification
TJC Accreditation, Medicare Approved, Utilization Review,
Pre-Admission Certification, State Licensure, Quality Assurance
Program

Key Personnel
CEO and President. . . . . David W Fields
Sales Director . . . . Cynthia L Paralta
cynthia.paralta@wellpoint.com
Media Contact . . . . Tony Felts
317-287-6036
tony.felts@wellpoint.com

546 UnitedHealthCare of Massachusetts

475 Kilvert Street
Warwick, RI 02886
Toll-Free: 888-735-5842
Fax: 781-419-8681
www.uhc.com
Subsidiary of: UnitedHealth Group
For Profit Organization: Yes
Number of Affiliated Hospitals: 105
Number of Primary Care Physicians: 8,000
Total Enrollment: 75,000,000

Healthplan and Services Defined
PLAN TYPE: HMO/PPO
Model Type: Network
Benefits Offered: Disease Management, Prescription, Wellness
Offers Demand Management Patient Information Service: Yes

Type of Coverage
Catastrophic Illness Benefit: None

Type of Payment Plans Offered
POS, FFS

Geographic Areas Served
Connecticut, Massachusetts, Maine, New Hampshire, Rhode Island

Subscriber Information
Average Monthly Fee Per Subscriber
(Employee + Employer Contribution):
Employee Only (Self): $150.00
Employee & 2 Family Members: $300.00

Network Qualifications
Pre-Admission Certification: Yes

Peer Review Type
Utilization Review: Yes
Second Surgical Opinion: Yes
Case Management: Yes

Publishes and Distributes Report Card: Yes

Accreditation Certification
NCQA
TJC Accreditation, Medicare Approved, Utilization Review,
Pre-Admission Certification, State Licensure, Quality Assurance
Program

Key Personnel
President/CEO . . . . Amy Knapp
CFO. . . . . Donald Powers
Marketing. . . . . Mark Butler
Medical Affairs . . . . Tony Kazlauskas
Sales . . . . James Moniz
Media Contact . . . . Debora Spano
401-732-7374
debora_m_spano@uhc.com

Average Claim Compensation
Physician's Fees Charged: 70%
Hospital's Fees Charged: 80%

Specialty Managed Care Partners
Enters into Contracts with Regional Business Coalitions: Yes

547 VSP: Vision Service Plan of Massachusetts

8 Faneuil Hall Market Place
Boston, MA 02109-6114
Phone: 617-854-7471

webmaster@vsp.com
www.vsp.com
Year Founded: 1955
Number of Primary Care Physicians: 26,000
Total Enrollment: 55,000,000

Healthplan and Services Defined
  PLAN TYPE: Vision
  Plan Specialty: Vision
  Benefits Offered: Vision

Type of Payment Plans Offered
  Capitated

Geographic Areas Served
  Statewide

Network Qualifications
  Pre-Admission Certification: Yes

Peer Review Type
  Utilization Review: Yes

Accreditation Certification
  Utilization Review, Quality Assurance Program

Health Insurance Coverage Status and Type of Coverage by Age

Category	All Persons		Under 18 years		Under 65 years		65 years and over	
	Number	%	Number	%	Number	%	Number	%
Total population	9,772	-	2,318	-	8,431	-	1,341	-
Covered by some type of health insurance	8,500 *(83)*	87.0 *(0.7)*	2,199 *(26)*	94.9 *(0.7)*	7,174 *(125)*	85.1 *(0.8)*	1,326 *(81)*	98.9 *(0.5)*
Covered by private health insurance	6,669 *(130)*	68.3 *(1.3)*	1,526 *(51)*	65.8 *(2.1)*	5,774 *(142)*	68.5 *(1.3)*	895 *(63)*	66.8 *(2.8)*
Employment based	5,811 *(146)*	59.5 *(1.4)*	1,419 *(50)*	61.2 *(2.1)*	5,259 *(145)*	62.4 *(1.4)*	552 *(52)*	41.2 *(3.2)*
Own employment based	2,754 *(69)*	28.2 *(0.7)*	5 *(4)*	0.2 *(0.2)*	2,322 *(71)*	27.5 *(0.7)*	432 *(43)*	32.2 *(2.6)*
Direct purchase	1,001 *(74)*	10.2 *(0.8)*	125 *(24)*	5.4 *(1.0)*	616 *(70)*	7.3 *(0.8)*	385 *(45)*	28.7 *(2.8)*
Covered by government health insurance	3,167 *(113)*	32.4 *(1.2)*	850 *(54)*	36.7 *(2.3)*	1,902 *(107)*	22.6 *(1.2)*	1,265 *(75)*	94.3 *(1.1)*
Covered by Medicaid	1,657 *(100)*	17.0 *(1.0)*	835 *(55)*	36.0 *(2.3)*	1,591 *(98)*	18.9 *(1.1)*	67 *(18)*	5.0 *(1.3)*
Also by private insurance	342 *(41)*	3.5 *(0.4)*	171 *(27)*	7.4 *(1.1)*	330 *(41)*	3.9 *(0.5)*	12 *(6)*	0.9 *(0.4)*
Covered by Medicare	1,613 *(70)*	16.5 *(0.7)*	22 *(9)*	0.9 *(0.4)*	352 *(33)*	4.2 *(0.4)*	1,261 *(74)*	94.1 *(1.1)*
Also by private insurance	968 *(58)*	9.9 *(0.6)*	4 *(3)*	0.2 *(0.1)*	135 *(21)*	1.6 *(0.3)*	834 *(58)*	62.2 *(2.9)*
Also by Medicaid	192 *(31)*	2.0 *(0.3)*	12 *(7)*	0.5 *(0.3)*	129 *(22)*	1.5 *(0.3)*	63 *(18)*	4.7 *(1.3)*
Covered by military health care	179 *(26)*	1.8 *(0.3)*	11 *(4)*	0.5 *(0.2)*	103 *(21)*	1.2 *(0.2)*	75 *(20)*	5.6 *(1.5)*
Not covered at any time during the year	1,271 *(69)*	13.0 *(0.7)*	119 *(17)*	5.1 *(0.7)*	1,257 *(69)*	14.9 *(0.8)*	15 *(7)*	1.1 *(0.5)*

Note: Numbers in thousands; figures cover 2010; standard error appears in parenthesis; (b) base less than 75,000; (x) not applicable
Source: U.S. Census Bureau, Current Population Survey, 2011 Annual Social and Economic Supplement. Table HI05. Health Insurance Coverage Status and Type of Coverage by State and Age for All People: 2010

Michigan

548 Aetna Health of Michigan

151 Farmington Avenue
RE52
Hartford, CT 06156
Toll-Free: 866-582-9629
www.aetna.com
For Profit Organization: Yes
Year Founded: 1988
Total Enrollment: 11,596,230

Healthplan and Services Defined
PLAN TYPE: PPO
Other Type: POS
Plan Specialty: PBM
Benefits Offered: Behavioral Health, Dental, Disease Management,
  Prescription, Vision
Offers Demand Management Patient Information Service: Yes

Type of Payment Plans Offered
DFFS

Geographic Areas Served
Statewide

Subscriber Information
Average Monthly Fee Per Subscriber
  (Employee + Employer Contribution):
    Employee Only (Self): $73.42
    Employee & 1 Family Member: $168.89

Network Qualifications
Pre-Admission Certification: Yes

Peer Review Type
Utilization Review: Yes

Publishes and Distributes Report Card: Yes

Key Personnel
CEO . . . . Ronald A Williams
President. . . . . Mark T Bertolini
SVP, General Counsel . . . . William J Casazza
EVP, CFO . . . . Joseph M Zubretsky
Head, M&A Integration . . . . Kay Mooney
SVP, Marketing. . . . . Robert E Mead
Chief Medical Officer . . . . Lonny Reisman, MD
SVP, Human Resources. Elease E Wright
SVP, CIO. . . . . Meg McCarthy

549 American Community Mutual Insurance Company

Under Reinsurance Agreement with Security Life

550 Assurant Employee Benefits: Michigan

3001 W Big Beaver Road
#330
Troy, MI 48084-3101
Phone: 248-649-4410
Fax: 248-643-7626
benefits@assurant.com
www.assurantemployeebenefits.com
Subsidiary of: Assurant, Inc
For Profit Organization: Yes
Number of Primary Care Physicians: 112,000
Total Enrollment: 47,000

Healthplan and Services Defined
PLAN TYPE: Multiple
Plan Specialty: Dental, Vision, Long & Short-Term Disability
Benefits Offered: Dental, Vision, Wellness, AD&D, Life, LTD, STD

Type of Coverage
Commercial, Indemnity, Individual Dental Plans

Geographic Areas Served
Statewide

Subscriber Information
Average Monthly Fee Per Subscriber
  (Employee + Employer Contribution):
    Employee Only (Self): Varies by plan

Key Personnel
Sales Manager . . . . Molly Dunn
Manager. . . . . Dave Braff
PR Specialist. . . . . Megan Hutchison
  816-556-7815
  megan.hutchison@assurant.com

551 Blue Care Network of Michigan: Corporate Headquarters

20500 Civic Center Drive
The Commons
Southfield, MI 48076
Toll-Free: 800-662-6667
Fax: 248-799-6327
www.mibcn.com
Mailing Address: PO Box 5184, Southfield, MI 48086
Subsidiary of: Blue Cross Blue Shield
Non-Profit Organization: Yes
Year Founded: 1998
Federally Qualified: Yes
Number of Affiliated Hospitals: 116
Number of Primary Care Physicians: 4,500
Number of Referral/Specialty Physicians: 13,500
Total Enrollment: 620,000
State Enrollment: 620,000

Healthplan and Services Defined
PLAN TYPE: HMO
Model Type: IPA, Network
Plan Specialty: Lab, Radiology
Benefits Offered: Behavioral Health, Disease Management,
  Prescription, Psychiatric, Wellness
Offers Demand Management Patient Information Service: Yes

Type of Coverage
Commercial, Individual, Supplemental Medicare
Catastrophic Illness Benefit: Covered

Type of Payment Plans Offered
POS

Geographic Areas Served
Statewide

Subscriber Information
Average Monthly Fee Per Subscriber
  (Employee + Employer Contribution):
    Employee Only (Self): Varies
    Employee & 1 Family Member: Varies
    Employee & 2 Family Members: Varies
    Medicare: Varies

Network Qualifications
Pre-Admission Certification: Yes

Peer Review Type
Case Management: Yes

Publishes and Distributes Report Card: Yes

Accreditation Certification
NCQA

Key Personnel
President/CEO . . . . Kevin L Klobucar
SVP, CFO . . . . Susan Kluge
SVP, Chief Medical Offc. . . . . Marc Keshishian, MD
General Counsel . . . . Lisa S DeMoss

Chief Information Officer . . . . William P Smith

Specialty Managed Care Partners
Enters into Contracts with Regional Business Coalitions: Yes

Employer References
General Motors, Ford Motor Company, State of Michigan, Federal Employee Program, Daimler Chrysler

---

552   Blue Care Network of Michigan: Medicare

20500 Civic Center Drive
P O Box 5043
Southfield, MI 48086-5043
Toll-Free: 800-430-3211
Fax: 248-799-6327
www.mibcn.com

Healthplan and Services Defined
PLAN TYPE: Medicare
Benefits Offered: Chiropractic, Disease Management, Home Care, Inpatient SNF, Physical Therapy, Podiatry, Prescription, Psychiatric, Wellness

Type of Coverage
Individual, Medicare

Geographic Areas Served
Available in Michigan within specific counties - contact Blue Care Network of Michigan for further information

Subscriber Information
Average Monthly Fee Per Subscriber
(Employee + Employer Contribution):
Employee Only (Self): Varies
Medicare: Varies
Average Annual Deductible Per Subscriber:
Employee Only (Self): Varies
Medicare: Varies
Average Subscriber Co-Payment:
Primary Care Physician: Varies
Non-Network Physician: Varies
Prescription Drugs: Varies
Hospital ER: Varies
Home Health Care: Varies
Home Health Care Max. Days/Visits Covered: Varies
Nursing Home: Varies
Nursing Home Max. Days/Visits Covered: Varies

Key Personnel
President/CEO . . . . Jeanne Carlson
SVP/CFO . . . . Susan Kluge
SVP/Chief Actuary Officer. David Nelson
Chief Medical Officer. . . . . Douglas Woll, MD

---

553   Blue Care Network: Ann Arbor

2311 Green Road
Ann Arbor, MI 48507
Toll-Free: 800-428-7361
Fax: 517-322-4315
www.mibcn.com
Non-Profit Organization: Yes
Year Founded: 1975
Federally Qualified: Yes
Number of Affiliated Hospitals: 116
Number of Primary Care Physicians: 4,500
Number of Referral/Specialty Physicians: 13,500
Total Enrollment: 620,000
State Enrollment: 620,000

Healthplan and Services Defined
PLAN TYPE: HMO
Model Type: Staff
Plan Specialty: Lab, Radiology
Benefits Offered: Behavioral Health, Dental, Disease Management, Prescription, Psychiatric, Wellness

---

Offers Demand Management Patient Information Service: Yes

Type of Coverage
Commercial, Individual, Supplemental Medicare
Catastrophic Illness Benefit: Varies per case

Type of Payment Plans Offered
POS, DFFS, Capitated, FFS, Combination FFS & DFFS

Geographic Areas Served
Clinton, Eaton, Ingham, Ionia, Jackson, Livingston, Shiawassee counties

Subscriber Information
Average Monthly Fee Per Subscriber
(Employee + Employer Contribution):
Employee Only (Self): Varies by plan
Employee & 1 Family Member: $365.40
Average Annual Deductible Per Subscriber:
Employee Only (Self): $0
Employee & 1 Family Member: $0
Employee & 2 Family Members: $0
Medicare: $0
Average Subscriber Co-Payment:
Primary Care Physician: $0
Home Health Care: $0
Home Health Care Max. Days/Visits Covered: Unlimited
Nursing Home: $0
Nursing Home Max. Days/Visits Covered: 45 days

Network Qualifications
Pre-Admission Certification: Yes

Peer Review Type
Utilization Review: Yes
Second Surgical Opinion: Yes
Case Management: Yes

Publishes and Distributes Report Card: Yes

Accreditation Certification
AAAHC, URAC, AAPI, NCQA
TJC Accreditation, Medicare Approved, Utilization Review, Pre-Admission Certification, State Licensure, Quality Assurance Program

Key Personnel
President/CEO BCBSMi . . . . Richard E Whitmer
President/CEO Blue Care . . . . Kevin L Seitz
CFO . . . . Mark R Bartlett
Chief Medical Offficer . . . . Thomas L Simmer, MD
Chief Information Officer. . . . . William P Smith

Average Claim Compensation
Physician's Fees Charged: 1%

Specialty Managed Care Partners
Enters into Contracts with Regional Business Coalitions: Yes

---

554   Blue Care Network: Flint

4520 Linden Creek Parkway
Suite A
Flint, MI 48507
Toll-Free: 800-654-3708
Phone: 810-720-6715
Fax: 810-720-6778
www.micbn.com
Subsidiary of: Blue Cross Blue Shield
Non-Profit Organization: Yes
Number of Affiliated Hospitals: 116
Number of Primary Care Physicians: 4,500
Number of Referral/Specialty Physicians: 13,500
Total Enrollment: 620,000
State Enrollment: 620,000

Healthplan and Services Defined
PLAN TYPE: HMO
Plan Specialty: Lab, Radiology

Benefits Offered: Behavioral Health, Disease Management,
Prescription, Psychiatric, Wellness

Type of Coverage
Commercial, Individual, Indemnity, Supplemental Medicare

Type of Payment Plans Offered
DFFS, Capitated

Publishes and Distributes Report Card: Yes

Key Personnel
Chief Executive Officer . . . . Richard E Whitmer
President/CEO Blue Care . . . . Kevin L Seitz
Chief Financial Officer . . . . Mark R Bartlett
Chief Medical Officer . . . . Thomas L Simmer, MD
General Counsel . . . . Lisa S DeMoss
Chief Information Officer . . . . William P Smith

555 Blue Care Network: Great Lakes, Muskegon Heights

611 Cascade W Parkway SE
Grand Rapids, MI 49546
Phone: 616-389-2060
Fax: 616-389-2115
www.mibcn.com
Non-Profit Organization: Yes
Year Founded: 1984
Federally Qualified: Yes
Number of Affiliated Hospitals: 116
Number of Primary Care Physicians: 4,500
Number of Referral/Specialty Physicians: 13,500
Total Enrollment: 620,000
State Enrollment: 620,000

Healthplan and Services Defined
PLAN TYPE: HMO
Model Type: IPA
Plan Specialty: Lab, Radiology
Benefits Offered: Behavioral Health, Dental, Disease Management,
Physical Therapy, Prescription, Psychiatric, Vision, Wellness

Type of Coverage
Commercial, Individual
Catastrophic Illness Benefit: Varies per case

Type of Payment Plans Offered
POS, Capitated, Combination FFS & DFFS

Geographic Areas Served
Muskegon, Newago, Oceana & Ottawa counties

Subscriber Information
Average Monthly Fee Per Subscriber
(Employee + Employer Contribution):
Employee Only (Self): Varies
Employee & 1 Family Member: Varies
Employee & 2 Family Members: Varies
Medicare: Varies
Average Annual Deductible Per Subscriber:
Employee Only (Self): $0
Employee & 1 Family Member: $0
Employee & 2 Family Members: $0
Medicare: $0
Average Subscriber Co-Payment:
Primary Care Physician: Varies
Non-Network Physician: Varies
Prescription Drugs: Varies
Hospital ER: Varies
Home Health Care: Varies
Nursing Home: Varies

Network Qualifications
Pre-Admission Certification: Yes

Peer Review Type
Utilization Review: Yes
Second Surgical Opinion: Yes

Publishes and Distributes Report Card: Yes

Key Personnel
President and CEO . . . . Kevin L Seitz
General Counsel . . . . Lisa S DeMoss
Chief Medical Officer . . . . Thomas L Simmer, MD
Chief Information Officer . . . . William P Smith

556 Blue Cross Blue Shield of Michigan

600 E Lafayette Blvd
Detroit, MI 48226-2998
Toll-Free: 877-469-2583
Phone: 313-225-9000
Fax: 313-225-6764
www.bcbsm.com
Non-Profit Organization: Yes
Number of Affiliated Hospitals: 159
Number of Primary Care Physicians: 30,000
Total Enrollment: 4,300,000
State Enrollment: 4,300,000

Healthplan and Services Defined
PLAN TYPE: PPO
Other Type: Major Medical
Model Type: IPA
Plan Specialty: Lab, Radiology
Benefits Offered: Behavioral Health, Disease Management, Home
Care, Prescription, Psychiatric, Wellness, Pharmacy

Type of Coverage
Commercial, Individual, Indemnity
Catastrophic Illness Benefit: Varies per case

Geographic Areas Served
Statewide/Michigan

Subscriber Information
Average Monthly Fee Per Subscriber
(Employee + Employer Contribution):
Employee Only (Self): Varies
Employee & 1 Family Member: Varies
Employee & 2 Family Members: Varies
Average Annual Deductible Per Subscriber:
Employee Only (Self): Varies

Network Qualifications
Pre-Admission Certification: Yes

Peer Review Type
Utilization Review: Yes
Second Surgical Opinion: No
Case Management: Yes

Publishes and Distributes Report Card: Yes

Accreditation Certification
TJC Accreditation, Medicare Approved, Utilization Review,
Pre-Admission Certification, State Licensure, Quality Assurance
Program

Key Personnel
President & CEO . . . . Daniel J Loepp
EVP, CFO. . . . . Mark R Bartlett
SVP, Health Care Value . . . . Susan L Barkell
SVP, Group Sales . . . . Kenneth R Dallafior
SVP, Subsidiary Operation . . . . Elizabeth R Harr
VP, Corporate Secretary . . . . Tricia A Keith
SVP, Business Efficiency . . . . Darrell E Middleton
VP, Treasurer . . . . Carolynn Walton
Chief Medical Officer . . . . Thomas L Simmer, MD
Chief Information Officer . . . . Joseph H Hohner

Specialty Managed Care Partners
Enters into Contracts with Regional Business Coalitions: Yes

557 Care Choices
Acquired by Priority Health

558 CareSource: Michigan

2900 West Road
Suite 201
East Lansing, MI 48823
Toll-Free: 800-390-7102
Phone: 517-349-9922
Fax: 517-349-5343
www.caresource-michigan.com
Non-Profit Organization: Yes
Year Founded: 1996
Number of Primary Care Physicians: 588
Number of Referral/Specialty Physicians: 3,983
Total Enrollment: 50,000
State Enrollment: 50,000

Healthplan and Services Defined
PLAN TYPE: HMO
Model Type: Network
Benefits Offered: Disease Management, Prescription, Wellness
Offers Demand Management Patient Information Service: Yes
DMPI Services Offered: 24-Hour Nurse Advice Line

Type of Coverage
Medicaid
Catastrophic Illness Benefit: Covered

Type of Payment Plans Offered
POS, DFFS, FFS, Combination FFS & DFFS

Geographic Areas Served
39 counties in Michigan

Subscriber Information
Average Subscriber Co-Payment:
Home Health Care Max. Days/Visits Covered: As necessary with pc
Nursing Home Max. Days/Visits Covered: 100/year

Network Qualifications
Pre-Admission Certification: Yes

Peer Review Type
Utilization Review: Yes

Publishes and Distributes Report Card: Yes

Accreditation Certification
TJC Accreditation, Medicare Approved, Utilization Review, Pre-Admission Certification, State Licensure, Quality Assurance Program

Key Personnel
President & CEO . . . . .Pamela Morris
Chief Operating Officer . . . . .Bobby Jones
EVP, External Affairs . . . . .Janet Grant
Chief Financial Officer .Tarlton Thomas, III
EVP, General Counsel. . . . . .Mark Chilson
Chief Medical Officer. . . . . .Craig Thiele, MD

Average Claim Compensation
Physician's Fees Charged: 40%
Hospital's Fees Charged: 35%

Specialty Managed Care Partners
Enters into Contracts with Regional Business Coalitions: Yes

559 CIGNA HealthCare of Michigan

400 Galleria Officenter
Suite 500
Southfield, MI 48034
Toll-Free: 866-438-2446
Phone: 248-226-9369
Fax: 248-226-9425
www.cigna.com
For Profit Organization: Yes

Healthplan and Services Defined
PLAN TYPE: PPO

Type of Coverage
Commercial

560 Cofinity

28588 Northwestern Highway
Southfield, MI 48034
Toll-Free: 800-831-1166
Fax: 888-499-3957
www.cofinity.net
Subsidiary of: Division of Aetna
For Profit Organization: Yes
Year Founded: 1979
Physician Owned Organization: Yes
Total Enrollment: 2,500,000

Healthplan and Services Defined
PLAN TYPE: PPO
Other Type: TPA
Model Type: Network
Plan Specialty: Behavioral Health, Chiropractic, Disease Management, EPO, Lab, Vision, Radiology, Worker's Compensation, UR, Medical Management, Medical Networks, Out-of-Network Claims Mgmt, Fraud & Abuse Mgmt, Credentialing Services
Benefits Offered: Dental, Prescription, Transplant, Worker's Compensation

Type of Coverage
Catastrophic Illness Benefit: Varies per case

Type of Payment Plans Offered
FFS

Geographic Areas Served
Statewide

Subscriber Information
Average Monthly Fee Per Subscriber
(Employee + Employer Contribution):
Employee Only (Self): $4.00
Employee & 1 Family Member: $4.00
Employee & 2 Family Members: $4.00
Average Subscriber Co-Payment:
Primary Care Physician: $15.00
Hospital ER: $50.00-75.00

Network Qualifications
Pre-Admission Certification: Yes

Peer Review Type
Utilization Review: Yes
Second Surgical Opinion: Yes
Case Management: Yes

Publishes and Distributes Report Card: No

Accreditation Certification
TJC Accreditation, Medicare Approved, Utilization Review, Pre-Admission Certification, State Licensure, Quality Assurance Program

Key Personnel
General Manager . . . . .Michael Cirrocchi
Products & Partnerships. . . . . .Kathy Edelman
Operations . . . . .Kelly Wright
Networks . . . . .Mark Granzier
Sales. . . . . .Doug Wilson

Average Claim Compensation
Physician's Fees Charged: 1%
Hospital's Fees Charged: 1%

Specialty Managed Care Partners
Gentiva
Enters into Contracts with Regional Business Coalitions: No

561 ConnectCare

4009 Orchard Drive
Suite 3021
Midland, MI 48640
Toll-Free: 888-646-2429
Phone: 989-839-1629
Fax: 989-839-1626
info@connectcare.com
www.connectcare.com
Subsidiary of: MidMichigan Health Network LLC
Non-Profit Organization: Yes
Year Founded: 1993
Physician Owned Organization: Yes
Owned by an Integrated Delivery Network (IDN): Yes
Federally Qualified: No
Number of Affiliated Hospitals: 4
Number of Primary Care Physicians: 113
Number of Referral/Specialty Physicians: 273
Total Enrollment: 17,000
State Enrollment: 36,000

Healthplan and Services Defined
 PLAN TYPE: PPO
 Model Type: Network
 Benefits Offered: Behavioral Health, Dental, Home Care, Inpatient
  SNF, Long-Term Care, Physical Therapy, Podiatry, Prescription,
  Psychiatric, Wellness

Type of Coverage
 Commercial, Indemnity

Type of Payment Plans Offered
 POS, DFFS

Geographic Areas Served
 Domiciled in central Michigan, with primary counties served
 including Clare, Gladwin, Gratiot, Isabella, Midland, Montcalm and
 Roscommon. Arrangement with national PPO's for coverage of
 downstate and those enrollees residing outside of Michigan

Subscriber Information
 Average Annual Deductible Per Subscriber:
  Employee Only (Self): $275.00
  Employee & 2 Family Members: $550.00

Network Qualifications
 Pre-Admission Certification: Yes

Peer Review Type
 Utilization Review: Yes
 Second Surgical Opinion: Yes
 Case Management: Yes

Accreditation Certification
 NCQA
 Quality Assurance Program

Key Personnel
 President/CEO . . . . .Brian Rodgers
  989-839-3269
  brian.rodgers@connectcare.com
 Financial Manager . . . . .Sara O'Dell
  989-839-1662
  sara.odell@connectcare.com
 Operations Director. . . . . .Janis Bond, RN CMCN
  989-839-1617
  janis.bond@connectcare.com
 Account Manager . . . . .Denise O'Keefe
  898-839-1612
  denise.okeefe@connectcare.com
 Medical Director . . . . .Dan Sorenson, MD
  989-839-1625
  dan.sorenson@connectcare.com

562 CoreSource: Michigan (NGS CoreSource)

27575 Harper Avenue
PO Box 7676
St Clair Shores, MI 48080
Toll-Free: 800-521-1555
Phone: 586-779-7676
www.coresource.com; www.ngs.com
Subsidiary of: Trustmark
Year Founded: 1980
Total Enrollment: 1,100,000

Healthplan and Services Defined
 PLAN TYPE: Multiple
 Other Type: TPA
 Model Type: Network
 Plan Specialty: Claims Administration, TPA
 Benefits Offered: Behavioral Health, Home Care, Prescription,
  Transplant

Type of Coverage
 Commercial

Geographic Areas Served
 Nationwide

Accreditation Certification
 Utilization Review, Pre-Admission Certification

563 Delta Dental: Corporate Headquarters

4100 Okemos Road
Okemos, MI 48864
Toll-Free: 800-482-8915
Phone: 517-349-6000
Fax: 517-347-5420
www.deltadentalmi.com
Secondary Address: 27500 Stansbury, Farmington Hills, MI 48334
Non-Profit Organization: Yes
Year Founded: 1957
Total Enrollment: 54,000,000

Healthplan and Services Defined
 PLAN TYPE: Dental
 Other Type: Dental PPO
 Model Type: Group
 Plan Specialty: Dental
 Benefits Offered: Dental

Type of Coverage
 Commercial

Type of Payment Plans Offered
 POS, Capitated, FFS

Geographic Areas Served
 Nationwide

Network Qualifications
 Pre-Admission Certification: Yes

Peer Review Type
 Utilization Review: Yes

Publishes and Distributes Report Card: Yes

Key Personnel
 Chief Executive Officer. . . . . .Thomas J Fleszar, DDS, MS
 Chief Operating Officer . . . . .Laura L Czelada, CPA
 Chief Information Officer . . . . .Brenda Laird
 Chief Marketing Officer. . . . . .Michael Clark
 SVP, Chief Science Offc. . . . . .Jed J. Jacobson, DDS/MPH
 Senior VP, Operations . . . . .Sherry L. Crisp
 SVP/Corp/Public Affairs . . . . .Nancy E. Hostetler
 Chief Admin Officer . . . . .Edward J Zobeck
 VP/Quality Assurance . . . . .Karen M Green
 VP, General Counsel . . . . .Jonathan S Groat, Esq
 VP, Chief Actuary . . . . .Toby L Hall
 VP, Chief Financial Offc. . . . . .Goran Jurkovic, CPA
 Pres/CEO, Renaissance Sys .Erick Paul

VP, Sales & Acct Mgmt . . . . Randy A Tasco
Communications Admin . . . . Ari B Adler
517-347-5292
aadler@deltadentalmi.com
Dir/Media & Public Affair . . . . Elizabeth Risberg
415-972-8423

Specialty Managed Care Partners
Enters into Contracts with Regional Business Coalitions: No

Employer References
General Motors Corp, State of Michigan, Michigan Public School Employee Retirement System, Daimler Chrysler Corp, Dow Chemical Company

564 Dencap Dental Plans

45 E Milwaukee Avenue
Detroit, MI 48202
Toll-Free: 800-875-2400
Phone: 313-972-1400
Fax: 313-972-4662
sales@dencap.com
www.dencap.com
Year Founded: 1984
Number of Primary Care Physicians: 200
State Enrollment: 20,000

Healthplan and Services Defined
PLAN TYPE: Dental
Model Type: Network
Plan Specialty: Dental
Benefits Offered: Dental

Type of Coverage
Commercial, Individual

Type of Payment Plans Offered
DFFS, FFS

Geographic Areas Served
Southeastern Michigan

Subscriber Information
Average Monthly Fee Per Subscriber
(Employee + Employer Contribution):
Employee Only (Self): Varies
Average Annual Deductible Per Subscriber:
Employee Only (Self): $0
Employee & 1 Family Member: $0
Employee & 2 Family Members: $0
Average Subscriber Co-Payment:
Primary Care Physician: 25%

Peer Review Type
Case Management: Yes

Publishes and Distributes Report Card: Yes

Accreditation Certification
Utilization Review, Quality Assurance Program

Key Personnel
President/CEO . . . . Joseph T Lentine
Provider Relations Dir. . . . . Frank Berge
fberge@dencap.com
Marketing. . . . . Roger Roberts
rroberts@dencap.com
Medical Affairs. . . . . James Feldman, DDS
Account Executive . . . . Precious Stitall
pstigall@dencap.com

Specialty Managed Care Partners
Midwest and Dentals, Great Expression

565 DenteMax

25925 Telegraph Road
Suite 400
Southfield, MI 48033

Toll-Free: 800-752-1547
Phone: 248-327-5200
Fax: 248-327-5201
customerservices@dentemax.com
www.dentemax.com
Subsidiary of: Blue Cross/Blue Shield of Michigan
For Profit Organization: Yes
Year Founded: 1985
Number of Primary Care Physicians: 113,000
Total Enrollment: 4,500,000

Healthplan and Services Defined
PLAN TYPE: Dental
Other Type: Dental PPO
Plan Specialty: Dental
Benefits Offered: Dental

Type of Coverage
Commercial, Individual
Catastrophic Illness Benefit: None

Type of Payment Plans Offered
DFFS

Geographic Areas Served
Nationwide

Subscriber Information
Average Monthly Fee Per Subscriber
(Employee + Employer Contribution):
Employee Only (Self): Varies by plan

Network Qualifications
Pre-Admission Certification: No

Peer Review Type
Utilization Review: Yes

Accreditation Certification
Quality Assurance Program

Key Personnel
President/CEO. . . . . John Doyle
Treasurer . . . . Craig Simundza
VP Operations . . . . Amy Frenzel
248-327-5242
afrenzel@dentemax.com
VP, Finance & Admin . . . . Richard J Werther
Dental Director. . . . . Glenn Melenyk
VP, Dental Network. . . . . Mike Miller
VP, Sales & Marketing . . . . Melissa Wagner
VP Sales/Marketing. . . . . Melissa Wagner
248-327-5230
mwagner@dentemax.com
Media Contact . . . . Andrea Pietrowsky
248-327-5247
apeitrowsky@dentemax.com

566 eHealthInsurance Services Inc.

11919 Foundation Place
Gold River, CA 95670
Toll-Free: 800-977-8860
info@ehealthinsurance.com
www.e.healthinsurance.com
Year Founded: 1997

Healthplan and Services Defined
PLAN TYPE: HMO/PPO
Benefits Offered: Dental, Life, STD

Type of Coverage
Commercial, Individual, Medicare

Geographic Areas Served
All 50 states in the USA and District of Columbia

Key Personnel
Chairman & CEO. . . . . Gary L. Lauer
EVP/Business & Corp. Dev.. . . . . Bruce Telkamp

EVP/Chief Technology . . . . Dr. Sheldon X. Wang
SVP & CFO . . . . Stuart M. Huizinga
Pres. of eHealth Gov. Sys . . . . Samuel C. Gibbs
SVP of Sales & Operations . . . . Robert S. Hurley
Director Public Relations . . . . Nate Purpura
    650-210-3115

567 Golden Dental Plans

29377 Hoover Road
Warren, MI 48093
Toll-Free: 800-451-5918
Phone: 586-573-8118
Fax: 586-573-8720
www.goldendentalplans.com
Secondary Address: 25601 Glendale, Redford, MI 48239
Year Founded: 1984
Number of Primary Care Physicians: 3,200
Total Enrollment: 130,000

Healthplan and Services Defined
  PLAN TYPE: Dental
  Other Type: Dental HMO
  Model Type: Network
  Plan Specialty: Dental
  Benefits Offered: Dental

Type of Payment Plans Offered
  DFFS

Geographic Areas Served
  Michigan, Illinois, Kentucky, Washington, DC, Maryland and
  Virginia

Accreditation Certification
  Utilization Review, Pre-Admission Certification

Key Personnel
  President/CEO . . . . Edward J Petersmarck
  Medical Affairs . . . . Gerald Yax, DDS
  Marketing . . . . Gary L Bingaman

568 Grand Valley Health Plan

829 Forest Hill Avenue SE
Grand Rapids, MI 49546
Phone: 616-949-2410
Fax: 616-949-4978
info@gvhp.com
www.gvhp.com
For Profit Organization: Yes
Year Founded: 1982
Number of Affiliated Hospitals: 7
Total Enrollment: 8,000
State Enrollment: 26,599

Healthplan and Services Defined
  PLAN TYPE: HMO
  Model Type: Staff
  Plan Specialty: Radiology
  Benefits Offered: Behavioral Health, Chiropractic, Disease
    Management, Physical Therapy, Podiatry, Prescription, Transplant,
    Vision, Wellness
  Offers Demand Management Patient Information Service: Yes

Type of Coverage
  Commercial

Type of Payment Plans Offered
  POS

Network Qualifications
  Pre-Admission Certification: Yes

Peer Review Type
  Utilization Review: Yes
  Second Surgical Opinion: Yes
  Case Management: Yes

Publishes and Distributes Report Card: Yes

Accreditation Certification
  NCQA
  TJC Accreditation

Key Personnel
  President and CEO . . . . Roland Palmer
  CFO . . . . Jack Heinen
  Medical Director . . . . James Kerby, MD
  Director Pharmacy Services . . . . Dave Ridout
  Marketing Director . . . . Pam Silva
  Marketing Manager . . . . Brian Mack
    616-949-2410
  Communications Manager . . . . Kristen Cichon
    616-949-2410

Specialty Managed Care Partners
  Enters into Contracts with Regional Business Coalitions: Yes

569 Great Lakes Health Plan

26957 Northwestern Highway
Suite 400
Southfield, MI 48033
Toll-Free: 800-903-5253
Phone: 248-559-5656
Fax: 248-559-4640
info@glhp.com
www.glhp.com
Subsidiary of: AmeriChoice, A UnitedHealth Group Company
For Profit Organization: Yes
Year Founded: 1994
Number of Affiliated Hospitals: 7
Number of Primary Care Physicians: 1,622
Number of Referral/Specialty Physicians: 4,928
Total Enrollment: 215,000
State Enrollment: 215,000

Healthplan and Services Defined
  PLAN TYPE: HMO
  Plan Specialty: Case Management
  Benefits Offered: Disease Management, Home Care, Prescription

Type of Coverage
  Medicare, Medicaid, MIChild

Type of Payment Plans Offered
  DFFS, Capitated

Geographic Areas Served
  Medicaid: Wayne, Oakland, Macomb, Washtenaw, Livingston,
  Lenawee, Calhoun, Hillsdale, Jackson, Berrien, Cass, Van Buren,
  Kalamazoo, St. Clair, Lapeer, Sanilac, Arenac, Huron, Tuscola,
  Saginaw, Alger, Baraga, Chippewa, Delta, Dickinson, Gogebic, Iron,
  Keweenaw, Houghton, Luce, Mackinac, Menominee, Marquette,
  Ontonogon, Schoolcraft. Commercial: Wayne, Oakland, Macomb,
  Washtenaw, Lapeer, Genesee, Calhoun, Jackson, Kalamazoo

Subscriber Information
  Average Monthly Fee Per Subscriber
    (Employee + Employer Contribution):
      Employee Only (Self): Varies by plan
  Average Subscriber Co-Payment:
    Home Health Care: $0
    Home Health Care Max. Days/Visits Covered: 180 days
    Nursing Home: 10%
    Nursing Home Max. Days/Visits Covered: Unlimited

Network Qualifications
  Pre-Admission Certification: Yes

Publishes and Distributes Report Card: No

Accreditation Certification
  TJC
  Utilization Review

Key Personnel
  President . . . . David Livingston

Chief Financial Officer . . . . .Guy Gauthier
Chief Information Officer. . . . . .Tim Holt
   248-331-8016
   tholt@glhp.com
Chief Medical Director . . . . .David Siegel, MD
Legal Counsel . . . . .Eric J Wexler, Esq
   248-331-4264
   ewexler@glhp.com
Disease Management . . . . .Janice Prewitt, RN/CPHQ
   248-331-4368
   jprewitt@glhp.com
Provider Services. . . . . .Sue Tomba
Human Resources . . . . .Aimee Taube
   248-331-4226
   atauve@glho.com
VP, Health Services . . . . .Rachel Godwin
VP, Customer Operations . . . . .Lisa Gray
Marketing Director . . . . .Dawn Siggett
Media Contact. . . . . .Jeff Smith
   952-931-5685
   jeff.smith@uhc.com

Specialty Managed Care Partners
  Rx America
  Enters into Contracts with Regional Business Coalitions: No

---

570 Great-West Healthcare Michigan
Acquired by CIGNA

---

571 Health Alliance Medicare
2850 West Grand Boulevard
Detroit, MI 48202
Toll-Free: 800-801-1770
www.hap.org/medicare
For Profit Organization: Yes
Total Enrollment: 383,000

Healthplan and Services Defined
  PLAN TYPE: Medicare
  Other Type: HMO/PPO, POS
  Benefits Offered: Chiropractic, Dental, Home Care, Inpatient SNF,
    Physical Therapy, Podiatry, Prescription, Psychiatric, Wellness,
    Worldwide Emergency, Fitness Benefits, Hearing Exams,
    Preventive Services, Eye Exams & Eyeglasses, Urgent Care, Hosp

Type of Coverage
  Individual, Medicare, Group Medicare Plans

Geographic Areas Served
  Michigan statewide

Subscriber Information
  Average Monthly Fee Per Subscriber
    (Employee + Employer Contribution):
      Employee Only (Self): Varies
      Medicare: Varies
  Average Annual Deductible Per Subscriber:
      Employee Only (Self): Varies
      Medicare: Varies
  Average Subscriber Co-Payment:
      Primary Care Physician: Varies
      Non-Network Physician: Varies
      Prescription Drugs: Varies
      Hospital ER: Varies
      Home Health Care: Varies
      Home Health Care Max. Days/Visits Covered: Varies
      Nursing Home: Varies
      Nursing Home Max. Days/Visits Covered: Varies

Key Personnel
  President/CEO . . . . .William Alvin
  CFO . . . . .Ronald Berry
  VP and General Counsel . . . . .Maurice E McMurray
  SVP, Chief Operating Offc . . . . .David M Scott

SVP, CMO . . . . .Mary Ann Tournoux
VP, Corporate Initiatives. . . . . .H Michael Flasch
SVP, Planning & Marketing. .Donald Hirt
VP, Information Tech . . . . .Christopher Pike

---

572 Health Alliance Plan
2850 W Grand Boulevard
Detroit, MI 48202
Toll-Free: 800-422-4641
Phone: 313-872-8100
Fax: 248-443-4424
msweb1@hap.org
www.hap.org
Non-Profit Organization: Yes
Year Founded: 1979
Number of Affiliated Hospitals: 157
Number of Primary Care Physicians: 18,000
Number of Referral/Specialty Physicians: 1,000
Total Enrollment: 500,000
State Enrollment: 500,000

Healthplan and Services Defined
  PLAN TYPE: HMO/PPO
  Other Type: EPO
  Model Type: Staff
  Benefits Offered: Disease Management, Prescription, Vision,
    Wellness, Alternative Medicine
  Offers Demand Management Patient Information Service: Yes
  DMPI Services Offered: Health Education Classes

Type of Coverage
  Commercial, Individual, Medicare

Type of Payment Plans Offered
  POS, Capitated, FFS, Combination FFS & DFFS

Geographic Areas Served
  Macomb, Monroe, Oakland, St Clair, Washtenaw & Wayne counties;
  Genesse, Livingston, Laper

Network Qualifications
  Pre-Admission Certification: Yes

Peer Review Type
  Utilization Review: Yes
  Second Surgical Opinion: No
  Case Management: Yes

Publishes and Distributes Report Card: Yes

Accreditation Certification
  NCQA
  TJC Accreditation, Medicare Approved, Utilization Review,
    Pre-Admission Certification, State Licensure, Quality Assurance
    Program

Key Personnel
  President/CEO . . . . .William Alvin
  CFO . . . . .Ronald Berry
  VP and General Counsel . . . . .Maurice E McMurray
  SVP, Chief Operating Offc . . . . .David M Scott
  SVP, CMO . . . . .Mary Ann Tournoux
  VP, Corporate Initiatives. . . . . .H Michael Flasch
  SVP, Planning & Marketing. .Donald Hirt
  VP, Information Tech . . . . .Christopher Pike

Specialty Managed Care Partners
  Enters into Contracts with Regional Business Coalitions: Yes

---

573 Health Plan of Michigan
777 Woodward Avenue
Suite 600
Detroit, MI 48226
Toll-Free: 888-773-2647
Fax: 313-202-0008
www.hpmich.com

Total Enrollment: 250,863
State Enrollment: 250,863
__Healthplan and Services Defined__
  __PLAN TYPE: HMO__
__Key Personnel__
  President/CEO . . . . David B Cotton, MD
  Chief Operating Officer . . . . Shery L Cotton
  EVP/CIO . . . . Thomas L Lauzon
  Chief Medical Officer . . . . Thomas A Raskauskas, MD
  VP/General Counsel . . . . Sean P Cotton, JD
  VP/Finance . . . . Jon Cotton
  VP/Operations . . . . Michael Cotton
  VP/Claims . . . . Nancy McNulty
  VP/Provider Services . . . . Raymond D Pitera
  Director/Quality Mgmt. . . . . Vicki Boyle, RN
  Director/Member Services . . . . Kelly Kramer
  Director/Care Management. . . . . Laurie Good, RN
  Director/Information Sys . . . . Paul Loffreda
  Medical Dir/Quality Mgmt. . . . . Hershel Moss, MD
  Acting Director/Pharmacy. . . . . Rene Acker, RPh

574 HealthPlus of Michigan: Flint

__2050 S Linden Road__
__Flint, MI 48532__
__Toll-Free: 800-332-9161__
__Phone: 810-230-2000__
__Fax: 810-230-2208__
customerservice@healthplus.org
__www.healthplus.org__
__Non-Profit Organization:__ Yes
__Year Founded:__ 1977
__Federally Qualified:__ Yes
__Number of Affiliated Hospitals:__ 29
__Number of Primary Care Physicians:__ 900
__Number of Referral/Specialty Physicians:__ 1,800
__Total Enrollment:__ 200,000
__State Enrollment:__ 200,000
__Healthplan and Services Defined__
  __PLAN TYPE: HMO__
  Model Type: Network
  Plan Specialty: Lab, Radiology
  Benefits Offered: Behavioral Health, Chiropractic, Complementary
    Medicine, Disease Management, Home Care, Inpatient SNF,
    Long-Term Care, Physical Therapy, Podiatry, Prescription,
    Psychiatric, Transplant, Vision, Wellness, Women's Health
  Offers Demand Management Patient Information Service: Yes

__Type of Coverage__
  Commercial, Individual, Medicare, Supplemental Medicare,
    Medicaid, Catastrophic, TPA
  Catastrophic Illness Benefit: Unlimited

__Type of Payment Plans Offered__
  POS, DFFS, Capitated, Combination FFS & DFFS

__Geographic Areas Served__
  Commercial Product: Bay, Genesee, Huron, Lapeer, Livingston,
    Midland, Northern Oakland counties, Saginaw, Sanilac, Shiawassee,
    Tuscola. Full counties: Arenac, Sanilac and St Clair

__Subscriber Information__
  Average Monthly Fee Per Subscriber
    (Employee + Employer Contribution):
      Employee Only (Self): Varies by plan
  Average Subscriber Co-Payment:
      Nursing Home Max. Days/Visits Covered: 730 days

__Network Qualifications__
  Pre-Admission Certification: Yes

__Peer Review Type__
  Utilization Review: Yes
  Second Surgical Opinion: Yes
  Case Management: Yes

__Publishes and Distributes Report Card:__ Yes
__Accreditation Certification__
  NCQA
  TJC Accreditation, Medicare Approved, Utilization Review,
    Pre-Admission Certification, State Licensure, Quality Assurance
    Program
__Key Personnel__
  President and CEO . . . . David Crosby
    810-230-2132
    dcrosby@healthplus.com
  VP Finance/Operations. . . . . Matthew Mendrygal
    810-230-2179
    mmendryg@healthplus.com
  General Counsel . . . . Dan E Champney, Esq
    810-230-2170
    dchampne@healthplus.com
  CIO . . . . Julie Boyer
    810-230-2061
    jboyer@healthplus.com
  Medical Director. . . . . John J Saalwaechter, MD
    810-230-2027
    jsaalwae@healthplus.com
  Pharmacy Director. Carrie Germain, RPh
    810-230-2027
    cgermain@healthplus.com
  Provider Services . . . . Elyse Berry
    810-230-2001
    eberry@healthplus.com
  Public Relations . . . . Richard Swenson
    810-230-2196
    rswenson@healthplus.com
  Compliance Officer. . . . . Theresa Schurman
    tschurma@healthplus.com
  Quality Improveovement. Laraine Yapo
    810-230-2167
    lyapo@healthplus.com
  Human Resources . . . . April Williamson
    810-230-2215
    awilliam@healthplus.com
  Marketing. . . . . Nancy Jenkins
    810-230-2183
    njenkins@healthplus.com
  Health Promotions . . . . Randy Jones
    810-230-2037
    rjones@healthplus.com
  VP/Government Programs. . . . . Christine Tomcala
    810-230-2173
    ctomcala@healthplus.com
  Sr Director/UR . . . . Meg Pointon
    800-345-9956
    mpointon@healthplus.com
__Specialty Managed Care Partners__
  American Healthways
  Enters into Contracts with Regional Business Coalitions: No
__Employer References__
  General Motors, Delphi, Covenant Health Partners

575 HealthPlus of Michigan: Saginaw

__5454 Hampton Place__
__Saginaw, MI 48604__
__Toll-Free: 800-942-8816__
__Phone: 989-797-4000__
__Fax: 989-797-4044__
__www.healthplus.org__
__Non-Profit Organization:__ Yes
__Number of Affiliated Hospitals:__ 29
__Number of Primary Care Physicians:__ 900
__Number of Referral/Specialty Physicians:__ 1,800
__Total Enrollment:__ 200,000

State Enrollment: 200,000

Healthplan and Services Defined
  PLAN TYPE: HMO
  Model Type: IPA
  Plan Specialty: Lab, Radiology
  Benefits Offered: Behavioral Health, Disease Management,
    Prescription, Psychiatric, Wellness, Women's Health

Type of Coverage
  Commercial, Individual, MIChild
  Catastrophic Illness Benefit: Covered

Type of Payment Plans Offered
  POS, Capitated, Combination FFS & DFFS

Geographic Areas Served
  Bay City, Saginaw & Tuscola counties

Network Qualifications
  Pre-Admission Certification: Yes

Publishes and Distributes Report Card: Yes

Accreditation Certification
  NCQA

Key Personnel
  CEO . . . . .David P Crosby
    810-230-2132
    dcrosby@healthplus.com
  CFO . . . . .Matthew Mendrygal
    810-230-2179
    mmendryg@healthplus.com
  CIO . . . . .Julie Boyer
    810-230-2061
    jboyer@healthplu.com
  Medical Director. . . . . .John J Saalwaechter, MD
    810-230-2027
    jsaalwae@healthplus.com
  Pharmacy Director. . . . . .Carrie Germain, RPh
    810-230-2027
    cgermain@healthplus.com
  Legal Counsel . . . . .Dan E Champney, Esq
    810-230-2170
    dchampne@healthplus.com
  Public Relations . . . . .Richard Swenson
    810-230-2196
    rswenson@healthplus.com
  Compliance Officer. . . . . .Theresa Schurman
    tschurman@healthplus.com
  Quality Improvement. . . . . .Laraine Yapo
    810-230-2167
    lyapo@healthplus.com
  Human Resources . . . . .April Williamson
    810-230-2215
    awilliam@healthplus.com
  Marketing. . . . . .Nancy Jenkins
    810-230-2183
    njenkins@healthplus.com
  Health Promotions . . . . .Randy Jones
    810-230-2037
    rjones@healthplus.com
  VP/Government Programs. . . . . .Christine Tomcala
    810-230-2173
    ctomcala@healthplus.com
  Sr Director/UR . . . . .Meg Pointon
    800-345-9956
    mpointon@healthplus.com

576 HealthPlus of Michigan: Troy
101 W Big Beaver Road
Suite 1400
Troy, MI 48084
Toll-Free: 800-332-9161
Phone: 248-687-1420

www.healthplus.org
Non-Profit Organization: Yes
Number of Affiliated Hospitals: 29
Number of Primary Care Physicians: 900
Number of Referral/Specialty Physicians: 1,800
Total Enrollment: 200,000
State Enrollment: 200,000

Healthplan and Services Defined
  PLAN TYPE: HMO
  Model Type: IPA
  Plan Specialty: Lab, Radiology
  Benefits Offered: Behavioral Health, Disease Management,
    Prescription, Psychiatric, Wellness, Women's Health

Type of Coverage
  Commercial, Individual, Medicare, MIChild
  Catastrophic Illness Benefit: Covered

Type of Payment Plans Offered
  POS, Capitated, Combination FFS & DFFS

Geographic Areas Served
  Bay City, Saginaw & Tuscola counties

Publishes and Distributes Report Card: Yes

Accreditation Certification
  NCQA

577 HealthPlus Senior Medicare Plan
5454 Hampton Place
Saginaw, MI 48604
Toll-Free: 800-942-8816
Phone: 989-797-4000
customerservice@healthplus.org
www.healthplus.org/medicare.aspx
Non-Profit Organization: Yes
Number of Affiliated Hospitals: 29
Number of Primary Care Physicians: 900
Number of Referral/Specialty Physicians: 1,800
Total Enrollment: 14,000
State Enrollment: 14,000

Healthplan and Services Defined
  PLAN TYPE: Medicare
  Benefits Offered: Chiropractic, Disease Management, Home Care,
    Inpatient SNF, Physical Therapy, Podiatry, Prescription, Psychiatric,
    Vision, Wellness

Type of Coverage
  Individual, Medicare, MIChild

Geographic Areas Served
  Health Plus Senior Medicare Coverage Plans available only within
  Michigan

Subscriber Information
  Average Monthly Fee Per Subscriber
    (Employee + Employer Contribution):
      Employee Only (Self): Varies
      Medicare: Varies
  Average Annual Deductible Per Subscriber:
      Employee Only (Self): Varies
      Medicare: Varies
  Average Subscriber Co-Payment:
      Primary Care Physician: Varies
      Non-Network Physician: Varies
      Prescription Drugs: Varies
      Hospital ER: Varies
      Home Health Care: Varies
      Home Health Care Max. Days/Visits Covered: Varies
      Nursing Home: Varies
      Nursing Home Max. Days/Visits Covered: Varies

Key Personnel
  President/CEO . . . . .David Crosby
  Communications Director . . . . .Rich Swenson

VP Health Care Services . . . . Laraine Yapo

578 Humana Health Insurance of Michigan

5555 Glenwood Hills Parkway
Suite 150
Grand Rapids, MI 49512
Toll-Free: 800-649-0059
Phone: 616-942-6701
Fax: 616-940-3655
www.humana.com
For Profit Organization: Yes
Total Enrollment: 112,011
State Enrollment: 47,400

Healthplan and Services Defined
  PLAN TYPE: HMO/PPO
  Plan Specialty: ASO
  Benefits Offered: Disease Management, Prescription, Wellness

Type of Coverage
  Commercial, Individual

Geographic Areas Served
  Michigan

Accreditation Certification
  URAC, NCQA, CORE

Key Personnel
  President . . . . Denise Christy
  Marketing. . . . . John Crusse

Specialty Managed Care Partners
  Caremark Rx

Employer References
  Tricare

579 M-Care

Acquired by Blue Care Network of Michigan

580 Meritain Health: Michigan

2370 Science Parkway
Okemos, MI 48864
Toll-Free: 800-748-0003
sales@meritain.com
www.meritain.com
For Profit Organization: Yes
Year Founded: 1983
Number of Affiliated Hospitals: 110
Number of Primary Care Physicians: 3,467
Number of Referral/Specialty Physicians: 5,720
Total Enrollment: 500,000
State Enrollment: 450,000

Healthplan and Services Defined
  PLAN TYPE: PPO
  Model Type: Network
  Plan Specialty: Dental, Disease Management, Vision, Radiology, UR
  Benefits Offered: Prescription
  Offers Demand Management Patient Information Service: Yes

Type of Coverage
  Commercial

Geographic Areas Served
  Nationwide

Subscriber Information
  Average Monthly Fee Per Subscriber
    (Employee + Employer Contribution):
      Employee Only (Self): Varies by plan

Accreditation Certification
  URAC

TJC Accreditation, Medicare Approved, Utilization Review,
    Pre-Admission Certification, State Licensure, Quality Assurance
    Program

Average Claim Compensation
  Physician's Fees Charged: 78%
  Hospital's Fees Charged: 90%

Specialty Managed Care Partners
  Express Scripts, LabOne, Interactive Health Solutions

581 Molina Healthcare: Michigan

100 West Big Beaver Raod
Suite 600
Troy, MI 48084
Toll-Free: 888-898-7969
Phone: 248-925-1700
www.molinahealthcare.com
For Profit Organization: Yes
Year Founded: 1980
Physician Owned Organization: Yes
Number of Affiliated Hospitals: 84
Number of Primary Care Physicians: 2,167
Number of Referral/Specialty Physicians: 6,184
Total Enrollment: 1,400,000

Healthplan and Services Defined
  PLAN TYPE: HMO
  Model Type: Network
  Benefits Offered: Chiropractic, Dental, Home Care, Inpatient SNF,
    Long-Term Care, Podiatry, Vision

Type of Coverage
  Commercial, Medicare, Supplemental Medicare, Medicaid

Accreditation Certification
  URAC, NCQA

582 OmniCare: A Coventry Health Care Plan

1333 Gratiot Avenue
Suite 400
Detroit, MI 48207
Toll-Free: 866-316-3784
Phone: 313-465-1500
www.omnicarehealthplan.com
Mailing Address: PO Box 7150, Claims Department, London, KY
  10742
Subsidiary of: Coventry Health Plans
Non-Profit Organization: Yes
Year Founded: 1973
Number of Affiliated Hospitals: 28
Number of Primary Care Physicians: 2,200
Total Enrollment: 50,000
State Enrollment: 50,000

Healthplan and Services Defined
  PLAN TYPE: HMO
  Model Type: IPA
  Benefits Offered: Disease Management, Prescription, Wellness
  Offers Demand Management Patient Information Service: Yes
  DMPI Services Offered: Foreign Language Service, Newsletter

Type of Coverage
  Commercial, Individual, Medicaid
  Catastrophic Illness Benefit: Varies per case

Type of Payment Plans Offered
  POS, DFFS, Capitated, FFS, Combination FFS & DFFS

Geographic Areas Served
  Macomb, Monroe, Oakland, Wayne, Washtenaw counties

Subscriber Information
  Average Monthly Fee Per Subscriber
    (Employee + Employer Contribution):
      Employee Only (Self): Varies by plan

Average Annual Deductible Per Subscriber:
    Employee Only (Self): $0
    Employee & 1 Family Member: $0
    Employee & 2 Family Members: $0
    Medicare: $0
Average Subscriber Co-Payment:
    Home Health Care: $0
    Home Health Care Max. Days/Visits Covered: Unlimited
    Nursing Home: $0
    Nursing Home Max. Days/Visits Covered: 30 days

Network Qualifications
Pre-Admission Certification: Yes

Peer Review Type
Utilization Review: Yes
Second Surgical Opinion: Yes
Case Management: Yes

Publishes and Distributes Report Card: Yes

Accreditation Certification
NCQA
TJC Accreditation, Medicare Approved, Utilization Review,
    Pre-Admission Certification, State Licensure, Quality Assurance
    Program

Key Personnel
President/CEO . . . . .Beverly Allen
CFO . . . . .Kenyata Rogers
SVP, Medicaid . . . . .Bobby Jones
Network Contracting .Marshall Katz, MD
In House Formulary . . . . .Esther Rose, RPh
Marketing . . . . .Velina Glass
Materials Management. . . . . .Solomon Payne
Medical Affairs . . . . .Robert Levine, MD
Member Services. . . . . .Marshall Howard
Provider Services . . . . .Sandra Hooks
Sales . . . . .Velina Glass

Average Claim Compensation
Physician's Fees Charged: 1%
Hospital's Fees Charged: 1%

Specialty Managed Care Partners
Enters into Contracts with Regional Business Coalitions: Yes

---

583   **Paramount Care of Michigan**

106 Park Place
Dundee, MI 48131-1016
Phone: 734-529-7800
Fax: 734-529-8896
www.paramounthealthcare.com
Subsidiary of: ProMedica Health System
For Profit Organization: Yes
Year Founded: 1988
Number of Affiliated Hospitals: 34
Number of Primary Care Physicians: 1,900
Total Enrollment: 187,000

Healthplan and Services Defined
PLAN TYPE: HMO/PPO
Benefits Offered: Disease Management, Prescription, Wellness

Type of Coverage
Commercial, Medicare

Geographic Areas Served
Southeast Michigan

Accreditation Certification
NCQA

Key Personnel
President . . . . .John C Randolph
    419-887-2500
VP, Finance . . . . .Jeff Martin
Managed Care Admin . . . . .Steve Gullett
Director, Marketing. . . . . .Jeff O'Connell

VP, Medical Services . . . . .John Meier
Member Relations . . . . .Karen Eichenberg

Specialty Managed Care Partners
Express Scripts

---

584   **Physicians Health Plan of Mid-Michigan**

PO Box 30377
Lansing, MI 48909-7877
Toll-Free: 888-892-0009
Phone: 517-364-8400
Fax: 517-364-8460
sales@phpmm.org
www.phpmm.org
Secondary Address: 1400 E Michigan Avenue, Lansing, MI 48912
Subsidiary of: Sparrow Health System
Non-Profit Organization: Yes
Year Founded: 1980
Owned by an Integrated Delivery Network (IDN): Yes
Number of Affiliated Hospitals: 38
Number of Primary Care Physicians: 1,063
Number of Referral/Specialty Physicians: 1,781
Total Enrollment: 68,942
State Enrollment: 68,942

Healthplan and Services Defined
PLAN TYPE: HMO
Model Type: IPA
Plan Specialty: Behavioral Health, Chiropractic, Dental, Disease
    Management, Lab, PBM, Vision, Radiology, UR
Benefits Offered: Behavioral Health, Chiropractic, Dental, Disease
    Management, Home Care, Inpatient SNF, Physical Therapy,
    Podiatry, Prescription, Psychiatric, Transplant, Vision, Wellness,
    AD&D, Life, STD, FSA

Type of Coverage
Commercial, Medicaid, Catastrophic, PPO, TPA
Catastrophic Illness Benefit: Unlimited

Type of Payment Plans Offered
POS, DFFS

Geographic Areas Served
Clinton, Eaton, Gratiot, Ionia, Ingham, Isabella, Montcalm, Saginaw
    and Shiawassee counties

Subscriber Information
Average Subscriber Co-Payment:
    Primary Care Physician: $10.00
    Non-Network Physician: 20%
    Prescription Drugs: $10.00/25.00/40.00
    Hospital ER: $50.00
    Home Health Care: $0
    Nursing Home: $0
    Nursing Home Max. Days/Visits Covered: 100

Network Qualifications
Pre-Admission Certification: Yes

Peer Review Type
Utilization Review: Yes
Second Surgical Opinion: Yes
Case Management: Yes

Publishes and Distributes Report Card: No

Accreditation Certification
NCQA
Medicare Approved, Utilization Review, Pre-Admission Certification,
    State Licensure, Quality Assurance Program

Key Personnel
President/CEO. . . . . .Scott Wilkerson
    517-364-8400
    scott.wilkerson@phpmm.org
CFO. . . . . .David Vis
    517-364-8370
    david.vis@phpmm.org

Pharmacy Management . . . . Ann Hunt-Fugate
517-364-8428
ann.hunt@phpmm.org
VP, Sales & Marketing . . . . Craig Lesley
517-364-8277
craig.lesley@phpmm.org
Market Research Coord . . . . Connie Scarpone
517-364-8266
Medical Director . . . . Howard Burgess
howard.burgess@phpmm.org
Community Services . . . . Larry Smith
517-364-8263
Provider Services . . . . Gary Gonzales
517-364-8461
gary.gonzales@phpmm.org

Specialty Managed Care Partners
United Behavioral Health
Enters into Contracts with Regional Business Coalitions: No

---

585 **Priority Health**
34505 West Twelve Mile Road
Farmington Hills, MI 48331
Toll-Free: 800-942-0954
Phone: 616-942-1820
Fax: 616-957-2529
ph-salessbd@priorityhealth.com
www.priorityhealth.com
Secondary Address: 250 East Eighth Street, Holland, MI 49423
Non-Profit Organization: Yes
Year Founded: 1986
Owned by an Integrated Delivery Network (IDN): Yes
Number of Affiliated Hospitals: 100
Number of Primary Care Physicians: 12,000
Number of Referral/Specialty Physicians: 12,000
State Enrollment: 146,000

Healthplan and Services Defined
PLAN TYPE: HMO/PPO
Other Type: POS
Model Type: Network
Plan Specialty: ASO, Behavioral Health, Chiropractic, Dental, Disease Management, EPO, Lab, MSO, PBM, Vision, Radiology
Benefits Offered: Behavioral Health, Chiropractic, Complementary Medicine, Dental, Disease Management, Home Care, Inpatient SNF, Long-Term Care, Physical Therapy, Podiatry, Prescription, Psychiatric, Transplant, Vision, Wellness, AD&D, Life, LTD, STD
Offers Demand Management Patient Information Service: Yes
DMPI Services Offered: Health Library

Type of Coverage
Commercial, Individual, Medicare, Medicaid

Type of Payment Plans Offered
POS, DFFS, Capitated, FFS, Combination FFS & DFFS

Publishes and Distributes Report Card: Yes

Accreditation Certification
URAC, NCQA

Key Personnel
President & CEO . . . . Kimberly K Horn
CFO . . . . Gregory Hawkins
VP, Government Programs . . . . Leon Lamoreaux
Claims . . . . Barry Cofield
VP, Network Strategy . . . . Michael Koziara
Chief Admin Officer . . . . Deborah Phillips
Chief Marketing Officer . . . . Joan Budden
Chief Medical Officer . . . . James F Byrne, MD
VP, Medical Operations . . . . Kim Suarez
CIO & VP, Enterprise Oper . . . . James S Slubowski
VP, Sales . . . . Mark J Zickel

Media Relations . . . . Amy Miller
616-464-8571
amy.miller@priorityhealth.com

Specialty Managed Care Partners
Principal, Fortis Time, Secure 1, US Life and Health
Enters into Contracts with Regional Business Coalitions: Yes

---

586 **Priority Health: Corporate Headquarters**
1231 E Beltline NE
Grand Rapids, MI 49525-4501
Toll-Free: 800-942-0954
Phone: 616-942-0954
Fax: 616-942-5651
rob.pocock@priorityhealth.com
www.priorityhealth.com
Non-Profit Organization: Yes
Year Founded: 1986
Physician Owned Organization: Yes
Owned by an Integrated Delivery Network (IDN): Yes
Federally Qualified: No
Number of Affiliated Hospitals: 5,000
Number of Referral/Specialty Physicians: 617,000
Total Enrollment: 596,220

Healthplan and Services Defined
PLAN TYPE: HMO
Model Type: IPA
Plan Specialty: ASO, Behavioral Health, Chiropractic, Dental, Disease Management, EPO, Lab, MSO, PBM, Vision, Radiology, UR
Benefits Offered: Behavioral Health, Chiropractic, Complementary Medicine, Dental, Disease Management, Home Care, Inpatient SNF, Long-Term Care, Physical Therapy, Podiatry, Prescription, Psychiatric, Transplant, Vision, Wellness, AD&D, Life, LTD, STD
Offers Demand Management Patient Information Service: No

Type of Coverage
Commercial, Individual, Indemnity, Medicare, Medicaid
Catastrophic Illness Benefit: Varies per case

Type of Payment Plans Offered
DFFS, Capitated, FFS, Combination FFS & DFFS

Geographic Areas Served
69 counties in Michigan

Subscriber Information
Average Monthly Fee Per Subscriber
(Employee + Employer Contribution):
Employee Only (Self): Varies
Employee & 1 Family Member: Varies
Employee & 2 Family Members: Varies
Medicare: Varies
Average Annual Deductible Per Subscriber:
Employee Only (Self): Varies
Employee & 1 Family Member: Varies
Employee & 2 Family Members: Varies
Medicare: Varies
Average Subscriber Co-Payment:
Primary Care Physician: Varies
Non-Network Physician: Varies
Prescription Drugs: Varies
Hospital ER: Varies
Home Health Care: Varies
Home Health Care Max. Days/Visits Covered: Varies
Nursing Home: Varies
Nursing Home Max. Days/Visits Covered: Varies

Network Qualifications
Pre-Admission Certification: No

Peer Review Type
Utilization Review: Yes
Case Management: Yes

Publishes and Distributes Report Card: No

Accreditation Certification

NCQA

Utilization Review, Pre-Admission Certification, State Licensure, Quality Assurance Program

Key Personnel

President and CEO . . . . .Kimberly K Horn
616-942-0954

Chief Financial Officer . . . . .Gregory Harwins

Chief Administative Offc. .Deborah Phillips

General Counsel. . . . . .Kimberly Thomas

Chief Information Officer . . . . .James S Slubowski

Dir, Pharmacy Programs .Steven Marciniak

Chief Marketing Officer. . . . . .Joan Budden

Director Communications .Robert Pocock

Chief Medical Officer/VP .Jim Byrne, MD

VP Sales/Client Services . . . . .Don Whitford

Specialty Managed Care Partners

Enters into Contracts with Regional Business Coalitions: Yes

National Federation of Independent Business

587 PriorityHealth Medicare Plans

1231 East Beltline Northeast
Grand Rapids, MI 49525-4501
Toll-Free: 888-389-6676
Phone: 616-464-8850
www.priorityhealth.com/medicare
Subsidiary of: PriorityHealth

Healthplan and Services Defined

PLAN TYPE: Medicare

Benefits Offered: Chiropractic, Dental, Disease Management, Home Care, Inpatient SNF, Physical Therapy, Podiatry, Prescription, Psychiatric, Vision, Wellness

Type of Coverage

Individual, Medicare

Geographic Areas Served

Medicare Plans available within Michigan only

Subscriber Information

Average Monthly Fee Per Subscriber
(Employee + Employer Contribution):
Employee Only (Self): Varies
Medicare: Varies

Average Annual Deductible Per Subscriber:
Employee Only (Self): Varies
Medicare: Varies

Average Subscriber Co-Payment:
Primary Care Physician: Varies
Non-Network Physician: Varies
Prescription Drugs: Varies
Hospital ER: Varies
Home Health Care: Varies
Home Health Care Max. Days/Visits Covered: Varies
Nursing Home: Varies
Nursing Home Max. Days/Visits Covered: Varies

Key Personnel

President and CEO . . . . .Kimberly K Horn
616-942-0954

Chief Financial Officer . . . . .Gregory Harwins

Chief Administative Offc. .Deborah Phillips

General Counsel. . . . . .Kimberly Thomas

Chief Information Officer . . . . .James S Slubowski

Dir, Pharmacy Programs. .Steven Marciniak

Chief Marketing Officer. . . . . .Joan Budden

Director Communications .Robert Pocock

Chief Medical Officer/VP .Jim Byrne, MD

VP Sales/Client Services . . . . .Don Whitford

588 SVS Vision

140 Macomb Place
Mount Clemens, MI 48043
Toll-Free: 800-787-4600
Phone: 586-468-7612
Fax: 586-468-7682
customerservice@svsvision.com
www.svsvision.com
For Profit Organization: Yes
Year Founded: 1974
Number of Primary Care Physicians: 1,135
Total Enrollment: 390,000

Healthplan and Services Defined

PLAN TYPE: Vision

Other Type: Vision Plan

Plan Specialty: Vision

Benefits Offered: Disease Management, Vision, Wellness, Services limited to vision care

Type of Payment Plans Offered

DFFS

Geographic Areas Served

Michigan; Illinois: Chicago; Indiana: Indianpolis; Kentucky: Louisville; Tennessee: Nashville; Missouri: Kansas City & St. Louis; Georgia: Atlanta; New York: Buffalo; Minnesota: St. Paul; Virginia: Norfolk

Subscriber Information

Average Monthly Fee Per Subscriber
(Employee + Employer Contribution):
Employee Only (Self): Varies by plan

Network Qualifications

Pre-Admission Certification: Yes

Peer Review Type

Utilization Review: Yes
Second Surgical Opinion: Yes
Case Management: Yes

Key Personnel

President/CEO . . . . .Ronald Dooley

CFO . . . . .Janice Gonzales-Basile

VP, Sales & Marketing . . . . .Catherine Walker
586-464-1573
cwalker@svsvision.com

Medical Affairs . . . . .Robert G Farrell, Jr

Media Contact. . . . . .Catherine Walker
586-464-1573
cwalker@svsvision.com

589 Total Health Care

3011 W Grand Boulevard
Suite 1600
Detroit, MI 48202
Toll-Free: 800-826-2862
Phone: 313-871-2000
Fax: 313-871-0196
thc@thc-online.com
www.totalhealthcareonline.com
Non-Profit Organization: Yes
Year Founded: 1973
Owned by an Integrated Delivery Network (IDN): Yes
Number of Affiliated Hospitals: 45
Number of Primary Care Physicians: 600
Number of Referral/Specialty Physicians: 1,500
Total Enrollment: 90,000
State Enrollment: 90,000

Healthplan and Services Defined

PLAN TYPE: HMO

Other Type: PPN, POS

Model Type: Staff

Plan Specialty: Lab, Radiology
Benefits Offered: Behavioral Health, Chiropractic, Complementary
Medicine, Disease Management, Home Care, Inpatient SNF,
Long-Term Care, Physical Therapy, Podiatry, Prescription,
Psychiatric, Transplant, Vision, Wellness, Worker's Compensation,
Alternative Treatments, Dur
Offers Demand Management Patient Information Service: Yes
DMPI Services Offered: Educational Classes and Programs, 24 hour
nurse line

Type of Coverage
Commercial, Individual, Medicare, Medicaid

Type of Payment Plans Offered
Combination FFS & DFFS

Geographic Areas Served
Wayne, Oakland, Macomb and Genesee counties

Subscriber Information
Average Monthly Fee Per Subscriber
(Employee + Employer Contribution):
Employee Only (Self): $67.12
Employee & 2 Family Members: $164.88
Average Subscriber Co-Payment:
Primary Care Physician: $10.00
Hospital ER: $40.00

Accreditation Certification
TJC, NCQA

Key Personnel
Executive Director . . . . .Lyle Algate
CFO. . . . . .Brian Efrusy
COO . . . . .Randy Narowitz
Claims Manager . . . . .Nancy Kowal
Compliance Officer . . . . .Karen Connolly
Pharmacy Director . . . . .Karen Bunio
Marketing Manager . . . . .Steven Slaga
Contracting Manager . . . . .Gary Francis
Medical Director. . . . . .Robyn James Arrington Jr, MD
Supervisor, Member Svcs. . . . . .Natalie Burke
Chief Information Officer .Sean Bumstead

Specialty Managed Care Partners
RxAmerica

Employer References
Federal Government, State of Michigan, American Airlines, Detroit
Board of Education, Wayne County Employees

590 Unicare: Michigan
3200 Greenfield Road
Dearborn, MI 48120
Phone: 313-336-5550
www.unicare.com
Subsidiary of: WellPoint Health Networks
For Profit Organization: Yes
Year Founded: 1995
Total Enrollment: 1,700,000

Healthplan and Services Defined
PLAN TYPE: HMO
Model Type: Network
Benefits Offered: Behavioral Health, Chiropractic, Complementary
Medicine, Dental, Disease Management, Home Care, Inpatient
SNF, Long-Term Care, Physical Therapy, Podiatry, Prescription,
Psychiatric, Transplant, Vision, Wellness, Life

Type of Coverage
Commercial, Individual, Supplemental Medicare, Medicaid

Geographic Areas Served
Illinois, Indiana, Kentucky, Ohio, Oklahoma, Michigan, Texas,
Nevada, Massachusetts, Virginia, and Wasington DC

Network Qualifications
Pre-Admission Certification: Yes

Peer Review Type
Utilization Review: Yes
Second Surgical Opinion: Yes
Case Management: Yes

Publishes and Distributes Report Card: Yes

Accreditation Certification
NCQA
TJC Accreditation, Utilization Review, Pre-Admission Certification,
State Licensure, Quality Assurance Program

Key Personnel
President. . . . . .Mark Weinberg
Media Contact . . . . .Tony Felts
317-287-6037
tony.felts@wellpoint.com

Specialty Managed Care Partners
WellPoint Pharmacy Management, WellPoint Dental Services,
WellPoint Behavioral Health
Enters into Contracts with Regional Business Coalitions: Yes

591 United Concordia: Michigan
Sheffield Office Park
3520 W Big Beaver, Suite 127
Troy, MI 48084
Toll-Free: 800-944-6432
Phone: 248-458-1581
Fax: 248-458-1136
ucproducer@ucci.com
www.secure.ucci.com
For Profit Organization: Yes
Year Founded: 1971
Number of Primary Care Physicians: 111,000
Total Enrollment: 8,000,000

Healthplan and Services Defined
PLAN TYPE: Dental
Plan Specialty: Dental
Benefits Offered: Dental

Type of Coverage
Commercial, Individual

Geographic Areas Served
Military personnel and their families, nationwide

592 UnitedHealthCare of Michigan
26957 Northwestern Highway
Suite 400
Southfield, MI 48034
Toll-Free: 800-842-3585
Fax: 248-936-1231
www.uhc.com
Subsidiary of: UnitedHealth Group
Year Founded: 1977
Number of Affiliated Hospitals: 4,200
Number of Primary Care Physicians: 460,000
Total Enrollment: 75,000,000
State Enrollment: 207,319

Healthplan and Services Defined
PLAN TYPE: HMO/PPO
Model Type: IPA, Group, Network
Plan Specialty: Lab, Radiology
Benefits Offered: Chiropractic, Dental, Physical Therapy,
Prescription, Wellness, AD&D, Life, LTD, STD
Offers Demand Management Patient Information Service: Yes

Type of Coverage
Commercial, Individual, Indemnity, Medicare

Geographic Areas Served
Statewide

Network Qualifications
Pre-Admission Certification: Yes

Peer Review Type
Utilization Review: Yes
Second Surgical Opinion: Yes
Case Management: Yes

Publishes and Distributes Report Card: Yes

Accreditation Certification
TJC, NCQA

Specialty Managed Care Partners
Enters into Contracts with Regional Business Coalitions: Yes

---

593   Upper Peninsula Health Plan

228 W Washington Street
Marquette, MI 49855
Toll-Free: 800-835-2556
Phone: 906-225-7500
uphpcsw@uphp.com
www.uphp.com
Total Enrollment: 25,278
State Enrollment: 25,278

Healthplan and Services Defined
PLAN TYPE: HMO

Type of Coverage
Medicaid

Key Personnel
Owner . . . . .Cynthia Nyquist
Chief Financial Officer . . . . .Greg Gustafson

---

594   VSP: Vision Service Plan of Michigan

2000 Town Center
Suite 1790
Southfield, MI 48075-1254
Phone: 248-350-2082
Fax: 248-350-1645
webmaster@vsp.com
www.vsp.com
Year Founded: 1955
Number of Primary Care Physicians: 26,000
Total Enrollment: 55,000,000

Healthplan and Services Defined
PLAN TYPE: Vision
Plan Specialty: Vision
Benefits Offered: Vision

Type of Payment Plans Offered
Capitated

Geographic Areas Served
Statewide

Network Qualifications
Pre-Admission Certification: Yes

Peer Review Type
Utilization Review: Yes

Accreditation Certification
Utilization Review, Quality Assurance Program

Key Personnel
President. . . . . .Bob Koval
CEO . . . . .Jay Alix

Health Insurance Coverage Status and Type of Coverage by Age

Category	All Persons		Under 18 years		Under 65 years		65 years and over	
	Number	%	Number	%	Number	%	Number	%
Total population	5,186	-	1,261	-	4,506	-	680	-
Covered by some type of health insurance	4,678 *(37)*	90.2 *(0.6)*	1,186 *(18)*	94.0 *(0.9)*	4,003 *(50)*	88.8 *(0.7)*	675 *(32)*	99.3 *(0.3)*
Covered by private health insurance	3,882 *(65)*	74.8 *(1.1)*	939 *(25)*	74.4 *(1.9)*	3,393 *(75)*	75.3 *(1.3)*	489 *(34)*	71.9 *(3.1)*
Employment based	3,204 *(72)*	61.8 *(1.2)*	854 *(23)*	67.7 *(1.8)*	3,050 *(75)*	67.7 *(1.3)*	154 *(20)*	22.6 *(2.7)*
Own employment based	1,599 *(46)*	30.8 *(0.8)*	9 *(3)*	0.7 *(0.3)*	1,483 *(49)*	32.9 *(0.9)*	115 *(15)*	16.9 *(2.0)*
Direct purchase	806 *(39)*	15.5 *(0.7)*	114 *(14)*	9.0 *(1.1)*	436 *(31)*	9.7 *(0.7)*	371 *(30)*	54.5 *(3.1)*
Covered by government health insurance	1,514 *(58)*	29.2 *(1.1)*	354 *(23)*	28.1 *(1.8)*	855 *(47)*	19.0 *(1.1)*	659 *(32)*	97.0 *(0.8)*
Covered by Medicaid	739 *(44)*	14.3 *(0.9)*	332 *(23)*	26.3 *(1.8)*	693 *(45)*	15.4 *(1.0)*	46 *(11)*	6.8 *(1.5)*
Also by private insurance	177 *(23)*	3.4 *(0.5)*	92 *(17)*	7.3 *(1.3)*	162 *(25)*	3.6 *(0.5)*	15 *(5)*	2.2 *(0.8)*
Covered by Medicare	763 *(35)*	14.7 *(0.7)*	7 *(4)*	0.5 *(0.3)*	107 *(14)*	2.4 *(0.3)*	656 *(32)*	96.5 *(0.9)*
Also by private insurance	505 *(33)*	9.7 *(0.6)*	3 *(2)*	0.2 *(0.2)*	34 *(8)*	0.8 *(0.2)*	471 *(32)*	69.3 *(2.9)*
Also by Medicaid	86 *(12)*	1.7 *(0.2)*	5 *(3)*	0.4 *(0.3)*	42 *(9)*	0.9 *(0.2)*	43 *(10)*	6.4 *(1.5)*
Covered by military health care	147 *(22)*	2.8 *(0.4)*	26 *(8)*	2.0 *(0.6)*	107 *(19)*	2.4 *(0.4)*	40 *(9)*	5.9 *(1.3)*
Not covered at any time during the year	509 *(30)*	9.8 *(0.6)*	75 *(11)*	6.0 *(0.9)*	504 *(30)*	11.2 *(0.7)*	5 *(2)*	0.7 *(0.3)*

Note: Numbers in thousands; figures cover 2010; standard error appears in parenthesis; (b) base less than 75,000; (x) not applicable
Source: U.S. Census Bureau, Current Population Survey, 2011 Annual Social and Economic Supplement. Table HI05. Health Insurance Coverage Status and Type of Coverage by State and Age for All People: 2010

Minnesota

595 Aetna Health of Minnesota

Partnered with eHealthInsurance Services Inc.

596 Araz Group

7201 West 78th Street
Suite 100
Bloomington, MN 55439
Toll-Free: 800-444-3005
Phone: 952-896-1200
Fax: 952-896-4888
info@araz.com
www.araz.com
Subsidiary of: America's PPO, HealthEZ
For Profit Organization: Yes
Year Founded: 1982
Number of Affiliated Hospitals: 260
Number of Primary Care Physicians: 18,000
Total Enrollment: 250,000
State Enrollment: 160,000

Healthplan and Services Defined
  PLAN TYPE: PPO
  Plan Specialty: UR
  Benefits Offered: Behavioral Health, Disease Management,
    Prescription, Worker's Compensation, AD&D, LTD, STD

Type of Coverage
  Commercial, Medicare

Geographic Areas Served
  Nationwide

Accreditation Certification
  Pre-Admission Certification

Key Personnel
  President/CEO . . . . Nazie Eftekhari
  CFO . . . . Josh Kutzler

Specialty Managed Care Partners
  Intracorp

597 Assurant Employee Benefits: Minnesota

6600 France Ave South
Suite 314
Minneapolis, MN 55435-1803
Phone: 952-920-8990
Fax: 952-920-8218
benefits@assurant.com
www.assurantemployeebenefits.com
Subsidiary of: Assurant, Inc
For Profit Organization: Yes
Number of Primary Care Physicians: 112,000
Total Enrollment: 47,000

Healthplan and Services Defined
  PLAN TYPE: Multiple
  Plan Specialty: Dental, Vision, Long & Short-Term Disability
  Benefits Offered: Dental, Vision, Wellness, AD&D, Life, LTD, STD

Type of Coverage
  Commercial, Indemnity, Individual Dental Plans

Geographic Areas Served
  Statewide

Subscriber Information
  Average Monthly Fee Per Subscriber
    (Employee + Employer Contribution):
      Employee Only (Self): Varies by plan

Key Personnel
  Principal . . . . Amie Benson

PR Specialist . . . . Megan Hutchison
  816-556-7815
  megan.hutchison@assurant.com

598 Avesis: Minnesota

904 Oak Pond Court
Sartell, MN 56377
Toll-Free: 888-363-1377
www.avesis.com
Year Founded: 1978
Number of Primary Care Physicians: 18,000
Total Enrollment: 2,000,000

Healthplan and Services Defined
  PLAN TYPE: PPO
  Other Type: Vision, Dental
  Model Type: Network
  Plan Specialty: Dental, Vision, Hearing
  Benefits Offered: Dental, Vision

Type of Coverage
  Commercial

Type of Payment Plans Offered
  POS, Capitated, Combination FFS & DFFS

Geographic Areas Served
  Nationwide and Puerto Rico

Publishes and Distributes Report Card: Yes

Accreditation Certification
  AAAHC
  TJC Accreditation

599 Blue Cross & Blue Shield of Minnesota

3535 Blue Cross Road
PO Box 64560
Saint Paul, MN 55164-0560
Toll-Free: 800-382-2000
Phone: 651-662-8000
Fax: 651-662-1657
www.bluecrossmn.com
Subsidiary of: Blue Cross Blue Shield
Non-Profit Organization: Yes
Year Founded: 1933
Owned by an Integrated Delivery Network (IDN): Yes
Number of Affiliated Hospitals: 30
Number of Primary Care Physicians: 8,000
Total Enrollment: 2,700,000
State Enrollment: 2,700,000

Healthplan and Services Defined
  PLAN TYPE: HMO
  Model Type: Network
  Plan Specialty: Medical
  Benefits Offered: Disease Management, Prescription, Wellness, Life

Type of Coverage
  Individual, Medicare, Supplemental Medicare

Geographic Areas Served
  Statewide

Network Qualifications
  Pre-Admission Certification: Yes

Peer Review Type
  Utilization Review: Yes
  Second Surgical Opinion: Yes

Publishes and Distributes Report Card: Yes

Accreditation Certification
  URAC, NCQA

Key Personnel
  President & CEO . . . . Patricia Geraghty
  SVP, Health Management . . . . James Eppel

SVP, Chief Legal Officer . . . . Scott Lynch
SVP, Public & Health Aff. . . . . Kathleen Mock
SVP, Corp Operations . . . . Patricia Riley
SVP, Chief Financial Offc . . . . Pamela Sedmak
VP, Community Relations . . . . Marsha Shotley
SVP, Chief Innovation Ofc. . . . . MaryAnn Stump
SVP, Human Resources . . . . Colleen Connors
SVP, Chief Info Officer . . . . Jay Levine

Specialty Managed Care Partners
Enters into Contracts with Regional Business Coalitions: No

Employer References
General Mills/Pillsbury, Northwest Airlines, Target

600 CIGNA HealthCare of Minnesota

11095 Viking Drive
Suite 520
Eden Prairie, MN 55344
Toll-Free: 866-438-2446
Phone: 952-996-2144
Fax: 952-996-2158
www.cigna.com
For Profit Organization: Yes
Total Enrollment: 64,977
State Enrollment: 53,490

Healthplan and Services Defined
PLAN TYPE: HMO
Benefits Offered: Disease Management, Prescription, Transplant, Wellness

Type of Coverage
Commercial

Type of Payment Plans Offered
POS, FFS

Geographic Areas Served
Minnesota

601 Delta Dental of Minnesota

3560 Delta Dental Drive
Eagan, MN 55122-3166
Toll-Free: 800-328-1188
Phone: 651-406-5900
Fax: 651-406-5934
www.deltadentalmn.org
Mailing Address: PO Box 9304, Minneapolis, MN 55440-9304
Non-Profit Organization: Yes
Year Founded: 1969
Number of Primary Care Physicians: 1,500
Total Enrollment: 54,000,000
State Enrollment: 3,500,000

Healthplan and Services Defined
PLAN TYPE: Dental
Other Type: Dental PPO
Model Type: Network
Plan Specialty: ASO, Dental
Benefits Offered: Dental

Type of Coverage
Commercial, Individual, Group
Catastrophic Illness Benefit: None

Geographic Areas Served
Minnesota, North Dakota

Subscriber Information
Average Monthly Fee Per Subscriber
(Employee + Employer Contribution):
Employee Only (Self): Varies
Employee & 1 Family Member: Varies
Employee & 2 Family Members: Varies
Average Annual Deductible Per Subscriber:

Employee Only (Self): Varies
Employee & 1 Family Member: Varies
Employee & 2 Family Members: Varies
Average Subscriber Co-Payment:
Prescription Drugs: $0
Home Health Care: $0
Nursing Home: $0

Key Personnel
President . . . . .David B Morse
CFO . . . . .Dani Fjelstad
Exec VP/Sales & Marketing . . . . Mark A Moksnes
Exec VP/Operations . . . . Norman C Storbakken
Media Contact . . . . .Ann Johnson
651-994-5248
ajohnson@deltadentalmn.org
Director Public Affairs . . . . .Elizabeth Risberg
415-972-8423

602 eHealthInsurance Services Inc.

11919 Foundation Place
Gold River, CA 95670
Toll-Free: 800-977-8860
info@ehealthinsurance.com
www.e.healthinsurance.com
Year Founded: 1997

Healthplan and Services Defined
PLAN TYPE: HMO/PPO
Benefits Offered: Dental, Life, STD

Type of Coverage
Commercial, Individual, Medicare

Geographic Areas Served
All 50 states in the USA and District of Columbia

Key Personnel
Chairman & CEO . . . . .Gary L. Lauer
EVP/Business & Corp. Dev. Bruce Telkamp
EVP/Chief Technology . . . . .Dr. Sheldon X. Wang
SVP & CFO . . . . .Stuart M. Huizinga
Pres. of eHealth Gov. Sys . . . . Samuel C. Gibbs
SVP of Sales & Operations . . . . Robert S. Hurley
Director Public Relations . . . . .Nate Purpura
650-210-3115

603 Evercare Health Plans

2920 Oakes Avenue
Anacortes, MN 98221
Toll-Free: 800-905-8671
Phone: 952-936-1300
Fax: 952-936-6902
www.evercareonline.com
Subsidiary of: Ovations/UnitedHealthcare Community Plan
Year Founded: 1987
Total Enrollment: 3,971
State Enrollment: 3,971

Healthplan and Services Defined
PLAN TYPE: Medicare

Type of Coverage
Medicare

Key Personnel
President . . . . .Wayne Cook
EVP/Field Operations . . . . William Pastore
Chief Financial Officer . . . . Scott Fries

604 Great-West Healthcare Minnesota

Acquired by CIGNA

605 Health Partners Medicare Plan

8170 33rd Avenue South
Bloomington, MN 55425
Toll-Free: 800-883-2177
Phone: 952-883-5000
http://medicare.healthpartners.com
Mailing Address: PO Box 1309, Bloomington, MN 55440-1309

Healthplan and Services Defined
PLAN TYPE: Medicare
Benefits Offered: Chiropractic, Dental, Disease Management, Home Care, Inpatient SNF, Physical Therapy, Podiatry, Prescription, Psychiatric, Vision, Wellness

Type of Coverage
Individual, Medicare

Geographic Areas Served
Available only within Minnesota

Subscriber Information
Average Monthly Fee Per Subscriber
(Employee + Employer Contribution):
Employee Only (Self): Varies
Medicare: Varies
Average Annual Deductible Per Subscriber:
Employee Only (Self): Varies
Medicare: Varies
Average Subscriber Co-Payment:
Primary Care Physician: Varies
Non-Network Physician: Varies
Prescription Drugs: Varies
Hospital ER: Varies
Home Health Care: Varies
Home Health Care Max. Days/Visits Covered: Varies
Nursing Home: Varies
Nursing Home Max. Days/Visits Covered: Varies

Key Personnel
President/CEO . . . . Mary Brainerd
EVP, Chief Admin Officer . . . . Kathy Cooney
SVP, General Counsel . . . . Barb Tretheway
CEO, Regions Hospital . . . . Brock Nelson
EVP, Chief Marketing Offc . . . . Andrea Walsh
Medical Director . . . . George Isham
Dir, Corp Communications . . . . Amy von Walter
952-883-5274
amy.e.vonwalter@healthpartners.com

606 HealthPartners

8170 33rd Avenue S
Bloomington, MN 55425
Toll-Free: 800-883-2177
Phone: 952-883-5000
Fax: 952-883-5380
www.healthpartners.com
Non-Profit Organization: Yes
Year Founded: 1957
Owned by an Integrated Delivery Network (IDN): Yes
Number of Affiliated Hospitals: 200
Number of Primary Care Physicians: 36,000
Number of Referral/Specialty Physicians: 650,000
Total Enrollment: 1,250,000
State Enrollment: 349,070

Healthplan and Services Defined
PLAN TYPE: HMO
Model Type: Staff, Network
Benefits Offered: Behavioral Health, Chiropractic, Dental, Disease Management, Home Care, Inpatient SNF, Physical Therapy, Prescription, Psychiatric, Transplant, Vision, Worker's Compensation, Durable Medical Equipment
Offers Demand Management Patient Information Service: Yes

DMPI Services Offered: HealthPartners Nurse Navigators, CareLine, BabyLine, Personalized Assistance Line

Type of Coverage
Commercial, Individual, Indemnity, Medicare, Supplemental Medicare, Medicaid
Catastrophic Illness Benefit: Unlimited

Type of Payment Plans Offered
POS, Combination FFS & DFFS

Geographic Areas Served
Iowa: Allamakee, Dickinson, Emmet, Howard, Osceola counties;
Minnesota: most counties

Subscriber Information
Average Monthly Fee Per Subscriber
(Employee + Employer Contribution):
Employee Only (Self): Varies by plan
Average Annual Deductible Per Subscriber:
Employee Only (Self): $150
Average Subscriber Co-Payment:
Primary Care Physician: $10.00-20

Peer Review Type
Utilization Review: Yes
Case Management: Yes

Key Personnel
President/CEO . . . . Mary Brainerd
EVP, Chief Admin Officer . . . . Kathy Cooney
SVP, General Counsel . . . . Barb Tretheway
CEO, Regions Hospital . . . . Brock Nelson
EVP, Chief Marketing Offc . . . . Andrea Walsh
Medical Director . . . . George Isham
Dir, Corp Communications . . . . Amy von Walter
952-883-5274
amy.e.vonwalter@healthpartners.com

Specialty Managed Care Partners
Alere, Accordant, RMS
Enters into Contracts with Regional Business Coalitions: Yes

Employer References
University of MN, St Paul Public Schools, The College of St Catherine

607 HSM: Healthcare Cost Management

7805 Hudson Road
Suite 190
St Paul, MN 55125
Toll-Free: 800-432-3640
Phone: 651-501-9635
Fax: 651-501-9644
info@hsminc.com
www.hsminc.com
For Profit Organization: Yes
Year Founded: 1985
Number of Referral/Specialty Physicians: 4,000

Healthplan and Services Defined
PLAN TYPE: PPO
Model Type: Network
Plan Specialty: Chiropractic, Disease Management
Benefits Offered: Chiropractic, Complementary Medicine, Disease Management, Physical Therapy, Accupuncture, Massage therapy, OT, Speech

Type of Coverage
Commercial, Indemnity, Medicare, Medicaid

Type of Payment Plans Offered
POS, DFFS, Capitated, FFS, Combination FFS & DFFS

Geographic Areas Served
North Dakota, South Dakota, Minnesota, Wisconsin, Illinois, Indiana, Ohio, Michigan, Kentucky, Iowa, Missouri, Montana, Idaho, Nebraska, Tennessee, Kansas, Oklahoma, Utah, Arkansas, Arizona, Georgia, Texas, Alabama

Peer Review Type
Utilization Review: Yes

Publishes and Distributes Report Card: Yes

Key Personnel
President/CEO............................David Olsen
Claims.................................Steve Oberg
Marketing..............................Jim Wieland
Clinical Services....................Rick Branson, DC
CIO....................................Jim Cassell
Clinical Management....................Karen Froyum

Specialty Managed Care Partners
Enters into Contracts with Regional Business Coalitions: Yes

---

608 Humana Health Insurance of Minnesota

505 Highway 169
Suite 560
Plymouth, MN 55441
Toll-Free: 877-367-6990
Phone: 763-543-6990
www.humana.com
For Profit Organization: Yes

Healthplan and Services Defined
PLAN TYPE: HMO/PPO

Type of Coverage
Commercial, Individual

Accreditation Certification
URAC, NCQA, CORE

---

609 Medica Health - Medicare Plan

401 Carlson Parkway
PO Box 9310
Minnetonka, MN 55440-9310
Toll-Free: 800-234-8819
Phone: 952-992-2345
centerforhealthyaging@medica.com
http://member.medica.com/C0/medicare/default.aspx

Healthplan and Services Defined
PLAN TYPE: Medicare
Benefits Offered: Chiropractic, Dental, Disease Management, Home
Care, Inpatient SNF, Physical Therapy, Podiatry, Prescription,
Psychiatric, Vision, Wellness

Type of Coverage
Individual, Medicare

Geographic Areas Served
Available within multiple states

Subscriber Information
Average Monthly Fee Per Subscriber
(Employee + Employer Contribution):
Employee Only (Self): Varies
Medicare: Varies
Average Annual Deductible Per Subscriber:
Employee Only (Self): Varies
Medicare: Varies
Average Subscriber Co-Payment:
Primary Care Physician: Varies
Non-Network Physician: Varies
Prescription Drugs: Varies
Hospital ER: Varies
Home Health Care: Varies
Home Health Care Max. Days/Visits Covered: Varies
Nursing Home: Varies
Nursing Home Max. Days/Visits Covered: Varies

Key Personnel
President/CEO............................David Tilford
EVP/CFO/CAO............................Aaron Reynolds
SVP/Operations.........................Jana L Johnson

SVP/Medical Officer....................Charles Faxio, MD
SVP/General Counsel....................Jim Jacobson
SVP/Communications.....................Rob Longendyke
SVP/CIO................................Scott Boher
SVP/Government Programs................Glenn E Andis
SVP/Healthcare Economics...............Mark Baird

---

610 Medica: Corporate Office

401 Carlson Parkway
Minnetonka, MN 55305
Toll-Free: 800-952-3455
Phone: 952-992-2900
Fax: 952-992-3700
www.medica.com
Secondary Address: 878 2nd Street South, Suite 160, Waite Park, MN
56387
Non-Profit Organization: Yes
Year Founded: 1975
Number of Affiliated Hospitals: 158
Number of Primary Care Physicians: 27,000
Total Enrollment: 1,600,000

Healthplan and Services Defined
PLAN TYPE: PPO
Model Type: IPA
Benefits Offered: Behavioral Health, Chiropractic, Disease
Management, Prescription

Type of Coverage
Commercial, Individual, Medicare

Type of Payment Plans Offered
FFS

Geographic Areas Served
Aitkin, Anoka, Becker, Beltrami, Benton, Blue Earth, Brown, Carlton,
Carver, Cass, Chisago, Clay, Clearwater, Cottonwood, Crow Wing,
Dakota, Dodge, Douglas, Fillmore, Goodhue, Grant, Hennepin,
Hubbard, Isanti, Itaska, Jackson, Kanabec, Koochiching, Lac Qui
Parle, Lake, Le Sueur, Lincoln, Lyon, Mahnomen, McLeod, Meeker,
Mille Lacs, Minneapolis, Morrison, Murray, Nicollet, Norman,
Olmsted, Otter Tail, Pine, Polk, Pope, Ramsey, Renville, Rice, Rock,
Scott

Subscriber Information
Average Monthly Fee Per Subscriber
(Employee + Employer Contribution):
Employee Only (Self): Varies by plan
Average Subscriber Co-Payment:
Primary Care Physician: $15.00
Non-Network Physician: Deductible + 20%
Hospital ER: $60.00
Home Health Care: 20%
Home Health Care Max. Days/Visits Covered: 180 visits/yr.
Nursing Home: 20%
Nursing Home Max. Days/Visits Covered: 120/yr.

Network Qualifications
Pre-Admission Certification: Yes

Peer Review Type
Utilization Review: Yes
Second Surgical Opinion: Yes
Case Management: Yes

Publishes and Distributes Report Card: Yes

Accreditation Certification
NCQA
TJC Accreditation, Medicare Approved, Utilization Review,
Pre-Admission Certification, State Licensure, Quality Assurance
Program

Key Personnel
President/CEO............................David Tilford
CFO....................................Aaron Reynolds
Sr VP/Government Programs...............Glenn E Andis

Sr VP/Finance. . . . . .Mark Baird
Chief Information Officer . . . . .Scott Booher
Medical Officer. . . . . .Charles Fazio, MD
Sr VP/Commercial Markets . . . . .Tom Henke
Sr VP/General Counsel . . . . .Jim Jacobson
Sr VP/Operations . . . . .Jana L Johnson
Sr VP/Human Resources . . . . .Deb Knutson
Sr VP/Marketing . . . . .Rob Longendyke

Average Claim Compensation
Physician's Fees Charged: 65%
Hospital's Fees Charged: 60%

611 Meritain Health: Minnesota

400 Highway 169 South
Suite 800
Minneapolis, MN 55426-1141
Toll-Free: 800-925-2272
Fax: 952-593-3750
sales@meritain.com
www.meritain.com
For Profit Organization: Yes
Year Founded: 1983
Number of Affiliated Hospitals: 110
Number of Primary Care Physicians: 3,467
Number of Referral/Specialty Physicians: 5,720
Total Enrollment: 500,000
State Enrollment: 450,000

Healthplan and Services Defined
   PLAN TYPE: PPO
   Model Type: Network
   Plan Specialty: Dental, Disease Management, Vision, Radiology, UR
   Benefits Offered: Prescription
   Offers Demand Management Patient Information Service: Yes

Type of Coverage
   Commercial

Geographic Areas Served
   Nationwide

Subscriber Information
   Average Monthly Fee Per Subscriber
      (Employee + Employer Contribution):
         Employee Only (Self): Varies by plan

Accreditation Certification
   URAC
   TJC Accreditation, Medicare Approved, Utilization Review,
      Pre-Admission Certification, State Licensure, Quality Assurance
      Program

Average Claim Compensation
   Physician's Fees Charged: 78%
   Hospital's Fees Charged: 90%

Specialty Managed Care Partners
   Express Scripts, LabOne, Interactive Health Solutions

612 Metropolitan Health Plan

400 South 4th Street
Suite 201
Minneapolis, MN 55415
Toll-Free: 800-647-0550
Phone: 612-348-3000
Fax: 612-904-4264
mhp@co.hennepin.mn.us
www.mhp4life.org
Subsidiary of: Hennepin County
Non-Profit Organization: Yes
Year Founded: 1983
Number of Affiliated Hospitals: 8
Number of Primary Care Physicians: 200

Number of Referral/Specialty Physicians: 275
Total Enrollment: 21,000
Healthplan and Services Defined
   PLAN TYPE: HMO
   Model Type: Network
   Benefits Offered: Behavioral Health, Chiropractic, Disease
      Management, Home Care, Inpatient SNF, Long-Term Care,
      Physical Therapy, Podiatry, Prescription, Psychiatric, Transplant,
      Vision
   Offers Demand Management Patient Information Service: Yes
   DMPI Services Offered: C.A.R.S. (Children Are Riding Safely)
      carseat prog, Interpretive Services, Cell Phone Program,
      Transportation Program, HealthConnection Nurse Line

Type of Coverage
   Medicaid

Type of Payment Plans Offered
   Combination FFS & DFFS

Geographic Areas Served
   Anoka, Carver, Hennepin, Mower, Polk and Scott counties

Subscriber Information
   Average Subscriber Co-Payment:
      Primary Care Physician: $0
      Non-Network Physician: $0
      Home Health Care: $0
      Nursing Home: $0

Peer Review Type
   Utilization Review: Yes
   Case Management: Yes

Key Personnel
   Executive Director . . . . .Sue Zuidema
   Chief Operating Officer . . . . .Cynthia MacDonald
   Chief Financial Officer . . . . .Tim Schultz
   Compliance Officer. . . . . .Christine Reiten
   Medical Director . . . . .Joseph C Horozaniecki, MD
   Chief Information Officer. .Sandy Hvizdos

Specialty Managed Care Partners
   United Behavioral Health, Delta Dental, Caremark Rx

Employer References
   Hennepin County

613 MHP North Star Plans

Grain Exchange Building
400 South Fourth Street, Suite 201
Minneapolis, MN 55415
Toll-Free: 888-562-8000
Phone: 612-347-8557
Fax: 612-904-4267
mhp@co.hennepin.mn.us
www.mhpnorthstarplans.org
Healthplan and Services Defined
   PLAN TYPE: Medicare
   Other Type: HMO/POS
   Benefits Offered: Chiropractic, Dental, Disease Management, Home
      Care, Inpatient SNF, Physical Therapy, Podiatry, Prescription,
      Psychiatric, Vision, Wellness

Type of Coverage
   Medicare, Supplemental Medicare

Geographic Areas Served
   Anoka, Carver, Dakota, Hennepin, Ramsey, Scott and Washington
   counties

Subscriber Information
   Average Monthly Fee Per Subscriber
      (Employee + Employer Contribution):
         Employee Only (Self): Varies
         Medicare: Varies
   Average Annual Deductible Per Subscriber:

Employee Only (Self): Varies
Medicare: Varies
Average Subscriber Co-Payment:
Primary Care Physician: Varies
Non-Network Physician: Varies
Prescription Drugs: Varies
Hospital ER: Varies
Home Health Care: Varies
Home Health Care Max. Days/Visits Covered: Varies
Nursing Home: Varies
Nursing Home Max. Days/Visits Covered: Varies

Key Personnel
Executive Director. . . . . .David R Johnson

614 OptumHealth Care Solutions: Physical Health

6300 Olson Memorial Highway
Golden Valley, MN 55427
Toll-Free: 866-427-6845
Phone: 763-595-3200
Fax: 763-595-3333
engage@optumhealth.com
www.optumhealth.com
For Profit Organization: Yes
Year Founded: 1987
Number of Primary Care Physicians: 29,000
Number of Referral/Specialty Physicians: 40,000
Total Enrollment: 60,000,000

Healthplan and Services Defined
PLAN TYPE: Multiple
Model Type: Network
Plan Specialty: Behavioral Health, Chiropractic, Dental, Vision, Worker's Compensation
Benefits Offered: Behavioral Health, Chiropractic, Complementary Medicine, Dental, Physical Therapy, Vision, Worker's Compensation, Alternative Medicine

Type of Coverage
Commercial, Medicare, Medicaid, Workers' Compensation, HSA

Type of Payment Plans Offered
POS, Capitated, FFS

Geographic Areas Served
Nationwide

Network Qualifications
Pre-Admission Certification: Yes

Peer Review Type
Utilization Review: Yes
Case Management: Yes

Publishes and Distributes Report Card: Yes

Accreditation Certification
URAC
Utilization Review, Quality Assurance Program

Key Personnel
CEO. . . . . .Dawn Owens
dawn.owens@optumhealth.com
COO . . . . .John Prince
john.prince@optumhealth.com
CFO. . . . . .Paul Emerson
paul.emerson@optumhealth.com
General Counsel . . . . .Timothy F Ryan
timothy.ryan@optumhealth.com
Chief Marketing Office. . . . . .W. Thomas McEnery
thomas.mcenery@optumhealth.com
Sr Human Capital Partner . . . . .David Sparkman
david.sparkman@optumhealth.com
Chief Medical Offier .Miles Snowden, MD
miles.snowden@optumhealth.com

Chief Client Officer . . . . .Russ Johannesson
russ.johannesson@optumhealth.com
Chief Information Officer . . . . .Rob Bohnenkamp
rob.bohnenkamp@optumhealth.com
Media Relations . . . . .Brian Kane
763-797-2229
brian.kane@optumhealth.com

Specialty Managed Care Partners
Enters into Contracts with Regional Business Coalitions: Yes

615 Patient Choice

401 Carlson Parkway
CP 217
Minnetonka, MN 55305
Toll-Free: 800-254-6254
Phone: 952-992-1700
Fax: 952-992-1730
info@pchealthcare.com
www.patientchoicehealthcare.com
Year Founded: 1997
Number of Affiliated Hospitals: 142
Total Enrollment: 80,000

Healthplan and Services Defined
PLAN TYPE: PPO
Model Type: Network
Plan Specialty: Tiering health care delivery networks

Type of Coverage
Commercial

Geographic Areas Served
Minnesota, North Dakota, South Dakota

Publishes and Distributes Report Card: Yes

Key Personnel
Dir, Health Plan Analysis . . . . .Gunnar Nelson
Director, Data Services . . . . .Christopher Passauer
Provider Value Management. . . . . .Lisa Spann
Communications Manager . . . . .Michelle Nied
952-992-1700
mnied@pchealthcare.com

Specialty Managed Care Partners
American Care Partner
Enters into Contracts with Regional Business Coalitions: Yes

616 PreferredOne

6105 Golden Hills Drive
Golden Valley, MN 55416
Toll-Free: 800-940-5049
Phone: 763-847-4000
Fax: 763-847-4010
www.preferredone.com
Mailing Address: PO Box 59052, Minneapolis, MN 55459-0052
For Profit Organization: Yes
Year Founded: 1984
Number of Affiliated Hospitals: 284
Number of Primary Care Physicians: 9,200
Number of Referral/Specialty Physicians: 11,350
Total Enrollment: 97,800
State Enrollment: 216,150

Healthplan and Services Defined
PLAN TYPE: HMO/PPO
Model Type: Network
Benefits Offered: Inpatient SNF, Physical Therapy, Podiatry, Prescription, Psychiatric, Transplant, Vision, Wellness, Durable Medical Equipment

Type of Coverage
Commercial, Individual
Catastrophic Illness Benefit: Varies per case

Type of Payment Plans Offered
Combination FFS & DFFS

Geographic Areas Served
Minnesota

Peer Review Type
Second Surgical Opinion: No

Accreditation Certification
URAC

Key Personnel
President/CEO . . . . Marcus Merz
EVP/Chief Marketing Off . . . . Paul Geiwitz
EVP/Chief Medical Officer . . . . John Frederick, MD
Marketing Director . . . . Dennis S. Fenster
763-847-3355
dennis.fenster@preferredone.com

---

617 Security Life Insurance Company of America
10901 Red Circle Drive
Minnetonka, MN 55343-9137
Toll-Free: 800-328-4667
Phone: 952-544-2121
Fax: 952-945-3419
www.securitylife.com
For Profit Organization: Yes
Total Enrollment: 55,000,000

Healthplan and Services Defined
PLAN TYPE: Multiple
Other Type: Dental, Vision
Plan Specialty: Dental, Vision
Benefits Offered: Dental, Vision

Type of Coverage
Commercial, Individual

Key Personnel
Chairman . . . . Stephen Beckman
Co-Chairman . . . . JS Beckman
Executive Vice President . . . . Stuart L Sorensen

---

618 UCare Medicare Plan
500 Stinson Blvd NE
Minneapolis, MN 55413
Toll-Free: 877-523-1518
Phone: 612-676-3500
conact@ucare.org
www.ucare.org/members/healthplans/ufs.html
Mailing Address: PO Box 52, Minneapolis, MN 55440-0052
Number of Primary Care Physicians: 16,000
Total Enrollment: 75,000

Healthplan and Services Defined
PLAN TYPE: Medicare
Benefits Offered: Chiropractic, Dental, Disease Management, Home Care, Inpatient SNF, Physical Therapy, Podiatry, Prescription, Psychiatric, Vision, Wellness

Type of Coverage
Individual, Medicare

Geographic Areas Served
Available only within Minnesota

Subscriber Information
Average Monthly Fee Per Subscriber
(Employee + Employer Contribution):
Employee Only (Self): Varies
Medicare: Varies
Average Annual Deductible Per Subscriber:
Employee Only (Self): Varies
Medicare: Varies

Average Subscriber Co-Payment:
Primary Care Physician: Varies
Non-Network Physician: Varies
Prescription Drugs: Varies
Hospital ER: Varies
Home Health Care: Varies
Home Health Care Max. Days/Visits Covered: Varies
Nursing Home: Varies
Nursing Home Max. Days/Visits Covered: Varies

Key Personnel
President and CEO . . . . Nancy J Feldman
Clinical & Quality Mgmt. Barry Baines, MD
SVP, Operations . . . . Laurie Heyer-Dean
SVP, Chief Medical Offc . . . . Russel J Kuzel, MD
SVP, Administration . . . . Hilary Marden-Resnik
SVP, Chief Financial Offc . . . . Beth Monsrud
SVP, Product Management. . . . . Thomas Mahowald
SVP, General Counsel. . . . . Mark Traynor
SVP, Marketing . . . . Ghita Worcester
Product Management. . . . . Patricia Ball
Information Systems. Robert G Beauchamp
Health Care Economics . . . . Jamie Carsello
Clinical & Quality Mgmt . . . . R Craig Christianson, MD
Business Services . . . . Renae Froemming
Sales . . . . Brian Eck

---

619 UCare Minnesota
500 Stinson Blvd NE
Minneapolis, MN 55413
Toll-Free: 866-457-7144
Phone: 612-676-6500
contact@ucare.org
www.ucare.org
Mailing Address: PO Box 52, Minneapolis, MN 55440-0052
Non-Profit Organization: Yes
Year Founded: 1984
Owned by an Integrated Delivery Network (IDN): Yes
Number of Affiliated Hospitals: 164
Number of Primary Care Physicians: 16,000
Number of Referral/Specialty Physicians: 9,367
Total Enrollment: 200,000

Healthplan and Services Defined
PLAN TYPE: HMO/PPO
Model Type: Network
Benefits Offered: Behavioral Health, Chiropractic, Dental, Disease Management, Home Care, Inpatient SNF, Physical Therapy, Podiatry, Prescription, Psychiatric, Transplant, Vision, Wellness, Durable Medical Equipment

Type of Coverage
Medicare, Supplemental Medicare, Medicaid, MinnesotaCare
Catastrophic Illness Benefit: Unlimited

Type of Payment Plans Offered
POS

Geographic Areas Served
Minnestota & western Wisconsin

Subscriber Information
Average Subscriber Co-Payment:
Home Health Care Max. Days/Visits Covered: Unlimited
Nursing Home Max. Days/Visits Covered: 100 days

Network Qualifications
Pre-Admission Certification: Yes

Peer Review Type
Utilization Review: Yes
Second Surgical Opinion: Yes
Case Management: Yes

Publishes and Distributes Report Card: Yes

Accreditation Certification

Medicare Approved, Utilization Review, Pre-Admission
Certification, State Licensure, Quality Assurance Program

Key Personnel

President and CEO . . . . Nancy J Feldman
Clinical & Quality Mgmt. . . . . Barry Baines, MD
SVP, Operations . . . . Laurie Heyer-Dean
SVP, Chief Medical Offc . . . . Russel J Kuzel, MD
SVP, Administration . . . . Hilary Marden-Resnik
SVP, Chief Financial Offc . . . . Beth Monsrud
SVP, Product Management. . . . . Thomas Mahowald
SVP, General Counsel. . . . . Mark Traynor
SVP, Marketing . . . . Ghita Worcester
Product Management. . . . . Patricia Ball
Information Systems. Robert G Beauchamp
Health Care Economics . . . . Jamie Carsello
Clinical & Quality Mgmt . . . . R Craig Christianson, MD
Business Services . . . . Renae Froemming
Sales . . . . Brian Eck

Specialty Managed Care Partners

Doral Dental, Chriocare, ProCare Rx, BHP
Enters into Contracts with Regional Business Coalitions: Yes

Employer References

Xcel Energy, State of Minnesota, City of Minneapolis, University of
Minnesota, Pentair

620   UnitedHealthCare of Minnesota

5901 Lincoln Drive
Edina, MN 55436
Toll-Free: 877-842-3210
www.uhc.com
Subsidiary of: UnitedHealth Group
Year Founded: 1977
Number of Affiliated Hospitals: 4,200
Number of Primary Care Physicians: 460,000
Total Enrollment: 75,000,000

Healthplan and Services Defined
   PLAN TYPE: HMO/PPO
Model Type: IPA, Group, Network
Plan Specialty: Lab, Radiology
Benefits Offered: Chiropractic, Dental, Physical Therapy,
Prescription, Wellness, AD&D, Life, LTD, STD
Offers Demand Management Patient Information Service: Yes

Type of Coverage
Commercial, Individual, Indemnity, Medicare

Geographic Areas Served
Nationwide and Puerto Rico

Network Qualifications
Pre-Admission Certification: Yes

Peer Review Type
Utilization Review: Yes
Second Surgical Opinion: Yes
Case Management: Yes

Publishes and Distributes Report Card: Yes

Accreditation Certification
TJC, NCQA

Key Personnel
CEO . . . . William W McGuire, MD
President/COO . . . . Stephen J Hemsley
Chief Exec Officer-UHC . . . . Robert J Sheehy
Senior Vice Preisdent. David S Wichmann
General Counsel . . . . David J Lubben

Specialty Managed Care Partners
Enters into Contracts with Regional Business Coalitions: Yes

621   UnitedHealthCare of Minnesota

5901 Lincoln Dr
Edina, MN 55436
Toll-Free: 877-842-3210
www.uhc.com
Subsidiary of: UnitedHealth Group
For Profit Organization: Yes
Total Enrollment: 75,000,000
State Enrollment: 283,106

Healthplan and Services Defined
   PLAN TYPE: HMO/PPO
Benefits Offered: Disease Management, Wellness

Type of Payment Plans Offered
DFFS

Geographic Areas Served
Statewide

Publishes and Distributes Report Card: Yes

Key Personnel
Marketing . . . . Elliot Holtz
Media Contact . . . . Mary McElrath-Jones
914-467-2039
mary_r_mcelrath-jones@uhc.com

622   UnitedHealthCare of Wisconsin: Central

5901 Lincoln Drive
Edina, MN 55436
Toll-Free: 800-842-3585
www.uhc.com
Secondary Address: 10701 W Research Drive, Milwaukee, WI 53226,
800-879-0071
Subsidiary of: UnitedHealth Group
For Profit Organization: Yes
Total Enrollment: 75,000,000
State Enrollment: 392,782

Healthplan and Services Defined
   PLAN TYPE: HMO/PPO
Benefits Offered: Disease Management, Prescription, Wellness

Type of Coverage
Commercial, Medicare, Medicaid

Geographic Areas Served
Statewide

Key Personnel
CEO . . . . William Felsing
CFO . . . . Glen Reinhard
Media Contact . . . . Greg Thompson
312-424-6913
gregory_a_thompson@uhc.com

623   VSP: Vision Service Plan of Minnesota

8400 Normandale Lake Blvd
#920
Minneapolis, MN 55437-1085
Phone: 952-921-2360
Fax: 952-921-2383
webmaster@vsp.com
www.vsp.com
Year Founded: 1955
Number of Primary Care Physicians: 26,000
Total Enrollment: 55,000,000

Healthplan and Services Defined
   PLAN TYPE: Vision
Plan Specialty: Vision
Benefits Offered: Vision

Type of Payment Plans Offered
Capitated

Geographic Areas Served
Statewide

Network Qualifications
Pre-Admission Certification: Yes

Peer Review Type
Utilization Review: Yes

Accreditation Certification
Utilization Review, Quality Assurance Program

Key Personnel
Manager................................Theresa Callanan

Health Insurance Coverage Status and Type of Coverage by Age

Category	All Persons		Under 18 years		Under 65 years		65 years and over	
	Number	%	Number	%	Number	%	Number	%
Total population	2,929	-	765	-	2,543	-	386	-
Covered by some type of health insurance	2,311 (37)	78.9 (1.3)	663 (17)	86.6 (2.8)	1,929 (38)	75.9 (1.4)	382 (23)	98.9 (0.7)
Covered by private health insurance	1,580 (41)	53.9 (1.5)	336 (19)	43.9 (2.3)	1,381 (39)	54.3 (1.3)	200 (17)	51.7 (4.5)
Employment based	1,324 (50)	45.2 (1.7)	309 (19)	40.4 (2.3)	1,221 (46)	48.0 (1.6)	102 (13)	26.5 (3.7)
Own employment based	734 (25)	25.1 (0.9)	2 (2)	0.3 (0.3)	655 (25)	25.8 (0.9)	79 (10)	20.4 (2.5)
Direct purchase	295 (32)	10.1 (1.1)	26 (10)	3.5 (1.3)	175 (31)	6.9 (1.2)	120 (21)	31.1 (5.3)
Covered by government health insurance	1,042 (48)	35.6 (1.6)	378 (34)	49.5 (4.7)	673 (37)	26.5 (1.5)	369 (24)	95.6 (1.3)
Covered by Medicaid	586 (59)	20.0 (2.1)	359 (36)	46.9 (5.0)	527 (54)	20.7 (2.2)	59 (9)	15.4 (2.5)
Also by private insurance	67 (18)	2.3 (0.6)	38 (16)	5.0 (2.1)	62 (18)	2.4 (0.7)	5 (4)	1.2 (1.1)
Covered by Medicare	446 (21)	15.2 (0.7)	0 (0)	0.0 (0.0)	77 (9)	3.0 (0.4)	369 (24)	95.6 (1.3)
Also by private insurance	207 (22)	7.1 (0.8)	0 (0)	0.0 (0.0)	20 (6)	0.8 (0.2)	187 (18)	48.4 (4.6)
Also by Medicaid	85 (12)	2.9 (0.4)	0 (0)	0.0 (0.0)	26 (8)	1.0 (0.3)	59 (9)	15.4 (2.5)
Covered by military health care	126 (30)	4.3 (1.0)	22 (7)	2.9 (0.9)	105 (26)	4.1 (1.0)	21 (8)	5.5 (2.0)
Not covered at any time during the year	618 (39)	21.1 (1.3)	102 (22)	13.4 (2.8)	614 (38)	24.1 (1.4)	4 (2)	1.1 (0.7)

Note: Numbers in thousands; figures cover 2010; standard error appears in parenthesis; (b) base less than 75,000; (x) not applicable
Source: U.S. Census Bureau, Current Population Survey, 2011 Annual Social and Economic Supplement. Table HI05. Health Insurance Coverage Status and Type of Coverage by State and Age for All People: 2010

Mississippi

624 Aetna Health of Mississippi

151 Farmington Avenue
Hartford, CT 06156
Toll-Free: 866-582-9629
www.aetna.com
For Profit Organization: Yes
Total Enrollment: 11,596,230

Healthplan and Services Defined
PLAN TYPE: PPO
Other Type: POS
Plan Specialty: EPO
Benefits Offered: Dental, Disease Management, Long-Term Care, Prescription, Wellness, Life, LTD, STD

Type of Coverage
Commercial, Individual

Type of Payment Plans Offered
POS, FFS

Geographic Areas Served
Statewide

Key Personnel
CEO . . . . .Ronald A Williams
President. . . . . .Mark T Bertolini
SVP, General Counsel . . . . .William J Casazza
EVP, CFO . . . . .Joseph M Zubretsky
Head, M&A Integration . . . . .Kay Mooney
SVP, Marketing. . . . . .Robert E Mead
Chief Medical Officer . . . . .Lonny Reisman, MD
SVP, Human Resources. .Elease E Wright
SVP, CIO. . . . . .Meg McCarthy

625 CIGNA HealthCare of Mississippi

3400 Players Club Pkwy
Suite 140
Memphis, TN 38125
Toll-Free: 866-438-2446
Phone: 901-748-4100
Fax: 901-748-4104
www.cigna.com
For Profit Organization: Yes
Year Founded: 1993
Total Enrollment: 64,997
State Enrollment: 53,490

Healthplan and Services Defined
PLAN TYPE: HMO
Model Type: IPA
Benefits Offered: Disease Management, Prescription, Transplant, Vision, Wellness
Offers Demand Management Patient Information Service: Yes

Type of Coverage
Commercial, Individual
Catastrophic Illness Benefit: Varies per case

Type of Payment Plans Offered
POS

Geographic Areas Served
Bolivar, Calhoun, Carroll, Chickasaw, Coahoma, Grenada, Leflore, Monroe, Montgomery, Tallahatchie, Tate, Tunica, Webster, Yalobusha counties

Publishes and Distributes Report Card: Yes

Accreditation Certification
NCQA
TJC Accreditation, Medicare Approved

Key Personnel
President/CEO. . . . . .David Mathis

CFO . . . . .Stuart Wright
Medical Affairs. . . . . .Frederick Buckwold
Member Services . . . . .Chuck Utterbeck

626 Delta Dental Insurance Company

1130 Sanctuary Parkway
Suite 600
Alpharetta, GA 30004
Toll-Free: 888-858-5252
Phone: 770-645-8700
Fax: 770-518-4757
4gasales@delta.org
www.deltadentalins.com
Mailing Address: PO Box 1809, Alpharetta, GA 30023-1809
Non-Profit Organization: Yes
Number of Primary Care Physicians: 198,000
Total Enrollment: 54,000,000

Healthplan and Services Defined
PLAN TYPE: Dental
Other Type: Dental PPO
Plan Specialty: Dental
Benefits Offered: Dental

Type of Coverage
Commercial

Type of Payment Plans Offered
POS, DFFS, FFS

Geographic Areas Served
Statewide

Key Personnel
CEO. . . . . .Gary D Radine
VP, Public & Govt Affairs . . . . .Jeff Album
415-972-8418
Dir/Media & Public Affair . . . . .Elizabeth Risberg
415-972-8423

627 eHealthInsurance Services Inc.

11919 Foundation Place
Gold River, CA 95670
Toll-Free: 800-977-8860
info@ehealthinsurance.com
www.e.healthinsurance.com
Year Founded: 1997

Healthplan and Services Defined
PLAN TYPE: HMO/PPO
Benefits Offered: Dental, Life, STD

Type of Coverage
Commercial, Individual, Medicare

Geographic Areas Served
All 50 states in the USA and District of Columbia

Key Personnel
Chairman & CEO . . . . .Gary L. Lauer
EVP/Business & Corp. Dev. . . . . .Bruce Telkamp
EVP/Chief Technology .Dr. Sheldon X. Wang
SVP & CFO . . . . .Stuart M. Huizinga
Pres. of eHealth Gov. Sys . . . . .Samuel C. Gibbs
SVP of Sales & Operations . . . . .Robert S. Hurley
Director Public Relations. . . . . .Nate Purpura
650-210-3115

628 Health Link PPO

808 Varsity Drive
Tupelo, MS 38801
Toll-Free: 888-855-2740
Phone: 662-377-3868
Fax: 662-377-7599

www.healthlinkppo.com
Non-Profit Organization: Yes
Year Founded: 1986
Number of Affiliated Hospitals: 30
Number of Primary Care Physicians: 1,500
Total Enrollment: 155,070

Healthplan and Services Defined
  PLAN TYPE: PPO
  Benefits Offered: Dental, Prescription, Transplant, Vision, Life, LTD, STD, Major Medical

Type of Coverage
  Commercial, Individual

Geographic Areas Served
  33 counties in Mississippi & Western Alabama

Accreditation Certification
  NCQA
  Medicare Approved, Utilization Review, Pre-Admission Certification, State Licensure, Quality Assurance Program

Key Personnel
  Vice President . . . . Wally Davis
  Health Link Manager . . . . Rose Harvey
  Marketing . . . . Len Grice
  Medical Affairs . . . . Homer Horton, MD
  Information Services . . . . Faye Perry

629 Humana Health Insurance of Mississippi

795 Woodlands Parkway
Suite 100
Ridgeland, MS 39157
Toll-Free: 800-224-4171
Phone: 601-956-8247
Fax: 601-956-1351
www.humana.com
For Profit Organization: Yes
Total Enrollment: 78,600
State Enrollment: 2,900

Healthplan and Services Defined
  PLAN TYPE: HMO/PPO
  Plan Specialty: ASO
  Benefits Offered: Disease Management, Prescription, Wellness

Type of Coverage
  Commercial, Individual, Medicare

Geographic Areas Served
  Alabama, Mississippi

Accreditation Certification
  URAC, NCQA

Key Personnel
  CEO . . . . Rick Remmers

Specialty Managed Care Partners
  Caremark Rx

Employer References
  Tricare

630 UnitedHealthCare of Mississippi

32 Millbranch Road
Suite 30
Hattiesburg, MS 39402
Toll-Free: 800-345-1520
Fax: 601-957-1306
mississippi_pr_team@uhc.com
www.uhc.com
Subsidiary of: UnitedHealth Group
For Profit Organization: Yes
Year Founded: 1992
Number of Affiliated Hospitals: 44

Number of Primary Care Physicians: 452
Total Enrollment: 75,000,000

Healthplan and Services Defined
  PLAN TYPE: HMO/PPO
  Model Type: IPA
  Benefits Offered: Dental, Disease Management, Prescription, Vision, Wellness, LTD, STD

Type of Coverage
  Commercial, Individual, Indemnity

Type of Payment Plans Offered
  FFS

Geographic Areas Served
  Statewide

Network Qualifications
  Pre-Admission Certification: Yes

Peer Review Type
  Utilization Review: Yes
  Second Surgical Opinion: Yes
  Case Management: Yes

Publishes and Distributes Report Card: Yes

Accreditation Certification
  NCQA
  TJC Accreditation, Medicare Approved, Utilization Review, Pre-Admission Certification, State Licensure, Quality Assurance Program

Key Personnel
  Chairman/CEO . . . . William McGuire, MD
  President . . . . Kim Dukes
  Media Contact . . . . Roger Rollman
  roger_f_rollman@uhc.com

Specialty Managed Care Partners
  Enters into Contracts with Regional Business Coalitions: Yes

631 Universal Health Care Group: Mississippi

385B Highland Colony Parkway
Suite 405
Ridgeland, MS 39157
Phone: 727-329-0640
www.univhc.com

Healthplan and Services Defined
  PLAN TYPE: Medicare

Type of Coverage
  Individual, Medicare, Supplemental Medicare, Medicaid

Health Insurance Coverage Status and Type of Coverage by Age

Category	All Persons		Under 18 years		Under 65 years		65 years and over	
	Number	%	Number	%	Number	%	Number	%
Total population	5,979	-	1,394	-	5,172	-	807	-
Covered by some type of health insurance	5,143 *(78)*	86.0 *(1.1)*	1,269 *(36)*	91.1 *(2.5)*	4,338 *(90)*	83.9 *(1.3)*	805 *(52)*	99.8 *(0.2)*
Covered by private health insurance	4,129 *(133)*	69.1 *(2.0)*	937 *(41)*	67.2 *(2.8)*	3,587 *(123)*	69.4 *(2.1)*	542 *(50)*	67.2 *(3.2)*
Employment based	3,406 *(119)*	57.0 *(1.8)*	837 *(43)*	60.1 *(3.0)*	3,154 *(123)*	61.0 *(2.1)*	252 *(32)*	31.2 *(2.8)*
Own employment based	1,804 *(73)*	30.2 *(1.1)*	1 *(1)*	0.1 *(0.1)*	1,612 *(76)*	31.2 *(1.3)*	192 *(25)*	23.7 *(2.4)*
Direct purchase	868 *(61)*	14.5 *(1.0)*	139 *(23)*	9.9 *(1.7)*	539 *(59)*	10.4 *(1.2)*	329 *(35)*	40.8 *(3.2)*
Covered by government health insurance	1,756 *(83)*	29.4 *(1.5)*	436 *(27)*	31.3 *(1.9)*	988 *(85)*	19.1 *(1.7)*	768 *(46)*	95.2 *(1.1)*
Covered by Medicaid	844 *(58)*	14.1 *(1.0)*	419 *(25)*	30.1 *(1.8)*	794 *(60)*	15.3 *(1.2)*	50 *(12)*	6.2 *(1.6)*
Also by private insurance	171 *(27)*	2.9 *(0.4)*	95 *(19)*	6.8 *(1.4)*	155 *(26)*	3.0 *(0.5)*	16 *(4)*	2.0 *(0.5)*
Covered by Medicare	979 *(49)*	16.4 *(0.9)*	8 *(6)*	0.6 *(0.4)*	211 *(40)*	4.1 *(0.8)*	768 *(46)*	95.2 *(1.1)*
Also by private insurance	560 *(49)*	9.4 *(0.8)*	0 *(0)*	0.0 *(0.0)*	55 *(16)*	1.1 *(0.3)*	505 *(45)*	62.6 *(3.4)*
Also by Medicaid	155 *(26)*	2.6 *(0.4)*	7 *(5)*	0.5 *(0.4)*	105 *(24)*	2.0 *(0.5)*	50 *(12)*	6.2 *(1.6)*
Covered by military health care	190 *(28)*	3.2 *(0.5)*	20 *(7)*	1.4 *(0.5)*	116 *(23)*	2.2 *(0.4)*	75 *(18)*	9.3 *(2.0)*
Not covered at any time during the year	835 *(65)*	14.0 *(1.1)*	124 *(35)*	8.9 *(2.5)*	834 *(65)*	16.1 *(1.3)*	2 *(2)*	0.2 *(0.2)*

Note: Numbers in thousands; figures cover 2010; standard error appears in parenthesis; (b) base less than 75,000; (x) not applicable
Source: U.S. Census Bureau, Current Population Survey, 2011 Annual Social and Economic Supplement. Table HI05. Health Insurance Coverage Status and Type of Coverage by State and Age for All People: 2010

Missouri

632 Aetna Health of Missouri

1 South Wacker Drive
Mail Stop F643
Chicago, IL 60606
Toll-Free: 866-582-9629
www.aetna.com
For Profit Organization: Yes
Year Founded: 1996
Federally Qualified: Yes
Total Enrollment: 10,885
State Enrollment: 10,885

Healthplan and Services Defined
PLAN TYPE: HMO
Other Type: POS
Model Type: Mixed
Benefits Offered: Behavioral Health, Chiropractic, Complementary
Medicine, Dental, Home Care, Inpatient SNF, Long-Term Care,
Physical Therapy, Podiatry, Prescription, Psychiatric, Transplant,
Vision, Wellness

Type of Coverage
Commercial, Medicare

Geographic Areas Served
Statewide

Accreditation Certification
NCQA

Key Personnel
President . . . . .Allan Ira Greenberg
CFO . . . . .Joan Barnicle
CMO . . . . .Haydee Muse
Pharmacy. . . . . .Eric Elliot

633 American Health Care Alliance

9229 Ward Parkway
Suite 300
Kansas City, MO 64114
Toll-Free: 800-870-6252
Fax: 816-523-1098
customerservice@ahappo.com
www.ahappo.com
Year Founded: 1990
Number of Affiliated Hospitals: 5,745
Number of Primary Care Physicians: 190,736
Number of Referral/Specialty Physicians: 285,353
Total Enrollment: 942,000
State Enrollment: 860,000

Healthplan and Services Defined
PLAN TYPE: PPO
Model Type: Network of PPOs
Benefits Offered: Behavioral Health, Chiropractic, Complementary
Medicine, Dental, Home Care, Physical Therapy, Podiatry,
Prescription, Psychiatric, Vision, Wellness
Offers Demand Management Patient Information Service: Yes

Geographic Areas Served
Nationwide

Subscriber Information
Average Annual Deductible Per Subscriber:
Employee Only (Self): Varies
Employee & 1 Family Member: Varies
Employee & 2 Family Members: Varies
Medicare: Varies
Average Subscriber Co-Payment:
Primary Care Physician: Varies
Non-Network Physician: Varies
Prescription Drugs: Varies

Hospital ER: Varies
Home Health Care: Varies
Nursing Home: Varies

Publishes and Distributes Report Card: Yes

Accreditation Certification
AAAHC, URAC, AAPI, NCQA
TJC Accreditation, Medicare Approved, Utilization Review,
Pre-Admission Certification, State Licensure

Key Personnel
Executive Vice President . . . . .Phil Mehelic
pmehelic@ahappo.com
Director Claims. . . . . .Rochelle Barrett
Director Client Service . . . . .Lisa Enslinger

634 Anthem Blue Cross & Blue Shield of Missouri

1831 Chestnut Street
Saint Louis, MO 63103
Toll-Free: 800-392-8740
Phone: 314-923-4444
moreinfo@bcbsmo.com
www.anthem.com
Secondary Address: 1000 W Nifong, Columbia, MO 65203
Subsidiary of: WellPoint
For Profit Organization: Yes
Year Founded: 1985
Owned by an Integrated Delivery Network (IDN): Yes
Number of Affiliated Hospitals: 35
Number of Primary Care Physicians: 4,000
Total Enrollment: 1,100,000
State Enrollment: 900,000

Healthplan and Services Defined
PLAN TYPE: PPO
Model Type: Group
Plan Specialty: Behavioral Health, Chiropractic, Disease
Management, Lab, PBM, Vision, Radiology, UR
Benefits Offered: Behavioral Health, Chiropractic, Disease
Management, Home Care, Inpatient SNF, Long-Term Care,
Physical Therapy, Podiatry, Prescription, Psychiatric, Transplant,
Wellness, AD&D

Type of Coverage
Individual, Indemnity, Medicare, Supplemental Medicare

Type of Payment Plans Offered
POS

Geographic Areas Served
St Louis City & County; 68 other counties

Subscriber Information
Average Annual Deductible Per Subscriber:
Employee Only (Self): $200.00
Employee & 1 Family Member: $400.00
Employee & 2 Family Members: $400.00
Medicare: $0
Average Subscriber Co-Payment:
Primary Care Physician: $0
Non-Network Physician: $0
Prescription Drugs: $7.00
Hospital ER: $0
Home Health Care: $0
Home Health Care Max. Days/Visits Covered: 100 visits/yr.
Nursing Home: $0
Nursing Home Max. Days/Visits Covered: 70/yr.

Network Qualifications
Pre-Admission Certification: Yes

Peer Review Type
Utilization Review: Yes
Second Surgical Opinion: Yes
Case Management: Yes

Accreditation Certification
NCQA
TJC Accreditation, Medicare Approved, Utilization Review,
　Pre-Admission Certification, State Licensure, Quality Assurance
　Program

Key Personnel
President . . . . Angela Braly
CFO . . . . Sandra Van Trease
Medical Affairs . . . . Joseph Hughenot
Information Systems . . . . Tom Ogdon
Provider Services . . . . Eleanor Bencic
Sales . . . . Ed Tenholder

Average Claim Compensation
Physician's Fees Charged: 1%
Hospital's Fees Charged: 65%

635　Assurant Employee Benefits: Corporate Headquarters

2323 Grand Boulevard
Kansas City, MO 64108
Toll-Free: 800-325-8385
Phone: 816-474-2345
Fax: 816-881-8996
benefits@assurant.com
www.assurantemployeebenefits.com
Subsidiary of: Assurant, Inc
For Profit Organization: Yes
Number of Primary Care Physicians: 112,000
Total Enrollment: 47,000

Healthplan and Services Defined
PLAN TYPE: Multiple
Other Type: Benefits Insurance
Plan Specialty: Dental, Vision, Long & Short-Term Disability
Benefits Offered: Dental, Vision, Wellness, AD&D, Life, LTD, STD

Type of Coverage
Commercial, Indemnity, Individual Dental Plans

Geographic Areas Served
Nationwide

Subscriber Information
Average Monthly Fee Per Subscriber
　(Employee + Employer Contribution):
　　Employee Only (Self): Varies by plan

Key Personnel
Interim President & CEO . . . . John S. Roberts
VP & General Counsel . . . . Kenneth D Bowen
SVP, Risk . . . . Dianna D Duvall
Vice President, Claims . . . . Sheryle L Ohme
SVP & CFO . . . . Miles B Yakre
VP, Marketing . . . . Joseph A Sevcik
SVP, Human Resources . . . . Sylvia Wagner
SVP & Chief Info Officer . . . . Karla J Schacht
Sr VP, Sales . . . . J Marc Warrington
PR Specialist . . . . Megan Hutchison
　816-556-7815
　megan.hutison@assurant.com
SVP, Investor Relations . . . . Melissa Kivett
　212-859-7029
　melissa.kivett@assurant.com

636　Blue Cross & Blue Shield of Kansas City

2301 Main Street
One Pershing Square
Kansas City, MO 64108
Toll-Free: 888-989-8842
Phone: 816-395-3558
Fax: 816-395-2035

www.bluekc.com
Non-Profit Organization: Yes
Year Founded: 1982
Number of Affiliated Hospitals: 56
Number of Primary Care Physicians: 1,189
Number of Referral/Specialty Physicians: 1,386
Total Enrollment: 1,000,000
State Enrollment: 1,000,000

Healthplan and Services Defined
PLAN TYPE: PPO
Model Type: Network
Benefits Offered: Behavioral Health, Chiropractic, Dental, Physical
　Therapy, Podiatry, Prescription, Psychiatric

Type of Coverage
Commercial, Individual, Medicare, Supplemental Medicare
Catastrophic Illness Benefit: Maximum $2M

Type of Payment Plans Offered
POS, FFS

Geographic Areas Served
32 counties in greater Kansas City, northwest Missouri and Johnson
　and Wyandotte counties in Kansas

Subscriber Information
Average Subscriber Co-Payment:
　Primary Care Physician: $10.00
　Non-Network Physician: Ded/coins.
　Prescription Drugs: $10.00/20.00/10.00
　Hospital ER: $50.00

Network Qualifications
Pre-Admission Certification: Yes

Peer Review Type
Utilization Review: Yes

Publishes and Distributes Report Card: No

Accreditation Certification
URAC, NCQA

Key Personnel
President & CEO . . . . Tom Bowser
President & CEO-Elect . . . . David Gentile
EVP, Community Affairs . . . . Peter Yelorda
CEO, Blue KC Subsidiaries . . . . John W Kennedy
EVP, Chief Mktg Officer . . . . Roger Foreman
Medical Affairs . . . . Frank DiTorro
Information Services . . . . Judy Bond
Media Contact . . . . Sue Johnson
　816-395-3566
　susan.johnson@bluekc.com

Specialty Managed Care Partners
Enters into Contracts with Regional Business Coalitions: Yes

637　BlueChoice
Acquired by Anthem Blue Cross & Blue Shield

638　Centene Corporation

7711 Carondelet Avenue
Suite 800
Saint Louis, MO 63105
Toll-Free: 800-225-2573
Phone: 314-725-4477
Fax: 314-558-2428
communication@centene.com
www.centene.com
For Profit Organization: Yes
Year Founded: 1984
Number of Affiliated Hospitals: 23
Number of Primary Care Physicians: 1,700
Total Enrollment: 1,450,000

Healthplan and Services Defined
PLAN TYPE: HMO
Benefits Offered: Behavioral Health, Disease Management,
Long-Term Care, Prescription, Psychiatric, Vision, Wellness
Offers Demand Management Patient Information Service: Yes
DMPI Services Offered: 24/7 Nurse Line

Type of Coverage
Medicaid, SCHIP

Geographic Areas Served
Arizona, Florida, Georgia, Indiana, Massachusetts, Ohio, South
Carolina, Texas, Wisonsin

Accreditation Certification
TJC Accreditation, Medicare Approved, Utilization Review,
Pre-Admission Certification, State Licensure, Quality Assurance
Program

Key Personnel
President, CEO. . . . . .Michael F Neidorff
Sr VP of Health Plans . . . . .Christopher D Bowers
SVP, Operations . . . . .Patricia J Darnley
EVP, Chief Admin Officer .Carol E Goldman
Sr VP/Strategy . . . . .Cary D Hobbs
Sr VP/Medical Affairs . . . . .Robert C Packman, MD
SVP, Specialty Business. . . . . .Jason M Harrold
Sr VP/Specialty Companies. . . . . .William N Scheffel
EVP, Corp Development. . . . . .Jesse N Hunter
EVP, Chief Info Officer. . . . . .Donald G Imholz
SVP, Investor Relations .Edmund E Kroll
EVP, Celtic Group Chair . . . . .Frederick J Manning
SVP, Chief Tech Officer . . . . .Glendon A Schuster
SVP, Public Affairs . . . . .Toni Simonetti
SVP, General Counsel. . . . . .Keith H Williamson

639 Children's Mercy Family Health Partners

PO Box 411806
Kansas City, MO 64179-1076
Toll-Free: 800-347-9363
Phone: 816-855-1888
Fax: 816-855-1890
membserv@fhp.org
www.fhp.org
Subsidiary of: Children's Mercy Family Health Partners
Non-Profit Organization: Yes
Year Founded: 1996
Owned by an Integrated Delivery Network (IDN): Yes
Number of Affiliated Hospitals: 31
Number of Primary Care Physicians: 200
Number of Referral/Specialty Physicians: 2,400
Total Enrollment: 49,976
State Enrollment: 49,976

Healthplan and Services Defined
PLAN TYPE: HMO
Model Type: Network, Medicaid
Benefits Offered: Behavioral Health, Dental, Disease Management,
Home Care, Inpatient SNF, Physical Therapy, Podiatry,
Prescription, Psychiatric, Vision, Wellness

Type of Coverage
Medicaid
Catastrophic Illness Benefit: None

Geographic Areas Served
Cass, Clay, Henry, Jackson, Johnson, Lafayette, Platte, Ray, St. Claire
counties in Missouri

Subscriber Information
Average Monthly Fee Per Subscriber
(Employee + Employer Contribution):
Employee Only (Self): $0.00
Employee & 1 Family Member: $0.00
Employee & 2 Family Members: $0.00

Peer Review Type
Utilization Review: Yes
Second Surgical Opinion: Yes
Case Management: Yes

Publishes and Distributes Report Card: Yes

Key Personnel
CEO. . . . . .Bob Finuf
CFO . . . . .Suzie Dunaway
Claims Manager . . . . .Doug Greg
Mgr, Community Relations. . . . . .Chris Beurman

Average Claim Compensation
Physician's Fees Charged: 50%
Hospital's Fees Charged: 60%

Specialty Managed Care Partners
Enters into Contracts with Regional Business Coalitions: Yes

Employer References
State of Missouri, Division of Medical Services, State of Kansas, SRS

640 CIGNA HealthCare of St. Louis

231 S Bemiston Avenue
Suite 500
Clayton, MO 63105
Toll-Free: 866-438-2446
Phone: 314-290-7300
Fax: 314-290-7303
www.cigna.com
For Profit Organization: Yes
Year Founded: 1984
Number of Affiliated Hospitals: 27
Total Enrollment: 8,049
State Enrollment: 8,049

Healthplan and Services Defined
PLAN TYPE: HMO
Other Type: POS
Model Type: IPA
Benefits Offered: Behavioral Health, Chiropractic, Dental, Physical
Therapy, Podiatry, Prescription, Psychiatric, Vision
Offers Demand Management Patient Information Service: Yes

Type of Coverage
Commercial
Catastrophic Illness Benefit: Varies per case

Type of Payment Plans Offered
POS, FFS

Geographic Areas Served
Franklin, Jefferson, Madison, Monroe, St. Charles, St. Clair, St. Louis
counties

Subscriber Information
Average Monthly Fee Per Subscriber
(Employee + Employer Contribution):
Employee Only (Self): Varies on plan
Average Annual Deductible Per Subscriber:
Employee Only (Self): $200.00
Employee & 1 Family Member: $200.00
Employee & 2 Family Members: $200.00
Average Subscriber Co-Payment:
Primary Care Physician: $10.00
Prescription Drugs: $5.00-10.00
Hospital ER: $50.00
Home Health Care: $0
Home Health Care Max. Days/Visits Covered: 60-120 days
Nursing Home: $0
Nursing Home Max. Days/Visits Covered: 60-120 days

Network Qualifications
Pre-Admission Certification: Yes

Peer Review Type
Utilization Review: Yes
Second Surgical Opinion: Yes

Case Management: Yes

Publishes and Distributes Report Card: Yes

Accreditation Certification
NCQA

Key Personnel
CEO . . . . .H Edward Hanway
CFO . . . . .Scott Duce
Director Network Development .David Bird
Medical Affairs. .Debbie Zimmerman, MD
Information Services . . . . .Jeff Robertson

Average Claim Compensation
Physician's Fees Charged: 85%
Hospital's Fees Charged: 75%

Specialty Managed Care Partners
Enters into Contracts with Regional Business Coalitions: Yes

---

641 Community Health Improvement Solutions
Heartland Health Business Plaza
137 N Belt Highway
Saint Joseph, MO 64506
Toll-Free: 800-990-9247
Phone: 816-271-1247
Fax: 816-271-1266
www.mychp.com
Subsidiary of: Aetna
Non-Profit Organization: Yes
Year Founded: 1995
Federally Qualified: Yes
Number of Affiliated Hospitals: 34
Number of Primary Care Physicians: 578
Number of Referral/Specialty Physicians: 2,203
Total Enrollment: 7,000
State Enrollment: 25,335

Healthplan and Services Defined
PLAN TYPE: HMO
Model Type: Group
Plan Specialty: ASO, Behavioral Health, Chiropractic, Disease
  Management, EPO, Lab, MSO, PBM, Vision, Radiology, Worker's
  Compensation, UR
Benefits Offered: Behavioral Health, Chiropractic, Complementary
  Medicine, Disease Management, Home Care, Inpatient SNF,
  Long-Term Care, Physical Therapy, Podiatry, Prescription,
  Psychiatric, Transplant, Vision, Wellness, Worker's Compensation,
  Life
Offers Demand Management Patient Information Service: Yes

Type of Coverage
Commercial, Individual, Indemnity, Catastrophic
Catastrophic Illness Benefit: Varies per case

Type of Payment Plans Offered
FFS, Combination FFS & DFFS

Geographic Areas Served
Northwest Missouri and Northeast Kansas

Publishes and Distributes Report Card: Yes

Accreditation Certification
NCQA
Medicare Approved, Utilization Review, State Licensure, Quality
  Assurance Program

Key Personnel
Plan Admin . . . . .Linda Bahrke
CFO. . . . . .Stan Vaughan
Claims . . . . .Marci Gillis
Marketing/Sales. . . . . .Ricard Pugh
Medical Affairs. . . . . .Robert Chabon, MD
Provider Services. . . . . .Audrey Shanley

Specialty Managed Care Partners
Heartland Regional Medical Centre, American Family

Enters into Contracts with Regional Business Coalitions: Yes

---

642 Cox Healthplans
Kelly Plaza
3200 S National, Building B
Springfield, MO 65807
Toll-Free: 800-664-1244
Phone: 417-269-4679
Fax: 417-269-4667
grouphealth@coxhealthplans.com
www.coxhealthplans.com
Mailing Address: PO Box 5750, Springfield, MO 65801-5750
Subsidiary of: CoxHealth
For Profit Organization: Yes
Number of Primary Care Physicians: 1,000
Number of Referral/Specialty Physicians: 5,000
Total Enrollment: 5,000
State Enrollment: 1,964

Healthplan and Services Defined
PLAN TYPE: HMO/PPO
Benefits Offered: Disease Management, Prescription, Wellness

Type of Coverage
Commercial, Individual

Type of Payment Plans Offered
POS

Geographic Areas Served
Missouri

Key Personnel
President & CEO . . . . .Jeff C Bond
Marketing . . . . .Kurt Scherer
Chief Financial Officer . . . . .Matthew Aug

Specialty Managed Care Partners
Caremark Rx

---

643 Delta Dental of Missouri
12399 Gravois Road
Saint Louis, MO 63127-1702
Toll-Free: 800-392-1167
Phone: 314-656-3000
Fax: 314-656-2900
service@ddpmo.org
www.deltadentalmo.com
Mailing Address: PO Box 8690, Saint Louis, MO 63126-0690
Subsidiary of: Delta Dental Plans Association
Non-Profit Organization: Yes
Year Founded: 1958
Owned by an Integrated Delivery Network (IDN): Yes
Number of Primary Care Physicians: 3,000
Total Enrollment: 54,000,000
State Enrollment: 1,400,000

Healthplan and Services Defined
PLAN TYPE: Dental
Other Type: Dental PPO
Model Type: Group
Plan Specialty: Dental
Benefits Offered: Dental

Type of Coverage
Commercial

Geographic Areas Served
Statewide

Subscriber Information
Average Monthly Fee Per Subscriber
  (Employee + Employer Contribution):
    Employee Only (Self): Varies
    Employee & 1 Family Member: Varies
    Employee & 2 Family Members: Varies

Medicare: Varies
Average Annual Deductible Per Subscriber:
  Employee Only (Self): Varies
  Employee & 1 Family Member: Varies
  Employee & 2 Family Members: Varies
  Medicare: Varies
Average Subscriber Co-Payment:
  Primary Care Physician: Varies
  Non-Network Physician: Varies
  Prescription Drugs: Varies
  Hospital ER: Varies
  Home Health Care: Varies
  Home Health Care Max. Days/Visits Covered: Varies
  Nursing Home: Varies
  Nursing Home Max. Days/Visits Covered: Varies

Network Qualifications
Pre-Admission Certification: Yes

Publishes and Distributes Report Card: No

Key Personnel
Chief Financial Officer. . . . . .David Haynes
SVP, COO . . . . .Pamela Martin
VP, Act & Underwriting . . . . .Rob Goren
VP, Board Relations . . . . .Janice M Lees
VP, Dental Affairs . . . . .Alcides O Martinez
Chief Marketing/Sales .Richard W Klassen
Chief Information Officer. .Karl A Mudra
Dir/Media & Public Affair . . . . .Elizabeth Risberg
  415-972-8423

Specialty Managed Care Partners
Enters into Contracts with Regional Business Coalitions: No

644 Dental Health Alliance

2323 Grand Boulevard
Kansas City, MO 64108
Toll-Free: 800-522-1313
Fax: 816-474-2638
www.dha.com
Subsidiary of: Union Security Insurance Company, Assurant Employee
  Benefits
Year Founded: 1994
Number of Primary Care Physicians: 74,000
Total Enrollment: 1,700,000

Healthplan and Services Defined
  PLAN TYPE: Dental
  Other Type: Dental PPO Network
  Model Type: Network, Dental PPO Network
  Plan Specialty: Dental
  Benefits Offered: Dental

Type of Coverage
  Commercial

Type of Payment Plans Offered
  POS, FFS, Combination FFS & DFFS

Geographic Areas Served
  Nationwide

Network Qualifications
  Pre-Admission Certification: No

Peer Review Type
  Utilization Review: Yes

Key Personnel
  President . . . . .Stacia Alnequist

645 eHealthInsurance Services Inc.

11919 Foundation Place
Gold River, CA 95670
Toll-Free: 800-977-8860
info@ehealthinsurance.com

www.e.healthinsurance.com
Year Founded: 1997

Healthplan and Services Defined
  PLAN TYPE: HMO/PPO
  Benefits Offered: Dental, Life, STD

Type of Coverage
  Commercial, Individual, Medicare

Geographic Areas Served
  All 50 states in the USA and District of Columbia

Key Personnel
  Chairman & CEO. . . . . .Gary L. Lauer
  EVP/Business & Corp. Dev. . . . . .Bruce Telkamp
  EVP/Chief Technology . . . . .Dr. Sheldon X. Wang
  SVP & CFO . . . . .Stuart M. Huizinga
  Pres. of eHealth Gov. Sys . . . . .Samuel C. Gibbs
  SVP of Sales & Operations . . . . .Robert S. Hurley
  Director Public Relations. .Nate Purpura
    650-210-3115

646 Essence Healthcare

13900 Riverport Drive
Maryland Heights, MO 63043
Phone: 314-209-2700
Fax: 314-209-2801
customerservice@essencehealthcare.com
www.essencehealthcare.com
Mailing Address: PO Box 12488, St. Louis, MO 63132
Subsidiary of: EGHC

Healthplan and Services Defined
  PLAN TYPE: Medicare
  Benefits Offered: Chiropractic, Dental, Disease Management, Home
    Care, Inpatient SNF, Physical Therapy, Podiatry, Prescription,
    Psychiatric, Vision, Wellness

Type of Coverage
  Individual, Medicare

Geographic Areas Served
  Available within select counties in Missouri and Illinois only

Subscriber Information
  Average Monthly Fee Per Subscriber
    (Employee + Employer Contribution):
      Employee Only (Self): Varies
      Medicare: Varies
  Average Annual Deductible Per Subscriber:
      Employee Only (Self): Varies
      Medicare: Varies
  Average Subscriber Co-Payment:
      Primary Care Physician: Varies
      Non-Network Physician: Varies
      Prescription Drugs: Varies
      Hospital ER: Varies
      Home Health Care: Varies
      Home Health Care Max. Days/Visits Covered: Varies
      Nursing Home: Varies
      Nursing Home Max. Days/Visits Covered: Varies

Key Personnel
  Chairmain & CEO. . . . . .Frank Ingari
  Executive Vice President . . . . .Debra Gribble, RN
  VP, Chief Operating Offc . . . . .Martha Butler, RN, MPH
  Chief Medical Officer . . . . .Deborah Zimmerman, MD
  VP, Human Resources. . . . . .Tom Murrill
  Chief Technology Officer . . . . .Tony Butler
  Media Contact . . . . .Andrew Shea
    314-209-2865
    ashea@essencecorp.com

647 GEHA-Government Employees Hospital Association

PO Box 4665
17306 E 24 Highway
Independence, MO 64051-4665
Toll-Free: 800-821-6136
Phone: 816-257-5500
Fax: 816-257-3333
cs.geha@geha.com
www.geha.com
Non-Profit Organization: Yes
Year Founded: 1939
Total Enrollment: 900,000

Healthplan and Services Defined
  PLAN TYPE: Multiple
  Benefits Offered: Dental, Disease Management, Prescription, Vision, Wellness
  Offers Demand Management Patient Information Service: Yes
  DMPI Services Offered: 24-Hour Health Advice Line

Type of Coverage
  Commercial, Medicare
  Catastrophic Illness Maximum Benefit: $5,000

Type of Payment Plans Offered
  FFS

Geographic Areas Served
  Nationwide

Subscriber Information
  Average Monthly Fee Per Subscriber
    (Employee + Employer Contribution):
      Employee Only (Self): $109.25
      Employee & 2 Family Members: $221.78
  Average Annual Deductible Per Subscriber:
      Employee Only (Self): $450.00
  Average Subscriber Co-Payment:
      Primary Care Physician: $10.00
      Non-Network Physician: $25.00
      Prescription Drugs: $5.00

Network Qualifications
  Pre-Admission Certification: Yes

Key Personnel
  President . . . . Richard Miles

Average Claim Compensation
  Hospital's Fees Charged: 85%

648 GHP Coventry Health Plan

550 Maryville Center Drive
Suite 300
St. Louis, MO 63141
Toll-Free: 800-755-3901
Phone: 314-506-1700
Fax: 866-465-9494
marketingghp@cvty.com
http://chcmissouri.coventryhealthcare.com
Non-Profit Organization: Yes
Year Founded: 1978
Number of Affiliated Hospitals: 100
Number of Primary Care Physicians: 4,000
Number of Referral/Specialty Physicians: 8,000
Total Enrollment: 330,000
State Enrollment: 330,000

Healthplan and Services Defined
  PLAN TYPE: HMO/PPO
  Other Type: POS
  Model Type: IPA

Benefits Offered: Behavioral Health, Chiropractic, Dental, Disease Management, Home Care, Inpatient SNF, Physical Therapy, Podiatry, Prescription, Psychiatric, Transplant, Vision, Wellness

Type of Coverage
  Commercial, Individual, Advantage

Geographic Areas Served
  St. Louis/Metro East Area, Mid-Missouri and Central and Southern Illinois

Accreditation Certification
  URAC

Key Personnel
  President & CEO . . . . Roman Kulich
  VP, Medical Affairs . . . . Scott Spradlin
  VP, Medicare. . . . . Thor Anderson

649 Great-West Healthcare Missouri

Acquired by CIGNA

650 Healthcare USA of Missouri

10 S Broadway
Suite 1200
Saint Louis, MO 63102
Toll-Free: 800-566-6444
Phone: 314-241-5300
Fax: 314-241-8010
smwijkowski@cvty.com
http://chcmedicaid-missouri.coventryhealthcare.com
Secondary Address: 2420 Hyde Park Road, Suite B, Provider Services Department, Jefferson City, MO 65109
Subsidiary of: Coventry Health Care
For Profit Organization: Yes
Year Founded: 1995
Total Enrollment: 185,375
State Enrollment: 185,375

Healthplan and Services Defined
  PLAN TYPE: HMO
  Model Type: Network
  Benefits Offered: Prescription
  Offers Demand Management Patient Information Service: Yes

Type of Coverage
  Medicaid

Type of Payment Plans Offered
  Combination FFS & DFFS

Geographic Areas Served
  Eastern, Central and Western Missouri

Network Qualifications
  Pre-Admission Certification: Yes

Peer Review Type
  Utilization Review: Yes
  Second Surgical Opinion: Yes
  Case Management: Yes

Publishes and Distributes Report Card: Yes

Accreditation Certification
  TJC Accreditation, Medicare Approved, Utilization Review, Pre-Admission Certification, State Licensure, Quality Assurance Program

Key Personnel
  President/CFO . . . . Claudia Bjerre
  Secretary . . . . Jennifer Handshy
  Executive Director. . . . . Ancelmo Lopes
  Director . . . . Becky Pierce
  Chief Medical Officer . . . . Mary Mason, MD

Specialty Managed Care Partners
  Enters into Contracts with Regional Business Coalitions: No

651 HealthLink HMO

12443 Olive Boulevard
St Louis, MO 63141
Toll-Free: 800-624-2356
Phone: 314-989-6000
www.healthlink.com
Subsidiary of: Wellpoint Health Networks
For Profit Organization: Yes
Year Founded: 1993
Number of Affiliated Hospitals: 129
Number of Primary Care Physicians: 2,705
Number of Referral/Specialty Physicians: 6,984
Total Enrollment: 1,000,000
State Enrollment: 395,996

Healthplan and Services Defined
  PLAN TYPE: HMO
  Model Type: IPA
  Plan Specialty: ASO, UR
  Benefits Offered: Behavioral Health, Chiropractic, Disease
    Management, Home Care, Physical Therapy, Podiatry,
    Prescription, Psychiatric, Transplant, Vision, Wellness
  Offers Demand Management Patient Information Service: Yes
  DMPI Services Offered: Heart Disease, Nurse Triage

Type of Coverage
  Commercial
  Catastrophic Illness Benefit: Varies per case

Type of Payment Plans Offered
  POS, DFFS, Combination FFS & DFFS

Geographic Areas Served
  Missouri, Illinois, Indiana, Arkansas, Kentucky, West Virginia

Subscriber Information
  Average Subscriber Co-Payment:
    Primary Care Physician: $10.00
    Prescription Drugs: $10/15/25
    Hospital ER: $50.00

Network Qualifications
  Pre-Admission Certification: Yes

Peer Review Type
  Utilization Review: Yes
  Second Surgical Opinion: No
  Case Management: Yes

Accreditation Certification
  URAC
  Utilization Review, Pre-Admission Certification, Quality Assurance
    Program

Key Personnel
  President/CEO.................................David Ott
    877-284-0101
    DOTT@healthlink.com
  General Manager.............................Bruce Gosser
    877-284-0101
    bgosser@healthlink.com
  VP Sales/Network Devel......................Donna Geringer
    877-284-0101
    dgeringer@healthlink.com
  Vice President/Marketing....................Courtney Walter
  Chief Medical Officer......................John Seidenfeld, MD
    877-284-0101
    seidenfj@healthlink.com
  Vice President/Planning ....Art Stengol
  Regional/VP Sales..........................Donna Geringer
    877-284-0101
    dgeringer@healthlink.com
  Media Contact ....Jon Mills
    jon.mills@wellpoint.com
  Media Contact ....Jill Becher
    jill.becher@wellpoint.com

Specialty Managed Care Partners
  WellPoint Pharmacy Management, Cigna Behavioral Health, Vision
    Service Plan
  Enters into Contracts with Regional Business Coalitions: Yes
  Gateway Purchases

Employer References
  Local fifty benefits service trust, Jefferson City Public Schools,
    ConAgra

652 Humana Health Insurance of Missouri

909 E Montclair
Suite 108
Springfield, MO 65807
Toll-Free: 800-951-0128
Phone: 417-882-3020
Fax: 417-882-2015
www.humana.com
For Profit Organization: Yes

Healthplan and Services Defined
  PLAN TYPE: HMO/PPO

Type of Coverage
  Commercial, Individual

Accreditation Certification
  URAC, NCQA, CORE

653 Med-Pay

1650 Battlefield
Suite 300
Springfield, MO 65804-3706
Toll-Free: 800-777-9087
Phone: 417-886-6886
Fax: 417-886-2276
sdemster@med-pay.com
www.med-pay.com
Year Founded: 1983
State Enrollment: 26,000

Healthplan and Services Defined
  PLAN TYPE: Other
  Other Type: TPA, HSA, HRA
  Model Type: Network
  Plan Specialty: ASO, Behavioral Health, Chiropractic, Dental,
    Disease Management, Lab, MSO, PBM, Vision, Radiology
  Benefits Offered: Behavioral Health, Chiropractic, Dental, Disease
    Management, Home Care, Inpatient SNF, Long-Term Care,
    Physical Therapy, Prescription, Transplant, Vision
  Offers Demand Management Patient Information Service: Yes

Type of Coverage
  Commercial, Individual

Accreditation Certification
  State of MO
  Utilization Review

Key Personnel
  President...................................Gordon Kinne
  Director Claims ....Pam Mathis
  Director Client Services...................Megan Broemmer

Specialty Managed Care Partners
  HCC, BCBS, Healthlink
  Enters into Contracts with Regional Business Coalitions: Yes

654 Mercy Health Medicare Plan

14528 South Outer 40
Suite 300
Chesterfield, MO 63017-5743
Toll-Free: 800-830-1918

Phone: 314-214-8100
Fax: 314-214-8101
www.mercyhealthplans.com
Non-Profit Organization: Yes

Healthplan and Services Defined
PLAN TYPE: Medicare
Benefits Offered: Chiropractic, Dental, Disease Management, Home Care, Inpatient SNF, Physical Therapy, Podiatry, Prescription, Psychiatric, Vision, Wellness

Type of Coverage
Individual, Medicare

Geographic Areas Served
Available within multiple states

Subscriber Information
Average Monthly Fee Per Subscriber
(Employee + Employer Contribution):
Employee Only (Self): Varies
Medicare: Varies
Average Annual Deductible Per Subscriber:
Employee Only (Self): Varies
Medicare: Varies
Average Subscriber Co-Payment:
Primary Care Physician: Varies
Non-Network Physician: Varies
Prescription Drugs: Varies
Hospital ER: Varies
Home Health Care: Varies
Home Health Care Max. Days/Visits Covered: Varies
Nursing Home: Varies
Nursing Home Max. Days/Visits Covered: Varies

Key Personnel
Interim CEO . . . . .Chris Knackstedt
EVP, COO. . . . . .Mike Treash
Executive Vice President . . . . .Janet Pursley
CFO, Treasurer. . . . . .George Schneider
VP, General Counsel . . . . .Charles Gilham
Chief Medical Officer . . . . Stephen Spurgeon, MD
VP, Human Resources. . . . . .Donna McDaniel
VP, Mission & Ethics . . . . .Michael Doyle
VP, Sales & Service. . . . . .Carl Schultz

655 Mercy Health Plans: Corporate Office
14528 South Outer 40
Suite 300
Chesterfield, MO 63017-5705
Toll-Free: 800-830-1918
Phone: 314-214-8100
Fax: 314-214-8101
www.mercyhealthplans.com
Secondary Address: 4520 South National, Springfield, MO 65810, 417-836-0450
Non-Profit Organization: Yes
Year Founded: 1994
Number of Primary Care Physicians: 8,500
Total Enrollment: 73,000

Healthplan and Services Defined
PLAN TYPE: HMO
Model Type: IPA
Benefits Offered: Behavioral Health, Chiropractic, Physical Therapy, Prescription, Vision

Type of Coverage
Commercial, Individual, Medicare, Supplemental Medicare, Medicaid

Geographic Areas Served
Eastern Central Missouri, Southwest Missouri, South Texas

Subscriber Information
Average Monthly Fee Per Subscriber
(Employee + Employer Contribution):
Employee Only (Self): Varies by plan
Average Annual Deductible Per Subscriber:
Employee Only (Self): $1000.00
Average Subscriber Co-Payment:
Primary Care Physician: $10.00
Non-Network Physician: $30.00
Prescription Drugs: $7-$12

Key Personnel
Interim CEO . . . . .Chris Knackstedt
EVP, COO. . . . . .Mike Treash
Executive Vice President . . . . .Janet Pursley
CFO, Treasurer. . . . . .George Schneider
VP, General Counsel . . . . .Charles Gilham
Chief Medical Officer . . . . Stephen Spurgeon, MD
VP, Human Resources. . . . . .Donna McDaniel
VP, Mission & Ethics . . . . .Michael Doyle
VP, Sales & Service. . . . . .Carl Schultz

656 Meritain Health: Missouri
9201 Watson Road
St. Louis, MO 63126
Toll-Free: 800-776-2452
Fax: 314-918-3535
sales@meritain.com
www.meritain.com
For Profit Organization: Yes
Year Founded: 1983
Number of Affiliated Hospitals: 110
Number of Primary Care Physicians: 3,467
Number of Referral/Specialty Physicians: 5,720
Total Enrollment: 500,000
State Enrollment: 450,000

Healthplan and Services Defined
PLAN TYPE: PPO
Model Type: Network
Plan Specialty: Dental, Disease Management, Vision, Radiology, UR
Benefits Offered: Prescription
Offers Demand Management Patient Information Service: Yes

Type of Coverage
Commercial

Geographic Areas Served
Nationwide

Subscriber Information
Average Monthly Fee Per Subscriber
(Employee + Employer Contribution):
Employee Only (Self): Varies by plan

Accreditation Certification
URAC
TJC Accreditation, Medicare Approved, Utilization Review, Pre-Admission Certification, State Licensure, Quality Assurance Program

Average Claim Compensation
Physician's Fees Charged: 78%
Hospital's Fees Charged: 90%

Specialty Managed Care Partners
Express Scripts, LabOne, Interactive Health Solutions

657 Mid America Health
Acquired by Coventry Health Care of Kansas

658 Molina Healthcare: Missouri
12400 Olive Blvd
Suite 100

St. Louis, MO 63141
Toll-Free: 800-875-0679
www.molinahealthcare.com
For Profit Organization: Yes
Year Founded: 1980
Physician Owned Organization: Yes
Number of Affiliated Hospitals: 84
Number of Primary Care Physicians: 2,167
Number of Referral/Specialty Physicians: 6,184
Total Enrollment: 1,400,000

Healthplan and Services Defined
  PLAN TYPE: HMO
  Model Type: Network
  Benefits Offered: Chiropractic, Dental, Home Care, Inpatient SNF,
    Long-Term Care, Podiatry, Vision

Type of Coverage
  Commercial, Medicare, Supplemental Medicare, Medicaid

Accreditation Certification
  URAC, NCQA

659 Ozark Health Plan

3335 E Ridgeview Street
Springfield, MO 65804
Toll-Free: 800-658-3518
Phone: 417-823-3910
Fax: 417-823-3706
www.ozarkhealthplan.com
Subsidiary of: Arcadian Health Plans

Healthplan and Services Defined
  PLAN TYPE: Medicare

Type of Coverage
  Medicare

660 Preferred Care Blue

Acquired by BlueCross BlueShield of Kansas City

661 UnitedHealthCare of Missouri

13655 Riverport Drive
Maryland Heights, MO 63043
Toll-Free: 800-627-0687
Phone: 314-592-7000
www.uhc.com
Subsidiary of: UnitedHealth Group
For Profit Organization: Yes
Total Enrollment: 75,000,000
State Enrollment: 60,000

Healthplan and Services Defined
  PLAN TYPE: HMO/PPO

Geographic Areas Served
  Statewide

Key Personnel
  Media Contact . . . . Greg Thompson
    312-424-6913
    gregory_a_thompson@uhc.com

Health Insurance Coverage Status and Type of Coverage by Age

Category	All Persons		Under 18 years		Under 65 years		65 years and over	
	Number	%	Number	%	Number	%	Number	%
Total population	971	-	215	-	814	-	157	-
Covered by some type of health insurance	795 *(16)*	81.9 *(1.2)*	196 *(4)*	91.2 *(1.5)*	640 *(21)*	78.7 *(1.5)*	155 *(10)*	98.4 *(0.8)*
Covered by private health insurance	606 *(27)*	62.4 *(2.4)*	131 *(10)*	60.7 *(4.8)*	513 *(28)*	63.0 *(2.6)*	93 *(10)*	59.0 *(5.5)*
Employment based	467 *(27)*	48.1 *(2.5)*	115 *(9)*	53.6 *(4.0)*	430 *(25)*	52.8 *(2.5)*	37 *(6)*	23.5 *(3.7)*
Own employment based	239 *(15)*	24.6 *(1.4)*	0 *(0)*	0.0 *(0.0)*	214 *(13)*	26.3 *(1.3)*	25 *(4)*	16.0 *(2.7)*
Direct purchase	146 *(14)*	15.1 *(1.4)*	14 *(4)*	6.7 *(1.9)*	87 *(15)*	10.7 *(1.7)*	59 *(8)*	37.6 *(4.3)*
Covered by government health insurance	327 *(19)*	33.7 *(2.1)*	86 *(10)*	39.9 *(4.4)*	175 *(14)*	21.6 *(1.9)*	151 *(10)*	96.1 *(1.0)*
Covered by Medicaid	135 *(13)*	13.9 *(1.4)*	76 *(8)*	35.1 *(3.9)*	123 *(12)*	15.1 *(1.6)*	12 *(3)*	7.5 *(2.0)*
Also by private insurance	24 *(4)*	2.4 *(0.5)*	14 *(3)*	6.3 *(1.5)*	22 *(4)*	2.7 *(0.5)*	2 *(1)*	1.2 *(0.7)*
Covered by Medicare	169 *(10)*	17.4 *(1.1)*	0 *(0)*	0.2 *(0.2)*	19 *(3)*	2.4 *(0.4)*	149 *(10)*	94.8 *(1.2)*
Also by private insurance	92 *(10)*	9.4 *(1.0)*	0 *(0)*	0.0 *(0.0)*	4 *(2)*	0.5 *(0.3)*	88 *(10)*	55.9 *(5.5)*
Also by Medicaid	18 *(4)*	1.9 *(0.4)*	0 *(0)*	0.2 *(0.2)*	7 *(2)*	0.8 *(0.2)*	11 *(3)*	7.1 *(2.0)*
Covered by military health care	69 *(11)*	7.1 *(1.1)*	11 *(4)*	5.2 *(1.6)*	45 *(7)*	5.5 *(0.9)*	24 *(7)*	15.1 *(4.0)*
Not covered at any time during the year	176 *(12)*	18.1 *(1.2)*	19 *(3)*	8.8 *(1.5)*	174 *(12)*	21.3 *(1.5)*	2 *(1)*	1.6 *(0.8)*

Note: Numbers in thousands; figures cover 2010; standard error appears in parenthesis; (b) base less than 75,000; (x) not applicable
Source: U.S. Census Bureau, Current Population Survey, 2011 Annual Social and Economic Supplement. Table HI05. Health Insurance Coverage Status and Type of Coverage by State and Age for All People: 2010

Montana

662 Aetna Health of Montana
Partnered with eHealthInsurance Services Inc.

663 Allegiance Life & Health Insurance Company
2806 South Garfield Street
PO Box 3507
Missoula, MT 59806-3507
Toll-Free: 800-737-3137
Phone: 406-523-3122
inquire@askallegiance.com
www.allegiancelifeandhealth.com
For Profit Organization: Yes
Year Founded: 2006

Healthplan and Services Defined
PLAN TYPE: HMO
Benefits Offered: Dental, Vision, Wellness, Pharmacy

Type of Coverage
Commercial, Individual

Geographic Areas Served
Montana

Key Personnel
Chairman...Dirk Visser

664 Blue Cross & Blue Shield of Montana
560 N Park Avenue
PO Box 4309
Helena, MT 59604-4309
Toll-Free: 800-447-7828
Phone: 406-437-5000
Fax: 406-444-8440
webdesk@bcbsmt.com
www.bcbsmt.com
Subsidiary of: Blue Cross Blue Shield Association
Non-Profit Organization: Yes
Year Founded: 1986
Owned by an Integrated Delivery Network (IDN): Yes
Federally Qualified: Yes
Number of Affiliated Hospitals: 58
Number of Primary Care Physicians: 1,900
Number of Referral/Specialty Physicians: 2,800
Total Enrollment: 236,000
State Enrollment: 236,000

Healthplan and Services Defined
PLAN TYPE: HMO
Model Type: Network
Plan Specialty: ASO, Behavioral Health, Chiropractic, Dental, Disease Management, EPO, Lab, MSO, PBM, Vision, Radiology, Worker's Compensation, UR
Benefits Offered: Behavioral Health, Chiropractic, Complementary Medicine, Dental, Disease Management, Home Care, Inpatient SNF, Long-Term Care, Physical Therapy, Podiatry, Prescription, Psychiatric, Transplant, Vision, Wellness, Worker's Compensation, AD&D, Life, LTD, ST
Offers Demand Management Patient Information Service: Yes

Type of Coverage
Commercial, Individual, Indemnity, Medicare, Supplemental Medicare, Catastrophic
Catastrophic Illness Benefit: Varies per case

Type of Payment Plans Offered
POS, DFFS, Capitated

Geographic Areas Served
Beaverhead, Big Horn, Blaine, Broadwater, Carbon, Carter, Cascade, Choteau, Custer, Deer Lodge, Flathead, Glacier, Hill, Jefferson, Lake, Lewis and Clark, Liberty, Lincoln, Madison, McCone, Meagher, Mineral, Missoula, Musselshell, Pondera, Ravalli, Sanders, Silver Bow, Stillwater, Sweet Grass, Teton, Wheatland, Yellowstone

Subscriber Information
Average Subscriber Co-Payment:
Primary Care Physician: $15
Non-Network Physician: Deductible
Hospital ER: $75.00
Home Health Care: No deductible
Home Health Care Max. Days/Visits Covered: 180 days
Nursing Home: $300 per admit co-pay
Nursing Home Max. Days/Visits Covered: 60 days

Network Qualifications
Pre-Admission Certification: Yes

Peer Review Type
Utilization Review: Yes
Second Surgical Opinion: Yes
Case Management: Yes

Publishes and Distributes Report Card: Yes

Key Personnel
President & CEO.............................Michael Frank
Chief Financial Officer.......................Mark Burzynski
Chief Information Officer.......................Patrick Law
Chief Marketing Officer....................Shannon Marsden
EVP Internal Operations.....................Fred Olson, MD
Corp Communications..........................Tim Warner
406-431-4366
tim_warner@bcbsmt.com

Specialty Managed Care Partners
Behavioral Health, Chiropractic, Dental, Disease Management, Home Care, Inpatient SNF, and more
Enters into Contracts with Regional Business Coalitions: Yes

Employer References
Montana University System, Evening Post Publishing Company, Costco Wholesale, State of Montana, Huntley Project Schools

665 CIGNA HealthCare of Montana
3900 East Mexico Avenue
Suite 1100
Denver, CO 80210
Toll-Free: 800-832-3211
Phone: 303-782-1500
Fax: 303-691-3197
www.cigna.com
For Profit Organization: Yes
Total Enrollment: 7,642
State Enrollment: 5,008

Healthplan and Services Defined
PLAN TYPE: HMO
Plan Specialty: Behavioral Health, Dental, Vision
Benefits Offered: Behavioral Health, Dental, Disease Management, Prescription, Transplant, Vision, Wellness, Life

Type of Coverage
Commercial

Type of Payment Plans Offered
POS, FFS

Geographic Areas Served
Montana

Key Personnel
Director At Cigna...........................Sallie Vanasdale
VP Provider Relations..........................William Cetti
VP Client Relations ....Gregg Prussing

666 **Delta Dental of Montana**
55 West 14th Street
Suite 101
Helena, MT 59601
Toll-Free: 800-547-1986
Phone: 406-449-0255
Fax: 406-495-0322
mtsales@delta.org
www.deltadentalins.com
Non-Profit Organization: Yes
Total Enrollment: 54,000,000

Healthplan and Services Defined
    PLAN TYPE: Dental
    Other Type: Dental PPO

Type of Coverage
    Commercial

Geographic Areas Served
    Statewide

Key Personnel
    VP, Public & Govt Affairs . . . . .Jeff Album
        415-972-8418
    Dir/Media & Public Affair . . . . .Elizabeth Risberg
        415-972-8423

667 **eHealthInsurance Services Inc.**
11919 Foundation Place
Gold River, CA 95670
Toll-Free: 800-977-8860
info@ehealthinsurance.com
www.e.healthinsurance.com
Year Founded: 1997

Healthplan and Services Defined
    PLAN TYPE: HMO/PPO
    Benefits Offered: Dental, Life, STD

Type of Coverage
    Commercial, Individual, Medicare

Geographic Areas Served
    All 50 states in the USA and District of Columbia

Key Personnel
    Chairman & CEO . . . . .Gary L. Lauer
    EVP/Business & Corp. Dev.. . . . . .Bruce Telkamp
    EVP/Chief Technology. . . . . .Dr. Sheldon X. Wang
    SVP & CFO . . . . .Stuart M. Huizinga
    Pres. of eHealth Gov. Sys . . . . .Samuel C. Gibbs
    SVP of Sales & Operations . . . . .Robert S. Hurley
    Director Public Relations. .Nate Purpura
        650-210-3115

668 **Great-West Healthcare Montana**
Acquired by CIGNA

669 **Health InfoNet**
1156 16th Street West
Suite 18
Billings, MT 59102
Toll-Free: 888-256-6556
Phone: 406-256-6556
Fax: 406-256-9466
info@healthinfonetmt.com
www.healthinfonetmt.com
Mailing Address: PO Box 20559, Billings, MT 59104-0559
Subsidiary of: Paradigm Group
For Profit Organization: Yes
Number of Affiliated Hospitals: 94
Number of Primary Care Physicians: 980

Number of Referral/Specialty Physicians: 1,793
Total Enrollment: 80,000
State Enrollment: 56,000

Healthplan and Services Defined
    PLAN TYPE: PPO
    Model Type: Open Panel & GeoExclusive
    Benefits Offered: Wellness, Provider Network Access

Type of Coverage
    Commercial, Individual, Private & Public Plans, Geo-specifi

Geographic Areas Served
    Montana, Wyoming, Colorado, North Dakota, South Dakota

Key Personnel
    CEO. . . . . .Robert L Hunter
    Principal, CIO . . . . .Jim McInerney
    CFO . . . . .Michael W Young
    CMO . . . . .Lionel Tapia, MD
    Provider Relations . . . . .John Larson
    Credentialing Specialist . . . . .Jen McGone
    PPO Services Director . . . . .Melody Heide
    Wellness & Disease Mgmt. . . . . .Tabatha Elsberry

Specialty Managed Care Partners
    Enters into Contracts with Regional Business Coalitions: Yes
    First Choice Health Network (Pacific NW)

670 **Humana Health Insurance of Montana**
1611 Alderson Avenue
Billings, MT 59102
Toll-Free: 800-967-2308
Phone: 406-238-7130
Fax: 406-238-0131
www.humana.com
For Profit Organization: Yes

Healthplan and Services Defined
    PLAN TYPE: HMO/PPO

Type of Coverage
    Commercial, Individual

Accreditation Certification
    URAC, NCQA, CORE

671 **Liberty Health Plan: Montana**
1001 S 24th Street West
Suite 312, Creekside III
Billings, MT 59102-6467
Toll-Free: 800-929-0996
Phone: 406-652-5345
Fax: 406-652-5345
customerservice.center@libertynorthwest.com
www.libertynorthwest.com
Secondary Address: 614 Ferguson Avenue, Suite 5, Bozeman, MT
    59718-6415
For Profit Organization: Yes
Year Founded: 1983

Healthplan and Services Defined
    PLAN TYPE: PPO
    Model Type: Group
    Plan Specialty: Worker's Compensation
    Benefits Offered: Prescription

Type of Payment Plans Offered
    POS, DFFS, FFS, Combination FFS & DFFS

Geographic Areas Served
    Statewide

Network Qualifications
    Pre-Admission Certification: Yes

Peer Review Type
    Case Management: Yes

Publishes and Distributes Report Card: No

Specialty Managed Care Partners
Enters into Contracts with Regional Business Coalitions: No

---

672 New West Health Services

2132 Broadwate Avenue
Unit A-1
Billings, MT 59102
Toll-Free: 800-500-3355
Phone: 406-255-0180
Fax: 406-457-2299
customerservice@nwhp.com
www.newwesthealth.com
Secondary Address: 1203 Highway 2 West, Suite 45, Kalispell, MT
59901-6071
Non-Profit Organization: Yes
Year Founded: 1998
Number of Affiliated Hospitals: 6
Number of Primary Care Physicians: 3,300
Total Enrollment: 43,000
State Enrollment: 43,000

Healthplan and Services Defined
PLAN TYPE: HMO/PPO
Plan Specialty: ASO
Benefits Offered: Prescription, Wellness

Type of Coverage
Commercial, Individual, Indemnity, Medicare, Supplemental
Medicare

Type of Payment Plans Offered
FFS

Geographic Areas Served
Montana

Key Personnel
CEO . . . . .David Kibbe
COO. . . . . .Ernie Humbert
CFO . . . . .Rick Gorenflo
Regional Team Sales Mgr . . . . .Mel Reinhardt
406-255-0186
Provider Services. . . . . .Suzann Jones
406-255-0184
VP, Strategic Growth. . . . . .Greg Loughlin
Medical Director . . . . .Robert Shepard
VP, Operations & CIO . . . . .Dory Hicks
VP, Provider Relations. . . . . .Tanya Ask
Sales & Marketing Dir . . . . .Lauretta Drean

Specialty Managed Care Partners
Caremark Rx

---

673 New West Medicare Plan

130 Neill Avenue
Helena, MT 59601
Toll-Free: 888-500-3355
Phone: 406-457-2200
Fax: 406-257-2600
www.newwesthealth.com
Secondary Address: 1203 Highway 2, Suite 45, Kalispell, MT
59901-6071
Total Enrollment: 43,000
State Enrollment: 43,000

Healthplan and Services Defined
PLAN TYPE: Medicare
Other Type: PPO
Benefits Offered: Chiropractic, Dental, Disease Management, Home
Care, Inpatient SNF, Physical Therapy, Podiatry, Prescription,
Psychiatric, Vision, Wellness

Type of Coverage
Individual, Medicare

Geographic Areas Served
Available within Montana only

Subscriber Information
Average Monthly Fee Per Subscriber
(Employee + Employer Contribution):
Employee Only (Self): Varies
Medicare: Varies
Average Annual Deductible Per Subscriber:
Employee Only (Self): Varies
Medicare: Varies
Average Subscriber Co-Payment:
Primary Care Physician: Varies
Non-Network Physician: Varies
Prescription Drugs: Varies
Hospital ER: Varies
Home Health Care: Varies
Home Health Care Max. Days/Visits Covered: Varies
Nursing Home: Varies
Nursing Home Max. Days/Visits Covered: Varies

Key Personnel
CEO . . . . .David Kibbe
COO. . . . . .Ernie Humbert
CFO . . . . .Rick Gorenflo
VP, Strategic Growth. . . . . .Greg Loughlin
Medical Director . . . . .Robert Shepard
VP, Operations & CIO . . . . .Dory Hicks
VP, Provider Relations. . . . . .Tanya Ask
Sales & Marketing Dir . . . . .Lauretta Drean

---

674 UnitedHealthCare of Montana

6465 S Greenwood Plaza Boulevard
Suite 300
Centennial, CO 80111
Toll-Free: 800-516-3344
Phone: 303-267-3300
Fax: 303-267-3597
www.uhc.com
Subsidiary of: UnitedHealth Group
For Profit Organization: Yes
Year Founded: 1986
Number of Affiliated Hospitals: 47
Number of Primary Care Physicians: 1,600
Number of Referral/Specialty Physicians: 3,500
Total Enrollment: 75,000,000
State Enrollment: 17,853

Healthplan and Services Defined
PLAN TYPE: HMO/PPO
Model Type: Mixed Model
Plan Specialty: MSO
Benefits Offered: Behavioral Health, Chiropractic, Complementary
Medicine, Dental, Disease Management, Home Care, Inpatient
SNF, Long-Term Care, Physical Therapy, Podiatry, Prescription,
Psychiatric, Transplant, Vision, Wellness, AD&D, Life

Type of Coverage
Commercial, Individual, Medicaid, Commercial Group

Type of Payment Plans Offered
DFFS, FFS, Combination FFS & DFFS

Geographic Areas Served
Statewide

Subscriber Information
Average Monthly Fee Per Subscriber
(Employee + Employer Contribution):
Employee Only (Self): Varies
Average Subscriber Co-Payment:
Primary Care Physician: $10
Prescription Drugs: $10/15/30

Hospital ER: $50

Network Qualifications
Pre-Admission Certification: Yes

Peer Review Type
Case Management: Yes

Publishes and Distributes Report Card: Yes

Accreditation Certification
URAC, NCQA
State Licensure, Quality Assurance Program

Average Claim Compensation
Physician's Fees Charged: 70%
Hospital's Fees Charged: 55%

Specialty Managed Care Partners
United Behavioral Health
Enters into Contracts with Regional Business Coalitions: No

Health Insurance Coverage Status and Type of Coverage by Age

Category	All Persons		Under 18 years		Under 65 years		65 years and over	
	Number	%	Number	%	Number	%	Number	%
Total population	1,788	-	458	-	1,569	-	219	-
Covered by some type of health insurance	1,551 *(21)*	86.7 *(0.8)*	411 *(8)*	89.7 *(1.5)*	1,335 *(21)*	85.1 *(0.9)*	216 *(13)*	98.6 *(0.9)*
Covered by private health insurance	1,300 *(30)*	72.7 *(1.4)*	305 *(11)*	66.5 *(2.6)*	1,150 *(27)*	73.3 *(1.4)*	150 *(13)*	68.7 *(3.7)*
Employment based	1,048 *(37)*	58.6 *(1.8)*	277 *(13)*	60.4 *(2.7)*	995 *(35)*	63.4 *(1.9)*	53 *(7)*	24.3 *(3.2)*
Own employment based	525 *(23)*	29.4 *(1.2)*	2 *(1)*	0.4 *(0.3)*	491 *(22)*	31.3 *(1.2)*	34 *(4)*	15.6 *(1.9)*
Direct purchase	286 *(16)*	16.0 *(0.9)*	41 *(6)*	9.1 *(1.3)*	182 *(16)*	11.6 *(1.0)*	105 *(9)*	47.9 *(2.7)*
Covered by government health insurance	492 *(19)*	27.5 *(1.1)*	139 *(10)*	30.4 *(2.1)*	283 *(17)*	18.0 *(1.1)*	209 *(13)*	95.7 *(1.2)*
Covered by Medicaid	202 *(13)*	11.3 *(0.8)*	121 *(9)*	26.4 *(2.0)*	183 *(13)*	11.7 *(0.8)*	19 *(3)*	8.8 *(1.3)*
Also by private insurance	48 *(7)*	2.7 *(0.4)*	21 *(4)*	4.7 *(0.8)*	40 *(5)*	2.6 *(0.3)*	8 *(3)*	3.5 *(1.4)*
Covered by Medicare	250 *(13)*	14.0 *(0.7)*	4 *(2)*	1.0 *(0.5)*	41 *(8)*	2.6 *(0.5)*	209 *(13)*	95.7 *(1.2)*
Also by private insurance	159 *(10)*	8.9 *(0.6)*	0 *(0)*	0.0 *(0.0)*	15 *(4)*	1.0 *(0.3)*	144 *(12)*	65.8 *(3.7)*
Also by Medicaid	36 *(5)*	2.0 *(0.3)*	4 *(2)*	1.0 *(0.5)*	17 *(4)*	1.1 *(0.2)*	19 *(3)*	8.8 *(1.3)*
Covered by military health care	105 *(12)*	5.9 *(0.7)*	24 *(5)*	5.2 *(1.0)*	88 *(11)*	5.6 *(0.7)*	17 *(4)*	7.9 *(1.8)*
Not covered at any time during the year	237 *(15)*	13.3 *(0.8)*	47 *(7)*	10.3 *(1.5)*	234 *(15)*	14.9 *(0.9)*	3 *(2)*	1.4 *(0.9)*

Note: Numbers in thousands; figures cover 2010; standard error appears in parenthesis; (b) base less than 75,000; (x) not applicable
Source: U.S. Census Bureau, Current Population Survey, 2011 Annual Social and Economic Supplement. Table HI05. Health Insurance Coverage Status and Type of Coverage by State and Age for All People: 2010

Nebraska

675 Aetna Health of Nebraska

151 Farmington Avenue
Hartford, CT 06156
Toll-Free: 866-582-9629
www.aetna.com
For Profit Organization: Yes
Total Enrollment: 11,596,230

Healthplan and Services Defined
  PLAN TYPE: PPO
  Other Type: POS
  Plan Specialty: EPO
  Benefits Offered: Dental, Disease Management, Long-Term Care, Prescription, Wellness, Life, LTD, STD

Type of Coverage
  Commercial, Individual

Type of Payment Plans Offered
  POS, FFS

Geographic Areas Served
  Statewide

Key Personnel
  CEO . . . . .Ronald A Williams
  President. . . . . .Mark T Bertolini
  SVP, General Counsel . . . . .William J Casazza
  EVP, CFO . . . . .Joseph M Zubretsky
  Head, M&A Integration . . . . Kay Mooney
  SVP, Marketing. . . . . .Robert E Mead
  Chief Medical Officer . . . . .Lonny Reisman, MD
  SVP, Human Resources. .Elease E Wright
  SVP, CIO. . . . . .Meg McCarthy

676 Ameritas Group

175 Fallbrook
Lincoln, NE 68521
Toll-Free: 800-776-9446
Phone: 402-309-2160
Fax: 402-309-2333
group@ameritas.com
www.ameritasgroup.com
Mailing Address: PO Box 81889, Lincoln, NE 68501
For Profit Organization: Yes
Year Founded: 1990
Number of Primary Care Physicians: 49,256
Number of Referral/Specialty Physicians: 16,508
Total Enrollment: 2,543,705
State Enrollment: 818,531

Healthplan and Services Defined
  PLAN TYPE: Dental
  Model Type: Staff
  Plan Specialty: ASO, Dental, Vision
  Benefits Offered: Dental, Vision

Type of Coverage
  Commercial, Individual

Type of Payment Plans Offered
  POS, DFFS, Capitated, Combination FFS & DFFS

Geographic Areas Served
  Nationwide

Peer Review Type
  Utilization Review: Yes
  Second Surgical Opinion: Yes
  Case Management: Yes

Publishes and Distributes Report Card: Yes

Accreditation Certification
  Medicare Approved

Key Personnel
  Chairman. . . . . .Lawrence J Arth
  President & CEO . . . . .JoAnn M Martin
  SVP, Group Marketing. . . . . .Karen Gustin

677 Blue Cross & Blue Shield of Nebraska

1919 Aksarben Drive
Omaha, NE 68180-0001
Toll-Free: 800-642-8980
Phone: 402-390-1820
Fax: 402-548-4355
www.nebraskablue.com
Secondary Address: 3707 N 118th Street, Member Services
  Headquarters, Omaha, NE 68164
Non-Profit Organization: Yes
Year Founded: 1974
Total Enrollment: 717,000
State Enrollment: 717,000

Healthplan and Services Defined
  PLAN TYPE: PPO
  Model Type: Network
  Benefits Offered: Behavioral Health, Chiropractic, Dental, Disease Management, Home Care, Inpatient SNF, Long-Term Care, Physical Therapy, Podiatry, Prescription, Psychiatric, Vision

Type of Coverage
  Commercial, Individual, Medicare, Supplemental Medicare

Publishes and Distributes Report Card: No

Key Personnel
  President . . . . .Steve S Martin
    402-982-7000
  EVP, CFO. . . . . .Lewis E Trowbridge
  EVP, COO . . . . .Steven H Grandfield
  VP, Ethical Practices . . . . .Sarah Waldman
  EVP, Chief Marketing Offc . . . . .Keith G Bushardt
  Dir, Corp Communications. . . . . .Andy Williams
    402-982-7779
    andy.williams@bcbsne.com
  Public Relations Spec . . . . .Nate Odgaard
    402-982-6528
    nathan.odgaard@bcbsne.com

678 CIGNA HealthCare of Nebraska

7400 West 110th Street
Suite 400
Overland Park, KS 66210
Toll-Free: 866-438-2446
Phone: 913-339-4700
www.cigna.com
For Profit Organization: Yes
Total Enrollment: 18,322
State Enrollment: 15,405

Healthplan and Services Defined
  PLAN TYPE: PPO
  Benefits Offered: Disease Management, Prescription, Transplant, Wellness

Type of Coverage
  Commercial

Type of Payment Plans Offered
  POS, FFS

Geographic Areas Served
  Nebraska

679 Coventry Health Care of Nebraska

15950 West Dodge Road
Omaha, NE 68118-4030

Toll-Free: 800-471-0240
Phone: 402-498-9030
http://chcnebraska.coventryhealthcare.com
For Profit Organization: Yes
Year Founded: 1985
Number of Affiliated Hospitals: 120
Number of Primary Care Physicians: 1,500
Number of Referral/Specialty Physicians: 3,500
Total Enrollment: 54,000
State Enrollment: 63,000

Healthplan and Services Defined
  PLAN TYPE: HMO/PPO
  Other Type: POS
  Model Type: IPA
  Benefits Offered: Behavioral Health, Chiropractic, Complementary
    Medicine, Dental, Disease Management, Home Care, Inpatient
    SNF, Long-Term Care, Physical Therapy, Podiatry, Prescription,
    Psychiatric, Transplant, Vision, Wellness

Type of Coverage
  Commercial

Type of Payment Plans Offered
  POS

Accreditation Certification
  URAC

Key Personnel
  Chief Executive Officer . . . . Kathy A Mallatt
  Executive Director . . . . Richard Cochran
  Director of Sales . . . . Mike Nelson
  Medical Director . . . . Joseph Blount

680 Delta Dental of Nebraska

11235 Davenport Street
Suite 105
Omaha, NE 68154
Toll-Free: 800-736-0710
Phone: 402-397-4878
Fax: 402-397-6401
www.deltadentalne.org
Non-Profit Organization: Yes
Year Founded: 1969
Total Enrollment: 54,000,000

Healthplan and Services Defined
  PLAN TYPE: Dental
  Other Type: Dental PPO
  Model Type: Network
  Plan Specialty: ASO, Dental
  Benefits Offered: Dental

Type of Coverage
  Commercial, Individual, Group
  Catastrophic Illness Benefit: None

Geographic Areas Served
  Statewide

Subscriber Information
  Average Monthly Fee Per Subscriber
    (Employee + Employer Contribution):
      Employee Only (Self): Varies
      Employee & 1 Family Member: Varies
      Employee & 2 Family Members: Varies
  Average Annual Deductible Per Subscriber:
      Employee Only (Self): Varies
      Employee & 1 Family Member: Varies
      Employee & 2 Family Members: Varies
  Average Subscriber Co-Payment:
      Prescription Drugs: $0
      Home Health Care: $0
      Nursing Home: $0

Key Personnel
  Dental Director . . . . Richard Hastreiter
  Chief Sales Officer . . . . Chris Earl
  Media Contact . . . . Barb Jensen
    402-397-4878
    bjensen@deltadentalne.org
  Director Public Affairs . . . . Elizabeth Risberg
    415-972-8423

681 eHealthInsurance Services Inc.

11919 Foundation Place
Gold River, CA 95670
Toll-Free: 800-977-8860
info@ehealthinsurance.com
www.e.healthinsurance.com
Year Founded: 1997

Healthplan and Services Defined
  PLAN TYPE: HMO/PPO
  Benefits Offered: Dental, Life, STD

Type of Coverage
  Commercial, Individual, Medicare

Geographic Areas Served
  All 50 states in the USA and District of Columbia

Key Personnel
  Chairman & CEO . . . . Gary L. Lauer
  EVP/Business & Corp. Dev . . . . Bruce Telkamp
  EVP/Chief Technology . . . . Dr. Sheldon X. Wang
  SVP & CFO . . . . Stuart M. Huizinga
  Pres. of eHealth Gov. Sys . . . . Samuel C. Gibbs
  SVP of Sales & Operations . . . . Robert S. Hurley
  Director Public Relations . . . . Nate Purpura
    650-210-3115

682 Humana Health Insurance of Nebraska

11420 Blondo Street
Suite 102
Omaha, NE 68164
Toll-Free: 800-941-1182
Phone: 402-496-3388
Fax: 402-498-2850
www.humana.com
For Profit Organization: Yes

Healthplan and Services Defined
  PLAN TYPE: HMO/PPO

Type of Coverage
  Commercial, Individual

Accreditation Certification
  URAC, NCQA, CORE

683 Midlands Choice

8420 W Dodge Road
Suite 210
Omaha, NE 68114-3492
Toll-Free: 800-605-8259
Phone: 402-390-8233
Fax: 402-390-7210
cs@midlandschoice.com
www.midlandschoice.com
Mailing Address: PO Box 5809, Troy, MI 48007-5809
For Profit Organization: Yes
Year Founded: 1993
Physician Owned Organization: Yes
Number of Affiliated Hospitals: 300
Number of Primary Care Physicians: 20,000
Total Enrollment: 615,000

Healthplan and Services Defined
  PLAN TYPE: PPO
  Model Type: PPO Network

Geographic Areas Served
  Iowa, Nebraska, eastern South Dakota and portions of Colorado,
  Wyoming, Kansas, Missouri, Illinois, Wisconsin and Minnesota

Accreditation Certification
  URAC

Key Personnel
  President/CEO...............................Thomas E Press
      402-390-7245
  Director, Finance ....Rick Poskevich
      402-390-1579
  VP Operations ....Greta R Vaught
      402-390-1589
  Dir, Prof Services ....Sharon K Rasmussen
      402-390-8394
  Legal Counsel ....Tim A Waggoner
      402-390-1554
  Dir, Businss Development....................Kelly L Nieman
      402-390-7257
  Dir, Medical Economics ....Daniel R McCulley
      402-390-7253
  VP, Client Services ....Linda M Sufficool
      402-390-8369
  Manager, Information Tech ....Matthew G Dill
      402-390-8392

Specialty Managed Care Partners
  Enters into Contracts with Regional Business Coalitions: No

684   Mutual of Omaha DentaBenefits

Mutual of Omaha Plaza
S-3
Omaha, NE 68175
Toll-Free: 800-775-6000
Phone: 402-351-4255
Fax: 402-351-2999
www.mutualofomaha.com
Subsidiary of: Mutual of Omaha
For Profit Organization: Yes
Year Founded: 1985
Number of Affiliated Hospitals: 3,999
Number of Primary Care Physicians: 216,781
Number of Referral/Specialty Physicians: 414,227
State Enrollment: 602,578

Healthplan and Services Defined
  PLAN TYPE: Dental
  Other Type: PPO
  Model Type: Network
  Benefits Offered: Behavioral Health, Chiropractic, Complementary
      Medicine, Dental, Disease Management, Home Care, Inpatient
      SNF, Long-Term Care, Physical Therapy, Podiatry, Prescription,
      Psychiatric, Transplant, Vision, Wellness

Type of Coverage
  Commercial, Individual

Type of Payment Plans Offered
  Combination FFS & DFFS

Geographic Areas Served
  All 50 States and DC except for Hawaii, Vermont and Wyoming

Network Qualifications
  Pre-Admission Certification: Yes

Peer Review Type
  Utilization Review: Yes
  Second Surgical Opinion: Yes
  Case Management: Yes

Publishes and Distributes Report Card: Yes

Accreditation Certification
  TJC Accreditation, Medicare Approved, Utilization Review,
      Pre-Admission Certification, State Licensure, Quality Assurance
      Program

Key Personnel
  President...................................Daniel P Neary
  EVP, General Counsel ....Richard C Anderi
  EVP, CFO.................................David A Diamond
  EVP, Group Benefits ....Daniel P Martin
  EVP, Customer Service ....Madeline R Rucker
  EVP, Corporate Services ....Stacy A Scholtz
  EVP, Chief Investment Ofc...................Richard A Witt
  EVP, Information Services ....James T Blackledge

Specialty Managed Care Partners
  Enters into Contracts with Regional Business Coalitions: No

Employer References
  National Rural Letter Carrier, Harrah's Entertainment, Sandia
      National Labs, Bechtel Nevada, Creighton University

685   Mutual of Omaha Health Plans

Mutual of Omaha Plaza
Omaha, NE 68175
Toll-Free: 800-228-0286
Phone: 402-342-7600
Fax: 402-351-3756
www.mutualofomaha.com
For Profit Organization: Yes
Year Founded: 1988
Number of Affiliated Hospitals: 43
Number of Primary Care Physicians: 673
Number of Referral/Specialty Physicians: 1,718
Total Enrollment: 54,418
State Enrollment: 28,978

Healthplan and Services Defined
  PLAN TYPE: HMO/PPO
  Other Type: POS
  Model Type: IPA
  Plan Specialty: ASO, Behavioral Health, Chiropractic, Disease
      Management, Lab, Vision, Radiology, UR
  Benefits Offered: Behavioral Health, Chiropractic, Disease
      Management, Home Care, Inpatient SNF, Long-Term Care,
      Physical Therapy, Podiatry, Prescription, Psychiatric, Transplant,
      Vision, Wellness, AD&D, Life, LTD, STD, Critical Illness, EAP

Type of Coverage
  Commercial, Individual, Indemnity, Medicare, Supplemental
      Medicare, Medicaid
  Catastrophic Illness Benefit: Covered

Type of Payment Plans Offered
  POS, Combination FFS & DFFS

Geographic Areas Served
  Iowa: Harrison, Mills & Pottawattamie counties; Nebraska: Burt,
      Butler, Cass, Colfas, Cuming, Oakota, Dixon, Filmore, Johnson,
      Lancaster, Madison, Otoe, Salone, Saunders, Seuard, Stanton, Dodge,
      Douglas, Sampy, Washington counties

Subscriber Information
  Average Monthly Fee Per Subscriber
      (Employee + Employer Contribution):
          Employee Only (Self): Varies by plan
  Average Annual Deductible Per Subscriber:
          Employee Only (Self): $0.00
  Average Subscriber Co-Payment:
          Primary Care Physician: $15.00
          Prescription Drugs: $15.00
          Hospital ER: $50.00
          Home Health Care: $25.00
          Home Health Care Max. Days/Visits Covered: Unlimited
          Nursing Home: $0.00

Nursing Home Max. Days/Visits Covered: 100 days

Network Qualifications
Pre-Admission Certification: Yes

Peer Review Type
Utilization Review: Yes
Second Surgical Opinion: No
Case Management: Yes

Publishes and Distributes Report Card: Yes

Accreditation Certification
URAC, NCQA
TJC Accreditation, Utilization Review, Pre-Admission Certification,
State Licensure, Quality Assurance Program

Key Personnel
President . . . . .Daniel P Neary
EVP, General Counsel . . . . .Richard C Anderi
EVP, CFO. . . . . .David A Diamond
EVP, Group Benefits . . . . .Daniel P Martin
EVP, Customer Service . . . . .Madeline R Rucker
EVP, Corporate Services .Stacy A Scholtz
EVP, Chief Investment Ofc. . . . . .Richard A Witt
EVP, Information Services . . . . .James T Blackledge

Average Claim Compensation
Physician's Fees Charged: 75%
Hospital's Fees Charged: 60%

Specialty Managed Care Partners
Enters into Contracts with Regional Business Coalitions: No

Employer References
Mutual of Omaha, Forest National Bank, Nebraska Furniture Mart,
Saint Joseph Hospital

---

686   UnitedHealthCare of Nebraska

2717 N 118th Circle
Suite 300
Omaha, NE 68164
Toll-Free: 800-284-0626
Phone: 402-445-5400
Fax: 402-445-5575
Nebraska_PR_Team@uhc.com
www.uhc.com
Secondary Address: 5105 Central Park Drive, Lincoln, NE 68164,
800-284-0626
Subsidary of: UnitedHealth Group
For Profit Organization: Yes
Year Founded: 1984
Number of Affiliated Hospitals: 41
Number of Primary Care Physicians: 516
Number of Referral/Specialty Physicians: 994
Total Enrollment: 75,000,000
State Enrollment: 44,000

Healthplan and Services Defined
PLAN TYPE: HMO/PPO
Model Type: Network
Plan Specialty: ASO, Behavioral Health, Chiropractic, Dental,
Disease Management, Lab, MSO, PBM, Vision, Radiology
Benefits Offered: Disease Management, Prescription, Wellness

Type of Coverage
Commercial, Medicare, Medicaid

Type of Payment Plans Offered
POS, DFFS, FFS

Geographic Areas Served
Iowa: Cass, Fremont, Harrison, Mills, Mononas, Page,
Pottawattsmie, Shelby, Woodbury counties; Nebraska: Buffalo, Burt,
Butler, Dodge, Douglas, Gage, Hale, Jefferson, Johnson, Lancaster,
Madison, Nemaha, Otoe, Pierce, Platte, Saline, Sarpy, Seward, &
Washington counties

Subscriber Information
Average Subscriber Co-Payment:
Primary Care Physician: $10.00
Non-Network Physician: Deductible
Prescription Drugs: $10.00
Hospital ER: $50.00

Network Qualifications
Pre-Admission Certification: Yes

Peer Review Type
Utilization Review: Yes
Second Surgical Opinion: Yes
Case Management: Yes

Publishes and Distributes Report Card: Yes

Accreditation Certification
TJC Accreditation, Medicare Approved, Utilization Review,
Pre-Admission Certification, State Licensure, Quality Assurance
Program

Key Personnel
President . . . . .Kathy Mauatt
Marketing . . . . .Sherry Helmke
Medical Affairs. . . . . .Deb Esser, MD
Member Services . . . . .Shelly Wedergren
Provider Services . . . . .Bob Starman
Sales. . . . . .Dorinda Card
Media Contact . . . . .Greg Thompson
312-424-6913
gregory_a_thompson@uhc.com

HMO/PPO DIRECTORY
NEVADA

Health Insurance Coverage Status and Type of Coverage by Age

Category	All Persons		Under 18 years		Under 65 years		65 years and over	
	Number	%	Number	%	Number	%	Number	%
Total population	2,639	-	669	-	2,335	-	304	-
Covered by some type of health insurance	2,076 *(39)*	78.7 *(1.4)*	552 *(15)*	82.5 *(2.0)*	1,778 *(42)*	76.1 *(1.6)*	298 *(19)*	98.1 *(0.8)*
Covered by private health insurance	1,662 *(46)*	63.0 *(1.7)*	416 *(18)*	62.2 *(2.6)*	1,510 *(45)*	64.7 *(1.8)*	152 *(14)*	49.9 *(3.3)*
Employment based	1,429 *(48)*	54.2 *(1.8)*	379 *(18)*	56.7 *(2.6)*	1,338 *(46)*	57.3 *(1.8)*	91 *(10)*	30.0 *(2.9)*
Own employment based	752 *(28)*	28.5 *(1.0)*	1 *(1)*	0.2 *(0.1)*	686 *(26)*	29.4 *(1.0)*	66 *(8)*	21.7 *(2.4)*
Direct purchase	255 *(23)*	9.7 *(0.9)*	46 *(9)*	6.9 *(1.3)*	183 *(20)*	7.8 *(0.9)*	73 *(11)*	23.9 *(3.2)*
Covered by government health insurance	667 *(30)*	25.3 *(1.1)*	183 *(17)*	27.4 *(2.5)*	382 *(26)*	16.4 *(1.1)*	285 *(20)*	93.6 *(1.5)*
Covered by Medicaid	259 *(22)*	9.8 *(0.8)*	145 *(16)*	21.7 *(2.4)*	232 *(21)*	9.9 *(0.9)*	27 *(6)*	8.9 *(2.0)*
Also by private insurance	52 *(10)*	2.0 *(0.4)*	23 *(7)*	3.5 *(1.0)*	40 *(9)*	1.7 *(0.4)*	12 *(4)*	3.8 *(1.4)*
Covered by Medicare	359 *(21)*	13.6 *(0.8)*	16 *(8)*	2.4 *(1.1)*	74 *(10)*	3.2 *(0.4)*	285 *(20)*	93.6 *(1.5)*
Also by private insurance	162 *(16)*	6.2 *(0.6)*	9 *(5)*	1.3 *(0.8)*	24 *(7)*	1.0 *(0.3)*	138 *(14)*	45.4 *(3.4)*
Also by Medicaid	54 *(9)*	2.0 *(0.3)*	1 *(1)*	0.2 *(0.1)*	27 *(5)*	1.1 *(0.2)*	27 *(6)*	8.9 *(2.0)*
Covered by military health care	179 *(20)*	6.8 *(0.7)*	33 *(8)*	4.9 *(1.1)*	125 *(17)*	5.3 *(0.7)*	54 *(10)*	17.9 *(3.0)*
Not covered at any time during the year	563 *(36)*	21.3 *(1.4)*	117 *(13)*	17.5 *(2.0)*	557 *(36)*	23.9 *(1.6)*	6 *(2)*	1.9 *(0.8)*

Note: Numbers in thousands; figures cover 2010; standard error appears in parenthesis; (b) base less than 75,000; (x) not applicable
Source: U.S. Census Bureau, Current Population Survey, 2011 Annual Social and Economic Supplement. Table HI05. Health Insurance Coverage Status and Type of Coverage by State and Age for All People: 2010

Nevada

687 Aetna Health of Nevada
2625 Shadelands Drive
Suite 240
Walnut Creek, CA 94598
Toll-Free: 866-582-9629
corporate.mailbox@aetna.com
www.aetna.com
For Profit Organization: Yes
Total Enrollment: 109,089

Healthplan and Services Defined
PLAN TYPE: HMO
Other Type: POS
Model Type: Network
Benefits Offered: Behavioral Health, Dental, Disease Management, Wellness

Geographic Areas Served
Statewide

Subscriber Information
Average Monthly Fee Per Subscriber
(Employee + Employer Contribution):
Employee Only (Self): $85.87
Employee & 1 Family Member: $213.80

Peer Review Type
Second Surgical Opinion: Yes

Key Personnel
President.....................................Cliff Kima
Chief Medical/Clinical.....................Richard Jones, MD

688 Amerigroup Nevada
7251 West Lake Mead Blvd
Suite 104
Las Vegas, NV 89128
Toll-Free: 877-543-7669
Phone: 702-486-5000
www.realsolutions.com
For Profit Organization: Yes
Year Founded: 2009
Total Enrollment: 1,900,000

Healthplan and Services Defined
PLAN TYPE: HMO

Type of Coverage
Medicaid, Nevada Child Health Assurance & Sta

689 Anthem Blue Cross & Blue Shield of Nevada
9133 West Russell Road
Las Vegas, NV 89148
Phone: 702-228-2583
Fax: 702-228-1259
www.anthem.com
Secondary Address: 5250 S Virginia Avenue, Reno, NV 89502
For Profit Organization: Yes
Year Founded: 1995
Number of Affiliated Hospitals: 27
Number of Primary Care Physicians: 3,474
Number of Referral/Specialty Physicians: 2,518
Total Enrollment: 14,000,000
State Enrollment: 154,503

Healthplan and Services Defined
PLAN TYPE: HMO/PPO
Model Type: IPA
Benefits Offered: Behavioral Health, Chiropractic, Complementary Medicine, Dental, Disease Management, Home Care, Inpatient
SNF, Long-Term Care, Physical Therapy, Podiatry, Prescription, Psychiatric, Transplant, Vision, Wellness, AD&D, Life, LTD, STD

Type of Coverage
Commercial, Individual, Indemnity, Medicare, Supplemental Medicare, Medicaid, Catastrophic

Geographic Areas Served
Statewide

Network Qualifications
Pre-Admission Certification: Yes

Peer Review Type
Utilization Review: Yes
Second Surgical Opinion: Yes
Case Management: Yes

Accreditation Certification
Medicare Approved, Utilization Review, Pre-Admission Certification, State Licensure, Quality Assurance Program

Key Personnel
Media Contact...............................Sally Kweskin
303-831-5899
sally.kweskin@anthem.com

690 Behavioral Healthcare Options, Inc.
2716-5 North Tenaya Way
Las Vegas, NV 89128
Toll-Free: 877-393-6094
Phone: 702-242-5864
Fax: 702-242-5864
www.behavioralhealthcareoptions.com
Subsidiary of: UnitedHealthcare
Year Founded: 1991
Number of Primary Care Physicians: 250
Total Enrollment: 600,000
State Enrollment: 600,000

Healthplan and Services Defined
PLAN TYPE: HMO/PPO
Model Type: Group
Plan Specialty: Behavioral Health
Benefits Offered: Behavioral Health, Psychiatric, Mental Health, Substance Abuse, EAP, Worklife Enhancement, Gambling Treatment

Type of Payment Plans Offered
POS, Capitated, FFS

Network Qualifications
Pre-Admission Certification: Yes

Accreditation Certification
TJC, URAC, NCQA
Utilization Review, Pre-Admission Certification

Key Personnel
President and CEO.......................Michael R Adams
Director Finance ....Brad Ellerman
VP/COO................................Carole A Fisher
Claims Supervisor.......................Tracey Toothcare
Director, Member Services ....Pam Smith
Director of New Business ....Harry Baut
Marketing.............................Carole A Fisher
Medical Director ....George Westerman, MD
Sr Systems Analyst.....................Albert Wu

691 CIGNA HealthCare of Nevada
PO Box 34886
Las Vegas, NV 89133-4886
Toll-Free: 866-438-2446
Fax: 602-861-8333
www.cigna.com
For Profit Organization: Yes

Healthplan and Services Defined
  PLAN TYPE: PPO

Type of Coverage
  Commercial

---

692 **Delta Dental of Nevada**

5920 South Rainbow Blvd
#10
Las Vegas, NV 89118
Toll-Free: 800-791-5653
Phone: 702-870-6860
Fax: 702-870-0644
nvsales@delta.org
www.deltadentalins.com
Non-Profit Organization: Yes
Total Enrollment: 54,000,000

Healthplan and Services Defined
  PLAN TYPE: Dental
  Other Type: Dental PPO

Type of Coverage
  Commercial

Geographic Areas Served
  Statewide

Key Personnel
  VP, Public & Govt Affairs ....Jeff Album
    415-972-8418
  Dir/Media & Public Affair...................Elizabeth Risberg
    415-972-8423

---

693 **eHealthInsurance Services Inc.**

11919 Foundation Place
Gold River, CA 95670
Toll-Free: 800-977-8860
info@ehealthinsurance.com
www.e.healthinsurance.com
Year Founded: 1997

Healthplan and Services Defined
  PLAN TYPE: HMO/PPO
  Benefits Offered: Dental, Life, STD

Type of Coverage
  Commercial, Individual, Medicare

Geographic Areas Served
  All 50 states in the USA and District of Columbia

Key Personnel
  Chairman & CEO ....Gary L. Lauer
  EVP/Business & Corp. Dev......................Bruce Telkamp
  EVP/Chief Technology...................Dr. Sheldon X. Wang
  SVP & CFO ....Stuart M. Huizinga
  Pres. of eHealth Gov. Sys ....Samuel C. Gibbs
  SVP of Sales & Operations...................Robert S. Hurley
  Director Public Relations........................Nate Purpura
    650-210-3115

---

694 **Great-West Healthcare of Nevada**

Acquired by CIGNA

---

695 **Health Plan of Nevada**

2716 N Tenaya Way
Las Vegas, NV 89128
Toll-Free: 800-777-1840
Phone: 702-242-7300
Fax: 702-242-7960
www.healthplanofnevada.com
Subsidiary of: AmeriChoice, A UnitedHealth Group Company

For Profit Organization: Yes
Year Founded: 1982
Total Enrollment: 418,000
State Enrollment: 25,576

Healthplan and Services Defined
  PLAN TYPE: HMO/PPO
  Other Type: POS, Medicare
  Benefits Offered: Disease Management, Prescription, Wellness

Type of Coverage
  Commercial, Individual, Medicare, Supplemental Medicare, Medicaid

Geographic Areas Served
  Mohave County

Accreditation Certification
  NCQA

Key Personnel
  President/CEO..........................Jonathan W Bunker
  Director Claims and Procedures.................Corrine Spaeth
    cspaeth@sierraheath.com
  Chief Information Offc.......................Robert Schaich
    rschaich@sierrahealth.com
  VP Member Services........................Sonya Winter
    swinter@sierrahealth.com
  VP Network Development.....................Scott Cassano
    scassono@sierrahealth.com
  Media Contact................................Jeff Smith
    952-931-5685
    jeff.smith@uhc.com

Specialty Managed Care Partners
  Express Scripts

---

696 **Hometown Health Plan**

830 Harvard Way
Reno, NV 89502
Toll-Free: 800-336-0123
Phone: 775-982-3232
Fax: 775-982-3741
customer_Service@hometownhealth.com
www.hometownhealth.com
Subsidiary of: Renown Health
Non-Profit Organization: Yes
Year Founded: 1988
Owned by an Integrated Delivery Network (IDN): Yes
Number of Affiliated Hospitals: 19
Number of Primary Care Physicians: 256
Number of Referral/Specialty Physicians: 8,917
Total Enrollment: 32,000
State Enrollment: 10,000

Healthplan and Services Defined
  PLAN TYPE: Multiple
  Model Type: Network
  Plan Specialty: ASO, Behavioral Health, Chiropractic, Dental, Disease Management, EPO, Lab, PBM, Vision, Radiology, Worker's Compensation, UR
  Benefits Offered: Behavioral Health, Chiropractic, Complementary Medicine, Dental, Disease Management, Home Care, Inpatient SNF, Physical Therapy, Podiatry, Prescription, Psychiatric, Transplant, Vision, Wellness, Worker's Compensation, AD&D, Life, LTD, STD, Accupuncture
  Offers Demand Management Patient Information Service: Yes

Type of Coverage
  Commercial, Medicare, Supplemental Medicare

Geographic Areas Served
  Statewide

Subscriber Information
  Average Monthly Fee Per Subscriber
    (Employee + Employer Contribution):
      Employee Only (Self): Varies

Employee & 1 Family Member: Varies
Employee & 2 Family Members: Varies
Medicare: Varies
Average Annual Deductible Per Subscriber:
Employee Only (Self): Varies
Employee & 1 Family Member: Varies
Employee & 2 Family Members: Varies
Medicare: Varies
Average Subscriber Co-Payment:
Primary Care Physician: Varies
Non-Network Physician: Varies
Prescription Drugs: Varies
Hospital ER: Varies
Home Health Care: Varies
Home Health Care Max. Days/Visits Covered: Varies
Nursing Home: Varies
Nursing Home Max. Days/Visits Covered: Varies

Accreditation Certification
TJC

Key Personnel
President/CEO ....Jim Miller
VP ....Troy Smith
Director Of Finance ....Jeff Brutcher
Marketing Director............................Ty Windfeldt
Medical Director.........................Linda Ash-Jackson
Customer Service Manager......................John Ormond
IR Director....................................Bob Farrer
Health Service Director ....Linda Keenan

697   Humana Health Insurance of Nevada

770 E Warm Springs Road
Suite 340
Las Vegas, NV 89119
Phone: 702-837-4401
Fax: 702-562-0134
www.humana.com
For Profit Organization: Yes

Healthplan and Services Defined
PLAN TYPE: HMO/PPO

Type of Coverage
Commercial, Individual

Accreditation Certification
URAC, NCQA, CORE

698   Liberty Dental Plan of Nevada

4775 S Durango Drive
Suite 200
Las Vegas, NV 89147
Toll-Free: 888-401-1128
Phone: 949-223-0007
Fax: 949-223-0011
www.libertydentalplan.com/nv
For Profit Organization: Yes

Healthplan and Services Defined
PLAN TYPE: Dental
Other Type: Dental HMO
Plan Specialty: Dental
Benefits Offered: Dental

Type of Coverage
Commercial

Key Personnel
Chairman & CEO ....Amir Neshat, DDS
President ....Randy Brecher
General Manager...............................Terry Allen
Dental Director.....................Charles Stirewalt, DMD
Dental Director ....Ralph Hargrave, DDS
Executive Vice President.......................John Carvelli

Chief Operating Officer ....Stu Gray
VP, Business Development.....................Bill Henderson
Dental Director ....Richard Hague, DMD
Chief Financial Officer..........................Maja Kapic
VP, Comm Business Dev ....Hugh Hazlewood
VP, Professional Services ....Lynda Bull
VP, Client Services........................Marsha Hazlewood

699   Nevada Preferred Healthcare Providers

639 Isbell Road
Suite 400
Las Vegas, NV 89509
Toll-Free: 800-776-6959
Phone: 775-356-1159
Fax: 775-356-5746
info@nevadapreferred.com
www.nvpp.com
Subsidiary of: Universal Health Network/Catholic Healthcare West
For Profit Organization: Yes
Year Founded: 1983
Owned by an Integrated Delivery Network (IDN): Yes
Number of Primary Care Physicians: 1,253
Number of Referral/Specialty Physicians: 2,162
Total Enrollment: 150,000
State Enrollment: 150,000

Healthplan and Services Defined
PLAN TYPE: PPO
Model Type: Network

Type of Payment Plans Offered
Capitated, FFS, Combination FFS & DFFS

Geographic Areas Served
Statewide

Network Qualifications
Pre-Admission Certification: Yes

Peer Review Type
Utilization Review: Yes
Second Surgical Opinion: Yes
Case Management: Yes

Publishes and Distributes Report Card: No

Accreditation Certification
Utilization Review, Pre-Admission Certification, State Licensure,
Quality Assurance Program

Key Personnel
Vice President ....Mary Hoover
Controller....................................Linda Barnes
Dir, Marketing & Bus Dev........................Jim Kroft

Average Claim Compensation
Physician's Fees Charged: 60%
Hospital's Fees Charged: 55%

Specialty Managed Care Partners
Enters into Contracts with Regional Business Coalitions: No

700   Nevada Preferred Healthcare Providers

639 Isbell Road
Suite 400
Reno, NV 89509
Toll-Free: 800-776-6959
Phone: 775-356-1159
Fax: 775-356-5746
info@nevadapreferred.com
www.universalhealthnet.com
Subsidiary of: Universal Health Network
Year Founded: 1991
Number of Affiliated Hospitals: 80
Number of Primary Care Physicians: 4,483
Total Enrollment: 150,000

State Enrollment: 150,000

Healthplan and Services Defined
 PLAN TYPE: HMO/PPO
 Other Type: EPO
 Model Type: Network
 Plan Specialty: EPO, Worker's Compensation
 Benefits Offered: Behavioral Health, Chiropractic, Home Care, Physical Therapy, Podiatry, Psychiatric, Transplant, Wellness, Worker's Compensation

Type of Payment Plans Offered
 POS, DFFS, FFS, Combination FFS & DFFS

Geographic Areas Served
 Comprehensive coverage for California, Louisiana, Nevada, South Carolina, Texas, Utah, Georgia, Washington, DC

Network Qualifications
 Pre-Admission Certification: Yes

Peer Review Type
 Utilization Review: Yes
 Second Surgical Opinion: Yes
 Case Management: Yes

Publishes and Distributes Report Card: No

Key Personnel
 CEO . . . . Mary Hoover
 Controller. . . . . Linda Barnes
 CFO . . . . David Challis
 Claims Supervisor . . . . Linda Barnett
 Network Management . . . . Char Robertson
 Marketing. . . . . Jim Kroft
 Provider Services . . . . Michelle Flores

Specialty Managed Care Partners
 Enters into Contracts with Regional Business Coalitions: Yes

Employer References
 State of Nevada, CCN, PPO USA GEHA, Valley Health System, Pepperpill

701   NevadaCare

10600 W Charleston Boulevard
Las Vegas, NV 89135-1014
Toll-Free: 800-447-9834
Phone: 702-304-5500
nevadacare@imxinc.com
www.nevadacare.com
Mailing Address: PO Box 379020, Las Vegas, NV 89137
Subsidiary of: Imxinc
For Profit Organization: Yes
Year Founded: 1991
Number of Primary Care Physicians: 4,000
Number of Referral/Specialty Physicians: 2,900
Total Enrollment: 3,000
State Enrollment: 19,642

Healthplan and Services Defined
 PLAN TYPE: HMO
 Model Type: Network
 Benefits Offered: Prescription

Type of Payment Plans Offered
 Combination FFS & DFFS

Geographic Areas Served
 Clark county and Reno/Sparks in Washoe counties

Network Qualifications
 Pre-Admission Certification: Yes

Peer Review Type
 Utilization Review: Yes

Publishes and Distributes Report Card: No

Accreditation Certification
 TJC Accreditation, Medicare Approved, Utilization Review, Pre-Admission Certification, State Licensure, Quality Assurance Program

Key Personnel
 President . . . . Todd Meek
 Public Affairs . . . . Larry Frank
 480-921-8944
 lawrencef@imxinc.com

702   PacifiCare of Nevada

700 E Warm Springs Road
Las Vegas, NV 89119
Phone: 702-269-7500
www.pacificare.com
Secondary Address: 5190 Neil Road, #420, Reno, NV 89502
Subsidiary of: UnitedHealthCare
Non-Profit Organization: Yes
Year Founded: 1992
Number of Affiliated Hospitals: 11
Number of Primary Care Physicians: 267
Number of Referral/Specialty Physicians: 805
Total Enrollment: 26,000
State Enrollment: 28,591

Healthplan and Services Defined
 PLAN TYPE: HMO
 Model Type: IPA, Network
 Plan Specialty: Behavioral Health, Chiropractic, Dental, Lab, Vision, Radiology
 Benefits Offered: Behavioral Health, Chiropractic, Dental, Inpatient SNF, Physical Therapy, Prescription, Vision
 Offers Demand Management Patient Information Service: Yes

Type of Coverage
 Commercial, Individual, Indemnity, Medicare, Supplemental Medicare
 Catastrophic Illness Benefit: Maximum $2M

Type of Payment Plans Offered
 Capitated, FFS

Accreditation Certification
 NCQA

Key Personnel
 CEO . . . . Howard Phanstiel
 CFO . . . . Gregory W Scott
 President. . . . . Brad Bowlus
 Executive Vice President. . . . . Jacqueline Kosecoff, PhD
 Director of Sales . . . . Bruce Huxghue

Employer References
 350 businesses in Nevada

703   Saint Mary's Health Plans

1510 Meadow Wood Lane
Reno, NV 89502
Toll-Free: 800-433-3077
Phone: 775-770-6000
Fax: 775-770-6253
www.saintmaryshealthplans.com
Subsidiary of: CHW
For Profit Organization: Yes
Year Founded: 1983
Number of Affiliated Hospitals: 21
Number of Primary Care Physicians: 4,000
Number of Referral/Specialty Physicians: 1,500
Total Enrollment: 15,000

Healthplan and Services Defined
 PLAN TYPE: HMO

Other Type: POS
Model Type: Group, Network
Plan Specialty: ASO, Behavioral Health, Chiropractic, Dental,
  Disease Management, EPO, MSO, PBM, Vision, Radiology,
  Worker's Compensation
Benefits Offered: Behavioral Health, Chiropractic, Complementary
  Medicine, Dental, Disease Management, Home Care, Inpatient
  SNF, Long-Term Care, Physical Therapy, Podiatry, Prescription,
  Psychiatric, Transplant, Vision, Wellness, Worker's Compensation,
  Routine PE, pre and

Type of Payment Plans Offered
POS, DFFS, FFS, Combination FFS & DFFS

Geographic Areas Served
Nevada and border communities in California and Arizona

Subscriber Information
Average Monthly Fee Per Subscriber
  (Employee + Employer Contribution):
    Employee Only (Self): Varies by plan
Average Subscriber Co-Payment:
  Nursing Home: Varies

Network Qualifications
Pre-Admission Certification: Yes

Peer Review Type
Utilization Review: Yes
Second Surgical Opinion: Yes
Case Management: Yes

Accreditation Certification
NCQA
TJC Accreditation, Medicare Approved, Pre-Admission Certification

Key Personnel
President/CEO . . . . M Donald Kowitz
Senior Director Oper. . . . . Lois Paynter
Claims Manager. . . . . Barbara Harkey
Network Contracting . . . . Lisa Gilbert
Credentialing Manager . . . . Kevin Brizendine
Director of Marketing . . . . Greg Johnson
Member Services Manager . . . . Casey Trump
Provider Services Manager. . . . . Kevin Brizendine
Manager Sales. . . . . Greg Johnson

704 UnitedHealthcare Nevada
2724 N Tenaya Way
Las Vegas, NV 89128
Phone: 702-242-7000
Fax: 702-242-7920
w3_hpnsd_sl@sierrahealth.com
www.uhcnevada.com
Mailing Address: PO Box 15645, Las Vegas, NV 89114-5645
For Profit Organization: Yes
Year Founded: 1984
Number of Affiliated Hospitals: 6
Number of Primary Care Physicians: 161
Total Enrollment: 580,000
State Enrollment: 107,963

Healthplan and Services Defined
  PLAN TYPE: HMO/PPO
  Other Type: POS
  Model Type: Network
  Benefits Offered: Prescription
  Offers Demand Management Patient Information Service: Yes

Type of Payment Plans Offered
POS, DFFS, Capitated, FFS

Geographic Areas Served
Clark County

Subscriber Information
Average Monthly Fee Per Subscriber
  (Employee + Employer Contribution):

Employee Only (Self): $39.00
Average Annual Deductible Per Subscriber:
  Employee Only (Self): $0
  Employee & 1 Family Member: $0
  Employee & 2 Family Members: $0
  Medicare: $0
Average Subscriber Co-Payment:
  Primary Care Physician: $0.00
  Prescription Drugs: $10.00
  Hospital ER: $50.00
  Home Health Care: Varies
  Home Health Care Max. Days/Visits Covered: Unlimited
  Nursing Home: Varies
  Nursing Home Max. Days/Visits Covered: 100 days

Peer Review Type
Case Management: Yes

Publishes and Distributes Report Card: Yes

Key Personnel
Market CEO . . . . Donald J Giancursio
Sr VP/CFO/Treasurer. . . . . Paul Palmer
Executive VP/Administrat . . . . William Godfrey
Vice President, PR . . . . Peter O'Neill
Sr VP/Program Office . . . . Larry Howard
President, Managed Health . . . . Jonathan Bunker
VP/Customer Service. . . . . Mike Montalvo
VP/Human Resources . . . . Daniel Kruger
CMO/VP Medical Affairs . . . . Christine Peterson, MD
Sr VP/Legal & Administ. . . . . Frank Collins
VP/Information Technology . . . . Robert Schaich
VP/Healthcare Quality/Ed . . . . Allan Ebbin, MD, MPH
Executive VP/Special Proj . . . . Marie Soldo
SVP, Public Relations . . . . Peter O'Neill
  702-242-7156
  peter.oneill@uhc.com
Manager, Public Relations . . . . Amanda Penn
  702-242-7784
  amanda.penn@uhc.com

Health Insurance Coverage Status and Type of Coverage by Age

Category	All Persons		Under 18 years		Under 65 years		65 years and over	
	Number	%	Number	%	Number	%	Number	%
Total population	1,302	-	277	-	1,130	-	172	-
Covered by some type of health insurance	1,168 (12)	89.7 (0.7)	262 (4)	94.5 (1.0)	996 (15)	88.2 (0.9)	172 (8)	100.0 (0.0)
Covered by private health insurance	1,011 (17)	77.6 (1.2)	229 (6)	82.5 (1.8)	911 (18)	80.6 (1.3)	100 (7)	58.0 (3.0)
Employment based	890 (18)	68.4 (1.3)	209 (6)	75.3 (2.0)	830 (18)	73.5 (1.4)	60 (6)	35.1 (3.0)
Own employment based	418 (10)	32.1 (0.8)	0 (0)	0.1 (0.1)	378 (10)	33.4 (0.8)	40 (4)	23.3 (2.0)
Direct purchase	139 (11)	10.7 (0.9)	28 (4)	10.0 (1.5)	95 (10)	8.5 (0.8)	44 (5)	25.4 (2.9)
Covered by government health insurance	290 (13)	22.3 (1.0)	49 (5)	17.6 (1.7)	126 (10)	11.1 (0.9)	165 (8)	96.1 (1.2)
Covered by Medicaid	85 (7)	6.5 (0.6)	44 (5)	16.0 (1.7)	80 (7)	7.0 (0.7)	5 (2)	3.0 (0.9)
Also by private insurance	23 (4)	1.8 (0.3)	13 (3)	4.8 (0.9)	22 (3)	2.0 (0.3)	0 (0)	0.3 (0.3)
Covered by Medicare	204 (10)	15.7 (0.8)	3 (2)	1.1 (0.5)	40 (5)	3.5 (0.5)	164 (8)	95.7 (1.1)
Also by private insurance	104 (7)	8.0 (0.6)	0 (0)	0.1 (0.1)	12 (3)	1.0 (0.2)	92 (7)	53.7 (2.9)
Also by Medicaid	18 (4)	1.4 (0.3)	2 (1)	0.5 (0.4)	13 (3)	1.1 (0.3)	5 (2)	3.0 (0.9)
Covered by military health care	39 (5)	3.0 (0.4)	3 (1)	1.0 (0.4)	20 (4)	1.8 (0.4)	19 (4)	11.2 (2.2)
Not covered at any time during the year	134 (10)	10.3 (0.7)	15 (3)	5.5 (1.0)	134 (10)	11.8 (0.9)	0 (0)	0.0 (0.0)

Note: Numbers in thousands; figures cover 2010; standard error appears in parenthesis; (b) base less than 75,000; (x) not applicable
Source: U.S. Census Bureau, Current Population Survey, 2011 Annual Social and Economic Supplement. Table HI05. Health Insurance Coverage Status and Type of Coverage by State and Age for All People: 2010

New Hampshire

705 Aetna Health of New Hampshire

Partnered with eHealthInsurance Services Inc.

706 Anthem Blue Cross & Blue Shield of New Hampshire

3000 Goffs Falls Road
Manchester, NH 03111-0001
Phone: 603-695-7000
www.anthem.com
Year Founded: 1942
Owned by an Integrated Delivery Network (IDN): Yes
Number of Affiliated Hospitals: 26
Number of Primary Care Physicians: 90
Number of Referral/Specialty Physicians: 3,608
Total Enrollment: 560,000
State Enrollment: 400,000

Healthplan and Services Defined
PLAN TYPE: HMO
Model Type: IPA, TPA
Plan Specialty: ASO, Behavioral Health, Chiropractic, Dental,
  Disease Management, EPO, Lab, MSO, PBM, Vision
Benefits Offered: Behavioral Health, Chiropractic, Dental, Disease
  Management, Home Care, Inpatient SNF, Physical Therapy,
  Prescription, Psychiatric, Transplant, Wellness, Life
Offers Demand Management Patient Information Service: Yes
DMPI Services Offered: Asthma, Diabetes, Cardiovascular, Healthy
  Babies, Lifestyle

Type of Coverage
Commercial, Individual

Geographic Areas Served
Maine, New Hampshire, Connecticut

Subscriber Information
Average Subscriber Co-Payment:
  Nursing Home: Varies

Network Qualifications
Pre-Admission Certification: Yes

Peer Review Type
Utilization Review: Yes
Case Management: Yes

Publishes and Distributes Report Card: Yes

Accreditation Certification
NCQA
Utilization Review, Quality Assurance Program

Key Personnel
President . . . . Lisa M Guertin
Dir, Commun & Comm Relat. Chris Dugan
Director, Govt Affairs . . . . Mark C Vatles
Provider Network Manager. Lance Milner
Media Contact. . . . . Chris Dugan
  603-695-7202
  chris.dugan@anthem.com

707 CIGNA HealthCare of New Hampshire

Two College Park Drive
Suite 250
Hooksett, NH 03106
Toll-Free: 866-438-2446
Phone: 603-268-7839
Fax: 603-268-7981
www.cigna.com
For Profit Organization: Yes
Year Founded: 1985
Physician Owned Organization: Yes

Owned by an Integrated Delivery Network (IDN): Yes
Federally Qualified: Yes
Number of Affiliated Hospitals: 26
Number of Primary Care Physicians: 1,055
Number of Referral/Specialty Physicians: 3,129
Total Enrollment: 23,559
State Enrollment: 23,559

Healthplan and Services Defined
PLAN TYPE: HMO
Other Type: POS
Model Type: Network
Plan Specialty: General Medical
Benefits Offered: Behavioral Health, Chiropractic, Complementary
  Medicine, Disease Management, Home Care, Inpatient SNF,
  Physical Therapy, Podiatry, Prescription, Psychiatric, Transplant,
  Vision, Wellness, Healthy babies, women's health, men's health
Offers Demand Management Patient Information Service: Yes

Type of Coverage
Commercial, Small Groups HMO All Network
Catastrophic Illness Benefit: Varies per case

Type of Payment Plans Offered
DFFS, Capitated, FFS, Combination FFS & DFFS

Geographic Areas Served
State of New Hampshire, all counties

Subscriber Information
Average Monthly Fee Per Subscriber
  (Employee + Employer Contribution):
    Employee Only (Self): Varies by plan
Average Subscriber Co-Payment:
    Primary Care Physician: $10.00
    Non-Network Physician: Not covered
    Prescription Drugs: $5/15/35
    Hospital ER: $50.00
    Home Health Care Max. Days/Visits Covered: Unlimited
    Nursing Home Max. Days/Visits Covered: 60 days per year

Network Qualifications
Pre-Admission Certification: Yes

Peer Review Type
Utilization Review: Yes
Second Surgical Opinion: Yes
Case Management: Yes

Publishes and Distributes Report Card: Yes

Accreditation Certification
TJC Accreditation, Medicare Approved, Utilization Review,
  Pre-Admission Certification, State Licensure, Quality Assurance
  Program

Key Personnel
Administration. . . . . William Bashan
Finance. . . . . Kerry Spencer
Claims. . . . . Ellie St Pierre
Credentialing . . . . Edna York
In-House Formulary . . . . Jim Demosthenes
Marketing. . . . . Deborah Wing
Medical Affairs . . . . Rob Hockmuth, MD
Provider Services . . . . Kathy Smith
Sales. . . . . Karynlee Harrington

708 Delta Dental Northeast

One Delta Drive
PO Box 2002
Concord, NH 03302-2002
Toll-Free: 800-537-1715
Phone: 603-223-1000
Fax: 603-223-1199
nedelta@nedelta.com
www.nedelta.com
Non-Profit Organization: Yes

Year Founded: 1961
Total Enrollment: 54,000,000
State Enrollment: 700,000

Healthplan and Services Defined
PLAN TYPE: Dental
Other Type: Dental PPO
Model Type: Network
Plan Specialty: ASO, Dental
Benefits Offered: Dental

Type of Coverage
Commercial, Individual, Group
Catastrophic Illness Benefit: None

Geographic Areas Served
Statewide

Subscriber Information
Average Monthly Fee Per Subscriber
(Employee + Employer Contribution):
Employee Only (Self): Varies
Employee & 1 Family Member: Varies
Employee & 2 Family Members: Varies
Average Annual Deductible Per Subscriber:
Employee Only (Self): Varies
Employee & 1 Family Member: Varies
Employee & 2 Family Members: Varies
Average Subscriber Co-Payment:
Prescription Drugs: $0
Home Health Care: $0
Nursing Home: $0

Key Personnel
President/CEO . . . . .Thomas Raffio
SVP, Operations . . . . .William H Lambrukos
VP, Information Systems . . . . .Michael D Bourbeau
Strategy Management . . . . .Linda J Roche
General Counsel . . . . .Kenneth L Robinson, Jr
VP, Marketing . . . . .Gene R Emery
VP, Human Resources . . . . .Connie M Roy-Czyzowski, SHPR
Dir, Corporate Relations . . . . .Barbara A McLaughlin
SVP, Finance . . . . .Helen T Biglin
Dir, Actuarial & Research . . . . .Laurence R Weissbrot, FSA
VP, Professional Relation . . . . .Shannon E Mills, DDS
Chief Dental Officer . . . . .Michael E Couret, DDS

709 eHealthInsurance Services Inc.

11919 Foundation Place
Gold River, CA 95670
Toll-Free: 800-977-8860
info@ehealthinsurance.com
www.e.healthinsurance.com
Year Founded: 1997

Healthplan and Services Defined
PLAN TYPE: HMO/PPO
Benefits Offered: Dental, Life, STD

Type of Coverage
Commercial, Individual, Medicare

Geographic Areas Served
All 50 states in the USA and District of Columbia

Key Personnel
Chairman & CEO . . . . .Gary L. Lauer
EVP/Business & Corp. Dev. .Bruce Telkamp
EVP/Chief Technology .Dr. Sheldon X. Wang
SVP & CFO . . . . .Stuart M. Huizinga
Pres. of eHealth Gov. Sys .Samuel C. Gibbs
SVP of Sales & Operations . . . . .Robert S. Hurley
Director Public Relations . . . . .Nate Purpura
650-210-3115

710 Harvard Pilgrim Health Care of New England

160 South River Road
Suite 201
Bedford, NH 03110
Toll-Free: 888-888-4742
www.harvardpilgrim.org
Non-Profit Organization: Yes
Year Founded: 1977
Number of Affiliated Hospitals: 135
Number of Primary Care Physicians: 28,000
Total Enrollment: 1,100,000
State Enrollment: 139,000

Healthplan and Services Defined
PLAN TYPE: Multiple
Model Type: Mixed

Geographic Areas Served
Massachusetts, New Hampshire and Maine

Accreditation Certification
NCQA

Key Personnel
President & CEO . . . . .Eric H Schultz
VP, New England Operation . . . . .Beth-Ann Roberts
SVP, Provider Network . . . . .Rick Weisblatt, PhD
VP, Marketing & Comm . . . . .Dana Rashti
VP, Customer Service . . . . .Lynn Bowman
Chief Information Officer . . . . .Deborah Norton
SVP, Sales & Cust Service . . . . .Vincent Capozzi
Dir, Media Relations . . . . .Sharon Torgerson
617-509-7458
sharon_torgerson@hphc.org

711 Humana Health Insurance of New Hampshire

1 New Hampshire Ave
Suite 125
Portsmouth, NH 03801
Phone: 603-766-4912
www.humana.com
For Profit Organization: Yes

Healthplan and Services Defined
PLAN TYPE: HMO/PPO

Type of Coverage
Commercial, Individual

Accreditation Certification
URAC, NCQA, CORE

712 MVP Health Care: New Hampshire

33 South Commercial Street
Suite 303
Manchester, NH 03101
Toll-Free: 866-687-6364
Phone: 603-647-7181
Fax: 603-647-9607
www.mvphealthcare.com
Non-Profit Organization: Yes
Year Founded: 1983
Number of Primary Care Physicians: 24,000
Total Enrollment: 750,000

Healthplan and Services Defined
PLAN TYPE: HMO/PPO
Model Type: IPA
Benefits Offered: Behavioral Health, Chiropractic, Complementary
Medicine, Dental, Disease Management, Home Care, Inpatient
SNF, Physical Therapy, Podiatry, Prescription, Psychiatric,

Transplant, Vision, Wellness, Worker's Compensation, Online Health Library

Type of Coverage
Commercial, Individual, Indemnity

Type of Payment Plans Offered
POS, DFFS, Capitated, FFS, Combination FFS & DFFS

Subscriber Information
Average Monthly Fee Per Subscriber
(Employee + Employer Contribution):
Employee Only (Self): Varies by plan
Average Annual Deductible Per Subscriber:
Employee Only (Self): Varies by plan

Accreditation Certification
NCQA

Key Personnel
President/CEO . . . . .David Oliker
EVP/COO . . . . .Chris Henchey
EVP/Rochester Operations. . . . . .Lisa A Brubaker
EVP/Network Management . . . . .Mark Fish
EVP/Planning. . . . . .Alfred Gatti
EVP/Chief Legal Officer. . . . . .Denise Gonick, Esq
EVP/Human Resources. . . . . .James Morrill

713 Northeast Community Care

49 Atlantic Place
South Portland, ME 04106-2316
Toll-Free: 800-998-3056
Phone: 207-773-3920
Fax: 207-773-3990
www.northeastcommunitycare.com
Subsidiary of: Arcadian Health Plans

Healthplan and Services Defined
PLAN TYPE: Medicare

Type of Coverage
Medicare

714 UnitedHealthCare of New Hampshire

1 Research Drive
Westborough, MA 01581
Toll-Free: 800-444-7855
www.uhc.com
Subsidiary of: UnitedHealth Group
For Profit Organization: Yes
Year Founded: 1986
Number of Affiliated Hospitals: 47
Number of Primary Care Physicians: 1,600
Number of Referral/Specialty Physicians: 3,500
Total Enrollment: 75,000,000

Healthplan and Services Defined
PLAN TYPE: HMO/PPO
Model Type: Mixed Model
Plan Specialty: MSO
Benefits Offered: Behavioral Health, Chiropractic, Complementary
Medicine, Dental, Disease Management, Home Care, Inpatient
SNF, Long-Term Care, Physical Therapy, Podiatry, Prescription,
Psychiatric, Transplant, Vision, Wellness, AD&D, Life

Type of Coverage
Commercial, Individual, Medicaid, Commercial Group

Type of Payment Plans Offered
DFFS, FFS, Combination FFS & DFFS

Geographic Areas Served
Statewide

Subscriber Information
Average Monthly Fee Per Subscriber
(Employee + Employer Contribution):
Employee Only (Self): Varies

Average Subscriber Co-Payment:
Primary Care Physician: $10
Prescription Drugs: $10/15/30
Hospital ER: $50

Network Qualifications
Pre-Admission Certification: Yes

Peer Review Type
Case Management: Yes

Publishes and Distributes Report Card: Yes

Accreditation Certification
URAC, NCQA
State Licensure, Quality Assurance Program

Average Claim Compensation
Physician's Fees Charged: 70%
Hospital's Fees Charged: 55%

Specialty Managed Care Partners
United Behavioral Health
Enters into Contracts with Regional Business Coalitions: No

HMO/PPO DIRECTORY

Health Insurance Coverage Status and Type of Coverage by Age

Category	All Persons		Under 18 years		Under 65 years		65 years and over	
	Number	%	Number	%	Number	%	Number	%
Total population	8,672	-	2,051	-	7,555	-	1,116	-
Covered by some type of health insurance	7,334 *(95)*	84.6 *(1.0)*	1,863 *(31)*	90.8 *(1.2)*	6,241 *(111)*	82.6 *(1.2)*	1,093 *(53)*	97.9 *(0.7)*
Covered by private health insurance	6,046 *(133)*	69.7 *(1.5)*	1,423 *(51)*	69.4 *(2.3)*	5,359 *(139)*	70.9 *(1.6)*	687 *(46)*	61.6 *(2.7)*
Employment based	5,403 *(134)*	62.3 *(1.5)*	1,340 *(54)*	65.3 *(2.5)*	4,951 *(136)*	65.5 *(1.7)*	452 *(36)*	40.5 *(2.8)*
Own employment based	2,601 *(67)*	30.0 *(0.7)*	3 *(2)*	0.1 *(0.1)*	2,245 *(67)*	29.7 *(0.8)*	356 *(30)*	31.9 *(2.3)*
Direct purchase	788 *(62)*	9.1 *(0.7)*	119 *(22)*	5.8 *(1.1)*	500 *(54)*	6.6 *(0.7)*	288 *(31)*	25.8 *(2.4)*
Covered by government health insurance	2,237 *(90)*	25.8 *(1.1)*	606 *(48)*	29.5 *(2.3)*	1,219 *(79)*	16.1 *(1.1)*	1,018 *(52)*	91.2 *(1.4)*
Covered by Medicaid	1,091 *(77)*	12.6 *(0.9)*	597 *(48)*	29.1 *(2.3)*	1,021 *(78)*	13.5 *(1.0)*	70 *(15)*	6.3 *(1.3)*
Also by private insurance	255 *(32)*	2.9 *(0.4)*	160 *(23)*	7.8 *(1.1)*	244 *(33)*	3.2 *(0.4)*	12 *(5)*	1.1 *(0.5)*
Covered by Medicare	1,234 *(55)*	14.2 *(0.6)*	9 *(4)*	0.4 *(0.2)*	216 *(24)*	2.9 *(0.3)*	1,018 *(52)*	91.2 *(1.4)*
Also by private insurance	689 *(47)*	7.9 *(0.5)*	4 *(3)*	0.2 *(0.1)*	76 *(17)*	1.0 *(0.2)*	613 *(43)*	54.9 *(2.7)*
Also by Medicaid	121 *(20)*	1.4 *(0.2)*	6 *(3)*	0.3 *(0.2)*	51 *(12)*	0.7 *(0.2)*	70 *(15)*	6.3 *(1.3)*
Covered by military health care	66 *(19)*	0.8 *(0.2)*	11 *(7)*	0.5 *(0.3)*	46 *(16)*	0.6 *(0.2)*	20 *(8)*	1.8 *(0.8)*
Not covered at any time during the year	1,338 *(91)*	15.4 *(1.0)*	188 *(24)*	9.2 *(1.2)*	1,314 *(90)*	17.4 *(1.2)*	24 *(7)*	2.1 *(0.7)*

Note: Numbers in thousands; figures cover 2010; standard error appears in parenthesis; (b) base less than 75,000; (x) not applicable
Source: U.S. Census Bureau, Current Population Survey, 2011 Annual Social and Economic Supplement. Table HI05. Health Insurance Coverage Status and Type of Coverage by State and Age for All People: 2010

New Jersey

715 Aetna Health of New Jersey

151 Farmington Avenue
Conveyer ASB2
Hartford, CT 06156
Toll-Free: 866-582-9629
www.aetna.com
For Profit Organization: Yes
Year Founded: 1981
Number of Affiliated Hospitals: 4,135
Number of Primary Care Physicians: 405,000
Number of Referral/Specialty Physicians: 684,000
Total Enrollment: 5,183,333
State Enrollment: 518,333

Healthplan and Services Defined
PLAN TYPE: HMO
Other Type: POS
Model Type: Network
Plan Specialty: ASO, Behavioral Health, Chiropractic, Dental,
Disease Management, Vision, Radiology, Worker's Compensation
Benefits Offered: Behavioral Health, Chiropractic, Complementary
Medicine, Dental, Disease Management, Home Care, Prescription,
Vision, Worker's Compensation
Offers Demand Management Patient Information Service: Yes

Type of Coverage
Commercial, Medicare

Type of Payment Plans Offered
POS, DFFS, Capitated, FFS, Combination FFS & DFFS

Geographic Areas Served
Statewide

Peer Review Type
Case Management: No

Publishes and Distributes Report Card: Yes

Key Personnel
CEO .... Ronald A Williams
President................................. Mark T Bertolini
SVP, General Counsel .... William J Casazza
EVP, CFO............................. Joseph M Zubretsky
Head, M&A Integration .... Kay Mooney
SVP, Marketing.......................... Robert E Mead
Chief Medical Officer .... Lonny Reisman, MD
SVP, Human Resources.................... Elease E Wright
SVP, CIO................................ Meg McCarthy

716 AmeriChoice by UnitedHealthCare

Four Gateway Center
100 Mulberry Street
Newark, NJ 07102
Toll-Free: 800-941-4647
Phone: 973-297-5500
www.americhoice.com
Subsidiary of: A UnitedHealth Group Company
For Profit Organization: Yes
Year Founded: 1989
Total Enrollment: 200,871
State Enrollment: 199,018

Healthplan and Services Defined
PLAN TYPE: HMO

Type of Coverage
Medicare, Medicaid, NJ Family Care

Geographic Areas Served
16 state area

Key Personnel
Chief Operating Officer .... Carolyn Magill

Finance Director............................... Phillip Franz
Chief Medical Officer .... Ebben Smith, MD
Member Services .... Dorothy Ward
Media Contact.............................. Jeff Smith
952-931-5685
jeff.smith@uhc.com

717 Amerigroup New Jersey

399 Thornall Street
9th Floor
Edison, NJ 08837
Toll-Free: 800-356-1561
Phone: 732-452-6000
www.amerigroupcorp.com
For Profit Organization: Yes
Year Founded: 1996
Total Enrollment: 1,900,000
State Enrollment: 105,000

Healthplan and Services Defined
PLAN TYPE: HMO

Type of Payment Plans Offered
Capitated

Geographic Areas Served
20 of the 21 counties in New Jersey

Accreditation Certification
Quality Assurance Program

Key Personnel
Manager, Communications .... Doug Blue
757-473-2737

718 AmeriHealth HMO

8000 Midlantic Drive
Suite 333
Mount Laurel, NJ 08054
Phone: 856-778-6500
Fax: 856-778-6551
www.amerihealth.com
Secondary Address: 485C US Highway 1 South, Suite 300, Iselin, NJ
08830-3052
For Profit Organization: Yes
Year Founded: 1995
Number of Affiliated Hospitals: 230
Number of Primary Care Physicians: 37,000
Number of Referral/Specialty Physicians: 36,496
Total Enrollment: 265,000
State Enrollment: 77,761

Healthplan and Services Defined
PLAN TYPE: HMO/PPO
Other Type: POS
Model Type: IPA, PPO
Benefits Offered: Dental, Disease Management, Prescription, Vision,
Wellness

Type of Coverage
Commercial, Individual, Medicare, Supplemental Medicare, Medicaid

Type of Payment Plans Offered
POS, DFFS, FFS

Geographic Areas Served
New Jersey, Delaware, Pennsylvania counties: Berks, Bucks, Chester,
Delaware, Lancaster, Lehigh, Montgomery, Northhampton,
Philadelphia

Subscriber Information
Average Monthly Fee Per Subscriber
(Employee + Employer Contribution):
Employee Only (Self): $190 per mo and up

Accreditation Certification
TJC, NCQA

Key Personnel
President and CEO ....William F Haggett
Media Contact ....Kate Wilhelmi
856-778-6552

Specialty Managed Care Partners
Enters into Contracts with Regional Business Coalitions: Yes

---

719   Assurant Employee Benefits: New Jersey

9 Campus Drive
Suite 3
Parsippany, NJ 07054-4412
Phone: 973-775-3125
benefits@assurant.com
www.assurantemployeebenefits.com
Subsidiary of: Assurant, Inc
For Profit Organization: Yes
Number of Primary Care Physicians: 112,000
Total Enrollment: 47,000

Healthplan and Services Defined
PLAN TYPE: Multiple
Plan Specialty: Dental, Vision, Long & Short-Term Disability
Benefits Offered: Dental, Vision, Wellness, AD&D, Life, LTD, STD

Type of Coverage
Commercial, Indemnity, Individual Dental Plans

Geographic Areas Served
Statewide

Subscriber Information
Average Monthly Fee Per Subscriber
(Employee + Employer Contribution):
Employee Only (Self): Varies by plan

Key Personnel
PR Specialist.............................Megan Hutchison
816-556-7815
megan.hutchison@assurant.com

---

720   Atlanticare Health Plans

1001 S Grand Street
Hammonton, NJ 08037-0941
Toll-Free: 800-272-5995
Phone: 609-567-9633
www.atlanticare.org
Non-Profit Organization: Yes
Year Founded: 1993
Number of Affiliated Hospitals: 36
Number of Primary Care Physicians: 15,009
Number of Referral/Specialty Physicians: 4,000
Total Enrollment: 150,000
State Enrollment: 150,000

Healthplan and Services Defined
PLAN TYPE: HMO/PPO
Model Type: IPA
Plan Specialty: ASO, Behavioral Health, Worker's Compensation,
UR

Type of Payment Plans Offered
Combination FFS & DFFS

Geographic Areas Served
Southeastern New Jersey

Subscriber Information
Average Subscriber Co-Payment:
Primary Care Physician: $10.00
Non-Network Physician: $20.00
Prescription Drugs: $15.00
Hospital ER: $50.00
Home Health Care: $60
Nursing Home: $120

Network Qualifications
Pre-Admission Certification: Yes

Peer Review Type
Utilization Review: Yes
Second Surgical Opinion: Yes
Case Management: Yes

Accreditation Certification
TJC, URAC, NCQA

Key Personnel
President ....George F Lynn

Specialty Managed Care Partners
Horizon BC/BS of NJ

---

721   Block Vision of New Jersey

325 Columbia Turnpike
Suite 303
Florham Park, NJ 07932
Toll-Free: 866-246-9589
Phone: 561-989-8100
Fax: 561-241-5126
www.blockvision.com
Year Founded: 1986
Number of Primary Care Physicians: 18,000
Total Enrollment: 300,000

Healthplan and Services Defined
PLAN TYPE: Vision
Model Type: Network
Plan Specialty: Vision
Benefits Offered: Vision
Offers Demand Management Patient Information Service: Yes

Type of Payment Plans Offered
Capitated

Geographic Areas Served
Nationwide

Key Personnel
President/CEO ....Andrew Alcorn
Member Services...........................Ilana Stone
Account Executive.........................Stacey Fiorina
866-246-9589
sfiorina@blockvision.com

---

722   CHN PPO

300 American Metro Blvd
Suite 300
Hamilton, NJ 08619
Toll-Free: 800-225-4246
Phone: 609-631-0414
marketing@conservgrp.com
www.csg-inc.net
Subsidiary of: Consolidated Services Group
For Profit Organization: Yes
Year Founded: 1986
Number of Affiliated Hospitals: 165
Number of Primary Care Physicians: 116,000
Number of Referral/Specialty Physicians: 57,550
Total Enrollment: 975,000

Healthplan and Services Defined
PLAN TYPE: PPO
Model Type: Network
Plan Specialty: Behavioral Health, Chiropractic, EPO, Lab, Vision,
Radiology, Worker's Compensation, UR
Benefits Offered: Behavioral Health, Chiropractic, Disease
Management, Home Care, Inpatient SNF, Long-Term Care,
Physical Therapy, Podiatry, Psychiatric, Transplant, Vision,
Wellness, Worker's Compensation

Type of Coverage
Catastrophic Illness Benefit: Varies per case

Type of Payment Plans Offered
POS, DFFS, FFS

Geographic Areas Served
Connecticut, New Jersey & New York

Subscriber Information
Average Monthly Fee Per Subscriber
(Employee + Employer Contribution):
Employee Only (Self): Varies
Employee & 1 Family Member: Varies
Employee & 2 Family Members: Varies
Medicare: Varies
Average Annual Deductible Per Subscriber:
Employee Only (Self): Varies
Employee & 1 Family Member: Varies
Employee & 2 Family Members: Varies
Medicare: Varies
Average Subscriber Co-Payment:
Primary Care Physician: Varies
Non-Network Physician: Varies
Prescription Drugs: Varies
Hospital ER: Varies
Home Health Care: Varies
Home Health Care Max. Days/Visits Covered: Varies
Nursing Home: Varies
Nursing Home Max. Days/Visits Covered: Varies

Network Qualifications
Pre-Admission Certification: Yes

Peer Review Type
Utilization Review: Yes
Second Surgical Opinion: Yes
Case Management: Yes

Accreditation Certification
URAC, AAPI
TJC Accreditation, Medicare Approved, Utilization Review,
Pre-Admission Certification, State Licensure, Quality Assurance
Program

Key Personnel
President/CEO...........................Michael A Morrone
Executive VP/COO ....Craig Goldstein
SVP, Utilization Mgmt Off....................John Miller, RN
SVP, Financial Operations.....................Lee Ann Iannelli
VP, Network Operations....................Cara Ianniello, RN
VP, Medical Case Mgmt..................Maria Longwoth, RN
Medial Director ....Robert A Ericksen
Chief Medical Officer ....William A Anthony, MD
VP, Human Resources ....Lawrence Lowry
SVP, Chief Info Officer ....Stan Tomasevich
VP, Client Services ....Missy Pudimott
missy.pudimott@chn.com
Vice President, Sales ....Steve Armenti

Average Claim Compensation
Physician's Fees Charged: 33%
Hospital's Fees Charged: 40%

Specialty Managed Care Partners
Enters into Contracts with Regional Business Coalitions: Yes

723 CIGNA HealthCare of New Jersey
499 Washington Boulevard
Suite 526
Jersey City, NJ 07310
Toll-Free: 866-438-2446
Phone: 201-533-7000
Fax: 201-533-7164
www.cigna.com
Secondary Address: Great-West Healthcare, now part of CIGNA, 1
Centennial Ave, 1st Floor, Piscataway, NJ 08855, 732-357-2900

For Profit Organization: Yes
Year Founded: 1978
Number of Affiliated Hospitals: 82
Number of Primary Care Physicians: 5,250
Number of Referral/Specialty Physicians: 12,240
Total Enrollment: 68,935
State Enrollment: 68,935

Healthplan and Services Defined
 PLAN TYPE: HMO
Other Type: POS
Model Type: Network, PPO, POS
Plan Specialty: ASO, Behavioral Health, Dental, Disease Management
Benefits Offered: Behavioral Health, Chiropractic, Dental, Disease
Management, Home Care, Physical Therapy, Podiatry, Prescription,
Psychiatric, Transplant, Vision, Wellness, Worker's Compensation

Type of Coverage
Commercial
Catastrophic Illness Benefit: Varies per case

Type of Payment Plans Offered
POS, FFS

Geographic Areas Served
Bergen, Essex, Hudson, Hunterdon, Middlesex, Monmouth, Morris,
Passaic, Somerset, Sussex, Union, Warren, Atlantic. Burlington,
Camden, Cape May, Cumberland, Gloucester, Ocean and Mercer
counties

Subscriber Information
Average Monthly Fee Per Subscriber
(Employee + Employer Contribution):
Employee Only (Self): Varies by plan
Average Subscriber Co-Payment:
Primary Care Physician: $10/15/20

Network Qualifications
Pre-Admission Certification: Yes

Peer Review Type
Utilization Review: Yes
Second Surgical Opinion: Yes
Case Management: Yes

Accreditation Certification
NCQA

Key Personnel
President....................................Charles Catalano
CFO..Michael Wise
VP Network ....Thomas Garvey
VP Medical Executive ....Don Nicoll, MD
Director Provider Services...................Ann Marie Castro
VP Sales ....Mike Mascolo

Specialty Managed Care Partners
Enters into Contracts with Regional Business Coalitions: Yes

724 Delta Dental of New Jersey & Connecticut
1639 Route 10
PO Box 222
Parsippany, NJ 07054-0222
Toll-Free: 800-452-9310
Phone: 973-285-4000
Fax: 973-285-4141
marketing@deltadentalnj.com
www.deltadentalnj.com
Non-Profit Organization: Yes
Year Founded: 1969
Total Enrollment: 54,000,000

Healthplan and Services Defined
 PLAN TYPE: Dental
Other Type: Dental HMO/PPO/POS
Model Type: Staff
Plan Specialty: Dental
Benefits Offered: Dental

Type of Coverage
Commercial

Type of Payment Plans Offered
POS, DFFS, Capitated, FFS, Combination FFS & DFFS

Geographic Areas Served
New Jersey and Connecticut

Key Personnel
President/CEO . . . . Walter VenBrunt
CFO. . . . . James Suleski
Senior Vice President . . . . Bruce Silverman
Vice President . . . . Scott Navarro, DDS
Vice President . . . . Mark Nadeau
Dir/Media & Public Affair . . . . Elizabeth Risberg
415-972-8423

725 eHealthInsurance Services Inc.
11919 Foundation Place
Gold River, CA 95670
Toll-Free: 800-977-8860
info@ehealthinsurance.com
www.e.healthinsurance.com
Year Founded: 1997

Healthplan and Services Defined
PLAN TYPE: HMO/PPO
Benefits Offered: Dental, Life, STD

Type of Coverage
Commercial, Individual, Medicare

Geographic Areas Served
All 50 states in the USA and District of Columbia

Key Personnel
Chairman & CEO . . . . Gary L. Lauer
EVP/Business & Corp. Dev. Bruce Telkamp
EVP/Chief Technology . . . . Dr. Sheldon X. Wang
SVP & CFO . . . . Stuart M. Huizinga
Pres. of eHealth Gov. Sys . . . . Samuel C. Gibbs
SVP of Sales & Operations . . . . Robert S. Hurley
Director Public Relations . . . . Nate Purpura
650-210-3115

726 Family Choice Health Alliance
401 Hackensack Avenue
Hackensack, NJ 07601
Toll-Free: 800-732-7892
Phone: 201-487-6002
customerservice@familychoicehealth.com
www.familychoicehealth.com
For Profit Organization: Yes
Year Founded: 1991
Number of Affiliated Hospitals: 51
Number of Primary Care Physicians: 10,000
State Enrollment: 115,000

Healthplan and Services Defined
PLAN TYPE: PPO
Model Type: Network
Benefits Offered: Chiropractic, Dental, Disease Management, Home
Care, Vision, Wellness

Type of Coverage
Commercial, Individual

Type of Payment Plans Offered
Combination FFS & DFFS

Geographic Areas Served
Statewide

Subscriber Information
Average Monthly Fee Per Subscriber
(Employee + Employer Contribution):
Employee Only (Self): Varies by plan

Average Annual Deductible Per Subscriber:
Employee Only (Self): $250.00
Average Subscriber Co-Payment:
Primary Care Physician: $10.00

Network Qualifications
Pre-Admission Certification: No

Peer Review Type
Utilization Review: Yes
Second Surgical Opinion: No
Case Management: No

Accreditation Certification
TJC Accreditation, Medicare Approved, Utilization Review,
Pre-Admission Certification, State Licensure, Quality Assurance
Program

Key Personnel
President/CEO . . . . Andrew H Baker
CFO. . . . . Jim Giacobello
Marketing. . . . . Karen Piotti
Medical Affairs . . . . Sheldon Ashley
Provider Services . . . . Jo-carol Leonard
Sales. . . . . Karen Piotti

Specialty Managed Care Partners
Enters into Contracts with Regional Business Coalitions: Yes

727 FC Diagnostic
401 Hackensack Avenue
Hackensack, NJ 07601
Toll-Free: 800-833-2132
Phone: 201-487-6001
customerservice@fcdiagnostic.com
www.fcdiagnostic.com
Year Founded: 1989
Number of Primary Care Physicians: 6,000

Healthplan and Services Defined
PLAN TYPE: PPO
Model Type: Network
Plan Specialty: Lab, Radiology
Benefits Offered: Physical Therapy, Diagnostic Imaging,
Laboratories, Rehabilitation

Geographic Areas Served
Nationwide

Accreditation Certification
Quality Assurance Program

Key Personnel
President/CEO . . . . Andrew H Baker
CFO. . . . . Jim Giacobello
Marketing. . . . . Karen Piotti
Provider Services . . . . Jo-carol Leonard
Sales. . . . . Karen Piotti

728 Great-West Healthcare of New Jersey
Acquired by CIGNA

729 HealthFirst New Jersey Medicare Plan
PO Box 12105
Newark, NJ 07101-3405
Toll-Free: 877-464-4365
Fax: 866-202-3874
webmaster@healthfirst.org
www.healthfirstnj.com
Non-Profit Organization: Yes
Number of Affiliated Hospitals: 21
Total Enrollment: 500,000
State Enrollment: 500,000

Healthplan and Services Defined
PLAN TYPE: Medicare

Type of Coverage
Medicare

Key Personnel

President & CEO	Patricia Wang, JD
EVP, COO	Daniel McCarthy
SVP, Business Development	Michael Honig
President/HealthFirst NJ	Terence L Byrd
SVP, General Counsel	Elizabeth St. Clair, Esq
SVP, CFO	Marybeth Tita
Dir, NJ Network Mgmt	Jessica Gamzon
VP, Compliance	Sonya L Henderson
Chief Marketing Officer	John Cheng
Dir, Medicaid Outreach	Anna Enriquez
VP, Medical Director	Deborah Hammond, MD
VP, Human Resources	Andrea Forino
SVP, Chief Info Officer	Steven Sakovits
Dir, Medicare Sales	Grace Santos
Director, Operations	John J Kirchner

730 Horizon Blue Cross & Blue Shield of New Jersey

3 Penn Plaza E
PO Box 820
Newark, NJ 07101-0820
Toll-Free: 800-355-2583
Phone: 973-466-4000
www.horizon-bcbsnj.com
Secondary Address: 33 Washington Street, Newark, NJ 07102
Non-Profit Organization: Yes
Year Founded: 1932
Number of Affiliated Hospitals: 65
Number of Primary Care Physicians: 961
Total Enrollment: 3,600,000
State Enrollment: 3,600,000

Healthplan and Services Defined
PLAN TYPE: HMO/PPO
Other Type: POS
Model Type: Staff, Network
Benefits Offered: Behavioral Health, Dental, Prescription, Psychiatric, Worker's Compensation
Offers Demand Management Patient Information Service: Yes

Type of Coverage
Commercial, Individual, Indemnity, Medicare
Catastrophic Illness Benefit: None

Type of Payment Plans Offered
POS, Combination FFS & DFFS

Geographic Areas Served
All of North, Central and Southern New Jersey

Subscriber Information
Average Monthly Fee Per Subscriber
(Employee + Employer Contribution):
Employee Only (Self): Varies by plan
Average Subscriber Co-Payment:
Primary Care Physician: 100% in network/70%
Non-Network Physician: Not covered
Prescription Drugs: $3.00/6.00
Hospital ER: $35.00
Home Health Care: $0
Nursing Home: $0

Network Qualifications
Pre-Admission Certification: Yes

Peer Review Type
Utilization Review: Yes
Second Surgical Opinion: Yes
Case Management: Yes

Accreditation Certification
AAAHC, URAC, NCQA

TJC Accreditation, Medicare Approved, Utilization Review, Pre-Admission Certification, State Licensure, Quality Assurance Program

Key Personnel

President/CEO	William J Marino
SVP, CFO & Treasurer	Robert J Pures
SVP, Gen Counsel & Secr	Linda Willett
EVP, COO	Robert A Marino
SVP, Service	Mark Barnard
SVP/Market Business Units	Christopher M Lepre
Pres\CEO, Horiz Health NJ	Christy W Bell
Dir, Public Affairs	Thomas W Rubino, Esq

973-468-8755
trubino@horizonblue.com

Mgr, Public Relations	Thomas Vincz

973-466-6625
thomas_vincz@horizonblue.com

Specialty Managed Care Partners
Enters into Contracts with Regional Business Coalitions: Yes

Employer References
Lesnevich & Marzano-Lesnevich

731 Horizon Healthcare of New Jersey
Acquired by Horizon Blue Cross & Blue Shield

732 Horizon NJ Health

210 Silvia Street
West Trenton, NJ 08628
Toll-Free: 877-765-4325
Phone: 609-538-0700
www.horizonnjhealth.com
Subsidiary of: Horizon Blue Cross Blue Shield of NJ
Year Founded: 1993
Total Enrollment: 467,000
State Enrollment: 467,000

Healthplan and Services Defined
PLAN TYPE: PPO
Model Type: Network
Benefits Offered: Dental, Disease Management, Prescription, Vision, Wellness

Type of Coverage
Individual, Medicaid

Geographic Areas Served
All 21 New Jersey counties

Accreditation Certification
URAC

Key Personnel

President & COO	Karen L Clark
Controller	James D'Alessio
Dir, Marketing & Comm	Len Kudgis
Chief Medical Officer	Philip M Bonaparte, MD
Media Contact	Carol Chernack

609-718-9290
carol_chernack@horizonnjhealth.com

733 Humana Health Insurance of New Jersey

1 International Blvd
Suite 400
Mahwah, NJ 07495
Toll-Free: 800-967-2370
Phone: 201-512-8818
www.humana.com
For Profit Organization: Yes

Healthplan and Services Defined
PLAN TYPE: HMO/PPO

Type of Coverage
  Commercial, Individual

Accreditation Certification
  URAC, NCQA, CORE

734 Managed Healthcare Systems of New Jersey
Acquired by Americhoice of New Jersey

735 One Call Medical
20 Waterview Boulevard
PO Box 614
Parsippany, NJ 07054
Toll-Free: 800-872-2875
Phone: 973-257-1000
Fax: 973-257-9284
webqcustomerservice@onecallmedical.com
www.onecallmedical.com
For Profit Organization: Yes
Year Founded: 1993

Healthplan and Services Defined
  PLAN TYPE: PPO
  Model Type: Network
  Benefits Offered: Worker's Compensation, Group Health

Type of Payment Plans Offered
  POS, DFFS, FFS, Combination FFS & DFFS

Geographic Areas Served
  Nationwide

Network Qualifications
  Pre-Admission Certification: Yes

Publishes and Distributes Report Card: No

Accreditation Certification
  Utilization Review, Quality Assurance Program

Key Personnel
  President & COO..............................Don Duford
  Chief Executive Officer.......................Kent Spafford
  Chief Financial Officer........................Warren Green
  VP, Business Development.......................Bob Zeccardi
    610-453-5910
  Business Development...........................Lori Lentz
    803-749-4101

Specialty Managed Care Partners
  Enters into Contracts with Regional Business Coalitions: No

736 Oxford Health Plans: New Jersey
111 Woods Avenue
Suite 2
Iselin, NJ 08830
Toll-Free: 800-201-6920
Phone: 732-623-1000
www.oxhp.com
For Profit Organization: Yes
Year Founded: 1985
Total Enrollment: 332,840
State Enrollment: 59,800

Healthplan and Services Defined
  PLAN TYPE: HMO
  Model Type: IPA
  Benefits Offered: Disease Management, Prescription, Wellness

Type of Coverage
  Commercial, Medicare

Type of Payment Plans Offered
  Capitated

Geographic Areas Served
  Sussex, Passaic, Bergen, Morris, Warren, Essex, Hudson, Union,
  Hunterdon, Somerset, Middlesex, Mercer, Monmouth, Ocean,
  Burlington, Camden, Gloucester, Salem, Cumberland, Atlantic, Cape
  May counties

Key Personnel
  President/CEO..............................Charles G Berg
  COO.......................................Steven H Black
  CFO.......................................Kurt B Thompson
  CMO.......................................Alan M Muney
  General Counsel..........................Daniel N Gregoire
  Provider Relations..........................Paul Conlin
  Sales/Marketing............................Kevin R Hill
  Member Relations........................Kevin Appleton
  Pharmacy Director........................Burton Orland
  Public Relations......................Maria Gordon Shydlo

737 QualCare
30 Knightbridge Road
Piscataway, NJ 08854
Toll-Free: 800-992-6613
Phone: 732-562-0833
Fax: 732-562-2833
info@qualcareinc.com
www.qualcareinc.com
For Profit Organization: Yes
Year Founded: 1993
Federally Qualified: Yes
Number of Affiliated Hospitals: 75
Number of Primary Care Physicians: 9,000
Number of Referral/Specialty Physicians: 14,000
Total Enrollment: 750,000
State Enrollment: 750,000

Healthplan and Services Defined
  PLAN TYPE: HMO/PPO
  Other Type: POS
  Model Type: Network
  Plan Specialty: ASO, Behavioral Health, Chiropractic, Dental,
    Disease Management, EPO, Lab, MSO, PBM, Vision, Radiology,
    Worker's Compensation, UR
  Benefits Offered: Behavioral Health, Chiropractic, Complementary
    Medicine, Dental, Disease Management, Home Care, Inpatient
    SNF, Long-Term Care, Physical Therapy, Podiatry, Prescription,
    Psychiatric, Transplant, Vision, Wellness, Worker's Compensation,
    AD&D, Life, LTD, ST
  Offers Demand Management Patient Information Service: Yes

Type of Coverage
  Commercial

Type of Payment Plans Offered
  FFS

Geographic Areas Served
  Statewide

Peer Review Type
  Utilization Review: Yes
  Second Surgical Opinion: Yes
  Case Management: Yes

Publishes and Distributes Report Card: Yes

Accreditation Certification
  AAAHC, TJC, AAPI, NCQA
  Medicare Approved, Utilization Review, State Licensure, Quality
    Assurance Program

Key Personnel
  President..................................Annette Catino
  CFO.......................................John McSorley
  VP/Marketing & Sales.......................Allison Hofmann
  Medical Director..........................Bruce Fisher, MD
  EVP, COO.................................Sharon Seitzman
  VP Provider Services..........................Kevin Joyce

VP Business Development . . . . Tim Ford
VP/Finance & Controller . . . . Janet Buggle
VP/Operations . . . . Charlene Renollet
VP/Medical Informatics . . . . Maureen Bueno
VP/Regional & Spec Accts . . . . Dawn Wright

Specialty Managed Care Partners
Multiplan

738 Rayant Insurance Company

3 Penn Plaza East
PP03C
Newark, NJ 07105
www.rayant.com
Subsidiary of: Horizon Healthcare Services
For Profit Organization: Yes
Total Enrollment: 21,000

Healthplan and Services Defined
PLAN TYPE: Dental
Plan Specialty: Dental
Benefits Offered: Dental

Geographic Areas Served
New York and Pennsylvania

Key Personnel
Chairman/President/CEO . . . . William J Marino
EVP/COO . . . . Robert A Marino
SVP Admin, CFO, Treasurer . . . . Robert J Pures
SVP/Information Tech . . . . Mark Barnard
VP, Chief Actuary . . . . Edward M Mailander
VP, Chief Medical Officer . . . . Richard G Popiel
VP, Chief Pharmacy Offc. . . . . Margaret M Johnson
SVP, General Counsel . . . . Linda A Willett

739 UnitedHealthCare of New Jersey

170 Wood Avenue South
3rd Floor
Iselin, NJ 08830
Toll-Free: 866-223-5802
Phone: 732-623-1000
www.uhc.com
For Profit Organization: Yes
Total Enrollment: 75,000,000
State Enrollment: 431,833

Healthplan and Services Defined
PLAN TYPE: HMO/PPO

Geographic Areas Served
Statewide

740 VSP: Vision Service Plan of New Jersey

1 Gatehall Drive
Suite 303
Parsippany, NJ 07054-4514
Phone: 973-538-2626
Fax: 973-538-0368
webmaster@vsp.com
www.vsp.com
Year Founded: 1955
Number of Primary Care Physicians: 26,000
Total Enrollment: 55,000,000

Healthplan and Services Defined
PLAN TYPE: Vision
Plan Specialty: Vision
Benefits Offered: Vision

Type of Payment Plans Offered
Capitated

Geographic Areas Served
Statewide

Network Qualifications
Pre-Admission Certification: Yes

Peer Review Type
Utilization Review: Yes

Accreditation Certification
Utilization Review, Quality Assurance Program

Key Personnel
Manager . . . . Karen Bennett

741 WellChoice

120 Wood Avenue S
Suite 200
Iselin, NJ 08830
Toll-Free: 888-476-8069
Phone: 888-476-6986
Fax: 888-592-3154
www.wellchoicenj.com
Subsidiary of: Wellpoint
For Profit Organization: Yes
Year Founded: 1998
Number of Affiliated Hospitals: 231
Number of Primary Care Physicians: 92,000
Total Enrollment: 12,317
State Enrollment: 12,317

Healthplan and Services Defined
PLAN TYPE: HMO

Geographic Areas Served
Northern and central New Jersey

Subscriber Information
Average Subscriber Co-Payment:
Primary Care Physician: $5.00 to 50.00

Key Personnel
President . . . . Dan McCarthy
Vice President/Sales . . . . Christopher Fallon

HMO/PPO DIRECTORY

NEW MEXICO

Health Insurance Coverage Status and Type of Coverage by Age

Category	All Persons		Under 18 years		Under 65 years		65 years and over	
	Number	%	Number	%	Number	%	Number	%
Total population	2,015	-	521	-	1,737	-	278	-
Covered by some type of health insurance	1,580 *(33)*	78.4 *(1.5)*	450 *(11)*	86.3 *(2.3)*	1,308 *(32)*	75.3 *(1.7)*	272 *(16)*	97.8 *(1.0)*
Covered by private health insurance	1,056 *(46)*	52.4 *(2.2)*	247 *(22)*	47.4 *(4.1)*	930 *(46)*	53.6 *(2.5)*	126 *(12)*	45.3 *(3.6)*
Employment based	934 *(42)*	46.4 *(2.1)*	233 *(20)*	44.8 *(3.9)*	840 *(42)*	48.4 *(2.3)*	94 *(11)*	33.7 *(3.2)*
Own employment based	480 *(21)*	23.8 *(1.0)*	1 *(1)*	0.2 *(0.2)*	413 *(22)*	23.8 *(1.2)*	67 *(8)*	24.2 *(2.4)*
Direct purchase	115 *(19)*	5.7 *(0.9)*	15 *(6)*	2.9 *(1.1)*	82 *(16)*	4.7 *(0.9)*	33 *(6)*	12.0 *(2.4)*
Covered by government health insurance	763 *(42)*	37.9 *(2.0)*	254 *(19)*	48.7 *(3.6)*	503 *(36)*	28.9 *(2.1)*	260 *(17)*	93.5 *(1.8)*
Covered by Medicaid	426 *(29)*	21.1 *(1.4)*	239 *(18)*	45.9 *(3.4)*	409 *(29)*	23.6 *(1.7)*	16 *(6)*	5.9 *(2.0)*
Also by private insurance	75 *(16)*	3.7 *(0.8)*	41 *(10)*	7.8 *(2.0)*	75 *(16)*	4.3 *(0.9)*	1 *(1)*	0.2 *(0.2)*
Covered by Medicare	303 *(20)*	15.0 *(1.0)*	0 *(0)*	0.0 *(0.0)*	47 *(8)*	2.7 *(0.4)*	256 *(17)*	92.1 *(2.0)*
Also by private insurance	120 *(11)*	6.0 *(0.6)*	0 *(0)*	0.0 *(0.0)*	9 *(3)*	0.5 *(0.2)*	111 *(11)*	39.9 *(3.4)*
Also by Medicaid	44 *(9)*	2.2 *(0.4)*	0 *(0)*	0.0 *(0.0)*	28 *(8)*	1.6 *(0.5)*	16 *(5)*	5.6 *(2.0)*
Covered by military health care	118 *(31)*	5.9 *(1.5)*	17 *(8)*	3.2 *(1.5)*	88 *(24)*	5.1 *(1.4)*	30 *(10)*	10.9 *(3.5)*
Not covered at any time during the year	435 *(32)*	21.6 *(1.5)*	71 *(12)*	13.7 *(2.3)*	429 *(31)*	24.7 *(1.7)*	6 *(3)*	2.2 *(1.0)*

Note: Numbers in thousands; figures cover 2010; standard error appears in parenthesis; (b) base less than 75,000; (x) not applicable
Source: U.S. Census Bureau, Current Population Survey, 2011 Annual Social and Economic Supplement. Table HI05. Health Insurance Coverage Status and Type of Coverage by State and Age for All People: 2010

New Mexico

742 Aetna Health of New Mexico

Partnered with eHealthInsurance Services Inc.

743 Amerigroup New Mexico

Two Park Square
6565 Americas Parkway NE, Suite 110
Albuquerque, NM 87110
Toll-Free: 888-997-2583
www.realsolutions.com
For Profit Organization: Yes
Year Founded: 2008
Total Enrollment: 1,900,000

Healthplan and Services Defined
PLAN TYPE: HMO

Type of Coverage
Medicare, Coordiation of Long Term Care Svcs.

744 Blue Cross & Blue Shield of New Mexico

5701 Balloon Fiesta Parkway
Albuquerque, NM 87113
Toll-Free: 800-835-8699
Phone: 505-291-3500
Fax: 505-816-5556
www.bcbsnm.com
Mailing Address: PO Box 27630, Albuquerque, NM 87125-7630
Subsidiary of: Health Care Service Corporation
Non-Profit Organization: Yes
Year Founded: 1940
Owned by an Integrated Delivery Network (IDN): Yes
Number of Affiliated Hospitals: 54
Number of Primary Care Physicians: 3,322
Number of Referral/Specialty Physicians: 6,742
Total Enrollment: 367,000
State Enrollment: 367,000

Healthplan and Services Defined
PLAN TYPE: HMO/PPO
Other Type: EPO, CDHP
Model Type: Network
Plan Specialty: ASO, Behavioral Health
Benefits Offered: Dental, Disease Management, Vision, Wellness, Medical, Case Management
Offers Demand Management Patient Information Service: Yes
DMPI Services Offered: Fully Insured

Type of Coverage
Commercial, Individual, Indemnity, Supplemental Medicare

Geographic Areas Served
Statewide

Network Qualifications
Pre-Admission Certification: Yes

Peer Review Type
Utilization Review: Yes
Second Surgical Opinion: Yes

Publishes and Distributes Report Card: Yes

Accreditation Certification
NCQA

Key Personnel
President . . . . Liz Watrin
CFO . . . . Kurt Shipley
VP, General Counsel . . . . Margaret McNett
VP Subscriber Services . . . . Linda Amburn
VP Health Care Management . . . . Tom Maclean
Marketing . . . . Bette Bolton
Materials Management . . . . Liz Carrillo

VP, Sales . . . . Jeff Newland
Media Contact . . . . Becky Kenny
505-816-2012
becky_kenny@bcbsnm.com

Specialty Managed Care Partners
Pharmacy Manager, Prime Theraputics

745 CIGNA HealthCare of New Mexico

6565 Americas Parkway
Suite 150
Albuquerque, NM 87110
Toll-Free: 866-438-2446
Fax: 505-872-2946
www.cigna.com
For Profit Organization: Yes
Year Founded: 1981
Owned by an Integrated Delivery Network (IDN): Yes

Healthplan and Services Defined
PLAN TYPE: HMO
Other Type: POS
Model Type: IPA
Plan Specialty: ASO, Behavioral Health, Chiropractic, Dental, Disease Management, EPO, Lab, MSO, PBM, Vision, Radiology, UR
Benefits Offered: Behavioral Health, Chiropractic, Dental, Disease Management, Home Care, Inpatient SNF, Physical Therapy, Podiatry, Prescription, Psychiatric, Transplant, Vision, Wellness, Life

Type of Coverage
Commercial

Type of Payment Plans Offered
FFS, Combination FFS & DFFS

Geographic Areas Served
Atlanta & Metro Area

Subscriber Information
Average Annual Deductible Per Subscriber:
Employee Only (Self): $0
Employee & 1 Family Member: $0
Employee & 2 Family Members: $0
Average Subscriber Co-Payment:
Primary Care Physician: $15.00
Non-Network Physician: Varies
Prescription Drugs: $10.00
Hospital ER: $50.00
Home Health Care: $0

Network Qualifications
Pre-Admission Certification: Yes

Peer Review Type
Utilization Review: Yes
Second Surgical Opinion: Yes
Case Management: Yes

Publishes and Distributes Report Card: Yes

Accreditation Certification
NCQA
TJC Accreditation, Utilization Review, Pre-Admission Certification, State Licensure, Quality Assurance Program

Specialty Managed Care Partners
Enters into Contracts with Regional Business Coalitions: No

746 Delta Dental of New Mexico

2500 Louisiana Boulevard NE
Suite 600
Albuquerque, NM 87110
Toll-Free: 877-395-9420
Phone: 505-855-7111
Fax: 505-883-7444

contact@deltadental.com
www.deltadentalnm.com
Non-Profit Organization: Yes
Year Founded: 1973
Number of Primary Care Physicians: 1,186
Total Enrollment: 54,000,000
State Enrollment: 200,000

Healthplan and Services Defined
    PLAN TYPE: Dental
    Other Type: Dental PPO
    Model Type: Group
    Plan Specialty: ASO, Dental, Vision
    Benefits Offered: Dental, Vision
    Offers Demand Management Patient Information Service: Yes

Type of Coverage
    Commercial

Geographic Areas Served
    Statewide

Network Qualifications
    Pre-Admission Certification: Yes

Publishes and Distributes Report Card: Yes

Key Personnel
    President and CEO.............................Walter S Bolic
    CFO..David Griswold
    CIO..Norma Cooper
    VP Marketing.................................Gail Davalos
    VP, Public & Govt Affairs....................Jeff Album
    415-972-8418

Specialty Managed Care Partners
    Enters into Contracts with Regional Business Coalitions: Yes

747 eHealthInsurance Services Inc.
11919 Foundation Place
Gold River, CA 95670
Toll-Free: 800-977-8860
info@ehealthinsurance.com
www.e.healthinsurance.com
Year Founded: 1997

Healthplan and Services Defined
    PLAN TYPE: HMO/PPO
    Benefits Offered: Dental, Life, STD

Type of Coverage
    Commercial, Individual, Medicare

Geographic Areas Served
    All 50 states in the USA and District of Columbia

Key Personnel
    Chairman & CEO..............................Gary L. Lauer
    EVP/Business & Corp. Dev....................Bruce Telkamp
    EVP/Chief Technology........................Dr. Sheldon X. Wang
    SVP & CFO...................................Stuart M. Huizinga
    Pres. of eHealth Gov. Sys...................Samuel C. Gibbs
    SVP of Sales & Operations...................Robert S. Hurley
    Director Public Relations...................Nate Purpura
    650-210-3115

748 Great-West Healthcare New Mexico
Acquired by CIGNA

749 Humana Health Insurance of New Mexico
4904 Alameda Blvd NE
Suite A
Albuquerque, NM 87113
Toll-Free: 800-681-0680
Phone: 505-468-0500
Fax: 505-468-0554

www.humana.com
For Profit Organization: Yes

Healthplan and Services Defined
    PLAN TYPE: HMO/PPO

Type of Coverage
    Commercial, Individual

Accreditation Certification
    URAC, NCQA, CORE

750 Lovelace Health Plan
4101 Indian School Road NE
Altura Office Complex
Albuquerque, NM 87110
Toll-Free: 800-808-7363
Phone: 505-727-5500
Fax: 505-262-7307
www.lovelacehealthplan.com
Mailing Address: PO Box 27107
Subsidiary of: Ardent
For Profit Organization: Yes
Year Founded: 1973
Owned by an Integrated Delivery Network (IDN): Yes
Number of Affiliated Hospitals: 39
Number of Primary Care Physicians: 7,000
Number of Referral/Specialty Physicians: 5,000
Total Enrollment: 163,000
State Enrollment: 68,674

Healthplan and Services Defined
    PLAN TYPE: HMO
    Model Type: Network
    Plan Specialty: ASO, Behavioral Health, Chiropractic, Disease
        Management, EPO, Lab, MSO, PBM, Vision, Radiology, UR
    Benefits Offered: Behavioral Health, Chiropractic, Complementary
        Medicine, Disease Management, Home Care, Inpatient SNF,
        Long-Term Care, Physical Therapy, Podiatry, Prescription,
        Psychiatric, Transplant, Vision, Wellness

Type of Coverage
    Commercial, Medicare
    Catastrophic Illness Benefit: Covered

Type of Payment Plans Offered
    POS, DFFS, FFS

Geographic Areas Served
    Statewide

Network Qualifications
    Pre-Admission Certification: No

Peer Review Type
    Utilization Review: Yes
    Second Surgical Opinion: No
    Case Management: Yes

Accreditation Certification
    NCQA
    TJC Accreditation, Medicare Approved, Utilization Review,
        Pre-Admission Certification, State Licensure, Quality Assurance
        Program

Key Personnel
    Chief Executive Officer......................Dennis Wilson
    Chief Operating Officer......................Rohan Reid
    Chief Financial Officer......................Frank Ulibarri
    AVP, Commercial Sales........................Douglas Gullino
    Asst VP, Underwriting........................Carole Henry
    Asst VP, Quality Health......................Linda Hubbard
    Chief Medical Officer........................Wayne M Casper, MD
    Director, Human Resources....................Patricia Harris
    Asst VP, Info Services.......................Bob Skinner
    Compliance Officer...........................Ann Greenberg
    Chief Sales Officer..........................Marlene Baca

Media Contact . . . . Susan Wilson
505-727-4440
susan.wilson@lovelace.com

Specialty Managed Care Partners
CIGNA Behavioral Health

751 Lovelace Medicare Health Plan
4101 Indian School Road Northeast
Suite 110
Albuquerque, NM 87110
Toll-Free: 800-808-7363
Phone: 505-727-LOVE
serena.lyons@lovelace.com
www.lovelacehealthplan.com
Number of Affiliated Hospitals: 40
Number of Referral/Specialty Physicians: 7,000
Total Enrollment: 200,000

Healthplan and Services Defined
PLAN TYPE: HMO/PPO
Plan Specialty: Medicare, Medicaid
Benefits Offered: Chiropractic, Dental, Disease Management, Home
Care, Inpatient SNF, Physical Therapy, Podiatry, Prescription,
Psychiatric, Vision, Wellness

Type of Coverage
Individual, Medicare

Geographic Areas Served
Available witin New Mexico only

Subscriber Information
Average Monthly Fee Per Subscriber
(Employee + Employer Contribution):
Employee Only (Self): Varies
Medicare: Varies
Average Annual Deductible Per Subscriber:
Employee Only (Self): Varies
Medicare: Varies
Average Subscriber Co-Payment:
Primary Care Physician: Varies
Non-Network Physician: Varies
Prescription Drugs: Varies
Hospital ER: Varies
Home Health Care: Varies
Home Health Care Max. Days/Visits Covered: Varies
Nursing Home: Varies
Nursing Home Max. Days/Visits Covered: Varies

Key Personnel
CEO . . . . .Dennis Wilson
COO . . . . .Rohan Reid
CFO . . . . .Frank Ulibarri
AVP, Commercial Sales . . . . .Douglas Gullino
Asst VP, Underwriting. .Carole Henry
Asst VP, Quality Health . . . . .Linda Hubbard
Marketing. . . . . .Serena Lyons
Medical Director . . . . .Jami Frost, MD
Dir, Human Resources. . . . . .Patricia Harris
Asst VP, Info Services. .Bob Skinner
VP Legal Operations . . . . .Angela Martinez
Chief Sales & Service Ofc . . . . .Marlene Baca

752 Molina Healthcare: New Mexico
8801 Horizon Boulevard NE
P.O. Box 3887
Albuquerque, NM 87113
Toll-Free: 800-377-9594
Phone: 505-342-4660
www.molinahealthcare.com
For Profit Organization: Yes
Number of Affiliated Hospitals: 60

Number of Primary Care Physicians: 1,511
Number of Referral/Specialty Physicians: 5,799
Total Enrollment: 1,400,000
State Enrollment: 83,000

Healthplan and Services Defined
PLAN TYPE: HMO
Benefits Offered: Disease Management, Wellness

Type of Coverage
Commercial, Medicare, Supplemental Medicare, Medicaid

Accreditation Certification
URAC, NCQA

Key Personnel
President . . . . .Ann Wehr, MD
888-562-5442
ann.wehr@molinahealthcare.com
COO . . . . .Lynn Allen
888-562-5442
lynn.allen@molinahealthcare.com
CFO . . . . .Todd Pilger
888-562-5442
todd.pilger@molinahealthcare.com
Chief Medical Officer . . . . .Eugene Sun, MD
505-342-4660
eugene.sun@molinahealthcare.com

753 Presbyterian Health Plan
2501 Buena Vista SE
Albuquerque, NM 87106
Toll-Free: 866-388-7737
Phone: 505-841-1234
Fax: 505-923-8163
info@phs.org
www.phs.org
Non-Profit Organization: Yes
Year Founded: 1985
Number of Affiliated Hospitals: 28
Number of Primary Care Physicians: 1,200
Number of Referral/Specialty Physicians: 4,850
Total Enrollment: 400,000
State Enrollment: 400,000

Healthplan and Services Defined
PLAN TYPE: HMO
Other Type: POS
Model Type: Contracted Network

Type of Coverage
Commercial, Medicare, Medicaid

Type of Payment Plans Offered
POS, DFFS, Capitated, FFS

Geographic Areas Served
State of New Mexico

Subscriber Information
Average Monthly Fee Per Subscriber
(Employee + Employer Contribution):
Employee Only (Self): Varies by plan
Average Subscriber Co-Payment:
Primary Care Physician: $10.00
Prescription Drugs: $0
Hospital ER: $50.00

Accreditation Certification
NCQA

Key Personnel
President . . . . .Dennis Batey, MD
Chief Financial Officer. .Lisa Farrell
VP, Chief Service Officer. . . . . .Jana Burdick
VP, Government Programs . . . . .Mary Eden
Exed Dir, Health Info . . . . .Cesar Goulart
VP, Chief Medical Officer. . . . . .Chuck Baumgart, MD

VP, Sales & Marketing . . . . Neal Spero

Employer References
State of New Mexico, Albuquerque Public Schools, Intel Corporation

754 Presbyterian Medicare Plans

PO Box 27489
Albuquerque, NM 87125-7489
Toll-Free: 800-347-4766
Phone: 505-923-8972
info@phs.org
www.phs.org

Healthplan and Services Defined
PLAN TYPE: Medicare
Benefits Offered: Chiropractic, Dental, Disease Management, Home Care, Inpatient SNF, Physical Therapy, Podiatry, Prescription, Psychiatric, Vision, Wellness

Type of Coverage
Individual, Medicare, Employer Group

Geographic Areas Served
Available within New Mexico only

Subscriber Information
Average Monthly Fee Per Subscriber
(Employee + Employer Contribution):
Employee Only (Self): Varies
Medicare: Varies
Average Annual Deductible Per Subscriber:
Employee Only (Self): Varies
Medicare: Varies
Average Subscriber Co-Payment:
Primary Care Physician: Varies
Non-Network Physician: Varies
Prescription Drugs: Varies
Hospital ER: Varies
Home Health Care: Varies
Home Health Care Max. Days/Visits Covered: Varies
Nursing Home: Varies
Nursing Home Max. Days/Visits Covered: Varies

Key Personnel
President . . . . Dennis Batey, MD
Chief Financial Officer . . . . Lisa Farrell
VP, Chief Service Officer . . . . Jana Burdick
VP, Government Programs . . . . Mary Eden
Exed Dir, Health Info . . . . Cesar Goulart
VP, Chief Medical Officer . . . . Chuck Baumgart, MD
VP, Sales & Marketing . . . . Neal Spero

755 United Concordia: New Mexico

6565 America's Parkway NE
Suite 200
Albuquerque, NM 87110
Toll-Free: 877-654-2124
Phone: 505-563-5869
Fax: 505-563-5867
ucproducer@ucci.com
www.secure.ucci.com
For Profit Organization: Yes
Year Founded: 1971
Number of Primary Care Physicians: 111,000
Total Enrollment: 8,000,000

Healthplan and Services Defined
PLAN TYPE: Dental
Plan Specialty: Dental
Benefits Offered: Dental

Type of Coverage
Commercial, Individual

Geographic Areas Served
Military personnel and their families, nationwide

756 UnitedHealthCare of New Mexico

8220 San Pedro NE
Albuquerque, NM 87113
Toll-Free: 866-573-2458
Phone: 505-449-4100
Fax: 505-449-4140
Colorado_PR_Team@uhc.com
www.uhc.com
Subsidiary of: UnitedHealth Group
For Profit Organization: Yes
Total Enrollment: 75,000,000
State Enrollment: 120,937

Healthplan and Services Defined
PLAN TYPE: HMO/PPO

Geographic Areas Served
Statewide

Key Personnel
Media Contact . . . . Will Shanley
will.shanley@uhc.com

Health Insurance Coverage Status and Type of Coverage by Age

Category	All Persons		Under 18 years		Under 65 years		65 years and over	
	Number	%	Number	%	Number	%	Number	%
Total population	19,289	-	4,418	-	16,766	-	2,523	-
Covered by some type of health insurance	16,403 *(135)*	85.0 *(0.7)*	4,069 *(53)*	92.1 *(1.0)*	13,959 *(140)*	83.3 *(0.7)*	2,443 *(80)*	96.9 *(0.9)*
Covered by private health insurance	12,096 *(200)*	62.7 *(1.0)*	2,654 *(97)*	60.1 *(2.1)*	10,787 *(193)*	64.3 *(1.1)*	1,308 *(71)*	51.9 *(2.2)*
Employment based	10,893 *(200)*	56.5 *(1.0)*	2,512 *(102)*	56.9 *(2.3)*	9,973 *(199)*	59.5 *(1.1)*	920 *(62)*	36.5 *(2.1)*
Own employment based	5,620 *(108)*	29.1 *(0.5)*	13 *(5)*	0.3 *(0.1)*	4,919 *(104)*	29.3 *(0.6)*	701 *(49)*	27.8 *(1.7)*
Direct purchase	1,490 *(96)*	7.7 *(0.5)*	232 *(32)*	5.2 *(0.7)*	1,037 *(90)*	6.2 *(0.5)*	453 *(36)*	18.0 *(1.3)*
Covered by government health insurance	6,405 *(195)*	33.2 *(1.0)*	1,721 *(101)*	38.9 *(2.3)*	4,075 *(186)*	24.3 *(1.1)*	2,330 *(78)*	92.4 *(1.1)*
Covered by Medicaid	3,917 *(186)*	20.3 *(1.0)*	1,665 *(101)*	37.7 *(2.3)*	3,582 *(181)*	21.4 *(1.1)*	335 *(33)*	13.3 *(1.3)*
Also by private insurance	734 *(60)*	3.8 *(0.3)*	269 *(34)*	6.1 *(0.8)*	669 *(60)*	4.0 *(0.4)*	65 *(18)*	2.6 *(0.7)*
Covered by Medicare	2,802 *(81)*	14.5 *(0.4)*	43 *(15)*	1.0 *(0.3)*	478 *(36)*	2.9 *(0.2)*	2,323 *(78)*	92.1 *(1.1)*
Also by private insurance	1,332 *(71)*	6.9 *(0.4)*	6 *(4)*	0.1 *(0.1)*	137 *(19)*	0.8 *(0.1)*	1,195 *(68)*	47.4 *(2.1)*
Also by Medicaid	508 *(39)*	2.6 *(0.2)*	23 *(10)*	0.5 *(0.2)*	179 *(24)*	1.1 *(0.1)*	329 *(33)*	13.0 *(1.3)*
Covered by military health care	312 *(49)*	1.6 *(0.3)*	40 *(14)*	0.9 *(0.3)*	236 *(46)*	1.4 *(0.3)*	76 *(18)*	3.0 *(0.7)*
Not covered at any time during the year	2,886 *(129)*	15.0 *(0.7)*	350 *(42)*	7.9 *(1.0)*	2,807 *(127)*	16.7 *(0.7)*	79 *(24)*	3.1 *(0.9)*

Note: Numbers in thousands; figures cover 2010; standard error appears in parenthesis; (b) base less than 75,000; (x) not applicable
Source: U.S. Census Bureau, Current Population Survey, 2011 Annual Social and Economic Supplement. Table HI05. Health Insurance Coverage Status and Type of Coverage by State and Age for All People: 2010

New York

757   Aetna Health of New York

151 Farmington Avenue
Conveyer ASB2
Hartford, CT 06156
Toll-Free: 866-582-9629
www.aetna.com
Year Founded: 1986
Number of Affiliated Hospitals: 61
Number of Primary Care Physicians: 2,691
Total Enrollment: 154,162
State Enrollment: 154,162

Healthplan and Services Defined
PLAN TYPE: PPO
Model Type: IPA, Network
Benefits Offered: Disease Management, Prescription, Wellness
Offers Demand Management Patient Information Service: Yes

Type of Coverage
Catastrophic Illness Benefit: Varies per case

Type of Payment Plans Offered
POS, Capitated

Geographic Areas Served
Statewide

Subscriber Information
Average Subscriber Co-Payment:
    Primary Care Physician: $2.00/5.00/10.00
    Non-Network Physician: Deductible
    Prescription Drugs: $2.00/5.00/10.00
    Hospital ER: $35.00

Network Qualifications
Pre-Admission Certification: Yes

Peer Review Type
Utilization Review: Yes
Second Surgical Opinion: No
Case Management: Yes

Publishes and Distributes Report Card: Yes

Accreditation Certification
NCQA
TJC Accreditation, Medicare Approved, Utilization Review,
    Pre-Admission Certification, State Licensure, Quality Assurance
    Program

Key Personnel
CEO . . . . .Ronald A Williams
President. . . . . .Mark T Bertolini
SVP, General Counsel .William J Casazza
EVP, CFO . . . . .Joseph M Zubretsky
Head, M&A Integration . . . . .Kay Mooney
SVP, Marketing. . . . . .Robert E Mead
Chief Medical Officer . . . . .Lonny Reisman, MD
SVP, Human Resources. . . . . .Elease E Wright
SVP, CIO. . . . . .Meg McCarthy

Specialty Managed Care Partners
Enters into Contracts with Regional Business Coalitions: Yes

758   Affinity Health Plan

2500 Halsey Street
Bronx, NY 10461
Phone: 718-794-7700
Fax: 718-794-7800
mainoffice@affinityplan.org
www.affinityplan.org
Non-Profit Organization: Yes
Year Founded: 1986
Number of Affiliated Hospitals: 60

Number of Primary Care Physicians: 1,400
Number of Referral/Specialty Physicians: 5,000
Total Enrollment: 134,837
State Enrollment: 134,837

Healthplan and Services Defined
PLAN TYPE: HMO
Model Type: Staff

Type of Coverage
Medicaid

Geographic Areas Served
NY Metropolitan Area

Accreditation Certification
TJC Accreditation, Medicare Approved, Utilization Review, State
    Licensure

Key Personnel
President/CEO . . . . .Maura Bluestone
EVP/CFO . . . . .Mark Corcoran
EVP/COO. . . . . .Robert Brown
VP, Compliance . . . . .Caron Cullen
SVP, Care Delivery . . . . .Joan Russo
VP, Marketing . . . . .Kelbourne J Ritter
VP, Corporate Services . . . . .Ann M Van Etten
VP, Medical Director . . . . .Munish Khaneja, MD
SVP, Community Connection . . . . .Abenna Abboa-Offei
SVP, Chief Inforamation . . . . .Robert Allen

759   AmeriChoice by UnitedHealthCare

77 Water Street
14th Floor
New York, NY 10005
Toll-Free: 800-493-4647
Phone: 212-898-8400
Fax: 347-438-3019
www.americhoice.com
Secondary Address: 1083 Coney Island Avenue, Brooklyn, NY 11230
Subsidiary of: UnitedHealth Group
For Profit Organization: Yes
Total Enrollment: 107,387

Healthplan and Services Defined
PLAN TYPE: HMO

Type of Coverage
Medicare, Medicaid

Key Personnel
Network Contracting . . . . .Lilli Brillstein
Marketing Director. . . . . .Jill Tobin
Sales Director. . . . . .Jill Tobin
Media Contact. . . . . .Jeff Smith
    952-931-5685
    jeff.smith@uhc.com

760   Amerigroup New York

360 West 31st Street
5th Floor
New York, NY 10001
Toll-Free: 877-472-8411
Phone: 212-563-5570
www.realsolutions.com
Secondary Address: 47 Mott Street, New York, NY 10013
For Profit Organization: Yes
Year Founded: 2005
Total Enrollment: 1,900,000

Healthplan and Services Defined
PLAN TYPE: HMO

Type of Coverage
Medicare, Medicaid, Expanded Medicaid, SCHIP, Managed L

Geographic Areas Served
New York City, boroughs of Brooklyn, Bronx, Manhattan, Queens, and Staten Island, and Putnam County

761 Atlantis Health Plan

45 Broadway
Suite 300
New York, NY 10006
Toll-Free: 866-747-8422
Phone: 212-747-0877
Fax: 212-747-0843
www.atlantishp.com
For Profit Organization: Yes
Year Founded: 1995
Total Enrollment: 30,000
State Enrollment: 30,000

Healthplan and Services Defined
PLAN TYPE: HMO

Type of Coverage
Commercial

Key Personnel
President/CEO/Chairman . . . . Sury Anand, MD
SVP, Operations . . . . Patrick Dodge
SVP, Health Services. . . . . Delia C Baquiran
Marketing Director . . . . David Stratton
   212-747-8276
   marketing@atlantishp.com
SVP, Information Tech. . . . . Abraham Wachsman

762 Blue Cross & Blue Shield of Western New York

257 West Genesee Street
Buffalo, NY 14202-2657
Toll-Free: 800-544-2583
Phone: 716-884-2800
Fax: 716-887-8993
www.bcbswny.com
Mailing Address: PO Box 80, Buffalo, NY 14240-0080
Non-Profit Organization: Yes
Year Founded: 1936
Total Enrollment: 555,405
State Enrollment: 197,194

Healthplan and Services Defined
PLAN TYPE: HMO/PPO
Other Type: POS, EPO
Plan Specialty: Lab
Benefits Offered: Dental, Disease Management, Prescription, Wellness

Type of Coverage
Commercial, Medicare, Supplemental Medicare, Medicaid

Geographic Areas Served
New York

Key Personnel
CEO . . . . Alphonso O'Neil-White
COO . . . . Stephen G Jepson
CFO. . . . . James Cardone
CMO . . . . John Gillsepie, MD
General Counsel . . . . Kenneth Sodaro
Provider Relations . . . . Lisa Meyers-Alessi
Member Relations. . . . . Pauline Cataldi
Pharmacy Director . . . . Renee Fleming
Public Relations . . . . Laura Perry
SVP, Chief Medical Offc . . . . Cynthia Ambres
VP, Information Systems . . . . Paul Stoddard

Public Relations. . . . . John F. Pitts
   716-887-8825
   pitts.john@bcbswny.com

Specialty Managed Care Partners
Wellpoint Pharmacy Management

763 BlueShield of Northeastern New York

30 Century Hill Drive
Latham, NY 12110
Toll-Free: 800-459-7587
Phone: 518-220-5700
www.bsneny.com
Mailing Address: PO Box 15013, Albany, NY 12212-5013
Non-Profit Organization: Yes
Year Founded: 1946
Total Enrollment: 193,498
State Enrollment: 72,563

Healthplan and Services Defined
PLAN TYPE: HMO/PPO
Other Type: POS, EPO
Benefits Offered: Disease Management, Prescription, Wellness

Type of Coverage
Commercial, Medicare, Supplemental Medicare, Medicaid

Type of Payment Plans Offered
POS, FFS

Geographic Areas Served
Albany, Clinton, Columbia, Essex, Fulton, Green, Montgomery, Schoharie, Schenectedy, Warren and Washington counties

Accreditation Certification
NCQA

Key Personnel
President & CEO . . . . Alphonso O'Neil-White
CMO. . . . . Steven E Szebenyi, MD
Public Relations . . . . Patrick Carrano
EVP, Operations. . . . . Cheryl Howe
CFO. . . . . Stephen Swift
Sr Dir, Public Relations . . . . Karen Merkel-Liberatore
   716-887-8811
   merkel-liberatore.karen@bsneny.com

Specialty Managed Care Partners
Wellpoint Pharmacy Management

764 CDPHP Medicare Plan

500 Patroon Creek Boulevard
Albany, NY 12206-1057
Toll-Free: 888-248-6522
Phone: 518-641-3950
www.cdphp.com
Year Founded: 1984
Total Enrollment: 400,000

Healthplan and Services Defined
PLAN TYPE: Medicare
Benefits Offered: Chiropractic, Dental, Disease Management, Home Care, Inpatient SNF, Physical Therapy, Podiatry, Prescription, Psychiatric, Vision, Wellness

Type of Coverage
Individual, Medicare

Geographic Areas Served
Available within New York state only

Subscriber Information
Average Monthly Fee Per Subscriber
  (Employee + Employer Contribution):
    Employee Only (Self): Varies
    Medicare: Varies
Average Annual Deductible Per Subscriber:
    Employee Only (Self): Varies

Medicare: Varies
Average Subscriber Co-Payment:
  Primary Care Physician: Varies
  Non-Network Physician: Varies
  Prescription Drugs: Varies
  Hospital ER: Varies
  Home Health Care: Varies
  Home Health Care Max. Days/Visits Covered: Varies
  Nursing Home: Varies
  Nursing Home Max. Days/Visits Covered: Varies

Key Personnel
President/CEO . . . . .John D Bennett, MD
SVP, Corp Administration . . . . Barbara A Downs, RN
SVP, Legal Affairs . . . . .Frederick B Galt
SVP, Govt Relations . . . . .Robert R Hinckley
SVP, CFO . . . . .Rolando J Portocarrero, CMA
SVP, Human Capital Mgmt . . . . Scott Klenk
Medical Director. . . . . Martin R Symansky, MD
Med Dir, Behavioral . . . . Kelly J Clark, MD
SVP, Marketing. . . . . .Brian J Morrissey
Medical Director . . . . Kirk R Panneton, MD
Senior Medical Director. . . . . .Clifford R Waldman, MD
SVP, Medical Affairs . . . . .Bruce D Nash, MD
SVP, Chief Info Officer . . . . .Linda Navarra
Vice President, Sales . . . . .Carole Montepare
Public Realtions Manager. . . . . .Kristin C Marshall
  518-641-5031
  kmarshall@cdphp.com
Public Realtions Spec . . . . .Julie K Tracy
  518-641-5126
  jtracy@cdphp.com

765 CDPHP: Capital District Physicians' Health Plan

500 Patroon Creek Boulevard
Albany, NY 12206
Toll-Free: 800-258-0477
Phone: 518-641-3000
Fax: 518-641-5005
www.cdphp.com
Non-Profit Organization: Yes
Year Founded: 1984
Number of Primary Care Physicians: 5,000
Total Enrollment: 350,000
State Enrollment: 350,000

Healthplan and Services Defined
  PLAN TYPE: HMO/PPO
  Other Type: POS, ASO
  Model Type: IPA
  Benefits Offered: Dental, Disease Management, Prescription,
    Wellness

Type of Coverage
  Commercial, Individual, Medicare, Medicaid

Geographic Areas Served
  Albany, Broome, Chenango, Columbia, Delaware, Dutchess, Essex,
  Fulton, Greene, Hamilton, Herkimer, Madison, Montgomery, Oneida,
  Orange, Ostego, Rensselaer, Saratoga, Schenectady, Schoharie,
  Tioga, Ulster, Warren, and Washington counties

Subscriber Information
  Average Monthly Fee Per Subscriber
    (Employee + Employer Contribution):
      Employee Only (Self): $64.41
      Employee & 2 Family Members: $175.47
  Average Subscriber Co-Payment:
    Primary Care Physician: $10
    Prescription Drugs: $5-20

Accreditation Certification
  NCQA

Key Personnel
President/CEO . . . . .John D Bennett, MD
SVP, Corp Administation . . . . Barbara A Downs, RN
SVP, Legal Affairs . . . . .Frederick B Galt
SVP, Govt Relations . . . . .Robert R Hinckley
SVP, CFO . . . . .Rolando J Portocarrero, CMA
SVP, Human Capital Mgmt . . . . Scott Klenk
Medical Director. . . . . Martin R Symansky, MD
Med Dir, Behavioral . . . . Kelly J Clark, MD
SVP, Marketing. . . . . .Brian J Morrissey
Medical Director . . . . Kirk R Panneton, MD
Senior Medical Director. . . . . .Clifford R Waldman, MD
SVP, Medical Affairs . . . . .Bruce D Nash, MD
SVP, Chief Info Officer . . . . .Linda Navarra
Vice President, Sales . . . . .Carole Montepare
Public Realtions Manager. . . . . .Kristin C Marshall
  518-641-5031
  kmarshall@cdphp.com
Public Realtions Spec . . . . .Julie K Tracy
  518-641-5126
  jtracy@cdphp.com

766 CIGNA HealthCare of New York

499 Washington Blvd
Suite 526
Jersey City, NJ 07310
Toll-Free: 866-438-2446
Phone: 201-533-7000
Fax: 201-533-7000
www.cigna.com
Secondary Address: Great-West Healthcare, now part of CIGNA, 50
  Main Street, 9th Floor, White Plains, NY 10606, 914-682-0159
For Profit Organization: Yes
Total Enrollment: 40,319
State Enrollment: 40,319

Healthplan and Services Defined
  PLAN TYPE: HMO
  Other Type: POS

Type of Coverage
  Commercial

767 Coalition America's National Preferred Provider Network

419 E Main Street
Middletown, NY 10940
Toll-Free: 800-557-1656
Phone: 845-343-1600
Fax: 845-344-3233
clientservices@coalitionamerica.com
www.nppn.com
For Profit Organization: Yes
Year Founded: 1993
Number of Affiliated Hospitals: 4,000
Number of Primary Care Physicians: 550,000
Number of Referral/Specialty Physicians: 90,000
Total Enrollment: 4,450,116
State Enrollment: 76,753

Healthplan and Services Defined
  PLAN TYPE: PPO
  Model Type: Network
  Benefits Offered: Prescription

Type of Payment Plans Offered
  DFFS, Capitated

Geographic Areas Served
  Nationwide

Subscriber Information
Average Monthly Fee Per Subscriber
(Employee + Employer Contribution):
Employee Only (Self): Varies
Employee & 1 Family Member: Varies
Employee & 2 Family Members: Varies
Medicare: Varies
Average Annual Deductible Per Subscriber:
Employee Only (Self): Varies
Employee & 1 Family Member: Varies
Employee & 2 Family Members: Varies
Medicare: Varies
Average Subscriber Co-Payment:
Primary Care Physician: Varies
Non-Network Physician: Varies
Prescription Drugs: Varies
Hospital ER: Varies
Home Health Care: Varies
Home Health Care Max. Days/Visits Covered: Varies
Nursing Home: Varies
Nursing Home Max. Days/Visits Covered: Varies

Publishes and Distributes Report Card: Yes

Accreditation Certification
TJC Accreditation, Medicare Approved, Utilization Review,
Pre-Admission Certification, State Licensure, Quality Assurance
Program

Key Personnel
Chairman . . . . Sean Smith
813-353-2300
CEO . . . . Scott Smith
President . . . . Mollie Brown
CFO . . . . Anthony R Levinson
COO . . . . Tina Ellex
Vice President. . . . . Larry Madlem
CIO . . . . Greg Comrie
Director, Marketing . . . . Libby Ricks
404-459-7201
libbyricks@coalitionamerica.com

Average Claim Compensation
Physician's Fees Charged: 1%
Hospital's Fees Charged: 1%

768 ConnectiCare of New York
175 Scott Swamp Road
PO Box 4050
Farmington, NY 06034-4050
Toll-Free: 800-846-8578
Phone: 860-674-2075
Fax: 860-674-2030
info@connecticare.com
www.connecticare.com
For Profit Organization: Yes
Year Founded: 1981
Number of Affiliated Hospitals: 126
Number of Primary Care Physicians: 22,000
Total Enrollment: 240,000

Healthplan and Services Defined
PLAN TYPE: HMO/PPO
Other Type: POS
Benefits Offered: Dental

Type of Coverage
Commercial, Individual, Medicare

Key Personnel
President . . . . Michael Wise
Media Contact. . . . . Stephen Jewett
publicrelations@connecticare.com

769 Davis Vision
159 Express Street
Plainview, NY 11803
Toll-Free: 800-328-4728
Phone: 516-932-9500
Fax: 800-933-9375
www.davisvision.com
https://idoc.davisvision.com
Subsidiary of: HVHC Inc.
For Profit Organization: Yes
Year Founded: 1964
Number of Primary Care Physicians: 30,000
Total Enrollment: 55,000,000

Healthplan and Services Defined
PLAN TYPE: Vision
Model Type: Network
Plan Specialty: Vision
Benefits Offered: Vision
Offers Demand Management Patient Information Service: Yes

Type of Payment Plans Offered
DFFS, Capitated, FFS

Geographic Areas Served
National & Puerto Rico, Guam, Saipan, Dominican Republic

Subscriber Information
Average Monthly Fee Per Subscriber
(Employee + Employer Contribution):
Employee Only (Self): Varies by plan
Medicare: Varies

Network Qualifications
Pre-Admission Certification: No

Peer Review Type
Utilization Review: Yes
Second Surgical Opinion: Yes
Case Management: Yes

Publishes and Distributes Report Card: Yes

Accreditation Certification
NCQA, COLTS Certification
TJC Accreditation

Key Personnel
President . . . . Steven Holden
COO/CFO . . . . Lawrence Gabel
EVP/CMO . . . . Tom Davis
Contracting Manager . . . . Heather Reynolds
Chief Marketing Officer . . . . Dale Paustian
Manager . . . . Michael O'Connor
Chief Information Officer . . . . Michael Thibdeau
SVP Provider Affairs . . . . Joseph Wende, OD
VP Business Development . . . . Robert Elsas

Average Claim Compensation
Physician's Fees Charged: 75%

Specialty Managed Care Partners
Enters into Contracts with Regional Business Coalitions: Yes

770 Delta Dental of the Mid-Atlantic
One Delta Drive
Mechanicsburg, PA 17055-6999
Toll-Free: 800-471-7091
Fax: 717-766-8719
www.deltadentalins.com
Non-Profit Organization: Yes
Total Enrollment: 54,000,000

Healthplan and Services Defined
PLAN TYPE: Dental
Other Type: Dental PPO

Type of Coverage
Commercial

Geographic Areas Served
Statewide

Key Personnel
President/CEO...............................Gary D Radine
VP, Public & Govt Affairs ....Jeff Album
415-972-8418
Dir/Media & Public Affair ....Elizabeth Risberg
415-972-8423

---

771 Dentcare Delivery Systems

333 Earle Ovington Boulevard
Uniondale, NY 11553-3608
Toll-Free: 800-468-0608
Phone: 516-542-2200
Fax: 516-794-3186
healthplex@aol.com
www.dentcaredeliverysystems.org
Non-Profit Organization: Yes
Year Founded: 1978
Number of Primary Care Physicians: 267
Number of Referral/Specialty Physicians: 175
State Enrollment: 295,841

Healthplan and Services Defined
PLAN TYPE: Dental
Model Type: IPA
Plan Specialty: Dental
Benefits Offered: Dental

Type of Coverage
Commercial, Individual
Catastrophic Illness Benefit: None

Type of Payment Plans Offered
FFS

Geographic Areas Served
Statewide

Subscriber Information
Average Annual Deductible Per Subscriber:
Employee Only (Self): $0
Employee & 1 Family Member: $0
Employee & 2 Family Members: $0
Medicare: $0

Accreditation Certification
NCQA
Utilization Review, Quality Assurance Program

Key Personnel
President.....................................Glenn J Sobel
516-794-3000
Treasurer.....................................Mary J Kelly
Secretary................................Nicole Mastantuono
Marketing..................................Bruce H Safran

---

772 eHealthInsurance Services Inc.

11919 Foundation Place
Gold River, CA 95670
Toll-Free: 800-977-8860
info@ehealthinsurance.com
www.e.healthinsurance.com
Year Founded: 1997

Healthplan and Services Defined
PLAN TYPE: HMO/PPO
Benefits Offered: Dental, Life, STD

Type of Coverage
Commercial, Individual, Medicare

Geographic Areas Served
All 50 states in the USA and District of Columbia

Key Personnel
Chairman & CEO ....Gary L. Lauer

EVP/Business & Corp. Dev.....................Bruce Telkamp
EVP/Chief Technology....................Dr. Sheldon X. Wang
SVP & CFO ....Stuart M. Huizinga
Pres. of eHealth Gov. Sys ....Samuel C. Gibbs
SVP of Sales & Operations ....Robert S. Hurley
Director Public Relations......................Nate Purpura
650-210-3115

---

773 Elderplan

6323 Seventh Avenue
Brooklyn, NY 11220
Toll-Free: 800-353-3765
Phone: 718-921-7979
Fax: 718-630-2565
info@elderplan.org
www.elderplan.org
Non-Profit Organization: Yes
Year Founded: 1985
Number of Affiliated Hospitals: 35
Number of Primary Care Physicians: 1,200
Number of Referral/Specialty Physicians: 3,800
Total Enrollment: 16,000
State Enrollment: 15,000

Healthplan and Services Defined
PLAN TYPE: Medicare
Other Type: Medicare Advantage
Model Type: Network
Plan Specialty: ASO, Behavioral Health, Chiropractic, Dental, Disease Management, EPO, Lab, Vision, Radiology
Benefits Offered: Behavioral Health, Chiropractic, Complementary Medicine, Dental, Disease Management, Home Care, Inpatient SNF, Long-Term Care, Physical Therapy, Podiatry, Prescription, Psychiatric, Transplant, Vision

Type of Coverage
Medicare

Type of Payment Plans Offered
FFS

Geographic Areas Served
Brooklyn, Bronx, Manhattan, Queens and Staten Island

Subscriber Information
Average Monthly Fee Per Subscriber
(Employee + Employer Contribution):
Medicare: No premium
Average Annual Deductible Per Subscriber:
Medicare: $0.00
Average Subscriber Co-Payment:
Primary Care Physician: $0.00 co-pay
Prescription Drugs: $5.00/9.00
Hospital ER: $50.00
Home Health Care: $0.00
Home Health Care Max. Days/Visits Covered: 365 days
Nursing Home Max. Days/Visits Covered: 200 days

Network Qualifications
Pre-Admission Certification: Yes

Peer Review Type
Utilization Review: Yes
Second Surgical Opinion: Yes
Case Management: Yes

Publishes and Distributes Report Card: No

Accreditation Certification
TJC Accreditation, Medicare Approved, Utilization Review, State Licensure, Quality Assurance Program

Key Personnel
President/CEO ....Eli S Feldman
CFO ....Joe Pinho
VP/Corporate Marketing/PR ....Janet Rothman
Medical Affairs ....Herbert Segal

Provider Services . . . . .Jim Berg
Dir, Public Relations . . . . .Audrey O Waters
        718-759-4677
        media@elderplan.org

Specialty Managed Care Partners
Health Plex, Maxore
Enters into Contracts with Regional Business Coalitions: Yes

---

774 Empire Blue Cross & Blue Shield
One Liberty Avenue
New York, NY 10006
Toll-Free: 800-261-5962
Phone: 212-476-1000
Fax: 518-367-4565
www.empireblue.com
Subsidiary of: A Subsidiary of Wellpoint
Non-Profit Organization: Yes
Year Founded: 1934
Owned by an Integrated Delivery Network (IDN): Yes
Number of Affiliated Hospitals: 200
Number of Primary Care Physicians: 66,000
Number of Referral/Specialty Physicians: 62,000
Total Enrollment: 171,028

Healthplan and Services Defined
  PLAN TYPE: HMO/PPO
  Other Type: EPO, POS
  Model Type: Network
  Plan Specialty: Behavioral Health, Vision, Radiology, Worker's
    Compensation
  Benefits Offered: Behavioral Health, Dental, Disease Management,
    Prescription, Psychiatric, Transplant, Vision, Wellness, Maternity
  Offers Demand Management Patient Information Service: Yes

Type of Coverage
  Individual, Medicare
  Catastrophic Illness Benefit: Varies per case

Type of Payment Plans Offered
  POS, DFFS

Geographic Areas Served
  28 eastern counties of New York

Network Qualifications
  Pre-Admission Certification: Yes

Peer Review Type
  Utilization Review: Yes
  Second Surgical Opinion: Yes
  Case Management: Yes

Publishes and Distributes Report Card: Yes

Accreditation Certification
  NCQA
  TJC Accreditation, State Licensure

Key Personnel
  President/CEO. . . . . .Michael A Stocker, MD
  Executive VP/COO . . . . .Gloria McCarthy
  Sr VP/Chief Financial Off. . . . . .John W Remshard
  Sr VP/Communications. . . . . .Deborah Loeb Bohren
  VP/Chief Actuary . . . . .Michael W Fedyna
  Sr VP/Sales & Marketing. . . . . .Jason Gorevic
  VP/Chief Infrastructure .Kenneth A Harth
  Sr VP/Human Resources . . . . .Robert W Lawrence
  Vice President/Operations . . . . .Elizabeth McManus
  Sr VP/General Counsel .Linda V Tiano, Esq
  Chief Medical Officer. . . . . .Alan E Sokolow, MD
  Public Relations Director. . . . . .Sally Kweskin
      303-831-5899
      sally.kweskin@anthem.com

Specialty Managed Care Partners
  Enters into Contracts with Regional Business Coalitions: Yes

---

775 Excellus Blue Cross Blue Shield: Central New York
333 Butternut Drive
Syracuse, NY 13214-1803
Toll-Free: 800-919-8809
Phone: 315-671-6400
www.excellusbcbs.com
Subsidiary of: Lifetime Healthcare Companies
Non-Profit Organization: Yes
Year Founded: 1985
Number of Affiliated Hospitals: 14
Number of Primary Care Physicians: 290
Number of Referral/Specialty Physicians: 677
Total Enrollment: 1,700,000
State Enrollment: 1,700,000

Healthplan and Services Defined
  PLAN TYPE: HMO
  Model Type: Network
  Plan Specialty: ASO, Behavioral Health, Chiropractic, Dental,
    Disease Management
  Benefits Offered: Behavioral Health, Chiropractic, Dental, Disease
    Management, Physical Therapy, Podiatry, Prescription, Psychiatric,
    Vision, Wellness

Type of Coverage
  Indemnity, Medicare, Supplemental Medicare

Type of Payment Plans Offered
  Capitated

Geographic Areas Served
  St. Lawrence, Jefferson, Lewis, Oswego, Onondaga, Cayuga,
  Tompkins, Courtland, Chenango, Broome, Tioga, Chemung, Schuyler
  and Steuben counties

Subscriber Information
  Average Monthly Fee Per Subscriber
    (Employee + Employer Contribution):
      Employee Only (Self): Varies by plan
  Average Subscriber Co-Payment:
    Primary Care Physician: $10.00
    Prescription Drugs: $10.00

Peer Review Type
  Second Surgical Opinion: No
  Case Management: Yes

Publishes and Distributes Report Card: Yes

Accreditation Certification
  NCQA
  TJC Accreditation, Medicare Approved, Utilization Review, State
    Licensure

Key Personnel
  President. . . . . .Arthur Vercillo, MD
  Sr Deputy General Counsel . . . . .Margaret M Cassady, Esq
  VP, Contracting. . . . . .Antonio V Vitagliano
  VP, Communications . . . . .Elizabeth Martin
  VP, Sales. . . . . .Todd Muscatello
  VP, Human Resources . . . . .Ellen Wilson

Specialty Managed Care Partners
  Enters into Contracts with Regional Business Coalitions: Yes

---

776 Excellus Blue Cross Blue Shield: Rochester Region
165 Court Street
Rochester, NY 14647
Toll-Free: 877-253-4797
Phone: 585-454-1700
www.excellusbcbs.com
Mailing Address: PO Box 22999, Rochester, NY 14692
Subsidiary of: Lifetime Healthcare Companies
Non-Profit Organization: Yes

Year Founded: 1985
Number of Affiliated Hospitals: 18
Number of Primary Care Physicians: 1,035
Number of Referral/Specialty Physicians: 2,082
Total Enrollment: 1,700,000
State Enrollment: 1,700,000

Healthplan and Services Defined
PLAN TYPE: HMO
Model Type: IPA
Benefits Offered: Disease Management, Prescription, Wellness
Offers Demand Management Patient Information Service: Yes

Type of Payment Plans Offered
POS, Combination FFS & DFFS

Geographic Areas Served
Livingston, Monroe, Ontario, Seneca, Wayne & Yates counties

Subscriber Information
Average Monthly Fee Per Subscriber
(Employee + Employer Contribution):
Employee Only (Self): $73.78
Employee & 1 Family Member: $365.24
Employee & 2 Family Members: $232.09
Medicare: $113.54
Average Annual Deductible Per Subscriber:
Employee Only (Self): $0
Employee & 1 Family Member: $0
Employee & 2 Family Members: $0
Medicare: $0
Average Subscriber Co-Payment:
Primary Care Physician: $15.00
Non-Network Physician: $0
Prescription Drugs: $0
Hospital ER: $50.00
Home Health Care: $0
Home Health Care Max. Days/Visits Covered: Unlimited
Nursing Home: $0
Nursing Home Max. Days/Visits Covered: 120-360 days

Publishes and Distributes Report Card: Yes

Accreditation Certification
NCQA
TJC Accreditation, Medicare Approved, Utilization Review, State Licensure, Quality Assurance Program

Key Personnel
President ....Kevin J McGurgan
VP, Human Resources ....Richard Nangreave
VP, Communications........................James Redmond
Regional VP, Sales ....Mary Beth O'Connor
VP, Chief Medical Officer.................Frank Dubeck, MD
General Counsel ....Lisa Santelli, Esq
VP, Contracting..........................Antonio V Vitagliano

777 Excellus Blue Cross Blue Shield: Utica Region

12 Rhoads Drive
Utica, NY 13502
Toll-Free: 877-757-3850
Phone: 585-454-1700
www.excellusbcbs.com
Subsidiary of: Lifetime Healthcare Companies
Non-Profit Organization: Yes
Total Enrollment: 1,700,000
State Enrollment: 1,700,000

Healthplan and Services Defined
PLAN TYPE: HMO
Benefits Offered: Disease Management, Wellness

Type of Coverage
Commercial, Medicare, Medicaid

Type of Payment Plans Offered
POS

Geographic Areas Served
Franklin, Cliton, Essex, Hamilton, Herkimer, Fulton, Oneida, Madision, Montgomery, Ostego and Delaware counties

Key Personnel
President ....Eve Van de Wal
Sr Deputy General Counsel ....Margaret M Cassady, Esq
VP, Communications.........................Stephanie Davis
VP, Chief Medical Officer.................Frank Dubeck, MD
VP, Provider Relations ....Kathy Horn
VP, Sales.................................Todd Muscatello

778 Fidelis Care

95-25 Queens Boulevard
Rego Park, NY 11374
Toll-Free: 888-343-3547
Phone: 718-896-6500
www.fideliscare.org
Secondary Address: 8 Southwoods Blvd, Albany, NY 12211
For Profit Organization: Yes
Year Founded: 1993
Number of Primary Care Physicians: 42,000
Total Enrollment: 625,000
State Enrollment: 625,000

Healthplan and Services Defined
PLAN TYPE: Multiple
Benefits Offered: Chiropractic, Dental, Disease Management, Home Care, Inpatient SNF, Physical Therapy, Podiatry, Prescription, Psychiatric, Vision, Wellness

Type of Coverage
Individual, Medicare, Medicaid

Geographic Areas Served
53 counties in New York State

Subscriber Information
Average Monthly Fee Per Subscriber
(Employee + Employer Contribution):
Employee Only (Self): Varies
Medicare: Varies
Average Annual Deductible Per Subscriber:
Employee Only (Self): Varies
Medicare: Varies
Average Subscriber Co-Payment:
Primary Care Physician: Varies
Non-Network Physician: Varies
Prescription Drugs: Varies
Hospital ER: Varies
Home Health Care: Varies
Home Health Care Max. Days/Visits Covered: Varies
Nursing Home: Varies
Nursing Home Max. Days/Visits Covered: Varies

Key Personnel
President/CEO ....Mark L Lane
SVP/Provider Relations........................David Thomas
Chief Information Officer ....Patrick Garland
VP/Information Technology ....John Olearczyk
Director Financial Ops ....Irene Amican
Director Info Technology.........................Don Martin
Network/Telecommunication ....Gary Crane
Chief Medical Officer....................Edward Anselm, MD
Director, Communications ....Darla Shattenkirk
518-445-3918
dshattenkirk@fideliscare.org
Public Relations Coord ....Jayson R White
518-445-3923
jwhite@fideliscare.org

779 GHI Medicare Plan

441 Ninth Avenue
New York, NY 10001-1681
Toll-Free: 800-611-8454
Phone: 877-244-4466
Fax: 845-340-1229
www.ghi.com
Mailing Address: PO Box 4296, Kingston, NY 12402
Subsidiary of: EmblemHealth
Year Founded: 1931
Total Enrollment: 53,000

Healthplan and Services Defined
PLAN TYPE: Medicare
Benefits Offered: Chiropractic, Dental, Disease Management, Home Care, Inpatient SNF, Physical Therapy, Podiatry, Prescription, Psychiatric, Vision, Wellness

Type of Coverage
Individual, Medicare

Geographic Areas Served
Available within New York state only

Subscriber Information
Average Monthly Fee Per Subscriber
(Employee + Employer Contribution):
Employee Only (Self): Varies
Medicare: Varies
Average Annual Deductible Per Subscriber:
Employee Only (Self): Varies
Medicare: Varies
Average Subscriber Co-Payment:
Primary Care Physician: Varies
Non-Network Physician: Varies
Prescription Drugs: Varies
Hospital ER: Varies
Home Health Care: Varies
Home Health Care Max. Days/Visits Covered: Varies
Nursing Home: Varies
Nursing Home Max. Days/Visits Covered: Varies

Key Personnel
CEO . . . . .Frank J Branchini
EVP, Health Care Oper . . . . .Daniel P Finke
EVP, CFO. . . . . .Michael D Fullwood
EVP, Chief Info Officer . . . . .John H Steber
SVP, Govt Relations. . . . . .David S Abernathy
SVP, Sales & Acct Mgmt. . . . . .George Babitsch
SVP . . . . .Fred Blickman
SVP, Dep General Counsel . . . . .Jeffrey D Chansler
SVP, Customer Service . . . . .Marilyn DeQuatro
SVP, Operations . . . . .Thomas K Dwyer
SVP, Network Mgmt. . . . . .Shawn M Fitzgibbon
SVP, Chief Medical Offc . . . . .William A Gillespie, MD
SVP, Govt Programs . . . . .William C Lamoreaux
SVP, Sales & Mktg . . . . .Charlene Maher
SVP, Public Affairs . . . . .Ilene D Margolin
SVP, Deputy Counsel. .William Mastro

780 Great-West Healthcare New York
Acquired by CIGNA

781 Group Health Incorporated (GHI)

441 Ninth Avenue
New York, NY 10001-1681
Toll-Free: 800-624-2414
Phone: 212-501-4444
Fax: 212-563-8561
www.ghi.com
Mailing Address: PO Box 3000, New York, NY 10016-3000
Subsidiary of: EmblemHealth

Non-Profit Organization: Yes
Year Founded: 1937
Number of Affiliated Hospitals: 230
Number of Primary Care Physicians: 15,529
Number of Referral/Specialty Physicians: 25,173
Total Enrollment: 1,601,000
State Enrollment: 2,475,666

Healthplan and Services Defined
PLAN TYPE: HMO/PPO
Model Type: Network
Plan Specialty: ASO, Behavioral Health, Dental, EPO
Benefits Offered: Behavioral Health, Chiropractic, Complementary Medicine, Dental, Disease Management, Home Care, Inpatient SNF, Physical Therapy, Podiatry, Prescription, Psychiatric, Transplant, Vision, Wellness

Type of Coverage
Commercial, Individual, Indemnity, Medicare, Supplemental Medicare, Medicaid

Type of Payment Plans Offered
DFFS

Geographic Areas Served
GHI operates statewide in New York. GHI HMO serves 26 eastern New York counties, including five New York City boroughs

Subscriber Information
Average Monthly Fee Per Subscriber
(Employee + Employer Contribution):
Employee Only (Self): $69.44
Average Annual Deductible Per Subscriber:
Employee & 2 Family Members: $214.30
Average Subscriber Co-Payment:
Primary Care Physician: $10.00
Prescription Drugs: $10.00/20.00/30.00

Peer Review Type
Utilization Review: Yes
Second Surgical Opinion: Yes
Case Management: Yes

Accreditation Certification
NCQA

Key Personnel
CEO . . . . .Frank J Branchini
EVP, Health Care Oper . . . . .Daniel P Finke
EVP, CFO. . . . . .Michael D Fullwood
EVP, Chief Info Officer . . . . .John H Steber
SVP, Govt Relations. . . . . .David S Abernathy
SVP, Sales & Acct Mgmt. . . . . .George Babitsch
SVP . . . . .Fred Blickman
SVP, Dep General Counsel . . . . .Jeffrey D Chansler
SVP, Customer Service . . . . .Marilyn DeQuatro
SVP, Operations . . . . .Thomas K Dwyer
SVP, Network Mgmt. . . . . .Shawn M Fitzgibbon
SVP, Chief Medical Offc . . . . .William A Gillespie, MD
SVP, Govt Programs . . . . .William C Lamoreaux
SVP, Sales & Mktg . . . . .Charlene Maher
SVP, Public Affairs . . . . .Ilene D Margolin
SVP, Deputy Counsel. .William Mastro

Specialty Managed Care Partners
Value Options, Express Scrips, Davis Vision, New York Medical Imaging, Multi-Plan, CCN

782 Guardian Life Insurance Company

7 Hanover Square
H-26-E
New York, NY 10004
Toll-Free: 888-482-7342
Phone: 212-598-8000
marketcc@glic.com
www.guardianlife.com
Subsidiary of: Guardian

For Profit Organization: Yes
Year Founded: 1860
Owned by an Integrated Delivery Network (IDN): Yes
Number of Affiliated Hospitals: 2,966
Number of Primary Care Physicians: 121,815
Number of Referral/Specialty Physicians: 193,137
Total Enrollment: 205,677

Healthplan and Services Defined
 PLAN TYPE: HMO/PPO
 Model Type: Network
 Plan Specialty: Chiropractic, Dental, Disease Management, Lab,
  PBM, Vision, Radiology, UR
 Benefits Offered: Behavioral Health, Chiropractic, Complementary
  Medicine, Dental, Disease Management, Home Care, Physical
  Therapy, Podiatry, Prescription, Psychiatric, Vision, Wellness,
  AD&D, Life, LTD, STD

Type of Coverage
 Commercial, Indemnity

Type of Payment Plans Offered
 Combination FFS & DFFS

Geographic Areas Served
 Nationwide

Subscriber Information
 Average Monthly Fee Per Subscriber
  (Employee + Employer Contribution):
   Employee Only (Self): Varies by plan

Peer Review Type
 Utilization Review: Yes
 Second Surgical Opinion: Yes
 Case Management: Yes

Publishes and Distributes Report Card: Yes

Accreditation Certification
 URAC, NCQA

Key Personnel
 President/CEO . . . . .Dennis J Manning
 CFO . . . . .Robert E Broatch
 Chief Information Officer . . . . .Dennis S Callahan
 Chief Actuary . . . . .Armand M De Palo
 Risk Management Products . . . . .Gary B Lenderink
 Chief Investment Officer . . . . .Thomas G Sorell
 Sr VP/Individual Markets . . . . .David W Allen
 Sr VP/Corporate Secretary . . . . .Joseph A Caruso
 Sr VP/Human Resources .James D Ranton
 Sr VP/Corporate Marketing . . . . .Nancy F Rogers
 Sr VP/Group Insurance . . . . .Richard A White
 Sr VP/General Counsel . . . . .John Peluso
 VP/Reinsurance . . . . .Jeremy Starr
 EVP/COO . . . . .K Rone Baldwin
 Public Relations . . . . .Richard Jones
  richard_jones@glic.com

Specialty Managed Care Partners
 Health Net
 Enters into Contracts with Regional Business Coalitions: Yes

---

783 **Health Plan of New York**
55 Water Street
New York, NY 10041
Toll-Free: 800-447-8255
Phone: 646-447-5900
Fax: 646-447-3011
www.hipusa.com
Subsidiary of: An Emblem Health Company
Total Enrollment: 1,200,000

Healthplan and Services Defined
 PLAN TYPE: HMO/PPO
 Other Type: POS, EPO, ASO

Benefits Offered: Chiropractic, Dental, Disease Management, Home
  Care, Inpatient SNF, Physical Therapy, Podiatry, Prescription,
  Psychiatric, Vision, Wellness

Type of Coverage
 Individual, Medicare

Geographic Areas Served
 New York, Connecticut, Massachusetts

Subscriber Information
 Average Monthly Fee Per Subscriber
  (Employee + Employer Contribution):
   Employee Only (Self): Varies
   Medicare: Varies
 Average Annual Deductible Per Subscriber:
   Employee Only (Self): Varies
   Medicare: Varies
 Average Subscriber Co-Payment:
   Primary Care Physician: Varies
   Non-Network Physician: Varies
   Prescription Drugs: Varies
   Hospital ER: Varies
   Home Health Care: Varies
   Home Health Care Max. Days/Visits Covered: Varies
   Nursing Home: Varies
   Nursing Home Max. Days/Visits Covered: Varies

Key Personnel
 Chairman/CEO . . . . .Anthony L Watson
 President/COO . . . . .Frank J Branchini
 SVP, Customer Service .Marilyn DeQuatro
 SVP, Operations . . . . .Thomas K Dwyer
 SVP, Network Mgmt . . . . .Shawn M Fitzgibbon
 SVP, Govt Relations . . . . .David S Abernathy
 EVP, CFO . . . . .Michael D Fullwood
 SVP, Govt Programs . . . . .William C Lamoreaux
 SVP, Sales & Marketing .Charlene Maher
 SVP, Dep General Counsel . . . . .William Mastro
 SVP, Chief Medical Offc . . . . .William A Gillespie, MD
 SVP . . . . .Fred Blickman
 EVP, Chief Info Officer .John H Steber
 SVP, Human Resources .Thomas A Nemeth
 SVP, Sales & Acct Mgmt . . . . .George Babitsch
 SVP, Public Affairs . . . . .Ilene D Margolin
 SVP, Finance . . . . .Michael Palmaterr

---

784 **HealthNow New York**
1901 Main Street
Buffalo, NY 14240
Toll-Free: 800-856-0480
Phone: 716-887-6900
Fax: 716-887-8981
www.healthnowny.com
Mailing Address: PO Box 15013, Albany, NY 12212-5013
Non-Profit Organization: Yes
Year Founded: 1936
Number of Affiliated Hospitals: 33
Number of Primary Care Physicians: 927
Number of Referral/Specialty Physicians: 2,059
Total Enrollment: 553,000
State Enrollment: 553,000

Healthplan and Services Defined
 PLAN TYPE: HMO
 Model Type: IPA
 Benefits Offered: Behavioral Health, Chiropractic, Disease
  Management, Home Care, Inpatient SNF, Physical Therapy,
  Podiatry, Prescription, Psychiatric, Transplant, Vision, Wellness

Type of Coverage
 Commercial, Individual, Indemnity, Medicare, Supplemental
  Medicare, Medicaid

Type of Payment Plans Offered
Capitated, FFS

Geographic Areas Served
Broome, Cayuga, Chenango, Cortland, Delaware, Franklin, Hamilton, Herkimer, Jefferson, Lewis, Madison, Oneida, Onondaga, Oswego, Otsego, St Lawrence and Tioga counties

Network Qualifications
Pre-Admission Certification: Yes

Peer Review Type
Utilization Review: Yes
Second Surgical Opinion: Yes
Case Management: Yes

Publishes and Distributes Report Card: Yes

Accreditation Certification
NCQA
Utilization Review, Pre-Admission Certification, State Licensure, Quality Assurance Program

Key Personnel
President/CEO . . . . Alphonso O'Neil-White
716-887-6948
Chair . . . . John Canavan
Vice Chair . . . . Donald Boswell
Sales Manager . . . . Brian Beaton
716-887-7993
beaton.brian@healthnow.org
Dir, Public Relations. . . . . Karen Merkel-Liberatore
716-887-8811
merkel-liberatore.karen@healthnow.org

Specialty Managed Care Partners
Integra, Quest Diagnostics, Prism, Alterna Health

---

785 Healthplex
333 Earle Ovington Boulevard
Suite 300
Uniondale, NY 11553
Toll-Free: 800-468-0608
Phone: 516-542-2200
Fax: 516-794-3186
info@healthplex.com
www.healthplex.com
For Profit Organization: Yes
Year Founded: 1977
Number of Primary Care Physicians: 2,855
Number of Referral/Specialty Physicians: 448
Total Enrollment: 2,000,000

Healthplan and Services Defined
PLAN TYPE: Dental
Other Type: Dental HMO/PPO
Model Type: IPA
Plan Specialty: Dental
Benefits Offered: Dental

Type of Coverage
Commercial, Individual, Indemnity

Type of Payment Plans Offered
POS, DFFS, Capitated, FFS, Combination FFS & DFFS

Geographic Areas Served
New Jersey & New York

Subscriber Information
Average Monthly Fee Per Subscriber
(Employee + Employer Contribution):
Employee Only (Self): $159.00
Employee & 1 Family Member: $264.00
Employee & 2 Family Members: $350.00
Average Annual Deductible Per Subscriber:
Employee Only (Self): $0
Employee & 1 Family Member: $0
Employee & 2 Family Members: $0

Network Qualifications
Pre-Admission Certification: No

Peer Review Type
Utilization Review: Yes
Second Surgical Opinion: Yes
Case Management: Yes

Accreditation Certification
NCQA
Utilization Review, Quality Assurance Program

Key Personnel
CEO . . . . Stephen Cuchel, DDS
President/Co-CEO . . . . Martin Kane
VP, Director . . . . Bruce Safran, DDS
CFO. . . . . Valerie Vignolia
VP. . . . . Sharon Zelkind, RDH
Dir. Government Services . . . . Sharon Zelkind, Rdh
Director IT. . . . . Chris Schmidt, MBA
Provider Services . . . . Ann Weeks

Specialty Managed Care Partners
Enters into Contracts with Regional Business Coalitions: Yes

---

786 Humana Health Insurance of New York
125 Wolf Road
Suite 501
Albany, NY 12205
Toll-Free: 800-951-0136
Phone: 518-435-0459
Fax: 518-435-0412
www.humana.com
Secondary Address: 160 Linden Oaks, Rochester, NY 14625
For Profit Organization: Yes
Total Enrollment: 81,000

Healthplan and Services Defined
PLAN TYPE: HMO/PPO

Type of Coverage
Commercial, Individual

Accreditation Certification
URAC, NCQA, CORE

---

787 Independent Health
511 Farber Lakes Drive
Buffalo, NY 14221
Toll-Free: 800-501-3439
Phone: 716-631-3001
Fax: 716-631-0430
wnyms@independenthealth.com
www.independenthealth.com
Non-Profit Organization: Yes
Year Founded: 1980
Number of Affiliated Hospitals: 35
Number of Primary Care Physicians: 1,125
Number of Referral/Specialty Physicians: 1,626
Total Enrollment: 365,000
State Enrollment: 365,000

Healthplan and Services Defined
PLAN TYPE: HMO
Model Type: IPA
Plan Specialty: EPO
Benefits Offered: Behavioral Health, Chiropractic, Dental, Disease Management, Home Care, Inpatient SNF, Physical Therapy, Podiatry, Prescription, Psychiatric, Transplant, Vision, Wellness

Type of Coverage
Commercial, Individual, Indemnity, Medicaid, Choice
Catastrophic Illness Benefit: Varies per case

Type of Payment Plans Offered
POS, Combination FFS & DFFS

Geographic Areas Served
Allegany, Cattaraugus, Chautauqua, Erie, Genesee, Niagara, Orleans & Wyoming counties of western New York

Subscriber Information
Average Monthly Fee Per Subscriber
(Employee + Employer Contribution):
Employee Only (Self): Varies by plan
Average Subscriber Co-Payment:
Primary Care Physician: $10.00
Prescription Drugs: $7.00
Hospital ER: $35.00
Home Health Care: $10.00
Home Health Care Max. Days/Visits Covered: 365 days
Nursing Home: $0
Nursing Home Max. Days/Visits Covered: 45 days

Network Qualifications
Pre-Admission Certification: Yes

Peer Review Type
Utilization Review: Yes
Second Surgical Opinion: Yes
Case Management: Yes

Publishes and Distributes Report Card: No

Accreditation Certification
TJC, NCQA
Utilization Review, Pre-Admission Certification, State Licensure, Quality Assurance Program

Key Personnel
President and CEO......................Michael W Cropp, MD
mcropp@independenthealth.com
Exec Dir, IH Foundation ....Carrie Meyer
Dir, Health Promotion ....Peggy Davis , RN
SVP, HR & Org Development...................Gord Cumming
SVP, Member Services ....Jill Syracuse
Dir, Pharmacy Services...................Martin Burruano, RPh
EVP, Chief Marketing Offc.......................John Rodgers
Chief Medical Officer ....Thomas J Foels, MD
Assoc Medical Director ....Kathleen Mylotte, MD
Assoc Medical Director ....Judith Feld, MD
Dir, Public Relations............................Frank Sava
716-635-3885
fsava@independenthealth.com

Specialty Managed Care Partners
Enters into Contracts with Regional Business Coalitions: No

---

788   Independent Health Medicare Plan
511 Farber Lakes Drive
Buffalo, NY 14221
Toll-Free: 800-958-4405
Phone: 716-631-5392
Fax: 716-631-0430
wnyms@independenthealth.com
www.independenthealth.com

Healthplan and Services Defined
PLAN TYPE: Medicare
Benefits Offered: Chiropractic, Dental, Disease Management, Home Care, Inpatient SNF, Physical Therapy, Podiatry, Prescription, Psychiatric, Vision, Wellness

Type of Coverage
Individual, Medicare

Geographic Areas Served
Available within New York state only

Subscriber Information
Average Monthly Fee Per Subscriber
(Employee + Employer Contribution):
Employee Only (Self): Varies
Medicare: Varies
Average Annual Deductible Per Subscriber:

Employee Only (Self): Varies
Medicare: Varies
Average Subscriber Co-Payment:
Primary Care Physician: Varies
Non-Network Physician: Varies
Prescription Drugs: Varies
Hospital ER: Varies
Home Health Care: Varies
Home Health Care Max. Days/Visits Covered: Varies
Nursing Home: Varies
Nursing Home Max. Days/Visits Covered: Varies

Key Personnel
President and CEO......................Michael W Cropp, MD
mcropp@independenthealth.com
Exec Dir, IH Foundation ....Carrie Meyer
Dir, Health Promotion ....Peggy Davis , RN
SVP, HR & Org Development...................Gord Cumming
SVP, Member Services ....Jill Syracuse
Dir, Pharmacy Services...................Martin Burruano, RPh
EVP, Chief Marketing Offc.......................John Rodgers
Chief Medical Officer ....Thomas J Foels, MD
Assoc Medical Director ....Kathleen Mylotte, MD
Assoc Medical Director ....Judith Feld, MD
Dir, Public Relations............................Frank Sava
716-635-3885
fsava@independenthealth.com

---

789   Island Group Administration, Inc.
3 Toilsome Lane
East Hampton, NY 11937
Toll-Free: 800-926-2306
Phone: 631-324-2306
Fax: 631-324-7021
lrkaplan@optonline.net
www.islandgroupadmin.com
For Profit Organization: Yes
Year Founded: 1990
Owned by an Integrated Delivery Network (IDN): No
Federally Qualified: No
Number of Affiliated Hospitals: 9,055
Number of Primary Care Physicians: 21,010
Total Enrollment: 52,000

Healthplan and Services Defined
PLAN TYPE: Multiple
Model Type: TPA
Plan Specialty: Dental, Vision, Radiology, Worker's Compensation, UR, Medical
Benefits Offered: Chiropractic, Dental, Disease Management, Home Care, Podiatry, Prescription, Psychiatric, Transplant, Vision, Wellness, Worker's Compensation, Medical, Hospital

Type of Coverage
Varies

Geographic Areas Served
Nationwide

Subscriber Information
Average Monthly Fee Per Subscriber
(Employee + Employer Contribution):
Employee Only (Self): Varies by plan

Peer Review Type
Utilization Review: Yes
Second Surgical Opinion: Yes
Case Management: Yes

Accreditation Certification
Utilization Review, Pre-Admission Certification, State Licensure

Key Personnel
President ....Alan Kaplan
CFO ....Rosemarie Nuzzi
COO ....Melissa King

Claims Supervisor............................Cindy Bacon, RN
Executive Vice President ....Lynn Kaplan
Credentialing ....Lynn Kaplan
QA/UR ....Lucille Dunne, RN
Provider Services...........................Ruthann Barron
Sales ....Alan Kaplan

Specialty Managed Care Partners
Standard Security; CareMark PBM

790 Liberty Health Advantage Medicare Plan

1 Huntington Quadrangle
Suite 3N01
Melville, NY 11747
Toll-Free: 866-542-4269
Phone: 631-777-1070
Fax: 866-542-6359
www.libertyhealthadvantage.com

Healthplan and Services Defined
  PLAN TYPE: Medicare
  Other Type: HMO
  Benefits Offered: Chiropractic, Dental, Disease Management, Home
    Care, Inpatient SNF, Physical Therapy, Podiatry, Prescription,
    Psychiatric, Vision, Wellness

Type of Coverage
  Individual, Medicare

Geographic Areas Served
  Available within New York state only

Subscriber Information
  Average Monthly Fee Per Subscriber
    (Employee + Employer Contribution):
      Employee Only (Self): Varies
      Medicare: Varies
  Average Annual Deductible Per Subscriber:
      Employee Only (Self): Varies
      Medicare: Varies
  Average Subscriber Co-Payment:
      Primary Care Physician: Varies
      Non-Network Physician: Varies
      Prescription Drugs: Varies
      Hospital ER: Varies
      Home Health Care: Varies
      Home Health Care Max. Days/Visits Covered: Varies
      Nursing Home: Varies
      Nursing Home Max. Days/Visits Covered: Varies

Key Personnel
  President ....Richard Koenigsberg
  SVP Business Development ....Jon Leeke
  VP/Behavioral Health........................Jim McCreath
  VP/Client Services ....Cindy Waterman
  Office Manager................................Stacey Carroll

791 MagnaCare

1 Penn Plaza
Suite 2000
New York, NY 10119
Toll-Free: 800-235-7267
Phone: 516-282-8000
providerrelations@magnacare.com
www.magnacare.com
Secondary Address: 825 East Gate Blvd, Garden City, NY 11530
For Profit Organization: Yes
Year Founded: 1990
Number of Affiliated Hospitals: 260
Number of Primary Care Physicians: 70,000
Number of Referral/Specialty Physicians: 58,000
Total Enrollment: 1,326,000
State Enrollment: 928,200

Healthplan and Services Defined
  PLAN TYPE: PPO
  Model Type: Network
  Plan Specialty: ASO, Behavioral Health, Chiropractic, Dental, Lab,
    Radiology, Worker's Compensation, UR
  Benefits Offered: Behavioral Health, Chiropractic, Dental, Home
    Care, Inpatient SNF, Physical Therapy, Podiatry, Prescription,
    Psychiatric, Worker's Compensation

Type of Coverage
  Leased Network Arrangement

Type of Payment Plans Offered
  DFFS

Geographic Areas Served
  New Jersey and New York

Subscriber Information
  Average Monthly Fee Per Subscriber
    (Employee + Employer Contribution):
      Employee Only (Self): Varies
  Average Subscriber Co-Payment:
      Primary Care Physician: $15.00
      Prescription Drugs: $10.00/20.00
      Home Health Care: Varies
      Home Health Care Max. Days/Visits Covered: Varies
      Nursing Home: Varies
      Nursing Home Max. Days/Visits Covered: Varies

Network Qualifications
  Pre-Admission Certification: Yes

Peer Review Type
  Utilization Review: Yes
  Second Surgical Opinion: No
  Case Management: Yes

Accreditation Certification
  TJC Accreditation, Utilization Review, Pre-Admission Certification,
    State Licensure, Quality Assurance Program

Key Personnel
  President/CEO...........................Joseph Berardo, Jr
  SVP, Operations...............................Terry Beach
  SVP, CFO ....Jim Cusumano
  SVP, Medical Economics.....................Matthew Fienman
  VP, General Counsel.......................Craig B Greenfield
  SVP, Marketing...............................Robert Post
  VP, Business Development ....Derek Moore
  SVP, Chief Medical Offc ....Catherine Marino, MD
  VP, Human Resources ....Julie Bank
  SVP, Information Systems.......................Arun Bhatia
  SVP, Sales & Acct Mgmt.....................Michael Jordan

Average Claim Compensation
  Physician's Fees Charged: 50%
  Hospital's Fees Charged: 60%

Specialty Managed Care Partners
  American Psych Systems, Intra State Choice Management
    Chiropractic

Employer References
  Local 947, District Council of Painters #9

792 Meritain Health: Corporate Headquarters

300 Corporate Parkway
Amherst, NY 14226
Toll-Free: 800-242-6226
Phone: 716-319-5725
sales@meritain.com
www.meritain.com
For Profit Organization: Yes
Year Founded: 1983
Number of Affiliated Hospitals: 110
Number of Primary Care Physicians: 3,467
Number of Referral/Specialty Physicians: 5,720

Total Enrollment: 500,000
State Enrollment: 450,000

Healthplan and Services Defined
  PLAN TYPE: PPO
  Model Type: Network
  Plan Specialty: Dental, Disease Management, Vision, Radiology, UR
  Benefits Offered: Prescription
  Offers Demand Management Patient Information Service: Yes

Type of Coverage
  Commercial

Geographic Areas Served
  Nationwide

Subscriber Information
  Average Monthly Fee Per Subscriber
    (Employee + Employer Contribution):
      Employee Only (Self): Varies by plan

Accreditation Certification
  URAC
  TJC Accreditation, Medicare Approved, Utilization Review,
    Pre-Admission Certification, State Licensure, Quality Assurance
    Program

Key Personnel
  CEO . . . . .Elliot Cooperstone
    ecooperstone@prodigyhealthgroup.com
  EVP/CFO . . . . .Vincent DiMura, CPA
    vince.dimura@meritain.com
  Regional President . . . . .Melissa Ellwood
    melissa.ellwood@meritain.com
  Regional President . . . . .Stephen H Heck
    steve.heck@meritain.com
  Regional President . . . . .Margie Mann
    margie.degrace@meritain.com
  SVP, Cost Management . . . . .Dale N Lyman
    dale.lyman@meritain.com
  Chief Medical Officer . . . . .Larry J Lutter, MD
    larry.lutter@meritain.com
  Regional President . . . . .Chris Reef
    reefc@wellbornhealthplans.com
  SVP/CIO . . . . .Peter Fianu
    peter.fianu@meritain.com
  Regional President . . . . .David Smith
    david.smith@meritain.com
  SVP, Sales . . . . .David C Parker
    dave.parker@mertain.com
  SVP, Corp Development . . . . .Todd Squilanti
    todd.squilanti@meritain.com
  SVP, Underwriting . . . . .John T Sullivan
    john.sullivan@meritain.com

Average Claim Compensation
  Physician's Fees Charged: 78%
  Hospital's Fees Charged: 90%

Specialty Managed Care Partners
  Express Scripts, LabOne, Interactive Health Solutions

793 MetroPlus Health Plan

160 Water Street
3rd Floor
New York, NY 10038
Toll-Free: 800-303-9626
Phone: 212-908-8600
Fax: 212-908-8601
www.metroplus.org
Subsidiary of: New York City Health Hospitals Corporation
Non-Profit Organization: Yes
Year Founded: 1985
Owned by an Integrated Delivery Network (IDN): Yes
Number of Affiliated Hospitals: 11
Number of Primary Care Physicians: 12,000

Total Enrollment: 332,128
State Enrollment: 332,128

Healthplan and Services Defined
  PLAN TYPE: HMO
  Model Type: Network
  Benefits Offered: Disease Management, Prescription, Wellness, Nurse
    management line, TeleHealth

Type of Coverage
  Medicaid, Child Health Plus, Family Health Pl

Geographic Areas Served
  Brooklyn, Bronx, Manhattan and Queens

Accreditation Certification
  TJC Accreditation

Key Personnel
  Chairman of the Board . . . . .Bernard Rosen
  Executive Director . . . . .Arnold Saperstein, MD
  Medical Affairs . . . . .Van Dunn, MD
  CIO . . . . .Michael Mattola
  Provider Services . . . . .Joseph Dicks

Specialty Managed Care Partners
  Enters into Contracts with Regional Business Coalitions: Yes

794 MultiPlan, Inc.

115 Fifth Avenue
New York, NY 10003
Toll-Free: 800-677-1098
Phone: 212-780-2000
Fax: 920-347-9230
sales@multiplan.com
www.multiplan.com
For Profit Organization: Yes
Year Founded: 1980
Physician Owned Organization: No
Owned by an Integrated Delivery Network (IDN): No
Federally Qualified: No
Number of Affiliated Hospitals: 5,000
Number of Primary Care Physicians: 772,000
Number of Referral/Specialty Physicians: 772,000
Total Enrollment: 19,000,000

Healthplan and Services Defined
  PLAN TYPE: PPO
  Model Type: Network
  Plan Specialty: Primary PPO Network
  Offers Demand Management Patient Information Service: No

Geographic Areas Served
  Nationwide

Accreditation Certification
  URAC, NCQA

Key Personnel
  CEO . . . . .Mark Tabak
    800-279-9776
  EVP, CFO . . . . .Dave Redmond
    800-279-9776
  EVP, COO . . . . .Michael Ferrante
    800-279-9776
  EVP, Chief Marketing Off . . . . .Warren Handelman
    800-279-9776
  VP, Corporate Medical Dir . . . . .Paul Goldstein, MD
    800-279-9776
  EVP, Sales & Acct Mgmt . . . . .Dale White
    800-279-9776
  Dir, Marketing & Comm . . . . .Pamela Walker
    800-253-4417
    pamela.walker@muliplan.com

795 MVP Health Care Medicare Plan

625 State Street
PO Box 2207
Schenectady, NY 12301-2207
Toll-Free: 800-777-4793
Phone: 518-370-4793
Fax: 518-370-0830
www.mvphealthcare.com
Non-Profit Organization: Yes

Healthplan and Services Defined
PLAN TYPE: Medicare
Benefits Offered: Chiropractic, Dental, Disease Management, Home
Care, Inpatient SNF, Physical Therapy, Podiatry, Prescription,
Psychiatric, Vision, Wellness

Type of Coverage
Commercial, Individual, Medicare

Geographic Areas Served
Available witin New York state only

Subscriber Information
Average Monthly Fee Per Subscriber
(Employee + Employer Contribution):
Employee Only (Self): Varies
Medicare: Varies
Average Annual Deductible Per Subscriber:
Employee Only (Self): Varies
Medicare: Varies
Average Subscriber Co-Payment:
Primary Care Physician: Varies
Non-Network Physician: Varies
Prescription Drugs: Varies
Hospital ER: Varies
Home Health Care: Varies
Home Health Care Max. Days/Visits Covered: Varies
Nursing Home: Varies
Nursing Home Max. Days/Visits Covered: Varies

Accreditation Certification
NCQA

Key Personnel
President/CEO . . . . .David Oliker
EVP/COO . . . . .Chris Henchey
EVP/Rochester Operations. . . . . .Lisa A Brubaker
EVP/Network Management . . . . .Mark Fish
EVP/Planning. . . . . .Alfred Gatti
EVP/Chief Legal Officer. . . . . .Denise Gonick, Esq
EVP/Human Resources. . . . . .James Morrill

796 MVP Health Care: Buffalo Region

6255 Sheridan Drive
Buffalo, NY 14221
Phone: 716-839-1366
Fax: 716-839-1795
www.mvphealthcare.com
Non-Profit Organization: Yes
Total Enrollment: 750,000

Healthplan and Services Defined
PLAN TYPE: HMO/PPO

Type of Coverage
Commercial, Individual

Accreditation Certification
NCQA

Key Personnel
President/CEO . . . . .David Oliker
EVP/COO . . . . .Chris Henchey
EVP/Rochester Operations. . . . . .Lisa A Brubaker
EVP/Network Management . . . . .Mark Fish
EVP/Planning. . . . . .Alfred Gatti

EVP/Chief Legal Officer. . . . . .Denise Gonick, Esq
EVP/Human Resources. . . . . .James Morrill

797 MVP Health Care: Central New York

4947 Commercial Drive
Suite 3
Yorkville, NY 13495
Toll-Free: 800-888-9635
Phone: 315-736-1625
Fax: 315-736-7002
www.mvphealthcare.com
Non-Profit Organization: Yes
Year Founded: 1983
Owned by an Integrated Delivery Network (IDN): Yes
Number of Affiliated Hospitals: 115
Number of Primary Care Physicians: 12,000
Number of Referral/Specialty Physicians: 7,371
Total Enrollment: 750,000

Healthplan and Services Defined
PLAN TYPE: HMO/PPO
Model Type: IPA
Plan Specialty: ASO
Benefits Offered: Behavioral Health, Chiropractic, Complementary
Medicine, Dental, Disease Management, Home Care, Inpatient
SNF, Physical Therapy, Podiatry, Prescription, Psychiatric,
Transplant, Vision, Wellness, Worker's Compensation
DMPI Services Offered: After Hours Phone Line, Health Central
(Library), Little Footprints Prenatal Program, Health Risk
Assestments, Adult and Childhood Immunizations

Type of Coverage
Commercial, Individual, Indemnity, Self Funded, Administrative
Service
Catastrophic Illness Benefit: Covered

Type of Payment Plans Offered
POS, DFFS, Capitated, FFS, Combination FFS & DFFS

Geographic Areas Served
In New York State: Albany, Broome, Cayuga, Chenango, Columbia,
Cortland, Oswego, Delaware, Dutchess, Fulton, Greene, Hamilton,
Herkimer, Lewis, Madison, Montgomery, Oneida, Onondaga, Orange,
Ostego, Putnam, Rensselaer, Saratoga, Schenectady, Schoharie, Tioga,
Ulster, Warren, Washington counties. In Vermont: Addison,
Bennington, Caledonia, Chittenden, Essex, Franklin, Gran Isle,
Lamoille, Orange, Rutland, Washington, Windham, Windsor

Subscriber Information
Average Monthly Fee Per Subscriber
(Employee + Employer Contribution):
Employee Only (Self): Varies by plan
Employee & 2 Family Members: $0
Average Annual Deductible Per Subscriber:
Employee Only (Self): $200
Employee & 1 Family Member: $200
Employee & 2 Family Members: $200 ind./500 family
Average Subscriber Co-Payment:
Primary Care Physician: $20.00
Non-Network Physician: $20.00
Prescription Drugs: $5.00/10.00
Hospital ER: $50.00
Home Health Care Max. Days/Visits Covered: Unlimited
Nursing Home Max. Days/Visits Covered: 45 days

Network Qualifications
Pre-Admission Certification: Yes

Peer Review Type
Utilization Review: Yes
Case Management: Yes

Publishes and Distributes Report Card: Yes

Accreditation Certification
NCQA

TJC Accreditation, Medicare Approved, Utilization Review, Pre-Admission Certification, State Licensure, Quality Assurance Program

Key Personnel
President/CEO ....David Oliker
EVP/COO ....Chris Henchey
EVP/Rochester Operations.....................Lisa A Brubaker
EVP/Network Management ....Mark Fish
EVP/Planning.................................Alfred Gatti
EVP/Chief Legal Officer...................Denise Gonick, Esq
EVP/Human Resources.........................James Morrill

Average Claim Compensation
Physician's Fees Charged: 75%
Hospital's Fees Charged: 65%

798 MVP Health Care: Corporate Office

625 State Street
PO Box 2207
Schenectady, NY 12301-2207
Toll-Free: 800-777-4793
Phone: 518-370-4793
Fax: 518-370-0830
www.mvphealthcare.com
Non-Profit Organization: Yes
Year Founded: 1983
Owned by an Integrated Delivery Network (IDN): Yes
Federally Qualified: Yes
Number of Affiliated Hospitals: 115
Number of Primary Care Physicians: 13,840
Number of Referral/Specialty Physicians: 7,371
Total Enrollment: 750,000

Healthplan and Services Defined
PLAN TYPE: HMO/PPO
Model Type: IPA
Plan Specialty: ASO
Benefits Offered: Behavioral Health, Chiropractic, Complementary Medicine, Dental, Disease Management, Home Care, Inpatient SNF, Physical Therapy, Podiatry, Prescription, Psychiatric, Transplant, Vision, Wellness, Worker's Compensation
DMPI Services Offered: After Hours Phone Line, Health Central (Library), Little Footprints Prenatal Program, Health Risk Assestments, Adult and Childhood Immunizations

Type of Coverage
Commercial, Individual, Indemnity, Self Funded, Administrative Service
Catastrophic Illness Benefit: Covered

Type of Payment Plans Offered
POS, DFFS, Capitated, FFS, Combination FFS & DFFS

Geographic Areas Served
In New York State: Albany, Cayuga, Cortland, Oswego, Columbia, Delaware, Dutchess, Fulton, Greene, Herkimer, Lewis, Madison, Montgomery, Oneida, Onondaga, Ostego, Putnam, Rensselaer, Rockland, Saratoga, Schenectady, Schoharie, Sullivan, Ulster, Warren, Westchwester counties. In Vermont: Addison, Bennington, Caledonia, Chittenden, Essex, Franklin, Gran Isle, Lamoille, Orange, Orleans, Rutland, Washington, Windham, Windsor counties

Subscriber Information
Average Monthly Fee Per Subscriber
(Employee + Employer Contribution):
Employee Only (Self): Varies by plan
Employee & 2 Family Members: $0
Average Annual Deductible Per Subscriber:
Employee Only (Self): $200
Employee & 1 Family Member: $200
Employee & 2 Family Members: $200 ind/500 family
Average Subscriber Co-Payment:
Primary Care Physician: $20.00
Non-Network Physician: $20.00

Prescription Drugs: $5.00/10.00
Hospital ER: $50.00
Home Health Care Max. Days/Visits Covered: Unlimited
Nursing Home Max. Days/Visits Covered: 45 days

Network Qualifications
Pre-Admission Certification: Yes

Peer Review Type
Utilization Review: Yes
Case Management: Yes

Publishes and Distributes Report Card: Yes

Accreditation Certification
NCQA
TJC Accreditation, Medicare Approved, Utilization Review, Pre-Admission Certification, State Licensure, Quality Assurance Program

Key Personnel
President/CEO ....David Oliker
EVP/COO ....Chris Henchey
EVP/Rochester Operations.....................Lisa A Brubaker
EVP/Network Management ....Karla Austen
Chief Financial Officer...........................Mark Fish
EVP/Planning.................................Alfred Gatti
EVP/Chief Legal Officer...................Denise Gonick, Esq
Chief Medical Officer ....Dennis Allen
EVP/Human Resources.........................James Morrill
Dir, Public Relations ....Gary Hughes
800-777-4793
hughesg@mvphealthcare.com

Average Claim Compensation
Physician's Fees Charged: 75%
Hospital's Fees Charged: 65%

799 MVP Health Care: Mid-State Region

120 Madison Street
AXA Tower 2, Suite 1000
Syracuse, NY 13202
Toll-Free: 800-568-3668
Phone: 315-436-3701
Fax: 315-426-3799
www.mvphealthcare.com
Non-Profit Organization: Yes
Total Enrollment: 750,000

Healthplan and Services Defined
PLAN TYPE: HMO/PPO

Type of Coverage
Commercial, Individual

Accreditation Certification
NCQA

Key Personnel
President/CEO ....David Oliker
EVP/COO ....Chris Henchey
EVP/Rochester Operations.....................Lisa A Brubaker
EVP/Network Management ....Mark Fish
EVP/Planning.................................Alfred Gatti
EVP/Chief Legal Officer...................Denise Gonick, Esq
EVP/Human Resources.........................James Morrill

800 MVP Health Care: Western New York

325 State Street
Schenectady, NY 12305
Toll-Free: 800-777-4793
Fax: 518-386-7800
www.mvphealthcare.com
Non-Profit Organization: Yes
Year Founded: 1979
Owned by an Integrated Delivery Network (IDN): Yes

Federally Qualified: Yes
Number of Affiliated Hospitals: 20
Number of Primary Care Physicians: 1,091
Number of Referral/Specialty Physicians: 4,500
Total Enrollment: 750,000

Healthplan and Services Defined
PLAN TYPE: HMO/PPO
Model Type: IPA
Plan Specialty: ASO, Behavioral Health, Chiropractic, Disease Management, Vision
Benefits Offered: Behavioral Health, Chiropractic, Dental, Disease Management, Home Care, Inpatient SNF, Physical Therapy, Podiatry, Prescription, Psychiatric, Transplant, Vision, Wellness
Offers Demand Management Patient Information Service: Yes
DMPI Services Offered: Diabetes, CHF, Cancer

Type of Coverage
Commercial, Individual, Medicare, Medicaid
Catastrophic Illness Benefit: Covered

Type of Payment Plans Offered
POS, DFFS, Capitated, FFS

Geographic Areas Served
Genesee, Livingston, Monroe, Ontario, Orleans, Seneca, Wayne, Wyoming, & Yates counties

Subscriber Information
Average Monthly Fee Per Subscriber
(Employee + Employer Contribution):
Employee Only (Self): Varies by plan
Average Annual Deductible Per Subscriber:
Employee Only (Self): $0
Employee & 1 Family Member: $0
Employee & 2 Family Members: $0
Medicare: $0
Average Subscriber Co-Payment:
Primary Care Physician: $5.00/10.00/15.00
Non-Network Physician: Not covered
Prescription Drugs: $10.00/20.00/35.00
Hospital ER: $50.00-100.00
Home Health Care: $10/day
Home Health Care Max. Days/Visits Covered: Varies
Nursing Home Max. Days/Visits Covered: 120/yr

Network Qualifications
Pre-Admission Certification: Yes

Peer Review Type
Utilization Review: Yes
Second Surgical Opinion: Yes
Case Management: Yes

Publishes and Distributes Report Card: Yes

Accreditation Certification
NCQA, HEDIS
TJC Accreditation

Key Personnel
President/CEO . . . . .David Oliker
EVP/COO . . . . .Chris Henchey
EVP/Rochester Operations .Lisa A Brubaker
EVP/Network Management . . . . .Karla Austen
Chief Financial Officer . . . . .Mark Fish
EVP/Planning . . . . .Alfred Gatti
EVP/Chief Legal Officer . . . . .Denise Gonick, Esq
Chief Medical Officer . . . . .Dennis Allen
EVP/Human Resources . . . . .James Morrill
Dir, Public Relations . . . . .Gary Hughes
800-777-4793
hughesg@mvphealthcare.com

Average Claim Compensation
Physician's Fees Charged: 1%

Specialty Managed Care Partners
MH, LandMark

Employer References
Eastman Kodak, Xerox, Federal Government, Monroe County Employees, New York State Employees

801 National Health Plan Corporation
11 Penn Plaza
Suite 330
New York, NY 10001
Toll-Free: 800-647-2677
Phone: 212-279-3232
Fax: 212-629-0749
www.nationalhealthplan.com
For Profit Organization: Yes
Year Founded: 1975
Number of Affiliated Hospitals: 2,500
Number of Primary Care Physicians: 250,000
Number of Referral/Specialty Physicians: 5,000
State Enrollment: 200,000

Healthplan and Services Defined
PLAN TYPE: PPO
Model Type: IPA, Group
Plan Specialty: ASO, Behavioral Health, Chiropractic, Dental, Disease Management, EPO, Lab, MSO, PBM, Vision, Radiology, Worker's Compensation
Benefits Offered: Prescription

Type of Coverage
Individual, Indemnity, Supplemental Medicare

Type of Payment Plans Offered
DFFS, FFS, Combination FFS & DFFS

Geographic Areas Served
Connecticut, New Jersey, New York & Pennsylvania; Prescriptions nationwide

Subscriber Information
Average Monthly Fee Per Subscriber
(Employee + Employer Contribution):
Employee & 2 Family Members: $8.00
Medicare: $6.25
Average Annual Deductible Per Subscriber:
Employee Only (Self): $0
Employee & 1 Family Member: $0
Employee & 2 Family Members: $0
Medicare: $0
Average Subscriber Co-Payment:
Primary Care Physician: $0
Non-Network Physician: Varies
Prescription Drugs: $1.00-5.00
Home Health Care: $0

Network Qualifications
Pre-Admission Certification: Yes

Peer Review Type
Utilization Review: Yes
Second Surgical Opinion: Yes
Case Management: Yes

Publishes and Distributes Report Card: No

Accreditation Certification
TJC Accreditation, Pre-Admission Certification

Key Personnel
President and CEO . . . . .David Konigsberg
Chairman . . . . .Alvin Konigsberg
Exec Vice President . . . . .David Zaback
Director Claims . . . . .Sharon Weinberg
In House Formulary . . . . .Alvin Konigsberg
Sales . . . . .David Konigsberg

Average Claim Compensation
Physician's Fees Charged: 10%
Hospital's Fees Charged: 10%

Specialty Managed Care Partners
Enters into Contracts with Regional Business Coalitions: No

802 National Medical Health Card
Acquired by SXC Health Solutions

803 Northeast Community Care
100 Elwood Davis Road
North Syracuse, NY 13212
Toll-Free: 866-395-4754
Phone: 315-461-4790
Fax: 315-461-4798
www.northeastcommunitycare.com
Subsidiary of: Arcadian Health Plans

Healthplan and Services Defined
PLAN TYPE: Medicare

Type of Coverage
Medicare

804 NOVA Healthcare Administrators
250 Essjay Road
Buffalo, NY 14221
Phone: 716-773-2122
Fax: 716-773-1276
www.novahealthcare.com
Subsidiary of: Acquired by Azeros Health Plans
For Profit Organization: Yes
Year Founded: 1982
Number of Affiliated Hospitals: 60
Number of Primary Care Physicians: 3,000
Total Enrollment: 80,000
State Enrollment: 100,000

Healthplan and Services Defined
PLAN TYPE: Other
Other Type: TPA
Plan Specialty: ASO, Dental
Benefits Offered: Dental, Disease Management, Prescription,
Wellness

Type of Coverage
Commercial, Indemnity

Geographic Areas Served
Nationwide

Network Qualifications
Pre-Admission Certification: Yes

Peer Review Type
Utilization Review: Yes
Second Surgical Opinion: Yes
Case Management: Yes

Key Personnel
President . . . . .Larry Thompson
Vice President . . . . .Kristy Long

Specialty Managed Care Partners
Express Scripts

805 Oxford Health Plans: New York
202 Canal Street
6th Floor
New York, NY 10013-4517
Phone: 212-801-3388
Fax: 212-805-3020
www.oxhp.com
Subsidiary of: UnitedHealthCare
For Profit Organization: Yes
Number of Affiliated Hospitals: 218

Number of Primary Care Physicians: 50,000
Total Enrollment: 1,500,000

Healthplan and Services Defined
PLAN TYPE: HMO
Benefits Offered: Behavioral Health, Chiropractic, Disease
Management, Inpatient SNF, Physical Therapy, Podiatry,
Psychiatric

Type of Coverage
Commercial, Medicare

Type of Payment Plans Offered
POS

Geographic Areas Served
Sullivan, Ulster, Dutchess, Putman, Orange, Rockland, Westchester,
Bergen, Bronx, Kings, Richmond, Queens, Nassau and Suffolk
counties

Subscriber Information
Average Monthly Fee Per Subscriber
(Employee + Employer Contribution):
Employee Only (Self): Varies by plan

Peer Review Type
Case Management: Yes

Publishes and Distributes Report Card: Yes

Accreditation Certification
NCQA

Key Personnel
Chairman and CEO . . . . .Charles G Berg
Public Relations . . . . .Maria Gordon Shydlo
Executive VP/CFO. . . . . .Kurt B Thompson
VP Claims . . . . .Micheal Santoro
Executive VP Sales/Marketing. . . . . .Kevin R Hill
Exec. VP/Chief Medical. . . . . .Alan M Muney, MD
Sr VP Chief Info Officer . . . . .Arthur L Gonzalez
VP Operations . . . . .Kevin Appleton
Sales . . . . .Kevin R Hill

806 Perfect Health Insurance Company
Acquired by GHI, an EmblemHealth Company

807 Quality Health Plans of New York
2805 Veterans Memorial Highway
Suite 17
Ronkonkoma, NY 11779
Toll-Free: 877-233-7058
www.qualityhealthplans.com
Year Founded: 2003
Physician Owned Organization: Yes
Total Enrollment: 19,000

Healthplan and Services Defined
PLAN TYPE: Medicare

Type of Coverage
Supplemental Medicare

Geographic Areas Served
13 counties in Florida

Key Personnel
President . . . . .Haider A Khan, MD
CEO & CMO . . . . .Nazeer H Khan, MD
COO. . . . . .Sabiha Khan, MBA
Medical Director . . . . .Trevor A Rose, MD, MS MMM
Reg Mgr, Network Services . . . . .Dawn R Smith
Director, Finance . . . . .David A Sherwin
Corp Services Manager . . . . .Farrah Sanabria, PHR
Director, Medical Affairs . . . . .Lisa Cierpka, RN
Dir, Business Development . . . . .Amber R Clements
Dir, Compliance. . . . . .Angela Hart
Medical Director. . . . . .Michael Yanuck, MD
Medical Director. . . . . .Richard Bonanno, MD

Media Contact . . . . Mike Worley
  866-747-2700
  mworley@qualityhealthplans.comm

808 Touchstone Health HMO

Church Street Station
PO Box 1265
White Plains, NY 10602
Toll-Free: 877-867-5750
Phone: 888-777-0204
Fax: 888-777-0374
information@touchstoneh.com
www.touchstoneh.com
Year Founded: 1980
Total Enrollment: 11,000

Healthplan and Services Defined
  PLAN TYPE: Medicare
  Benefits Offered: Chiropractic, Dental, Disease Management, Home
    Care, Inpatient SNF, Physical Therapy, Podiatry, Prescription,
    Psychiatric, Vision, Wellness

Type of Coverage
  Individual, Medicare, Supplemental Medicare

Geographic Areas Served
  New York state only

Subscriber Information
  Average Monthly Fee Per Subscriber
    (Employee + Employer Contribution):
      Employee Only (Self): Varies
      Medicare: Varies
  Average Annual Deductible Per Subscriber:
    Employee Only (Self): Varies
    Medicare: Varies
  Average Subscriber Co-Payment:
    Primary Care Physician: Varies
    Non-Network Physician: Varies
    Prescription Drugs: Varies
    Hospital ER: Varies
    Home Health Care: Varies
    Home Health Care Max. Days/Visits Covered: Varies
    Nursing Home: Varies
    Nursing Home Max. Days/Visits Covered: Varies

Key Personnel
  President/CEO . . . . Bryan D Birch
  Chief Administrative Offc . . . . Robert Caione
  General Counsel/Secretary . . . . Edward C Fargis
  Chief Marketing Officer . . . . Steven V Calabrese
  Chief Medical Officer . . . . Roger London, MD

809 United Concordia: New York

420 Fifth Avenue
Third Floor
New York, NY 10018
Toll-Free: 800-235-6753
Phone: 212-921-0394
Fax: 212-921-0539
nysales@ucci.com
www.secure.ucci.com
Secondary Address: 159 Express Street, Plainview, NY 11803,
  516-827-6720
For Profit Organization: Yes
Year Founded: 1971
Number of Primary Care Physicians: 111,000
Total Enrollment: 8,000,000

Healthplan and Services Defined
  PLAN TYPE: Dental
  Plan Specialty: Dental
  Benefits Offered: Dental

Type of Coverage
  Commercial, Individual

Geographic Areas Served
  Military personnel and their families, nationwide

810 UnitedHealthCare of New York

5015 Campuswood Drive
Suite 303
East Syracuse, NY 13057
Toll-Free: 800-339-5380
Phone: 315-433-5700
www.uhc.com
Secondary Address: 2 Penn Plaza, 7th Floor, New York, NY 10121,
  212-216-6400
Subsidiary of: UnitedHealth Group
For Profit Organization: Yes
Year Founded: 1987
Federally Qualified: Yes
Number of Affiliated Hospitals: 170
Number of Primary Care Physicians: 8,500
Number of Referral/Specialty Physicians: 2,225
Total Enrollment: 75,000,000
State Enrollment: 222,000

Healthplan and Services Defined
  PLAN TYPE: HMO/PPO
  Model Type: IPA
  Benefits Offered: Disease Management, Prescription, Wellness
  Offers Demand Management Patient Information Service: Yes

Type of Payment Plans Offered
  DFFS, Capitated

Geographic Areas Served
  New York, New Jersey & Fairfield County, Connecticut

Network Qualifications
  Pre-Admission Certification: Yes

Peer Review Type
  Utilization Review: Yes
  Second Surgical Opinion: Yes
  Case Management: Yes

Publishes and Distributes Report Card: Yes

Accreditation Certification
  TJC Accreditation, Medicare Approved, Utilization Review,
    Pre-Admission Certification, State Licensure, Quality Assurance
    Program

Key Personnel
  President . . . . Sharon Seitzman
  CFO . . . . Dan Gollman
  In House Formulary . . . . Ann Marie O'Brien
  Marketing . . . . Barbara Willis
  Medical Affairs . . . . Lillian Grillo
  Member Services . . . . Timothy Stover
  Provider Services . . . . William Lamoreux
  Sales . . . . Gregory Choy
  Media Contact . . . . Mary McElrath-Jones
    914-467-2039
    mary_r_mcelrath-jones@uhc.com

Specialty Managed Care Partners
  Enters into Contracts with Regional Business Coalitions: Yes

811 Univera Healthcare

205 Park Club Lane
Buffalo, NY 14221-5239
Toll-Free: 800-427-8490
Phone: 716-847-1480
Fax: 716-847-1257
www.univerahealthcare.com
Mailing Address: PO Box 23000, Rochester, NY 14692

Subsidiary of: The Lifetime Healthcare Companies
Non-Profit Organization: Yes
Number of Affiliated Hospitals: 35
Number of Primary Care Physicians: 5,700
Total Enrollment: 1,700,000
State Enrollment: 1,700,000

Healthplan and Services Defined
  PLAN TYPE: HMO
  Model Type: Network
  Plan Specialty: ASO, Behavioral Health, Chiropractic, Dental,
    Disease Management, EPO, Lab, MSO, PBM, Vision, Radiology,
    Worker's Compensation, UR
  Benefits Offered: Behavioral Health, Chiropractic, Complementary
    Medicine, Dental, Disease Management, Home Care, Inpatient
    SNF, Long-Term Care, Physical Therapy, Podiatry, Prescription,
    Psychiatric, Transplant, Vision, Wellness, Worker's Compensation,
    Life

Type of Coverage
  Commercial, Individual, Medicare

Geographic Areas Served
  Allegany, Cattaraugus, Chautauqua, Erie, Genesee, Niagara, Orleans
  and Wyoming counties

Subscriber Information
  Average Monthly Fee Per Subscriber
    (Employee + Employer Contribution):
      Employee Only (Self): Varies by plan
  Average Subscriber Co-Payment:
      Primary Care Physician: Varies
      Prescription Drugs: Varies

Publishes and Distributes Report Card: Yes

Accreditation Certification
  NCQA

Key Personnel
  President . . . . Arthur Wingerter
  Chief Executive Officer. . . . . David H Klein
  Chief Financial Officer . . . . Emil D Duda
  VP Network Contracting . . . . Lisa Meyers-Alessi
  VP, Chief Medical Officer . . . . Robert Holzhauer
  Regional Medical Officer. . . . . Richard Vienne, DO
  VP, Sales . . . . Pamela J Pawenski
  VP, Communications. . . . . Peter B Kates
    716-857-4495
    peter.kates@univerahealthcare.com

812 Universal American Medicare Plans
6 International Drive
Rye Brook, NY 10573-1068
Toll-Free: 866-714-3976
www.universalamerican.com
Total Enrollment: 2,000,000

Healthplan and Services Defined
  PLAN TYPE: Medicare
  Benefits Offered: Prescription

Type of Coverage
  Individual, Medicare

Geographic Areas Served
  Available in multiple states

Subscriber Information
  Average Monthly Fee Per Subscriber
    (Employee + Employer Contribution):
      Employee Only (Self): Varies
      Medicare: Varies
  Average Annual Deductible Per Subscriber:
      Employee Only (Self): Varies
      Medicare: Varies
  Average Subscriber Co-Payment:
      Primary Care Physician: Varies

  Non-Network Physician: Varies
  Prescription Drugs: Varies
  Hospital ER: Varies

Key Personnel
  Chairman & CEO . . . . Richard A Barasch
  EVP, Chief Financial Offc. . . . . Robert A Waegelein, CPA
  SVP, Corporate Developmnt. . . . . Gary M Jacobs
  Chief Operating Officer. . . . . Jason J Israel
  Pres, Medicare Advantage. . . . . Theodore M Carpenter, Jr
  Pres, Medicare Part D . . . . John Wardle
  SVP, Health Quality . . . . Robert M Hayes

813 Vytra Health Plans
395 N Service Road
PO Box 9091
Melville, NY 11747-9091
Toll-Free: 800-406-0806
Phone: 631-694-4000
Fax: 631-719-0911
memberservices@vytra.com
www.vytra.com
Subsidiary of: HIP Health Plan
Non-Profit Organization: Yes
Year Founded: 1985
Number of Affiliated Hospitals: 38
Number of Primary Care Physicians: 1,500
Number of Referral/Specialty Physicians: 10,000
Total Enrollment: 200,000
State Enrollment: 76,213

Healthplan and Services Defined
  PLAN TYPE: HMO/PPO
  Other Type: POS
  Model Type: IPA
  Plan Specialty: ASO, Chiropractic, Dental, Disease Management,
    EPO, Vision, Radiology
  Benefits Offered: Behavioral Health, Chiropractic, Complementary
    Medicine, Dental, Disease Management, Home Care, Inpatient
    SNF, Physical Therapy, Podiatry, Prescription, Psychiatric,
    Transplant, Vision, Wellness

Type of Payment Plans Offered
  Capitated

Geographic Areas Served
  Nassau, Queens, Suffolk counties and Long Island

Subscriber Information
  Average Monthly Fee Per Subscriber
    (Employee + Employer Contribution):
      Employee Only (Self): Varies by plan
  Average Subscriber Co-Payment:
      Primary Care Physician: $10.00
      Non-Network Physician: 25%
      Prescription Drugs: $5.00
      Hospital ER: $25.00
      Nursing Home: $0.00
      Nursing Home Max. Days/Visits Covered: 45 days

Accreditation Certification
  URAC, NCQA
  TJC Accreditation, Medicare Approved, Utilization Review,
    Pre-Admission Certification, State Licensure, Quality Assurance
    Program

Key Personnel
  President/CEO . . . . Tom McAteer, Jr
  COO . . . . Michael G Murphy
  CFO. . . . . Roy Goldman
  Marketing . . . . William A Bennett
  Chief Medical Officer. . . . . Jerry Royer, MD, MBA
  Human Resources . . . . Donna McDaniel
  Information Services. . . . . Garth Womack

SVP, Public Affairs . . . . Ilene Margolin
646-447-0098
imargolin@emblemhealth.com

Specialty Managed Care Partners
Health Care, Multi Plan

Health Insurance Coverage Status and Type of Coverage by Age

Category	All Persons		Under 18 years		Under 65 years		65 years and over	
	Number	%	Number	%	Number	%	Number	%
Total population	9,248	-	2,328	-	8,099	-	1,149	-
Covered by some type of health insurance	7,673 *(112)*	83.0 *(1.0)*	2,114 *(37)*	90.8 *(1.2)*	6,536 *(122)*	80.7 *(1.1)*	1,137 *(52)*	98.9 *(0.6)*
Covered by private health insurance	5,558 *(127)*	60.1 *(1.4)*	1,183 *(60)*	50.8 *(2.5)*	4,835 *(122)*	59.7 *(1.5)*	723 *(51)*	62.9 *(2.5)*
Employment based	4,774 *(134)*	51.6 *(1.4)*	1,091 *(60)*	46.9 *(2.5)*	4,415 *(123)*	54.5 *(1.5)*	360 *(38)*	31.3 *(3.0)*
Own employment based	2,713 *(85)*	29.3 *(0.9)*	2 *(2)*	0.1 *(0.1)*	2,424 *(77)*	29.9 *(0.9)*	289 *(32)*	25.2 *(2.6)*
Direct purchase	927 *(74)*	10.0 *(0.8)*	133 *(23)*	5.7 *(1.0)*	519 *(49)*	6.4 *(0.6)*	409 *(46)*	35.6 *(3.2)*
Covered by government health insurance	3,163 *(178)*	34.2 *(1.8)*	1,085 *(74)*	46.6 *(3.1)*	2,066 *(177)*	25.5 *(2.1)*	1,097 *(55)*	95.5 *(1.3)*
Covered by Medicaid	1,583 *(75)*	17.1 *(0.8)*	941 *(54)*	40.4 *(2.3)*	1,469 *(74)*	18.1 *(0.9)*	114 *(18)*	9.9 *(1.5)*
Also by private insurance	199 *(34)*	2.2 *(0.4)*	101 *(22)*	4.3 *(1.0)*	170 *(32)*	2.1 *(0.4)*	29 *(10)*	2.5 *(0.8)*
Covered by Medicare	1,334 *(64)*	14.4 *(0.7)*	3 *(3)*	0.1 *(0.1)*	239 *(28)*	2.9 *(0.3)*	1,095 *(54)*	95.3 *(1.3)*
Also by private insurance	751 *(54)*	8.1 *(0.6)*	3 *(3)*	0.1 *(0.1)*	69 *(15)*	0.9 *(0.2)*	681 *(52)*	59.3 *(2.6)*
Also by Medicaid	194 *(25)*	2.1 *(0.3)*	3 *(3)*	0.1 *(0.1)*	80 *(13)*	1.0 *(0.2)*	114 *(18)*	9.9 *(1.5)*
Covered by military health care	565 *(184)*	6.1 *(2.0)*	172 *(61)*	7.4 *(2.6)*	494 *(169)*	6.1 *(2.1)*	72 *(20)*	6.2 *(1.8)*
Not covered at any time during the year	1,575 *(89)*	17.0 *(1.0)*	213 *(27)*	9.2 *(1.2)*	1,563 *(90)*	19.3 *(1.1)*	13 *(7)*	1.1 *(0.6)*

Note: Numbers in thousands; figures cover 2010; standard error appears in parenthesis; (b) base less than 75,000; (x) not applicable
Source: U.S. Census Bureau, Current Population Survey, 2011 Annual Social and Economic Supplement. Table HI05. Health Insurance Coverage Status and Type of Coverage by State and Age for All People: 2010

North Carolina

814 Aetna Health of the Carolinas

11675 Great Oaks Way
Suite 330
Alpharetta, GA 30022
Toll-Free: 866-582-9629
www.aetna.com
For Profit Organization: Yes
Year Founded: 1995
Total Enrollment: 18,960

Healthplan and Services Defined
PLAN TYPE: HMO
Other Type: POS
Benefits Offered: Prescription

Type of Coverage
Commercial, Individual

Type of Payment Plans Offered
POS, DFFS, FFS

Geographic Areas Served
Statewide

Peer Review Type
Case Management: Yes

Accreditation Certification
NCQA

Key Personnel
President/CEO . . . . .William H Donaldson
General Manager . . . . .Rick Kelly
Sales. . . . . .Brian O'Shields

Employer References
NC Baptist Hospital

815 Assurant Employee Benefits: North Carolina

6302 Fairview Road
Suite 209
Charlotte, NC 28210-2254
Phone: 704-553-7609
Fax: 704-553-7821
benefits@assurant.com
www.assurantemployeebenefits.com
Subsidiary of: Assurant, Inc
For Profit Organization: Yes
Number of Primary Care Physicians: 112,000
Total Enrollment: 47,000

Healthplan and Services Defined
PLAN TYPE: Multiple
Plan Specialty: Dental, Vision, Long & Short-Term Disability
Benefits Offered: Dental, Vision, Wellness, AD&D, Life, LTD, STD

Type of Coverage
Commercial, Indemnity, Individual Dental Plans

Geographic Areas Served
Statewide

Subscriber Information
Average Monthly Fee Per Subscriber
(Employee + Employer Contribution):
Employee Only (Self): Varies by plan

Key Personnel
Sales Agent . . . . .Heather Omeo
PR Specialist. . . . . .Megan Hutchison
816-556-7815
megan.hutchison@assurant.com

816 Blue Cross & Blue Shield of North Carolina

5901 Chapel Hill Road
Durham, NC 27707
Toll-Free: 800-324-4973
Phone: 919-765-7347
Fax: 919-765-7288
www.bcbsnc.com
Mailing Address: PO Box 2291, Durham, NC 27702-2291
Non-Profit Organization: Yes
Year Founded: 1933
Number of Affiliated Hospitals: 113
Number of Primary Care Physicians: 5,200
Number of Referral/Specialty Physicians: 20,000
Total Enrollment: 3,718,355
State Enrollment: 3,718,355

Healthplan and Services Defined
PLAN TYPE: HMO/PPO
Model Type: Network
Plan Specialty: ASO, Behavioral Health, Chiropractic, Dental,
Disease Management, Lab, PBM, Vision, Radiology, UR
Benefits Offered: Behavioral Health, Chiropractic, Complementary
Medicine, Dental, Disease Management, Home Care, Inpatient
SNF, Long-Term Care, Physical Therapy, Podiatry, Prescription,
Psychiatric, Transplant, Vision, Wellness, AD&D, Life, LTD, STD
Offers Demand Management Patient Information Service: Yes
DMPI Services Offered: Health Line Blue Nurseline, VitaBlue, Optic
Blue, Atl Med Blue, Active Blue Magazine

Type of Coverage
Commercial, Individual, Supplemental Medicare

Type of Payment Plans Offered
POS, DFFS, FFS, Combination FFS & DFFS

Geographic Areas Served
Blue Cross and Blue Shield of North Carolina is licensed to do
business in all 100 counties in North Carolina

Subscriber Information
Average Monthly Fee Per Subscriber
(Employee + Employer Contribution):
Employee Only (Self): Varies by plan
Average Annual Deductible Per Subscriber:
Employee Only (Self): $250.00
Employee & 1 Family Member: $500.00
Employee & 2 Family Members: $500.00
Average Subscriber Co-Payment:
Primary Care Physician: $15.00
Prescription Drugs: $10.00/20.00/30.00
Hospital ER: $100.00
Home Health Care: 10%
Home Health Care Max. Days/Visits Covered: 20 days
Nursing Home: 10%
Nursing Home Max. Days/Visits Covered: 60 days

Network Qualifications
Pre-Admission Certification: Yes

Peer Review Type
Utilization Review: Yes
Second Surgical Opinion: Yes
Case Management: Yes

Accreditation Certification
NCQA
State Licensure

Key Personnel
President & CEO. . . . . .J Bradley Wilson
Chief Financial Officer. . . . . .Gerald Petkau
EVP/General Counsel . . . . .Maureen K O'Connor
SVP/Chief Info Officer . . . . .Alan Hughes
SVP/Human Resources Offc . . . . .Fara M Palumbo
Sr VP Sales/Marketing . . . . .John T Roos
john.roos@bcbsnc.com
SVP/Chief Medical Officer . . . . .Don W Bradley, MD

Average Claim Compensation
Physician's Fees Charged: 43%
Hospital's Fees Charged: 35%

Specialty Managed Care Partners
Magellan Behavioral Health (MH), Health Dialog (24-hour nurseline), Merck-Medco (pharmacy), Ceridian Benefits Services (COBRA), Chiropractic Network of the Carolinas, OptiCare Eye Health Network (vision)

817 Catalyst RX

4020 Wake Forest Road
Suite 102
Raleigh, NC 27609
Toll-Free: 800-323-6640
Phone: 301-548-2900
rxcsinfo@catalystrx.com
www.catalystrx.com
Subsidiary of: Catalyst Health Solutions
For Profit Organization: Yes
Year Founded: 1994
Total Enrollment: 5,000,000
State Enrollment: 325,000

Healthplan and Services Defined
PLAN TYPE: PPO
Model Type: Network
Plan Specialty: PBM
Benefits Offered: Prescription

Geographic Areas Served
Nationwide

Subscriber Information
Average Subscriber Co-Payment:
Prescription Drugs: $12.00

Accreditation Certification
Utilization Review, State Licensure

Key Personnel
Chief Executive Officer . . . . .David T Blair
301-548-2901
President & COO . . . . .Richard Bates
Treasurer & CFO. . . . . .Hai Tran
htran@chsi.com
General Counsel. . . . . .Bruce Metge
Mgr, Sales Administration . . . . .Ronelle Rondon
301-548-2900
media@catalysthealthsolutions.com

Employer References
Progress Energy, BB&T, SC Local Government Assurance Group, General Shale, Hickory Springs Manufacturing

818 CIGNA HealthCare of North Carolina

11016 Rushmore Drive
Suite 300
Charlotte, NC 28277
Toll-Free: 800-888-4973
Phone: 704-586-0708
Fax: 704-586-7181
www.cigna.com
Secondary Address: 701 Corporate Center Drive, Raleigh, NC 27607, 919-854-7000
For Profit Organization: Yes
Year Founded: 1992
Number of Primary Care Physicians: 20,100
Number of Referral/Specialty Physicians: 9,000
Total Enrollment: 29,583
State Enrollment: 29,583

Healthplan and Services Defined
PLAN TYPE: HMO
Other Type: POS
Model Type: IPA, Network
Benefits Offered: Behavioral Health, Chiropractic, Complementary Medicine, Dental, Disease Management, Home Care, Physical Therapy, Podiatry, Prescription, Psychiatric, Transplant, Vision, Wellness
DMPI Services Offered: 24 hour Health Information Line, Health Information Library, Automated ReferralLine

Type of Coverage
Commercial

Type of Payment Plans Offered
POS

Geographic Areas Served
Buncombe, Cabarrus, Caldwell, Catawba, Cleveland, Gaston, Henderson, Lincoln, Mecklenburg, Rowan, Stanly and Union counties

Subscriber Information
Average Monthly Fee Per Subscriber
(Employee + Employer Contribution):
Employee Only (Self): Varies by plan

Network Qualifications
Pre-Admission Certification: Yes

Peer Review Type
Utilization Review: Yes
Second Surgical Opinion: Yes
Case Management: Yes

Publishes and Distributes Report Card: Yes

Accreditation Certification
NCQA

Key Personnel
President . . . . .David M Cordani
Regional Vice President. .Joseph C Gregor
Sr VP/Marketing . . . . .James Lyski
President/Middle Markets .Matt Manders
Regional Vice President . . . . .Edgar A Miranda
President/National Accts . . . . .Noel Obourn
Chief Counsel . . . . .John Perlstein
Sr VP/Chief Underwriting .Jonathan Rubin
Executive VP/Operations . . . . .Scott A Storrer
President, Southeast Reg. . . . . .Michael W Triplett, Sr
President, Small Bus Seg. .Dennis Wilson
President, Group Ins . . . . .Gregory Wolf
Sr VP/Sales . . . . .Gary Kirkner
Sr VP/Marketing . . . . .Jay Menario
Chief Financial Officer . . . . .Peter J Vogt

819 CoreSource: North Carolina

5200 77 Center Drive
Suite 400
Charlotte, NC 28217
Toll-Free: 800-327-5462
Phone: 704-554-44400
www.coresource.com
Subsidiary of: Trustmark
Year Founded: 1980
Total Enrollment: 1,100,000

Healthplan and Services Defined
PLAN TYPE: Multiple
Other Type: TPA
Model Type: Network
Plan Specialty: Claims Administration, TPA
Benefits Offered: Behavioral Health, Home Care, Prescription, Transplant

Type of Coverage
Commercial

Geographic Areas Served
Nationwide

Accreditation Certification
Utilization Review, Pre-Admission Certification

820 Crescent Preferred Provider Organization

1200 Ridgefield Boulevard
Suite 215
Asheville, NC 28806
Toll-Free: 800-707-7726
Phone: 828-670-9145
Fax: 828-670-9155
information@crescentppo.com
www.crescentppo.com
Non-Profit Organization: Yes
Year Founded: 1999
Physician Owned Organization: Yes
Number of Affiliated Hospitals: 15
Number of Primary Care Physicians: 1,900
Number of Referral/Specialty Physicians: 2,400
Total Enrollment: 40,000
State Enrollment: 40,000

Healthplan and Services Defined
PLAN TYPE: PPO
Benefits Offered: Disease Management, Prescription, Wellness, Case Management, UR, TPA Services

Type of Coverage
Commercial, Individual

Geographic Areas Served
16 counties in Western North Carolina

Peer Review Type
Utilization Review: Yes
Case Management: Yes

Key Personnel
CEO . . . . .Myrna Harris
VP, Operations . . . . .Jennifer Moore
Pharmacy Benfits Coord. . . . . .Michelle Rumfelt
Provider Relations. . . . . .Deana Gardner
Client Services Coord . . . . .Delane Stiles
VP, Marketing . . . . .Keith Challenger
Director, Business Dev. . . . . .Stephen Harris, PhD
Medical Director. . . . . .Andrew Price, MD
CFO . . . . .Tara Pressley
Director, Health Mgmt . . . . .Jackie Dula
Credentialing Coordinator . . . . .Sandra Price
VP, Client Services. . . . . .Pat Hensley
VP, TPA Services. . . . . .Georgia Sasscer

821 Delta Dental of North Carolina

343 East Six Forks Road
Suite 180
Raleigh, NC 27609
Toll-Free: 800-662-8856
Fax: 919-832-6549
enrollmentnc@deltadentalnc.org
www.deltadentalnc.org
Non-Profit Organization: Yes
Number of Primary Care Physicians: 198,000
Total Enrollment: 54,000,000

Healthplan and Services Defined
PLAN TYPE: Dental
Other Type: Dental PPO
Plan Specialty: Dental
Benefits Offered: Dental

Type of Coverage
Commercial

Type of Payment Plans Offered
POS, DFFS, FFS

Geographic Areas Served
Statewide

Key Personnel
President & CEO. . . . . .Robert Rosenthal
Dir/Media & Public Affair . . . . .Elizabeth Risberg
415-972-8423

822 eHealthInsurance Services Inc.

11919 Foundation Place
Gold River, CA 95670
Toll-Free: 800-977-8860
info@ehealthinsurance.com
www.e.healthinsurance.com
Year Founded: 1997

Healthplan and Services Defined
PLAN TYPE: HMO/PPO
Benefits Offered: Dental, Life, STD

Type of Coverage
Commercial, Individual, Medicare

Geographic Areas Served
All 50 states in the USA and District of Columbia

Key Personnel
Chairman & CEO . . . . .Gary L. Lauer
EVP/Business & Corp. Dev. . . . . .Bruce Telkamp
EVP/Chief Technology . . . . .Dr. Sheldon X. Wang
SVP & CFO . . . . .Stuart M. Huizinga
Pres. of eHealth Gov. Sys . . . . .Samuel C. Gibbs
SVP of Sales & Operations . . . . .Robert S. Hurley
Director Public Relations. .Nate Purpura
650-210-3115

823 FirstCarolinaCare

42 Memorial Drive
Pinehurst, NC 28374
Toll-Free: 800-574-8556
Phone: 910-715-8100
Fax: 910-715-8101
www.firstcarolinacare.com
Subsidiary of: FirstHealth of the Carolinas
Total Enrollment: 13,000
State Enrollment: 13,000

Healthplan and Services Defined
PLAN TYPE: HMO
Offers Demand Management Patient Information Service: Yes
DMPI Services Offered: Nurse Helpline

Key Personnel
Executive Director . . . . .Kenneth Lewis
Executive Director . . . . .Charles Frock
Corporate Communications. . . . . .Emily Sloan
910-715-5376

824 Great-West Healthcare North Carolina

Acquired by CIGNA

825 Humana Health Insurance of North Carolina

2000 Regency Pkwy
Suite 470
Cary, NC 27518
Toll-Free: 866-653-7295
Phone: 919-465-1367
Fax: 919-468-8556
www.humana.com
For Profit Organization: Yes
Total Enrollment: 494,200
State Enrollment: 17,400

Healthplan and Services Defined
  PLAN TYPE: HMO/PPO
  Plan Specialty: ASO
  Benefits Offered: Disease Management, Prescription, Wellness

Type of Coverage
  Commercial, Individual

Geographic Areas Served
  North Carolina, South Carolina, Virginia

Accreditation Certification
  URAC, NCQA, CORE

Key Personnel
  President . . . . .Alan Guzzino

Specialty Managed Care Partners
  Caremark Rx

Employer References
  Tricare

---

826 MedCost

165 Kimel Park Drive
Winston Salem, NC 27103
Toll-Free: 800-824-7406
Phone: 336-760-3090
Fax: 336-760-1506
cscustsvc@medcost.com
www.medcost.com
Subsidiary of: Carolinas HealthCare System
For Profit Organization: Yes
Year Founded: 1983
Number of Affiliated Hospitals: 191
Number of Primary Care Physicians: 12,349
Number of Referral/Specialty Physicians: 21,295
Total Enrollment: 670,000
State Enrollment: 670,000

Healthplan and Services Defined
  PLAN TYPE: PPO
  Model Type: Network
  Plan Specialty: UR, PPO Network, Maternity Management, Case
    Management, Nurse Coaching
  Benefits Offered: Home Care, Inpatient SNF, Long-Term Care,
    Physical Therapy, Podiatry, Psychiatric, Transplant, Vision,
    Wellness, Medical, Hospice, Durable Medical Equipment

Type of Coverage
  Commercial

Type of Payment Plans Offered
  FFS

Geographic Areas Served
  North Carolina and South Carolina

Subscriber Information
  Average Subscriber Co-Payment:
    Primary Care Physician: Varies
    Non-Network Physician: Varies
    Prescription Drugs: Varies
    Hospital ER: Varies
    Home Health Care: Varies
    Home Health Care Max. Days/Visits Covered: Varies
    Nursing Home: Varies
    Nursing Home Max. Days/Visits Covered: Varies

Peer Review Type
  Utilization Review: Yes
  Second Surgical Opinion: Yes
  Case Management: Yes

Publishes and Distributes Report Card: Yes

Accreditation Certification
  URAC

Key Personnel
  President/CEO . . . . .Bill Ketner

Vice President. . . . . .Suzanne Young
Vice President . . . . .Latha Hafer
Director Claims . . . . .Wanda Owen
Network Management. . . . . .Paul Stetson
Vice President. . . . . .Diana Brackins
Dir Information Systems. . . . . .Kevin Barnette

---

827 Mid Atlantic Medical Services: North Carolina

The Atrium at 77 South
4421 Stuart Andrews Blvd, Suite 600
Charlotte, NC 28217
Toll-Free: 800-469-8471
Phone: 704-529-1211
Fax: 704-529-6078
www.mamsiunitedhealthcare.com
Secondary Address: 627 Davis Drive, Suite 100, Morrisville, NC
27560
Subsidiary of: UnitedHealthCare/UnitedHealth Group
Federally Qualified: Yes
Number of Primary Care Physicians: 45,000
Total Enrollment: 50,000,000

Healthplan and Services Defined
  PLAN TYPE: HMO/PPO
  Benefits Offered: Behavioral Health, Dental, Disease Management,
    Home Care, Prescription, Psychiatric, Vision, Wellness, AD&D,
    Life, STD, Hospice, discounts on value-added services such as laser
    vision correction, acupuncture, chiropractic services, massage

Accreditation Certification
  NCQA

Key Personnel
  President/CEO . . . . .Thomas P Barbera

Specialty Managed Care Partners
  HomeCall, FirstCall, HomeCall Pharmaceutical Services, HomeCall
    Hospice Services

---

828 OptiCare Managed Vision

112 Zebulon Court
PO Box 7548
Rocky Mount, NC 27804
Toll-Free: 800-334-3937
Phone: 252-451-2270
Fax: 800-980-4002
sales@opticare.net
www.opticare.com
For Profit Organization: Yes
Year Founded: 1955
Number of Primary Care Physicians: 20,000
Total Enrollment: 1,000,000

Healthplan and Services Defined
  PLAN TYPE: Vision
  Model Type: Network
  Plan Specialty: Vision
  Benefits Offered: Vision

Type of Coverage
  Commercial, Medicare, Supplemental Medicare, Medicaid

Type of Payment Plans Offered
  POS, DFFS, Capitated, FFS, Combination FFS & DFFS

Geographic Areas Served
  Nationwide

Peer Review Type
  Utilization Review: Yes
  Case Management: Yes

Accreditation Certification
  AAAHC, NCQA, State Licensure

Key Personnel

President, Managed Care . . . . David Lavely
SVP, Finance . . . . George Verrastro
SVP, Regulatory Affairs . . . . Larry Keeley
VP, Operations . . . . Tara Price
VP, Quality Management . . . . Connie Cook
VP, Managed Care . . . . John Davis
VP Provider Affairs . . . . Jeremy Myers
VP Business Development . . . . John Davis
Medical Director . . . . Milan R. Genge
National Medical Director . . . . Mark Ruchman
Medical Director . . . . David Robert Haas
SVP, Information Systems . . . . Juan Marrero
Medical Director . . . . Shawn C Putman
Sales . . . . Marigene McHale

Employer References

Wilmer-Hutchins Independent School D+strict

829 Preferred Care Select

Acquired by Blue Cross & Blue Shield

830 Southeast Community Care

4600 Marriott Drive
Suite 100
Raleigh, NC 27612
Toll-Free: 877-268-3866
Phone: 919-781-8000
Fax: 919-781-8088
www.southeastcommunitycare.com
Subsidiary of: Arcadian Health Plans

Healthplan and Services Defined
  PLAN TYPE: Medicare

Type of Coverage
  Medicare

831 United Concordia: North Carolina

2601 Weston Parkway
Suite 103
Cary, NC 25713
Toll-Free: 888-303-8224
Phone: 919-678-8060
Fax: 909-677-7850
ucproducer@ucci.com
www.secure.ucci.com
For Profit Organization: Yes
Year Founded: 1971
Number of Primary Care Physicians: 111,000
Total Enrollment: 8,000,000

Healthplan and Services Defined
  PLAN TYPE: Dental
  Plan Specialty: Dental
  Benefits Offered: Dental

Type of Coverage
  Commercial, Individual

Geographic Areas Served
  Military personnel and their families, nationwide

832 UnitedHealthCare of North Carolina

1001 Winstead Drive
Suite 200
Cary, NC 27513
Toll-Free: 800-362-0655
Fax: 919-677-9012
carolinaprteam@uhc.com
www.uhc.com

Secondary Address: 6101 Carnegie Blvd, Suite 500, Charlotte, NC 28209, 704-442-4145
Subsidiary of: UnitedHealth Group
For Profit Organization: Yes
Year Founded: 1985
Number of Affiliated Hospitals: 107
Number of Primary Care Physicians: 4,364
Number of Referral/Specialty Physicians: 7,182
Total Enrollment: 75,000,000
State Enrollment: 357,768

Healthplan and Services Defined
  PLAN TYPE: HMO/PPO
  Model Type: IPA
  Benefits Offered: Disease Management, Prescription, Wellness
  Offers Demand Management Patient Information Service: Yes

Type of Coverage
  Catastrophic Illness Benefit: Maximum $2M

Type of Payment Plans Offered
  POS, DFFS, FFS, Combination FFS & DFFS

Geographic Areas Served
  All 100 counties within North Carolina, with operational provider networks in these 57 counties: Alamance, Alexander, Bladen, Brunswick, Buncombe, Burke, Cabarrus, Caldwell, Caswell, Catawba, Cleveland, Columbus, Cumberland, Davidson, Davie, Duplin,Durham, Forsyth, Franklin, Gaston, Guilford, Harnett, Haywood, Henderson, Hoke, Irepell, Jackson, Lee, Lincoln, Madison, McDowell, Mecklenburg, Moore, New Hanover, Onslow, Orange, Pender, Person, Polk, Randolph, Richmond

Subscriber Information
  Average Subscriber Co-Payment:
      Primary Care Physician: $10.00
      Non-Network Physician: 20%
      Prescription Drugs: $10.00
      Hospital ER: $35.00
      Home Health Care: $0
      Home Health Care Max. Days/Visits Covered: 30 days
      Nursing Home: 20%
      Nursing Home Max. Days/Visits Covered: 30 days

Network Qualifications
  Pre-Admission Certification: Yes

Peer Review Type
  Utilization Review: Yes
  Second Surgical Opinion: No
  Case Management: Yes

Publishes and Distributes Report Card: Yes

Accreditation Certification
  TJC Accreditation, Utilization Review, Pre-Admission Certification, State Licensure, Quality Assurance Program

Key Personnel

President/CEO . . . . Frank J Branchini
COO . . . . Donna Lynne
CFO . . . . Joseph Capezza
Claims . . . . Howard Greenburg
Network Contracting . . . . Caroline Green
Credentialing . . . . Caroline Green
Dental . . . . John Baackes
In House Formulary . . . . Steve Kessler
Marketing . . . . David Henderson
Materials Management . . . . Joseph Capezza
Medical Affairs . . . . Aran Ron, MD
Member Services . . . . Marilyn DeQuatro
Information Systems . . . . Philip Berman
Provider Services . . . . Caroline Greene
Sales . . . . David Henderson
Media Contact . . . . Roger Rollman
  roger_f_rollman@uhc.com

833 WellPath: A Coventry Health Care Plan

2801 Slater Road
Suite 200
Morrisville, NC 27560
Toll-Free: 800-935-7284
Phone: 919-419-3868
Fax: 919-419-3871
wpmembers@cvty.com
http://chcnorthcarolina.coventryhealthcare.com
Secondary Address: 2815 Coliseum Center Drive, Suite 550,
Charlotte, NC 28217
Subsidiary of: Coventry Health Care
For Profit Organization: Yes
Year Founded: 1995
Number of Affiliated Hospitals: 65
Number of Primary Care Physicians: 24,000
Number of Referral/Specialty Physicians: 5,000
Total Enrollment: 160,000
State Enrollment: 160,000

Healthplan and Services Defined
PLAN TYPE: HMO
Model Type: Network
Plan Specialty: Chiropractic, Vision
Benefits Offered: Prescription

Type of Coverage
Medicare
Catastrophic Illness Benefit: Unlimited

Type of Payment Plans Offered
POS, Capitated, FFS

Geographic Areas Served
North Carolina: Alamance, Buncombe, Burke, Cabarrus, Carteret,
Caswell, Catawba, Chatham, Cleveland, Columbus, Craven,
Cumberland, Davidson, Davie, Durham, Forsyth, Franklin, Gaston,
Granville, Guilford, Harnett, Iredell, Johnston, Lee, Lincoln,
Mecklenburg, Moore, Nash, Orange, Person, Randolph, Robeson,
Rockingham, Rowan, Scotland, Stanly, Stokes, Surry, Union, Vance,
Wake, Wilson, Warren & Yadkin; South Carolina: Anderson,
Cherokee, Chester, Greenville, Lancaster

Subscriber Information
Average Monthly Fee Per Subscriber
(Employee + Employer Contribution):
Employee Only (Self): Varies by plan
Average Subscriber Co-Payment:
Primary Care Physician: $10.00
Prescription Drugs: $15.00
Hospital ER: $50.00
Home Health Care: $0
Home Health Care Max. Days/Visits Covered: Unlimited
Nursing Home: $0
Nursing Home Max. Days/Visits Covered: 60 days

Network Qualifications
Pre-Admission Certification: Yes

Peer Review Type
Utilization Review: Yes
Second Surgical Opinion: Yes
Case Management: Yes

Publishes and Distributes Report Card: Yes

Accreditation Certification
URAC
TJC Accreditation, Medicare Approved, Utilization Review,
Pre-Admission Certification, State Licensure, Quality Assurance
Program

Key Personnel
President/CEO . . . . .Ann Lore
CFO . . . . .Dewey Brown
COO . . . . .Linda Chirichella
In House Formulary. . . . . .Marvin McBride, MD

Marketing. . . . . .Mike King
Materials Management . . . . .Dave Messinger
Medical Affairs . . . . .Dan Barco, MD
Information Systems . . . . .Dan Plonski
Provider Services. . . . . .Tammy Mapes

Specialty Managed Care Partners
Magellan Health, Avefif

Health Insurance Coverage Status and Type of Coverage by Age

Category	All Persons		Under 18 years		Under 65 years		65 years and over	
	Number	%	Number	%	Number	%	Number	%
Total population	635	-	148	-	551	-	84	-
Covered by some type of health insurance	552 *(7)*	86.9 *(0.9)*	133 *(3)*	89.8 *(1.7)*	468 *(8)*	85.0 *(1.0)*	83 *(4)*	99.5 *(0.5)*
Covered by private health insurance	477 *(10)*	75.2 *(1.4)*	108 *(4)*	73.0 *(2.4)*	415 *(9)*	75.3 *(1.3)*	62 *(4)*	74.4 *(3.6)*
Employment based	375 *(12)*	59.2 *(1.7)*	93 *(4)*	63.1 *(2.6)*	346 *(12)*	62.7 *(1.9)*	30 *(4)*	35.5 *(3.5)*
Own employment based	201 *(9)*	31.7 *(1.3)*	0 *(0)*	0.2 *(0.2)*	180 *(9)*	32.7 *(1.4)*	21 *(2)*	25.1 *(2.0)*
Direct purchase	115 *(10)*	18.1 *(1.6)*	18 *(3)*	12.0 *(2.1)*	75 *(8)*	13.7 *(1.4)*	39 *(4)*	47.1 *(5.1)*
Covered by government health insurance	166 *(7)*	26.2 *(1.1)*	37 *(4)*	25.3 *(2.8)*	88 *(6)*	15.9 *(1.2)*	79 *(5)*	93.8 *(1.5)*
Covered by Medicaid	60 *(5)*	9.5 *(0.8)*	31 *(4)*	20.7 *(2.5)*	56 *(5)*	10.1 *(1.0)*	5 *(2)*	5.5 *(1.8)*
Also by private insurance	19 *(3)*	3.0 *(0.5)*	8 *(2)*	5.1 *(1.2)*	16 *(3)*	2.9 *(0.5)*	3 *(1)*	3.8 *(1.4)*
Covered by Medicare	90 *(5)*	14.2 *(0.8)*	1 *(0)*	0.5 *(0.2)*	12 *(2)*	2.1 *(0.4)*	79 *(5)*	93.8 *(1.5)*
Also by private insurance	61 *(4)*	9.6 *(0.7)*	0 *(0)*	0.3 *(0.2)*	3 *(1)*	0.6 *(0.2)*	58 *(4)*	68.8 *(3.8)*
Also by Medicaid	8 *(2)*	1.2 *(0.3)*	1 *(0)*	0.4 *(0.1)*	3 *(1)*	0.6 *(0.2)*	5 *(2)*	5.5 *(1.8)*
Covered by military health care	31 *(4)*	5.0 *(0.7)*	7 *(1)*	4.8 *(0.9)*	27 *(4)*	4.9 *(0.8)*	4 *(1)*	5.2 *(1.6)*
Not covered at any time during the year	83 *(6)*	13.1 *(0.9)*	15 *(3)*	10.2 *(1.7)*	83 *(5)*	15.0 *(1.0)*	0 *(0)*	0.5 *(0.5)*

Note: Numbers in thousands; figures cover 2010; standard error appears in parenthesis; (b) base less than 75,000; (x) not applicable
Source: U.S. Census Bureau, Current Population Survey, 2011 Annual Social and Economic Supplement. Table HI05. Health Insurance Coverage Status and Type of Coverage by State and Age for All People: 2010

North Dakota

834   Aetna Health of North Dakota
Partnered with eHealthInsurance Services Inc.

835   CIGNA HealthCare of North Dakota
525 W Monroe Street
Suite 300
Chicago, IL 60661
Toll-Free: 866-438-2446
Phone: 312-648-2460
Fax: 312-648-3617
www.cigna.com
For Profit Organization: Yes
Year Founded: 1986

Healthplan and Services Defined
  PLAN TYPE: HMO
  Other Type: POS
  Model Type: IPA, Network
  Plan Specialty: ASO, Behavioral Health, Dental
  Benefits Offered: Behavioral Health, Complementary Medicine, Dental, Disease Management, Prescription, Transplant, Vision, Wellness

Type of Coverage
  Commercial, Indemnity

Type of Payment Plans Offered
  POS, DFFS, FFS

Geographic Areas Served
  Illinois: Bureau, Coles, Cook, DuPage, Grundy, Kane, Kankakee, Lake, LaSalle, Livingston, Madison, Massac, McHenry, Monroe, Saint Clair, Shelby, Vermilion, Will counties

Network Qualifications
  Pre-Admission Certification: Yes

Peer Review Type
  Utilization Review: Yes

Publishes and Distributes Report Card: Yes

Accreditation Certification
  NCQA
  TJC Accreditation, Medicare Approved, Utilization Review, Pre-Admission Certification, State Licensure, Quality Assurance Program

836   Delta Dental of North Dakota
3560 Delta Dental Drive
Eagan, MN 55122-3166
Toll-Free: 800-328-1188
Phone: 651-406-5900
Fax: 651-406-5934
www.deltadentalins.com
Mailing Address: PO Box 9304, Minneapolis, MN 55440-9304
Non-Profit Organization: Yes
Year Founded: 1969
Number of Primary Care Physicians: 1,500
Total Enrollment: 54,000,000

Healthplan and Services Defined
  PLAN TYPE: Dental
  Other Type: Dental PPO
  Model Type: Network
  Plan Specialty: ASO, Dental
  Benefits Offered: Dental

Type of Coverage
  Commercial, Individual, Group
  Catastrophic Illness Benefit: None

Geographic Areas Served
  Minnesota, North Dakota

Subscriber Information
  Average Monthly Fee Per Subscriber
    (Employee + Employer Contribution):
      Employee Only (Self): Varies
      Employee & 1 Family Member: Varies
      Employee & 2 Family Members: Varies
  Average Annual Deductible Per Subscriber:
      Employee Only (Self): Varies
      Employee & 1 Family Member: Varies
      Employee & 2 Family Members: Varies
  Average Subscriber Co-Payment:
      Prescription Drugs: $0
      Home Health Care: $0
      Nursing Home: $0

Key Personnel
  President . . . . David B Morse
  CFO . . . . Dani Fjelstad
  Exec VP/Sales & Marketing . . . . Mark A Moksnes
  Exec VP/Operations . . . . Norman C Storbakken
  Media Contact . . . . Ann Johnson
    651-994-5248
    ajohnson@deltadentalmn.org
  Dir/Media & Public Affair . . . . Elizabeth Risberg
    415-972-8423

837   eHealthInsurance Services Inc.
11919 Foundation Place
Gold River, CA 95670
Toll-Free: 800-977-8860
info@ehealthinsurance.com
www.e.healthinsurance.com
Year Founded: 1997

Healthplan and Services Defined
  PLAN TYPE: HMO/PPO
  Benefits Offered: Dental, Life, STD

Type of Coverage
  Commercial, Individual, Medicare

Geographic Areas Served
  All 50 states in the USA and District of Columbia

Key Personnel
  Chairman & CEO . . . . Gary L. Lauer
  EVP/Business & Corp. Dev. . . . . Bruce Telkamp
  EVP/Chief Technology . . . . Dr. Sheldon X. Wang
  SVP & CFO . . . . Stuart M. Huizinga
  Pres. of eHealth Gov. Sys . . . . Samuel C. Gibbs
  SVP of Sales & Operations . . . . Robert S. Hurley
  Director Public Relations . . . . Nate Purpura
    650-210-3115

838   Great-West Healthcare North Dakota
Acquired by CIGNA

839   Heart of America Health Plan
810 S Main Avenue
Rugby, ND 58368
Toll-Free: 800-525-5661
Phone: 701-776-5848
Fax: 701-776-5425
hoahp@gondtc.com
www.hoahp.com
Non-Profit Organization: Yes
Year Founded: 1982
Number of Affiliated Hospitals: 1
Number of Primary Care Physicians: 15
Number of Referral/Specialty Physicians: 500

Total Enrollment: 1,000
State Enrollment: 2,049

Healthplan and Services Defined
  PLAN TYPE: HMO
  Model Type: Group
  Benefits Offered: Behavioral Health, Disease Management,
    Psychiatric, Wellness, LTD, substance abuse, maternity

Type of Coverage
  Supplemental Medicare

Type of Payment Plans Offered
  POS, DFFS

Geographic Areas Served
  North Central North Dakota: Pierce, Rolette, Bottineau,
  McHenry,ÆTowner, Ward and Renville counties in North Dakota and
  portions of Benson, Wells, Sheridan, McLean, Mountrail and Burke
  counties

Subscriber Information
  Average Annual Deductible Per Subscriber:
    Employee Only (Self): $600
    Employee & 1 Family Member: $0
    Employee & 2 Family Members: $0
    Medicare: $0
  Average Subscriber Co-Payment:
    Primary Care Physician: $10.00
    Non-Network Physician: 20%
    Prescription Drugs: $0.00
    Hospital ER: $30.00

Accreditation Certification
  TJC Accreditation

Key Personnel
  President . . . . Robert Keller
  Executive Director/CFO . . . . Mary Ann Jaeger
  Member Services . . . . Sharon Pederson
  Provider Services . . . . Sharon Pederson

Average Claim Compensation
  Physician's Fees Charged: 1%
  Hospital's Fees Charged: 1%

Employer References
  Federal Employee Plan

---

840 Humana Health Insurance of North Dakota
11420 Blondo Street
Suite 102
Omaha, NE 68164
Toll-Free: 800-941-1182
Phone: 402-496-3388
Fax: 402-498-2850
www.humana.com
For Profit Organization: Yes

Healthplan and Services Defined
  PLAN TYPE: HMO/PPO

Type of Coverage
  Commercial, Individual

Accreditation Certification
  URAC, NCQA, CORE

---

841 Medica: North Dakota
1711 Gold Drive South
Suite 210
Fargo, ND 57104
Toll-Free: 800-371-1613
mary.ames@medica.com
www.medica.com
Non-Profit Organization: Yes
Year Founded: 1974

Number of Affiliated Hospitals: 158
Number of Primary Care Physicians: 24,000
Total Enrollment: 1,600,000

Healthplan and Services Defined
  PLAN TYPE: HMO
  Model Type: IPA
  Benefits Offered: Behavioral Health, Chiropractic, Dental, Disease
    Management, Prescription, Wellness, AD&D, Life, LTD, STD
  Offers Demand Management Patient Information Service: Yes

Type of Coverage
  Medicare
  Catastrophic Illness Benefit: Covered

Type of Payment Plans Offered
  Capitated, FFS, Combination FFS & DFFS

Geographic Areas Served
  Aitkin, Anoka, Becker, Beltrami, Benton, Big Stone, Blue Earth,
  Brown, Carlton, Carver, Cass, Chisago, Clay, Clearwater,
  Cottonwood, Crow Wing, Dakota, Dodge, Douglas, Fillmore,
  Goodhue, Grant, Hennepin, Hubbard, Isanti, Itaska, Kanabec,
  Kandiyohi, Koochiching, Jackson, Lac Qui Parle, Lake, Le Sueur,
  Lincoln, Lyon, Mahnomen, McLeod, Meeker, Mille Lacs, Morrison,
  Murray, Nicollet, Norman, Olnsted, Otter Tail, Pine, Polk, Pope,
  Ramsey, Renville, Rice, Rock, Scott

Subscriber Information
  Average Monthly Fee Per Subscriber
    (Employee + Employer Contribution):
      Employee Only (Self): Varies by plan
  Average Subscriber Co-Payment:
    Primary Care Physician: $15.00
    Non-Network Physician: Deductible + 20%
    Prescription Drugs: $11.00
    Hospital ER: $60.00
    Home Health Care: 20%
    Nursing Home: 20%

Network Qualifications
  Pre-Admission Certification: Yes

Peer Review Type
  Utilization Review: Yes
  Second Surgical Opinion: Yes
  Case Management: Yes

Publishes and Distributes Report Card: Yes

Accreditation Certification
  NCQA
  TJC Accreditation, Medicare Approved, Utilization Review,
    Pre-Admission Certification, State Licensure, Quality Assurance
    Program

Key Personnel
  President/CEO. . . . . David Tilford
    david.tilford@medica.com
  CFO. . . . . Aaron Reynolds
  Sr VP/Government Programs . . . . Glenn E Andis
  Sr VP/Finance. . . . . Mark Baird
  Chief Information Officer . . . . Scott Booher
  Medical Officer. . . . . Charles Fazio, MD
  Sr VP/Commercial Markets . . . . Tom Henke
  Sr VP/General Counsel . . . . Jim Jacobson
  Sr VP/Operations . . . . Jana L Johnson
  Sr VP/Human Resources . . . . Deb Knutson
  Sr VP/Marketing . . . . Rob Longendyke

Average Claim Compensation
  Physician's Fees Charged: 65%
  Hospital's Fees Charged: 60%

Specialty Managed Care Partners
  Express Scrips, Vision Service Plan, National Healthcare Resources,
    Cigna Behavioral Resources
  Enters into Contracts with Regional Business Coalitions: Yes

Employer References
Construction Industry Laborers Welfare Fund-Jefferson City, District 9 Machinists (Missouri/Welfare Plan), Government Employees Hospital Association/GEHA, Missouri Highway & Transportation Department/Highway Patrol

842   Noridian Insurance Services

4510 13th Avenue
Fargo, ND 58103
Toll-Free: 888-838-3106
Phone: 701-297-1595
www.mynisi.com
Mailing Address: PO Box 1872, Fargo, ND 58107-1872
For Profit Organization: Yes
Total Enrollment: 434,000

Healthplan and Services Defined
   PLAN TYPE: PPO
   Benefits Offered: Dental, Long-Term Care, AD&D, Life, LTD, STD

Type of Coverage
   Commercial, Indemnity

Geographic Areas Served
   North Dakota and northwest Minnesota

Key Personnel
   Worksite Benefit Consult . . . . Maggy Penderson
   LT Care Consulting Spec . . . . Rhonda Peterson

843   UnitedHealthCare of North Dakota

5901 Lincoln Drive
Edina, MN 55436
Toll-Free: 800-525-9432
Phone: 952-992-5315
Fax: 952-992-4190
www.uhc.com
Subsidiary of: UnitedHealth Group
For Profit Organization: Yes
Year Founded: 1977
Number of Affiliated Hospitals: 4,200
Number of Primary Care Physicians: 460,000
Total Enrollment: 75,000,000

Healthplan and Services Defined
   PLAN TYPE: HMO/PPO
   Model Type: Network
   Plan Specialty: Lab, Radiology
   Benefits Offered: Behavioral Health, Dental, Disease Management, Home Care, Physical Therapy, Prescription, Psychiatric, Wellness, AD&D, Life, LTD, STD

Type of Coverage
   Commercial, Individual, Indemnity, Medicare
   Catastrophic Illness Benefit: Varies per case

Geographic Areas Served
   Statewide

Publishes and Distributes Report Card: Yes

Accreditation Certification
   TJC Accreditation, Medicare Approved

Specialty Managed Care Partners
   Enters into Contracts with Regional Business Coalitions: Yes

Health Insurance Coverage Status and Type of Coverage by Age

Category	All Persons		Under 18 years		Under 65 years		65 years and over	
	Number	%	Number	%	Number	%	Number	%
Total population	11,349	-	2,690	-	9,856	-	1,493	-
Covered by some type of health insurance	9,795 *(105)*	86.3 *(0.8)*	2,468 *(35)*	91.7 *(1.0)*	8,328 *(99)*	84.5 *(0.9)*	1,467 *(64)*	98.3 *(0.7)*
Covered by private health insurance	7,661 *(205)*	67.5 *(1.7)*	1,744 *(68)*	64.8 *(2.5)*	6,783 *(175)*	68.8 *(1.8)*	878 *(60)*	58.8 *(3.0)*
Employment based	6,827 *(199)*	60.2 *(1.7)*	1,635 *(70)*	60.8 *(2.6)*	6,247 *(180)*	63.4 *(1.8)*	580 *(49)*	38.8 *(2.8)*
Own employment based	3,519 *(98)*	31.0 *(0.8)*	8 *(4)*	0.3 *(0.1)*	3,099 *(85)*	31.4 *(0.8)*	420 *(35)*	28.1 *(2.0)*
Direct purchase	897 *(78)*	7.9 *(0.7)*	115 *(20)*	4.3 *(0.7)*	585 *(54)*	5.9 *(0.5)*	312 *(44)*	20.9 *(2.7)*
Covered by government health insurance	3,334 *(127)*	29.4 *(1.1)*	908 *(62)*	33.8 *(2.2)*	1,928 *(128)*	19.6 *(1.3)*	1,405 *(64)*	94.1 *(1.1)*
Covered by Medicaid	1,609 *(118)*	14.2 *(1.1)*	858 *(63)*	31.9 *(2.3)*	1,528 *(113)*	15.5 *(1.1)*	81 *(16)*	5.4 *(1.1)*
Also by private insurance	263 *(28)*	2.3 *(0.2)*	155 *(21)*	5.7 *(0.8)*	243 *(29)*	2.5 *(0.3)*	19 *(6)*	1.3 *(0.4)*
Covered by Medicare	1,717 *(67)*	15.1 *(0.6)*	39 *(16)*	1.4 *(0.6)*	314 *(34)*	3.2 *(0.3)*	1,403 *(64)*	93.9 *(1.1)*
Also by private insurance	861 *(57)*	7.6 *(0.5)*	8 *(8)*	0.3 *(0.3)*	45 *(15)*	0.5 *(0.1)*	816 *(59)*	54.6 *(2.9)*
Also by Medicaid	172 *(23)*	1.5 *(0.2)*	18 *(7)*	0.7 *(0.3)*	92 *(20)*	0.9 *(0.2)*	81 *(16)*	5.4 *(1.1)*
Covered by military health care	301 *(49)*	2.7 *(0.4)*	39 *(12)*	1.4 *(0.4)*	207 *(39)*	2.1 *(0.4)*	94 *(27)*	6.3 *(1.8)*
Not covered at any time during the year	1,554 *(91)*	13.7 *(0.8)*	222 *(26)*	8.3 *(1.0)*	1,528 *(91)*	15.5 *(0.9)*	26 *(10)*	1.7 *(0.7)*

Note: Numbers in thousands; figures cover 2010; standard error appears in parenthesis; (b) base less than 75,000; (x) not applicable
Source: U.S. Census Bureau, Current Population Survey, 2011 Annual Social and Economic Supplement. Table HI05. Health Insurance Coverage Status and Type of Coverage by State and Age for All People: 2010

Ohio

844 Aetna Health of Ohio
1 South Wacker Drive
Mail Stop F643
Chicago, IL 60606
Toll-Free: 866-582-9629
www.aetna.com
For Profit Organization: Yes
Year Founded: 1930
Number of Affiliated Hospitals: 25
Total Enrollment: 159,375
State Enrollment: 159,375

Healthplan and Services Defined
  PLAN TYPE: HMO
  Other Type: POS
  Model Type: IPA
  Benefits Offered: Disease Management, Wellness

Type of Payment Plans Offered
  POS

Geographic Areas Served
  Statewide

Subscriber Information
  Average Subscriber Co-Payment:
    Primary Care Physician: $5.00
    Prescription Drugs: $5.00
    Hospital ER: $25.00
    Home Health Care: $25.00
    Home Health Care Max. Days/Visits Covered: Unlimited

Network Qualifications
  Pre-Admission Certification: No

Peer Review Type
  Utilization Review: Yes
  Second Surgical Opinion: Yes
  Case Management: Yes

Publishes and Distributes Report Card: Yes

Accreditation Certification
  NCQA
  TJC Accreditation, Utilization Review, Pre-Admission Certification,
    State Licensure, Quality Assurance Program

Specialty Managed Care Partners
  Enters into Contracts with Regional Business Coalitions: Yes

845 Amerigroup Ohio
10123 Alliance Road
Suites 140 & 320
Cincinnati, OH 45242
Toll-Free: 800-324-8680
www.realsolutions.com
For Profit Organization: Yes
Year Founded: 2006
Total Enrollment: 1,900,000

Healthplan and Services Defined
  PLAN TYPE: HMO

Type of Coverage
  Medicaid, SCHIP

846 Anthem Blue Cross & Blue Shield of Ohio
4361 Irwin Simpson Road
Building II
Mason, OH 45040
Toll-Free: 800-442-1832
Phone: 513-872-8100
www.anthem.com

Secondary Address: 86 Columbus Road, Athens, OH 45701
For Profit Organization: Yes
Year Founded: 1944
Owned by an Integrated Delivery Network (IDN): Yes
Number of Affiliated Hospitals: 568
Number of Primary Care Physicians: 25,000
Number of Referral/Specialty Physicians: 61,728
Total Enrollment: 3,000,000
State Enrollment: 3,000,000

Healthplan and Services Defined
  PLAN TYPE: PPO
  Plan Specialty: ASO, Behavioral Health, Chiropractic, Dental,
    Disease Management, Lab, PBM, Vision, Radiology, Worker's
    Compensation, UR
  Benefits Offered: Behavioral Health, Chiropractic, Dental, Disease
    Management, Home Care, Inpatient SNF, Physical Therapy,
    Podiatry, Prescription, Psychiatric, Transplant, Vision, Wellness,
    Worker's Compensation
  Offers Demand Management Patient Information Service: Yes
  DMPI Services Offered: Iris Program, Care Wise (24/7 Nurse Line),
    Dental, Vision

Type of Coverage
  Commercial, Individual, Indemnity, Medicare

Type of Payment Plans Offered
  POS, DFFS, Capitated, FFS

Subscriber Information
  Average Monthly Fee Per Subscriber
  (Employee + Employer Contribution):
    Employee Only (Self): Proprietary
    Employee & 1 Family Member: Proprietary
    Employee & 2 Family Members: Proprierary
    Medicare: Proprietary
  Average Annual Deductible Per Subscriber:
    Employee Only (Self): Proprietary
    Employee & 1 Family Member: Proprietary
    Employee & 2 Family Members: Proprietary
    Medicare: Proprietary

Network Qualifications
  Pre-Admission Certification: Yes

Peer Review Type
  Utilization Review: Yes
  Second Surgical Opinion: Yes
  Case Management: Yes

Accreditation Certification
  URAC, NCQA
  TJC Accreditation, Medicare Approved, Utilization Review,
    Pre-Admission Certification, State Licensure, Quality Assurance
    Program

Key Personnel
  President . . . . Erin Hoeflinger
  Marketing Director . . . . Shelley Hahn
  Medical Director . . . . Barry Malinowski, MD
  Media Contact . . . . Kim Ashley
    513-682-8863
    kim.ashley@anthem.com

Specialty Managed Care Partners
  Anthem Dental, Anthem Prescription Management LLC, Anthem
    Vision, Anthem Life

847 Assurant Employee Benefits: Ohio
312 Elm Street
Suite 1500
Cincinnati, OH 45202-2769
Phone: 513-621-1924
Fax: 513-621-4553
benefits@assurant.com
www.assurantemployeebenefits.com
Subsidiary of: Assurant, Inc

For Profit Organization: Yes
Number of Primary Care Physicians: 112,000
Total Enrollment: 47,000

Healthplan and Services Defined
   PLAN TYPE: Multiple
   Plan Specialty: Dental, Vision, Long & Short-Term Disability
   Benefits Offered: Dental, Vision, Wellness, AD&D, Life, LTD, STD

Type of Coverage
   Commercial, Indemnity, Individual Dental Plans

Geographic Areas Served
   Statewide

Subscriber Information
   Average Monthly Fee Per Subscriber
     (Employee + Employer Contribution):
      Employee Only (Self): Varies by plan

Key Personnel
   Business Manager . . . . .Maureen Seubert
   PR Specialist. . . . . .Megan Hutchison
     816-556-7815
     megan.hutchison@assurant.com

848   Aultcare Corporation

2600 6th Street SW
Canton, OH 44710
Toll-Free: 800-344-8858
Phone: 330-438-6360
Fax: 330-438-2911
www.aultcare.com
Non-Profit Organization: Yes
Year Founded: 1985
Number of Affiliated Hospitals: 14
Number of Primary Care Physicians: 3,500
Number of Referral/Specialty Physicians: 6,800
Total Enrollment: 500,000
State Enrollment: 5,151

Healthplan and Services Defined
   PLAN TYPE: HMO/PPO
   Model Type: Network
   Benefits Offered: Dental, Disease Management, Vision, Worker's
     Compensation, STD, Flexible Spending Accounts

Type of Coverage
   Commercial, Individual

Geographic Areas Served
   Carroll, Holmes, Stark, Summit, Tuscarawas and Wayne counties

Network Qualifications
   Pre-Admission Certification: Yes

Peer Review Type
   Utilization Review: Yes
   Second Surgical Opinion: Yes
   Case Management: Yes

Accreditation Certification
   NCQA

Key Personnel
   President/CEO. . . . . .Rick Haines
   CFO. . . . . .George Film
   Director Claims . . . . .Frank Hayden
   Marketing . . . . .Dan Pearce
   Medical Affairs . . . . .Meade Perlman, MD
   Chairman. . . . . .William Alford

Employer References
   Maytag, Timken Company

849   CareSource

320 North Main Street
Dayton, OH 45402-2016

Phone: 937-224-3300
Fax: 937-425-0864
www.caresource.com
Mailing Address: PO Box 8738, Dayton, OH 45401-8738
Non-Profit Organization: Yes
Year Founded: 1989
Total Enrollment: 840,000
State Enrollment: 501,086

Healthplan and Services Defined
   PLAN TYPE: HMO
   Model Type: IPA
   Benefits Offered: Disease Management, Wellness

Type of Coverage
   Medicaid

Type of Payment Plans Offered
   Capitated

Geographic Areas Served
   Ohio and Michigan

Key Personnel
   President & CEO . . . . .Pamela Morris
     937-531-2201
     pamela.morris@csmg-online.com
   Chief Financial Officer . . . . .Tarlton Thomas
   Chief Operating Officer . . . . .Bobby Jones
   SVP, Care Management . . . . .Pam Tropiano
     937-531-2033
     pam.tropiano@csmg-online.com
   SVP, Bus Dev & Reg Affair . . . . .Janet Grant
   Director, Communications. . . . . .Jenny Michael
   EVP, General Counsel. . . . . .Mark Chilson
   EVP, Business Development. . . . . .Janet Grant
   Chief Medical Officer. . . . . .Craig Thiele, MD
   Director of Communication. . . . . .Jenny Michael
     937-531-2910
     jenny.michael@caresource.com

850   CIGNA HealthCare of Ohio

3 Summit Park Drive
Suite 250
Independence, OH 44131
Toll-Free: 866-438-2446
Phone: 216-642-1700
Fax: 216-642-1820
www.cigna.com
Secondary Address: 440 Polaris Parkway, Suite 300, Columbus, OH
43240
For Profit Organization: Yes

Healthplan and Services Defined
   PLAN TYPE: PPO

Type of Coverage
   Commercial

851   CoreSource: Ohio

5200 Upper Metro Place
Suite 300
Dublin, OH 43017
Toll-Free: 800-282-3920
Phone: 614-336-9604
www.coresource.com
Subsidiary of: Trustmark
Year Founded: 1980
Total Enrollment: 1,100,000

Healthplan and Services Defined
   PLAN TYPE: Multiple
   Other Type: TPA
   Model Type: Network

Plan Specialty: Claims Administration, TPA
Benefits Offered: Behavioral Health, Home Care, Prescription,
Transplant

Type of Coverage
Commercial

Geographic Areas Served
Nationwide

Accreditation Certification
Utilization Review, Pre-Admission Certification

852   Delta Dental of Michigan, Ohio and Indiana

550 Polaris Parkway
Suite 550
Westerville, OH 43082
Toll-Free: 800-537-5527
Phone: 614-890-1117
Fax: 614-890-1274
www.deltadentaloh.com
Secondary Address: 6000 Lombardo, Suite 140, Seven Hills, OH
44131
Non-Profit Organization: Yes
Year Founded: 1960
Total Enrollment: 54,000,000
State Enrollment: 952,000

Healthplan and Services Defined
PLAN TYPE: Dental
Other Type: Dental PPO
Plan Specialty: Dental
Benefits Offered: Dental

Type of Coverage
Commercial

Type of Payment Plans Offered
POS

Geographic Areas Served
Indiana, Ohio and Michigan

Network Qualifications
Pre-Admission Certification: Yes

Peer Review Type
Second Surgical Opinion: Yes
Case Management: No

Publishes and Distributes Report Card: Yes

Accreditation Certification
Utilization Review

Key Personnel
President/CEO . . . . Thomas Fleszar, DDS
517-349-6000
tfleszar@ddpmi.com
CFO . . . . Laura L Czelada, CPA
VP/Chief Actuary . . . . William T Billard
VP/Administration . . . . Judge Patrick T Cahill
VP/Operations . . . . Sherry L Crisp
VP/Corporate Affairs. . . . . Nancy E Hostetier
Dental Director . . . . Jed J Jacobson, DDS
VP/Sales . . . . Charles D Floyd, CEBS
VP/Marketing . . . . E Craig Lesley
Communications Admin . . . . Ari B Adler
517-347-5292
aadler@deltadentalmi.com
Dir/Media & Public Affair . . . . Elizabeth Risberg
415-972-8423

Specialty Managed Care Partners
Enters into Contracts with Regional Business Coalitions: Yes

853   eHealthInsurance Services Inc.

11919 Foundation Place
Gold River, CA 95670
Toll-Free: 800-977-8860
info@ehealthinsurance.com
www.e.healthinsurance.com
Year Founded: 1997

Healthplan and Services Defined
PLAN TYPE: HMO/PPO
Benefits Offered: Dental, Life, STD

Type of Coverage
Commercial, Individual, Medicare

Geographic Areas Served
All 50 states in the USA and District of Columbia

Key Personnel
Chairman & CEO . . . . Gary L. Lauer
EVP/Business & Corp. Dev. . . . . Bruce Telkamp
EVP/Chief Technology . . . . Dr. Sheldon X. Wang
SVP & CFO . . . . Stuart M. Huizinga
Pres. of eHealth Gov. Sys . . . . Samuel C. Gibbs
SVP of Sales & Operations . . . . Robert S. Hurley
Director Public Relations. Nate Purpura
650-210-3115

854   Emerald Health PPO

Acquired by HealthSmart

855   EyeMed Vision Care

4000 Luxottica Place
Mason, OH 45040
Toll-Free: 866-939-3633
Phone: 513-765-4321
Fax: 513-765-6388
http://portal.eyemedvisioncare.com
For Profit Organization: Yes
Year Founded: 1988
Total Enrollment: 159,000,000

Healthplan and Services Defined
PLAN TYPE: Vision
Plan Specialty: Vision
Benefits Offered: Vision

Type of Coverage
Commercial

Key Personnel
SVP, General Counsel . . . . Michael Boxer
SVP, Human Resources . . . . Mildred Curtis

856   Health Maintenance Plan

Acquired by Anthem BlueCross & BlueShield of Ohio

857   HealthSpan

Pictoria Tower 1
225 Pictoria Drive, Suite 320
Cincinnati, OH 45246
Toll-Free: 888-914-7726
Phone: 513-551-1400
Fax: 513-551-1469
dpwoods@health-partners.org
www.healthspannetwork.com
Subsidiary of: Mercy Health Partners
For Profit Organization: Yes
Year Founded: 1991
Physician Owned Organization: Yes
Number of Affiliated Hospitals: 86

Number of Primary Care Physicians: 8,400
Total Enrollment: 108,000
State Enrollment: 81,760

Healthplan and Services Defined
  PLAN TYPE: PPO
  Benefits Offered: Disease Management, Wellness

Type of Coverage
  Commercial, Individual

Geographic Areas Served
  Indiana, Kentucky, Ohio

Peer Review Type
  Utilization Review: Yes
  Case Management: Yes

Accreditation Certification
  URAC

Key Personnel
  President & CEO . . . . .Kenneth Page
  VP Operations . . . . .Barbara Eisenhardt
  CMO . . . . .Anthony Behler, MD
  Director . . . . .Barbara Durr
  Director . . . . .Jane Hawkins
  Marketing Director . . . . .Dawn Woods
  Member Services . . . . .Chris Crapsey
  Member Services . . . . .Diane Oliver
  Information Systems . . . . .Melissa Mehring
  Provider Services . . . . .Barbara Durr
  Media Contact . . . . .Dawn Woods, APR
    513-675-3885
    dpwoods@health-partners.org

858 HMO Health Ohio
2060 East 9th Street
Cleveland, OH 44115
Toll-Free: 800-523-8558
Phone: 216-687-7000
Fax: 216-687-6585
www.medmutual.com
Mailing Address: PO Box 94917, Cleveland, OH 44101-4917
Subsidiary of: Medical Mutual of Ohio
Year Founded: 1978
Number of Primary Care Physicians: 21
State Enrollment: 55,000

Healthplan and Services Defined
  PLAN TYPE: HMO
  Model Type: Staff
  Benefits Offered: Prescription
  Offers Demand Management Patient Information Service: Yes

Type of Payment Plans Offered
  DFFS, Capitated, FFS, Combination FFS & DFFS

Geographic Areas Served
  Ohio

Network Qualifications
  Pre-Admission Certification: Yes

Publishes and Distributes Report Card: Yes

Accreditation Certification
  NCQA

Key Personnel
  President/CEO . . . . .Rick Chiricosta
  Chief Communications Offc .Jared Chaney
  Chief Legal Officer. . . . . .Pat Dugan
  EVP, Chief Managed Care . . . . George Stadtlander
  EVP, CFO. . . . . .Dennis Janscy
  EVP, Chief Experience Ofc . . . . .Sue Tyler
  VP, Govt Relations .Joseph F Gibbons, Jr
  Dir, Community Relations .Debra Green
  VP, New Market Dev. .Lincoln LaFayette
  Chief Diversity Officer. . . . . .Patricia Lattimore

Chief Medical Officer . . . . .Robert Rzewnicki
VP, Internal Audit. . . . . .Kathy Golovan
Chief Information Officer . . . . .Kenneth Sidon
VP, Healthcare Finance . . . . .Kevin S Lauterjung
SVP, Business Development . . . . .Jeff Perry
Mgr, Media Relations. . . . . .Ed Byers
    216-687-2685
VP, Finance . . . . .Steffany Matticola

Specialty Managed Care Partners
  Enters into Contracts with Regional Business Coalitions: Yes

859 Humana Health Insurance of Ohio
655 Eden Park Drive
Cincinnati, OH 45202
Toll-Free: 800-777-6940
Phone: 513-684-7439
www.humana.com
Secondary Address: 4690 Munson Street NW, Suite D, Canton, OH
  44718
For Profit Organization: Yes
Year Founded: 1979
Owned by an Integrated Delivery Network (IDN): Yes
Number of Affiliated Hospitals: 12
Number of Primary Care Physicians: 3,121
Total Enrollment: 100,000
State Enrollment: 404,052

Healthplan and Services Defined
  PLAN TYPE: HMO/PPO
  Model Type: Group
  Plan Specialty: ASO, Dental, Vision, Radiology, Worker's
    Compensation
  Benefits Offered: Behavioral Health, Chiropractic, Disease
    Management, Inpatient SNF, Physical Therapy, Podiatry,
    Prescription, Psychiatric, Transplant, Vision, Wellness
  Offers Demand Management Patient Information Service: Yes

Type of Coverage
  Commercial, Individual, Medicare, Medicaid

Type of Payment Plans Offered
  POS, DFFS, Capitated, FFS, Combination FFS & DFFS

Geographic Areas Served
  Cincinnati, Dayton Southern Ohio, Northern Kentucky and
  Southeastern Indiana

Subscriber Information
  Average Subscriber Co-Payment:
    Home Health Care: $0
    Nursing Home: $0

Network Qualifications
  Pre-Admission Certification: Yes

Peer Review Type
  Utilization Review: Yes
  Case Management: Yes

Publishes and Distributes Report Card: No

Accreditation Certification
  URAC, NCQA, CORE
  Utilization Review, Pre-Admission Certification, State Licensure,
    Quality Assurance Program

Key Personnel
  President/CEO . . . . .Michael B McCallister
  Chief Operating Officer .James E Murray
  VP/Chief Actuary . . . . .John M Bertko, FSA
  Chief Financial Officer .James H Bloem
  Chief Informatin Officer . . . . .Bruce J Goodman
  Chief Human Resources Off . . . . .Bonita C Hathcock
  General Counsel . . . . .Arthur P Hipwell
  Sr VP/Corporate Devel. . . . . .Thomas J Liston
  Chief Innovation Officer . . . . .Jonathan T Lord, MD
  Sr VP/Government Relation . . . . .Heidi S Margulis

Vice President/Controller. . . . . .Steven E McCulley
Sr VP/Chief Marketing Officer . . . . .Steven O Moya

Specialty Managed Care Partners
Enters into Contracts with Regional Business Coalitions: No

---

860 Interplan Health Group
Acquired by HealthSmart

---

861 Kaiser Permanente Health Plan Ohio
1001 Lakeside Avenue
Suite 1200
Cleveland, OH 44114
Toll-Free: 800-686-7100
Phone: 216-621-7100
Fax: 216-621-7354
renee.m.deluca@kp.org
www.kaiserpermanente.org
Non-Profit Organization: Yes
Year Founded: 1964
Owned by an Integrated Delivery Network (IDN): Yes
Number of Affiliated Hospitals: 35
Number of Primary Care Physicians: 15,129
Total Enrollment: 110,000
State Enrollment: 134,949

Healthplan and Services Defined
PLAN TYPE: HMO
Model Type: Staff
Plan Specialty: Dental, Disease Management, Vision
Benefits Offered: Disease Management, Prescription, Wellness

Type of Coverage
Individual, Medicare

Type of Payment Plans Offered
POS

Geographic Areas Served
Cuyahoga, Geauga, Lake, Lorain, Medina, Portage, Stark, Summit and Wayne counties

Subscriber Information
Average Monthly Fee Per Subscriber
(Employee + Employer Contribution):
Employee Only (Self): Varies by plan
Average Subscriber Co-Payment:
Primary Care Physician: $5.00-10.00
Non-Network Physician: Not covered
Prescription Drugs: $5.00-10.00
Hospital ER: $35.00-45.00
Home Health Care Max. Days/Visits Covered: Unlimited
Nursing Home Max. Days/Visits Covered: 100/year

Network Qualifications
Pre-Admission Certification: Yes

Peer Review Type
Utilization Review: Yes
Second Surgical Opinion: Yes
Case Management: Yes

Publishes and Distributes Report Card: Yes

Accreditation Certification
NCQA
TJC Accreditation, Medicare Approved, Utilization Review,
Pre-Admission Certification, State Licensure, Quality Assurance
Program

Key Personnel
Regional President. . . . . .Patricia D Kennedy-Scott
President & Med Director . . . . .Ronald Louis Copeland, MD
Media Relation Specialist . . . . .Renee M Deluca
216-479-5079

Media Contact . . . . .Renee DeLuca
216-479-5079
renee.m.deluca@kp.org

Specialty Managed Care Partners
Federal Government, City of Cleveland, State of Ohio, Chrysler
Enters into Contracts with Regional Business Coalitions: No

---

862 Medical Mutual of Ohio
2060 E 9th Street
Cleveland, OH 44115-9831
Toll-Free: 800-700-2583
Phone: 216-687-7000
www.medmutual.com
Year Founded: 1934
Number of Affiliated Hospitals: 202
Number of Primary Care Physicians: 7,728
Number of Referral/Specialty Physicians: 18,736
Total Enrollment: 1,107,000

Healthplan and Services Defined
PLAN TYPE: HMO/PPO
Model Type: Group, Network, PPO, TPA, HMO
Benefits Offered: Dental, Prescription, Vision, Wellness, Life, Health

Type of Coverage
Commercial, Individual

Geographic Areas Served
Ohio, seven other states via subsidiaries

Network Qualifications
Pre-Admission Certification: Yes

Peer Review Type
Utilization Review: Yes
Second Surgical Opinion: Yes
Case Management: Yes

Publishes and Distributes Report Card: Yes

Accreditation Certification
NCQA

Key Personnel
President/CEO . . . . .Rick Chiricosta
Chief Communications Offc . . . . .Jared Chaney
Chief Legal Officer. . . . . .Pat Dugan
EVP, Chief Managed Care . . . . .George Stadtlander
EVP, CFO. . . . . .Dennis Jansey
EVP, Chief Experience Ofc . . . . .Sue Tyler
VP, Govt Relations .Joseph F Gibbons, Jr
Dir, Community Relations .Debra Green
VP, New Market Dev. . . . . .Lincoln LaFayette
Chief Diversity Officer. . . . . .Patricia Lattimore
Chief Medical Officer . . . . .Robert Rzewnicki
VP, Internal Audit. . . . . .Kathy Golovan
Chief Information Officer . . . . .Kenneth Sidon
VP, Healthcare Finance . . . . .Kevin S Lauterjung
SVP, Business Development .Jeff Perry
Mgr, Media Relations. . . . . .Ed Byers
216-687-2685
VP, Finance . . . . .Steffany Matticola

---

863 Medical Mutual of Ohio Medicare Plan
2060 East Ninth Street
Cleveland, OH 44115
Toll-Free: 800-700-2583
Phone: 216-687-7000
www.medmutual.com

Healthplan and Services Defined
PLAN TYPE: Medicare
Benefits Offered: Chiropractic, Dental, Disease Management, Home
Care, Inpatient SNF, Physical Therapy, Podiatry, Prescription,
Psychiatric, Vision, Wellness

Type of Coverage
Individual, Medicare

Geographic Areas Served
Available within Ohio only

Subscriber Information
Average Monthly Fee Per Subscriber
(Employee + Employer Contribution):
Employee Only (Self): Varies
Medicare: Varies
Average Annual Deductible Per Subscriber:
Employee Only (Self): Varies
Medicare: Varies
Average Subscriber Co-Payment:
Primary Care Physician: Varies
Non-Network Physician: Varies
Prescription Drugs: Varies
Hospital ER: Varies
Home Health Care: Varies
Home Health Care Max. Days/Visits Covered: Varies
Nursing Home: Varies
Nursing Home Max. Days/Visits Covered: Varies

Key Personnel
President/CEO . . . . .Rick Chiricosta
Chief Communications Offc . . . . .Jared Chaney
Chief Legal Officer. . . . . .Pat Dugan
EVP, Chief Managed Care . . . . .George Stadtlander
EVP, CFO . . . . .Dennis Janscy
EVP, Chief Experience Ofc .Sue Tyler
VP, Govt Relations . . . . .Joseph F Gibbons, Jr
Dir, Community Relations . . . . .Debra Green
VP, New Market Dev . . . . .Lincoln LaFayette
Chief Diversity Officer. . . . . .Patricia Lattimore
Chief Medical Officer .Robert Rzewnicki
VP, Internal Audit. . . . . .Kathy Golovan
Chief Information Officer .Kenneth Sidon
VP, Healthcare Finance . . . . .Kevin S Lauterjung
SVP, Business Development . . . . .Jeff Perry
Mgr, Media Relations. . . . . .Ed Byers
216-687-2685
VP, Finance . . . . .Steffany Matticola

864 Meritain Health: Ohio

24651 Center Ridge Road
2nd Floor, Ste 200, Point 6 Office Bldg
Westlake, OH 44145
Toll-Free: 800-356-6226
sales@meritain.com
www.meritain.com
For Profit Organization: Yes
Year Founded: 1983
Number of Affiliated Hospitals: 110
Number of Primary Care Physicians: 3,467
Number of Referral/Specialty Physicians: 5,720
Total Enrollment: 500,000
State Enrollment: 450,000

Healthplan and Services Defined
PLAN TYPE: PPO
Model Type: Network
Plan Specialty: Dental, Disease Management, Vision, Radiology, UR
Benefits Offered: Prescription
Offers Demand Management Patient Information Service: Yes

Type of Coverage
Commercial

Geographic Areas Served
Nationwide

Subscriber Information
Average Monthly Fee Per Subscriber
(Employee + Employer Contribution):

Employee Only (Self): Varies by plan

Accreditation Certification
URAC
TJC Accreditation, Medicare Approved, Utilization Review,
Pre-Admission Certification, State Licensure, Quality Assurance
Program

Average Claim Compensation
Physician's Fees Charged: 78%
Hospital's Fees Charged: 90%

Specialty Managed Care Partners
Express Scripts, LabOne, Interactive Health Solutions

865 Molina Healthcare: Ohio

PO Box 349020
Columbus, OH 43234-9020
Toll-Free: 800-642-4168
www.molinahealthcare.com
For Profit Organization: Yes
Year Founded: 1980
Physician Owned Organization: Yes
Number of Affiliated Hospitals: 84
Number of Primary Care Physicians: 2,167
Number of Referral/Specialty Physicians: 6,184
Total Enrollment: 1,400,000

Healthplan and Services Defined
PLAN TYPE: HMO
Model Type: Network
Benefits Offered: Chiropractic, Dental, Home Care, Inpatient SNF,
Long-Term Care, Podiatry, Vision

Type of Coverage
Commercial, Medicare, Supplemental Medicare, Medicaid

Accreditation Certification
URAC, NCQA

866 Mount Carmel Health Plan Inc (MediGold)

6150 East Broad Street
Suite EE320
Columbus, OH 43213-1574
Toll-Free: 800-964-4525
Phone: 614-234-5000
Fax: 614-234-5985
www.medigold.com
Non-Profit Organization: Yes
Year Founded: 1997
Federally Qualified: Yes
Number of Affiliated Hospitals: 23
Number of Primary Care Physicians: 1,050
Number of Referral/Specialty Physicians: 1,850
Total Enrollment: 28,125
State Enrollment: 28,125

Healthplan and Services Defined
PLAN TYPE: Medicare
Model Type: Network, Medicare
Benefits Offered: Behavioral Health, Chiropractic, Dental, Disease
Management, Home Care, Inpatient SNF, Physical Therapy,
Podiatry, Prescription, Psychiatric, Vision, Wellness, Medical, OP
Services, Drug Coverage

Type of Coverage
Individual, Medicare
Catastrophic Illness Benefit: Unlimited

Type of Payment Plans Offered
Combination FFS & DFFS

Geographic Areas Served
Clark, Delaware, Fairfield, Fayette, Franklin, Greene, Knox, Licking,
Madison, Montgomery, Pickaway, Ross, Union counties

Peer Review Type
Utilization Review: Yes
Second Surgical Opinion: Yes
Case Management: Yes

Key Personnel
President . . . . .Thomas A Sullivan
VP/Sales, Mktg, Comm. . . . . .Bryan A James
Executive Director/Sales .Mark Woessner
Director, Sales/Marketing . . . . .Linda Wells
Materials Management . . . . .Edward Martin
Manager Medical Affairs .Christy Barnes
Member Services. . . . . .Mona Delvalle
Information Services. . . . . .Adam Yanchak
Director Provider Services . . . . .Leslie Colvin
Sales Director. . . . . .Melissa Lewis

869   Ohio State University Health Plan Inc.

700 Ackerman Road
Suite 440
Columbus, OH 43202
Toll-Free: 800-678-6269
Phone: 614-292-4700
Fax: 614-292-1166
www.osuhealthplan.com
Non-Profit Organization: Yes
Year Founded: 1991
Number of Affiliated Hospitals: 95
Number of Primary Care Physicians: 3,250
Number of Referral/Specialty Physicians: 7,950
Total Enrollment: 52,000
State Enrollment: 52,000

Healthplan and Services Defined
PLAN TYPE: Multiple
Model Type: IPA
Plan Specialty: ASO, Behavioral Health, Disease Management, EPO
Benefits Offered: Behavioral Health, Chiropractic, Complementary
   Medicine, Dental, Disease Management, Home Care, Inpatient
   SNF, Physical Therapy, Podiatry, Prescription, Psychiatric,
   Transplant, Vision, Wellness
Offers Demand Management Patient Information Service: Yes
DMPI Services Offered: Faculty and Staff Assistance Program,
   University Health Connection

Type of Payment Plans Offered
DFFS, Capitated, Combination FFS & DFFS

Geographic Areas Served
Ohio State University employees and their dependents

Subscriber Information
Average Annual Deductible Per Subscriber:
    Employee Only (Self): $0
    Employee & 1 Family Member: $0
    Employee & 2 Family Members: $0
    Medicare: $0
Average Subscriber Co-Payment:
    Primary Care Physician: $15.00
    Non-Network Physician: 30%
    Prescription Drugs: 20% (generic)
    Hospital ER: $75.00
    Home Health Care: 20%
    Home Health Care Max. Days/Visits Covered: Unlimited
    Nursing Home: $0
    Nursing Home Max. Days/Visits Covered: 60 days

Network Qualifications
Pre-Admission Certification: Yes

Peer Review Type
Utilization Review: Yes
Second Surgical Opinion: No
Case Management: Yes

Publishes and Distributes Report Card: No
Accreditation Certification
NCQA
TJC Accreditation, Medicare Approved, Utilization Review,
   Pre-Admission Certification, State Licensure, Quality Assurance
   Program

Key Personnel
Chief Executive Officer . . . . .Scott Streator
Interim Finance Director . . . . .Richard Schrock
Chief Operating Officer. . . . . .Tom Jones
Medical Director. . . . . .Bruce Wall, MD
Assoc Exec Dir, Client Sv. .Judy Kadja
Medical Mgmt Director . . . . .Lorena Owings
Pharmacy Director . . . . .Brian Lehman
Dir, Comm & Marketing . . . . .Joni Bentz Seal
Dir, Provider Relations. . . . . .Maureen Cahill
Dir, Comm & Marketing . . . . .Joni Bentz Seal
   614-292-4405
   joni.seal@osumc.edu

Specialty Managed Care Partners
Enters into Contracts with Regional Business Coalitions: No

Employer References
Ohio State University

870   OhioHealth Group

445 Hutchinson Avenue
Suite 550
Columbus, OH 43235
Toll-Free: 800-455-4460
Phone: 614-566-0056
www.ohiohealthgroup.com
For Profit Organization: Yes
Year Founded: 1985
Physician Owned Organization: Yes
Number of Affiliated Hospitals: 68
Number of Primary Care Physicians: 5,900
Number of Referral/Specialty Physicians: 10,000
Total Enrollment: 100,000
State Enrollment: 100,000

Healthplan and Services Defined
PLAN TYPE: PPO
Model Type: TPA
Benefits Offered: Disease Management, Prescription, Wellness

Type of Coverage
Commercial, Individual

Geographic Areas Served
Ohio

Peer Review Type
Utilization Review: Yes
Case Management: Yes

Key Personnel
CEO. . . . . .Randy Hoffman
COO. . . . . .Ron Kadylak
CFO. . . . . .Kathy Savenko
CMO . . . . .Bruce A Wall
Marketing. . . . . .Ed Piela
Member Relations . . . . .Lora Heddleston
Pharmacy Director. . . . . .Maria Eileen Murpht

871   Paramount Elite Medicare Plan

1901 Indian Wood Circle
PO Box 928
Maumee, OH 43537
Toll-Free: 800-462-3589
Phone: 419-887-2500
Fax: 419-887-2014

www.paramounthealthcare.com
Year Founded: 1988
Number of Affiliated Hospitals: 34
Number of Primary Care Physicians: 1,900
Total Enrollment: 187,000

Healthplan and Services Defined
  PLAN TYPE: Medicare
  Benefits Offered: Chiropractic, Dental, Disease Management, Home
    Care, Inpatient SNF, Physical Therapy, Podiatry, Prescription,
    Psychiatric, Vision

Type of Coverage
  Individual, Medicare

Geographic Areas Served
  Paramount Elite is available to persons currently enrolled in
  Medicare Parts A and B who permanently reside in Lucas or Wood
  counties in Ohio, or, within Monroe County in Michigan

Subscriber Information
  Average Monthly Fee Per Subscriber
    (Employee + Employer Contribution):
      Employee Only (Self): Varies
      Medicare: Varies
  Average Annual Deductible Per Subscriber:
      Employee Only (Self): Varies
      Medicare: Varies
  Average Subscriber Co-Payment:
      Primary Care Physician: Varies
      Non-Network Physician: Varies
      Prescription Drugs: Varies
      Hospital ER: Varies
      Home Health Care: Varies
      Home Health Care Max. Days/Visits Covered: Varies
      Nursing Home: Varies
      Nursing Home Max. Days/Visits Covered: Varies

Key Personnel
  President . . . . .John C Randolph
    419-887-2500
  VP, Finance . . . . .Jeff Martin
  Managed Care Admin . . . . .Steve Gullett
  Director, Marketing. . . . . .Jeff O'Connell
  VP, Medical Services . . . . .John Meier
  Member Relations . . . . .Karen Eichenberg

872   Paramount Health Care

1901 Indian Wood Circle
Maumee, OH 43537
Toll-Free: 800-462-3589
Phone: 419-887-2500
Fax: 419-887-2031
www.paramounthealthcare.org
Mailing Address: PO Box 928, Toledo, OH 43697-0928
Subsidiary of: ProMedica Health System
For Profit Organization: Yes
Year Founded: 1988
Number of Affiliated Hospitals: 34
Number of Primary Care Physicians: 1,900
Number of Referral/Specialty Physicians: 900
Total Enrollment: 187,000

Healthplan and Services Defined
  PLAN TYPE: HMO/PPO
  Model Type: Network
  Benefits Offered: Prescription

Geographic Areas Served
  Northwest Ohio

Subscriber Information
  Average Monthly Fee Per Subscriber
    (Employee + Employer Contribution):
      Employee Only (Self): Varies by plan
  Average Annual Deductible Per Subscriber:

      Employee Only (Self): Varies
      Employee & 1 Family Member: Varies
      Employee & 2 Family Members: Varies
  Average Subscriber Co-Payment:
      Primary Care Physician: Varies
      Prescription Drugs: Varies
      Hospital ER: $25.00
      Home Health Care: $0
      Home Health Care Max. Days/Visits Covered: Unlimited
      Nursing Home: $0
      Nursing Home Max. Days/Visits Covered: 100 days

Network Qualifications
  Pre-Admission Certification: Yes

Peer Review Type
  Second Surgical Opinion: Yes

Publishes and Distributes Report Card: Yes

Accreditation Certification
  URAC, NCQA

Key Personnel
  President . . . . .John C Randolph
    419-887-2500
  VP, Finance . . . . .Jeff Martin
  Managed Care Admin . . . . .Steve Gullett
  Director, Marketing. . . . . .Jeff O'Connell
  VP, Medical Services . . . . .John Meier
  Member Relations . . . . .Karen Eichenberg

873   Prime Time Health Medicare Plan

214 Dartmouth Ave SW
Canton, OH 44710
Toll-Free: 800-577-5084
Phone: 330-363-7407
www.primetimehealthplan.com
Mailing Address: PO Box 6905, Canton, OH 44706
Subsidiary of: Aultcare

Healthplan and Services Defined
  PLAN TYPE: Medicare
  Benefits Offered: Chiropractic, Dental, Disease Management, Home
    Care, Inpatient SNF, Physical Therapy, Podiatry, Prescription,
    Psychiatric, Vision, Wellness

Type of Coverage
  Individual, Medicare, Medicaid

Geographic Areas Served
  Stark, Carroll, Columbiana, Holmes, Harrison, Jefferson, Mahoning,
  Tuscarawas and Wayne counties

Subscriber Information
  Average Monthly Fee Per Subscriber
    (Employee + Employer Contribution):
      Employee Only (Self): Varies
      Medicare: Varies
  Average Annual Deductible Per Subscriber:
      Employee Only (Self): Varies
      Medicare: Varies
  Average Subscriber Co-Payment:
      Primary Care Physician: Varies
      Non-Network Physician: Varies
      Prescription Drugs: Varies
      Hospital ER: Varies
      Home Health Care: Varies
      Home Health Care Max. Days/Visits Covered: Varies
      Nursing Home: Varies
      Nursing Home Max. Days/Visits Covered: Varies

Key Personnel
  President/CEO. . . . . .Rick Haines
  Chief Financial Officer. .George Film
  Medical Director. . . . . .Gregory Haban

874 S&S Healthcare Strategies

1385 Kemper Meadow Drive
Cincinnati, OH 45240
Toll-Free: 800-717-2872
Phone: 513-772-8866
Fax: 513-772-9174
info@ss-healthcare.com
www.ss-healthcare.com
Subsidiary of: International Managed Care Strategies (IMCS)
Year Founded: 1994

Healthplan and Services Defined
PLAN TYPE: PPO
Model Type: Network
Benefits Offered: Dental, Prescription, Vision

Type of Payment Plans Offered
POS, DFFS, FFS

Network Qualifications
Pre-Admission Certification: Yes

Peer Review Type
Second Surgical Opinion: No
Case Management: No

Publishes and Distributes Report Card: Yes

Key Personnel
President/CEO.............................Gale Schweitzer
Information Services.........................Michael Ward

Specialty Managed Care Partners
Enters into Contracts with Regional Business Coalitions: Yes

875 SummaCare Health Plan

10 North Main Street
Akron, OH 44308
Toll-Free: 800-996-8411
Phone: 330-996-8410
Fax: 330-996-8454
individualinfo@summacare.com
www.summacare.com
Mailing Address: PO Box 3620, Akron, OH 44309
Subsidiary of: Summa Health System
For Profit Organization: Yes
Year Founded: 1993
Physician Owned Organization: Yes
Number of Affiliated Hospitals: 50
Number of Primary Care Physicians: 6,000
Number of Referral/Specialty Physicians: 2,733
Total Enrollment: 155,000
State Enrollment: 155,000

Healthplan and Services Defined
PLAN TYPE: HMO/PPO
Other Type: POS
Model Type: IPA, PPO, POS
Plan Specialty: ASO, Behavioral Health, Chiropractic, Dental,
Disease Management, EPO
Benefits Offered: Behavioral Health, Chiropractic, Complementary
Medicine, Dental, Disease Management, Home Care, Inpatient
SNF, Physical Therapy, Podiatry, Prescription, Psychiatric,
Transplant, Vision, Wellness, AD&D, Life
Offers Demand Management Patient Information Service: Yes
DMPI Services Offered: Nurses Line

Type of Coverage
Catastrophic Illness Benefit: Covered

Type of Payment Plans Offered
POS, DFFS, FFS

Geographic Areas Served
Northeast Ohio: Cuyahoga, Geauga, Medina, Portage, Stark,
Summit, Wayne, Tuscarawas, Ashtabula, Caroll, Mahoning, Trumbull
& Lorain counties

Subscriber Information
Average Monthly Fee Per Subscriber
(Employee + Employer Contribution):
Employee Only (Self): Proprietary
Average Annual Deductible Per Subscriber:
Employee Only (Self): $0
Employee & 1 Family Member: $0
Employee & 2 Family Members: $0
Medicare: $45.00
Average Subscriber Co-Payment:
Primary Care Physician: $5.00/10.00
Prescription Drugs: $5.00/10.00
Hospital ER: $50.00
Home Health Care: $0 if in-network
Home Health Care Max. Days/Visits Covered: 30 days
Nursing Home: $0 if in-network
Nursing Home Max. Days/Visits Covered: 100 days

Network Qualifications
Pre-Admission Certification: Yes

Peer Review Type
Utilization Review: Yes
Second Surgical Opinion: Yes
Case Management: Yes

Accreditation Certification
NCQA
TJC Accreditation, Medicare Approved, Utilization Review,
Pre-Admission Certification, State Licensure, Quality Assurance
Program

Key Personnel
President/CEO.............................Martin P Hauser
330-996-8410
hauserm@summacare.com
CFO.............................Ernie Humbert
330-996-8410
humberte@summacare.com
COO.............................Claude Vincenti
330-996-8410
vincentic@summacare.com
Director Operations.....................Kevin Armbruster
330-996-8410
armbrusterk@summacare.com
Contracting Coordinator.........................Anne Armao
330-996-8410
armaoa@summacare.com
Manager Credentialing.......................Janna Kennedy
330-996-8410
kennedyj@summacare.com
QA/UR.............................Nancy Markle
330-996-8410
marklen@summacare.com
Director Pharmacy...........................Tracy Dankoff
330-996-8410
dankofft@summacare.com
VP Sales and Marketing.......................Kevin Cavalier
330-996-8410
cavalierk@summacare.com
Manager Public Relations.....................Tracie Babarick
330-996-8410
babarickt@summacare.com
Chief Medical Officer.......................Tere Koenig, MD
330-996-8410
koenigt@summacare.com
Director Operations.........................Kevin Armbruster
330-996-8410
armbrusterk@summacare.com
Information Systems.........................Claude Vincenti
vincentic@summacare.com
Director Provider Relations.....................Anne Armao
330-996-8410
armaoa@summacare.com

VP Health Service Mgr. . . . . .Kevin Cavalier
  330-996-8410
  cavalierk@summacare.com
Dir, Public Relations . . . . .Mike Bernstein
  330-375-7930

Specialty Managed Care Partners
  Enters into Contracts with Regional Business Coalitions: Yes
  Akron Regional Development Board, Canton Regional Chamber of
  Commerce, Home Builders Association

Employer References
  Goodyear, Summa Health System, Cuyahoga County, University of
  Akron, Akron Public Schools

876 SummaCare Medicare Advantage Plan
10 North Main Street
Akron, OH 44308
Toll-Free: 800-996-8411
Phone: 330-996-8410
Fax: 330-996-8454
individualinfo@summacare.com
www.summacare.com
Mailing Address: PO Box 3620, Akron, OH 44309
Subsidiary of: Summa Health System
For Profit Organization: Yes
Year Founded: 1993
Physician Owned Organization: Yes
Number of Affiliated Hospitals: 50
Number of Primary Care Physicians: 6,000
Number of Referral/Specialty Physicians: 3,596
Total Enrollment: 26,000
State Enrollment: 73,724

Healthplan and Services Defined
  PLAN TYPE: Medicare
  Model Type: IPA, PPO, POS
  Benefits Offered: Behavioral Health, Chiropractic, Complementary
    Medicine, Dental, Disease Management, Home Care, Inpatient
    SNF, Physical Therapy, Podiatry, Prescription, Psychiatric,
    Transplant, Vision, Wellness, AD&D, Life
  Offers Demand Management Patient Information Service: Yes
  DMPI Services Offered: Nurses Line

Type of Coverage
  Medicare
  Catastrophic Illness Benefit: Covered

Type of Payment Plans Offered
  POS, DFFS, FFS

Geographic Areas Served
  Northeast Ohio: Cuyahoga, Geauga, Medina, Portage, Stark,
  Summit, Wayne, Tuscarawas, Ashtabula, Caroll, Mahoning, Trumbull
  & Lorain counties

Subscriber Information
  Average Monthly Fee Per Subscriber
    (Employee + Employer Contribution):
      Employee Only (Self): Proprietary
  Average Annual Deductible Per Subscriber:
      Employee Only (Self): $0
      Employee & 1 Family Member: $0
      Employee & 2 Family Members: $0
      Medicare: $45.00
  Average Subscriber Co-Payment:
      Primary Care Physician: $5.00/10.00
      Prescription Drugs: $5.00/10.00
      Hospital ER: $50.00
      Home Health Care: $0 if in-network
      Home Health Care Max. Days/Visits Covered: 30 days
      Nursing Home: $0 if in-network
      Nursing Home Max. Days/Visits Covered: 100 days

Network Qualifications
  Pre-Admission Certification: Yes

Peer Review Type
  Utilization Review: Yes
  Second Surgical Opinion: Yes
  Case Management: Yes

Accreditation Certification
  NCQA
  TJC Accreditation, Medicare Approved, Utilization Review,
    Pre-Admission Certification, State Licensure, Quality Assurance
    Program

Key Personnel
  President/CEO. . . . . .Martin P Hauser
    330-996-8410
    hauserm@summacare.com
  CFO . . . . .Ernie Humbert
    330-996-8410
    humberte@summacare.com
  COO. . . . . .Claude Vincenti
    330-996-8410
    vincentic@summacare.com
  Director Operations . . . . .Kevin Armbruster
    330-996-8410
    armbrusterk@summacare.com
  Contracting Coordinator. . . . . .Anne Armao
    330-996-8410
    armaoa@summacare.com
  Manager Credentialing. . . . . .Janna Kennedy
    330-996-8410
    kennedyj@summacare.com
  QA/UR . . . . .Nancy Markle
    330-996-8410
    marklen@summacare.com
  Director Pharmacy. . . . . .Tracy Dankoff
    330-996-8410
    dankofft@summacare.com
  VP Sales and Marketing . . . . .Kevin Cavalier
    330-996-8410
    cavalierk@summacare.com
  Manager Public Relations .Tracie Babarick
    330-996-8410
    babarickt@summacare.com
  Chief Medical Officer. . . . . .Tere Koenig, MD
    330-996-8410
    koenigt@summacare.com
  Director Operations . . . . .Kevin Armbruster
    330-996-8410
    armbrusterk@summacare.com
  Information Systems . . . . .Claude Vincenti
    vincentic@summacare.com
  Director Provider Relations .Anne Armao
    330-996-8410
    armaoa@summacare.com
  VP Health Service Mgr. . . . . .Kevin Cavalier
    330-996-8410
    cavalierk@summacare.com
  Dir, Public Relations . . . . .Mike Bernstein
    330-375-7930

Specialty Managed Care Partners
  Enters into Contracts with Regional Business Coalitions: Yes
  Akron Regional Development Board, Canton Regional Chamber of
  Commerce, Home Builders Association

Employer References
  Goodyear, Summa Health System, Cuyahoga County, University of
  Akron, Akron Public Schools

877 Superior Dental Care
6683 Centerville Business Parkway
Dayton, OH 45459
Toll-Free: 800-762-3159

Phone: 937-438-0283
Fax: 937-291-8695
www.superiordental.com
Year Founded: 1986
Physician Owned Organization: Yes
Number of Primary Care Physicians: 4,200
Number of Referral/Specialty Physicians: 10,000
State Enrollment: 135,000

Healthplan and Services Defined
　PLAN TYPE: Dental
　Model Type: IPA
　Plan Specialty: Dental
　Benefits Offered: Dental, Vision, Ceridian Products

Type of Payment Plans Offered
　FFS

Geographic Areas Served
　Ohio, Kentucky

Subscriber Information
　Average Monthly Fee Per Subscriber
　　(Employee + Employer Contribution):
　　　Employee Only (Self): $18.00
　　　Employee & 1 Family Member: $38.00
　　　Employee & 2 Family Members: $56.00

Publishes and Distributes Report Card: Yes

Key Personnel
　President/Dental Director . . . . Richard W Portune, DDS
　CEO . . . . Rebecca York
　Secretary . . . . Roger E Clark, DDS
　Treasurer . . . . Douglas R Hoefling, DDS
　Director . . . . Dennis A Burns, DDS
　Director . . . . L Don Schumaker, DDS
　Director . . . . James L Sims, DDS
　Chief Marketing Officer . . . . Traci Harrell
　CFO . . . . Wendy Glover
　VP/Dental Director . . . . Richard W Portune, DDS

878　SuperMed One
3768 Avon Lake Rd
Litchfield, OH 44253
Toll-Free: 800-722-7331
Phone: 216-687-7000
Fax: 216-687-7274
sm1@insuredonebenefits.com
www.supermedone.com
Subsidiary of: Medical Mutual of Ohio
Non-Profit Organization: Yes
Year Founded: 1934
Number of Affiliated Hospitals: 150
Number of Primary Care Physicians: 3,977
Number of Referral/Specialty Physicians: 6,761

Healthplan and Services Defined
　PLAN TYPE: PPO
　Model Type: IPA, Group, Network
　Benefits Offered: Prescription
　Offers Demand Management Patient Information Service: Yes

Type of Coverage
　Commercial
　Catastrophic Illness Benefit: Varies per case

Type of Payment Plans Offered
　POS, Combination FFS & DFFS

Geographic Areas Served
　Statewide

Network Qualifications
　Pre-Admission Certification: Yes

Peer Review Type
　Utilization Review: Yes

Second Surgical Opinion: Yes
　Case Management: Yes

Publishes and Distributes Report Card: Yes

Accreditation Certification
　NCQA
　TJC Accreditation, Medicare Approved, Utilization Review,
　　Pre-Admission Certification, State Licensure, Quality Assurance
　　Program

Key Personnel
　President/CEO . . . . Rick Chiricosta
　Chief Communications Offc . . . . Jared Chaney
　Chief Legal Officer . . . . Pat Dugan
　EVP, Chief Managed Care . . . . George Stadtlander
　EVP, CFO . . . . Dennis Janscy
　EVP, Chief Experience Ofc . . . . Sue Tyler
　VP, Govt Relations . . . . Joseph F Gibbons, Jr
　Dir, Community Relations . . . . Debra Green
　VP, New Market Dev . . . . Lincoln LaFayette
　Chief Diversity Officer . . . . Patricia Lattimore
　Chief Medical Officer . . . . Robert Rzewnicki
　VP, Internal Audit . . . . Kathy Golovan
　Chief Information Officer . . . . Kenneth Sidon
　VP, Healthcare Finance . . . . Kevin S Lauterjung
　SVP, Business Development . . . . Jeff Perry
　Mgr, Media Relations . . . . Ed Byers
　　216-687-2685
　VP, Finance . . . . Steffany Matticola

Specialty Managed Care Partners
　Enters into Contracts with Regional Business Coalitions: Yes

879　The Dental Care Plus Group
100 Crowne Point Place
Cincinnati, OH 45241
Toll-Free: 800-367-9466
Phone: 513-554-1100
Fax: 513-554-3187
info@dentalcareplus.com
www.dentalcareplus.com
For Profit Organization: Yes
Year Founded: 1988
Physician Owned Organization: Yes
Number of Primary Care Physicians: 4,179
Number of Referral/Specialty Physicians: 850
Total Enrollment: 269,392

Healthplan and Services Defined
　PLAN TYPE: Dental
　Model Type: IPA
　Plan Specialty: Dental
　Benefits Offered: Dental, Vision

Type of Coverage
　Dental & Vision Insurance

Type of Payment Plans Offered
　POS

Geographic Areas Served
　Ohio, Kentucky, Indiana

Subscriber Information
　Average Monthly Fee Per Subscriber
　　(Employee + Employer Contribution):
　　　Employee Only (Self): $23.50
　　　Employee & 1 Family Member: $45.85
　　　Employee & 2 Family Members: $82.28
　Average Annual Deductible Per Subscriber:
　　　Employee Only (Self): $50.00
　　　Employee & 1 Family Member: $50.00
　　　Employee & 2 Family Members: $50.00

Peer Review Type
　Utilization Review: Yes

Key Personnel
  President and CEO............................Anthony A Cook
    513-554-1100
  CFO.................................Robert C Hodgkins, Jr
  Chief Sales/Marketing ....Ann Young
  Dir, Corp Communications ....Allison Dubbs
    513-554-1100

---

880 The Health Plan of the Upper Ohio Valley

100 Lillian Gish Boulevard
Massillon, OH 44648
Toll-Free: 877-236-2289
Phone: 330-834-2200
Fax: 330-830-5634
information@healthplan.org
www.healthplan.org
Non-Profit Organization: Yes
Year Founded: 1979
Federally Qualified: Yes
Number of Affiliated Hospitals: 63
Number of Primary Care Physicians: 4,000
Number of Referral/Specialty Physicians: 1,000
Total Enrollment: 380,000
State Enrollment: 380,000

Healthplan and Services Defined
  PLAN TYPE: HMO/PPO
  Other Type: POS
  Model Type: IPA
  Plan Specialty: ASO, Disease Management, Worker's Compensation, UR, TPA
  Benefits Offered: Behavioral Health, Chiropractic, Disease Management, Home Care, Inpatient SNF, Physical Therapy, Podiatry, Prescription, Psychiatric, Transplant, Vision, Worker's Compensation, AD&D, Life, LTD, STD
  Offers Demand Management Patient Information Service: No

Type of Coverage
  Individual, Medicare, Medicaid
  Catastrophic Illness Benefit: Unlimited

Type of Payment Plans Offered
  POS, DFFS

Geographic Areas Served
  Eastern Ohio, Northern & Central West Virginia

Subscriber Information
  Average Monthly Fee Per Subscriber
    (Employee + Employer Contribution):
      Employee Only (Self): Varies
      Medicare: Varies
  Average Annual Deductible Per Subscriber:
      Employee Only (Self): Varies
      Medicare: Varies
  Average Subscriber Co-Payment:
      Primary Care Physician: Varies
      Non-Network Physician: Varies
      Prescription Drugs: Varies
      Hospital ER: Varies
      Home Health Care: Varies
      Home Health Care Max. Days/Visits Covered: Varies
      Nursing Home: Varies
      Nursing Home Max. Days/Visits Covered: Varies

Network Qualifications
  Pre-Admission Certification: Yes

Peer Review Type
  Utilization Review: Yes
  Second Surgical Opinion: Yes
  Case Management: Yes

Publishes and Distributes Report Card: Yes

Accreditation Certification
  NCQA

TJC Accreditation, Medicare Approved, Utilization Review, Pre-Admission Certification, State Licensure, Quality Assurance Program

Key Personnel
  CFO......................................John Yeager
  COO.....................................Patricia Fast
  President/CEO ....Phil Wright
  Treasurer.................................Jeffrey Knight

---

881 Unison Health Plan of Ohio

2800 Corporate Exchange Drive
Suite 200
Columbus, OH 43231
Toll-Free: 877-886-4733
Phone: 614-890-6850
Fax: 877-877-7697
www.unisonhealthplan.com
Subsidiary of: AmeriChoice, A UnitedHealth Group Company
Total Enrollment: 103,000

Healthplan and Services Defined
  PLAN TYPE: HMO

Key Personnel
  Chief Executive Officer........................Jeff Corzine
  Finance Director ....Tim Brinkley
  Marketing Director...........................Jackie Lewis
  Chief Medical Officer ....Linda Post, MD
  Provider Services ....Suzanne Pierce
  Media Contact...............................Jeff Smith
    952-931-5685
    jeff.smith@uhc.com

---

882 UnitedHealthCare of Ohio: Columbus

9200 Worthington Road
Westerville, OH 43082
Toll-Free: 800-328-8835
Phone: 614-410-7000
www.uhc.com
Subsidiary of: UnitedHealth Group
For Profit Organization: Yes
Year Founded: 1980
Number of Affiliated Hospitals: 34
Number of Primary Care Physicians: 2,442
Number of Referral/Specialty Physicians: 3,304
Total Enrollment: 75,000,000
State Enrollment: 82,000

Healthplan and Services Defined
  PLAN TYPE: HMO/PPO
  Model Type: IPA
  Plan Specialty: Dental, Vision
  Benefits Offered: Disease Management, Prescription, Wellness

Geographic Areas Served
  Statewide

Subscriber Information
  Average Subscriber Co-Payment:
    Primary Care Physician: $15.00
    Prescription Drugs: $15.00

Accreditation Certification
  NCQA

Key Personnel
  CEO......................................Tom Brady
    614-410-7102
  CFO...................................Ralph O'Brien
  Regional Dir/Operations.......................Leslie Worley
  Medical Affairs.......................Steve Richardson, MD
  Provider Services...........................Lyn Flanagan
  Sales...................................Christine Kyle

Media Contact .... Debora Spano
debora_m_spano@uhc.com

Peer Review Type
Utilization Review: Yes

Accreditation Certification
Utilization Review, Quality Assurance Program

Key Personnel
President .... Rob Lynch

883 UnitedHealthCare of Ohio: Dayton & Cincinnati

9050 Centre Point Drive
Suite 400
West Chester, OH 45069
Toll-Free: 800-861-4037
Phone: 513-603-6200
Fax: 3
www.uhc.com
Subsidiary of: UnitedHealth Group
For Profit Organization: Yes
Year Founded: 1980
Number of Affiliated Hospitals: 34
Number of Primary Care Physicians: 2,442
Number of Referral/Specialty Physicians: 3,304
Total Enrollment: 75,000,000
State Enrollment: 82,000

Healthplan and Services Defined
PLAN TYPE: HMO/PPO
Model Type: IPA
Plan Specialty: Dental, Vision
Benefits Offered: Disease Management, Prescription, Wellness

Geographic Areas Served
Statewide

Subscriber Information
Average Subscriber Co-Payment:
Primary Care Physician: $15.00
Prescription Drugs: $15.00

Accreditation Certification
NCQA

Key Personnel
CEO .... Tom Brady
614-410-7000
CFO .... Ralph O'Brien
Regional Dir/Operations .... Leslie Worley
VP Network Management .... Lyn Flanagan
Medical Affairs .... Steve Richardson, MD
VP Network Management & P .... Lyn Flanagan
Sales .... Christine Kyle
Media Contact .... Debora Spano
debora_m_spano@uhc.com

884 VSP: Vision Service Plan of Ohio

4450 Belden Village Street NW
#808
Canton, OH 44718-2552
Phone: 330-759-4877
webmaster@vsp.com
www.vsp.com
Year Founded: 1955
Number of Primary Care Physicians: 26,000
Total Enrollment: 55,000,000

Healthplan and Services Defined
PLAN TYPE: Vision
Plan Specialty: Vision
Benefits Offered: Vision

Type of Payment Plans Offered
Capitated

Geographic Areas Served
Statewide

Network Qualifications
Pre-Admission Certification: Yes

Health Insurance Coverage Status and Type of Coverage by Age

Category	All Persons		Under 18 years		Under 65 years		65 years and over	
	Number	%	Number	%	Number	%	Number	%
Total population	3,673	-	954	-	3,170	-	503	-
Covered by some type of health insurance	3,049 *(49)*	83.0 *(1.3)*	840 *(18)*	88.1 *(1.6)*	2,547 *(52)*	80.3 *(1.5)*	502 *(22)*	99.8 *(0.2)*
Covered by private health insurance	2,298 *(64)*	62.6 *(1.7)*	535 *(29)*	56.0 *(3.0)*	2,014 *(63)*	63.5 *(1.9)*	285 *(19)*	56.6 *(3.1)*
Employment based	2,026 *(59)*	55.2 *(1.6)*	495 *(24)*	51.9 *(2.6)*	1,853 *(58)*	58.5 *(1.7)*	173 *(19)*	34.3 *(3.4)*
Own employment based	1,085 *(47)*	29.5 *(1.2)*	4 *(3)*	0.4 *(0.3)*	946 *(41)*	29.9 *(1.2)*	138 *(18)*	27.5 *(3.1)*
Direct purchase	350 *(32)*	9.5 *(0.9)*	43 *(11)*	4.5 *(1.2)*	190 *(29)*	6.0 *(0.9)*	160 *(15)*	31.7 *(2.8)*
Covered by government health insurance	1,277 *(54)*	34.8 *(1.5)*	428 *(30)*	44.9 *(3.1)*	783 *(48)*	24.7 *(1.6)*	494 *(22)*	98.2 *(0.7)*
Covered by Medicaid	596 *(42)*	16.2 *(1.1)*	377 *(28)*	39.5 *(3.0)*	540 *(39)*	17.0 *(1.2)*	57 *(13)*	11.3 *(2.6)*
Also by private insurance	145 *(24)*	4.0 *(0.6)*	90 *(17)*	9.4 *(1.9)*	126 *(21)*	4.0 *(0.7)*	19 *(7)*	3.9 *(1.3)*
Covered by Medicare	578 *(30)*	15.7 *(0.8)*	10 *(7)*	1.1 *(0.7)*	90 *(18)*	2.9 *(0.6)*	487 *(21)*	96.9 *(0.9)*
Also by private insurance	295 *(21)*	8.0 *(0.6)*	1 *(1)*	0.1 *(0.1)*	20 *(6)*	0.6 *(0.2)*	274 *(20)*	54.5 *(3.4)*
Also by Medicaid	79 *(15)*	2.1 *(0.4)*	9 *(6)*	1.0 *(0.7)*	27 *(9)*	0.8 *(0.3)*	52 *(11)*	10.4 *(2.2)*
Covered by military health care	268 *(53)*	7.3 *(1.5)*	57 *(19)*	6.0 *(2.0)*	198 *(41)*	6.3 *(1.3)*	70 *(16)*	13.8 *(3.2)*
Not covered at any time during the year	624 *(50)*	17.0 *(1.3)*	114 *(15)*	11.9 *(1.6)*	623 *(50)*	19.7 *(1.5)*	1 *(1)*	0.2 *(0.2)*

Note: Numbers in thousands; figures cover 2010; standard error appears in parenthesis; (b) base less than 75,000; (x) not applicable
Source: U.S. Census Bureau, Current Population Survey, 2011 Annual Social and Economic Supplement. Table HI05. Health Insurance Coverage Status and Type of Coverage by State and Age for All People: 2010

Oklahoma

885 Aetna Health of Oklahoma

2777 Stemmons Freeway
Suite 300
Dallas, TX 75207
Toll-Free: 866-582-9629
www.aetna.com
For Profit Organization: Yes
Year Founded: 1998
Number of Affiliated Hospitals: 3,589
Number of Primary Care Physicians: 49,000
Number of Referral/Specialty Physicians: 300,000
Total Enrollment: 31,363
State Enrollment: 31,363

Healthplan and Services Defined
 PLAN TYPE: HMO
 Other Type: POS
 Model Type: IPA
 Benefits Offered: Behavioral Health, Chiropractic, Dental, Disease
  Management, Home Care, Inpatient SNF, Long-Term Care,
  Physical Therapy, Podiatry, Prescription, Psychiatric, Transplant,
  Vision, Wellness, AD&D, Life, LTD, STD, Alternative Heatlh
  Care programs, Informed H

Type of Coverage
 Commercial

Type of Payment Plans Offered
 DFFS, Capitated, FFS

Geographic Areas Served
 Statewide

Subscriber Information
 Average Subscriber Co-Payment:
  Primary Care Physician: $20.00
  Non-Network Physician: $30.00
  Prescription Drugs: $15/30/60
  Hospital ER: $150.00

Peer Review Type
 Second Surgical Opinion: Yes
 Case Management: Yes

Accreditation Certification
 NCQA

Key Personnel
 General Manager......................Melissa Heim-lawrence
 Sr Vice President ....Bill Roth
 Business Development..........................Brian Forbes
 Medical Director..........................David Valdez, MD
 Sales Manager ....Jeff Miller

886 Assurant Employee Benefits: Oklahoma

22323 E 62nd Street South
Broken Arrow, OK 74014-2006
Phone: 918-355-4150
benefits@assurant.com
www.assurantemployeebenefits.com
Subsidiary of: Assurant, Inc
For Profit Organization: Yes
Number of Primary Care Physicians: 112,000
Total Enrollment: 47,000

Healthplan and Services Defined
 PLAN TYPE: Multiple
 Plan Specialty: Dental, Vision, Long & Short-Term Disability
 Benefits Offered: Dental, Vision, Wellness, AD&D, Life, LTD, STD

Type of Coverage
 Commercial, Indemnity, Individual Dental Plans

Geographic Areas Served
 Statewide

Subscriber Information
 Average Monthly Fee Per Subscriber
  (Employee + Employer Contribution):
   Employee Only (Self): Varies by plan

Key Personnel
 Branch Manager............................Robert Burkeen
 PR Specialist............................Megan Hutchison
  816-556-7815
  megan.hutchison@assurant.com

887 Blue Cross & Blue Shield of Oklahoma

1215 S Boulder Avenue
PO Box 3283
Tulsa, OK 74102
Phone: 918-560-3500
www.bcbsok.com
Secondary Address: 3401 NW 63rd, PO Box 60545, Oklahoma City,
 OK 73146-0545
Non-Profit Organization: Yes
Year Founded: 1940
Number of Affiliated Hospitals: 88
Number of Primary Care Physicians: 1,551
Number of Referral/Specialty Physicians: 6,000
Total Enrollment: 600,000
State Enrollment: 600,000

Healthplan and Services Defined
 PLAN TYPE: HMO/PPO
 Model Type: IPA
 Plan Specialty: ASO, Behavioral Health, Chiropractic, Dental,
  Disease Management, Lab, MSO, PBM, Vision, Radiology, UR
 Benefits Offered: Behavioral Health, Chiropractic, Dental, Disease
  Management, Home Care, Inpatient SNF, Long-Term Care,
  Physical Therapy, Podiatry, Prescription, Psychiatric, Transplant,
  Vision, Worker's Compensation, Life, LTD, STD

Type of Coverage
 Commercial, Individual, Indemnity, Supplemental Medicare

Type of Payment Plans Offered
 POS, FFS

Geographic Areas Served
 State wide

Subscriber Information
 Average Annual Deductible Per Subscriber:
  Employee Only (Self): $500.00
 Average Subscriber Co-Payment:
  Primary Care Physician: $10.00
  Prescription Drugs: 10/20/30%

Network Qualifications
 Pre-Admission Certification: Yes

Peer Review Type
 Utilization Review: Yes
 Second Surgical Opinion: Yes
 Case Management: Yes

Accreditation Certification
 URAC

Key Personnel
 President ....Bert Marshall
 EVP Subsidiary ....Michael Rhoads
 Executive VP/Internal Ops.....................Jerry L Hudson
 General Counsel ....Jacqueline Haglund
 VP/Benefits Admin......................Nequita K Hanna
 Chief Information Officer ....Jerry D Scherer
 VP Marketing ....Lisa Putt
 Chief Medical Officer......................Joseph Nicholson
 Chief Medical Director....................Charles Knife

Media Contact . . . . Nicole Amend
918-551-3339
namend@bcbsok.com

Specialty Managed Care Partners
Enters into Contracts with Regional Business Coalitions: Yes

Employer References
Federal Employee Program, The Williams Companies, OneOK, Helmerich & Payne, Bank of Oklahoma

---

888 BlueLincs HMO
Acquired by BlueCross BlueShield of Oklahoma

---

889 CIGNA HealthCare of Oklahoma
1640 Dallas Parkway
4th Floor
Plano, TX 75093
Toll-Free: 866-438-2446
Phone: 972-863-4300
www.cigna.com
For Profit Organization: Yes
Year Founded: 1992
Number of Primary Care Physicians: 1,000
State Enrollment: 22,300

Healthplan and Services Defined
PLAN TYPE: HMO/PPO
Model Type: IPA
Benefits Offered: Disease Management, Prescription, Transplant, Wellness, Womens and Mens Health Programs
Offers Demand Management Patient Information Service: Yes
DMPI Services Offered: Language Links Service, 24 hour health information line, Health Information Library, Automated ReferralLine

Type of Coverage
Commercial

Type of Payment Plans Offered
POS

Geographic Areas Served
Creek, Lincoln, Mayes, Muskogee, Okmulgee, Osage, Rogers, Tulsa and Washington counties

---

890 CommunityCare Managed Healthcare Plans of Oklahoma
218 West Sixth Street
Tulsa, OK 74119
Toll-Free: 800-278-7563
Phone: 918-594-5200
Fax: 918-594-5210
ccare@ccok.com
www.ccok.com
For Profit Organization: Yes
Number of Affiliated Hospitals: 30
Number of Primary Care Physicians: 3,000
Number of Referral/Specialty Physicians: 1,300
Total Enrollment: 250,000
State Enrollment: 250,000

Healthplan and Services Defined
PLAN TYPE: HMO/PPO
Other Type: POS
Benefits Offered: Disease Management, Prescription, Vision, Wellness, Womens health, EAP
Offers Demand Management Patient Information Service: Yes
DMPI Services Offered: 24 hour nurse line

Type of Coverage
Commercial, Medicare, Supplemental Medicare

Type of Payment Plans Offered
POS

Geographic Areas Served
Arkansas, Kansas, Missouri, Oklahoma

Key Personnel
CEO . . . . Richard Todd
COO . . . . Nancy Horstmann
VP, CFO . . . . John Thomas
CMO . . . . Jack Sommers, MD
General Counsel . . . . Rem Beitel
Provider Relations . . . . Kelly Ross
Marketing . . . . Cindy Giddings
Member Relations . . . . Pat Hall
Pharmacy Director . . . . Melanie Maxwell
Public Relations . . . . Betsy Panturf
VP . . . . William Hancock

Specialty Managed Care Partners
PrecisionRX

---

891 CommunityCare Medicare Plan
218 W 6th Street
Tulsa, OK 74119
Toll-Free: 800-278-7563
Phone: 918-594-5200
Fax: 918-594-5209
ccare@ccok.com
www.ccok.com/CommunityCare%20Medicare/

Healthplan and Services Defined
PLAN TYPE: Medicare
Benefits Offered: Chiropractic, Dental, Disease Management, Home Care, Inpatient SNF, Physical Therapy, Podiatry, Prescription, Psychiatric, Vision, Wellness

Type of Coverage
Individual, Medicare

Geographic Areas Served
Available within Oklahoma only

Subscriber Information
Average Monthly Fee Per Subscriber
(Employee + Employer Contribution):
Employee Only (Self): Varies
Medicare: Varies
Average Annual Deductible Per Subscriber:
Employee Only (Self): Varies
Medicare: Varies
Average Subscriber Co-Payment:
Primary Care Physician: Varies
Non-Network Physician: Varies
Prescription Drugs: Varies
Hospital ER: Varies
Home Health Care: Varies
Home Health Care Max. Days/Visits Covered: Varies
Nursing Home: Varies
Nursing Home Max. Days/Visits Covered: Varies

Key Personnel
President . . . . Richard W Todd
Vice President . . . . William H Hancock
VP/CFO . . . . John Thomas
Human Resources Director . . . . Candia Fields

---

892 Delta Dental of Oklahoma
16 NW 63rd Street
Suite 201
Oklahoma City, OK 73116
Toll-Free: 800-522-0188
Phone: 405-607-2100
customerservice@deltadentalok.org
www.deltadentalok.org

Mailing Address: PO Box 54709, Oklahoma City, OK 73154-1709
Non-Profit Organization: Yes
Year Founded: 1973
Total Enrollment: 54,000,000
State Enrollment: 700,000

Healthplan and Services Defined
 PLAN TYPE: Dental
 Other Type: Dental PPO
 Model Type: Network
 Plan Specialty: ASO, Dental
 Benefits Offered: Dental

Type of Coverage
 Commercial, Individual, Group
 Catastrophic Illness Benefit: None

Geographic Areas Served
 Statewide

Subscriber Information
 Average Monthly Fee Per Subscriber
  (Employee + Employer Contribution):
   Employee Only (Self): Varies
   Employee & 1 Family Member: Varies
   Employee & 2 Family Members: Varies
 Average Annual Deductible Per Subscriber:
   Employee Only (Self): Varies
   Employee & 1 Family Member: Varies
   Employee & 2 Family Members: Varies
 Average Subscriber Co-Payment:
   Prescription Drugs: $0
   Home Health Care: $0
   Nursing Home: $0

Key Personnel
 Chief Executive Officer . . . . .John Gladden
 Dir, Corporate Comm . . . . .Thomas J Searls
  405-607-2100
  corpcomm@deltadentalok.org
 Dir/Media & Public Affair . . . . .Elizabeth Risberg
  415-972-8423

893 eHealthInsurance Services Inc.
11919 Foundation Place
Gold River, CA 95670
Toll-Free: 800-977-8860
info@ehealthinsurance.com
www.e.healthinsurance.com
Year Founded: 1997

Healthplan and Services Defined
 PLAN TYPE: HMO/PPO
 Benefits Offered: Dental, Life, STD

Type of Coverage
 Commercial, Individual, Medicare

Geographic Areas Served
 All 50 states in the USA and District of Columbia

Key Personnel
 Chairman & CEO . . . . .Gary L. Lauer
 EVP/Business & Corp. Dev. .Bruce Telkamp
 EVP/Chief Technology . . . . .Dr. Sheldon X. Wang
 SVP & CFO . . . . .Stuart M. Huizinga
 Pres. of eHealth Gov. Sys .Samuel C. Gibbs
 SVP of Sales & Operations . . . . .Robert S. Hurley
 Director Public Relations. . . . . .Nate Purpura
  650-210-3115

894 Great-West Healthcare Oklahoma
Acquired by CIGNA

895 Humana Health Insurance of Oklahoma
7104 S Sheridan
Suite 10A
Tulsa, OK 74136
Toll-Free: 800-681-0637
Phone: 918-477-9357
Fax: 918-499-2297
www.humana.com
For Profit Organization: Yes

Healthplan and Services Defined
 PLAN TYPE: HMO/PPO

Type of Coverage
 Commercial, Individual

Accreditation Certification
 URAC, NCQA, CORE

896 Mercy Health Plans: Oklahoma
14528 South Outer 40
Suite 300
Chesterfield, MO 63017-5743
Toll-Free: 800-830-1918
Phone: 314-214-8100
Fax: 314-810-8101
www.mercyhealthplans.com
Non-Profit Organization: Yes
Total Enrollment: 73,000

Healthplan and Services Defined
 PLAN TYPE: HMO

Type of Coverage
 Commercial, Individual

Key Personnel
 Interim CEO . . . . .Chris Knackstedt
 EVP, COO . . . . .Mike Treash
 Executive Vice President . . . . .Janet Pursley
 CFO, Treasurer . . . . .George Schneider
 VP, General Counsel . . . . .Charles Gilham
 Chief Medical Officer . . . . .Stephen Spurgeon, MD
 VP, Human Resources . . . . .Donna McDaniel
 VP, Mission & Ethics . . . . .Michael Doyle
 VP, Sales & Service. . . . . .Carl Schultz

897 PacifiCare of Oklahoma
7666 E 61st Street
Suite 500
Tulsa, OK 74133
Phone: 918-459-1100
Fax: 918-459-1450
www.pacificare.com
Subsidiary of: UnitedHealthCare
For Profit Organization: Yes
Year Founded: 1985
Owned by an Integrated Delivery Network (IDN): Yes
Number of Affiliated Hospitals: 15
Number of Primary Care Physicians: 474
Total Enrollment: 43,000
State Enrollment: 78,785

Healthplan and Services Defined
 PLAN TYPE: HMO
 Model Type: Network
 Plan Specialty: ASO, Behavioral Health, Chiropractic, Dental,
  Disease Management, EPO, Lab, MSO, PBM, Vision, Radiology,
  Worker's Compensation
 Benefits Offered: Prescription
 Offers Demand Management Patient Information Service: Yes

Type of Coverage
   Commercial, Individual, Indemnity, Medicare, Supplemental
      Medicare
   Catastrophic Illness Benefit: Covered

Type of Payment Plans Offered
   POS, Combination FFS & DFFS

Geographic Areas Served
   Tulsa, Canadian, Cleveland, Creek, Grady, Kingfisher, Lincoln,
   Logan, Mayes, McClain, Muskogee, Okfuskee, Oklahoma,
   Okmulgee, Osage, Pawnee, Payne, Pottawatomie, Rogers, Seminole,
   Wagoner, & Washington counties

Subscriber Information
   Average Monthly Fee Per Subscriber
      (Employee + Employer Contribution):
         Employee Only (Self): Varies by plan
   Average Subscriber Co-Payment:
      Primary Care Physician: $10.00
      Hospital ER: $50.00
      Home Health Care: $10.00
      Home Health Care Max. Days/Visits Covered: Unlimited

Network Qualifications
   Pre-Admission Certification: Yes

Peer Review Type
   Utilization Review: Yes
   Second Surgical Opinion: No
   Case Management: Yes

Publishes and Distributes Report Card: Yes

Accreditation Certification
   NCQA
   TJC Accreditation, Medicare Approved, Pre-Admission Certification,
      State Licensure, Quality Assurance Program

Key Personnel
   President/CEO . . . . .George H Becker, Jr
   CFO. . . . . .Daniel J Comrie
   Marketing . . . . .Victor J Pluto
   Medical Affairs. . . . . .Steve Sanders, DO

898   UnitedHealthCare of Oklahoma

5800 Granite Parkway
Suite 700
Plano, TX 75024
Toll-Free: 800-458-5653
Fax: 469-633-8856
www.uhc.com
Subsidiary of: UnitedHealth Group
For Profit Organization: Yes
Year Founded: 1986
Number of Affiliated Hospitals: 4,500
Number of Primary Care Physicians: 470,000
Total Enrollment: 75,000,000
State Enrollment: 177,243

Healthplan and Services Defined
   PLAN TYPE: HMO/PPO
   Model Type: IPA
   Benefits Offered: Dental, Disease Management, Prescription,
      Wellness, AD&D, Life, LTD, STD

Type of Coverage
   Commercial, Individual, Medicare

Geographic Areas Served
   Statewide

Network Qualifications
   Pre-Admission Certification: Yes

Publishes and Distributes Report Card: Yes

Accreditation Certification
   NCQA

Specialty Managed Care Partners
   Enters into Contracts with Regional Business Coalitions: Yes

Health Insurance Coverage Status and Type of Coverage by Age

Category	All Persons		Under 18 years		Under 65 years		65 years and over	
	Number	%	Number	%	Number	%	Number	%
Total population	3,777	-	855	-	3,261	-	516	-
Covered by some type of health insurance	3,165 (42)	83.8 (1.1)	766 (14)	89.6 (1.5)	2,650 (52)	81.3 (1.3)	515 (33)	99.8 (0.2)
Covered by private health insurance	2,585 (64)	68.4 (1.7)	534 (28)	62.5 (3.3)	2,206 (69)	67.6 (1.9)	379 (30)	73.5 (3.4)
Employment based	2,112 (62)	55.9 (1.7)	474 (29)	55.5 (3.4)	1,953 (67)	59.9 (1.9)	159 (25)	30.7 (4.2)
Own employment based	1,133 (33)	30.0 (0.9)	1 (1)	0.1 (0.1)	1,031 (40)	31.6 (1.1)	102 (18)	19.8 (3.0)
Direct purchase	532 (42)	14.1 (1.1)	80 (11)	9.4 (1.3)	293 (27)	9.0 (0.8)	240 (28)	46.4 (5.2)
Covered by government health insurance	1,100 (54)	29.1 (1.4)	281 (22)	32.8 (2.6)	598 (37)	18.3 (1.2)	502 (32)	97.3 (0.8)
Covered by Medicaid	521 (34)	13.8 (0.9)	272 (22)	31.8 (2.6)	475 (33)	14.6 (1.0)	46 (11)	8.9 (2.4)
Also by private insurance	107 (13)	2.8 (0.3)	40 (12)	4.7 (1.4)	85 (14)	2.6 (0.4)	22 (7)	4.2 (1.4)
Covered by Medicare	589 (31)	15.6 (0.8)	0 (0)	0.0 (0.0)	92 (12)	2.8 (0.4)	497 (31)	96.2 (1.0)
Also by private insurance	394 (28)	10.4 (0.7)	0 (0)	0.0 (0.0)	31 (6)	1.0 (0.2)	363 (29)	70.3 (3.4)
Also by Medicaid	75 (14)	2.0 (0.4)	0 (0)	0.0 (0.0)	29 (7)	0.9 (0.2)	46 (11)	8.9 (2.4)
Covered by military health care	119 (25)	3.2 (0.6)	9 (5)	1.0 (0.6)	65 (11)	2.0 (0.4)	54 (19)	10.5 (3.3)
Not covered at any time during the year	612 (42)	16.2 (1.1)	89 (13)	10.4 (1.5)	611 (42)	18.7 (1.3)	1 (1)	0.2 (0.2)

Note: Numbers in thousands; figures cover 2010; standard error appears in parenthesis; (b) base less than 75,000; (x) not applicable
Source: U.S. Census Bureau, Current Population Survey, 2011 Annual Social and Economic Supplement. Table HI05. Health Insurance Coverage Status and Type of Coverage by State and Age for All People: 2010

Oregon

899 Aetna Health of Oregon
Partnered with eHealthInsurance Services Inc.

900 Assurant Employee Benefits: Oregon
1515 SW 5th Avenue
Suite 645
Portland, OR 97201-5445
Phone: 503-228-4511
Fax: 503-228-4286
benefits@assurant.com
www.assurantemployeebenefits.com
Subsidiary of: Assurant, Inc
For Profit Organization: Yes
Number of Primary Care Physicians: 112,000
Total Enrollment: 47,000

Healthplan and Services Defined
  PLAN TYPE: Multiple
  Plan Specialty: Dental, Vision, Long & Short-Term Disability
  Benefits Offered: Dental, Vision, Wellness, AD&D, Life, LTD, STD

Type of Coverage
  Commercial, Indemnity, Individual Dental Plans

Geographic Areas Served
  Statewide

Subscriber Information
  Average Monthly Fee Per Subscriber
    (Employee + Employer Contribution):
      Employee Only (Self): Varies by plan

Key Personnel
  Account Manager . . . . Sarah Trinh
  PR Specialist. . . . . Megan Hutchison
    816-556-7815
    megan.hutchison@assurant.com

901 Atrio Health Plans
2270 NW Aviation Drive
Suite 3
Roseburg, OR 97470
Toll-Free: 877-672-8620
Phone: 541-672-8620
Fax: 541-672-8670
memberservices@atriohp.com
www.atriohp.com

Healthplan and Services Defined
  PLAN TYPE: Medicare
  Other Type: HMO, PPO
  Benefits Offered: Chiropractic, Dental, Disease Management, Home
    Care, Inpatient SNF, Physical Therapy, Podiatry, Prescription,
    Psychiatric, Vision, Wellness

Type of Coverage
  Individual, Medicare

Geographic Areas Served
  Douglas, Klamath & Washington counties in Oregon

Subscriber Information
  Average Monthly Fee Per Subscriber
    (Employee + Employer Contribution):
      Employee Only (Self): Varies
      Medicare: Varies
  Average Annual Deductible Per Subscriber:
      Employee Only (Self): Varies
      Medicare: Varies
  Average Subscriber Co-Payment:
      Primary Care Physician: Varies
      Non-Network Physician: Varies

Prescription Drugs: Varies
Hospital ER: Varies
Home Health Care: Varies
Home Health Care Max. Days/Visits Covered: Varies
Nursing Home: Varies
Nursing Home Max. Days/Visits Covered: Varies

Key Personnel
  Chief Executive Officer . . . . Pamela M.K. Johnson
  Board of Directors . . . . William C Guest III
  Board of Directors . . . . David J Davis
  Board of Directors . . . . William J Moriatry, MD
  Board of Directors . . . . Laurence Sharp, MD
  Board of Directors . . . . Joni M Mostert

902 CareOregon Health Plan
315 SW Fifth Avenue
Suite 900
Portland, OR 97204
Toll-Free: 800-224-4840
Phone: 503-416-4100
www.careoregon.org
Non-Profit Organization: Yes
Year Founded: 1993
Number of Affiliated Hospitals: 33
Number of Primary Care Physicians: 950
Number of Referral/Specialty Physicians: 3,000
Total Enrollment: 131,096
State Enrollment: 131,096

Healthplan and Services Defined
  PLAN TYPE: Medicare

Type of Coverage
  Medicare

Geographic Areas Served
  20 counties in Oregon

Key Personnel
  Chief Executive Officer . . . . David E Ford

903 CareSource Mid Rogue Health Plan
740 SE 7th Street
Grants Pass, OR 97526
Toll-Free: 888-460-0185
Phone: 541-471-4106
Fax: 541-471-1524
www.caresourcehp.com
Secondary Address: 1390 Biddle Road, Suite 105, Medford, OR 97504
Year Founded: 1995

Healthplan and Services Defined
  PLAN TYPE: Medicare
  Benefits Offered: Chiropractic, Dental, Disease Management, Home
    Care, Inpatient SNF, Physical Therapy, Podiatry, Prescription,
    Psychiatric, Vision, Wellness

Type of Coverage
  Individual, Medicare

Geographic Areas Served
  Available within Oregon only

Subscriber Information
  Average Monthly Fee Per Subscriber
    (Employee + Employer Contribution):
      Employee Only (Self): Varies
      Medicare: Varies
  Average Annual Deductible Per Subscriber:
      Employee Only (Self): Varies
      Medicare: Varies
  Average Subscriber Co-Payment:
      Primary Care Physician: Varies
      Non-Network Physician: Varies

Prescription Drugs: Varies
Hospital ER: Varies
Home Health Care: Varies
Home Health Care Max. Days/Visits Covered: Varies
Nursing Home: Varies
Nursing Home Max. Days/Visits Covered: Varies

Key Personnel
Director . . . . .Cynthia Ackerman
Chief Executive Officer . . . . .Doug Flow
Chief Executive Officer. . . . . .Jan Buffa
Medical Director . . . . .Chris Kirk
Marketing Director . . . . .Freddy Senhauser
Medicare Advantage Spec . . . . .Grace Ely

904   CIGNA HealthCare of Oregon

121 SW Morrison
Suite 525
Portland, OR 97204
Toll-Free: 800-274-0143
Phone: 503-224-0143
Fax: 505-262-3867
www.cigna.com
For Profit Organization: Yes
Total Enrollment: 126,000

Healthplan and Services Defined
PLAN TYPE: PPO
Model Type: Gatekeeper/ConsumerDriven
Benefits Offered: Behavioral Health, Dental, Prescription, Medical

Type of Coverage
Commercial

Type of Payment Plans Offered
POS, FFS

Geographic Areas Served
Oregon & Southwest Washington

Key Personnel
President & General Mgr . . . . .Chris Blanton

905   Clear One Health Plans

Acquired by PacificSource Health Plans

906   eHealthInsurance Services Inc.

11919 Foundation Place
Gold River, CA 95670
Toll-Free: 800-977-8860
info@ehealthinsurance.com
www.e.healthinsurance.com
Year Founded: 1997

Healthplan and Services Defined
PLAN TYPE: HMO/PPO
Benefits Offered: Dental, Life, STD

Type of Coverage
Commercial, Individual, Medicare

Geographic Areas Served
All 50 states in the USA and District of Columbia

Key Personnel
Chairman & CEO . . . . .Gary L. Lauer
EVP/Business & Corp. Dev. .Bruce Telkamp
EVP/Chief Technology . . . . .Dr. Sheldon X. Wang
SVP & CFO . . . . .Stuart M. Huizinga
Pres. of eHealth Gov. Sys . . . . .Samuel C. Gibbs
SVP of Sales & Operations . . . . .Robert S. Hurley
Director Public Relations. . . . . .Nate Purpura
     650-210-3115

907   FamilyCare Health Medicare Plan

825 NE Multnomah
Suite 300
Portland, OR 97232
Toll-Free: 800-458-9518
Phone: 503-222-2880
Fax: 503-222-2392
www.familycareinc.org
For Profit Organization: Yes
Year Founded: 1984
Total Enrollment: 2,000

Healthplan and Services Defined
PLAN TYPE: Medicare
Benefits Offered: Chiropractic, Dental, Disease Management, Home Care, Inpatient SNF, Physical Therapy, Podiatry, Prescription, Psychiatric, Vision, Wellness

Type of Coverage
Individual, Medicare, Medicaid

Geographic Areas Served
Clackamas, Clatsop, Morrow, Multnomah, Umatilla and Washington counties

Subscriber Information
Average Monthly Fee Per Subscriber
  (Employee + Employer Contribution):
    Employee Only (Self): Varies
    Medicare: Varies
Average Annual Deductible Per Subscriber:
    Employee Only (Self): Varies
    Medicare: Varies
Average Subscriber Co-Payment:
    Primary Care Physician: Varies
    Non-Network Physician: Varies
    Prescription Drugs: Varies
    Hospital ER: Varies
    Home Health Care: Varies
    Home Health Care Max. Days/Visits Covered: Varies
    Nursing Home: Varies
    Nursing Home Max. Days/Visits Covered: Varies

Key Personnel
President/CEO. . . . . .Jeff Heatherington

908   Great-West Healthcare Oregon

Acquired by CIGNA

909   Health Net Health Plan of Oregon

13221 SW 68th Parkway
Suite 200
Tigard, OR 97223
Toll-Free: 888-802-7001
Phone: 503-213-5279
service@healthnet.com
www.healthnet.com
Subsidiary of: Health Net
For Profit Organization: Yes
Number of Affiliated Hospitals: 39
Number of Primary Care Physicians: 4,400
Number of Referral/Specialty Physicians: 6,000
Total Enrollment: 123,000
State Enrollment: 17,100

Healthplan and Services Defined
PLAN TYPE: HMO/PPO
Model Type: IPA
Benefits Offered: Behavioral Health, Chiropractic, Complementary Medicine, Dental, Disease Management, Home Care, Inpatient SNF, Physical Therapy, Podiatry, Prescription, Psychiatric, Transplant, Vision, Wellness

Type of Coverage
Commercial, Individual, Indemnity, Supplemental Medicare

Type of Payment Plans Offered
POS, DFFS, Capitated, FFS, Combination FFS & DFFS

Geographic Areas Served
18 Oregon counties

Subscriber Information
Average Subscriber Co-Payment:
Primary Care Physician: $25.00
Non-Network Physician: 50%
Hospital ER: $100.00

Key Personnel
President . . . . .Chris Ellertson
Claims . . . . .Kitty Oreskovich
Network Contracting . . . . .Gerry Weiner
Credentialing . . . . .Renee Claborn
Dental. . . . . .Kitty Oreskovich
In-House Formulary . . . . .Renee Claborn
Marketing. . . . . .Richard Skayhan
Materials Management . . . . .Richard Skayhan
Provider Services. . . . . .Gerry Weiner
Sales . . . . .Greg O'Hanlon
Director, Communications . . . . .Amy Sheyer
818-676-8304
amy.l.sheyer@healthnet.com

Average Claim Compensation
Physician's Fees Charged: 30%
Hospital's Fees Charged: 35%

Specialty Managed Care Partners
Mhn, Vsp, Chp

Employer References
COSTCO, Willamette ESD

910 Humana Health Insurance of Oregon

1498 SE Tech Center Place
Suite 300
Vancouver, WA 98683
Toll-Free: 800-781-4203
Phone: 360-253-7523
Fax: 360-253-7524
www.humana.com
For Profit Organization: Yes

Healthplan and Services Defined
PLAN TYPE: HMO/PPO

Type of Coverage
Commercial, Individual

Accreditation Certification
URAC, NCQA, CORE

911 Kaiser Permanente Health Plan Northwest

500 NE Multnomah Street
Suite 100
Portland, OR 97232
Toll-Free: 800-813-2000
Phone: 503-813-2000
david.t.northfield@kp.org
www.kaiserpermanente.org
Subsidiary of: Kaiser Foundation Health Plan
Non-Profit Organization: Yes
Year Founded: 1945
Owned by an Integrated Delivery Network (IDN): Yes
Number of Affiliated Hospitals: 35
Number of Primary Care Physicians: 15,129
Number of Referral/Specialty Physicians: 11,000
Total Enrollment: 471,000
State Enrollment: 471,000

Healthplan and Services Defined
PLAN TYPE: HMO
Model Type: Group
Plan Specialty: Behavioral Health, Disease Management, Lab, Vision, Radiology, Worker's Compensation
Benefits Offered: Behavioral Health, Chiropractic, Complementary Medicine, Dental, Disease Management, Home Care, Inpatient SNF, Physical Therapy, Prescription, Psychiatric, Transplant, Vision, Wellness, Worker's Compensation

Type of Coverage
Commercial, Individual, Medicare, Medicaid

Type of Payment Plans Offered
POS, Capitated

Geographic Areas Served
Northwestern Oregon & Southwestern Washington

Subscriber Information
Average Monthly Fee Per Subscriber
(Employee + Employer Contribution):
Employee Only (Self): Varies
Employee & 1 Family Member: Varies
Employee & 2 Family Members: Varies
Medicare: Varies
Average Subscriber Co-Payment:
Primary Care Physician: Varies
Non-Network Physician: Varies
Prescription Drugs: Varies
Hospital ER: Varies
Home Health Care: Varies
Home Health Care Max. Days/Visits Covered: Varies
Nursing Home: Varies
Nursing Home Max. Days/Visits Covered: Varies

Network Qualifications
Pre-Admission Certification: Yes

Peer Review Type
Utilization Review: Yes

Publishes and Distributes Report Card: Yes

Accreditation Certification
TJC, NCQA

Key Personnel
Regional President. . . . . .Andrew R McCulloch
Exec Medical Director . . . . .Sharon M Higgins, MD
Dental Director & CEO. . . . . .John J Snyder, DMD
Media Contact . . . . .David Northfield
503-813-4235
david.t.northfield@kp.org

Specialty Managed Care Partners
Complementary Health Plan

Employer References
Federal Employees, State of Oregon, Oregon PERS, State of Washington

912 Liberty Health Plan: Corporate Office

650 NE Holladay Street
PO Box 4555
Portland, OR 97232-2045
Toll-Free: 800-275-5600
Phone: 503-239-5800
Fax: 503-736-7303
customerservice.center@libertynorthwest.com
www.libertynorthwest.com
For Profit Organization: Yes
Year Founded: 1983

Healthplan and Services Defined
PLAN TYPE: PPO
Model Type: Group
Plan Specialty: Worker's Compensation
Benefits Offered: Prescription

Type of Payment Plans Offered
POS, DFFS, FFS, Combination FFS & DFFS

Geographic Areas Served
Baker, Benton, Clackamas, Columbia, Coos, Crook, Curry, Deschutes, Douglas, Gilliam, Grant, Harney, Hood River, Jackson, Jefferson, Josephine, Klamath, Lake, Lane, Lincoln counties

Network Qualifications
Pre-Admission Certification: Yes

Peer Review Type
Case Management: Yes

Publishes and Distributes Report Card: No

Key Personnel
President/CEO . . . . Matt Nickerson
CFO . . . . Jim McKittrick
Controller . . . . Mary Augustyn
Vice Presdient, Claims . . . . Margie Cooper
Vp/Corporate Marketing . . . . Beth Shia
   503-736-7003
   beth.shia@libertynorthwest.com
VP/Public Affairs . . . . Brian Boe
   503-736-7027
   brian.boe@libertynorthwest.com
Medical Affairs . . . . Chris Fassenfelt
Member Services . . . . Phil Wentz
Information Systems . . . . Jim Scott
Media Contact . . . . Christopher Goetcheus
   774-279-5923
   christopher.goetcheus@libertynorthwest.c

Specialty Managed Care Partners
Enters into Contracts with Regional Business Coalitions: No

913 Lifewise Health Plan of Oregon

2020 SW Fourth Street
Suite 1000
Portland, OR 97201
Toll-Free: 800-596-3440
Phone: 503-295-6707
Fax: 503-279-5295
www.lifewiseor.com
Secondary Address: 815 SW Bond, Bend, OR 97702
For Profit Organization: Yes
Number of Primary Care Physicians: 9,000
Total Enrollment: 1,500,000
State Enrollment: 82,000

Healthplan and Services Defined
PLAN TYPE: PPO

Key Personnel
President/CEO . . . . Majd El-Azma
Mgr, Operations . . . . Amber Elgin
VP, Healthcare Delivery . . . . Allison Bechtol
VP, Underwriting . . . . Sharon Howe
VP, Sales & Marketing . . . . David Lechner
Communications Team Lead . . . . Deanna Strunk
   541-318-2071
   deana.strunk@lifewisehealth.com

914 Managed HealthCare Northwest

PO Box 4629
Portland, OR 97208-4629
Toll-Free: 800-648-6356
Phone: 503-413-5800
Fax: 503-413-5801
www.mhninc.com
Secondary Address: 422 East Burnside Street, #215, Portland, OR 97214
Subsidiary of: CareMark PPO/MHN PPO/CareMark Comp

For Profit Organization: Yes
Year Founded: 1988
Number of Affiliated Hospitals: 22
Number of Primary Care Physicians: 1,435
Number of Referral/Specialty Physicians: 4,236
Total Enrollment: 129,120
State Enrollment: 129,120

Healthplan and Services Defined
PLAN TYPE: PPO
Model Type: Network
Plan Specialty: Worker's Compensation, MCO, Precertification, Utilization Review, Case Management
Benefits Offered: Worker's Compensation, MCO, Precertification, Utilization Review, Case Management

Type of Coverage
Commercial, Individual, Group Workers' Comp, MCO

Geographic Areas Served
Oregon: Clackamas, Columbia, Coos, Hood River, Lane, Marion, Multnomah, Polk, Wasco, Washington & Yamhill counties; Washington: Clark, Klickitat & Skamania counties

Network Qualifications
Pre-Admission Certification: Yes

Peer Review Type
Utilization Review: Yes
Second Surgical Opinion: Yes
Case Management: Yes

Publishes and Distributes Report Card: No

Key Personnel
President and CEO . . . . Dolores Russell
Marketing Manager . . . . Jody Ordway
Commercial Care Mgmt . . . . Jan Munro
Workers' Comp MCO . . . . Rhea Schnitzer
IS Director, Finance Dir . . . . David Pyle
Provider Relations Dir . . . . Jennifer Kirk

Specialty Managed Care Partners
Enters into Contracts with Regional Business Coalitions: Yes

Employer References
City of Portland, SAIF Corporation, Adventist Medical Center, Legacy Health System

915 ODS Health Plan

601 Southwest Second Avenue
Portland, OR 97204-3154
Toll-Free: 877-299-9062
Phone: 503-228-6554
www.odscompanies.com
Mailing Address: PO Box 40384, Portland, OR 97240-0384
Year Founded: 1955
Total Enrollment: 1,500,000
State Enrollment: 1,500,000

Healthplan and Services Defined
PLAN TYPE: Multiple
Other Type: PPO, POS, Dental
Benefits Offered: Chiropractic, Dental, Disease Management, Home Care, Inpatient SNF, Physical Therapy, Podiatry, Prescription, Psychiatric, Vision, Wellness

Type of Coverage
Commercial, Individual, Medicare

Geographic Areas Served
Available within Oregon only

Subscriber Information
Average Monthly Fee Per Subscriber
  (Employee + Employer Contribution):
   Employee Only (Self): Varies
   Medicare: Varies
Average Annual Deductible Per Subscriber:
   Employee Only (Self): Varies

Medicare: Varies
Average Subscriber Co-Payment:
Primary Care Physician: Varies
Non-Network Physician: Varies
Prescription Drugs: Varies
Hospital ER: Varies
Home Health Care: Varies
Home Health Care Max. Days/Visits Covered: Varies
Nursing Home: Varies
Nursing Home Max. Days/Visits Covered: Varies

Key Personnel
President/CEO . . . . .Robert Gootee
Senior Vice President . . . . .Tracie Murphy
Senior Vice President. . . . . .Robin Richardson
Senior Vice President. . . . . .Steve Wynne
SVP, Dental Services . . . . .Bill Ten Pas
VP, Corp Communications . . . . .Jonathan Nicholas
503-219-3673

916 PacifiCare of Oregon
5 Centerpointe Drive
Suite 600
Lake Oswego, OR 97035
Toll-Free: 800-922-1444
Phone: 503-603-7355
Fax: 503-624-5162
www.pacificare.com
Mailing Address: PO Box 6090, Cypress, CA 90630-0092
Subsidiary of: UnitedHealthCare
For Profit Organization: Yes
Year Founded: 1985
Number of Affiliated Hospitals: 25
Number of Primary Care Physicians: 4,200
Total Enrollment: 29,000
State Enrollment: 49,455

Healthplan and Services Defined
PLAN TYPE: HMO
Model Type: Mixed
Benefits Offered: Behavioral Health, Chiropractic, Complementary
Medicine, Dental, Disease Management, Home Care, Inpatient
SNF, Physical Therapy, Podiatry, Prescription, Psychiatric,
Transplant, Vision, Wellness, Life, LTD, STD

Type of Coverage
Commercial, Individual, Indemnity, Medicare

Accreditation Certification
NCQA

Key Personnel
CEO. . . . . .Randy Wardlow
Medical Director . . . . .Bill Hopper, MD

917 PacificSource Health Plans: Corporate Headquarters
110 International Way
Springfield, OR 97477
Toll-Free: 800-624-6052
Phone: 541-686-1242
Fax: 541-485-0915
www.pacificsource.com
Secondary Address: 2965 NE Conners Avenue, Bend, OR 97701
Non-Profit Organization: Yes
Year Founded: 1933
Number of Primary Care Physicians: 34,000
Total Enrollment: 280,000

Healthplan and Services Defined
PLAN TYPE: HMO/PPO

Benefits Offered: Dental, Disease Management, Prescription, Vision,
Wellness

Type of Coverage
Commercial, Individual

Type of Payment Plans Offered
POS, Combination FFS & DFFS

Geographic Areas Served
Oregon and Idaho

Key Personnel
President & CEO. . . . . .Ken Provencher
EVP, COO . . . . .Sujata Sanghvi
EVP, CFO . . . . .Peter Davidson
SVP, Director ID & WA . . . . .Dave Self
VP, Large Group & ASO .Steve Schmidt
VP, Administration . . . . .Paul Wynkoop
VP, Finance & Controller. . . . . .Kari Patterson
VP, Business Development .Lisz Zenev
Reg VP, Marketing Officer . . . . .Troy Kirk
SVP, Chief Medical Offc . . . . .Steven D Marks, MD
SVP, Chief Info Officer . . . . .Erick Doolen
VP, Provider Network .Peter McGarry
VP, Actuarial . . . . .Victor Paguia
Media Contact. . . . . .Colleen Thompson
541-684-5453
cthompson@pacificsource.com

Specialty Managed Care Partners
Caremark Rx

918 Providence Health Plans
3601 SW Murray Boulevard
Suite 109
Beaverton, OR 97005
Toll-Free: 877-245-4077
Phone: 503-215-7550
Fax: 503-215-7543
www.providence.org/healthplans
Mailing Address: PO Box 4327, Portland, OR 97208-4327
Subsidiary of: Providence Health Systems
Non-Profit Organization: Yes
Year Founded: 1985
Number of Affiliated Hospitals: 31
Number of Primary Care Physicians: 1,366
Number of Referral/Specialty Physicians: 3,042
Total Enrollment: 350,000
State Enrollment: 350,000

Healthplan and Services Defined
PLAN TYPE: HMO/PPO
Model Type: IPA, Group, PHO
Plan Specialty: Disease Management, EPO, Vision, UR
Benefits Offered: Behavioral Health, Chiropractic, Complementary
Medicine, Disease Management, Home Care, Inpatient SNF,
Physical Therapy, Podiatry, Prescription, Psychiatric, Transplant,
Vision, Wellness
Offers Demand Management Patient Information Service: Yes
DMPI Services Offered: 24 Hour Telephone Advice Nurse, Website,
Fitness Wellness Classes, Resource Telephone Service, Discounted
Vision Service

Type of Coverage
Commercial, Medicare, Medicaid

Type of Payment Plans Offered
POS, FFS

Geographic Areas Served
Oregon: Benton, Clackamas, Crook, Deschules, Grant, Harney,
Jefferson, Josephine, Lake, Marion, Multnomah, Tillamook,
Washington, Wheeler, and Yamhill; WA: Clark and Skamania

Subscriber Information
Average Monthly Fee Per Subscriber
(Employee + Employer Contribution):
Employee Only (Self): Varies by plan
Average Subscriber Co-Payment:
Home Health Care Max. Days/Visits Covered: 30 days
Nursing Home Max. Days/Visits Covered: 60 days

Network Qualifications
Pre-Admission Certification: Yes

Peer Review Type
Utilization Review: Yes
Second Surgical Opinion: Yes
Case Management: Yes

Publishes and Distributes Report Card: Yes

Accreditation Certification
NCQA
Medicare Approved, Utilization Review, Pre-Admission
Certification, State Licensure, Quality Assurance Program

Key Personnel
Chief Executive Officer . . . . .Jack Friedman
Chief Operating Officer . . . . .Michael White
Chief Service Officer . . . . .Alison Schrupp
Dir, Mission Integration . . . . .Margaret Pastro, SP
Dir, Regulatory Compl . . . . .Carrie Smith
Chief Sales & Mktg Offc . . . . .Barbara Christensen

Average Claim Compensation
Physician's Fees Charged: 55%
Hospital's Fees Charged: 48%

Specialty Managed Care Partners
PBH Behavioral Health, ARGUS (PBM), Complementary Health
Care, Well Partner
Enters into Contracts with Regional Business Coalitions: No

Employer References
Providence Health System, PeaceHealth, Portland Public School
District, Oregon PERS, Tektonix

919   Regence Blue Cross & Blue Shield of Oregon
100 SW Market Street
Portland, OR 97201
Toll-Free: 800-452-7278
Phone: 503-225-5221
Fax: 503-225-5274
dmglass@regence.com
www.or.regence.com
Mailing Address: PO Box 1071, Portland, OR 97207
Subsidiary of: The Regence Group
Non-Profit Organization: Yes
Year Founded: 1941
Owned by an Integrated Delivery Network (IDN): Yes
Number of Affiliated Hospitals: 48
Number of Primary Care Physicians: 10,425
Total Enrollment: 2,500,000
State Enrollment: 800,000

Healthplan and Services Defined
PLAN TYPE: PPO
Model Type: IPA
Benefits Offered: Behavioral Health, Dental, Disease Management,
Prescription, Vision, Wellness, Hearing Care, Local Gym
Memberships, Weight Loss Programs, Child Health & Safety
Products

Type of Coverage
Commercial, Individual, Indemnity, Medicare, Supplemental
Medicare
Catastrophic Illness Benefit: Maximum $2M

Type of Payment Plans Offered
POS, DFFS, Capitated, FFS, Combination FFS & DFFS

Geographic Areas Served
All Oregon and Clark County, WA

Subscriber Information
Average Annual Deductible Per Subscriber:
Employee Only (Self): $250.00
Average Subscriber Co-Payment:
Primary Care Physician: $15.00/100.00
Prescription Drugs: $10/30/50
Hospital ER: $100.00
Home Health Care: $180 days

Network Qualifications
Pre-Admission Certification: Yes

Peer Review Type
Utilization Review: Yes
Second Surgical Opinion: Yes
Case Management: Yes

Publishes and Distributes Report Card: Yes

Accreditation Certification
NCQA
TJC Accreditation, Medicare Approved, Pre-Admission Certification,
State Licensure

Key Personnel
President/CEO . . . . .Mark B. Ganz
Execuive VP/Health Care . . . . .Bill Barr
SVP, Chief Info Officer . . . . .Cheron Vail
Chief Marketing Executive . . . . .Mohan Nair
SVP, Healthcare Services . . . . .John Stellmon
EVP, Chief Legal Officer . . . . .Kerry Barnett
Chief Financial Officer . . . . .Vince Price
Sr VP/Human Resources . . . . .Tom Kennedy
EVP, Chief Marketing Exec . . . . .Mohan Nair
SVP, Enterprise Mgmt . . . . .Jo Ann Long
Chief Medical Officer .Dennis Chong, MD
President, Regence WA . . . . .Johnathan Hensley
President, Regence UT . . . . .Robert A Hatch
President, Regence ID . . . . .Scott Kreiling
President, Regence OR . . . . .Jared L Short
Oregon Media Inquiries . . . . .Samantha Meese
503-225-5332
sxmeese@regence.com
Vice President . . . . .Peggy Maguire

Specialty Managed Care Partners
Magellan, Ceres Behavioral, Advance Masters, Northwest Mental
Health, Alternare, Heart Masters

920   Samaritan Health Plan
815 Northwest 9th Street
Corvallis, OR 97330
Toll-Free: 800-832-4580
Fax: 541-768-4482
advantage@samhealth.org
www.samhealth.org/shplans
Mailing Address: PO Box 1510, Corvallis, OR 97339
Year Founded: 1993
Total Enrollment: 30,000
State Enrollment: 30,000

Healthplan and Services Defined
PLAN TYPE: Multiple
Benefits Offered: Chiropractic, Dental, Disease Management, Home
Care, Inpatient SNF, Physical Therapy, Podiatry, Prescription,
Psychiatric, Vision, Wellness

Type of Coverage
Individual, Medicare

Geographic Areas Served
Available within Oregon only

Subscriber Information
  Average Monthly Fee Per Subscriber
    (Employee + Employer Contribution):
      Employee Only (Self): Varies
      Medicare: Varies
  Average Annual Deductible Per Subscriber:
      Employee Only (Self): Varies
      Medicare: Varies
  Average Subscriber Co-Payment:
      Primary Care Physician: Varies
      Non-Network Physician: Varies
      Prescription Drugs: Varies
      Hospital ER: Varies
      Home Health Care: Varies
      Home Health Care Max. Days/Visits Covered: Varies
      Nursing Home: Varies
      Nursing Home Max. Days/Visits Covered: Varies

Key Personnel
  President & CEO . . . . .Larry A Mullins, DHA
  CEO. . . . . .Kelley C Kaiser, MPH
  COO . . . . .Kim R Whitley, MPA
  CFO . . . . .Ronald S Stevens, MBA
  Medical Director . . . . .Rick Wopat, MD

921 Trillium Community Health Plan

UO Riverfront Research Park
1800 Millrace Drive
Eugene, OR 97403
Toll-Free: 800-910-3906
Phone: 541-282-2455
Fax: 541-984-5685
customerservice@trilliumchp.com
www.trilliumchp.com
Mailing Address: PO Box 11756, Eugene, OR 97440-3956
Subsidiary of: Lane Individual Practice Association (LIPA)

Healthplan and Services Defined
  PLAN TYPE: Medicare
  Benefits Offered: Chiropractic, Dental, Disease Management, Home
    Care, Inpatient SNF, Physical Therapy, Podiatry, Prescription,
    Psychiatric, Vision, Wellness

Type of Coverage
  Individual, Medicare, Sprout Healthy KidsConnect

Geographic Areas Served
  Available within Oregon only

Subscriber Information
  Average Monthly Fee Per Subscriber
    (Employee + Employer Contribution):
      Employee Only (Self): Varies
      Medicare: Varies
  Average Annual Deductible Per Subscriber:
      Employee Only (Self): Varies
      Medicare: Varies
  Average Subscriber Co-Payment:
      Primary Care Physician: Varies
      Non-Network Physician: Varies
      Prescription Drugs: Varies
      Hospital ER: Varies
      Home Health Care: Varies
      Home Health Care Max. Days/Visits Covered: Varies
      Nursing Home: Varies
      Nursing Home Max. Days/Visits Covered: Varies

Key Personnel
  President . . . . .Thomas K Wuest, MD
  Chief Financial Officer . . . . .David L Cole
  Chief Medical Officer .Robert R Wheeler
  Chief Admin Officer . . . . .Kent M Noah
  Governmental Affairs . . . . .Rhonda J Busek
  Secretary. . . . . .Terry W Coplin

Board of Directors/CEO. . . . . .Peter Fletcher Davidson
Board of Directors .Dean Raymond Kortge
Board of Directors . . . . .Mary Frances Theresa Spilde
Medicare Director. . . . . .Shannon Conley
Medical Directori . . . . .John Sattenspiel
Medicare Compliance Dir. . . . . .Cheryl Lund
Enrollment Specialist. . . . . .Billie Stoltz
Claims Analyst. . . . . .Terri Maack

922 United Concordia: Oregon

121 Southwest Salmon Street
Suite 1132
Portland, OR 97024
Toll-Free: 888-815-8224
Phone: 503-471-1466
Fax: 503-471-1442
ucproducer@ucci.com
www.secure.ucci.com
For Profit Organization: Yes
Year Founded: 1971
Number of Primary Care Physicians: 111,000
Total Enrollment: 8,000,000

Healthplan and Services Defined
  PLAN TYPE: Dental
  Plan Specialty: Dental
  Benefits Offered: Dental

Type of Coverage
  Commercial, Individual

Geographic Areas Served
  Military personnel and their families, nationwide

923 UnitedHealthCare of Oregon

5 Centerpointe Drive
Suite 600
Lake Oswego, OR 97035
Toll-Free: 800-922-1444
www.uhc.com
Subsidiary of: UnitedHealth Group
For Profit Organization: Yes
Total Enrollment: 75,000,000
State Enrollment: 231,125

Healthplan and Services Defined
  PLAN TYPE: HMO/PPO

Geographic Areas Served
  Statewide

Key Personnel
  Chief Executive Officer . . . . .David Hansen
  Marketing . . . . .Lya Selby
  Medical Director . . . . .Roger Muller, MD
  Media Contact . . . . .Will Shanley
    will.shanley@uhc.com

924 VSP: Vision Service Plan of Oregon

121 SW Morrison Street
Suite 1050
Portland, OR 97024-3119
Phone: 503-232-8187
webmaster@vsp.com
www.vsp.com
Year Founded: 1955
Number of Primary Care Physicians: 26,000
Total Enrollment: 55,000,000

Healthplan and Services Defined
  PLAN TYPE: Vision
  Plan Specialty: Vision

Benefits Offered: Vision

Type of Payment Plans Offered
Capitated

Geographic Areas Served
Statewide

Network Qualifications
Pre-Admission Certification: Yes

Peer Review Type
Utilization Review: Yes

Accreditation Certification
Utilization Review, Quality Assurance Program

Key Personnel

Manager	Steve Hanks
Mgr Information Security	Douglas Ljung
Manager	Jennifer Aberg

925 Willamette Dental Insurance

6950 NE Campus Way
Hillsboro, OR 97124
Toll-Free: 800-460-7644
Phone: 503-952-2000
Fax: 503-952-2200
info@willamettedental.com
www.willamettedental.com
Subsidiary of: Willamette Dental Group
For Profit Organization: Yes
Year Founded: 1970
Number of Primary Care Physicians: 245

Healthplan and Services Defined
PLAN TYPE: Dental
Model Type: Staff
Plan Specialty: Dental
Benefits Offered: Dental

Type of Payment Plans Offered
POS, FFS

Geographic Areas Served
Oregon: Washington: Idaho: Nevada

Network Qualifications
Pre-Admission Certification: Yes

Peer Review Type
Case Management: Yes

Publishes and Distributes Report Card: No

Key Personnel

President/CEO	Steve Petruzelli
COO	Yuen Chin
CFO	Wee Chin
Marketing	Doug Wohlman
VP, Human Resources	Chris Holgerson
VP Marketing	Doug Wohlman
Information Services	Don Mason
VP, Operations	April Kniess

Specialty Managed Care Partners
Enters into Contracts with Regional Business Coalitions: No

Health Insurance Coverage Status and Type of Coverage by Age

Category	All Persons		Under 18 years		Under 65 years		65 years and over	
	Number	%	Number	%	Number	%	Number	%
Total population	12,453	-	2,747	-	10,461	-	1,993	-
Covered by some type of health insurance	11,085 *(115)*	89.0 *(0.7)*	2,521 *(42)*	91.8 *(1.4)*	9,108 *(140)*	87.1 *(0.9)*	1,978 *(66)*	99.3 *(0.3)*
Covered by private health insurance	8,986 *(152)*	72.2 *(1.1)*	1,816 *(61)*	66.1 *(2.1)*	7,595 *(156)*	72.6 *(1.2)*	1,391 *(74)*	69.8 *(2.3)*
Employment based	7,606 *(167)*	61.1 *(1.2)*	1,721 *(59)*	62.6 *(2.0)*	6,904 *(166)*	66.0 *(1.3)*	702 *(52)*	35.2 *(2.1)*
Own employment based	3,972 *(87)*	31.9 *(0.6)*	2 *(2)*	0.1 *(0.1)*	3,465 *(86)*	33.1 *(0.7)*	508 *(39)*	25.5 *(1.7)*
Direct purchase	1,746 *(83)*	14.0 *(0.7)*	175 *(28)*	6.4 *(1.0)*	964 *(72)*	9.2 *(0.7)*	782 *(52)*	39.2 *(2.2)*
Covered by government health insurance	3,920 *(107)*	31.5 *(0.9)*	882 *(57)*	32.1 *(2.1)*	2,038 *(96)*	19.5 *(0.9)*	1,882 *(66)*	94.5 *(0.9)*
Covered by Medicaid	1,778 *(94)*	14.3 *(0.8)*	864 *(56)*	31.4 *(2.1)*	1,679 *(94)*	16.1 *(0.9)*	99 *(18)*	5.0 *(0.9)*
Also by private insurance	372 *(37)*	3.0 *(0.3)*	165 *(22)*	6.0 *(0.8)*	339 *(36)*	3.2 *(0.3)*	33 *(10)*	1.6 *(0.5)*
Covered by Medicare	2,210 *(74)*	17.7 *(0.6)*	6 *(5)*	0.2 *(0.2)*	330 *(36)*	3.2 *(0.3)*	1,879 *(66)*	94.3 *(0.9)*
Also by private insurance	1,412 *(76)*	11.3 *(0.6)*	0 *(0)*	0.0 *(0.0)*	116 *(19)*	1.1 *(0.2)*	1,296 *(74)*	65.0 *(2.5)*
Also by Medicaid	217 *(31)*	1.7 *(0.2)*	6 *(5)*	0.2 *(0.2)*	117 *(22)*	1.1 *(0.2)*	99 *(18)*	5.0 *(0.9)*
Covered by military health care	296 *(42)*	2.4 *(0.3)*	25 *(10)*	0.9 *(0.4)*	175 *(27)*	1.7 *(0.3)*	120 *(25)*	6.0 *(1.2)*
Not covered at any time during the year	1,368 *(93)*	11.0 *(0.7)*	226 *(39)*	8.2 *(1.4)*	1,353 *(90)*	12.9 *(0.9)*	15 *(6)*	0.7 *(0.3)*

Note: Numbers in thousands; figures cover 2010; standard error appears in parenthesis; (b) base less than 75,000; (x) not applicable
Source: U.S. Census Bureau, Current Population Survey, 2011 Annual Social and Economic Supplement. Table HI05. Health Insurance Coverage Status and Type of Coverage by State and Age for All People: 2010

Pennsylvania

926 Aetna Health of Pennsylvania
151 Farmington Avenue
Conveyer ASB2
Hartford, CT 06156
Toll-Free: 866-582-9629
www.aetna.com
For Profit Organization: Yes
Year Founded: 1987
Number of Affiliated Hospitals: 52
Number of Primary Care Physicians: 1,524
Number of Referral/Specialty Physicians: 3,928
Total Enrollment: 409,265
State Enrollment: 409,265

Healthplan and Services Defined
PLAN TYPE: HMO
Other Type: POS
Model Type: IPA
Benefits Offered: Disease Management, Prescription, Wellness
Offers Demand Management Patient Information Service: Yes

Geographic Areas Served
Statewide

Network Qualifications
Pre-Admission Certification: Yes

Peer Review Type
Utilization Review: Yes
Second Surgical Opinion: Yes
Case Management: Yes

Publishes and Distributes Report Card: Yes

Accreditation Certification
URAC, NCQA

Key Personnel
CEO . . . . .Ronald A Williams
President. . . . . .Mark T Bertolini
SVP, General Counsel . . . . .William J Casazza
EVP, CFO . . . . .Joseph M Zubretsky
Head, M&A Integration . . . . .Kay Mooney
SVP, Marketing. . . . . .Robert E Mead
Chief Medical Officer . . . . .Lonny Reisman, MD
SVP, Human Resources. . . . . .Elease E Wright
SVP, CIO. . . . . .Meg McCarthy

Specialty Managed Care Partners
Enters into Contracts with Regional Business Coalitions: Yes

927 American Health Care Group
1910 Cochran Road
Manor Oak One, Suite 405
Pittsburgh, PA 15220
Phone: 412-563-8800
Fax: 412-563-8319
info@american-healthcare.net
www.american-healthcare.net
For Profit Organization: Yes
Year Founded: 1996
Number of Affiliated Hospitals: 30
Total Enrollment: 60,000

Healthplan and Services Defined
PLAN TYPE: HMO/PPO
Model Type: Network
Plan Specialty: ASO, Chiropractic, Dental, MSO, Worker's Compensation
Benefits Offered: Behavioral Health, Chiropractic, Complementary Medicine, Dental, Disease Management, Home Care, Inpatient SNF, Long-Term Care, Physical Therapy, Podiatry, Prescription, Psychiatric, Transplant, Vision, Wellness, Worker's Compensation, Offers a variety of
Offers Demand Management Patient Information Service: Yes
DMPI Services Offered: PPO Network, Workers Complaint, Customize Network Development, Information Systems

Type of Payment Plans Offered
FFS

Geographic Areas Served
Pennsylvania, Eastern Ohio, Northwestern Virgina

Peer Review Type
Utilization Review: Yes
Second Surgical Opinion: Yes
Case Management: Yes

Accreditation Certification
State Licensure

Key Personnel
President/CEO. . . . . .Robert E Hagan
  bhagan@american-healthcare.net
Marketing Manager . . . . .Mary Double
  mdouble@american-healthcare.net
Financial Operations .Lynn Hagan
  lhagan@american-healthcare.net
Chief Medical Officer . . . . .Joseph C Maroon, MD
Medical Management Svcs . . . . .Sarah Doyle Steranka
  ssteranka@american-healthcare.net
Wellness Program Manager . . . . .Liz Kanche
  lhkanche@american-healthcare.net
Health Benefit Services . . . . .Erin E Hart
  ehart@american-healthcare.net

928 American WholeHealth Network
46040 Center Oak Plaza
Suite 130
Sterling, PA 20166
Toll-Free: 800-274-7526
Phone: 703-547-5100
Fax: 703-547-5573
ContactUs1@awhinc.com
www.americanwholehealth.com
Secondary Address: Healthways, Inc., 701 Cool Springs Blvd, Franklin, TN 37067
Subsidiary of: Healthways, Inc.
For Profit Organization: Yes
Year Founded: 1975
Owned by an Integrated Delivery Network (IDN): Yes
Number of Referral/Specialty Physicians: 4,000
Total Enrollment: 3,100,000

Healthplan and Services Defined
PLAN TYPE: PPO
Model Type: IPA, Network
Plan Specialty: Chiropractic, MSO, Physical Therapy
Benefits Offered: Chiropractic, Complementary Medicine, Disease Management, Physical Therapy, Wellness

Type of Payment Plans Offered
POS, DFFS, FFS

Geographic Areas Served
Arizona, California, Connecticut, Delaware, Florida, Georgia, Massachusetts, Maryland, Minnesota, North Carolina, New Jersey, Nevada, New York, Pennsylvania, Rhode Island, South Carolina, Tennessee and Washington, DC

Subscriber Information
Average Monthly Fee Per Subscriber
  (Employee + Employer Contribution):
    Employee Only (Self): Varies
    Employee & 1 Family Member: Varies
    Employee & 2 Family Members: Varies
    Medicare: Varies

Average Annual Deductible Per Subscriber:
  Employee Only (Self): Varies
  Employee & 1 Family Member: Varies
  Employee & 2 Family Members: Varies
  Medicare: Varies

Network Qualifications
Pre-Admission Certification: Yes

Peer Review Type
Utilization Review: Yes
Case Management: Yes

Accreditation Certification
URAC
Utilization Review, Pre-Admission Certification, Quality Assurance
Program

Key Personnel
President and CEO . . . . William P Dorney, Dr
VP/Operations . . . . Vincent J Love
Controller . . . . Lori Piccioni
Director . . . . Walter Channing, Jr
Director . . . . H Tomkins O'Connor
Director . . . . Sam Havens
Information Technology . . . . Billie York
Sales . . . . William Dorney, MD
Media Contact . . . . Melissa Wyllie
  615-614-4466
  melissa.wyllie@healthways.com

Specialty Managed Care Partners
Enters into Contracts with Regional Business Coalitions: Yes

929 Americhoice of Pennsylvania

The Wanamaker Building
100 Penn Square E, Suite 900
Philadelphia, PA 19107
Phone: 215-832-4500
Fax: 215-832-4644
www.americhoice.com
Subsidiary of: UnitedHealth Group
For Profit Organization: Yes
Year Founded: 1988
Number of Affiliated Hospitals: 42
Number of Primary Care Physicians: 1,100
Number of Referral/Specialty Physicians: 3,400
Total Enrollment: 71,000
State Enrollment: 110,736

Healthplan and Services Defined
PLAN TYPE: Multiple
Model Type: IPA
Benefits Offered: Disease Management, Prescription, Wellness

Type of Coverage
Medicare, Supplemental Medicare, Medicaid

Type of Payment Plans Offered
DFFS, Capitated, Combination FFS & DFFS

Geographic Areas Served
Bucks, Chester, Delaware, Montgomery & Philadelphia counties

Accreditation Certification
NCQA
TJC Accreditation, Medicare Approved, Utilization Review,
Pre-Admission Certification, State Licensure, Quality Assurance
Program

Key Personnel
CEO . . . . Ernest Montiletto
President . . . . Rick Jelinek
Acting CFO . . . . Andy Bhugra

930 AmeriHealth Medicare Plan

1901 Market Street
Philadelphia, PA 19101-8951
Toll-Free: 800-898-3492
www.amerihealth.com/amerihealth65/index.html
Secondary Address: 580 Swedesford Road, Wayne, PA 19087

Healthplan and Services Defined
PLAN TYPE: Medicare
Other Type: POS
Benefits Offered: Chiropractic, Dental, Disease Management, Home
Care, Inpatient SNF, Physical Therapy, Podiatry, Prescription,
Psychiatric, Vision, Wellness

Type of Coverage
Individual, Medicare

Geographic Areas Served
Available within mutliple states

Subscriber Information
Average Monthly Fee Per Subscriber
  (Employee + Employer Contribution):
    Employee Only (Self): Varies
    Medicare: Varies
Average Annual Deductible Per Subscriber:
    Employee Only (Self): Varies
    Medicare: Varies
Average Subscriber Co-Payment:
    Primary Care Physician: Varies
    Non-Network Physician: Varies
    Prescription Drugs: Varies
    Hospital ER: Varies
    Home Health Care: Varies
    Home Health Care Max. Days/Visits Covered: Varies
    Nursing Home: Varies
    Nursing Home Max. Days/Visits Covered: Varies

Key Personnel
President . . . . Judith Roman
VP Provider Relations . . . . Paul E Portsmore, Jr
CEO . . . . Joseph A Frick
VP Deputy General Counsel . . . . Lilton R Taliaferro, Jr
VP Marketing . . . . Susan L Sendlewski
VP Medical Director . . . . Allan B Goldstein
Media Contact . . . . Kate Wilhelmi
  856-778-6552

931 Assurant Employee Benefits: Pennsylvania

436 7th Avenue
Suite 2900
Pittsburgh, PA 15219-1829
Phone: 412-471-1020
Fax: 412-471-3614
benefits@assurant.com
www.assurantemployeebenefits.com
Subsidiary of: Assurant, Inc
For Profit Organization: Yes
Number of Primary Care Physicians: 112,000
Total Enrollment: 47,000

Healthplan and Services Defined
PLAN TYPE: Multiple
Plan Specialty: Dental, Vision, Long & Short-Term Disability
Benefits Offered: Dental, Vision, Wellness, AD&D, Life, LTD, STD

Type of Coverage
Commercial, Indemnity, Individual Dental Plans

Geographic Areas Served
Statewide

Subscriber Information
Average Monthly Fee Per Subscriber
  (Employee + Employer Contribution):
    Employee Only (Self): Varies by plan

Key Personnel
Manager . . . . .Ray Brady
PR Specialist. . . . . .Megan Hutchison
816-556-7815
megan.hutchison@assurant.com

---

932 Berkshire Health Partners

50 Commerce Drive
Wyomissing, PA 19610
Toll-Free: 866-257-0445
Phone: 610-372-8044
Fax: 484-334-7027
zimmermann@bhp.org
www.bhp.org
Non-Profit Organization: Yes
Year Founded: 1986
Physician Owned Organization: Yes
Number of Affiliated Hospitals: 16
Number of Primary Care Physicians: 825
Number of Referral/Specialty Physicians: 3,120
Total Enrollment: 60,353
State Enrollment: 60,353

Healthplan and Services Defined
PLAN TYPE: PPO
Model Type: Preferred Provider
Plan Specialty: PPO
Benefits Offered: Large provider network, claims repricing, case
mgmt, wellness and disease mgmt and short term disability case
mgmt

Type of Coverage
Commercial, Individual, Indemnity, Catastrophic, Self-Funded -ASO,
Fully-Insured
Catastrophic Illness Benefit: Varies per case

Type of Payment Plans Offered
FFS

Geographic Areas Served
Berks, Upper Bucks, Lancaster, Lehigh, Montgomery, Northampton,
Schuylkill counties in PA

Subscriber Information
Average Monthly Fee Per Subscriber
(Employee + Employer Contribution):
Employee Only (Self): Varies
Average Annual Deductible Per Subscriber:
Employee Only (Self): Varies
Employee & 2 Family Members: Varies
Average Subscriber Co-Payment:
Primary Care Physician: Varies
Prescription Drugs: Varies
Hospital ER: Varies
Nursing Home Max. Days/Visits Covered: Varies

Peer Review Type
Utilization Review: Yes
Second Surgical Opinion: Yes
Case Management: Yes

Accreditation Certification
URAC, NCQA

Key Personnel
President & CEO. . . . . .Charles Wills
610-372-8044
Director Operations. . . . . .Tanya Glouner
Claims Manager . . . . .Lori Calpino
Marketing/Sales . . . . .Natalie Zimmerman
Dir, Medical Management . . . . .Dawn Dreibelbis
Mgr, Medical Management . . . . .Robin Riegner
Provider Services. . . . . .Tanya Glouner
Dir, Business Development. . . . . .Natalie Zimmerman
610-372-8044
zimmermann@bhp.org

Specialty Managed Care Partners
Enters into Contracts with Regional Business Coalitions: Yes
PPHN, Unity

---

933 Blue Cross of Northeastern Pennsylvania

19 N Main Street
Wilkes Barre, PA 18711-0302
Toll-Free: 800-822-8753
Phone: 570-200-4300
Fax: 570-200-6888
www.bcnepa.com
Non-Profit Organization: Yes
Year Founded: 1938
Number of Affiliated Hospitals: 30
Total Enrollment: 600,000
State Enrollment: 600,000

Healthplan and Services Defined
PLAN TYPE: HMO/PPO
Other Type: EPO
Model Type: IPA
Plan Specialty: Dental, Vision
Benefits Offered: Dental, Disease Management, Prescription, Vision,
Wellness

Type of Coverage
Commercial, Individual

Geographic Areas Served
Northeast Pennsylvania

Network Qualifications
Pre-Admission Certification: Yes

Peer Review Type
Second Surgical Opinion: Yes

Publishes and Distributes Report Card: Yes

Accreditation Certification
URAC, NCQA

Key Personnel
CEO . . . . .Denise Cesare
CFO. . . . . .Michael Gallagher
COO . . . . .Cathy Stitzer
VP of Customer Service . . . . .Edward Fennel
Officer . . . . .Trish Savitsky
Manager . . . . .Alan Pawlenok
Information Technology. . . . . .Paul Fort
Medical Affairs .Carmella Sabastian, MD
Project Manager . . . . .Linda Moharsky

Specialty Managed Care Partners
Enters into Contracts with Regional Business Coalitions: Yes

---

934 Blue Ridge Health Network

PO Box 674
Schuylkill Haven, PA 17972
Toll-Free: 800-730-0134
Phone: 570-628-2236
Fax: 570-628-1880
contact_us@blueridgehealthnetwork.com
www.blueridgehealthnetwork.com
Year Founded: 1995
Number of Affiliated Hospitals: 15
Number of Primary Care Physicians: 1,395
Number of Referral/Specialty Physicians: 5,125
Total Enrollment: 50,000
State Enrollment: 50,000

Healthplan and Services Defined
PLAN TYPE: PPO
Model Type: Network
Plan Specialty: Advantage Plus
Benefits Offered: Chiropractic, Prescription

Offers Demand Management Patient Information Service: Yes

Type of Coverage
Catastrophic Illness Benefit: Maximum $1M

Geographic Areas Served
Carbon, Lebanon, Monroe, Schuylkill, Luzerne, Columbia, Northumberland, Montour

Subscriber Information
Average Annual Deductible Per Subscriber:
Employee Only (Self): $500.00
Employee & 1 Family Member: $1000.00
Employee & 2 Family Members: $1000.00
Average Subscriber Co-Payment:
Primary Care Physician: $20.00-25.00
Non-Network Physician: 30%
Prescription Drugs: $15.00-40.00
Hospital ER: $50.00
Home Health Care: Yes
Home Health Care Max. Days/Visits Covered: 90 visits
Nursing Home: Yes
Nursing Home Max. Days/Visits Covered: 90 days

Network Qualifications
Pre-Admission Certification: Yes

Peer Review Type
Utilization Review: Yes
Second Surgical Opinion: No
Case Management: Yes

Accreditation Certification
TJC Accreditation, Medicare Approved, Utilization Review, Pre-Admission Certification, State Licensure, Quality Assurance Program

Key Personnel
President/CEO . . . . Robert Jones
CFO. . . . . .Lisa A Laudeman

Average Claim Compensation
Physician's Fees Charged: 51%
Hospital's Fees Charged: 34%

Specialty Managed Care Partners
Enters into Contracts with Regional Business Coalitions: Yes

935   Bravo Health: Pennsylvania
1500 Spring Garden Street
Suite 800
Philadelphia, PA 19130
Toll-Free: 800-291-0396
www.bravohealth.com
Secondary Address: Foster Plaza - 5, 651 Holiday Drive, 4th Floor, Pittsburgh, PA 15220
Year Founded: 1996
Number of Primary Care Physicians: 30,000
Total Enrollment: 360,000

Healthplan and Services Defined
PLAN TYPE: Medicare

Type of Coverage
Medicare, Supplemental Medicare

Geographic Areas Served
Delaware, Maryland, Pennslyvania, Texas, Washington DC, New Jersey

Key Personnel
SVP, Executive Director . . . . .Jason Feuerman

936   Capital Blue Cross
2500 Elmerton Avenue
Harrisburg, PA 17177
Toll-Free: 800-962-2242

Phone: 717-541-7000
Fax: 717-541-6915
www.capbluecross.com
Secondary Address: 1221 West Hamilton Street, Allentown, PA 18101
Non-Profit Organization: Yes
Year Founded: 1938
Number of Affiliated Hospitals: 37
Number of Primary Care Physicians: 11,000
Total Enrollment: 121,000
State Enrollment: 116,465

Healthplan and Services Defined
PLAN TYPE: HMO/PPO
Benefits Offered: Home Care, Inpatient SNF, Physical Therapy, Prescription, Psychiatric, Transplant, Wellness

Type of Coverage
Commercial

Type of Payment Plans Offered
FFS

Geographic Areas Served
A 21-county area in central Pennsylvania and the Lehigh Valley

Peer Review Type
Second Surgical Opinion: Yes
Case Management: Yes

Accreditation Certification
TJC Accreditation, Medicare Approved, Utilization Review, Pre-Admission Certification, State Licensure, Quality Assurance Program

Key Personnel
Chief Executive Officer . . . . .William Lehr, Jr
Sr Exec Vice President . . . . .Ronald Drnevich
Pres, Capital BlueCross . . . . .Gary St. Hilaire
SVP, Sales & Marketing . . . . .Marc Backon
Media Relations Spec. . . . . .Joe Butera
717-541-6139
joe.butera@capbluecross.com

937   Central Susquehanna Healthcare Providers
1 Hospital Drive
Lewisburg, PA 17837
Toll-Free: 866-890-2747
Phone: 570-522-4034
Fax: 570-522-4072
rferry@evanhospital.com
www.cshpnetwork.com
Subsidiary of: Evangelical Community Hosptial
Non-Profit Organization: Yes
Year Founded: 1987
Number of Affiliated Hospitals: 8
Number of Primary Care Physicians: 274
Number of Referral/Specialty Physicians: 825
Total Enrollment: 12,700
State Enrollment: 12,700

Healthplan and Services Defined
PLAN TYPE: PPO
Model Type: Network
Benefits Offered: Behavioral Health, Home Care, Inpatient SNF, Long-Term Care, Physical Therapy, Podiatry, Prescription, Psychiatric, Transplant, Vision, Wellness

Type of Coverage
Commercial, Individual, Indemnity, Medicaid
Catastrophic Illness Benefit: Maximum $2M

Type of Payment Plans Offered
DFFS, Combination FFS & DFFS

Geographic Areas Served
Central Pennsylvania

Network Qualifications
Pre-Admission Certification: No

Key Personnel
President and CEO . . . . Michael O'Keese
Director. . . . . Kelly Geise
    570-522-4035
    kgeise@evanhospital.com
Contract Analyst . . . . Rahmaire Brooks
    570-522-4073
    rbrooks@evanhospital.com
Credentialing . . . . Lisa Featherman
    570-522-2798
    lfeatherman@evanhospital.com
Managed Care Coordinator . . . . Renee Ferry
    570-522-4034
    rferry@evanhospital.com
Media Contact . . . . Liz Hendricks
    570-522-4160
    lhendricks@evanhospital.com

Average Claim Compensation
Physician's Fees Charged: 25%
Hospital's Fees Charged: 16%

938   CIGNA HealthCare of Pennsylvania
Acquired by CIGNA

939   CIGNA: Corporate Headquarters
2 Liberty Place
1601 Chestnut Street
Philadelphia, PA 19192-1550
Toll-Free: 866-438-2446
www.cigna.com
For Profit Organization: Yes
Year Founded: 1989
Number of Affiliated Hospitals: 5,400
Number of Primary Care Physicians: 612,000
Total Enrollment: 11,000,000
State Enrollment: 11,969

Healthplan and Services Defined
  PLAN TYPE: HMO
  Other Type: POS
  Benefits Offered: Disease Management, Transplant, Wellness

Type of Coverage
Commercial

Type of Payment Plans Offered
POS

Geographic Areas Served
Nationwide

Publishes and Distributes Report Card: Yes

Key Personnel
President & CEO. . . . . David M Cordani
President, CIGNA Intl. . . . . William L Atwell
President, US Service. Matthew G Manders
Acting CFO . . . . Thomas A McCarthy
EVP, Human Resources . . . . John M Murabito
EVP, General Counsel. . . . . Carol Ann Petren
President, US Commercial . . . . Bertram Scott
EVP, Chief Information Of. . . . . Michael D Woeller
VP, Chief Accounting Offc . . . . Marty T Hoeltzel

940   CoreSource: Pennsylvania
1280 North Plum Street
Lancaster, PA 17601
Toll-Free: 800-223-3943
Phone: 717-295-9201
www.coresource.com

Subsidiary of: Trustmark
Year Founded: 1980
Total Enrollment: 1,100,000

Healthplan and Services Defined
  PLAN TYPE: Multiple
  Other Type: TPA
  Model Type: Network
  Plan Specialty: Claims Administration, TPA
  Benefits Offered: Behavioral Health, Home Care, Prescription, Transplant

Type of Coverage
Commercial

Geographic Areas Served
Nationwide

Accreditation Certification
Utilization Review, Pre-Admission Certification

941   Delta Dental of the Mid-Atlantic
One Delta Drive
Mechanicsburg, PA 17055-6999
Toll-Free: 800-471-7091
Fax: 717-766-8719
www.deltadentalins.com
Non-Profit Organization: Yes
Total Enrollment: 54,000,000

Healthplan and Services Defined
  PLAN TYPE: Dental
  Other Type: Dental PPO

Type of Coverage
Commercial

Geographic Areas Served
Statewide

Key Personnel
President/CEO. . . . . Gary D Radine
VP, Public & Govt Affairs . . . . Jeff Album
    415-972-8418
Dir/Media & Public Affair . . . . Elizabeth Risberg
    415-972-8423

942   Devon Health Services
1100 First Avenue
Suite 100
King of Prussia, PA 19406
Toll-Free: 800-431-2273
Fax: 800-221-0002
marketing@devonhealth.com
www.devonhealth.com
For Profit Organization: Yes
Year Founded: 1991
Physician Owned Organization: Yes
Number of Affiliated Hospitals: 638
Number of Primary Care Physicians: 20,000
Number of Referral/Specialty Physicians: 325,000
Total Enrollment: 3,000,000
State Enrollment: 3,000,000

Healthplan and Services Defined
  PLAN TYPE: PPO
  Model Type: Network
  Plan Specialty: Chiropractic, Dental, Lab, Vision, Radiology, Worker's Compensation, Group Health & Pharmacy Plans
  Benefits Offered: Dental, Inpatient SNF, Physical Therapy, Vision, Worker's Compensation, Group Health & Pharmacy Plans

Type of Coverage
Commercial

Type of Payment Plans Offered
DFFS, FFS, Combination FFS & DFFS

Geographic Areas Served
Pennsylvania, New Jersey, New York, Ohio, Delaware and Maryland

Subscriber Information
Average Subscriber Co-Payment:
Primary Care Physician: $10.00-20.00
Hospital ER: $25-50.00
Home Health Care: Varies
Nursing Home: Varies

Network Qualifications
Pre-Admission Certification: Yes

Publishes and Distributes Report Card: No

Key Personnel
President . . . . .Charles Falcone
800-431-2273
CEO . . . . .John A Bennett, MD
800-431-2273
Chief Legal Counsel . . . . .Galen Hawk
VP Operations. . . . . .Andrea Fisher
800-431-2273
VP, Network Development . . . . .Bill Bruce
800-431-2273
VP, Client Services . . . . .Mike Tosti
800-431-2273
Chief Financial Officer . . . . .Francis Lutz
VP, Sales. . . . . .Jeff Penn
800-431-2273
Dir, Marketing & Comm . . . . .Darren Behuniak
800-431-2273
dbehuniak@devonhealth.com

Average Claim Compensation
Physician's Fees Charged: 55%
Hospital's Fees Charged: 58%

Specialty Managed Care Partners
Medimpact
Enters into Contracts with Regional Business Coalitions: Yes

Employer References
Mid-Jersey trucking Industry & Local 701 Welfare Fund,
Pennsylvania Public School Health Care Trust, International
Brotherhood of Teamsters

943   eHealthInsurance Services Inc.

11919 Foundation Place
Gold River, CA 95670
Toll-Free: 800-977-8860
info@ehealthinsurance.com
www.e.healthinsurance.com
Year Founded: 1997

Healthplan and Services Defined
PLAN TYPE: HMO/PPO
Benefits Offered: Dental, Life, STD

Type of Coverage
Commercial, Individual, Medicare

Geographic Areas Served
All 50 states in the USA and District of Columbia

Key Personnel
Chairman & CEO . . . . .Gary L. Lauer
EVP/Business & Corp. Dev. . . . . .Bruce Telkamp
EVP/Chief Technology . . . . .Dr. Sheldon X. Wang
SVP & CFO . . . . .Stuart M. Huizinga
Pres. of eHealth Gov. Sys . . . . .Samuel C. Gibbs
SVP of Sales & Operations . . . . .Robert S. Hurley
Director Public Relations. . . . . .Nate Purpura
650-210-3115

944   EHP

PO Box 8737
Lancaster, PA 17604-8737
Toll-Free: 888-498-9648
Phone: 717-735-7760
Fax: 717-399-1693
information@ehpservices.com
www.ehpservices.com
Subsidiary of: Significa Insurance Group
Non-Profit Organization: Yes
Year Founded: 1996
Number of Affiliated Hospitals: 179
Number of Primary Care Physicians: 49,000

Healthplan and Services Defined
PLAN TYPE: PPO
Plan Specialty: Offers EHP Healthy Benefits including discounts for
members to health clubs.
Benefits Offered: Disease Management, Wellness

Geographic Areas Served
Berks, Lancaster & York counties

Subscriber Information
Average Monthly Fee Per Subscriber
(Employee + Employer Contribution):
Employee Only (Self): $3.00

Key Personnel
President/CEO . . . . .Larry W Rodabaugh
Provider Services . . . . .Kris Danz

945   EHP Signifia

PO Box 7777
Lancaster, PA 17604-7777
Toll-Free: 800-423-8877
Phone: 717-581-1245
info@significa-ins.com
www.ehpsignifica.com
Subsidiary of: Significa Insurance Group
Non-Profit Organization: Yes
Number of Affiliated Hospitals: 179
Number of Primary Care Physicians: 49,000

Healthplan and Services Defined
PLAN TYPE: PPO

Type of Coverage
Commercial

946   First Priority Health

Acquired by Blue Cross of NE Pennsylvania

947   Gateway Health Plan

US Steel Tower, 41st Floor
600 Grant Street
Pittsburgh, PA 15219-2704
Toll-Free: 877-428-3929
Phone: 412-255-4640
Fax: 412-255-4670
www.gatewayhealthplan.com
For Profit Organization: Yes
Year Founded: 1992
Number of Affiliated Hospitals: 135
Number of Primary Care Physicians: 8,000
Number of Referral/Specialty Physicians: 4,650
Total Enrollment: 244,000
State Enrollment: 244,000

Healthplan and Services Defined
PLAN TYPE: HMO
Other Type: Medicaid

Model Type: Network

Plan Specialty: Dental, Disease Management, Vision, UR, Prospective Care Managment

Benefits Offered: Chiropractic, Dental, Disease Management, Home Care, Inpatient SNF, Physical Therapy, Podiatry, Prescription, Transplant, Vision, Wellness

Type of Coverage

Medicare, Medicaid

Type of Payment Plans Offered

DFFS, Capitated, FFS

Geographic Areas Served

Allegheny, Armstrong, Beaver, Berks, Blair, Butler, Cambria, Clarion, Cumberland, Dauphin, Erie, Fayette, Greene, Indiana, Jefferson, Lawrence, Lehigh, Mercer, Montour, Northumberland, Schulkill, Somerset, Washington and Westmoreland counties

Peer Review Type

Utilization Review: Yes

Second Surgical Opinion: Yes

Case Management: Yes

Accreditation Certification

NCQA

Utilization Review, State Licensure, Quality Assurance Program

Key Personnel

President/CEO . . . . .Michael Blackwood

Physician Advisor . . . . .Ronald Mohan, MD

Medical Director . . . . .Maria E Moutinho, MD

Pediatric Physician Adv . . . . .Barbara Negrini, MD

Chief Medical Officer .Michael Madden, MD

Medical Director . . . . .Caesar A DeLeo, MD

Physician Advisor . . . . .Shawn C Files, MD

Medical Director . . . . .Edwin J Kairis, MD

Medical Director . . . . .Renee Miskimmin, MD

Specialty Managed Care Partners

Clarity Vision, Dental Benefit Providers, National Imaging Association, Merck-Medco

948 Geisinger Health Plan

100 North Academy Avenue

Danville, PA 17822-3040

Toll-Free: 800-498-9731

Phone: 570-271-8771

Fax: 570-271-7218

media@thehealthplan.com

www.thehealthplan.com

Mailing Address: PO Box 8200, Danville, PA 17821-8200

Non-Profit Organization: Yes

Year Founded: 1985

Number of Affiliated Hospitals: 89

Number of Primary Care Physicians: 3,696

Number of Referral/Specialty Physicians: 24,397

Total Enrollment: 250,000

Healthplan and Services Defined

PLAN TYPE: HMO/PPO

Benefits Offered: Chiropractic, Dental, Disease Management, Home Care, Inpatient SNF, Physical Therapy, Podiatry, Prescription, Psychiatric, Vision, Wellness

Type of Coverage

Commercial, Individual, Medicare, Supplemental Medicare, CHIP

Geographic Areas Served

Adams, Bedford, Berks, Blair, Bradford, Cambria, Cameron, Carbon, Centre, Clearfield, Clinton, Columbia, Cumberland, Dauphin, Elk, Fulton, Huntingdon, Jefferson, Juanita, Lackawanna, Lancaster, Lebanon, Lehigh, Luzerne, Lycoming, Miffin, Monroe, Montour, Northumberland, Northampton, Perry, Pike, Potter, Schuyikill, Somerset, Snyder, Sullivan, Susquehana, Tioga, Union, Wayne, York counties

Subscriber Information

Average Monthly Fee Per Subscriber (Employee + Employer Contribution):

Employee Only (Self): Varies

Medicare: Varies

Average Annual Deductible Per Subscriber:

Employee Only (Self): Varies

Medicare: Varies

Average Subscriber Co-Payment:

Primary Care Physician: Varies

Non-Network Physician: Varies

Prescription Drugs: Varies

Hospital ER: Varies

Home Health Care: Varies

Home Health Care Max. Days/Visits Covered: Varies

Nursing Home: Varies

Nursing Home Max. Days/Visits Covered: Varies

Accreditation Certification

NCQA

Key Personnel

CEO . . . . .Jean Haynes, RN

COO . . . . .Richard Kwei

CFO . . . . .George Schneider, CPA

VP, Chief Medical Offc . . . . .Duane E Davis, MD

Assoc Chief Legal Officer . . . . .David J Weader, JD

Chief Sales Officer . . . . .Joseph Haddock, MHA

Dir, Group & Brand Mktg . . . . .Lisa D Hartman

570-271-8135

949 Great-West Healthcare Pennsylvania

Acquired by CIGNA

950 Health Partners Medicare Plan

901 Market Street

Suite 500

Philadelphia, PA 19107

Toll-Free: 800-553-0784

Phone: 215-426-4372

sroberts@healthpart.com

www.healthpart.com

Non-Profit Organization: Yes

Physician Owned Organization: Yes

Total Enrollment: 154,000

State Enrollment: 154,000

Healthplan and Services Defined

PLAN TYPE: Medicare

Benefits Offered: Chiropractic, Dental, Disease Management, Home Care, Inpatient SNF, Physical Therapy, Podiatry, Prescription, Psychiatric, Vision, Wellness

Type of Coverage

Medicare, Medicaid

Geographic Areas Served

Available within Pennsylvania only

Subscriber Information

Average Monthly Fee Per Subscriber (Employee + Employer Contribution):

Employee Only (Self): Varies

Medicare: Varies

Average Annual Deductible Per Subscriber:

Employee Only (Self): Varies

Medicare: Varies

Average Subscriber Co-Payment:

Primary Care Physician: Varies

Non-Network Physician: Varies

Prescription Drugs: Varies

Hospital ER: Varies

Home Health Care: Varies

Home Health Care Max. Days/Visits Covered: Varies

Nursing Home: Varies
Nursing Home Max. Days/Visits Covered: Varies

Key Personnel
President/CEO . . . . William George
SVP/COO . . . . Elaine Markezin
SVP Business Development . . . . Judy B Harrington
SVP/Compliance/Resources . . . . Vicki Sessoms
SVP/Pharmacy Business . . . . Don Daddario
SVP/Operations . . . . Debra A Kircher
SVP/Chief Medical Officer . . . . Mary K Stom, MD
SVP, CFO. . . . . Martin J Brill
Senior Communications Spc . . . . Felicia R Phillips
   215-991-4580
   fphillips@healthpart.com

951   HealthAmerica
5473 Village Common Drive
Erie, PA 16501
Toll-Free: 800-255-4281
Phone: 814-878-1700
Fax: 814-878-1820
www.healthamerica.cvty.com
Secondary Address: 3721 TecPort Drive, PO Box 67103, Harrisburg,
   PA 17106-6445
Subsidiary of: A Coventry Health Care Plan
For Profit Organization: Yes
Year Founded: 1994
Number of Affiliated Hospitals: 36
Number of Primary Care Physicians: 370
Number of Referral/Specialty Physicians: 605
Total Enrollment: 500,000

Healthplan and Services Defined
  PLAN TYPE: Multiple
  Other Type: HMO, POS, Medicare
  Model Type: IPA, Network
  Plan Specialty: ASO, Behavioral Health, Disease Management
  Benefits Offered: Chiropractic, Dental, Disease Management, Home
    Care, Inpatient SNF, Physical Therapy, Podiatry, Prescription,
    Psychiatric, Transplant, Vision, Wellness

Type of Coverage
  Commercial, Indemnity
  Catastrophic Illness Benefit: Maximum $1M

Type of Payment Plans Offered
  POS, DFFS, Capitated, Combination FFS & DFFS

Geographic Areas Served
  Pennsylvania and Ohio

Subscriber Information
  Average Monthly Fee Per Subscriber
    (Employee + Employer Contribution):
      Employee Only (Self): $170.42
      Employee & 1 Family Member: $525.00
      Employee & 2 Family Members: $525.00
  Average Subscriber Co-Payment:
      Primary Care Physician: $10.00
      Prescription Drugs: $10.00/25.00
      Hospital ER: $35.00
      Nursing Home: $0

Network Qualifications
  Minimum Years of Practice: 3
  Pre-Admission Certification: Yes

Peer Review Type
  Utilization Review: Yes
  Second Surgical Opinion: Yes
  Case Management: Yes

Accreditation Certification
  NCQA, 3yr excellent

Key Personnel
President. . . . . Thomas P McDonough
Executive VP . . . . Harvey C DeMovick, Jr
CEO. . . . . Dale B Wolf
Executive VP/CFO. . . . . Shawn M Guertin
Marketing . . . . Alfred Dore, Jr
Medical Affairs . . . . John Bauers, MD
Director Health Plan Operations . . . . Patricia Carns
Information Systems. . . . . Patricia Carns
Provider Services . . . . Patricia Carns

Specialty Managed Care Partners
  Enters into Contracts with Regional Business Coalitions: Yes

952   HealthAmerica Pennsylvania
3721 TecPort Drive
PO Box 67103
Harrisburg, PA 17106-7103
Toll-Free: 800-788-7895
Phone: 717-540-4260
http://healthamerica.coventryhealthcare.com
Secondary Address: 11 Stanwix Street, Suite 2300, Pittsburgh, PA
   15222
Subsidiary of: Coventry Health Care
For Profit Organization: Yes
Year Founded: 1974
Owned by an Integrated Delivery Network (IDN): Yes
Number of Affiliated Hospitals: 127
Number of Primary Care Physicians: 3,915
Number of Referral/Specialty Physicians: 8,358
Total Enrollment: 500,000
State Enrollment: 395,000

Healthplan and Services Defined
  PLAN TYPE: Multiple
  Model Type: Network
  Plan Specialty: ASO, Behavioral Health, Chiropractic, Dental,
    Disease Management, Lab, Vision, Radiology
  Benefits Offered: Behavioral Health, Chiropractic, Complementary
    Medicine, Dental, Disease Management, Home Care, Inpatient
    SNF, Physical Therapy, Podiatry, Prescription, Psychiatric,
    Transplant, Vision, Wellness
  Offers Demand Management Patient Information Service: Yes

Type of Coverage
  Commercial, Medicare, Medicaid

Type of Payment Plans Offered
  Capitated, FFS

Geographic Areas Served
  Central Pennsylvania-Clinton, Lycomuing, Centre, Blair, Huntington,
  Franklin, Adams, Cumberland, Perry, Juniata, Mifflin, Union, Snyder,
  Dauphin, York, Northumberland, Erie, Crawford, Warren, Venangom,
  Forest; Ohio-Thumbull, Mahoning, Columbiana, Jefferson, Harrison,
  Belmont

Subscriber Information
  Average Monthly Fee Per Subscriber
    (Employee + Employer Contribution):
      Employee Only (Self): Proprietary
      Employee & 1 Family Member: Proprietary
      Employee & 2 Family Members: Proprietary
      Medicare: Proprietary
  Average Annual Deductible Per Subscriber:
      Employee Only (Self): Proprietary
      Employee & 1 Family Member: Proprietary
      Employee & 2 Family Members: Proprietary
      Medicare: Proprietary
  Average Subscriber Co-Payment:
      Primary Care Physician: $10.00
      Non-Network Physician: $20.00
      Prescription Drugs: $10.00/20.00
      Hospital ER: Varies

Home Health Care Max. Days/Visits Covered: 120
Nursing Home Max. Days/Visits Covered: 100

Network Qualifications
Pre-Admission Certification: Yes

Peer Review Type
Utilization Review: Yes
Case Management: Yes

Accreditation Certification
TJC, NCQA
Medicare Approved, Utilization Review, Pre-Admission
Certification, State Licensure, Quality Assurance Program

Key Personnel
CEO . . . . .Timothy E Nolan
Executive VP . . . . .Mary Lou Osborne
CFO . . . . .Stephen Dengler
VP/Sales . . . . .Darin Hayes
VP/Health Services . . . . .Angel Oddo
VP/Quality and Cost Mgmt . . . . .Joshua Bennett, MD
Regional Director NWPA . . . . .Eric Hays
VP/Medical Affairs . . . . .Eugene Sun, MD
VP/Medicare Operations . . . . .Pauline Degenfelder
VP Business Development .Jayne Olshanski

Specialty Managed Care Partners
ValueOptions, CareMark, Dominion Dental (WPA) Delta Dental
(EPA), Quest Diagnostics (EPA) LabCorp (WPA), National Vision
Administrators (NVA)

Employer References
Federal Government, Penn State University, US Airways, City of
Pittsburgh, General Motors

---

953 Highmark Blue Cross & Blue Shield

501 Penn Avenue Place
Pittsburgh, PA 15222-3099
Toll-Free: 800-294-9568
Phone: 412-544-7000
Fax: 412-544-8368
cynthia.dellecker@highmark.com
www.highmarkbcbs.com
Mailing Address: PO Box 226, Pittsburgh, PA 15222
For Profit Organization: Yes
Year Founded: 1996
Owned by an Integrated Delivery Network (IDN): Yes
Number of Affiliated Hospitals: 50
Number of Primary Care Physicians: 1,200
Number of Referral/Specialty Physicians: 4,552
Total Enrollment: 4,700,000
State Enrollment: 4,700,000

Healthplan and Services Defined
PLAN TYPE: HMO/PPO
Model Type: IPA
Benefits Offered: Dental, Disease Management, Prescription, Vision,
Wellness
Offers Demand Management Patient Information Service: Yes

Type of Coverage
Commercial, Individual
Catastrophic Illness Benefit: Unlimited

Type of Payment Plans Offered
POS, DFFS, Capitated, FFS, Combination FFS & DFFS

Geographic Areas Served
Allegheny, Armstrong, Beaver, Bedford, Blair, Butler, Cambria,
Clarion, Clearfield, Crawford, Erie, Fayette, Forest, Greene,
Huntingdon, Indiana, Jefferson, Lawrence, McKean, Mercer,
Somerset, Venango, Washington, Cameron, Elk, Potter, Warren and
Westmoreland counties

Subscriber Information
Average Monthly Fee Per Subscriber
(Employee + Employer Contribution):

Employee Only (Self): $205.00
Employee & 1 Family Member: $620.00
Employee & 2 Family Members: $470.00
Medicare: $39.50
Average Annual Deductible Per Subscriber:
Employee Only (Self): $0
Employee & 1 Family Member: $0
Employee & 2 Family Members: $0
Medicare: $0
Average Subscriber Co-Payment:
Primary Care Physician: $5.00
Non-Network Physician: $0
Prescription Drugs: $2.00/8.00
Hospital ER: $25.00
Home Health Care: $0
Home Health Care Max. Days/Visits Covered: Varies
Nursing Home: $0
Nursing Home Max. Days/Visits Covered: 100 days

Network Qualifications
Pre-Admission Certification: Yes

Peer Review Type
Utilization Review: Yes
Second Surgical Opinion: No
Case Management: Yes

Publishes and Distributes Report Card: No

Accreditation Certification
URAC, NCQA
Medicare Approved, Pre-Admission Certification, State Licensure

Key Personnel
Chairman of the Board .J Robert Baum, PhD
President/CEO . . . . .Kenneth R Melani, MD
EVP, Chief Financial Offc . . . . .Nanette P DeTurk
EVP, Chief Legal Officer . . . . .Maureen Hogel
EVP, Vision Services . . . . .David L Holmberg
EVP, Government Services. . . . . .David M O'Brien
SVP, Chief Audit Exec. . . . . .Elizabeth A Farbacher
EVP, Comm & Strategy . . . . .Thomas Kerr
EVP, Subsidiary Business . . . . .Daniel J Lebish
EVP, Health Services . . . . .Deborah L Rice
Client Svcs, Enrollment . . . . .Nadina Bowman
Provider Relations . . . . .Bill Jarrett
Public Relations . . . . .Aaron Billger
412-544-7826
aaron.billger@highmark.com

Average Claim Compensation
Physician's Fees Charged: 50%
Hospital's Fees Charged: 61%

Specialty Managed Care Partners
Enters into Contracts with Regional Business Coalitions: No

---

954 Highmark Blue Shield

1800 Center Street
Camp Hill, PA 17011
Toll-Free: 866-856-6166
Phone: 412-544-7000
webmaster@highmark.com
www.highmarkblueshield.com
Mailing Address: PO Box 890173, Camp Hill, PA 17089-0173
Non-Profit Organization: Yes
Year Founded: 1932
Total Enrollment: 600,000
State Enrollment: 375,300

Healthplan and Services Defined
PLAN TYPE: PPO
Model Type: Network
Benefits Offered: Disease Management, Prescription, Wellness
Offers Demand Management Patient Information Service: Yes

Type of Payment Plans Offered
POS, DFFS, Combination FFS & DFFS

Geographic Areas Served
Statewide

Network Qualifications
Pre-Admission Certification: Yes

Peer Review Type
Second Surgical Opinion: Yes

Publishes and Distributes Report Card: Yes

Accreditation Certification
URAC, NCQA

Key Personnel
President and CEO .Kenneth R Melani, MD
Chairperson . . . . .J Robert Baum
EVP, Chief Legal Officer. . . . . .Maureen Hogel
EVP, Chief Financial Offc . . . . .Nanette P DeTurk
EVP, Vision Services .David L Holmberg
EVP/Government Services. . . . . .David M O'Brien
SVP/Chief Auditor . . . . .Elizabeth A Farbacher
EVP/Chief Strategy Offc . . . . .Thomas Kerr
EVP/Subsidiary Business. . . . . .Daniel J Lebish
EVP/Health Services . . . . .Deborah L Rice
Public Relations . . . . .Aaron Billger
    412-544-7826
    aaron.billger@highmark.com
Corp Media Relations . . . . .Michael Weinstein
    412-544-7903
    michael.weinstein@highmark.com

Specialty Managed Care Partners
Enters into Contracts with Regional Business Coalitions: Yes

955 Humana Health Insurance of Pennsylvania

5000 Ritter Road
Suite 101
Mechanicsburg, PA 17055
Toll-Free: 866-355-5861
Phone: 717-766-6040
Fax: 717-795-1951
www.humana.com
Secondary Address: 1000 Cliff Mine Road, Suite 420, Pittsburgh, PA
15108
For Profit Organization: Yes

Healthplan and Services Defined
PLAN TYPE: HMO/PPO

Type of Coverage
Commercial, Individual

Accreditation Certification
URAC, NCQA, CORE

956 Independence Blue Cross

1901 Market Street
Philadelphia, PA 19103
Toll-Free: 800-555-1514
Phone: 215-636-9559
www.ibx.com
Non-Profit Organization: Yes
Year Founded: 1938
Number of Affiliated Hospitals: 159
Number of Primary Care Physicians: 38,053
Total Enrollment: 3,300,000
State Enrollment: 3,300,000

Healthplan and Services Defined
PLAN TYPE: HMO/PPO
Other Type: POS
Benefits Offered: Dental, Disease Management, Prescription, Vision,
Wellness, Life

Type of Coverage
Commercial, Individual, Medicare, Supplemental Medicare

Type of Payment Plans Offered
POS, FFS

Geographic Areas Served
Philadelphia and southeastern Pennsylvania

Key Personnel
Chairman of the Board .M Walter D'Alessio
President & CEO. . . . . .Joseph A Frick
Executive Vice President. . . . . .Christopher Butler
EVP, Health Markets . . . . .Daniel J Hilferty
SVP, Chief Admin Officer. . . . . .Yvette D Bright
SVP, Corp & Public Affair. . . . . .Christopher Cashman
SVP, Provider Networks . . . . .Douglas L Chaet
SVP, Underwriting. . . . . .Kathryn A Galareau, FSA
SVP, Marketing Services. . . . . .John R Janney, Jr
SVP, Chief Financial Offc . . . . .Alan Krigstein
EVP Health Services . . . . .I Steven Udvarhelyi, MD
SVP, Internal Audit . . . . .Karen Lessin
SVP, Chief Info Officer . . . . .Carolyn W Luther
Senior Vice President . . . . .Richard J Neeson
SVP, Operations . . . . .Stephen R Roker
SPV, Chief Marketing .Linda M Taylor
SVP, General Counsel . . . . .Paul A Tufano, Esq

Specialty Managed Care Partners
Caremark Rx

957 InterGroup Services Corporation

Valleybrooke III, 101 Lindenwood Drive
Suite 150
Malvern, PA 19355
Toll-Free: 800-537-9389
Phone: 610-640-0646
Fax: 610-647-5383
www.igs-ppo.com
Secondary Address: 401 Shady Avenue, Suite B108, Pittsburgh, PA
15206
For Profit Organization: Yes
Year Founded: 1985
Number of Affiliated Hospitals: 320
Number of Primary Care Physicians: 26,000
Number of Referral/Specialty Physicians: 62,000
Total Enrollment: 700,000

Healthplan and Services Defined
PLAN TYPE: PPO
Model Type: Network
Plan Specialty: ASO, Behavioral Health, Chiropractic, EPO, Lab,
MSO, PBM, Vision, Radiology, Worker's Compensation
Benefits Offered: Behavioral Health, Disease Management,
Prescription, Wellness, Worker's Compensation

Type of Coverage
Commercial

Geographic Areas Served
Delaware, New Jersey, Pennsylvania, West Virginia

Network Qualifications
Pre-Admission Certification: Yes

Key Personnel
President . . . . .John George
    800-537-9389
CFO . . . . .Caren Ryan
    800-537-9389
CEO/COO . . . . .G Martin Dudley
    800-537-9389
    mdudley@igs-ppo.com
Manager Claims Repricing. . . . . .Jennifer McNatt
    800-537-9389
    jmcnatt@igs-ppo.com

Network Contracting.........................Gregory Dudley
  800-537-9389
  gdudley@igs-ppo.com
Marketing ....Joe McLaughlin
  800-537-9389
  jmclaughlin@igs-ppo.com
Member Services.........................Joe McLaughlin
  800-537-9389
  jmclaughlin@igs-ppo.com
Dir Information Systems.....................Gregory Dudley
  800-537-9389
  gdudley@igs-ppo.com
VP Provider Relations.......................Gregory Dudley
  800-537-9389
  gdudley@igs-ppo.com

Specialty Managed Care Partners
Chiropractic Network

958   Keystone Health Plan Central
Acquired by Capital Blue Cross

959   Keystone Health Plan East
Acquired by Independence Blue Cross

960   Mid Atlantic Medical Services: Pennsylvania
2 West Rolling Crossroads
Suite 11
Baltimore, MD 21228
Toll-Free: 800-782-1966
Phone: 410-869-7400
Fax: 410-869-7583
masales99@uhc.com
www.mamsiunitedhealthcare.com
Subsidiary of: United Healthcare/United Health Group
Year Founded: 1986
Number of Affiliated Hospitals: 342
Number of Primary Care Physicians: 3,276
Total Enrollment: 180,000

Healthplan and Services Defined
  PLAN TYPE: HMO/PPO
  Model Type: IPA, Network
  Benefits Offered: Disease Management, Prescription, Wellness

Type of Payment Plans Offered
  Combination FFS & DFFS

Geographic Areas Served
  Delaware, Maryland, North Carolina, Pennsylvania, Virginia, Washington DC, West Virginia

Network Qualifications
  Pre-Admission Certification: Yes

Peer Review Type
  Utilization Review: Yes
  Second Surgical Opinion: Yes
  Case Management: Yes

Publishes and Distributes Report Card: No

Accreditation Certification
  TJC, NCQA

Specialty Managed Care Partners
  Enters into Contracts with Regional Business Coalitions: Yes

961   Penn Highlands Health Plan
820 Parish Street
Pittsburgh, PA 15220
Toll-Free: 888-722-0805
Phone: 814-536-7525
Fax: 814-534-1544

mgbarret@conemaugh.org
www.pennhighlands.com
Subsidiary of: Conemaugh Health Plan, Highlands Preferred Physicians
Non-Profit Organization: Yes
Year Founded: 1985
Number of Affiliated Hospitals: 7
Number of Primary Care Physicians: 425
Number of Referral/Specialty Physicians: 4,100
Total Enrollment: 18,500
State Enrollment: 18,500

Healthplan and Services Defined
  PLAN TYPE: PPO
  Model Type: IPA
  Plan Specialty: ASO, Behavioral Health, Disease Management, EPO, Lab, MSO, Radiology, Worker's Compensation, UR
  Benefits Offered: Behavioral Health, Chiropractic, Disease Management, Home Care, Inpatient SNF, Long-Term Care, Physical Therapy, Podiatry, Psychiatric, Transplant, Wellness, Worker's Compensation
  Offers Demand Management Patient Information Service: Yes

Type of Coverage
  Commercial

Type of Payment Plans Offered
  POS, DFFS, Combination FFS & DFFS

Geographic Areas Served
  Bedford, Blair, Cambria and Somerset counties

Subscriber Information
  Average Annual Deductible Per Subscriber:
    Employee & 2 Family Members: $200.00
  Average Subscriber Co-Payment:
    Primary Care Physician: $10.00
    Non-Network Physician: 50%
    Hospital ER: $50.00

Network Qualifications
  Pre-Admission Certification: Yes

Peer Review Type
  Utilization Review: Yes
  Second Surgical Opinion: No
  Case Management: Yes

Publishes and Distributes Report Card: Yes

Accreditation Certification
  AAAHC, URAC
  TJC Accreditation, Medicare Approved, Pre-Admission Certification, State Licensure

Key Personnel
  President ....Renee A Staib
  CFO ....Ed De Pasquale
  Medical Director ....Richard S Wozniak, MD
  Provider Services ....Robert Schalles

Average Claim Compensation
  Physician's Fees Charged: 1%
  Hospital's Fees Charged: 1%

Specialty Managed Care Partners
  Enters into Contracts with Regional Business Coalitions: No

962   Preferred Care
1300 Virginia Drive
Suite 315
Fort Washington, PA 19034
Toll-Free: 800-222-3085
Phone: 215-639-6208
Fax: 215-639-2674
info@preferredcareinc.net
www.preferredcareinc.net
For Profit Organization: Yes
Year Founded: 1985
Number of Affiliated Hospitals: 51

Number of Primary Care Physicians: 4,030
Number of Referral/Specialty Physicians: 10,960
Total Enrollment: 186,425
State Enrollment: 146,000

Healthplan and Services Defined
PLAN TYPE: PPO
Other Type: TPA
Model Type: Group, Network
Plan Specialty: Chiropractic, PBM
Benefits Offered: Behavioral Health, Chiropractic, Dental, Physical
    Therapy, Podiatry, Vision, Life

Type of Payment Plans Offered
DFFS, Capitated, FFS

Geographic Areas Served
Delaware, New Jersey, New York, Pennsylvania: (Bucks, Chester,
    Delaware, Lehigh, Montgomery, Philadelphia & Northhampton
    counties)

Network Qualifications
Pre-Admission Certification: Yes

Peer Review Type
Utilization Review: Yes
Second Surgical Opinion: Yes
Case Management: Yes

Publishes and Distributes Report Card: No

Accreditation Certification
TJC Accreditation, Medicare Approved, Utilization Review,
    Pre-Admission Certification, State Licensure, Quality Assurance
    Program

Key Personnel
President . . . . .Richard Wehr
PPO President . . . . .Richard Matthew
Manager Claims . . . . .Maureen Rensom
Contracting. . . . . .Carole Chapman
Credentialing . . . . .Carol Chapman
Marketing . . . . .Patricia McGovern
Medical Affairs. . . . . .H Newton Spencer
QA/UR. . . . . .Carol Chapman

Specialty Managed Care Partners
Mental Health Consultants, Foot Care Network
Enters into Contracts with Regional Business Coalitions: No

---

963   Preferred Health Care

Sterling Center 20-D
East Roseville Road
Lancaster, PA 17604
Phone: 717-560-9290
Fax: 717-560-2312
info@phcunity.com
www.phcunity.com
Non-Profit Organization: Yes
Year Founded: 1984
Number of Affiliated Hospitals: 19
Number of Primary Care Physicians: 1,900
Total Enrollment: 80,316

Healthplan and Services Defined
PLAN TYPE: PPO
Model Type: Network
Offers Demand Management Patient Information Service: Yes

Type of Payment Plans Offered
FFS

Geographic Areas Served
Lancaster, Chester, York, Tioga, Bradford and Potter counties

Subscriber Information
Average Subscriber Co-Payment:
    Primary Care Physician: 20%
    Non-Network Physician: 30%-40%

Home Health Care: 20%

Peer Review Type
Utilization Review: Yes
Case Management: Yes

Accreditation Certification
TJC Accreditation, Medicare Approved, Utilization Review,
    Pre-Admission Certification, State Licensure, Quality Assurance
    Program

Key Personnel
President/CEO . . . . .Eric E Buck
    717-560-9290
    ebuck@phcunity.com
VP Operations . . . . .Sherry Wolgemuth
    swolgemuth@phcunity.com
Medical Director . . . . .David Bowers, MD
    dbowers@phcunity.com
Network Affairs Rep . . . . .Roger Milner
    rmilner@phcuinity.com
Media Contact . . . . .Roger Milner
    717-560-9290
    rmilner@phcunity.com

---

964   Preferred Healthcare System

PO Box 1015
Duncansville, PA 16635
Toll-Free: 800-238-9900
Phone: 814-317-5063
Fax: 814-317-5139
mfrucella.preferred@altanticbbn.net
www.phsppo.com
For Profit Organization: Yes
Year Founded: 1985
Physician Owned Organization: Yes
Number of Affiliated Hospitals: 14
Number of Primary Care Physicians: 150
Number of Referral/Specialty Physicians: 448
Total Enrollment: 20,000

Healthplan and Services Defined
PLAN TYPE: PPO
Model Type: Network
Plan Specialty: ASO, Behavioral Health, Chiropractic, Dental,
    Disease Management, EPO, PBM, Vision, Worker's Compensation,
    Health
Benefits Offered: Behavioral Health, Chiropractic, Complementary
    Medicine, Dental, Disease Management, Home Care, Inpatient
    SNF, Long-Term Care, Physical Therapy, Podiatry, Prescription,
    Psychiatric, Transplant, Vision, Wellness, AD&D, Life, STD,
    Durable Medical Equipment

Type of Coverage
Commercial, Individual, Indemnity
Catastrophic Illness Benefit: Maximum $1M

Type of Payment Plans Offered
Combination FFS & DFFS

Geographic Areas Served
Clearfield, Centre, Cambria, Blair, Huntingdon, Mifflin, Bedford,
    Fulton, Sommerset and Juniata counties

Subscriber Information
Average Monthly Fee Per Subscriber
    (Employee + Employer Contribution):
        Employee Only (Self): Varies
        Employee & 1 Family Member: Varies
        Employee & 2 Family Members: Varies
        Medicare: Varies
Average Annual Deductible Per Subscriber:
        Employee Only (Self): Varies
        Employee & 1 Family Member: Varies
        Employee & 2 Family Members: Varies
        Medicare: Varies

Average Subscriber Co-Payment:
Prescription Drugs: Varies
Hospital ER: Varies
Home Health Care: Varies
Home Health Care Max. Days/Visits Covered: Varies
Nursing Home: Varies
Nursing Home Max. Days/Visits Covered: Varies

Network Qualifications
Pre-Admission Certification: Yes

Peer Review Type
Utilization Review: Yes
Second Surgical Opinion: Yes

Publishes and Distributes Report Card: No

Accreditation Certification
TJC Accreditation, Utilization Review, Pre-Admission Certification, State Licensure, Quality Assurance Program

Key Personnel
President . . . . .Maureen Frucella
Chief Executive Officer .Brian Brumbaugh
Utilization Review . . . . .Jessie E Bradfield

Average Claim Compensation
Physician's Fees Charged: 70%
Hospital's Fees Charged: 70%

Specialty Managed Care Partners
Enters into Contracts with Regional Business Coalitions: Yes

965 Prime Source Health Network

409 South 2nd Street
Suite 3F
Harrisburg, PA 17104-1612
Toll-Free: 800-842-1768
Phone: 717-851-6800
Fax: 717-851-6775
www.primesourcehealthnetwork.com
Subsidiary of: South Central Preferred Health Network
Non-Profit Organization: Yes
Year Founded: 1992
Number of Affiliated Hospitals: 16
Number of Primary Care Physicians: 6,150
Number of Referral/Specialty Physicians: 1,275
Total Enrollment: 33,000
State Enrollment: 33,000

Healthplan and Services Defined
PLAN TYPE: PPO
Model Type: PHO
Plan Specialty: Behavioral Health, Chiropractic, Radiology
Benefits Offered: Behavioral Health, Chiropractic, Home Care, Inpatient SNF, Long-Term Care, Physical Therapy, Podiatry, Psychiatric, Transplant

Type of Coverage
Catastrophic Illness Benefit: None

Type of Payment Plans Offered
Capitated

Geographic Areas Served
Cumberland, Dauphin, Lebanon, Perry and Northern York counties

Subscriber Information
Average Monthly Fee Per Subscriber
(Employee + Employer Contribution):
Employee Only (Self): $6.75 per employee

Network Qualifications
Pre-Admission Certification: No

Peer Review Type
Utilization Review: Yes

Key Personnel
Executive Director . . . . .Robin Scherer
Director Claims . . . . .Shawntel Hoover

Average Claim Compensation
Physician's Fees Charged: 64%
Hospital's Fees Charged: 70%

966 SelectCare Access Corporation

Manor Oak Township, Suite 605
1910 Cochran Road
Pittsburgh, PA 15220
Toll-Free: 800-922-4966
Phone: 412-922-2803
Fax: 412-922-3071
www.mcoa.com
Secondary Address: 250 East Broad Street, Suite 600, Columbus, OH 43215
Subsidiary of: Managed Care of America, Inc.
For Profit Organization: Yes
Year Founded: 1991
Number of Affiliated Hospitals: 55
Number of Primary Care Physicians: 1,375
Number of Referral/Specialty Physicians: 3,609
Total Enrollment: 15,700

Healthplan and Services Defined
PLAN TYPE: PPO
Model Type: Network
Benefits Offered: Prescription

Type of Payment Plans Offered
POS, DFFS, FFS, Combination FFS & DFFS

Geographic Areas Served
Statewide

Network Qualifications
Pre-Admission Certification: No

Peer Review Type
Utilization Review: Yes
Second Surgical Opinion: No
Case Management: Yes

Accreditation Certification
TJC Accreditation, Utilization Review, State Licensure

Key Personnel
President/CFO . . . . .Phyllis Shehab
412-922-0780
COO . . . . .Richard Adams
412-922-0780
rladams@mcoa.com
Legal Counsel . . . . .Charles E Davidson
412-922-0780
cedavidson@mcoa.com
Credentialing . . . . .Jane Kwiecinski
412-922-0780
ljkwiecinski@mcoa.com
VP Marketing . . . . .Dennis Casey
412-922-0780
Dir. Provider Services . . . . .Tracey M Shank
412-922-0780
tmshank@mcoa.com

967 South Central Preferred

1803 Mount Rose Avenue
B-5
York, PA 17403
Toll-Free: 800-842-1768
Phone: 717-851-6800
Fax: 717-851-6775
www.scphealth.com
Subsidiary of: WellSpan
Non-Profit Organization: Yes
Year Founded: 1992
Number of Affiliated Hospitals: 16

Number of Primary Care Physicians: 6,150
Total Enrollment: 56,000
State Enrollment: 56,000

Healthplan and Services Defined
PLAN TYPE: PPO
Benefits Offered: Wellness, Self-funded Administration & PPO
Network, EAP

Type of Coverage
Commercial, Individual

Geographic Areas Served
South Central Pennsylvania

Peer Review Type
Utilization Review: Yes
Case Management: Yes

Key Personnel
COO . . . . .Jim Cochran
Finance . . . . .Bill Smith
CMO . . . . .Neal Friedman
Provider Relations. . . . . .Jane Grove
Marketing . . . . .Andy Seebold
aseebold@wellspan.org
Claims. . . . . .Deb Kehres
Customer Service. . . . . .Rebecca Timmermans

Specialty Managed Care Partners
Express Scripts

---

968 Susquehanna EHP Significa

PO Box 7777
Lancaster, PA 17604-7777
Toll-Free: 800-432-8877
Phone: 717-581-1245
www.sh-ehpsig.com
Subsidiary of: Significa Insurance Group
Non-Profit Organization: Yes
Number of Affiliated Hospitals: 179
Number of Primary Care Physicians: 49,000

Healthplan and Services Defined
PLAN TYPE: PPO

Type of Coverage
Commercial

Geographic Areas Served
Bradford, Centre, Clinton, Columbia, Lycoming, Montour,
Northumberland, Snyder, Tioga and Union counties in Pennsylvania

---

969 Susquehanna Health Care

109 North Mulberry Street
Berwick, PA 18603-4706
Phone: 570-759-1702
Fax: 570-759-2559
For Profit Organization: Yes
Year Founded: 1985
Physician Owned Organization: Yes
Number of Affiliated Hospitals: 33
Number of Primary Care Physicians: 1,090
Total Enrollment: 45,000
State Enrollment: 45,000

Healthplan and Services Defined
PLAN TYPE: PPO
Model Type: Network
Benefits Offered: Prescription

Type of Coverage
Catastrophic Illness Benefit: Maximum $2M

Geographic Areas Served
Central & Northeastern Pennsylvania, 17 counties

Subscriber Information
Average Monthly Fee Per Subscriber
(Employee + Employer Contribution):
Employee Only (Self): $140
Employee & 1 Family Member: $275
Employee & 2 Family Members: $410
Average Annual Deductible Per Subscriber:
Employee Only (Self): $500
Average Subscriber Co-Payment:
Primary Care Physician: $30.00
Non-Network Physician: $52.00
Hospital ER: $75.00
Home Health Care: 15%
Home Health Care Max. Days/Visits Covered: 100 days
Nursing Home Max. Days/Visits Covered: 30/confinement

Network Qualifications
Pre-Admission Certification: Yes

Peer Review Type
Utilization Review: Yes
Second Surgical Opinion: Yes

Publishes and Distributes Report Card: No

Accreditation Certification
Medicare Approved, Utilization Review, Pre-Admission Certification,
State Licensure, Quality Assurance Program

Key Personnel
President/CEO . . . . .Steven P. Johnson, Jr
Communications Director . . . . .Kendall Marcocci

Specialty Managed Care Partners
Enters into Contracts with Regional Business Coalitions: Yes

---

970 Unison Health Plan of Pennsylvania

1001 Brinton Road
Unison Plaza
Pittsburgh, PA 15221
Toll-Free: 800-600-9007
Phone: 412-858-4000
www.unisonhealthplan.com
Subsidiary of: AmeriChoice, A UnitedHealth Group Company
Total Enrollment: 160,000

Healthplan and Services Defined
PLAN TYPE: Multiple
Benefits Offered: Chiropractic, Dental, Disease Management, Home
Care, Inpatient SNF, Physical Therapy, Podiatry, Prescription,
Psychiatric, Vision, Wellness

Type of Coverage
Individual, Medicare

Geographic Areas Served
Available within Pennsylvania, South Carolina, Ohio, and Tennesse

Subscriber Information
Average Monthly Fee Per Subscriber
(Employee + Employer Contribution):
Employee Only (Self): Varies
Medicare: Varies
Average Annual Deductible Per Subscriber:
Employee Only (Self): Varies
Medicare: Varies
Average Subscriber Co-Payment:
Primary Care Physician: Varies
Non-Network Physician: Varies
Prescription Drugs: Varies
Hospital ER: Varies
Home Health Care: Varies
Home Health Care Max. Days/Visits Covered: Varies
Nursing Home: Varies
Nursing Home Max. Days/Visits Covered: Varies

Key Personnel
President/Pennsylvania . . . . .Jennifer Kessler

SVP/Medical Operations . . . . .Shirley Blevins
Chief Operating Officer . . . . .Fred Madill
SVP/General Counsel . . . . .David Thomas
Compliance Officer . . . . .John G Beck
President/South Carolina . . . . .Dan Gallagher
President/Ohio . . . . .Scott A Bowers
President/Tennessee . . . . .Matthew Moore
VP/Medicare Products . . . . .Keith Volberg
VP/Network Administration. . . . . .Healther Cianfrocco
VP, National Marketing . . . . .Brandon Moser
   412-473-4630
   brandon.moser@unisonhealthplan.com

971 United Concordia

4401 Deer Path Road
Harrisburg, PA 17110
Toll-Free: 800-972-4191
Phone: 717-260-6800
Fax: 717-433-9871
ucproducer@ucci.com
www.secure.ucci.com
For Profit Organization: Yes
Year Founded: 1971
Number of Primary Care Physicians: 111,000
Total Enrollment: 8,000,000

Healthplan and Services Defined
 PLAN TYPE: Dental
 Plan Specialty: Dental
 Benefits Offered: Dental

Type of Coverage
 Commercial, Individual

Geographic Areas Served
 Military personnel and their families, nationwide

Key Personnel
 Chairman & CEO . . . . .Daniel Lebish
 SVP, Finance . . . . .Daniel Wright
 SVP, Sales & Marketing . . . . .Sharon Muscarella

972 UnitedHealthCare of Pennsylvania

300 Oxford Drive
Suite 350
Monroeville, PA 15146
Toll-Free: 800-307-7820
www.uhc.com
Subsidiary of: UnitedHealth Group
For Profit Organization: Yes
Total Enrollment: 75,000,000
State Enrollment: 283,106

Healthplan and Services Defined
 PLAN TYPE: HMO/PPO
 Benefits Offered: Disease Management, Wellness

Type of Payment Plans Offered
 DFFS

Geographic Areas Served
 Statewide

Publishes and Distributes Report Card: Yes

Key Personnel
 Marketing . . . . .Elliot Holtz
 Media Contact . . . . .Mary McElrath-Jones
   914-467-2039
   mary_r_mcelrath-jones@uhc.com

973 UPMC Health Plan

1 Chatham Center
112 Washington Place

Pittsburgh, PA 15219
Toll-Free: 866-778-6073
Phone: 412-434-1200
Fax: 412-454-7711
hponeline@upmc.edu
www.upmchealthplan.com
Subsidiary of: University of Pittsburgh Medical Center
For Profit Organization: Yes
Year Founded: 1996
Physician Owned Organization: Yes
Number of Affiliated Hospitals: 80
Number of Primary Care Physicians: 7,600
Total Enrollment: 101,000
State Enrollment: 209,211

Healthplan and Services Defined
 PLAN TYPE: Multiple
 Benefits Offered: Behavioral Health, Chiropractic, Complementary
   Medicine, Dental, Disease Management, Home Care, Inpatient
   SNF, Physical Therapy, Podiatry, Prescription, Psychiatric,
   Transplant, Vision, Wellness

Type of Coverage
 Commercial, Individual, Medicare, Medicaid

Type of Payment Plans Offered
 POS

Geographic Areas Served
 26 counties in western Pennsylvania

Subscriber Information
 Average Monthly Fee Per Subscriber
   (Employee + Employer Contribution):
     Employee Only (Self): Varies
     Employee & 1 Family Member: Varies
     Employee & 2 Family Members: Varies
     Medicare: Varies
 Average Annual Deductible Per Subscriber:
     Employee Only (Self): Varies
     Employee & 1 Family Member: Varies
     Employee & 2 Family Members: Varies
     Medicare: Varies
 Average Subscriber Co-Payment:
     Primary Care Physician: Varies
     Non-Network Physician: Varies
     Prescription Drugs: Varies
     Hospital ER: Varies
     Home Health Care: Varies
     Home Health Care Max. Days/Visits Covered: Varies
     Nursing Home: Varies
     Nursing Home Max. Days/Visits Covered: Varies

Accreditation Certification
 NCQA

Key Personnel
 President . . . . .Diane P Holder
 CFO . . . . .Scott Lammie
 COO . . . . .Mary Beth Jenkins
 VP, Medicare . . . . .Cathy Batteer
 VP, Network/Provider Rel . . . . .Sandra E McAnallen
 VP, Quality, Audit, Fraud . . . . .William Gedmen, CPA
 CEO, Askesis Dev Group . . . . .Sharon Hicks
 VP, Health Economics . . . . .Pamela Peele, PhD
 VP, Marketing & Comm .Jeffrey Nelson
 VP Business Development . . . . .Anthony Benevento
 VP, Medical Affairs. .Michael Culyba, MD
 VP, Human Resources . . . . .Sharon Czyzewski
 Chief Medical Officer . . . . .Anne Boland Docimo, MD
 President, UPMC For You . . . . .John Lovelace
 VP, Sales & Marketing . . . . .Anthony Benevento
 Dir, Public Relations .Gina Pferdehirt
   412-454-4953
   pferdehirtgm@upmc.edu
 VP, Pharmacy . . . . .Chronis Manolis, RPh

974 Val-U-Health
Acquired by Value Behavioral Health of PA

975 Valley Preferred
1605 N Cedar Crest Blvd
Suite 411
Allentown, PA 18104-2351
Toll-Free: 800-955-6620
Phone: 610-969-0480
Fax: 610-969-0439
info@valleypreferred.com
www.valleypreferred.com
Non-Profit Organization: Yes
Year Founded: 1994
Physician Owned Organization: Yes
Federally Qualified: Yes
Number of Affiliated Hospitals: 18
Number of Primary Care Physicians: 778
Number of Referral/Specialty Physicians: 2,977
Total Enrollment: 174,309
State Enrollment: 174,209

Healthplan and Services Defined
PLAN TYPE: Multiple
Model Type: PHO

Geographic Areas Served
Lehigh, Northampton, Berks, Bucks, Montgomery, Dauphin,
Schuylkill, Columbia, Luzerne, Carbon and Lackawanna counties

Accreditation Certification
TJC

Key Personnel
Interim Exec Director . . . . Jack A Lenhart
Medical Director . . . . Jack A Lenhart
Dir, Info Technology . . . . Louis W Bottitta
GLVIPA Coordinator . . . . Maryann Curcio
General Manager. . . . . Laura J Mertz
Admin, Health Services . . . . Christina Lewisr
Provider Relations . . . . Patricia A Sank

Specialty Managed Care Partners
Enters into Contracts with Regional Business Coalitions: No
NPRHCC

976 Value Behavioral Health of Pennsylvania
520 Pleasant Valley Road
Trafford, PA 15085
Toll-Free: 877-615-8503
Phone: 724-744-6361
Fax: 724-744-6379
vbhpawebmaster@valueoptions.com
www.vbh-pa.com
Subsidiary of: A ValueOptions Company
For Profit Organization: Yes
Year Founded: 1983
Physician Owned Organization: Yes
Number of Affiliated Hospitals: 1,225
Number of Referral/Specialty Physicians: 6,000
Total Enrollment: 22,000,000

Healthplan and Services Defined
PLAN TYPE: PPO
Model Type: Network
Plan Specialty: ASO, Behavioral Health, UR
Benefits Offered: Behavioral Health, Psychiatric, EAP

Type of Coverage
Commercial, Indemnity, Medicaid

Type of Payment Plans Offered
POS, DFFS, Combination FFS & DFFS

Geographic Areas Served
Armstrong, Beaver, Butler, Cambria, Crawford, Erie, Fayette, Greene,
Indiana, Lawrence, Mercer, Venango, Washington and Westmoreland
counties

Peer Review Type
Case Management: Yes

Publishes and Distributes Report Card: Yes

Accreditation Certification
URAC, NCQA

Key Personnel
President and CEO . . . . Dr Ronald Dozoretz
COO . . . . John Hill
CFO . . . . Ed Hackett
Director, Marketing/Sales . . . . Lisa Todd

Health Insurance Coverage Status and Type of Coverage by Age

Category	All Persons		Under 18 years		Under 65 years		65 years and over	
	Number	%	Number	%	Number	%	Number	%
Total population	na	na	na	na	na	na	na	na
Covered by some type of health insurance	na	na	na	na	na	na	na	na
Covered by private health insurance	na	na	na	na	na	na	na	na
Employment based	na	na	na	na	na	na	na	na
Own employment based	na	na	na	na	na	na	na	na
Direct purchase	na	na	na	na	na	na	na	na
Covered by government health insurance	na	na	na	na	na	na	na	na
Covered by Medicaid	na	na	na	na	na	na	na	na
Also by private insurance	na	na	na	na	na	na	na	na
Covered by Medicare	na	na	na	na	na	na	na	na
Also by private insurance	na	na	na	na	na	na	na	na
Also by Medicaid	na	na	na	na	na	na	na	na
Covered by military health care	na	na	na	na	na	na	na	na
Not covered at any time during the year	na	na	na	na	na	na	na	na

Note: Numbers in thousands; figures cover 2010; standard error appears in parenthesis; (b) base less than 75,000; (x) not applicable; (na) not available
Source: U.S. Census Bureau, Current Population Survey, 2011 Annual Social and Economic Supplement. Table HI05. Health Insurance Coverage Status and Type of Coverage by State and Age for All People: 2010

Puerto Rico

977 CIGNA HealthCare of Puerto Rico
Hato Rey Tower
268 Munoz Rivera Avenue, Suite 700
San Juan, PR 00918
Toll-Free: 866-438-2446
www.cigna.com
For Profit Organization: Yes

Healthplan and Services Defined
    PLAN TYPE: PPO

Type of Coverage
    Commercial

978 First Medical Health Plan
Ext Villa Caparra Mar Buch 530
Guaynabo, PR 00968
Toll-Free: 888-364-7535
www.firstmedicalpr.com
For Profit Organization: Yes
Year Founded: 1977
Number of Affiliated Hospitals: 16
Total Enrollment: 180,000
State Enrollment: 180,000

Healthplan and Services Defined
    PLAN TYPE: Multiple

Key Personnel
    President . . . . Francisco Javier Artau Feliciano

979 Humana Health Insurance of Puerto Rico
383 Franklin Delano Roosevelt Ave
San Juan, PR 00918
Toll-Free: 866-836-6162
Phone: 502-301-1903
Fax: 888-899-8319
www.humana.com
For Profit Organization: Yes
Total Enrollment: 370,000

Healthplan and Services Defined
    PLAN TYPE: HMO/PPO

Type of Coverage
    Commercial, Individual

Accreditation Certification
    URAC, NCQA, CORE

980 Medical Card System (MCS)
Bird Ponce De Leon #255
Suite 1600, Floor 9
San Juan, PR 00917
Toll-Free: 888-758-1616
Phone: 787-758-2500
Fax: 787-250-0380
www.mcs.com.pr
For Profit Organization: Yes
Year Founded: 1983
Number of Affiliated Hospitals: 57
Total Enrollment: 300,000

Healthplan and Services Defined
    PLAN TYPE: Multiple
    Model Type: Group, Network
    Plan Specialty: ASO, Behavioral Health, Chiropractic, Dental,
        Disease Management, EPO, Lab, MSO, PBM, Vision, Radiology
    Benefits Offered: Behavioral Health, Chiropractic, Complementary
        Medicine, Dental, Disease Management, Home Care, Inpatient

SNF, Physical Therapy, Podiatry, Prescription, Psychiatric,
Transplant, Vision, Wellness, Life, LTD

Type of Coverage
    Commercial, Individual, Indemnity, Medicare, Supplemental
        Medicare, Medicaid, Catastrophic

Type of Payment Plans Offered
    POS, Capitated

Geographic Areas Served
    Puerto Rico

Subscriber Information
    Average Monthly Fee Per Subscriber
        (Employee + Employer Contribution):
            Employee Only (Self): Varies
            Employee & 1 Family Member: Varies
            Employee & 2 Family Members: Varies
            Medicare: Varies
    Average Annual Deductible Per Subscriber:
            Employee Only (Self): Varies
            Employee & 1 Family Member: Varies
            Employee & 2 Family Members: Varies
            Medicare: Varies
    Average Subscriber Co-Payment:
            Primary Care Physician: Varies
            Non-Network Physician: Varies
            Prescription Drugs: Varies
            Hospital ER: Varies
            Home Health Care: Varies
            Home Health Care Max. Days/Visits Covered: Varies
            Nursing Home: Varies
            Nursing Home Max. Days/Visits Covered: Varies

Network Qualifications
    Pre-Admission Certification: Yes

Peer Review Type
    Utilization Review: Yes
    Second Surgical Opinion: Yes
    Case Management: Yes

Accreditation Certification
    Medicare Approved, Pre-Admission Certification, State Licensure

Key Personnel
    Co-CEO, CFO . . . . Mark A Rishell
    Co-CEO, MCS President. . . . . Julio F Julia
    Chief Actuary Officer . . . . Scott Allen
    Chief Legal Officer. . . . . Maritza I Munich
    VP, Chief Audit Executive . . . . Un Tian See
    MCS HMO President . . . . Jose Mirabal
    MCS HMO Vice President . . . . Lilia Sabater
    Controller . . . . Brendan Shanahan
    VP, Finance . . . . David Schaffer
    VP, Underwriting . . . . Eduardo Zetina
    Chief Medical Officer . . . . Ines Hernandez, MD
    VP, Business Development . . . . Roberto Pando
    Chief Information Officer . . . . Ivars Blums
    VP, Service & Renewals . . . . Carmen Molina
    VP, Individual Sales . . . . Richard Luna

Employer References
    Sensormatic, El Nuevo Dia, Pan Pepin, Nypro Puerto Rico, Cardinal
        Health

981 MMM Healthcare
350 Chardon Ave
Suite 500, Torre Chardon
San Juan, PR 00918-2101
Toll-Free: 866-333-5470
Phone: 787-622-3000
Fax: 787-629-2399
www.mmm-pr.com
Year Founded: 2001
Total Enrollment: 126,000

Healthplan and Services Defined
  PLAN TYPE: Multiple

Type of Coverage
  Individual, Medicare

Geographic Areas Served
  Puerto Rico

Key Personnel
  CEO...Richard Shinto
  President ....Lcdo. Orlando Gonzalez

982 PMC Medicare Choice

350 Chardon Ave
Suite 500, Torre Chardon
San Juan, PR 00918-2101
Toll-Free: 877-568-0808
Phone: 787-622-3000
Fax: 787-999-1762
www.pmcpr.org
Secondary Address: Jose Mercado Avenue, Gatsby Plaza Building,
  2nd Floor, Caguas, PR
For Profit Organization: Yes
Year Founded: 2004
Total Enrollment: 53,000

Healthplan and Services Defined
  PLAN TYPE: Medicare

Type of Coverage
  Medicare

Geographic Areas Served
  Puerto Rico

Key Personnel
  Chief Executive Officer ....Richard Shinto, MD
  President...........................Orlando Gonzalez, Esq

983 Triple-S Salud Blue Cross Blue Shield of Puerto Rico

1441 F D Roosevelt Avenue
Guaynabo, PR 00920
Phone: 787-774-6060
Fax: 787-706-2833
servicioalcliente@ssspr.com
www.ssspr.com
Mailing Address: PO Box 363628, San Juan, PR 00936-3628
Year Founded: 1959
Total Enrollment: 100,000
State Enrollment: 100,000

Healthplan and Services Defined
  PLAN TYPE: Multiple
  Benefits Offered: Chiropractic, Dental, Disease Management, Home
    Care, Inpatient SNF, Physical Therapy, Podiatry, Prescription,
    Psychiatric, Vision, Wellness

Type of Coverage
  Individual, Medicare, Supplemental Medicare

Geographic Areas Served
  Puerto Rico

Subscriber Information
  Average Monthly Fee Per Subscriber
    (Employee + Employer Contribution):
      Employee Only (Self): Varies
      Employee & 1 Family Member: Varies
      Employee & 2 Family Members: Varies
      Medicare: Varies
  Average Annual Deductible Per Subscriber:
      Employee Only (Self): Varies
      Employee & 1 Family Member: Varies
      Employee & 2 Family Members: Varies

Medicare: Varies
  Average Subscriber Co-Payment:
      Primary Care Physician: Varies
      Non-Network Physician: Varies
      Prescription Drugs: Varies
      Hospital ER: Varies
      Home Health Care: Varies
      Home Health Care Max. Days/Visits Covered: Varies
      Nursing Home: Varies
      Nursing Home Max. Days/Visits Covered: Varies

Key Personnel
  President..........................Jesus R Sanchez Colon
  Vice President.......................Jose Hawayek Alemany
  Secretary.......................Ing. Jorge Fuentes Benejam
  Media Contact ....Vivian Lopez
    787-749-4112
    vivian.lopez@ssspr.com

984 UnitedHealthCare of Puerto Rico

5901 Lincoln Drive
Edina, MN 55436
Toll-Free: 800-842-3585
www.uhc.com
Subsidiary of: UnitedHealth Group
Year Founded: 1977
Number of Affiliated Hospitals: 4,200
Number of Primary Care Physicians: 460,000
Total Enrollment: 75,000,000

Healthplan and Services Defined
  PLAN TYPE: HMO/PPO
  Model Type: IPA, Group, Network
  Plan Specialty: Lab, Radiology
  Benefits Offered: Chiropractic, Dental, Physical Therapy,
    Prescription, Wellness, AD&D, Life, LTD, STD
  Offers Demand Management Patient Information Service: Yes

Type of Coverage
  Commercial, Individual, Indemnity, Medicare

Geographic Areas Served
  Statewide

Network Qualifications
  Pre-Admission Certification: Yes

Peer Review Type
  Utilization Review: Yes
  Second Surgical Opinion: Yes
  Case Management: Yes

Publishes and Distributes Report Card: Yes

Accreditation Certification
  TJC, NCQA

Specialty Managed Care Partners
  Enters into Contracts with Regional Business Coalitions: Yes

Health Insurance Coverage Status and Type of Coverage by Age

Category	All Persons		Under 18 years		Under 65 years		65 years and over	
	Number	%	Number	%	Number	%	Number	%
Total population	1,048	-	226	-	896	-	151	-
Covered by some type of health insurance	928 *(12)*	88.6 *(0.9)*	214 *(4)*	94.7 *(1.0)*	779 *(14)*	86.9 *(1.0)*	149 *(9)*	98.6 *(0.7)*
Covered by private health insurance	707 *(16)*	67.5 *(1.4)*	148 *(6)*	65.7 *(2.7)*	623 *(17)*	69.5 *(1.5)*	84 *(8)*	55.4 *(3.3)*
Employment based	615 *(17)*	58.7 *(1.5)*	138 *(6)*	61.3 *(2.7)*	573 *(17)*	63.9 *(1.6)*	42 *(5)*	27.9 *(2.7)*
Own employment based	302 *(10)*	28.8 *(0.9)*	0 *(0)*	0.0 *(0.0)*	272 *(10)*	30.4 *(0.9)*	29 *(4)*	19.4 *(2.1)*
Direct purchase	100 *(9)*	9.5 *(0.8)*	8 *(2)*	3.5 *(0.9)*	53 *(7)*	5.9 *(0.8)*	47 *(6)*	31.0 *(2.9)*
Covered by government health insurance	347 *(15)*	33.1 *(1.4)*	84 *(6)*	37.2 *(2.7)*	203 *(12)*	22.6 *(1.4)*	144 *(9)*	95.2 *(1.1)*
Covered by Medicaid	174 *(11)*	16.7 *(1.1)*	80 *(6)*	35.3 *(2.6)*	166 *(11)*	18.5 *(1.3)*	9 *(2)*	5.8 *(1.0)*
Also by private insurance	32 *(4)*	3.1 *(0.4)*	16 *(3)*	7.1 *(1.2)*	32 *(4)*	3.5 *(0.5)*	1 *(1)*	0.4 *(0.3)*
Covered by Medicare	174 *(9)*	16.6 *(0.9)*	2 *(1)*	0.8 *(0.3)*	31 *(4)*	3.4 *(0.4)*	144 *(9)*	95.0 *(1.1)*
Also by private insurance	86 *(8)*	8.2 *(0.7)*	1 *(0)*	0.2 *(0.2)*	7 *(2)*	0.8 *(0.2)*	79 *(7)*	52.0 *(3.2)*
Also by Medicaid	27 *(3)*	2.6 *(0.3)*	1 *(1)*	0.6 *(0.3)*	19 *(3)*	2.1 *(0.3)*	9 *(2)*	5.7 *(1.0)*
Covered by military health care	39 *(6)*	3.7 *(0.5)*	5 *(2)*	2.0 *(0.7)*	27 *(5)*	3.0 *(0.6)*	11 *(3)*	7.5 *(1.6)*
Not covered at any time during the year	119 *(9)*	11.4 *(0.9)*	12 *(2)*	5.3 *(1.0)*	117 *(9)*	13.1 *(1.0)*	2 *(1)*	1.4 *(0.7)*

Note: Numbers in thousands; figures cover 2010; standard error appears in parenthesis; (b) base less than 75,000; (x) not applicable
Source: U.S. Census Bureau, Current Population Survey, 2011 Annual Social and Economic Supplement. Table HI05. Health Insurance Coverage Status and Type of Coverage by State and Age for All People: 2010

Rhode Island

985 Aetna Health of Rhode Island
Partnered with eHealthInsurance Services Inc.

986 Blue Cross & Blue Shield of Rhode Island
500 Exchange Street
Providence, RI 02903-2699
Toll-Free: 800-564-0888
Phone: 401-459-1000
Fax: 401-459-1333
www.bcbsri.com
Non-Profit Organization: Yes
Year Founded: 1939
Total Enrollment: 600,000

Healthplan and Services Defined
PLAN TYPE: HMO
Model Type: Staff
Benefits Offered: Disease Management, Wellness

Type of Payment Plans Offered
DFFS

Peer Review Type
Case Management: Yes

Publishes and Distributes Report Card: Yes

Key Personnel
President & CEO . . . . Peter Andruszkiewicz
COO . . . . William K Wray
General Counsel/CAO . . . . Michele B Lederberg
VP, Human Resources . . . . Eric Gasbaro
Chief Marketing Officer . . . . Shanna Marzilli
SVP/Chief Medical Officer . . . . Gus Manocchia, MD
Dir, Media Relations . . . . Kimberly Reingold
  401-459-5611
  kimberly.reingold@bcbsri.org

987 CIGNA HealthCare of Rhode Island
Three Newton Executive Park
2223 Washington Street
Newton, MA 02462
Toll-Free: 866-438-2446
Phone: 617-630-4300
Fax: 617-630-4380
www.cigna.com
For Profit Organization: Yes

Healthplan and Services Defined
PLAN TYPE: PPO

Type of Coverage
Commercial

988 CVS CareMark
One CVS Drive
Woonsocket, RI 02895
Toll-Free: 800-552-8159
Phone: 401-765-1500
www.cvscaremark.com
Mailing Address: PO Box 832407, CareMark Customer Service, Richardson, TX 75083
For Profit Organization: Yes
Year Founded: 1963
Owned by an Integrated Delivery Network (IDN): Yes
Number of Primary Care Physicians: 60,000
Total Enrollment: 75,000,000

Healthplan and Services Defined
PLAN TYPE: Other
Other Type: PBM
Model Type: Staff
Plan Specialty: Disease Management, PBM
Benefits Offered: Disease Management, Prescription

Type of Payment Plans Offered
POS, DFFS, FFS

Geographic Areas Served
Nationwide

Peer Review Type
Second Surgical Opinion: Yes
Case Management: Yes

Publishes and Distributes Report Card: Yes

Key Personnel
Chairman & CEO . . . . Thomas M. Ryan
Pres & COO, CVS Caremark . . . . Larry J. Merlo
EVP, Chief Financial Offc . . . . David M Denton
SVP, Controller . . . . Laird Daniels
President, Pharmacy Svcs . . . . Per Lofberg
EVP, Chief Marketing Offc . . . . Helena B Foulkes
PBM Chief Operating Offc . . . . Johathan C. Roberts
EVP & Chief Medical Off. . . . . Troyen A. Brennan, MD
SVP, Chief Human Resource . . . . Lisa Bisaccia
SVP, Chief Info Officer . . . . Stuart M. McGuigan
EVP, Sales & Acct Svcs . . . . David Joyner
Dir, Public Relations . . . . Christine Cramer
  401-770-3317
  ckcramer@cvs.com
EVP, Chief Legal Officer . . . . Douglas A. Sgarro

Specialty Managed Care Partners
Enters into Contracts with Regional Business Coalitions: Yes

989 Delta Dental of Rhode Island
10 Charles Street
Providence, RI 02904-2208
Toll-Free: 800-598-6684
Phone: 401-752-6000
Fax: 401-752-6060
email@deltadentalri.com
www.deltadentalri.com
Mailing Address: PO Box 1517, Providence, RI 02901-1517
Non-Profit Organization: Yes
Year Founded: 1959
Total Enrollment: 54,000,000
State Enrollment: 620,000

Healthplan and Services Defined
PLAN TYPE: Dental
Other Type: Dental PPO
Plan Specialty: Dental
Benefits Offered: Dental

Type of Coverage
Commercial

Geographic Areas Served
Statewide

Peer Review Type
Case Management: Yes

Publishes and Distributes Report Card: Yes

Key Personnel
President & CEO . . . . Joseph A Nagle
VP, Chief Financial Offc . . . . Richard A Fritz
VP, Chief Actuary . . . . Craig W Lewis
VP, Sales, Altus Dental . . . . Joseph Perroni
VP, External Affairs . . . . Kathryn M Shanley
VP, Operations . . . . Stephen J Sperandio
VP, Chief Info Officer . . . . Thomas D Chase
VP, Sales, Delta Dental . . . . Angelo Pezzullo

Corporate Communications . . . . Mary Sommer
   401-752-6265
   msommer@deltadentalri.com
Dir/Media & Public Affair . . . . Elizabeth Risberg
   415-972-8423

990   eHealthInsurance Services Inc.

11919 Foundation Place
Gold River, CA 95670
Toll-Free: 800-977-8860
info@ehealthinsurance.com
www.e.healthinsurance.com
Year Founded: 1997

Healthplan and Services Defined
  PLAN TYPE: HMO/PPO
  Benefits Offered: Dental, Life, STD

Type of Coverage
  Commercial, Individual, Medicare

Geographic Areas Served
  All 50 states in the USA and District of Columbia

Key Personnel
  Chairman & CEO . . . . Gary L. Lauer
  EVP/Business & Corp. Dev. . . . . Bruce Telkamp
  EVP/Chief Technology . . . . Dr. Sheldon X. Wang
  SVP & CFO . . . . Stuart M. Huizinga
  Pres. of eHealth Gov. Sys . . . . Samuel C. Gibbs
  SVP of Sales & Operations . . . . Robert S. Hurley
  Director Public Relations. . . . . Nate Purpura
   650-210-3115

991   Humana Health Insurance of Rhode Island

1 International Blvd
Suite 400
Mahwah, NJ 07495
Toll-Free: 800-967-2370
Phone: 201-512-8818
www.humana.com
For Profit Organization: Yes

Healthplan and Services Defined
  PLAN TYPE: HMO/PPO

Type of Coverage
  Commercial, Individual

Accreditation Certification
  URAC, NCQA, CORE

992   Neighborhood Health Plan of Rhode Island

299 Promenade Street
Providence, RI 02908
Toll-Free: 800-963-1001
Phone: 401-459-6000
Fax: 401-459-6175
www.nhpri.org
Non-Profit Organization: Yes
Number of Primary Care Physicians: 700
Number of Referral/Specialty Physicians: 1,700
Total Enrollment: 76,000
State Enrollment: 76,000

Healthplan and Services Defined
  PLAN TYPE: HMO
  Model Type: Network
  Benefits Offered: Disease Management, Wellness

Type of Coverage
  Medicaid

Peer Review Type
  Case Management: Yes

Publishes and Distributes Report Card: Yes

Key Personnel
  CEO . . . . Mark Reynolds
  Chief Financial Officer . . . . T. Clark Phillip, Jr
  COO . . . . Nancy Coburn
  Chief Medical Officer . . . . L. McTyeire Johnston, MD

993   Tufts Health Plan: Rhode Island

1 West Exchange Place
Providence, RI 02903
Toll-Free: 800-462-0224
Phone: 401-272-3499
www.tuftshealthplan.com
Non-Profit Organization: Yes
Year Founded: 1979
Number of Affiliated Hospitals: 90
Number of Primary Care Physicians: 25,000
Number of Referral/Specialty Physicians: 12,500
Total Enrollment: 737,411

Healthplan and Services Defined
  PLAN TYPE: HMO/PPO
  Model Type: IPA
  Plan Specialty: ASO, Behavioral Health, Chiropractic, Disease
   Management, EPO, Lab, PBM, Vision, Radiology, UR, Pharmacy
  Benefits Offered: Behavioral Health, Chiropractic, Complementary
   Medicine, Disease Management, Home Care, Inpatient SNF,
   Physical Therapy, Podiatry, Prescription, Psychiatric, Transplant,
   Vision, Wellness

Type of Coverage
  Commercial, Individual, Medicare, Supplemental Medicare

Type of Payment Plans Offered
  POS, DFFS, FFS, Combination FFS & DFFS

Geographic Areas Served
  Massachusetts, New Hampshire and Rhode Island

Subscriber Information
  Average Monthly Fee Per Subscriber
   (Employee + Employer Contribution):
    Employee Only (Self): $190.00-220.00
    Employee & 2 Family Members: $800.00-950.00
    Medicare: $150.00
  Average Annual Deductible Per Subscriber:
    Employee Only (Self): $1000.00
    Employee & 1 Family Member: $500.00
    Employee & 2 Family Members: $3000.00
  Average Subscriber Co-Payment:
    Primary Care Physician: $10.00
    Non-Network Physician: 20%
    Prescription Drugs: $10/20/35
    Hospital ER: $50.00
    Home Health Care: $0
    Home Health Care Max. Days/Visits Covered: 120 days
    Nursing Home: $0
    Nursing Home Max. Days/Visits Covered: 120 days

Network Qualifications
  Pre-Admission Certification: No

Peer Review Type
  Utilization Review: Yes
  Case Management: Yes

Publishes and Distributes Report Card: Yes

Accreditation Certification
  TJC, AAPI, NCQA

Key Personnel
  Principal . . . . Mark Cenachetti
  Account Executive . . . . Sarah Nowicki

Average Claim Compensation
  Physician's Fees Charged: 75%
  Hospital's Fees Charged: 70%

Specialty Managed Care Partners
  Advance PCS, Private Healthe Care Systems

Employer References
  Commonwealth of Massachuestts, Fleet Boston, Roman Catholic
    Archdiocese of Boston, City of Boston, State Street Corporation

994 UnitedHealthCare of Rhode Island

475 Kilvert Street
Warwick, RI 02886
Toll-Free: 800-447-1245
Phone: 401-737-6900
Fax: 401-732-7211
RhodeIsland_PR_Team@uhc.com
www.uhc.com
Subsidiary of: UnitedHealth Group
For Profit Organization: Yes
Year Founded: 1983
Owned by an Integrated Delivery Network (IDN): Yes
Number of Affiliated Hospitals: 13
Number of Primary Care Physicians: 2,278
Total Enrollment: 75,000,000
State Enrollment: 92,000

Healthplan and Services Defined
  PLAN TYPE: HMO/PPO
  Model Type: IPA
  Plan Specialty: Behavioral Health, Chiropractic, Dental, Disease
    Management, Lab, PBM, Vision, Radiology
  Benefits Offered: Prescription
  Offers Demand Management Patient Information Service: Yes

Type of Coverage
  Commercial

Type of Payment Plans Offered
  Combination FFS & DFFS

Geographic Areas Served
  Rhode Island & Southeastern Massachusetts

Publishes and Distributes Report Card: Yes

Accreditation Certification
  NCQA

Key Personnel
  CFO.....................................Donald H Powers
  In House Formulary........................Scott E Enos, RPh
  Marketing ....James Moniz, Jr
  Materials Management ....Diane McDole
  Medical Affairs ....William Corrao, MD
  Media Contact ....Debora Spano
    debora_m_spano@uhc.com

Specialty Managed Care Partners
  G Tec, State of RI

Health Insurance Coverage Status and Type of Coverage by Age

Category	All Persons		Under 18 years		Under 65 years		65 years and over	
	Number	%	Number	%	Number	%	Number	%
Total population	4,526	-	1,070	-	3,878	-	649	-
Covered by some type of health insurance	3,596 (58)	79.4 (1.1)	917 (26)	85.8 (2.1)	2,957 (56)	76.3 (1.3)	639 (41)	98.5 (0.6)
Covered by private health insurance	2,675 (75)	59.1 (1.6)	601 (33)	56.2 (2.9)	2,325 (74)	60.0 (1.8)	351 (31)	54.1 (3.8)
Employment based	2,263 (76)	50.0 (1.7)	541 (31)	50.6 (2.7)	2,101 (76)	54.2 (1.9)	162 (26)	24.9 (3.5)
Own employment based	1,215 (45)	26.8 (1.0)	0 (0)	0.0 (0.0)	1,101 (45)	28.4 (1.0)	114 (17)	17.5 (2.5)
Direct purchase	420 (37)	9.3 (0.8)	52 (14)	4.9 (1.3)	219 (31)	5.6 (0.8)	201 (21)	31.0 (3.0)
Covered by government health insurance	1,452 (65)	32.1 (1.3)	389 (32)	36.3 (3.0)	833 (50)	21.5 (1.3)	619 (41)	95.5 (1.2)
Covered by Medicaid	625 (44)	13.8 (1.0)	359 (33)	33.6 (3.0)	575 (47)	14.8 (1.2)	50 (18)	7.7 (2.7)
Also by private insurance	98 (20)	2.2 (0.4)	59 (14)	5.5 (1.3)	85 (18)	2.2 (0.5)	13 (7)	2.1 (1.0)
Covered by Medicare	788 (45)	17.4 (0.9)	18 (9)	1.7 (0.8)	171 (20)	4.4 (0.5)	617 (40)	95.1 (1.3)
Also by private insurance	379 (29)	8.4 (0.6)	4 (4)	0.3 (0.3)	50 (13)	1.3 (0.3)	329 (29)	50.7 (3.5)
Also by Medicaid	104 (19)	2.3 (0.4)	15 (7)	1.4 (0.7)	56 (11)	1.4 (0.3)	48 (18)	7.4 (2.7)
Covered by military health care	226 (33)	5.0 (0.7)	28 (10)	2.7 (0.9)	163 (26)	4.2 (0.7)	63 (16)	9.8 (2.2)
Not covered at any time during the year	930 (51)	20.6 (1.1)	152 (22)	14.2 (2.1)	920 (51)	23.7 (1.3)	10 (4)	1.5 (0.6)

Note: Numbers in thousands; figures cover 2010; standard error appears in parenthesis; (b) base less than 75,000; (x) not applicable
Source: U.S. Census Bureau, Current Population Survey, 2011 Annual Social and Economic Supplement. Table HI05. Health Insurance Coverage Status and Type of Coverage by State and Age for All People: 2010

South Carolina

995 Aetna Health of the Carolinas
11675 Great Oaks Way
Suite 330
Alpharetta, GA 30022
Toll-Free: 866-582-9629
www.aetna.com
For Profit Organization: Yes
Total Enrollment: 18,960

Healthplan and Services Defined
  PLAN TYPE: HMO
  Other Type: POS
  Plan Specialty: EPO
  Benefits Offered: Dental, Disease Management, Long-Term Care,
    Prescription, Wellness, Life, LTD, STD

Type of Coverage
  Commercial, Individual

Type of Payment Plans Offered
  POS, FFS

Geographic Areas Served
  Statewide

996 Assurant Employee Benefits: South Carolina
5 Foot Point Road
Columbia, SC 29209-0846
Phone: 803-782-2132
benefits@assurant.com
www.assurantemployeebenefits.com
Subsidiary of: Assurant, Inc
For Profit Organization: Yes
Number of Primary Care Physicians: 112,000
Total Enrollment: 47,000

Healthplan and Services Defined
  PLAN TYPE: Multiple
  Plan Specialty: Dental, Vision, Long & Short-Term Disability
  Benefits Offered: Dental, Vision, Wellness, AD&D, Life, LTD, STD

Type of Coverage
  Commercial, Indemnity, Individual Dental Plans

Geographic Areas Served
  Statewide

Subscriber Information
  Average Monthly Fee Per Subscriber
    (Employee + Employer Contribution):
      Employee Only (Self): Varies by plan

Key Personnel
  Manager . . . . Dan Pruitt
  PR Specialist. . . . . Megan Hutchison
    816-556-7815
    megan.hutchison@assurant.com

997 Blue Cross & Blue Shield of South Carolina
I-20 Alpine Road
Columbia, SC 29219
Toll-Free: 800-288-2227
Phone: 803-264-2508
Fax: 803-264-0206
www.bcbssc.com
For Profit Organization: Yes
Year Founded: 1946
Number of Affiliated Hospitals: 64
Number of Primary Care Physicians: 3,434
Number of Referral/Specialty Physicians: 5,473
Total Enrollment: 950,000
State Enrollment: 950,000

Healthplan and Services Defined
  PLAN TYPE: HMO/PPO
  Model Type: Network
  Plan Specialty: ASO, Behavioral Health, Chiropractic, Dental,
    Disease Management, EPO, Lab, PBM, Vision, Radiology, UR
  Benefits Offered: Behavioral Health, Chiropractic, Complementary
    Medicine, Dental, Disease Management, Physical Therapy,
    Podiatry, Prescription, Psychiatric, Transplant, Vision, Wellness
  Offers Demand Management Patient Information Service: Yes

Type of Coverage
  Commercial, Individual, Medicare

Type of Payment Plans Offered
  POS, DFFS, Capitated, FFS, Combination FFS & DFFS

Geographic Areas Served
  Statewide

Network Qualifications
  Pre-Admission Certification: Yes

Peer Review Type
  Utilization Review: Yes
  Second Surgical Opinion: Yes

Publishes and Distributes Report Card: Yes

Accreditation Certification
  NCQA
  TJC Accreditation, Utilization Review, Pre-Admission Certification,
    State Licensure, Quality Assurance Program

Key Personnel
  Chairman. . . . . Ed Sellers
  President . . . . David Pankau
  EVP/COO . . . . Thomas Faulds
  VP/Managed Care Services . . . . Robert Leichtle
  SVP/Actuarial Services. . . . . William R Schrader
  Media/Press Relations . . . . Dale Rish
  Small Group & Indiv Oper. . . . . Terry Peace
  Marketing . . . . Mike Griggs
  Medical Affairs . . . . John Little
  Information Systems . . . . Stephen Wiggins
  Sales . . . . Mike Griggs
  Media Contact . . . . Elizabeth Hammond
    803-264-4626

Specialty Managed Care Partners
  Enters into Contracts with Regional Business Coalitions: Yes

998 BlueChoice Health Plan of South Carolina
PO Box 6170
Columbia, SC 29223
Toll-Free: 800-327-3183
Phone: 803-786-8466
Fax: 803-754-6386
ann.weldon@bluechoicesc.com
www.bluechoicesc.com
Secondary Address: 4101 Percival Road, Columbia, SC 29229
Subsidiary of: Blue Cross Blue Shield of South Carolina
For Profit Organization: Yes
Year Founded: 1984
Owned by an Integrated Delivery Network (IDN): Yes
Federally Qualified: Yes
Number of Affiliated Hospitals: 68
Number of Primary Care Physicians: 7,700
Number of Referral/Specialty Physicians: 4,199
Total Enrollment: 205,000
State Enrollment: 205,000

Healthplan and Services Defined
  PLAN TYPE: Multiple
  Model Type: IPA
  Plan Specialty: ASO, Disease Management, EPO, PBM, Vision, UR
  Benefits Offered: Behavioral Health, Chiropractic, Complementary
    Medicine, Dental, Disease Management, Home Care, Inpatient

SNF, Physical Therapy, Podiatry, Prescription, Psychiatric, Transplant, Vision, Wellness, AD&D, Life, LTD, STD, EAP
Offers Demand Management Patient Information Service: Yes

Type of Coverage
Commercial, Individual, Medicare, Medicaid, Medicare Advantage
Catastrophic Illness Benefit: Maximum $2M

Type of Payment Plans Offered
POS, DFFS, Combination FFS & DFFS

Geographic Areas Served
South Carolina

Subscriber Information
Average Annual Deductible Per Subscriber:
    Employee Only (Self): $0
    Employee & 1 Family Member: $0
    Employee & 2 Family Members: $0
Average Subscriber Co-Payment:
    Primary Care Physician: $15.00
    Non-Network Physician: $25.00
    Prescription Drugs: $3 tier
    Hospital ER: 10%
    Home Health Care: 10%
    Home Health Care Max. Days/Visits Covered: Unlimited
    Nursing Home Max. Days/Visits Covered: 120 days

Network Qualifications
Pre-Admission Certification: Yes

Peer Review Type
Utilization Review: Yes
Second Surgical Opinion: Yes
Case Management: Yes

Publishes and Distributes Report Card: Yes

Accreditation Certification
NCQA
Quality Assurance Program

Key Personnel
President/COO . . . . .Mary P Mazzola-Spivey
    803-786-8466
Finance Director . . . . .Timothy L Vaughn
    803-786-8466
VP Operations . . . . .Toni Hankins
Assistant VP Operations . . . . .Toni J Hankins
    803-786-8466
VP Health Care Network . . . . .Ann T Burnett
    803-786-8466
Chief Medical Officer .Laura B Long, MD
    803-786-8466
In House Formulary . . . . .Laura B Long, MD
VP Marketing . . . . .Bill Ferguson
    803-786-8466
QA/UR . . . . .Laura B Long, MD
Medical Affairs. . . . . .Laura B Long, MD
Manager Info. Services . . . . .Mark Rush
    803-786-8466
VP Health Network . . . . .Ann T Burnett
    803-786-8466
VP Sales. . . . . .Bill Ferguson
    803-786-8466

Average Claim Compensation
Physician's Fees Charged: 65%
Hospital's Fees Charged: 65%

Specialty Managed Care Partners
Companion Benefit Alternatives (CBA)

Employer References
Alltel Corporation, Bank of America, Kimberley Clark, BellSouth, United Parcel Service

---

999 # Carolina Care Plan

201 Executive Center Drive
Suite 300
Columbia, SC 29210
Toll-Free: 800-868-6734
Phone: 803-750-7400
Fax: 803-750-7474
www.carolinacareplan.com
Secondary Address: 3535 Pelham Road, Suite 102, Greenville, SC 29615
Subsidiary of: A Medical Mutual of Ohio Company
For Profit Organization: Yes
Year Founded: 1984
Number of Affiliated Hospitals: 61
Number of Primary Care Physicians: 7,332
Total Enrollment: 123,000
State Enrollment: 123,000

Healthplan and Services Defined
  PLAN TYPE: HMO
  Other Type: POS
  Benefits Offered: Chiropractic, Dental, Disease Management, Home Care, Inpatient SNF, Physical Therapy, Podiatry, Prescription, Psychiatric, Vision, Wellness

Type of Coverage
Commercial, Individual, Medicare

Geographic Areas Served
South Carolina

Subscriber Information
Average Monthly Fee Per Subscriber
  (Employee + Employer Contribution):
    Employee Only (Self): Varies
    Employee & 1 Family Member: Varies
    Employee & 2 Family Members: Varies
    Medicare: Varies
Average Annual Deductible Per Subscriber:
    Employee Only (Self): Varies
    Employee & 1 Family Member: Varies
    Employee & 2 Family Members: Varies
    Medicare: Varies
Average Subscriber Co-Payment:
    Primary Care Physician: Varies
    Non-Network Physician: Varies
    Prescription Drugs: Varies
    Hospital ER: Varies
    Home Health Care: Varies
    Home Health Care Max. Days/Visits Covered: Varies
    Nursing Home: Varies
    Nursing Home Max. Days/Visits Covered: Varies

Accreditation Certification
URAC

Key Personnel
President. . . . . .Carson Meehan
VP/COO/Medical Affairs . . . . .Belinda Cox, RN/CPHQ
VP/CFO. . . . . .Mark T Corcoran
Medical Director . . . . .Edward D Hutt, MD
VP Network Management .Donald Pifer
Marketing. . . . . .Robert M Dickes
Pharmacy Director. . . . . .Jim Shelley, PhD
Compliance Officer . . . . .Pat Mack
Manager, Media Relations . . . . .Ed Byers
    216-687-2685
Sr Communications Spec. . . . . .Kasey Stround
    803-561-7707

Specialty Managed Care Partners
Express Scripts

Employer References
South Carolina Bar, South Carolina Home Builders Association, Low County Manufactures Council, South Carolina Federal Employees

1000 CIGNA HealthCare of South Carolina

250 Commonwealth Drive
Suite 110
Greenville, SC 29615
Toll-Free: 800-962-8811
Phone: 864-987-1350
Fax: 864-987-1389
www.cigna.com
For Profit Organization: Yes
Year Founded: 1987
Number of Primary Care Physicians: 8,100
Total Enrollment: 14,341
State Enrollment: 14,341

Healthplan and Services Defined
  PLAN TYPE: HMO
  Model Type: IPA
  Benefits Offered: Chiropractic, Complementary Medicine, Dental,
  Disease Management, Home Care, Inpatient SNF, Long-Term
  Care, Podiatry, Prescription, Psychiatric, Transplant, Vision,
  Wellness

Type of Coverage
  Commercial

Type of Payment Plans Offered
  POS

Key Personnel
  President/CEO ....H Edward Hanaway
  Executive VP/CFO ....Michael W Bell
  Ex VP Operations/Tech.......................Scott A Storrer
  Chairman Audit Committee.................Robert H Campbell
  Corporate Governance ....Marilyn Ware
  Finance Committee...........................Peter N Larson

1001 Delta Dental of South Carolina

1320 Main Street
Suite 650
Columbia, SC 29201
Toll-Free: 800-529-3268
Fax: 803-731-0273
www.deltadentalsc.com
Non-Profit Organization: Yes
Year Founded: 1969
Total Enrollment: 54,000,000

Healthplan and Services Defined
  PLAN TYPE: Dental
  Other Type: Dental PPO
  Model Type: Network
  Plan Specialty: ASO, Dental
  Benefits Offered: Dental

Type of Coverage
  Commercial, Individual, Group
  Catastrophic Illness Benefit: None

Geographic Areas Served
  Statewide

Subscriber Information
  Average Monthly Fee Per Subscriber
    (Employee + Employer Contribution):
      Employee Only (Self): Varies
      Employee & 1 Family Member: Varies
      Employee & 2 Family Members: Varies
  Average Annual Deductible Per Subscriber:
      Employee Only (Self): Varies
      Employee & 1 Family Member: Varies
      Employee & 2 Family Members: Varies
  Average Subscriber Co-Payment:
      Prescription Drugs: $0
      Home Health Care: $0
      Nursing Home: $0

1002 eHealthInsurance Services Inc.

11919 Foundation Place
Gold River, CA 95670
Toll-Free: 800-977-8860
info@ehealthinsurance.com
www.e.healthinsurance.com
Year Founded: 1997

Healthplan and Services Defined
  PLAN TYPE: HMO/PPO
  Benefits Offered: Dental, Life, STD

Type of Coverage
  Commercial, Individual, Medicare

Geographic Areas Served
  All 50 states in the USA and District of Columbia

Key Personnel
  Chairman & CEO ....Gary L. Lauer
  EVP/Business & Corp. Dev.....................Bruce Telkamp
  EVP/Chief Technology....................Dr. Sheldon X. Wang
  SVP & CFO ....Stuart M. Huizinga
  Pres. of eHealth Gov. Sys ....Samuel C. Gibbs
  SVP of Sales & Operations ....Robert S. Hurley
  Director Public Relations........................Nate Purpura
    650-210-3115

1003 Great-West Healthcare South Carolina

Acquired by CIGNA

1004 Humana Health Insurance of South Carolina

1220 Bower Parkway
Suite E8
Columbia, SC 29212
Toll-Free: 877-486-2622
Phone: 803-865-7663
Fax: 803-865-1760
www.humana.com
Secondary Address: 420 The Parkway, Suite M, Greer, SC 29650
For Profit Organization: Yes

Healthplan and Services Defined
  PLAN TYPE: HMO/PPO

Type of Coverage
  Commercial, Individual

Accreditation Certification
  URAC, NCQA, CORE

1005 InStil Health

17 Technology
Columbia, SC 29023
Toll-Free: 877-446-7845
instilhealth@myinstil.com
www.myinstil.com
Mailing Address: PO Box 100294, Mail Code AG-790, Columbia, SC
  29202-3294
Total Enrollment: 30,000

Healthplan and Services Defined
  PLAN TYPE: Medicare

Type of Coverage
  Medicare, Supplemental Medicare

Key Personnel
  President & CEO ....Bruce Hughes
    803-763-7130
    bruce.hughes@palmettoGBA.com
  Dir, Operations Oversight ....Dee Yurko
    803-763-5888
    dee.yurko@myinstil.com

Dir, Billing & Finance . . . . Jennifer Pendleton
803-763-6623
jennifer.pendleton@myinstil.com

1006 Kanawha Healthcare Solutions
Acquired by Humana, Inc.

1007 Medical Mutual Services
PO Box 1640
Columbia, SC 29202-1640
Toll-Free: 800-773-1445
Phone: 803-214-3384
Fax: 803-214-3388
www.supermednetwork.com
Subsidiary of: SuperMed Network
Total Enrollment: 144,000

Healthplan and Services Defined
    PLAN TYPE: PPO

Type of Coverage
    Commercial, Self Funded, Insurance Companies

Geographic Areas Served
    South Carolina, Georgia, Ohio

Key Personnel
    Director Sales/Marketing . . . . Dee Nash
        dee.nash@medmutual.com

1008 Select Health of South Carolina
4390 Belle Oaks Drive
Suite 400
North Charleston, SC 29405
Toll-Free: 800-741-6605
Phone: 843-569-1759
Fax: 843-569-7228
www.selecthealthofsc.com
Mailing Address: PO Box 40849, Charleston, SC 29423
Subsidiary of: AmeriHealth Mercy
For Profit Organization: Yes
Total Enrollment: 200,000
State Enrollment: 200,000

Healthplan and Services Defined
    PLAN TYPE: HMO
    Model Type: Medicaid
    Plan Specialty: Medicaid
    Benefits Offered: Medicaid

Type of Coverage
    Medicaid

Peer Review Type
    Case Management: Yes

Publishes and Distributes Report Card: Yes

Accreditation Certification
    URAC

Key Personnel
    President/CEO . . . . J Michael Jernigan
    Executive Director . . . . Cindy Helling
    CFO . . . . Rob Aubrey
    Dir, Data & Tech Services . . . . John McFadden
    Dir, Human Resources . . . . Michelle Powell
    Dir, Network Management . . . . Peggy Vickery
    Dir, Provider Relations . . . . Philip Fairchild
    Dir, Quaility Improvement . . . . Rebecca Engelman, RN
    Regional Dir Marketing . . . . Tina Davis
    Community Liason Director . . . . Terry J Davenport
    Chief Medical Officer . . . . Fred Volkman, MD
    Medical Director . . . . Stuart Hamilton, MD
    Assoc Medical Director . . . . James G Baldwin, MD

Medical Director . . . . William Burnham, MD
Reg Dir, Marketing . . . . Lillian Suarez
Dir, Communications . . . . Tracy Pou
Dir, Member Services . . . . Kevin Vaughn

1009 Southeast Community Care
7301 Rivers Avenue
Suite 100
North Charleston, SC 29406-4650
Toll-Free: 888-998-3055
Phone: 843-553-9996
Fax: 843-553-9821
www.southeastcommunitycare.com
Subsidiary of: Arcadian Health Plans

Healthplan and Services Defined
    PLAN TYPE: Medicare

Type of Coverage
    Medicare

1010 Unison Health Plan of South Carolina
100 Executive Center Drive
Suite A-3
Columbia, SC 29210
Phone: 803-798-6210
Fax: 866-657-9443
www.unisonhealthplan.com
Total Enrollment: 39,000

Healthplan and Services Defined
    PLAN TYPE: HMO

Key Personnel
    Chief Executive Officer . . . . Dan Gallagher
    Finance Director . . . . Jeff Skobel
    Operations Director . . . . Mary Ann Kelleher
    Chief Medical Officer . . . . Brenna DeLaine, MD
    Media Contact . . . . Jeff Smith
        952-931-5685
        jeff.smith@uhc.com

1011 UnitedHealthCare of South Carolina
107 Westpark Blvd
Suite 110
Columbia, SC 29210
Toll-Free: 800-660-5378
Phone: 803-551-1170
Fax: 803-454-1340
www.uhc.com
Subsidiary of: UnitedHealth Group
For Profit Organization: Yes
Total Enrollment: 75,000,000
State Enrollment: 148,404

Healthplan and Services Defined
    PLAN TYPE: HMO/PPO

Geographic Areas Served
    Statewide

Key Personnel
    Media Contact . . . . Roger Rollman
        roger_f_rollman@uhc.com

1012 VSP: Vision Service Plan of South Carolina
11 Brendan Way
Suite B33
Greenville, SC 26915-3612
Phone: 864-421-0707
webmaster@vsp.com

409

www.vsp.com
Year Founded: 1955
Number of Primary Care Physicians: 26,000
Total Enrollment: 55,000,000

Healthplan and Services Defined
 PLAN TYPE: Vision
 Plan Specialty: Vision
 Benefits Offered: Vision

Type of Payment Plans Offered
 Capitated

Geographic Areas Served
 Statewide

Network Qualifications
 Pre-Admission Certification: Yes

Peer Review Type
 Utilization Review: Yes

Accreditation Certification
 Utilization Review, Quality Assurance Program

Key Personnel
 Manager . . . . .Warren Laird

Health Insurance Coverage Status and Type of Coverage by Age

Category	All Persons		Under 18 years		Under 65 years		65 years and over	
	Number	%	Number	%	Number	%	Number	%
Total population	806	-	196	-	697	-	110	-
Covered by some type of health insurance	701 *(9)*	87.0 *(0.8)*	183 *(2)*	93.4 *(1.1)*	592 *(11)*	85.0 *(1.0)*	110 *(6)*	99.7 *(0.3)*
Covered by private health insurance	570 *(15)*	70.7 *(1.7)*	135 *(6)*	69.0 *(3.0)*	495 *(15)*	71.1 *(1.7)*	75 *(7)*	68.5 *(4.2)*
Employment based	453 *(17)*	56.2 *(2.1)*	122 *(7)*	62.1 *(3.5)*	431 *(17)*	61.9 *(2.2)*	22 *(4)*	20.4 *(3.4)*
Own employment based	233 *(9)*	28.9 *(1.1)*	0 *(0)*	0.0 *(0.0)*	217 *(9)*	31.2 *(1.1)*	16 *(3)*	14.3 *(2.7)*
Direct purchase	140 *(13)*	17.4 *(1.6)*	18 *(4)*	9.2 *(1.8)*	81 *(10)*	11.6 *(1.4)*	59 *(7)*	53.9 *(5.5)*
Covered by government health insurance	250 *(10)*	31.0 *(1.3)*	68 *(5)*	34.6 *(2.4)*	143 *(8)*	20.5 *(1.2)*	107 *(6)*	97.7 *(1.0)*
Covered by Medicaid	103 *(8)*	12.8 *(1.0)*	60 *(5)*	30.4 *(2.4)*	94 *(8)*	13.5 *(1.1)*	9 *(2)*	7.8 *(2.2)*
Also by private insurance	27 *(4)*	3.4 *(0.5)*	16 *(3)*	8.0 *(1.3)*	23 *(3)*	3.3 *(0.5)*	4 *(2)*	3.8 *(1.4)*
Covered by Medicare	129 *(7)*	16.0 *(0.9)*	5 *(2)*	2.5 *(1.2)*	23 *(5)*	3.3 *(0.7)*	107 *(6)*	97.1 *(1.1)*
Also by private insurance	78 *(7)*	9.6 *(0.9)*	0 *(0)*	0.2 *(0.2)*	5 *(2)*	0.8 *(0.2)*	72 *(7)*	65.8 *(4.4)*
Also by Medicaid	22 *(4)*	2.7 *(0.5)*	5 *(2)*	2.5 *(1.2)*	13 *(3)*	1.9 *(0.5)*	9 *(2)*	7.8 *(2.2)*
Covered by military health care	61 *(7)*	7.5 *(0.9)*	10 *(2)*	5.3 *(1.2)*	44 *(6)*	6.3 *(0.8)*	17 *(3)*	15.1 *(2.4)*
Not covered at any time during the year	105 *(7)*	13.0 *(0.8)*	13 *(2)*	6.6 *(1.1)*	105 *(7)*	15.0 *(1.0)*	0 *(0)*	0.3 *(0.3)*

Note: Numbers in thousands; figures cover 2010; standard error appears in parenthesis; (b) base less than 75,000; (x) not applicable
Source: U.S. Census Bureau, Current Population Survey, 2011 Annual Social and Economic Supplement. Table HI05. Health Insurance Coverage Status and Type of Coverage by State and Age for All People: 2010

South Dakota

1013 Aetna Health of South Dakota

Partnered with eHealthInsurance Services Inc.

1014 Americas PPO

7201 W 78th Street
Suite 100
Bloomington, MN 55439
Toll-Free: 800-948-9451
Phone: 952-896-1200
Fax: 952-896-4888
www.americaspo.com
Subsidiary of: Araz Group Inc
For Profit Organization: Yes
Year Founded: 1982
Physician Owned Organization: No
Number of Affiliated Hospitals: 260
Number of Primary Care Physicians: 18,000
Number of Referral/Specialty Physicians: 71,000
State Enrollment: 245,000

Healthplan and Services Defined
  PLAN TYPE: PPO
  Model Type: Staff, Group
  Benefits Offered: Behavioral Health, Wellness, Worker's
    Compensation, Maternity
  Offers Demand Management Patient Information Service: No

Type of Coverage
  Commercial, Individual, Medicaid
  Catastrophic Illness Benefit: Maximum $1M

Type of Payment Plans Offered
  DFFS, Capitated

Geographic Areas Served
  Minnesota, South Dakota, North Dakota, Western Wisconsin

Subscriber Information
  Average Monthly Fee Per Subscriber
    (Employee + Employer Contribution):
      Employee Only (Self): Varies by plan
  Average Annual Deductible Per Subscriber:
    Employee Only (Self): $500.00
    Employee & 1 Family Member: $500.00
    Employee & 2 Family Members: $750.00
  Average Subscriber Co-Payment:
    Primary Care Physician: $15.00
    Non-Network Physician: $500.00-1000.00
    Prescription Drugs: $10.00/15.00
    Hospital ER: $150.00
    Nursing Home: Varies

Network Qualifications
  Pre-Admission Certification: Yes

Peer Review Type
  Utilization Review: Yes
  Case Management: Yes

Publishes and Distributes Report Card: No

Accreditation Certification
  URAC
  TJC Accreditation, Utilization Review, Pre-Admission Certification,
    State Licensure, Quality Assurance Program

Key Personnel
  President . . . . Amir Eftekhari
  CEO . . . . Nazie Eftekhari
  Executive Vice President. . . . . Elizabeth Vetter
  Marketing . . . . Tim Bode
  Sales. . . . . Wendy Olson

Specialty Managed Care Partners
  Enters into Contracts with Regional Business Coalitions: Yes

1015 Avera Health Plans

3816 South Elmwood Ave
Suite 100
Sioux Falls, SD 57105-6538
Toll-Free: 888-322-2115
Phone: 605-322-4545
Fax: 605-322-4540
service@averahealthplans.com
www.averahealthplans.com
Subsidiary of: Avera Health
Total Enrollment: 18,000
State Enrollment: 29,748

Healthplan and Services Defined
  PLAN TYPE: HMO
  Benefits Offered: Disease Management, Prescription, Wellness,
    Health Education, EAP

Type of Coverage
  Commercial, Individual

Type of Payment Plans Offered
  POS

Geographic Areas Served
  South Dakota and areas of North Dakota, Minnesota, Iowa and
    Nebraska

Key Personnel
  Chairman . . . . Rodney Fouberg
  President & CEO. . . . . John Porter
  SVP, Hospital Operations . . . . Judy Blauwet

1016 CIGNA HealthCare of South Dakota

525 West Monroe Street
Suite 300
Chicago, IL 60661-3629
Toll-Free: 866-438-2446
Phone: 312-648-2460
Fax: 312-648-3617
www.cigna.com
For Profit Organization: Yes
Total Enrollment: 8,135
State Enrollment: 6,570

Healthplan and Services Defined
  PLAN TYPE: PPO
  Benefits Offered: Disease Management, Prescription, Transplant,
    Wellness

Type of Coverage
  Commercial

Type of Payment Plans Offered
  POS, FFS

Geographic Areas Served
  South Dakota

1017 DakotaCare

2600 W. 49th Street
P.O. Box 7406
Sioux Falls, SD 57117-7406
Toll-Free: 800-325-5598
Phone: 605-334-4000
Fax: 605-331-5254
customer-service@dakotacare.com
www.dakotacare.com
Subsidiary of: Dakotacare Administrative Services
For Profit Organization: Yes
Year Founded: 1986
Physician Owned Organization: Yes
Number of Affiliated Hospitals: 74
Number of Primary Care Physicians: 825

Number of Referral/Specialty Physicians: 950
Total Enrollment: 118,600
State Enrollment: 24,310

Healthplan and Services Defined
  PLAN TYPE: HMO
  Model Type: IPA
  Plan Specialty: ASO, Behavioral Health, Chiropractic, Dental, Disease Management, Lab, PBM, Vision, Radiology, UR
  Benefits Offered: Behavioral Health, Chiropractic, Complementary Medicine, Dental, Disease Management, Home Care, Inpatient SNF, Physical Therapy, Podiatry, Prescription, Psychiatric, Transplant, Vision, Wellness, AD&D, Life, LTD, STD
  Offers Demand Management Patient Information Service: No

Type of Payment Plans Offered
  POS, FFS

Geographic Areas Served
  HMO: all counties in South Dakota; TPA: Nationwide

Subscriber Information
  Average Monthly Fee Per Subscriber
    (Employee + Employer Contribution):
      Employee Only (Self): Varies by plan
  Average Annual Deductible Per Subscriber:
    Employee & 1 Family Member: $1500
  Average Subscriber Co-Payment:
    Primary Care Physician: $25.00
    Non-Network Physician: $25.00
    Hospital ER: $150.00

Network Qualifications
  Pre-Admission Certification: Yes

Peer Review Type
  Utilization Review: Yes
  Case Management: Yes

Publishes and Distributes Report Card: No

Accreditation Certification
  Utilization Review, Pre-Admission Certification, State Licensure, Quality Assurance Program

Key Personnel
  CEO . . . . .Kirk Zimmer
    605-334-4000
    kzimmer@dakotacare.com
  Government Affairs . . . . .Dean Krogman
    dkrogman@dakotacare.com
  Asst VP, Process Improv .Trish Zimmer
    tzimmer@dakotacare.com
  Enrollment . . . . .Melissa Powell
    mpowell@dakotacare.com
  COBRA . . . . .Joanne Curry
    jcurry@dakotacare.com
  Director, TPA Services .Marti Thompson
    mthompso@dakotacare.com
  VP, Chief Marketing Offc .Tom Nicholson
    tnichols@dakotacare.com
  Compliance/Quality . . . . .Jacqueline Cole
    jcole@dakotacare.com
  Medical Director . . . . .Paul Amundson, MD
    pamundso@dakotacare.com
  Dir, Customer Service . . . . .Jill Jaacks
    jjaacks@dakotacare.com
  VP, Provider Services . . . . .Scott Jamison
    sjamison@dakotacare.com
  Director, Marketing . . . . .Greg Jasmer
    gjasmer@dakotacare.com

Specialty Managed Care Partners
  Prescription benefits - CVS Caremark, Chiropractic - CASD, Transplant - Optum, Dental Benefits - Companion Life, Life Insurance Benefits - Companion Life, Sun Life Standard, STD/LTD - Companion Life
  Enters into Contracts with Regional Business Coalitions: No

1018 Delta Dental of South Dakota

720 N Euclid Avenue
Pierre, SD 57501
Toll-Free: 800-627-3961
Fax: 605-224-0909
sales@deltadentalsd.com
www.deltadentalsd.com
Mailing Address: PO Box 1157, Pierre, SD 57501
Non-Profit Organization: Yes
Year Founded: 1963
Total Enrollment: 54,000,000
State Enrollment: 204,000

Healthplan and Services Defined
  PLAN TYPE: Dental
  Other Type: Dental PPO
  Model Type: Network
  Plan Specialty: ASO, Dental
  Benefits Offered: Dental

Type of Coverage
  Commercial, Individual, Group
  Catastrophic Illness Benefit: None

Geographic Areas Served
  Statewide

Subscriber Information
  Average Monthly Fee Per Subscriber
    (Employee + Employer Contribution):
      Employee Only (Self): Varies
      Employee & 1 Family Member: Varies
      Employee & 2 Family Members: Varies
  Average Annual Deductible Per Subscriber:
    Employee Only (Self): Varies
    Employee & 1 Family Member: Varies
    Employee & 2 Family Members: Varies
  Average Subscriber Co-Payment:
    Prescription Drugs: $0
    Home Health Care: $0
    Nursing Home: $0

Key Personnel
  President & CEO . . . . .Scott Jones
  VP, Operations . . . . .Mick Heckenlable
  VP, Finance . . . . .Kirby Scott
  VP, Underwriting . . . . .Jeff Miller
  VP, Professional Services . . . . .Nance Orsbon
  VP, Information Tech. . . . . .Gene Tetzlaff
  Dir/Media & Public Affair . . . . .Elizabeth Risberg
    415-972-8423

1019 eHealthInsurance Services Inc.

11919 Foundation Place
Gold River, CA 95670
Toll-Free: 800-977-8860
info@ehealthinsurance.com
www.e.healthinsurance.com
Year Founded: 1997

Healthplan and Services Defined
  PLAN TYPE: HMO/PPO
  Benefits Offered: Dental, Life, STD

Type of Coverage
  Commercial, Individual, Medicare

Geographic Areas Served
  All 50 states in the USA and District of Columbia

Key Personnel
  Chairman & CEO . . . . .Gary L. Lauer
  EVP/Business & Corp. Dev. .Bruce Telkamp
  EVP/Chief Technology .Dr. Sheldon X. Wang
  SVP & CFO . . . . .Stuart M. Huizinga
  Pres. of eHealth Gov. Sys . . . . .Samuel C. Gibbs

SVP of Sales & Operations . . . . Robert S. Hurley
Director Public Relations. . . . . Nate Purpura
650-210-3115

1020 First Choice of the Midwest
100 S Spring Avenue
Suite 220
Sioux Falls, SD 57104
Toll-Free: 888-246-9949
Phone: 605-332-5955
Fax: 605-332-5953
info@1choicem.com
www.1choicem.com
Mailing Address: PO Box 5078, Sioux Falls, SD 57117
For Profit Organization: Yes
Year Founded: 1997
Owned by an Integrated Delivery Network (IDN): Yes
Number of Referral/Specialty Physicians: 6,924
Total Enrollment: 87,000
State Enrollment: 25,000

Healthplan and Services Defined
PLAN TYPE: PPO
Model Type: Network, Open Staff
Plan Specialty: ASO, Behavioral Health, Chiropractic, Disease
   Management, EPO, Lab, Radiology, Worker's Compensation
Benefits Offered: Behavioral Health, Chiropractic, Complementary
   Medicine, Home Care, Inpatient SNF, Long-Term Care, Physical
   Therapy, Podiatry, Prescription, Psychiatric, Transplant, Vision,
   Wellness, Worker's Compensation, Durable Medical Equipment

Type of Payment Plans Offered
DFFS

Geographic Areas Served
Colorado, Iowa, North Dakota, Nebraska, Utah, South Dakota,
Minnesota, Montana, Wyoming, and Idaho

Network Qualifications
Pre-Admission Certification: No

Accreditation Certification
TJC, NCQA

Average Claim Compensation
Physician's Fees Charged: 85%
Hospital's Fees Charged: 90%

Specialty Managed Care Partners
Enters into Contracts with Regional Business Coalitions: Yes

1021 Great-West Healthcare South Dakota
Acquired by CIGNA

1022 Humana Health Insurance of South Dakota
11420 Blondo Street
Suite 102
Omaha, NE 68164
Toll-Free: 800-941-1182
Phone: 402-496-3388
Fax: 402-498-2850
www.humana.com
For Profit Organization: Yes

Healthplan and Services Defined
PLAN TYPE: HMO/PPO

Type of Coverage
Commercial, Individual

Accreditation Certification
URAC, NCQA, CORE

1023 Medica: South Dakota
110 South Phillips Ave
Suite 200
Sioux Falls, SD 57104
Toll-Free: 800-841-6753
neducafb@medica.com
www.medica.com
Non-Profit Organization: Yes
Year Founded: 1991
Total Enrollment: 1,600,000

Healthplan and Services Defined
PLAN TYPE: HMO
Model Type: IPA
Benefits Offered: Behavioral Health, Chiropractic, Complementary
   Medicine, Dental, Disease Management, Home Care, Inpatient
   SNF, Physical Therapy, Podiatry, Prescription, Psychiatric,
   Transplant, Vision, Wellness, Worker's Compensation, Nurse line
   chat, visiting nurse, wo

Type of Coverage
Commercial, Individual, Medicare, Medicaid

Type of Payment Plans Offered
POS

Geographic Areas Served
Minnesota, Wisconsin, North Dakota, South Dakota

Accreditation Certification
NCQA

Key Personnel
President/CEO. . . . . .David Tilford
Sr VP/Government Programs .Glenn Andis
Sr VP/Finance. . . . . .Mark Baird
Sr VP/Chief Info Officer . . . . .Scott Booher
Sr VP/Chief Medical Off . . . . .Charles Fazio, MD
Sr VP/Commercial Markets . . . . .Tom Henke
Sr VP/General Counsel . . . . .Jim Jacobson
Sr VP/Operations . . . . .Jana L Johnson
Sr VP/Human Resources . . . . .Deb Knutson
Sr VP/Marketing . . . . .Rob Longendyke
Exec VP/CFO . . . . .Aaron Reynolds

1024 UnitedHealthCare of South Dakota
5901 Lincoln Drive
Edina, MN 55436
Toll-Free: 877-842-3210
www.uhc.com
Subsidiary of: UnitedHealth Group
Year Founded: 1977
Number of Affiliated Hospitals: 4,200
Number of Primary Care Physicians: 460,000
Total Enrollment: 75,000,000

Healthplan and Services Defined
PLAN TYPE: HMO/PPO
Model Type: IPA, Group, Network
Plan Specialty: Lab, Radiology
Benefits Offered: Chiropractic, Dental, Physical Therapy,
   Prescription, Wellness, AD&D, Life, LTD, STD
Offers Demand Management Patient Information Service: Yes

Type of Coverage
Commercial, Individual, Indemnity, Medicare

Geographic Areas Served
Statewide

Network Qualifications
Pre-Admission Certification: Yes

Peer Review Type
Utilization Review: Yes
Second Surgical Opinion: Yes
Case Management: Yes

Publishes and Distributes Report Card: Yes

Accreditation Certification
TJC, NCQA

Specialty Managed Care Partners
Enters into Contracts with Regional Business Coalitions: Yes

1025 Wellmark Blue Cross & Blue Shield of South Dakota

1601 W Madison Street
Sioux Falls, SD 57104
Toll-Free: 800-831-4818
Phone: 605-373-7200
Fax: 605-373-7498
www.wellmark.com
For Profit Organization: Yes
Owned by an Integrated Delivery Network (IDN): Yes
Number of Affiliated Hospitals: 6,000
Number of Primary Care Physicians: 600,000
Total Enrollment: 199,000
State Enrollment: 275,053

Healthplan and Services Defined
PLAN TYPE: PPO
Model Type: Network
Plan Specialty: ASO, Behavioral Health, Chiropractic, Dental, Disease Management, EPO, Lab, PBM, Vision, Radiology, UR
Benefits Offered: Behavioral Health, Chiropractic, Complementary Medicine, Dental, Disease Management, Home Care, Inpatient SNF, Physical Therapy, Podiatry, Prescription, Psychiatric, Transplant, Vision, Wellness, AD&D, Life, LTD, STD

Type of Coverage
Commercial, Individual, Indemnity, Medicare, Supplemental Medicare, Medicaid, Catastrophic
Catastrophic Illness Benefit: Maximum $1M

Geographic Areas Served
South Dakota, Iowa

Publishes and Distributes Report Card: Yes

Accreditation Certification
AAAHC, TJC, URAC, NCQA

Key Personnel
Chairman/CEO . . . . John D Forsyth
President/COO Wellmark SD . . . . Philip M Davis
Media Contact . . . . Rob Schweers
515-248-5683
schweers@wellmark.com

Specialty Managed Care Partners
American Health Ways

HMO/PPO DIRECTORY
TENNESSEE

Health Insurance Coverage Status and Type of Coverage by Age

Category	All Persons		Under 18 years		Under 65 years		65 years and over	
	Number	%	Number	%	Number	%	Number	%
Total population	6,311	-	1,476	-	5,527	-	784	-
Covered by some type of health insurance	5,381 *(85)*	85.3 *(1.1)*	1,360 *(29)*	92.1 *(1.5)*	4,604 *(90)*	83.3 *(1.2)*	777 *(55)*	99.1 *(0.5)*
Covered by private health insurance	3,882 *(104)*	61.5 *(1.5)*	860 *(43)*	58.3 *(2.5)*	3,489 *(114)*	63.1 *(1.8)*	393 *(48)*	50.1 *(4.8)*
Employment based	3,319 *(114)*	52.6 *(1.7)*	769 *(41)*	52.1 *(2.6)*	3,141 *(119)*	56.8 *(2.0)*	177 *(30)*	22.6 *(3.3)*
Own employment based	1,758 *(65)*	27.9 *(1.0)*	0 *(0)*	0.0 *(0.0)*	1,631 *(70)*	29.5 *(1.2)*	127 *(24)*	16.2 *(2.7)*
Direct purchase	686 *(74)*	10.9 *(1.1)*	107 *(20)*	7.2 *(1.3)*	438 *(49)*	7.9 *(0.9)*	249 *(40)*	31.7 *(4.4)*
Covered by government health insurance	2,221 *(85)*	35.2 *(1.4)*	613 *(36)*	41.6 *(2.4)*	1,468 *(85)*	26.6 *(1.6)*	753 *(54)*	96.1 *(1.2)*
Covered by Medicaid	1,098 *(75)*	17.4 *(1.2)*	538 *(34)*	36.4 *(2.6)*	1,038 *(73)*	18.8 *(1.4)*	60 *(15)*	7.6 *(1.7)*
Also by private insurance	162 *(25)*	2.6 *(0.4)*	77 *(14)*	5.2 *(0.9)*	151 *(24)*	2.7 *(0.4)*	10 *(6)*	1.3 *(0.8)*
Covered by Medicare	993 *(58)*	15.7 *(0.9)*	14 *(8)*	1.0 *(0.5)*	243 *(22)*	4.4 *(0.4)*	750 *(53)*	95.7 *(1.3)*
Also by private insurance	424 *(43)*	6.7 *(0.7)*	0 *(0)*	0.0 *(0.0)*	58 *(9)*	1.1 *(0.2)*	366 *(44)*	46.7 *(4.3)*
Also by Medicaid	136 *(20)*	2.1 *(0.3)*	11 *(6)*	0.7 *(0.4)*	76 *(16)*	1.4 *(0.3)*	60 *(15)*	7.6 *(1.7)*
Covered by military health care	355 *(95)*	5.6 *(1.5)*	77 *(38)*	5.2 *(2.5)*	296 *(102)*	5.4 *(1.8)*	59 *(16)*	7.5 *(1.9)*
Not covered at any time during the year	930 *(70)*	14.7 *(1.1)*	116 *(22)*	7.9 *(1.5)*	923 *(69)*	16.7 *(1.2)*	7 *(4)*	0.9 *(0.5)*

Note: Numbers in thousands; figures cover 2010; standard error appears in parenthesis; (b) base less than 75,000; (x) not applicable
Source: U.S. Census Bureau, Current Population Survey, 2011 Annual Social and Economic Supplement. Table HI05. Health Insurance Coverage Status and Type of Coverage by State and Age for All People: 2010

Tennessee

1026 Aetna Health of Tennessee
11675 Great Oaks Way
Suite 500
Alpharetta, GA 30022
Toll-Free: 866-582-9629
www.aetna.com
For Profit Organization: Yes
Year Founded: 1982
Number of Affiliated Hospitals: 11
Number of Primary Care Physicians: 355
Total Enrollment: 24,054
State Enrollment: 24,054

Healthplan and Services Defined
PLAN TYPE: HMO
Other Type: POS
Model Type: Group
Benefits Offered: Behavioral Health, Disease Management,
Prescription, Wellness
Offers Demand Management Patient Information Service: Yes

Type of Coverage
Commercial

Geographic Areas Served
Statewide

Subscriber Information
Average Monthly Fee Per Subscriber
(Employee + Employer Contribution):
Employee Only (Self): $56.09
Employee & 2 Family Members: $199.61
Medicare: $56.09
Average Annual Deductible Per Subscriber:
Employee Only (Self): None
Employee & 1 Family Member: None
Employee & 2 Family Members: None
Medicare: None
Average Subscriber Co-Payment:
Primary Care Physician: $20.00
Prescription Drugs: $10/20
Hospital ER: $50.00
Home Health Care: $0
Home Health Care Max. Days/Visits Covered: Unlimited
Nursing Home: $0
Nursing Home Max. Days/Visits Covered: Unlimited

Publishes and Distributes Report Card: Yes

Accreditation Certification
NCQA
TJC Accreditation, Medicare Approved, Utilization Review,
Pre-Admission Certification, State Licensure, Quality Assurance
Program

Key Personnel
President/CEO...............................Robert Wolfkiel
CFO......................................Chris Sluder
Network Manager ....Barbara Robinson
Account Executive...........................Mike Watson

Employer References
Federal Employees Health Plan

1027 Amerigroup Tennessee
22 Century Blvd
Suite 310
Nashville, TN 37214
Toll-Free: 866-311-4287
www.realsolutions.com
For Profit Organization: Yes
Year Founded: 2007

Total Enrollment: 1,900,000

Healthplan and Services Defined
PLAN TYPE: HMO
Type of Coverage
TennCare
Geographic Areas Served
Middle Tennessee

1028 Assurant Employee Benefits: Tennessee
6055 Primacy Parkway
Suite 330
Memphis, TN 38119-5724
Phone: 901-685-3111
benefits@assurant.com
www.assurantemployeebenefits.com
Subsidiary of: Assurant, Inc
For Profit Organization: Yes
Number of Primary Care Physicians: 112,000
Total Enrollment: 47,000

Healthplan and Services Defined
PLAN TYPE: Multiple
Plan Specialty: Dental, Vision, Long & Short-Term Disability
Benefits Offered: Dental, Vision, Wellness, AD&D, Life, LTD, STD

Type of Coverage
Commercial, Indemnity, Individual Dental Plans

Geographic Areas Served
Statewide

Subscriber Information
Average Monthly Fee Per Subscriber
(Employee + Employer Contribution):
Employee Only (Self): Varies by plan

Key Personnel
Manager ....Craig Wright
PR Specialist............................Megan Hutchison
816-556-7815
megan.hutchison@assurant.com

1029 Baptist Health Services Group
350 N Humphreys Boulevard
4th Floor
Memphis, TN 38120
Toll-Free: 800-522-2474
Phone: 901-227-2474
Fax: 901-227-2420
bhsginfo@bmhcc.org
www.bhsgonline.org
Subsidiary of: Baptist Memorial Health Care Corporation
Non-Profit Organization: Yes
Year Founded: 1984
Number of Affiliated Hospitals: 52
Number of Primary Care Physicians: 1,007
Number of Referral/Specialty Physicians: 2,073
Total Enrollment: 423,244

Healthplan and Services Defined
PLAN TYPE: Other
Model Type: Network, Provider Spons. Network
Plan Specialty: Worker's Compensation
Offers Demand Management Patient Information Service: No

Geographic Areas Served
E Arkansas, SW Kentucky, N Mississipi, SE Missouri, and W
Tennessee

Subscriber Information
Average Monthly Fee Per Subscriber
(Employee + Employer Contribution):
Employee Only (Self): n/a
Average Annual Deductible Per Subscriber:

Employee Only (Self): n/a
Average Subscriber Co-Payment:
Primary Care Physician: n/a

Publishes and Distributes Report Card: No

Key Personnel
CEO . . . . .David R Elliott
System Director, Sales . . . . .Kim Manning

Average Claim Compensation
Physician's Fees Charged: 1%
Hospital's Fees Charged: 1%

Specialty Managed Care Partners
Enters into Contracts with Regional Business Coalitions: Yes

1030 Blue Cross & Blue Shield of Tennessee

1 Cameron Hill Circle
Chattanooga, TN 37402
Toll-Free: 800-565-9140
Phone: 423-755-5600
Fax: 423-535-6255
www.bcbst.com
Secondary Address: 85 North Danny Thomas Blvd, Memphis, TN
38103-2398
Non-Profit Organization: Yes
Year Founded: 1945
Number of Affiliated Hospitals: 130
Number of Primary Care Physicians: 2,490
Number of Referral/Specialty Physicians: 15,000
Total Enrollment: 3,000,000
State Enrollment: 3,000,000

Healthplan and Services Defined
PLAN TYPE: HMO/PPO
Benefits Offered: Dental, Disease Management, Vision, Wellness

Type of Coverage
Medicaid

Key Personnel
President & CEO . . . . .Vicky Gregg
EVP, CFO . . . . .John Giblin
EVP, President Govt Bus . . . . .Steve Coulter, MD
EVP, Pres Commercial Bus. .Joan Harp
SVP, Chief Info Officer . . . . .Nick Coussoule
SVP, People Services . . . . .Ron Harr
SVP, Treasurer . . . . .Chris Hunter
SVP, Chief Strategy Offc . . . . .Bob Worthington
SVP, Chief Compliance . . . . .Bill Young

Specialty Managed Care Partners
Magellen Health Services

Employer References
State, local and government employees

1031 Cariten Healthcare

1420 Centerpoint Boulevard
Knoxville, TN 37932
Toll-Free: 800-793-1495
Phone: 865-470-7470
Fax: 865-670-7255
www.cariten.com
Secondary Address: 101 Medtech Parkway, Suite 404, Johnson City,
TN 37604
Subsidiary of: A Humana Affiliate
For Profit Organization: Yes
Year Founded: 1985
Number of Affiliated Hospitals: 60
Number of Primary Care Physicians: 1,500
Number of Referral/Specialty Physicians: 6,000
Total Enrollment: 73,000
State Enrollment: 14,477

Healthplan and Services Defined
PLAN TYPE: Multiple
Other Type: HMO/POS
Plan Specialty: Behavioral Health, Chiropractic, Disease
Management, Vision, Radiology, Worker's Compensation, UR
Benefits Offered: Behavioral Health, Chiropractic, Disease
Management, Home Care, Inpatient SNF, Long-Term Care,
Physical Therapy, Podiatry, Prescription, Psychiatric, Transplant,
Vision, Wellness, Worker's Compensation, EAP, Voc Rehab

Type of Coverage
Commercial, Medicare, Medicaid, Catastrophic
Catastrophic Illness Benefit: Covered

Type of Payment Plans Offered
POS, DFFS, Capitated, FFS, Combination FFS & DFFS

Geographic Areas Served
28 counties in East Tennessee

Subscriber Information
Average Monthly Fee Per Subscriber
(Employee + Employer Contribution):
Medicare: Varies
Average Annual Deductible Per Subscriber:
Medicare: Varies
Average Subscriber Co-Payment:
Primary Care Physician: $20.00
Prescription Drugs: $10/20/35
Hospital ER: $100.00
Home Health Care Max. Days/Visits Covered: 100 days
Nursing Home Max. Days/Visits Covered: 100 days

Network Qualifications
Pre-Admission Certification: Yes

Peer Review Type
Utilization Review: Yes
Case Management: Yes

Publishes and Distributes Report Card: Yes

Accreditation Certification
URAC, NCQA

Key Personnel
President and CEO . . . . .Anthony L Spezia
CFO . . . . .Jeff Collake
Director Operations . . . . .Linda Lyle
COO . . . . .Douglas E Haaland
Network Contracting Mgr . . . . .Pat Gillespie
Dir, Provider Relations . . . . .Pat Gillespie
Director, Pharmacy. .John Cuifo, DPh
Chairman. . . . . .Larry Martin
Vice Chairman .Francis H Olmstead, Jr
Materials Management . . . . .Mary Cogar
Medical Director . . . . .George Andrews, MD
Member Services Manager . . . . .Theresa Christian-Wills
VP/MIS . . . . .Barry Robbins
Marketing Director. . . . . .Christy Newman
Sales Manager . . . . .Lisa Johnson

Average Claim Compensation
Physician's Fees Charged: 25%
Hospital's Fees Charged: 30%

Specialty Managed Care Partners
Express Scripts
Enters into Contracts with Regional Business Coalitions: Yes
Healthcare 21 Business Coalition

1032 Cariten Preferred

1420 Centerpoint Boulevard
Knoxville, TN 37932
Toll-Free: 800-793-1495
Phone: 865-470-7470
Fax: 865-670-7255
www.cariten.com

Secondary Address: 6101 Enterprise Park Drive, Suite 600, Chattanooga, TN 37416
Subsidiary of: A Humana Affiliate
For Profit Organization: Yes
Year Founded: 1985
Number of Affiliated Hospitals: 69
Number of Primary Care Physicians: 20,016
Total Enrollment: 50,919
State Enrollment: 50,919

Healthplan and Services Defined
  PLAN TYPE: PPO
  Plan Specialty: Behavioral Health, Chiropractic, Disease Management, Vision, Radiology, Worker's Compensation, UR
  Benefits Offered: Behavioral Health, Chiropractic, Disease Management, Home Care, Inpatient SNF, Long-Term Care, Physical Therapy, Podiatry, Prescription, Psychiatric, Transplant, Vision, Wellness, Worker's Compensation, AD&D, Life, LTD, STD, EAP, Voc Rehab

Type of Coverage
  Commercial, Medicare, Medicaid

Type of Payment Plans Offered
  POS, DFFS, Capitated, Combination FFS & DFFS

Geographic Areas Served
  35 counties in East Tennessee

Peer Review Type
  Utilization Review: Yes
  Case Management: Yes

Accreditation Certification
  URAC, NCQA

Key Personnel
  President/CEO . . . . Lance Hunsinger
  CFO . . . . Jeff Collake
  Director Operations . . . . Linda Lyle
  COO . . . . Douglas E Haaland
  Dir, Provider Relations . . . . Pat Gillespie
  Network Contracting Mgr . . . . Pat Gillespie
  Director, Pharmacy . . . . John Cuifo, DPh
  Marketing Director . . . . Christy Newman
  Materials Management . . . . Mary Cogar
  Medical Director . . . . George Andrews, MD
  Member Services Manager . . . . Theresa Christian-Wills
  Information Systems . . . . Barry Robbins, VPMIS
  Sales Manager . . . . Lisa Johnson

Specialty Managed Care Partners
  ProCare Rx

1033 CIGNA HealthCare of Tennessee

1111 Market Street
Chattanooga, TN 37402
Toll-Free: 866-438-2446
Phone: 423-321-5550
Fax: 423-321-4861
www.cigna.com
Secondary Address: 3400 Players Club Parkway, Suite 140, Memphis, TN 38125, 901-748-4100
For Profit Organization: Yes
Year Founded: 1988
Owned by an Integrated Delivery Network (IDN): Yes
Number of Affiliated Hospitals: 300
Number of Primary Care Physicians: 15,200
Total Enrollment: 229,356
State Enrollment: 229,356

Healthplan and Services Defined
  PLAN TYPE: HMO
  Other Type: POS
  Model Type: Network

Plan Specialty: ASO, Behavioral Health, Chiropractic, Dental, Disease Management, EPO, Lab, MSO, PBM, Vision, Radiology, UR
Benefits Offered: Behavioral Health, Chiropractic, Complementary Medicine, Dental, Disease Management, Home Care, Long-Term Care, Physical Therapy, Podiatry, Prescription, Psychiatric, Transplant, Vision, Wellness, AD&D, Life, LTD, STD, Women's and Men's Health Programs
Offers Demand Management Patient Information Service: Yes
DMPI Services Offered: Language Links Service, 24 hour Health Information Line, Health Information Library, Automated ReferralLine

Type of Coverage
  Commercial, Indemnity, Medicare, Supplemental Medicare, Medicaid, Catastrophic
  Catastrophic Illness Benefit: Varies per case

Type of Payment Plans Offered
  DFFS

Geographic Areas Served
  Fayette, Shelby, Tipton, Benton, Carroll, Chester, Crockett, Decatur, Dyer, Gibson, Hardin, Haywood, Henderson, Henry, Lake, Lauderdale, Madison, McNairy, Obion and Tipton counties of Tennessee

Network Qualifications
  Pre-Admission Certification: Yes

Peer Review Type
  Second Surgical Opinion: Yes

Publishes and Distributes Report Card: Yes

Accreditation Certification
  AAAHC, TJC, URAC, AAPI, NCQA

Key Personnel
  CEO . . . . Ed Hanaway
  Sr Contract Negotiator . . . . Chuck Utterback
  Marketing . . . . Patrick Hoffman

Specialty Managed Care Partners
  Enters into Contracts with Regional Business Coalitions: No

1034 Delta Dental of Tennessee

240 Venture Circle
Nashville, TN 37228-1699
Toll-Free: 800-233-3104
Fax: 615-244-8108
www.deltadentaltn.com
Non-Profit Organization: Yes
Year Founded: 1965
Total Enrollment: 1,200,000

Healthplan and Services Defined
  PLAN TYPE: Dental
  Other Type: Dental PPO
  Model Type: Network
  Plan Specialty: ASO, Dental, Fully-Insured
  Benefits Offered: Dental

Type of Coverage
  Commercial, Individual, Group
  Catastrophic Illness Benefit: None

Geographic Areas Served
  Statewide

Subscriber Information
  Average Monthly Fee Per Subscriber
    (Employee + Employer Contribution):
      Employee Only (Self): Varies
      Employee & 1 Family Member: Varies
      Employee & 2 Family Members: Varies
  Average Annual Deductible Per Subscriber:
      Employee Only (Self): Varies
      Employee & 1 Family Member: Varies
      Employee & 2 Family Members: Varies

Average Subscriber Co-Payment:
    Prescription Drugs: $0
    Home Health Care: $0
    Nursing Home: $0

Accreditation Certification
  Website Annual Report

Key Personnel
  President & CEO .... Phil Wenk
  SVP, Operations .... Kaye Martin
  SVP, Employee Relations .... Pam Dishman
  SVP, CFO .... Tom Perry

1035 eHealthInsurance Services Inc.

11919 Foundation Place
Gold River, CA 95670
Toll-Free: 800-977-8860
info@ehealthinsurance.com
www.e.healthinsurance.com
Year Founded: 1997

Healthplan and Services Defined
  PLAN TYPE: HMO/PPO
  Benefits Offered: Dental, Life, STD

Type of Coverage
  Commercial, Individual, Medicare

Geographic Areas Served
  All 50 states in the USA and District of Columbia

Key Personnel
  Chairman & CEO .... Gary L. Lauer
  EVP/Business & Corp. Dev. .... Bruce Telkamp
  EVP/Chief Technology .... Dr. Sheldon X. Wang
  SVP & CFO .... Stuart M. Huizinga
  Pres. of eHealth Gov. Sys .... Samuel C. Gibbs
  SVP of Sales & Operations .... Robert S. Hurley
  Director Public Relations .... Nate Purpura
    650-210-3115

1036 Health Choice LLC

1661 International Place
Suite 150
Memphis, TN 38120
Toll-Free: 888-821-5625
Phone: 901-821-6700
Fax: 901-821-4900
info@myhealthchoice.com
www.myhealthchoice.com
Year Founded: 1985
Number of Affiliated Hospitals: 24
Number of Primary Care Physicians: 1,408
Total Enrollment: 518,000
State Enrollment: 518,000

Healthplan and Services Defined
  PLAN TYPE: PPO
  Model Type: PHO
  Plan Specialty: ASO, Behavioral Health, Chiropractic, Disease Management, EPO, Lab, MSO, PBM, Radiology, Worker's Compensation, UR

Type of Payment Plans Offered
  DFFS, FFS, Combination FFS & DFFS

Geographic Areas Served
  Tennessee: Shelby, Tipton, Fayette; Arkansas: Crittenden, Cross; Mississippi: Tunica, Desoto; Missouri: Pemiscott

Network Qualifications
  Pre-Admission Certification: Yes

Peer Review Type
  Utilization Review: Yes
  Second Surgical Opinion: Yes

Case Management: Yes

Accreditation Certification
  AAAHC
  TJC Accreditation, Medicare Approved, Utilization Review, Pre-Admission Certification, State Licensure, Quality Assurance Program

Key Personnel
  President/CEO .... Bill Breen
    901-821-6700
    breenb@myhealthchoice.com
  COO .... Jan Dickson
    901-821-6700
    dicksonj@myhealthchoice.com
  Manager Contracting .... Pat Abernathy
    801-821-6720
    abernathyp@myhealthchoice.com
  CEO MetroCare .... Jonna Elzen
    901-360-1360
  VP Customer Development .... Wayne Lohman
    901-821-6712
    lohmanw@myhealthchoice.com
  Chief Medical Officer .... Gail Thurmond, MD
    901-821-6733
    thurmondg@myhealthchoice.com
  Director Member Services .... Diana Hampton
    901-821-6742
    hamptond@myhealthchoice.com
  VP Info Systems .... Marty Robbins
    901-821-6734
    robbinsm@myhealthchoice.com
  Director Provider Services .... Carole Caylor
    901-255-9810
    caylorc@myhealthchoice.com

Specialty Managed Care Partners
  Lakeside Behavioral Health, Med Impact PEM
  Memphis Business Group On Health

Employer References
  City of Memphis Employees, Shelby County Government, Memphis Light Gas and Water, Methodist HealthCare Associates, St. Jude Children's Hospital

1037 HealthPartners

1804 Highway 45 Bypass
Suite 400
Jackson, TN 38305
Toll-Free: 800-694-7888
Phone: 731-512-1500
Fax: 731-661-0176
www.hptpa.com
Subsidiary of: West Tennessee Healthcare
Non-Profit Organization: Yes
Number of Affiliated Hospitals: 127
Number of Primary Care Physicians: 3,357
Total Enrollment: 48,477
State Enrollment: 48,477

Healthplan and Services Defined
  PLAN TYPE: PPO
  Other Type: TPA
  Plan Specialty: Worker's Compensation
  Benefits Offered: Dental, Disease Management, Prescription, Wellness
  Offers Demand Management Patient Information Service: Yes
  DMPI Services Offered: Classes and Events

Type of Coverage
  Commercial, Individual

Geographic Areas Served
  18 counties in West Tennessee

Peer Review Type
Utilization Review: Yes
Case Management: Yes

Key Personnel
CEO . . . . .Jim Dockins
President . . . . .Bill Jones
COO . . . . .Jeff Coley
CFO . . . . .Norma Shipp
CMO. . . . . .Dr Paul Caudill
Provider Relations. . . . . .Dan Rainer
Marketing. . . . . .Sherri Kilburn
Member Relations . . . . .Candace Yates

Specialty Managed Care Partners
Express Scripts

1038 HealthSpring Prescription Drug Plan
44 Vantage Way
Suite 300
Nashville, TN 37228
Toll-Free: 866-593-4468
Phone: 615-291-7000
www.healthspring.com

Healthplan and Services Defined
PLAN TYPE: Medicare
Benefits Offered: Prescription

Type of Coverage
Individual, Medicare

Geographic Areas Served
Available within multiple states

Subscriber Information
Average Monthly Fee Per Subscriber
(Employee + Employer Contribution):
Employee Only (Self): Varies
Medicare: Varies
Average Annual Deductible Per Subscriber:
Employee Only (Self): Varies
Medicare: Varies
Average Subscriber Co-Payment:
Primary Care Physician: Varies
Non-Network Physician: Varies
Prescription Drugs: Varies
Hospital ER: Varies
Home Health Care: Varies
Home Health Care Max. Days/Visits Covered: Varies
Nursing Home: Varies
Nursing Home Max. Days/Visits Covered: Varies

Key Personnel
President. . . . . .M Shawn Morris

1039 HealthSpring: Corporate Offices
9009 Carothers Parkway
Suite 501
Franklin, TN 37067
Toll-Free: 866-593-4468
Phone: 615-291-7000
Fax: 615-401-4566
info@myhealthspring.com
www.healthspring.com
Secondary Address: 44 Vantage Way, Suite 300, Nashville, TN
37228-1513
For Profit Organization: Yes
Year Founded: 1995
Number of Affiliated Hospitals: 42
Number of Primary Care Physicians: 4,300
Total Enrollment: 345,000
State Enrollment: 17,844

Healthplan and Services Defined
PLAN TYPE: Medicare
Model Type: Network
Plan Specialty: ASO, EPO
Benefits Offered: Behavioral Health, Chiropractic, Disease
Management, Home Care, Inpatient SNF, Physical Therapy,
Podiatry, Prescription, Psychiatric, Transplant, Vision

Type of Coverage
Commercial, Medicare, Supplemental Medicare, Catastrophic,
Medicare PPO
Catastrophic Illness Benefit: Covered

Type of Payment Plans Offered
POS, DFFS, Capitated, Combination FFS & DFFS

Geographic Areas Served
Tennessee, Northern Mississippi, Northern Georgia

Subscriber Information
Average Monthly Fee Per Subscriber
(Employee + Employer Contribution):
Employee Only (Self): Varies by plan
Medicare: $0
Average Subscriber Co-Payment:
Primary Care Physician: Varies by plan

Network Qualifications
Minimum Years of Practice: 3
Pre-Admission Certification: Yes

Peer Review Type
Utilization Review: Yes
Case Management: Yes

Accreditation Certification
AAAHC, URAC

Key Personnel
Chairman/CEO . . . . .Herbert Fritch
President. . . . . .Michael Mirt
EVP/CFO. . . . . .Karey Witty
SVP/General Counsel . . . . .J Gentry Barden
SVP/Chief Actuary . . . . .David L Terry, Jr
EVP/COO . . . . .Mark Tullock
Chief Strategy Officer. . . . . .Sharad Mansukani, MD
SVP/Chief Medical Officer . . . . .Dirk O Wales, MD
Corp Mgr, Media Relations . . . . .Jolene Sharp
615-234-6710
jolene.sharp@healthspring.com

Average Claim Compensation
Physician's Fees Charged: 65%
Hospital's Fees Charged: 80%

Specialty Managed Care Partners
Magellaw, Black Vision, MedImpact

Employer References
Lifeway, Ingram Industries, AmSouth Banks

1040 Humana Health Insurance of Tennessee
6075 Poplar Avenue
Suite 221
Memphis, TN 38119
Toll-Free: 877-365-1197
Phone: 901-820-5738
Fax: 920-632-0760
www.humana.com
Secondary Address: 320 Seven Springs Way, Suite 200, Brentwood,
TN 37027
For Profit Organization: Yes
Total Enrollment: 172,000
State Enrollment: 35,800

Healthplan and Services Defined
PLAN TYPE: HMO/PPO
Plan Specialty: ASO
Benefits Offered: Disease Management, Prescription, Wellness

Type of Coverage
Commercial, Individual

Geographic Areas Served
Tennessee

Accreditation Certification
URAC, NCQA, CORE

Key Personnel
CEO . . . . .Rick Remmers

Specialty Managed Care Partners
Caremark Rx

Employer References
Tricare

1041 Initial Group

6556 Jocelyn Hollow Road
Nashville, TN 37205
Toll-Free: 866-511-0933
Phone: 615-352-8722
Fax: 615-352-8782
information@initialgroup.com
www.initialgroup.com
Mailing Address: PO Box 3818, Knoxville, TN 37927-3818
Subsidiary of: Baptist Health System of East Tennessee
For Profit Organization: Yes
Year Founded: 1994
Number of Affiliated Hospitals: 75
Number of Primary Care Physicians: 5,000
Number of Referral/Specialty Physicians: 4,000
Total Enrollment: 200,000
State Enrollment: 106,364

Healthplan and Services Defined
PLAN TYPE: PPO
Model Type: Network
Plan Specialty: Behavioral Health, Lab, Radiology, Worker's
Compensation
Benefits Offered: Behavioral Health, Home Care, Inpatient SNF,
Physical Therapy, Podiatry, Psychiatric, Transplant, Wellness,
Worker's Compensation, Life, LTD

Type of Coverage
Commercial, Medicare
Catastrophic Illness Benefit: Covered

Type of Payment Plans Offered
POS

Geographic Areas Served
Eastern Tennessee

Subscriber Information
Average Monthly Fee Per Subscriber
(Employee + Employer Contribution):
Employee Only (Self): Varies by plan
Average Annual Deductible Per Subscriber:
Employee Only (Self): $250.00
Employee & 2 Family Members: $500.00
Average Subscriber Co-Payment:
Primary Care Physician: $15.00
Prescription Drugs: $5.00/10.00
Hospital ER: $30.00
Home Health Care: $30.00

Network Qualifications
Pre-Admission Certification: Yes

Peer Review Type
Utilization Review: Yes
Second Surgical Opinion: Yes
Case Management: Yes

Accreditation Certification
URAC

TJC Accreditation, Medicare Approved, Utilization Review,
Pre-Admission Certification, State Licensure, Quality Assurance
Program

Key Personnel
President/CEO . . . . .Lisa J Wear
865-546-1893
COO . . . . .Cheryl Wilburn
865-546-1893
Marketing . . . . .Mark Field
865-546-1893
Information Services . . . . .Julles Tarkett
865-546-1893
Provider Services . . . . .Meredith Leeger
865-546-1893
Sales/Marketing. . . . . .Mark Field
865-546-1893

Specialty Managed Care Partners
Health System

1042 John Deere Health

2033 Madowview Lane
Suite 300
Kingsport, TN 37660
Toll-Free: 888-432-3373
Phone: 423-378-5122
Fax: 865-690-2741
u.s.employeebenefits@johndeere.com
www.johndeerehealth.com
Subsidiary of: Healty Directions
For Profit Organization: Yes
Year Founded: 1985
Number of Affiliated Hospitals: 26
Number of Primary Care Physicians: 1,126
Number of Referral/Specialty Physicians: 1,581
Total Enrollment: 551,309
State Enrollment: 251,418

Healthplan and Services Defined
PLAN TYPE: HMO/PPO
Other Type: HSA
Model Type: IPA
Benefits Offered: Disease Management, Prescription, Wellness
Offers Demand Management Patient Information Service: Yes

Type of Coverage
Commercial, Medicare, Medicaid

Type of Payment Plans Offered
POS, DFFS

Geographic Areas Served
Tennessee and Virginia

Network Qualifications
Pre-Admission Certification: Yes

Peer Review Type
Utilization Review: Yes

Publishes and Distributes Report Card: Yes

Accreditation Certification
NCQA
TJC Accreditation, Medicare Approved, Utilization Review,
Pre-Admission Certification, State Licensure, Quality Assurance
Program

Key Personnel
President/CEO. . . . . .Lowell Crawford
Manager. . . . . .Garland Scott

Specialty Managed Care Partners
Enters into Contracts with Regional Business Coalitions: Yes

1043 Signature Health Alliance

2630 Elm Hill Pike
Suite 117
Nashville, TN 37214
Toll-Free: 800-264-3060
Phone: 615-872-8796
Fax: 615-872-8938
info@signaturehealth.com
www.signaturehealth.com
Mailing Address: PO Box 22419, Nashville, TN 37202-2419
Subsidiary of: Bluegrass Family Health
For Profit Organization: Yes
Year Founded: 1984
Number of Affiliated Hospitals: 191
Number of Primary Care Physicians: 20,000
Number of Referral/Specialty Physicians: 13,192
Total Enrollment: 80,000
State Enrollment: 379,224

Healthplan and Services Defined
PLAN TYPE: PPO
Model Type: Network

Geographic Areas Served
Statewide

Accreditation Certification
State Licensure

Key Personnel
Principal.................................Susan Aldreridge
Vice President...............................Mindy Brown
Director ....Deona Mitchel
Marketing ....Victoria Prendergast
    vprendergast@signaturehealth.com

Specialty Managed Care Partners
Enters into Contracts with Regional Business Coalitions: Yes

1044 UnitedHealthCare of Tennessee

10 Cadillac Drive
Suite 200
Brentwood, TN 37027
Toll-Free: 800-695-1273
Phone: 615-372-3622
Fax: 615-372-3564
www.uhc.com
Secondary Address: 633 Chestnut Street, Suite 1010, Chattanooga, TN
    37450, 800-945-0143
Subsidiary of: UnitedHealth Group
For Profit Organization: Yes
Year Founded: 1992
Number of Affiliated Hospitals: 137
Number of Primary Care Physicians: 4,000
Number of Referral/Specialty Physicians: 3,369
Total Enrollment: 75,000,000
State Enrollment: 270,665

Healthplan and Services Defined
PLAN TYPE: HMO/PPO
Model Type: Fully Integrated
Plan Specialty: ASO, Behavioral Health, Chiropractic, Dental,
    Disease Management, EPO, Lab, MSO, PBM, Vision, Radiology,
    UR
Benefits Offered: Dental, Prescription, Vision, AD&D, Life, LTD,
    STD
Offers Demand Management Patient Information Service: Yes

Type of Coverage
Commercial, Individual, Indemnity, Medicare
Catastrophic Illness Benefit: Covered

Geographic Areas Served
Statewide

Network Qualifications
Pre-Admission Certification: Yes

Accreditation Certification
NCQA

Key Personnel
Media Contact...............................Roger Rollman
    roger_f_rollman@uhc.com

Specialty Managed Care Partners
United Health Group, Spectra, United Behavioral Health
Enters into Contracts with Regional Business Coalitions: Yes

1045 Windsor Medicare Extra

7100 Commerce Way
Suite 285
Brentwood, TN 37027
Toll-Free: 800-316-2273
Phone: 615-782-7800
Fax: 615-782-7828
www.windsormedicareextra.com
Total Enrollment: 75,000

Healthplan and Services Defined
PLAN TYPE: Medicare
Benefits Offered: Chiropractic, Dental, Disease Management, Home
    Care, Inpatient SNF, Physical Therapy, Podiatry, Prescription,
    Psychiatric, Vision, Wellness

Type of Coverage
Individual, Medicare

Geographic Areas Served
Available only within Tennessee

Subscriber Information
Average Monthly Fee Per Subscriber
    (Employee + Employer Contribution):
        Employee Only (Self): Varies
        Medicare: Varies
Average Annual Deductible Per Subscriber:
        Employee Only (Self): Varies
        Medicare: Varies
Average Subscriber Co-Payment:
        Primary Care Physician: Varies
        Non-Network Physician: Varies
        Prescription Drugs: Varies
        Hospital ER: Varies
        Home Health Care: Varies
        Home Health Care Max. Days/Visits Covered: Varies
        Nursing Home: Varies
        Nursing Home Max. Days/Visits Covered: Varies

Key Personnel
President ....Michael Bailey
Chairman/CEO...............................Philip Hertik
EVP/CFO ....Willis E Jones, III
VP, Admin & Claims........................Robin Bradley
VP, Network Services...............Jenifer L Mariencheckr, RN
CEO, Windsor HomeCare Net ....Bart Cunningham
VP, Marketing ....John Sowell
    615-782-7938
    jsowell@windsorhealthgroup.com
Chief Medical Officer ....James Bracikowski, MD
VP, Customer Service ....Pat Sheridan
Chief Infomation Officer ....Steve Yates
VP, Information Tech.........................Barry Shermer
VP, Sales...................................Gary W Adkins
Media Contact ....John Sowell
    615-782-7938
    jsowell@windsorhealthgroup.com

Health Insurance Coverage Status and Type of Coverage by Age

Category	All Persons		Under 18 years		Under 65 years		65 years and over	
	Number	%	Number	%	Number	%	Number	%
Total population	25,154	-	7,073	-	22,628	-	2,526	-
Covered by some type of health insurance	18,973 *(216)*	75.4 *(0.8)*	5,920 *(65)*	83.7 *(0.9)*	16,548 *(234)*	73.1 *(0.9)*	2,425 *(84)*	96.0 *(0.7)*
Covered by private health insurance	13,867 *(301)*	55.1 *(1.1)*	3,329 *(99)*	47.1 *(1.4)*	12,645 *(310)*	55.9 *(1.2)*	1,222 *(76)*	48.4 *(2.3)*
Employment based	12,385 *(290)*	49.2 *(1.1)*	3,137 *(98)*	44.3 *(1.4)*	11,627 *(290)*	51.4 *(1.2)*	758 *(61)*	30.0 *(2.2)*
Own employment based	6,444 *(145)*	25.6 *(0.6)*	13 *(6)*	0.2 *(0.1)*	5,865 *(148)*	25.9 *(0.6)*	579 *(48)*	22.9 *(1.8)*
Direct purchase	1,545 *(103)*	6.1 *(0.4)*	214 *(28)*	3.0 *(0.4)*	1,019 *(91)*	4.5 *(0.4)*	526 *(47)*	20.8 *(1.6)*
Covered by government health insurance	7,026 *(173)*	27.9 *(0.7)*	2,959 *(96)*	41.8 *(1.3)*	4,714 *(136)*	20.8 *(0.6)*	2,312 *(82)*	91.5 *(1.0)*
Covered by Medicaid	3,980 *(138)*	15.8 *(0.6)*	2,736 *(99)*	38.7 *(1.4)*	3,692 *(132)*	16.3 *(0.6)*	288 *(27)*	11.4 *(1.1)*
Also by private insurance	453 *(40)*	1.8 *(0.2)*	253 *(29)*	3.6 *(0.4)*	384 *(37)*	1.7 *(0.2)*	69 *(16)*	2.7 *(0.6)*
Covered by Medicare	2,852 *(90)*	11.3 *(0.4)*	64 *(17)*	0.9 *(0.2)*	550 *(38)*	2.4 *(0.2)*	2,302 *(82)*	91.1 *(1.1)*
Also by private insurance	1,199 *(73)*	4.8 *(0.3)*	11 *(4)*	0.2 *(0.1)*	93 *(15)*	0.4 *(0.1)*	1,106 *(72)*	43.8 *(2.2)*
Also by Medicaid	502 *(38)*	2.0 *(0.2)*	29 *(11)*	0.4 *(0.2)*	218 *(25)*	1.0 *(0.1)*	284 *(27)*	11.3 *(1.1)*
Covered by military health care	1,027 *(90)*	4.1 *(0.4)*	207 *(35)*	2.9 *(0.5)*	757 *(80)*	3.3 *(0.4)*	271 *(29)*	10.7 *(1.1)*
Not covered at any time during the year	6,181 *(196)*	24.6 *(0.8)*	1,153 *(67)*	16.3 *(0.9)*	6,081 *(191)*	26.9 *(0.9)*	101 *(17)*	4.0 *(0.7)*

Note: Numbers in thousands; figures cover 2010; standard error appears in parenthesis; (b) base less than 75,000; (x) not applicable
Source: U.S. Census Bureau, Current Population Survey, 2011 Annual Social and Economic Supplement. Table HI05. Health Insurance Coverage Status and Type of Coverage by State and Age for All People: 2010

Texas

1046 Aetna Health of Texas
2777 Stemmons Freeway
Suite 300
Dallas, TX 75207
Toll-Free: 866-582-9629
www.aetna.com
Year Founded: 1997
Number of Affiliated Hospitals: 8
Number of Primary Care Physicians: 21,166
Total Enrollment: 294,566
State Enrollment: 294,566

Healthplan and Services Defined
PLAN TYPE: HMO
Other Type: POS
Model Type: IPA
Benefits Offered: Dental, Disease Management, Prescription,
Transplant, Vision, Wellness, AD&D, Life, LTD, STD, Alternative
Health Care Program, Informed Health Line, Women's Health
Programs, National Medical Excellence Program

Type of Payment Plans Offered
POS, FFS

Geographic Areas Served
Statewide

Subscriber Information
Average Subscriber Co-Payment:
Primary Care Physician: $15.00
Non-Network Physician: $25.00
Prescription Drugs: $15/25/40
Hospital ER: $100.00

Peer Review Type
Second Surgical Opinion: Yes
Case Management: Yes

Publishes and Distributes Report Card: Yes

Accreditation Certification
NCQA
TJC Accreditation, Medicare Approved, Utilization Review,
Pre-Admission Certification, State Licensure, Quality Assurance
Program

Key Personnel
CFO . . . . .David Oster
VP/San Antonio. . . . . .Lynne McKirdy
Medical Affairs. . . . . .Jay Lawrence, MD
Director/Sales. . . . . .Alex Herrera
210-515-2671
HerraA@aetna.com

1047 Alliance Regional Health Network
1501 S. Coulter
Amarillo, TX 79175
Toll-Free: 800-687-8007
Phone: 806-351-5151
Fax: 806-354-1122
www.nwtexashealthcare.com/alliance-ppo-network
Subsidiary of: Northwest Texas Healthcare System
For Profit Organization: Yes
Year Founded: 1986
Number of Affiliated Hospitals: 25
Number of Primary Care Physicians: 1,000
Number of Referral/Specialty Physicians: 900
Total Enrollment: 80,000
State Enrollment: 79,500

Healthplan and Services Defined
PLAN TYPE: PPO
Model Type: Network

Plan Specialty: Behavioral Health, Radiology
Benefits Offered: Disease Management, Wellness, Worker's
Compensation, Occupational therapy

Geographic Areas Served
Amraillo, Lubbock and the Panhandle region

Network Qualifications
Pre-Admission Certification: Yes

Accreditation Certification
Medicare Approved, Utilization Review, State Licensure, Quality
Assurance Program

Key Personnel
CEO. . . . . .Frank Lopez
806-354-1000
Network Contracting . . . . .Diana Avila
806-351-5151
Credentialing Coordinator . . . . .Patsy Smith
806-351-5153
PSmith@nwths.com
Director of Sales . . . . .Scott Carlisle
806-351-5155
SCarlise@nwths.com
Medical Affairs . . . . .Pablo Diaz-Esquivel, MD
Member Services . . . . .Chris Grigo
806-351-5152
Provider Services . . . . .Diana Avila
Sales. . . . . .Scott Carlisle

Employer References
City of Amarillo, Affilate Foods, Potter County, TPMHMR/State
Center, Boys Ranch

1048 American PPO
433 East Las Colinas Blvd
Suite 1050
Irving, TX 75039
Toll-Free: 877-223-3372
Phone: 972-717-5200
Fax: 972-717-5209
www.americanppo.com
For Profit Organization: Yes
Year Founded: 2000
Number of Affiliated Hospitals: 305
Number of Primary Care Physicians: 10,000
Number of Referral/Specialty Physicians: 13,000

Healthplan and Services Defined
PLAN TYPE: PPO
Model Type: Network
Benefits Offered: Behavioral Health, Chiropractic, Dental, Disease
Management, Home Care, Inpatient SNF, Long-Term Care,
Physical Therapy, Prescription, Vision
Offers Demand Management Patient Information Service: Yes

Type of Coverage
Commercial

Type of Payment Plans Offered
Combination FFS & DFFS

Geographic Areas Served
Arkansas, Louisiana, Mississippi, Missouri, Oklahoma, Tennessee and
Texas

Key Personnel
Sales/Marketing Director . . . . .Shelly Dowdy
877-223-3372
americanppo@aol.com
Plan/Business Dev Dir . . . . .Carmen Khorram
877-223-3372
americanppo@aol.com
Network Development Dir . . . . .Heather Brumley
877-223-3372
americanppo@aol.com

Specialty Managed Care Partners
Enters into Contracts with Regional Business Coalitions: Yes

1049 Amerigroup Texas

3800 Buffalo Speedway
Suite 400
Houston, TX 77098
Toll-Free: 800-252-8263
www.realsolutions.com
Secondary Address: 823 Congress Avenue, Suite 400, Austin, TX 78701
For Profit Organization: Yes
Total Enrollment: 1,900,000

Healthplan and Services Defined
  PLAN TYPE: HMO

Type of Coverage
Medicare, Medicaid, SCHIP, SSI

Geographic Areas Served
Austin, Corpus Christi, Dallas, Fort Worth, San Antonio, Houston and surrounding counties

1050 Assurant Employee Benefits: Texas

2745 Dallas Parkway
Suite 500
Plano, TX 75093-8900
Phone: 214-258-1020
benefits@assurant.com
www.assurantemployeebenefits.com
Subsidiary of: Assurant, Inc
For Profit Organization: Yes
Number of Primary Care Physicians: 112,000
Total Enrollment: 47,000

Healthplan and Services Defined
  PLAN TYPE: Multiple
  Plan Specialty: Dental, Vision, Long & Short-Term Disability
  Benefits Offered: Dental, Vision, Wellness, AD&D, Life, LTD, STD

Type of Coverage
Commercial, Indemnity, Individual Dental Plans

Geographic Areas Served
Statewide

Subscriber Information
Average Monthly Fee Per Subscriber
  (Employee + Employer Contribution):
    Employee Only (Self): Varies by plan

Key Personnel
Vice President.........................Greg Dowling
General Manager ....Dottie Panchuk
Manager ....Luc Sterck
PR Specialist.........................Megan Hutchison
  816-556-7815
  megan.hutchison@assurant.com

1051 Avesis: Texas

8000 IH 10 West
Suite 600
San Antonio, TX 78230
Toll-Free: 866-884-4986
Phone: 210-366-8071
www.avesis.com
Year Founded: 1978
Number of Primary Care Physicians: 18,000
Total Enrollment: 2,000,000

Healthplan and Services Defined
  PLAN TYPE: PPO
  Other Type: Vision, Dental

Model Type: Network
Plan Specialty: Dental, Vision, Hearing
Benefits Offered: Dental, Vision

Type of Coverage
Commercial

Type of Payment Plans Offered
POS, Capitated, Combination FFS & DFFS

Geographic Areas Served
Nationwide and Puerto Rico

Publishes and Distributes Report Card: Yes

Accreditation Certification
AAAHC
TJC Accreditation

Key Personnel
Insurance Broker.........................Rebecca Jolly

1052 Block Vision of Texas

4100 Alpha Road
Suite 910
Dallas, TX 75244
Toll-Free: 800-914-9795
Phone: 972-991-8816
Fax: 972-991-4704
www.blockvision.com
Year Founded: 1996
State Enrollment: 4,000,000

Healthplan and Services Defined
  PLAN TYPE: Vision
  Model Type: Staff
  Plan Specialty: Vision
  Benefits Offered: Vision, Wellness

Type of Coverage
Commercial, Medicare, Medicaid, CHIP

Type of Payment Plans Offered
Combination FFS & DFFS

Geographic Areas Served
All Texas counties

Publishes and Distributes Report Card: No

Accreditation Certification
NCQA
State Licensure

Key Personnel
VP/COO ....Joy Schreiber
  jschreiber@blockvision.com
Medical Affairs ....Barry Davis
Account Executive.........................Stuart Bowie
  800-914-9795
  sbowie@blockvision.com
Account Exec, Texas ....April Sanchez
  512-699-2049
  asanchez@blockvision.com

Specialty Managed Care Partners
Parkland Community Health Plan, Seton Health Plan, Aetna, Amerigroup, Community Health Plan, Texas Childrens Hospital & Health Plan

1053 Blue Cross & Blue Shield of Texas

1001 E Lookout Drive
Richardson, TX 75082
Toll-Free: 800-521-2227
Phone: 972-766-6900
Fax: 972-766-8253
www.bcbstx.com
Mailing Address: P.O. Box 660044, Dallas, TX 75226-0044
Subsidiary of: Health Care Service Corp

Non-Profit Organization: Yes
Year Founded: 1929
Number of Affiliated Hospitals: 451
Number of Primary Care Physicians: 38,000
Total Enrollment: 3,645,891
State Enrollment: 310,853

Healthplan and Services Defined
 PLAN TYPE: HMO/PPO
 Other Type: POS
 Benefits Offered: Disease Management, Wellness
 Offers Demand Management Patient Information Service: Yes

Type of Coverage
 Commercial, Individual, Medicare, Medicaid

Type of Payment Plans Offered
 POS

Geographic Areas Served
 Southwest Texas

Publishes and Distributes Report Card: Yes

Key Personnel
 President. . . . . .Darren Rodgers
 SVP, Finace & CFO. . . . . .Denise Buiak
 VP, Chief Medical Officer. . . . . .Eduardo Sanchez
 VP Network Management . . . . .Shannon Stansbury
 Sales & Marketing Dir. . . . . .Jack Smith
 Media Contact . . . . .Margaret Jarvis
 972-766-7165
 margaret_jarvis@bcbstx.com

Specialty Managed Care Partners
 Magellen Behavioral Health

1054 Blue Cross & Blue Shield of Texas: Houston

2425 W Loop Fwy South
Suite 1000
Houston, TX 77027
Toll-Free: 800-235-0796
Phone: 713-354-7000
Fax: 713-663-1297
www.bcbstx.com
Subsidiary of: Health Care Services Corp
For Profit Organization: Yes
Year Founded: 1984
Number of Affiliated Hospitals: 451
Number of Primary Care Physicians: 3,800
Total Enrollment: 4,000,000
State Enrollment: 2,720,162

Healthplan and Services Defined
 PLAN TYPE: HMO/PPO
 Model Type: Staff, IPA
 Benefits Offered: Behavioral Health, Disease Management, Physical
  Therapy, Prescription, Psychiatric, Wellness, Care van

Type of Coverage
 Commercial
 Catastrophic Illness Benefit: Unlimited

Type of Payment Plans Offered
 POS, DFFS, Capitated, FFS, Combination FFS & DFFS

Geographic Areas Served
 All 254 Texas counties

Subscriber Information
 Average Monthly Fee Per Subscriber
  (Employee + Employer Contribution):
   Employee Only (Self): Varies by plan
 Average Subscriber Co-Payment:
   Home Health Care Max. Days/Visits Covered: 60 days
   Nursing Home Max. Days/Visits Covered: 60 days

Network Qualifications
 Pre-Admission Certification: Yes

Peer Review Type
 Utilization Review: Yes
 Second Surgical Opinion: Yes
 Case Management: Yes

Publishes and Distributes Report Card: Yes

Accreditation Certification
 NCQA
 TJC Accreditation, Medicare Approved, Utilization Review,
  Pre-Admission Certification, State Licensure, Quality Assurance
  Program

Key Personnel
 Director . . . . .Art Chitty
 Manager. . . . . .Betty Bialaszewsky
 Administrator . . . . .Eric Bing
 Media Contact . . . . .Margaret Jarvis
 972-766-7165
 margaret_jarvis@bcbstx.com

Average Claim Compensation
 Physician's Fees Charged: 1%
 Hospital's Fees Charged: 1%

Specialty Managed Care Partners
 Magellen Behavioral Health
 Enters into Contracts with Regional Business Coalitions: Yes

Employer References
 Brinker International, Brookshire Grocery, City of Houston,
  Continental Airlines, Pilgrim's Pride

1055 Bravo Health: Texas

7551 Callaghan Road
Suite 310
San Antonio, TX 78229
Toll-Free: 888-454-0061
www.bravohealth.com
Secondary Address: 4141 Pinnacle Street, Suite 109, El Paso, TX
79902
Year Founded: 1996
Number of Primary Care Physicians: 30,000
Total Enrollment: 360,000

Healthplan and Services Defined
 PLAN TYPE: Medicare

Type of Coverage
 Medicare, Supplemental Medicare

Geographic Areas Served
 Delaware, Maryland, Pennslyvania, Texas, Washington DC, New
 Jersey

Key Personnel
 SVP, Executive Director . . . . .Patrick Feyen

1056 Brazos Valley Health Network

3115 Pine Avenue
Suite 10
Waco, TX 76708
Phone: 254-202-5320
Fax: 254-202-5310
Non-Profit Organization: Yes
Year Founded: 1992
Number of Affiliated Hospitals: 10
Number of Primary Care Physicians: 305
Number of Referral/Specialty Physicians: 174
Total Enrollment: 65,300
State Enrollment: 78,139

Healthplan and Services Defined
 PLAN TYPE: PPO
 Other Type: PHO
 Model Type: Network
 Benefits Offered: Dental

Type of Payment Plans Offered
DFFS, Combination FFS & DFFS

Geographic Areas Served
Texas: Bell, Bosque, Brazos, Coryell, Falls, Hamilton, Hill, Limestone, McLennan, Milam, Robertson & Washington

Network Qualifications
Pre-Admission Certification: Yes

Peer Review Type
Utilization Review: Yes

Publishes and Distributes Report Card: No

Key Personnel
Executive Director . . . . .Donald K Reeves
Medical Director . . . . .Dr James E Grey
Assoc Medical Director. . . . . .Dr Gerard A Marrorquin
Nurse Manager . . . . .Judy Johnson

Specialty Managed Care Partners
Enters into Contracts with Regional Business Coalitions: No

1057 CIGNA HealthCare of North Texas

1640 Dallas Parkway
4th Floor
Plano, TX 75093
Toll-Free: 866-438-2446
Phone: 972-863-4300
Fax: 866-530-3585
www.cigna.com
For Profit Organization: Yes
Year Founded: 1980
Number of Affiliated Hospitals: 59
Number of Primary Care Physicians: 1,454
Number of Referral/Specialty Physicians: 3,279
Total Enrollment: 111,877
State Enrollment: 111,877

Healthplan and Services Defined
PLAN TYPE: HMO/PPO
Model Type: Staff, IPA
Benefits Offered: Behavioral Health, Dental, Disease Management, Physical Therapy, Prescription, Psychiatric, Transplant, Vision, Wellness, Language Line Service, 24 hour Health Information LIne, automated ReferralLine, Women's Health
Offers Demand Management Patient Information Service: Yes
DMPI Services Offered: Health Information Library

Type of Coverage
Commercial

Type of Payment Plans Offered
POS, DFFS, Capitated, FFS, Combination FFS & DFFS

Geographic Areas Served
All of Northern Texas including Dallas, Tyler, El Paso and Waco

Network Qualifications
Pre-Admission Certification: Yes

Peer Review Type
Utilization Review: Yes
Second Surgical Opinion: Yes
Case Management: Yes

Publishes and Distributes Report Card: Yes

Accreditation Certification
NCQA
Medicare Approved, Utilization Review, Pre-Admission Certification, State Licensure, Quality Assurance Program

Key Personnel
President . . . . .David Cordani

Specialty Managed Care Partners
Quest
Enters into Contracts with Regional Business Coalitions: Yes

1058 CIGNA HealthCare of South Texas

2700 Post Oak
Suite 700
Houston, TX 77056
Toll-Free: 866-438-2446
Phone: 713-576-4300
Fax: 866-530-3585
www.cigna.com
Secondary Address: 7600 North Capital of Texas Highway, Suite 335, Austin, TX 78731, 512-338-7100
For Profit Organization: Yes
Year Founded: 1982
Number of Affiliated Hospitals: 92
Number of Primary Care Physicians: 2,517
Number of Referral/Specialty Physicians: 7,947
Total Enrollment: 111,877
State Enrollment: 111,877

Healthplan and Services Defined
PLAN TYPE: HMO
Other Type: POS
Model Type: Staff, IPA, Group
Plan Specialty: ASO, Behavioral Health, Chiropractic, Dental, Disease Management, Lab, Vision, Radiology, UR
Benefits Offered: Behavioral Health, Chiropractic, Complementary Medicine, Dental, Disease Management, Home Care, Long-Term Care, Physical Therapy, Prescription, Psychiatric, Transplant, Vision, Wellness, Worker's Compensation, AD&D, Life, LTD, STD, Women's and Men's Heal
Offers Demand Management Patient Information Service: Yes
DMPI Services Offered: Language Line Service, 24 hour Health Information Line, Health Information Library, Automated ReferralLine

Type of Coverage
Commercial, Individual, Indemnity

Type of Payment Plans Offered
POS, DFFS, Capitated, FFS, Combination FFS & DFFS

Geographic Areas Served
All of Southern Texas including Houston, Austin, Beaumont/Port Arthur, Corpus Christi, San Antonio and Lufkin

Subscriber Information
Average Monthly Fee Per Subscriber
(Employee + Employer Contribution):
Employee Only (Self): Varies
Employee & 1 Family Member: Varies
Employee & 2 Family Members: Varies
Medicare: Varies
Average Annual Deductible Per Subscriber:
Employee Only (Self): Varies
Employee & 1 Family Member: Varies
Employee & 2 Family Members: Varies
Medicare: Varies
Average Subscriber Co-Payment:
Hospital ER: $75.00
Home Health Care Max. Days/Visits Covered: Unlimited
Nursing Home Max. Days/Visits Covered: Unlimited

Network Qualifications
Pre-Admission Certification: Yes

Peer Review Type
Utilization Review: Yes
Second Surgical Opinion: Yes
Case Management: Yes

Publishes and Distributes Report Card: Yes

Accreditation Certification
NCQA
Utilization Review, Pre-Admission Certification, State Licensure, Quality Assurance Program

Average Claim Compensation
Physician's Fees Charged: 1%

Hospital's Fees Charged: 1%

Specialty Managed Care Partners
Quest
Enters into Contracts with Regional Business Coalitions: Yes

1059 Community First Health Plans

12238 Silicon Drive
Suite 100
San Antonio, TX 78249
Toll-Free: 800-434-2347
Phone: 210-227-2347
Fax: 210-358-6170
www.cfhp.com
Secondary Address: Avenida Guadalupe, 1401 Guadalupe Street, Suite 222, San Antonio, TX 78207
Subsidiary of: University Health System
Non-Profit Organization: Yes
Year Founded: 1995
Total Enrollment: 110,000
State Enrollment: 110,000

Healthplan and Services Defined
PLAN TYPE: HMO/PPO
Benefits Offered: Disease Management, Wellness

Type of Coverage
Commercial, Medicaid, CHIP

Geographic Areas Served
Bexar and surrounding seven counties

Key Personnel
Interim CEO . . . . Theresa Scepanski
COO. . . . . Patrina Fowler
Senior Medical Director . . . . Shelia Owens-Collins, MD
Dir, Compliance & Reg Aff. . . . . Marion Richardson
Dir, Network Management . . . . Martin Jiminez
Admin Dir, Strat Planning. . . . . Carol Huber
Admin Dir, Member Rel . . . . Mary Helen Gonzalez
Claims Manager. . . . . Norma Doria
Dir, Network Management . . . . Martin Jiminez
Mgr, Clinical Pharmacy . . . . Ramie Ramirez
Credentialing Manager . . . . Paul Maldonado
Underwriting Manager. . . . . Eric Ashihundu
Communications Director. . . . . Catherine Zambrano-Chavez
210-358-6173
czambrano-chavez@cfhp.com

1060 Concentra: Corporate Office

5080 Spectrum Drive
Suite 1200 West
Addison, TX 75001
Toll-Free: 800-232-3550
Phone: 972-364-8000
Fax: 972-387-0019
www.concentra.com
For Profit Organization: Yes
Number of Affiliated Hospitals: 300
Total Enrollment: 30,000

Healthplan and Services Defined
PLAN TYPE: HMO/PPO

Key Personnel
Chief Executive Officer . . . . James M. Greenwood
President & COO . . . . W. Keith Newton
Executive VP, COO . . . . Thomas E. Kiraly
SVP, Reimbursement . . . . Gregory M. Gilbert
EVP, General Counsel . . . . Mark A Solls
Pres, Medical Centers . . . . Ted Bucknam
Pres, Health Solutions . . . . A Michael McCollum
SVP, Therapy Director. . . . . Gary C Zigenfus, PT
SVP, Chief Marketing Off. . . . . John A. deLorimer

---

SVP, Human Resources. . . . . Tammy S Steele
EVP/Chief Medical Officer. . . . . W Tom Fogarty, MD
SVP, Accounting . . . . Su Zan Nelson
Senior VP, CIO . . . . Suzanne C. Kosub
SVP, Medical Operations . . . . John R Anderson, DO
Senior VP, Sales . . . . Jay B. Blakey
SVP, Medical Operations . . . . William R Lewis, MD

1061 Delta Dental of Texas

317 RR 620 South
Suite 301
Austin, TX 78734
Toll-Free: 800-852-8952
Phone: 512-306-9570
Fax: 512-306-9573
aus-txsales@delta.org
www.deltadentalins.com
Mailing Address: PO Box 1809, Alpharetta, GA 30023-1809
Non-Profit Organization: Yes
Total Enrollment: 54,000,000

Healthplan and Services Defined
PLAN TYPE: Dental
Other Type: Dental PPO

Type of Coverage
Commercial

Geographic Areas Served
Statewide

Key Personnel
VP, Public & Govt Affairs . . . . Jeff Album
415-972-8418
Dir/Media & Public Affair . . . . Elizabeth Risberg
415-972-8423

1062 Dental Solutions Plus

12946 Dairy Ashford Road
Suite 360
Sugarland, TX 77478
Toll-Free: 866-912-7131
Phone: 713-313-7155
Fax: 713-313-7155
info@dentalsolutionsplus.com
www.dentalsolutionsplus.com
Subsidiary of: First Continental Life & Accident Insurance
For Profit Organization: Yes
Year Founded: 1986

Healthplan and Services Defined
PLAN TYPE: Dental
Plan Specialty: Dental
Benefits Offered: Dental

Subscriber Information
Average Annual Deductible Per Subscriber:
Employee Only (Self): $0
Employee & 1 Family Member: $0
Employee & 2 Family Members: $0
Medicare: $0
Average Subscriber Co-Payment:
Primary Care Physician: $9.00

Key Personnel
President/CEO . . . . James Taylor
CFO . . . . Patrick Stoner
COO. . . . . Rick Barrett

1063 Dental Source: Dental Health Care Plans

12946 Dairy Ashford
Suite 360
Sugar Land, TX 77478

Toll-Free: 877-493-6282
Fax: 281-313-7155
www.densource.com
For Profit Organization: Yes
Number of Primary Care Physicians: 149
State Enrollment: 1,500

Healthplan and Services Defined
  PLAN TYPE: Dental
  Model Type: Network
  Plan Specialty: Dental, Vision
  Benefits Offered: Dental, Vision

Type of Coverage
  Commercial, Individual, Indemnity

Geographic Areas Served
  Kansas and Missouri

Key Personnel
  President/CEO . . . . .James A Taylor
  CFO . . . . .Patrick Stoner
  COO. . . . . .Rick Barrett
  Director Sales/Marketing . . . . .Mark Groves

1064 eHealthInsurance Services Inc.
11919 Foundation Place
Gold River, CA 95670
Toll-Free: 800-977-8860
info@ehealthinsurance.com
www.e.healthinsurance.com
Year Founded: 1997

Healthplan and Services Defined
  PLAN TYPE: HMO/PPO
  Benefits Offered: Dental, Life, STD

Type of Coverage
  Commercial, Individual, Medicare

Geographic Areas Served
  All 50 states in the USA and District of Columbia

Key Personnel
  Chairman & CEO . . . . .Gary L. Lauer
  EVP/Business & Corp. Dev. . . . . .Bruce Telkamp
  EVP/Chief Technology . . . . .Dr. Sheldon X. Wang
  SVP & CFO . . . . .Stuart M. Huizinga
  Pres. of eHealth Gov. Sys . . . . .Samuel C. Gibbs
  SVP of Sales & Operations . . . . .Robert S. Hurley
  Director Public Relations . . . . .Nate Purpura
    650-210-3115

1065 First Care Health Plans
12940 N Highway 183
Corporate Offices
Austin, TX 78750
Toll-Free: 800-431-7731
Phone: 806-784-4300
Fax: 512-257-6037
questions@firstcare.com
www.firstcare.com
Secondary Address: 1901 West Loop 289, Suite 9, Lubbock, TX
  79407
Subsidiary of: SHA LLC, Covenant Health System, Hendrick Health
  System
For Profit Organization: Yes
Year Founded: 1985
Owned by an Integrated Delivery Network (IDN): Yes
Number of Affiliated Hospitals: 82
Number of Primary Care Physicians: 1,100
Number of Referral/Specialty Physicians: 2,005
Total Enrollment: 130,000
State Enrollment: 130,000

Healthplan and Services Defined
  PLAN TYPE: Multiple
  Model Type: IPA
  Plan Specialty: ASO, Behavioral Health, Chiropractic, Dental,
    Disease Management, EPO, Lab, PBM, Vision, Radiology, UR
  Benefits Offered: Behavioral Health, Chiropractic, Complementary
    Medicine, Dental, Disease Management, Home Care, Inpatient
    SNF, Physical Therapy, Podiatry, Prescription, Psychiatric,
    Transplant, Vision, Wellness, Life, HSC

Type of Coverage
  Commercial, Individual, Indemnity, Medicare, Medicaid, Catastrophic
  Catastrophic Illness Benefit: Unlimited

Type of Payment Plans Offered
  Combination FFS & DFFS

Geographic Areas Served
  108 counties in North, Central and West Texas

Subscriber Information
  Average Monthly Fee Per Subscriber
    (Employee + Employer Contribution):
      Employee Only (Self): Varies by plan
      Medicare: Varies
  Average Annual Deductible Per Subscriber:
      Employee Only (Self): $0
      Employee & 1 Family Member: $0
      Employee & 2 Family Members: $0
      Medicare: Varies
  Average Subscriber Co-Payment:
      Primary Care Physician: $10.00
      Non-Network Physician: $10.00
      Prescription Drugs: $10/20/35
      Hospital ER: $50.00
      Home Health Care: $0
      Home Health Care Max. Days/Visits Covered: Unlimited
      Nursing Home: $0
      Nursing Home Max. Days/Visits Covered: 100 days

Network Qualifications
  Pre-Admission Certification: Yes

Peer Review Type
  Utilization Review: Yes
  Second Surgical Opinion: No
  Case Management: Yes

Publishes and Distributes Report Card: Yes

Accreditation Certification
  TJC Accreditation, Medicare Approved, Utilization Review,
    Pre-Admission Certification, State Licensure, Quality Assurance
    Program

Key Personnel
  CEO. . . . . .Cliff Frank
  VP, Sales. . . . . .Steven Abalos
  Manager TPA Services . . . . .Ken Cook
  Abilene Region Sales . . . . .Becky West
    bwest@firstcare.com
  Amarillo Region Sales. . . . . .Dana Nicklaus
    amamarketing@firstcare.com
  Lubbock Region Sales . . . . .Cannon Allen
    806-783-9654
    khamsmith@daains.com
  Waco Region Sales . . . . .Dan Mayfield
    254-761-5802
    dmayfield@firstcare.com

Specialty Managed Care Partners
  PBM, Comp Care, MH Net
  Enters into Contracts with Regional Business Coalitions: No

1066 Galaxy Health Network
631 106th Street
Arlington, TX 76011
Toll-Free: 800-975-3322

Phone: 817-633-5822
Fax: 817-633-5729
contracting@ghn-mci.com
www.galaxyhealth.net
Mailing Address: PO Box 201425, Arlington, TX 76006
For Profit Organization: Yes
Year Founded: 1993
Number of Affiliated Hospitals: 2,700
Number of Primary Care Physicians: 400,000
Number of Referral/Specialty Physicians: 47,000
Total Enrollment: 3,200,000
State Enrollment: 3,200,000

Healthplan and Services Defined
   PLAN TYPE: PPO
   Model Type: Network
   Benefits Offered: Prescription
   Offers Demand Management Patient Information Service: Yes

Type of Coverage
   Catastrophic Illness Benefit: Varies per case

Type of Payment Plans Offered
   POS, DFFS, FFS, Combination FFS & DFFS

Geographic Areas Served
   National

Subscriber Information
   Average Monthly Fee Per Subscriber
      (Employee + Employer Contribution):
         Employee Only (Self): Varies by plan
   Average Annual Deductible Per Subscriber:
         Employee Only (Self): $500.00
         Employee & 1 Family Member: $1000.00
         Employee & 2 Family Members: $1000.00
   Average Subscriber Co-Payment:
         Primary Care Physician: $10.00

Network Qualifications
   Pre-Admission Certification: Yes

Peer Review Type
   Utilization Review: Yes
   Second Surgical Opinion: Yes
   Case Management: Yes

Publishes and Distributes Report Card: Yes

Accreditation Certification
   Utilization Review, Pre-Admission Certification, State Licensure,
      Quality Assurance Program

Key Personnel
   President and CEO . . . . .P.J. Shane, Jr
      pjshaneyjr@ghn-mci.com
   Executive Vice President . . . . Dan Shadle
      dshadle@ghn-mci.com
   Administrative Manager . . . . .Venus Warner
      vmathews@ghn-mci.com
   Dir, Network Operations . . . . .Susdey Sud
      susdeys@ghn-mci.com
   Chief Technology Offier . . . . .Stephen Ferraro
      sferraro@ghn-mci.com
   Manager, Info Services . . . . .Brandie Santillan
      bsantillan@ghn-mci.com
   Vice President, Sales . . . . .Stacey Hollinger
      shollinger@ghn-mci.com

Specialty Managed Care Partners
   Enters into Contracts with Regional Business Coalitions: Yes

1067 Great-West Healthcare Texas
Acquired by CIGNA

1068 HAS-Premier Providers
Acquired by Texas True Choice

1069 Healthcare Partners of East Texas
Acquired by Viant

1070 HealthSmart Preferred Care
2002 West Loop 289
Suite 110
Lubbock, TX 79407
Toll-Free: 888-744-6638
Phone: 806-473-2400
Fax: 806-473-2425
info.his@healthsmart.com
www.healthsmart.com
Secondary Address: 222 West Las Colinas Blvd, Suite 600N, Irving,
   TX 75039
Non-Profit Organization: Yes
Year Founded: 1983
Number of Affiliated Hospitals: 63
Number of Primary Care Physicians: 400,000
Total Enrollment: 470,623
State Enrollment: 394,011

Healthplan and Services Defined
   PLAN TYPE: PPO
   Model Type: Network
   Plan Specialty: ASO, EPO, UR
   Benefits Offered: Behavioral Health, Disease Management, Physical
      Therapy, Wellness
   Offers Demand Management Patient Information Service: Yes
   DMPI Services Offered: Nurse Triage

Type of Coverage
   Catastrophic Illness Benefit: Varies per case

Type of Payment Plans Offered
   POS, DFFS, FFS, Combination FFS & DFFS

Geographic Areas Served
   36 counties in North Central Texas, including Greater Dallas/ Fort
      Worth area. National coverage available

Subscriber Information
   Average Monthly Fee Per Subscriber
      (Employee + Employer Contribution):
         Employee Only (Self): Varies
         Employee & 1 Family Member: Varies
         Employee & 2 Family Members: Varies
         Medicare: Varies
   Average Annual Deductible Per Subscriber:
         Employee Only (Self): Varies
         Employee & 1 Family Member: Varies
         Employee & 2 Family Members: Varies
         Medicare: Varies
   Average Subscriber Co-Payment:
         Primary Care Physician: Varies
         Non-Network Physician: Varies
         Hospital ER: Varies
         Home Health Care: Varies
         Home Health Care Max. Days/Visits Covered: Varies
         Nursing Home: Varies
         Nursing Home Max. Days/Visits Covered: Varies

Network Qualifications
   Minimum Years of Practice: 1
   Pre-Admission Certification: Yes

Peer Review Type
   Utilization Review: Yes
   Second Surgical Opinion: Yes
   Case Management: Yes

Publishes and Distributes Report Card: Yes

Accreditation Certification
   URAC
   Medicare Approved, Utilization Review, Pre-Admission Certification,
      State Licensure, Quality Assurance Program

Key Personnel

Chairman . . . . Daniel D Crowley
President . . . . James M Pennington
SVP/Chief Financial Offc . . . . William Dembereckyj
Chief Sales Officer . . . . Alex N Arnet
SVP, Sales . . . . Charles Busch
SVP/Benefit Solutions . . . . Marc Zech
SVP/Pharmacy Analytics . . . . Eileen Romansky
SVP/Account Management . . . . Lovie Pollinger
SVP/Network Development . . . . Marci Conlin
SVP/Care Mgmt Solutions . . . . Pamela Coffey
SVP/Information Systems . . . . Jason Bielss
VP/General Counsel . . . . James Kelly

Specialty Managed Care Partners

Enters into Contracts with Regional Business Coalitions: Yes

Employer References

Garland ISD, Richardson ISD, Nokia, Tenet Health System, Gulf Stream Aerospace

---

1071 HealthSpring of Texas

2900 North Loop West
Suite 1300
Houston, TX 77092
Toll-Free: 888-501-1115
Phone: 832-553-3300
infotxhs@myhealthspring.com
www.healthspring.com
Secondary Address: 105 Decker Court, Suite 1000, Irving, TX 75062
For Profit Organization: Yes
Year Founded: 2000

Healthplan and Services Defined
  PLAN TYPE: Medicare

Type of Coverage
Medicare, Medicaid

Geographic Areas Served
Houston, Golden Triangle & Valley / North Texas & Lubbock

Key Personnel

President . . . . Scott Huebner
Corp Mgr, Media Relations . . . . Jolene Sharp
  615-234-6710
  jolene.sharp@healthspring.com

1072 HMO Blue Texas

1001 E Lookout Drive
Richarson, TX 75082
Toll-Free: 877-299-2377
Phone: 972-766-6900
www.hmobluetexas.com
Mailing Address: PO Box 660044, Dallas, TX 75266-0044
Subsidiary of: A subsidiary of Blue Cross/Blue Shield of Texas
Non-Profit Organization: Yes
Year Founded: 1944
Number of Affiliated Hospitals: 451
Number of Primary Care Physicians: 38,000
Total Enrollment: 3,800,000

Healthplan and Services Defined
  PLAN TYPE: HMO
  Benefits Offered: Behavioral Health, Disease Management, Inpatient SNF, Prescription, Psychiatric, Wellness, Mayo Clinic Online Resources, Women's health

Type of Coverage
Commercial, Individual, Medicare

Geographic Areas Served
All 254 Texas counties

Subscriber Information
Average Monthly Fee Per Subscriber
  (Employee + Employer Contribution):
    Employee Only (Self): Varies by plan
Average Annual Deductible Per Subscriber:
  Employee Only (Self): $0
  Employee & 1 Family Member: $0
  Employee & 2 Family Members: $0
  Medicare: $0
Average Subscriber Co-Payment:
  Primary Care Physician: $25.00
  Non-Network Physician: $30.00
  Prescription Drugs: $10/25/40
  Hospital ER: $100.00

Accreditation Certification
NCQA

Key Personnel

President/CEO . . . . Patricia Jemmingway-Hall
News Media Contact . . . . Margaret Jarvis
  972-766-7165
  margaret_jarvis@bcbtx.com

Employer References
University of Texas

1073 Horizon Health Corporation

2941 South Lake Vista Drive
Lewisville, TX 75057
Toll-Free: 800-931-4646
Phone: 972-420-8200
Fax: 972-420-8252
cindy.novak@horizonhealth.com
www.horizonhealth.com
Subsidiary of: Psychiatric Solutions
For Profit Organization: Yes
Year Founded: 1975
Number of Affiliated Hospitals: 2,000
Number of Primary Care Physicians: 17,000
Number of Referral/Specialty Physicians: 18,531
Total Enrollment: 120,000

Healthplan and Services Defined
  PLAN TYPE: PPO
  Model Type: Staff
  Plan Specialty: Behavioral Health, UR
  Benefits Offered: Behavioral Health, Psychiatric, Rehabilitation Services

Type of Coverage
Commercial, Indemnity

Type of Payment Plans Offered
POS, DFFS, Capitated, FFS, Combination FFS & DFFS

Geographic Areas Served
All 50 United States, Canada, Puerto Rico, Mexico, England, and the Virgin Islands

Subscriber Information
Average Monthly Fee Per Subscriber
  (Employee + Employer Contribution):
    Employee & 2 Family Members: Varies by plan

Network Qualifications
Pre-Admission Certification: Yes

Peer Review Type
Utilization Review: Yes
Case Management: Yes

Publishes and Distributes Report Card: Yes

Accreditation Certification
URAC, NCQA

Key Personnel

President . . . . Linda Laitner
Vice President/EAP . . . . Dorothy Harrison

VP/Managed Care Division . . . . Paul Patti
Business Affairs Director . . . . Susan Bellofatto
   407-915-0025
Network Director . . . . Lupe Rivero
   407-915-0025
Network Manager . . . . Julie Harmon, MHA
   407-915-0025
VP Marketing . . . . Robert Kramer
   972-420-8200
Dir Quality Management . . . . Jane Baker
Medical Director . . . . William Eckbert, MD
   407-915-0025
Implementation/Member Management . . . . Ruth Scott
   407-915-0025
Director IS . . . . Richard Hippert
   407-915-0025
Provider Services . . . . Lupe Rivero
   407-915-0025
VP Sales/Acct Management . . . . Steve Hart
   407-915-0025

Specialty Managed Care Partners
Enters into Contracts with Regional Business Coalitions: Yes
Employer Health Coalition

Employer References
American Greetings, Saint Gobain Corporation, Broodwing,
Jeld-Wen, The Pep Boys

1074 Humana Health Insurance of Corpus Christi

1801 S Alameda Street
Suite 100
Corpus Christi, TX 78404
Toll-Free: 800-533-5758
Phone: 361-866-1400
Fax: 361-866-1429
www.humana.com
For Profit Organization: Yes
Year Founded: 1983
Number of Affiliated Hospitals: 2,800
Number of Primary Care Physicians: 320,000
Total Enrollment: 172,000

Healthplan and Services Defined
  PLAN TYPE: HMO/PPO
  Model Type: IPA
  Benefits Offered: Disease Management, Prescription, Wellness

Type of Coverage
  Commercial, Individual

Type of Payment Plans Offered
  POS, DFFS, Capitated

Geographic Areas Served
  Arkansas, Kleberg, Nueces & San Patricio counties

Network Qualifications
  Pre-Admission Certification: Yes

Publishes and Distributes Report Card: No

Accreditation Certification
  URAC, NCQA, CORE

Key Personnel
  President/CEO Humana . . . . Mike McCallister
  Corporate Communications . . . . Ross McLaren
  CEO/Humana Texas . . . . Gary Goldstein, MD

Specialty Managed Care Partners
Enters into Contracts with Regional Business Coalitions: No

1075 Humana Health Insurance of San Antonio

8431 Fredericksburg Road
Suite 170
San Antonio, TX 78229

Toll-Free: 800-611-1456
Phone: 210-617-5100
www.humana.com
Secondary Address: 500 West Main Street, Corporate Offices,
  Louisville, KY 40202
For Profit Organization: Yes
Year Founded: 1983
Number of Affiliated Hospitals: 2,800
Number of Primary Care Physicians: 330,000
Total Enrollment: 172,000

Healthplan and Services Defined
  PLAN TYPE: HMO/PPO
  Model Type: Network
  Benefits Offered: Disease Management, Prescription, Wellness
  Offers Demand Management Patient Information Service: Yes

Type of Coverage
  Commercial, Individual
  Catastrophic Illness Benefit: Covered

Geographic Areas Served
  Bexar County; Medina, Comal, Wilson, Guadalupe, Karnes, Bandera,
  Kendall, Atascosa, Frio, Blanco

Subscriber Information
  Average Monthly Fee Per Subscriber
    (Employee + Employer Contribution):
      Employee Only (Self): Varies by plan
  Average Annual Deductible Per Subscriber:
    Employee Only (Self): $200.00
    Employee & 1 Family Member: $600.00
    Employee & 2 Family Members: $600.00
  Average Subscriber Co-Payment:
    Primary Care Physician: $10.00
    Non-Network Physician: Not covered
    Hospital ER: $50.00
    Home Health Care: $0
    Home Health Care Max. Days/Visits Covered: 30 visits
    Nursing Home Max. Days/Visits Covered: 30 days

Network Qualifications
  Pre-Admission Certification: Yes

Peer Review Type
  Utilization Review: Yes
  Second Surgical Opinion: Yes
  Case Management: Yes

Publishes and Distributes Report Card: Yes

Accreditation Certification
  URAC, NCQA, CORE
  TJC Accreditation, Medicare Approved, Utilization Review,
    Pre-Admission Certification, State Licensure, Quality Assurance
    Program

Key Personnel
  President/CEO Humana . . . . Mike McCallister
  Corporate Communications . . . . Ross McLaren
  CEO/Humana Texas . . . . Gary Goldstein, MD

Average Claim Compensation
  Physician's Fees Charged: 80%
  Hospital's Fees Charged: 80%

Specialty Managed Care Partners
  Enters into Contracts with Regional Business Coalitions: Yes

1076 Interplan Health Group
Acquired by HealthSmart

1077 KelseyCare Advantage

8900 Lakes at 610 Drive
Suite 1100
Houston, TX 77054

Toll-Free: 866-302-9336
Phone: 713-442-2273
www.kelseycareadvantage.com

Healthplan and Services Defined
  PLAN TYPE: Medicare
  Other Type: HMO/POS
  Benefits Offered: Disease Management, Prescription, Wellness

Type of Coverage
  Medicare, Medicare Advantage

Key Personnel
  President . . . . .Barbara L Tyer

1078 Legacy Health Plan

120 East Harris
San Angelo, TX 76903
Toll-Free: 800-839-7198
Phone: 325-658-7104
www.legacyhealthplan.com
Year Founded: 2004
Total Enrollment: 1,000

Healthplan and Services Defined
  PLAN TYPE: HMO

Geographic Areas Served
  Coke, Coleman, Concho, Crockett, Edwards, Irion, Kimble, Kinney,
  Mason, McCulloch, Menard, Reagan, Runnels, Schleicher, Sterling,
  Sutton, Tom Green, Val Verde counties

1079 Medical Care Referral Group

4100 Rio Bravo
Suite 211
El Paso, TX 79902
Toll-Free: 800-424-9919
Phone: 915-532-2408
Fax: 915-532-1772
www.mcrg.net
Subsidiary of: Assured Benefits Administration
For Profit Organization: Yes
Year Founded: 1985
Number of Affiliated Hospitals: 8
Number of Primary Care Physicians: 190
Number of Referral/Specialty Physicians: 560
State Enrollment: 65,000

Healthplan and Services Defined
  PLAN TYPE: PPO
  Model Type: Network
  Plan Specialty: IUO
  Benefits Offered: Behavioral Health, Chiropractic, Dental, Disease
    Management, Home Care, Inpatient SNF, Physical Therapy,
    Podiatry, Prescription, Psychiatric, Transplant, Vision, Wellness,
    Worker's Compensation, AD&D, Life, LTD, STD

Geographic Areas Served
  El Paso

Network Qualifications
  Pre-Admission Certification: Yes

Peer Review Type
  Utilization Review: Yes
  Second Surgical Opinion: Yes
  Case Management: Yes

Publishes and Distributes Report Card: No

Accreditation Certification
  Utilization Review, Pre-Admission Certification, State Licensure,
    Quality Assurance Program

Key Personnel
  President and CEO . . . . .Joseph Halow
    914-532-2100
    jhalow@assurebenefitsadmin.com
  Executive VP . . . . .Lorri Halo
  VP Administration . . . . .Eddie Garcia
  Benefits Administration . . . . .Angie Carrasco
    acarrasco@assurebenefitsadmin.com
  Marketing. . . . . .Sueann Austin
    saustin@assurebenefitsadmin.com
  Medical Affairs . . . . .George Halow, MD

Specialty Managed Care Partners
  Enters into Contracts with Regional Business Coalitions: No

1080 Mercy Health Plans: Texas

5901 McPherson
Suite 1 & 2B, Centre Plaza
Laredo, TX 78041
Toll-Free: 800-617-3433
Phone: 956-723-2144
Fax: 956-723-8246
www.mercyhealthplans.com
Non-Profit Organization: Yes
Total Enrollment: 73,000

Healthplan and Services Defined
  PLAN TYPE: HMO

Type of Coverage
  Commercial, Individual

1081 MHNet Behavioral Health

4006 Beltline Road
Suite 205
Addison, TX 78501
Toll-Free: 800-866-7242
Phone: 972-588-2623
Fax: 972-931-1938
servicenow@mhnet.com
www.mhnet.com
For Profit Organization: Yes
Year Founded: 1985
Number of Affiliated Hospitals: 134
Number of Referral/Specialty Physicians: 2,000
Total Enrollment: 5,000,000

Healthplan and Services Defined
  PLAN TYPE: Multiple
  Model Type: IPA
  Plan Specialty: Behavioral Health, Employee Assistance Programs
    and Managed Behavioral Health Care
  Benefits Offered: Behavioral Health, Psychiatric
  Offers Demand Management Patient Information Service: Yes
  DMPI Services Offered: Psychiatric Illness

Type of Payment Plans Offered
  POS, DFFS, Capitated, FFS, Combination FFS & DFFS

Geographic Areas Served
  Nationwide

Network Qualifications
  Minimum Years of Practice: 1
  Pre-Admission Certification: Yes

Peer Review Type
  Utilization Review: Yes
  Second Surgical Opinion: Yes
  Case Management: Yes

Publishes and Distributes Report Card: Yes

Accreditation Certification
  NCQA

Key Personnel
Chief Operating Officer . . . . Kevin Middleton, PsyD
Controller . . . . Bill Scheerer, CPA
Dir, Operations Support . . . . Talitha Appenzeller, MBA
Natl Dir, Quality Mgmt . . . . Jacki Roschbach, MSS
Corporate Medical Dir . . . . Peter Harris, MD, PhD

Average Claim Compensation
Physician's Fees Charged: 30%
Hospital's Fees Charged: 30%

Specialty Managed Care Partners
Enters into Contracts with Regional Business Coalitions: Yes

1082 Molina Healthcare: Texas

84 N E Loop 410
Suite 200
San Antonio, TX 78216
Toll-Free: 877-665-4622
www.molinahealthcare.com
Secondary Address: 15115 Park Row Blvd, Suite 110, Houston, TX
77084
For Profit Organization: Yes
Year Founded: 1980
Physician Owned Organization: Yes
Number of Affiliated Hospitals: 84
Number of Primary Care Physicians: 2,167
Number of Referral/Specialty Physicians: 6,184
Total Enrollment: 1,400,000

Healthplan and Services Defined
PLAN TYPE: HMO
Model Type: Network
Benefits Offered: Chiropractic, Dental, Home Care, Inpatient SNF,
Long-Term Care, Podiatry, Vision

Type of Coverage
Commercial, Medicare, Supplemental Medicare, Medicaid

Accreditation Certification
URAC, NCQA

1083 Ora Quest Dental Plans

12946 Dairy Ashford
Suite 360
Sugar Land, TX 77478
Toll-Free: 800-660-6064
Phone: 281-313-7170
Fax: 281-313-7155
info@oraquest.com
www.oraquest.com
For Profit Organization: Yes

Healthplan and Services Defined
PLAN TYPE: Dental
Other Type: Dental HMO
Model Type: Network
Plan Specialty: Dental
Benefits Offered: Dental

Type of Coverage
Commercial, Individual, Medicare, Medicaid

Subscriber Information
Average Annual Deductible Per Subscriber:
Employee Only (Self) $0

Key Personnel
President/CEO . . . . .James Taylor
CFO . . . . .Patrick Stoner
COO. . . . . .Rick Barrett

1084 PacifiCare of Texas

5001 LBJ Freeway
Tower II Bldg, Suite 600
Dallas, TX 75244-6130
Toll-Free: 800-825-9355
Phone: 972-866-1693
Fax: 210-474-5048
www.pacificare.com
Secondary Address: 1800 West Loop South, #350, Houston, TX 77027
Subsidiary of: UnitedHealthCare
For Profit Organization: Yes
Year Founded: 1986
Number of Primary Care Physicians: 4,800
Total Enrollment: 146,000
State Enrollment: 47,755

Healthplan and Services Defined
PLAN TYPE: HMO
Model Type: IPA, Group, Network
Benefits Offered: Behavioral Health, Disease Management,
Prescription, Psychiatric, 24 hour nurse line
Offers Demand Management Patient Information Service: Yes

Type of Coverage
Commercial, Individual, Indemnity, Medicare
Catastrophic Illness Benefit: Varies per case

Type of Payment Plans Offered
POS, DFFS, FFS, Combination FFS & DFFS

Geographic Areas Served
Greater San Antonio, Houston, Dallas/Ft. Worth, Metroplex and
Galveston

Subscriber Information
Average Monthly Fee Per Subscriber
(Employee + Employer Contribution):
Employee Only (Self): Varies by plan
Medicare: $0
Average Annual Deductible Per Subscriber:
Employee Only (Self): $0
Employee & 1 Family Member: $0
Employee & 2 Family Members: $0
Medicare: $0
Average Subscriber Co-Payment:
Primary Care Physician: $10.00
Prescription Drugs: $5.00/10.00
Hospital ER: $50.00
Home Health Care Max. Days/Visits Covered: Unlimited as necc.
Nursing Home: $0
Nursing Home Max. Days/Visits Covered: 100 days

Peer Review Type
Second Surgical Opinion: Yes
Case Management: Yes

Publishes and Distributes Report Card: Yes

Accreditation Certification
NCQA
TJC Accreditation, Medicare Approved, Utilization Review,
Pre-Admission Certification, State Licensure, Quality Assurance
Program

Key Personnel
Chairman/CEO Health Sys. . . . . .Howard Phanstiel
CFO . . . . .Greg Scott
President/CEO Health Plan . . . . .Brad Bowlus
Exec VP/Specialty Comp . . . . .Jacqueline Kosecoff
Exec VP/Enterprise Svce. . . . . .Sharon Garrett
Exec VP/General Counsel . . . . .Joseph Konowiecki
Exec VP/Major Accounts . . . . .James Frey
Exec VP/Cheif Med Officer. . . . . .Sam Ho
President/CEO Beh Health . . . . .Jerome V Vaccaro, MD
Sr VP/Human Resources .Carol Black

Average Claim Compensation
Physician's Fees Charged: 1%

Specialty Managed Care Partners
Enters into Contracts with Regional Business Coalitions: Yes

1085 Parkland Community Health Plan

2777 N Stemmons Freeway
Suite 1750
Dallas, TX 75207
Phone: 214-266-2100
Fax: 214-266-2150
webmaster@parklandhmo.org
www.parklandhmo.com
Secondary Address: Claims Department, PO Box 610088, Phoenix,
AZ 85082
Non-Profit Organization: Yes
Year Founded: 1996
Number of Affiliated Hospitals: 30
Number of Primary Care Physicians: 1,900
Total Enrollment: 170,000

Healthplan and Services Defined
PLAN TYPE: HMO
Model Type: Network
Benefits Offered: Behavioral Health, Chiropractic, Home Care,
Inpatient SNF, Physical Therapy, Podiatry, Prescription,
Psychiatric, Transplant, Vision, Durable Medical Equipment
Offers Demand Management Patient Information Service: Yes
DMPI Services Offered: Nurse Line

Type of Coverage
Medicaid, CHIP, KIDSfirst

Type of Payment Plans Offered
POS, FFS

Geographic Areas Served
Dallas, Collin, Ellis, Hunt, Kaufman, Navarro and Rockwall counties

Network Qualifications
Pre-Admission Certification: Yes

Peer Review Type
Utilization Review: Yes
Second Surgical Opinion: Yes
Case Management: Yes

Accreditation Certification
Utilization Review, Pre-Admission Certification, State Licensure,
Quality Assurance Program

Specialty Managed Care Partners
Comprehensive Behavioral Care, Block Vision

1086 SafeGuard Health Enterprises: Texas

95 Enterprise
Suite 200
Aliso Viejo, CA 92656
Toll-Free: 800-880-1800
www.safeguard.net
Subsidiary of: MetLife
For Profit Organization: Yes
Year Founded: 1974
Number of Primary Care Physicians: 2,073
Number of Referral/Specialty Physicians: 2,030
Total Enrollment: 1,800,000

Healthplan and Services Defined
PLAN TYPE: Dental
Other Type: Dental HMO
Model Type: IPA
Plan Specialty: ASO, Dental, Vision
Benefits Offered: Dental, Vision

Type of Coverage
Individual, Indemnity, Medicaid

Type of Payment Plans Offered
DFFS, Capitated

Geographic Areas Served
California, Texas, Florida

Subscriber Information
Average Annual Deductible Per Subscriber:
Employee Only (Self): $50.00
Employee & 1 Family Member: $100.00
Employee & 2 Family Members: $150.00

Network Qualifications
Pre-Admission Certification: Yes

Peer Review Type
Utilization Review: Yes

Publishes and Distributes Report Card: No

Key Personnel
Chairman/CEO . . . . .James E Buncher
949-425-4500
President/COO . . . . .Stephen J Baker
SVP/CFO . . . . .Dennis L Gates
VP/CIO . . . . .Michael J Lauffenburger
SVP/General Counsel .Ronald I Brendzel
Dir/Human Resources . . . . .William Wolff
Director . . . . .Jack R Anderson

Specialty Managed Care Partners
Enters into Contracts with Regional Business Coalitions: Yes

Employer References
State of California, Boeing, County of Los Angeles, Farmers
Insurance, Automobile Club

1087 Scott & White Health Plan

2401 S 31st Street
Temple, TX 76508
Toll-Free: 800-321-7947
Phone: 254-298-3000
Fax: 254-298-3011
swhpques@swmail.sw.org
www.swhp.org
Secondary Address: 3000 Briarcrest, Suite 422, Bryan, TX 77802
Non-Profit Organization: Yes
Year Founded: 1979
Owned by an Integrated Delivery Network (IDN): Yes
Number of Affiliated Hospitals: 18
Number of Primary Care Physicians: 1,000
Total Enrollment: 202,000
State Enrollment: 202,000

Healthplan and Services Defined
PLAN TYPE: HMO
Other Type: POS, CDHP
Model Type: Group
Benefits Offered: Behavioral Health, Dental, Disease Management,
Home Care, Inpatient SNF, Long-Term Care, Physical Therapy,
Podiatry, Prescription, Psychiatric, Transplant, Vision
Offers Demand Management Patient Information Service: Yes
DMPI Services Offered: Secondary prevention of Coronary Artery
Disease, Pediatric Asthma, Diabetes Mellitius, Congestive Heart
Failure, Hypertension

Type of Coverage
Commercial, Individual, Medicare, Medicare cost
Catastrophic Illness Benefit: Covered

Type of Payment Plans Offered
DFFS, Capitated

Geographic Areas Served
Bastrop, Bell, Blanco, Bosque, Brazos, Burleson, Burnet, Caldwell,
Coryell, Falls, Grimes, Hamilton, Hays, Hill, Hood, Johnson,
Lampasas, Lee, Llano, Madison, McLennan, Milam, Mills, Robertson,
San Saba, Somervell, Travis, Walker, Washington & Williamson;
Portions of Austin, Erath, Leon & Waller

Subscriber Information
Average Monthly Fee Per Subscriber
(Employee + Employer Contribution):
Employee Only (Self): Varies by plan
Average Annual Deductible Per Subscriber:
Employee Only (Self): $0.00
Employee & 1 Family Member: $0.00
Employee & 2 Family Members: $0.00
Average Subscriber Co-Payment:
Primary Care Physician: $10.00
Prescription Drugs: $5.00/20.00/50.00
Hospital ER: $75.00
Home Health Care: $10.00
Nursing Home: $0

Network Qualifications
Pre-Admission Certification: No

Peer Review Type
Utilization Review: Yes
Second Surgical Opinion: No
Case Management: Yes

Publishes and Distributes Report Card: Yes

Accreditation Certification
NCQA
TJC Accreditation, Medicare Approved, Utilization Review, State
Licensure, Quality Assurance Program

Key Personnel
Chief Executive Officer . . . . Allan Einboden
CFO . . . . Harvy Littman
Assod Exec Dir/MIS . . . . Troy Stillwagon
Chief Medical Director. . . . . Marylou Buyse
Dir, Sales & Marketing . . . . Sandy Gerik
Manager, Media Relations . . . . Katherine Voss
254-724-4097
kvoss@swmail.sw.org
Manager, Media Relations . . . . Scott Clark
254-724-9724
sdclark@swmail.sw.org

Average Claim Compensation
Physician's Fees Charged: 57%
Hospital's Fees Charged: 43%

Employer References
Texas A&M, ERS, Wiliamson County

1088 Script Care, Ltd.
6380 Folsom Drive
Suite 100
Beaumont, TX 77706
Toll-Free: 800-880-9988
Phone: 409-833-9061
Fax: 409-832-3109
customerservice@scriptcare.com
www.scriptcare.com
Year Founded: 1989
Number of Primary Care Physicians: 60,000

Healthplan and Services Defined
PLAN TYPE: PPO
Other Type: PBM
Plan Specialty: PBM
Benefits Offered: Prescription

Type of Payment Plans Offered
Capitated, FFS

Geographic Areas Served
National

Subscriber Information
Average Subscriber Co-Payment:
Prescription Drugs: Variable

Peer Review Type
Case Management: Yes

Key Personnel
President . . . . Jim Brown
Vice President. . . . . Steve Holiday
COO . . . . Kathy Cannon
Office Manager. . . . . Mary Alice Stuart
Manager . . . . Pam Boehme
Manager . . . . Rachel Tate
VP Sales/Marketing. . . . . Kevin Brown
Director, Account Manager . . . . Rachel Tate
Provider Relations . . . . Lisa Gutierrez

1089 Seton Health Plan
1201 W 38th Street
Austin, TX 78705-1006
Phone: 512-324-3125
Fax: 512-324-3359
shpproviderservices@seton.org
www.setonhealthplan.com
Subsidiary of: Seton Family of Hospitals
For Profit Organization: Yes
Number of Affiliated Hospitals: 20
Number of Primary Care Physicians: 1,900
Total Enrollment: 15,000

Healthplan and Services Defined
PLAN TYPE: HMO
Benefits Offered: Disease Management, Prescription, Wellness

Type of Coverage
Commercial

Geographic Areas Served
Central Texas

Key Personnel
Vice President . . . . Carol Medford

1090 TexanPlus Medicare Advantage HMO
4888 Loop Central
Suite 300
Houston, TX 77081
Toll-Free: 888-800-0760
Fax: 713-843-6740
www.universalamerican.com
Subsidiary of: Universal American
For Profit Organization: Yes
Total Enrollment: 42,000

Healthplan and Services Defined
PLAN TYPE: Medicare
Benefits Offered: Chiropractic, Dental, Disease Management, Home
Care, Inpatient SNF, Physical Therapy, Podiatry, Prescription,
Psychiatric, Vision, Wellness

Type of Coverage
Individual, Medicare

Geographic Areas Served
Available only within Texas

Subscriber Information
Average Monthly Fee Per Subscriber
(Employee + Employer Contribution):
Employee Only (Self): Varies
Medicare: Varies
Average Annual Deductible Per Subscriber:
Employee Only (Self): Varies
Medicare: Varies
Average Subscriber Co-Payment:
Primary Care Physician: Varies
Non-Network Physician: Varies
Prescription Drugs: Varies

Hospital ER: Varies
Home Health Care: Varies
Home Health Care Max. Days/Visits Covered: Varies
Nursing Home: Varies
Nursing Home Max. Days/Visits Covered: Varies

Key Personnel
Chairman & CEO . . . . Richard A Barasch
EVP/COO . . . . Gary W Bryant
EVP/CFO . . . . Robert Waegelein, CPA
SVP, Corp Development . . . . Gary Jacobs
COO . . . . Jason Israel
President & CEO Med Advan . . . . Theodore Carpenter

1091 Texas Community Care

9111 Jollyville Road
Suite 102
Austin, TX 78759
Toll-Free: 888-686-9548
Phone: 512-795-8092
Fax: 512-795-2371
www.texascommunitycare.com
Secondary Address: 7500 Viscount Blvd, Suite 292, El Paso, TX 79925
Subsidiary of: Arcadian Health Plan, Inc.
Total Enrollment: 230,000

Healthplan and Services Defined
PLAN TYPE: Medicare
Benefits Offered: Chiropractic, Dental, Disease Management, Home Care, Inpatient SNF, Physical Therapy, Podiatry, Prescription, Psychiatric, Vision, Wellness

Type of Coverage
Individual, Medicare

Geographic Areas Served
Available only within Texas

Subscriber Information
Average Monthly Fee Per Subscriber
(Employee + Employer Contribution):
Employee Only (Self): Varies
Medicare: Varies
Average Annual Deductible Per Subscriber:
Employee Only (Self): Varies
Medicare: Varies
Average Subscriber Co-Payment:
Primary Care Physician: Varies
Non-Network Physician: Varies
Prescription Drugs: Varies
Hospital ER: Varies
Home Health Care: Varies
Home Health Care Max. Days/Visits Covered: Varies
Nursing Home: Varies
Nursing Home Max. Days/Visits Covered: Varies

Key Personnel
Chairman/CEO . . . . John H Austin, MD
President . . . . Nancy Freeman
Chief Financial Officer . . . . Ken Zimmerman, MBA
Senior Medical Director . . . . Gary R Herzberg, MD
Senior Medical Executive . . . . Jeffrey McManus, MD
SVP/Business Management . . . . Cheryl Perkins, RN
VP/Network Management . . . . Peter G Goll
VP/Development . . . . Chase Milbrandt, MBA
VP/Sales & Marketing . . . . Garrison Rios
VP/Health Services . . . . Laurie Wilson, RN
Media Contact . . . . Nilsa Lennig
510-817-1016
nlennig@arcadianhealth.com

1092 Texas True Choice
Acquired by MultiPlan

1093 Unicare: Texas

3820 American Drive
Plano, TX 75075-6126
Toll-Free: 800-333-2203
Phone: 972-599-3888
Fax: 972-599-6267
www.unicare.com
Secondary Address: 106 East Sixth Street, Suite 333, Austin, TX 78701
Subsidiary of: WellPoint
For Profit Organization: Yes
Year Founded: 1995
Total Enrollment: 38,000

Healthplan and Services Defined
PLAN TYPE: HMO/PPO
Model Type: Network
Plan Specialty: Dental, EPO, Lab, Radiology
Benefits Offered: Dental, Inpatient SNF, Long-Term Care, Prescription, Transplant, Wellness, AD&D, Life, LTD, STD, EAP

Type of Coverage
Individual, Indemnity, Medicare, Supplemental Medicare

Geographic Areas Served
Illinois, Indiana, Ohio, Michigan, Texas, Nevada, Massachusetts, Virginia, Washington DC, Oklahoma

Network Qualifications
Pre-Admission Certification: Yes

Peer Review Type
Utilization Review: Yes
Second Surgical Opinion: Yes
Case Management: Yes

Publishes and Distributes Report Card: No

Accreditation Certification
NCQA
TJC Accreditation, Utilization Review, Pre-Admission Certification, State Licensure, Quality Assurance Program

Key Personnel
President/CEO . . . . David W Fields
Medical Director . . . . Neal Fischer, MD
Sales Director . . . . Mike Ryan
mike.ryan@wellpoint.com
Media Contact . . . . Tony Felts
317-287-6036
tony.felts@wellpoint.com

Specialty Managed Care Partners
Wellpoint Pharmacy Management, Wellpoint Dental Services, Wellpoint Behavioral Health
Enters into Contracts with Regional Business Coalitions: No

1094 United Concordia: Texas

8214 Westchester Drive
Suite 600
Dallas, TX 72552
Toll-Free: 877-722-8224
Phone: 214-378-6410
Fax: 214-378-6306
ucproducer@ucci.com
www.secure.ucci.com
Secondary Address: 11200 Westheimer, Suite 820, Houston, TX 77042, 888-828-6432
For Profit Organization: Yes
Year Founded: 1971
Number of Primary Care Physicians: 111,000
Total Enrollment: 8,000,000

Healthplan and Services Defined
PLAN TYPE: Dental
Plan Specialty: Dental
Benefits Offered: Dental

Type of Coverage
  Commercial, Individual

Geographic Areas Served
  Military personnel and their families, nationwide

1095 UnitedHealthCare of Texas

1250 Capital Of TX Hwy South
Bldg 1, Suite 400
Austin, TX 78746
Toll-Free: 877-294-1429
www.uhc.com
Secondary Address: 6200 Northwest Pkwy, Suite 107, San Antonio,
  TX 78249, 210-478-4800
Subsidiary of: UnitedHealth Group
For Profit Organization: Yes
Year Founded: 1986
Number of Affiliated Hospitals: 4,500
Number of Primary Care Physicians: 470,000
Total Enrollment: 75,000,000
State Enrollment: 1,862,466

Healthplan and Services Defined
  PLAN TYPE: HMO/PPO
  Model Type: IPA
  Benefits Offered: Dental, Disease Management, Prescription,
    Wellness, AD&D, Life, LTD, STD

Type of Coverage
  Commercial, Individual, Medicare

Geographic Areas Served
  79 counties in Texas

Network Qualifications
  Pre-Admission Certification: Yes

Publishes and Distributes Report Card: Yes

Accreditation Certification
  NCQA

Key Personnel
  Media Contact . . . . .Kim Whitaker
    469-633-8536
    kim_t_whitaker@uhc.com

Specialty Managed Care Partners
  Enters into Contracts with Regional Business Coalitions: Yes

1096 USA Managed Care Organization

1250 S Capital of Texas Highway
Bldg 3, Suite 500
Austin, TX 78746
Toll-Free: 800-872-0020
Phone: 512-306-0201
Fax: 512-306-1374
info@usamco.com
www.usamco.com
Secondary Address: 7301 North 16th Street, #201, Phoenix, AZ 85020
For Profit Organization: Yes
Year Founded: 1984
Number of Affiliated Hospitals: 5,000
Number of Primary Care Physicians: 430,000
Total Enrollment: 5,427,579
State Enrollment: 1,118,582

Healthplan and Services Defined
  PLAN TYPE: PPO
  Model Type: Group
  Plan Specialty: Behavioral Health, Chiropractic, Dental, Disease
    Management, EPO, Lab, PBM, Vision, Radiology, Worker's
    Compensation, UR
  Benefits Offered: Prescription, Worker's Compensation

Type of Coverage
  Commercial

Type of Payment Plans Offered
  POS, DFFS, FFS, Combination FFS & DFFS

Geographic Areas Served
  USA MCO is a National Preferred Provider network

Network Qualifications
  Pre-Admission Certification: Yes

Peer Review Type
  Utilization Review: Yes
  Second Surgical Opinion: Yes
  Case Management: Yes

Publishes and Distributes Report Card: No

Accreditation Certification
  TJC Accreditation, Pre-Admission Certification, State Licensure,
    Quality Assurance Program

Key Personnel
  President and CEO . . . . .George Bogle
    800-872-0820
  CFO . . . . .Joseph Dulin
  COO . . . . .Mike Bogle
  VP, Marketing . . . . .Sarah Beatty
  Medical Director . . . . .James E Gerace
  VP, Human Resources .Tammy Greene
  Chief Information Officer . . . . .Jim Mahoney
  VP, Sales . . . . .Sean Graff

Average Claim Compensation
  Physician's Fees Charged: 34%
  Hospital's Fees Charged: 32%

1097 UTMB HealthCare Systems

301 University Boulevard
Galveston, TX 77550
Toll-Free: 877-238-8543
Phone: 409-766-4064
Fax: 409-797-8001
www.utmbhcs.org
Mailing Address: PO Box 16809, Galveston, TX 77552
Subsidiary of: University of Texas Medical Branch
Non-Profit Organization: Yes
Year Founded: 1994
Total Enrollment: 1,000

Healthplan and Services Defined
  PLAN TYPE: HMO

Type of Coverage
  Commercial, Medicare, Medicaid, CHIP

Geographic Areas Served
  SE Texas

Key Personnel
  Chief Executive Officer . . . . .Donna Sollenberger
  Executive Director . . . . .Donna Johnson
  Vice President . . . . .DK Norman

1098 Valley Baptist Health Plan

2005 Ed Carey Drive
Harlingen, TX 78550
Toll-Free: 800-829-6440
Phone: 956-389-2260
Fax: 956-389-2281
vhp.customerservice@valleybaptist.net
www.valleyhealthplans.com
Subsidiary of: Valley Baptist Insurance Company
Non-Profit Organization: Yes
Total Enrollment: 22,000
State Enrollment: 12,004

Healthplan and Services Defined
  PLAN TYPE: HMO

Benefits Offered: Chiropractic, Dental, Disease Management, Home Care, Inpatient SNF, Physical Therapy, Podiatry, Prescription, Psychiatric, Transplant, Vision, Wellness, Durable Medical Equipment

Type of Coverage
Commercial

Type of Payment Plans Offered
POS

Geographic Areas Served
Texas

Subscriber Information
Average Monthly Fee Per Subscriber
  (Employee + Employer Contribution):
    Employee Only (Self): Varies
    Employee & 1 Family Member: Varies
    Employee & 2 Family Members: Varies
    Medicare: Varies
Average Annual Deductible Per Subscriber:
    Employee Only (Self): Varies
    Employee & 1 Family Member: Varies
    Employee & 2 Family Members: Varies
    Medicare: Varies
Average Subscriber Co-Payment:
    Primary Care Physician: Varies
    Non-Network Physician: Varies
    Prescription Drugs: Varies
    Hospital ER: Varies
    Home Health Care: Varies
    Home Health Care Max. Days/Visits Covered: Varies
    Nursing Home: Varies
    Nursing Home Max. Days/Visits Covered: Varies

Key Personnel
President/CEO . . . . James G Springfield
EVP/COO . . . . James Eastham, MD/FACC
SVP/CFO . . . . Randy McLelland
SVP/CIO . . . . Jim Barbaglia
VP/Corporate Services . . . . Jim Salyer
VP/Governmental Affairs . . . . Linda McKenna
SVP/Chief Legal Officer . . . . Manny Vela
SVP/Human Resources . . . . Irma Pye

Specialty Managed Care Partners
Express Scripts

1099 VSP: Vision Service Plan of Texas

4265 San Felipe Street
#1100
Houston, TX 77027-2920
Phone: 713-960-6680
webmaster@vsp.com
www.vsp.com
Year Founded: 1955
Number of Primary Care Physicians: 26,000
Total Enrollment: 55,000,000

Healthplan and Services Defined
  PLAN TYPE: Vision
  Plan Specialty: Vision
  Benefits Offered: Vision

Type of Payment Plans Offered
  Capitated

Geographic Areas Served
  Statewide

Network Qualifications
  Pre-Admission Certification: Yes

Peer Review Type
  Utilization Review: Yes

Accreditation Certification
  Utilization Review, Quality Assurance Program

Key Personnel
  Manager . . . . Thomas Barber

1100 WellPoint NextRx

5450 North Riverside Drive
Fort Worth, TX 76137
Toll-Free: 888-809-6084
Phone: 800-293-2202
www.wellpointnextrx.com
Secondary Address: 8990 Duke Blvd, Suite 3-600, Box 21, Austin, TX 78701-3942
Subsidiary of: WellPoint
For Profit Organization: Yes
Year Founded: 1993
Total Enrollment: 300,000

Healthplan and Services Defined
  PLAN TYPE: Multiple
  Model Type: Network
  Plan Specialty: PBM
  Benefits Offered: Prescription

Type of Coverage
  Commercial

Geographic Areas Served
  Nationwide

Accreditation Certification
  URAC
  Pre-Admission Certification

Key Personnel
  General Manager . . . . Michael Nameth
  VP/CFO . . . . Sally Sharma
  Marketing . . . . Jacqueline Dart
  VP Info. Systems . . . . Prudence Kaui
  National Sales Director . . . . Jeff Turner
    706-369-1300

Employer References
  Blue Cross of California, Blue Cross and Blue Shield of Georgia, United Wisconsin

Health Insurance Coverage Status and Type of Coverage by Age

Category	All Persons		Under 18 years		Under 65 years		65 years and over	
	Number	%	Number	%	Number	%	Number	%
Total population	2,829	-	881	-	2,533	-	296	-
Covered by some type of health insurance	2,443 (36)	86.4 (1.1)	780 (17)	88.6 (1.6)	2,148 (41)	84.8 (1.2)	295 (18)	99.5 (0.5)
Covered by private health insurance	2,087 (56)	73.8 (1.8)	643 (26)	73.0 (2.6)	1,922 (54)	75.9 (1.7)	165 (18)	55.5 (5.6)
Employment based	1,858 (64)	65.7 (2.1)	596 (28)	67.7 (3.0)	1,759 (62)	69.4 (2.0)	99 (18)	33.4 (5.8)
Own employment based	793 (31)	28.0 (1.0)	1 (1)	0.1 (0.1)	724 (27)	28.6 (0.9)	68 (14)	23.1 (4.5)
Direct purchase	281 (31)	9.9 (1.1)	50 (11)	5.7 (1.3)	205 (30)	8.1 (1.2)	76 (11)	25.8 (3.7)
Covered by government health insurance	652 (39)	23.0 (1.4)	194 (22)	22.1 (2.6)	366 (34)	14.5 (1.4)	285 (18)	96.3 (1.4)
Covered by Medicaid	268 (29)	9.5 (1.0)	156 (18)	17.7 (2.1)	252 (28)	9.9 (1.1)	16 (7)	5.4 (2.4)
Also by private insurance	79 (17)	2.8 (0.6)	41 (10)	4.7 (1.2)	76 (17)	3.0 (0.7)	2 (2)	0.8 (0.5)
Covered by Medicare	351 (28)	12.4 (1.0)	23 (11)	2.6 (1.3)	65 (17)	2.6 (0.7)	285 (18)	96.3 (1.4)
Also by private insurance	172 (17)	6.1 (0.6)	1 (1)	0.2 (0.2)	17 (5)	0.7 (0.2)	155 (18)	52.2 (5.7)
Also by Medicaid	31 (9)	1.1 (0.3)	1 (1)	0.2 (0.2)	15 (5)	0.6 (0.2)	16 (7)	5.4 (2.4)
Covered by military health care	108 (22)	3.8 (0.8)	18 (6)	2.0 (0.7)	67 (18)	2.7 (0.7)	40 (9)	13.6 (3.0)
Not covered at any time during the year	386 (30)	13.6 (1.1)	101 (14)	11.4 (1.6)	384 (30)	15.2 (1.2)	1 (1)	0.5 (0.5)

Note: Numbers in thousands; figures cover 2010; standard error appears in parenthesis; (b) base less than 75,000; (x) not applicable
Source: U.S. Census Bureau, Current Population Survey, 2011 Annual Social and Economic Supplement. Table HI05. Health Insurance Coverage Status and Type of Coverage by State and Age for All People: 2010

Utah

1101 Aetna Health of Utah
Partnered with eHealthInsurance Services Inc.

1102 Altius Health Plans
10421 S Jordan Parkway
Suite 400
South Jordan, UT 84095
Toll-Free: 800-377-4161
Phone: 801-355-1234
utahcustomerservice@ahplans.com
www.altiushealthplans.com
Subsidiary of: Coventry Health Care
For Profit Organization: Yes
Year Founded: 1998
Number of Affiliated Hospitals: 46
Number of Primary Care Physicians: 3,800
Number of Referral/Specialty Physicians: 1,850
Total Enrollment: 148,000
State Enrollment: 84,000

Healthplan and Services Defined
PLAN TYPE: Multiple
Model Type: Group, POS
Plan Specialty: Behavioral Health, Chiropractic, Disease
    Management, Lab, PBM, Vision, Radiology, UR
Benefits Offered: Behavioral Health, Chiropractic, Dental, Disease
    Management, Home Care, Inpatient SNF, Physical Therapy,
    Podiatry, Prescription, Psychiatric, Transplant, Vision, Wellness
Offers Demand Management Patient Information Service: Yes

Type of Coverage
Commercial, Catastrophic
Catastrophic Illness Benefit: Unlimited

Type of Payment Plans Offered
POS, DFFS

Geographic Areas Served
Utah, Idaho and Wyoming

Subscriber Information
Average Monthly Fee Per Subscriber
    (Employee + Employer Contribution):
        Employee Only (Self): Varies
        Employee & 1 Family Member: Varies
        Employee & 2 Family Members: Varies
        Medicare: Varies
Average Annual Deductible Per Subscriber:
        Employee Only (Self): Varies
        Employee & 1 Family Member: Varies
        Employee & 2 Family Members: Varies
        Medicare: Varies
Average Subscriber Co-Payment:
        Primary Care Physician: $15.00
        Non-Network Physician: 70%
        Prescription Drugs: Varies
        Hospital ER: Varies
        Home Health Care: Varies
        Home Health Care Max. Days/Visits Covered: 60 visits
        Nursing Home: Varies
        Nursing Home Max. Days/Visits Covered: 60 visits

Network Qualifications
Pre-Admission Certification: Yes

Peer Review Type
Utilization Review: Yes
Second Surgical Opinion: Yes
Case Management: Yes

Publishes and Distributes Report Card: Yes
Accreditation Certification
TJC Accreditation, Medicare Approved, Utilization Review,
    Pre-Admission Certification, State Licensure, Quality Assurance
    Program

Key Personnel
Chief Executive Officer . . . . Todd Treptin
CFO . . . . Brett Clay
Director, Human Resources . . . . Lani Anderson
Marketing Executive . . . . Deborah Rosenhan
VP Chief Medical Officer . . . . Dennis T Harston, MD
Information Services . . . . Russell Nelson

Specialty Managed Care Partners
Horizon Behavioral Health, ESI

Employer References
Federal Government, State of Utah, Davis County School District,
    Wells Fargo, DMBA

1103 CIGNA HealthCare of Utah
Acquired by CIGNA

1104 Delta Dental of Utah
257 East 200 South
Suite 375
Salt Lake City, UT 84111
Toll-Free: 800-453-5577
Phone: 801-575-5168
Fax: 801-575-5171
utsales@delta.org
www.deltadentalins.com
Non-Profit Organization: Yes
Total Enrollment: 54,000,000

Healthplan and Services Defined
PLAN TYPE: Dental
Other Type: Dental PPO

Type of Coverage
Commercial

Geographic Areas Served
Statewide

Key Personnel
Dir/Media & Public Affair . . . . Elizabeth Risberg
    415-972-8423

1105 Educators Mutual
852 E Arrowhead Lane
Murray, UT 84107-5298
Toll-Free: 800-662-5851
Phone: 801-262-7475
Fax: 801-269-9734
cs@educatorsmutual.com
www.educatorsmutual.com
Non-Profit Organization: Yes
Year Founded: 1935
Physician Owned Organization: Yes
Federally Qualified: Yes
Number of Affiliated Hospitals: 25
Number of Primary Care Physicians: 3,500
Total Enrollment: 6,000
State Enrollment: 65,000

Healthplan and Services Defined
PLAN TYPE: HMO/PPO
Model Type: Network
Plan Specialty: Behavioral Health, Chiropractic, Disease
    Management, Radiology, UR

Benefits Offered: Behavioral Health, Chiropractic, Complementary
Medicine, Dental, Disease Management, Home Care, Inpatient
SNF, Physical Therapy, Podiatry, Prescription, Psychiatric,
Transplant, Vision, Wellness, AD&D, Life, LTD, STD
Offers Demand Management Patient Information Service: Yes
DMPI Services Offered: Wellness Web

Type of Coverage
Commercial, Individual

Type of Payment Plans Offered
POS

Geographic Areas Served
Box Elder, Cache, Davis, Salt Lake, Weber counties

Subscriber Information
Average Monthly Fee Per Subscriber
(Employee + Employer Contribution):
Employee Only (Self): Varies by plan
Average Annual Deductible Per Subscriber:
Employee Only (Self): $0
Employee & 1 Family Member: $0
Employee & 2 Family Members: $0
Medicare: $0
Average Subscriber Co-Payment:
Primary Care Physician: $5.00
Prescription Drugs: 30%
Hospital ER: $25.00
Home Health Care: $0
Nursing Home: $0

Network Qualifications
Pre-Admission Certification: Yes

Peer Review Type
Utilization Review: Yes
Second Surgical Opinion: No
Case Management: Yes

Publishes and Distributes Report Card: Yes

Accreditation Certification
TJC Accreditation, Utilization Review, Pre-Admission Certification,
State Licensure, Quality Assurance Program

Key Personnel
CEO . . . . Andy Galano
CFO . . . . David Glauser
Press Contact . . . . Nicole Santiago
801-481-9482
Director of Claims . . . . Ilene Wind
Controller . . . . David Leonard, CPA
Marketing . . . . Tom Busby
Chief Information Officer . . . . Ted Peck

Specialty Managed Care Partners
Enters into Contracts with Regional Business Coalitions: No

1106   eHealthInsurance Services Inc.
11919 Foundation Place
Gold River, CA 95670
Toll-Free: 800-977-8860
info@ehealthinsurance.com
www.e.healthinsurance.com
Year Founded: 1997

Healthplan and Services Defined
PLAN TYPE: HMO/PPO
Benefits Offered: Dental, Life, STD

Type of Coverage
Commercial, Individual, Medicare

Geographic Areas Served
All 50 states in the USA and District of Columbia

Key Personnel
Chairman & CEO . . . . Gary L. Lauer
EVP/Business & Corp. Dev. . . . . Bruce Telkamp
EVP/Chief Technology . . . . Dr. Sheldon X. Wang

SVP & CFO . . . . Stuart M. Huizinga
Pres. of eHealth Gov. Sys . . . . Samuel C. Gibbs
SVP of Sales & Operations . . . . Robert S. Hurley
Director Public Relations . . . . Nate Purpura
650-210-3115

1107   Humana Health Insurance of Utah
9815 South Monroe Street
Suite 300
Sandy, UT 84070
Toll-Free: 800-884-8328
Phone: 801-256-6200
Fax: 801-256-0782
www.humana.com
For Profit Organization: Yes

Healthplan and Services Defined
PLAN TYPE: HMO/PPO

Type of Coverage
Commercial, Individual

Accreditation Certification
URAC, NCQA, CORE

1108   Meritain Health: Utah
Sorenson Park Building #7
4246 S Riverboat Road, Suite 200
Taylorsville, UT 84123
Phone: 801-261-5511
sales@meritain.com
www.meritain.com
For Profit Organization: Yes
Year Founded: 1983
Number of Affiliated Hospitals: 110
Number of Primary Care Physicians: 3,467
Number of Referral/Specialty Physicians: 5,720
Total Enrollment: 500,000
State Enrollment: 450,000

Healthplan and Services Defined
PLAN TYPE: PPO
Model Type: Network
Plan Specialty: Dental, Disease Management, Vision, Radiology, UR
Benefits Offered: Prescription
Offers Demand Management Patient Information Service: Yes

Type of Coverage
Commercial

Geographic Areas Served
Nationwide

Subscriber Information
Average Monthly Fee Per Subscriber
(Employee + Employer Contribution):
Employee Only (Self): Varies by plan

Accreditation Certification
URAC
TJC Accreditation, Medicare Approved, Utilization Review,
Pre-Admission Certification, State Licensure, Quality Assurance
Program

Key Personnel
Regional President . . . . David Smith

Average Claim Compensation
Physician's Fees Charged: 78%
Hospital's Fees Charged: 90%

Specialty Managed Care Partners
Express Scripts, LabOne, Interactive Health Solutions

1109 Molina Healthcare: Utah

7050 Union Park Center
Suite 200
Midvale, UT 84047
Toll-Free: 888-483-0760
Phone: 801-858-0400
www.molinahealthcare.com
For Profit Organization: Yes
Year Founded: 1980
Physician Owned Organization: Yes
Number of Affiliated Hospitals: 84
Number of Primary Care Physicians: 2,167
Number of Referral/Specialty Physicians: 6,184
Total Enrollment: 1,400,000

Healthplan and Services Defined
   PLAN TYPE: HMO
   Model Type: Network
   Benefits Offered: Chiropractic, Dental, Home Care, Inpatient SNF,
      Long-Term Care, Podiatry, Vision

Type of Coverage
   Commercial, Medicare, Supplemental Medicare, Medicaid

Accreditation Certification
   URAC, NCQA

1110 Opticare of Utah

1901 W Parkway Boulevard
Salt Lake City, UT 84119-1907
Toll-Free: 800-393-2273
Phone: 801-886-2020
Fax: 801-954-0054
service@opticareofutah.com
www.opticareofutah.com
For Profit Organization: Yes
Year Founded: 1985
Number of Primary Care Physicians: 17
Number of Referral/Specialty Physicians: 40
Total Enrollment: 150,000
State Enrollment: 150,000

Healthplan and Services Defined
   PLAN TYPE: Vision
   Other Type: Optical
   Model Type: Network
   Plan Specialty: Vision
   Benefits Offered: Vision

Type of Payment Plans Offered
   POS, Capitated, FFS

Geographic Areas Served
   Statewide

Subscriber Information
   Average Subscriber Co-Payment:
      Primary Care Physician: Varies

Network Qualifications
   Pre-Admission Certification: Yes

Peer Review Type
   Utilization Review: Yes
   Second Surgical Opinion: Yes
   Case Management: Yes

Key Personnel
   Chief Executive Officer . . . . Aaron Schubach
      801-886-2020
      aaron@opticareofutah.com
   President. . . . . Stephen Schubach
      801-243-1290
      stephen@opticareofutah.com

Chief Financial Officer . . . . Ken Acker
   801-886-2020
   ken@opticareofutah.com
Office Manager . . . . Brittany Acker
   801-886-2020
   brittany@opticareofutah.com
Large Group Enrollment . . . . Jared Jensen
   jared@opticareofutah.com
Claims Processing . . . . Stacie Merrill
   stacie@opticareofutah.com
Provider Relations . . . . Michelle Anderson
   801-886-2020
   michelle@standardoptical.net
Director of Sales . . . . Nicole Monroe
   801-869-2018
   nicolem@opticareofutah.com

Specialty Managed Care Partners
   Enters into Contracts with Regional Business Coalitions: Yes

Employer References
   State of Utah Employees

1111 Public Employees Health Program

560 East 200 South
Salt Lake City, UT 84102
Toll-Free: 800-765-7347
Phone: 801-366-7555
Fax: 801-366-7596
www.pehp.org
Secondary Address: Southern Utah Branch Office, 165 North 100 East
   #9, St. George, UT 84770
Subsidiary of: Utah Retirement Systems
Non-Profit Organization: Yes
Year Founded: 1977
Number of Affiliated Hospitals: 49
Number of Primary Care Physicians: 12,000
Number of Referral/Specialty Physicians: 2,900
Total Enrollment: 177,854
State Enrollment: 177,854

Healthplan and Services Defined
   PLAN TYPE: PPO
   Model Type: Network
   Plan Specialty: Behavioral Health, Chiropractic, Dental, Disease
      Management, Lab, PBM, Vision, Radiology, UR
   Benefits Offered: Behavioral Health, Chiropractic, Dental, Disease
      Management, Home Care, Physical Therapy, Podiatry, Prescription,
      Psychiatric, Transplant, Vision, Wellness, AD&D, Life, LTD

Type of Coverage
   Supplemental Medicare, Children's Health Insurance Program
   Catastrophic Illness Benefit: None

Type of Payment Plans Offered
   FFS

Geographic Areas Served
   Utah's public employees and their families

Subscriber Information
   Average Monthly Fee Per Subscriber
      (Employee + Employer Contribution):
         Employee Only (Self): Varies by plan
         Employee & 1 Family Member: $583.00
   Average Annual Deductible Per Subscriber:
         Employee Only (Self): $0
         Employee & 1 Family Member: $0
         Employee & 2 Family Members: $0
         Medicare: $0
   Average Subscriber Co-Payment:
         Primary Care Physician: $15.00
         Non-Network Physician: 15.00 + 30%
         Prescription Drugs: 20%
         Hospital ER: $80.00

Home Health Care Max. Days/Visits Covered: Unlimited

Network Qualifications
Pre-Admission Certification: No

Peer Review Type
Utilization Review: Yes
Second Surgical Opinion: Yes
Case Management: Yes

Publishes and Distributes Report Card: Yes

Accreditation Certification
TJC Accreditation, Medicare Approved, State Licensure

Key Personnel
Director . . . . .Jeffrey L Jensen, CPA
Finance Director . . . . .Steven Y Broadhead, CPA
Healthcare Services Dir . . . . .G Steve Baker
General Services Director . . . . .R Scott Hansen
Medical Director . . . . .Cynthia Jones, MD
Administrative Assistant. . . . . .Karen M Ridges

Average Claim Compensation
Physician's Fees Charged: 70%
Hospital's Fees Charged: 80%

Specialty Managed Care Partners
Managed Mental Healthcare, Chiropratic Health Plan, IHC Auesst
Enters into Contracts with Regional Business Coalitions: Yes

Employer References
State of Utah, Jordon School District, Salt Lake County, Salt Lake City, Utah School Boards Association

1112 Regence Blue Cross & Blue Shield of Utah

2890 E Cottonwood Parkway
Salt Lake City, UT 84121
Toll-Free: 800-624-6519
Phone: 801-333-2000
Fax: 801-476-9138
www.ut.regence.com
Mailing Address: PO Box 1071, Portland, OR 97207
Subsidiary of: Blue Cross Blue Shield National Association
For Profit Organization: Yes
Year Founded: 1942
Physician Owned Organization: Yes
Owned by an Integrated Delivery Network (IDN): Yes
Number of Affiliated Hospitals: 44
Number of Primary Care Physicians: 4,350
Total Enrollment: 320,000
State Enrollment: 231,824

Healthplan and Services Defined
PLAN TYPE: PPO
Model Type: Network
Plan Specialty: ASO, Behavioral Health, Chiropractic, Dental, Disease Management, MSO, PBM, Vision, Radiology, UR
Benefits Offered: Behavioral Health, Chiropractic, Complementary Medicine, Dental, Disease Management, Home Care, Inpatient SNF, Physical Therapy, Podiatry, Prescription, Psychiatric, Transplant, Vision, Wellness, AD&D, Life, LTD, STD

Type of Coverage
Individual, Supplemental Medicare
Catastrophic Illness Benefit: Varies per case

Geographic Areas Served
Statewide

Subscriber Information
Average Monthly Fee Per Subscriber
(Employee + Employer Contribution):
Employee Only (Self): Varies by plan
Average Annual Deductible Per Subscriber:
Employee Only (Self): $250.00 per person
Employee & 1 Family Member: $250.00 per person
Employee & 2 Family Members: $250.00 per person
Average Subscriber Co-Payment:

Primary Care Physician: Varies by plan
Non-Network Physician: Varies
Prescription Drugs: $5.00/20%
Hospital ER: $50.00
Home Health Care: 20%
Nursing Home: 20%

Network Qualifications
Pre-Admission Certification: Yes

Peer Review Type
Utilization Review: Yes
Second Surgical Opinion: No
Case Management: Yes

Publishes and Distributes Report Card: Yes

Accreditation Certification
Ambest
TJC Accreditation, Medicare Approved, Utilization Review, Pre-Admission Certification, State Licensure, Quality Assurance Program

Key Personnel
President. . . . . .Robert A Hatch
Chief Information Officer .Cheron Vail
Chief Marketing Exec . . . . .Mohan Nair
Chief Legal Officer . . . . .Kerry Barnett
Vice President/Sales . . . . .Alfred S Tredway
Media Contact . . . . .J Kevin Bischoff
801-333-5285
kbischoff@regence.com
VP, Provider Relations . . . . .Bryon Clawson
Media Contact. . . . . .Mike Tatko
208-798-2221
mtatkoid@regence.com

Average Claim Compensation
Physician's Fees Charged: 30%
Hospital's Fees Charged: 21%

Specialty Managed Care Partners
Enters into Contracts with Regional Business Coalitions: Yes

1113 SelectHealth

5381 Green Street
Murray, UT 84123
Toll-Free: 800-538-5038
Phone: 801-442-5000
http://selecthealth.org
Subsidiary of: Intermountain Healthcare
Non-Profit Organization: Yes
Total Enrollment: 402,000

Healthplan and Services Defined
PLAN TYPE: HMO

Type of Coverage
Commercial, Individual

Accreditation Certification
NCQA

Key Personnel
President/CEO . . . . .Patricia R Richards
Media Contact . . . . .Spencer Sutherland
801-442-7960

1114 Total Dental Administrators

969 East Murray Holladay Road
Suite 4E
Salt Lake City, UT 84117
Toll-Free: 800-880-3536
Phone: 801-268-8740
Fax: 801-268-9873
www.tdadental.com

Healthplan and Services Defined
  PLAN TYPE: Dental

Key Personnel
  President...................................Jane Morrison
  VP, Operations.............................Jeremy Spencer

1115 UnitedHealthCare of Utah
  2525 Lake Park Blvd
  Salt Lake City, UT 84120
  Toll-Free: 800-624-2942
  www.uhc.com
  Subsidiary of: UnitedHealth Group
  For Profit Organization: Yes
  Total Enrollment: 75,000,000
  State Enrollment: 109,709

Healthplan and Services Defined
  PLAN TYPE: HMO/PPO

Geographic Areas Served
  Statewide

Key Personnel
  Media Contact ....Will Shanley
    will.shanley@uhc.com

1116 University Health Plans
  127 S 500 E
  Suite 360
  Salt Lake City, UT 84102
  Toll-Free: 888-271-5870
  Phone: 801-587-6480
  Fax: 801-587-6433
  uuhp@hsc.utah.edu
  http://uhealthplan.utah.edu
  Non-Profit Organization: Yes
  Number of Affiliated Hospitals: 28
  Number of Primary Care Physicians: 1,750
  Total Enrollment: 86,000
  State Enrollment: 50,000

Healthplan and Services Defined
  PLAN TYPE: HMO/PPO
  Benefits Offered: Disease Management, Wellness

Type of Coverage
  Commercial, Medicare, Medicaid

Geographic Areas Served
  Utah

Key Personnel
  CEO...Vicky Wilson
  COO...Vicky Wilson
  CMO.....................................Dean Smart, MD
  Provider Relations............................Collin Davis
  Marketing ....Vicky Wilson
  Provider Services............................Todd Randall
    801-587-6602
    todd.randall@hsc.utah.edu

Health Insurance Coverage Status and Type of Coverage by Age

Category	All Persons		Under 18 years		Under 65 years		65 years and over	
	Number	%	Number	%	Number	%	Number	%
Total population	622	-	120	-	542	-	81	-
Covered by some type of health insurance	563 *(7)*	90.5 *(0.8)*	115 *(2)*	95.9 *(1.1)*	483 *(8)*	89.2 *(0.9)*	80 *(5)*	99.4 *(0.4)*
Covered by private health insurance	423 *(11)*	68.0 *(1.6)*	76 *(3)*	63.2 *(2.5)*	373 *(11)*	68.8 *(1.7)*	50 *(4)*	62.4 *(3.7)*
Employment based	365 *(12)*	58.7 *(1.7)*	69 *(3)*	57.8 *(2.4)*	342 *(11)*	63.2 *(1.8)*	23 *(3)*	28.5 *(3.6)*
Own employment based	186 *(6)*	29.9 *(1.0)*	0 *(0)*	0.0 *(0.0)*	171 *(6)*	31.6 *(1.0)*	15 *(2)*	18.8 *(2.5)*
Direct purchase	66 *(5)*	10.6 *(0.8)*	7 *(1)*	5.5 *(1.2)*	34 *(4)*	6.2 *(0.8)*	32 *(4)*	39.8 *(3.6)*
Covered by government health insurance	234 *(9)*	37.6 *(1.5)*	54 *(3)*	44.6 *(2.6)*	156 *(8)*	28.8 *(1.5)*	78 *(5)*	97.1 *(1.1)*
Covered by Medicaid	146 *(7)*	23.4 *(1.2)*	52 *(3)*	43.0 *(2.5)*	135 *(7)*	25.0 *(1.4)*	10 *(2)*	12.5 *(2.7)*
Also by private insurance	35 *(4)*	5.6 *(0.6)*	14 *(2)*	11.2 *(1.6)*	32 *(4)*	5.9 *(0.7)*	3 *(1)*	3.9 *(1.4)*
Covered by Medicare	96 *(5)*	15.4 *(0.8)*	0 *(0)*	0.1 *(0.1)*	17 *(2)*	3.2 *(0.4)*	78 *(5)*	97.1 *(1.1)*
Also by private insurance	52 *(4)*	8.4 *(0.7)*	0 *(0)*	0.1 *(0.1)*	4 *(1)*	0.7 *(0.2)*	49 *(4)*	60.1 *(3.5)*
Also by Medicaid	20 *(3)*	3.3 *(0.5)*	0 *(0)*	0.0 *(0.0)*	10 *(2)*	1.9 *(0.3)*	10 *(2)*	12.5 *(2.7)*
Covered by military health care	25 *(4)*	4.0 *(0.6)*	2 *(1)*	1.8 *(0.7)*	14 *(3)*	2.7 *(0.5)*	10 *(3)*	12.7 *(3.1)*
Not covered at any time during the year	59 *(5)*	9.5 *(0.8)*	5 *(1)*	4.1 *(1.1)*	59 *(5)*	10.8 *(0.9)*	0 *(0)*	0.6 *(0.4)*

Note: Numbers in thousands; figures cover 2010; standard error appears in parenthesis; (b) base less than 75,000; (x) not applicable
Source: U.S. Census Bureau, Current Population Survey, 2011 Annual Social and Economic Supplement. Table HI05. Health Insurance Coverage Status and Type of Coverage by State and Age for All People: 2010

Vermont

1117 Aetna Health of Vermont

Partnered with eHealthInsurance Services Inc.

1118 Blue Cross & Blue Shield of Vermont

445 Industrial Lane
Berlin, VT 05602
Toll-Free: 800-247-2583
Phone: 802-223-6131
Fax: 802-223-4229
customerservice@bcbsvt.com
www.bcbsvt.com
Mailing Address: PO Box 186, Montpelier, VT 05601
Non-Profit Organization: Yes
Year Founded: 1944
Number of Affiliated Hospitals: 16
Number of Primary Care Physicians: 681
Number of Referral/Specialty Physicians: 2,802
Total Enrollment: 180,000
State Enrollment: 54,023

Healthplan and Services Defined
 PLAN TYPE: PPO
 Model Type: Network
 Plan Specialty: Behavioral Health, Chiropractic, Disease
  Management, PBM, Vision, UR
 Benefits Offered: Behavioral Health, Chiropractic, Physical Therapy,
  Prescription, Psychiatric, Vision, AD&D, Life, LTD, STD,
  Alternative Healthcare discounts, Vermont Medigap Blue

Type of Coverage
 Commercial, Individual, Indemnity, Medicare, Supplemental
  Medicare, Catastrophic
 Catastrophic Illness Benefit: Maximum $1M

Type of Payment Plans Offered
 Capitated

Geographic Areas Served
 Vermont

Subscriber Information
 Average Monthly Fee Per Subscriber
  (Employee + Employer Contribution):
   Employee Only (Self): Varies by plan
 Average Annual Deductible Per Subscriber:
   Employee Only (Self): $400.00
   Employee & 1 Family Member: $400.00
   Employee & 2 Family Members: $200.00
 Average Subscriber Co-Payment:
   Primary Care Physician: $10.00
   Prescription Drugs: $10.00/20.00/35.00
   Hospital ER: $50.00
   Home Health Care: $40.00

Network Qualifications
 Pre-Admission Certification: Yes

Peer Review Type
 Utilization Review: Yes
 Second Surgical Opinion: No
 Case Management: Yes

Publishes and Distributes Report Card: No

Accreditation Certification
 Utilization Review, State Licensure, Quality Assurance Program

Key Personnel
 President and CEO..............................Don George
 VP, External Affairs..........................Kevin Goddard
 VP, Planning..................................Catherine Hamilton, PhD
 VP, General Counsel...........................Christopher R Gannon
 VP, Sales & Marketing.........................David Krupa
 VP, Treasurer & CFO...........................John Trifone
 VP, Operations................................Douglas L Warren
 VP Sales and Marketing........................David Krupa
 Dir, Govt & Public Rel........................Leigh Tofferi
  802-223-6131
  webmail@bcbsvt.com

Average Claim Compensation
 Physician's Fees Charged: 85%
 Hospital's Fees Charged: 92%

Specialty Managed Care Partners
 Magellan, Restat
 Enters into Contracts with Regional Business Coalitions: Yes

1119 CIGNA HealthCare of Vermont

30 Main Street
Burlington, VT 05401
Toll-Free: 866-438-2446
Fax: 802-658-9212
www.cigna.com
For Profit Organization: Yes

Healthplan and Services Defined
 PLAN TYPE: PPO

Type of Coverage
 Commercial

1120 Delta Dental of Vermont

135 College Street
Burlington, VT 05401-8384
Toll-Free: 800-955-2030
Phone: 502-736-5000
Fax: 802-865-4430
nedental@nedental.com
www.nedental.com
Non-Profit Organization: Yes
Year Founded: 1961
Total Enrollment: 54,000,000

Healthplan and Services Defined
 PLAN TYPE: Dental
 Other Type: Dental PPO
 Model Type: Network
 Plan Specialty: ASO, Dental
 Benefits Offered: Dental

Type of Coverage
 Commercial, Individual, Group
 Catastrophic Illness Benefit: None

Geographic Areas Served
 Statewide

Subscriber Information
 Average Monthly Fee Per Subscriber
  (Employee + Employer Contribution):
   Employee Only (Self): Varies
   Employee & 1 Family Member: Varies
   Employee & 2 Family Members: Varies
 Average Annual Deductible Per Subscriber:
   Employee Only (Self): Varies
   Employee & 1 Family Member: Varies
   Employee & 2 Family Members: Varies
 Average Subscriber Co-Payment:
   Prescription Drugs: $0
   Home Health Care: $0
   Nursing Home: $0

1121 eHealthInsurance Services Inc.

11919 Foundation Place
Gold River, CA 95670
Toll-Free: 800-977-8860
info@ehealthinsurance.com

www.e.healthinsurance.com
Year Founded: 1997

Healthplan and Services Defined
  PLAN TYPE: HMO/PPO
  Benefits Offered: Dental, Life, STD

Type of Coverage
  Commercial, Individual, Medicare

Geographic Areas Served
  All 50 states in the USA and District of Columbia

Key Personnel
  Chairman & CEO . . . . .Gary L. Lauer
  EVP/Business & Corp. Dev. .Bruce Telkamp
  EVP/Chief Technology . . . . .Dr. Sheldon X. Wang
  SVP & CFO . . . . .Stuart M. Huizinga
  Pres. of eHealth Gov. Sys .Samuel C. Gibbs
  SVP of Sales & Operations . . . . .Robert S. Hurley
  Director Public Relations. . . . . .Nate Purpura
    650-210-3115

1122 MVP Health Care: Vermont

66 Knight Lane
Suite 10
Williston, VT 05495
Toll-Free: 800-380-3530
Phone: 802-264-6500
Fax: 802-264-6555
www.mvphealthcare.com
Non-Profit Organization: Yes
Year Founded: 1983
Federally Qualified: Yes
Number of Affiliated Hospitals: 81
Number of Primary Care Physicians: 3,091
Number of Referral/Specialty Physicians: 5,504
Total Enrollment: 750,000

Healthplan and Services Defined
  PLAN TYPE: HMO/PPO
  Model Type: IPA
  Plan Specialty: ASO, EPO
  Benefits Offered: Behavioral Health, Chiropractic, Complementary
    Medicine, Dental, Disease Management, Home Care, Inpatient
    SNF, Physical Therapy, Podiatry, Prescription, Psychiatric,
    Transplant, Vision, Wellness, Worker's Compensation
  Offers Demand Management Patient Information Service: No
  DMPI Services Offered: After Hours Phone Line, Health Central
    (Library), Little Footprints Prenatal Program, Health Risk
    Assessments, Adult and Childhood Immunizations

Type of Coverage
  Commercial, Individual, Indemnity, Self Funded, Administrative
    Service
  Catastrophic Illness Benefit: Covered

Type of Payment Plans Offered
  POS, DFFS, Capitated, FFS, Combination FFS & DFFS

Geographic Areas Served
  VT

Subscriber Information
  Average Annual Deductible Per Subscriber:
    Employee Only (Self): $200/400

Peer Review Type
  Utilization Review: Yes
  Case Management: Yes

Publishes and Distributes Report Card: Yes

Accreditation Certification
  NCQA
  TJC Accreditation, Medicare Approved, Utilization Review,
    Pre-Admission Certification, State Licensure, Quality Assurance
    Program

Key Personnel
  President/CEO . . . . .David Oliker
  EVP/COO . . . . .Chris Henchey
  EVP/Rochester Operations. . . . . .Lisa A Brubaker
  EVP/Network Management . . . . .Mark Fish
  EVP/Planning. . . . . .Alfred Gatti
  EVP/Chief Legal Officer. . . . . .Denise Gonick, Esq
  EVP/Human Resources. . . . . .James Morrill

Average Claim Compensation
  Physician's Fees Charged: 75%
  Hospital's Fees Charged: 65%

1123 UnitedHealthCare of Vermont

1 Research Drive
Westborough, MA 01581
Toll-Free: 800-444-7855
www.uhc.com
Subsidiary of: UnitedHealth Group
For Profit Organization: Yes
Year Founded: 1986
Number of Affiliated Hospitals: 47
Number of Primary Care Physicians: 1,600
Number of Referral/Specialty Physicians: 3,500
Total Enrollment: 75,000,000

Healthplan and Services Defined
  PLAN TYPE: HMO/PPO
  Model Type: Mixed Model
  Plan Specialty: MSO
  Benefits Offered: Behavioral Health, Chiropractic, Complementary
    Medicine, Dental, Disease Management, Home Care, Inpatient
    SNF, Long-Term Care, Physical Therapy, Podiatry, Prescription,
    Psychiatric, Transplant, Vision, Wellness, AD&D, Life

Type of Coverage
  Commercial, Individual, Medicaid, Commercial Group

Type of Payment Plans Offered
  DFFS, FFS, Combination FFS & DFFS

Geographic Areas Served
  Statewide

Subscriber Information
  Average Monthly Fee Per Subscriber
    (Employee + Employer Contribution):
      Employee Only (Self): Varies
    Average Subscriber Co-Payment:
      Primary Care Physician: $10
      Prescription Drugs: $10/15/30
      Hospital ER: $50

Network Qualifications
  Pre-Admission Certification: Yes

Peer Review Type
  Case Management: Yes

Publishes and Distributes Report Card: Yes

Accreditation Certification
  URAC, NCQA
  State Licensure, Quality Assurance Program

Average Claim Compensation
  Physician's Fees Charged: 70%
  Hospital's Fees Charged: 55%

Specialty Managed Care Partners
  United Behavioral Health
  Enters into Contracts with Regional Business Coalitions: No

Health Insurance Coverage Status and Type of Coverage by Age

Category	All Persons		Under 18 years		Under 65 years		65 years and over	
	Number	%	Number	%	Number	%	Number	%
Total population	7,771	-	1,867	-	6,884	-	887	-
Covered by some type of health insurance	6,675 (77)	85.9 (0.8)	1,713 (29)	91.7 (1.2)	5,801 (87)	84.3 (0.9)	874 (48)	98.6 (0.5)
Covered by private health insurance	5,486 (113)	70.6 (1.3)	1,326 (43)	71.0 (2.0)	4,944 (111)	71.8 (1.4)	542 (39)	61.1 (3.0)
Employment based	4,768 (110)	61.4 (1.3)	1,218 (38)	65.3 (1.8)	4,440 (104)	64.5 (1.3)	328 (28)	37.0 (2.7)
Own employment based	2,348 (66)	30.2 (0.8)	5 (3)	0.2 (0.1)	2,102 (61)	30.5 (0.8)	246 (23)	27.7 (2.3)
Direct purchase	765 (68)	9.8 (0.9)	112 (24)	6.0 (1.3)	521 (59)	7.6 (0.9)	244 (27)	27.5 (2.4)
Covered by government health insurance	2,126 (81)	27.4 (1.1)	543 (35)	29.1 (1.9)	1,299 (72)	18.9 (1.0)	827 (49)	93.3 (1.4)
Covered by Medicaid	645 (57)	8.3 (0.8)	360 (33)	19.3 (1.8)	590 (50)	8.6 (0.7)	54 (18)	6.1 (1.9)
Also by private insurance	120 (17)	1.5 (0.2)	68 (14)	3.7 (0.8)	113 (17)	1.6 (0.3)	7 (5)	0.8 (0.6)
Covered by Medicare	968 (52)	12.5 (0.7)	9 (6)	0.5 (0.3)	149 (21)	2.2 (0.3)	819 (48)	92.3 (1.6)
Also by private insurance	539 (38)	6.9 (0.5)	3 (2)	0.2 (0.1)	49 (8)	0.7 (0.1)	490 (38)	55.3 (3.0)
Also by Medicaid	84 (22)	1.1 (0.3)	0 (0)	0.0 (0.0)	32 (8)	0.5 (0.1)	52 (17)	5.8 (1.9)
Covered by military health care	744 (63)	9.6 (0.8)	186 (24)	9.9 (1.3)	633 (58)	9.2 (0.8)	112 (22)	12.6 (2.4)
Not covered at any time during the year	1,096 (64)	14.1 (0.8)	154 (23)	8.3 (1.2)	1,083 (64)	15.7 (0.9)	13 (5)	1.4 (0.5)

Note: Numbers in thousands; figures cover 2010; standard error appears in parenthesis; (b) base less than 75,000; (x) not applicable
Source: U.S. Census Bureau, Current Population Survey, 2011 Annual Social and Economic Supplement. Table HI05. Health Insurance Coverage Status and Type of Coverage by State and Age for All People: 2010

Virginia

1124 Aetna Health of Virginia

151 Farmington Avenue
Conveyer ASB2
Hartford, CT 06156
Toll-Free: 866-582-9629
www.aetna.com
For Profit Organization: Yes
Year Founded: 1984
Number of Affiliated Hospitals: 119
Number of Primary Care Physicians: 6,908
Number of Referral/Specialty Physicians: 12,502
Total Enrollment: 211,156

Healthplan and Services Defined
PLAN TYPE: HMO
Other Type: POS
Model Type: IPA
Benefits Offered: Behavioral Health, Dental, Disease Management, Prescription, Vision, Wellness, Life
Offers Demand Management Patient Information Service: Yes

Type of Coverage
Commercial, Individual, Medicare

Type of Payment Plans Offered
POS, DFFS

Geographic Areas Served
Statewide

Subscriber Information
Average Annual Deductible Per Subscriber:
Employee Only (Self): Varies
Employee & 1 Family Member: Varies
Employee & 2 Family Members: Varies
Medicare: Varies

Network Qualifications
Pre-Admission Certification: Yes

Peer Review Type
Utilization Review: No
Second Surgical Opinion: Yes
Case Management: Yes

Publishes and Distributes Report Card: Yes

Accreditation Certification
NCQA
TJC Accreditation, Utilization Review, Pre-Admission Certification, State Licensure, Quality Assurance Program

Key Personnel
CEO & President . . . . .Mark T Bertolini
SVP, General Counsel . . . . .William J Casazza
SEVP, CFO. . . . . .Joseph M Zubretsky
Head, M&A Integration . . . . .Kay Mooney
SVP, Marketing. . . . . .Robert E Mead
Chief Medical Officer .Lonny Reisman, MD
SVP, Human Resources. . . . . .Elease E Wright
SVP, CIO. . . . . .Meg McCarthy

Specialty Managed Care Partners
Enters into Contracts with Regional Business Coalitions: Yes

1125 Amerigroup Corporation

2815 Hartland Road
Suite 200
Merrifield, VA 22043
Toll-Free: 800-600-4441
Phone: 757-490-6900
mpsweb@amerigroupcorp.com
www.amerigroupcorp.com
For Profit Organization: Yes

Year Founded: 1994
Number of Primary Care Physicians: 3,066
Total Enrollment: 1,900,000

Healthplan and Services Defined
PLAN TYPE: HMO
Benefits Offered: Disease Management

Type of Coverage
Medicaid

Geographic Areas Served
11 counties in Northern Virginia

Accreditation Certification
URAC, NCQA

Key Personnel
Chairman/President/CEO. .James G Carlson
EVP, General Counsel . . . . .Stanley F Baldwin
sbaldwi@amerigroupcorp.com
EVP, Public Policy Inst . . . . .Nancy L Grden
EVP, CFO. . . . . .James W Truess
EVP, COO . . . . .Richard C Zoretic
Chief Compliance Officer. . . . . .John R Finley
SVP, Chief Accounting Ofc . . . . .Margaret M Roomsburg
EVP, General Counsel . . . . .Nicholas Pace
EVP, Chief Medical Offc . . . . .Mary McCluskey
EVP, Human Resources . . . . .Linda Whitley-Taylor
EVP, Chief Info Officer. .Leon A Root, Jr
EVP, External Relations . . . . .John E Littel
Corporate Communications. . . . . .Tara Wall
757-321-3592
twall01@amerigroupcorp.com

1126 Anthem Blue Cross & Blue Shield of Virginia

2015 Staples Mill Road
PO Box 27401
Richmond, VA 23230
Toll-Free: 800-421-1880
Phone: 804-354-7000
Fax: 804-354-3610
www.anthem.com
Secondary Address: 602 South Jefferson Street, Roanoke, VA 24011
For Profit Organization: Yes
Year Founded: 1980
Number of Affiliated Hospitals: 125
Number of Primary Care Physicians: 2,700
Number of Referral/Specialty Physicians: 5,700
Total Enrollment: 2,800,000
State Enrollment: 2,800,000

Healthplan and Services Defined
PLAN TYPE: HMO
Model Type: IPA
Plan Specialty: Lab, Radiology
Benefits Offered: Behavioral Health, Dental, Disease Management, Prescription, Vision, Wellness, Life, Alternative Medicine

Type of Coverage
Commercial, Individual, Medicare
Catastrophic Illness Benefit: Unlimited

Type of Payment Plans Offered
Capitated

Geographic Areas Served
Chesapeake, Norfolk, Petersburg, Richmond, Virginia Beach, Suffolk, South Hampton Road and surrounding counties

Subscriber Information
Average Subscriber Co-Payment:
Primary Care Physician: $5.00/10.00
Prescription Drugs: $5.00/10.00
Hospital ER: $25.00
Home Health Care Max. Days/Visits Covered: 100 days

Peer Review Type
Case Management: Yes

Publishes and Distributes Report Card: Yes

Accreditation Certification
TJC Accreditation, Medicare Approved, Utilization Review, Pre-Admission Certification, State Licensure, Quality Assurance Program

Key Personnel
President . . . . C Burke King
Media Contact . . . . Scott Golden
804-354-5252
scott.golden@anthem.com

Specialty Managed Care Partners
Enters into Contracts with Regional Business Coalitions: Yes

Employer References
Commonwealth of Virginia, GE

1127 CareFirst Blue Cross & Blue Shield of Virginia
10455 & 10453 Mill Run Circle
Owings Mills, MD 21117
Toll-Free: 888-579-8969
Phone: 401-581-3000
www.carefirst.com
Subsidiary of: CareFirst, Inc.
Non-Profit Organization: Yes
Year Founded: 1985
Number of Affiliated Hospitals: 165
Number of Primary Care Physicians: 4,500
Number of Referral/Specialty Physicians: 15,068
Total Enrollment: 3,400,000

Healthplan and Services Defined
PLAN TYPE: HMO/PPO
Model Type: IPA
Plan Specialty: ASO, Behavioral Health, Dental, Vision
Benefits Offered: Behavioral Health, Chiropractic, Dental, Disease Management, Home Care, Physical Therapy, Podiatry, Prescription, Psychiatric, Transplant, Vision, Wellness

Type of Coverage
Commercial, Individual

Type of Payment Plans Offered
POS

Geographic Areas Served
Maryland, Delaware and Washington DC areas

Accreditation Certification
NCQA

Key Personnel
President/CEO . . . . Chester Burrell
EVP, CFO . . . . G Mark Chaney
Chief Marketing Officer . . . . Gregory A Devou
Executive VP/Operations . . . . Leon Kaplan
Exec VP/General Counsel . . . . John A Picciotto, Esq
Chief of Staff . . . . Sharon J Vecchioni
EVP/Medical Systems . . . . David D Wolf
SVP/Public Policy . . . . Maria Tildon

1128 Carilion Health Plans
213 South Jefferson Street
Suite 1409
Roanoke, VA 24011
Toll-Free: 800-779-2285
Phone: 540-857-5200
Fax: 540-857-5343
direct@carilion.com
www.carilionmedicare.com

Subsidiary of: Carilion Health Systems
For Profit Organization: Yes
Year Founded: 1997
Number of Affiliated Hospitals: 12
Number of Primary Care Physicians: 800
Number of Referral/Specialty Physicians: 140

Healthplan and Services Defined
PLAN TYPE: Medicare
Other Type: HMO, POS
Model Type: Network
Plan Specialty: ASO, EPO, Vision, UR
Benefits Offered: Behavioral Health, Chiropractic, Dental, Disease Management, Home Care, Physical Therapy, Podiatry, Prescription, Psychiatric, Transplant, Vision, Wellness

Type of Coverage
Commercial

Type of Payment Plans Offered
POS, DFFS

Geographic Areas Served
Virginia counties: Bedford, Botetourt, Craig, Franklin, Patrick, Pulsaki, Giles, Henry, Roanoke, Floyd, Rockbridge, Montgomery, Tazewell and Wythe

Subscriber Information
Average Subscriber Co-Payment:
Primary Care Physician: $15.00
Prescription Drugs: $20.00
Hospital ER: $50.00

Peer Review Type
Utilization Review: Yes
Case Management: Yes

Key Personnel
President and CEO . . . . Carolyn Chrisman
540-857-5206
COO . . . . James Gore
540-857-5370
Mgr Contract/Compliance . . . . Mel Elkin
540-857-5317
Dir Utilization Mgmt . . . . Peggy Callahan, BSN
540-857-5203
Quality Management . . . . Ruth Ellen Ayers
540-857-5232
Chief Medical Officer . . . . Rome Walker, MD
540-857-5237
Manager Benefit Services . . . . Scottie Krupa
540-857-5223
Dir Information Mgmt . . . . Mattie Tenzer
540-857-5226
Provider Relations Manager . . . . Lynn Rock
540-857-5202

Specialty Managed Care Partners
Express Scripts PBM

1129 CIGNA HealthCare of Virginia
1 James Center
901 E Cary St, Suite 2000
Richmond, VA 23219
Toll-Free: 866-438-2446
Phone: 804-344-2693
Fax: 804-560-3946
www.cigna.com
Secondary Address: 3130 Chaparrell Drive, Suite 104, Roanoke, VA 24018, 800-797-7964
For Profit Organization: Yes
Year Founded: 1984
Number of Affiliated Hospitals: 25
Number of Primary Care Physicians: 1,737
Total Enrollment: 324,600
State Enrollment: 28,460

Healthplan and Services Defined
PLAN TYPE: HMO
Model Type: IPA, Network
Benefits Offered: Behavioral Health, Disease Management, Prescription, Psychiatric, Transplant, Vision, Wellness, Women's and Men's Health
Offers Demand Management Patient Information Service: Yes
DMPI Services Offered: Language Line Service, 24 hour Health Information Line, Health Information Library

Type of Coverage
Commercial, Individual

Geographic Areas Served
Amelia, Caroline, Charles City, Chesterfield, Cumberland, Dinwiddie, Gloucester, Goochland, Greensville, Hanover, Henrico, Isle of Wight, James City, King and Queen, King William, Louisa, Matthews, Middlesex, New Kent, Nottoway, Powhatan, Prince George, Surry, Sussex, York

Publishes and Distributes Report Card: Yes

Accreditation Certification
NCQA
TJC Accreditation, Pre-Admission Certification, State Licensure, Quality Assurance Program

Key Personnel
President and General Manager . . . . Matthew Manders
Sales . . . . Susan Schick

Specialty Managed Care Partners
Cole Managed Vision
Enters into Contracts with Regional Business Coalitions: Yes

1130 Coventry Health Care Virginia

9881 Mayland Drive
Richmond, VA 23233
Toll-Free: 800-424-0077
Phone: 804-747-3700
Fax: 804-762-9349
http://chcvirginia.coventryhealthcare.com
Secondary Address: 1000 Research Park Blvd, Suite 200, Charlottesville, VA 22911
For Profit Organization: Yes
Year Founded: 1985
Number of Affiliated Hospitals: 132
Number of Primary Care Physicians: 12,000
Number of Referral/Specialty Physicians: 2,854
Total Enrollment: 200,000
State Enrollment: 200,000

Healthplan and Services Defined
PLAN TYPE: HMO/PPO
Other Type: POS
Plan Specialty: ASO, Behavioral Health, Chiropractic, Disease Management, Lab, Vision, Radiology, Worker's Compensation, UR
Benefits Offered: Chiropractic, Disease Management, Home Care, Inpatient SNF, Physical Therapy, Podiatry, Prescription, Transplant, Vision, Wellness

Type of Coverage
Commercial, Medicare, Medicaid, Catastrophic
Catastrophic Illness Benefit: Unlimited

Type of Payment Plans Offered
DFFS

Geographic Areas Served
Virginia counties: Albemarle, Alleghany, Amelia, Bath, Botetourt, Buckingham, Caroline, Charles City, Charlotte, Chesterfield, Craig, Culpeper, Cumberland, Dinwiddie, Essex, Floyd, Fluvanna, Giles, Goochland, Greene, Halifax, Hanover, Henrico, JamesCity, King & Queen, King William, Lancaster, Louisa, Lunenberg, Madison, Mathews, Mecklenburg, Middlesex, Montgomery, Nelson, New

Kent, Northumberland, Nottoway, Orange, Pittsylvania, Powhatan, Prince Edward, and more

Subscriber Information
Average Annual Deductible Per Subscriber:
Employee Only (Self): $0
Employee & 1 Family Member: $0
Employee & 2 Family Members: $0
Average Subscriber Co-Payment:
Primary Care Physician: $10.00
Non-Network Physician: Varies
Prescription Drugs: $10/20/45
Hospital ER: $50.00
Home Health Care: $0
Home Health Care Max. Days/Visits Covered: 90 days
Nursing Home: $0
Nursing Home Max. Days/Visits Covered: 100 days

Peer Review Type
Second Surgical Opinion: No

Publishes and Distributes Report Card: Yes

Accreditation Certification
NCQA
TJC Accreditation, Medicare Approved, Utilization Review, Pre-Admission Certification, State Licensure, Quality Assurance Program

Specialty Managed Care Partners
PHCSN, Caremark, Senterea, Colevision
Enters into Contracts with Regional Business Coalitions: Yes

1131 Delta Dental of Virginia

4818 Starkey Road
Roanoke, VA 24018
Toll-Free: 800-237-6060
Phone: 540-989-8000
Fax: 540-774-7574
www.deltadentalva.com
Secondary Address: 4860 Cox Road, Suite 130, Glen Allen, VA 23060
Non-Profit Organization: Yes
Year Founded: 1964
Total Enrollment: 54,000,000

Healthplan and Services Defined
PLAN TYPE: Dental
Other Type: Dental PPO/POS
Model Type: Dental Model
Plan Specialty: Dental
Benefits Offered: Dental

Type of Coverage
Commercial, Group Coverage

Type of Payment Plans Offered
FFS

Geographic Areas Served
Statewide

Key Personnel
President . . . . George A Levicki, DDS
VP Finance . . . . Michael Wise
VP Marketing . . . . PV Davies, II
VP Information Services . . . . Oscar Bryant
Dir/Media & Public Affair . . . . Elizabeth Risberg
415-972-8423

1132 Dominion Dental Services

115 S Union Street
Suite 300
Alexandria, VA 22314
Toll-Free: 888-681-5100
Phone: 703-518-5000
Fax: 703-518-8849

www.dominiondental.com

Mailing Address: PO Box 1126, Claims/Utilization, Elk Grove Village, IL 60009

For Profit Organization: Yes

Year Founded: 1996

Physician Owned Organization: Yes

Number of Primary Care Physicians: 46,000

Total Enrollment: 24,000,000

State Enrollment: 400,000

Healthplan and Services Defined
  PLAN TYPE: Dental
  Plan Specialty: Dental
  Benefits Offered: Dental

Type of Coverage
  Commercial, Individual

Type of Payment Plans Offered
  DFFS, Capitated, Combination FFS & DFFS

Geographic Areas Served
  Maryland, Delaware, Pennsylvania, District of Columbia, Virginia and New Jersey

Network Qualifications
  Pre-Admission Certification: Yes

Peer Review Type
  Utilization Review: Yes
  Case Management: Yes

Publishes and Distributes Report Card: No

Accreditation Certification
  NCQA

Key Personnel
  President . . . . .Mitch McGlynn
  COO . . . . .Michael Davis
  VP, Professional Services . . . . .Lori Hayes
  VP, Accounting . . . . .Kara Greenhouse, CPA
  Dental Director . . . . .Wayne Silverman, DDS
  VP, Business Development . . . . .Jay Rausch
    703-518-5000
  Member Services. . . . . .Lori Hayes
  VP, Sales & Marketing. . . . . .Thomas McGlynn
  Media Contact . . . . .Jeff Schwab
    703-518-5000

Specialty Managed Care Partners
  Enters into Contracts with Regional Business Coalitions: Yes

1133 eHealthInsurance Services Inc.

11919 Foundation Place

Gold River, CA 95670

Toll-Free: 800-977-8860

info@ehealthinsurance.com

www.e.healthinsurance.com

Year Founded: 1997

Healthplan and Services Defined
  PLAN TYPE: HMO/PPO
  Benefits Offered: Dental, Life, STD

Type of Coverage
  Commercial, Individual, Medicare

Geographic Areas Served
  All 50 states in the USA and District of Columbia

Key Personnel
  Chairman & CEO . . . . .Gary L. Lauer
  EVP/Business & Corp. Dev. . . . . .Bruce Telkamp
  EVP/Chief Technology . . . . .Dr. Sheldon X. Wang
  SVP & CFO . . . . .Stuart M. Huizinga
  Pres. of eHealth Gov. Sys . . . . .Samuel C. Gibbs
  SVP of Sales & Operations . . . . .Robert S. Hurley
  Director Public Relations. .Nate Purpura
    650-210-3115

1134 EPIC Pharmacy Network

8703 Studley Road

Suite B

Mechanicsville, VA 23116-2016

Toll-Free: 800-876-3742

Phone: 804-559-4597

Fax: 804-559-2038

www.epicrx.com

Mailing Address: PO Box 1750, Mechanicsville, VA 23116-2016

Subsidiary of: EPIC Pharmacies, Inc.

For Profit Organization: Yes

Year Founded: 1992

Number of Primary Care Physicians: 1,400

Healthplan and Services Defined
  PLAN TYPE: PPO
  Plan Specialty: PBM
  Benefits Offered: Prescription

Geographic Areas Served
  Mid Atlantic states

Key Personnel
  CEO and President . . . . .Angelo C Voxakis, PharmD
    800-965-3742
  VP, Contracts. . . . . .Thomas E Scono, RPh
  Executive Vice President . . . . .Mark P Barwig
  Executive Vice President . . . . .Patrick M Berryman

1135 Humana Health Insurance of Virginia

4551 Cox Road

Suite 200

Glen Allen, VA 23060

Toll-Free: 800-350-7213

Phone: 804-290-4252

Fax: 804-290-0184

www.humana.com

Secondary Address: 3800 Electric Road, Suite 406, Roanoke, VA 24018

For Profit Organization: Yes

Healthplan and Services Defined
  PLAN TYPE: HMO/PPO

Type of Coverage
  Commercial, Individual

Accreditation Certification
  URAC, NCQA, CORE

1136 Magellan Medicaid Administration

4300 Cox Road

Glen Allen, VA 23060

Toll-Free: 800-884-2822

Phone: 804-965-7400

Fax: 804-527-6849

info-fhsc@magellanhealth.com

www.magellanmedicaid.com

Subsidiary of: Magellan Health

Non-Profit Organization: Yes

Year Founded: 1968

Healthplan and Services Defined
  PLAN TYPE: Medicare
  Benefits Offered: Disease Management, Prescription, Wellness

Type of Coverage
  Medicaid

Key Personnel
  President. . . . . .Tim Nolan

1137 Mid Atlantic Medical Services: Virginia

3951 Westerre Parkway
Suite 260
Richmond, VA 23233
Toll-Free: 800-504-2562
Phone: 804-967-2384
Fax: 804-270-9216
masales99@uhc.com
www.mamsiunitedhealthcare.com
Secondary Address: 21515 Ridgetop Circle, #330, Sterling, VA 20166
Subsidiary of: United Healthcare/United Health Group
Year Founded: 1986
Number of Affiliated Hospitals: 342
Number of Primary Care Physicians: 3,276
Total Enrollment: 180,000

Healthplan and Services Defined
  PLAN TYPE: HMO/PPO
  Model Type: IPA, Network
  Benefits Offered: Disease Management, Prescription, Wellness

Type of Payment Plans Offered
  Combination FFS & DFFS

Geographic Areas Served
  Delaware, Maryland, North Carolina, Pennsylvania, Virginia, Washington DC, West Virginia

Network Qualifications
  Pre-Admission Certification: Yes

Peer Review Type
  Utilization Review: Yes
  Second Surgical Opinion: Yes
  Case Management: Yes

Publishes and Distributes Report Card: No

Accreditation Certification
  TJC, NCQA

Specialty Managed Care Partners
  Enters into Contracts with Regional Business Coalitions: Yes

1138 National Capital PPO

4825 Mark Center Drive
Suite 750
Alexandria, VA 22150
Toll-Free: 800-624-2356
Phone: 703-933-2660
www.ncppo.com
Secondary Address: 12443 Olive Blvd, HealthLink HQ, St. Louis, MO 63141
Subsidiary of: HealthLink, WellPoint
For Profit Organization: Yes
Year Founded: 1987
Physician Owned Organization: Yes
Federally Qualified: Yes
Number of Affiliated Hospitals: 100
Number of Primary Care Physicians: 23,000
Total Enrollment: 100,000
State Enrollment: 44,458

Healthplan and Services Defined
  PLAN TYPE: PPO
  Model Type: Network
  Plan Specialty: Dental, Disease Management, Worker's Compensation
  Benefits Offered: Behavioral Health, Dental, Disease Management, Wellness
  Offers Demand Management Patient Information Service: Yes

Type of Coverage
  Commercial, Individual, Labour and Union

Type of Payment Plans Offered
  FFS

Geographic Areas Served
  Southern and Eastern Virginia, Delaware and portions of New Jersey and Pennsylvania

Publishes and Distributes Report Card: Yes

Accreditation Certification
  TJC Accreditation, Medicare Approved, Utilization Review, Pre-Admission Certification, State Licensure, Quality Assurance Program

Key Personnel
  Regional Vice President . . . . .Jeanell Austin
  CFO. . . . . .Kathy Chandra
  Manager, Network Services. . . . . .Brenda Faust-Thomas

Average Claim Compensation
  Physician's Fees Charged: 40%
  Hospital's Fees Charged: 33%

Specialty Managed Care Partners
  Unicare, Health Link
  Enters into Contracts with Regional Business Coalitions: Yes

1139 Optima Health Plan

4417 Corporation Lane
Virginia Beach, VA 23462-3162
Toll-Free: 877-552-7401
Phone: 757-687-6030
Fax: 757-687-6031
members@optimahealth.com
www.optimahealth.com
Secondary Address: 1604 Santa Rosa Road, Suite 100, Richmond, VA 23229
Subsidiary of: Sentara Health Plans
Non-Profit Organization: Yes
Year Founded: 1984
Federally Qualified: Yes
Number of Affiliated Hospitals: 12
Number of Primary Care Physicians: 15,000
Number of Referral/Specialty Physicians: 3,870
Total Enrollment: 415,000
State Enrollment: 415,000

Healthplan and Services Defined
  PLAN TYPE: HMO/PPO
  Other Type: POS
  Model Type: Network
  Plan Specialty: ASO, Behavioral Health, Chiropractic, Dental, PBM, Vision
  Benefits Offered: Behavioral Health, Chiropractic, Complementary Medicine, Dental, Disease Management, Home Care, Inpatient SNF, Long-Term Care, Physical Therapy, Podiatry, Prescription, Psychiatric, Transplant, Vision, Wellness
  Offers Demand Management Patient Information Service: Yes
  DMPI Services Offered: After hours nurse triage

Type of Coverage
  Commercial, Individual, Medicare, Medicaid
  Catastrophic Illness Benefit: Covered

Type of Payment Plans Offered
  FFS

Geographic Areas Served
  Selected counties in Virginia

Subscriber Information
  Average Monthly Fee Per Subscriber
    (Employee + Employer Contribution):
      Employee Only (Self): Varies by plan
      Medicare: Varies
  Average Annual Deductible Per Subscriber:
      Employee Only (Self): $0
      Employee & 1 Family Member: $0
      Employee & 2 Family Members: $0
      Medicare: Varies

Average Subscriber Co-Payment:
    Primary Care Physician: $15.00
    Non-Network Physician: 70 %
    Prescription Drugs: 50/20%
    Hospital ER: 80%
    Home Health Care: 80%

Network Qualifications
  Pre-Admission Certification: Yes

Peer Review Type
  Utilization Review: Yes
  Second Surgical Opinion: No
  Case Management: Yes

Accreditation Certification
  URAC, NCQA

Key Personnel
  President & CEO . . . . .Michael M Dudley
  SVP/Chief Operating Offc . . . . .Darlene A Mastin
  SVP/Chief Financial Offc . . . . .Andy Hilbert
  SVP, Sales & Marketing. .John DeGruttola
  VP, Medical Director .George Heuser, MD

Specialty Managed Care Partners
  Cole Vision, American Specialty Health, Doral Dental, Sentara
    Mental Health
  Enters into Contracts with Regional Business Coalitions: Yes

Employer References
  City of Virginia Beach, City of Norfolk, Bank of America, Nexcom,
    CHKD

1140 Peninsula Health Care

11870 Merchants Walk
#200
Newport News, VA 23606-3315
Toll-Free: 800-421-1880
Phone: 804-358-7390
Fax: 804-354-4140
www.anthem.com
Mailing Address: PO Box 26623, Richmond, VA 23285-0031
For Profit Organization: Yes
Year Founded: 1994
Number of Affiliated Hospitals: 6
Number of Primary Care Physicians: 225
Number of Referral/Specialty Physicians: 475
Total Enrollment: 53,000
State Enrollment: 55,017

Healthplan and Services Defined
  PLAN TYPE: HMO/PPO
  Model Type: IPA
  Benefits Offered: Prescription
  Offers Demand Management Patient Information Service: Yes

Type of Coverage
  Commercial, Individual, Medicaid

Geographic Areas Served
  Virginia counties: Essex, Gloucester, Hampton, Isle of Wight, James
    City, King and Queen, Mathews

Network Qualifications
  Pre-Admission Certification: Yes

Peer Review Type
  Utilization Review: Yes

Publishes and Distributes Report Card: Yes

Accreditation Certification
  NCQA
  TJC Accreditation, Medicare Approved, Utilization Review,
    Pre-Admission Certification, State Licensure, Quality Assurance
    Program

Key Personnel
  President . . . . .CB King

Chief Financial Officer . . . . .Sally Hartman
Administrative Secretary . . . . .Rachel Kampfe
Specialty Managed Care Partners
  Enters into Contracts with Regional Business Coalitions: Yes

1141 Piedmont Community Health Plan

1937 Thomson Drive
Lynchburg, VA 24501
Toll-Free: 800-400-7247
Phone: 434-947-4463
Fax: 434-947-3670
cservice@pchp.net
www.pchp.net
For Profit Organization: Yes
Year Founded: 1995
Physician Owned Organization: Yes
Number of Primary Care Physicians: 350
Total Enrollment: 30,000
State Enrollment: 30,000

Healthplan and Services Defined
  PLAN TYPE: PPO
  Other Type: POS
  Benefits Offered: Disease Management, Prescription, Wellness

Type of Payment Plans Offered
  POS

Geographic Areas Served
  Cities of Lynchburg and Bedford and the counties of Albemarle,
    Amherst, Appomattox, Bedford, Buchkingham, Campbell,
    Cumberland, Lunenburg, Nottoway and Price Edward

Key Personnel
  CEO. . . . . .Alan Wood
  COO. . . . . .Brenda Grant
  CFO . . . . .Jacqueline Mosby
  CMO . . . . .Dr David Smith
  Provider Relations . . . . .Dana Neiswander
  Marketing . . . . .Cheryl Midkiff
  Member Relations . . . . .Pam Moon
  Corp Media Contact . . . . .Cheryl Midkiff
    cservice@pchp.net

Specialty Managed Care Partners
  Caremark Rx

1142 Southeast Community Care

5700 Lake Wright Drive
#110
Norfolk, VA 23502
Toll-Free: 800-653-2924
Phone: 757-461-6344
Fax: 877-267-8399
www.southeastcommunitycare.com
Subsidiary of: Arcadian Health Plans

Healthplan and Services Defined
  PLAN TYPE: Medicare

Type of Coverage
  Medicare

1143 Trigon Health Care

Acquired by Anthem

1144 United Concordia: Virginia

Fair Oaks Center
11320 Random Hills Road, Suite 620
Fairfax, VA 22030
ucproducer@ucci.com
www.secure.ucci.com

For Profit Organization: Yes
Year Founded: 1971
Number of Primary Care Physicians: 111,000
Total Enrollment: 8,000,000

Healthplan and Services Defined
PLAN TYPE: Dental
Plan Specialty: Dental
Benefits Offered: Dental

Type of Coverage
Commercial, Individual

Geographic Areas Served
Military personnel and their families, nationwide

1145 UnitedHealthCare of Virginia
9020 Stoney Point Parkway
Suite 400
Richmond, VA 23235
Toll-Free: 800-357-0978
Phone: 804-267-5200
www.uhc.com
Secondary Address: 12018 Sunrise Valley Drive, Suite 400, Reston, VA 20191, 571-262-2245
Subsidiary of: UnitedHealth Group
For Profit Organization: Yes
Total Enrollment: 75,000,000

Healthplan and Services Defined
PLAN TYPE: HMO/PPO

Geographic Areas Served
Statewide

Key Personnel
Media Contact . . . . Debora Spano
debora_m_spano@uhc.com

1146 Virginia Health Network
7400 Beaufont Springs Drive
Suite 505
Richmond, VA 23225-5517
Toll-Free: 800-989-3837
Phone: 804-320-3837
Fax: 804-320-5984
scampbell@vhn.com
www.vhn.com
For Profit Organization: Yes
Year Founded: 1988
Physician Owned Organization: No
Federally Qualified: No
Number of Affiliated Hospitals: 85
Number of Primary Care Physicians: 3,934
Number of Referral/Specialty Physicians: 8,566
Total Enrollment: 88,366
State Enrollment: 88,366

Healthplan and Services Defined
PLAN TYPE: PPO
Model Type: Network
Plan Specialty: Worker's Compensation, Medical PPO
Offers Demand Management Patient Information Service: No

Type of Coverage
Commercial

Geographic Areas Served
Hampton Roads, the Greater Richmond area, Northern Virginia, Charlottesville, Fredericksburg, Southwest Virginia

Network Qualifications
Pre-Admission Certification: Yes

Publishes and Distributes Report Card: No
Accreditation Certification
Medicare; State License
TJC Accreditation, Medicare Approved, Utilization Review, State Licensure

Key Personnel
President/CEO . . . . James W Brittain
804-320-3837
jbrittain@vhn.com
Claims . . . . Bobbie Jo Crawford
bjcrawford@vhn.com
Credentialing . . . . Sheron Campbell
scampbell@vhn.com
Information Systems . . . . DeVonna Flora
dflora@vhn.com
VP Marketing . . . . James L Gore
jgore@vhn.com
Information Services . . . . Sandy Bartal
sbartal@vhn.com
Information Systems . . . . DeVonna Flora
dflora@vhn.com

Average Claim Compensation
Physician's Fees Charged: 79%
Hospital's Fees Charged: 67%

Specialty Managed Care Partners
Enters into Contracts with Regional Business Coalitions: Yes

1147 Virginia Premier Health Plan
600 East Broad Street, Suite 400
PO Box 5307
Richmond, VA 23220
Toll-Free: 800-727-7536
Phone: 804-819-5151
Fax: 804-819-5187
www.virginiapremier.com
Secondary Address: 2322 Blue Stone Hills Drive, Suite 220, Harrisonburg, VA 22801
For Profit Organization: Yes
Year Founded: 1995
Number of Affiliated Hospitals: 49
Number of Primary Care Physicians: 1,151
Number of Referral/Specialty Physicians: 4,450
Total Enrollment: 143,725
State Enrollment: 81,803

Healthplan and Services Defined
PLAN TYPE: HMO
Model Type: IPA
Plan Specialty: PBM, UR
Benefits Offered: Behavioral Health, Dental, Prescription, Psychiatric, Vision

Type of Coverage
Individual, Medicaid

Geographic Areas Served
counties: Accomack, Albemarle, Amelia, Augusta, Bedford, Botetourt, Brunswick, Caroline, Charles City, Chesterfield, Culpeper, Cumberland, Dinwiddie, Franklin, Giles, Goochland, Green, Greensville, Henrico, Henry, King George, King William, Louisa, Lunenburg, Madison, Mecklenburg, Montgomery, Kent, Northampton, Nottoway, Orange, Patrick, Prince Edward, Prince George, Pulaski, Roanoke, Rockbridge, Rockingham, Southampton, Spotsylvania, Stafford, Surry, Sussex

Accreditation Certification
TJC, URAC, NCQA

Key Personnel
President/CEO . . . . James S Parrot
Dir Business Development . . . . Terone B Greene
Medical Director . . . . Melvin Pinn, MD

Dir Provider Relations . . . . Patrick McMahon
Director, Finance . . . . Tim Carpenter, CPA
VP/Medical Management . . . . Linda Hines, MS/RN
Director of Human Res . . . . Tonya Woodson
Director of Claims . . . . Mike Parker
Dir/Quality Improvement . . . . Jamie McPherson, MPA/BSN
Director of Systems Dev . . . . David Summers
Director of Operations . . . . Constance Goodman
Enrollment Manager . . . . Ryan McCarthy
Information Systems Dir . . . . Derrick D Lee

Specialty Managed Care Partners
AmeriHealth Mercy, Vision Services Plan, Doral Dental of Virginia

Health Insurance Coverage Status and Type of Coverage by Age

Category	All Persons		Under 18 years		Under 65 years		65 years and over	
	Number	%	Number	%	Number	%	Number	%
Total population	6,723	-	1,610	-	5,844	-	880	-
Covered by some type of health insurance	5,797 (69)	86.2 (1.0)	1,515 (22)	94.1 (0.9)	4,926 (70)	84.3 (1.0)	870 (48)	99.0 (0.6)
Covered by private health insurance	4,444 (109)	66.1 (1.7)	890 (49)	55.3 (2.9)	3,854 (103)	66.0 (1.8)	590 (49)	67.1 (3.1)
Employment based	3,724 (107)	55.4 (1.6)	812 (45)	50.4 (2.6)	3,456 (101)	59.1 (1.7)	268 (29)	30.4 (3.0)
Own employment based	2,053 (58)	30.5 (0.8)	3 (2)	0.2 (0.1)	1,854 (56)	31.7 (0.8)	199 (20)	22.6 (2.2)
Direct purchase	794 (61)	11.8 (0.9)	73 (15)	4.5 (0.9)	449 (42)	7.7 (0.7)	346 (37)	39.3 (2.9)
Covered by government health insurance	2,276 (113)	33.8 (1.6)	766 (45)	47.6 (2.8)	1,447 (105)	24.8 (1.8)	829 (46)	94.3 (1.3)
Covered by Medicaid	1,017 (64)	15.1 (0.9)	636 (40)	39.5 (2.5)	935 (63)	16.0 (1.1)	81 (14)	9.2 (1.6)
Also by private insurance	175 (26)	2.6 (0.4)	92 (20)	5.7 (1.2)	149 (26)	2.6 (0.5)	26 (9)	2.9 (1.0)
Covered by Medicare	940 (52)	14.0 (0.8)	9 (6)	0.6 (0.4)	112 (17)	1.9 (0.3)	827 (46)	94.1 (1.4)
Also by private insurance	561 (50)	8.3 (0.8)	0 (0)	0.0 (0.0)	12 (5)	0.2 (0.1)	549 (48)	62.4 (3.2)
Also by Medicaid	116 (14)	1.7 (0.2)	6 (5)	0.4 (0.3)	35 (10)	0.6 (0.2)	81 (14)	9.2 (1.6)
Covered by military health care	583 (105)	8.7 (1.5)	139 (43)	8.7 (2.7)	479 (106)	8.2 (1.8)	104 (18)	11.9 (2.0)
Not covered at any time during the year	927 (66)	13.8 (1.0)	95 (15)	5.9 (0.9)	918 (65)	15.7 (1.0)	9 (5)	1.0 (0.6)

Note: Numbers in thousands; figures cover 2010; standard error appears in parenthesis; (b) base less than 75,000; (x) not applicable
Source: U.S. Census Bureau, Current Population Survey, 2011 Annual Social and Economic Supplement. Table HI05. Health Insurance Coverage Status and Type of Coverage by State and Age for All People: 2010

Washington

1148 Aetna Health of Washington

Partnered with eHealthInsurance Services Inc.

1149 Assurant Employee Benefits: Washington

1512 Plaza
Building 600
Seattle, WA 98101
Phone: 206-441-3133
Fax: 206-728-2509
benefits@assurant.com
www.assurantemployeebenefits.com
Subsidiary of: Assurant, Inc
For Profit Organization: Yes
Number of Primary Care Physicians: 112,000
Total Enrollment: 47,000

Healthplan and Services Defined
PLAN TYPE: Multiple
Plan Specialty: Dental, Vision, Long & Short-Term Disability
Benefits Offered: Dental, Vision, Wellness, AD&D, Life, LTD, STD

Type of Coverage
Commercial, Indemnity, Individual Dental Plans

Geographic Areas Served
Statewide

Subscriber Information
Average Monthly Fee Per Subscriber
(Employee + Employer Contribution):
Employee Only (Self): Varies by plan

Key Personnel
Manager . . . . Ernie Albino
Manager. . . . . Tim Kennedy
PR Specialist. . . . . Megan Hutchison
816-556-7815
megan.hutchison@assurant.com

1150 Asuris Northwest Health

528 E. Spokane Falls Blvd.
Suite 301
Spokane, WA 99202
Toll-Free: 888-344-5593
Phone: 509-922-8072
Fax: 509-922-8264
wa_rnh_info@asurius.com
www.asurisnorthwesthealth.com
Mailing Address: Po Box 91130, Seattle, WA 98111-9230
Subsidiary of: Regence Group
Non-Profit Organization: Yes
Year Founded: 1998
Number of Affiliated Hospitals: 40
Number of Primary Care Physicians: 19,000

Healthplan and Services Defined
PLAN TYPE: Multiple
Model Type: Network, TPA
Plan Specialty: ASO, Behavioral Health, Chiropractic, Disease
Management, Lab, Vision, Radiology
Benefits Offered: Chiropractic, Dental, Disease Management, Home
Care, Inpatient SNF, Physical Therapy, Podiatry, Prescription,
Psychiatric, Vision, Wellness, AD&D, Life, LTD, STD

Type of Coverage
Individual, Medicare, Supplemental Medicare, Medicaid, Other
Public Programs

Geographic Areas Served
Eastern Washington

Subscriber Information
Average Monthly Fee Per Subscriber
(Employee + Employer Contribution):
Employee Only (Self): Varies
Employee & 1 Family Member: Varies
Employee & 2 Family Members: Varies
Medicare: Varies
Average Annual Deductible Per Subscriber:
Employee Only (Self): Varies
Employee & 1 Family Member: Varies
Employee & 2 Family Members: Varies
Medicare: Varies
Average Subscriber Co-Payment:
Primary Care Physician: Varies
Non-Network Physician: Varies
Prescription Drugs: Varies
Hospital ER: Varies
Home Health Care: Varies
Home Health Care Max. Days/Visits Covered: Varies
Nursing Home: Varies
Nursing Home Max. Days/Visits Covered: Varies

Network Qualifications
Pre-Admission Certification: No

Peer Review Type
Utilization Review: Yes
Second Surgical Opinion: Yes

Accreditation Certification
TJC Accreditation, Medicare Approved, State Licensure

Key Personnel
President . . . . Brady Cass
CEO. . . . . Mark Ganz
Regional Manager . . . . Tony Kahmann
Media Contact. . . . . Mike Tatko
208-798-2221
mtatkoid@regence.com

Average Claim Compensation
Physician's Fees Charged: 80%
Hospital's Fees Charged: 80%

1151 CIGNA HealthCare of Washington

701 Fifth Avenue
Suite 4900
Seattle, WA 98104
Toll-Free: 866-438-2446
Phone: 206-625-8892
Fax: 206-625-8880
www.cigna.com
Secondary Address: Great-West Healthcare, now part of CIGNA, 155
108th Avenue NE, Suite 800, Belleview, WA 98004, 425-372-0600
For Profit Organization: Yes
Total Enrollment: 120,000
State Enrollment: 49,135

Healthplan and Services Defined
PLAN TYPE: PPO
Model Type: Gatekeeper/ConsumerDriven
Benefits Offered: Behavioral Health, Dental, Prescription, Medical

Type of Coverage
Commercial

Type of Payment Plans Offered
POS, FFS

Geographic Areas Served
Washington - Statewide

Key Personnel
President & General Mgr . . . . Chris Blanton

1152 Community Health Plan of Washington

720 Olive Way
Suite 300
Seattle, WA 98101-1830
Toll-Free: 800-440-1561
Phone: 206-521-8833
Fax: 206-521-8834
customercare@chpw.org
www.chpw.org
Non-Profit Organization: Yes
Year Founded: 1992
Number of Affiliated Hospitals: 100
Number of Primary Care Physicians: 2,365
Number of Referral/Specialty Physicians: 13,571
Total Enrollment: 270,000
State Enrollment: 270,000

Healthplan and Services Defined
  PLAN TYPE: Multiple
  Benefits Offered: Disease Management, Prescription, Wellness

Type of Coverage
  Commercial, Individual, Medicare, Medicaid

Geographic Areas Served
  38 counties in Washington State

Subscriber Information
  Average Monthly Fee Per Subscriber
    (Employee + Employer Contribution):
      Employee Only (Self): Varies
      Employee & 1 Family Member: Varies
      Employee & 2 Family Members: Varies
      Medicare: Varies
  Average Annual Deductible Per Subscriber:
      Employee Only (Self): Varies
      Employee & 1 Family Member: Varies
      Employee & 2 Family Members: Varies
      Medicare: Varies
  Average Subscriber Co-Payment:
      Primary Care Physician: Varies
      Non-Network Physician: Varies
      Prescription Drugs: Varies
      Hospital ER: Varies
      Home Health Care: Varies
      Home Health Care Max. Days/Visits Covered: Varies
      Nursing Home: Varies
      Nursing Home Max. Days/Visits Covered: Varies

Key Personnel
  CEO . . . . .Lance Hunsinger
  Chief Admin Officer . . . . .Marilee McGuire
  CFO . . . . .Alan Lederman
  SVP/CMO . . . . .Dr Christopher Mathews
  SVP Business Development . . . . .Howard Springer
  VP/Human Resources . . . . .Laura Boyd
  VP/Strategy & Analytics .Stacy Kessel
  VP/General Counsel . . . . .Wade Harman
  Director, Marketing . . . . .David Kinard
    206-613-8949
    david.kinard@chpw.org

Specialty Managed Care Partners
  Express Scripts

1153 Delta Dental of Washington

9706 Fourth Avenue NE
Seattle, WA 98115-2157
Toll-Free: 800-367-4104
Phone: 206-522-1300
cservice@deltadentalwa.com
www.deltadentalwa.com
Non-Profit Organization: Yes

Year Founded: 1954
Total Enrollment: 54,000,000
State Enrollment: 2,000,000

Healthplan and Services Defined
  PLAN TYPE: Dental
  Other Type: Dental PPO
  Model Type: Network
  Plan Specialty: ASO, Dental
  Benefits Offered: Dental

Type of Coverage
  Commercial, Individual, Group
  Catastrophic Illness Benefit: None

Geographic Areas Served
  Statewide

Subscriber Information
  Average Monthly Fee Per Subscriber
    (Employee + Employer Contribution):
      Employee Only (Self): Varies
      Employee & 1 Family Member: Varies
      Employee & 2 Family Members: Varies
  Average Annual Deductible Per Subscriber:
      Employee Only (Self): Varies
      Employee & 1 Family Member: Varies
      Employee & 2 Family Members: Varies
  Average Subscriber Co-Payment:
      Prescription Drugs: $0
      Home Health Care: $0
      Nursing Home: $0

Key Personnel
  President & CEO . . . . .Jim Dwyer
  SVP, Underwriting & Act . . . . .John Bursett
  VP, Corporate Development. . . . . .Thomas Gates
  Dental Director . . . . .Ron Inge, DDS
  VP, Human Resources . . . . .Larry Leopold
  VP, Sales & Marketing . . . . .Kristin Merlo
  VP, Chief Infomation Offc . . . . .John Poli
  Public Relations . . . . .Sean Pickard
    206-528-2304
    spickard@deltadentawa.com
  Dir/Media & Public Affair . . . . .Elizabeth Risberg
    415-972-8423

1154 Dental Health Services of Washington

Northlake Plaza
936 N 34th Street, Suite 208
Seattle, WA 98103
Toll-Free: 800-248-8108
Phone: 206-633-2300
Fax: 206-624-8755
www.dentalhealthservices.com
For Profit Organization: Yes
Year Founded: 1984

Healthplan and Services Defined
  PLAN TYPE: Dental

Geographic Areas Served
  Washington State

1155 eHealthInsurance Services Inc.

11919 Foundation Place
Gold River, CA 95670
Toll-Free: 800-977-8860
info@ehealthinsurance.com
www.e.healthinsurance.com
Year Founded: 1997

Healthplan and Services Defined
  PLAN TYPE: HMO/PPO
  Benefits Offered: Dental, Life, STD

Type of Coverage
Commercial, Individual, Medicare

Geographic Areas Served
All 50 states in the USA and District of Columbia

Key Personnel
Chairman & CEO . . . . Gary L. Lauer
EVP/Business & Corp. Dev. . . . . Bruce Telkamp
EVP/Chief Technology . . . . Dr. Sheldon X. Wang
SVP & CFO . . . . Stuart M. Huizinga
Pres. of eHealth Gov. Sys . . . . Samuel C. Gibbs
SVP of Sales & Operations . . . . Robert S. Hurley
Director Public Relations . . . . Nate Purpura
650-210-3115

1156 Great-West Healthcare of Washington
Acquired by CIGNA

1157 Group Health Cooperative
320 Westlake Ave N
Suite 100
Seattle, WA 98109
Toll-Free: 888-901-4636
Phone: 206-448-4140
info@ghc.org
www.ghc.org
Mailing Address: PO Box 34590, Seattle, WA 98124
Non-Profit Organization: Yes
Year Founded: 1947
Owned by an Integrated Delivery Network (IDN): Yes
Number of Affiliated Hospitals: 34
Number of Primary Care Physicians: 6,000
Total Enrollment: 600,000

Healthplan and Services Defined
PLAN TYPE: Multiple
Model Type: Staff
Plan Specialty: Behavioral Health, Chiropractic, Disease Management
Benefits Offered: Behavioral Health, Chiropractic, Disease Management, Home Care, Inpatient SNF, Long-Term Care, Physical Therapy, Podiatry, Prescription, Psychiatric, Transplant, Vision, Wellness
Offers Demand Management Patient Information Service: Yes

Type of Coverage
Commercial, Individual, Indemnity, Medicare, Supplemental Medicare, Medicaid
Catastrophic Illness Benefit: Varies per case

Type of Payment Plans Offered
POS

Geographic Areas Served
Washington State and Northern Idaho

Subscriber Information
Average Monthly Fee Per Subscriber
(Employee + Employer Contribution):
Employee Only (Self): Varies by plan
Average Annual Deductible Per Subscriber:
Employee Only (Self): $0
Employee & 1 Family Member: $0
Employee & 2 Family Members: $0
Medicare: $0
Average Subscriber Co-Payment:
Primary Care Physician: $10.00
Prescription Drugs: $10.00
Hospital ER: $100.00
Home Health Care Max. Days/Visits Covered: Covered in full

Network Qualifications
Pre-Admission Certification: Yes

Peer Review Type
Utilization Review: Yes
Second Surgical Opinion: Yes
Case Management: Yes

Publishes and Distributes Report Card: Yes

Accreditation Certification
TJC, NCQA
Medicare Approved, Utilization Review, Pre-Admission Certification, State Licensure, Quality Assurance Program

Key Personnel
President/CEO . . . . Scott Armstrong
CFO . . . . Jim Truess
EVP, General Counsel . . . . Rick Woods
Exec VP/Group Practic Div . . . . James Hereford
Executive Vice President . . . . Janet Liang
Exec VP/Public Affairs. . . . . Pam MacEwan
Exec VP/Sales & Marketing . . . . Maureen McLaughlin
Exec VP/Puget Sound Reg . . . . Peter Morgan
EVP, CFO . . . . Richard Magnuson
Exec VP/General Counsel . . . . Rick Woods
Chief Medical Executive . . . . Michael Soman, MD
Exec Medical Director . . . . Brenda Bruns, MD
EVP, Group Practice . . . . Peter Morgan
EVP, Health Division . . . . Robert O'Brien
EVP, Grp Hlth Permanente . . . . Marc West
Sr Media Consultant . . . . Katie McCarthy
206-448-2149
mccarthy.kx@ghc.org
Media Relations Manager. . . . . Mike Foley
206-448-4148
foley.m@ghc.org

Specialty Managed Care Partners
Seattle Health Care
Enters into Contracts with Regional Business Coalitions: Yes

Employer References
State of Washington, Federal Employees, Safeco, Wells Fargo, Nordstorm

1158 Humana Health Insurance of Washington
1498 SE Tech Center Place
Suite 300
Vancouver, WA 98683
Toll-Free: 800-781-4203
Phone: 360-253-7523
Fax: 360-253-7524
www.humana.com
For Profit Organization: Yes

Healthplan and Services Defined
PLAN TYPE: HMO/PPO

Type of Coverage
Commercial, Individual

Accreditation Certification
URAC, NCQA, CORE

1159 Liberty Health Plan: Washington
22425 E Appleway Avenue
Liberty Lake, WA 99019-9514
Toll-Free: 800-926-7324
Phone: 509-944-2209
Fax: 509-944-2019
customerservice.center@libertynorthwest.com
www.libertynorthwest.com
Secondary Address: 1191 Second Avenue, Safeco Center, Seattle, WA 98101-2997
For Profit Organization: Yes
Year Founded: 1983

Healthplan and Services Defined
  PLAN TYPE: PPO
  Model Type: Group
  Plan Specialty: Worker's Compensation
  Benefits Offered: Prescription

Type of Payment Plans Offered
  POS, DFFS, FFS, Combination FFS & DFFS

Geographic Areas Served
  Statewide

Network Qualifications
  Pre-Admission Certification: Yes

Peer Review Type
  Case Management: Yes

Publishes and Distributes Report Card: No

Specialty Managed Care Partners
  Enters into Contracts with Regional Business Coalitions: No

---

1160   Lifewise Health Plan of Washington

7001 220th Street SW
Bldg 1
Mountlake Terrace, WA 98043
Toll-Free: 800-592-6804
www.lifewisewa.org
Mailing Address: PO Box 91509, Seattle, WA 98111-9159
Total Enrollment: 1,500,000
State Enrollment: 87,000

Healthplan and Services Defined
  PLAN TYPE: PPO

Accreditation Certification
  URAC

Key Personnel
  Media Relations Manager . . . . Eric Earling
    425-918-3297
    eric.earling@lifewisehealth.com

1161   Molina Healthcare: Washington

21540 30th Drive SE
Suite 400
Bothell, WA 98021
Toll-Free: 800-869-7175
Phone: 425-424-1100
Fax: 425-487-8987
www.molinahealthcare.com
Secondary Address: 5709 W Sunset Highway, Suite 200, Spokane,
  WA 99224-9795
For Profit Organization: Yes
Year Founded: 1995
Number of Affiliated Hospitals: 81
Number of Primary Care Physicians: 2,714
Number of Referral/Specialty Physicians: 5,325
Total Enrollment: 1,400,000
State Enrollment: 263,795

Healthplan and Services Defined
  PLAN TYPE: HMO
  Model Type: Hybrid
  Benefits Offered: Behavioral Health, Disease Management,
    Prescription, Psychiatric, Transplant, Wellness
  Offers Demand Management Patient Information Service: Yes
  DMPI Services Offered: 24/7 Nurse Line

Type of Coverage
  Commercial, Medicare, Supplemental Medicare, Medicaid, SCHIP

Type of Payment Plans Offered
  Capitated, FFS

Geographic Areas Served
  Adams, Benton, Chelon, Clallam, Columbia, Cowlitz, Douglas,
  Franklin, Garfield, Grant, Grays Harbor, Island, King, Kitsap, Lewis,
  Lincoln, Mason, Okanogan, Pacific, Pend Oreirlle, Pierce, San Juan,
  Skagit, Snohomish, Spokane, Thurston, Walla Walla, Whatconm,
  Whitman, Yakima

Subscriber Information
  Average Monthly Fee Per Subscriber
    (Employee + Employer Contribution):
      Employee Only (Self): Varies by plan
  Average Annual Deductible Per Subscriber:
    Employee Only (Self): $150.00
  Average Subscriber Co-Payment:
    Primary Care Physician: $15.00
    Hospital ER: $100.00

Network Qualifications
  Minimum Years of Practice: 5
  Pre-Admission Certification: Yes

Peer Review Type
  Utilization Review: Yes
  Second Surgical Opinion: Yes
  Case Management: Yes

Accreditation Certification
  URAC, NCQA
  TJC Accreditation, Medicare Approved, Utilization Review,
    Pre-Admission Certification, State Licensure, Quality Assurance
    Program

Key Personnel
  President and CEO. . . . . J Mario Molina, MD
  CFO. . . . . John C Molina, JD
  Exec VP/General Counsel . . . . Mark L Andrews
  Exec VP/Health Plan Ops . . . . Terry Bayer, JD
  Exec VP/Shared Services . . . . Sheila K Shapiro
  Exec VP/Chief Medical Off . . . . . William P Bracciodieta, MD/MBA
  Exec VP/Public Policy . . . . George S Goldstein, PhD
  Exec VP/Reseach & Devel . . . . Martha Bernadette, MD
  Chief Information Officer . . . . Rick Click

Specialty Managed Care Partners
  VGP Vision, RxAmerica Pharmacy
  Enters into Contracts with Regional Business Coalitions: Yes

---

1162   PacifiCare Benefit Administrators

7525 SE 24th Street
PO Box 9005, Suite 200
Mercer Island, WA 98040
Toll-Free: 800-829-2925
Phone: 206-236-2500
Fax: 206-230-7484
pamela.nygaard@phs.com
www.pacificare.com
Subsidiary of: UnitedHealthCare
For Profit Organization: Yes
Year Founded: 1986
Owned by an Integrated Delivery Network (IDN): Yes
Number of Affiliated Hospitals: 14
Number of Primary Care Physicians: 5,000
Total Enrollment: 240,000
State Enrollment: 7,550

Healthplan and Services Defined
  PLAN TYPE: PPO
  Model Type: Network
  Plan Specialty: ASO, Behavioral Health, Chiropractic, Dental,
    Disease Management, Lab, PBM, Radiology, UR, Acupuncture,
    Naturopathy
  Benefits Offered: Behavioral Health, Chiropractic, Dental, Disease
    Management, Home Care, Inpatient SNF, Long-Term Care,
    Physical Therapy, Podiatry, Prescription, Psychiatric, Transplant,
    Wellness

Offers Demand Management Patient Information Service: Yes
DMPI Services Offered: HealthBeat Magazine

Type of Coverage
Commercial, Individual, Indemnity, Medicare, Supplemental
    Medicare, Medicaid, Catastrophic
Catastrophic Illness Benefit: Maximum $2M

Type of Payment Plans Offered
DFFS, FFS

Geographic Areas Served
Alaska, California, Oregon & Washington

Subscriber Information
Average Annual Deductible Per Subscriber:
    Employee Only (Self): $100.00
    Employee & 2 Family Members: $300.00
Average Subscriber Co-Payment:
    Primary Care Physician: $10.00
    Non-Network Physician: $10.00
    Prescription Drugs: $5.00/10.00
    Hospital ER: $50.00
    Home Health Care: $100.00
    Home Health Care Max. Days/Visits Covered: 50 days

Network Qualifications
Pre-Admission Certification: Yes

Peer Review Type
Utilization Review: Yes
Second Surgical Opinion: Yes

Publishes and Distributes Report Card: Yes

Accreditation Certification
NCQA

Key Personnel
Chairman.................................Howard Phanstiel
CFO ....Greg Scott
CEO ....Brad Bowlus
Executive Vice President ....Jacqueline Kosecoff
General Counsel ....Joseph Konowiecki
Chief Medical Officer ....Sam Ho
Sr VP/Human Resources ....Carol Black

Specialty Managed Care Partners
Enters into Contracts with Regional Business Coalitions: Yes

1163 PacifiCare of Washington

7525 SE 24th
Suite 200
Mercer Island, WA 98040
Toll-Free: 800-829-2925
Phone: 206-236-2500
Fax: 206-236-3099
www.pacificare.com
Subsidiary of: UnitedHealthCare
For Profit Organization: Yes
Year Founded: 1986
Number of Affiliated Hospitals: 14
Number of Primary Care Physicians: 5,000
Number of Referral/Specialty Physicians: 640
Total Enrollment: 45,000
State Enrollment: 52,186

Healthplan and Services Defined
PLAN TYPE: HMO
Model Type: Network
Plan Specialty: PBM
Benefits Offered: Behavioral Health, Disease Management,
    Prescription, Psychiatric, Wellness
Offers Demand Management Patient Information Service: Yes
DMPI Services Offered: HealthBeat Magazine

Type of Coverage
Commercial, Individual, Indemnity, Medicare

Type of Payment Plans Offered
Combination FFS & DFFS

Geographic Areas Served
Eight counties statewide

Subscriber Information
Average Subscriber Co-Payment:
    Hospital ER: $50.00
    Home Health Care: Varies
    Nursing Home: Varies

Peer Review Type
Case Management: Yes

Accreditation Certification
Utilization Review, Quality Assurance Program

Key Personnel
Chairman.................................Howard Phanstiel
CFO ....Don Costa
CEO ....Brad Bowlus
Executive Vice President ....Jacqueline Kosecoff
General Counsel ....Joseph Konowiecki
Chief Medical Officer ....Sam Ho
Sr VP/Human Resources ....Carol Black
Chief Information Officer......................Mary Cox
Sales Manager ....Debbie Huntington

1164 Premera Blue Cross

7001 220th SW
Building 1
Montlake Terrace, WA 98043
Toll-Free: 800-722-1471
Phone: 425-918-4000
Fax: 425-918-5575
www.premera.com
Secondary Address: 3900 East Sprague, Building 1, Spokane, WA
99202
For Profit Organization: Yes
Year Founded: 1933
Number of Affiliated Hospitals: 100
Number of Primary Care Physicians: 20,000
Total Enrollment: 1,300,000
State Enrollment: 1,300,000

Healthplan and Services Defined
PLAN TYPE: PPO
Other Type: EPO
Benefits Offered: Dental, Disease Management, Long-Term Care

Type of Coverage
Indemnity, Supplemental Medicare

Geographic Areas Served
Washington and Alaska

Subscriber Information
Average Monthly Fee Per Subscriber
    (Employee + Employer Contribution):
    Employee Only (Self): Varies by plan

Accreditation Certification
NCQA

Key Personnel
President/CEO ....H R Brereton Barlow
Exec VP/Strategic Dev.............................Brian Ancell
SVP/Operations ....Kacey Kemp
SVP, Healthcare Delivery......................Richard Maturi
SVP/Congressional Affairs.......................Jack McRae
EVP/COO ....Kent Marquardt
Chief Legal Officer ....Yori Milo
SVP, Chief Medical Offc...................Roki Chauhan, MD
SVP, Human Resources......................Barbara Magusin
SVP, Chief Info Officer ....Kirsten Simonitsch
SVP, General Counsel...........................John Pierce

Media Relations Manager . . . . Eric Earling
425-918-3297
eric.earling@premera.com

1165 Puget Sound Health Partners

32129 Weyerhaeuser Way S
Suite 201
Federal Way, WA 98001
Toll-Free: 866-789-7747
Phone: 253-779-8830
www.ourpshp.com
Secondary Address: 319 7th Ave SE, Suite 202, Olympia, WA 98501
Year Founded: 2007

Healthplan and Services Defined
  PLAN TYPE: Medicare

Type of Coverage
  Medicare

Key Personnel
  Chief Executive Officer . . . . April Golenor
    253-517-4312
    april.g@ourpshp.com
  Chief Operating Officer. . . . . Christine Tomcala
    253-517-4339
    christine.t@ourpshp.com
  Chief Financial Officer. . . . . Zachary Smulski, MBA
    253-517-4336
    zachary.s@ourpshp.com
  Dir, Network Development. . . . . Christine Turner
    253-517-4334
    chris.t@ourpshp.com
  Dir, Marketing & Comm. . . . . Kim Heuss
    253-517-4305
    kim.h@ourpshp.com
  Dir, Business Development . . . . Diana Elser
    253-517-4344
    diana.e@ourpshp.com
  Chief Medical Officer . . . . Hugh Straley, MD
    253-517-4325
    hugh.s@ourpshp.com

1166 Regence Blue Shield

1800 Ninth Avenue
Seattle, WA 98101
Toll-Free: 800-222-6129
Phone: 206-464-3600
Fax: 206-525-9795
www.wa.regence.com
Secondary Address: 12728 19th Avenue SE, Suite 101, Everett, WA 98208
Non-Profit Organization: Yes
Number of Primary Care Physicians: 19,702
Total Enrollment: 1,117,128
State Enrollment: 21,633

Healthplan and Services Defined
  PLAN TYPE: PPO
  Model Type: Network
  Benefits Offered: Dental, Disease Management, Prescription, Vision, Wellness

Type of Payment Plans Offered
  POS, Combination FFS & DFFS

Geographic Areas Served
  Walla Walla, Clallam, Mason, Columbia, Pacific, Cowlitz, Pierce, Grays Harbor, Snohomish, Thurston, King, Wahkiakum, Kitsap, Lewis, Jefferson, Yakima, Klickitat, Skamania, Whatcom, Skagit, Island and San Juan counties

Subscriber Information
  Average Subscriber Co-Payment:

Primary Care Physician: Varies
Non-Network Physician: Varies
Prescription Drugs: Varies
Hospital ER: Varies
Home Health Care: Varies
Home Health Care Max. Days/Visits Covered: Varies
Nursing Home: Varies
Nursing Home Max. Days/Visits Covered: Varies

Network Qualifications
  Pre-Admission Certification: Yes

Peer Review Type
  Utilization Review: No
  Second Surgical Opinion: Yes
  Case Management: Yes

Publishes and Distributes Report Card: No

Accreditation Certification
  TJC Accreditation

Key Personnel
  President . . . . Jonathan Hensley
  Director of Public Policy . . . . Nancy Ellison
  VP/Provider Services . . . . Audrey Nudd
  Vice President . . . . Maureen Tressel Lewis
  Media Contact . . . . Rachelle Cunningham
    206-332-3713
    rmcunni@regence.com

Specialty Managed Care Partners
  Enters into Contracts with Regional Business Coalitions: No

1167 Spokane Community Care

1330 N Washington Street
#3500
Spokane, WA 992010
Toll-Free: 800-573-8600
Phone: 509-325-8004
Fax: 509-325-8003
www.spokanecommunitycare.com
Subsidiary of: Arcadian Health Plans

Healthplan and Services Defined
  PLAN TYPE: Medicare

Type of Coverage
  Medicare

1168 Sterling Health Plans

2219 Rimland Drive
PO Box 1917
Bellingham, WA 98227-1917
Toll-Free: 888-858-8551
Fax: 888-858-8552
www.sterlingplans.com
Subsidiary of: Sterling Life Insurance Company

Healthplan and Services Defined
  PLAN TYPE: Medicare
  Benefits Offered: Chiropractic, Dental, Disease Management, Home Care, Inpatient SNF, Long-Term Care, Physical Therapy, Podiatry, Prescription, Psychiatric, Vision, Wellness, Life

Type of Coverage
  Commercial, Individual, Medicare, Supplemental Medicare

Geographic Areas Served
  Nationwide

Subscriber Information
  Average Monthly Fee Per Subscriber
  (Employee + Employer Contribution):
    Employee Only (Self): Varies
    Medicare: Varies
  Average Annual Deductible Per Subscriber:

Employee Only (Self): Varies
Medicare: Varies
Average Subscriber Co-Payment:
Primary Care Physician: Varies
Non-Network Physician: Varies
Prescription Drugs: Varies
Hospital ER: Varies
Home Health Care: Varies
Home Health Care Max. Days/Visits Covered: Varies
Nursing Home: Varies
Nursing Home Max. Days/Visits Covered: Varies

Key Personnel
President/CEO . . . . Michael A Muchnicki
Chief Financial Officer . . . . David Goltz
Chief Marketing Officer . . . . Ron Bendes
Medical Director . . . . James Jacobson
Dir, Human Resources. . . . . Harriet Ziegler
Mgr, Information Tech . . . . Tom Cahill
Sr Mgr, Sales & Mktg . . . . Gib Kassing

1169 United Concordia: Washington

2200 Sixth Avenue
Suite 804
Seattle, WA 98121-1849
Toll-Free: 888-245-8224
Fax: 206-728-2740
ucproducer@ucci.com
www.secure.ucci.com
For Profit Organization: Yes
Year Founded: 1971
Number of Primary Care Physicians: 111,000
Total Enrollment: 8,000,000

Healthplan and Services Defined
PLAN TYPE: Dental
Plan Specialty: Dental
Benefits Offered: Dental

Type of Coverage
Commercial, Individual

Geographic Areas Served
Military personnel and their families, nationwide

1170 UnitedHealthCare of Washington

7525 SE 24th Street
Suite 200
Mercer Island, WA 98040
Toll-Free: 800-516-3344
Phone: 206-236-2500
www.uhc.com
Subsidiary of: UnitedHealth Group
For Profit Organization: Yes
Total Enrollment: 75,000,000
State Enrollment: 624,000

Healthplan and Services Defined
PLAN TYPE: HMO/PPO

Geographic Areas Served
Statewide

Key Personnel
Chief Executive Officer . . . . David Hansen
Vice President, Network . . . . Deborah Mcquade
Marketing . . . . Lya Selby
Senior Medical Director . . . . Roger Muller, MD
Media Contact . . . . Will Shanley
will.shanley@uhc.com

1171 VSP: Vision Service Plan of Washington

600 University Street
Suite 2004
Seattle, WA 98101-1176
Phone: 206-623-5178
Fax: 206-621-7515
webmaster@vsp.com
www.vsp.com
Year Founded: 1955
Number of Primary Care Physicians: 26,000
Total Enrollment: 55,000,000

Healthplan and Services Defined
PLAN TYPE: Vision
Plan Specialty: Vision
Benefits Offered: Vision

Type of Payment Plans Offered
Capitated

Geographic Areas Served
Statewide

Network Qualifications
Pre-Admission Certification: Yes

Peer Review Type
Utilization Review: Yes

Accreditation Certification
Utilization Review, Quality Assurance Program

Key Personnel
Manager . . . . Phyllis Moore

Health Insurance Coverage Status and Type of Coverage by Age

Category	All Persons		Under 18 years		Under 65 years		65 years and over	
	Number	%	Number	%	Number	%	Number	%
Total population	1,807	-	401	-	1,563	-	245	-
Covered by some type of health insurance	1,564 *(32)*	86.5 *(1.4)*	390 *(8)*	97.3 *(0.8)*	1,321 *(35)*	84.5 *(1.7)*	243 *(14)*	99.1 *(0.4)*
Covered by private health insurance	1,119 *(47)*	61.9 *(2.4)*	253 *(19)*	63.0 *(4.5)*	979 *(50)*	62.6 *(2.9)*	140 *(12)*	57.2 *(3.6)*
Employment based	1,047 *(48)*	57.9 *(2.5)*	244 *(19)*	60.8 *(4.4)*	943 *(50)*	60.3 *(2.9)*	104 *(12)*	42.3 *(4.0)*
Own employment based	537 *(24)*	29.7 *(1.2)*	1 *(1)*	0.4 *(0.4)*	461 *(26)*	29.5 *(1.5)*	76 *(9)*	31.1 *(3.0)*
Direct purchase	74 *(10)*	4.1 *(0.6)*	7 *(3)*	1.7 *(0.8)*	35 *(8)*	2.2 *(0.5)*	39 *(7)*	15.8 *(2.6)*
Covered by government health insurance	684 *(32)*	37.8 *(1.8)*	176 *(17)*	43.9 *(4.3)*	449 *(30)*	28.7 *(1.9)*	235 *(15)*	96.0 *(1.5)*
Covered by Medicaid	330 *(25)*	18.3 *(1.4)*	163 *(18)*	40.7 *(4.5)*	314 *(24)*	20.1 *(1.6)*	16 *(4)*	6.5 *(1.7)*
Also by private insurance	53 *(11)*	2.9 *(0.6)*	30 *(6)*	7.6 *(1.5)*	50 *(10)*	3.2 *(0.6)*	3 *(2)*	1.3 *(0.9)*
Covered by Medicare	341 *(19)*	18.8 *(1.1)*	2 *(2)*	0.5 *(0.5)*	107 *(12)*	6.8 *(0.8)*	234 *(15)*	95.6 *(1.6)*
Also by private insurance	166 *(13)*	9.2 *(0.8)*	0 *(0)*	0.0 *(0.0)*	34 *(8)*	2.2 *(0.5)*	132 *(14)*	54.0 *(4.3)*
Also by Medicaid	46 *(7)*	2.5 *(0.4)*	0 *(0)*	0.0 *(0.0)*	30 *(5)*	1.9 *(0.3)*	16 *(4)*	6.5 *(1.7)*
Covered by military health care	97 *(13)*	5.4 *(0.7)*	17 *(4)*	4.4 *(0.9)*	77 *(12)*	4.9 *(0.7)*	20 *(6)*	8.1 *(2.3)*
Not covered at any time during the year	244 *(26)*	13.5 *(1.4)*	11 *(3)*	2.7 *(0.8)*	241 *(26)*	15.5 *(1.7)*	2 *(1)*	0.9 *(0.4)*

Note: Numbers in thousands; figures cover 2010; standard error appears in parenthesis; (b) base less than 75,000; (x) not applicable
Source: U.S. Census Bureau, Current Population Survey, 2011 Annual Social and Economic Supplement. Table HI05. Health Insurance Coverage Status and Type of Coverage by State and Age for All People: 2010

West Virginia

1172 Aetna Health of West Virginia

151 Farmington Avenue
RE52
Hartford, CT 06156
Toll-Free: 866-582-9629
www.aetna.com
For Profit Organization: Yes
Year Founded: 1985
Number of Affiliated Hospitals: 76
Number of Primary Care Physicians: 3,000
Number of Referral/Specialty Physicians: 4,000
Total Enrollment: 11,596,230

Healthplan and Services Defined
PLAN TYPE: PPO
Other Type: POS
Model Type: Group
Benefits Offered: Behavioral Health, Chiropractic, Dental, Disease
   Management, Physical Therapy, Prescription, Vision
Offers Demand Management Patient Information Service: Yes

Type of Coverage
Commercial, Individual

Type of Payment Plans Offered
Capitated

Geographic Areas Served
Statewide

Publishes and Distributes Report Card: Yes

Key Personnel
CEO . . . . Ronald A Williams
President. . . . . Mark T Bertolini
SVP, General Counsel . . . . William J Casazza
EVP, CFO . . . . Joseph M Zubretsky
Head, M&A Integration . . . . Kay Mooney
SVP, Marketing. . . . . Robert E Mead
Chief Medical Officer . . . . Lonny Reisman, MD
SVP, Human Resources. . . . . Elease E Wright
SVP, CIO. . . . . Meg McCarthy

Specialty Managed Care Partners
Enters into Contracts with Regional Business Coalitions: Yes

1173 CIGNA HealthCare of West Virginia

3101 Park Lane Drive
Pittsburgh, PA 15275
Toll-Free: 866-438-2446
Phone: 412-747-4410
Fax: 412-747-4416
www.cigna.com
For Profit Organization: Yes
Total Enrollment: 35,316
State Enrollment: 27,783

Healthplan and Services Defined
PLAN TYPE: PPO
Benefits Offered: Disease Management, Prescription, Transplant,
   Wellness

Type of Coverage
Commercial

Type of Payment Plans Offered
POS, FFS

Geographic Areas Served
West Virginia

Key Personnel
CMO . . . . Z Colette Edwards, MD

1174 Coventry Health Care of West Virginia

500 Virginia Street E
Suite 400
Charleston, WV 25301
Toll-Free: 888-388-1744
Phone: 304-348-2900
Fax: 304-348-2948
www.chcwestvirginia.coventryhealthcare.com
Secondary Address: The Wagner Building, 2001 Main Street, Suite
   201, Wheeling, WV 26003
For Profit Organization: Yes
Year Founded: 1995
Number of Affiliated Hospitals: 135
Number of Primary Care Physicians: 14,700
Total Enrollment: 100,000
State Enrollment: 100,000

Healthplan and Services Defined
PLAN TYPE: HMO/PPO
Benefits Offered: Behavioral Health, Disease Management,
   Prescription, Vision, Wellness

Type of Coverage
Commercial, Medicare, Medicaid

Geographic Areas Served
All 55 West Virginia counties

Peer Review Type
Case Management: Yes

Publishes and Distributes Report Card: Yes

Accreditation Certification
URAC

Key Personnel
President/CEO . . . . Cosby Davis
   434-951-2580
   cmdavis@cvty.com
Chief Medical Director. . . . . Rod McKinney
   304-348-2911
   rdmckinney@cvty.com
VP Marketing . . . . Roger Stewart
   304-348-2008
   rpstewart@cvty.com

1175 Delta Dental of the Mid-Atlantic

One Delta Drive
Mechanicsburg, PA 17055-6999
Toll-Free: 800-471-7091
Fax: 717-766-8719
www.deltadentalins.com
Non-Profit Organization: Yes
Total Enrollment: 54,000,000

Healthplan and Services Defined
PLAN TYPE: Dental
Other Type: Dental PPO

Type of Coverage
Commercial

Geographic Areas Served
Statewide

Key Personnel
President/CEO. . . . . Gary D Radine
VP, Public & Govt Affairs . . . . Jeff Album
   415-972-8418
Dir/Media & Public Affair . . . . Elizabeth Risberg
   415-972-8423

1176 eHealthInsurance Services Inc.

11919 Foundation Place
Gold River, CA 95670
Toll-Free: 800-977-8860
info@ehealthinsurance.com
www.e.healthinsurance.com
Year Founded: 1997

Healthplan and Services Defined
PLAN TYPE: HMO/PPO
Benefits Offered: Dental, Life, STD

Type of Coverage
Commercial, Individual, Medicare

Geographic Areas Served
All 50 states in the USA and District of Columbia

Key Personnel
Chairman & CEO .... Gary L. Lauer
EVP/Business & Corp. Dev. .... Bruce Telkamp
EVP/Chief Technology .... Dr. Sheldon X. Wang
SVP & CFO .... Stuart M. Huizinga
Pres. of eHealth Gov. Sys .... Samuel C. Gibbs
SVP of Sales & Operations .... Robert S. Hurley
Director Public Relations .... Nate Purpura
650-210-3115

1177 Great-West Healthcare West Virginia

Acquired by CIGNA

1178 Humana Health Insurance of West Virginia

4202A Maccorkle Ave SE
Charleston, WV 25304
Toll-Free: 800-951-0130
Phone: 304-925-0972
Fax: 304-925-0976
www.humana.com
For Profit Organization: Yes

Healthplan and Services Defined
PLAN TYPE: HMO/PPO

Type of Coverage
Commercial, Individual

Accreditation Certification
URAC, NCQA

Key Personnel
Branch Mgr/Executive Dir .... Charles Showalter
Manager .... John Vogel

1179 Mid Atlantic Medical Services: West Virginia

4 Taft Court
Second Floor
Rockville, MD 20850
Toll-Free: 800-884-5188
Phone: 301-545-5300
Fax: 301-545-5380
masales99@uhc.com
www.mamsiunitedhealthcare.com
Subsidiary of: United Healthcare/United Health Group
Year Founded: 1986
Number of Affiliated Hospitals: 342
Number of Primary Care Physicians: 3,276
Total Enrollment: 180,000

Healthplan and Services Defined
PLAN TYPE: HMO/PPO
Model Type: IPA, Network
Benefits Offered: Disease Management, Prescription, Wellness

Type of Payment Plans Offered
Combination FFS & DFFS

Geographic Areas Served
Delaware, Maryland, North Carolina, Pennsylvania, Virginia, Washington DC, West Virginia

Network Qualifications
Pre-Admission Certification: Yes

Peer Review Type
Utilization Review: Yes
Second Surgical Opinion: Yes
Case Management: Yes

Publishes and Distributes Report Card: No

Accreditation Certification
TJC, NCQA

Specialty Managed Care Partners
Enters into Contracts with Regional Business Coalitions: Yes

1180 Mountain Health Trust/Physician Assured Access System

405 Capitol Street
Suite 406
Charleston, WV 25301
Toll-Free: 800-449-8466
Phone: 304-345-0436
Fax: 304-345-1581
mountainhealthtrust/contact.asp
www.mountainhealthtrust.com
Year Founded: 1996

Healthplan and Services Defined
PLAN TYPE: HMO
Benefits Offered: Disease Management, Wellness

Type of Coverage
Medicaid

Geographic Areas Served
Statewide

1181 Mountain State Blue Cross Blue Shiled

PO Box 1948
Parkersburg, WV 26102
Toll-Free: 888-809-9121
Phone: 304-424-7701
Fax: 304-347-7696
mscomm@highmark.com
www.highmarkbcbswv.com
Mailing Address: PO Box 7026, Customer Service, Wheeling, WV 26003
Subsidiary of: A Highmark Affiliate
For Profit Organization: Yes
Year Founded: 1932
Number of Affiliated Hospitals: 65
Number of Primary Care Physicians: 1,400
Number of Referral/Specialty Physicians: 3,200
Total Enrollment: 400,000
State Enrollment: 400,000

Healthplan and Services Defined
PLAN TYPE: PPO
Model Type: Network, PPO, POS, TPA
Plan Specialty: ASO, Behavioral Health, Chiropractic, EPO, Lab, Radiology, UR, Case Management
Benefits Offered: Behavioral Health, Chiropractic, Home Care, Inpatient SNF, Long-Term Care, Physical Therapy, Podiatry, Prescription, Psychiatric, Transplant

Type of Coverage
Commercial, Individual, Supplemental Medicare

Type of Payment Plans Offered
POS, DFFS

Geographic Areas Served
All 55 counties in West Virginia and Washington county, Ohio

Network Qualifications
Pre-Admission Certification: Yes

Peer Review Type
Utilization Review: Yes
Second Surgical Opinion: Yes
Case Management: Yes

Publishes and Distributes Report Card: No

Accreditation Certification
URAC

Key Personnel
President.....................................J Fred Earley
SVP, Operations ....JoAnn Morrison
SVP, Finance..............................J Mark Sengewaltt
VP Claims...................................Tom Alderson
304-347-7682
thomas.alderson@msbcbs.com

Specialty Managed Care Partners
WV University, Charleston Area Medical Center (CAMC)
Enters into Contracts with Regional Business Coalitions: No

1182 SelectNet Plus, Inc.
602 Virginia Street, East
Charleston, WV 25301
Toll-Free: 800-647-0873
Phone: 304-556-4769
Fax: 304-353-8748
valorie.raines@wellsfargo.com
Mailing Address: PO Box 3262, Charleston, WV 25332-3262
Subsidiary of: A subsidiary of Wells Fargo Third Party Administrators Inc.
For Profit Organization: Yes
Year Founded: 1987
Physician Owned Organization: No
Federally Qualified: No
Number of Affiliated Hospitals: 85
Number of Primary Care Physicians: 1,989
Number of Referral/Specialty Physicians: 3,820
Total Enrollment: 65,000
State Enrollment: 50,000

Healthplan and Services Defined
PLAN TYPE: PPO
Model Type: Regional Provider Network
Offers Demand Management Patient Information Service: No

Type of Coverage
Catastrophic Illness Benefit: Varies per case

Geographic Areas Served
Kentucky, Virgina, Ohio, Tennessee, Pennsylvania, Maryland, West Virginia

Subscriber Information
Average Monthly Fee Per Subscriber
(Employee + Employer Contribution):
Employee Only (Self): Pepm or % of savings
Average Annual Deductible Per Subscriber:
Employee Only (Self): Def by access client
Average Subscriber Co-Payment:
Primary Care Physician: Def by access client

Network Qualifications
Pre-Admission Certification: No

Publishes and Distributes Report Card: No

Key Personnel
SVP/Managed Care............................Jennings Hart
304-556-4792
jennings.hart@wellsfargo.com
Assistant Vice President.......................Valerie Raines
304-556-4769
valorie.raines@wellsfargo.com
Assistant Vice President ....Valorie Raines
304-556-4769
valorie.raines@wellsfargo.com

Specialty Managed Care Partners
Self-Funded Employers, Third Party Claims, Third Party Claims Administrators

1183 Unicare: West Virginia
1207 Quarrier Street
Charleston, WV 25304
Phone: 304-347-1962
www.unicare.com
Year Founded: 1985
Number of Affiliated Hospitals: 102
Number of Primary Care Physicians: 3,500
Number of Referral/Specialty Physicians: 8,000
Total Enrollment: 80,000

Healthplan and Services Defined
PLAN TYPE: HMO/PPO
Model Type: Network
Benefits Offered: Chiropractic, Dental, Physical Therapy, Prescription, Vision

Type of Coverage
Medicare, Supplemental Medicare

Geographic Areas Served
Massachusetts, Southern New Hampshire & Rhode Island

Subscriber Information
Average Monthly Fee Per Subscriber
(Employee + Employer Contribution):
Employee Only (Self): Varies
Employee & 1 Family Member: Varies
Employee & 2 Family Members: Varies
Medicare: Varies
Average Annual Deductible Per Subscriber:
Employee Only (Self): Varies
Employee & 1 Family Member: Varies
Employee & 2 Family Members: Varies
Medicare: Varies
Average Subscriber Co-Payment:
Primary Care Physician: Varies
Non-Network Physician: Varies
Prescription Drugs: Varies
Hospital ER: Varies
Home Health Care: Varies
Home Health Care Max. Days/Visits Covered: Varies
Nursing Home: Varies
Nursing Home Max. Days/Visits Covered: Varies

Network Qualifications
Pre-Admission Certification: Yes

Peer Review Type
Utilization Review: Yes
Second Surgical Opinion: Yes
Case Management: Yes

Publishes and Distributes Report Card: No

Accreditation Certification
TJC Accreditation, Medicare Approved, Utilization Review, Pre-Admission Certification, State Licensure, Quality Assurance Program

Key Personnel
Principal.................................Melissa Coffman
Sales Director ....Jay Staszewski
    jay.staszewski@wellpoint.com
Media Contact ....Tony Felts
    317-287-6036
    tony.felts@wellpoint.com

1184 UnitedHealthCare of West Virginia

5901 Lincoln Drive
Edina, MN 55436
Toll-Free: 866-432-5992
www.uhc.com
Subsidiary of: UnitedHealth Group
Year Founded: 1977
Number of Affiliated Hospitals: 4,200
Number of Primary Care Physicians: 460,000
Total Enrollment: 75,000,000

Healthplan and Services Defined
  PLAN TYPE: HMO/PPO
  Model Type: IPA, Group, Network
  Plan Specialty: Lab, Radiology
  Benefits Offered: Chiropractic, Dental, Physical Therapy,
    Prescription, Wellness, AD&D, Life, LTD, STD
  Offers Demand Management Patient Information Service: Yes

Type of Coverage
  Commercial, Individual, Indemnity, Medicare

Geographic Areas Served
  Statewide

Network Qualifications
  Pre-Admission Certification: Yes

Peer Review Type
  Utilization Review: Yes
  Second Surgical Opinion: Yes
  Case Management: Yes

Publishes and Distributes Report Card: Yes

Accreditation Certification
  TJC, NCQA

Specialty Managed Care Partners
  Enters into Contracts with Regional Business Coalitions: Yes

Health Insurance Coverage Status and Type of Coverage by Age

Category	All Persons		Under 18 years		Under 65 years		65 years and over	
	Number	%	Number	%	Number	%	Number	%
Total population	5,610	-	1,283	-	4,770	-	840	-
Covered by some type of health insurance	5,084 *(61)*	90.6 *(0.8)*	1,224 *(15)*	95.4 *(0.7)*	4,252 *(65)*	89.1 *(0.9)*	832 *(35)*	99.1 *(0.6)*
Covered by private health insurance	4,170 *(96)*	74.3 *(1.5)*	930 *(26)*	72.5 *(1.8)*	3,581 *(87)*	75.1 *(1.5)*	590 *(44)*	70.2 *(3.6)*
Employment based	3,470 *(99)*	61.9 *(1.6)*	894 *(26)*	69.7 *(1.9)*	3,240 *(94)*	67.9 *(1.7)*	230 *(24)*	27.4 *(2.5)*
Own employment based	1,674 *(53)*	29.8 *(0.9)*	2 *(2)*	0.2 *(0.1)*	1,528 *(51)*	32.0 *(1.0)*	146 *(16)*	17.4 *(1.7)*
Direct purchase	714 *(56)*	12.7 *(1.0)*	40 *(8)*	3.1 *(0.6)*	316 *(32)*	6.6 *(0.7)*	398 *(44)*	47.5 *(4.4)*
Covered by government health insurance	1,751 *(68)*	31.2 *(1.2)*	399 *(28)*	31.1 *(2.2)*	946 *(57)*	19.8 *(1.2)*	805 *(33)*	95.8 *(1.0)*
Covered by Medicaid	839 *(57)*	15.0 *(1.0)*	381 *(27)*	29.7 *(2.1)*	801 *(53)*	16.8 *(1.1)*	39 *(14)*	4.6 *(1.7)*
Also by private insurance	201 *(27)*	3.6 *(0.5)*	91 *(16)*	7.1 *(1.3)*	191 *(27)*	4.0 *(0.6)*	10 *(5)*	1.2 *(0.6)*
Covered by Medicare	930 *(36)*	16.6 *(0.6)*	11 *(6)*	0.8 *(0.4)*	127 *(14)*	2.7 *(0.3)*	803 *(33)*	95.6 *(1.1)*
Also by private insurance	607 *(44)*	10.8 *(0.8)*	1 *(1)*	0.1 *(0.1)*	47 *(10)*	1.0 *(0.2)*	560 *(40)*	66.7 *(3.2)*
Also by Medicaid	101 *(17)*	1.8 *(0.3)*	6 *(4)*	0.5 *(0.3)*	63 *(10)*	1.3 *(0.2)*	39 *(14)*	4.6 *(1.7)*
Covered by military health care	172 *(29)*	3.1 *(0.5)*	20 *(8)*	1.6 *(0.7)*	107 *(21)*	2.3 *(0.4)*	64 *(18)*	7.7 *(2.0)*
Not covered at any time during the year	526 *(46)*	9.4 *(0.8)*	59 *(9)*	4.6 *(0.7)*	519 *(45)*	10.9 *(0.9)*	7 *(5)*	0.9 *(0.6)*

Note: Numbers in thousands; figures cover 2010; standard error appears in parenthesis; (b) base less than 75,000; (x) not applicable
Source: U.S. Census Bureau, Current Population Survey, 2011 Annual Social and Economic Supplement. Table HI05. Health Insurance Coverage Status and Type of Coverage by State and Age for All People: 2010

Wisconsin

1185 ABRI Health Plan, Inc.
2400 S. 102nd Street
Suite 105
West Allis, WI 53227
Toll-Free: 888-999-2404
Phone: 414-847-1779
Fax: 414-847-1778
contactabri@abrihealthplan.com
www.abrihealthplan.com
Subsidiary of: Acquired by Molina Healthcare
Year Founded: 2004
Total Enrollment: 24,000

Healthplan and Services Defined
  PLAN TYPE: Multiple

Type of Coverage
  Individual, Medicare, Supplemental Medicare, Medicaid

Key Personnel
  President . . . . .Stephen Harris
  CEO . . . . .Ron Scasny
  Chairman . . . . .Maria Padilla

1186 Aetna Health of Wisconsin
Partnered with eHealthInsurance Services Inc.

1187 Anthem Blue Cross & Blue Shield of Wisconsin
N17 W23430 Riverwood Drive
Waukesha, WI 53188
Phone: 414-459-5000
www.anthem.com
Secondary Address: 216 Pinnacle Way, Suite 100, Eau Claire, WI 54701

Healthplan and Services Defined
  PLAN TYPE: HMO/PPO
  Benefits Offered: Dental, Vision, Life

Type of Coverage
  Commercial, Individual, Medicare

Key Personnel
  President. . . . . .Larry Screiber
  Network Contracting. . . . . .John Foley
  Medical Officer. . . . . .Michael Jaeger, MD
  Media Contact . . . . .Scott Larrivee
    262-523-4746
    scott.larrivee@bcbswi.com

1188 Assurant Employee Benefits: Wisconsin
125 N Executive Drive
Suite 305
Brookfield, WI 53005-6070
Phone: 262-798-0280
Fax: 262-785-1838
benefits@assurant.com
www.assurantemployeebenefits.com
Subsidiary of: Assurant, Inc
For Profit Organization: Yes
Number of Primary Care Physicians: 112,000
Total Enrollment: 47,000

Healthplan and Services Defined
  PLAN TYPE: Multiple
  Plan Specialty: Dental, Vision, Long & Short-Term Disability
  Benefits Offered: Dental, Vision, Wellness, AD&D, Life, LTD, STD

Type of Coverage
  Commercial, Indemnity, Individual Dental Plans

Geographic Areas Served
  Statewide

Subscriber Information
  Average Monthly Fee Per Subscriber
    (Employee + Employer Contribution):
      Employee Only (Self): Varies by plan

Key Personnel
  Branch Manager. . . . . .Jay Curle
  Director . . . . .Ed Rapee
  PR Specialist. . . . . .Megan Hutchison
    816-556-7815
    megan.hutchison@assurant.com

1189 Care Plus Dental Plans
1135 South 16th Street
Milwaukee, WI 53204
Toll-Free: 800-318-7007
Phone: 414-645-4540
Fax: 414-771-7640
www.careplusdentalplans.com
Subsidiary of: Dental Associates Ltd
Non-Profit Organization: Yes
Year Founded: 1983
Physician Owned Organization: Yes
Number of Primary Care Physicians: 51
Total Enrollment: 200,000

Healthplan and Services Defined
  PLAN TYPE: Dental
  Model Type: Staff
  Plan Specialty: Dental
  Benefits Offered: Dental, Prescription

Type of Coverage
  Commercial, Individual

Type of Payment Plans Offered
  Capitated

Geographic Areas Served
  Appleton, Fond Du Lac, Green Bay, Greenville, Kenosha, Milwaukee & Waukesha

Peer Review Type
  Utilization Review: Yes

Key Personnel
  President/CEO . . . . .Michael Bania
  CFO . . . . .Kurt Schmidt
  Dental. . . . . .Charles Leonarduzzi
  Marketing . . . . .John Krause

1190 ChiroCare of Wisconsin
2825 N Mayfair Road
Suite 106
Wauwatosa, WI 53222
Toll-Free: 800-397-1541
Phone: 414-476-4733
Fax: 414-476-4517
ccwiweb@chirocarewi.com
www.chirocarewi.com
Non-Profit Organization: Yes
Year Founded: 1986
Number of Primary Care Physicians: 401
Total Enrollment: 150,000

Healthplan and Services Defined
  PLAN TYPE: PPO
  Model Type: IPA, Network
  Plan Specialty: Chiropractic, Complimentary Medicine Networks
  Benefits Offered: Chiropractic

Type of Coverage
Commercial, Indemnity, Medicare, Supplemental Medicare, Medicaid

Type of Payment Plans Offered
POS, DFFS, Capitated, FFS, Combination FFS & DFFS

Geographic Areas Served
Statewide

Network Qualifications
Pre-Admission Certification: Yes

Peer Review Type
Utilization Review: Yes
Second Surgical Opinion: Yes
Case Management: Yes

Accreditation Certification
Quality Assurance Program

Key Personnel
President/CEO . . . . .Jeffrey Nienhaus
414-476-4733
jnienhaus@chirocarewi.com
Director Operations . . . . .Esther Guerrero
eguerrero@chirocarewi.com
Network Contracting . . . . .Hans Hildebrand
hhildebrand@chirocarewi.com
Credentialing . . . . .Hans Hildebrand
hhildebrand@chirocarewi.com
Sales Executive . . . . .Jeffrey Nienhaus
jnienhaus@chirocarewi.com
Provider Service Manager . . . . .Hans Hildebrand
hhildebrand@chirocarewi.com

1191 CIGNA HealthCare of Wisconsin
2675 North Mayfair Road
Suite 210
Wauwatosa, WI 53226
Toll-Free: 866-438-2446
Phone: 414-256-3310
Fax: 414-256-3328
www.cigna.com
For Profit Organization: Yes
Total Enrollment: 72,853
State Enrollment: 53,255

Healthplan and Services Defined
PLAN TYPE: PPO
Benefits Offered: Disease Management, Prescription, Transplant, Wellness

Type of Coverage
Commercial

Type of Payment Plans Offered
POS, FFS

Geographic Areas Served
Wisconsin

Key Personnel
CMO . . . . .Aslam Khan, MD

1192 Dean Health Plan
1277 Deming Way
Madison, WI 53717
Toll-Free: 800-279-1301
Phone: 608-828-1301
Fax: 608-827-4212
www.deancare.com
For Profit Organization: Yes
Year Founded: 1983
Physician Owned Organization: Yes
Federally Qualified: Yes
Number of Affiliated Hospitals: 26

Number of Primary Care Physicians: 1,500
Total Enrollment: 247,881
Healthplan and Services Defined
PLAN TYPE: Multiple
Model Type: Network
Benefits Offered: Behavioral Health, Chiropractic, Dental, Disease Management, Home Care, Inpatient SNF, Physical Therapy, Podiatry, Prescription, Psychiatric, Transplant, Vision, Wellness
Offers Demand Management Patient Information Service: Yes
DMPI Services Offered: On Call Nurse Line

Type of Coverage
Commercial, Individual, Indemnity, Medicare, Supplemental Medicare, Medicaid

Type of Payment Plans Offered
Capitated

Geographic Areas Served
20 counties in Southern Wisconsin

Subscriber Information
Average Monthly Fee Per Subscriber
(Employee + Employer Contribution):
Employee Only (Self): Varies
Employee & 1 Family Member: Varies
Employee & 2 Family Members: Varies
Medicare: Varies
Average Annual Deductible Per Subscriber:
Employee Only (Self): Varies
Employee & 1 Family Member: Varies
Employee & 2 Family Members: Varies
Medicare: Varies
Average Subscriber Co-Payment:
Primary Care Physician: Varies
Non-Network Physician: Varies
Prescription Drugs: Varies
Hospital ER: Varies
Home Health Care: Varies
Home Health Care Max. Days/Visits Covered: Varies
Nursing Home: Varies
Nursing Home Max. Days/Visits Covered: Varies

Network Qualifications
Pre-Admission Certification: Yes

Peer Review Type
Utilization Review: Yes

Publishes and Distributes Report Card: Yes

Accreditation Certification
NCQA 'Excellent'

Key Personnel
CEO . . . . .Robert Palmer
608-836-1400
President . . . . .Lon Sprecher
Market Intelligence Spec. . . . . .Rick Loerke
608-827-4050
rick.loerke@deancare.com

Specialty Managed Care Partners
Enters into Contracts with Regional Business Coalitions: No

Employer References
State of Wisconsin Employees

1193 Delta Dental of Wisconsin
2801 Hoover Road
PO Box 828
Stevens Point, WI 54481
Toll-Free: 800-236-3712
Phone: 715-344-6087
Fax: 715-343-7623
www.deltadentalwi.com
Non-Profit Organization: Yes
Year Founded: 1962

Total Enrollment: 54,000,000

Healthplan and Services Defined
  PLAN TYPE: Dental
  Other Type: Dental PPO
  Model Type: Network
  Plan Specialty: Dental, Vision
  Benefits Offered: Dental, Vision

Type of Coverage
  Commercial

Type of Payment Plans Offered
  POS, FFS

Geographic Areas Served
  Statewide

Network Qualifications
  Pre-Admission Certification: Yes

Peer Review Type
  Case Management: Yes

Publishes and Distributes Report Card: No

Key Personnel
  President/CEO . . . . .Dennis Brown
  Claims . . . . .Karen Johnson
  Marketing . . . . .Gary Rogers
  Dir/Media & Public Affair .Elizabeth Risberg
    415-972-8423

Specialty Managed Care Partners
  Enters into Contracts with Regional Business Coalitions: No

1194 Dental Protection Plan
7130 W Greenfield Avenue
West Allis, WI 53214-4708
Phone: 414-258-2500
www.mydentalprotectionplan.com
Year Founded: 1987

Healthplan and Services Defined
  PLAN TYPE: Dental
  Other Type: Dental HMO
  Plan Specialty: Dental
  Benefits Offered: Dental

Geographic Areas Served
  Nationwide

Subscriber Information
  Average Monthly Fee Per Subscriber
    (Employee + Employer Contribution):
      Employee Only (Self): $35/year

Peer Review Type
  Case Management: Yes

Publishes and Distributes Report Card: Yes

1195 eHealthInsurance Services Inc.
11919 Foundation Place
Gold River, CA 95670
Toll-Free: 800-977-8860
info@ehealthinsurance.com
www.e.healthinsurance.com
Year Founded: 1997

Healthplan and Services Defined
  PLAN TYPE: HMO/PPO
  Benefits Offered: Dental, Life, STD

Type of Coverage
  Commercial, Individual, Medicare

Geographic Areas Served
  All 50 states in the USA and District of Columbia

Key Personnel
  Chairman & CEO . . . . .Gary L. Lauer

EVP/Business & Corp. Dev. .Bruce Telkamp
EVP/Chief Technology .Dr. Sheldon X. Wang
SVP & CFO . . . . .Stuart M. Huizinga
Pres. of eHealth Gov. Sys .Samuel C. Gibbs
SVP of Sales & Operations . . . . .Robert S. Hurley
Director Public Relations. . . . . .Nate Purpura
  650-210-3115

1196 Great-West Healthcare Wisconsin
Acquired by CIGNA

1197 Group Health Cooperative of Eau Claire
2503 North Hillcrest Parkway
Altoona, WI 54702
Toll-Free: 888-203-7770
Phone: 715-552-4300
Fax: 715-836-7683
www.group-health.com
Mailing Address: PO Box 3217, Eau Claire, WI 54702
Non-Profit Organization: Yes
Year Founded: 1976
Number of Affiliated Hospitals: 57
Number of Primary Care Physicians: 7,700
Number of Referral/Specialty Physicians: 3,800
Total Enrollment: 95,000
State Enrollment: 95,000

Healthplan and Services Defined
  PLAN TYPE: HMO
  Model Type: Network
  Benefits Offered: Dental, Disease Management, Prescription,
    Wellness, Comprehensive Health
  Offers Demand Management Patient Information Service: Yes
  DMPI Services Offered: FirstCare Nurseline

Type of Coverage
  Commercial, Medicaid, SSI
  Catastrophic Illness Benefit: Varies per case

Geographic Areas Served
  Barron, Buffalo, Chippewa, Clark, Dunn, Eau Claire, Jackson, Pepin,
  Rusk, Sawyer, Taylor, Trempealeau, Washburn, Ashland, Bayfield,
  Douglas, Burnett, Polk, St. Croix, Pierce, LaCrosse, Monroe, Juneau,
  Veronn, Crawford, Richland, Sauk, Columbia, Grant, Iowa, Lafayette,
  Green counties

Peer Review Type
  Utilization Review: Yes
  Second Surgical Opinion: Yes
  Case Management: Yes

Publishes and Distributes Report Card: Yes

Accreditation Certification
  AAAHC
  TJC Accreditation, Medicare Approved, Utilization Review, State
    Licensure, Quality Assurance Program

Key Personnel
  General Manager & CEO. . . . . .Peter Farrow
  Chief Medical Officer . . . . .Lon Blaser, DO
  Chief Operating Officer. .Darin McFadden
  Chief Financial Officer. . . . . .Heidi Liedl

Specialty Managed Care Partners
  CMS, OMNE
  Enters into Contracts with Regional Business Coalitions: Yes

1198 Group Health Cooperative of South Central Wisconsin
1265 John Q Hammons Drive
Madison, WI 53717
Toll-Free: 800-605-4327

Phone: 608-828-4853
Fax: 608-828-9333
member_services@ghcscw.com
https://ghcscw.com
Mailing Address: PO Box 44971, Madison, WI 53744-4971
Non-Profit Organization: Yes
Year Founded: 1976
Owned by an Integrated Delivery Network (IDN): Yes
Federally Qualified: Yes
Number of Affiliated Hospitals: 4
Number of Primary Care Physicians: 100
Number of Referral/Specialty Physicians: 735
Total Enrollment: 61,000
State Enrollment: 48,202

Healthplan and Services Defined
PLAN TYPE: HMO
Model Type: Staff
Plan Specialty: Dental, Lab, Vision, Radiology
Benefits Offered: Disease Management, Physical Therapy,
  Prescription, Vision, Wellness
Offers Demand Management Patient Information Service: Yes

Type of Coverage
Commercial, Medicare, Medicaid

Type of Payment Plans Offered
DFFS, Capitated

Geographic Areas Served
Dane County & one zip code adjoining Dane County, Jefferson,
Green and Rock counties

Subscriber Information
Average Monthly Fee Per Subscriber
  (Employee + Employer Contribution):
    Employee Only (Self): Varies by plan
Average Annual Deductible Per Subscriber:
    Employee Only (Self): $0
    Employee & 1 Family Member: $0
    Employee & 2 Family Members: $0
    Medicare: $0
Average Subscriber Co-Payment:
    Primary Care Physician: $0
    Non-Network Physician: $0
    Prescription Drugs: $0
    Hospital ER: $0
    Home Health Care: $0
    Home Health Care Max. Days/Visits Covered: Unlimited
    Nursing Home: $0
    Nursing Home Max. Days/Visits Covered: 100 days

Publishes and Distributes Report Card: Yes

Accreditation Certification
AAAHC, NCQA
Medicare Approved, Utilization Review, Pre-Admission
  Certification, State Licensure, Quality Assurance Program

Key Personnel
President . . . . Kenneth N. Machtau
Board of Directors . . . . Robert Matthew, MD
Board of Directors . . . . Mark Huth, MD
Medical Affairs . . . . Michael Ostrov, MD

Specialty Managed Care Partners
UW Hospitals
Enters into Contracts with Regional Business Coalitions: Yes

1199 Gundersen Lutheran Health Plan
3190 Gundersen Drive
Onalaska, WI 54650
Toll-Free: 800-362-9567
Phone: 608-782-7300
Fax: 608-775-8091
hpcustomerservice@gundluth.org

www.ghealthplan.org
Secondary Address: Mail: 1836 South Avenue, NCA2-01, LaCrosse,
  WI 54650
Subsidiary of: Gunderson Lutheran Health System
Non-Profit Organization: Yes
Year Founded: 1995
Physician Owned Organization: Yes
Federally Qualified: Yes
Number of Affiliated Hospitals: 14
Number of Primary Care Physicians: 850
Number of Referral/Specialty Physicians: 200
Total Enrollment: 90,000
State Enrollment: 90,000

Healthplan and Services Defined
PLAN TYPE: HMO
Other Type: POS
Model Type: Network
Plan Specialty: ASO, Behavioral Health, Chiropractic, Disease
  Management, Lab, PBM, Radiology, UR
Benefits Offered: Behavioral Health, Chiropractic, Disease
  Management, Home Care, Inpatient SNF, Physical Therapy,
  Podiatry, Prescription, Psychiatric, Transplant, Vision, Wellness,
  AD&D
Offers Demand Management Patient Information Service: Yes
DMPI Services Offered: Nurse Advisor Line

Type of Coverage
Commercial, Individual, Medicare

Geographic Areas Served
Western Wisconsin

Subscriber Information
Average Monthly Fee Per Subscriber
  (Employee + Employer Contribution):
    Employee Only (Self): Varies
Average Annual Deductible Per Subscriber:
    Employee & 2 Family Members: Varies

Accreditation Certification
Pre-Admission Certification

Key Personnel
CEO . . . . Jeffrey E Thompson, MD
SVP, Business Services. . . . . Jerry Arndt
Chief Financial Officer . . . . Daryl Applebury
Managed Care COO. . . . . Pat Kohn
Medical Vice President . . . . Marilu Blintz, MD
Vice President . . . . Jan DeHann
Medical Vice President . . . . Michael J Dolan, MD
Chief Quality Officer. . . . . Jean Krause
Chief Bus Dev Officer. . . . . Pamela Maas
Chief Learning Officer. . . . . Mary Ellen McCartney
EVP, Chief Medical Off . . . . Julio Bird, MD
Exec Dir, Human Resources. . . . . Monty Clark
Vice President, Nursing. . . . . Mary Lu Gerke, PhD
Chief Govt Relations . . . . Joan Curran
Compliance Director. . . . . Jenny Noren
  jjnoren@gundluth.org

1200 Health Tradition
1808 East Main Street
Onalaska, WI 54602-0188
Toll-Free: 888-459-3020
Phone: 608-781-9692
www.healthtradition.com
Mailing Address: PO Box 188, La Crosse, WI 54602-0188
For Profit Organization: Yes
Year Founded: 1986
Number of Affiliated Hospitals: 17
Number of Primary Care Physicians: 800
Number of Referral/Specialty Physicians: 100
Total Enrollment: 34,000

State Enrollment: 40,000

Healthplan and Services Defined
PLAN TYPE: HMO
Model Type: Group
Benefits Offered: Disease Management, Prescription, Wellness
Offers Demand Management Patient Information Service: Yes
DMPI Services Offered: 24 hour nurse line

Type of Coverage
Medicare, Medicaid
Catastrophic Illness Benefit: Maximum $2M

Type of Payment Plans Offered
POS, Combination FFS & DFFS

Geographic Areas Served
Iowa: Allamakee; Minnesota: Houston; Buffalo, Crawford, Fillmore, Jackson, La Crosse, Monroe, Trempealeau, Vernon, Winneshiek, Winona counties

Subscriber Information
Average Monthly Fee Per Subscriber
(Employee + Employer Contribution):
Employee Only (Self): Varies by plan
Average Annual Deductible Per Subscriber:
Employee Only (Self): $50.00
Employee & 1 Family Member: $100.00
Employee & 2 Family Members: $150.00
Average Subscriber Co-Payment:
Primary Care Physician: $0
Prescription Drugs: $11.00
Hospital ER: $25.00-50.00
Home Health Care: $0
Home Health Care Max. Days/Visits Covered: 345 days
Nursing Home: $0
Nursing Home Max. Days/Visits Covered: 60 days

Network Qualifications
Pre-Admission Certification: Yes

Peer Review Type
Utilization Review: Yes
Second Surgical Opinion: Yes
Case Management: Yes

Publishes and Distributes Report Card: No

Accreditation Certification
TJC Accreditation, Medicare Approved, Utilization Review, Pre-Admission Certification, State Licensure, Quality Assurance Program

Key Personnel
Director of Operations .Beverly Larson, RN
Executive Director . . . . .Steven M Kunes
Medical Direcctor . . . . .Alan Krumholz, MD
Director/Sales & Market .Michael Eckstein

Average Claim Compensation
Physician's Fees Charged: 85%
Hospital's Fees Charged: 85%

Specialty Managed Care Partners
Franciscon Scam Health Care
Enters into Contracts with Regional Business Coalitions: No

1201 HealthEOS
Acquired by MultiPlan

1202 Humana Health Insurance of Wisconsin
N19 W24133 Riverwood Drive
Suite 300
Waukesha, WI 53188
Toll-Free: 800-289-0260
Phone: 262-951-2300
Fax: 920-632-9508
www.humana.com

Subsidiary of: Humana
For Profit Organization: Yes
Year Founded: 1985
Physician Owned Organization: Yes
Number of Affiliated Hospitals: 23
Number of Primary Care Physicians: 1,300
Number of Referral/Specialty Physicians: 320,000
Total Enrollment: 49,000

Healthplan and Services Defined
PLAN TYPE: HMO/PPO
Model Type: IPA, Network
Plan Specialty: UR
Benefits Offered: Behavioral Health, Chiropractic, Dental, Disease Management, Home Care, Inpatient SNF, Physical Therapy, Podiatry, Prescription, Psychiatric, Transplant, Vision, Wellness, Worker's Compensation, AD&D, Life, LTD
Offers Demand Management Patient Information Service: Yes

Type of Coverage
Commercial, Individual

Type of Payment Plans Offered
POS, DFFS, Capitated, FFS, Combination FFS & DFFS

Geographic Areas Served
Dodge, Jefferson, Kenosha, Milwaukee, Ozaukee, Racine, Sheboygan, Walworth, Washington, Fond du Luc, Green, Montowoe, Rock & Waukesha counties

Subscriber Information
Average Subscriber Co-Payment:
Home Health Care Max. Days/Visits Covered: 40 days
Nursing Home Max. Days/Visits Covered: 100 days

Network Qualifications
Pre-Admission Certification: Yes

Peer Review Type
Utilization Review: Yes
Second Surgical Opinion: Yes
Case Management: Yes

Accreditation Certification
AAAHC, URAC, NCQA, CORE

Key Personnel
President/CEO. . . . . .Michael Derdinski
CFO . . . . .Gary Hovila, CPA
Director Network Development . . . . .Titus Muzi
Director of QI. . . . . .Patrice Thor, RN
Pharmacy Manager . . . . .Dennis Oleg, PhD
Marketing . . . . .David Fee
Materials Management . . . . .Maryann Herman
Medical Director. . . . . .Albert Tzeel, MD
Manager Customer Service . . . . .Anne Andryczyk
Medical Management Dir . . . . .Patrice Thor, RN
Sales. . . . . .Scott Austin

Specialty Managed Care Partners
Aurora Behavioral, Chirotech, Accordant, Health Service

1203 Managed Health Services
10700 W Research Drive
Wauwatosa, WI 53226
Toll-Free: 888-713-6180
Phone: 414-773-4000
Fax: 414-345-4624
www.mhswi.com
For Profit Organization: Yes
Year Founded: 1984
Number of Affiliated Hospitals: 57
Number of Primary Care Physicians: 5,500
Number of Referral/Specialty Physicians: 1,255
Total Enrollment: 130,000
State Enrollment: 164,700

Healthplan and Services Defined
PLAN TYPE: HMO
Model Type: IPA, Network
Benefits Offered: Disease Management, Prescription, Wellness
Offers Demand Management Patient Information Service: Yes

Type of Coverage
Medicare, Medicaid
Catastrophic Illness Benefit: Varies per case

Type of Payment Plans Offered
POS, FFS

Geographic Areas Served
22 counties in Wisconsin, Northern Indiana, and Illinois, Racine, Kenosha; Indiana: Indianapolis; Illinois: Chicago

Subscriber Information
Average Monthly Fee Per Subscriber
(Employee + Employer Contribution):
Employee Only (Self): Varies
Employee & 1 Family Member: Varies
Employee & 2 Family Members: Varies
Medicare: Varies
Average Annual Deductible Per Subscriber:
Employee Only (Self): Varies
Employee & 1 Family Member: Varies
Employee & 2 Family Members: Varies
Medicare: Varies
Average Subscriber Co-Payment:
Primary Care Physician: $10.00/15.00
Non-Network Physician: 100%
Prescription Drugs: $5.00/10.00
Hospital ER: $25.00
Home Health Care: $0

Network Qualifications
Pre-Admission Certification: Yes

Peer Review Type
Utilization Review: Yes

Publishes and Distributes Report Card: Yes

Accreditation Certification
NCQA
TJC Accreditation, Medicare Approved, Utilization Review, Pre-Admission Certification, State Licensure, Quality Assurance Program

Key Personnel
President & CEO . . . . .Sherry Husa
SVP, Govt Relations . . . . .Sandra S Tunis
VP, Network Management . . . . .Paul Sabin
VP, Finance . . . . .Christopher Scott
VP, Member Services . . . . .Danielle Brazee
Asst Plan Controller . . . . .Stephen Moore
Mgr, Human Resources . . . . .Jean Bellante
VP, Medical Management . . . . .Pamala Rundhaug

Specialty Managed Care Partners
Enters into Contracts with Regional Business Coalitions: Yes

1204　Medical Associates Health Plan: East

1000 Langworthy
Dubuque, IA 52001
Toll-Free: 800-648-6868
Phone: 563-584-3000
www.mahealthcare.com
For Profit Organization: Yes
Year Founded: 1982
Number of Affiliated Hospitals: 7
Number of Primary Care Physicians: 169
Total Enrollment: 45,000
State Enrollment: 8,527

Healthplan and Services Defined
PLAN TYPE: HMO

Other Type: POS, EPO
Model Type: Network
Benefits Offered: Behavioral Health, Chiropractic, Complementary Medicine, Disease Management, Home Care, Inpatient SNF, Physical Therapy, Podiatry, Prescription, Psychiatric, Transplant, Vision, Wellness

Type of Coverage
Commercial, Medicare, Supplemental Medicare

Geographic Areas Served
counties: Crawford, Grant, Iowa, Lafayette

Accreditation Certification
TJC, NCQA

Key Personnel
CEO . . . . .Alan Avery
Medical Director . . . . .Mike Grund, MD
CFO . . . . .Ronald Fahey

1205　MercyCare Health Plans

3430 Palmer Drive
PO Box 2770
Janesville, WI 53547-2770
Toll-Free: 800-752-3431
Phone: 608-741-6891
Fax: 608-752-3751
mcash@mhsjvl.org
www.mercycarehealthplans.com
For Profit Organization: Yes
Year Founded: 1994
Number of Affiliated Hospitals: 180
Number of Primary Care Physicians: 440
Total Enrollment: 30,000

Healthplan and Services Defined
PLAN TYPE: HMO
Model Type: Network
Benefits Offered: Disease Management, Prescription, Wellness
Offers Demand Management Patient Information Service: Yes

Type of Coverage
Medicare, Medicaid
Catastrophic Illness Benefit: Unlimited

Type of Payment Plans Offered
POS, Combination FFS & DFFS

Geographic Areas Served
Wisconsin: Green, Jefferson, Rock, Walworth; Illinois: McHenry

Subscriber Information
Average Monthly Fee Per Subscriber
(Employee + Employer Contribution):
Employee Only (Self): Vaires by plan
Average Annual Deductible Per Subscriber:
Employee Only (Self): $0
Employee & 1 Family Member: $0
Employee & 2 Family Members: $0
Average Subscriber Co-Payment:
Primary Care Physician: $15.00
Non-Network Physician: 100%
Prescription Drugs: $5.00/15.00
Hospital ER: $35.00
Home Health Care: $0
Home Health Care Max. Days/Visits Covered: 40 days
Nursing Home: $0
Nursing Home Max. Days/Visits Covered: 120 days

Network Qualifications
Pre-Admission Certification: Yes

Peer Review Type
Utilization Review: Yes
Second Surgical Opinion: Yes
Case Management: Yes

Publishes and Distributes Report Card: Yes

Accreditation Certification
NCQA
TJC Accreditation, Medicare Approved, Utilization Review, Pre-Admission Certification, State Licensure, Quality Assurance Program

Key Personnel
Chief Executive Officer . . . . .Javon R Bea
CFO . . . . .Matt Hicks
VP/COO . . . . .Joseph Nemeth
Compliance Audit and Data .Barb Johnson
Director Sales and Networks . . . . .Duwayne Severson

Average Claim Compensation
Physician's Fees Charged: 75%
Hospital's Fees Charged: 75%

Specialty Managed Care Partners
Enters into Contracts with Regional Business Coalitions: No

1206 Network Health Plan of Wisconsin

1570 Midway Place
PO Box 120
Menasha, WI 54952
Toll-Free: 800-826-0940
Phone: 920-720-1300
Fax: 920-720-1909
www.networkhealth.com
Subsidiary of: Affinity Health System
For Profit Organization: Yes
Year Founded: 1982
Number of Affiliated Hospitals: 14
Number of Primary Care Physicians: 1,400
Total Enrollment: 118,000
State Enrollment: 67,812

Healthplan and Services Defined
PLAN TYPE: HMO/PPO
Model Type: Group, Network
Plan Specialty: Behavioral Health, Chiropractic, Disease Management
Benefits Offered: Disease Management, Prescription, Wellness

Type of Coverage
Commercial, Medicare, Medicaid

Type of Payment Plans Offered
POS, Combination FFS & DFFS

Geographic Areas Served
16 counties in Wisconsin. Brown, Calumet, Dodge, Door, Fond du Lac, Green Lake, Kewaunee, Manitowoc, Marquette, Outagamie, Portage, Shawano, Sheboygan, Waupaca, Waushara, Winnebago counties

Subscriber Information
Average Monthly Fee Per Subscriber
(Employee + Employer Contribution):
Employee Only (Self): Varies
Employee & 1 Family Member: Varies
Employee & 2 Family Members: Varies
Medicare: Varies
Average Annual Deductible Per Subscriber:
Employee Only (Self): Varies
Employee & 1 Family Member: Varies
Employee & 2 Family Members: Varies
Medicare: Varies
Average Subscriber Co-Payment:
Primary Care Physician: $10.00
Prescription Drugs: $5.00-7.00
Home Health Care: $0

Network Qualifications
Pre-Admission Certification: Yes

Peer Review Type
Utilization Review: Yes
Second Surgical Opinion: No
Case Management: Yes

Publishes and Distributes Report Card: Yes

Accreditation Certification
NCQA
TJC Accreditation, Medicare Approved, Utilization Review, Pre-Admission Certification, State Licensure, Quality Assurance Program

Key Personnel
President. . . . . .Sheila Jenkins
Dir, Millennium Products . . . . .Deborah Anderson
VP, Medicare Products. .Marcia Broeren
VP, Sales . . . . .William O'Brien
Dir, Web Strategy . . . . .Valerie Pfeiffer
Medical Director. . . . . .Edward Scanlan, MD
Dir, Business Development . . . . .Donald Schumann
Chief Operating Officer . . . . .Tim Temperly
Dir, Information Systems . . . . .Dave Bloedorn
Dir, Finance. . . . . .Gerry Demmer
Mgr, Provider Data Svcs . . . . .Barb Gore
Mgr, Customer Service. . . . . .Peggy Huss
Mgr, Medicare Operations . . . . .Kathleen Krentz
Mgr, Product Development . . . . .Maureen Lawson
Mgr, Medicare Sales. . . . . .Joan Merwin
Marketing Communications .Maria Heim
920-720-1752
mheim@affinityhealth.org
Mgr, Care Management . . . . .Dawn Rady

Specialty Managed Care Partners
Enters into Contracts with Regional Business Coalitions: Yes

1207 Physicians Plus Insurance Corporation

22 E Mifflin Street
Suite 200
Madison, WI 53703
Toll-Free: 800-545-5015
Phone: 608-282-8900
Fax: 608-258-1902
ppicinfo@pplusic.com
www.pplusic.com
Mailing Address: PO Box 2078, Madison, WI 53701-2078
Subsidiary of: Meriter Health Services
For Profit Organization: Yes
Year Founded: 1986
Physician Owned Organization: Yes
Number of Affiliated Hospitals: 24
Number of Primary Care Physicians: 3,000
Number of Referral/Specialty Physicians: 2,117
Total Enrollment: 112,000
State Enrollment: 112,000

Healthplan and Services Defined
PLAN TYPE: HMO/PPO
Other Type: POS
Model Type: Network
Plan Specialty: Behavioral Health, Chiropractic, Dental, Disease Management, Lab, X-Ray
Benefits Offered: Behavioral Health, Chiropractic, Dental, Disease Management, Home Care, Inpatient SNF, Physical Therapy, Podiatry, Prescription, Transplant, Vision, Wellness, Durable Medical Equipment

Type of Coverage
Individual, Supplemental Medicare, Commercial Small Group, Large Group
Catastrophic Illness Benefit: Covered

Type of Payment Plans Offered
Capitated, FFS, Combination FFS & DFFS

Geographic Areas Served
South central Wisconsin

Subscriber Information
Average Monthly Fee Per Subscriber
(Employee + Employer Contribution):
Employee Only (Self): Varies by plan
Average Annual Deductible Per Subscriber:
Employee Only (Self): Varies by plan
Employee & 1 Family Member: $0
Employee & 2 Family Members: $0
Medicare: $0
Average Subscriber Co-Payment:
Primary Care Physician: Varies by plan
Hospital ER: $100.00
Home Health Care Max. Days/Visits Covered: 100 visits
Nursing Home Max. Days/Visits Covered: 100 days

Network Qualifications
Pre-Admission Certification: Yes

Peer Review Type
Utilization Review: Yes
Second Surgical Opinion: Yes
Case Management: Yes

Publishes and Distributes Report Card: Yes

Accreditation Certification
State Licensure, Quality Assurance Program

Key Personnel
President/CEO . . . . Micahel A Mohoney
President . . . . Linda Hoff
VP, Operations. . . . . Terri Lowek
VP, Finance . . . . Dawn Witek
Chief Pharmacy Officer . . . . Bill Reay
VP, Sales & Mktg Officer . . . . Scott T Kowalski
Sr Dir, Provider Network . . . . Mary D Strasser
Manager, Marketing. . . . . Scott Shoemaker
608-260-7116
scott.shoemaker@pplusic.com

Average Claim Compensation
Physician's Fees Charged: 70%
Hospital's Fees Charged: 75%

Specialty Managed Care Partners
Enters into Contracts with Regional Business Coalitions: No

1208   Prevea Health Network

2710 Executive Drive
Green Bay, WI 54304
Toll-Free: 866-640-7444
Phone: 920-272-1100
Fax: 920-272-1120
preveappoinfo@prevea.com
www.preveappo.com
Mailing Address: PO Box 13397, Green Bay, WI 54307-3397
For Profit Organization: Yes
Year Founded: 1996
Number of Affiliated Hospitals: 14
Number of Primary Care Physicians: 1,602
Total Enrollment: 119,712
State Enrollment: 15,706

Healthplan and Services Defined
PLAN TYPE: PPO
Model Type: Group
Plan Specialty: UR
Benefits Offered: Behavioral Health, Chiropractic, Disease
Management, Home Care, Prescription, Transplant, Wellness,
Durable Medical Equipment

Type of Coverage
Commercial, Supplemental Medicare

Geographic Areas Served
counties: Brown, Door, Kewaunee, Manitowoc, Marinette, Oconto

Subscriber Information
Average Annual Deductible Per Subscriber:
Employee Only (Self): $0
Employee & 1 Family Member: $0
Employee & 2 Family Members: $0
Medicare: $0
Average Subscriber Co-Payment:
Primary Care Physician: $0

Accreditation Certification
Pre-Admission Certification

Key Personnel
CEO . . . . Mark Minsloff
CFO . . . . Kathy Michulsky
Credentialing Coordinator . . . . Holly Mock
Health Promotions Coord. . . . . Candy Blaney
Client Support Coord . . . . Deb Rhode
Client Services . . . . Cherie Heath
Provider Network Coord . . . . Trisha Paulson

Specialty Managed Care Partners
Express Scripts

1209   Security Health Plan of Wisconsin

1515 Saint Joseph Avenue
PO Box 8000
Marshfield, WI 54449-8000
Toll-Free: 800-472-2363
Phone: 715-221-9555
Fax: 715-221-9500
www.securityhealth.org
Secondary Address: 3610 Oakwood Mall Drive, Suite 203, Eau Claire,
WI 54701
Non-Profit Organization: Yes
Year Founded: 1986
Physician Owned Organization: Yes
Number of Affiliated Hospitals: 42
Number of Primary Care Physicians: 4,100
Total Enrollment: 187,000
State Enrollment: 187,000

Healthplan and Services Defined
PLAN TYPE: Multiple
Model Type: Network
Plan Specialty: Behavioral Health, Chiropractic, Disease
Management, EPO, Lab, PBM, Vision, Radiology, Worker's
Compensation, UR
Benefits Offered: Behavioral Health, Chiropractic, Complementary
Medicine, Dental, Disease Management, Home Care, Inpatient
SNF, Long-Term Care, Podiatry, Prescription, Psychiatric,
Transplant, Vision, Wellness, Worker's Compensation, AD&D,
Durable Medical Equipment
Offers Demand Management Patient Information Service: Yes
DMPI Services Offered: Nurse Line, Health Information Line

Type of Coverage
Commercial, Individual, Indemnity, Medicare, Supplemental
Medicare, Medicaid, TPA
Catastrophic Illness Benefit: Covered

Type of Payment Plans Offered
Capitated, FFS

Geographic Areas Served
Northern, Western and Central Wisconsin

Subscriber Information
Average Monthly Fee Per Subscriber
(Employee + Employer Contribution):
Employee Only (Self): Varies by plan
Average Annual Deductible Per Subscriber:
Employee Only (Self): $200.00

Employee & 2 Family Members: $100.00
Medicare: $0
Average Subscriber Co-Payment:
Primary Care Physician: $20.00
Non-Network Physician: $20.00
Prescription Drugs: $3.00
Hospital ER: $50.00
Home Health Care: $0
Home Health Care Max. Days/Visits Covered: 40 days
Nursing Home: $0
Nursing Home Max. Days/Visits Covered: 30 days

Network Qualifications
Pre-Admission Certification: No

Peer Review Type
Utilization Review: Yes

Publishes and Distributes Report Card: Yes

Accreditation Certification
NCQA
Medicare Approved, Pre-Admission Certification

Key Personnel
Chief Administrative Off . . . . Steve Youso
Utilization Management . . . . Lawrence McFarlane, MBA, MD
Disease Management . . . . Michele L Bachhuber, MD
Technology Assessment . . . . Andrea Hillerud, MD
Behavioral Health Until . . . . Edward J Krall, MD

Specialty Managed Care Partners
Enters into Contracts with Regional Business Coalitions: Yes

1210 Trilogy Health Insurance

18000 West Sarah Lane
Brookfield, WI 53045
Toll-Free: 866-429-3242
Phone: 262-432-9150
www.trilogycares.com
For Profit Organization: Yes
Total Enrollment: 5,000

Healthplan and Services Defined
PLAN TYPE: PPO
Other Type: HSA
Benefits Offered: Disease Management, Prescription, Wellness
Offers Demand Management Patient Information Service: Yes
DMPI Services Offered: 24-Hour Nurse Line

Type of Coverage
Commercial

Key Personnel
President/CEO . . . . Bill Felsing

1211 UnitedHealthCare of Wisconsin: Central

5901 Lincoln Drive
Edina, WI 55436
Toll-Free: 800-842-3585
www.uhc.com
Secondary Address: 10701 W Research Drive, Milwaukee, WI 53226,
800-879-0071
Subsidiary of: UnitedHealth Group
For Profit Organization: Yes
Total Enrollment: 75,000,000
State Enrollment: 392,782

Healthplan and Services Defined
PLAN TYPE: HMO/PPO
Benefits Offered: Disease Management, Prescription, Wellness

Type of Coverage
Commercial, Medicare, Medicaid

Geographic Areas Served
Statewide

Key Personnel
CEO . . . . William Felsing
CFO . . . . Glen Reinhard
Media Contact . . . . Greg Thompson
312-424-6913
gregory_a_thompson@uhc.com

1212 Unity Health Insurance

840 Carolina Street
Sauk City, WI 53583
Toll-Free: 800-362-3310
Phone: 608-643-2491
Fax: 608-643-2564
marketing@unityhealth.com
www.unityhealth.com
Subsidiary of: University Health Care Inc
For Profit Organization: Yes
Year Founded: 1994
Number of Affiliated Hospitals: 44
Number of Primary Care Physicians: 908
Number of Referral/Specialty Physicians: 3,227
Total Enrollment: 90,000
State Enrollment: 75,000

Healthplan and Services Defined
PLAN TYPE: Multiple
Model Type: Network
Benefits Offered: Behavioral Health, Chiropractic, Dental, Disease
Management, Home Care, Inpatient SNF, Physical Therapy,
Podiatry, Prescription, Psychiatric, Transplant, Vision, Wellness

Type of Coverage
Commercial, Individual, Medicaid

Type of Payment Plans Offered
POS, DFFS, FFS, Combination FFS & DFFS

Geographic Areas Served
20 counties in southwestern and south central Wisconsin

Network Qualifications
Pre-Admission Certification: Yes

Peer Review Type
Utilization Review: Yes
Second Surgical Opinion: Yes
Case Management: Yes

Publishes and Distributes Report Card: Yes

Accreditation Certification
NCQA
Medicare Approved, Utilization Review, Pre-Admission Certification,
State Licensure, Quality Assurance Program

Key Personnel
CEO/Chairman of the Board . . . . Terry Bolz
Vice President Finance . . . . Radovan Bursac
Vice President Operations . . . . Gail Midlikowski
General Counsel . . . . David Diercks
VP, Network Development . . . . Brian Collien
Director, Quality Care . . . . Elaine Rosenblatt
Pharmacy Director . . . . Pat Cory
VP, Finance, CFO . . . . Jim Hiveley
Medical Director . . . . Mary Pak, MD

Specialty Managed Care Partners
Behavioral Health Consultation System, UW Hospital and Clinics,
APS Healthcare
Enters into Contracts with Regional Business Coalitions: No

Employer References
University of Wisconsin Medical Foundation, Middleton Cross Plains
School District, Rockwell Automation, Brakebush Brothers, Epic
Systemss Corporation

1213 Vision Insurance Plan of America

6737 W Washington Street
Suite 2202, PO Box 44077
West Allis, WI 53214-4077
Toll-Free: 800-883-5747
Phone: 414-475-1875
Fax: 414-475-1599
VIPA@visionplans.com
www.visionplans.com
Total Enrollment: 5,000,000

Healthplan and Services Defined
  PLAN TYPE: Vision
  Plan Specialty: Vision
  Benefits Offered: Vision

Geographic Areas Served
  Nationwide

Key Personnel
  President . . . . .Thomas Witter
    twitter@visionplans.com
  Compliance Officer . . . . .Dana Bagnall
    dbagnall@visionplans.com
  VP, Sales & Marketing . . . . .Mark Wallner
    mwallner@visionplans.com
  Account Executive . . . . .Laurie Kohls
    lkohls@visionplans.com
  Account Services . . . . .Jesse Rulli
    jrulli@visionplans.com

1214 Wisconsin Physician's Service

1717 W Broadway
PO Box 8190
Madison, WI 53708-8190
Toll-Free: 888-915-5477
Phone: 608-221-4711
Fax: 608-223-3626
member@wpsic.com
www.wpsic.com
Secondary Address: 208 E Olin Avenue, Individual Sales: PO Box
  8190, Madison, WI 53713
Non-Profit Organization: Yes
Year Founded: 1946
Owned by an Integrated Delivery Network (IDN): Yes
Number of Affiliated Hospitals: 129
Number of Primary Care Physicians: 14,500
Total Enrollment: 175,000
State Enrollment: 223,000

Healthplan and Services Defined
  PLAN TYPE: PPO
  Model Type: Network
  Plan Specialty: ASO, Behavioral Health, Chiropractic, Dental,
    Disease Management, EPO, Lab, PBM, Vision, Radiology,
    Worker's Compensation, UR, Rational Med
  Benefits Offered: Behavioral Health, Chiropractic, Dental, Disease
    Management, Home Care, Inpatient SNF, Physical Therapy,
    Podiatry, Prescription, Psychiatric, Transplant, Vision, Wellness,
    AD&D, Life, LTD, STD
  Offers Demand Management Patient Information Service: Yes

Type of Coverage
  Commercial, Individual, Indemnity, Medicare, Supplemental
    Medicare, Catastrophic
  Catastrophic Illness Benefit: Varies per case

Type of Payment Plans Offered
  POS, DFFS

Subscriber Information
  Average Annual Deductible Per Subscriber:
      Employee Only (Self): $0
      Employee & 1 Family Member: $0

Employee & 2 Family Members: $0
  Medicare: $0

Peer Review Type
  Case Management: Yes

Publishes and Distributes Report Card: Yes

Accreditation Certification
  AAAHC, URAC
  Medicare Approved, Utilization Review, State Licensure, Quality
    Assurance Program

Key Personnel
  President and CEO . . . . .Jim Riordan
  EVP/COO . . . . .Bill Bathke
  Dir, Treasury & Govt Oper . . . . .Lyle David
  Executive Director . . . . .Leni Siker
  Executive Director . . . . .Jon Flora
  VP, Regulatory Services . . . . .Susan Caldwell
  Dir, Pharmacy Services . . . . .David Armstrong
  Dir, Reinsurance Services . . . . .Tim Healy
  SVP, Sales & Marketing . . . . .Tom Olson

Specialty Managed Care Partners
  Delta Dental
  Enters into Contracts with Regional Business Coalitions: Yes

Employer References
  US Department of Defense

HMO/PPO DIRECTORY
WYOMING

Health Insurance Coverage Status and Type of Coverage by Age

Category	All Persons		Under 18 years		Under 65 years		65 years and over	
	Number	%	Number	%	Number	%	Number	%
Total population	537	-	133	-	476	-	60	-
Covered by some type of health insurance	444 *(6)*	82.7 *(0.9)*	120 *(2)*	89.8 *(1.5)*	384 *(8)*	80.7 *(1.1)*	60 *(5)*	98.6 *(0.8)*
Covered by private health insurance	364 *(10)*	67.8 *(1.6)*	85 *(4)*	63.7 *(2.8)*	323 *(11)*	67.8 *(1.8)*	41 *(4)*	67.5 *(4.2)*
Employment based	313 *(11)*	58.3 *(1.8)*	78 *(4)*	58.3 *(2.7)*	294 *(11)*	61.7 *(1.8)*	19 *(3)*	32.0 *(4.0)*
Own employment based	166 *(6)*	31.0 *(1.0)*	0 *(0)*	0.1 *(0.1)*	149 *(5)*	31.4 *(0.9)*	17 *(2)*	28.1 *(3.8)*
Direct purchase	53 *(4)*	9.8 *(0.7)*	7 *(1)*	5.1 *(0.7)*	29 *(4)*	6.1 *(0.7)*	23 *(3)*	38.7 *(4.7)*
Covered by government health insurance	143 *(9)*	26.7 *(1.8)*	47 *(4)*	35.2 *(2.9)*	87 *(7)*	18.3 *(1.7)*	56 *(5)*	92.9 *(1.6)*
Covered by Medicaid	65 *(6)*	12.0 *(1.2)*	42 *(4)*	31.5 *(2.8)*	62 *(6)*	12.9 *(1.3)*	3 *(1)*	5.1 *(1.4)*
Also by private insurance	14 *(2)*	2.5 *(0.4)*	9 *(2)*	6.8 *(1.3)*	12 *(2)*	2.6 *(0.4)*	1 *(1)*	2.2 *(1.1)*
Covered by Medicare	63 *(5)*	11.7 *(0.9)*	0 *(0)*	0.0 *(0.0)*	6 *(2)*	1.4 *(0.3)*	56 *(5)*	92.9 *(1.6)*
Also by private insurance	39 *(4)*	7.2 *(0.7)*	0 *(0)*	0.0 *(0.0)*	2 *(1)*	0.3 *(0.1)*	37 *(4)*	61.8 *(4.2)*
Also by Medicaid	6 *(1)*	1.1 *(0.2)*	0 *(0)*	0.0 *(0.0)*	3 *(1)*	0.6 *(0.2)*	3 *(1)*	5.1 *(1.4)*
Covered by military health care	33 *(5)*	6.1 *(1.0)*	5 *(2)*	4.0 *(1.2)*	24 *(5)*	5.0 *(1.0)*	9 *(2)*	14.7 *(3.2)*
Not covered at any time during the year	93 *(5)*	17.3 *(0.9)*	14 *(2)*	10.2 *(1.5)*	92 *(5)*	19.3 *(1.1)*	1 *(0)*	1.4 *(0.8)*

Note: Numbers in thousands; figures cover 2010; standard error appears in parenthesis; (b) base less than 75,000; (x) not applicable
Source: U.S. Census Bureau, Current Population Survey, 2011 Annual Social and Economic Supplement. Table HI05. Health Insurance Coverage Status and Type of Coverage by State and Age for All People: 2010

Wyoming

1215 Aetna Health of Wyoming
Partnered with eHealthInsurance Services Inc.

1216 Blue Cross & Blue Shield of Wyoming
4000 House Avenue
Cheyenne, WY 82001
Toll-Free: 800-442-2376
Phone: 307-634-1393
Fax: 307-634-5742
www.bcbswy.com
Mailing Address: PO Box 2266, Cheyenne, WY 82003
Non-Profit Organization: Yes
Year Founded: 1976
Total Enrollment: 100,000
State Enrollment: 100,000

Healthplan and Services Defined
PLAN TYPE: PPO
Benefits Offered: Disease Management, Physical Therapy, Wellness

Type of Coverage
Commercial, Individual, Medicare, Medicaid

Type of Payment Plans Offered
FFS

Geographic Areas Served
Wyoming

Key Personnel
President & CEO .... Tim J Crilly
Chairman .... Cliff Kirk
Vice Chairman. .... Thomas Lockhart
Sales Representative .... Granger Gallegos

Specialty Managed Care Partners
Prime Therapeutics

Employer References
Tricare

1217 CIGNA HealthCare of Wyoming
3900 East Mexico Avenue
#1100
Denver, CO 80210
Phone: 303-782-1500
Fax: 303-691-3197
www.cigna.com
For Profit Organization: Yes
Total Enrollment: 11,234
State Enrollment: 3,334

Healthplan and Services Defined
PLAN TYPE: PPO
Plan Specialty: Behavioral Health, Dental, Vision
Benefits Offered: Behavioral Health, Dental, Disease Management, Prescription, Transplant, Vision, Wellness, Life

Type of Coverage
Commercial

Type of Payment Plans Offered
POS, FFS

Geographic Areas Served
Wyoming

Key Personnel
Director At Cigna .... Sallie Vanasdale
VP Provider Realations .... William Cetti
VP Client Relations .... Gregg Prussing

1218 Delta Dental of Wyoming
320 West 25th Street
Suite 100
Cheyenne, WY 82001
Toll-Free: 800-735-3379
Phone: 307-632-3313
Fax: 307-632-7309
www.deltadentalwy.org
Mailing Address: PO Box 29, Cheyenne, WY 82003-0029
Non-Profit Organization: Yes
Total Enrollment: 54,000,000

Healthplan and Services Defined
PLAN TYPE: Dental
Other Type: Dental PPO
Model Type: Network
Plan Specialty: ASO, Dental
Benefits Offered: Dental

Type of Coverage
Commercial, Individual, Group
Catastrophic Illness Benefit: None

Geographic Areas Served
Statewide

Subscriber Information
Average Monthly Fee Per Subscriber
(Employee + Employer Contribution):
Employee Only (Self): Varies
Employee & 1 Family Member: Varies
Employee & 2 Family Members: Varies
Average Annual Deductible Per Subscriber:
Employee Only (Self): Varies
Employee & 1 Family Member: Varies
Employee & 2 Family Members: Varies
Average Subscriber Co-Payment:
Prescription Drugs: $0
Home Health Care: $0
Nursing Home: $0

Key Personnel
Executive Director. .... Jeanne Thobro
CEO .... Kerry Hall

1219 eHealthInsurance Services Inc.
11919 Foundation Place
Gold River, CA 95670
Toll-Free: 800-977-8860
info@ehealthinsurance.com
www.e.healthinsurance.com
Year Founded: 1997

Healthplan and Services Defined
PLAN TYPE: HMO/PPO
Benefits Offered: Dental, Life, STD

Type of Coverage
Commercial, Individual, Medicare

Geographic Areas Served
All 50 states in the USA and District of Columbia

Key Personnel
Chairman & CEO .... Gary L. Lauer
EVP/Business & Corp. Dev. .... Bruce Telkamp
EVP/Chief Technology .... Dr. Sheldon X. Wang
SVP & CFO .... Stuart M. Huizinga
Pres. of eHealth Gov. Sys .... Samuel C. Gibbs
SVP of Sales & Operations .... Robert S. Hurley
Director Public Relations. .... Nate Purpura
650-210-3115

1220 Humana Health Insurance of Wyoming

1611 Alderson Avenue
Billings, MT 59102
Toll-Free: 800-967-2370
Phone: 201-512-8818
www.humana.com
For Profit Organization: Yes

Healthplan and Services Defined
PLAN TYPE: HMO/PPO

Type of Coverage
Commercial, Individual

Accreditation Certification
URAC, NCQA, CORE

1221 UnitedHealthCare of Wyoming

6465 S Greenwood Plaza Boulevard
Suite 300
Centennial, CO 80111
Toll-Free: 800-516-3344
Phone: 303-267-3300
Fax: 303-267-3597
www.uhc.com
Subsidiary of: UnitedHealth Group
For Profit Organization: Yes
Year Founded: 1986
Number of Affiliated Hospitals: 47
Number of Primary Care Physicians: 1,600
Number of Referral/Specialty Physicians: 3,500
Total Enrollment: 75,000,000
State Enrollment: 21,919

Healthplan and Services Defined
PLAN TYPE: HMO/PPO
Model Type: Mixed Model
Plan Specialty: MSO
Benefits Offered: Behavioral Health, Chiropractic, Complementary
Medicine, Dental, Disease Management, Home Care, Inpatient
SNF, Long-Term Care, Physical Therapy, Podiatry, Prescription,
Psychiatric, Transplant, Vision, Wellness, AD&D, Life

Type of Coverage
Commercial, Individual, Medicaid, Commercial Group

Type of Payment Plans Offered
DFFS, FFS, Combination FFS & DFFS

Geographic Areas Served
Statewide

Subscriber Information
Average Monthly Fee Per Subscriber
(Employee + Employer Contribution):
Employee Only (Self): Varies
Average Subscriber Co-Payment:
Primary Care Physician: $10
Prescription Drugs: $10/15/30
Hospital ER: $50

Network Qualifications
Pre-Admission Certification: Yes

Peer Review Type
Case Management: Yes

Publishes and Distributes Report Card: Yes

Accreditation Certification
URAC, NCQA
State Licensure, Quality Assurance Program

Average Claim Compensation
Physician's Fees Charged: 70%
Hospital's Fees Charged: 55%

Specialty Managed Care Partners
United Behavioral Health

Enters into Contracts with Regional Business Coalitions: No

1222 WINhealth Partners

1200 East 20th Street
Suite A
Cheyenne, WY 82001
Toll-Free: 800-868-7670
Phone: 307-773-1300
Fax: 307-638-7701
service@winhealthpartners.org
www.winhealthpartners.org
Non-Profit Organization: Yes
Year Founded: 1996
Total Enrollment: 11,000
State Enrollment: 9,864

Healthplan and Services Defined
PLAN TYPE: Multiple
Plan Specialty: Lab, Radiology
Benefits Offered: Behavioral Health, Chiropractic, Disease
Management, Home Care, Inpatient SNF, Physical Therapy,
Prescription, Vision, Wellness, Durable Medical Equipment

Type of Coverage
Individual, Medicare

Subscriber Information
Average Monthly Fee Per Subscriber
(Employee + Employer Contribution):
Medicare: Varies
Average Annual Deductible Per Subscriber:
Employee Only (Self): $500.00
Medicare: Varies
Average Subscriber Co-Payment:
Primary Care Physician: $20.00
Prescription Drugs: $10/15/40
Hospital ER: $75.00

Peer Review Type
Case Management: Yes

Publishes and Distributes Report Card: Yes

Accreditation Certification
TJC, NCQA

Key Personnel
President . . . . Dick Torkelson, MD
Medical Director . . . . John Glode, MD
Executive Director/CEO . . . . Beth Wasson
Systems Administrator . . . . Keri Fox
Chief Information Officer . . . . Michael Hofmeister

Employer References
United Medical Center, Wyoming Employees Federal Credit Union

Appendix A: Glossary of Terms

A

Access
A person's ability to obtain healthcare services.

Acute Care
Medical treatment rendered to people whose illnesses or medical problems are short-term or don't require long-term continuing care. Acute care facilities are hospitals that mainly treat people with short-term health problems.

Aggregate Indemnity
The maximum amount of payment provided by an insurer for each covered service for a group of insured people.

Aid to Families with Dependent Children (AFDC)
A state-based federal assistance program that provided cash payments to needy children (and their caretakers), who met certain income requirements. AFDC has now been replaced by a new block grant program, but the requirements, or criteria, can still be used for determining eligibility for Medicaid.

Alliance
Large businesses, small businesses, and individuals who form a group for insurance coverage.

All-payer System
A proposed healthcare system in which, no matter who is paying, prices for health services and payment methods are the same. Federal or state government, a private insurance company, a self-insured employer plan, an individual, or any other payer would pay the same rates. Also called Multiple Payer system.

Ambulatory Care
All health services that are provided on an out-patient basis, that don't require overnight care. Also called out-patient care.

Ancillary Services
Supplemental services, including laboratory, radiology and physical therapy, that are provided along with medical or hospital care.

B

Beneficiary
A person who is eligible for or receiving benefits under an insurance policy or plan.

Benefits
The services that members are entitled to receive based on their health plan.

Blue Cross/Blue Shield
Non-profit, tax-exempt insurance service plans that cover hospital care, physician care and related services. Blue Cross and Blue Shield are separate organizations that have different benefits, premiums and policies. These organizations are in all states, and The Blue Cross and Blue Shield Association of America is their national organization.

Board Certified
Status granted to a medical specialist who completes required training and passes and examination in his/her specialized area. Individuals who have met all requirements, but have not completed the exam are referred to as "board eligible."

Board Eligible
Reference to medical specialists who have completed all required training but have not completed the exam in his/her specialized area.

C

Cafeteria Plan
This benefit plan gives employees a set amount of funds that they can choose to spend on a different benefit options, such as health insurance or retirement savings

Capitation
A fixed prepayment, per patient covered, to a healthcare provider to deliver medical services to a particular group of patients. The payment is the same no matter how many services or what type of services each patient actually gets. Under capitation, the provider is financially responsible.

Care Guidelines
A set of medical treatments for a particular condition or group of patients that has been reviewed and endorsed by a national organization, such as the Agency for Healthcare Policy Research.

Carrier
A private organization, usually an insurance company, that finances healthcare.

Carve-out
Medical services that are separated out and contracted for independently from any other benefits.

Case management
Intended to improve health outcomes or control costs, services and education are tailored to a patient's needs, which are designed to improve health outcomes and/or control costs

Catastrophic Health Insurance
Health insurance that provides coverage for treating severe or lengthy illnesses or disability.

CHAMPUS
(Civilian Health and Medical Program of the Uniformed Services) A health plan that serves the dependents of active duty military personnel and retired military personnel and their dependents.

Chronic Care
Treatment given to people whose health problems are long-term and continuing. Nu nursing homes, mental hospitals and rehabilitation facilities are chronic care facilities.

Chronic Disease
A medical problem that will not improve, that lasts a lifetime, or recurs.

Claims

Bills for services. Doctors, hospitals, labs and other providers send billed claims to health insurance plans, and what the plans pay are called paid claims.

COBRA

(Consolidated Omnibus Budget Reconciliation Act of 1985) Designed to provide health coverage to workers between jobs, this legal act lets workers who leave a company buy health insurance from that company at the employer's group rate rather than an individual rate.

Co-insurance

A cost-sharing requirement under some health insurance policies in which the insured person pays some of the costs of covered services.

Cooperatives/Co-ops

HMOs that are managed by the members of the health plan or insurance purchasing arrangements in which businesses or other groups join together to gain the buying power of large employers or groups.

Co-pay

Flat fees or payments (often $5-10) that a patient pays for each doctor visit or prescription.

Cost Containment

The method of preventing healthcare costs from increasing beyond a set level by controlling or reducing inefficiency and waste in the healthcare system.

Cost Sharing

An insurance policy requires the insured person to pay a portion of the costs of covered services. Deductibles, co-insurance and co-payments are cost sharing.

Cost Shifting

When one group of patients does not pay for services, such as uninsured or Medicare patients, healthcare providers pass on the costs for these health services to other groups of patients.

Coverage

A person's healthcare costs are paid by their insurance or by the government..

Covered services

Treatments or other services for which a health plan pays at least part of the charge.

D

Deductible

The amount of money, or value of certain services (such as one physician visit), a patient or family must pay before costs (or percentages of costs) are covered by the health plan or insurance company, usually per year.

Diagnostic related groups (DRGs)

A system for classifying hospital stays according to the diagnosis of the medical problem being treated, for the purposes of payment.

Direct access

The ability to see a doctor or receive a medical service without a referral from your primary care physician.

Disease management

Programs for people who have chronic illnesses, such as asthma or diabetes, that try to encourage them to have a healthy lifestyle, to take medications as prescribed, and that coordinate care.

Disposable Personal Income

The amount of a person's income that is left over after money has been spent on basic necessities such as rent, food, and clothing.

E

Early and Periodic Screening, Diagnosis, and Treatment Program (EPSDT)

As part of the Medicaid program, the law requires that all states have a program for eligible children under age 21 to receive a medical assessment, medical treatments and other measures to correct any problems and treat chronic conditions.

Elective

A healthcare procedure that is not an emergency and that the patient and doctor plan in advance.

Emergency

A medical condition that starts suddenly and requires immediate care.

Employee Retirement Income Security Act (ERISA)

A Federal act, passed in 1974, that established new standards for employer-funded health benefit and pension programs. Companies that have self-funded health benefit plans operating under ERISA are not subject to state insurance regulations and healthcare legislation.

Employer Contribution

The contribution is the money a company pays for its employees' healthcare. Exclusions
Health conditions that are explicitly not covered in an insurance package and that your insurance will not pay for.

Exclusive Provider Organizations (EPO)/Exclusive Provider Arrangement (EPA)

An indemnity or service plan that provides benefits only if those hospitals or doctors with which it contracts provide the medical services, with some exceptions for emergency and out-of-area services.

F

Federal Employee Health Benefit Program (FEP)

Health insurance program for Federal workers and their dependents, established in 1959 under the Federal Employees Health Benefits Act. Federal employees may choose to participate in one of two or more plans.

Fee-for-Service

Physicians or other providers bill separately for each patient encounter or service they provide. This method of billing means the insurance company pays all or some set percentage of the fees that hospitals and doctors set and charge. Expenditures increase if the increaseThis is still the main system of paying for healthcare services in the United States.

First Dollar Coverage

A system in which the insurer pays for all employee out-of-pocket healthcare costs. Under first dollar coverage, the beneficiary has no deductible and no co-payments.

Flex plan

An account that lets workers set aside pretax dollars to pay for medical benefits, childcare, and other services.

Formulary

A list of medications that a managed care company encourages or requires physicians to prescribe as necessary in order to reduce costs.

G

Gag clause

A contractual agreement between a managed care organization and a provider that restricts what the provider can say about the managed care company

Gatekeeper

The person in a managed care organization, often a primary care provider, who controls a patient's access to healthcare services and whose approval is required for referrals to other services or other specialists.

General Practice

Physicians without specialty training who provide a wide range of primary healthcare services to patients.

Global Budgeting

A way of containing hospital costs in which participating hospitals share a budget, agreeing together to set the maximum amount of money that will be paid for healthcare.

Group Insurance

Health insurance offered through business, union trusts or other groups and associations. The most common system of health insurance in the United States, in which the cost of insurance is based on the age, sex, health status and occupation of the people in the group.

Group model HMO

An HMO that contracts with an independent group practice to provide medical services

Guaranteed Issue

The requirement that an insurance plan accept everyone who applies for coverage and guarantee the renewal of that coverage as long as the covered person pays the policy premium.

H

Healthcare Benefits

The specific services and procedures covered by a health plan or insurer.

Healthcare Financing Administration (HCFA)

The federal government agency within the Department of Health and Human Services that directs the Medicare and Medicaid programs. HCFA also does research to support these programs and oversees more than a quarter of all healthcare costs in the United States.

Health Insurance

Financial protection against the healthcare costs caused by treating disease or accidental injury.

Health Insurance Portability and Accountability Act (HIPAA)

Also known as Kennedy-Kassebaum law, this guarantees that people who lose their group health insurance will have access to individual insurance, regardless of pre-existing medical problems. The law also allows employees to secure health insurance from their new employer when they switch jobs even if they have a pre-existing medical condition.

Health Insurance Purchasing Cooperatives (HIPCs)

Public or private organizations that get health insurance coverage for certain populations of people, combining everyone in a specific geographic region and basing insurance rates on the people in that area.

Health Maintenance Organization (HMO)

A health plan provides comprehensive medical services to its members for a fixed, prepaid premium. Members must use participating providers and are enrolled for a fixed period of time. HMOs can do business either on a for-profit or not-for-profit basis.

Health Plan Employer Data and Information Set (HEDIS)

Performance measures designed by the National Committee for Quality Assurance to give participating managed health plans and employers to information about the value of their healthcare and trends in their health plan performance compared with other health plans.

Home healthcare

Skilled nurses and trained aides who provide nursing services and related care to someone at home.

Hospice Care

Care given to terminally ill patients. Hospital Alliances Groups of hospitals that join together to cut their costs by purchasing services and equipment in volume.

I

Indemnity Insurance

A system of health insurance in which the insurer pays for the costs of covered services after care has been given, and which usually defines the maximum amounts which will be paid for covered services. This is the most common type of insurance in the United States.

Independent Practice Association (IPA)

A group of private physicians who join together in an association to contract with a managed care organization.

Indigent Care
Care provided, at no cost, to people who do not have health insurance or are not covered by Medicare, Medicaid, or other public programs.

In-patient
A person who has been admitted to a hospital or other health facility, for a period of at least 24 hours.

Integrated Delivery System (IDS)
An organization that usually includes a hospital, a large medical group, and an insurer such as an HMO or PPO.

Integrated Provider (IP)
A group of providers that offer comprehensive and coordinated care, and usually provides a range of medical care facilities and service plans including hospitals, group practices, a health plan and other related healthcare services.

J

Joint Commission on the Accreditation of Healthcare Organizations (JCAHO)
A national private, non-profit organization that accredits healthcare organizations and agencies and sets guidelines for operation for these facilities.

L

Limitations
A "cap" or limit on the amount of services that may be provided. It may be the maximum cost or number of days that a service or treatment is covered.

Limited Service Hospital
A hospital, often located in a rural area, that provides a limited set of medical and surgical services.

Long-term Care
Healthcare, personal care and social services provided to people who have a chronic illness or disability and do not have full functional capacity. This care can take place in an institution or at home, on a long-term basis.

M

Malpractice Insurance
Coverage for medical professionals which pays the costs of legal fees and/or any damages assessed by the court in a lawsuit brought against a professional who has been charged with negligence.

Managed care
This term describes many types of health insurance, including HMOs and PPOs. They control the use of health services by their members so that they can contain healthcare costs and/or improve the quality of care.

Mandate
Law requiring that a health plan or insurance carrier must offer a particular procedure or type of coverage.

Means Test
An assessment of a person's or family's income or assets so that it can be determined if they are eligible to receive public support, such as Medicaid.

Medicaid
An insurance program for people with low incomes who are unable to afford healthcare. Although funded by the federal government, Medicaid is administered by each state. Following very broad federal guidelines, states determine specific benefits and amounts of payment for providers.

Medical IRAs
Personal accounts which, like individual retirement plans, allow a person to accumulate funds for future use. The money in these accounts must be used to pay for medical services. The employee decides how much money he or she will spend on healthcare.

Medically Indigent
A person who does not have insurance and is not covered by Medicaid, Medicare or other public programs.

Medicare
A federal program of medical care benefits created in 1965 designed for those over age 65 or permanently disabled. Medicare consists of two separate programs: A and B. Medicare Part A, which is automatic at age 65, covers hospital costs and is financed largely by employer payroll taxes. Medicare Part B covers outpatient care and is financed through taxes and individual payments toward a premium.

Medicare Supplements or Medigap
A privately-purchased health insurance policy available to Medicare beneficiaries to cover costs of care that Medicare does not pay. Some policies cover additional costs, such as preventive care, prescription drugs, or at-home care.

Member
The person enrolled in a health plan.

N

National Committee on Quality Assurance (NCQA)
An independent national organization that reviews and accredits managed care plans and measures the quality of care offered by managed care plans.

Network
A group of affiliated contracted healthcare providers (physicians, hospitals, testing centers, rehabilitation centers etc.), such as an HMO, PPO, or Point of Service plan.

Non-contributory Plan
A group insurance plan that requires no payment from employees for their healthcare coverage.

Non-participating Provider
A healthcare provider who is not part of a health plan. Usually patients must pay their own healthcare costs to see a non-participating provider.

Nurse practitioner

A nurse specialist who provides primary and/or specialty care to patients. In some states nurse practitioners do not have to be supervised by a doctor.

O

Open Enrollment Period

A specified period of time during which people are allowed to change health plans.

Open Panel

A right included in an HMO, which allows the covered person to get non-emergency covered services from a specialist without getting a referral from the primary care physician or gatekeeper.

Out of Pocket costs or expenditures

The amount of money that a person must pay for his or her healthcare, including: deductibles, co-pays, payments for services that are not covered, and/or health insurance premiums that are not paid by his or her employer.

Outcomes

Measures of the effectiveness of particular kinds of medical treatment. This refers to what is quantified to determine if a specific treatment or type of service works.

Out of Pocket Maximum

The maximum amount that a person must pay under a plan or insurance contract.

Outpatient Care

Healthcare services that do not require a patient to receive overnight care in a hospital.

P

Participating Physician or Provider

Healthcare providers who have contracted with a managed care plan to provide eligible healthcare services to members of that plan.

Payer

The organization responsible for the costs of healthcare services. A payer may be private insurance, the government, or an employer's self-funded plan.

Peer Review Organization (PRO or PSRO)

An agency that monitors the quality and appropriateness of medical care delivered to Medicare and Medicaid patients. Healthcare professionals in these agencies review other professionals with similar training and experience. [See Quality Improvement Organizations]

Percent of Poverty

A term that describes the income level a person or family must have to be eligible for Medicaid.

Physician Assistant

A health professional who provides primary and/or specialty care to patients under the supervision of a physician.

Physician Hospital Organizations (PHOs)

An organization that contracts with payers on behalf of one or more hospitals and affiliated physicians. Physicians still own their practices.

Play or Pay

This system would provide coverage for all people by requiring employers either to provide health insurance for their employees and dependents (play) or pay a contribution to a publicly-provided system that covers uninsured or unemployed people without private insurance (pay).

Point of Service (POS)

A type of insurance where each time healthcare services are needed, the patient can choose from different types of provider systems (indemnity plan, PPO or HMO). Usually, members are required to pay more to see PPO or non-participating providers than to see HMO providers.

Portability

A person's ability to keep his or her health coverage during times of change in health status or personal situation (such as change in employment or unemployment, marriage or divorce) or while moving between health plans.

Postnatal Care

Healthcare services received by a woman immediately following the delivery of her child

Pre-authorization

The process where, before a patient can be admitted to the hospital or receive other types of specialty services, the managed care company must approve of the proposed service in order to cover it.

Pre-existing Condition

A medical condition or diagnosis that began before coverage began under a current plan or insurance contract. The insurance company may provide coverage but will specifically exclude treatment for such a condition from that person's coverage for a certain period of time, often six months to a year.

Preferred Provider Organization (PPO)

A type of insurance in which the managed care company pays a higher percentage of the costs when a preferred (in-plan) provider is used. The participating providers have agreed to provide their services at negotiated discount fees.

Premium

The amount paid periodically to buy health insurance coverage. Employers and employees usually share the cost of premiums.

Premium Cap

The maximum amount of money an insurance company can charge for coverage.

Premium Tax

A state tax on insurance premiums.

Prepaid Group Practice

A type of HMO where participating providers receive a fixed payment in advance for providing particular healthcare services.

Preventive Care
Healthcare services that prevent disease or its consequences. It includes primary prevention to keep people from getting sick (such as immunizations), secondary prevention to detect early disease (such as Pap smears) and tertiary prevention to keep ill people or those at high risk of disease from getting sicker (such as helping someone with lung disease to quit smoking).

Primary Care
Basic or general routine office medical care, usually from an internist, obstetrician-gynecologist, family practitioner, or pediatrician.

Primary care provider (PCP)
The health professional who provides basic healthcare services. The PCP may control patients' access to the rest of the healthcare system through referrals.

Private Insurance
Health insurance that is provided by insurance companies such as commercial insurers and Blue Cross plans, self-funded plans sponsored by employers, HMOs or other managed care arrangements.

Provider
An individual or institution who provides medical care, including a physician, hospital, skilled nursing facility, or intensive care facility.

Provider-Sponsored Organization (PSO)
Healthcare providers (physicians and/or hospitals) who form an affiliation to act as insurer for an enrolled population.

Q

Quality Assessment
Measurement of the quality of care.

Quality Assurance and Quality Improvement
A systematic process to improve quality of healthcare by monitoring quality, finding out what is not working, and fixing the problems of healthcare delivery.

Quality Improvement Organization (QIO)
An organization contracting with HCFA to review the medical necessity and quality of care provided to Medicare beneficiaries.

Quality of care
How well health services result in desired health outcomes.

R

Rate Setting
These programs were developed by several states in the 1970's to establish in advance the amount that hospitals would be paid no matter how high or low their costs actually were in any particular year. (Also known as hospital rate setting or prospective reimbursement programs)

Referral system
The process through which a primary care provider authorizes a patient to see a specialist to receive additional care.

Reimbursement
The amount paid to providers for services they provide to patients.

Risk
The responsibility for profiting or losing money based on the cost of healthcare services provided. Traditionally, health insurance companies have carried the risk. Under capitation, healthcare providers bear risk.

S

Self-insured
A type of insurance arrangement where employers, usually large employers, pay for medical claims out of their own funds rather than contracting with an insurance company for coverage. This puts the employer at risk for its employees' medical expenses rather than an insurance company.

Single Payer System
A healthcare reform proposal in which healthcare costs are paid by taxes rather than by the employer and employee. All people would have coverage paid by the government.

Socialized Medicine
A healthcare system in which providers are paid by the government, and healthcare facilities are run by the government.

Staff Model HMO
A type of managed care where physicians are employees of the health plan, usually in the health plan's own health center or facility.

Standard Benefit Package
A defined set of benefits provided to all people covered under a health plan.

T

Third Party Administrator (TPA)
An organization that processes health plan claims but does not carry any insurance risk.

Third Party Payer
An organization other than the patient or healthcare provider involved in the financing of personal health services.

U

Uncompensated Care
Healthcare provided to people who cannot pay for it and who are not covered by any insurance. This includes both charity care which is not billed and the cost of services that were billed but never paid.

Underinsured
People who have some type of health insurance but not enough insurance to cover their the cost of necessary healthcare. This includes people who have very high deductibles of $1000 to $5000 per year, or insurance policies that have specific exclusions for costly services.

Underwriting
This process is the basis of insurance. It analyzes the health status and history, claims experience (cost), age and general health risks of the individual or group who is applying for insurance coverage.

Uninsured
People who do not have health insurance of any type. Over 80 percent of the uninsured are working adults and their family members.

Universal Coverage
This refers to the proposal that all people could get health insurance, regardless of the way that the system is financed.

Utilization Review
A program designed to help reduce unnecessary medical expenses by studying the appropriateness of when certain services are used and by how many patients they are used.

Utilization
How many times people use particular healthcare services during particular periods of time.

V

Vertical Integration
A healthcare system that includes the entire range of healthcare services from out-patient to hospital and long-term care.

W

Waiting Period
The amount of time a person must wait from the date he or she is accepted into a health plan (or from when he or she applies) until the insurance becomes effective and he or she can receive benefits.

Withhold
A percentage of providers' fees that managed care companies hold back from providers which is only given to them if the amount of care they provide (or that the entire plan provides) is under a budgeted amount for each quarter or the whole year.

Worker's Compensation Coverage
States require employers to provide coverage to compensate employees for work-related injuries or disabilities.

Source: Public Broadcasting Service, http://www.pbs.org/ healthcarecrisis/glossary.htm. Reprinted with permission of www.issuestv.com and www.pbs.com.

Appendix B: Industry Websites

Alliance of Community Health Plans (ACHP)

http://www.achp.org

Offers information on health care so that it is safe, effective, patient-centered, timely, efficient and equitable. Members use this web site to collaborate, share strategies and work toward solutions to some of health care's biggest challenges.

America's Health Insurance Plans (AHIP)

http://www.ahip.org

AHIP is a national trade association representing nearly 1,300 member companies providing health insurance coverage to more than 200 million Americans.

American Academy of Medical Administrators (AAMA)

http://www.aameda.org

Supports individuals involved in medical administration at the executive - or middle-management levels. Promotes educational courses for the training of persons in medical administration. Conducts research. Offers placement service.

American Accreditation Healthcare Commission/URAC

http://www.urac.org

URAC (Utilization Review Accreditation Commission) is a 501(c)(3) non-profit charitable organization founded in 1990 to establish standards for the managed care industry. URAC's broad-based membership includes representation from all the constituencies affected by managed care - employers, consumers, regulators, health care providers, and the workers' compensation and managed care industries.

American Association of Healthcare Administrative Management (AAHAM)

http://www.aaham.org

A professional organization in healthcare administrative management that offers information, education and advocacy in the areas of reimbursement, admitting and registration, data management, medical records, patient relations and more. Founded in 1968, AAHAM represents a broad-based constituency of healthcare professionals through a comprehensive program of legislative and regulatory monitoring and its participation in industry groups such as ANSI, DISA and NUBC.

American Association of Integrated Healthcare Delivery Systems (AAIHDS)

http://www.aaihds.org

AAIHDS was founded in 1993 as a non-profit organization dedicated to the educational advancement of provider-based managed care professionals involved in integrated healthcare delivery.

American Association of Preferred Provider Organizations (AAPPO)

http://www.aappo.org

A national association of preferred provider organizations (PPOs) and affiliate organizations, established in 1983 to advance awareness of the benefits - greater access, choice and flexibility - that PPOs bring to American health care.

American College of Health Care Administrators (ACHCA)

http://achca.org

Founded in 1962, ACHCA provides superior educational programming, professional certification, and career development opportunities for its members. It identifies, recognizes, and supports long term care leaders, advocating for their mission and promoting excellence in their profession.

American College of Healthcare Executives (ACHE)

http://www.ache.org

International professional society of more than 30,000 healthcare executives, including credentialing and educational programs and sponsors the Congress on Healthcare Management. ACHE's publishing division, Health Administration Press, is one of the largest publishers of books.

American College of Physician Executives (ACPE)

http://www.acpe.org

Supports physicians whose primary professional responsibility is the management of healthcare organizations. Provides for continuing education and certification of the physician executive. Offers specialized career planning, counseling, recruitment and placement services, and research and information data on physician managers.

American Health Care Association (AHCA)

http://www.ahcancal.org

A non-profit federation of affiliated state health organizations, representing more than 10,000 non-profit and for-profit assisted living, nursing facility, developmentally-disabled, and subacute care providers that care for more than 1.5 million elderly and disabled individuals nationally.

American Health Planning Association (AHPA)

http://www.ahpanet.org

A non-profit public interest organization that brings together individuals and organizations interested in the availability, affordability and equitable distribution of health services. AHPA supports community participation in health policy formulation and in the organization and operation of local health services.

American Health Quality Association (AHQA)

http://www.ahqa.org

The American Health Quality Association represents Quality Improvement Organizations (QIOs) and professionals working to improve the quality of health care in communities across America. QIOs share information about best practices with physicians, hospitals, nursing homes, home health agencies, and others. Working together with health care providers, QIOs identify opportunities and provide assistance for improvement.

American Medical Association (AMA)

http://www.ama-assn.org

Founded more than 150 years ago, the AMA's work includes the development and promotion of standards in medical practice, research, and education. This site offers medical information for physicians, medical students, other health professionals, and patients.

American Medical Directors Association (AMDA)

http://www.amda.com

A professional association of medical directors, attending physicians, and others practicing in the long term care continuum, that provides education, advocacy, information, and professional development to promote the delivery of quality long term care medicine.

American Medical Group Association (AMGA)
http://www.amga.org
Association that supports various medical groups and organized systems of care at the national level.

Association of Family Medicine Residency Directors (AFMRD)
http://www.afmrd.org
Provides representation for residency directors at a national level and provides a political voice for them to appropriate arenas. Promotes cooperation and communication between residency programs and different branches of the family medicine specialty. Dedicated to improving of education of family physicians. Provides a network for mutual assistance among FP, residency directors.

Association of Family Practice Administrators (AFPA)
http://www.uams.edu/afpa/afpa1.htm
Promotes professionalism in family practice administration. Serves as a network for sharing of information and fellowship among members. Provides technical assistance to members and functions as a liaison to related professional organizations.

Association of Healthcare Internal Auditors (AHIA)
http://www.ahia.org
Promotes cost containment and increased productivity in health care institutions through internal auditing. Serves as a forum for the exchange of experience, ideas, and information among members; provides continuing professional education courses and informs members of developments in health care internal auditing. Offers employment clearinghouse services.

Case Management Society of America (CMSA)
http://www.cmsa.org
Information for the case management profession.

Centers for Medicare and Medicaid Services (CMS)
http://cms.hhs.gov
Formerly known as the Health Care Financing Administration (HCFA), this is the federal agency that administers Medicare, Medicaid and the State Children's Health Insurance Program (SCHIP). CMS provides health insurance for over 74 million Americans through these programs.

College of Healthcare Information Management Executives (CHIME)
http://www.cio-chime.org
Serves the professional development needs of healthcare CIOs, and advocating the more effective use of information management within healthcare.

Electronic Healthcare Network Accreditation Commission (EHNAC)
http://www.ehnac.org
A federally-recognized standards development organization and non-profit accrediting body designed to improve transactional quality, operational efficiency and data security in healthcare.

Healthcare Financial Management Association (HFMA)
http://www.hfma.org
HFMA is a membership organization for healthcare financial management executives and leaders. The association brings perspective and clarity to the industry's complex issues for the

purpose of preparing members to succeed. Programs, publications and partnerships enhance the capabilities that strengthen not only individuals careers, but also the organizations from which members come.

Healthcare Information and Management Systems Society (HIMSS)
http://www.himss.org
The healthcare industry's membership organization exclusively focused on providing global leadership for the optimal use of healthcare information technology (IT) and management systems. HIMSS represents more than 20,000 individual members and over 300 corporate members leads healthcare public policy and industry practices through its advocacy, educational and professional development initiatives designed to promote information and management systems' contributions to ensuring quality patient care.

Healthfinder.gov
http://www.healthfinder.gov
A comprehensive guide to resources for health information from the federal government and related agencies.

The Joint Commission (JC)
http://www.jointcommission.org
An independent, not-for-profit organization, JC accredits and certifies more than 15,000 health care organizations and programs in the United States which is recognized nationwide as a symbol of quality that reflects an organization's commitment to meeting certain performance standards.

Managed Care Information Center (MCIC)
http://www.managedcaremarketplace.com
An online yellow pages for companies providing services to Managed Care Organizations (MCO), hospitals and physician groups. There are more than three dozen targeted categories, offering information on vendors from claims processing to transportation services to health care compliance.

National Association for Healthcare Quality (NAHQ)
http://www.nahq.org
Provides vital research, education, networking, certification and professional practice resources, designed to empower healthcare quality professionals from every specialty. This leading resource for healthcare quality professionals is an essential connection for leadership, excellence and innovation in healthcare quality.

National Association for Health Care Recruitment (NAHCR)
http://www.nahcr.com
Supports individuals employed directly by hospitals and other health care organizations which are involved in the practice of professional health care recruitment. Promotes sound principles of professional healthcare recruitment. Provides financial assistance to aid members in planning and implementing regional educational programs. Offers technical assistance and consultation services. Compiles statistics.

National Association Medical Staff Services (NAMSS)
http://www.namss.org
Supports individuals involved in the management and administration of health care provider services. Seeks to enhance the knowledge and experience of medical staff services professionals and promote the certification of those involved in the profession.

National Association of Dental Plans (NADP)
http://www.nadp.org

Promotes and advances the dental benefits industry to improve consumer access to affordable, quality dental care.

National Association of Insurance Commissoners (NAIC)
http://www.naic.org
The mission of the NAIC is to assist state insurance regulators, individually and collectively, in serving the public interest and achieving the following fundamental insurance regulatory goals in a responsive, efficient and cost effective manner, consistent with the wishes of its members: protect the public interest; promote competitive markets; facilitate the fair and equitable treatment of insurance consumers; promote the reliability, solvency and financial solidity of insurance institutions; and support and improve state regulation of insurance.
The NAIC also provides links to State Insurance Department web sites *(http://www.naic.org/state_web_map.htm)*.

The National Association of Managed Care Regulators (NAMCR)
http://www.namcr.org
Includes both regulator members and associate industry members. Established in 1975, NAMCR provides expertise and a forum for discussion to state regulators and managed care companies about current issues facing managed care. NAMCR has also provided expertise to the National Association of Insurance Commissioners (NAIC) in preparation of NAIC Model Acts used by many states.

National Association of State Medicaid Directors (NASMD)
http://www.nasmd.org
Promotes effective Medicaid policy and program administration; works with the federal government on issues through technical advisory groups. Conducts forums on policy and technical issues.

National Committee for Quality Assurance (NCQA)
http://www.ncqa.org
The National Committee for Quality Assurance (NCQA) is a private, not-for-profit organization dedicated to assessing and reporting on the quality of managed care plans. Their efforts are organized around two activities, accreditation and performance measurement, which are complementary strategies for producing information to guide choice.

National Institute for Health Care Management Research and Educational Foundation (NIHCM Foundation)
http://www.nihcm.org

A nonprofit, nonpartisan group that conducts research on health care issues. The Foundation disseminates research findings and analysis and holds forums and briefings for policy makers, the health care industry, consumers, the government, and the media to increase understanding of issues affecting the health care system.

National Quality Forum (NQF)
http://www.qualityforum.org
A not-for-profit membership organization created to develop and implement a national strategy for health care quality measurement and reporting, Prompted by the impact of health care quality on patient outcomes, workforce productivity, and health care costs. NQF has broad participation from all parts of the health care system, including national, state, regional, and local groups representing consumers, public and private purchasers, employers, health care professionals, provider organizations.,health plans, accrediting bodies, labor unions, supporting industries, and organizations.

National Society of Certified Healthcare Business Consultants (NSCHBC)
http://www.ichbc.org
The NSCHBC is a national organization dedicated to serving the needs of consultants who provide ethical, confidential and professional advice to the healthcare industry. Membership by successful completion of certification examination only.

Professional Association of Health Care Office Management (PAHCOM)
http://www.pahcom.com
Supports office managers of small group and solo medical practices. Operates certification program for healthcare office managers.

U.S. Food and Drug Administration (USFDA)
http://www.fda.gov
A department of the U.S. Department of Health and Human Services, the Food and Drug Administration provides information regarding health, medicine and nutrition. Their MedWatch Safety Information and Adverse Event Reporting Program serves both healthcare professionals and the public. MedWatch provides clinical information about safety issues involving medical products, including prescription and over-the-counter drugs, biologics, dietary supplements, and medical devices *(http://www.fda.gov/medwatch)*.

Plan Index

Aetna Health of Ohio Chicago, IL, 844
Aetna Health of Oklahoma Dallas, TX, 885
Aetna Health of Pennsylvania Hartford, CT, 926
Aetna Health of Tennessee Alpharetta, GA, 1026
Aetna Health of Texas Dallas, TX, 1046
Aetna Health of the Carolinas Alpharetta, GA, 814, 995
Aetna Health of Virginia Hartford, CT, 1124
Aetna Health, Inc. Corporate Headquarters Hartford, CT, 217
Affinity Health Plan Bronx, NY, 758
Alameda Alliance for Health Alameda, CA, 81
Allegiance Life & Health Insurance Company Missoula, MT, 663
Alliant Health Plans Calhoun, GA, 310
AlohaCare Honolulu, HI, 333
American Denticare Little Rock, AR, 65
American Health Care Group Pittsburgh, PA, 927
American Postal Workers Union (APWU) Health Plan Glen Burnie, MD, 498
American Republic Insurance Company Des Moines, IA, 419
American Specialty Health San Diego, CA, 82
AmeriChoice by UnitedHealthcare Rocky Hill, CT, 219
AmeriChoice by UnitedHealthCare Newark, NJ, 716
AmeriChoice by UnitedHealthCare New York, NY, 759
Amerigroup Corporation Merrifield, VA, 1125
Amerigroup Florida Tampa, FL, 256
Amerigroup Georgia Atlanta, GA, 311
Amerigroup Maryland Hanover, MD, 499
Amerigroup Nevada Las Vegas, NV, 688
Amerigroup New Jersey Edison, NJ, 717
Amerigroup New Mexico Albuquerque, NM, 743
Amerigroup New York New York, NY, 760
Amerigroup Ohio Cincinnati, OH, 845
Amerigroup Tennessee Nashville, TN, 1027
Amerigroup Texas Houston, TX, 1049
AmeriHealth HMO Wilmington, DE, 232
AmeriHealth HMO Mount Laurel, NJ, 718
Anthem Blue Cross & Blue Sheild of Indiana Indianapolis, IN, 391
Anthem Blue Cross & Blue Shield Connecticut North Haven, CT, 220
Anthem Blue Cross & Blue Shield of Colorado Denver, CO, 192
Anthem Blue Cross & Blue Shield of Indiana Indianapolis, IN, 392
Anthem Blue Cross & Blue Shield of Kentucky Louisville, KY, 456
Anthem Blue Cross & Blue Shield of Maine Augusta, ME, 488
Anthem Blue Cross & Blue Shield of Nevada Las Vegas, NV, 689
Anthem Blue Cross & Blue Shield of New Hampshire Manchester, NH, 706
Anthem Blue Cross & Blue Shield of Virginia Richmond, VA, 1126
Anthem Blue Cross & Blue Shield of Wisconsin Waukesha, WI, 1187
Arcadian Health Plans Oakland, CA, 83
Arizona Physicians IPA Phoenix, AZ, 33
Arnett Health Plans Lafayette, IN, 394
Athens Area Health Plan Select Athens, GA, 313
Atlanticare Health Plans Hammonton, NJ, 720
Atlantis Health Plan New York, NY, 761
Aultcare Corporation Canton, OH, 848
Avera Health Plans Sioux Falls, SD, 1015
AvMed Health Plan: Corporate Office Miami, FL, 259
AvMed Health Plan: Fort Lauderdale Fort Lauderdale, FL, 260
AvMed Health Plan: Gainesville Gainesville, FL, 261
AvMed Health Plan: Jacksonville Jacksonville, FL, 262
AvMed Health Plan: Orlando Orlando, FL, 263
AvMed Health Plan: Tampa Tampa, FL, 264

Beech Street Corporation: Western Region Lake Forest, CA, 89
Behavioral Healthcare Options, Inc. Las Vegas, NV, 690
Blue Care Network of Michigan: Corporate Headquarters Southfield, MI, 551
Blue Care Network: Ann Arbor Ann Arbor, MI, 553
Blue Care Network: Flint Flint, MI, 554
Blue Care Network: Great Lakes, Muskegon Heights Grand Rapids, MI, 555
Blue Cross & Blue Shield of Alabama Birmingham, AL, 5
Blue Cross & Blue Shield of Arizona Phoenix, AZ, 36
Blue Cross & Blue Shield of Delaware Wilmington, DE, 233
Blue Cross & Blue Shield of Florida: Jacksonville Jacksonville, FL, 266
Blue Cross & Blue Shield of Florida: Pensacola Pensacola, FL, 267
Blue Cross & Blue Shield of Georgia Atlanta, GA, 315

Blue Cross & Blue Shield of Illinois Chicago, IL, 359
Blue Cross & Blue Shield of Kansas Topeka, KS, 436
Blue Cross & Blue Shield of Louisiana Baton Rouge, LA, 472
Blue Cross & Blue Shield of Massachusetts Boston, MA, 527
Blue Cross & Blue Shield of Minnesota Saint Paul, MN, 599
Blue Cross & Blue Shield of Montana Helena, MT, 664
Blue Cross & Blue Shield of New Mexico Albuquerque, NM, 744
Blue Cross & Blue Shield of North Carolina Durham, NC, 816
Blue Cross & Blue Shield of Oklahoma Tulsa, OK, 887
Blue Cross & Blue Shield of Rhode Island Providence, RI, 986
Blue Cross & Blue Shield of South Carolina Columbia, SC, 997
Blue Cross & Blue Shield of Tennessee Chattanooga, TN, 1030
Blue Cross & Blue Shield of Texas Richardson, TX, 1053
Blue Cross & Blue Shield of Texas: Houston Houston, TX, 1054
Blue Cross & Blue Shield of Western New York Buffalo, NY, 762
Blue Cross of Idaho Health Service, Inc. Meridian, ID, 345
Blue Cross of Northeastern Pennsylvania Wilkes Barre, PA, 933
Blue Shield of California San Francisco, CA, 91
BlueChoice St. Louis, MO, 637
Bluegrass Family Health Lexington, KY, 457
BlueLincs HMO Tulsa, OK, 888
BlueShield of Northeastern New York Latham, NY, 763
Boston Medical Center Healthnet Plan Boston, MA, 528
Brand New Day HMO Signal Hill, CA, 92

CalOptima Orange, CA, 96
Capital Blue Cross Harrisburg, PA, 936
Capital Health Plan Tallahassee, FL, 268
Cardinal Health Alliance Muncie, IN, 396
Care 1st Health Plan: Arizona Phoenix, AZ, 37
Care 1st Health Plan: California Monterey Park, CA, 97
Care Choices Farmington Hills, MI, 557
CareFirst Blue Cross & Blue Shield of Virginia Owings Mills, MD, 1127
CareFirst Blue Cross Blue Shield Washington, DC, 244
CarePlus Health Plans, Inc Doral, FL, 269
CareSource Dayton, OH, 849
CareSource: Michigan East Lansing, MI, 558
Carolina Care Plan Columbia, SC, 999
Catalyst Health Solutions Inc Rockville, MD, 503
CDPHP: Capital District Physicians' Health Plan Albany, NY, 765
CenCal Health: The Regional Health Authority Santa Barbara, CA, 99
Centene Corporation Saint Louis, MO, 638
Central California Alliance for Health Scotts Valley, CA, 100
CHA Health Lexington, KY, 458
Charter Oak Health Plan Hartford, CT, 221
Children's Mercy Family Health Partners Kansas City, MO, 639
Chinese Community Health Plan San Francisco, CA, 102
CIGNA HealthCare of Alaska Denver, CO, 21
CIGNA HealthCare of Arizona Phoenix, AZ, 38
CIGNA HealthCare of Arkansas Memphis, TN, 69
CIGNA HealthCare of California Glendale, CA, 105
CIGNA HealthCare of Colorado Denver, CO, 197
CIGNA HealthCare of Connecticut Hartford, CT, 222
CIGNA HealthCare of Delaware Blue Bell, PA, 234
CIGNA HealthCare of Florida Lake Mary, FL, 270
CIGNA HealthCare of Georgia Atlanta, GA, 316
CIGNA HealthCare of Hawaii San Francisco, CA, 334
CIGNA HealthCare of Illinois Chicago, IL, 361
CIGNA HealthCare of Indiana Carmel, IN, 397
CIGNA HealthCare of Iowa Chicago, IL, 421
CIGNA HealthCare of Kansas Overland Park, KS, 437
CIGNA HealthCare of Kentucky Franklin, TN, 459
CIGNA HealthCare of Louisiana Houston, TX, 474
CIGNA HealthCare of Maine South Portland, ME, 489
CIGNA HealthCare of Minnesota Eden Prairie, MN, 600
CIGNA HealthCare of Mississippi Memphis, TN, 625
CIGNA HealthCare of Montana Denver, CO, 665
CIGNA HealthCare of New Hampshire Hooksett, NH, 707
CIGNA HealthCare of New Jersey Jersey City, NJ, 723
CIGNA HealthCare of New Mexico Albuquerque, NM, 745
CIGNA HealthCare of New York Jersey City, NJ, 766
CIGNA HealthCare of North Carolina Charlotte, NC, 818
CIGNA HealthCare of North Dakota Chicago, IL, 835

CIGNA HealthCare of North Texas Plano, TX, 1057
CIGNA HealthCare of Northern California San Francisco, CA, 106
CIGNA HealthCare of Oklahoma Plano, TX, 889
CIGNA HealthCare of Pennsylvania Blue Bell, PA, 938
CIGNA HealthCare of South Carolina Greenville, SC, 1000
CIGNA HealthCare of South Texas Houston, TX, 1058
CIGNA HealthCare of Southern California Irvine, CA, 107
CIGNA HealthCare of St. Louis Clayton, MO, 640
CIGNA HealthCare of Tennessee Chattanooga, TN, 1033
CIGNA HealthCare of the Mid-Atlantic Columbia, MD, 245, 504
CIGNA HealthCare of Utah Salt Lake City, UT, 1103
CIGNA HealthCare of Virginia Richmond, VA, 1129
CIGNA: Corporate Headquarters Philadelphia, PA, 939
Citizens Choice Healthplan Cerritos, CA, 108
Colorado Access Denver, CO, 199
Colorado Choice Health Plans Alamosa, CO, 200
Colorado Health Partnerships Colorado Springs, CO, 201
Community First Health Plans San Antonio, TX, 1059
Community Health Group Chula Vista, CA, 110
Community Health Improvement Solutions Saint Joseph, MO, 641
Community Health Plan of Los Angeles County Monterey Park, CA, 111
CommunityCare Managed Healthcare Plans of Oklahoma Tulsa, OK, 890
Concentra: Corporate Office Addison, TX, 1060
ConnectiCare Farmington, CT, 223
ConnectiCare of Massachusetts Farmington, CT, 530
ConnectiCare of New York Farmington, NY, 768
Contra Costa Health Plan Martinez, CA, 113
Coventry Health Care of Delaware Wilmington, DE, 235
Coventry Health Care of Florida Sunrise, FL, 274
Coventry Health Care of GA Atlanta, GA, 319
Coventry Health Care of Iowa Urbandale, IA, 422
Coventry Health Care of Kansas Kansas City, KS, 439
Coventry Health Care of Louisiana Metairie, LA, 475
Coventry Health Care of Nebraska Omaha, NE, 679
Coventry Health Care of West Virginia Charleston, WV, 1174
Coventry Health Care Virginia Richmond, VA, 1130
Coventry Health Care: Corporate Headquarters Bethesda, MD, 506
Coventry Medicare London, KY, 460
Cox Healthplans Springfield, MO, 642

DakotaCare Sioux Falls, SD, 1017
DC Chartered Health Plan Washington, DC, 246
Denver Health Medical Plan Inc Denver, CO, 203

Educators Mutual Murray, UT, 1105
eHealthInsurance Services Inc. Gold River,, CA, 9, 22, 42, 72, 121, 204, 237, 248, 277, 321, 335, 348, 367, 400, 424, 441, 462, 478, 490, 510, 532, 566, 602, 627, 645, 667, 681, 693, 709, 725, 747, 772, 822, 837, 853, 893, 906, 943, 990, 1002, 1019
eHealthInsurance Services Inc. Corporate Office Mountainview,, CA, 122
Empire Blue Cross & Blue Shield New York, NY, 774
Excellus Blue Cross Blue Shield: Central New York Syracuse, NY, 775
Excellus Blue Cross Blue Shield: Rochester Region Rochester, NY, 776
Excellus Blue Cross Blue Shield: Utica Region Utica, NY, 777

Fallon Community Health Plan Worcester, MA, 533
First Commonwealth Chicago, IL, 368
First Priority Health Wilkes Barre, PA, 946
FirstCarolinaCare Pinehurst, NC, 823
Florida Health Care Plan Holly Hill, FL, 279

Gateway Health Plan Pittsburgh, PA, 947
Geisinger Health Plan Danville, PA, 948
GHP Coventry Health Plan St. Louis, MO, 648
Grand Valley Health Plan Grand Rapids, MI, 568
Graphic Arts Benefit Corporation Greenbelt, MD, 511
Great Lakes Health Plan Southfield, MI, 569
Great-West Healthcare Alabama Atlanta, GA, 10
Great-West Healthcare Alaska Denver, CO, 23
Great-West Healthcare Arizona Scottsdale, AZ, 45
Great-West Healthcare California Irvine, CA, 127
Great-West Healthcare Colorado Greenwood Village, CO, 205
Great-West Healthcare Connecticut Hartford, CT, 225

Great-West Healthcare Delaware Bluebell, PA, 238
Great-West Healthcare Florida Tampa, FL, 281
Great-West Healthcare Georgia Atlanta, GA, 322
Great-West Healthcare Hawaii Oakland, CA, 336
Great-West Healthcare Illinois Rosemont, IL, 370
Great-West Healthcare Indiana Indianapolis, IN, 403, 404
Great-West Healthcare Iowa Chicago, IL, 425
Great-West Healthcare Kansas Overland Park, KS, 442
Great-West Healthcare Los Angeles Glendale, CA, 128
Great-West Healthcare Maine South Portland, ME, 491
Great-West Healthcare Michigan Southfield, MI, 570
Great-West Healthcare Minnesota Eden Prairie, MN, 604
Great-West Healthcare Missouri St. Louis, MO, 649
Great-West Healthcare Montana Bellevue, WA, 668
Great-West Healthcare New Mexico Scottsdale, AZ, 748
Great-West Healthcare New York White Plains, NY, 780
Great-West Healthcare North Carolina Charlotte, NC, 824
Great-West Healthcare North Dakota Chicago, IL, 838
Great-West Healthcare Northern California Walnut Creek, CA, 129
Great-West Healthcare of Idaho Denver, CO, 349
Great-West Healthcare of Maryland Bethesda, MD, 512
Great-West Healthcare of Massachusetts Waltham, MA, 535
Great-West Healthcare of Nevada Henderson, NV, 694
Great-West Healthcare of New Jersey Piscataway, NJ, 728
Great-West Healthcare of Washington Belleview, WA, 1156
Great-West Healthcare Oklahoma Dallas, TX, 894
Great-West Healthcare Oregon Portland, OR, 908
Great-West Healthcare Pennsylvania Piscataway, NJ, 949
Great-West Healthcare South Carolina Greenville, NC, 1003
Great-West Healthcare South Dakota Chicago, IL, 1021
Great-West Healthcare Texas Dallas, TX, 1067
Great-West Healthcare West Virginia Pittsburgh, OH, 1177
Great-West Healthcare Wisconsin Wauwatosa, WI, 1196
Great-West PPO Greenwood Village, CO, 206
Great-West/One Health Plan Greenwood Village, CO, 207
Group Health Cooperative of Eau Claire Altoona, WI, 1197
Group Health Cooperative of South Central Wisconsin Madison, WI, 1198
Group Health Incorporated (GHI) New York, NY, 781
Guardian Life Insurance Company New York, NY, 782
Gundersen Lutheran Health Plan Onalaska, WI, 1199

Harvard University Group Health Plan Cambridge, MA, 537
Health Alliance Medical Plans Urbana, IL, 371
Health Alliance Plan Detroit, MI, 572
Health Care Service Corporation Chicago, IL, 373
Health Choice Arizona Phoenix, AZ, 46
Health First Health Plans Rockledge, FL, 282
Health Maintenance Plan Cincinnati, OH, 856
Health Net Health Plan of Oregon Tigard, OR, 909
Health Net of Arizona Tempe, AZ, 47
Health Net of the Northeast Shelton, CT, 226
Health Net: Corporate Headquarters Woodland Hills, CA, 132
Health New England Springfield, MA, 538
Health Plan of Michigan Detroit, MI, 573
Health Plan of Nevada Las Vegas, NV, 695
Health Plan of New York New York, NY, 783
Health Plan of New York: Connecticut New York, NY, 227
Health Plan of New York: Massachusetts New York, NY, 539
Health Plan of San Joaquin French Camp, CA, 133
Health Plan of San Mateo South San Francisco, CA, 134
Health Plus of Louisiana Shreveport, LA, 479
Health Tradition Onalaska, WI, 1200
Healthcare USA of Missouri Saint Louis, MO, 650
HealthLink HMO St Louis, MO, 651
HealthNow New York Buffalo, NY, 784
HealthPartners Bloomington, MN, 606
HealthPlus of Michigan: Flint Flint, MI, 574
HealthPlus of Michigan: Saginaw Saginaw, MI, 575
HealthPlus of Michigan: Troy Troy, MI, 576
Healthy & Well Kids in Iowa Des Moines, IA, 426
Healthy Indiana Plan Indianapolis, IN, 406
Heart of America Health Plan Rugby, ND, 839
Highmark Blue Cross & Blue Shield Pittsburgh, PA, 953

HMO Blue Texas Richarson, TX, 1072
HMO Colorado Denver, CO, 208
HMO Health Ohio Cleveland, OH, 858
Horizon Blue Cross & Blue Shield of New Jersey Newark, NJ, 730
Horizon Healthcare of New Jersey Newark, NJ, 731
Humana Health Insurance of Alabama Huntsville, AL, 13
Humana Health Insurance of Alaska Vancouver, WA, 24
Humana Health Insurance of Arizona Phoenix, AZ, 48
Humana Health Insurance of Connecticut Mahwah, NJ, 228
Humana Health Insurance of Corpus Christi Corpus Christi, TX, 1074
Humana Health Insurance of D.C. Mahwah, NJ, 249
Humana Health Insurance of Delaware Mahwah, NJ, 239
Humana Health Insurance of Georgia Atlanta, GA, 323
Humana Health Insurance of Hawaii Honolulu, HI, 339
Humana Health Insurance of Idaho Meridian, ID, 350
Humana Health Insurance of Illinois Chicago, IL, 377
Humana Health Insurance of Indiana Indianapolis, IN, 407
Humana Health Insurance of Iowa Davenport, IA, 427
Humana Health Insurance of Jacksonville Jacksonville, FL, 286
Humana Health Insurance of Kansas Overland Park, MO, 444
Humana Health Insurance of Kentucky Louisville, KY, 463
Humana Health Insurance of Little Rock Little Rock, AR, 74
Humana Health Insurance of Louisiana Metairie, LA, 480
Humana Health Insurance of Maryland Mahwah, NJ, 513
Humana Health Insurance of Massachusetts Mahwah, NJ, 541
Humana Health Insurance of Michigan Grand Rapids, MI, 578
Humana Health Insurance of Minnesota Plymouth, MN, 608
Humana Health Insurance of Mississippi Ridgeland, MS, 629
Humana Health Insurance of Missouri Springfield, MO, 652
Humana Health Insurance of Montana Billings, MT, 670
Humana Health Insurance of Nebraska Omaha, NE, 682
Humana Health Insurance of Nevada Las Vegas, NV, 697
Humana Health Insurance of New Hampshire Portsmouth, NH, 711
Humana Health Insurance of New Jersey Mahwah, NJ, 733
Humana Health Insurance of New Mexico Albuquerque, NM, 749
Humana Health Insurance of New York Albany, NY, 786
Humana Health Insurance of North Carolina Cary, NC, 825
Humana Health Insurance of North Dakota Omaha, NE, 840
Humana Health Insurance of Northern California Walnut Creek, CA, 135
Humana Health Insurance of Ohio Cincinnati, OH, 859
Humana Health Insurance of Oklahoma Tulsa, OK, 895
Humana Health Insurance of Oregon Vancouver, WA, 910
Humana Health Insurance of Orlando Alamonte Springs, FL, 287
Humana Health Insurance of Pennsylvania Mechanicsburg, PA, 955
Humana Health Insurance of Puerto Rico San Juan, PR, 979
Humana Health Insurance of Rhode Island Mahwah, NJ, 991
Humana Health Insurance of San Antonio San Antonio, TX, 1075
Humana Health Insurance of South Carolina Columbia, SC, 1004
Humana Health Insurance of South Dakota Omaha, NE, 1022
Humana Health Insurance of Southern California Carlsbad, CA, 136
Humana Health Insurance of Tampa - Pinellas Tampa, FL, 288
Humana Health Insurance of Tennessee Memphis, TN, 1040
Humana Health Insurance of Utah Sandy, UT, 1107
Humana Health Insurance of Virginia Glen Allen, VA, 1135
Humana Health Insurance of Washington Vancouver, WA, 1158
Humana Health Insurance of West Virginia Charleston, WV, 1178
Humana Health Insurance of Wisconsin Waukesha, WI, 1202
Humana Health Insurance of Wyoming Billings, MT, 1220
Humana Health Insurnace of Colorado Colorado Springs, CO, 209

IHC: Intermountain Healthcare Health Plan Salt Lake City, UT, 351
Independence Blue Cross Philadelphia, PA, 956
Independent Health Buffalo, NY, 787
Inland Empire Health Plan San Bernardino, CA, 137

JMH Health Plan Miami, FL, 289
John Deere Health Kingsport, TN, 1042

Kaiser Permanente Health Plan Northwest Portland, OR, 911
Kaiser Permanente Health Plan of Colorado Denver, CO, 210
Kaiser Permanente Health Plan of Hawaii Honolulu, HI, 340
Kaiser Permanente Health Plan of Northern California Oakland, CA, 140
Kaiser Permanente Health Plan of Southern California Pasadena, CA, 141

Kaiser Permanente Health Plan of the Mid-Atlantic States Rockville, MD, 514
Kaiser Permanente Health Plan Ohio Cleveland, OH, 861
Kaiser Permanente Health Plan: Corporate Office Oakland, CA, 142
Kaiser Permanente of Georgia Atlanta, GA, 324
Kern Family Health Care Bakersfield, CA, 144
Keystone Health Plan Central Harrisburg, PA, 958
Keystone Health Plan East Philadelphia, PA, 959

L.A. Care Health Plan Los Angeles, CA, 145
Lakeside Community Healthcare Network Glendale, CA, 146
Landmark Healthplan of California Sacramento, CA, 147
Legacy Health Plan San Angelo, TX, 1078
Leon Medical Centers Health Plan Miami, FL, 290
Los Angeles County Public Healthcare Los Angeles, CA, 149
Lovelace Health Plan Albuquerque, NM, 750
Lovelace Medicare Health Plan Albuquerque, NM, 751

Managed Health Services Wauwatosa, WI, 1203
Managed Healthcare Systems of New Jersey Newark, NJ, 734
Maricopa Integrated Health System/Maricopa Health Plan Phoenix, AZ, 50
Medica: North Dakota Fargo, ND, 841
Medica: South Dakota Sioux Falls, SD, 1023
Medical Associates Health Plan Dubuque, IA, 378
Medical Associates Health Plan: East Dubuque, IA, 1204
Medical Associates Health Plan: West Dubuque, IA, 428
Medical Mutual of Ohio Cleveland, OH, 862
Mercy Health Network Des Moines, IA, 429
Mercy Health Plans: Arkansas Little Rock, AR, 75
Mercy Health Plans: Corporate Office Chesterfield, MO, 655
Mercy Health Plans: Kansas Chesterfield, MO, 445
Mercy Health Plans: Oklahoma Chesterfield, MO, 896
Mercy Health Plans: Texas Laredo, TX, 1080
MercyCare Health Plans Janesville, WI, 1205
MetroPlus Health Plan New York, NY, 793
Metropolitan Health Plan Minneapolis, MN, 612
Mid America Health Kansas City, MO, 657
Mid Atlantic Medical Services: Corporate Office Rockville, MD, 516
Mid Atlantic Medical Services: DC Rockville, MD, 250
Mid Atlantic Medical Services: Delaware Baltimore, MD, 240
Mid Atlantic Medical Services: North Carolina Charlotte, NC, 827
Mid Atlantic Medical Services: Pennsylvania Baltimore, MD, 960
Mid Atlantic Medical Services: Virginia Richmond, VA, 1137
Mid Atlantic Medical Services: West Virginia Rockville, MD, 1179
Molina Healthcare: Corporate Office Long Beach, CA, 155
Molina Healthcare: Florida Miami, FL, 292
Molina Healthcare: Michigan Troy, MI, 581
Molina Healthcare: Missouri St. Louis, MO, 658
Molina Healthcare: New Mexico Albuquerque, NM, 752
Molina Healthcare: Ohio Columbus, OH, 865
Molina Healthcare: Texas San Antonio, TX, 1082
Molina Healthcare: Utah Midvale, UT, 1109
Molina Healthcare: Washington Bothell, WA, 1161
Mountain Health Trust/Physician Assured Access System Charleston, WV, 1180
Mutual of Omaha Health Plans Omaha, NE, 685
MVP Health Care: Buffalo Region Buffalo, NY, 796
MVP Health Care: Central New York Yorkville, NY, 797
MVP Health Care: Corporate Office Schenectady, NY, 798
MVP Health Care: Mid-State Region Syracuse, NY, 799
MVP Health Care: New Hampshire Manchester, NH, 712
MVP Health Care: Vermont Williston, VT, 1122
MVP Health Care: Western New York Schenectady, NY, 800

Nationwide Better Health Columbus, OH, 867
Neighborhood Health Partnership Miami, FL, 293
Neighborhood Health Plan Boston, MA, 542
Neighborhood Health Plan of Rhode Island Providence, RI, 992
Network Health Plan of Wisconsin Menasha, WI, 1206
Nevada Preferred Healthcare Providers Reno, NV, 700
NevadaCare Las Vegas, NV, 701
New West Health Services Billings, MT, 672

OmniCare: A Coventry Health Care Plan Detroit, MI, 582
On Lok Lifeways San Francisco, CA, 157
Optima Health Plan Virginia Beach, VA, 1139
Optimum Choice Rockville, MD, 519
OSF Healthcare Peoria, IL, 379
Oxford Health Plans: Corporate Headquarters Trumbull, CT, 229
Oxford Health Plans: New Jersey Iselin, NJ, 736
Oxford Health Plans: New York New York, NY, 805

PacifiCare Health Systems Cypress, CA, 164
PacifiCare of Arizona Phoeniz, AZ, 54
PacifiCare of California Cypress, CA, 165
PacifiCare of Colorado Greenwood Village, CO, 211
PacifiCare of Nevada Las Vegas, NV, 702
PacifiCare of Oklahoma Tulsa, OK, 897
PacifiCare of Oregon Lake Oswego, OR, 916
PacifiCare of Texas Dallas, TX, 1084
PacifiCare of Washington Mercer Island, WA, 1163
PacificSource Health Plans: Corporate Headquarters Springfield, OR, 917
PacificSource Health Plans: Idaho Boise, ID, 353
Paramount Care of Michigan Dundee, MI, 583
Paramount Health Care Maumee, OH, 872
Parkland Community Health Plan Dallas, TX, 1085
Passport Health Plan Louisville, KY, 466
Peninsula Health Care Newport News, VA, 1140
PersonalCare Champaign, IL, 381
Phoenix Health Plan Phoenix, AZ, 55
Physicians Health Plan of Mid-Michigan Lansing, MI, 584
Physicians Health Plan of Northern Indiana Fort Wayne, IN, 411
Physicians Plus Insurance Corporation Madison, WI, 1207
Pima Health System Tucson, AZ, 56
Preferred Medical Plan Coral Gables, FL, 297
Preferred Plus of Kansas Wichita, KS, 449
PreferredOne Golden Valley, MN, 616
Presbyterian Health Plan Albuquerque, NM, 753
Priority Health Farmington Hills, MI, 585
Priority Health: Corporate Headquarters Grand Rapids, MI, 586
Priority Partners Health Plans Glen Burnie, MD, 520
Providence Health Plans Beaverton, OR, 918

QualCare Piscataway, NJ, 737
QualChoice/QCA Health Plan Little Rock, AR, 76
Quality Plan Administrators Washington, DC, 251

Rocky Mountain Health Plans Grand Junction, CO, 213

Saint Mary's Health Plans Reno, NV, 703
San Francisco Health Plan San Francisco, CA, 173
Sanford Health Plan Sioux Falls, SD, 430
Santa Clara Family Health Plan Campbell, CA, 174
SCAN Health Plan Long Beach, CA, 175
Scott & White Health Plan Temple, TX, 1087
Select Health of South Carolina North Charleston, SC, 1008
SelectHealth Murray, UT, 1113
Seton Health Plan Austin, TX, 1089
Sharp Health Plan San Diego, CA, 176
Southeastern Indiana Health Organization Columbus, IN, 413
SummaCare Health Plan Akron, OH, 875

Tenet Choices Kenner, LA, 483
The Health Plan of the Upper Ohio Valley Massillon, OH, 880
Total Health Care Detroit, MI, 589
Total Health Choice Miami, FL, 300
Trigon Health Care Richmond, VA, 1143
Tufts Health Plan Watertown, MA, 544
Tufts Health Plan: Rhode Island Providence, RI, 993

UCare Minnesota Minneapolis, MN, 619
Unicare: Illinois Chicago, IL, 385
Unicare: Kansas Topeka, KS, 452
Unicare: Massachusetts Andover, MA, 545
Unicare: Michigan Dearborn, MI, 590
Unicare: Texas Plano, TX, 1093

Unicare: West Virginia Charleston, WV, 1183
Unison Health Plan of Delaware Greenville, DE, 241
Unison Health Plan of Ohio Columbus, OH, 881
Unison Health Plan of South Carolina Columbia, SC, 1010
Unison Health Plan of the Capital Area Washington, DC, 252
UnitedHealthcare Nevada Las Vegas, NV, 704
UnitedHealthCare of Alabama Birmingham, AL, 16
UnitedHealthCare of Alaska Tigard, OR, 28
UnitedHealthCare of Arizona Phoenix, AZ, 61
UnitedHealthCare of Arkansas Little Rock, AR, 78
UnitedHealthCare of Colorado Centennial, CO, 215
UnitedHealthCare of Connecticut Hartford, CT, 230
UnitedHealthCare of Florida Jacksonville, FL, 302
UnitedHealthCare of Georgia Norcross, GA, 330
UnitedHealthCare of Hawaii Cypress, CA, 341
UnitedHealthCare of Idaho Cypress, CA, 356
UnitedHealthCare of Illinois Chicago, IL, 386
UnitedHealthCare of Indiana Indianapolis, IN, 414
UnitedHealthCare of Iowa Des Moines, IA, 431
UnitedHealthCare of Kansas Overland Park, KS, 453
UnitedHealthCare of Kentucky Lexington, KY, 469
UnitedHealthCare of Louisiana Metairie, LA, 484
UnitedHealthCare of Maine Edina, MN, 495
UnitedHealthCare of Massachusetts Warwick, RI, 546
UnitedHealthCare of Michigan Southfield, MI, 592
UnitedHealthCare of Minnesota Edina, MN, 620, 621
UnitedHealthCare of Mississippi Hattiesburg, MS, 630
UnitedHealthCare of Missouri Maryland Heights, MO, 661
UnitedHealthCare of Montana Centennial, CO, 674
UnitedHealthCare of Nebraska Omaha, NE, 686
UnitedHealthCare of New Hampshire Westborough, MA, 714
UnitedHealthCare of New Jersey Iselin, NJ, 739
UnitedHealthCare of New Mexico Albuquerque, NM, 756
UnitedHealthcare of New York East Syracuse, NY, 810
UnitedHealthCare of North Carolina Cary, NC, 832
UnitedHealthCare of North Dakota Edina, MN, 843
UnitedHealthCare of Northern California Cypress, CA, 182
UnitedHealthCare of Ohio: Columbus Westerville, OH, 882
UnitedHealthCare of Ohio: Dayton & Cincinnati West Chester, OH, 883
UnitedHealthCare of Oklahoma Plano, TX, 898
UnitedHealthCare of Oregon Lake Oswego, OR, 923
UnitedHealthCare of Pennsylvania Monroeville, PA, 972
UnitedHealthCare of Puerto Rico Edina, MN, 984
UnitedHealthCare of Rhode Island Warwick, RI, 994
UnitedHealthCare of South Carolina Columbia, SC, 1011
UnitedHealthCare of South Dakota Edina, MN, 1024
UnitedHealthCare of South Florida Sunrise, FL, 303
UnitedHealthCare of Southern California Cypress, CA, 183
UnitedHealthCare of Tennessee Brentwood, TN, 1044
UnitedHealthCare of Texas Austin, TX, 1095
UnitedHealthCare of the District of Columbia Bethesda, MD, 253
UnitedHealthCare of the Mid-Atlantic Elkridge, MD, 242, 523
UnitedHealthCare of Utah Salt Lake City, UT, 1115
UnitedHealthCare of Vermont Westborough, MA, 1123
UnitedHealthCare of Virginia Richmond, VA, 1145
UnitedHealthCare of Washington Mercer Island, WA, 1170
UnitedHealthCare of West Virginia Edina, MN, 1184
UnitedHealthCare of Wisconsin: Central Edina, MN, 622
UnitedHealthCare of Wisconsin: Central Edina, WI, 1211
UnitedHealthCare of Wyoming Centennial, CO, 1221
Univera Healthcare Buffalo, NY, 811
University Family Care Health Plan Tucson, AZ, 62
University Health Plans Salt Lake City, UT, 1116
Upper Peninsula Health Plan Marquette, MI, 593
UTMB HealthCare Systems Galveston, TX, 1097

Valley Baptist Health Plan Harlingen, TX, 1098
Vantage Health Plan Monroe, LA, 485
Ventura County Health Care Plan Ventura, CA, 184
Virginia Premier Health Plan Richmond, VA, 1147
VIVA Health Birmingham, AL, 17
Vytra Health Plans Melville, NY, 813

Welborn Health Plans Evansville, IN, 416
WellChoice Iselin, NJ, 741
Wellmark Health Plan of Iowa Des Moines, IA, 432
WellPath: A Coventry Health Care Plan Morrisville, NC, 833
WellPoint: Corporate Office Indianapolis, IN, 417
Western Health Advantage Sacramento, CA, 189

Medicare

American Pioneer Life Insurance Co Lake Mary, FL, 255
AmeriHealth Medicare Plan Philadelphia, PA, 930
Arcadian Community Care Shreveport, LA, 471
Arkansas Community Care Little Rock, AR, 67
Arta Medicare Health Plan Irvine, CA, 84
Atrio Health Plans Roseburg, OR, 901
AvMed Medicare Preferred Miami, FL, 265

Banner MediSun Medicare Plan Sun City, AZ, 35
Blue Care Network of Michigan: Medicare Southfield, MI, 552
Blue Cross and Blue Shield Association Chicago, IL, 360
Bravo Health: Corporate Headquarters Baltimore, MD, 502
Bravo Health: Pennsylvania Philadelphia, PA, 935
Bravo Health: Texas San Antonio, TX, 1055

CareMore Health Plan Cerritos, CA, 98
CareOregon Health Plan Portland, OR, 902
CareSource Mid Rogue Health Plan Grants Pass, OR, 903
Carilion Health Plans Roanoke, VA, 1128
CDPHP Medicare Plan Albany, NY, 764
Central Health Medicare Plan Diamond Bar, CA, 101
Citrus Health Care Tampa, FL, 271
CommunityCare Medicare Plan Tulsa, OK, 891

Desert Canyon Community Care Prescott, AZ, 41

Easy Choice Health Plan Long Beach, CA, 120
Elderplan Brooklyn, NY, 773
Essence Healthcare Maryland Heights, MO, 646
Evercare Health Plans Anacortes, MN, 603

Fallon Community Medicare Plan Worcester, MA, 534
FamilyCare Health Medicare Plan Portland, OR, 907
First Medical Health Plan of Florida Miami, FL, 278
Freedom Health, Inc Tampa, FL, 280

GEMCare Health Plan Bakersfield, CA, 125
GHI Medicare Plan New York, NY, 779

Health Alliance Medicare Urbana, IL, 372
Health Alliance Medicare Detroit, MI, 571
Health First Medicare Plans Rockledge, FL, 283
Health Net Medicare Plan Woodland Hills, CA, 131
Health Partners Medicare Plan Bloomington, MN, 605
Health Partners Medicare Plan Philadelphia, PA, 950
HealthFirst New Jersey Medicare Plan Newark, NJ, 729
HealthPlus Senior Medicare Plan Saginaw, MI, 577
HealthSpring of Alabama Birmingham, AL, 12
HealthSpring of Illinois Rosemont, IL, 375
HealthSpring of Texas Houston, TX, 1071
HealthSpring Prescription Drug Plan Nashville, TN, 1038
HealthSpring: Corporate Offices Franklin, TN, 1039
HealthSun Health Plans Miami, FL, 285
Humana Benefit Plan of Illinois Peoria, IL, 376
Humana Medicare Plan Louisville, KY, 464

Independent Health Medicare Plan Buffalo, NY, 788
InStil Health Columbia, SC, 1005

Kaiser Permanente Medicare Plan Oakland, CA, 143
KelseyCare Advantage Houston, TX, 1077

Liberty Health Advantage Medicare Plan Melville, NY, 790

Magellan Medicaid Administration Glen Allen, VA, 1136

MD Care Healthplan Signal Hill, CA, 152
Medica Health - Medicare Plan Minnetonka, MN, 609
Medica HealthCare Plans, Inc Coral Gables, FL, 291
Medical Mutual of Ohio Medicare Plan Cleveland, OH, 863
Mercy Care Plan/Mercy Care Advantage Phoenix, AZ, 51
Mercy Health Medicare Plan Chesterfield, MO, 654
MHP North Star Plans Minneapolis, MN, 613
Mount Carmel Health Plan Inc (MediGold) Columbus, OH, 866
MVP Health Care Medicare Plan Schenectady, NY, 795

New West Medicare Plan Helena, MT, 673
Northeast Community Care South Portland, ME, 494, 713
Northeast Community Care North Syracuse, NY, 803

Optimum HealthCare, Inc Tampa, FL, 294
Ozark Health Plan Springfield, MO, 659

Paramount Elite Medicare Plan Maumee, OH, 871
Partnership HealthPlan of California Fairfield, CA, 166
Peoples Health Metairie, LA, 482
PMC Medicare Choice San Juan, PR, 982
Presbyterian Medicare Plans Albuquerque, NM, 754
Prime Time Health Medicare Plan Canton, OH, 873
PriorityHealth Medicare Plans Grand Rapids, MI, 587
Puget Sound Health Partners Federal Way, WA, 1165

Quality Health Plans Tampa, FL, 298
Quality Health Plans of New York Ronkonkoma, NY, 807

Secure Horizons Hot Springs, AR, 77
Southeast Community Care Macon, GA, 328
Southeast Community Care Raleigh, NC, 830
Southeast Community Care North Charleston, SC, 1009
Southeast Community Care Norfolk, VA, 1142
Spokane Community Care Spokane, WA, 1167
Sterling Health Plans Bellingham, WA, 1168
SummaCare Medicare Advantage Plan Akron, OH, 876

TexanPlus Medicare Advantage HMO Houston, TX, 1090
Texas Community Care Austin, TX, 1091
Touchstone Health HMO White Plains, NY, 808
Trillium Community Health Plan Eugene, OR, 921
Tufts Health Medicare Plan Watertown, MA, 543

UCare Medicare Plan Minneapolis, MN, 618
Universal American Medicare Plans Rye Brook, NY, 812
Universal Health Care Group St Petersburg, FL, 304
Universal Health Care Group: Mississippi Ridgeland, MS, 631

Vantage Medicare Advantage Monroe, LA, 486

WellCare Health Plans Tampa, FL, 307
Windsor Medicare Extra Brentwood, TN, 1045

Multiple

ABRI Health Plan, Inc. West Allis, WI, 1185
Advance Insurance Company of Kansas Topeka, KS, 433
Altius Health Plans South Jordan, UT, 1102
Americhoice of Pennsylvania Philadelphia, PA, 929
Arizona Foundation for Medical Care Phoenix, AZ, 32
Arkansas Blue Cross and Blue Shield Little Rock, AR, 66
Assurant Employee Benefits: Alabama Birmingham, AL, 2
Assurant Employee Benefits: California Sacramento, CA, 85
Assurant Employee Benefits: Colorado Greenwood Village, CO, 193
Assurant Employee Benefits: Corporate Headquarters Kansas City, MO, 635
Assurant Employee Benefits: Florida Tampa, FL, 257
Assurant Employee Benefits: Georgia Atlanta, GA, 312
Assurant Employee Benefits: Illinois Oakbrook Terrace, IL, 358
Assurant Employee Benefits: Kansas Shawnee Mission, KS, 435
Assurant Employee Benefits: Massachusetts Marlborough, MA, 525
Assurant Employee Benefits: Michigan Troy, MI, 550
Assurant Employee Benefits: Minnesota Minneapolis, MN, 597

Assurant Employee Benefits: New Jersey Parsippany, NJ, 719
Assurant Employee Benefits: North Carolina Charlotte, NC, 815
Assurant Employee Benefits: Ohio Cincinnati, OH, 847
Assurant Employee Benefits: Oklahoma Broken Arrow, OK, 886
Assurant Employee Benefits: Oregon Portland, OR, 900
Assurant Employee Benefits: Pennsylvania Pittsburgh, PA, 931
Assurant Employee Benefits: South Carolina Columbia, SC, 996
Assurant Employee Benefits: Tennessee Memphis, TN, 1028
Assurant Employee Benefits: Texas Plano, TX, 1050
Assurant Employee Benefits: Washington Seattle, WA, 1149
Assurant Employee Benefits: Wisconsin Brookfield, WI, 1188
Asuris Northwest Health Spokane, WA, 1150

Beta Health Plan Denver, CO, 195
BlueChoice Health Plan of South Carolina Columbia, SC, 998

Calais Health Baton Rouge, LA, 473
Cariten Healthcare Knoxville, TN, 1031
ChiroSource Inc Concord, CA, 104
Clear One Health Plans Bend, OR, 905
Community Health Plan of Washington Seattle, WA, 1152
CompBenefits Corporation Roswell, GA, 318
CompBenefits: Alabama Birmingham, AL, 7
CompBenefits: Florida Miami, FL, 272
CompBenefits: Illinois Chicago, IL, 363
CompCare: Comprehensive Behavioral Care Tampa, FL, 273
CoreSource: Arizona Tucson, AZ, 39
CoreSource: Arkansas Little Rock, AR, 70
CoreSource: Corporate Headquarters Lake Forest, IL, 364
CoreSource: Kansas (FMH CoreSource) Overland Park, KS, 438
CoreSource: Maryland Baltimore, MD, 505
CoreSource: Michigan (NGS CoreSource) St Clair Shores, MI, 562
CoreSource: North Carolina Charlotte, NC, 819
CoreSource: Ohio Dublin, OH, 851
CoreSource: Pennsylvania Lancaster, PA, 940

Dean Health Plan Madison, WI, 1192
Denta-Chek of Maryland Columbia, MD, 508

Fidelis Care Rego Park, NY, 778
First Care Health Plans Austin, TX, 1065
First Medical Health Plan Guaynabo, PR, 978

GEHA-Government Employees Hospital Association Independence, MO, 647
Golden West Dental & Vision Plan Oxnard, CA, 126
Group Health Cooperative Seattle, WA, 1157

Harvard Pilgrim Health Care Wellesley, MA, 536
Harvard Pilgrim Health Care of New England Bedford, NH, 710
Harvard Pilgrim Health Care: Maine Portland, ME, 492
HealthAmerica Erie, PA, 951
HealthAmerica Pennsylvania Harrisburg, PA, 952
Hometown Health Plan Reno, NV, 696

Inter Valley Health Plan Pomona, CA, 138
Island Group Administration, Inc. East Hampton, NY, 789

Magellan Health Services: Corporate Headquarters Columbia, MD, 515
Martin's Point HealthCare Portland, ME, 493
Medical Card System (MCS) San Juan, PR, 980
MHNet Behavioral Health Addison, TX, 1081
Mid Atlantic Psychiatric Services (MAMSI) Rockville, MD, 517
MMM Healthcare San Juan, PR, 981

National Medical Health Card Port Washington, NY, 802

ODS Alaska Anchorage, AK, 26
ODS Health Plan Portland, OR, 915
Ohio State University Health Plan Inc. Columbus, OH, 869
OptumHealth Care Solutions: Physical Health Golden Valley, MN, 614

Pacific Foundation for Medical Care Santa Rosa, CA, 160
PacifiCare Dental and Vision Administrators Santa Ana, CA, 163
Physical Therapy Provider Network Calabasas, CA, 167

Physicians United Plan Winter Park, FL, 295
Preferred Care Partners Miami, FL, 296
Preferred Mental Health Management Wichita, KS, 448
Primary Health Plan Boise, ID, 354

Regence BlueShield of Idaho Lewiston, ID, 355

Samaritan Health Plan Corvallis, OR, 920
Security Health Plan of Wisconsin Marshfield, WI, 1209
Security Life Insurance Company of America Minnetonka, MN, 617
Spectera Columbia, MD, 521

Triple-S Salud Blue Cross Blue Shield of Puerto Rico Guaynabo, PR, 983

Unison Health Plan of Pennsylvania Pittsburgh, PA, 970
Unity Health Insurance Sauk City, WI, 1212
UPMC Health Plan Pittsburgh, PA, 973

Valley Preferred Allentown, PA, 975
Vista Healthplan of South Florida, Inc Sunrise, FL, 305

WellPoint NextRx Fort Worth, TX, 1100
WINhealth Partners Cheyenne, WY, 1222

PPO

Aetna Health of Alaska Hartford, CT, 18
Aetna Health of Arkansas Hartford, CT, 64
Aetna Health of Hawaii Hartford, CT, 332
Aetna Health of Idaho Hartford, CT, 344
Aetna Health of Iowa Hartford, CT, 418
Aetna Health of Kansas Hartford, CT, 434
Aetna Health of Kentucky Hartford, CT, 455
Aetna Health of Louisiana Hartford, CT, 470
Aetna Health of Michigan Hartford, CT, 548
Aetna Health of Minnesota Hartford, CT, 595
Aetna Health of Mississippi Hartford, CT, 624
Aetna Health of Montana Hartford, CT, 662
Aetna Health of Nebraska Hartford, CT, 675
Aetna Health of New Hampshire Hartford, CT, 705
Aetna Health of New Mexico Hartford, CT, 742
Aetna Health of New York Hartford, CT, 757
Aetna Health of North Dakota Hartford, CT, 834
Aetna Health of Oregon Hartford, CT, 899
Aetna Health of Rhode Island Hartford, CT, 985
Aetna Health of South Dakota Hartford, CT, 1013
Aetna Health of Utah Hartford, CT, 1101
Aetna Health of Vermont Hartford, CT, 1117
Aetna Health of Washington Hartford, CT, 1148
Aetna Health of West Virginia Hartford, CT, 1172
Aetna Health of Wisconsin Hartford, CT, 1186
Aetna Health of Wyoming Hartford, CT, 1215
Alere Health Altanta, GA, 309
Alliance PPO, LLC Rockville, MD, 497
Alliance Regional Health Network Amarillo, TX, 1047
Alliant Health Plans Calhoun, GA, 310
American Community Mutual Insurance Company Livonia, MI, 549
American Health Care Alliance Kansas City, MO, 633
American Health Care Group Pittsburgh, PA, 927
American Health Network of Indiana Indianapolis, IN, 390
American Postal Workers Union (APWU) Health Plan Glen Burnie, MD, 498
American PPO Irving, TX, 1048
American WholeHealth Network Sterling, PA, 928
Americas PPO Bloomington, MN, 1014
AmeriHealth HMO Wilmington, DE, 232
AmeriHealth HMO Mount Laurel, NJ, 718
Anthem Blue Cross & Blue Shield Connecticut North Haven, CT, 220
Anthem Blue Cross & Blue Shield of Colorado Denver, CO, 192
Anthem Blue Cross & Blue Shield of Indiana Indianapolis, IN, 392
Anthem Blue Cross & Blue Shield of Maine Augusta, ME, 488
Anthem Blue Cross & Blue Shield of Missouri Saint Louis, MO, 634
Anthem Blue Cross & Blue Shield of Nevada Las Vegas, NV, 689

Anthem Blue Cross & Blue Shield of Ohio Mason, OH, 846
Anthem Blue Cross & Blue Shield of Wisconsin Waukesha, WI, 1187
Araz Group Bloomington, MN, 596
Arcadian Health Plans Oakland, CA, 83
Arkansas Managed Care Organization Little Rock, AR, 68
Atlanticare Health Plans Hammonton, NJ, 720
Aultcare Corporation Canton, OH, 848
Avalon Healthcare Tampa, FL, 258
Avesis: Corporate Headquarters Phoenix, AZ, 34
Avesis: Georgia Snellville, GA, 314
Avesis: Indiana Lawrenceburg, IN, 395
Avesis: Iowa Des Moines, IA, 420
Avesis: Maryland Owings Mills, MD, 500
Avesis: Massachusetts North Andover, MA, 526
Avesis: Minnesota Sartell, MN, 598
Avesis: Texas San Antonio, TX, 1051

Basic Chiropractic Health Plan Stockton, CA, 86
Beech Street Corporation: Alabama Alpharetta, GA, 3
Beech Street Corporation: Corporate Office Lake Forest, CA, 87
Beech Street Corporation: Northeast Region Lake Forest, CA, 88
Beech Street: Alaska Lake Forest, CA, 19
Behavioral Health Systems Birmingham, AL, 4
Behavioral Healthcare Options, Inc. Las Vegas, NV, 690
Berkshire Health Partners Wyomissing, PA, 932
BEST Life and Health Insurance Co. Irvine, CA, 90
Blue Cross & Blue Shield of Arizona Phoenix, AZ, 36
Blue Cross & Blue Shield of Delaware Wilmington, DE, 233
Blue Cross & Blue Shield of Florida: Jacksonville Jacksonville, FL, 266
Blue Cross & Blue Shield of Florida: Pensacola Pensacola, FL, 267
Blue Cross & Blue Shield of Illinois Chicago, IL, 359
Blue Cross & Blue Shield of Kansas City Kansas City, MO, 636
Blue Cross & Blue Shield of Louisiana Baton Rouge, LA, 472
Blue Cross & Blue Shield of Nebraska Omaha, NE, 677
Blue Cross & Blue Shield of New Mexico Albuquerque, NM, 744
Blue Cross & Blue Shield of North Carolina Durham, NC, 816
Blue Cross & Blue Shield of Oklahoma Tulsa, OK, 887
Blue Cross & Blue Shield of South Carolina Columbia, SC, 997
Blue Cross & Blue Shield of Tennessee Chattanooga, TN, 1030
Blue Cross & Blue Shield of Texas Richardson, TX, 1053
Blue Cross & Blue Shield of Texas: Houston Houston, TX, 1054
Blue Cross & Blue Shield of Vermont Berlin, VT, 1118
Blue Cross & Blue Shield of Western New York Buffalo, NY, 762
Blue Cross & Blue Shield of Wyoming Cheyenne, WY, 1216
Blue Cross Blue Shield of Michigan Detroit, MI, 556
Blue Cross of Idaho Health Service, Inc. Meridian, ID, 345
Blue Cross of Northeastern Pennsylvania Wilkes Barre, PA, 933
Blue Cross Preferred Care Birmingham, AL, 6
Blue Ridge Health Network Schuylkill Haven, PA, 934
Blue Shield of California San Francisco, CA, 91
Bluegrass Family Health Lexington, KY, 457
BlueShield of Northeastern New York Latham, NY, 763
Boulder Valley Individual Practice Association Boulder, CO, 196
Brazos Valley Health Network Waco, TX, 1056

California Foundation for Medical Care Riverside, CA, 95
Capital Blue Cross Harrisburg, PA, 936
Cardinal Health Alliance Muncie, IN, 396
CareFirst Blue Cross & Blue Shield of Virginia Owings Mills, MD, 1127
CareFirst Blue Cross Blue Shield Washington, DC, 244
Cariten Preferred Knoxville, TN, 1032
Catalyst RX Raleigh, NC, 817
CCN: Alaska San Diego, CA, 20
CDPHP: Capital District Physicians' Health Plan Albany, NY, 765
Central Susquehanna Healthcare Providers Lewisburg, PA, 937
ChiroCare of Wisconsin Wauwatosa, WI, 1190
Chiropractic Health Plan of California Concord, CA, 103
CHN PPO Hamilton, NJ, 722
CIGNA HealthCare of Arizona Phoenix, AZ, 38
CIGNA HealthCare of Idaho Seattle, WA, 346
CIGNA HealthCare of Massachusetts Newton, MA, 529
CIGNA HealthCare of Michigan Southfield, MI, 559
CIGNA HealthCare of Nebraska Overland Park, KS, 678

CIGNA HealthCare of Nevada Las Vegas, NV, 691
CIGNA HealthCare of North Texas Plano, TX, 1057
CIGNA HealthCare of Ohio Independence, OH, 850
CIGNA HealthCare of Oklahoma Plano, TX, 889
CIGNA HealthCare of Oregon Portland, OR, 904
CIGNA HealthCare of Puerto Rico San Juan, PR, 977
CIGNA HealthCare of Rhode Island Newton, MA, 987
CIGNA HealthCare of South Dakota Chicago, IL, 1016
CIGNA HealthCare of the Mid-Atlantic Columbia, MD, 245, 504
CIGNA HealthCare of Utah Salt Lake City, UT, 1103
CIGNA HealthCare of Vermont Burlington, VT, 1119
CIGNA HealthCare of Washington Seattle, WA, 1151
CIGNA HealthCare of West Virginia Pittsburgh, PA, 1173
CIGNA HealthCare of Wisconsin Wauwatosa, WI, 1191
CIGNA HealthCare of Wyoming Denver, CO, 1217
CNA Insurance Companies: Colorado Littleton, CO, 198
CNA Insurance Companies: Georgia Duluth, GA, 317
CNA Insurance Companies: Illinois Chicago, IL, 362
Coalition America's National Preferred Provider Network Middletown, NY, 767
Coastal Healthcare Administrators Salinas, CA, 109
Cofinity Southfield, MI, 560
Community First Health Plans San Antonio, TX, 1059
CommunityCare Managed Healthcare Plans of Oklahoma Tulsa, OK, 890
Concentra: Corporate Office Addison, TX, 1060
ConnectCare Midland, MI, 561
ConnectiCare Farmington, CT, 223
ConnectiCare of Massachusetts Farmington, CT, 530
ConnectiCare of New York Farmington, NY, 768
CorVel Corporation Irvine, CA, 114
Coventry Health Care of Delaware Wilmington, DE, 235
Coventry Health Care of Florida Sunrise, FL, 274
Coventry Health Care of GA Atlanta, GA, 319
Coventry Health Care of Iowa Urbandale, IA, 422
Coventry Health Care of Kansas Kansas City, KS, 439
Coventry Health Care of Nebraska Omaha, NE, 679
Coventry Health Care of West Virginia Charleston, WV, 1174
Coventry Health Care Virginia Richmond, VA, 1130
Coventry Health Care: Corporate Headquarters Bethesda, MD, 506
Coventry Medicare London, KY, 460
Cox Healthplans Springfield, MO, 642
Crescent Preferred Provider Organization Asheville, NC, 820

Deaconess Health Plans Evansville, IN, 398
Devon Health Services King of Prussia, PA, 942
Dimension Health PPO Miami Lakes, FL, 276

Educators Mutual Murray, UT, 1105
eHealthInsurance Services Inc. Gold River,, CA, 9, 22, 42, 72, 121, 204, 237, 248, 277, 321, 335, 348, 367, 400, 424, 441, 462, 478, 490, 510, 532, 566, 602, 627, 645, 667, 681, 693, 709, 725, 747, 772, 822, 837, 853, 893, 906, 943, 990, 1002, 1019
eHealthInsurance Services Inc. Corporate Office Mountainview,, CA, 122
EHP Lancaster, PA, 944
EHP Signifia Lancaster, PA, 945
Emerald Health PPO Cleveland, OH, 854
Empire Blue Cross & Blue Shield New York, NY, 774
Encore Health Network Indianapolis, IN, 402
EPIC Pharmacy Network Mechanicsville, VA, 1134

Fallon Community Health Plan Worcester, MA, 533
Family Choice Health Alliance Hackensack, NJ, 726
FC Diagnostic Hackensack, NJ, 727
First Choice of the Midwest Sioux Falls, SD, 1020
First Health Downers Grove, IL, 369
Fortified Provider Network Scottsdale, AZ, 44
Foundation for Medical Care for Kern & Santa Barbara County Bakersfield, CA, 123
Foundation for Medical Care for Mendocino and Lake Counties Ukiah, CA, 124

Galaxy Health Network Arlington, TX, 1066
Geisinger Health Plan Danville, PA, 948

GHP Coventry Health Plan St. Louis, MO, 648
Graphic Arts Benefit Corporation Greenbelt, MD, 511
Great-West Healthcare Alabama Atlanta, GA, 10
Great-West Healthcare Alaska Denver, CO, 23
Great-West Healthcare Arizona Scottsdale, AZ, 45
Great-West Healthcare California Irvine, CA, 127
Great-West Healthcare Colorado Greenwood Village, CO, 205
Great-West Healthcare Connecticut Hartford, CT, 225
Great-West Healthcare Delaware Bluebell, PA, 238
Great-West Healthcare Florida Tampa, FL, 281
Great-West Healthcare Georgia Atlanta, GA, 322
Great-West Healthcare Hawaii Oakland, CA, 336
Great-West Healthcare Illinois Rosemont, IL, 370
Great-West Healthcare Indiana Indianapolis, IN, 403, 404
Great-West Healthcare Iowa Chicago, IL, 425
Great-West Healthcare Kansas Overland Park, KS, 442
Great-West Healthcare Los Angeles Glendale, CA, 128
Great-West Healthcare Maine South Portland, ME, 491
Great-West Healthcare Michigan Southfield, MI, 570
Great-West Healthcare Minnesota Eden Prairie, MN, 604
Great-West Healthcare Missouri St. Louis, MO, 649
Great-West Healthcare Montana Bellevue, WA, 668
Great-West Healthcare New Mexico Scottsdale, AZ, 748
Great-West Healthcare New York White Plains, NY, 780
Great-West Healthcare North Carolina Charlotte, NC, 824
Great-West Healthcare North Dakota Chicago, IL, 838
Great-West Healthcare Northern California Walnut Creek, CA, 129
Great-West Healthcare of Idaho Denver, CO, 349
Great-West Healthcare of Maryland Bethesda, MD, 512
Great-West Healthcare of Massachusetts Waltham, MA, 535
Great-West Healthcare of Nevada Henderson, NV, 694
Great-West Healthcare of New Jersey Piscataway, NJ, 728
Great-West Healthcare of Washington Belleview, WA, 1156
Great-West Healthcare Oklahoma Dallas, TX, 894
Great-West Healthcare Oregon Portland, OR, 908
Great-West Healthcare Pennsylvania Piscataway, NJ, 949
Great-West Healthcare South Carolina Greenville, NC, 1003
Great-West Healthcare South Dakota Chicago, IL, 1021
Great-West Healthcare Texas Dallas, TX, 1067
Great-West Healthcare West Virginia Pittsburgh, OH, 1177
Great-West Healthcare Wisconsin Wauwatosa, WI, 1196
Great-West PPO Greenwood Village, CO, 206
Great-West/One Health Plan Greenwood Village, CO, 207
Group Health Incorporated (GHI) New York, NY, 781
Guardian Life Insurance Company New York, NY, 782

HAS-Premier Providers Addison, TX, 1068
Hawaii Medical Assurance Association Honolulu, HI, 337
Hawaii Medical Services Association Honolulu, HI, 338
Health Alliance Medical Plans Urbana, IL, 371
Health Alliance Plan Detroit, MI, 572
Health Care Service Corporation Chicago, IL, 373
Health Choice LLC Memphis, TN, 1036
Health Choice of Alabama Birmingham, AL, 11
Health InfoNet Billings, MT, 669
Health Link PPO Tupelo, MS, 628
Health Net Health Plan of Oregon Tigard, OR, 909
Health Partners of Kansas Wichita, KS, 443
Health Plan of Nevada Las Vegas, NV, 695
Health Plan of New York New York, NY, 783
Health Plan of New York: Connecticut New York, NY, 227
Health Plan of New York: Massachusetts New York, NY, 539
Healthcare Partners of East Texas Longview, TX, 1069
Healthchoice Orlando Orlando, FL, 284
HealthEOS De Pere, WI, 1201
HealthPartners Jackson, TN, 1037
HealthSmart Preferred Care Lisle, IL, 374
HealthSmart Preferred Care Lubbock, TX, 1070
HealthSpan Cincinnati, OH, 857
Highmark Blue Cross & Blue Shield Pittsburgh, PA, 953
Highmark Blue Shield Camp Hill, PA, 954
Horizon Blue Cross & Blue Shield of New Jersey Newark, NJ, 730
Horizon Health Corporation Lewisville, TX, 1073

Horizon Healthcare of New Jersey Newark, NJ, 731
Horizon NJ Health West Trenton, NJ, 732
HSM: Healthcare Cost Management St Paul, MN, 607
Humana Health Insurance of Alabama Huntsville, AL, 13
Humana Health Insurance of Alaska Vancouver, WA, 24
Humana Health Insurance of Arizona Phoenix, AZ, 48
Humana Health Insurance of Connecticut Mahwah, NJ, 228
Humana Health Insurance of Corpus Christi Corpus Christi, TX, 1074
Humana Health Insurance of D.C. Mahwah, NJ, 249
Humana Health Insurance of Delaware Mahwah, NJ, 239
Humana Health Insurance of Georgia Atlanta, GA, 323
Humana Health Insurance of Hawaii Honolulu, HI, 339
Humana Health Insurance of Idaho Meridian, ID, 350
Humana Health Insurance of Illinois Chicago, IL, 377
Humana Health Insurance of Indiana Indianapolis, IN, 407
Humana Health Insurance of Iowa Davenport, IA, 427
Humana Health Insurance of Jacksonville Jacksonville, FL, 286
Humana Health Insurance of Kansas Overland Park, MO, 444
Humana Health Insurance of Kentucky Louisville, KY, 463
Humana Health Insurance of Little Rock Little Rock, AR, 74
Humana Health Insurance of Louisiana Metairie, LA, 480
Humana Health Insurance of Maryland Mahwah, NJ, 513
Humana Health Insurance of Massachusetts Mahwah, NJ, 541
Humana Health Insurance of Michigan Grand Rapids, MI, 578
Humana Health Insurance of Minnesota Plymouth, MN, 608
Humana Health Insurance of Mississippi Ridgeland, MS, 629
Humana Health Insurance of Missouri Springfield, MO, 652
Humana Health Insurance of Montana Billings, MT, 670
Humana Health Insurance of Nebraska Omaha, NE, 682
Humana Health Insurance of Nevada Las Vegas, NV, 697
Humana Health Insurance of New Hampshire Portsmouth, NH, 711
Humana Health Insurance of New Jersey Mahwah, NJ, 733
Humana Health Insurance of New Mexico Albuquerque, NM, 749
Humana Health Insurance of New York Albany, NY, 786
Humana Health Insurance of North Carolina Cary, NC, 825
Humana Health Insurance of North Dakota Omaha, NE, 840
Humana Health Insurance of Northern California Walnut Creek, CA, 135
Humana Health Insurance of Ohio Cincinnati, OH, 859
Humana Health Insurance of Oklahoma Tulsa, OK, 895
Humana Health Insurance of Oregon Vancouver, WA, 910
Humana Health Insurance of Orlando Alamonte Springs, FL, 287
Humana Health Insurance of Pennsylvania Mechanicsburg, PA, 955
Humana Health Insurance of Puerto Rico San Juan, PR, 979
Humana Health Insurance of Rhode Island Mahwah, NJ, 991
Humana Health Insurance of San Antonio San Antonio, TX, 1075
Humana Health Insurance of South Carolina Columbia, SC, 1004
Humana Health Insurance of South Dakota Omaha, NE, 1022
Humana Health Insurance of Tampa - Pinellas Tampa, FL, 288
Humana Health Insurance of Tennessee Memphis, TN, 1040
Humana Health Insurance of Utah Sandy, UT, 1107
Humana Health Insurance of Virginia Glen Allen, VA, 1135
Humana Health Insurance of Washington Vancouver, WA, 1158
Humana Health Insurance of West Virginia Charleston, WV, 1178
Humana Health Insurance of Wisconsin Waukesha, WI, 1202
Humana Health Insurance of Wyoming Billings, MT, 1220
Humana Health Insurnace of Colorado Colorado Springs, CO, 209

Independence Blue Cross Philadelphia, PA, 956
Initial Group Nashville, TN, 1041
InterGroup Services Corporation Malvern, PA, 957
Interplan Health Group Stockton, CA, 139
Interplan Health Group Cleveland, OH, 860
Interplan Health Group Irving, TX, 1076

John Deere Health Kingsport, TN, 1042

Kanawha Healthcare Solutions Lancaster, SC, 1006
Keystone Health Plan East Philadelphia, PA, 959

Landmark Healthplan of California Sacramento, CA, 147
Liberty Health Plan: Alaska Anchorage, AK, 25
Liberty Health Plan: Corporate Office Portland, OR, 912
Liberty Health Plan: Idaho Boise, ID, 352

UnitedHealthCare of Arkansas Little Rock, AR, 78
UnitedHealthCare of Colorado Centennial, CO, 215
UnitedHealthCare of Connecticut Hartford, CT, 230
UnitedHealthCare of Florida Jacksonville, FL, 302
UnitedHealthCare of Georgia Norcross, GA, 330
UnitedHealthCare of Hawaii Cypress, CA, 341
UnitedHealthCare of Idaho Cypress, CA, 356
UnitedHealthCare of Illinois Chicago, IL, 386
UnitedHealthCare of Indiana Indianapolis, IN, 414
UnitedHealthCare of Iowa Des Moines, IA, 431
UnitedHealthCare of Kansas Overland Park, KS, 453
UnitedHealthCare of Kentucky Lexington, KY, 469
UnitedHealthCare of Louisiana Metairie, LA, 484
UnitedHealthCare of Maine Edina, MN, 495
UnitedHealthCare of Massachusetts Warwick, RI, 546
UnitedHealthCare of Michigan Southfield, MI, 592
UnitedHealthCare of Minnesota Edina, MN, 620, 621
UnitedHealthCare of Mississippi Hattiesburg, MS, 630
UnitedHealthCare of Missouri Maryland Heights, MO, 661
UnitedHealthCare of Montana Centennial, CO, 674
UnitedHealthCare of Nebraska Omaha, NE, 686
UnitedHealthCare of New Hampshire Westborough, MA, 714
UnitedHealthCare of New Jersey Iselin, NJ, 739
UnitedHealthCare of New Mexico Albuquerque, NM, 756
UnitedHealthCare of New York East Syracuse, NY, 810
UnitedHealthCare of North Carolina Cary, NC, 832
UnitedHealthCare of North Dakota Edina, MN, 843
UnitedHealthCare of Northern California Cypress, CA, 182
UnitedHealthCare of Ohio: Columbus Westerville, OH, 882
UnitedHealthCare of Ohio: Dayton & Cincinnati West Chester, OH, 883
UnitedHealthCare of Oklahoma Plano, TX, 898
UnitedHealthCare of Oregon Lake Oswego, OR, 923
UnitedHealthCare of Pennsylvania Monroeville, PA, 972
UnitedHealthCare of Puerto Rico Edina, MN, 984
UnitedHealthCare of Rhode Island Warwick, RI, 994
UnitedHealthCare of South Carolina Columbia, SC, 1011
UnitedHealthCare of South Dakota Edina, MN, 1024
UnitedHealthCare of South Florida Sunrise, FL, 303
UnitedHealthCare of Southern California Cypress, CA, 183
UnitedHealthCare of Tennessee Brentwood, TN, 1044
UnitedHealthCare of Texas Austin, TX, 1095
UnitedHealthCare of the District of Columbia Bethesda, MD, 253
UnitedHealthCare of the Mid-Atlantic Elkridge, MD, 242, 523
UnitedHealthCare of Utah Salt Lake City, UT, 1115
UnitedHealthCare of Vermont Westborough, MA, 1123
UnitedHealthCare of Virginia Richmond, VA, 1145
UnitedHealthCare of Washington Mercer Island, WA, 1170
UnitedHealthCare of West Virginia Edina, MN, 1184
UnitedHealthCare of Wisconsin: Central Edina, MN, 622
UnitedHealthCare of Wisconsin: Central Edina, WI, 1211
UnitedHealthCare of Wyoming Centennial, CO, 1221
University Health Alliance Honolulu, HI, 342

University Health Plans Salt Lake City, UT, 1116
USA Managed Care Organization Austin, TX, 1096

Val-U-Health Belle Vernon, PA, 974
Value Behavioral Health of Pennsylvania Trafford, PA, 976
Virginia Health Network Richmond, VA, 1146
Vytra Health Plans Melville, NY, 813

Wellmark Blue Cross & Blue Shield of South Dakota Sioux Falls, SD, 1025
Wisconsin Physician's Service Madison, WI, 1214

Vision

Block Vision of New Jersey Florham Park, NJ, 721
Block Vision of Texas Dallas, TX, 1052

Davis Vision Plainview, NY, 769

EyeMed Vision Care Mason, OH, 855

March Vision Care Los Angeles, CA, 151

OptiCare Managed Vision Rocky Mount, NC, 828
Opticare of Utah Salt Lake City, UT, 1110
Outlook Vision Service Mesa, AZ, 53

Preferred Vision Care Overland Park, KS, 450

Superior Vision Services, Inc. Rancho Cordova, CA, 178
SVS Vision Mount Clemens, MI, 588

Vision Insurance Plan of America West Allis, WI, 1213
Vision Plan of America Los Angeles, CA, 185
VSP: Vision Service Plan Rancho Cordova, CA, 186
VSP: Vision Service Plan of Arizona Phoenix, AZ, 63
VSP: Vision Service Plan of California San Francisco, CA, 187
VSP: Vision Service Plan of Colorado Denver, CO, 216
VSP: Vision Service Plan of Florida Tampa, FL, 306
VSP: Vision Service Plan of Georgia Norcross, GA, 331
VSP: Vision Service Plan of Hawaii Honolulu, HI, 343
VSP: Vision Service Plan of Illinois Chicago, IL, 387
VSP: Vision Service Plan of Indiana Indianpolis, IN, 415
VSP: Vision Service Plan of Kansas Shawnee Mission, KS, 454
VSP: Vision Service Plan of Massachusetts Boston, MA, 547
VSP: Vision Service Plan of Michigan Southfield, MI, 594
VSP: Vision Service Plan of Minnesota Minneapolis, MN, 623
VSP: Vision Service Plan of New Jersey Parsippany, NJ, 740
VSP: Vision Service Plan of Ohio Canton, OH, 884
VSP: Vision Service Plan of Oregon Portland, OR, 924
VSP: Vision Service Plan of South Carolina Greenville, SC, 1012
VSP: Vision Service Plan of Texas Houston, TX, 1099
VSP: Vision Service Plan of Washington Seattle, WA, 1171

Personnel Index

A

Angeli, Raymond Blue Cross & Blue Shield of Illinois, 359
Angerami, John CNA Insurance Companies: Colorado, 198
Angerami, John CNA Insurance Companies: Georgia, 317
Angerami, John CNA Insurance Companies: Illinois, 362
Annunziata, Russell SXC Health Solutions Corp, 383
Anselm, Edward, MD Fidelis Care, 778
Anthony, William A, MD CHN PPO, 722
Antigua, Paul Health Plan of San Joaquin, 133
Apfel, Mark, MD Foundation for Medical Care for Mendocino and Lake Counties, 124
Apgar, Frank, MD Arcadian Health Plans, 83
Apolinsky, Craig Alere Health, 309
Appel, Frank Coventry Health Care of Florida, 274
Appenzeller, Talitha, MBA MHNet Behavioral Health, 1081
Applebury, Daryl Gundersen Lutheran Health Plan, 1199
Appleton, Kevin Oxford Health Plans: New Jersey, 736
Appleton, Kevin Oxford Health Plans: New York, 805
Arca, Albert Preferred Medical Plan, 297
Arcidiacono, Susan Inland Empire Health Plan, 137
Arfin, Ronald Managed Healthcare Systems of New Jersey, 734
Armao, Anne SummaCare Health Plan, 875
Armao, Anne SummaCare Medicare Advantage Plan, 876
Armbruster, Kevin SummaCare Health Plan, 875
Armbruster, Kevin SummaCare Medicare Advantage Plan, 876
Armenti, Steve CHN PPO, 722
Armstrong, C Michael Priority Partners Health Plans, 520
Armstrong, Cathleen HealthSCOPE Benefits, 73
Armstrong, David Wisconsin Physician's Service, 1214
Armstrong, Richard, MD QualChoice/QCA Health Plan, 76
Armstrong, Scott Group Health Cooperative, 1157
Arndt, Jerry Gundersen Lutheran Health Plan, 1199
Arnesen, Kayla Rocky Mountain Health Plans, 213
Arneson, Linda M Delta Dental of Colorado, 202
Arnet, Alex N HealthSmart Preferred Care, 1070
Arnett, Julia UnitedHealthCare of Iowa, 431
Arnold, Roy, MD Welborn Health Plans, 416
Arrington, Robyn, MD Total Health Choice, 300
Arrington Jr, Robyn James, MD Total Health Care, 589
Arth, Lawrence J Ameritas Group, 676
Ash-Jackson, Linda Hometown Health Plan, 696
Ashby, Darren HealthSCOPE Benefits, 73
Asher, Chris Southeastern Indiana Health Organization, 413
Asher, Drew Coventry Health Care: Corporate Headquarters, 506
Ashihundu, Eric Community First Health Plans, 1059
Ashley, Kim Anthem Blue Cross & Blue Shield of Ohio, 846
Ashley, Sheldon Family Choice Health Alliance, 726
Ask, Tanya New West Health Services, 672
Ask, Tanya New West Medicare Plan, 673
Astorga, Tony M Blue Cross & Blue Shield of Arizona, 36
Atkins, Nancy Bluegrass Family Health, 457
Atwell, William L CIGNA: Corporate Headquarters, 939
Atwood, Michael D, MD Blue Cross & Blue Shield of Kansas, 436
Aubrey, Rob Select Health of South Carolina, 1008
Auer, Bill Kaiser Permanente of Georgia, 324
Aug, Matthew Cox Healthplans, 642
Augustyn, Mary Liberty Health Plan: Corporate Office, 912
Austen, Karla MVP Health Care: Corporate Office, 798
Austen, Karla MVP Health Care: Western New York, 800
Austin, Jeanell National Capital PPO, 1138
Austin, John, MD Arkansas Community Care, 67
Austin, John H, MD Texas Community Care, 1091
Austin, Scott Humana Health Insurance of Wisconsin, 1202
Austin, Sueann Medical Care Referral Group, 1079
Authur Pierce, Ena Bravo Health: Corporate Headquarters, 502
Avery, Alan Medical Associates Health Plan, 378
Avery, Alan Medical Associates Health Plan: West, 428
Avery, Alan Medical Associates Health Plan: East, 1204
Avila, Diana Alliance Regional Health Network, 1047
Avner, Kenneth Health Care Service Corporation, 373
Ayers, Kay AvMed Health Plan: Corporate Office, 259
Ayers, Kay AvMed Health Plan: Gainesville, 261
Ayers, Kay AvMed Health Plan: Orlando, 263

Ayers, Ruth Ellen Carilion Health Plans, 1128

B

Baackes, John UnitedHealthCare of North Carolina, 832
Babarick, Tracie SummaCare Health Plan, 875
Babarick, Tracie SummaCare Medicare Advantage Plan, 876
Babitsch, George GHI Medicare Plan, 779
Babitsch, George Group Health Incorporated (GHI), 781
Babitsch, George Health Plan of New York, 783
Baca, Mari Health Plan of San Mateo, 134
Baca, Marlene Lovelace Health Plan, 750
Baca, Marlene Lovelace Medicare Health Plan, 751
Bachhuber, Michele L, MD Security Health Plan of Wisconsin, 1209
Backon, Marc Capital Blue Cross, 936
Bacon, Cindy, RN Island Group Administration, Inc., 789
Bagnall, Dana Vision Insurance Plan of America, 1213
Bahrke, Linda Community Health Improvement Solutions, 641
Bailey, Jim Arkansas Blue Cross and Blue Shield, 66
Bailey, Michael Windsor Medicare Extra, 1045
Bailey, S Graham Blue Cross & Blue Shield of Kansas, 436
Baines, Barry, MD UCare Medicare Plan, 618
Baines, Barry, MD UCare Minnesota, 619
Baird, Mark Medica Health - Medicare Plan, 609
Baird, Mark Medica: Corporate Office, 610
Baird, Mark Medica: North Dakota, 841
Baird, Mark Medica: South Dakota, 1023
Bajaj, Sandeep Physicians United Plan, 295
Baker, Andrew H Family Choice Health Alliance, 726
Baker, Andrew H FC Diagnostic, 727
Baker, Brendan CareMore Health Plan, 98
Baker, G Steve Public Employees Health Program, 1111
Baker, Jane Horizon Health Corporation, 1073
Baker, Stephen J SafeGuard Health Enterprises: Corporate Office, 172
Baker, Stephen J SafeGuard Health Enterprises: Florida, 299
Baker, Stephen J SafeGuard Health Enterprises: Texas, 1086
Balash, Robert Advantage Health Solutions, 388
Baldwin, James G, MD Select Health of South Carolina, 1008
Baldwin, K Rone Guardian Life Insurance Company, 782
Baldwin, Stanley F Amerigroup Corporation, 1125
Ball, Donald, Jr VSP: Vision Service Plan, 186
Ball, Patricia UCare Medicare Plan, 618
Ball, Patricia UCare Minnesota, 619
Banda, Kay Arizona Foundation for Medical Care, 32
Banda, Kay Preferred Therapy Providers, 57
Bania, Michael Care Plus Dental Plans, 1189
Bank, Julie MagnaCare, 791
Banner, Rio, MD AlohaCare, 333
Baquiran, Delia C Atlantis Health Plan, 761
Barasch, Richard A American Pioneer Life Insurance Co, 255
Barasch, Richard A Universal American Medicare Plans, 812
Barasch, Richard A TexanPlus Medicare Advantage HMO, 1090
Barbaglia, Jim Valley Baptist Health Plan, 1098
Barber, Thomas VSP: Vision Service Plan of Texas, 1099
Barbera, Thomas P Mid Atlantic Medical Services: Delaware, 240
Barbera, Thomas P Alliance PPO, LLC, 497
Barbera, Thomas P Mid Atlantic Psychiatric Services (MAMSI), 517
Barbera, Thomas P Optimum Choice, 519
Barbera, Thomas P Mid Atlantic Medical Services: North Carolina, 827
Barco, Dan, MD WellPath: A Coventry Health Care Plan, 833
Barden, J Gentry HealthSpring: Corporate Offices, 1039
Barkell, Susan L Blue Cross Blue Shield of Michigan, 556
Barker, David S Southeastern Indiana Health Organization, 413
Barker, Jean Kaiser Permanente Health Plan of Colorado, 210
Barlow, H R Brereton Premera Blue Cross, 1164
Barnard, Mark Horizon Blue Cross & Blue Shield of New Jersey, 730
Barnard, Mark Rayant Insurance Company, 738
Barnes, Christy Ohio Health Choice, 868
Barnes, Linda Nevada Preferred Healthcare Providers, 699, 700
Barnes, Scott HealthSCOPE Benefits, 73
Barnett, Kerry Regence Blue Cross & Blue Shield of Oregon, 919
Barnett, Kerry Regence Blue Cross & Blue Shield of Utah, 1112
Barnett, Kerry E Regence BlueShield of Idaho, 355

Barnett, Linda Nevada Preferred Healthcare Providers, 700
Barnette, Kevin MedCost, 826
Barnhart, Mark Cardinal Health Alliance, 396
Barnicle, Joan Aetna Health of Missouri, 632
Barr, Bill Regence BlueShield of Idaho, 355
Barr, Bill Regence Blue Cross & Blue Shield of Oregon, 919
Barr, Paula Preferred Health Plan Inc, 467
Barrett, Marie Alameda Alliance for Health, 81
Barrett, Rick DINA Dental Plans, 477
Barrett, Rick Dental Solutions Plus, 1062
Barrett, Rick Dental Source: Dental Health Care Plans, 1063
Barrett, Rick Ora Quest Dental Plans, 1083
Barrett, Rochelle American Health Care Alliance, 633
Barrington, Christina Health Alliance Medical Plans, 371
Barron, Ruthann Island Group Administration, Inc., 789
Bartal, Sandy Virginia Health Network, 1146
Bartlett, Karen Premera Blue Cross Blue Shield of Alaska, 27
Bartlett, Mark R Blue Care Network: Ann Arbor, 553
Bartlett, Mark R Blue Care Network: Flint, 554
Bartlett, Mark R Blue Cross Blue Shield of Michigan, 556
Bartlett, Tom Beech Street Corporation: Corporate Office, 87
Barwig, Mark P EPIC Pharmacy Network, 1134
Bashan, William CIGNA HealthCare of New Hampshire, 707
Basher, Kathy Humana Health Insurance of Orlando, 287
Baskin, Tery, PharmD National Medical Health Card, 802
Batchlor, Elaine, MD L.A. Care Health Plan, 145
Bates, Debbie, MD UnitedHealthCare of Louisiana, 484
Bates, Richard Catalyst Health Solutions Inc, 503
Bates, Richard Catalyst RX, 817
Batey, Dennis, MD Presbyterian Health Plan, 753
Batey, Dennis, MD Presbyterian Medicare Plans, 754
Bathke, Bill Wisconsin Physician's Service, 1214
Batteer, Cathy UPMC Health Plan, 973
Battista, Jeanette Delta Dental of Illinois, 365
Bauer Jones, Stacy Sanford Health Plan, 430
Bauers, John, MD HealthAmerica, 951
Baughman, Chris Health Plan of San Mateo, 134
Baum, J Robert, PhD Highmark Blue Cross & Blue Shield, 953
Baum, J Robert Highmark Blue Shield, 954
Baumgart, Chuck, MD Presbyterian Health Plan, 753
Baumgart, Chuck, MD Presbyterian Medicare Plans, 754
Baut, Harry Behavioral Healthcare Options, Inc., 690
Baxter, Raymond J, PhD Kaiser Permanente Health Plan of Northern
   California, 140
Baxter, Raymond J, PhD Kaiser Permanente Health Plan of Southern
   California, 141
Baxter, Raymond J, PhD Kaiser Permanente Health Plan: Corporate Office,
   142
Baxter, Raymond J, PhD Kaiser Permanente Medicare Plan, 143
Bayer, Gregory A, PhD United Behavioral Health, 180
Bayer, Terry, JD Molina Healthcare: Washington, 1161
Bayer, Terry T, JD Molina Healthcare: Corporate Office, 155
Bayham, Alan, RPh Tenet Choices, 483
Bea, Javon R MercyCare Health Plans, 1205
Beach, Terry MagnaCare, 791
Beall, Tom Florida Health Care Plan, 279
Beargeon, Steve California Foundation for Medical Care, 95
Beaton, Brian HealthNow New York, 784
Beatty, Sarah USA Managed Care Organization, 1096
Beauchaine, David HealthSpring of Alabama, 12
Beauchamp, Christy Preferred Therapy Providers, 57
Beauchamp, Robert, MD UnitedHealthCare of Arizona, 61
Beauchamp, Robert G UCare Medicare Plan, 618
Beauchamp, Robert G UCare Minnesota, 619
Beaulieu, Matt Assurant Employee Benefits: Florida, 257
Beaver, Brandon Medfocus Radiology Network, 153
Becher, Jill HealthLink HMO, 651
Bechtol, Allison Lifewise Health Plan of Oregon, 913
Beck, Greg Superior Vision Services, Inc., 178
Beck, John G Unison Health Plan of Pennsylvania, 970
Becker, George H, Jr PacifiCare of Oklahoma, 897
Beckman, JS Security Life Insurance Company of America, 617

Beckman, Stephen Security Life Insurance Company of America, 617
Beebe, Laurie Health New England, 538
Behler, Anthony, MD HealthSpan, 857
Behnke, David Delta Dental of Illinois, 365
Behuniak, Darren Devon Health Services, 942
Beitel, Rem CommunityCare Managed Healthcare Plans of Oklahoma, 890
Beitelman, Angela Health Alliance Medical Plans, 371
Belek, Marilynn, DMD Delta Dental of California, 115
Bell, Christy W Horizon Blue Cross & Blue Shield of New Jersey, 730
Bell, Jill J Passport Health Plan, 466
Bell, Michael W CIGNA HealthCare of Connecticut, 222
Bell, Michael W CIGNA HealthCare of Maine, 489
Bell, Michael W CIGNA HealthCare of South Carolina, 1000
Bell, Paul Preferred Medical Plan, 297
Bellah, Ann Pueblo Health Care, 212
Bellante, Jean Managed Health Services, 1203
Bellofatto, Susan Horizon Health Corporation, 1073
Bellone, Lauren Pacific Health Alliance, 161
Belrose, David United Concordia: Alabama, 15
Belski, Krystyna, MD Stanislaus Foundation for Medical Care, 177
Bencic, Eleanor Anthem Blue Cross & Blue Shield of Missouri, 634
Bendes, Ron Sterling Health Plans, 1168
Benedetto, Frank CIGNA HealthCare of Arizona, 38
Benevento, Anthony UPMC Health Plan, 973
Benjamin, Brian, DDS Liberty Dental Plan, 148
Bennett, George E First Health, 369
Bennett, John A, MD Devon Health Services, 942
Bennett, John D, MD CDPHP Medicare Plan, 764
Bennett, John D, MD CDPHP: Capital District Physicians' Health Plan, 765
Bennett, Joshua, MD HealthAmerica Pennsylvania, 952
Bennett, Karen VSP: Vision Service Plan of New Jersey, 740
Bennett, William A Vytra Health Plans, 813
Bennof, Mike SXC Health Solutions Corp, 383
Benson, Amie Assurant Employee Benefits: Minnesota, 597
Benson, Donald T. Great-West Healthcare Texas, 1067
Bentz Seal, Joni Ohio State University Health Plan Inc., 869
Berardo, Joseph, Jr MagnaCare, 791
Berding, Ronald J Coventry Health Care of Florida, 274
Beres, Mark, CPA Nationwide Better Health, 867
Berg, Al VSP: Vision Service Plan, 186
Berg, Charles G WellCare Health Plans, 307
Berg, Charles G Oxford Health Plans: New Jersey, 736
Berg, Charles G Oxford Health Plans: New York, 805
Berg, Jim Elderplan, 773
Berge, Frank Dencap Dental Plans, 564
Bergman, Jane CoreSource: Arizona, 39
Berkowitz, Mona Pima Health System, 56
Berman, Cliff SXC Health Solutions Corp, 383
Berman, Philip UnitedHealthCare of North Carolina, 832
Bernadett, MD, Martha Molina Healthcare: Corporate Office, 155
Bernadette, Martha, MD Molina Healthcare: Washington, 1161
Bernard, Desi Quality Plan Administrators, 251
Bernard, Milton, DDS Quality Plan Administrators, 251
Bernauer, Judu PacifiCare Health Systems, 164
Berneking, Vicky Deaconess Health Plans, 398
Bernstein, Mike SummaCare Health Plan, 875
Bernstein, Mike SummaCare Medicare Advantage Plan, 876
Berrigan, Karen Delta Dental of Arizona, 40
Berry, Elyse HealthPlus of Michigan: Flint, 574
Berry, Melody OSF HealthPlans, 380
Berry, Ronald Health Alliance Medicare, 571
Berry, Ronald Health Alliance Plan, 572
Berry, Steven BlueLincs HMO, 888
Berryman, Patrick M EPIC Pharmacy Network, 1134
Bertko, John, FSA MAAA Humana Health Insurance of Arizona, 48
Bertko, John M Humana Medicare Plan, 464
Bertko, John M, FSA Humana Health Insurance of Ohio, 859
Bertolini, Mark T Aetna Health of Alabama, 1
Bertolini, Mark T Aetna Health of Alaska, 18
Bertolini, Mark T Aetna Health of Arkansas, 64
Bertolini, Mark T Aetna Health of Colorado, 190
Bertolini, Mark T Aetna Health, Inc. Corporate Headquarters, 217

Booher, Scott Medica: Corporate Office, 610
Booher, Scott Medica: North Dakota, 841
Booher, Scott Medica: South Dakota, 1023
Boone, Michael Novasys Health, 52
Boreing, Donna Lee Anthem Blue Cross & Blue Shield of Colorado, 192
Borer, Dorinda Unison Health Plan of Delaware, 241
Borg, Stanley, DO Blue Cross & Blue Shield of Illinois, 359
Boris, Lily, MD Alameda Alliance for Health, 81
Borrajero, Maritza Neighborhood Health Partnership, 293
Borup, Lynn Colorado Choice Health Plans, 200
Bossier, Donna Tenet Choices, 483
Boswell, Donald HealthNow New York, 784
Bottitta, Louis W Valley Preferred, 975
Bottrill, Lorry Health Net of Arizona, 47
Bottrill, Lorry Mercy Care Plan/Mercy Care Advantage, 51
Bouchard, Angelee F, Esq Health Net: Corporate Headquarters, 132
Bouharoun, Khalil DC Chartered Health Plan, 246
Bourbeau, Michael D Delta Dental Northeast, 708
Bowen, Kenneth D Assurant Employee Benefits: Corporate Headquarters, 635
Bowen, Kenneth W, Jr QualChoice/QCA Health Plan, 76
Bowers, Christopher D Centene Corporation, 638
Bowers, David, MD Preferred Health Care, 963
Bowers, Scott A Unison Health Plan of Pennsylvania, 970
Bowie, Stuart Block Vision of Texas, 1052
Bowlus, Brad Secure Horizons, 77
Bowlus, Brad PacifiCare of Nevada, 702
Bowlus, Brad PacifiCare of Texas, 1084
Bowlus, Brad PacifiCare Benefit Administrators, 1162
Bowlus, Brad PacifiCare of Washington, 1163
Bowman, Lynn Harvard Pilgrim Health Care: Maine, 492
Bowman, Lynn Harvard Pilgrim Health Care, 536
Bowman, Lynn Harvard Pilgrim Health Care of New England, 710
Bowman, Nadina Highmark Blue Cross & Blue Shield, 953
Bowser, Tom Blue Cross & Blue Shield of Kansas City, 636
Boxer, Michael EyeMed Vision Care, 855
Boyd, Laura Community Health Plan of Washington, 1152
Boyer, Julie HealthPlus of Michigan: Flint, 574
Boyer, Julie HealthPlus of Michigan: Saginaw, 575
Boyer, Kent Great-West Healthcare of Massachusetts, 535
Boyle, Vicki, RN Health Plan of Michigan, 573
Bracciodieta, William P, MD/MBA Molina Healthcare: Washington, 1161
Bracikowski, James, MD Windsor Medicare Extra, 1045
Brackins, Diana MedCost, 826
Bracy, Bob HealthSCOPE Benefits, 73
Bradfield, Jessie E Preferred Healthcare System, 964
Bradford, Dale Martin's Point HealthCare, 493
Bradley, Don W, MD Blue Cross & Blue Shield of North Carolina, 816
Bradley, Robin Windsor Medicare Extra, 1045
Bradshaw, John Interplan Health Group, 1076
Brady, Ray Assurant Employee Benefits: Pennsylvania, 931
Brady, Tom UnitedHealthCare of Ohio: Columbus, 882
Brady, Tom UnitedHealthCare of Ohio: Dayton & Cincinnati, 883
Braff, Dave Assurant Employee Benefits: Michigan, 550
Brainerd, Mary Health Partners Medicare Plan, 605
Brainerd, Mary HealthPartners, 606
Braly, Angela Anthem Blue Cross & Blue Shield of Missouri, 634
Braly, Angela F WellPoint: Corporate Office, 417
Bramson, James United Concordia: Alabama, 15
Branchick, Vivian C, RN Los Angeles County Public Healthcare, 149
Branchini, Frank J GHI Medicare Plan, 779
Branchini, Frank J Group Health Incorporated (GHI), 781
Branchini, Frank J Health Plan of New York, 783
Branchini, Frank J UnitedHealthCare of North Carolina, 832
Brandenburg, Heather Chinese Community Health Plan, 102
Brandon, Marie Premier Access Insurance/Access Dental, 169
Brandstetter, Tamara Delta Dental of Idaho, 347
Branson, Rick, DC HSM: Healthcare Cost Management, 607
Branstetter, Phil Inland Empire Health Plan, 137
Brantner, Linda Delta Dental of Kansas, 440
Braswell, Judi Behavioral Health Systems, 4
Brazee, Danielle Managed Health Services, 1203
Brecher, Randy Liberty Dental Plan, 148

Brecher, Randy Pacific Dental Benefits, 159
Brecher, Randy Liberty Dental Plan of Nevada, 698
Breen, Bill Health Choice LLC, 1036
Breidenbach, William R Health Plans, Inc., 540
Brendzel, Ronald I SafeGuard Health Enterprises: Corporate Office, 172
Brendzel, Ronald I SafeGuard Health Enterprises: Florida, 299
Brendzel, Ronald I SafeGuard Health Enterprises: Texas, 1086
Brennan, Martin Pacific Dental Benefits, 159
Brennan, Troyen A., MD CVS CareMark, 988
Brewer, Charles UnitedHealthCare of Louisiana, 484
Briard, Mike Vantage Health Plan, 485
Brickson, Gretchen, MPH On Lok Lifeways, 157
Bridges, David Arkansas Blue Cross and Blue Shield, 66
Bright, Yvette D Independence Blue Cross, 956
Brill, Joel V, MD Action Healthcare Management Services, 30
Brill, Martin J Health Partners Medicare Plan, 950
Brillstein, Lilli AmeriChoice by UnitedHealthCare, 759
Brinkerhoff, James J Assurant Employee Benefits: Alabama, 2
Brinkley, Tim Unison Health Plan of Ohio, 881
Brinson, Beverlie Kaiser Permanente Health Plan of the Mid-Atlantic States, 514
Britt, Brian Keystone Health Plan Central, 958
Brittain, James W Virginia Health Network, 1146
Brizendine, Kevin Saint Mary's Health Plans, 703
Broadhead, Steven Y, CPA Public Employees Health Program, 1111
Broatch, Robert E Guardian Life Insurance Company, 782
Brocksome, Stephen J Blue Cross of Idaho Health Service, Inc., 345
Broderick, Peter, MD Stanislaus Foundation for Medical Care, 177
Brodsky, Mitchell Care 1st Health Plan: California, 97
Brodt, Carolyn Primecare Dental Plan, 170
Broemmer, Megan Med-Pay, 653
Broeren, Marcia Network Health Plan of Wisconsin, 1206
Brook, Fred Assurant Employee Benefits: California, 85
Brooks, G. Remmington, MD Kern Family Health Care, 144
Brooks, Gary VSP: Vision Service Plan, 186
Brooks, Rahmaire Central Susquehanna Healthcare Providers, 937
Brower, Dwight, MD Blue Cross & Blue Shield of Louisiana, 472
Brown, Adrian Health Choice Arizona, 46
Brown, D'Ln Foundation for Medical Care for Kern & Santa Barbara County, 123
Brown, Dennis Delta Dental of Wisconsin, 1193
Brown, Dewey WellPath: A Coventry Health Care Plan, 833
Brown, Frank L, MD Trigon Health Care, 1143
Brown, Jim Script Care, Ltd., 1088
Brown, Julie Humana Health Insurance of Orlando, 287
Brown, Kevin Script Care, Ltd., 1088
Brown, Marc Kaiser Permanente Health Plan of Northern California, 140
Brown, Mary Kim, RN-BC Action Healthcare Management Services, 30
Brown, Mike Arkansas Blue Cross and Blue Shield, 66
Brown, Mindy Signature Health Alliance, 1043
Brown, Mollie Coalition America's National Preferred Provider Network, 767
Brown, Patricia M.C. Priority Partners Health Plans, 520
Brown, Paul F Blue Cross and Blue Shield Association, 360
Brown, Robert Affinity Health Plan, 758
Brown, Robert Clear One Health Plans, 905
Brown, Sandy Health Plus of Louisiana, 479
Browning, Francis QualChoice/QCA Health Plan, 76
Brubaker, Lisa A MVP Health Care: New Hampshire, 712
Brubaker, Lisa A MVP Health Care Medicare Plan, 795
Brubaker, Lisa A MVP Health Care: Buffalo Region, 796
Brubaker, Lisa A MVP Health Care: Central New York, 797
Brubaker, Lisa A MVP Health Care: Corporate Office, 798
Brubaker, Lisa A MVP Health Care: Mid-State Region, 799
Brubaker, Lisa A MVP Health Care: Western New York, 800
Brubaker, Lisa A MVP Health Care: Vermont, 1122
Bruce, Bill Devon Health Services, 942
Bruce, Reagan Interplan Health Group, 139
Bruce, Reagan HealthSmart Preferred Care, 374
Brueckner, Stefen Humana Health Insurance of Illinois, 377
Brumley, Heather American PPO, 1048
Brunnemer, James A Arnett Health Plans, 394
Bruns, Brenda, MD Group Health Cooperative, 1157

Brutcher, Jeff Hometown Health Plan, 696
Bryant, Gary W, CPA American Pioneer Life Insurance Co, 255
Bryant, Gary W TexanPlus Medicare Advantage HMO, 1090
Bryant, Oscar Delta Dental of Virginia, 1131
Bucher, George Coventry Health Care of Louisiana, 475
Buck, Eric E Preferred Health Care, 963
Buckert, Greg, MD, MPH CalOptima, 96
Bucknam, Ted Concentra: Corporate Office, 1060
Buckwold, Frederick CIGNA HealthCare of Arkansas, 69
Buckwold, Frederick CIGNA HealthCare of Mississippi, 625
Budden, Joan Priority Health, 585
Budden, Joan Priority Health: Corporate Headquarters, 586
Budden, Joan PriorityHealth Medicare Plans, 587
Bueno, Maureen QualCare, 737
Buffa, Jan CareSource Mid Rogue Health Plan, 903
Buggle, Janet QualCare, 737
Buiak, Denise Blue Cross & Blue Shield of Texas, 1053
Bujak, Denise Blue Cross & Blue Shield of Illinois, 359
Bujak, Denise Health Care Service Corporation, 373
Bulger, Chris Bluegrass Family Health, 457
Bull, Lynda Liberty Dental Plan of Nevada, 698
Bullock, Doug Blue Cross of Idaho Health Service, Inc., 345
Bumstead, Sean Total Health Care, 589
Buncher, James E SafeGuard Health Enterprises: Corporate Office, 172
Buncher, James E SafeGuard Health Enterprises: Florida, 299
Buncher, James E SafeGuard Health Enterprises: Texas, 1086
Bundgus, Burt Emerald Health PPO, 854
Bunio, Karen Total Health Care, 589
Bunker, Jonathan UnitedHealthcare Nevada, 704
Bunker, Jonathan W Health Plan of Nevada, 695
Burdick, Jana Presbyterian Health Plan, 753
Burdick, Jana Presbyterian Medicare Plans, 754
Burgess, Howard Physicians Health Plan of Mid-Michigan, 584
Burgos, Gilbert, MD Care Choices, 557
Burk, Gail Beta Health Plan, 195
Burke, Natalie Total Health Care, 589
Burke, Richard, Sr UnitedHealthCare of Alabama, 16
Burke, Richard P Fallon Community Health Plan, 533
Burke, Richard P Fallon Community Medicare Plan, 534
Burkeen, Robert Assurant Employee Benefits: Oklahoma, 886
Burnett, Ann T BlueChoice Health Plan of South Carolina, 998
Burnett, Janet Welborn Health Plans, 416
Burnham, William, MD Select Health of South Carolina, 1008
Burns, Dennis A, DDS Superior Dental Care, 877
Burns, Heather Welborn Health Plans, 416
Burrell, Chester CareFirst Blue Cross Blue Shield, 244
Burrell, Chester CareFirst Blue Cross & Blue Shield of Virginia, 1127
Burruano, Martin, RPh Independent Health, 787
Burruano, Martin, RPh Independent Health Medicare Plan, 788
Burrus, William American Postal Workers Union (APWU) Health Plan, 498
Bursac, Radovan Unity Health Insurance, 1212
Bursett, John Delta Dental of Washington, 1153
Burton, David Great-West/One Health Plan, 207
Burzynski, Mark Blue Cross & Blue Shield of Montana, 664
Busby, Tom Educators Mutual, 1105
Buscetto, Greg SXC Health Solutions Corp, 383
Busch, Charles HealthSmart Preferred Care, 1070
Busek, Rhonda J Trillium Community Health Plan, 921
Bushardt, Keith G Blue Cross & Blue Shield of Nebraska, 677
Butera, Joe Capital Blue Cross, 936
Butera, Joe Keystone Health Plan Central, 958
Butler, Christopher Independence Blue Cross, 956
Butler, Mark UnitedHealthCare of Massachusetts, 546
Butler, Martha, RN, MPH Essence Healthcare, 646
Butler, Tony Essence Healthcare, 646
Butts, Wayne Western Dental Services, 188
Buxton, Brad Blue Cross & Blue Shield of Illinois, 359
Buyse, Marylou Scott & White Health Plan, 1087
Byers, Ed HMO Health Ohio, 858
Byers, Ed Medical Mutual of Ohio, 862
Byers, Ed Medical Mutual of Ohio Medicare Plan, 863
Byers, Ed SuperMed One, 878

Byers, Ed Carolina Care Plan, 999
Byrd, Angie Preferred Mental Health Management, 448
Byrd, Terence L HealthFirst New Jersey Medicare Plan, 729
Byrne, James F, MD Priority Health, 585
Byrne, Jim, MD Priority Health: Corporate Headquarters, 586
Byrne, Jim, MD PriorityHealth Medicare Plans, 587

C

Cagan, Laird, MD Boulder Valley Individual Practice Association, 196
Cahill, Judge Patrick T Delta Dental of Michigan, Ohio and Indiana, 399, 852
Cahill, Maureen Ohio State University Health Plan Inc., 869
Cahill, Tom Sterling Health Plans, 1168
Caione, Robert Touchstone Health HMO, 808
Calabrese, Steven V Touchstone Health HMO, 808
Caldwell, Susan Wisconsin Physician's Service, 1214
Callahan, Dennis S Guardian Life Insurance Company, 782
Callahan, Peggy, BSN Carilion Health Plans, 1128
Callanan, Theresa VSP: Vision Service Plan of Minnesota, 623
Calpino, Lori Berkshire Health Partners, 932
Camancho, Jill Western Health Advantage, 189
Campbell, Juan A Health New England, 538
Campbell, Raedina Preferred Health Systems Insurance Company, 447
Campbell, Raedina Preferred Plus of Kansas, 449
Campbell, Robert H CIGNA HealthCare of South Carolina, 1000
Campbell, Sheron Virginia Health Network, 1146
Campos, Alina, MD Leon Medical Centers Health Plan, 290
Canavan, John HealthNow New York, 784
Cannon, John, III WellPoint: Corporate Office, 417
Cannon, Kathy Script Care, Ltd., 1088
Cantrell, Dawn Blue Cross & Blue Shield of Louisiana, 472
Capezza, Joseph UnitedHealthCare of North Carolina, 832
Capezza, Joseph C, CPA Health Net: Corporate Headquarters, 132
Caplan, Jesse M, Esq Fallon Community Health Plan, 533
Caplan, Jesse M, Esq Fallon Community Medicare Plan, 534
Capozzi, Vincent Harvard Pilgrim Health Care: Maine, 492
Capozzi, Vincent Harvard Pilgrim Health Care, 536
Capozzi, Vincent Harvard Pilgrim Health Care of New England, 710
Cappel, Lawrence, PhD Pacific Health Alliance, 161
Card, Dorinda UnitedHealthCare of Nebraska, 686
Cardone, James Blue Cross & Blue Shield of Western New York, 762
Carliner, David Bravo Health: Corporate Headquarters, 502
Carlisle, Douglas Humana Health Insurance of Illinois, 377
Carlisle, Scott Alliance Regional Health Network, 1047
Carlos, Clayton, MPA Kern Family Health Care, 144
Carlson, Danita Central California Alliance for Health, 100
Carlson, James G Amerigroup Corporation, 1125
Carlson, Jeanne Blue Care Network of Michigan: Medicare, 552
Carlson, Lisa Sanford Health Plan, 430
Carns, Patricia HealthAmerica, 951
Carpenter, Marie UnitedHealthCare of the Mid-Atlantic, 523
Carpenter, Sara Alliant Health Plans, 310
Carpenter, Theodore TexanPlus Medicare Advantage HMO, 1090
Carpenter, Theodore M, Jr American Pioneer Life Insurance Co, 255
Carpenter, Theodore M, Jr Universal American Medicare Plans, 812
Carpenter, Tim, CPA Virginia Premier Health Plan, 1147
Carrano, Patrick BlueShield of Northeastern New York, 763
Carrasco, Angie Medical Care Referral Group, 1079
Carrillo, Liz Blue Cross & Blue Shield of New Mexico, 744
Carriveau, Lavon CIGNA HealthCare of Arizona, 38
Carroll, Bill CIGNA HealthCare of Arizona, 38
Carroll, Jim CONCERN: Employee Assistance Program, 112
Carroll, Stacey Liberty Health Advantage Medicare Plan, 790
Carrollux, Milton Blue Cross & Blue Shield of Illinois, 359
Carsazza, William Aetna Health of Colorado, 190
Carsello, Jamie UCare Medicare Plan, 618
Carsello, Jamie UCare Minnesota, 619
Carson, Chris Magellan Health Services Arizona, 49
Carson, Kim Healthy & Well Kids in Iowa, 426
Carter, David W Magellan Health Services: Corporate Headquarters, 515
Carter, Julie PacifiCare of Arizona, 54
Carter, Trudi, MD CalOptima, 96
Caruncho, Joseph L Preferred Care Partners, 296

Caruso, Joseph A Guardian Life Insurance Company, 782
Carvelli, John Liberty Dental Plan, 148
Carvelli, John Liberty Dental Plan of Nevada, 698
Casazza, William J Aetna Health of Alabama, 1
Casazza, William J Aetna Health of Alaska, 18
Casazza, William J Aetna Health of Arkansas, 64
Casazza, William J Aetna Health, Inc. Corporate Headquarters, 217
Casazza, William J Aetna Health, Inc. Medicare Plan, 218
Casazza, William J Aetna Health of Delaware, 231
Casazza, William J Aetna Health District of Columbia, 243
Casazza, William J Aetna Health of Hawaii, 332
Casazza, William J Aetna Health of Idaho, 344
Casazza, William J Aetna Health of Iowa, 418
Casazza, William J Aetna Health of Kansas, 434
Casazza, William J Aetna Health of Kentucky, 455
Casazza, William J Aetna Health of Louisiana, 470
Casazza, William J Aetna Health of Maine, 487
Casazza, William J Aetna Health of Maryland, 496
Casazza, William J Aetna Health of Massachusetts, 524
Casazza, William J Aetna Health of Michigan, 548
Casazza, William J Aetna Health of Minnesota, 595
Casazza, William J Aetna Health of Mississippi, 624
Casazza, William J Aetna Health of Montana, 662
Casazza, William J Aetna Health of Nebraska, 675
Casazza, William J Aetna Health of New Hampshire, 705
Casazza, William J Aetna Health of New Jersey, 715
Casazza, William J Aetna Health of New Mexico, 742
Casazza, William J Aetna Health of New York, 757
Casazza, William J Aetna Health of North Dakota, 834
Casazza, William J Aetna Health of Oregon, 899
Casazza, William J Aetna Health of Pennsylvania, 926
Casazza, William J Aetna Health of Rhode Island, 985
Casazza, William J Aetna Health of South Dakota, 1013
Casazza, William J Aetna Health of Utah, 1101
Casazza, William J Aetna Health of Vermont, 1117
Casazza, William J Aetna Health of Virginia, 1124
Casazza, William J Aetna Health of Washington, 1148
Casazza, William J Aetna Health of West Virginia, 1172
Casazza, William J Aetna Health of Wisconsin, 1186
Casazza, William J Aetna Health of Wyoming, 1215
Casberg, Jeff, RPh ConnectiCare, 223
Casberg, Jeff ConnectiCare of Massachusetts, 530
Casey, Dennis Anthem Blue Cross & Blue Sheild of Indiana, 391
Casey, Dennis SelectCare Access Corporation, 966
Casey, Dennis W Anthem Blue Cross & Blue Shield of Indiana, 392
Casey, Steven California Dental Network, 94
Cashman, Christopher Independence Blue Cross, 956
Casper, Steven Medfocus Radiology Network, 153
Casper, Wayne M, MD Lovelace Health Plan, 750
Cass, Brady Asuris Northwest Health, 1150
Cass, Danielle Kaiser Permanente Health Plan: Corporate Office, 142
Cassady, Margaret M, Esq Excellus Blue Cross Blue Shield: Central New York, 775
Cassady, Margaret M, Esq Excellus Blue Cross Blue Shield: Utica Region, 777
Cassano, Scott Health Plan of Nevada, 695
Cassell, Jim HSM: Healthcare Cost Management, 607
Cassidy, Andrew Avalon Healthcare, 258
Cassidy, Christine Fallon Community Health Plan, 533
Cassidy, Christine Fallon Community Medicare Plan, 534
Castillo, Mayra Vision Plan of America, 185
Castleberry, Mike HealthSCOPE Benefits, 73
Castro, Ann Marie CIGNA HealthCare of New Jersey, 723
Catalano, Charles CIGNA HealthCare of New Jersey, 723
Cataldi, Pauline Blue Cross & Blue Shield of Western New York, 762
Cataldo, Jeanette Chiropractic Health Plan of California, 103
Cataldo, Jeanette ChiroSource Inc, 104
Cataldo, Jeanette Preferred Utilization Management Inc, 168
Cataldo, Ronald, DC Chiropractic Health Plan of California, 103
Cataldo, Ronald, DC Preferred Utilization Management Inc, 168
Cataldo, Ronald S, DC Chiropractic Health Plan of California, 103
Cataldo, Ronald S, DC ChiroSource Inc, 104

Cataldo, Todd Chiropractic Health Plan of California, 103
Cataldo, Todd ChiroSource Inc, 104
Catino, Annette QualCare, 737
Cato, Rose Anne QualChoice/QCA Health Plan, 76
Caudill, Dr Paul HealthPartners, 1037
Caufield, Mary, MD CIGNA HealthCare of Georgia, 316
Cavalier, Kevin SummaCare Health Plan, 875
Cavalier, Kevin SummaCare Medicare Advantage Plan, 876
Caylor, Carole Health Choice LLC, 1036
Cega, Sam Preferred Therapy Providers, 57
Cenachetti, Mark Tufts Health Plan: Rhode Island, 993
Cesare, Denise Blue Cross of Northeastern Pennsylvania, 933
Cesare, Denise First Priority Health, 946
Cetti, William CIGNA HealthCare of Alaska, 21
Cetti, William CIGNA HealthCare of Colorado, 197
Cetti, William CIGNA HealthCare of Montana, 665
Cetti, William CIGNA HealthCare of Wyoming, 1217
Chabon, Robert, MD Community Health Improvement Solutions, 641
Chaet, Douglas L Independence Blue Cross, 956
Chagolla, Lilia Central California Alliance for Health, 100
Chaitkin, Paul, MD First Commonwealth, 368
Challenger, Keith Crescent Preferred Provider Organization, 820
Challis, David Nevada Preferred Healthcare Providers, 700
Chambers, Mary Beth Blue Cross & Blue Shield of Kansas, 436
Chambers, Richard CalOptima, 96
Champney, Dan E, Esq HealthPlus of Michigan: Flint, 574
Champney, Dan E, Esq HealthPlus of Michigan: Saginaw, 575
Chandler, Greg Blue Cross & Blue Shield of Georgia, 315
Chandler, H Jody Blue Cross & Blue Shield of Arizona, 36
Chandler Holt, Jane Blue Cross & Blue Shield of Kansas, 436
Chandra, Kathy National Capital PPO, 1138
Chaney, G Mark CareFirst Blue Cross & Blue Shield of Virginia, 1127
Chaney, Jared HMO Health Ohio, 858
Chaney, Jared Medical Mutual of Ohio, 862
Chaney, Jared Medical Mutual of Ohio Medicare Plan, 863
Chaney, Jared SuperMed One, 878
Chaney, Mark CareFirst Blue Cross Blue Shield, 244
Channing, Walter, Jr American WholeHealth Network, 928
Chansler, Jeffrey D GHI Medicare Plan, 779
Chansler, Jeffrey D Group Health Incorporated (GHI), 781
Chapman, Barbara Harvard Pilgrim Health Care, 536
Chapman, Carol Preferred Care, 962
Chapman, Carole Preferred Care, 962
Chapman, Heidi UnitedHealthCare of Louisiana, 484
Chapman, Ronald W, MD Partnership HealthPlan of California, 166
Chase, Deb Priority Partners Health Plans, 520
Chase, Michael D, MD Kaiser Permanente Health Plan of Colorado, 210
Chase, Thomas D Delta Dental of Rhode Island, 989
Chauhan, Roki, MD Premera Blue Cross Blue Shield of Alaska, 27
Chauhan, Roki, MD Premera Blue Cross, 1164
Cheng, John HealthFirst New Jersey Medicare Plan, 729
Cheng, Michael Hawaii Medical Services Association, 338
Chernack, Carol Horizon NJ Health, 732
Chernis, Bob Central California Alliance for Health, 100
Chica, Manuel Leon Medical Centers Health Plan, 290
Chickering, Marcelle Wellmark Health Plan of Iowa, 432
Chilson, Mark CareSource: Michigan, 558
Chilson, Mark CareSource, 849
Chin, Wee Willamette Dental Insurance, 925
Chin, Yuen Willamette Dental Insurance, 925
Chirichella, Linda Avesis: Corporate Headquarters, 34
Chirichella, Linda WellPath: A Coventry Health Care Plan, 833
Chiricosta, Rick HMO Health Ohio, 858
Chiricosta, Rick Medical Mutual of Ohio, 862
Chiricosta, Rick Medical Mutual of Ohio Medicare Plan, 863
Chiricosta, Rick SuperMed One, 878
Chitty, Art Blue Cross & Blue Shield of Texas: Houston, 1054
Choate, Eddie Delta Dental of Arkansas, 71
Chong, Dennis, MD Regence Blue Cross & Blue Shield of Oregon, 919
Chow, Edward, MD Chinese Community Health Plan, 102
Chowning, Betty CHA Health, 458
Choy, Gregory UnitedHealthCare of New York, 810

Chrisman, Carolyn Carilion Health Plans, 1128
Christensen, Barbara Providence Health Plans, 918
Christian, Todd, MBA Nationwide Better Health, 867
Christian-Wills, Theresa Cariten Healthcare, 1031
Christian-Wills, Theresa Cariten Preferred, 1032
Christianson, Blair HMO Colorado, 208
Christianson, R Craig, MD UCare Medicare Plan, 618
Christianson, R Craig, MD UCare Minnesota, 619
Christie, Edward J Magellan Health Services: Corporate Headquarters, 515
Christy, Denise Humana Health Insurance of Michigan, 578
Christy, Paul Physicians United Plan, 295
Chu, Benjamin K, MPH Kaiser Permanente Health Plan of Southern California, 141
Chung, Richard S, MD Hawaii Medical Services Association, 338
Churchill, David Assurant Employee Benefits: Colorado, 193
Cianchette Maker, Andrea Martin's Point HealthCare, 493
Cianciolo, Kirk AvMed Health Plan: Corporate Office, 259
Cianfrocco, Healther Unison Health Plan of Pennsylvania, 970
Cichon, Kristen Grand Valley Health Plan, 568
Cierpka, Lisa, RN Quality Health Plans, 298
Cierpka, Lisa, RN Quality Health Plans of New York, 807
Ciorletti, Julia Bravo Health: Corporate Headquarters, 502
Cirrocchi, Michael Cofinity, 560
Claborn, Renee Health Net Health Plan of Oregon, 909
Clancy, Mike Southeastern Indiana Health Organization, 413
Clarey, Patricia T Health Net: Corporate Headquarters, 132
Clark, Alan Southeastern Indiana Health Organization, 413
Clark, Debby American Specialty Health, 82
Clark, John, MD Pacific Health Alliance, 161
Clark, Karen Managed Healthcare Systems of New Jersey, 734
Clark, Karen L Horizon NJ Health, 732
Clark, Kelly J, MD CDPHP Medicare Plan, 764
Clark, Kelly J, MD CDPHP: Capital District Physicians' Health Plan, 765
Clark, Michael Delta Dental: Corporate Headquarters, 563
Clark, Monty Gundersen Lutheran Health Plan, 1199
Clark, Roger E, DDS Superior Dental Care, 877
Clark, Scott Total Dental Administrators, 59
Clark, Scott Scott & White Health Plan, 1087
Clarren, Steven N American Community Mutual Insurance Company, 549
Clawson, Bryon Regence Blue Cross & Blue Shield of Utah, 1112
Clay, Brett Altius Health Plans, 1102
Clemente, Gina Managed Health Network, 150
Clements, Amber R Quality Health Plans, 298
Clements, Amber R Quality Health Plans of New York, 807
Clemons, Gordon CorVel Corporation, 114
Clepper, Frank Delta Dental of Kansas, 440
Click, Rick Arcadian Health Plans, 83
Click, Rick Molina Healthcare: Washington, 1161
Clothier, Brad Preferred Health Systems Insurance Company, 447
Clothier, Brad Preferred Plus of Kansas, 449
Cobb, Lisa Interplan Health Group, 139, 1076
Coburn, Nancy Neighborhood Health Plan of Rhode Island, 992
Cochran, Jim South Central Preferred, 967
Cochran, Richard Coventry Health Care of Nebraska, 679
Coffey, Pamela HealthSmart Preferred Care, 1070
Coffman, Melissa Unicare: West Virginia, 1183
Cofield, Barry Priority Health, 585
Cogar, Mary Cariten Healthcare, 1031
Cogar, Mary Cariten Preferred, 1032
Cohen, Gerald Coventry Health Care of Florida, 274
Cohen, William Avesis: Corporate Headquarters, 34
Cohn, Josh Avesis: Corporate Headquarters, 34
Coil, Gerald V Health Net Medicare Plan, 131
Colantuono, Robin AmeriHealth HMO, 232
Colbourne, William A Blue Cross and Blue Shield Association, 360
Cole, David L Trillium Community Health Plan, 921
Cole, Jacqueline DakotaCare, 1017
Coley, Christopher, MD Harvard University Group Health Plan, 537
Coley, Jeff HealthPartners, 1037
Collake, Jeff Cariten Healthcare, 1031
Collake, Jeff Cariten Preferred, 1032
Collien, Brian Unity Health Insurance, 1212

Collins, Denis Pacific Health Alliance, 161
Collins, Fiona, DDS Delta Dental of Colorado, 202
Collins, Frank UnitedHealthcare Nevada, 704
Collins, Joseph, MD Health First Health Plans, 282
Collins, R Dennis, MD Santa Clara Family Health Plan, 174
Colquette, Monica Humana Health Insurance of Jacksonville, 286
Colvin, Leslie Ohio Health Choice, 868
Comer, William M, Jr American Specialty Health, 82
Commander, Richard Fallon Community Health Plan, 533
Commander, Richard Fallon Community Medicare Plan, 534
Comrie, Dan J Citrus Health Care, 271
Comrie, Daniel J PacifiCare of Oklahoma, 897
Comrie, Greg Coalition America's National Preferred Provider Network, 767
Conley, Shannon Trillium Community Health Plan, 921
Conlin, Marci HealthSmart Preferred Care, 1070
Conlin, Paul Oxford Health Plans: New Jersey, 736
Connelly, Mike PacifiCare Health Systems, 164
Connolly, Karen Total Health Care, 589
Connors, Colleen Blue Cross & Blue Shield of Minnesota, 599
Consie, Mary Maricopa Integrated Health System/Maricopa Health Plan, 50
Consie, Mary University Family Care Health Plan, 62
Constantine, Timothy J Blue Cross & Blue Shield of Delaware, 233
Conte, Sue Capital Health Plan, 268
Cook, Anthony A The Dental Care Plus Group, 879
Cook, Bill Blue Cross & Blue Shield of Georgia, 315
Cook, Connie OptiCare Managed Vision, 828
Cook, Ken First Care Health Plans, 1065
Cook, Larry N, MD Passport Health Plan, 466
Cook, Wayne Evercare Health Plans, 603
Cooney, Kathy Health Partners Medicare Plan, 605
Cooney, Kathy HealthPartners, 606
Cooper, Christina C WellCare Health Plans, 307
Cooper, Margie Liberty Health Plan: Corporate Office, 912
Cooper, Norma Delta Dental of New Mexico, 746
Cooper, Richard Arkansas Blue Cross and Blue Shield, 66
Cooper, Sunny San Francisco Health Plan, 173
Cooper, Walter W WellCare Health Plans, 307
Cooperstone, Elliot Meritain Health: Corporate Headquarters, 792
Copeland, Ronald Louis, MD Kaiser Permanente Health Plan Ohio, 861
Coplin, Terry W Trillium Community Health Plan, 921
Corbett, Rick P Superior Vision Services, Inc., 178
Corbin, Andrew C Advance Insurance Company of Kansas, 433
Corbin, Andrew C. Blue Cross & Blue Shield of Kansas, 436
Corcoran, Mark Affinity Health Plan, 758
Corcoran, Mark T Carolina Care Plan, 999
Cordani, David CIGNA HealthCare of Connecticut, 222
Cordani, David CIGNA HealthCare of North Texas, 1057
Cordani, David M CIGNA HealthCare of North Carolina, 818
Cordani, David M CIGNA: Corporate Headquarters, 939
Cordier, Susan Care 1st Health Plan: Arizona, 37
Cormany, Doug Preferred Care Partners, 296
Corral, Melissa D Northeast Georgia Health Partners, 326
Corrao, William, MD UnitedHealthCare of Rhode Island, 994
Corrigan, Rob CoreSource: Corporate Headquarters, 364
Cory, Pat Unity Health Insurance, 1212
Corzine, Jeff Unison Health Plan of Ohio, 881
Costa, Don PacifiCare of Washington, 1163
Costal, Steffanie Care 1st Health Plan: Arizona, 37
Costrich, Timothy D, MD CHA Health, 458
Coto, Ramon Neighborhood Health Partnership, 293
Cotton, David B, MD Health Plan of Michigan, 573
Cotton, Jon Health Plan of Michigan, 573
Cotton, Michael Health Plan of Michigan, 573
Cotton, Michael L Alere Health, 309
Cotton, Sean P, JD Health Plan of Michigan, 573
Cotton, Shery L Health Plan of Michigan, 573
Couch, Beth North Alabama Managed Care Inc, 14
Couch, Jim QualChoice/QCA Health Plan, 76
Coulter, Steve, MD Blue Cross & Blue Shield of Tennessee, 1030
Courchaine, Dolph M-Care, 579
Couret, Michael E, DDS Delta Dental Northeast, 708
Course, Steve BEST Life and Health Insurance Co., 90

Coussoule, Nick Blue Cross & Blue Shield of Tennessee, 1030
Covas, Sergie Total Health Choice, 300
Covington, David Magellan Health Services Arizona, 49
Covne, Michael W CNA Insurance Companies: Colorado, 198
Covne, Michael W CNA Insurance Companies: Georgia, 317
Covne, Michael W CNA Insurance Companies: Illinois, 362
Coward, Grace Quality Plan Administrators, 251
Cowdrey, Lori Health Alliance Medical Plans, 371
Cox, Belinda, RN/CPHQ Carolina Care Plan, 999
Cox, Karen ProviDRs Care Network, 451
Cox, Mary PacifiCare of Washington, 1163
Cox, Mel HealthSCOPE Benefits, 73
Cox, Susan Spectera, 521
Cox, Susan E Spectera, 521
Coyle, John W Trigon Health Care, 1143
Coyne, Frank C Blue Cross and Blue Shield Association, 360
Cragin, John Boston Medical Center Healthnet Plan, 528
Craig, Peter B Emerald Health PPO, 854
Cramer, Christine CVS CareMark, 988
Cramer, Samuel, MD Anthem Blue Cross & Blue Sheild of Indiana, 391
Crane, Gary Fidelis Care, 778
Cranston, Chad Total Dental Administrators, 59
Crapsey, Chris HealthSpan, 857
Crawford, Bobbie Jo Virginia Health Network, 1146
Crawford, Lowell John Deere Health, 1042
Creech, Helen AvMed Health Plan: Gainesville, 261
Crilly, Tim J Blue Cross & Blue Shield of Wyoming, 1216
Crisafi, Joe, CPA CompCare: Comprehensive Behavioral Care, 273
Crisp, Sherry L Delta Dental of Michigan, Ohio and Indiana, 399, 852
Crisp, Sherry L. Delta Dental: Corporate Headquarters, 563
Crockett, Gary, Esq CalOptima, 96
Croffy, Bruce, MD Blue Cross of Idaho Health Service, Inc., 345
Crooms, John, Jr. Delta Dental of California, 115
Cropp, Michael W, MD Independent Health, 787
Cropp, Michael W, MD Independent Health Medicare Plan, 788
Crosby, David HealthPlus of Michigan: Flint, 574
Crosby, David HealthPlus Senior Medicare Plan, 577
Crosby, David P HealthPlus of Michigan: Saginaw, 575
Crosby, Lynette Delta Dental of California, 115
Cross, Gregory Blue Cross & Blue Shield of Louisiana, 472
Croswell, Thomas A Tufts Health Medicare Plan, 543
Croswell, Thomas A Tufts Health Plan, 544
Crouch, Jeff Blue Cross of Idaho Health Service, Inc., 345
Crow, Randall A QualChoice/QCA Health Plan, 76
Crowley, Daniel D HealthSmart Preferred Care, 1070
Crowley, Mike Wellmark Health Plan of Iowa, 432
Crusse, John Humana Health Insurance of Michigan, 578
Cuchel, Stephen, DDS Healthplex, 785
Cueny, Doug AvMed Health Plan: Fort Lauderdale, 260
Cuifo, John, DPh Cariten Healthcare, 1031
Cuifo, John, DPh Cariten Preferred, 1032
Culberson, Lynne Dental Network of America, 366
Cullen, Caron Affinity Health Plan, 758
Culyba, Michael, MD UPMC Health Plan, 973
Cumming, Gord Independent Health, 787
Cumming, Gord Independent Health Medicare Plan, 788
Cummings, Scott Care 1st Health Plan: Arizona, 37
Cummins, Susan Anthem Blue Cross & Blue Sheild of Indiana, 391
Cunningham, Alec WellCare Health Plans, 307
Cunningham, Bart Windsor Medicare Extra, 1045
Cunningham, Kim, SPHR CalOptima, 96
Cunningham, Rachelle Regence Blue Shield, 1166
Cunningham, Steve UnitedHealthCare of Louisiana, 484
Curcio, Maryann Valley Preferred, 975
Curcio, Trina L Val-U-Health, 974
Curle, Jay Assurant Employee Benefits: Wisconsin, 1188
Curley, Jay Blue Cross & Blue Shield of Massachusetts, 527
Curran, Joan Gundersen Lutheran Health Plan, 1199
Currier, Cecile CONCERN: Employee Assistance Program, 112
Curry, Donald M CIGNA HealthCare of Massachusetts, 529
Curry, Joanne DakotaCare, 1017
Curtis, Mildred EyeMed Vision Care, 855

Cushman, William H American Pioneer Life Insurance Co, 255
Custer, Timothy J Dental Network of America, 366
Cusumano, Jim MagnaCare, 791
Cutsinger, Jennifer Southeastern Indiana Health Organization, 413
Cymerys, Ed Blue Shield of California, 91
Cymerys, Edward PacifiCare Health Systems, 164
Czelada, Laura L, CPA Delta Dental of Michigan, Ohio and Indiana, 399
Czelada, Laura L, CPA Delta Dental: Corporate Headquarters, 563
Czelada, Laura L, CPA Delta Dental of Michigan, Ohio and Indiana, 852
Czyzewski, Sharon UPMC Health Plan, 973

D

D'Alessio, James Horizon NJ Health, 732
D'Alessio, M Walter Independence Blue Cross, 956
Dabuni, Ziad, MD Lakeside Community Healthcare Network, 146
Daddario, Don Health Partners Medicare Plan, 950
Dallafior, Kenneth R Blue Cross Blue Shield of Michigan, 556
Daly, Marilyn Neighborhood Health Plan, 542
Daly Lauenstein, Teri Community Health Plan of Los Angeles County, 111
Daniels, Joni S QualChoice/QCA Health Plan, 76
Daniels, Laird CVS CareMark, 988
Dankoff, Tracy SummaCare Health Plan, 875
Dankoff, Tracy SummaCare Medicare Advantage Plan, 876
Danz, Kris EHP, 944
Darnley, Patricia J Centene Corporation, 638
Dart, Jacqueline WellPoint NextRx, 1100
Datko, Rita Sharp Health Plan, 176
Dauner, Beth PCC Preferred Chiropractic Care, 446
Dauner, Marlon R Preferred Health Systems Insurance Company, 447
Dauner, Marlon R Preferred Plus of Kansas, 449
Davalos, Gail Delta Dental of New Mexico, 746
Dave, Santosh Beech Street Corporation: Corporate Office, 87
Davenport, Becky Kern Family Health Care, 144
Davenport, Terry J Select Health of South Carolina, 1008
David, Lyle Wisconsin Physician's Service, 1214
Davidson, Alphonzo L, DDS Quality Plan Administrators, 251
Davidson, Charles E SelectCare Access Corporation, 966
Davidson, Peter PacificSource Health Plans: Corporate Headquarters, 917
Davidson, Peter Fletcher Trillium Community Health Plan, 921
Davies, Matthew UnitedHealthCare of Florida, 302
Davies, PV, II Delta Dental of Virginia, 1131
Davila, Juan Blue Shield of California, 91
Davis, Barry Block Vision of Texas, 1052
Davis, Ben Dental Benefit Providers, 509
Davis, Benton UnitedHealthCare of Arizona, 61
Davis, Collin University Health Plans, 1116
Davis, Cosby Coventry Health Care of West Virginia, 1174
Davis, David J Atrio Health Plans, 901
Davis, DeDe Passport Health Plan, 466
Davis, Duane E, MD Geisinger Health Plan, 948
Davis, James Delta Dental of Arizona, 40
Davis, John OptiCare Managed Vision, 828
Davis, Joyzelle Anthem Blue Cross & Blue Shield of Colorado, 192
Davis, Michael Dominion Dental Services, 1132
Davis, Patrisha L Coventry Health Care: Corporate Headquarters, 506
Davis, Philip M Wellmark Blue Cross & Blue Shield of South Dakota, 1025
Davis, Stephanie Excellus Blue Cross Blue Shield: Utica Region, 777
Davis, Thomas Coventry Health Care of GA, 319
Davis, Tina Select Health of South Carolina, 1008
Davis, Tom Davis Vision, 769
Davis, Wally Health Link PPO, 628
Dawes, Christopher Santa Clara Family Health Plan, 174
Dawson, Bob HealthSpring of Alabama, 12
Day, Stephen Delta Dental of Kentucky, 461
De Palo, Armand M Guardian Life Insurance Company, 782
De Pasquale, Ed Penn Highlands Health Plan, 961
De Rosa, Chris CIGNA HealthCare of Southern California, 107
DeBerry, Ron Arkansas Blue Cross and Blue Shield, 66
Debner, Donna L Citrus Health Care, 271
DeBold, Cheryl HAS-Premier Providers, 1068
Decamp, Cody R Western Dental Services, 188
Decker, Camissa Health Plus of Louisiana, 479

Decker, Chad Health Resources, Inc., 405
Degenfelder, Pauline HealthAmerica Pennsylvania, 952
DeGruttola, John Optima Health Plan, 1139
DeHann, Jan Gundersen Lutheran Health Plan, 1199
Dehls Cornell, Lois Tufts Health Medicare Plan, 543
Dehls Cornell, Lois Tufts Health Plan, 544
DeLaine, Brenna, MD Unison Health Plan of South Carolina, 1010
DeLeo, Caesar A, MD Gateway Health Plan, 947
deLorimer, John A. Concentra: Corporate Office, 1060
DeLuca, Renee Kaiser Permanente Health Plan Ohio, 861
Deluca, Renee M Kaiser Permanente Health Plan Ohio, 861
Delvalle, Mona Ohio Health Choice, 868
Dembereckyj, Bill Interplan Health Group, 139, 1076
Dembereckyj, William HealthSmart Preferred Care, 1070
Demilio, Mark S Magellan Health Services Indiana, 408
Demmer, Gerry Network Health Plan of Wisconsin, 1206
DeMonteverde, Michelle CIGNA HealthCare of Southern California, 107
DeMontmollin, Stephen J AvMed Health Plan: Corporate Office, 259
DeMoss, Lisa S Blue Care Network of Michigan: Corporate Headquarters, 551
DeMoss, Lisa S Blue Care Network: Flint, 554
DeMoss, Lisa S Blue Care Network: Great Lakes, Muskegon Heights, 555
Demosthenes, Jim CIGNA HealthCare of New Hampshire, 707
DeMovick, Harvey C, Jr Coventry Health Care of Kansas, 439
DeMovick, Harvey C, Jr HealthAmerica, 951
Dempsey, Francis P American Community Mutual Insurance Company, 549
Dengler, Stephen HealthAmerica Pennsylvania, 952
Denton, David M CVS CareMark, 988
DeQuatro, Marilyn GHI Medicare Plan, 779
DeQuatro, Marilyn Group Health Incorporated (GHI), 781
DeQuatro, Marilyn Health Plan of New York, 783
DeQuatro, Marilyn UnitedHealthCare of North Carolina, 832
Derdinski, Michael Humana Health Insurance of Wisconsin, 1202
Derr, Joanne Neighborhood Health Plan, 542
Desai, A.K., MD, MPH Universal Health Care Group, 304
Deters, Beth Deaconess Health Plans, 398
DeTurk, Nanette P Highmark Blue Cross & Blue Shield, 953
DeTurk, Nanette P Highmark Blue Shield, 954
Deus, Frank N, MD Peoples Health, 482
Devaux, Deborah Blue Cross & Blue Shield of Massachusetts, 527
DeVeydt, Wayne S WellPoint: Corporate Office, 417
DeVille, Greg Beech Street Corporation: Alabama, 3
DeVille, Greg Beech Street: Alaska, 19
Devou, Gregory A CareFirst Blue Cross & Blue Shield of Virginia, 1127
DeVries, George American Specialty Health, 82
Dewester, Gerald American Health Network of Indiana, 390
Dhaliwal, Amarjit, MD Stanislaus Foundation for Medical Care, 177
Diamond, David A Mutual of Omaha DentaBenefits, 684
Diamond, David A Mutual of Omaha Health Plans, 685
Diaz, Norma Community Health Group, 110
Diaz-Esquivel, Pablo, MD Alliance Regional Health Network, 1047
Dickes, Robert M Carolina Care Plan, 999
Dicks, Joseph MetroPlus Health Plan, 793
Dickson, Jan Health Choice LLC, 1036
Diehs, Creta Dimension Health PPO, 276
Diercks, David Unity Health Insurance, 1212
Dill, Matthew G Midlands Choice, 683
Dillard, Gray Arkansas Blue Cross and Blue Shield, 66
DiMarco, Arthur Perfect Health Insurance Company, 806
DiMura, Vincent, CPA Meritain Health: Corporate Headquarters, 792
Dishman, Pam Delta Dental of Tennessee, 1034
Disser, E J Preferred Vision Care, 450
Disser, Michele G, RN Preferred Vision Care, 450
Disser, P J Preferred Vision Care, 450
DiTorro, Frank Blue Cross & Blue Shield of Kansas City, 636
Dockins, Jim HealthPartners, 1037
Dodge, Patrick Atlantis Health Plan, 761
Dodt, Sandy Preferred Therapy Providers, 57
Doerr, R Chris Blue Cross & Blue Shield of Florida: Jacksonville, 266
Doerr, R Chris Blue Cross & Blue Shield of Florida: Pensacola, 267
Doherty, Michelle American Pioneer Life Insurance Co, 255
Dolan, Michael J, MD Gundersen Lutheran Health Plan, 1199
Dolatowski, Tom ODS Alaska, 26

Dolloff, Gaylee Health Partners of Kansas, 443
Dolsky, Mark G Blue Cross & Blue Shield of Kansas, 436
Donaldson, William H Aetna Health of the Carolinas, 814
Donigan, Heyward Premera Blue Cross Blue Shield of Alaska, 27
Donohoe, Cindy Great-West Healthcare of Massachusetts, 535
Donohue, Fay Dentaquest, 531
Donovan, Leann Denver Health Medical Plan Inc, 203
Donovan, Raymond Athens Area Health Plan Select, 313
Doolen, Erick PacificSource Health Plans: Corporate Headquarters, 917
Dooley, Ronald SVS Vision, 588
Dopps, Brad, DC PCC Preferred Chiropractic Care, 446
Dopps, John, DC PCC Preferred Chiropractic Care, 446
Dopps, Mark, DC PCC Preferred Chiropractic Care, 446
Dopps, Robert, DC PCC Preferred Chiropractic Care, 446
Dore, Alfred, Jr HealthAmerica, 951
Doria, Norma Community First Health Plans, 1059
Dorman-Rodriguez, Deborah Health Care Service Corporation, 373
Dorney, William, MD American WholeHealth Network, 928
Dorney, William P, Dr American WholeHealth Network, 928
Dorr, Marjorie Anthem Blue Cross & Blue Shield Connecticut, 220
Dorr, Marjorie Anthem Blue Cross & Blue Shield of Maine, 488
Double, Mary American Health Care Group, 927
Dougan, Gary Pacific Dental Benefits, 159
Douglass, Lee Arkansas Blue Cross and Blue Shield, 66
Dowd Gurber, Tara Health Care Service Corporation, 373
Dowdy, Shelly American PPO, 1048
Dowling, Greg Assurant Employee Benefits: Texas, 1050
Downey, Ellen American Community Mutual Insurance Company, 549
Downey, Ellen M Care Choices, 557
Downs, Barbara A, RN CDPHP Medicare Plan, 764
Downs, Barbara A, RN CDPHP: Capital District Physicians' Health Plan, 765
Doyle, Anne Fallon Community Health Plan, 533
Doyle, Anne Fallon Community Medicare Plan, 534
Doyle, John Dental Network of America, 366
Doyle, John DenteMax, 565
Doyle, Michael Mercy Health Plans: Kansas, 445
Doyle, Michael Mercy Health Medicare Plan, 654
Doyle, Michael Mercy Health Plans: Corporate Office, 655
Doyle, Michael Mercy Health Plans: Oklahoma, 896
Doyle Steranka, Sarah American Health Care Group, 927
Dozoretz, Dr Ronald Value Behavioral Health of Pennsylvania, 976
Draper, Gene Foundation for Medical Care for Mendocino and Lake Counties, 124
Drean, Lauretta New West Health Services, 672
Drean, Lauretta New West Medicare Plan, 673
Dreibelbis, Dawn Berkshire Health Partners, 932
Dreyfus, Andrew Blue Cross & Blue Shield of Massachusetts, 527
Drnevich, Ronald Capital Blue Cross, 936
Druker, Michele Wellmark Health Plan of Iowa, 432
Dubbs, Allison The Dental Care Plus Group, 879
Dubeck, Frank, MD Excellus Blue Cross Blue Shield: Rochester Region, 776
Dubeck, Frank, MD Excellus Blue Cross Blue Shield: Utica Region, 777
Duce, Scott CIGNA HealthCare of St. Louis, 640
DuCharme, James Harvard Pilgrim Health Care, 536
Duda, Emil D Univera Healthcare, 811
Dudley, G Martin InterGroup Services Corporation, 957
Dudley, Gregory InterGroup Services Corporation, 957
Dudley, Michael M Optima Health Plan, 1139
Duer, Linda Primary Health Plan, 354
Duford, Don One Call Medical, 735
Dugan, Chris Anthem Blue Cross & Blue Shield of Maine, 488
Dugan, Chris Anthem Blue Cross & Blue Shield of New Hampshire, 706
Dugan, Pat HMO Health Ohio, 858
Dugan, Pat Medical Mutual of Ohio, 862
Dugan, Pat Medical Mutual of Ohio Medicare Plan, 863
Dugan, Pat SuperMed One, 878
Dukes, Kim UnitedHealthCare of Mississippi, 630
Dula, Jackie Crescent Preferred Provider Organization, 820
Dulin, Joseph USA Managed Care Organization, 1096
Dunaway, George CompBenefits Corporation, 318
Dunaway, Suzie Children's Mercy Family Health Partners, 639
Duncan, Pat Rocky Mountain Health Plans, 213

Dunk, Jeanne Care Choices, 557
Dunlop, Richard UnitedHealthCare of Kentucky, 469
Dunn, Molly Assurant Employee Benefits: Michigan, 550
Dunn, Van, MD MetroPlus Health Plan, 793
Dunn, Zon Superior Vision Services, Inc., 178
Dunn-Malhotra, Ellen Health Plan of San Mateo, 134
Dunne, Lucille, RN Island Group Administration, Inc., 789
Durr, Barbara HealthSpan, 857
Duvall, Dianna D Assurant Employee Benefits: Corporate Headquarters, 635
Dworak, Jerry Blue Cross of Idaho Health Service, Inc., 345
Dwyer, Jim Delta Dental of Washington, 1153
Dwyer, Thomas K GHI Medicare Plan, 779
Dwyer, Thomas K Group Health Incorporated (GHI), 781
Dwyer, Thomas K Health Plan of New York, 783
Dykes, Cathy Southeastern Indiana Health Organization, 413

E

Earl, Chris Delta Dental of Nebraska, 680
Earley, J Fred Mountain State Blue Cross Blue Shiled, 1181
Earling, Eric Premera Blue Cross Blue Shield of Alaska, 27
Earling, Eric Lifewise Health Plan of Washington, 1160
Earling, Eric Premera Blue Cross, 1164
Early, Karen Blue Cross of Idaho Health Service, Inc., 345
Eastham, James, MD/FACC Valley Baptist Health Plan, 1098
Ebbin, Allan, MD, MPH UnitedHealthcare Nevada, 704
Ebenkamp, Bob Delta Dental of Kansas, 440
Ebert, Mike OneNet PPO, 518
Ebert, Thomas H, MD Health New England, 538
Eck, Brian UCare Medicare Plan, 618
Eck, Brian UCare Minnesota, 619
Eckbert, William, MD Horizon Health Corporation, 1073
Eckrich, Nancy CoreSource: Corporate Headquarters, 364
Eckstein, Michael Health Tradition, 1200
Edelman, Kathy Cofinity, 560
Edelstein, Marc, MD AvMed Health Plan: Orlando, 263
Eden, Mary Presbyterian Health Plan, 753
Eden, Mary Presbyterian Medicare Plans, 754
Eder, Dennis SCAN Health Plan, 175
Edmondson, Mike BlueLincs HMO, 888
Edmondson, Robert E On Lok Lifeways, 157
Edmunds, Daryl CIGNA HealthCare of Colorado, 197
Edwards, Joe HealthSCOPE Benefits, 73
Edwards, Kathy Cardinal Health Alliance, 396
Edwards, Z Colette, MD CIGNA HealthCare of West Virginia, 1173
Edynak, Eugene, MD JMH Health Plan, 289
Efrusy, Brian Total Health Care, 589
Eftekhari, Amir Americas PPO, 1014
Eftekhari, Nazie Araz Group, 596
Eftekhari, Nazie Americas PPO, 1014
Egan, Rob Tufts Health Medicare Plan, 543
Egan, Rob Tufts Health Plan, 544
Egbert, Jeff Abrazo Advantage Health Plan, 29
Eichenberg, Karen Paramount Care of Michigan, 583
Eichenberg, Karen Paramount Elite Medicare Plan, 871
Eichenberg, Karen Paramount Health Care, 872
Einboden, Allan Scott & White Health Plan, 1087
Eisenhardt, Barbara HealthSpan, 857
El-Azma, Majd Lifewise Health Plan of Oregon, 913
Elgin, Amber Lifewise Health Plan of Oregon, 913
Elkin, Mel Carilion Health Plans, 1128
Eller, Kim Peoples Health, 482
Eller, Kim Tenet Choices, 483
Ellerman, Brad Behavioral Healthcare Options, Inc., 690
Ellertson, Chris Health Net Health Plan of Oregon, 909
Ellex, Tina Coalition America's National Preferred Provider Network, 767
Elliot, Eric Aetna Health of Missouri, 632
Elliot, Jennifer Preferred Health Systems Insurance Company, 447
Elliot, Jennifer Preferred Plus of Kansas, 449
Elliott, David R Baptist Health Services Group, 1029
Elliott, Rick UnitedHealthCare of Georgia, 330
Ellis, Lyndle BlueLincs HMO, 888
Ellison, Amy Delta Dental of Kansas, 440

Ellison, Nancy Regence Blue Shield, 1166
Ellwood, Melissa Meritain Health: Corporate Headquarters, 792
Elsas, Robert Davis Vision, 769
Elsberry, Tabatha Health InfoNet, 669
Elser, Diana Puget Sound Health Partners, 1165
Elzen, Jonna Health Choice LLC, 1036
Ely, Grace CareSource Mid Rogue Health Plan, 903
Emerson, Jeff D Magellan Health Services Indiana, 408
Emerson, Paul OptumHealth Care Solutions: Physical Health, 614
Emery, Gene R Delta Dental Northeast, 708
Emmer, Dan Horizon Healthcare of New Jersey, 731
Emory, Charles, PhD Horizon Healthcare of New Jersey, 731
Engelhard, Michael P CalOptima, 96
Engelman, Rebecca, RN Select Health of South Carolina, 1008
England, Pat Kanawha Healthcare Solutions, 1006
England, Patricia Kanawha Healthcare Solutions, 1006
English, George Blue Cross & Blue Shield of Delaware, 233
Enos, Deborah C Neighborhood Health Plan, 542
Enos, Scott E, RPh UnitedHealthCare of Rhode Island, 994
Enriquez, Anna HealthFirst New Jersey Medicare Plan, 729
Enslinger, Lisa American Health Care Alliance, 633
Ensner, Lynda Welborn Health Plans, 416
Eppel, James Blue Cross & Blue Shield of Minnesota, 599
Epstein, Tom Blue Shield of California, 91
Erba, John Dell UnitedHealthCare of the Mid-Atlantic, 523
Ericksen, Jack Blue Cross and Blue Shield Association, 360
Ericksen, Robert A CHN PPO, 722
Erickson, David W Molina Healthcare: Corporate Office, 155
Erickson, Gary Partnership HealthPlan of California, 166
Erkenbrack, Steven Rocky Mountain Health Plans, 213
Ertel, Al Alliant Health Plans, 310
Ervin, Candace Advantage Health Solutions, 388
Esser, Deb, MD UnitedHealthCare of Nebraska, 686
Eudell, Nasia Quality Plan Administrators, 251
Evans, Bill Nationwide Better Health, 867
Evans, Nichole Health Alliance Medical Plans, 371
Everett, Junetta Delta Dental of Kansas, 440

F

Fahey, Ronald Medical Associates Health Plan: East, 1204
Fahnestock, George Preferred Health Systems Insurance Company, 447
Fahnestock, George Preferred Plus of Kansas, 449
Faine, Nora, MD Sharp Health Plan, 176
Fairchild, Philip Select Health of South Carolina, 1008
Falcone, Charles Devon Health Services, 942
Falhman, Robert Arcadian Health Plans, 83
Faller, Keith Anthem Blue Cross & Blue Sheild of Indiana, 391
Fallon, Christopher WellChoice, 741
Fallon, John, MD Blue Cross & Blue Shield of Massachusetts, 527
Fandricch, William Blue Cross & Blue Shield of Massachusetts, 527
Farasce, Theresa UnitedHealthCare of the Mid-Atlantic, 523
Farbacher, Elizabeth A Highmark Blue Cross & Blue Shield, 953
Farbacher, Elizabeth A Highmark Blue Shield, 954
Farell, James OSF Healthcare, 379
Fargis, Edward C Touchstone Health HMO, 808
Farnsley, John HealthSmart Preferred Care, 374
Farrante, Michael HealthEOS, 1201
Farrell, Barbara Bluegrass Family Health, 457
Farrell, James Humana Benefit Plan of Illinois, 376
Farrell, James G OSF Healthcare, 379
Farrell, Lisa Presbyterian Health Plan, 753
Farrell, Lisa Presbyterian Medicare Plans, 754
Farrell, Paul Coventry Health Care of GA, 319
Farrell, Robert G, Jr SVS Vision, 588
Farren, Linda Perfect Health Insurance Company, 806
Farrer, Bob Hometown Health Plan, 696
Farrow, Peter Group Health Cooperative of Eau Claire, 1197
Fasano, Phil Kaiser Permanente Health Plan of Northern California, 140
Fasano, Phil Kaiser Permanente Health Plan of Southern California, 141
Fasano, Phil Kaiser Permanente Health Plan: Corporate Office, 142
Fasano, Phil Kaiser Permanente Medicare Plan, 143
Fassenfelt, Chris Liberty Health Plan: Corporate Office, 912

Fast, Patricia The Health Plan of the Upper Ohio Valley, 880
Faulds, Thomas Blue Cross & Blue Shield of South Carolina, 997
Faulkner II, R. Blaine First Health, 369
Faust-Thomas, Brenda National Capital PPO, 1138
Faxio, Charles, MD Medica Health - Medicare Plan, 609
Fay, George R CNA Insurance Companies: Colorado, 198
Fay, George R CNA Insurance Companies: Georgia, 317
Fay, George R CNA Insurance Companies: Illinois, 362
Fay, Michael D Wellmark Health Plan of Iowa, 432
Fazio, Charles, MD Medica: Corporate Office, 610
Fazio, Charles, MD Medica: North Dakota, 841
Fazio, Charles, MD Medica: South Dakota, 1023
Feagin, Card VIVA Health, 17
Featherman, Lisa Central Susquehanna Healthcare Providers, 937
Federico, Francesco, MD Lakeside Community Healthcare Network, 146
Fedyna, Michael W Empire Blue Cross & Blue Shield, 774
Fee, David Humana Health Insurance of Wisconsin, 1202
Feeny, Kathy Secure Horizons, 77
Fein, Harvey A Molina Healthcare: Corporate Office, 155
Feingold, Orrin HealthEOS, 1201
Feld, Judith, MD Independent Health, 787
Feld, Judith, MD Independent Health Medicare Plan, 788
Feldman, Eli S Elderplan, 773
Feldman, James, DDS Dencap Dental Plans, 564
Feldman, Karen Golden West Dental & Vision Plan, 126
Feldman, Nancy J UCare Medicare Plan, 618
Feldman, Nancy J UCare Minnesota, 619
Felix, Carl Bluegrass Family Health, 457
Felix, John Henry Hawaii Medical Assurance Association, 337
Felsing, Bill Trilogy Health Insurance, 1210
Felsing, William UnitedHealthCare of Wisconsin: Central, 622
Felts, Tony Unicare: Illinois, 385
Felts, Tony Anthem Blue Cross & Blue Sheild of Indiana, 391
Felts, Tony Unicare: Kansas, 452
Felts, Tony Unicare: Massachusetts, 545
Felts, Tony Unicare: Michigan, 590
Felts, Tony Unicare: Texas, 1093
Felts, Tony Unicare: West Virginia, 1183
Fennel, Edward Blue Cross of Northeastern Pennsylvania, 933
Fenster, Dennis S. PreferredOne, 616
Ferguson, Bill BlueChoice Health Plan of South Carolina, 998
Fernandez, Albert UnitedHealthCare of South Florida, 303
Fernandez, Luis Leon Medical Centers Health Plan, 290
Ferrante, Michael MultiPlan, Inc., 794
Ferraro, Stephen Galaxy Health Network, 1066
Ferreira, Alice AmeriChoice by UnitedHealthcare, 219
Ferry, Renee Central Susquehanna Healthcare Providers, 937
Feruck, Dan Aetna Health of Georgia, 308
Feruck, Dan Humana Health Insurance of Georgia, 323
Feuerman, Jason Bravo Health: Corporate Headquarters, 502
Feuerman, Jason Bravo Health: Pennsylvania, 935
Feyen, Patrick Bravo Health: Corporate Headquarters, 502
Feyen, Patrick Bravo Health: Texas, 1055
Fianu, Peter Meritain Health: Corporate Headquarters, 792
Fickling, William, Jr Beech Street: Alaska, 19
Fickling, William A, Jr Beech Street Corporation: Alabama, 3
Field, Mark Initial Group, 1041
Fielder, Barry, PharmD QualChoice/QCA Health Plan, 76
Fields, Candia CommunityCare Medicare Plan, 891
Fields, David Unicare: Illinois, 385
Fields, David Unicare: Kansas, 452
Fields, David W Unicare: Massachusetts, 545
Fields, David W Unicare: Texas, 1093
Fields, Heidi Blue Shield of California, 91
Fields, Karen Pima Health System, 56
Fienman, Matthew MagnaCare, 791
Fifer Ferry, Karen Boston Medical Center Healthnet Plan, 528
Fike, Randy HealthSpring of Illinois, 375
Files, Shawn C, MD Gateway Health Plan, 947
Film, George Aultcare Corporation, 848
Film, George Prime Time Health Medicare Plan, 873
Findlay, Janet VSP: Vision Service Plan of California, 187

Fingers, David Humana Health Insurnace of Colorado, 209
Finke, Daniel P GHI Medicare Plan, 779
Finke, Daniel P Group Health Incorporated (GHI), 781
Finley, John R Amerigroup Corporation, 1125
Finuf, Bob Children's Mercy Family Health Partners, 639
Fiore, Paula Harvard University Group Health Plan, 537
Fiorina, Stacey Block Vision of New Jersey, 721
Fischer, Greg AvMed Health Plan: Corporate Office, 259
Fischer, Neal, MD Unicare: Texas, 1093
Fish, Mark MVP Health Care: New Hampshire, 712
Fish, Mark MVP Health Care Medicare Plan, 795
Fish, Mark MVP Health Care: Buffalo Region, 796
Fish, Mark MVP Health Care: Central New York, 797
Fish, Mark MVP Health Care: Corporate Office, 798
Fish, Mark MVP Health Care: Mid-State Region, 799
Fish, Mark MVP Health Care: Western New York, 800
Fish, Mark MVP Health Care: Vermont, 1122
Fisher, Andrea Devon Health Services, 942
Fisher, Bruce, MD QualCare, 737
Fisher, Carole A Behavioral Healthcare Options, Inc., 690
Fisher, Larry CompBenefits Corporation, 318
Fisher, Mark Mercy Care Plan/Mercy Care Advantage, 51
Fisher, Marsha ProviDRs Care Network, 451
Fisher, Tammy San Francisco Health Plan, 173
Fitzgerald, Kevin R, MD Rocky Mountain Health Plans, 213
Fitzgibbon, Shawn M GHI Medicare Plan, 779
Fitzgibbon, Shawn M Group Health Incorporated (GHI), 781
Fitzgibbon, Shawn M Health Plan of New York, 783
Fitzpatrick, Maria Coventry Health Care: Corporate Headquarters, 506
Fjelstad, Dani Delta Dental of Minnesota, 601
Fjelstad, Dani Delta Dental of North Dakota, 836
Flachbart, Ray Blue Cross of Idaho Health Service, Inc., 345
Flanagan, Lyn UnitedHealthCare of Ohio: Columbus, 882
Flanagan, Lyn UnitedHealthCare of Ohio: Dayton & Cincinnati, 883
Flanagan, Shannon Behavioral Health Systems, 4
Flanders McGinnis, Gretchen, MSPH Colorado Access, 199
Flasch, H Michael Health Alliance Medicare, 571
Flasch, H Michael Health Alliance Plan, 572
Fleischer, Steven Block Vision, 501
Fleischer, Stuart F National Medical Health Card, 802
Fleming, Katie Health First Health Plans, 282
Fleming, Renee Blue Cross & Blue Shield of Western New York, 762
Fleszar, Thomas, DDS Delta Dental of Michigan, Ohio and Indiana, 399, 852
Fleszar, Thomas J, DDS, MS Delta Dental: Corporate Headquarters, 563
Flora, DeVonna Virginia Health Network, 1146
Flora, Jon Wisconsin Physician's Service, 1214
Florentine, Mauro Humana Health Insurance of Orlando, 287
Flores, Michelle Nevada Preferred Healthcare Providers, 700
Flores-Witte, Amanda Alameda Alliance for Health, 81
Flow, Doug CareSource Mid Rogue Health Plan, 903
Flowers, Sandra D Arizona Foundation for Medical Care, 32
Floyd, Charles D, CEBS Delta Dental of Michigan, Ohio and Indiana, 399, 852
Fluegel, Brad M WellPoint: Corporate Office, 417
Flynn, Barbara, RN Central California Alliance for Health, 100
Flynn, Susan M Val-U-Health, 974
Flynn, Tom Fortified Provider Network, 44
Foels, Thomas J, MD Independent Health, 787
Foels, Thomas J, MD Independent Health Medicare Plan, 788
Fogarty, W Tom, MD Concentra: Corporate Office, 1060
Foley, John Anthem Blue Cross & Blue Shield of Wisconsin, 1187
Foley, Mike Group Health Cooperative, 1157
Folick, Jeff Bravo Health: Corporate Headquarters, 502
Foos, John AmeriHealth HMO, 232
Foos, John G Keystone Health Plan East, 959
Foose, Jon QualChoice/QCA Health Plan, 76
Forbes, Brian Aetna Health of Oklahoma, 885
Ford, David E CareOregon Health Plan, 902
Ford, Milam Blue Cross & Blue Shield of Louisiana, 472
Ford, Tim QualCare, 737
Foreman, Cory UnitedHealthCare of Colorado, 215
Foreman, Roger Blue Cross & Blue Shield of Kansas City, 636
Forino, Andrea HealthFirst New Jersey Medicare Plan, 729

Forney, Drew S Blue Cross of Idaho Health Service, Inc., 345
Forrest, Rochelle, RN Encore Health Network, 402
Forston, Debbie Health Plus of Louisiana, 479
Forsyth, John Wellmark Health Plan of Iowa, 432
Forsyth, John D Wellmark Blue Cross & Blue Shield of South Dakota, 1025
Fort, Glenda Healthcare Partners of East Texas, 1069
Fort, Paul Blue Cross of Northeastern Pennsylvania, 933
Fortner, Scott Central California Alliance for Health, 100
Foss, Robert E Mid Atlantic Medical Services: Delaware, 240
Foss, Robert E Alliance PPO, LLC, 497
Foss, Robert E Mid Atlantic Psychiatric Services (MAMSI), 517
Foss, Robert E Optimum Choice, 519
Foster, Martin G Health Care Service Corporation, 373
Foster, Michael C CareMore Health Plan, 98
Fouberg, Rodney Avera Health Plans, 1015
Foulkes, Helena B CVS CareMark, 988
Fouts, Dr. Terry Great-West Healthcare Oklahoma, 894
Fouts, Terry, MD Great-West Healthcare Delaware, 238
Fouts, Terry, MD Great-West Healthcare of Massachusetts, 535
Fouts, Terry, MD Great-West Healthcare South Dakota, 1021
Fouts, Terry, MD Great-West Healthcare Wisconsin, 1196
Fowler, Patrina Community First Health Plans, 1059
Fowlie, Kate Contra Costa Health Plan, 113
Fox, Alissa Blue Cross and Blue Shield Association, 360
Fox, Jacque PCC Preferred Chiropractic Care, 446
Fox, Keri WINhealth Partners, 1222
Francis, Gary Total Health Care, 589
Frank, Cliff First Care Health Plans, 1065
Frank, Larry NevadaCare, 701
Frank, Michael Blue Cross & Blue Shield of Montana, 664
Frantz, Jim Health Plus of Louisiana, 479
Franz, Phillip AmeriChoice by UnitedHealthCare, 716
Fraser, David Assurant Employee Benefits: Massachusetts, 525
Frederick, John, MD PreferredOne, 616
Frederickson, Paula Partnership HealthPlan of California, 166
Freeman, Jerome, MD Sanford Health Plan, 430
Freeman, Joanna, CPa Superior Vision Services, Inc., 178
Freeman, Nancy Arkansas Community Care, 67
Freeman, Nancy Texas Community Care, 1091
Frenzel, Amy DenteMax, 565
Frey, James Secure Horizons, 77
Frey, James PacifiCare of California, 165
Frey, James PacifiCare of Texas, 1084
Frick, Joseph AmeriHealth HMO, 232
Frick, Joseph A AmeriHealth Medicare Plan, 930
Frick, Joseph A Independence Blue Cross, 956
Frick, Joseph A Keystone Health Plan East, 959
Frieden, Regena Blue Cross & Blue Shield of Arizona, 36
Friedley, Pat Behavioral Health Systems, 4
Friedman, Jack Providence Health Plans, 918
Friedman, Neal South Central Preferred, 967
Friedman, Robert, MD Primary Health Plan, 354
Fries, Scott Evercare Health Plans, 603
Fritch, Herbert HealthSpring: Corporate Offices, 1039
Fritz, James S Bluegrass Family Health, 457
Fritz, Richard A Delta Dental of Rhode Island, 989
Frock, Charles FirstCarolinaCare, 823
Froemming, Renae UCare Medicare Plan, 618
Froemming, Renae UCare Minnesota, 619
Frost, Jami, MD Lovelace Medicare Health Plan, 751
Froyen, Scott Wellmark Health Plan of Iowa, 432
Froyum, Karen HSM: Healthcare Cost Management, 607
Frucella, Maureen Preferred Healthcare System, 964
Fuentes Benejam, Ing. Jorge Triple-S Salud Blue Cross Blue Shield of Puerto Rico, 983
Fuhrman, James Pacific Dental Benefits, 159
Fuller, Patty Health Plus of Louisiana, 479
Fullwood, Michael D GHI Medicare Plan, 779
Fullwood, Michael D Group Health Incorporated (GHI), 781
Fullwood, Michael D Health Plan of New York, 783
Fulton, Richard Premier Access Insurance/Access Dental, 169
Furlough, Joyce CareMore Health Plan, 98

Fusco, Dave Anthem Blue Cross & Blue Shield Connecticut, 220

G

Gabel, Lawrence Davis Vision, 769
Gadinsky, Pam Coventry Health Care of Florida, 274
Gaebel, John Pacific Dental Benefits, 159
Gage, Deborah Beech Street Corporation: Corporate Office, 87
Gage Lofgren, Diane Kaiser Permanente Health Plan of Northern California, 140
Gage Lofgren, Diane Kaiser Permanente Health Plan of Southern California, 141
Gage Lofgren, Diane Kaiser Permanente Health Plan: Corporate Office, 142
Gage Lofgren, Diane Kaiser Permanente Medicare Plan, 143
Gailey, Vernice CIGNA HealthCare of Georgia, 316
Gaines, Carol HealthSCOPE Benefits, 73
Gaines, Nici C Passport Health Plan, 466
Galano, Andy Educators Mutual, 1105
Galareau, Kathryn A, FSA Independence Blue Cross, 956
Galica, Michael, MD Health Plans, Inc., 540
Gallagher, Adeline Perfect Health Insurance Company, 806
Gallagher, Dan Unison Health Plan of Pennsylvania, 970
Gallagher, Dan Unison Health Plan of South Carolina, 1010
Gallagher, Michael Blue Cross of Northeastern Pennsylvania, 933
Gallagher, Michael, Sr First Priority Health, 946
Gallagher, Michael P AvMed Health Plan: Corporate Office, 259
Gallagher, Michael P AvMed Health Plan: Jacksonville, 262
Gallaher, Cindy Trustmark Companies, 384
Gallegos, Granger Blue Cross & Blue Shield of Wyoming, 1216
Gallegos, Rene Colorado Access, 199
Galt, Frederick B CDPHP Medicare Plan, 764
Galt, Frederick B CDPHP: Capital District Physicians' Health Plan, 765
Gammarino, Stephen W Blue Cross and Blue Shield Association, 360
Gamzon, Jessica HealthFirst New Jersey Medicare Plan, 729
Gannon, Christopher R Blue Cross & Blue Shield of Vermont, 1118
Ganz, Mark Asuris Northwest Health, 1150
Ganz, Mark B Regence BlueShield of Idaho, 355
Ganz, Mark B. Regence Blue Cross & Blue Shield of Oregon, 919
Garcia, Carolina M Leon Medical Centers Health Plan, 290
Garcia, Eddie Medical Care Referral Group, 1079
Garcia, Joseph Community Health Group, 110
Garcia, Nancy Preferred Medical Plan, 297
Gardner, Deana Crescent Preferred Provider Organization, 820
Garg, Angeli Santa Clara Family Health Plan, 174
Garland, Patrick Fidelis Care, 778
Garrett, Sharon Secure Horizons, 77
Garrett, Sharon PacifiCare of Texas, 1084
Garrison, Larry F Health First Medicare Plans, 283
Garvey, Thomas CIGNA HealthCare of New Jersey, 723
Garzelli, Lisa Foundation for Medical Care for Kern & Santa Barbara County, 123
Gasbaro, Eric Blue Cross & Blue Shield of Rhode Island, 986
Gastineau, Mark Blue Shield of California, 91
Gates, Dennis L SafeGuard Health Enterprises: Corporate Office, 172
Gates, Dennis L SafeGuard Health Enterprises: Florida, 299
Gates, Dennis L SafeGuard Health Enterprises: Texas, 1086
Gates, Thomas Delta Dental of Washington, 1153
Gatti, Alfred MVP Health Care: New Hampshire, 712
Gatti, Alfred MVP Health Care Medicare Plan, 795
Gatti, Alfred MVP Health Care: Buffalo Region, 796
Gatti, Alfred MVP Health Care: Central New York, 797
Gatti, Alfred MVP Health Care: Corporate Office, 798
Gatti, Alfred MVP Health Care: Mid-State Region, 799
Gatti, Alfred MVP Health Care: Western New York, 800
Gatti, Alfred MVP Health Care: Vermont, 1122
Gaucher, Ellen J Wellmark Health Plan of Iowa, 432
Gauen, Steve HAS-Premier Providers, 1068
Gaulstrand, Paul Spectera, 521
Gauthier, Guy Great Lakes Health Plan, 569
Gavras, Jonathan, MD UnitedHealthCare of South Florida, 303
Gavras, Jonathan B, MD Blue Cross & Blue Shield of Florida: Jacksonville, 266
Gedmen, William, CPA UPMC Health Plan, 973

Gore, Barb Network Health Plan of Wisconsin, 1206
Gore, James Carilion Health Plans, 1128
Gore, James L Virginia Health Network, 1146
Goren, Rob Delta Dental of Missouri, 643
Gorenflo, Rick New West Health Services, 672
Gorenflo, Rick New West Medicare Plan, 673
Gorevic, Jason Empire Blue Cross & Blue Shield, 774
Gorman, Preston Bluegrass Family Health, 457
Gormley, Kate San Francisco Health Plan, 173
Gorner, Ed Care 1st Health Plan: California, 97
Goss, Phil, CPA Trustmark Companies, 384
Gosser, Bruce HealthLink HMO, 651
Goulart, Cesar Presbyterian Health Plan, 753
Goulart, Cesar Presbyterian Medicare Plans, 754
Goulet, Ken WellPoint: Corporate Office, 417
Graff, Sean USA Managed Care Organization, 1096
Graham, William J Harvard Pilgrim Health Care, 536
Grandfield, Steven H Blue Cross & Blue Shield of Nebraska, 677
Granger, Helen Calais Health, 473
Granow, Les Arcadian Health Plans, 83
Grant, Brenda Piedmont Community Health Plan, 1141
Grant, Chris Kaiser Permanente Health Plan of Northern California, 140
Grant, Chris Kaiser Permanente Health Plan of Southern California, 141
Grant, Chris Kaiser Permanente Health Plan: Corporate Office, 142
Grant, Chris Kaiser Permanente Medicare Plan, 143
Grant, Janet CareSource: Michigan, 558
Grant, Janet CareSource, 849
Granzier, Mark Cofinity, 560
Grassy, Richard PersonalCare, 381
Graves, Teri Health Plus of Louisiana, 479
Gray, Lisa Great Lakes Health Plan, 569
Gray, Lorraine CIGNA HealthCare of Delaware, 234
Gray, Stu Liberty Dental Plan, 148
Gray, Stu Liberty Dental Plan of Nevada, 698
Gray, Walter Care 1st Health Plan: California, 97
Graye, Mitchell T.G. Great-West PPO, 206
Graye, Mitchell T.G. Great-West/One Health Plan, 207
Grden, Nancy L Amerigroup Corporation, 1125
Greczyn, Robert J, Jr Preferred Care Select, 829
Green, Caroline UnitedHealthCare of North Carolina, 832
Green, Debra HMO Health Ohio, 858
Green, Debra Medical Mutual of Ohio, 862
Green, Debra Medical Mutual of Ohio Medicare Plan, 863
Green, Debra SuperMed One, 878
Green, Dolores L California Foundation for Medical Care, 95
Green, Karen M Delta Dental: Corporate Headquarters, 563
Green, Warren One Call Medical, 735
Greenberg, Allan Ira Aetna Health of Missouri, 632
Greenberg, Ann Lovelace Health Plan, 750
Greenburg, Howard UnitedHealthCare of North Carolina, 832
Greene, Caroline UnitedHealthCare of North Carolina, 832
Greene, Richard Arcadian Health Plans, 83
Greene, Tammy USA Managed Care Organization, 1096
Greene, Terone B Virginia Premier Health Plan, 1147
Greenfield, Craig B MagnaCare, 791
Greenhouse, Kara, CPA Dominion Dental Services, 1132
Greenwood, James M. Concentra: Corporate Office, 1060
Greg, Doug Children's Mercy Family Health Partners, 639
Gregg, Vicky Blue Cross & Blue Shield of Tennessee, 1030
Gregoire, Daniel N Magellan Health Services Indiana, 408
Gregoire, Daniel N Magellan Health Services: Corporate Headquarters, 515
Gregoire, Daniel N Oxford Health Plans: New Jersey, 736
Gregoire, John San Francisco Health Plan, 173
Gregor, Joseph C CIGNA HealthCare of North Carolina, 818
Gregory, Rhian Neighborhood Health Plan, 542
Greifer, Cliff Beech Street Corporation: Corporate Office, 87
Grey, Dr James E Brazos Valley Health Network, 1056
Grgurina, John F, Jr San Francisco Health Plan, 173
Gribble, Debra, RN Essence Healthcare, 646
Grice, Len Health Link PPO, 628
Griffin, Julie Alere Health, 309
Griffin, Robert, MD Arkansas Blue Cross and Blue Shield, 66

Griggs, Ken Preferred Health Systems Insurance Company, 447
Griggs, Ken Preferred Plus of Kansas, 449
Griggs, Mike Blue Cross & Blue Shield of South Carolina, 997
Grigo, Chris Alliance Regional Health Network, 1047
Grillo, Lillian UnitedHealthCare of New York, 810
Grimes, MD, Alan UnitedHealthCare of Indiana, 414
Griswold, David Delta Dental of New Mexico, 746
Groat, Jonathan S, Esq Delta Dental: Corporate Headquarters, 563
Grooms, Ed HealthSCOPE Benefits, 73
Gross, Don Mida Dental Plan, 154
Grossman, Robert S, MD Citrus Health Care, 271
Grouel, Gus Medfocus Radiology Network, 153
Grove, Jane South Central Preferred, 967
Groves, Mark Dental Source: Dental Health Care Plans, 1063
Gruenbaum, Samuel H Western Dental Services, 188
Grund, MD, Mike Medical Associates Health Plan: East, 1204
Guengerich, Gary Dentaquest, 531
Guenther, Bret Dentistat, 119
Guerra-Garcia, H., MD Unison Health Plan of Delaware, 241
Guerrero, Esther ChiroCare of Wisconsin, 1190
Guertin, Lisa M Anthem Blue Cross & Blue Shield of New Hampshire, 706
Guertin, Shawn M HealthAmerica, 951
Guest III, William C Atrio Health Plans, 901
Guffey, CJ American Postal Workers Union (APWU) Health Plan, 498
Gullett, Steve Paramount Care of Michigan, 583
Gullett, Steve Paramount Elite Medicare Plan, 871
Gullett, Steve Paramount Health Care, 872
Gullino, Douglas Lovelace Health Plan, 750
Gullino, Douglas Lovelace Medicare Health Plan, 751
Gunawardane, Gamini, PhD Care 1st Health Plan: California, 97
Gustafson, Greg Upper Peninsula Health Plan, 593
Gustavel, Jack Blue Cross of Idaho Health Service, Inc., 345
Gustin, Karen Ameritas Group, 676
Gutierrez, Lisa Script Care, Ltd., 1088
Gutierrez, Melissa, CLU Nationwide Better Health, 867
Guyette, Michael Blue Cross & Blue Shield of Florida: Jacksonville, 266
Guzzino, Alan Humana Health Insurance of Jacksonville, 286
Guzzino, Alan Humana Health Insurance of North Carolina, 825

H

Haaland, Douglas E Cariten Healthcare, 1031
Haaland, Douglas E Cariten Preferred, 1032
Haas, David Robert OptiCare Managed Vision, 828
Haban, Gregory Prime Time Health Medicare Plan, 873
Hackett, Ed Value Behavioral Health of Pennsylvania, 976
Hackworth, John, PhD Health Plan of San Joaquin, 133
Haddock, Joseph, MHA Geisinger Health Plan, 948
Haefner, Larry A CNA Insurance Companies: Colorado, 198
Haefner, Larry A CNA Insurance Companies: Georgia, 317
Haefner, Larry A CNA Insurance Companies: Illinois, 362
Hafer, Latha MedCost, 826
Hagan, Lynn American Health Care Group, 927
Hagan, Robert E American Health Care Group, 927
Haggett, William F AmeriHealth HMO, 718
Haglund, Jacqueline Blue Cross & Blue Shield of Oklahoma, 887
Hague, Richard, DMD, MPA Liberty Dental Plan, 148
Hague, Richard, DMD Liberty Dental Plan of Nevada, 698
Hahn, Shelley Anthem Blue Cross & Blue Shield of Ohio, 846
Haillyer, Jeff HAS-Premier Providers, 1068
Haines, Rick Aultcare Corporation, 848
Haines, Rick Prime Time Health Medicare Plan, 873
Hairston, Don AvMed Health Plan: Orlando, 263
Hairston, Donald AvMed Health Plan: Gainesville, 261
Hale, Bill Beech Street Corporation: Northeast Region, 88
Hale, Kathy Healthcare Partners of East Texas, 1069
Hale, William Beech Street Corporation: Alabama, 3
Hale, William Beech Street: Alaska, 19
Hall, David Dental Benefit Providers, 509
Hall, Kerry Delta Dental of Wyoming, 1218
Hall, Pat CommunityCare Managed Healthcare Plans of Oklahoma, 890
Hall, Toby L Delta Dental: Corporate Headquarters, 563
Halo, Lorri Medical Care Referral Group, 1079

Halow, George, MD Medical Care Referral Group, 1079
Halow, Joseph Medical Care Referral Group, 1079
Halpern, Steven, MD CIGNA HealthCare of Northern California, 106
Halpern, Steven, MD CIGNA HealthCare of Southern California, 107
Halvorson, George C Kaiser Permanente Health Plan of Northern California, 140
Halvorson, George C Kaiser Permanente Health Plan of Southern California, 141
Halvorson, George C Kaiser Permanente Health Plan: Corporate Office, 142
Halvorson, George C Kaiser Permanente Medicare Plan, 143
Hamilton, Catherine, PhD Blue Cross & Blue Shield of Vermont, 1118
Hamilton, Coleen Arizona Foundation for Medical Care, 32
Hamilton, Stuart, MD Select Health of South Carolina, 1008
Hammer, Kenneth J, DDS,MBA CompBenefits Corporation, 318
Hammond, Deborah, MD HealthFirst New Jersey Medicare Plan, 729
Hammond, Elizabeth Blue Cross & Blue Shield of South Carolina, 997
Hammond, Gerry Total Health Choice, 300
Hampton, Diana Health Choice LLC, 1036
Hanaway, Ed CIGNA HealthCare of Tennessee, 1033
Hanaway, H Edward CIGNA HealthCare of South Carolina, 1000
Hancock, William CommunityCare Managed Healthcare Plans of Oklahoma, 890
Hancock, William H CommunityCare Medicare Plan, 891
Handa, Angela Health First Health Plans, 282
Handelman, Warren MultiPlan, Inc., 794
Handelman, Warren HealthEOS, 1201
Handler, Elisabeth Santa Clara Family Health Plan, 174
Handshuh, Ana Physicians United Plan, 295
Handshy, Jennifer Healthcare USA of Missouri, 650
Hankins, Toni BlueChoice Health Plan of South Carolina, 998
Hankins, Toni J BlueChoice Health Plan of South Carolina, 998
Hanks, Steve VSP: Vision Service Plan of Oregon, 924
Hanley, Sheila, MD Anthem Blue Cross & Blue Shield of Maine, 488
Hanna, Gabriel J DC Chartered Health Plan, 246
Hanna, Nequita K Blue Cross & Blue Shield of Oklahoma, 887
Hannan, Claire L, CPA PacifiCare Dental and Vision Administrators, 163
Hannon, Richard M Blue Cross & Blue Shield of Arizona, 36
Hannum, Ed AvMed Health Plan: Corporate Office, 259
Hannum, Ed AvMed Health Plan: Gainesville, 261
Hannum, Edwin AvMed Health Plan: Corporate Office, 259
Hannum, Edwin AvMed Health Plan: Orlando, 263
Hannum, Edwin AvMed Health Plan: Tampa, 264
Hansen, David UnitedHealthCare of Alaska, 28
Hansen, David UnitedHealthCare of Oregon, 923
Hansen, David UnitedHealthCare of Washington, 1170
Hansen, P Gunnar, Jr Clear One Health Plans, 905
Hansen, R Scott Public Employees Health Program, 1111
Hanserd, Brenda Care 1st Health Plan: Arizona, 37
Hanson, Kerry, MD Premier Access Insurance/Access Dental, 169
Hanus, Phil CHA Health, 458
Hanway, H Edward CIGNA HealthCare of Connecticut, 222
Hanway, H Edward CIGNA HealthCare of Illinois, 361
Hanway, H Edward CIGNA HealthCare of Maine, 489
Hanway, H Edward CIGNA HealthCare of St. Louis, 640
Harding, Cheryl Delta Dental of Iowa, 423
Hardwick, Debi Coastal Healthcare Administrators, 109
Hargrave, Ralph, DDS Liberty Dental Plan of Nevada, 698
Harkey, Barbara Saint Mary's Health Plans, 703
Harman, Wade Community Health Plan of Washington, 1152
Harmon, Julie, MHA Horizon Health Corporation, 1073
Harp, Joan Blue Cross & Blue Shield of Tennessee, 1030
Harper, Wesley A, DDS Delta Dental of Arizona, 40
Harr, Elizabeth R Blue Cross Blue Shield of Michigan, 556
Harr, Ron Blue Cross & Blue Shield of Tennessee, 1030
Harrell, Traci Superior Dental Care, 877
Harrington, Judy B Health Partners Medicare Plan, 950
Harrington, Karynlee CIGNA HealthCare of New Hampshire, 707
Harris, Dave Anthem Blue Cross & Blue Shield of Colorado, 192
Harris, Irwin E, MD, MBA CenCal Health: The Regional Health Authority, 99
Harris, Myrna Crescent Preferred Provider Organization, 820
Harris, Patricia Lovelace Health Plan, 750
Harris, Patricia Lovelace Medicare Health Plan, 751

Harris, Peter, MD, PhD MHNet Behavioral Health, 1081
Harris, Robert T, MD Preferred Care Select, 829
Harris, Stephen, PhD Crescent Preferred Provider Organization, 820
Harris, Stephen ABRI Health Plan, Inc., 1185
Harris, Terry Beech Street Corporation: Corporate Office, 87
Harrison, Dorothy Horizon Health Corporation, 1073
Harrold, Jason M Centene Corporation, 638
Harston, Dennis T, MD Altius Health Plans, 1102
Hart, Angela Quality Health Plans, 298
Hart, Angela Quality Health Plans of New York, 807
Hart, Erin E American Health Care Group, 927
Hart, Jennings SelectNet Plus, Inc., 1182
Hart, Marci Arnett Health Plans, 394
Hart, Richard, MD Aetna Health of Georgia, 308
Hart, Sam ODS Alaska, 26
Hart, Steve Horizon Health Corporation, 1073
Harth, Kenneth A Empire Blue Cross & Blue Shield, 774
Hartman, Lisa D Geisinger Health Plan, 948
Hartman, Sally Peninsula Health Care, 1140
Harvey, Rose Health Link PPO, 628
Harwins, Gregory Priority Health: Corporate Headquarters, 586
Harwins, Gregory PriorityHealth Medicare Plans, 587
Hastreiter, Richard Delta Dental of Nebraska, 680
Hatch, Robert A Regence Blue Cross & Blue Shield of Oregon, 919
Hatch, Robert A Regence Blue Cross & Blue Shield of Utah, 1112
Hatfield, Lance Blue Cross of Idaho Health Service, Inc., 345
Hathcock, Bonita Humana Health Insurance of Arizona, 48
Hathcock, Bonita C Humana Health Insurance of Kentucky, 463
Hathcock, Bonita C Humana Health Insurance of Ohio, 859
Hathcock, Bonnie Humana Health Insurance of Illinois, 377
Hathcock, Bonnie Humana Health Insurance of Iowa, 427
Hauser, Martin P SummaCare Health Plan, 875
Hauser, Martin P SummaCare Medicare Advantage Plan, 876
Havens, Sam American WholeHealth Network, 928
Hawayek Alemany, Jose Triple-S Salud Blue Cross Blue Shield of Puerto Rico, 983
Hawk, Galen Devon Health Services, 942
Hawkins, Gregory M-Care, 579
Hawkins, Gregory Priority Health, 585
Hawkins, Jane HealthSpan, 857
Hay, Jeffrey Lakeside Community Healthcare Network, 146
Hayburn, Marty Blue Cross & Blue Shield of Delaware, 233
Haydel, Augustavia J L.A. Care Health Plan, 145
Hayden, Frank Aultcare Corporation, 848
Hayden Cook, Melissa Sharp Health Plan, 176
Hayes, Darin HealthAmerica Pennsylvania, 952
Hayes, Jane Health Alliance Medical Plans, 371
Hayes, Lori Dominion Dental Services, 1132
Hayes, Robert M Universal American Medicare Plans, 812
Haynes, David Delta Dental of Missouri, 643
Haynes, Jean, RN Geisinger Health Plan, 948
Hays, Eric HealthAmerica Pennsylvania, 952
Hazelip, Tina Deaconess Health Plans, 398
Hazlewood, Hugh Liberty Dental Plan of Nevada, 698
Hazlewood, Marsha Liberty Dental Plan, 148
Hazlewood, Marsha Liberty Dental Plan of Nevada, 698
Headley, Jay CIGNA HealthCare of Arizona, 38
Healy, Tim Wisconsin Physician's Service, 1214
Heath, Cherie Prevea Health Network, 1208
Heatherington, Jeff FamilyCare Health Medicare Plan, 907
Hebert, Laura Calais Health, 473
Heck, Stephen H Meritain Health: Corporate Headquarters, 792
Heckel, Keith Wellmark Health Plan of Iowa, 432
Heckenlable, Mick Delta Dental of South Dakota, 1018
Heckman, Lauralee Health Net of the Northeast, 226
Heddleston, Lora OhioHealth Group, 870
Hefner, Juanell Managed Health Network, 150
Heide, Melody Health InfoNet, 669
Heim, Maria Network Health Plan of Wisconsin, 1206
Heim-lawrence, Melissa Aetna Health of Oklahoma, 885
Heinen, Jack Grand Valley Health Plan, 568
Heiser, Donna CoreSource: Corporate Headquarters, 364

Held, Dana Anthem Blue Cross & Blue Shield of Colorado, 192
Helling, Cindy Select Health of South Carolina, 1008
Helmer, Richard, MD Central California Alliance for Health, 100
Helmer, MD, Richard A Molina Healthcare: Corporate Office, 155
Helmke, Sherry UnitedHealthCare of Nebraska, 686
Helstrom, Roxane Sharp Health Plan, 176
Heltz, Sabrina Blue Cross & Blue Shield of Louisiana, 472
Helwig, Jon First Commonwealth, 368
Hemingway Hall, Patricia Blue Cross & Blue Shield of Illinois, 359
Hemingway Hall, Patricia A Health Care Service Corporation, 373
Hemmele, Christi Preferred Therapy Providers, 57
Hemmingsen-Souza, Lori, RN Superior Vision Services, Inc., 178
Hemsley, Stephen J UnitedHealthCare of Minnesota, 620
Henchel, Beth Denver Health Medical Plan Inc, 203
Henchey, Chris MVP Health Care: New Hampshire, 712
Henchey, Chris MVP Health Care Medicare Plan, 795
Henchey, Chris MVP Health Care: Buffalo Region, 796
Henchey, Chris MVP Health Care: Central New York, 797
Henchey, Chris MVP Health Care: Corporate Office, 798
Henchey, Chris MVP Health Care: Mid-State Region, 799
Henchey, Chris MVP Health Care: Western New York, 800
Henchey, Chris MVP Health Care: Vermont, 1122
Henderson, Bill Liberty Dental Plan, 148
Henderson, Bill Liberty Dental Plan of Nevada, 698
Henderson, David UnitedHealthCare of North Carolina, 832
Henderson, Pamela Care Choices, 557
Henderson, Sonya L HealthFirst New Jersey Medicare Plan, 729
Hendricks, Liz Central Susquehanna Healthcare Providers, 937
Henke, Tom Medica: Corporate Office, 610
Henke, Tom Medica: North Dakota, 841
Henke, Tom Medica: South Dakota, 1023
Henning, William, MD Inland Empire Health Plan, 137
Henry, Aaron S Physicians United Plan, 295
Henry, Carole Lovelace Health Plan, 750
Henry, Carole Lovelace Medicare Health Plan, 751
Henry, Debra M Blue Cross of Idaho Health Service, Inc., 345
Henry, Lisa Arkansas Community Care, 67
Hensley, Johatnan Regence Blue Cross & Blue Shield of Oregon, 919
Hensley, Jonathan Regence Blue Shield, 1166
Hensley, Nicole Deaconess Health Plans, 398
Hensley, Pat Crescent Preferred Provider Organization, 820
Herbert, Michael Delta Dental of Kansas, 440
Herdes, Meridith Beech Street Corporation: Corporate Office, 87
Hereford, James Group Health Cooperative, 1157
Herman, Maryann Humana Health Insurance of Wisconsin, 1202
Herman, Roberta Harvard Pilgrim Health Care, 536
Hernandez, Henry Leon Medical Centers Health Plan, 290
Hernandez, Ines, MD Medical Card System (MCS), 980
Heron, Rick Western Health Advantage, 189
Herrera, Alex Aetna Health of Texas, 1046
Herron, Judith CompBenefits Corporation, 318
Hertik, Philip Windsor Medicare Extra, 1045
Herzberg, Gary R, MD Texas Community Care, 1091
Hess, Kimberley Superior Vision Services, Inc., 178
Heuer, Max Arkansas Blue Cross and Blue Shield, 66
Heuser, George, MD Optima Health Plan, 1139
Heuss, Kim Puget Sound Health Partners, 1165
Heyer-Dean, Laurie UCare Medicare Plan, 618
Heyer-Dean, Laurie UCare Minnesota, 619
Hiam, Robert P Hawaii Medical Services Association, 338
Hicks, Dory New West Health Services, 672
Hicks, Dory New West Medicare Plan, 673
Hicks, Jim Great-West/One Health Plan, 207
Hicks, Matt MercyCare Health Plans, 1205
Hicks, Sharon UPMC Health Plan, 973
Higgins, Catherine, CPA Boulder Valley Individual Practice Association, 196
Higgins, Sharon M, MD Kaiser Permanente Health Plan Northwest, 911
Higgins-Mays, Kimberley San Francisco Health Plan, 173
Hilbert, Andy Optima Health Plan, 1139
Hildebrand, Hans ChiroCare of Wisconsin, 1190
Hilferty, Daniel J Independence Blue Cross, 956
Hill, Jerry On Lok Lifeways, 157

Hill, John Value Behavioral Health of Pennsylvania, 976
Hill, Kevin R Oxford Health Plans: New Jersey, 736
Hill, Kevin R Oxford Health Plans: New York, 805
Hill, Terri Nationwide Better Health, 867
Hillebert, Jaxene Preferred Therapy Providers, 57
Hillerud, Andrea, MD Security Health Plan of Wisconsin, 1209
Hillman, Lori Health Net: Corporate Headquarters, 132
Himes, BJ QualChoice/QCA Health Plan, 76
Hinckley, Robert R CDPHP Medicare Plan, 764
Hinckley, Robert R CDPHP: Capital District Physicians' Health Plan, 765
Hinek, James Coventry Health Care of Delaware, 235
Hines, Linda, MS/RN Virginia Premier Health Plan, 1147
Hingst, Jeanne ProviDRs Care Network, 451
Hinrichsen, Julie Blue Cross & Blue Shield of Kansas, 436
Hinshaw, Deborah Athens Area Health Plan Select, 313
Hippert, Richard Horizon Health Corporation, 1073
Hipwell, Art Humana Health Insurance of Illinois, 377
Hipwell, Art Humana Health Insurance of Iowa, 427
Hipwell, Arthur Humana Health Insurance of Arizona, 48
Hipwell, Arthur P Humana Health Insurance of Ohio, 859
Hirst, Nancy Phoenix Health Plan, 55
Hirt, Donald Health Alliance Medicare, 571
Hirt, Donald Health Alliance Plan, 572
Hiveley, Jim Unity Health Insurance, 1212
Ho, Sam Secure Horizons, 77
Ho, Sam PacifiCare Health Systems, 164
Ho, Sam PacifiCare of Colorado, 211
Ho, Sam PacifiCare of Texas, 1084
Ho, Sam PacifiCare Benefit Administrators, 1162
Ho, Sam PacifiCare of Washington, 1163
Hobbs, Cary D Centene Corporation, 638
Hobgood, Mark Healthcare Partners of East Texas, 1069
Hochberg, Stanley, MD Boston Medical Center Healthnet Plan, 528
Hockmuth, Dr Rob CIGNA HealthCare of Massachusetts, 529
Hockmuth, Rob, MD CIGNA HealthCare of New Hampshire, 707
Hodgin, Ace PacifiCare of Arizona, 54
Hodgkins, Robert C, Jr The Dental Care Plus Group, 879
Hoefling, Douglas R, DDS Superior Dental Care, 877
Hoeflinger, Erin Anthem Blue Cross & Blue Shield of Ohio, 846
Hoeltzel, Marty T CIGNA: Corporate Headquarters, 939
Hoff, Linda Physicians Plus Insurance Corporation, 1207
Hoffman, Joseph Anthem Blue Cross & Blue Shield of Colorado, 192
Hoffman, Patrick CIGNA HealthCare of Tennessee, 1033
Hoffman, Randy PersonalCare, 381
Hoffman, Randy OhioHealth Group, 870
Hofmann, Allison QualCare, 737
Hofmeister, Michael WINhealth Partners, 1222
Hogan, Michael, MD Coventry Health Care of Florida, 274
Hogel, Maureen Highmark Blue Cross & Blue Shield, 953
Hogel, Maureen Highmark Blue Shield, 954
Hoges, Deb Health Plans, Inc., 540
Hohner, Joseph H Blue Cross Blue Shield of Michigan, 556
Holden, Steven Davis Vision, 769
Holder, Diane P UPMC Health Plan, 973
Holgerson, Chris Willamette Dental Insurance, 925
Holiday, Steve Script Care, Ltd., 1088
Hollinger, Stacey Galaxy Health Network, 1066
Hollman, Monye, MD Blue Cross & Blue Shield of Georgia, 315
Hollman, Wayne, MD Blue Cross & Blue Shield of Georgia, 315
Holmberg, David L Highmark Blue Cross & Blue Shield, 953
Holmberg, David L Highmark Blue Shield, 954
Hologood, Mark Healthcare Partners of East Texas, 1069
Holt, Shawn Physicians United Plan, 295
Holt, Tim Great Lakes Health Plan, 569
Holtz, Elliot UnitedHealthCare of Minnesota, 621
Holzhauer, Robert Univera Healthcare, 811
Holzner, Charles, MD CareMore Health Plan, 98
Honig, Michael HealthFirst New Jersey Medicare Plan, 729
Hooker, Dennis Blue Cross & Blue Shield of Illinois, 359
Hooks, Sandra OmniCare: A Coventry Health Care Plan, 582
Hoops, Alan CareMore Health Plan, 98
Hoover, Mary Nevada Preferred Healthcare Providers, 699, 700

Jackson, Laura Wellmark Health Plan of Iowa, 432
Jackson, Marianne Blue Shield of California, 91
Jacobs, Gary TexanPlus Medicare Advantage HMO, 1090
Jacobs, Gary M American Pioneer Life Insurance Co, 255
Jacobs, Gary M Universal American Medicare Plans, 812
Jacobs, Richard, MD Health Net of Arizona, 47
Jacobs, Seth A, Esq Blue Shield of California, 91
Jacobson, James Sterling Health Plans, 1168
Jacobson, Jed J, DDS Delta Dental of Michigan, Ohio and Indiana, 399, 852
Jacobson, Jed J., DDS/MPH Delta Dental: Corporate Headquarters, 563
Jacobson, Jim Medica Health - Medicare Plan, 609
Jacobson, Jim Medica: Corporate Office, 610
Jacobson, Jim Medica: North Dakota, 841
Jacobson, Jim Medica: South Dakota, 1023
Jacques, Douglas A, Esq SCAN Health Plan, 175
Jaeger, Mary Ann Heart of America Health Plan, 839
Jaeger, Michael, MD Anthem Blue Cross & Blue Shield of Wisconsin, 1187
Jamal, Asif JMH Health Plan, 289
Jamali, M Nicole, MD Easy Choice Health Plan, 120
James, Bryan A Ohio Health Choice, 868
Jamison, Scott DakotaCare, 1017
Jan, Janet Care 1st Health Plan: California, 97
Jankowski, Ray CalOptima, 96
Jankowski, Tim VSP: Vision Service Plan, 186
Janney, John R, Jr Independence Blue Cross, 956
Janscy, Dennis HMO Health Ohio, 858
Janscy, Dennis Medical Mutual of Ohio, 862
Janscy, Dennis Medical Mutual of Ohio Medicare Plan, 863
Janscy, Dennis SuperMed One, 878
Jarrett, Bill Highmark Blue Cross & Blue Shield, 953
Jarvis, Alfred Anthem Blue Cross & Blue Shield Connecticut, 220
Jarvis, Margaret Blue Cross & Blue Shield of Texas, 1053
Jarvis, Margaret Blue Cross & Blue Shield of Texas: Houston, 1054
Jarvis, Margaret HMO Blue Texas, 1072
Jasmer, Greg DakotaCare, 1017
Javier Artau Feliciano, Francisco First Medical Health Plan, 978
Jehle, Christopher Total Dental Administrators, 59
Jelinek, Rick Americhoice of Pennsylvania, 929
Jemmingway-Hall, Patricia HMO Blue Texas, 1072
Jenkins, Harry American Pioneer Life Insurance Co, 255
Jenkins, Mary Beth UPMC Health Plan, 973
Jenkins, Nancy HealthPlus of Michigan: Flint, 574
Jenkins, Nancy HealthPlus of Michigan: Saginaw, 575
Jenkins, Sheila Network Health Plan of Wisconsin, 1206
Jennifer, Jackie Horizon Healthcare of New Jersey, 731
Jennings, Julie American Specialty Health, 82
Jennings, Reynold Tenet Choices, 483
Jensen, Barb Delta Dental of Nebraska, 680
Jensen, Jared Opticare of Utah, 1110
Jensen, Jeffrey L, CPA Public Employees Health Program, 1111
Jepson, Stephen G Blue Cross & Blue Shield of Western New York, 762
Jernigan, J Michael Select Health of South Carolina, 1008
Jesse, Sandra L Blue Cross & Blue Shield of Massachusetts, 527
Jewett, Stephen ConnectiCare, 223
Jewett, Stephen ConnectiCare of Massachusetts, 530
Jewett, Stephen ConnectiCare of New York, 768
Jhaveri, Vishu J, MD Blue Cross & Blue Shield of Arizona, 36
Jiminez, Marissa L.A. Care Health Plan, 145
Jiminez, Martin Community First Health Plans, 1059
Joe, David Western Dental Services, 188
Johankin, William Primary Health Plan, 354
Johannesson, Russ OptumHealth Care Solutions: Physical Health, 614
Johnson, Ann Delta Dental of Minnesota, 601
Johnson, Ann Delta Dental of North Dakota, 836
Johnson, Barb MercyCare Health Plans, 1205
Johnson, Bendel Health Plus of Louisiana, 479
Johnson, David UnitedHealthCare of Arkansas, 78
Johnson, David R MHP North Star Plans, 613
Johnson, Donna UTMB HealthCare Systems, 1097
Johnson, Elizabeth H, MD Martin's Point HealthCare, 493
Johnson, Greg Saint Mary's Health Plans, 703
Johnson, Jana L Medica Health - Medicare Plan, 609

Johnson, Jana L Medica: Corporate Office, 610
Johnson, Jana L Medica: North Dakota, 841
Johnson, Jana L Medica: South Dakota, 1023
Johnson, Judy Inter Valley Health Plan, 138
Johnson, Judy Brazos Valley Health Network, 1056
Johnson, Karen Delta Dental of Wisconsin, 1193
Johnson, Lisa Cariten Healthcare, 1031
Johnson, Lisa Cariten Preferred, 1032
Johnson, Margaret M Rayant Insurance Company, 738
Johnson, Pamela M.K. Atrio Health Plans, 901
Johnson, Richard, PharmD Central California Alliance for Health, 100
Johnson, Ron Outlook Vision Service, 53
Johnson, Sandra Health Partners of Kansas, 443
Johnson, Scott Health Plus of Louisiana, 479
Johnson, Steven P., Jr Susquehanna Health Care, 969
Johnson, Sue Blue Cross & Blue Shield of Kansas City, 636
Johnson, Susan HealthSCOPE Benefits, 73
Johnson, Vicki Physicians Health Plan of Northern Indiana, 411
Johnston, L. McTyeire, MD Neighborhood Health Plan of Rhode Island, 992
Johnston, Ross HealthSCOPE Benefits, 73
Johnston, Steve, JD Healthcare Partners of East Texas, 1069
Joiner, Stephen CIGNA HealthCare of Georgia, 316
Jokisch, Mark Phoenix Health Plan, 55
Jolly, Rebecca Avesis: Texas, 1051
Jones, Bill HealthPartners, 1037
Jones, Bobby CareSource: Michigan, 558
Jones, Bobby OmniCare: A Coventry Health Care Plan, 582
Jones, Bobby CareSource, 849
Jones, Brooks Care 1st Health Plan: California, 97
Jones, Cynthia, MD Public Employees Health Program, 1111
Jones, David A, Jr Humana Health Insurance of Iowa, 427
Jones, Julie Preferred Therapy Providers, 57
Jones, P Gary, MD Vantage Health Plan, 485
Jones, Randy HealthPlus of Michigan: Flint, 574
Jones, Randy HealthPlus of Michigan: Saginaw, 575
Jones, Richard, MD Aetna Health of Nevada, 687
Jones, Richard Guardian Life Insurance Company, 782
Jones, Richard W Humana Health Insurnace of Colorado, 209
Jones, Robert Blue Ridge Health Network, 934
Jones, Scott Delta Dental of South Dakota, 1018
Jones, Suzann New West Health Services, 672
Jones, Tom Ohio State University Health Plan Inc., 869
Jones, Willis E, III Windsor Medicare Extra, 1045
Jones, Jr, David A Humana Health Insurance of Georgia, 323
Jordan, Michael MagnaCare, 791
Joseph, Charles Blue Cross & Blue Shield of Florida: Jacksonville, 266
Joseph, Peter Coventry Health Care of Florida, 274
Joyce, Kevin QualCare, 737
Joyner, David CVS CareMark, 988
Joyner, David S Blue Shield of California, 91
Julia, Julio F Medical Card System (MCS), 980
Jurak, Joseph Beta Health Plan, 195
Jurkovic, Goran, CPA Delta Dental: Corporate Headquarters, 563
Justice, Billy Vantage Health Plan, 485

K

Kaczor, William J, Jr American Postal Workers Union (APWU) Health Plan, 498
Kadja, Judy Ohio State University Health Plan Inc., 869
Kadota, Rudy, MD Kaiser Permanente Health Plan of Colorado, 210
Kadylak, Ron OhioHealth Group, 870
Kaegi, R John Blue Cross & Blue Shield of Florida: Jacksonville, 266
Kagehiro, Jan Kaiser Permanente Health Plan of Hawaii, 340
Kahmann, Tony Asuris Northwest Health, 1150
Kahn, Howard A L.A. Care Health Plan, 145
Kairis, Edwin J, MD Gateway Health Plan, 947
Kaiser, Kelley C, MPH Samaritan Health Plan, 920
Kakiuchi, Hideo Premier Access Insurance/Access Dental, 169
Kalahiki, Linda University Health Alliance, 342
Kalekos, Peggy Coastal Healthcare Administrators, 109
Kalmer, James American Pioneer Life Insurance Co, 255
Kampfe, Rachel Peninsula Health Care, 1140

Kanach, Chuck Bravo Health: Corporate Headquarters, 502
Kanche, Liz American Health Care Group, 927
Kane, Brian OptumHealth Care Solutions: Physical Health, 614
Kane, Ed Harvard Pilgrim Health Care: Maine, 492
Kane, Martin Healthplex, 785
Kaneshiro, Lance University Health Alliance, 342
Kant, Dennis Universal Health Care Group, 304
Kantor, Johathan D CNA Insurance Companies: Colorado, 198
Kantor, Johathan D CNA Insurance Companies: Georgia, 317
Kantor, Johathan D CNA Insurance Companies: Illinois, 362
Kao, John CareMore Health Plan, 98
Kapic, Maja Liberty Dental Plan, 148
Kapic, Maja Liberty Dental Plan of Nevada, 698
Kaplan, Alan Island Group Administration, Inc., 789
Kaplan, Leon CareFirst Blue Cross & Blue Shield of Virginia, 1127
Kaplan, Lynn Island Group Administration, Inc., 789
Kappel, James Anthem Blue Cross & Blue Shield of Indiana, 392
Karajia, Paul Wellmark Health Plan of Iowa, 432
Karr, Brian Magellan Health Services Arizona, 49
Kasitz, Todd Preferred Health Systems Insurance Company, 447
Kasitz, Todd Preferred Plus of Kansas, 449
Kasper, Michael Coventry Health Care of Louisiana, 475
Kassing, Gib Sterling Health Plans, 1168
Kasuba, Pual, MD Tufts Health Medicare Plan, 543
Kasuba, Pual, MD Tufts Health Plan, 544
Kates, Peter B Univera Healthcare, 811
Katz, Ben CIGNA HealthCare of Northern California, 106
Katz, Marshall, MD OmniCare: A Coventry Health Care Plan, 582
Kaui, Prudence WellPoint NextRx, 1100
Kawamura, Marilyn Kaiser Permanente Health Plan of the Mid-Atlantic
    States, 514
Kaye, Michael PTPN, 171
Kaye, Mitchel Physical Therapy Provider Network, 167
Kaye, Thomas, RPH BlueLincs HMO, 888
Kazlauskas, Tony UnitedHealthCare of Massachusetts, 546
Keeley, Larry OptiCare Managed Vision, 828
Keenan, Linda Hometown Health Plan, 696
Kehres, Deb South Central Preferred, 967
Keith, Tricia A Blue Cross Blue Shield of Michigan, 556
Kelleher, Mary Ann Unison Health Plan of South Carolina, 1010
Keller, Brian Blue Cross & Blue Shield of Louisiana, 472
Keller, Robert Heart of America Health Plan, 839
Keller, Shannon Delta Dental of Arizona, 40
Kellogg, Terry Blue Cross Preferred Care, 6
Kellogg, Terry D Blue Cross & Blue Shield of Alabama, 5
Kelly, James HealthSmart Preferred Care, 1070
Kelly, Mary J Dentcare Delivery Systems, 771
Kelly, Rick Aetna Health of the Carolinas, 814
Kelly, Scott R Health Net: Corporate Headquarters, 132
Kemp, Kacey Premera Blue Cross, 1164
Kenargy, Robert Preferred Health Systems Insurance Company, 447
Kenargy, Robert Preferred Plus of Kansas, 449
Kendrick, Morgan Blue Cross & Blue Shield of Georgia, 315
Kennedy, Janna SummaCare Health Plan, 875
Kennedy, Janna SummaCare Medicare Advantage Plan, 876
Kennedy, John W Blue Cross & Blue Shield of Kansas City, 636
Kennedy, Tim Assurant Employee Benefits: Washington, 1149
Kennedy, Tom Regence Blue Cross & Blue Shield of Oregon, 919
Kennedy-Scott, Patricia D Kaiser Permanente Health Plan Ohio, 861
Kenny, Becky Blue Cross & Blue Shield of New Mexico, 744
Kerby, James, MD Grand Valley Health Plan, 568
Kerlin, Mary Partnership HealthPlan of California, 166
Kerr, Thomas Highmark Blue Cross & Blue Shield, 953
Kerr, Thomas Highmark Blue Shield, 954
Keshishian, Marc, MD Blue Care Network of Michigan: Corporate
    Headquarters, 551
Kessel, Stacy Community Health Plan of Washington, 1152
Kessler, James Health New England, 538
Kessler, Jennifer Unison Health Plan of Pennsylvania, 970
Kessler, Steve UnitedHealthCare of North Carolina, 832
Ketner, Bill MedCost, 826
Ketron, Mike Southeastern Indiana Health Organization, 413

Ketterman, Laura Citrus Health Care, 271
Kettlewell, Kelly SXC Health Solutions Corp, 383
Khan, Asiam, MD CIGNA HealthCare of Indiana, 397
Khan, Aslam, MD CIGNA HealthCare of Wisconsin, 1191
Khan, Haider A, MD Quality Health Plans, 298
Khan, Haider A, MD Quality Health Plans of New York, 807
Khan, Nazeer H, MD Quality Health Plans, 298
Khan, Nazeer H, MD Quality Health Plans of New York, 807
Khan, Sabiha, MBA Quality Health Plans, 298
Khan, Sabiha, MBA Quality Health Plans of New York, 807
Khaneja, Munish, MD Affinity Health Plan, 758
Khorram, Carmen American PPO, 1048
Kibbe, David New West Health Services, 672
Kibbe, David New West Medicare Plan, 673
Kidd, Wyndham BlueLincs HMO, 888
Kieckhefer, Robert Blue Cross & Blue Shield of Illinois, 359
Kieffer, Brad Health Net Dental, 130
Kieffer, Brad Health Net: Corporate Headquarters, 132
Kilburn, Sherri HealthPartners, 1037
Kilgallon, Tim Alere Health, 309
Kim, Ken, MD CareMore Health Plan, 98
Kima, Cliff Aetna Health of Nevada, 687
Kimrey, Tom Dental Network of America, 366
Kinard, David Community Health Plan of Washington, 1152
Kincannon, Elizabeth, MD Kaiser Permanente Health Plan of Colorado, 210
King, C Burke Anthem Blue Cross & Blue Shield of Virginia, 1126
King, CB Peninsula Health Care, 1140
King, Kathy Foundation for Medical Care for Mendocino and Lake Counties,
    124
King, Melissa Island Group Administration, Inc., 789
King, Mike WellPath: A Coventry Health Care Plan, 833
Kinne, Gordon Med-Pay, 653
Kiraly, Thomas E. Concentra: Corporate Office, 1060
Kircher, Debra A Health Partners Medicare Plan, 950
Kirchner, John J HealthFirst New Jersey Medicare Plan, 729
Kirk, Chris CareSource Mid Rogue Health Plan, 903
Kirk, Cliff Blue Cross & Blue Shield of Wyoming, 1216
Kirk, Jennifer Managed HealthCare Northwest, 914
Kirk, Troy PacificSource Health Plans: Corporate Headquarters, 917
Kirkner, Gary CIGNA HealthCare of North Carolina, 818
Kirkpatrick, Mercy Leon Medical Centers Health Plan, 290
Kirsch, Kenneth W, DDS Western Dental Services, 188
Kissner, Lawrence J UnitedHealthCare of South Florida, 303
Kivett, Melissa Assurant Employee Benefits: Corporate Headquarters, 635
Kjerstad, Rick, CEBS Superior Vision Services, Inc., 178
Klammer, Thomas P Landmark Healthplan of California, 147
Klasner, John Anthem Blue Cross & Blue Sheild of Indiana, 391
Klassen, Richard W Delta Dental of Missouri, 643
Kleaver, Ellwood Primary Health Plan, 354
Klein, David H Univera Healthcare, 811
Klein, Gary, RPh Florida Health Care Plan, 279
Kleinner, Richard Coventry Health Care of Kansas, 439
Klenk, Scott CDPHP Medicare Plan, 764
Klenk, Scott CDPHP: Capital District Physicians' Health Plan, 765
Kline, Teresa CHA Health, 458
Klobucar, Kevin L Blue Care Network of Michigan: Corporate Headquarters,
    551
Kloystermeyer, Roy Florida Health Care Plan, 279
Kludt, John, MD Blue Cross & Blue Shield of Georgia, 315
Kluge, Susan Blue Care Network of Michigan: Corporate Headquarters, 551
Kluge, Susan Blue Care Network of Michigan: Medicare, 552
Knackstedt, Chris Mercy Health Plans: Kansas, 445
Knackstedt, Chris Great-West Healthcare of Massachusetts, 535
Knackstedt, Chris Mercy Health Medicare Plan, 654
Knackstedt, Chris Mercy Health Plans: Corporate Office, 655
Knackstedt, Chris Mercy Health Plans: Oklahoma, 896
Knapp, Amy UnitedHealthCare of Massachusetts, 546
Knapp Pinnas, Susan AvMed Health Plan: Corporate Office, 259
Kneidel, Kara, MBA Nationwide Better Health, 867
Kniess, April Willamette Dental Insurance, 925
Knife, Charles Blue Cross & Blue Shield of Oklahoma, 887
Knight, Jeffrey The Health Plan of the Upper Ohio Valley, 880

Knight, Summer Capital Health Plan, 268
Knight, Terry VIVA Health, 17
Knighton, Larry Health Plus of Louisiana, 479
Knispel, John Amerigroup Florida, 256
Knox, Ronald Kaiser Permanente Health Plan of Northern California, 140
Knox, Ronald Kaiser Permanente Health Plan of Southern California, 141
Knox, Ronald Kaiser Permanente Health Plan: Corporate Office, 142
Knox, Ronald Kaiser Permanente Medicare Plan, 143
Knutson, Deb Medica: Corporate Office, 610
Knutson, Deb Medica: North Dakota, 841
Knutson, Deb Medica: South Dakota, 1023
Koenig, Tere, MD SummaCare Health Plan, 875
Koenig, Tere, MD SummaCare Medicare Advantage Plan, 876
Koenigsberg, Richard Liberty Health Advantage Medicare Plan, 790
Kohls, Laurie Vision Insurance Plan of America, 1213
Kohlscheen, Jennifer Boulder Valley Individual Practice Association, 196
Kohn, Pat Gundersen Lutheran Health Plan, 1199
Koizumi, Noreen, PharmD Community Health Group, 110
Kollefrath, James Physicians United Plan, 295
Kolodgy, Robert Blue Cross and Blue Shield Association, 360
Konigsberg, Alvin National Health Plan Corporation, 801
Konigsberg, David National Health Plan Corporation, 801
Konkel, Nicole HealthEOS, 1201
Konowiecki, Joseph Secure Horizons, 77
Konowiecki, Joseph PacifiCare of Texas, 1084
Konowiecki, Joseph PacifiCare Benefit Administrators, 1162
Konowiecki, Joseph PacifiCare of Washington, 1163
Kordella, Robert National Medical Health Card, 802
Korn, Allan M, MD Blue Cross and Blue Shield Association, 360
Kortge, Dean Raymond Trillium Community Health Plan, 921
Korth, Susan First Health, 369
Kosecoff, Jacqueline Secure Horizons, 77
Kosecoff, Jacqueline, PhD PacifiCare of Nevada, 702
Kosecoff, Jacqueline PacifiCare of Texas, 1084
Kosecoff, Jacqueline PacifiCare Benefit Administrators, 1162
Kosecoff, Jacqueline PacifiCare of Washington, 1163
Kosior, Robert A Health New England, 538
Kosub, Suzanne C. Concentra: Corporate Office, 1060
Kotin, Anthony M, MD Magellan Health Services Indiana, 408
Kotin, Anthony M, MD Magellan Health Services: Corporate Headquarters, 515
Koval, Bob VSP: Vision Service Plan of Michigan, 594
Kovaleski, Kerry Arizona Foundation for Medical Care, 32
Kowal, Nancy Total Health Care, 589
Kowalski, Scott T Physicians Plus Insurance Corporation, 1207
Kowitz, M Donald Saint Mary's Health Plans, 703
Koziara, Michael Priority Health, 585
Koziara, Mike Care Choices, 557
Krall, Edward J, MD Security Health Plan of Wisconsin, 1209
Kramer, Kelly Health Plan of Michigan, 573
Kramer, Robert Horizon Health Corporation, 1073
Kramer, Ryan VIVA Health, 17
Krause, Jean Gundersen Lutheran Health Plan, 1199
Krause, John Care Plus Dental Plans, 1189
Kraymer, Lisa Santa Clara Family Health Plan, 174
Kreiling, Scott Regence BlueShield of Idaho, 355
Kreiling, Scott Regence Blue Cross & Blue Shield of Oregon, 919
Krentz, Kathleen Network Health Plan of Wisconsin, 1206
Krigstein, Alan Independence Blue Cross, 956
Kroft, Jim Nevada Preferred Healthcare Providers, 699, 700
Krogman, Dean DakotaCare, 1017
Kroll, Edmund E Centene Corporation, 638
Krueger, Linda Beta Health Plan, 195
Kruger, Daniel UnitedHealthcare Nevada, 704
Krugman, Mark E, MD Orange County Foundation for Medical Care, 158
Krumholz, Alan, MD Health Tradition, 1200
Krupa, David Blue Cross & Blue Shield of Vermont, 1118
Krupa, Scottie Carilion Health Plans, 1128
Krzyzewski, Kristen Bravo Health: Corporate Headquarters, 502
Kudgis, Len Horizon NJ Health, 732
Kuester, Cynthia Health Resources, Inc., 405

Kujawa, Kevin American Specialty Health, 82
Kuk, Kenneth U. Kanawha Healthcare Solutions, 1006
Kukla, Steven Mercy Health Network, 429
Kulich, Roman GHP Coventry Health Plan, 648
Kulton, Michelle Landmark Healthplan of California, 147
Kunes, Steven M Health Tradition, 1200
Kunis, Suzanne Magellan Health Services: Corporate Headquarters, 515
Kunkle, Jeff Athens Area Health Plan Select, 313
Kunz, Eileen, MPH On Lok Lifeways, 157
Kurpad, Umesh Tufts Health Medicare Plan, 543
Kurpad, Umesh Tufts Health Plan, 544
Kusserow, Paul B Humana Health Insurance of Kentucky, 463
Kuter, Daniel UnitedHealthCare of Iowa, 431
Kutz, Kathryn Health Plan of San Joaquin, 133
Kutzler, Josh Araz Group, 596
Kuzel, Russel J, MD UCare Medicare Plan, 618
Kuzel, Russel J, MD UCare Minnesota, 619
Kwei, Richard Geisinger Health Plan, 948
Kweskin, Sally Anthem Blue Cross & Blue Shield of Nevada, 689
Kweskin, Sally Empire Blue Cross & Blue Shield, 774
Kwiecinski, Jane SelectCare Access Corporation, 966
Kyle, Christine UnitedHealthCare of Ohio: Columbus, 882
Kyle, Christine UnitedHealthCare of Ohio: Dayton & Cincinnati, 883

L

Lacombe, Philip M Health New England, 538
Ladig, Curt Delta Dental of Kentucky, 461
Lady, Shirley S Blue Cross and Blue Shield Association, 360
LaFayette, Lincoln HMO Health Ohio, 858
LaFayette, Lincoln Medical Mutual of Ohio, 862
LaFayette, Lincoln Medical Mutual of Ohio Medicare Plan, 863
LaFayette, Lincoln SuperMed One, 878
Lages, Adolphus, OD Vision Plan of America, 185
Lagrone, Karen Blue Cross & Blue Shield of Louisiana, 472
Laird, Brenda Delta Dental: Corporate Headquarters, 563
Laird, Warren VSP: Vision Service Plan of South Carolina, 1012
Laitner, Linda Horizon Health Corporation, 1073
Lambrukos, William H Delta Dental Northeast, 708
Lamirault, Ingrid Alameda Alliance for Health, 81
Lamm, Roy QualChoice/QCA Health Plan, 76
Lammie, Scott UPMC Health Plan, 973
Lamoreaux, Leon Priority Health, 585
Lamoreaux, William C GHI Medicare Plan, 779
Lamoreaux, William C Group Health Incorporated (GHI), 781
Lamoreaux, William C Health Plan of New York, 783
Lamoreux, William UnitedHealthCare of New York, 810
Lancaster, Kathy Kaiser Permanente Health Plan of Northern California, 140
Lancaster, Kathy Kaiser Permanente Health Plan of Southern California, 141
Lancaster, Kathy Kaiser Permanente Health Plan: Corporate Office, 142
Lancaster, Kathy Kaiser Permanente Medicare Plan, 143
Landis, Robert J CompCare: Comprehensive Behavioral Care, 273
Landry, Joanne Neighborhood Health Plan, 542
Landry, Laura Blue Cross & Blue Shield of Louisiana, 472
Lane, Jack Harvard Pilgrim Health Care, 536
Lane, Kim Health Care Service Corporation, 373
Lane, Mark L Fidelis Care, 778
Lang, James Anthem Blue Cross & Blue Shield of Colorado, 192
Lang, James Anthem Blue Cross & Blue Shield of Maine, 488
Langer, Carolyn Harvard Pilgrim Health Care, 536
Langley, Leon Tenet Choices, 483
Langlois, Darrell Blue Cross & Blue Shield of Louisiana, 472
Lapetina, Antoinette Perfect Health Insurance Company, 806
Laporte, Todd, CPA Employers Dental Services, 43
Lapp, Roger L SCAN Health Plan, 175
Larrivee, Scott Anthem Blue Cross & Blue Shield of Wisconsin, 1187
Larson, Beverly, RN Health Tradition, 1200
Larson, John Health InfoNet, 669
Larson, Peter N CIGNA HealthCare of South Carolina, 1000
Lathem, Janet Northeast Georgia Health Partners, 326
Lattimore, Patricia HMO Health Ohio, 858
Lattimore, Patricia Medical Mutual of Ohio, 862
Lattimore, Patricia Medical Mutual of Ohio Medicare Plan, 863

Lattimore, Patricia SuperMed One, 878

Latts, Dr Lisa Anthem Blue Cross & Blue Shield of Colorado, 192

Lau, Sandra Western Dental Services, 188

Laudeman, Lisa A Blue Ridge Health Network, 934

Lauer, Gary L. eHealthInsurance Services Inc., 9

Lauffenburger, Michael J SafeGuard Health Enterprises: Corporate Office, 172

Lauffenburger, Michael J SafeGuard Health Enterprises: Florida, 299

Lauffenburger, Michael J SafeGuard Health Enterprises: Texas, 1086

Lauterjung, Kevin S HMO Health Ohio, 858

Lauterjung, Kevin S Medical Mutual of Ohio, 862

Lauterjung, Kevin S Medical Mutual of Ohio Medicare Plan, 863

Lauterjung, Kevin S SuperMed One, 878

Lauzon, Thomas L Health Plan of Michigan, 573

Lavely, David OptiCare Managed Vision, 828

Law, Patrick Blue Cross & Blue Shield of Montana, 664

Law, Scott D WellCare Health Plans, 307

Lawhead, Jean Delta Dental of Colorado, 202

Lawrence, Jay, MD Aetna Health of Texas, 1046

Lawrence, Robert W Empire Blue Cross & Blue Shield, 774

Lawson, Maureen Network Health Plan of Wisconsin, 1206

Lazar, Heidi BEST Life and Health Insurance Co., 90

Le, Curt Contra Costa Health Plan, 113

Leamon, Cheryl WellPoint: Corporate Office, 417

Leathers, Jr., Fred Blue Cross & Blue Shield of Georgia, 315

Lebish, Daniel United Concordia, 971

Lebish, Daniel J Highmark Blue Cross & Blue Shield, 953

Lebish, Daniel J Highmark Blue Shield, 954

Lechner, David Lifewise Health Plan of Oregon, 913

LeClaire, Brian Humana Health Insurance of Kentucky, 463

Lederberg, Michele B Blue Cross & Blue Shield of Rhode Island, 986

Lederman, Alan Community Health Plan of Washington, 1152

Lee, Amy Chinese Community Health Plan, 102

Lee, Chad University Health Alliance, 342

Lee, Cheryl Physicians Health Plan of Northern Indiana, 411

Lee, Derrick D Virginia Premier Health Plan, 1147

Lee, Howard K, MD University Health Alliance, 342

Lee, Yolanda Chinese Community Health Plan, 102

Leeger, Meredith Initial Group, 1041

Leeke, Jon Liberty Health Advantage Medicare Plan, 790

Lees, Janice M Delta Dental of Missouri, 643

Lehman, Brian Ohio State University Health Plan Inc., 869

Lehr, William, Jr Capital Blue Cross, 936

Leichtle, Robert Blue Cross & Blue Shield of South Carolina, 997

Lem, Cindy Health Plan of San Mateo, 134

Lenderink, Gary B Guardian Life Insurance Company, 782

Lenhart, Jack A Valley Preferred, 975

Lenihamy, Kevin Blue Cross & Blue Shield of Georgia, 315

Leninhan, Kevin Blue Cross & Blue Shield of Georgia, 315

Lennig, Nilsa Texas Community Care, 1091

Lentine, Joseph T Dencap Dental Plans, 564

Lentz, Lori One Call Medical, 735

Leonard, David, CPA Educators Mutual, 1105

Leonard, Jo-carol Family Choice Health Alliance, 726

Leonard, Jo-carol FC Diagnostic, 727

Leonardo, Connie Maricopa Integrated Health System/Maricopa Health Plan, 50

Leonardo, Connie University Family Care Health Plan, 62

Leonarduzzi, Charles Care Plus Dental Plans, 1189

Leong, Daryl Care 1st Health Plan: California, 97

Leopold, Larry Delta Dental of Washington, 1153

Lepre, Christopher M Horizon Blue Cross & Blue Shield of New Jersey, 730

Lerer, Rene, MD Magellan Health Services Indiana, 408

Lerer, Rene, MD Magellan Health Services: Corporate Headquarters, 515

Lescault, Tom SCAN Health Plan, 175

Lesley, Craig Physicians Health Plan of Mid-Michigan, 584

Lesley, E Craig Delta Dental of Michigan, Ohio and Indiana, 399, 852

Lessin, Karen Independence Blue Cross, 956

Lessin, Leeba CareMore Health Plan, 98

Levicki, George A, DDS Delta Dental of Virginia, 1131

Levin, Howard, OD Block Vision, 501

Levine, Jay Blue Cross & Blue Shield of Minnesota, 599

Levine, Robert, MD OmniCare: A Coventry Health Care Plan, 582

Levinson, Anthony R Coalition America's National Preferred Provider Network, 767

Levinson, Donald M CIGNA HealthCare of Maine, 489

Levy, Laurel Aetna Health of Georgia, 308

Lewis, Catherine Medfocus Radiology Network, 153

Lewis, Craig W Delta Dental of Rhode Island, 989

Lewis, Denise Arkansas Managed Care Organization, 68

Lewis, DiJuana Anthem Blue Cross & Blue Shield Connecticut, 220

Lewis, Dijuana WellPoint: Corporate Office, 417

Lewis, DiJuana Anthem Blue Cross & Blue Shield of Maine, 488

Lewis, Jackie Unison Health Plan of Ohio, 881

Lewis, Jennifer Spectera, 521

Lewis, Kenneth FirstCarolinaCare, 823

Lewis, Melissa Ohio Health Choice, 868

Lewis, William R, MD Concentra: Corporate Office, 1060

Lewis-Clapper, Caskie Magellan Health Services Indiana, 408

Lewis-Clapper, Caskie Magellan Health Services: Corporate Headquarters, 515

Lewisr, Christina Valley Preferred, 975

Li, Grace, MHA On Lok Lifeways, 157

Liang, Janet Kaiser Permanente Health Plan of Hawaii, 340

Liang, Janet Group Health Cooperative, 1157

Liang, Louise L, MD Kaiser Permanente Health Plan of Northern California, 140

Liang, Louise L, MD Kaiser Permanente Health Plan of Southern California, 141

Liang, Louise L, MD Kaiser Permanente Health Plan: Corporate Office, 142

Liang, Louise L, MD Kaiser Permanente Medicare Plan, 143

Liedl, Heidi Group Health Cooperative of Eau Claire, 1197

Liepins, Janis Fallon Community Health Plan, 533

Liepins, Janis Fallon Community Medicare Plan, 534

Lile III, J Matt, RHU American Denticare, 65

Lin, Gary H Harvard Pilgrim Health Care, 536

Lindemann, Bob CNA Insurance Companies: Colorado, 198

Lindemann, Bob CNA Insurance Companies: Georgia, 317

Lindemann, Bob CNA Insurance Companies: Illinois, 362

Lindgren, Charles Dimension Health PPO, 276

Lindsay, Mark UnitedHealthCare of Kentucky, 469

Lindsey, Claudia Anthem Blue Cross & Blue Shield Connecticut, 220

Lindsey, Claudia Anthem Blue Cross & Blue Shield of Maine, 488

Lindsey, James California Dental Network, 94

Linfield, Rob Liberty Dental Plan, 148

Linse-weiss, Mickey Florida Health Care Plan, 279

Liston, Thomas Humana Health Insurance of Arizona, 48

Liston, Thomas J Humana Health Insurance of Kentucky, 463

Liston, Thomas J Humana Medicare Plan, 464

Liston, Thomas J Humana Health Insurance of Ohio, 859

Liston, Tom Humana Health Insurance of Illinois, 377

Liston, Tom Humana Health Insurance of Iowa, 427

Littel, John E Amerigroup Corporation, 1125

Little, John Blue Cross & Blue Shield of South Carolina, 997

Little, Karen CIGNA HealthCare of Georgia, 316

Littman, Harvy Scott & White Health Plan, 1087

Livermore, Arnold Blue Cross & Blue Shield of Florida: Pensacola, 267

Livermore, Duke Blue Cross & Blue Shield of Florida: Jacksonville, 266

Livermore, Duke Blue Cross & Blue Shield of Florida: Pensacola, 267

Livingston, David Great Lakes Health Plan, 569

Livingston, Pam Cardinal Health Alliance, 396

Ljung, Douglas VSP: Vision Service Plan of Oregon, 924

Lockhart, Thomas Blue Cross & Blue Shield of Wyoming, 1216

Lockwood, Kristi Superior Vision Services, Inc., 178

Loder, Sandra Clear One Health Plans, 905

Loeb Bohren, Deborah Empire Blue Cross & Blue Shield, 774

Loepp, Daniel J Blue Cross Blue Shield of Michigan, 556

Loerke, Rick Dean Health Plan, 1192

Lofberg, Per CVS CareMark, 988

Loffreda, Paul Health Plan of Michigan, 573

Lohman, Wayne Health Choice LLC, 1036

London, Dr Robert Anthem Blue Cross & Blue Shield of Colorado, 192

London, Roger, MD Touchstone Health HMO, 808

Long, Jo Ann Regence Blue Cross & Blue Shield of Oregon, 919

Long, Kristy NOVA Healthcare Administrators, 804

Long, Laura B, MD BlueChoice Health Plan of South Carolina, 998
Longendyke, Rob Medica Health - Medicare Plan, 609
Longendyke, Rob Medica: Corporate Office, 610
Longendyke, Rob Medica: North Dakota, 841
Longendyke, Rob Medica: South Dakota, 1023
Longwoth, Maria, RN CHN PPO, 722
Lonsdale, Winston AvMed Health Plan: Fort Lauderdale, 260
Lonsdale, Winston AvMed Health Plan: Tampa, 264
Loosn, Richard Chinese Community Health Plan, 102
Lopes, Ancelmo Healthcare USA of Missouri, 650
Lopez, Frank Alliance Regional Health Network, 1047
Lopez, Vivian Triple-S Salud Blue Cross Blue Shield of Puerto Rico, 983
Lopez Duarte, Milori Vision Plan of America, 185
Lopez-Casiro, Rosie Preferred Medical Plan, 297
Lopez-Fernandez, Orlando, Jr, MD Preferred Care Partners, 296
Lord, Jack, MD Humana Health Insurance of Illinois, 377
Lord, Jack, MD Humana Health Insurance of Iowa, 427
Lord, Jonathan, MD Humana Health Insurance of Arizona, 48
Lord, Jonathan T, MD Humana Health Insurance of Ohio, 859
Lore, Ann WellPath: A Coventry Health Care Plan, 833
Lotterman, Brad United Behavioral Health, 180
Lotvin, Alan M, MD Magellan Health Services: Corporate Headquarters, 515
Loughlin, Greg New West Health Services, 672
Loughlin, Greg New West Medicare Plan, 673
Louie, Deena Chinese Community Health Plan, 102
Louie, Deena San Francisco Health Plan, 173
Louie, Irene Chinese Community Health Plan, 102
Loux, Pamela Arkansas Managed Care Organization, 68
Love, Vincent J American WholeHealth Network, 928
Lovelace, John UPMC Health Plan, 973
Lowe, Art Bluegrass Family Health, 457
Lowek, Terri Physicians Plus Insurance Corporation, 1207
Lowery Born, Beryl Blue Cross & Blue Shield of Kansas, 436
Lowery-Born, Beryl Advance Insurance Company of Kansas, 433
Loweth, William B HAS-Premier Providers, 1068
Lowry, Joel Neil, CPA DC Chartered Health Plan, 246
Lowry, Lawrence CHN PPO, 722
Lowry, Shawn Foundation for Medical Care for Mendocino and Lake Counties, 124
Lubben, David J UnitedHealthCare of Minnesota, 620
Lucas, Stephanie Block Vision, 501
Ludy, Jeff Universal Health Care Group, 304
Luebke, Art Kaiser Permanente Health Plan of Colorado, 210
Lufrano, Robert I, MD Blue Cross & Blue Shield of Florida: Jacksonville, 266
Lufrano, Robert I, MD Blue Cross & Blue Shield of Florida: Pensacola, 267
Lukach, Melissa Blue Cross & Blue Shield of Delaware, 233
Lukas, Catherine Harvard University Group Health Plan, 537
Lukens, Kay PCC Preferred Chiropractic Care, 446
Lum, Alison, PharmD San Francisco Health Plan, 173
Luman, R Lyle, MBA CenCal Health: The Regional Health Authority, 99
Luna, Richard Medical Card System (MCS), 980
Lund, Cheryl Trillium Community Health Plan, 921
Luptowski, Marybeth CIGNA HealthCare of Georgia, 316
Luther, Carolyn W Independence Blue Cross, 956
Lutter, Larry J, MD Meritain Health: Corporate Headquarters, 792
Lutz, Francis Devon Health Services, 942
Lyle, Linda Cariten Healthcare, 1031
Lyle, Linda Cariten Preferred, 1032
Lyman, Dale N Meritain Health: Corporate Headquarters, 792
Lynch, Kevin, MS Los Angeles County Public Healthcare, 149
Lynch, Michael Humana Health Insurance of Jacksonville, 286
Lynch, Rob VSP: Vision Service Plan, 186
Lynch, Rob VSP: Vision Service Plan of Ohio, 884
Lynch, Scott Blue Cross & Blue Shield of Minnesota, 599
Lynch, Stephen D Health Net Medicare Plan, 131
Lynn, George F Atlanticare Health Plans, 720
Lynne, Donna, DrPH Kaiser Permanente Health Plan of Colorado, 210
Lynne, Donna UnitedHealthCare of North Carolina, 832
Lyons, Serena Lovelace Medicare Health Plan, 751
Lyski, James CIGNA HealthCare of North Carolina, 818

M

Maack, Terri Trillium Community Health Plan, 921
Maas, Pamela Gundersen Lutheran Health Plan, 1199
MacDonald, Cynthia Metropolitan Health Plan, 612
MacEwan, Pam Group Health Cooperative, 1157
Machtau, Kenneth N. Group Health Cooperative of South Central Wisconsin, 1198
Mack, Brian Grand Valley Health Plan, 568
Mack, Pat Carolina Care Plan, 999
Mackail, Christopher Mid Atlantic Medical Services: Corporate Office, 516
Mackenzie, Laurida Spectera, 521
Mackin, John T, Jr American Pioneer Life Insurance Co, 255
Mackin, Koko Blue Cross & Blue Shield of Alabama, 5
Mackin, Koko Blue Cross Preferred Care, 6
MacKinnon, Elinor Blue Shield of California, 91
Mackler, Robert, MA Pacific Health Alliance, 161
Maclean, Tom Blue Cross & Blue Shield of New Mexico, 744
Macomber, Steve Blue Cross & Blue Shield of Florida: Pensacola, 267
Madden, Kathleen ConnectiCare, 223
Madden, Michael, MD Gateway Health Plan, 947
Madill, Fred Unison Health Plan of Pennsylvania, 970
Madlem, Larry Coalition America's National Preferred Provider Network, 767
Maesaka, Clifford Delta Dental of Kentucky, 461
Magby, Kathy UnitedHealthCare of Louisiana, 484
Magill, Carolyn AmeriChoice by UnitedHealthCare, 716
Maginnis, John Blue Cross & Blue Shield of Louisiana, 472
Magnuson, Richard Group Health Cooperative, 1157
Maguire, Peggy Regence Blue Cross & Blue Shield of Oregon, 919
Magusin, Barbara Premera Blue Cross Blue Shield of Alaska, 27
Magusin, Barbara Premera Blue Cross, 1164
Maher, Charlene GHI Medicare Plan, 779
Maher, Charlene Group Health Incorporated (GHI), 781
Maher, Charlene Health Plan of New York, 783
Maher, Dan Pacific Dental Benefits, 159
Mahmood, Alec Health Net of Arizona, 47
Mahoney, Jim USA Managed Care Organization, 1096
Mahowald, Thomas UCare Medicare Plan, 618
Mahowald, Thomas UCare Minnesota, 619
Mailander, Edward M Rayant Insurance Company, 738
Mailer, Wendy Contra Costa Health Plan, 113
Maisel, Garry Western Health Advantage, 189
Majcher, Justin Dental Network of America, 366
Maldonado, Anna Maria Care 1st Health Plan: Arizona, 37
Maldonado, Paul Community First Health Plans, 1059
Malinowski, Barry, MD Anthem Blue Cross & Blue Shield of Ohio, 846
Malko, Elizabeth, MD Fallon Community Health Plan, 533
Malko, Elizabeth, MD Fallon Community Medicare Plan, 534
Mallatt, Kathy A Coventry Health Care of Nebraska, 679
Mallea, Dan Blue Cross & Blue Shield of Alabama, 5
Malloy, Mark Coventry Health Care of Delaware, 235
Maloney, Sheila Santa Clara Family Health Plan, 176
Maltz, Allen P Blue Cross & Blue Shield of Massachusetts, 527
Manchandia, Mahesh Primecare Dental Plan, 170
Manchee, Nancy Pacific Foundation for Medical Care, 160
Manders, Matt CIGNA HealthCare of North Carolina, 818
Manders, Matthew CIGNA HealthCare of Virginia, 1129
Manders, Matthew G CIGNA: Corporate Headquarters, 939
Mann, Margie Meritain Health: Corporate Headquarters, 792
Manning, Dennis J Guardian Life Insurance Company, 782
Manning, Frederick J Centene Corporation, 638
Manning, Kim Baptist Health Services Group, 1029
Manobianco, Steve Managed Healthcare Systems of New Jersey, 734
Manocchia, Gus, MD Blue Cross & Blue Shield of Rhode Island, 986
Manolis, Chronis, RPh UPMC Health Plan, 973
Manos, Paul, DDS Mida Dental Plan, 154
Manson, Dennis Preferred Health Systems Insurance Company, 447
Manson, Dennis Preferred Plus of Kansas, 449
Mansukani, Sharad, MD HealthSpring: Corporate Offices, 1039
Mapes, Tammy WellPath: A Coventry Health Care Plan, 833
March, Cabrini T, MD March Vision Care, 151
March, Glenville A, Jr, MD March Vision Care, 151
Marciniak, Steven Priority Health: Corporate Headquarters, 586

Mead, Robert E Aetna Health of Idaho, 344
Mead, Robert E Aetna Health of Iowa, 418
Mead, Robert E Aetna Health of Kansas, 434
Mead, Robert E Aetna Health of Kentucky, 455
Mead, Robert E Aetna Health of Louisiana, 470
Mead, Robert E Aetna Health of Maine, 487
Mead, Robert E Aetna Health of Maryland, 496
Mead, Robert E Aetna Health of Massachusetts, 524
Mead, Robert E Aetna Health of Michigan, 548
Mead, Robert E Aetna Health of Minnesota, 595
Mead, Robert E Aetna Health of Mississippi, 624
Mead, Robert E Aetna Health of Montana, 662
Mead, Robert E Aetna Health of Nebraska, 675
Mead, Robert E Aetna Health of New Hampshire, 705
Mead, Robert E Aetna Health of New Jersey, 715
Mead, Robert E Aetna Health of New Mexico, 742
Mead, Robert E Aetna Health of New York, 757
Mead, Robert E Aetna Health of North Dakota, 834
Mead, Robert E Aetna Health of Oregon, 899
Mead, Robert E Aetna Health of Pennsylvania, 926
Mead, Robert E Aetna Health of Rhode Island, 985
Mead, Robert E Aetna Health of South Dakota, 1013
Mead, Robert E Aetna Health of Utah, 1101
Mead, Robert E Aetna Health of Vermont, 1117
Mead, Robert E Aetna Health of Virginia, 1124
Mead, Robert E Aetna Health of Washington, 1148
Mead, Robert E Aetna Health of West Virginia, 1172
Mead, Robert E Aetna Health of Wisconsin, 1186
Mead, Robert E Aetna Health of Wyoming, 1215
Medford, Carol Seton Health Plan, 1089
Meehan, Carson Coventry Health Care of Louisiana, 475
Meehan, Carson Carolina Care Plan, 999
Meek, Todd NevadaCare, 701
Meese, Samantha Regence Blue Cross & Blue Shield of Oregon, 919
Mehelic, Phil American Health Care Alliance, 633
Mehring, Melissa HealthSpan, 857
Meier, John Paramount Care of Michigan, 583
Meier, John Paramount Elite Medicare Plan, 871
Meier, John Paramount Health Care, 872
Meisel, Stephen, MD Medfocus Radiology Network, 153
Melani, Kenneth R, MD Highmark Blue Cross & Blue Shield, 953
Melani, Kenneth R, MD Highmark Blue Shield, 954
Melenyk, Glenn DenteMax, 565
Memezes, Bob San Francisco Health Plan, 173
Menario, Jay CIGNA HealthCare of North Carolina, 818
Mendez, Ernest HAS-Premier Providers, 1068
Mendis, Paul, MD Neighborhood Health Plan, 542
Mendrygal, Matthew HealthPlus of Michigan: Flint, 574
Mendrygal, Matthew HealthPlus of Michigan: Saginaw, 575
Menezes, Bob San Francisco Health Plan, 173
Mense, D Craig CNA Insurance Companies: Colorado, 198
Mense, D Craig CNA Insurance Companies: Georgia, 317
Mense, D Craig CNA Insurance Companies: Illinois, 362
Meoli, Angela Coventry Health Care of GA, 319
Meoli, Angela Coventry Health Care of Louisiana, 475
Merkel-Liberatore, Karen BlueShield of Northeastern New York, 763
Merkel-Liberatore, Karen HealthNow New York, 784
Merlo, Kristin Delta Dental of Washington, 1153
Merlo, Larry J. CVS CareMark, 988
Merrick, Mayra Citizens Choice Healthplan, 108
Merrill, Stacie Opticare of Utah, 1110
Mertz, Laura J Valley Preferred, 975
Merwin, Joan Network Health Plan of Wisconsin, 1206
Merz, Marcus PreferredOne, 616
Messina, Elizabeth A Blue Cross & Blue Shield of Arizona, 36
Messinger, Dave WellPath: A Coventry Health Care Plan, 833
Metge, Bruce Catalyst Health Solutions Inc, 503
Metge, Bruce Catalyst RX, 817
Metz, R Douglas, DC American Specialty Health, 82
Meyer, Carol Los Angeles County Public Healthcare, 149
Meyer, Carrie Independent Health, 787
Meyer, Carrie Independent Health Medicare Plan, 788

Meyers-Alessi, Lisa Blue Cross & Blue Shield of Western New York, 762
Meyers-Alessi, Lisa Univera Healthcare, 811
Meyerson, Tamara Preferred Medical Plan, 297
Mggarry, Peter Clear One Health Plans, 905
Michael, Jenny CareSource, 849
Michulsky, Kathy Prevea Health Network, 1208
Middleton, Darrell E Blue Cross Blue Shield of Michigan, 556
Middleton, Kevin, PsyD MHNet Behavioral Health, 1081
Midkiff, Cheryl Piedmont Community Health Plan, 1141
Midlikowski, Gail Unity Health Insurance, 1212
Milbrandt, Chase Arcadian Health Plans, 83
Milbrandt, Chase, MBA Texas Community Care, 1091
Miles, Richard GEHA-Government Employees Hospital Association, 647
Miller, Amy Priority Health, 585
Miller, Cynthia S WellPoint: Corporate Office, 417
Miller, Deborah A SCAN Health Plan, 175
Miller, Fred, Md Pima Health System, 56
Miller, Gil Bravo Health: Corporate Headquarters, 502
Miller, Jeff Aetna Health of Oklahoma, 885
Miller, Jeff Delta Dental of South Dakota, 1018
Miller, Jim Hometown Health Plan, 696
Miller, John, RN CHN PPO, 722
Miller, Jolee Deaconess Health Plans, 398
Miller, Mike Dental Network of America, 366
Miller, Mike DenteMax, 565
Miller, Sandra H Anthem Blue Cross & Blue Sheild of Indiana, 391
Miller, Steve Blue Cross & Blue Shield of Georgia, 315
Mills, Jon HealthLink HMO, 651
Mills, Randy Southeastern Indiana Health Organization, 413
Mills, Shannon E, DDS Delta Dental Northeast, 708
Milner, Lance Anthem Blue Cross & Blue Shield of New Hampshire, 706
Milner, Roger Preferred Health Care, 963
Milo, Yoram Premera Blue Cross Blue Shield of Alaska, 27
Milo, Yori Premera Blue Cross, 1164
Mims, Pamela C Florida Health Care Plan, 279
Minsloff, Mark Prevea Health Network, 1208
Mirabal, Jose Medical Card System (MCS), 980
Miranda, Edgar A CIGNA HealthCare of North Carolina, 818
Mirt, Michael HealthSpring: Corporate Offices, 1039
Miskimmin, Renee, MD Gateway Health Plan, 947
Mitchel, Deona Signature Health Alliance, 1043
Mitchell, George K, MD Arkansas Blue Cross and Blue Shield, 66
Mitchell, Kathy CoreSource: Arizona, 39
Mitchell, Michael Interplan Health Group, 860
Mitchell, Tracy Arizona Foundation for Medical Care, 32
Mitchum, Rick Preferred Health Plan Inc, 467
Mitten, Anthony Arizona Foundation for Medical Care, 32
Mitten, Daniel Arizona Foundation for Medical Care, 32
Mixer, Mark Alliant Health Plans, 310
Miyasato, Gwen S Hawaii Medical Services Association, 338
Mizell, Cynthia Blue Cross Preferred Care, 6
Mock, Holly Prevea Health Network, 1208
Mock, Kathleen Blue Cross & Blue Shield of Minnesota, 599
Mockus, Jennifer, RN Central California Alliance for Health, 100
Moffat, James, MD AvMed Health Plan: Fort Lauderdale, 260
Moffat, James, MD AvMed Health Plan: Orlando, 263
Moffat, James, MD AvMed Health Plan: Tampa, 264
Mohan, Ronald, MD Gateway Health Plan, 947
Moharsky, Linda Blue Cross of Northeastern Pennsylvania, 933
Mohoney, Micahel A Physicians Plus Insurance Corporation, 1207
Moksnes, Mark A Delta Dental of Minnesota, 601
Moksnes, Mark A Delta Dental of North Dakota, 836
Molina, Carmen Medical Card System (MCS), 980
Molina, J Mario, MD Molina Healthcare: Corporate Office, 155
Molina, J Mario, MD Molina Healthcare: Washington, 1161
Molina, John C, JD Molina Healthcare: Corporate Office, 155
Molina, John C, JD Molina Healthcare: Washington, 1161
Monez, Sue Partnership HealthPlan of California, 166
Monfiletto, Sandra Martin's Point HealthCare, 493
Moniz, James UnitedHealthCare of Massachusetts, 546
Moniz, James, Jr UnitedHealthCare of Rhode Island, 994
Monkhouse, Cheryl Blue Cross & Blue Shield of Georgia, 315

Monroe, Nicole Opticare of Utah, 1110
Monroe, Wayne Mid Atlantic Medical Services: Corporate Office, 516
Monsrud, Beth UCare Medicare Plan, 618
Monsrud, Beth UCare Minnesota, 619
Montalvo, Mike UnitedHealthcare Nevada, 704
Montenegro, Teresa Health Partners of Kansas, 443
Montepare, Carole CDPHP Medicare Plan, 764
Montepare, Carole CDPHP: Capital District Physicians' Health Plan, 765
Montes, Denese Arkansas Managed Care Organization, 68
Montgomery, Jamie Deaconess Health Plans, 398
Montgomery, Richard Western Dental Services, 188
Montiletto, Ernest Americhoice of Pennsylvania, 929
Moon, Pam Piedmont Community Health Plan, 1141
Mooney, Kay Aetna Health of Alabama, 1
Mooney, Kay Aetna Health of Alaska, 18
Mooney, Kay Aetna Health of Arkansas, 64
Mooney, Kay Aetna Health, Inc. Corporate Headquarters, 217
Mooney, Kay Aetna Health, Inc. Medicare Plan, 218
Mooney, Kay Aetna Health of Delaware, 231
Mooney, Kay Aetna Health District of Columbia, 243
Mooney, Kay Aetna Health of Hawaii, 332
Mooney, Kay Aetna Health of Idaho, 344
Mooney, Kay Aetna Health of Iowa, 418
Mooney, Kay Aetna Health of Kansas, 434
Mooney, Kay Aetna Health of Kentucky, 455
Mooney, Kay Aetna Health of Louisiana, 470
Mooney, Kay Aetna Health of Maine, 487
Mooney, Kay Aetna Health of Maryland, 496
Mooney, Kay Aetna Health of Massachusetts, 524
Mooney, Kay Aetna Health of Michigan, 548
Mooney, Kay Aetna Health of Minnesota, 595
Mooney, Kay Aetna Health of Mississippi, 624
Mooney, Kay Aetna Health of Montana, 662
Mooney, Kay Aetna Health of Nebraska, 675
Mooney, Kay Aetna Health of New Hampshire, 705
Mooney, Kay Aetna Health of New Jersey, 715
Mooney, Kay Aetna Health of New Mexico, 742
Mooney, Kay Aetna Health of New York, 757
Mooney, Kay Aetna Health of North Dakota, 834
Mooney, Kay Aetna Health of Oregon, 899
Mooney, Kay Aetna Health of Pennsylvania, 926
Mooney, Kay Aetna Health of Rhode Island, 985
Mooney, Kay Aetna Health of South Dakota, 1013
Mooney, Kay Aetna Health of Utah, 1101
Mooney, Kay Aetna Health of Vermont, 1117
Mooney, Kay Aetna Health of Virginia, 1124
Mooney, Kay Aetna Health of Washington, 1148
Mooney, Kay Aetna Health of West Virginia, 1172
Mooney, Kay Aetna Health of Wisconsin, 1186
Mooney, Kay Aetna Health of Wyoming, 1215
Moore, Dan Superior Vision Services, Inc., 178
Moore, Derek MagnaCare, 791
Moore, James OSF Healthcare, 379
Moore, James OSF HealthPlans, 380
Moore, Jennifer Crescent Preferred Provider Organization, 820
Moore, Macon Peoples Health, 482
Moore, Matthew Unison Health Plan of Pennsylvania, 970
Moore, Phyllis VSP: Vision Service Plan of California, 187
Moore, Phyllis VSP: Vision Service Plan of Washington, 1171
Moore, Stephen Physical Therapy Provider Network, 167
Moore, Stephen Managed Health Services, 1203
Moore, Tim CIGNA HealthCare of Arkansas, 69
Moorman, Deborah Aetna Health of Georgia, 308
Morand, Mary Ann ProviDRs Care Network, 451
Morgan, Daniel VSP: Vision Service Plan of California, 187
Morgan, Lesley CHA Health, 458
Morgan, Melanie A CoreSource: Corporate Headquarters, 364
Morgan, Peter Group Health Cooperative, 1157
Morgan, Todd Partnership HealthPlan of California, 166
Moriatry, William J, MD Atrio Health Plans, 901
Morrill, James MVP Health Care: New Hampshire, 712
Morrill, James MVP Health Care Medicare Plan, 795

Morrill, James MVP Health Care: Buffalo Region, 796
Morrill, James MVP Health Care: Central New York, 797
Morrill, James MVP Health Care: Corporate Office, 798
Morrill, James MVP Health Care: Mid-State Region, 799
Morrill, James MVP Health Care: Western New York, 800
Morrill, James MVP Health Care: Vermont, 1122
Morris, Brett A Health Net of Arizona, 47
Morris, M Shawn HealthSpring Prescription Drug Plan, 1038
Morris, Pamela CareSource: Michigan, 558
Morris, Pamela CareSource, 849
Morrison, Jane Total Dental Administrators, 1114
Morrison, JoAnn Mountain State Blue Cross Blue Shiled, 1181
Morrison, Marion Health Plus of Louisiana, 479
Morrissey, Brian J CDPHP Medicare Plan, 764
Morrissey, Brian J CDPHP: Capital District Physicians' Health Plan, 765
Morrone, Michael A CHN PPO, 722
Morse, David B Delta Dental of Minnesota, 601
Morse, David B Delta Dental of North Dakota, 836
Morton, Robert Secure Health PPO Newtork, 327
Mosby, Jacqueline Piedmont Community Health Plan, 1141
Moscaritolo, Eileen CalOptima, 96
Moscovic, David Basic Chiropractic Health Plan, 86
Moser, Brandon Unison Health Plan of Pennsylvania, 970
Moss, Hershel, MD Health Plan of Michigan, 573
Mostert, Joni M Atrio Health Plans, 901
Motamed, Thomas F CNA Insurance Companies: Colorado, 198
Motamed, Thomas F CNA Insurance Companies: Georgia, 317
Motamed, Thomas F CNA Insurance Companies: Illinois, 362
Motter, Eric, MBA Nationwide Better Health, 867
Moutinho, Maria E, MD Gateway Health Plan, 947
Moya, Steve Humana Health Insurance of Illinois, 377
Moya, Steve Humana Health Insurance of Iowa, 427
Moya, Steven Humana Health Insurance of Arizona, 48
Moya, Steven O Humana Health Insurance of Kansas, 444
Moya, Steven O Humana Medicare Plan, 464
Moya, Steven O Humana Health Insurance of Ohio, 859
Mroue, Carole Care Choices, 557
Muchnicki, Michael A Sterling Health Plans, 1168
Mudra, Karl A Delta Dental of Missouri, 643
Muller, Roger, MD UnitedHealthCare of Alaska, 28
Muller, Roger, MD UnitedHealthCare of Oregon, 923
Muller, Roger, MD UnitedHealthCare of Washington, 1170
Mullins, Larry A, DHA Samaritan Health Plan, 920
Mummery, Ray, MD Dimension Health PPO, 276
Muney, Alan M Oxford Health Plans: New Jersey, 736
Muney, Alan M, MD Oxford Health Plans: New York, 805
Munich, Maritza I Medical Card System (MCS), 980
Munro, Jan Managed HealthCare Northwest, 914
Murabito, John M CIGNA: Corporate Headquarters, 939
Murpht, Maria Eileen OhioHealth Group, 870
Murphy, Michael G Vytra Health Plans, 813
Murphy, Terry Arizona Foundation for Medical Care, 32
Murphy, Tracie ODS Health Plan, 915
Murray, Charles University Health Alliance, 342
Murray, James Humana Health Insurance of Arizona, 48
Murray, James E Humana Health Insurance of Tampa - Pinellas, 288
Murray, James E Humana Health Insurance of Kansas, 444
Murray, James E Humana Health Insurance of Kentucky, 463
Murray, James E Humana Medicare Plan, 464
Murray, James E Humana Health Insurance of Ohio, 859
Murray, Jim Humana Health Insurance of Illinois, 377
Murray, Jim Humana Health Insurance of Iowa, 427
Murray, Tara Blue Cross & Blue Shield of Massachusetts, 527
Murrell, Warren Peoples Health, 482
Murrill, Tom Essence Healthcare, 646
Muscarella, Sharon United Concordia, 971
Muscatello, Todd Excellus Blue Cross Blue Shield: Central New York, 775
Muscatello, Todd Excellus Blue Cross Blue Shield: Utica Region, 777
Muse, Haydee Aetna Health of Missouri, 632
Muzi, Titus Humana Health Insurance of Wisconsin, 1202
Myers, Issac Advantage Health Solutions, 388
Myers, Jeremy OptiCare Managed Vision, 828

Myers, Michael R GEMCare Health Plan, 125
Myers, Wendy, MD Florida Health Care Plan, 279
Mylotte, Kathleen, MD Independent Health, 787
Mylotte, Kathleen, MD Independent Health Medicare Plan, 788

N

Nacol, John Pacific Foundation for Medical Care, 160
Nadeau, Mark Delta Dental of New Jersey & Connecticut, 224, 724
Nagle, Joseph A Delta Dental of Rhode Island, 989
Nair, Mohan Regence Blue Cross & Blue Shield of Oregon, 919
Nair, Mohan Regence Blue Cross & Blue Shield of Utah, 1112
Nameth, Michael WellPoint NextRx, 1100
Nangreave, Richard Excellus Blue Cross Blue Shield: Rochester Region, 776
Napier, Annette Vantage Health Plan, 485
Narowitz, Randy Total Health Care, 589
Narula, Mohender Primecare Dental Plan, 170
Nash, Bruce D, MD CDPHP Medicare Plan, 764
Nash, Bruce D, MD CDPHP: Capital District Physicians' Health Plan, 765
Nash, Dee Medical Mutual Services, 1007
Nava, Rachael Central California Alliance for Health, 100
Navarra, Linda CDPHP Medicare Plan, 764
Navarra, Linda CDPHP: Capital District Physicians' Health Plan, 765
Navarro, Scott, DDS Delta Dental of New Jersey & Connecticut, 224, 724
Navran, Susan Blue Cross & Blue Shield of Arizona, 36
Neary, Daniel P Mutual of Omaha DentaBenefits, 684
Neary, Daniel P Mutual of Omaha Health Plans, 685
Needleman, Phillip Vision Plan of America, 185
Needleman, Stuart, OD Vision Plan of America, 185
Neely, Marc Great-West Healthcare Delaware, 238
Neeson, Richard J Independence Blue Cross, 956
Negrini, Barbara, MD Gateway Health Plan, 947
Neidorff, Michael F Centene Corporation, 638
Neira, Alma Preferred Therapy Providers, 57
Neiswander, Dana Piedmont Community Health Plan, 1141
Nelles, Roslind American Pioneer Life Insurance Co, 255
Nelson, Amy Dentaquest, 531
Nelson, Brock Health Partners Medicare Plan, 605
Nelson, Brock HealthPartners, 606
Nelson, David Blue Care Network of Michigan: Medicare, 552
Nelson, Gunnar Patient Choice, 615
Nelson, Jeffrey UPMC Health Plan, 973
Nelson, Josh Great-West/One Health Plan, 207
Nelson, Mike Coventry Health Care of Nebraska, 679
Nelson, Russell Altius Health Plans, 1102
Nelson, Sandy Wellmark Health Plan of Iowa, 432
Nelson, Su Zan Concentra: Corporate Office, 1060
Nelson, William IHC: Intermountain Healthcare Health Plan, 351
Nemeth, Joseph MercyCare Health Plans, 1205
Nemeth, Thomas A Health Plan of New York, 783
Nenni, Angie Delta Dental of Kentucky, 461
Neshat, Amir, DDS Liberty Dental Plan, 148
Neshat, Amir, DDS Liberty Dental Plan of Nevada, 698
Nethery, Regina C Humana Medicare Plan, 464
New, Deborah Anthem Blue Cross & Blue Shield of Colorado, 192
New, Deborah Anthem Blue Cross & Blue Shield Connecticut, 220
New, Deborah Anthem Blue Cross & Blue Shield of Indiana, 391
New, Deborah Anthem Blue Cross & Blue Shield of Indiana, 392
New, Deborah Anthem Blue Cross & Blue Shield of Maine, 488
Newland, Jeff Blue Cross & Blue Shield of New Mexico, 744
Newman, Christy Cariten Healthcare, 1031
Newman, Christy Cariten Preferred, 1032
Newman, Kermit Lakeside Community Healthcare Network, 146
Newsome, Rick Kaiser Permanente Health Plan of Colorado, 210
Newton, Cecil San Francisco Health Plan, 173
Newton, Dean Delta Dental of Kansas, 440
Newton, W. Keith Concentra: Corporate Office, 1060
Nguyen, Minh N MD Care Healthplan, 152
Nguyen, Ted Calais Health, 473
Nicholas, Jonathan ODS Health Plan, 915
Nichols, Sandra, MD UnitedHealthCare of Northern California, 182
Nichols, Sandra, MD UnitedHealthCare of Southern California, 183
Nicholson, Joseph Blue Cross & Blue Shield of Oklahoma, 887

Nicholson, Tom DakotaCare, 1017
Nickerson, Matt Liberty Health Plan: Corporate Office, 912
Nicklaus, Dana First Care Health Plans, 1065
Nicoll, Don, MD CIGNA HealthCare of New Jersey, 723
Nied, Michelle Patient Choice, 615
Niederberger, Jane Anthem Blue Cross & Blue Sheild of Indiana, 391
Nieman, Kelly L Midlands Choice, 683
Nienhaus, Jeffrey ChiroCare of Wisconsin, 1190
Nissenbaum, Richard, RPh Humana Health Insurance of Tampa - Pinellas, 288
Noah, Kent M Trillium Community Health Plan, 921
Nobile, Paul Unicare: Illinois, 385
Nolan, Tim Magellan Health Services: Corporate Headquarters, 515
Nolan, Tim Magellan Medicaid Administration, 1136
Nolan, Timothy E HealthAmerica Pennsylvania, 952
Noland, Tom Humana Health Insurance of Illinois, 377
Noland, Tom Humana Health Insurance of Iowa, 427
Nonal, Timothy Coventry Health Care of Delaware, 235
Norato, Mark Coventry Health Care of GA, 319
Noren, Jenny Gundersen Lutheran Health Plan, 1199
Norman, DK UTMB HealthCare Systems, 1097
Norman, Gordon K, MD/MBA Alere Health, 309
Northfield, David Kaiser Permanente Health Plan Northwest, 911
Norton, Deborah Harvard Pilgrim Health Care: Maine, 492
Norton, Deborah Harvard Pilgrim Health Care, 536
Norton, Deborah Harvard Pilgrim Health Care of New England, 710
Nota-Kirby, Betsy M-Care, 579
Novello, James Arcadian Health Plans, 83
Novick, Nancy Phoenix Health Plan, 55
Nowakowski, Richard M-Care, 579
Nowicki, Sarah Tufts Health Plan: Rhode Island, 993
Nudd, Audrey Regence Blue Shield, 1166
Nussbaum, Samuel R, MD WellPoint: Corporate Office, 417
Nuzzi, Rosemarie Island Group Administration, Inc., 789
Nyquist, Cynthia Upper Peninsula Health Plan, 593

O

O'Brien, Ann Marie UnitedHealthCare of New York, 810
O'Brien, Cyndie Inter Valley Health Plan, 138
O'Brien, David M Highmark Blue Cross & Blue Shield, 953
O'Brien, David M Highmark Blue Shield, 954
O'Brien, Lauren CIGNA HealthCare of Georgia, 316
O'Brien, Ralph UnitedHealthCare of Ohio: Columbus, 882
O'Brien, Ralph UnitedHealthCare of Ohio: Dayton & Cincinnati, 883
O'Brien, Robert Group Health Cooperative, 1157
O'Brien, Tim Blue Cross & Blue Shield of Massachusetts, 527
O'Brien, William Network Health Plan of Wisconsin, 1206
O'Connell, Jeff Paramount Care of Michigan, 583
O'Connell, Jeff Paramount Elite Medicare Plan, 871
O'Connell, Jeff Paramount Health Care, 872
O'Connor, H Tomkins American WholeHealth Network, 928
O'Connor, Mary Beth Excellus Blue Cross Blue Shield: Rochester Region, 776
O'Connor, Maureen K Blue Cross & Blue Shield of North Carolina, 816
O'Connor, Maureen K Preferred Care Select, 829
O'Connor, Michael Davis Vision, 769
O'Connor, Sharon CorVel Corporation, 114
O'Dell, Sara ConnectCare, 561
O'Drobinak, James P Universal Health Care Group, 304
O'Gorman, Scott Boston Medical Center Healthnet Plan, 528
O'Hanlon, Greg Health Net Health Plan of Oregon, 909
O'Keefe, Denise ConnectCare, 561
O'Keese, Michael Central Susquehanna Healthcare Providers, 937
O'Loughlin, William B Blue Cross and Blue Shield Association, 360
O'Neil-White, Alphonso Blue Cross & Blue Shield of Western New York, 762
O'Neil-White, Alphonso BlueShield of Northeastern New York, 763
O'Neil-White, Alphonso HealthNow New York, 784
O'Neill, Charles Avalon Healthcare, 258
O'Neill, Peter UnitedHealthcare Nevada, 704
O'Shields, Brian Aetna Health of the Carolinas, 814
Oakley, Donald VSP: Vision Service Plan, 186
Oaks, Joe Health Choice of Alabama, 11
Oberg, Steve HSM: Healthcare Cost Management, 607

Obourn, Noel CIGNA HealthCare of North Carolina, 818
Oddo, Angel HealthAmerica Pennsylvania, 952
Odgaard, Nate Blue Cross & Blue Shield of Nebraska, 677
Odom, Karen HAS-Premier Providers, 1068
Odzer, Randall United Behavioral Health, 180
Ogdon, Tom Anthem Blue Cross & Blue Shield of Missouri, 634
Ogle, Jane Santa Clara Family Health Plan, 174
Ohman, Daniel Laurence UnitedHealthCare of Georgia, 330
Ohme, Sheryle L Assurant Employee Benefits: Corporate Headquarters, 635
Olearczyk, John Fidelis Care, 778
Oleg, Dennis, PhD Humana Health Insurance of Wisconsin, 1202
Oliker, David MVP Health Care: New Hampshire, 712
Oliker, David MVP Health Care Medicare Plan, 795
Oliker, David MVP Health Care: Buffalo Region, 796
Oliker, David MVP Health Care: Central New York, 797
Oliker, David MVP Health Care: Corporate Office, 798
Oliker, David MVP Health Care: Mid-State Region, 799
Oliker, David MVP Health Care: Western New York, 800
Oliker, David MVP Health Care: Vermont, 1122
Oliver, Diane HealthSpan, 857
Olmstead, Francis H, Jr Cariten Healthcare, 1031
Olsen, David HSM: Healthcare Cost Management, 607
Olshanski, Jayne HealthAmerica Pennsylvania, 952
Olson, David W Health Net Medicare Plan, 131
Olson, Fred, MD Blue Cross & Blue Shield of Montana, 664
Olson, Michael Fortified Provider Network, 44
Olson, Tom Wisconsin Physician's Service, 1214
Olson, Wendy Americas PPO, 1014
Olsten, Dan Martin's Point HealthCare, 493
Olzawski, Elaine, RN BlueLincs HMO, 888
Omeo, Heather Assurant Employee Benefits: North Carolina, 815
Onorati, Annette C, Esq Preferred Care Partners, 296
Ordway, Jody Managed HealthCare Northwest, 914
Oreskovich, Kitty Health Net Health Plan of Oregon, 909
Orland, Burton Oxford Health Plans: New Jersey, 736
Ormond, John Hometown Health Plan, 696
Orsbon, Nance Delta Dental of South Dakota, 1018
Ortega, Janice Peoples Health, 482
Ortego, Janice Tenet Choices, 483
Ortiz, Diana Blue Cross & Blue Shield of Delaware, 233
Osborne, Mary Lou HealthAmerica Pennsylvania, 952
Osenar, Peter Interplan Health Group, 139, 1076
Osenar, Peter R Emerald Health PPO, 854
Osgood, Teena Fallon Community Health Plan, 533
Osgood, Teena Fallon Community Medicare Plan, 534
Osmick, Mary Jane American Specialty Health, 82
Osorio, Rosemary Dimension Health PPO, 276
Osowski, Henry SCAN Health Plan, 175
Oster, David Aetna Health of Texas, 1046
Ostrov, Michael, MD Group Health Cooperative of South Central Wisconsin, 1198
Ott, David HealthLink HMO, 651
Outten, Cornelia Interplan Health Group, 139
Owen, Wanda MedCost, 826
Owens, Dawn Dental Benefit Providers, 509
Owens, Dawn OptumHealth Care Solutions: Physical Health, 614
Owens-Collins, Shelia, MD Community First Health Plans, 1059
Owings, Lorena Ohio State University Health Plan Inc., 869
Ownbey, Ron Delta Dental of Arkansas, 71

P

Pace, Carolyn Health Net of Arizona, 47
Pace, Nicholas Amerigroup Corporation, 1125
Packman, Robert C, MD Centene Corporation, 638
Padilla, Maria ABRI Health Plan, Inc., 1185
Page, Kenneth HealthSpan, 857
Pagliaro, Brian P Tufts Health Medicare Plan, 543
Pagliaro, Brian P Tufts Health Plan, 544
Paguia, Victor PacificSource Health Plans: Corporate Headquarters, 917
Pair, Judy Alliant Health Plans, 310
Pak, Mary, MD Unity Health Insurance, 1212
Palenske, Frederick D Blue Cross & Blue Shield of Kansas, 436

Palmaterr, Michael Health Plan of New York, 783
Palmer, Cynthia Colorado Choice Health Plans, 200
Palmer, Elaine Wellmark Health Plan of Iowa, 432
Palmer, Paul UnitedHealthcare Nevada, 704
Palmer, Paula VSP: Vision Service Plan of Colorado, 216
Palmer, Paula VSP: Vision Service Plan of Hawaii, 343
Palmer, Robert Dean Health Plan, 1192
Palmer, Roland Grand Valley Health Plan, 568
Palumbo, Fara M Blue Cross & Blue Shield of North Carolina, 816
Palumbo, Pam PacifiCare Health Systems, 164
Panchuk, Dottie Assurant Employee Benefits: Texas, 1050
Pando, Roberto Medical Card System (MCS), 980
Pankau, David Blue Cross & Blue Shield of South Carolina, 997
Panneton, Kirk R, MD CDPHP Medicare Plan, 764
Panneton, Kirk R, MD CDPHP: Capital District Physicians' Health Plan, 765
Panturf, Betsy CommunityCare Managed Healthcare Plans of Oklahoma, 890
Paralta, Cynthia L Unicare: Massachusetts, 545
Pardi, Cherie Health Choice of Alabama, 11
Parietti, Dan WellCare Health Plans, 307
Park, Jeffrey SXC Health Solutions Corp, 383
Parker, David C Meritain Health: Corporate Headquarters, 792
Parker, James Anthem Blue Cross & Blue Shield of Maine, 488
Parker, Katrina W CNA Insurance Companies: Colorado, 198
Parker, Katrina W CNA Insurance Companies: Georgia, 317
Parker, Katrina W CNA Insurance Companies: Illinois, 362
Parker, Mike Virginia Premier Health Plan, 1147
Parker, Robert, MD Health Alliance Medical Plans, 371
Parker, Ted Interplan Health Group, 139
Parker, Ted HealthSmart Preferred Care, 374
Parker, Ted Interplan Health Group, 1076
Parrot, James S Virginia Premier Health Plan, 1147
Parrott, Chris Total Dental Administrators, 59
Paskowski, Robert S Arnett Health Plans, 394
Pass, Kathy Pacific Foundation for Medical Care, 160
Passauer, Christopher Patient Choice, 615
Pastore, William Evercare Health Plans, 603
Pastro, Margaret, SP Providence Health Plans, 918
Patberg, Elizabeth Deaconess Health Plans, 398
Patel, Nilesh Pacific Dental Benefits, 159
Patel, Prakash R, MD Magellan Health Services: Corporate Headquarters, 515
Patel, Sandip Universal Health Care Group, 304
Patmas, Michael, MD Clear One Health Plans, 905
Patterson, Kari PacificSource Health Plans: Corporate Headquarters, 917
Patti, Paul Horizon Health Corporation, 1073
Paul, Erick Delta Dental: Corporate Headquarters, 563
Paul, Katherine Delta Dental of Colorado, 202
Paulson, Trisha Prevea Health Network, 1208
Paustian, Dale Davis Vision, 769
Pawenski, Pamela J Univera Healthcare, 811
Pawlenok, Alan Blue Cross of Northeastern Pennsylvania, 933
Payne, Donna Arizona Physicians IPA, 33
Payne, Solomon OmniCare: A Coventry Health Care Plan, 582
Paynter, Lois Saint Mary's Health Plans, 703
Payson, Norman, MD Oxford Health Plans: Corporate Headquarters, 229
Peabody, Laura S Harvard Pilgrim Health Care, 536
Peace, Terry Blue Cross & Blue Shield of South Carolina, 997
Pearce, Dan Aultcare Corporation, 848
Pearl, Robert M, MD Kaiser Permanente Health Plan of Northern California, 140
Pearl, Robert M, MD Kaiser Permanente Health Plan of the Mid-Atlantic States, 514
Pearson, Christy Healthchoice Orlando, 284
Peck, Ted Educators Mutual, 1105
Peddie, Gidget Managed Health Network, 150
Pederson, Sharon Heart of America Health Plan, 839
Peele, Pamela, PhD UPMC Health Plan, 973
Pellegrino, Nicholas E Health First Medicare Plans, 283
Pelly, Cameron Premera Blue Cross Blue Shield of Alaska, 27
Pels Beck, Leslie Sharp Health Plan, 176
Peluso, John Guardian Life Insurance Company, 782
Penderson, Maggy Noridian Insurance Services, 842
Pendleton, Jennifer InStil Health, 1005

Prussing, Gregg CIGNA HealthCare of Alaska, 21
Prussing, Gregg CIGNA HealthCare of Colorado, 197
Prussing, Gregg CIGNA HealthCare of Montana, 665
Prussing, Gregg CIGNA HealthCare of Wyoming, 1217
Przesiek, David Fallon Community Health Plan, 533
Przesiek, David Fallon Community Medicare Plan, 534
Ptacek, Scott Bravo Health: Corporate Headquarters, 502
Pudimott, Missy CHN PPO, 722
Puente, Mark Bravo Health: Corporate Headquarters, 502
Pugh, Ricard Community Health Improvement Solutions, 641
Puglisi, Jennifer Leon Medical Centers Health Plan, 290
Pures, Robert Horizon Healthcare of New Jersey, 731
Pures, Robert J Horizon Blue Cross & Blue Shield of New Jersey, 730
Pures, Robert J Rayant Insurance Company, 738
Purpura, Nate eHealthInsurance Services Inc., 9
Pursley, Janet Mercy Health Plans: Kansas, 445
Pursley, Janet Mercy Health Medicare Plan, 654
Pursley, Janet Mercy Health Plans: Corporate Office, 655
Pursley, Janet Mercy Health Plans: Oklahoma, 896
Putiak, Mike Peoples Health, 482
Putiak, Mike Tenet Choices, 483
Putman, Shawn C OptiCare Managed Vision, 828
Putnam, Harold Neighborhood Health Plan, 542
Putt, Lisa Blue Cross & Blue Shield of Oklahoma, 887
Putz, Jeff Blue Cross & Blue Shield of Delaware, 233
Pye, Irma Valley Baptist Health Plan, 1098
Pyle, David Managed HealthCare Northwest, 914

Q

Quinlinvan, Keith Kern Family Health Care, 144
Quinn, Su Welborn Health Plans, 416
Quinn, Tom Medfocus Radiology Network, 153

R

Radhe, Brenda Humana Health Insurance of Orlando, 287
Radine, Gary Delta Dental of California, 115
Radine, Gary D Delta Dental of Alabama, 8
Radine, Gary D Delta Dental of the Mid-Atlantic, 236, 247
Radine, Gary D Delta Dental of Georgia, 320
Radine, Gary D Delta Dental Insurance Company, 476
Radine, Gary D Delta Dental of the Mid-Atlantic, 507
Radine, Gary D Delta Dental Insurance Company, 626
Radine, Gary D Delta Dental of the Mid-Atlantic, 770, 941, 1175
Radner, Marc J SCAN Health Plan, 175
Rady, Dawn Network Health Plan of Wisconsin, 1206
Raffio, Thomas Delta Dental Northeast, 708
Rainer, Dan HealthPartners, 1037
Raines, Valerie SelectNet Plus, Inc., 1182
Raines, Valorie SelectNet Plus, Inc., 1182
Rains, Cheryl VSP: Vision Service Plan of Georgia, 331
Rajamannar, Raja Humana Health Insurance of Kentucky, 463
Rakestraw, Rita CIGNA HealthCare of Georgia, 316
Raley, Karen Arkansas Blue Cross and Blue Shield, 66
Ramirez, Ramie Community First Health Plans, 1059
Ramsey, Garry Bluegrass Family Health, 457
Randall, Todd University Health Plans, 1116
Randolph, John C Paramount Care of Michigan, 583
Randolph, John C Paramount Elite Medicare Plan, 871
Randolph, John C Paramount Health Care, 872
Randolph, Kimberly Basic Chiropractic Health Plan, 86
Ranton, James D Guardian Life Insurance Company, 782
Rapee, Ed Assurant Employee Benefits: Wisconsin, 1188
Rashti, Dana Harvard Pilgrim Health Care: Maine, 492
Rashti, Dana Harvard Pilgrim Health Care, 536
Rashti, Dana Harvard Pilgrim Health Care of New England, 710
Raskauskas, Thomas A, MD Health Plan of Michigan, 573
Rasmussen, Sharon K Midlands Choice, 683
Rausch, Jay Dominion Dental Services, 1132
Rausch, Joy Superior Vision Services, Inc., 178
Ray, Mary Delta Dental of Alabama, 8
Raybuck, Gregg E Alere Health, 309

Reagan, Michael Fortified Provider Network, 44
Reamer, Michael Avesis: Corporate Headquarters, 34
Reay, Bill Physicians Plus Insurance Corporation, 1207
Records, Paul Kaiser Permanente Health Plan of Northern California, 140
Records, Paul Kaiser Permanente Health Plan of Southern California, 141
Records, Paul Kaiser Permanente Health Plan: Corporate Office, 142
Records, Paul Kaiser Permanente Medicare Plan, 143
Redmond, Dave MultiPlan, Inc., 794
Redmond, James Excellus Blue Cross Blue Shield: Rochester Region, 776
Redmund, David Beech Street Corporation: Corporate Office, 87
Reed, Philip J Colorado Access, 199
Reef, Chris Meritain Health: Indiana, 409
Reef, Chris Welborn Health Plans, 416
Reef, Chris Meritain Health: Kentucky, 465
Reef, Chris Meritain Health: Corporate Headquarters, 792
Reese, Dennis, CPA Martin's Point HealthCare, 493
Reese Furgerson, Cindy, RN QualChoice/QCA Health Plan, 76
Reeves, Donald K Brazos Valley Health Network, 1056
Reid, Allan Health Resources, Inc., 405
Reid, Rohan Lovelace Health Plan, 750
Reid, Rohan Lovelace Medicare Health Plan, 751
Reimer, Eric Magellan Health Services Indiana, 408
Reinecke, Mark, MD Humana Health Insurance of Orlando, 287
Reingold, Kimberly Blue Cross & Blue Shield of Rhode Island, 986
Reinhard, Glen UnitedHealthCare of Wisconsin: Central, 622
Reinhardt, Mel New West Health Services, 672
Reinke, John Blue Shield of California, 91
Reisman, Lonny, MD Aetna Health of Alabama, 1
Reisman, Lonny, MD Aetna Health of Alaska, 18
Reisman, Lonny, MD Aetna Health of Arkansas, 64
Reisman, Lonny, MD Aetna Health, Inc. Corporate Headquarters, 217
Reisman, Lonny, MD Aetna Health, Inc. Medicare Plan, 218
Reisman, Lonny, MD Aetna Health of Delaware, 231
Reisman, Lonny, MD Aetna Health District of Columbia, 243
Reisman, Lonny, MD Aetna Health of Hawaii, 332
Reisman, Lonny, MD Aetna Health of Idaho, 344
Reisman, Lonny, MD Aetna Health of Iowa, 418
Reisman, Lonny, MD Aetna Health of Kansas, 434
Reisman, Lonny, MD Aetna Health of Kentucky, 455
Reisman, Lonny, MD Aetna Health of Louisiana, 470
Reisman, Lonny, MD Aetna Health of Maine, 487
Reisman, Lonny, MD Aetna Health of Maryland, 496
Reisman, Lonny, MD Aetna Health of Massachusetts, 524
Reisman, Lonny, MD Aetna Health of Michigan, 548
Reisman, Lonny, MD Aetna Health of Minnesota, 595
Reisman, Lonny, MD Aetna Health of Mississippi, 624
Reisman, Lonny, MD Aetna Health of Montana, 662
Reisman, Lonny, MD Aetna Health of Nebraska, 675
Reisman, Lonny, MD Aetna Health of New Hampshire, 705
Reisman, Lonny, MD Aetna Health of New Jersey, 715
Reisman, Lonny, MD Aetna Health of New Mexico, 742
Reisman, Lonny, MD Aetna Health of New York, 757
Reisman, Lonny, MD Aetna Health of North Dakota, 834
Reisman, Lonny, MD Aetna Health of Oregon, 899
Reisman, Lonny, MD Aetna Health of Pennsylvania, 926
Reisman, Lonny, MD Aetna Health of Rhode Island, 985
Reisman, Lonny, MD Aetna Health of South Dakota, 1013
Reisman, Lonny, MD Aetna Health of Utah, 1101
Reisman, Lonny, MD Aetna Health of Vermont, 1117
Reisman, Lonny, MD Aetna Health of Virginia, 1124
Reisman, Lonny, MD Aetna Health of Washington, 1148
Reisman, Dennis, MD Aetna Health of West Virginia, 1172
Reisman, Lonny, MD Aetna Health of Wisconsin, 1186
Reisman, Lonny, MD Aetna Health of Wyoming, 1215
ReismanD, Lonny Aetna Health of Colorado, 190
Reitan, Colleen Blue Cross & Blue Shield of Illinois, 359
Reitan, Colleen Health Care Service Corporation, 373
Reiten, Christine Metropolitan Health Plan, 612
Reitz, Mike Blue Cross & Blue Shield of Louisiana, 472
Rekart, Thomas Bravo Health: Corporate Headquarters, 502
Rekart, Tom Spectera, 521
Remmers, Rick Humana Health Insurance of Mississippi, 629

Romansky, Eilene Interplan Health Group, 860
Romasco, Robert G CIGNA HealthCare of Maine, 489
Romza, John SXC Health Solutions Corp, 383
Ron, Aran, MD UnitedHealthCare of North Carolina, 832
Rondon, Ronelle Catalyst RX, 817
Roomsburg, Margaret M Amerigroup Corporation, 1125
Roos, John T Blue Cross & Blue Shield of North Carolina, 816
Roos, John T Preferred Care Select, 829
Roosevelt, James, Jr Tufts Health Medicare Plan, 543
Roosevelt, James, Jr Tufts Health Plan, 544
Root, Leon A, Jr Amerigroup Corporation, 1125
Root, Paula, MD BlueLincs HMO, 888
Roschbach, Jacki, MSS MHNet Behavioral Health, 1081
Rose, Brian Preferred Health Systems Insurance Company, 447
Rose, Brian Preferred Plus of Kansas, 449
Rose, Carolyn Health Choice Arizona, 46
Rose, Esther, RPh OmniCare: A Coventry Health Care Plan, 582
Rose, Joan, MPH Lakeside Community Healthcare Network, 146
Rose, MD, Trevor A, MS MMM Quality Health Plans, 298
Rose, MD, Trevor A, MS MMM Quality Health Plans of New York, 807
Rose-Long, Jennifer Advance Insurance Company of Kansas, 433
Rosen, Bernard MetroPlus Health Plan, 793
Rosenblatt, Elaine Unity Health Insurance, 1212
Rosenhan, Deborah Altius Health Plans, 1102
Rosenthal, Dan UnitedHealthCare of Northern California, 182
Rosenthal, Dan UnitedHealthCare of South Florida, 303
Rosenthal, Daniel Neighborhood Health Partnership, 293
Rosenthal, David S, MD Harvard University Group Health Plan, 537
Rosenthal, Robert Delta Dental of North Carolina, 821
Ross, Kelly CommunityCare Managed Healthcare Plans of Oklahoma, 890
Ross, Michael Total Health Choice, 300
Ross, Patrick Arcadian Health Plans, 83
Rosse, Claire, RN Nationwide Better Health, 867
Roth, Bill Aetna Health of Oklahoma, 885
Rothbart, Marc, BSN Southeastern Indiana Health Organization, 413
Rothenberg, Nancy Physical Therapy Provider Network, 167
Rothenberg, Nancy PTPN, 171
Rothman, Janet Elderplan, 773
Rothrock, Kirk CompBenefits Corporation, 318
Rountree, Virginia Pima Health System, 56
Routh, Charles, MD Cardinal Health Alliance, 396
Rowan, Michael Care 1st Health Plan: California, 97
Rowe, John W, MD Aetna Health of Indiana, 389
Roxstrom, Tony Western Dental Services, 188
Roy, Denis J Wellmark Health Plan of Iowa, 432
Roy-Czyzowski, Connie M, SHPR Delta Dental Northeast, 708
Royer, Jerry, MD, MBA Vytra Health Plans, 813
Rubin, Jonathan CIGNA HealthCare of North Carolina, 818
Rubin, Jonathan N Magellan Health Services: Corporate Headquarters, 515
Rubino, Thomas M, Esq Horizon Healthcare of New Jersey, 731
Rubino, Thomas W, Esq Horizon Blue Cross & Blue Shield of New Jersey, 730
Rubinstein, Richard San Francisco Health Plan, 173
Rubretsky, Joseph Aetna Health of Colorado, 190
Ruchman, Mark OptiCare Managed Vision, 828
Rucker, Madeline R Mutual of Omaha DentaBenefits, 684
Rucker, Madeline R Mutual of Omaha Health Plans, 685
Rudd, Lori Health Alliance Medical Plans, 371
Ruhlmann, John L Coventry Health Care: Corporate Headquarters, 506
Ruiz-Topinka, Conchita AvMed Health Plan: Corporate Office, 259
Ruiz-Topinka, Conchita AvMed Health Plan: Fort Lauderdale, 260
Ruiz-Topinka, Conchita AvMed Health Plan: Gainesville, 261
Ruiz-Topinka, Conchita AvMed Health Plan: Jacksonville, 262
Ruiz-Topinka, Conchita AvMed Health Plan: Orlando, 263
Ruiz-Topinka, Conchita AvMed Health Plan: Tampa, 264
Rulli, Jesse Vision Insurance Plan of America, 1213
Rumfelt, Michelle Crescent Preferred Provider Organization, 820
Rundhaug, Pamala Managed Health Services, 1203
Runnoe, Phil, DDS Western Dental Services, 188
Rupp, Tammy Care Choices, 557
Ruppert, Greg Peoples Health, 482
Rush, Mark BlueChoice Health Plan of South Carolina, 998

Russell, Dolores Managed HealthCare Northwest, 914
Russell, Elizabeth Delta Dental of California, 115
Russell, Elizabeth S SCAN Health Plan, 175
Russell, Nichelle North Alabama Managed Care Inc, 14
Russo, Joan Affinity Health Plan, 758
Russo, Pamela United Behavioral Health, 180
Russo, Patricia A Trigon Health Care, 1143
Ruth, Kevin Dental Benefit Providers, 509
Ruthven, Courtney Preferred Mental Health Management, 448
Ruthven, Les, PhD Preferred Mental Health Management, 448
Ryan, Caren InterGroup Services Corporation, 957
Ryan, John Novasys Health, 52
Ryan, Kevin HealthSCOPE Benefits, 73
Ryan, Mike Unicare: Texas, 1093
Ryan, Thomas M. CVS CareMark, 988
Ryan, Tim CHA Health, 458
Ryan, Timothy F OptumHealth Care Solutions: Physical Health, 614
Rzewnicki, Robert HMO Health Ohio, 858
Rzewnicki, Robert Medical Mutual of Ohio, 862
Rzewnicki, Robert Medical Mutual of Ohio Medicare Plan, 863
Rzewnicki, Robert SuperMed One, 878

S

Saalwaechter, John J, MD HealthPlus of Michigan: Flint, 574
Saalwaechter, John J, MD HealthPlus of Michigan: Saginaw, 575
Sabastian, Carmella, MD Blue Cross of Northeastern Pennsylvania, 933
Sabater, Lilia Medical Card System (MCS), 980
Sabatino, Ezio ConnectiCare, 223
Sabin, Paul Managed Health Services, 1203
Sabolik, Jim HealthSmart Preferred Care, 374
Sack, Robert, MD Magellan Health Services Arizona, 49
Sacks, Joel Denta-Chek of Maryland, 508
Sacks, Robert D Denta-Chek of Maryland, 508
Sade, Nikki ProviDRs Care Network, 451
Sadler, Robin Kaiser Permanente Health Plan of Colorado, 210
Safran, Bruce, DDS Healthplex, 785
Safran, Bruce H Dentcare Delivery Systems, 771
Sakovits, Steven HealthFirst New Jersey Medicare Plan, 729
Salazar, Deanna Blue Cross & Blue Shield of Arizona, 36
Salm, Gordon Health Alliance Medical Plans, 371
Saltarelli, Wendy Boulder Valley Individual Practice Association, 196
Salyards, Keith Foundation for Medical Care for Kern & Santa Barbara County, 123
Salyer, Jim Valley Baptist Health Plan, 1098
Samples, Dana Chinese Community Health Plan, 102
Sanabria, Farrah, PHR Quality Health Plans, 298
Sanabria, Farrah, PHR Quality Health Plans of New York, 807
Sanchez, April Block Vision of Texas, 1052
Sanchez, Eduardo Blue Cross & Blue Shield of Texas, 1053
Sanchez, Ester M California Foundation for Medical Care, 95
Sanchez, Javier CalOptima, 96
Sanchez Colon, Jesus R Triple-S Salud Blue Cross Blue Shield of Puerto Rico, 983
Sanders, Scott B First Commonwealth, 368
Sanders, Steve, DO PacifiCare of Oklahoma, 897
Sandoval, Lisa A, CPA Colorado Choice Health Plans, 200
Sands, Mark Phoenix Health Plan, 55
Sanghvi, Sujata PacificSource Health Plans: Corporate Headquarters, 917
Sank, Patricia A Valley Preferred, 975
Santelli, Lisa, Esq Excellus Blue Cross Blue Shield: Rochester Region, 776
Santiago, Nicole Educators Mutual, 1105
Santillan, Brandie Galaxy Health Network, 1066
Santoro, Micheal Oxford Health Plans: New York, 805
Santos, Grace HealthFirst New Jersey Medicare Plan, 729
Saperstein, Arnold, MD MetroPlus Health Plan, 793
Sarrel, Lloyd CoreSource: Corporate Headquarters, 364
Sasscer, Georgia Crescent Preferred Provider Organization, 820
Sassi, Brian A WellPoint: Corporate Office, 417
Sattenspiel, John Trillium Community Health Plan, 921
Sauter, Toni PersonalCare, 381
Sava, Frank Independent Health, 787
Sava, Frank Independent Health Medicare Plan, 788

Savenko, Kathy OhioHealth Group, 870
Savitsky, Trish Blue Cross of Northeastern Pennsylvania, 933
Saxinger Norwig, Debye Avalon Healthcare, 258
Scanlan, Edward, MD Network Health Plan of Wisconsin, 1206
Scarborough, Bianca California Foundation for Medical Care, 95
Scarbrough, Stephanie Healthchoice Orlando, 284
Scarpone, Connie Physicians Health Plan of Mid-Michigan, 584
Scasny, Ron ABRI Health Plan, Inc., 1185
Scavone, Cindy AvMed Health Plan: Fort Lauderdale, 260
Scepanski, Theresa Community First Health Plans, 1059
Schacht, Karla J Assurant Employee Benefits: Corporate Headquarters, 635
Schaffer, David Medical Card System (MCS), 980
Schaffer, Ian A Managed Health Network, 150
Schaich, Robert Health Plan of Nevada, 695
Schaich, Robert UnitedHealthcare Nevada, 704
Schalles, Robert Penn Highlands Health Plan, 961
Schandel, David Florida Health Care Plan, 279
Scheele, Robb Humana Health Insurnace of Colorado, 209
Scheerer, Bill, CPA MHNet Behavioral Health, 1081
Scheff, Jonathan H, MD/MBA Health Net Medicare Plan, 131
Scheffel, William N Centene Corporation, 638
Schellinger, Ellen, MA Sanford Health Plan, 430
Scherer, Jerry D Blue Cross & Blue Shield of Oklahoma, 887
Scherer, Kurt Cox Healthplans, 642
Scherer, Robin Prime Source Health Network, 965
Scherier, Russell J Delta Dental of Colorado, 202
Schexnayder, Todd Blue Cross & Blue Shield of Louisiana, 472
Schick, Susan CIGNA HealthCare of Virginia, 1129
Schievelbein, Karen Dental Benefit Providers, 509
Schmidt, Bradley Bright Now! Dental, 93
Schmidt, Chester, MD Priority Partners Health Plans, 520
Schmidt, Chris, MBA Healthplex, 785
Schmidt, Dave SCAN Health Plan, 175
Schmidt, Kurt Care Plus Dental Plans, 1189
Schmidt, Steve PacificSource Health Plans: Corporate Headquarters, 917
Schneider, George Mercy Health Plans: Kansas, 445
Schneider, George Mercy Health Medicare Plan, 654
Schneider, George Mercy Health Plans: Corporate Office, 655
Schneider, George Mercy Health Plans: Oklahoma, 896
Schneider, George, CPA Geisinger Health Plan, 948
Schnipper, Ida ConnectiCare of Massachusetts, 530
Schnitzer, Rhea Managed HealthCare Northwest, 914
Scholtz, Stacy A Mutual of Omaha DentaBenefits, 684
Scholtz, Stacy A Mutual of Omaha Health Plans, 685
Schotz, Michael Interplan Health Group, 139
Schrader, Elana, MD Blue Cross & Blue Shield of Florida: Jacksonville, 266
Schrader, Michael CenCal Health: The Regional Health Authority, 99
Schrader, Michael Boston Medical Center Healthnet Plan, 528
Schrader, William R Blue Cross & Blue Shield of South Carolina, 997
Schreiber, Joy Block Vision of Texas, 1052
Schreiner, Rob, MD Kaiser Permanente of Georgia, 324
Schrock, Richard Ohio State University Health Plan Inc., 869
Schrupp, Alison Providence Health Plans, 918
Schubach, Aaron Opticare of Utah, 1110
Schubach, Stephen Opticare of Utah, 1110
Schuchmann, Pace Assurant Employee Benefits: Georgia, 312
Schultz, Carl Mercy Health Plans: Kansas, 445
Schultz, Carl Mercy Health Medicare Plan, 654
Schultz, Carl Mercy Health Plans: Corporate Office, 655
Schultz, Carl Mercy Health Plans: Oklahoma, 896
Schultz, Eric Harvard Pilgrim Health Care, 536
Schultz, Eric H Harvard Pilgrim Health Care: Maine, 492
Schultz, Eric H Harvard Pilgrim Health Care of New England, 710
Schultz, Mary Ann Blue Cross & Blue Shield of Illinois, 359
Schultz, Tim Metropolitan Health Plan, 612
Schultze-Evans, Jill Dental Benefit Providers: California, 117
Schumacher-Konick, Tamara Citrus Health Care, 271
Schumaker, L Don, DDS Superior Dental Care, 877
Schumann, Donald Network Health Plan of Wisconsin, 1206
Schunhoff, John F, PhD Los Angeles County Public Healthcare, 149
Schurman, Theresa HealthPlus of Michigan: Flint, 574
Schurman, Theresa HealthPlus of Michigan: Saginaw, 575

Schuster, Glendon A Centene Corporation, 638
Schwab, Jeff Dominion Dental Services, 1132
Schwab, Timothy, MD SCAN Health Plan, 175
Schwarz, Jon UnitedHealthCare of South Florida, 303
Schweers, Rob Wellmark Health Plan of Iowa, 432
Schweers, Rob Wellmark Blue Cross & Blue Shield of South Dakota, 1025
Schweitzer, Gale S&S Healthcare Strategies, 874
Schweppe, Richard CorVel Corporation, 114
Scoggens, Alan Texas True Choice, 1092
Scono, Thomas E, RPh EPIC Pharmacy Network, 1134
Scott, Barry Quality Plan Administrators, 251
Scott, Bertram CIGNA: Corporate Headquarters, 939
Scott, Christopher Managed Health Services, 1203
Scott, Cory Coventry Health Care of GA, 319
Scott, David M Health Alliance Medicare, 571
Scott, David M Health Alliance Plan, 572
Scott, Garland John Deere Health, 1042
Scott, Greg Secure Horizons, 77
Scott, Greg PacifiCare of Colorado, 211
Scott, Greg PacifiCare of Texas, 1084
Scott, Greg PacifiCare Benefit Administrators, 1162
Scott, Gregory W PacifiCare Health Systems, 164
Scott, Gregory W PacifiCare of Nevada, 702
Scott, Jim Liberty Health Plan: Corporate Office, 912
Scott, Kirby Delta Dental of South Dakota, 1018
Scott, Peggy Blue Cross & Blue Shield of Louisiana, 472
Scott, Ruth Horizon Health Corporation, 1073
Screiber, Larry Anthem Blue Cross & Blue Shield of Wisconsin, 1187
Seabert, Pat, RN Care 1st Health Plan: Arizona, 37
Searls, Thomas J Delta Dental of Oklahoma, 892
Sedita-Igneri, Jessica Care 1st Health Plan: Arizona, 37
Sedmak, Pamela Blue Cross & Blue Shield of Minnesota, 599
See, Kyle Assurant Employee Benefits: California, 85
Seebold, Andy South Central Preferred, 967
Segal, David Neighborhood Health Plan, 542
Segal, Herbert Elderplan, 773
Seidenfeld, John, MD HealthLink HMO, 651
Seidman, Rob Blue Cross & Blue Shield of Georgia, 315
Seiler, Dr Eleanor Anthem Blue Cross & Blue Shield Connecticut, 220
Seitz, Kevin L Blue Care Network: Ann Arbor, 553
Seitz, Kevin L Blue Care Network: Flint, 554
Seitz, Kevin L Blue Care Network: Great Lakes, Muskegon Heights, 555
Seitzman, Sharon QualCare, 737
Seitzman, Sharon UnitedHealthCare of New York, 810
Selby, Lya UnitedHealthCare of Alaska, 28
Selby, Lya UnitedHealthCare of Oregon, 923
Selby, Lya UnitedHealthCare of Washington, 1170
Self, Dave PacificSource Health Plans: Idaho, 353
Self, Dave PacificSource Health Plans: Corporate Headquarters, 917
Self, David Primary Health Plan, 354
Sellars, Ann Calais Health, 473
Sellers, Ed Blue Cross & Blue Shield of South Carolina, 997
Sementi, Darcy PersonalCare, 381
Sendlewski, Susan L AmeriHealth Medicare Plan, 930
Sengewaltt, J Mark Mountain State Blue Cross Blue Shiled, 1181
Senhauser, Freddy CareSource Mid Rogue Health Plan, 903
Serota, Scott P Blue Cross and Blue Shield Association, 360
Serrano, Patricia First Medical Health Plan of Florida, 278
Sessler, Raymond Boston Medical Center Healthnet Plan, 528
Sessoms, Vicki Health Partners Medicare Plan, 950
Settle, Scott Emerald Health PPO, 854
Seubert, Maureen Assurant Employee Benefits: Ohio, 847
Sevcik, Joseph A Assurant Employee Benefits: Corporate Headquarters, 635
Severson, Duwayne MercyCare Health Plans, 1205
Sewell, Geoffrey S, MD Kaiser Permanente Health Plan of Hawaii, 340
Sewell, Ronald Southeastern Indiana Health Organization, 413
Sewert, Dan, III National Better Living Association, 325
Sgarro, Douglas A. CVS CareMark, 988
Shadle, Dan Galaxy Health Network, 1066
Shafer, Deborah Partnership HealthPlan of California, 166
Shanahan, Brendan Medical Card System (MCS), 980
Shane, P.J., Jr Galaxy Health Network, 1066

Shank, Tracey M SelectCare Access Corporation, 966
Shanley, Audrey Community Health Improvement Solutions, 641
Shanley, Kathryn M Delta Dental of Rhode Island, 989
Shanley, Will UnitedHealthCare of Alaska, 28
Shanley, Will UnitedHealthCare of Arizona, 61
Shanley, Will UnitedHealthCare of Northern California, 182
Shanley, Will UnitedHealthCare of Southern California, 183
Shanley, Will UnitedHealthCare of Colorado, 215
Shanley, Will UnitedHealthCare of New Mexico, 756
Shanley, Will UnitedHealthCare of Oregon, 923
Shanley, Will UnitedHealthCare of Utah, 1115
Shanley, Will UnitedHealthCare of Washington, 1170
Shapiro, Lauralee W Blue Cross & Blue Shield of Florida: Jacksonville, 266
Shapiro, Sheila K Molina Healthcare: Washington, 1161
Shapiro, Stanley CompBenefits Corporation, 318
Sharma, Sally WellPoint NextRx, 1100
Sharp, Jolene HealthSpring of Illinois, 375
Sharp, Jolene HealthSpring: Corporate Offices, 1039
Sharp, Jolene HealthSpring of Texas, 1071
Sharp, Laurence, MD Atrio Health Plans, 901
Shattenkirk, Darla Fidelis Care, 778
Shaver, Tona Keystone Health Plan Central, 958
Shea, Andrew Essence Healthcare, 646
Sheehy, Joseph, MD Southeastern Indiana Health Organization, 413
Sheehy, Robert J UnitedHealthCare of Minnesota, 620
Sheets, Cindy Mount Carmel Health Plan Inc (MediGold), 866
Shehab, Phyllis SelectCare Access Corporation, 966
Shelby, Cindy Contra Costa Health Plan, 113
Shell, Scott Novasys Health, 52
Shelley, Jim, PhD Carolina Care Plan, 999
Shepard, Robert New West Health Services, 672
Shepard, Robert New West Medicare Plan, 673
Sheridan, Pat Windsor Medicare Extra, 1045
Shermer, Barry Windsor Medicare Extra, 1045
Sherwin, David A Quality Health Plans, 298
Sherwin, David A Quality Health Plans of New York, 807
Sheyer, Amy Health Net Medicare Plan, 131
Sheyer, Amy Health Net Health Plan of Oregon, 909
Shia, Beth Liberty Health Plan: Corporate Office, 912
Shiblaq, Marwan, MBA Nationwide Better Health, 867
Shields, Guy Landmark Healthplan of California, 147
Shin, Amy On Lok Lifeways, 157
Shinto, Richard MMM Healthcare, 981
Shinto, Richard, MD PMC Medicare Choice, 982
Shipley, Kurt Blue Cross & Blue Shield of New Mexico, 744
Shipp, Norma HealthPartners, 1037
Shirlely, Michael Blue Cross of Idaho Health Service, Inc., 345
Shoemaker, Scott Physicians Plus Insurance Corporation, 1207
Sholder, Marty CCN: Alaska, 20
Shonkoff, Fredi Blue Cross & Blue Shield of Massachusetts, 527
Shoptaw, Robert L Arkansas Blue Cross and Blue Shield, 66
Shorman, Hays, Gary D. Blue Cross & Blue Shield of Kansas, 436
Short, Jared L Regence Blue Cross & Blue Shield of Oregon, 919
Short, Pam Northeast Georgia Health Partners, 326
Short, Steve Arkansas Blue Cross and Blue Shield, 66
Shotley, Marsha Blue Cross & Blue Shield of Minnesota, 599
Showalter, Charles Humana Health Insurance of West Virginia, 1178
Shulman, Steven J Magellan Health Services Indiana, 408
Sick, Christine AmeriHealth HMO, 232
Sidener, Debby Welborn Health Plans, 416
Sidon, Kenneth HMO Health Ohio, 858
Sidon, Kenneth Medical Mutual of Ohio, 862
Sidon, Kenneth Medical Mutual of Ohio Medicare Plan, 863
Sidon, Kenneth SuperMed One, 878
Siegel, Bernard, MD Lakeside Community Healthcare Network, 146
Siegel, David, MD Great Lakes Health Plan, 569
Siewert, Timothy National Better Living Association, 325
Sigel, Deena Phoenix Health Plan, 55
Siggett, Dawn Great Lakes Health Plan, 569
Siker, Leni Wisconsin Physician's Service, 1214
Silva, Pam Grand Valley Health Plan, 568
Silverman, Bruce Delta Dental of New Jersey & Connecticut, 224, 724

Silverman, Wayne, DDS Dominion Dental Services, 1132
Simmer, Thomas L, MD Blue Care Network: Ann Arbor, 553
Simmer, Thomas L, MD Blue Care Network: Flint, 554
Simmer, Thomas L, MD Blue Care Network: Great Lakes, Muskegon Heights, 555
Simmer, Thomas L, MD Blue Cross Blue Shield of Michigan, 556
Simonetti, Toni Centene Corporation, 638
Simonitsch, Kirsten Premera Blue Cross Blue Shield of Alaska, 27
Simonitsch, Kirsten Premera Blue Cross, 1164
Simpson, Edward F, Jr Florida Health Care Plan, 279
Simpson, Jeanne Foundation for Medical Care for Kern & Santa Barbara County, 123
Sims, James L, DDS Superior Dental Care, 877
Simundza, Craig Dental Network of America, 366
Simundza, Craig DenteMax, 565
Singer, Anne Preferred Therapy Providers, 57
Siren, Pam Neighborhood Health Plan, 542
Sisco-Creed, Shirley, RN ProviDRs Care Network, 451
Sivori, John P Health Net Medicare Plan, 131
Sivori, John P Health Net: Corporate Headquarters, 132
Sizer, John, MD Interplan Health Group, 139
Skayhan, Richard Health Net Health Plan of Oregon, 909
Skinner, Bob Lovelace Health Plan, 750
Skinner, Bob Lovelace Medicare Health Plan, 751
Skobel, Jeff Unison Health Plan of South Carolina, 1010
Slaga, Steven Total Health Care, 589
Slavik, Kevin, RPh/MHA Blue Cross & Blue Shield of Illinois, 359
Sloan, Beverly HMO Colorado, 208
Sloan, Emily FirstCarolinaCare, 823
Slubowski, James S Priority Health, 585
Slubowski, James S Priority Health: Corporate Headquarters, 586
Slubowski, James S PriorityHealth Medicare Plans, 587
Sluder, Chris Aetna Health of Tennessee, 1026
Small, Brian Blue Cross & Blue Shield of Louisiana, 472
Smallie, Don, DC Basic Chiropractic Health Plan, 86
Smart, Dean, MD University Health Plans, 1116
Smiley, Andrea Magellan Health Services Arizona, 49
Smiley, Bruce Encircle Network, 401
Smiley, Bruce Encore Health Network, 402
Smith, Bill South Central Preferred, 967
Smith, Carrie Providence Health Plans, 918
Smith, Clare CoreSource: Corporate Headquarters, 364
Smith, Darnell Blue Cross & Blue Shield of Florida: Jacksonville, 266
Smith, David Meritain Health: Corporate Headquarters, 792
Smith, David Meritain Health: Utah, 1108
Smith, Dawn R Quality Health Plans, 298
Smith, Dawn R Quality Health Plans of New York, 807
Smith, DeWitt Perfect Health Insurance Company, 806
Smith, Dr David Piedmont Community Health Plan, 1141
Smith, Ebben, MD AmeriChoice by UnitedHealthCare, 716
Smith, Eric Capital Health Plan, 268
Smith, Francis S DC Chartered Health Plan, 246
Smith, Jack Blue Cross & Blue Shield of Texas, 1053
Smith, James F National Medical Health Card, 802
Smith, Jeff Arizona Physicians IPA, 33
Smith, Jeff Unison Health Plan of Delaware, 241
Smith, Jeff Unison Health Plan of the Capital Area, 252
Smith, Jeff Healthy Indiana Plan, 406
Smith, Jeff Great Lakes Health Plan, 569
Smith, Jeff Health Plan of Nevada, 695
Smith, Jeff AmeriChoice by UnitedHealthCare, 716, 759
Smith, Jeff Unison Health Plan of Ohio, 881
Smith, Jeff Unison Health Plan of South Carolina, 1010
Smith, Joseph Arkansas Blue Cross and Blue Shield, 66
Smith, Katherine Premier Access Insurance/Access Dental, 169
Smith, Kathy CIGNA HealthCare of New Hampshire, 707
Smith, Larry Physicians Health Plan of Mid-Michigan, 584
Smith, Leslie Lyles DC Chartered Health Plan, 246
Smith, Michael Anthem Blue Cross & Blue Shield of Colorado, 192
Smith, Nancy Humana Health Insurance of Orlando, 287
Smith, Pam Behavioral Healthcare Options, Inc., 690
Smith, Patsy Alliance Regional Health Network, 1047

Smith, Roy Bright Now! Dental, 93

Smith, Scott Kaiser Permanente Health Plan of Colorado, 210

Smith, Scott Coalition America's National Preferred Provider Network, 767

Smith, Sean Coalition America's National Preferred Provider Network, 767

Smith, Troy Hometown Health Plan, 696

Smith, William P Blue Care Network of Michigan: Corporate Headquarters, 551

Smith, William P Blue Care Network: Ann Arbor, 553

Smith, William P Blue Care Network: Flint, 554

Smith, William P Blue Care Network: Great Lakes, Muskegon Heights, 555

Smith-boykin, Laverne UnitedHealthCare of the Mid-Atlantic, 523

Smokler, Jeff Blue Cross and Blue Shield Association, 360

Smulski, Zachary, MBA Puget Sound Health Partners, 1165

Smyth, Glen Anthem Blue Cross & Blue Shield Connecticut, 220

Snead, Thomas G, Jr Trigon Health Care, 1143

Snowden, Miles, MD OptumHealth Care Solutions: Physical Health, 614

Snyder, John J, DMD Kaiser Permanente Health Plan Northwest, 911

Sobel, Glenn J Dentcare Delivery Systems, 771

Sobocinski, Vincent CIGNA HealthCare of Delaware, 234

Sodaro, Kenneth Blue Cross & Blue Shield of Western New York, 762

Soistman, Francis S, Jr Coventry Health Care of Kansas, 439

Sokolow, Alan E, MD Empire Blue Cross & Blue Shield, 774

Soldo, Marie UnitedHealthcare Nevada, 704

Sollenberger, Donna UTMB HealthCare Systems, 1097

Solls, Mark A Concentra: Corporate Office, 1060

Soloman, Carol A Peoples Health, 482

Solomon, Carol A Tenet Choices, 483

Soman, Michael, MD Group Health Cooperative, 1157

Sommer, Mary Delta Dental of Rhode Island, 989

Sommers, Jack, MD CommunityCare Managed Healthcare Plans of Oklahoma, 890

Soni, Nirali, RPh, CDE Care 1st Health Plan: Arizona, 37

Sonnenshine, Stephanie Central California Alliance for Health, 100

Soonthornsima, Ob Blue Cross & Blue Shield of Louisiana, 472

Sorberg, Beth UnitedHealthCare of Colorado, 215

Sorell, Thomas G Guardian Life Insurance Company, 782

Sorensen, Stuart L Security Life Insurance Company of America, 617

Sorenson, Charles, Jr MD IHC: Intermountain Healthcare Health Plan, 351

Sorenson, Dan, MD ConnectCare, 561

Sorrell, Carol, RN Kern Family Health Care, 144

Southam, Arthur M, MD Kaiser Permanente Health Plan of Northern California, 140

Southam, Arthur M, MD Kaiser Permanente Health Plan of Southern California, 141

Southam, Arthur M, MD Kaiser Permanente Health Plan: Corporate Office, 142

Southam, Arthur M, MD Kaiser Permanente Medicare Plan, 143

Souza, Frank Central California Alliance for Health, 100

Sowell, John Windsor Medicare Extra, 1045

Sowers, Chuck Mercy Care Plan/Mercy Care Advantage, 51

Spaeth, Corrine Health Plan of Nevada, 695

Spafford, Kent One Call Medical, 735

Spahn, Gloria Chiropractic Health Plan of California, 103

Spahn, Glorie ChiroSource Inc, 104

Spalding, George E, Jr, CPA National Better Living Association, 325

Spalding, Susan National Better Living Association, 325

Spann, Lisa Patient Choice, 615

Spano, Debora UnitedHealthCare of the Mid-Atlantic, 523

Spano, Debora UnitedHealthCare of Massachusetts, 546

Spano, Debora UnitedHealthCare of Ohio: Columbus, 882

Spano, Debora UnitedHealthCare of Ohio: Dayton & Cincinnati, 883

Spano, Debora UnitedHealthCare of Rhode Island, 994

Spano, Debora UnitedHealthCare of Virginia, 1145

Sparkman, David OptumHealth Care Solutions: Physical Health, 614

Sparks, Alison Pacific Health Alliance, 161

Sparks, Kevin Mid America Health, 657

Spencer, Eric E, MBA Easy Choice Health Plan, 120

Spencer, H Newton Preferred Care, 962

Spencer, Jeremy Total Dental Administrators, 1114

Spencer, Kerry CIGNA HealthCare of New Hampshire, 707

Spencer, Selden, MD Healthy & Well Kids in Iowa, 426

Sperandio, Stephen J Delta Dental of Rhode Island, 989

Spero, Neal Presbyterian Health Plan, 753

Spero, Neal Presbyterian Medicare Plans, 754

Spezia, Anthony L Cariten Healthcare, 1031

Spilde, Mary Frances Theresa Trillium Community Health Plan, 921

Spoor, Martha Great-West/One Health Plan, 207

Spradlin, Scott GHP Coventry Health Plan, 648

Sprecher, Lon Dean Health Plan, 1192

Springer, Barbara B, JD Delta Dental of Colorado, 202

Springer, Howard Community Health Plan of Washington, 1152

Springfield, James G Valley Baptist Health Plan, 1098

Spurgeon, Stephen, MD Mercy Health Plans: Kansas, 445

Spurgeon, Stephen, MD Mercy Health Medicare Plan, 654

Spurgeon, Stephen, MD Mercy Health Plans: Corporate Office, 655

Spurgeon, Stephen, MD Mercy Health Plans: Oklahoma, 896

Squarok, John, CPA American Pioneer Life Insurance Co, 255

Squilanti, Todd Meritain Health: Corporate Headquarters, 792

St Pierre, Ellie CIGNA HealthCare of New Hampshire, 707

St. Clair, Elizabeth, Esq HealthFirst New Jersey Medicare Plan, 729

St. Hilaire, Gary Capital Blue Cross, 936

Stade, Monika Healthcare Partners of East Texas, 1069

Stadler, Mark Great-West Healthcare of Massachusetts, 535

Stadtlander, George HMO Health Ohio, 858

Stadtlander, George Medical Mutual of Ohio, 862

Stadtlander, George Medical Mutual of Ohio Medicare Plan, 863

Stadtlander, George SuperMed One, 878

Staib, Renee A Penn Highlands Health Plan, 961

Stalmeyer, Jan Mid America Health, 657

Stambaugh, Elizabeth, SPHR Employers Dental Services, 43

Stanislaw, Sherry L SCAN Health Plan, 175

Stanley, Christopher, MD UnitedHealthCare of Colorado, 215

Stanley, David A Passport Health Plan, 466

Stansbury, Shannon Blue Cross & Blue Shield of Texas, 1053

Starck, Daniel J CorVel Corporation, 114

Starman, Bob UnitedHealthCare of Nebraska, 686

Starr, Jeremy Guardian Life Insurance Company, 782

Starr, Maureen Interplan Health Group, 139

Stasi, Joe Mid America Health, 657

Staszewski, Jay Unicare: West Virginia, 1183

Steber, John H GHI Medicare Plan, 779

Steber, John H Group Health Incorporated (GHI), 781

Steber, John H Health Plan of New York, 783

Steckbeck, Marie, MBA Colorado Access, 199

Steele, Tammy S Concentra: Corporate Office, 1060

Steines, Brian Abrazo Advantage Health Plan, 29

Stelben, John Coventry Health Care: Corporate Headquarters, 506

Stellmon, John Regence Blue Cross & Blue Shield of Oregon, 919

Stelzer, Elizabeth Nationwide Better Health, 867

Stengol, Art HealthLink HMO, 651

Stephens, Deborah L Behavioral Health Systems, 4

Stephenson, George, II Foundation for Medical Care for Kern & Santa Barbara County, 123

Sterck, Luc Assurant Employee Benefits: Texas, 1050

Sterler, Lowell Blue Cross & Blue Shield of Florida: Jacksonville, 266

Stern, Kyle Spectera, 521

Sternbergh, John S Preferred Care Select, 829

Stetson, Paul MedCost, 826

Stevans, Joel, DC Landmark Healthplan of California, 147

Stevens, Christopher Dental Network of America, 366

Stevens, Linda VSP: Vision Service Plan of Indiana, 415

Stevens, Ronald S, MBA Samaritan Health Plan, 920

Stewart, Doug CIGNA HealthCare of Northern California, 106

Stewart, Doug CIGNA HealthCare of Southern California, 107

Stewart, Roger Coventry Health Care of West Virginia, 1174

Stiles, Delane Crescent Preferred Provider Organization, 820

Stillwagon, Troy Scott & White Health Plan, 1087

Stinde, Mary Ellen PersonalCare, 381

Stine, Kristen Assurant Employee Benefits: Kansas, 435

Stirewalt, Charles, DDS Bright Now! Dental, 93

Stirewalt, Charles, DMD Liberty Dental Plan of Nevada, 698

Stitall, Precious Dencap Dental Plans, 564

Stitzer, Cathy Blue Cross of Northeastern Pennsylvania, 933

Stivers, Mary Preferred Health Plan Inc, 467

Stobbe, Greg First Commonwealth, 368

Stocker, Michael A, MD Empire Blue Cross & Blue Shield, 774
Stoddard, Paul Blue Cross & Blue Shield of Western New York, 762
Stohler, Dona American Health Network of Indiana, 390
Stokes, Raplh CIGNA HealthCare of Georgia, 316
Stoltz, Billie Trillium Community Health Plan, 921
Stom, Mary K, MD Health Partners Medicare Plan, 950
Stone, Ilana Block Vision of New Jersey, 721
Stone, W Randy L.A. Care Health Plan, 145
Stonehouse, Steve CNA Insurance Companies: Colorado, 198
Stonehouse, Steve CNA Insurance Companies: Georgia, 317
Stonehouse, Steve CNA Insurance Companies: Illinois, 362
Stoner, Patrick DINA Dental Plans, 477
Stoner, Patrick Dental Solutions Plus, 1062
Stoner, Patrick Dental Source: Dental Health Care Plans, 1063
Stoner, Patrick Ora Quest Dental Plans, 1083
Stoner, Roberta Health First Health Plans, 282
Storbakken, Norman C Delta Dental of Minnesota, 601
Storbakken, Norman C Delta Dental of North Dakota, 836
Storrer, Scott A CIGNA HealthCare of North Carolina, 818
Storrer, Scott A CIGNA HealthCare of South Carolina, 1000
Stovall, Dennis Preferred Health Plan Inc, 467
Stover, Timothy UnitedHealthCare of New York, 810
Straley, Hugh, MD Puget Sound Health Partners, 1165
Straley, Peter F Health New England, 538
Strange, Kyle Behavioral Health Systems, 4
Strasser, Mary D Physicians Plus Insurance Corporation, 1207
Stratton, David Atlantis Health Plan, 761
Strauss, Art Harvard University Group Health Plan, 537
Streator, Scott Ohio State University Health Plan Inc., 869
Streicher, Mikelle, RN Florida Health Care Plan, 279
Stround, Kasey Carolina Care Plan, 999
Strunk, Deanna Lifewise Health Plan of Oregon, 913
Stuart, Mary Alice Script Care, Ltd., 1088
Stuart, Randall L AvMed Health Plan: Corporate Office, 259
Stump, MaryAnn Blue Cross & Blue Shield of Minnesota, 599
Stumpf, David UnitedHealthCare of Illinois, 386
Suarez, Kim Priority Health, 585
Suarez, Lillian Select Health of South Carolina, 1008
Sud, Susdey Galaxy Health Network, 1066
Sufficool, Linda M Midlands Choice, 683
Suleski, James Delta Dental of New Jersey & Connecticut, 224, 724
Sullivan, Heidi Arcadian Health Plans, 83
Sullivan, John T Meritain Health: Corporate Headquarters, 792
Sullivan, Maureen E Blue Cross and Blue Shield Association, 360
Sullivan, Thomas A Ohio Health Choice, 868
Summers, David Virginia Premier Health Plan, 1147
Sun, Eugene, MD Molina Healthcare: New Mexico, 752
Sun, Eugene, MD HealthAmerica Pennsylvania, 952
Susanin, Timothy S WellCare Health Plans, 307
Sutherland, Spencer SelectHealth, 1113
Sutherlin, Graham QualChoice/QCA Health Plan, 76
Swackhamer, Merlin SCAN Health Plan, 175
Swayze, Jim Rocky Mountain Health Plans, 213
Sweatman, Paul Assurant Employee Benefits: Illinois, 358
Swenson, Rich HealthPlus Senior Medicare Plan, 577
Swenson, Richard HealthPlus of Michigan: Flint, 574
Swenson, Richard HealthPlus of Michigan: Saginaw, 575
Swift, Stephen BlueShield of Northeastern New York, 763
Sylvers, Sandy Pacific Foundation for Medical Care, 160
Symansky, Martin R, MD CDPHP Medicare Plan, 764
Symansky, Martin R, MD CDPHP: Capital District Physicians' Health Plan, 765
Syracuse, Jill Independent Health, 787
Syracuse, Jill Independent Health Medicare Plan, 788
Szebenyi, Steven E, MD BlueShield of Northeastern New York, 763
Szerlong, Tim CNA Insurance Companies: Colorado, 198
Szerlong, Tim CNA Insurance Companies: Georgia, 317
Szerlong, Tim CNA Insurance Companies: Illinois, 362

T

Tabak, Mark MultiPlan, Inc., 794
Tabak, Mark HealthEOS, 1201

Tabakin, Scott Bravo Health: Corporate Headquarters, 502
Tagli, Hugo Blue Cross & Blue Shield of Illinois, 359
Taliaferro, Lilton R, Jr AmeriHealth Medicare Plan, 930
Tallent, John Medical Associates Health Plan, 378
Tallent, John Medical Associates Health Plan: West, 428
Tamayo, Jonathan Community Health Group, 110
Tamme, Bernard Preferred Health Plan Inc, 467
Tanquary, Patricia, MPH, PhD Contra Costa Health Plan, 113
Tapia, Lionel, MD Health InfoNet, 669
Taravaglia, Laura Humana Health Insurance of Jacksonville, 286
Tarkett, Julles Initial Group, 1041
Tasco, Randy A Delta Dental: Corporate Headquarters, 563
Tatar, Margaret CalOptima, 96
Tate, Rachel Script Care, Ltd., 1088
Tatko, Mike Regence Blue Cross & Blue Shield of Utah, 1112
Tatko, Mike Asuris Northwest Health, 1150
Taube, Aimee Great Lakes Health Plan, 569
Taylor, Greg Magellan Health Services Arizona, 49
Taylor, James DINA Dental Plans, 477
Taylor, James Dental Solutions Plus, 1062
Taylor, James Ora Quest Dental Plans, 1083
Taylor, James A Dental Source: Dental Health Care Plans, 1063
Taylor, Linda M Independence Blue Cross, 956
Teal, Jan Advantage Health Solutions, 388
Telkamp, Bruce eHealthInsurance Services Inc., 9
Temperly, Tim Network Health Plan of Wisconsin, 1206
Temple, Carolyn J Foundation for Medical Care for Kern & Santa Barbara County, 123
Ten Pas, Bill ODS Health Plan, 915
Tenholder, Ed Anthem Blue Cross & Blue Shield of Missouri, 634
Tenzer, Mattie Carilion Health Plans, 1128
Terry, David L, Jr HealthSpring: Corporate Offices, 1039
Terry, Donna Pima Health System, 56
Tetzlaff, Gene Delta Dental of South Dakota, 1018
Thibdeau, Michael Davis Vision, 769
Thiele, Craig, MD CareSource: Michigan, 558
Thiele, Craig, MD CareSource, 849
Thiele, Shawn Magellan Health Services Arizona, 49
Thierer, Mark A SXC Health Solutions Corp, 383
Thobro, Jeanne Delta Dental of Wyoming, 1218
Thomas, Betty Arnett Health Plans, 394
Thomas, David Fidelis Care, 778
Thomas, David Unison Health Plan of Pennsylvania, 970
Thomas, J Grover, Jr Trustmark Companies, 384
Thomas, John CommunityCare Managed Healthcare Plans of Oklahoma, 890
Thomas, John CommunityCare Medicare Plan, 891
Thomas, Kimberly Priority Health: Corporate Headquarters, 586
Thomas, Kimberly PriorityHealth Medicare Plans, 587
Thomas, Marshall, MD Colorado Access, 199
Thomas, Milton, MD Mid America Health, 657
Thomas, Tarlton, III CareSource: Michigan, 558
Thomas, Tarlton CareSource, 849
Thompson, Colleen PacificSource Health Plans: Idaho, 353
Thompson, Colleen Clear One Health Plans, 905
Thompson, Colleen PacificSource Health Plans: Corporate Headquarters, 917
Thompson, Greg UnitedHealthCare of Illinois, 386
Thompson, Greg UnitedHealthCare of Indiana, 414
Thompson, Greg UnitedHealthCare of Iowa, 431
Thompson, Greg UnitedHealthCare of Kansas, 453
Thompson, Greg UnitedHealthCare of Kentucky, 469
Thompson, Greg UnitedHealthCare of Wisconsin: Central, 622
Thompson, Greg UnitedHealthCare of Missouri, 661
Thompson, Greg UnitedHealthCare of Nebraska, 686
Thompson, Jeffrey E, MD Gundersen Lutheran Health Plan, 1199
Thompson, Kurt Oxford Health Plans: Corporate Headquarters, 229
Thompson, Kurt B Oxford Health Plans: New Jersey, 736
Thompson, Kurt B Oxford Health Plans: New York, 805
Thompson, Larry NOVA Healthcare Administrators, 804
Thompson, Margita Health Net: Corporate Headquarters, 132
Thompson, Margita Managed Health Network, 150
Thompson, Marti DakotaCare, 1017
Thompson, Paula HealthSCOPE Benefits, 73

Thon, Carolyn Health Plan of San Mateo, 134
Thor, Patrice, RN Humana Health Insurance of Wisconsin, 1202
Thurman, Kathy Care 1st Health Plan: Arizona, 37
Thurmond, Gail, MD Health Choice LLC, 1036
Tian See, Un Medical Card System (MCS), 980
Tiano, Linda V, Esq Health Net of the Northeast, 226
Tiano, Linda V, Esq Empire Blue Cross & Blue Shield, 774
Tibbetts, Cheryl ProviDRs Care Network, 451
Tildon, Maria CareFirst Blue Cross & Blue Shield of Virginia, 1127
Tilford, David Medica Health - Medicare Plan, 609
Tilford, David Medica: Corporate Office, 610
Tilford, David Medica: North Dakota, 841
Tilford, David Medica: South Dakota, 1023
Tilton, Jon W, DDS Delta Dental of Kansas, 440
Timmermans, Rebecca South Central Preferred, 967
Timmons, Clay HealthSmart Preferred Care, 374
Timms, Dennis BlueLincs HMO, 888
Tita, Marybeth HealthFirst New Jersey Medicare Plan, 729
Tobin, Jill AmeriChoice by UnitedHealthCare, 759
Tobin, Michael E American Community Mutual Insurance Company, 549
Todd, Lisa Value Behavioral Health of Pennsylvania, 976
Todd, Richard CommunityCare Managed Healthcare Plans of Oklahoma, 890
Todd, Richard W CommunityCare Medicare Plan, 891
Todoroff, Cheri, MPH Los Angeles County Public Healthcare, 149
Todoroff, Christopher M Humana Health Insurance of Kentucky, 463
Todt, Blair W WellCare Health Plans, 307
Tofferi, Leigh Blue Cross & Blue Shield of Vermont, 1118
Tomasevich, Stan CHN PPO, 722
Tomba, Sue Great Lakes Health Plan, 569
Tomcala, Christine HealthPlus of Michigan: Flint, 574
Tomcala, Christine HealthPlus of Michigan: Saginaw, 575
Tomcala, Christine Puget Sound Health Partners, 1165
Toothcare, Tracey Behavioral Healthcare Options, Inc., 690
Torgerson, Sharon Harvard Pilgrim Health Care: Maine, 492
Torgerson, Sharon Harvard Pilgrim Health Care, 536
Torgerson, Sharon Harvard Pilgrim Health Care of New England, 710
Torkelson, Dick, MD WINhealth Partners, 1222
Torres, Maria Access Dental Services, 79
Tosti, Mike Devon Health Services, 942
Totterdale, Matt Anthem Blue Cross & Blue Sheild of Indiana, 391
Tough, Steven D Health Net: Corporate Headquarters, 132
Tournoux, Mary Ann Health Alliance Medicare, 571
Tournoux, Mary Ann Health Alliance Plan, 572
Townsend, Michelle Arkansas Managed Care Organization, 68
Tracy, Julie K CDPHP Medicare Plan, 764
Tracy, Julie K CDPHP: Capital District Physicians' Health Plan, 765
Tran, Anna Care 1st Health Plan: California, 97
Tran, Hai Catalyst Health Solutions Inc, 503
Tran, Hai Catalyst RX, 817
Tran, Thomas L WellCare Health Plans, 307
Tran, Tom ConnectiCare of Massachusetts, 530
Trapani, Lisa Bravo Health: Corporate Headquarters, 502
Trask, Anna Boston Medical Center Healthnet Plan, 528
Traylor, Thomas Boston Medical Center Healthnet Plan, 528
Traynor, Mark UCare Medicare Plan, 618
Traynor, Mark UCare Minnesota, 619
Treash, Mike Mercy Health Plans: Kansas, 445
Treash, Mike Mercy Health Medicare Plan, 654
Treash, Mike Mercy Health Plans: Corporate Office, 655
Treash, Mike Mercy Health Plans: Oklahoma, 896
Trebino, Tricia Tufts Health Medicare Plan, 543
Trebino, Tricia Tufts Health Plan, 544
Tredway, Alfred S Regence Blue Cross & Blue Shield of Utah, 1112
Treptin, Todd Altius Health Plans, 1102
Tressel Lewis, Maureen Regence Blue Shield, 1166
Tretheway, Barb Health Partners Medicare Plan, 605
Tretheway, Barb HealthPartners, 606
Treves, Daniel Western Dental Services, 188
Trifone, John Blue Cross & Blue Shield of Vermont, 1118
Trinh, Sarah Assurant Employee Benefits: Oregon, 900
Triplett, Michael W, Sr CIGNA HealthCare of North Carolina, 818
Triplett, Mike CIGNA HealthCare of the Mid-Atlantic, 504

Trombley, Amy Health New England, 538
Tropiano, Pam CareSource, 849
Trowbridge, Lewis E Blue Cross & Blue Shield of Nebraska, 677
Truess, James W Amerigroup Corporation, 1125
Truess, Jim Group Health Cooperative, 1157
Trump, Casey Saint Mary's Health Plans, 703
Truong, Vy CalOptima, 96
Trybual, John VSP: Vision Service Plan of Illinois, 387
Tsang, Steve Chinese Community Health Plan, 102
Tsang, Tom Chinese Community Health Plan, 102
Tucker, JC Chinese Community Health Plan, 102
Tudor, John, MD Great-West/One Health Plan, 207
Tufano, Paul A, Esq Independence Blue Cross, 956
Tull, Debra Landmark Healthplan of California, 147
Tuller, Edwin Care Choices, 557
Tullock, Mark HealthSpring: Corporate Offices, 1039
Tunis, Sandra S Managed Health Services, 1203
Turner, Christine Puget Sound Health Partners, 1165
Turner, Jeff WellPoint NextRx, 1100
Turner, Jim Humana Health Insurance of Kentucky, 463
Turner, Shannon R, JD Passport Health Plan, 466
Tyer, Barbara L KelseyCare Advantage, 1077
Tyler, Sue HMO Health Ohio, 858
Tyler, Sue Medical Mutual of Ohio, 862
Tyler, Sue Medical Mutual of Ohio Medicare Plan, 863
Tyler, Sue SuperMed One, 878
Tyre, Janie Santa Clara Family Health Plan, 174
Tyson, Bernard J Kaiser Permanente Health Plan of Northern California, 140
Tyson, Bernard J Kaiser Permanente Health Plan of Southern California, 141
Tyson, Bernard J Kaiser Permanente Health Plan: Corporate Office, 142
Tyson, Bernard J Kaiser Permanente Medicare Plan, 143
Tzeel, Albert, MD Humana Health Insurance of Wisconsin, 1202

U

Uchrin, Mike Health Choice Arizona, 46
Udvarhelyi, I Steven, MD Independence Blue Cross, 956
Ueoka, Jamie Care 1st Health Plan: California, 97
Uhm, Alex UnitedHealthCare of Southern California, 183
Ulibarri, Frank UnitedHealthCare of Alabama, 16
Ulibarri, Frank Lovelace Health Plan, 750
Ulibarri, Frank Lovelace Medicare Health Plan, 751
Uma, Chet Inland Empire Health Plan, 137
Underhill, David Nationwide Better Health, 867
Underwood, Thomas D Alere Health, 309
Utterback, Chuck CIGNA HealthCare of Tennessee, 1033
Utterbeck, Chuck CIGNA HealthCare of Arkansas, 69
Utterbeck, Chuck CIGNA HealthCare of Mississippi, 625

V

Vaccaro, Jerome V, MD Secure Horizons, 77
Vaccaro, Jerome V, MD PacifiCare Dental and Vision Administrators, 163
Vaccaro, Jerome V, MD PacifiCare of Texas, 1084
Vachon, Jennifer Blue Cross and Blue Shield Association, 360
Vagts, Joyce ConnectiCare, 223
Vail, Cheron Regence Blue Cross & Blue Shield of Oregon, 919
Vail, Cheron Regence Blue Cross & Blue Shield of Utah, 1112
Valdez, David, MD Aetna Health of Oklahoma, 885
Valine, Roger VSP: Vision Service Plan of Illinois, 387
Van De Beek, Diane Exline CIGNA HealthCare of Delaware, 234
Van de Wal, Eve Excellus Blue Cross Blue Shield: Utica Region, 777
Van Etten, Ann M Affinity Health Plan, 758
Van Horn, Eric CareMore Health Plan, 98
Van Lowe, Yvonne CIGNA HealthCare of the Mid-Atlantic, 504
Van Ribbink, Steve Hawaii Medical Services Association, 338
Van Trease, Sandra Anthem Blue Cross & Blue Shield of Missouri, 634
Van Vessem, Nancy, MD Capital Health Plan, 268
Vanasdale, Sallie CIGNA HealthCare of Alaska, 21
Vanasdale, Sallie CIGNA HealthCare of Colorado, 197
Vanasdale, Sallie CIGNA HealthCare of Montana, 665
Vanasdale, Sallie CIGNA HealthCare of Wyoming, 1217
Vance, Ronald Sagamore Health Network, 412

Vance Jr, Ron CIGNA HealthCare of the Mid-Atlantic, 504
VanClees, Kathleen Managed Healthcare Systems of New Jersey, 734
Vander Pluym, Joan Outlook Vision Service, 53
Vangeison, Keith Beech Street Corporation: Corporate Office, 87
Vatles, Mark C Anthem Blue Cross & Blue Shield of New Hampshire, 706
Vaughan, Stan Community Health Improvement Solutions, 641
Vaughn, Kevin Select Health of South Carolina, 1008
Vaughn, Timothy L BlueChoice Health Plan of South Carolina, 998
Vaught, Greta R Midlands Choice, 683
Vavrina, Robert T, Jr Preferred Care Select, 829
Vecchioni, Sharon J CareFirst Blue Cross & Blue Shield of Virginia, 1127
Vela, Manny Valley Baptist Health Plan, 1098
Velasco, Christie Pueblo Health Care, 212
Velazquez, Ralph, MD OSF HealthPlans, 380
VenBrunt, Walter Delta Dental of New Jersey & Connecticut, 224, 724
Vercillo, Arthur, MD Excellus Blue Cross Blue Shield: Central New York, 775
Verrastro, George OptiCare Managed Vision, 828
Verre, Mark ConnectiCare, 223
Vetter, Elizabeth Americas PPO, 1014
Vezzosi, Greg CNA Insurance Companies: Colorado, 198
Vezzosi, Greg CNA Insurance Companies: Georgia, 317
Vezzosi, Greg CNA Insurance Companies: Illinois, 362
Vickery, Peggy Select Health of South Carolina, 1008
Vienne, Richard, DO Univera Healthcare, 811
Vieth, George W, Jr Landmark Healthplan of California, 147
Vignolia, Valerie Healthplex, 785
Villani, Dale Magellan Health Services Arizona, 49
Vincenti, Claude SummaCare Health Plan, 875
Vincenti, Claude SummaCare Medicare Advantage Plan, 876
Vincz, Thomas Horizon Blue Cross & Blue Shield of New Jersey, 730
Vis, David Physicians Health Plan of Mid-Michigan, 584
Viscuso, Ernest A Block Vision, 501
Visser, Dirk Allegiance Life & Health Insurance Company, 663
Vitagliano, Antonio V Excellus Blue Cross Blue Shield: Central New York, 775
Vitagliano, Antonio V Excellus Blue Cross Blue Shield: Rochester Region, 776
Vo, Frank Easy Choice Health Plan, 120
Vogel, John Humana Health Insurance of West Virginia, 1178
Vogt, Peter J CIGNA HealthCare of North Carolina, 818
Volberg, Keith Unison Health Plan of Pennsylvania, 970
Volk, Kim ODS Alaska, 26
Volkman, Fred, MD Select Health of South Carolina, 1008
von Walter, Amy Health Partners Medicare Plan, 605
von Walter, Amy HealthPartners, 606
von Zychlin, Claus Mount Carmel Health Plan Inc (MediGold), 866
Voss, Katherine Scott & White Health Plan, 1087
Voxakis, Angelo C, PharmD EPIC Pharmacy Network, 1134

W

Wachsman, Abraham Atlantis Health Plan, 761
Wachtel, Steve CNA Insurance Companies: Colorado, 198
Wachtel, Steve CNA Insurance Companies: Georgia, 317
Wachtel, Steve CNA Insurance Companies: Illinois, 362
Wade, Katie CIGNA HealthCare of the Mid-Atlantic, 504
Waegelein, Robert, CPA TexanPlus Medicare Advantage HMO, 1090
Waegelein, Robert A American Pioneer Life Insurance Co, 255
Waegelein, Robert A, CPA Universal American Medicare Plans, 812
Waggoner, Devon UnitedHealthCare of Northern California, 182
Waggoner, Devon UnitedHealthCare of Southern California, 183
Waggoner, Tim A Midlands Choice, 683
Wagner, Barry AvMed Health Plan: Gainesville, 261
Wagner, Melissa DenteMax, 565
Wagner, Sylvia Assurant Employee Benefits: Corporate Headquarters, 635
Wakefield, Walter W UnitedHealthCare of Kentucky, 469
Waldman, Clifford R, MD CDPHP Medicare Plan, 764
Waldman, Clifford R, MD CDPHP: Capital District Physicians' Health Plan, 765
Waldman, Sarah Blue Cross & Blue Shield of Nebraska, 677
Waldron, Neil Rocky Mountain Health Plans, 213
Wales, Dirk O, MD HealthSpring: Corporate Offices, 1039
Walker, Ann Marie Delta Dental of Illinois, 365
Walker, Catherine SVS Vision, 588

Walker, George Anthem Blue Cross & Blue Sheild of Indiana, 391
Walker, Pamela MultiPlan, Inc., 794
Walker, Rome, MD Carilion Health Plans, 1128
Walker, William, MD Contra Costa Health Plan, 113
Walko, Nancy American Pioneer Life Insurance Co, 255
Wall, Bruce, MD Ohio State University Health Plan Inc., 869
Wall, Bruce A OhioHealth Group, 870
Wall, Tara Amerigroup Corporation, 1125
Wallace, C Wayne BlueLincs HMO, 888
Wallbaum, Chuck PersonalCare, 381
Wallner, Mark Block Vision, 501
Wallner, Mark Vision Insurance Plan of America, 1213
Walsh, Andrea Health Partners Medicare Plan, 605
Walsh, Andrea HealthPartners, 606
Walsh, Kate Boston Medical Center Healthnet Plan, 528
Walter, Courtney HealthLink HMO, 651
Walters, Laurel Rocky Mountain Health Plans, 213
Walton, Carolynn Blue Cross Blue Shield of Michigan, 556
Wang, Dr. Sheldon X. eHealthInsurance Services Inc., 9
Wang, Patricia, JD HealthFirst New Jersey Medicare Plan, 729
Ward, Dorothy AmeriChoice by UnitedHealthCare, 716
Ward, Julie UnitedHealthCare of Illinois, 386
Ward, Karin J QualChoice/QCA Health Plan, 76
Ward, Michael S&S Healthcare Strategies, 874
Ward, Thomas First Priority Health, 946
Wardle, John Universal American Medicare Plans, 812
Wardlow, Randy PacifiCare of Oregon, 916
Ware, Marilyn CIGNA HealthCare of South Carolina, 1000
Warner, Tim Blue Cross & Blue Shield of Montana, 664
Warner, Venus Galaxy Health Network, 1066
Warren, Dennis Blue Cross of Idaho Health Service, Inc., 345
Warren, Douglas L Blue Cross & Blue Shield of Vermont, 1118
Warren, Jessica Preferred Health Systems Insurance Company, 447
Warren, Jessica Preferred Plus of Kansas, 449
Warrington, J Marc Assurant Employee Benefits: Corporate Headquarters, 635
Warrren, Ann Community Health Group, 110
Wasson, Beth WINhealth Partners, 1222
Waterman, Cindy Liberty Health Advantage Medicare Plan, 790
Waters, Audrey O Elderplan, 773
Waters, Bill AvMed Health Plan: Fort Lauderdale, 260
Waters, Bill AvMed Health Plan: Orlando, 263
Watkins, Robert E DC Chartered Health Plan, 246
Watrin, Liz Blue Cross & Blue Shield of New Mexico, 744
Watson, Anthony L Health Plan of New York, 783
Watson, Mike Aetna Health of Tennessee, 1026
Watson, Roger Superior Vision Services, Inc., 178
Watson, Ruth CalOptima, 96
Weader, David J, JD Geisinger Health Plan, 948
Wear, Lisa J Initial Group, 1041
Weatherford, Michael Santa Clara Family Health Plan, 174
Weaver, Emily University Health Alliance, 342
Weaver, Karen CIGNA HealthCare of Iowa, 421
Weaver, Lois Val-U-Health, 974
Webb, Traci Central California Alliance for Health, 100
Webb, W Larry Athens Area Health Plan Select, 313
Weber, Chuck CareMore Health Plan, 98
Weber, Deanna Emerald Health PPO, 854
Weber, Tim Wellmark Health Plan of Iowa, 432
Webster, Daryl Premier Access Insurance/Access Dental, 169
Wedemeyer, David Care 1st Health Plan: California, 97
Wedergren, Shelly UnitedHealthCare of Nebraska, 686
Weeks, Ann Healthplex, 785
Weeks, Cynthia Employers Dental Services, 43
Wehr, Ann, MD Molina Healthcare: New Mexico, 752
Wehr, Ann O WellCare Health Plans, 307
Wehr, Richard Preferred Care, 962
Weiman, Debbie PersonalCare, 381
Weimer, Kurt A CIGNA HealthCare of Arizona, 38
Weinberg, Mark Unicare: Michigan, 590
Weinberg, Sharon National Health Plan Corporation, 801
Weiner, Gerry Health Net Health Plan of Oregon, 909

Weingarten, Jorge, Md Care 1st Health Plan: California, 97
Weinper, Michael Physical Therapy Provider Network, 167
Weinper, Michael, PT PTPN, 171
Weinstein, Audrey M Block Vision, 501
Weinstein, Burt Pacific Dental Benefits, 159
Weinstein, Michael Highmark Blue Shield, 954
Weisblatt, Rick, PhD Harvard Pilgrim Health Care: Maine, 492
Weisblatt, Rick, PhD Harvard Pilgrim Health Care, 536
Weisblatt, Rick, PhD Harvard Pilgrim Health Care of New England, 710
Weiss, Bruce, MD AvMed Health Plan: Gainesville, 261
Weiss, Peter J, MD Health First Health Plans, 282
Weissberg, Jed, MD Kaiser Permanente Health Plan of Northern California, 140
Weissberg, Jed, MD Kaiser Permanente Health Plan of Southern California, 141
Weissberg, Jed, MD Kaiser Permanente Health Plan: Corporate Office, 142
Weissberg, Jed, MD Kaiser Permanente Medicare Plan, 143
Weissbrot, Laurence R, FSA Delta Dental Northeast, 708
Weisz, Jeffery A, MD Kaiser Permanente Health Plan of Southern California, 141
Welch, Peter CIGNA HealthCare of Northern California, 106
Wells, David AvMed Health Plan: Orlando, 263
Wells, Linda Ohio Health Choice, 868
Welsh, Wilfred Quality Plan Administrators, 251
Wende, Joseph, OD Davis Vision, 769
Wenk, Phil Delta Dental of Tennessee, 1034
Wentz, Phil Liberty Health Plan: Corporate Office, 912
Werther, Richard J DenteMax, 565
Werthwein, Norman Beech Street Corporation: Alabama, 3
Werthwein, Norman Beech Street: Alaska, 19
West, Becky First Care Health Plans, 1065
West, Colleen First Health, 369
West, Ed Anthem Blue Cross & Blue Shield of Indiana, 392
West, Marc Group Health Cooperative, 1157
Westen, B Curtis, Esq Health Net Medicare Plan, 131
Westerman, George, MD Behavioral Healthcare Options, Inc., 690
Westfall, Laurie Care Choices, 557
Wexler, Eric J, Esq Great Lakes Health Plan, 569
Whaley, Don American Dental Group, 191
Whalley, John W PacifiCare Dental and Vision Administrators, 163
Wheeler, Robert R Trillium Community Health Plan, 921
Whelan, Martin Delta Dental of California, 115
Whitaker, Kim UnitedHealthCare of Texas, 1095
Whitaker, Suzanne M, APR Peoples Health, 482
White, Dale MultiPlan, Inc., 794
White, Dale HealthEOS, 1201
White, Jayson R Fidelis Care, 778
White, Jeff Citrus Health Care, 271
White, Mark Arkansas Blue Cross and Blue Shield, 66
White, Michael Providence Health Plans, 918
White, Richard A Guardian Life Insurance Company, 782
White, Robert American Specialty Health, 82
Whited, Amy D Kaiser Permanente Health Plan of Colorado, 210
Whitehead, Daryl Arkansas Managed Care Organization, 68
Whitehouse, David, MD United Behavioral Health, 180
Whiteside, Ronald Mount Carmel Health Plan Inc (MediGold), 866
Whitford, Don Priority Health: Corporate Headquarters, 586
Whitford, Don PriorityHealth Medicare Plans, 587
Whitley, Kim R, MPA Samaritan Health Plan, 920
Whitley-Taylor, Linda Amerigroup Corporation, 1125
Whitmer, Richard E Blue Care Network: Ann Arbor, 553
Whitmer, Richard E Blue Care Network: Flint, 554
Whittington, Michael Calais Health, 473
Wichmann, David S UnitedHealthCare of Minnesota, 620
Widmann, Janet Blue Shield of California, 91
Wieland, Jim HSM: Healthcare Cost Management, 607
Wiffler, Thomas UnitedHealthCare of Illinois, 386
Wiggins, Stephen Blue Cross & Blue Shield of South Carolina, 997
Wilburn, Cheryl Initial Group, 1041
Wild, Joseph Aetna Health of Georgia, 308
Wilhelmi, Kate AmeriHealth HMO, 232, 718
Wilhelmi, Kate AmeriHealth Medicare Plan, 930

Wilkerson, Scott Physicians Health Plan of Mid-Michigan, 584
Willett, Linda Horizon Blue Cross & Blue Shield of New Jersey, 730
Willett, Linda A Rayant Insurance Company, 738
Williams, Andy Blue Cross & Blue Shield of Nebraska, 677
Williams, Doyle Dentaquest, 531
Williams, Liz Keystone Health Plan East, 959
Williams, Ronald A Aetna Health of Alabama, 1
Williams, Ronald A Aetna Health of Alaska, 18
Williams, Ronald A Aetna Health of Arkansas, 64
Williams, Ronald A Aetna Health of Colorado, 190
Williams, Ronald A Aetna Health, Inc. Corporate Headquarters, 217
Williams, Ronald A Aetna Health, Inc. Medicare Plan, 218
Williams, Ronald A Aetna Health of Delaware, 231
Williams, Ronald A Aetna Health District of Columbia, 243
Williams, Ronald A Aetna Health of Hawaii, 332
Williams, Ronald A Aetna Health of Idaho, 344
Williams, Ronald A Aetna Health of Iowa, 418
Williams, Ronald A Aetna Health of Kansas, 434
Williams, Ronald A Aetna Health of Kentucky, 455
Williams, Ronald A Aetna Health of Louisiana, 470
Williams, Ronald A Aetna Health of Maine, 487
Williams, Ronald A Aetna Health of Maryland, 496
Williams, Ronald A Aetna Health of Massachusetts, 524
Williams, Ronald A Aetna Health of Michigan, 548
Williams, Ronald A Aetna Health of Minnesota, 595
Williams, Ronald A Aetna Health of Mississippi, 624
Williams, Ronald A Aetna Health of Montana, 662
Williams, Ronald A Aetna Health of Nebraska, 675
Williams, Ronald A Aetna Health of New Hampshire, 705
Williams, Ronald A Aetna Health of New Jersey, 715
Williams, Ronald A Aetna Health of New Mexico, 742
Williams, Ronald A Aetna Health of New York, 757
Williams, Ronald A Aetna Health of North Dakota, 834
Williams, Ronald A Aetna Health of Oregon, 899
Williams, Ronald A Aetna Health of Pennsylvania, 926
Williams, Ronald A Aetna Health of Rhode Island, 985
Williams, Ronald A Aetna Health of South Dakota, 1013
Williams, Ronald A Aetna Health of Utah, 1101
Williams, Ronald A Aetna Health of Vermont, 1117
Williams, Ronald A Aetna Health of Washington, 1148
Williams, Ronald A Aetna Health of West Virginia, 1172
Williams, Ronald A Aetna Health of Wisconsin, 1186
Williams, Ronald A Aetna Health of Wyoming, 1215
Williams, Sandra Aetna Health of Georgia, 308
Williamson, April HealthPlus of Michigan: Flint, 574
Williamson, April HealthPlus of Michigan: Saginaw, 575
Williamson, Jane, RN HealthSmart Preferred Care, 374
Williamson, Keith H Centene Corporation, 638
Williamson, Lynn, MD Coventry Health Care of Louisiana, 475
Willis, Barbara UnitedHealthCare of New York, 810
Willoughby, Brenda North Alabama Managed Care Inc, 14
Wills, Charles Berkshire Health Partners, 932
Wilson, Dawn Preferred Therapy Providers, 57
Wilson, Dennis Lovelace Health Plan, 750
Wilson, Dennis Lovelace Medicare Health Plan, 751
Wilson, Dennis CIGNA HealthCare of North Carolina, 818
Wilson, Doug Cofinity, 560
Wilson, Ellen Excellus Blue Cross Blue Shield: Central New York, 775
Wilson, J Bradley Blue Cross & Blue Shield of North Carolina, 816
Wilson, J Bradley Preferred Care Select, 829
Wilson, Laurie, RN Texas Community Care, 1091
Wilson, M Haley QualChoice/QCA Health Plan, 76
Wilson, Michael Texas True Choice, 1092
Wilson, Peter W CNA Insurance Companies: Colorado, 198
Wilson, Peter W CNA Insurance Companies: Georgia, 317
Wilson, Peter W CNA Insurance Companies: Illinois, 362
Wilson, Robert AvMed Health Plan: Fort Lauderdale, 260
Wilson, Roger G Blue Cross and Blue Shield Association, 360
Wilson, Ryan CHA Health, 458
Wilson, Susan Lovelace Health Plan, 750
Wilson, Vicky University Health Plans, 1116
Wind, Ilene Educators Mutual, 1105

Windfeldt, **Ty** Hometown Health Plan, 696
Wing, **Deborah** CIGNA HealthCare of New Hampshire, 707
Wingerter, **Arthur** Univera Healthcare, 811
Winsett, **Claudia** Welborn Health Plans, 416
Winter, **Sonya** Health Plan of Nevada, 695
Wise, **Allen F** Coventry Health Care: Corporate Headquarters, 506
Wise, **Duell** Coventry Health Care of Florida, 274
Wise, **Michael** ConnectiCare, 223
Wise, **Michael** ConnectiCare of Massachusetts, 530
Wise, **Michael** CIGNA HealthCare of New Jersey, 723
Wise, **Michael** ConnectiCare of New York, 768
Wise, **Michael** Delta Dental of Virginia, 1131
Witek, **Dawn** Physicians Plus Insurance Corporation, 1207
Witt, **Richard A** Mutual of Omaha DentaBenefits, 684
Witt, **Richard A** Mutual of Omaha Health Plans, 685
Witter, **Thomas** Vision Insurance Plan of America, 1213
Witty, **Karey** HealthSpring: Corporate Offices, 1039
Woeller, **Michael D** CIGNA: Corporate Headquarters, 939
Woessner, **Mark** Ohio Health Choice, 868
Wohlman, **Doug** Willamette Dental Insurance, 925
Wolf, **Dale** CCN: Alaska, 20
Wolf, **Dale B** Coventry Health Care of Kansas, 439
Wolf, **Dale B** Coventry Health Care: Corporate Headquarters, 506
Wolf, **Dale B** HealthAmerica, 951
Wolf, **David D** CareFirst Blue Cross & Blue Shield of Virginia, 1127
Wolf, **Gregory** CIGNA HealthCare of North Carolina, 818
Wolf, **Jan** Central California Alliance for Health, 100
Wolff, **William** SafeGuard Health Enterprises: Corporate Office, 172
Wolff, **William** SafeGuard Health Enterprises: Florida, 299
Wolff, **William** SafeGuard Health Enterprises: Texas, 1086
Wolfkiel, **Robert** Aetna Health of Tennessee, 1026
Wolgemuth, **Sherry** Preferred Health Care, 963
Woll, **Douglas, MD** Blue Care Network of Michigan: Medicare, 552
Womack, **Garth** Vytra Health Plans, 813
Wong, **Josie, RN** Care 1st Health Plan: California, 97
Wong, **Sue** On Lok Lifeways, 157
Wong, **Van** San Francisco Health Plan, 173
Wong, **Winston, MD** CareFirst Blue Cross Blue Shield, 244
Woo, **Herbert** Care 1st Health Plan: California, 97
Wood, **Alan** Piedmont Community Health Plan, 1141
Woodard, **Bob** Kern Family Health Care, 144
Woodley, **Pamela** Aetna Health of Georgia, 308
Woods, **Dawn** HealthSpan, 857
Woods, **Rick** Group Health Cooperative, 1157
Woodson, **Tonya** Virginia Premier Health Plan, 1147
Woodsone, **Will** Premier Access Insurance/Access Dental, 169
Woodward, **Frances** Bravo Health: Corporate Headquarters, 502
Wopat, **Rick, MD** Samaritan Health Plan, 920
Worcester, **Ghita** UCare Medicare Plan, 618
Worcester, **Ghita** UCare Minnesota, 619
Worley, **Leslie** UnitedHealthCare of Ohio: Columbus, 882
Worley, **Leslie** UnitedHealthCare of Ohio: Dayton & Cincinnati, 883
Worley, **Mike** Quality Health Plans, 298
Worley, **Mike** Quality Health Plans of New York, 807
Worthington, **Bob** Blue Cross & Blue Shield of Tennessee, 1030
Woske, **Wendy** CIGNA HealthCare of Arizona, 38
Woys, **James E** Health Net Medicare Plan, 131
Woys, **James E** Health Net: Corporate Headquarters, 132
Wozniak, **Richard S, MD** Penn Highlands Health Plan, 961
Wray, **William K** Blue Cross & Blue Shield of Rhode Island, 986
Wright, **Craig** Assurant Employee Benefits: Tennessee, 1028
Wright, **Daniel** United Concordia, 971
Wright, **Dawn** QualCare, 737
Wright, **Elease E** Aetna Health of Alabama, 1
Wright, **Elease E** Aetna Health of Alaska, 18
Wright, **Elease E** Aetna Health of Arkansas, 64
Wright, **Elease E** Aetna Health, Inc. Corporate Headquarters, 217
Wright, **Elease E** Aetna Health, Inc. Medicare Plan, 218
Wright, **Elease E** Aetna Health of Delaware, 231
Wright, **Elease E** Aetna Health District of Columbia, 243
Wright, **Elease E** Aetna Health of Hawaii, 332
Wright, **Elease E** Aetna Health of Idaho, 344

Wright, **Elease E** Aetna Health of Iowa, 418
Wright, **Elease E** Aetna Health of Kansas, 434
Wright, **Elease E** Aetna Health of Kentucky, 455
Wright, **Elease E** Aetna Health of Louisiana, 470
Wright, **Elease E** Aetna Health of Maine, 487
Wright, **Elease E** Aetna Health of Maryland, 496
Wright, **Elease E** Aetna Health of Massachusetts, 524
Wright, **Elease E** Aetna Health of Michigan, 548
Wright, **Elease E** Aetna Health of Minnesota, 595
Wright, **Elease E** Aetna Health of Mississippi, 624
Wright, **Elease E** Aetna Health of Montana, 662
Wright, **Elease E** Aetna Health of Nebraska, 675
Wright, **Elease E** Aetna Health of New Hampshire, 705
Wright, **Elease E** Aetna Health of New Jersey, 715
Wright, **Elease E** Aetna Health of New Mexico, 742
Wright, **Elease E** Aetna Health of New York, 757
Wright, **Elease E** Aetna Health of North Dakota, 834
Wright, **Elease E** Aetna Health of Oregon, 899
Wright, **Elease E** Aetna Health of Pennsylvania, 926
Wright, **Elease E** Aetna Health of Rhode Island, 985
Wright, **Elease E** Aetna Health of South Dakota, 1013
Wright, **Elease E** Aetna Health of Utah, 1101
Wright, **Elease E** Aetna Health of Vermont, 1117
Wright, **Elease E** Aetna Health of Virginia, 1124
Wright, **Elease E** Aetna Health of Washington, 1148
Wright, **Elease E** Aetna Health of West Virginia, 1172
Wright, **Elease E** Aetna Health of Wisconsin, 1186
Wright, **Elease E** Aetna Health of Wyoming, 1215
Wright, **Ellen** Foundation for Medical Care for Kern & Santa Barbara County, 123
Wright, **Kelly** Cofinity, 560
Wright, **Phil** The Health Plan of the Upper Ohio Valley, 880
Wright, **Stuart** CIGNA HealthCare of Arkansas, 69
Wright, **Stuart** CIGNA HealthCare of Mississippi, 625
Wright, **William, MD** Kaiser Permanente Health Plan of Colorado, 210
Wu, **Albert** Behavioral Healthcare Options, Inc., 690
Wuest, **Thomas K, MD** Trillium Community Health Plan, 921
Wyllie, **Melissa** American WholeHealth Network, 928
Wynkoop, **Paul** PacificSource Health Plans: Corporate Headquarters, 917
Wynn, **Jene** Care Choices, 557
Wynne, **Steve** ODS Health Plan, 915
Wyss, **Tom** Coventry Health Care of Florida, 274

Y

Yakre, **Miles B** Assurant Employee Benefits: Corporate Headquarters, 635
Yalowitz, **David, MD** UnitedHealthCare of the Mid-Atlantic, 523
Yancey, **Betty** Coastal Healthcare Administrators, 109
Yanchak, **Adam** Ohio Health Choice, 868
Yander, **Leslie** Calais Health, 473
Yang, **Anna** Western Dental Services, 188
Yanuck, **Michael, MD** Quality Health Plans, 298
Yanuck, **Michael, MD** Quality Health Plans of New York, 807
Yapo, **Laraine** HealthPlus of Michigan: Flint, 574
Yapo, **Laraine** HealthPlus of Michigan: Saginaw, 575
Yapo, **Laraine** HealthPlus Senior Medicare Plan, 577
Yates, **C. Alan, MD** Stanislaus Foundation for Medical Care, 177
Yates, **Candace** HealthPartners, 1037
Yates, **Libba** VIVA Health, 17
Yates, **Steve** Windsor Medicare Extra, 1045
Yax, **Gerald, DDS** Golden Dental Plans, 567
Yeager, **John** The Health Plan of the Upper Ohio Valley, 880
Yeager, **Mark E** American Pioneer Life Insurance Co, 255
Yeager, **Sarah** Anthem Blue Cross & Blue Shield Connecticut, 220
Yelorda, **Peter** Blue Cross & Blue Shield of Kansas City, 636
Yong, **Eben** Health Plan of San Mateo, 134
York, **Billie** American WholeHealth Network, 928
York, **Edna** CIGNA HealthCare of New Hampshire, 707
York, **Linda** Advantage Health Solutions, 388
York, **Rebecca** Superior Dental Care, 877
Young, **Ann** The Dental Care Plus Group, 879
Young, **Bill** Blue Cross & Blue Shield of Tennessee, 1030
Young, **Fred, MD** Athens Area Health Plan Select, 313

Membership Enrollment Index

400,000	CDPHP Medicare Plan, 764
400,000	Dimension Health PPO, 276
400,000	Mountain State Blue Cross Blue Shiled, 1181
400,000	Preferred Mental Health Management, 448
400,000	Presbyterian Health Plan, 753
390,000	Dental Alternatives Insurance Services, 116
390,000	SVS Vision, 588
383,000	Health Alliance Medicare, 571
380,000	The Health Plan of the Upper Ohio Valley, 880
370,000	Humana Health Insurance of Puerto Rico, 979
370,000	Ohio Health Choice, 868
367,000	Blue Cross & Blue Shield of New Mexico, 744
365,000	Independent Health, 787
360,561	Sagamore Health Network, 412
360,000	Bravo Health: Corporate Headquarters, 502
360,000	Bravo Health: Pennsylvania, 935
360,000	Bravo Health: Texas, 1055
350,000	CDPHP: Capital District Physicians' Health Plan, 765
350,000	Providence Health Plans, 918
345,000	HealthSpring: Corporate Offices, 1039
338,000	Pacific Health Alliance, 161
332,840	Oxford Health Plans: New Jersey, 736
332,128	MetroPlus Health Plan, 793
330,000	GHP Coventry Health Plan, 648
328,000	PacifiCare of Colorado, 211
324,600	CIGNA HealthCare of Virginia, 1129
320,000	First Medical Health Plan of Florida, 278
320,000	Regence Blue Cross & Blue Shield of Utah, 1112
316,465	Health Alliance Medical Plans, 371
316,000	Preferred Network Access, 382
315,440	Western Dental Services, 188
310,000	Coventry Health Care of Florida, 274
300,000	AvMed Health Plan: Corporate Office, 259
300,000	AvMed Health Plan: Fort Lauderdale, 260
300,000	AvMed Health Plan: Gainesville, 261
300,000	AvMed Health Plan: Jacksonville, 262
300,000	AvMed Health Plan: Orlando, 263
300,000	AvMed Health Plan: Tampa, 264
300,000	Block Vision of New Jersey, 721
300,000	First Commonwealth, 368
300,000	Medical Card System (MCS), 980
300,000	Mercy Care Plan/Mercy Care Advantage, 51
300,000	Pacific Foundation for Medical Care, 160
300,000	WellPoint NextRx, 1100
294,566	Aetna Health of Texas, 1046
291,000	Care 1st Health Plan: California, 97
280,000	PacificSource Health Plans: Corporate Headquarters, 917
280,000	PacificSource Health Plans: Idaho, 353
270,000	CNA Insurance Companies: Colorado, 198
270,000	CNA Insurance Companies: Georgia, 317
270,000	CNA Insurance Companies: Illinois, 362
270,000	Community Health Plan of Washington, 1152
269,392	The Dental Care Plus Group, 879
265,000	AmeriHealth HMO, 718, 232
257,819	Kaiser Permanente of Georgia, 324
255,494	Health Alliance Medicare, 372
250,863	Health Plan of Michigan, 573
250,000	Araz Group, 596
250,000	CommunityCare Managed Healthcare Plans of Oklahoma, 890
250,000	Geisinger Health Plan, 948
250,000	Lakeside Community Healthcare Network, 146
250,000	Wellmark Health Plan of Iowa, 432
247,881	Dean Health Plan, 1192
244,000	Gateway Health Plan, 947
240,890	Boston Medical Center Healthnet Plan, 528
240,000	ConnectiCare, 223
240,000	ConnectiCare of Massachusetts, 530
240,000	ConnectiCare of New York, 768
240,000	PacifiCare Benefit Administrators, 1162
238,976	Preferred Care Blue, 660
236,000	Blue Cross & Blue Shield of Montana, 664
234,072	CIGNA HealthCare of California, 105
230,000	Texas Community Care, 1091
229,356	CIGNA HealthCare of Tennessee, 1033
223,795	Kaiser Permanente Health Plan of Hawaii, 340
220,000	M-Care, 579
215,000	Great Lakes Health Plan, 569
211,156	Aetna Health District of Columbia, 243
211,156	Aetna Health of Maryland, 496
211,156	Aetna Health of Virginia, 1124
205,677	Guardian Life Insurance Company, 782
205,000	BlueChoice Health Plan of South Carolina, 998
204,077	Great-West Healthcare California, 127
203,856	Great-West Healthcare Texas, 1067
202,000	Scott & White Health Plan, 1087
200,871	AmeriChoice by UnitedHealthCare, 716
200,473	Golden West Dental & Vision Plan, 126
200,000	Arkansas Managed Care Organization, 68
200,000	Care Plus Dental Plans, 1189
200,000	Community Health Plan of Los Angeles County, 111
200,000	Coventry Health Care Virginia, 1130
200,000	Health Resources, Inc., 405
200,000	HealthPlus of Michigan: Flint, 574
200,000	HealthPlus of Michigan: Saginaw, 575
200,000	HealthPlus of Michigan: Troy, 576
200,000	Initial Group, 1041
200,000	Lovelace Medicare Health Plan, 751
200,000	Select Health of South Carolina, 1008
200,000	UCare Minnesota, 619
200,000	Vytra Health Plans, 813
199,000	Wellmark Blue Cross & Blue Shield of South Dakota, 1025
194,944	CIGNA HealthCare of Florida, 270
193,498	BlueShield of Northeastern New York, 763
190,000	CHA Health, 458
190,000	Central California Alliance for Health, 100
187,000	Paramount Care of Michigan, 583
187,000	Paramount Elite Medicare Plan, 871
187,000	Paramount Health Care, 872
187,000	Premera Blue Cross Blue Shield of Alaska, 27
187,000	Security Health Plan of Wisconsin, 1209
186,425	Preferred Care, 962
186,000	Neighborhood Health Plan, 542
185,375	Healthcare USA of Missouri, 650
185,000	American Community Mutual Insurance Company, 549
185,000	Priority Partners Health Plans, 520
180,000	Blue Cross & Blue Shield of Vermont, 1118
180,000	First Medical Health Plan, 978
180,000	Mid Atlantic Medical Services: DC, 250
180,000	Mid Atlantic Medical Services: Delaware, 240
180,000	Mid Atlantic Medical Services: Pennsylvania, 960
180,000	Mid Atlantic Medical Services: Virginia, 1137
180,000	Mid Atlantic Medical Services: West Virginia, 1179
180,000	Rocky Mountain Health Plans, 213
178,000	Fallon Community Health Plan, 533
177,854	Public Employees Health Program, 1111
175,000	Arizona Foundation for Medical Care, 32
175,000	Wisconsin Physician's Service, 1214
174,309	Valley Preferred, 975
172,000	Humana Health Insurance of Corpus Christi, 1074
172,000	Humana Health Insurance of San Antonio, 1075
172,000	Humana Health Insurance of Tennessee, 1040
171,028	Empire Blue Cross & Blue Shield, 774
170,000	Parkland Community Health Plan, 1085
169,000	Health Net of the Northeast, 226
163,000	Lovelace Health Plan, 750
161,000	Mid Atlantic Medical Services: Corporate Office, 516
160,000	Colorado Health Partnerships, 201
160,000	Unison Health Plan of Pennsylvania, 970
160,000	WellPath: A Coventry Health Care Plan, 833
159,730	Passport Health Plan, 466
159,375	Aetna Health of Ohio, 844
155,070	Health Link PPO, 628
155,000	SummaCare Health Plan, 875
154,162	Aetna Health of New York, 757

22,417	Aetna Health of Maine, 487
22,000	Valley Baptist Health Plan, 1098
21,580	Great-West Healthcare Kansas, 442
21,000	Metropolitan Health Plan, 612
21,000	Rayant Insurance Company, 738
20,000	Preferred Healthcare System, 964
19,468	Kanawha Healthcare Solutions, 1006
19,000	Quality Health Plans, 298
19,000	Quality Health Plans of New York, 807
18,960	Aetna Health of the Carolinas, 995, 814
18,588	CIGNA HealthCare of Illinois, 361
18,556	Great-West Healthcare Minnesota, 604
18,500	Penn Highlands Health Plan, 961
18,335	Great-West Healthcare Oklahoma, 894
18,322	CIGNA HealthCare of Nebraska, 678
18,000	Avera Health Plans, 1015
17,000	ConnectCare, 561
17,000	Primecare Dental Plan, 170
16,852	Great-West Healthcare South Carolina, 1003
16,000	Elderplan, 773
15,700	SelectCare Access Corporation, 966
15,153	American Health Network of Indiana, 390
15,000	Alliant Health Plans, 310
15,000	Denver Health Medical Plan Inc, 203
15,000	Saint Mary's Health Plans, 703
15,000	Seton Health Plan, 1089
14,600	Inter Valley Health Plan, 138
14,341	CIGNA HealthCare of South Carolina, 1000
14,000	HealthPlus Senior Medicare Plan, 577
14,000	Primary Health Plan, 354
14,000	Vantage Health Plan, 485
14,000	Vantage Medicare Advantage, 486
13,582	Chinese Community Health Plan, 102
13,000	FirstCarolinaCare, 823
12,700	Central Susquehanna Healthcare Providers, 937
12,317	WellChoice, 741
12,000	Health Plans, Inc., 540
12,000	Medica HealthCare Plans, Inc, 291
11,745	Great-West Healthcare West Virginia, 1177
11,234	CIGNA HealthCare of Wyoming, 1217
11,121	Aetna Health of Massachusetts, 524
11,000	Touchstone Health HMO, 808
11,000	WINhealth Partners, 1222
10,885	Aetna Health of Missouri, 632
10,816	Great-West Healthcare New Mexico, 748
10,315	CIGNA HealthCare of Massachusetts, 529

10,231	Southeastern Indiana Health Organization, 413
10,082	Great-West Healthcare Iowa, 425
10,000	Denta-Chek of Maryland, 508
10,000	Total Health Choice, 300
9,848	CIGNA HealthCare of Kansas, 437
9,678	CIGNA HealthCare of Indiana, 397
9,000	Perfect Health Insurance Company, 806
8,184	Great-West Healthcare Maine, 491
8,147	Great-West Healthcare Alabama, 10
8,135	CIGNA HealthCare of South Dakota, 1016
8,097	Humana Health Insurance of Alaska, 24
8,049	CIGNA HealthCare of St. Louis, 640
8,000	Arnett Health Plans, 394
8,000	Easy Choice Health Plan, 120
8,000	Grand Valley Health Plan, 568
8,000	Graphic Arts Benefit Corporation, 511
7,642	CIGNA HealthCare of Montana, 665
7,000	Arkansas Community Care, 67
7,000	Community Health Improvement Solutions, 641
7,000	Pima Health System, 56
6,443	Harvard University Group Health Plan, 537
6,343	CIGNA HealthCare of Maine, 489
6,000	Avalon Healthcare, 258
6,000	Educators Mutual, 1105
5,000	Colorado Choice Health Plans, 200
5,000	Cox Healthplans, 642
5,000	Trilogy Health Insurance, 1210
4,970	Great-West Healthcare Montana, 668
3,971	Evercare Health Plans, 603
3,000	Abrazo Advantage Health Plan, 29
3,000	Central Health Medicare Plan, 101
3,000	NevadaCare, 701
2,718	Great-West Healthcare Delaware, 238
2,407	CIGNA HealthCare of Hawaii, 334
2,375	Val-U-Health, 974
2,000	FamilyCare Health Medicare Plan, 907
1,685	Great-West Healthcare South Dakota, 1021
1,003	CCN: Alaska, 20
1,000	Heart of America Health Plan, 839
1,000	Legacy Health Plan, 1078
1,000	On Lok Lifeways, 157
1,000	UTMB HealthCare Systems, 1097
984	CIGNA HealthCare of Delaware, 234
884	Great-West Healthcare North Dakota, 838
368	Great-West Healthcare Hawaii, 336

Primary Care Physician Index

26,000	VSP: Vision Service Plan of Arizona, 63	15,059	Sagamore Health Network, 412
26,000	VSP: Vision Service Plan of California, 187	15,009	Atlanticare Health Plans, 720
26,000	VSP: Vision Service Plan of Colorado, 216	15,000	CHA Health, 458
26,000	VSP: Vision Service Plan of Florida, 306	15,000	Optima Health Plan, 1139
26,000	VSP: Vision Service Plan of Georgia, 331	14,700	Coventry Health Care of West Virginia, 1174
26,000	VSP: Vision Service Plan of Hawaii, 343	14,500	Wisconsin Physician's Service, 1214
26,000	VSP: Vision Service Plan of Illinois, 387	14,000	Encircle Network, 401
26,000	VSP: Vision Service Plan of Indiana, 415	13,840	MVP Health Care: Corporate Office, 798
26,000	VSP: Vision Service Plan of Kansas, 454	13,729	Kaiser Permanente Health Plan of Southern California, 141
26,000	VSP: Vision Service Plan of Massachusetts, 547	13,000	Arizona Foundation for Medical Care, 32
26,000	VSP: Vision Service Plan of Michigan, 594	12,349	MedCost, 826
26,000	VSP: Vision Service Plan of Minnesota, 623	12,000	Coventry Health Care Virginia, 1130
26,000	VSP: Vision Service Plan of New Jersey, 740	12,000	MVP Health Care: Central New York, 797
26,000	VSP: Vision Service Plan of Ohio, 884	12,000	MetroPlus Health Plan, 793
26,000	VSP: Vision Service Plan of Oregon, 924	12,000	Priority Health, 585
26,000	VSP: Vision Service Plan of South Carolina, 1012	12,000	Public Employees Health Program, 1111
26,000	VSP: Vision Service Plan of Texas, 1099	11,500	Care Choices, 557
26,000	VSP: Vision Service Plan of Washington, 1171	11,300	CIGNA HealthCare of Connecticut, 222
25,000	Anthem Blue Cross & Blue Shield of Ohio, 846	11,000	Behavioral Health Systems, 4
25,000	Tufts Health Plan, 544	11,000	Capital Blue Cross, 936
25,000	Tufts Health Plan: Rhode Island, 993	10,500	Preferred Mental Health Management, 448
24,000	Coventry Health Care of Delaware, 235	10,425	Regence Blue Cross & Blue Shield of Oregon, 919
24,000	MVP Health Care: New Hampshire, 712	10,032	Aetna Health of Maryland, 496
24,000	Medica: North Dakota, 841	10,000	American PPO, 1048
24,000	Spectera, 521	10,000	Family Choice Health Alliance, 726
24,000	WellPath: A Coventry Health Care Plan, 833	10,000	Keystone Health Plan East, 959
23,000	National Capital PPO, 1138	10,000	Preferred Vision Care, 450
22,000	ConnectiCare of Massachusetts, 530	9,200	PreferredOne, 616
22,000	ConnectiCare of New York, 768	9,000	Blue Cross Preferred Care, 6
21,166	Aetna Health of Texas, 1046	9,000	Lifewise Health Plan of Oregon, 913
21,070	Humana Health Insurance of Illinois, 377	9,000	Parkview Total Health, 410
21,010	Island Group Administration, Inc., 789	9,000	QualCare, 737
20,266	Blue Cross & Blue Shield of Massachusetts, 527	8,986	PacifiCare Dental and Vision Administrators, 163
20,100	CIGNA HealthCare of North Carolina, 818	8,977	Blue Cross & Blue Shield of Florida: Jacksonville, 266
20,016	Cariten Preferred, 1032	8,500	Mercy Health Plans: Corporate Office, 655
20,000	Devon Health Services, 942	8,500	UnitedHealthCare of New York, 810
20,000	Midlands Choice, 683	8,400	HealthSpan, 857
20,000	OptiCare Managed Vision, 828	8,271	PacifiCare of California, 165
20,000	Premera Blue Cross, 1164	8,100	CIGNA HealthCare of South Carolina, 1000
20,000	Signature Health Alliance, 1043	8,000	Blue Cross & Blue Shield of Minnesota, 599
19,702	Regence Blue Shield, 1166	8,000	Gateway Health Plan, 947
19,000	Asuris Northwest Health, 1150	8,000	UnitedHealthCare of Massachusetts, 546
19,000	Blue Cross & Blue Shield of Georgia, 315	7,932	Ohio Health Choice, 868
18,000	Americas PPO, 1014	7,728	Medical Mutual of Ohio, 862
18,000	Araz Group, 596	7,700	BlueChoice Health Plan of South Carolina, 998
18,000	Avesis: Corporate Headquarters, 34	7,700	Group Health Cooperative of Eau Claire, 1197
18,000	Avesis: Georgia, 314	7,600	UPMC Health Plan, 973
18,000	Avesis: Indiana, 395	7,500	Aetna Health of Massachusetts, 524
18,000	Avesis: Iowa, 420	7,332	Carolina Care Plan, 999
18,000	Avesis: Maryland, 500	7,000	HealthEOS, 1201
18,000	Avesis: Massachusetts, 526	7,000	Lovelace Health Plan, 750
18,000	Avesis: Minnesota, 598	6,908	Aetna Health of Virginia, 1124
18,000	Avesis: Texas, 1051	6,560	SCAN Health Plan, 175
18,000	Block Vision, 501	6,150	Prime Source Health Network, 965
18,000	Block Vision of New Jersey, 721	6,150	South Central Preferred, 967
18,000	Health Alliance Plan, 572	6,000	Dimension Health PPO, 276
17,000	Coventry Health Care of GA, 319	6,000	FC Diagnostic, 727
17,000	Horizon Health Corporation, 1073	6,000	Group Health Cooperative, 1157
17,000	Oxford Health Plans: Corporate Headquarters, 229	6,000	Orange County Foundation for Medical Care, 158
16,000	CIGNA HealthCare of Georgia, 316	6,000	SummaCare Health Plan, 875
16,000	UCare Medicare Plan, 618	6,000	SummaCare Medicare Advantage Plan, 876
16,000	UCare Minnesota, 619	5,900	OhioHealth Group, 870
15,529	Group Health Incorporated (GHI), 781	5,800	Nationwide Better Health, 867
15,200	CIGNA HealthCare of Tennessee, 1033	5,700	Univera Healthcare, 811
15,129	Kaiser Permanente Health Plan Northwest, 911	5,580	ConnectiCare, 223
15,129	Kaiser Permanente Health Plan Ohio, 861	5,500	Managed Health Services, 1203
15,129	Kaiser Permanente Health Plan of Colorado, 210	5,250	CIGNA HealthCare of New Jersey, 723
15,129	Kaiser Permanente Health Plan of Hawaii, 340	5,200	Blue Cross & Blue Shield of North Carolina, 816
15,129	Kaiser Permanente Health Plan of Northern California, 140	5,000	CDPHP: Capital District Physicians' Health Plan, 765
15,129	Kaiser Permanente Health Plan of the Mid-Atlantic States, 514	5,000	Denver Health Medical Plan Inc, 203
15,129	Kaiser Permanente Health Plan: Corporate Office, 142	5,000	First Medical Health Plan of Florida, 278
15,129	Kaiser Permanente of Georgia, 324	5,000	Initial Group, 1041

5,000	M-Care, 579
5,000	PacifiCare Benefit Administrators, 1162
5,000	PacifiCare of Washington, 1163
5,000	Vista Healthplan of South Florida, Inc, 305
4,800	Coventry Health Care of Kansas, 439
4,800	PacifiCare of Texas, 1084
4,538	Health Choice of Alabama, 11
4,500	Blue Care Network of Michigan: Corporate Headquarters, 551
4,500	Blue Care Network: Ann Arbor, 553
4,500	Blue Care Network: Flint, 554
4,500	Blue Care Network: Great Lakes, Muskegon Heights, 555
4,500	CareFirst Blue Cross & Blue Shield of Virginia, 1127
4,500	CareFirst Blue Cross Blue Shield, 244
4,500	ProviDRs Care Network, 451
4,483	Nevada Preferred Healthcare Providers, 700
4,465	Horizon Healthcare of New Jersey, 731
4,425	Preferred Care Select, 829
4,400	Health Net Health Plan of Oregon, 909
4,364	UnitedHealthCare of North Carolina, 832
4,350	Regence Blue Cross & Blue Shield of Utah, 1112
4,310	Health New England, 538
4,300	HealthSpring: Corporate Offices, 1039
4,200	PacifiCare of Oregon, 916
4,200	Superior Dental Care, 877
4,179	The Dental Care Plus Group, 879
4,100	Security Health Plan of Wisconsin, 1209
4,030	Preferred Care, 962
4,000	Anthem Blue Cross & Blue Shield of Missouri, 634
4,000	GHP Coventry Health Plan, 648
4,000	NevadaCare, 701
4,000	Saint Mary's Health Plans, 703
4,000	The Health Plan of the Upper Ohio Valley, 880
4,000	UnitedHealthCare of Tennessee, 1044
3,977	SuperMed One, 878
3,934	Virginia Health Network, 1146
3,915	HealthAmerica Pennsylvania, 952
3,800	Altius Health Plans, 1102
3,800	Blue Cross & Blue Shield of Texas: Houston, 1054
3,696	Geisinger Health Plan, 948
3,600	Pacific Dental Benefits, 159
3,555	L.A. Care Health Plan, 145
3,532	Anthem Blue Cross & Blue Shield of Indiana, 392
3,500	Aultcare Corporation, 848
3,500	CalOptima, 96
3,500	Coventry Health Care of Iowa, 422
3,500	Educators Mutual, 1105
3,500	Humana Health Insurance of Louisiana, 480
3,500	PCC Preferred Chiropractic Care, 446
3,500	Unicare: Massachusetts, 545
3,500	Unicare: West Virginia, 1183
3,474	Anthem Blue Cross & Blue Shield of Nevada, 689
3,467	Meritain Health: Corporate Headquarters, 792
3,467	Meritain Health: Indiana, 409
3,467	Meritain Health: Kentucky, 465
3,467	Meritain Health: Louisiana, 481
3,467	Meritain Health: Michigan, 580
3,467	Meritain Health: Minnesota, 611
3,467	Meritain Health: Missouri, 656
3,467	Meritain Health: Ohio, 864
3,467	Meritain Health: Utah, 1108
3,464	Humana Health Insurance of Georgia, 323
3,434	Blue Cross & Blue Shield of South Carolina, 997
3,400	CNA Insurance Companies: Colorado, 198
3,400	CNA Insurance Companies: Georgia, 317
3,400	CNA Insurance Companies: Illinois, 362
3,400	Medfocus Radiology Network, 153
3,357	HealthPartners, 1037
3,322	Blue Cross & Blue Shield of New Mexico, 744
3,300	New West Health Services, 672
3,276	Great-West PPO, 206
3,276	Mid Atlantic Medical Services: DC, 250
3,276	Mid Atlantic Medical Services: Delaware, 240

3,276	Mid Atlantic Medical Services: Pennsylvania, 960
3,276	Mid Atlantic Medical Services: Virginia, 1137
3,276	Mid Atlantic Medical Services: West Virginia, 1179
3,276	Mid Atlantic Psychiatric Services (MAMSI), 517
3,276	Optimum Choice, 519
3,250	Ohio State University Health Plan Inc., 869
3,200	Golden Dental Plans, 567
3,200	Humana Health Insurance of Jacksonville, 286
3,200	QualChoice/QCA Health Plan, 76
3,121	Humana Health Insurance of Ohio, 859
3,091	MVP Health Care: Vermont, 1122
3,066	Amerigroup Corporation, 1125
3,000	Aetna Health of West Virginia, 1172
3,000	AlohaCare, 333
3,000	Boston Medical Center Healthnet Plan, 528
3,000	Care 1st Health Plan: California, 97
3,000	CommunityCare Managed Healthcare Plans of Oklahoma, 890
3,000	Delta Dental of Missouri, 643
3,000	Health Alliance Medicare, 372
3,000	JMH Health Plan, 289
3,000	NOVA Healthcare Administrators, 804
3,000	Pacific Foundation for Medical Care, 160
3,000	Physicians Plus Insurance Corporation, 1207
2,963	Beech Street Corporation: Alabama, 3
2,855	Healthplex, 785
2,811	Humana Health Insurnace of Colorado, 209
2,800	Neighborhood Health Plan, 542
2,714	Molina Healthcare: Washington, 1161
2,705	HealthLink HMO, 651
2,700	Anthem Blue Cross & Blue Shield of Virginia, 1126
2,700	Delta Dental of Arizona, 40
2,700	Health Net Dental, 130
2,691	Aetna Health of New York, 757
2,594	Coastal Healthcare Administrators, 109
2,559	UnitedHealthCare of the District of Columbia, 253
2,559	UnitedHealthCare of the Mid-Atlantic, 523, 242
2,558	Rocky Mountain Health Plans, 213
2,517	CIGNA HealthCare of South Texas, 1058
2,500	Emerald Health PPO, 854
2,500	UnitedHealthCare of South Florida, 303
2,500	Wellmark Health Plan of Iowa, 432
2,490	Blue Cross & Blue Shield of Tennessee, 1030
2,476	Delta Dental of California, 115
2,442	UnitedHealthCare of Ohio: Columbus, 882
2,442	UnitedHealthCare of Ohio: Dayton & Cincinnati, 883
2,365	Community Health Plan of Washington, 1152
2,316	Southeastern Indiana Health Organization, 413
2,300	San Francisco Health Plan, 173
2,292	Aetna Health of Colorado, 190
2,278	UnitedHealthCare of Rhode Island, 994
2,251	Trigon Health Care, 1143
2,212	Anthem Blue Cross & Blue Shield of Kentucky, 456
2,200	Healthcare Partners of East Texas, 1069
2,200	OmniCare: A Coventry Health Care Plan, 582
2,200	UnitedHealthCare of Georgia, 330
2,167	Molina Healthcare: Corporate Office, 155
2,167	Molina Healthcare: Florida, 292
2,167	Molina Healthcare: Michigan, 581
2,167	Molina Healthcare: Missouri, 658
2,167	Molina Healthcare: Ohio, 865
2,167	Molina Healthcare: Texas, 1082
2,167	Molina Healthcare: Utah, 1109
2,133	ChiroSource Inc, 104
2,091	WellCare Health Plans, 307
2,073	SafeGuard Health Enterprises: Corporate Office, 172
2,073	SafeGuard Health Enterprises: Florida, 299
2,073	SafeGuard Health Enterprises: Texas, 1086
2,061	AvMed Health Plan: Corporate Office, 259
2,032	CIGNA HealthCare of the Mid-Atlantic, 245, 504
2,011	Golden West Dental & Vision Plan, 126
2,000	Access Dental Services, 79
2,000	CIGNA HealthCare of Indiana, 397

670	Aetna Health of Minnesota, 595
637	First Priority Health, 946
600	Humana Health Insurance of Tampa - Pinellas, 288
600	Preferred Medical Plan, 297
600	Total Health Care, 589
600	Total Health Choice, 300
588	CareSource: Michigan, 558
578	Community Health Improvement Solutions, 641
535	BlueChoice, 637
525	Clear One Health Plans, 905
516	UnitedHealthCare of Nebraska, 686
500	CIGNA HealthCare of Colorado, 197
500	Humana Health Insurance of Arizona, 48
500	Northeast Georgia Health Partners, 326
500	Preferred Health Plan Inc, 467
498	North Alabama Managed Care Inc, 14
488	Community Health Group, 110
485	OSF HealthPlans, 380
480	Beta Health Plan, 195
474	PacifiCare of Oklahoma, 897
469	Aetna Health of Georgia, 308
455	Kanawha Healthcare Solutions, 1006
452	UnitedHealthCare of Mississippi, 630
440	MercyCare Health Plans, 1205
438	BlueLincs HMO, 888
430	Harvard University Group Health Plan, 537
425	Penn Highlands Health Plan, 961
423	Primary Health Plan, 354
416	Preferred Plus of Kansas, 449
401	ChiroCare of Wisconsin, 1190
400	Health Choice Arizona, 46
400	Omni IPA/Medcore Medical Group, 156
370	HealthAmerica, 951
356	UnitedHealthCare of Louisiana, 484
355	Aetna Health of Tennessee, 1026
350	Foundation for Medical Care for Mendocino & Lake Counties, 124
350	Piedmont Community Health Plan, 1141
350	Pima Health System, 56
328	AvMed Health Plan: Fort Lauderdale, 260
310	CIGNA HealthCare of Utah, 1103
305	Brazos Valley Health Network, 1056
300	Arnett Health Plans, 394
300	Bright Now! Dental, 93
300	CIGNA HealthCare of Arkansas, 69
300	Denta-Chek of Maryland, 508
300	Lakeside Community Healthcare Network, 146
300	Phoenix Health Plan, 55
300	Welborn Health Plans, 416
290	Excellus Blue Cross Blue Shield: Central New York, 775

274	Central Susquehanna Healthcare Providers, 937
274	PersonalCare, 381
267	AvMed Health Plan: Jacksonville, 262
267	Dentcare Delivery Systems, 771
267	PacifiCare of Nevada, 702
256	Hometown Health Plan, 696
250	Behavioral Healthcare Options, Inc., 690
250	Humana Health Insurance of Orlando, 287
245	Pueblo Health Care, 212
245	Willamette Dental Insurance, 925
240	AvMed Health Plan: Tampa, 264
240	Blue Cross & Blue Shield of Florida: Pensacola, 267
228	Health First Health Plans, 282
225	Peninsula Health Care, 1140
219	AvMed Health Plan: Gainesville, 261
213	Kern Family Health Care, 144
210	OSF Healthcare, 379
200	Cardinal Health Alliance, 396
200	Children's Mercy Family Health Partners, 639
200	Dencap Dental Plans, 564
200	Metropolitan Health Plan, 612
197	Health Plan of San Mateo, 134
190	Medical Care Referral Group, 1079
180	Health Plan of San Joaquin, 133
175	Quality Plan Administrators, 251
169	Medical Associates Health Plan: East, 1204
161	UnitedHealthcare Nevada, 704
160	Chinese Community Health Plan, 102
150	Contra Costa Health Plan, 113
150	Preferred Healthcare System, 964
149	Dental Source: Dental Health Care Plans, 1063
140	Val-U-Health, 974
124	Maricopa Integrated Health System/Maricopa Health Plan, 50
120	Capital Health Plan, 268
113	ConnectCare, 561
110	Anthem Blue Cross & Blue Sheild of Indiana, 391
100	Group Health Cooperative of South Central Wisconsin, 1198
92	Boulder Valley Individual Practice Association, 196
90	Anthem Blue Cross & Blue Shield of New Hampshire, 706
71	Florida Health Care Plan, 279
70	American Denticare, 65
51	Care Plus Dental Plans, 1189
21	HMO Health Ohio, 858
17	Opticare of Utah, 1110
15	Heart of America Health Plan, 839
12	Beech Street: Alaska, 19
11	CCN: Alaska, 20
10	On Lok Lifeways, 157

Referral/Specialty Physician Index

4,791	Inter Valley Health Plan, 138
4,722	Southeastern Indiana Health Organization, 413
4,678	Beech Street Corporation: Alabama, 3
4,650	Gateway Health Plan, 947
4,552	Highmark Blue Cross & Blue Shield, 953
4,500	CIGNA HealthCare of Connecticut, 222
4,500	Landmark Healthplan of California, 147
4,500	MVP Health Care: Western New York, 800
4,500	UnitedHealthCare of South Florida, 303
4,450	Virginia Premier Health Plan, 1147
4,430	Pacific Foundation for Medical Care, 160
4,374	Aetna Health of Arizona, 31
4,236	Managed HealthCare Northwest, 914
4,199	BlueChoice Health Plan of South Carolina, 998
4,151	Advantage Health Solutions, 388
4,100	Penn Highlands Health Plan, 961
4,000	Aetna Health of West Virginia, 1172
4,000	American WholeHealth Network, 928
4,000	Atlanticare Health Plans, 720
4,000	HSM: Healthcare Cost Management, 607
4,000	Initial Group, 1041
4,000	Preferred Mental Health Management, 448
4,000	UnitedHealthCare of Georgia, 330
3,983	CareSource: Michigan, 558
3,952	Anthem Blue Cross & Blue Shield of Kentucky, 456
3,928	Aetna Health of Pennsylvania, 926
3,884	M-Care, 579
3,870	Optima Health Plan, 1139
3,820	SelectNet Plus, Inc., 1182
3,800	Elderplan, 773
3,800	Group Health Cooperative of Eau Claire, 1197
3,800	Health Net of Arizona, 47
3,700	Primecare Dental Plan, 170
3,660	Dimension Health PPO, 276
3,653	Humana Health Insurnace of Colorado, 209
3,609	SelectCare Access Corporation, 966
3,608	Anthem Blue Cross & Blue Shield of New Hampshire, 706
3,596	SummaCare Medicare Advantage Plan, 876
3,504	Fallon Community Health Plan, 533
3,500	Coventry Health Care of Nebraska, 679
3,500	UnitedHealthCare of Colorado, 215
3,500	UnitedHealthCare of Montana, 674
3,500	UnitedHealthCare of New Hampshire, 714
3,500	UnitedHealthCare of Vermont, 1123
3,500	UnitedHealthCare of Wyoming, 1221
3,400	Americhoice of Pennsylvania, 929
3,369	UnitedHealthCare of Tennessee, 1044
3,304	UnitedHealthCare of Ohio: Columbus, 882
3,304	UnitedHealthCare of Ohio: Dayton & Cincinnati, 883
3,279	CIGNA HealthCare of North Texas, 1057
3,276	Great-West/One Health Plan, 207
3,276	Perfect Health Insurance Company, 806
3,241	Coastal Healthcare Administrators, 109
3,227	Unity Health Insurance, 1212
3,200	Mountain State Blue Cross Blue Shiled, 1181
3,180	CIGNA HealthCare of Arizona, 38
3,129	CIGNA HealthCare of New Hampshire, 707
3,120	Berkshire Health Partners, 932
3,042	Providence Health Plans, 918
3,000	CareOregon Health Plan, 902
3,000	Health New England, 538
3,000	Preferred Therapy Providers, 57
2,977	Valley Preferred, 975
2,900	NevadaCare, 701
2,900	Public Employees Health Program, 1111
2,854	Coventry Health Care Virginia, 1130
2,802	Blue Cross & Blue Shield of Vermont, 1118
2,800	Blue Cross & Blue Shield of Montana, 664
2,733	SummaCare Health Plan, 875
2,705	PacifiCare Dental and Vision Administrators, 163
2,681	Health Choice of Alabama, 11
2,518	Anthem Blue Cross & Blue Shield of Nevada, 689

2,427	Humana Health Insurance of Louisiana, 480
2,400	Children's Mercy Family Health Partners, 639
2,400	Crescent Preferred Provider Organization, 820
2,400	PacifiCare of Colorado, 211
2,309	Santa Clara Family Health Plan, 174
2,225	UnitedHealthCare of New York, 810
2,221	Healthchoice Orlando, 284
2,219	Blue Cross & Blue Shield of Louisiana, 472
2,203	Community Health Improvement Solutions, 641
2,200	Encore Health Network, 402
2,162	Nevada Preferred Healthcare Providers, 699
2,117	Physicians Plus Insurance Corporation, 1207
2,082	Excellus Blue Cross Blue Shield: Rochester Region, 776
2,073	Baptist Health Services Group, 1029
2,070	Mid America Health, 657
2,059	HealthNow New York, 784
2,030	SafeGuard Health Enterprises: Corporate Office, 172
2,030	SafeGuard Health Enterprises: Florida, 299
2,030	SafeGuard Health Enterprises: Texas, 1086
2,005	First Care Health Plans, 1065
2,000	BlueChoice, 637
2,000	CIGNA HealthCare of Indiana, 397
2,000	MHNet Behavioral Health, 1081
1,983	UnitedHealthCare of Indiana, 414
1,983	UnitedHealthCare of Kentucky, 469
1,913	Healthcare Partners of East Texas, 1069
1,870	Preferred Health Systems Insurance Company, 447
1,850	Altius Health Plans, 1102
1,850	Mount Carmel Health Plan Inc (MediGold), 866
1,820	Community Health Group, 110
1,800	HealthPlus Senior Medicare Plan, 577
1,800	HealthPlus of Michigan: Flint, 574
1,800	HealthPlus of Michigan: Saginaw, 575
1,800	HealthPlus of Michigan: Troy, 576
1,793	Health InfoNet, 669
1,791	PacifiCare Health Systems, 164
1,781	Physicians Health Plan of Mid-Michigan, 584
1,718	Mutual of Omaha Health Plans, 685
1,700	Neighborhood Health Plan of Rhode Island, 992
1,700	Pacific Dental Benefits, 159
1,668	CIGNA HealthCare of Arkansas, 69
1,626	Independent Health, 787
1,604	Anthem Blue Cross & Blue Shield of Maine, 488
1,581	John Deere Health, 1042
1,566	IHC: Intermountain Healthcare Health Plan, 351
1,500	Lakeside Community Healthcare Network, 146
1,500	Pacific Health Alliance, 161
1,500	Preferred Health Plan Inc, 467
1,500	Saint Mary's Health Plans, 703
1,500	Total Health Care, 589
1,466	PacifiCare of California, 165
1,427	Kanawha Healthcare Solutions, 1006
1,400	Health Plan of San Joaquin, 133
1,400	Interplan Health Group, 860
1,400	Western Dental Services, 188
1,386	Blue Cross & Blue Shield of Kansas City, 636
1,300	CommunityCare Managed Healthcare Plans of Oklahoma, 890
1,275	Prime Source Health Network, 965
1,275	ProviDRs Care Network, 451
1,255	Managed Health Services, 1203
1,213	BlueLincs HMO, 888
1,200	Aetna Health of Georgia, 308
1,200	CIGNA HealthCare of Maine, 489
1,200	Physical Therapy Provider Network, 167
1,200	Total Health Choice, 300
1,197	Preferred Plus of Kansas, 449
1,174	Physicians Health Plan of Northern Indiana, 411
1,133	OSF HealthPlans, 380
1,014	North Alabama Managed Care Inc, 14
1,000	Bluegrass Family Health, 457
1,000	Health Alliance Plan, 572
1,000	The Health Plan of the Upper Ohio Valley, 880

1,000	Welborn Health Plans, 416	**400**	Dental Health Services of California, 118
994	UnitedHealthCare of Nebraska, 686	**400**	Kern Family Health Care, 144
950	DakotaCare, 1017	**363**	Anthem Blue Cross & Blue Sheild of Indiana, 391
924	Delta Dental of California, 115	**350**	Blue Cross & Blue Shield of Florida: Pensacola, 267
900	Alliance Regional Health Network, 1047	**317**	Maricopa Integrated Health System/Maricopa Health Plan, 50
900	Paramount Health Care, 872	**275**	Metropolitan Health Plan, 612
877	UnitedHealthCare of Louisiana, 484	**273**	ConnectCare, 561
850	The Dental Care Plus Group, 879	**250**	Delta Dental of Kansas, 440
826	Blue Cross & Blue Shield of Delaware, 233	**250**	Preferred Network Access, 382
825	Central Susquehanna Healthcare Providers, 937	**241**	Florida Health Care Plan, 279
805	PacifiCare of Nevada, 702	**215**	Cardinal Health Alliance, 396
797	CIGNA HealthCare of Florida, 270	**210**	Contra Costa Health Plan, 113
775	AvMed Health Plan: Orlando, 263	**200**	Denta-Chek of Maryland, 508
735	Group Health Cooperative of South Central Wisconsin, 1198	**200**	Gundersen Lutheran Health Plan, 1199
733	Golden West Dental & Vision Plan, 126	**186**	Capital Health Plan, 268
731	Coventry Health Care of Kansas, 439	**175**	Dentcare Delivery Systems, 771
711	PersonalCare, 381	**174**	Brazos Valley Health Network, 1056
677	Excellus Blue Cross Blue Shield: Central New York, 775	**171**	Boulder Valley Individual Practice Association, 196
640	PacifiCare of Washington, 1163	**165**	Vision Plan of America, 185
605	HealthAmerica, 951	**144**	Chinese Community Health Plan, 102
596	AvMed Health Plan: Gainesville, 261	**140**	Carilion Health Plans, 1128
594	First Commonwealth, 368	**120**	Beta Health Plan, 195
564	AvMed Health Plan: Fort Lauderdale, 260	**100**	Health Tradition, 1200
560	Medical Care Referral Group, 1079	**100**	On Lok Lifeways, 157
555	Deaconess Health Plans, 398	**99**	Calais Health, 473
550	AvMed Health Plan: Tampa, 264	**68**	Beech Street: Alaska, 19
537	Health First Health Plans, 282	**60**	American Dental Group, 191
500	Heart of America Health Plan, 839	**60**	Harvard University Group Health Plan, 537
487	Primary Health Plan, 354	**50**	OSF Healthcare, 379
475	Peninsula Health Care, 1140	**40**	Opticare of Utah, 1110
448	Healthplex, 785	**35**	Northeast Georgia Health Partners, 326
448	Preferred Healthcare System, 964	**25**	American Denticare, 65
416	Bright Now! Dental, 93	**19**	CCN: Alaska, 20

General Reference

American Environmental Leaders: From Colonial Times to the Present
An African Biographical Dictionary
An Encyclopedia of Human Rights in the United States
Encyclopedia of African-American Writing
Encyclopedia of Gun Control & Gun Rights
Encyclopedia of Invasions & Conquests
Encyclopedia of Prisoners of War & Internment
Encyclopedia of Religion & Law in America
Encyclopedia of Rural America
Encyclopedia of the United States Cabinet, 1789-2010
Encyclopedia of War Journalism
Encyclopedia of Warrior Peoples & Fighting Groups
From Suffrage to the Senate: America's Political Women
Nations of the World
Political Corruption in America
Speakers of the House of Representatives, 1789-2009
The Environmental Debate: A Documentary History
The Evolution Wars: A Guide to the Debates
The Religious Right: A Reference Handbook
The Value of a Dollar: 1860-2009
The Value of a Dollar: Colonial Era
University & College Museums, Galleries & Related Facilities
US Land & Natural Resource Policy
Weather America
Working Americans 1770-1869 Vol. IX: Revol. War to the Civil War
Working Americans 1880-1999 Vol. I: The Working Class
Working Americans 1880-1999 Vol. II: The Middle Class
Working Americans 1880-1999 Vol. III: The Upper Class
Working Americans 1880-1999 Vol. IV: Their Children
Working Americans 1880-2003 Vol. V: At War
Working Americans 1880-2005 Vol. VI: Women at Work
Working Americans 1880-2006 Vol. VII: Social Movements
Working Americans 1880-2007 Vol. VIII: Immigrants
Working Americans 1880-2009 Vol. X: Sports & Recreation
Working Americans 1880-2010 Vol. XI: Inventors & Entrepreneurs
Working Americans 1880-2011 Vol. XII: Musicians
World Cultural Leaders of the 20th & 21st Centuries

Business Information

Directory of Business Information Resources
Directory of Mail Order Catalogs
Directory of Venture Capital & Private Equity Firms
Environmental Resource Handbook
Food & Beverage Market Place
Grey House Homeland Security Directory
Grey House Performing Arts Directory
Hudson's Washington News Media Contacts Directory
New York State Directory
Sports Market Place Directory
The Rauch Guides – Industry Market Research Reports

Statistics & Demographics

America's Top-Rated Cities
America's Top-Rated Small Towns & Cities
America's Top-Rated Smaller Cities
Comparative Guide to American Hospitals
Comparative Guide to American Suburbs
Comparative Guide to Health in America
Profiles of... Series – State Handbooks

Health Information

Comparative Guide to American Hospitals
Comparative Guide to Health in America
Complete Directory for Pediatric Disorders
Complete Directory for People with Chronic Illness
Complete Directory for People with Disabilities
Complete Mental Health Directory
Directory of Health Care Group Purchasing Organizations
Directory of Hospital Personnel
HMO/PPO Directory
Medical Device Register
Older Americans Information Directory

Education Information

Charter School Movement
Comparative Guide to American Elementary & Secondary Schools
Complete Learning Disabilities Directory
Educators Resource Directory
Special Education

Financial Ratings Series

TheStreet.com Ratings Guide to Bond & Money Market Mutual Funds
TheStreet.com Ratings Guide to Common Stocks
TheStreet.com Ratings Guide to Exchange-Traded Funds
TheStreet.com Ratings Guide to Stock Mutual Funds
TheStreet.com Ratings Ultimate Guided Tour of Stock Investing
Weiss Ratings Consumer Box Set
Weiss Ratings Guide to Banks & Thrifts
Weiss Ratings Guide to Credit Unions
Weiss Ratings Guide to Health Insurers
Weiss Ratings Guide to Life & Annuity Insurers
Weiss Ratings Guide to Property & Casualty Insurers

Bowker's Books In Print®Titles

Books In Print®
Books In Print® Supplement
American Book Publishing Record® Annual
American Book Publishing Record® Monthly
Books Out Loud™
Bowker's Complete Video Directory™
Children's Books In Print®
Complete Directory of Large Print Books & Serials™
El-Hi Textbooks & Serials In Print®
Forthcoming Books®
Law Books & Serials In Print™
Medical & Health Care Books In Print™
Publishers, Distributors & Wholesalers of the US™
Subject Guide to Books In Print®
Subject Guide to Children's Books In Print®

Canadian General Reference

Associations Canada
Canadian Almanac & Directory
Canadian Environmental Resource Guide
Canadian Parliamentary Guide
Financial Services Canada
Governments Canada
Libraries Canada
The History of Canada

Grey House Publishing

4919 Route 22, PO Box 56, Amenia NY 12501-0056 | (800) 562-2139 | www.greyhouse.com | books@greyhouse.com